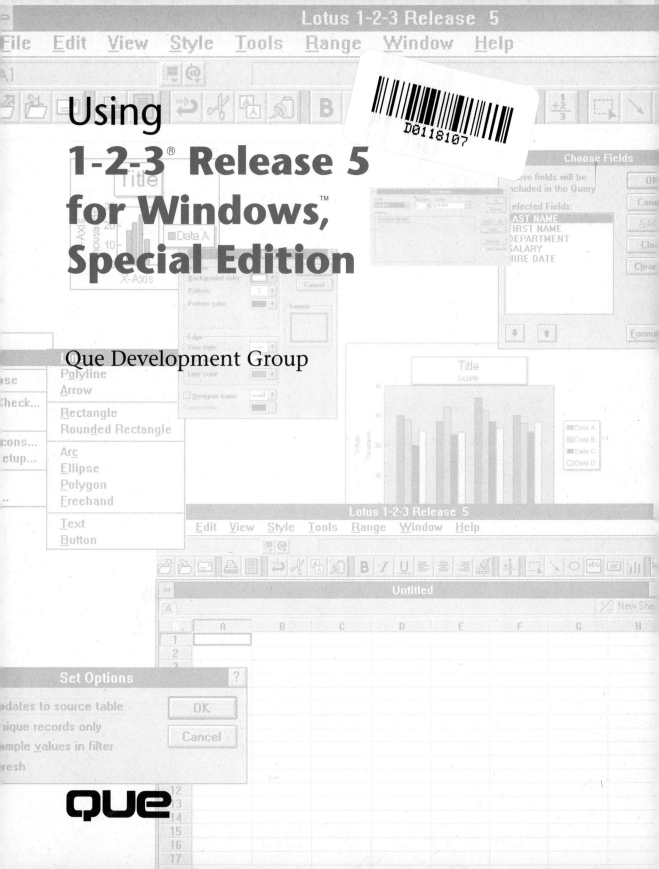

Using
1-2-3® Release 5
for Windows,™
Special Edition

Que Development Group

Using 1-2-3 Release 5 for Windows, Special Edition

Library of Congress Catalog No.: 94-66718

ISBN: 1-56529-743-1

97 96 95   10 9 8 7 6 5

Interpretation of the printing code: the rightmost double-digit number is the year of the book's printing; the rightmost single-digit number, the number of the book's printing. For example, a printing code of 94-1 shows that the first printing of the book occurred in 1994.

Publisher: David P. Ewing

Associate Publisher: Don Roche, Jr.

Managing Editor: Michael Cunningham

Product Marketing Manager: Greg Wiegand

Credits

Publishing Manager
Nancy Stevenson

Acquisitions Editor
Thomas F. Godfrey III

Product Directors
Joyce J. Nielsen
Kathie-Jo Arnoff

Product Development
Robin Drake
Janice A. Snyder

Production Editor
Mike La Bonne

Copy Editors
Geneil Breeze
Judy Brunetti
Patrick Kanouse
Susan Ross Moore
Katherine Murray
Kathy Simpson
Heather Stith

Technical Editors
Edward Hanley
Lee Mosqueda
Phil Sabotin
Michael Watson
Warren Estep

Acquisitions Coordinator
Deborah Abshier

Editorial Assistant
Jill L. Stanley

Technical Specialist
Cari Ohm

Book Designer
Amy Peppler-Adams

Graphic Image Specialists
Teresa Forrester
Tim Montgomery
Dennis Sheehan
Sue VandeWalle

Production Team
Steve Adams
Stephen Carlin
Maxine Dillingham
Chad Dressler
Aren Howell
Bob LaRoche
Beth Lewis
G. Alan Palmore
Clair Schwinler
Mike Thomas
Donna Winter

Indexer
Johnna VanHoose

Composed in *Stone Serif* and *MCPdigital* by Que Corporation

About the Authors

Rebecca Bridges Altman got her bachelor's degree in economics from Stanford University in 1981 and has run her own computer training and consulting business in Cupertino, California for 12 years. She has been revision author for a number of Que books, including *Using 1-2-3 for Windows*; *Using 1-2-3 Release 3.1*, Second Edition; *Using 1-2-3 Release 2.2*; and *Using Symphony*, 2nd Edition. She coauthored *Using 1-2-3 Release 4 for Windows*, Special Edition. She has also authored books on PageMaker, Microsoft Works, Harvard Graphics, and Harvard Graphics for Windows.

Dan Fingerman is president of Computer Insights, a Lotus Authorized Training Company, in Berkeley, California. Dan's company provides consulting, training, programming, and technical writing, based on a strong foundation in microcomputers and adult education. In over a decade, Dan has trained more than 15,000 people in both the private and public sectors, as well as at the university level, to use microcomputer technology. He has authored books on Ami Pro and WordPerfect for Windows, and has produced LearnKey training videos on Ami Pro. Dan received his undergraduate degree from MIT and has a master's degree and advanced graduate studies in education, specializing in the training of adults. He can be reached directly on CompuServe at 71172,532.

Jane Hosie-Bounar has worked with Lotus products since 1987, when she started work as a free-lance technical editor and technical writer. Since then, she has been a consultant for a number of companies, including Lotus Development, Dragon Systems, and J.A.M. Associates. She has written and/or edited many courses for Lotus products, including 1-2-3, Notes, Ami Pro, Improv, and SmartSuite. She has also worked as a trainer, testing software courses for business users, and as developmental editor for the Lotus Notes ViP documentation group. Hosie-Bonar also writes fiction, and her first novel, *Life Belts*, was published by Delacorte Press in 1993.

Cathy Kenny is an associate technical editor for *PC World Lotus Edition*. Before joining *PC World*, Kenny produced training materials for a microcomputer training company in Boston. She has also served as technical editor on more than 100 books for Que and Howard W. Sams.

John Kilroy is a quality assurance engineer at Lotus Development Corporation. He has been a member of both Windows and DOS spreadsheet product teams, including 1-2-3 for DOS Releases 2.4 and 3.4; and 1-2-3 for Windows

Releases 1.0, 4.0, and 5. He has a bachelor of science in business administration from the University of New Hampshire and a certificate in computer technology from the Lowell Institute School at MIT.

Sherri-Ann Lancton has her own training and consulting practice in Boulder, CO. She authored the *Microsoft Word 2.0 SureSteps* book for Que. Sherri spends part of her time in the classroom training users on all levels of word processing and spreadsheet use. The rest of the time, she writes course materials and documentation for her own training and for other trainers and clients.

Lisa Mosley is a technical writer at Lotus Development, where she has written extensively about 1-2-3 for seven years, primarily about @ functions and macros. She has written reference manuals and on-line help for every release of 1-2-3 for Windows, and developed animated movies for the Multimedia Release of 1-2-3.

Katherine Murray is the author of over 30 books and the president of reVisions Plus, Inc., a writing, editing, and desktop publishing company that specializes in the production of computer-related materials.

Joyce J. Nielsen is a senior product development specialist for Que Corporation, where she focuses on the development of spreadsheet, database, and word processing books. Before joining Que five years ago, Nielsen worked as a research analyst for a shopping mall developer, where she began using 1-2-3 in 1984 to develop and document 1-2-3 business applications used nationwide. She is the author of *1-2-3 Release 4 for Windows Quick Reference*, *1-2-3 Release 2.4 Quick Reference*, and *1-2-3 Release 3.4 Quick Reference*; and contributing author to many other Que titles, such as *Using 1-2-3 Release 4 for DOS*, Special Edition. Nielsen received a bachelor of science degree in Quantitative Business Analysis from Indiana University.

Dick Purcell is chairman of a new company in Boulder, CO, that markets and licenses software he has developed for graphic analysis of business plans entered in spreadsheets. For over a decade, he has conducted hundreds of courses in more than 40 states on use of spreadsheets and graphic analysis for business planning and decision-making, under sponsorship of the American Institute of Certified Public Accountants. For 3 1/2 years he served the governor of Ohio as executive director of the Governor's Business and Employment Council. He is author of *Understanding a Company's Finances—A Graphic Approach*, published by Houghton Mifflin Company, and of *Scrapbook Earth*, an illustrated science-based history and future of Earth and humankind. He holds a BS from MIT and an MBA from Harvard.

Robert L. Weberg is a senior systems analyst for Continental Bank in Chicago. He develops applications and business systems in Ami Pro, Lotus 1-2-3, Paradox, and Lotus Notes. Robert resides with his wife in the Bartlett, IL, area.

Christie Williams is a free-lance writer and editor in the Boston, MA area with more than 12 years of experience in developing, writing, editing, and producing computer books, courseware, documentation, and articles. She has written several books on word processing software, developed numerous courses for Lotus Development Corporation, contributed articles to *PC World Lotus Edition* and *InfoWorld*, and written documentation for both large and small software companies.

Majie Zeller is an independent curriculum developer and technical writer. After several years in arts management, she began working as a free-lance technical editor at Lotus Development Corporation in 1988. Since that time, she has been a curriculum developer, editor, writer, and trainer for a number of companies and consulting firms, including J.A.M. Associates, Communitec, Inc., and Learn PC. She has written or edited courses about many Lotus products, including 1-2-3 for DOS, Windows, and Macintosh, Improv, Notes, Ami Pro, and Freelance Graphics.

Trademark Acknowledgments

We'd Like To Hear from You!

As part of our continuing effort to produce books of the highest possible quality, Que would like to hear your comments. To stay competitive, we *really* want you, as a computer book reader and user, to let us know what you like or dislike most about this book or other Que products.

You can mail comments, ideas, or suggestions for improving future editions to the address below, or send us a fax at (317) 581-4663. For the on-line inclined, Macmillan Computer Publishing now has a forum on CompuServe (type **GO QUEBOOKS** at any prompt) through which our staff and authors are available for questions and comments. In addition to exploring our forum, please feel free to contact me personally on CompuServe at 70724,1467 to discuss your opinions of this book.

Thanks in advance—your comments will help us to continue publishing the best books available on computer topics in today's market.

Don Roche, Jr.
Associate Publisher
Que Corporation
201 W. 103rd Street
Indianapolis, IN 46290

Contents at a Glance

Everyday Worksheet Tasks

Working with Charts

Optimizing 1-2-3

Analyzing the Worksheet

Managing Databases

Integrating 1-2-3

Customizing 1-2-3

Automating with Macros

Appendixes

Contents

12 Modifying Charts   397

13 Formatting Charts   427

V Managing Databases 695

23 Creating a Database 697

24 Entering and Editing Data in a Database 709

25 Sorting Data 723

Introduction

When Lotus 1-2-3 was introduced, DOS was the major operating system for personal computers. As the computer industry has grown and matured, however, so have the needs of computer users. More powerful hardware, operating systems, and operating environments—such as Microsoft Windows—are in use today, as are more powerful software packages—such as 1-2-3 Release 5 for Windows.

Whether you are new to spreadsheets or are an experienced 1-2-3 user, this book is for you. Following the Que tradition, *Using 1-2-3 Release 5 for Windows*, Special Edition, leads you through the basics of spreadsheets and into the intermediate and advanced features of 1-2-3 Release 5 for Windows. This book provides the most extensive tutorial and reference coverage available for the new 1-2-3 Release 5 for Windows.

Que's unprecedented experience with 1-2-3 and 1-2-3 users has helped produce this high-quality, highly informative book. But a book such as *Using 1-2-3 Release 5 for Windows*, Special Edition, doesn't develop overnight. This book represents long hours of work from a team of expert authors and dedicated editors.

The experts who worked on this book include managers, consultants, trainers, experienced 1-2-3 users, and Lotus product design and documentation professionals. They know firsthand the many ways people use 1-2-3 daily and are familiar with what you expect when turning to *Using 1-2-3 Release 5 for Windows*, Special Edition. They know how to answer your questions about 1-2-3 quickly, clearly, and completely. The authors of this book have used 1-2-3 and have taught others how to use 1-2-3 to build many types of applications—from accounting and general business applications to scientific applications. This experience, combined with the editorial expertise of the world's leading computer-book publisher, brings you outstanding tutorial and reference information.

The authors of *Using 1-2-3 Release 5 for Windows*, Special Edition wrote new sections and new chapters covering the new features of 1-2-3 Release 5 for Windows. If you have used a previous version of 1-2-3, you can easily find and learn what makes 1-2-3 Release 5 so different from earlier versions of 1-2-3. You learn more than what the new features of Release 5 are: *Using 1-2-3 Release 5 for Windows,* Special Edition explains the exact benefits of the new features to your work. You learn, for example, that you can easily copy range styles to multiple locations in the worksheet by using the Fast Format feature. You learn also that you can open more than one worksheet file at a time from the File Open dialog box. And if you need a professionally designed spreadsheet template, *Using 1-2-3 Release 5 for Windows*, Special Edition shows you how to use and customize the SmartMaster templates provided with Release 5 to quickly create applications for common business tasks, such as budgets and financial statements.

In addition to enhancements added to this book based on the new features of 1-2-3 Release 5 for Windows, the design and overall structure of this book also have been greatly improved. User cautions and notes are emphasized with colored bars throughout the text, and tips are presented in the margins. Special cross-references within chapters enable you to follow alternative learning paths by providing quick access to related topics in other chapters. Within the text, the actual 1-2-3 Release 5 for Windows SmartIcons appear in the margin to highlight text that describes and uses the SmartIcons. The inside back cover of *Using 1-2-3 Release 5 for Windows*, Special Edition, in- cludes an "Action Index," which enables you to quickly find the information that you need to complete common procedures. A tear-out card in the back of this book includes the 1-2-3 Release 5 for Windows screen with parts of the screen labeled and a listing of common shortcut keys.

Don Roche Jr. (Publishing Director of this book), Joyce Nielsen (Product Di- rector), and the authors have also made this edition of *Using 1-2-3* easier to use. They have divided many of the long chapters from the previous edition into shorter chapters, giving you more logical chapter breaks and making it easier and faster to find information. Many chapters in this book also have been restructured to make them even easier to follow than in previous edi- tions. The result of these efforts is a comprehensive tutorial and reference, written in the easy-to-follow style expected from Que books.

Who Should Read This Book?

For both beginning and experienced users of 1-2-3, this introduction provides a road map to using this book. To help you find the information you need, turn to the section, "A Quick Tour of This Book." Whether you are a new or experienced user, use this introduction as a reference to the organization and conventions of *Using 1-2-3 Release 5 for Windows,* Special Edition.

Using 1-2-3 Release 5 for Windows, Special Edition, is written and organized to meet the needs of a wide range of readers, from those who have just started to use 1-2-3 to those who are experienced 1-2-3 users who have upgraded to 1-2-3 Release 5 for Windows.

If you are just beginning to use 1-2-3, this book helps you learn the basics so that you can quickly begin using 1-2-3 for your needs. In particular, Part I, "Everyday Worksheet Tasks," teaches basic concepts for understanding 1-2-3: commands, special uses of the keyboard and mouse, features of the 1-2-3 Release 5 for Windows screen, and methods for creating and modifying 1-2-3 worksheets.

> **Note**
>
> Release 5 and previous 1-2-3 versions often differ in the wording of prompts in menus and dialog boxes. This book shows only the Release 5 version in the screens and in the text.

If you are an experienced 1-2-3 user and have upgraded to 1-2-3 Release 5 for Windows, you learn about the new features of Release 5 and how to apply them as you develop worksheet applications.

Whether you are a beginning 1-2-3 user or a user who has upgraded to Release 5, *Using 1-2-3 Release 5 for Windows,* Special Edition, provides the tips and techniques necessary to help you get the most from the program.

A Quick Tour of This Book

If you flip quickly through this book, you can get a better sense of its organization and layout. The book is organized to follow the natural flow of learning and using 1-2-3. The following sections describe the organization of this book.

Part I: Everyday Worksheet Tasks

Chapter 1, "Getting Around in 1-2-3 and Windows," introduces the general concepts you need to understand 1-2-3 for Windows as a spreadsheet program. You learn how to manipulate and display multiple windows as well as use menus, dialog boxes, SmartIcons, and the mouse to improve your efficiency.

Chapter 2, "Navigating and Selecting in 1-2-3 for Windows," introduces the concepts of worksheets and files and teaches you how to move the cell pointer around the worksheet. You also learn how to work with ranges of data in the worksheet.

Chapter 3, "Entering and Editing Data," shows you how to enter and edit data in the worksheet, how to fill ranges with a series of data, and how to find and replace data. This chapter also covers how to erase cells and ranges, spell check your data, and use the Undo feature. In addition, you learn how to insert and delete cells, rows, and columns.

Chapter 4, "Working with Formulas," discusses how to create, enter, and correct errors in worksheet formulas. In addition, you learn how to specify the method and order of recalculation and how to handle unwanted circular references in the worksheet.

Chapter 5, "Using Functions," explains how to enter functions. The chapter provides a description of all the functions available in the following 1-2-3 Release 5 for Windows function categories: Calendar, Database, Engineering, Financial, Information, Logical, Lookup, Mathematical, Statistical, and Text.

Chapter 6, "Moving or Copying Data," shows you a variety of techniques for moving and copying worksheet data. These include drag-and-drop, which allows you simply to drag information from one location to another, and using the Windows Clipboard together with 1-2-3 commands to reposition information on your worksheet.

Chapter 7, "Reorganizing Worksheets," explains how you can organize your data more efficiently by using the multiple-worksheet feature to include up to 256 worksheets in a single worksheet file. You learn how to insert, rename, delete, and group worksheets in a multiple-worksheet file.

Chapter 8, "Managing Files," covers the commands related to creating, saving, closing, opening, deleting, and listing files. You also learn how to change directories and protect files. In addition, this chapter teaches you how to transfer files among different programs and how to send mail.

Chapter 9, "Formatting Worksheets," shows you how to change the way data appears on-screen, including the way values, formulas, and text display. You also learn how to set column widths and row heights, suppress the display of zeros, and how to use fast format, named styles, and style galleries to quickly format data.

Chapter 10, "Printing Worksheets," shows you how to specify a print range, preview reports before you print them, print reports of different sizes, and enhance reports with page-setup options. You also learn how to stop and suspend printing and how to print a text file to disk.

Part II: Working with Charts

Chapter 11, "Creating Charts," teaches you the different methods for creating charts from worksheet data. You learn how to create charts automatically from data in a worksheet file and how to define a chart's data ranges manually. In addition, you learn how to add charts to worksheet files.

Chapter 12, "Modifying Charts," explains how to manipulate the elements in a chart, including resizing the whole chart or parts of the chart, adding and deleting elements, editing the titles and legends, and other tasks.

Chapter 13, "Formatting Charts," covers how to change colors and patterns, number format, and text attributes, as well as how to annotate a chart. You also learn to preview and print charts.

Chapter 14, "Building Complex Charts and Mapping Data," shows you how to create the more complicated chart types offered by 1-2-3 for Windows (2Y-axis, XY, Mixed, and HLCO), as well as how to import graphics into a chart. You also learn how to use the exciting new mapping feature to illustrate worksheet data.

Part III: Optimizing 1-2-3

Chapter 15, "Managing the Worksheet Display," shows you how to choose worksheet display preferences, freeze worksheet titles, split and scroll worksheet windows, display worksheets in perspective view, magnify and restore the worksheet display, and hide columns, rows, and ranges.

Chapter 16, "Adding Graphics to Worksheets," covers how to add text boxes, lines, arrows, ellipses, and other graphic elements to a chart. You also learn how to rearrange graphic objects in the worksheet.

Chapter 17, "Developing Business Presentations," focuses on using spreadsheet-publishing techniques to create computer, slide, and overhead presentations. Examples include how to combine text, graphics, and clip art effectively on a single page.

Part IV: Analyzing the Worksheet

Chapter 18, "Manipulating and Analyzing Data," covers how to combine whole and partial units of text, use formulas that make decisions, analyze and obtain data from tables, and create what-if tables.

Chapter 19, "Linking and Consolidating Worksheets," discusses the benefits of using multiple-worksheet files, and shows you how to enter formulas that link worksheets and files, and how to combine and consolidate worksheets.

Chapter 20, "Auditing Worksheets," shows you how to use the Audit feature to find all formulas in a worksheet, formulas that refer to data in a selected range, the cells that a formula references, formulas with circular references, and cells that contain a link to another file.

Chapter 21, "Solving Problems with Solver and Backsolver," shows you how to use Solver and Backsolver to find and evaluate solutions to "what-if" scenarios. Examples illustrate how Solver and Backsolver are used in practical business situations.

Chapter 22, "Managing Multiple Solutions with the Version Manager," shows you how to use the Version Manager feature to keep track of the changing information in worksheets—and how to share this information with others. You learn how to create and display different versions of data in a named range and how to group versions together into scenarios.

Part V: Managing Databases

Chapter 23, "Creating a Database," introduces the simplified 1-2-3 Release 5 for Windows database features. This chapter presents the essential concepts and methods for defining, designing, and creating a 1-2-3 database.

Chapter 24, "Entering and Editing Data in a Database," shows you how to add and delete database records, edit records, insert and delete fields, move a field, and divide and combine fields.

Chapter 25, "Sorting Data," discusses how to sort data in a worksheet according to one, two, or more columns or data. This chapter also explains how to restore worksheet data to its original order if you make a mistake when sorting or need a copy of the original data prior to sorting.

Chapter 26, "Finding and Extracting Data," explains how to search a worksheet to find data. You learn the ways you can list, extract, and delete records in a 1-2-3 database. Also, the chapter explains the different methods for defining the criteria upon which to conduct a search.

Chapter 27, "Understanding Advanced Data Management," covers some of the more advanced database features such as joining multiple databases and using cross tabs and aggregates. You also learn how to create frequency distributions, perform regression analysis, and analyze matrixes.

Chapter 28, "Retrieving Data from External Databases," explains how to create a query table from data in an external database, update or add data to an external table from 1-2-3, create a new external table, and import data from other programs to a 1-2-3 worksheet and "parse" it into columns.

Part VI: Integrating 1-2-3

Chapter 29, "Using 1-2-3 with the Lotus SmartSuite," shows you how to use the Clipboard to perform basic copy-and-paste operations between applications. The chapter also explains how to use the more advanced DDE and OLE capabilities of Lotus SmartSuite applications (1-2-3 for Windows, Ami Pro, Approach, Freelance Graphics, and cc:Mail) to dynamically link data between applications.

Chapter 30, "Using 1-2-3 with Lotus Notes," shows you how to use 1-2-3 effectively with Lotus Notes—a "groupware" application that manages data and information for many users. You learn how to create a Notes Shared file in 1-2-3, how to import a 1-2-3 spreadsheet into a Notes View, how to export a Notes View to 1-2-3, how to create a 1-2-3 linked or embedded object in Notes, and how to use Application Field Exchange with 1-2-3.

Chapter 31, "Integrating 1-2-3 with DOS and Mainframe Applications," explains how to copy and paste information between 1-2-3 and DOS applications, save 1-2-3 worksheets in file formats readable by other applications, and transfer data to and from 1-2-3 and DOS or mainframe applications by using text files.

Part VII: Customizing 1-2-3

Chapter 32, "Customizing the 1-2-3 for Windows Screen," teaches you how to customize the 1-2-3 screen by controlling which elements appear on the 1-2-3 screen, controlling the appearance of the worksheet frame and grid, changing the screen's color scheme, and modifying the desktop.

Chapter 33, "Creating Custom SmartIcon Palettes," shows you how to use and customize 1-2-3's SmartIcons. Specifically, you learn how to switch SmartIcon palettes, hide and display SmartIcons, move and rearrange SmartIcons, create custom SmartIcons, and create custom SmartIcon palettes.

Chapter 34, "Working with Templates and Creating Custom Dialog Boxes," shows you how to use the SmartMaster templates, use and design custom templates, create autoloading worksheets, and design custom dialog boxes for use with 1-2-3 macros.

Part VIII: Automating with Macros

Chapter 35, "Writing 1-2-3 for Windows Macros," is an introduction to the powerful macro capabilities of 1-2-3. This chapter teaches you how to plan, create, format, name, and run macros, as well as how to document and protect macros.

Chapter 36, "Recording and Modifying Macros," teaches you how to record macros automatically, add macro buttons to a worksheet, avoid common macro errors, and translate macros from earlier versions of 1-2-3 for Windows.

Chapter 37, "Using Advanced Macro Techniques," explains the powerful macro commands available in the 1-2-3 Release 5 for Windows macro language. The chapter also includes a reference list of all the macro commands and some examples of their uses.

Chapter 38, "Exploring a Corporate Macro Example," examines a macro-driven application that builds on the lessons learned in the two preceding chapters. This chapter describes the macros used to create an expense report application.

Appendixes

Appendix A, "1-2-3 for Windows Support Services," explains where to get additional support on 1-2-3 for Windows via telephone, fax, or modem.

Appendix B, "SmartIcons Listing," includes a table that lists each of the SmartIcons you'll encounter in 1-2-3 for Windows. The SmartIcons are arranged by the menu (or in some cases, submenu) to which their functions correspond.

Appendix C, "Index of Common Problems," includes a table that categorizes the most common 1-2-3 for Windows problems and provides page numbers referencing the location of solutions to these problems in this book.

Reference Card

In the back of this book is a tear-out reference card that lists 1-2-3 Release 5 for Windows shortcut keys and elements of the 1-2-3 Release 5 for Windows screen.

Conventions Used in This Book

Certain conventions are used in *Using 1-2-3 Release 5 for Windows*, Special Edition, to help you more easily use this book and understand 1-2-3's concepts. The following sections include examples of these conventions to help you distinguish among the different elements.

Special Typefaces and Representations

Special typefaces in *Using 1-2-3 Release 5 for Windows*, Special Edition, include the following:

Type	Meaning
italics	New terms or phrases when initially defined; function and macro command syntax
boldface	Information you are asked to type, including 1-2-3 Release 5 for Windows menu and dialog-box options that appear underlined on-screen, the first character of 1-2-3 Classic commands, and the slash (/) and colon (:) that precede 1-2-3 Classic commands
`special type`	Direct quotations of words that appear on-screen or in a figure; menu command prompts

Elements printed in uppercase include range names such as SALES, functions such as @FIND, and cell references such as A:B19. Also presented in uppercase letters are DOS commands such as CHKDSK and file names such as STATUS.WK4. Mode and status indicators such as Ready and End are printed in initial cap, as they appear on-screen.

In most cases, keys are represented as they appear on the keyboard. The arrow keys usually are represented by name (for example, *the up-arrow key*). The Print Screen key is abbreviated PrtSc; Page Up is PgUp; Insert is Ins; and so on. On your keyboard, these key names may be spelled out or abbreviated differently.

When two keys appear together with a plus sign, such as Shift+Ins, press and hold the first key as you press the second key. When two keys appear together without a plus sign, such as End Home, press and release the first key before you press the second key.

The function keys, F1 through F10, are used for special situations in 1-2-3. In the text, the name of the function key is usually listed with the function key number, such as Edit (F2).

Tip
This paragraph format suggests easier or alternative methods of executing a procedure.

> **Note**
>
> This paragraph format indicates additional information that may help you avoid problems or that should be considered in using the described features.

> **Caution**
>
> This paragraph format warns the reader of hazardous procedures (for example, activities that delete files).

Margin Icons

 Icons appear in the margin to indicate that the procedure described in the text includes instructions for using the appropriate SmartIcons in 1-2-3 Release 5 for Windows.

Special Sections

Using 1-2-3 Release 5 for Windows, Special Edition, uses cross-references to help you access other parts of the book. Beside the relevant paragraphs, related tasks you may need to perform are listed in the margin by section name and page number.

In addition, troubleshooting sections are provided in most chapters to help you find solutions to common problems encountered with the 1-2-3 procedures covered in that section of the book.

Macro Conventions

Conventions that pertain to macros deserve special mention:

- Single-character macro names (Ctrl+*letter* combinations) appear with the backslash (\) and single-character name in lowercase: \a. The \ indicates that you press and hold the Ctrl key as you press the A key.

- Representations of direction keys such as {DOWN} and {NEXTSHEET}, function keys such as {CALC}, and editing keys such as {DEL} appear in uppercase letters and surrounded by curly braces.

- 1-2-3 for Windows' macro commands are enclosed within curly braces—such as {GET-LABEL} and {EDIT-COPY}—when used in a syntax line or within a macro; the same commands generally appear without braces in the text.

- The Enter key is represented by the tilde (~).

Part I

Everyday
Worksheet Tasks

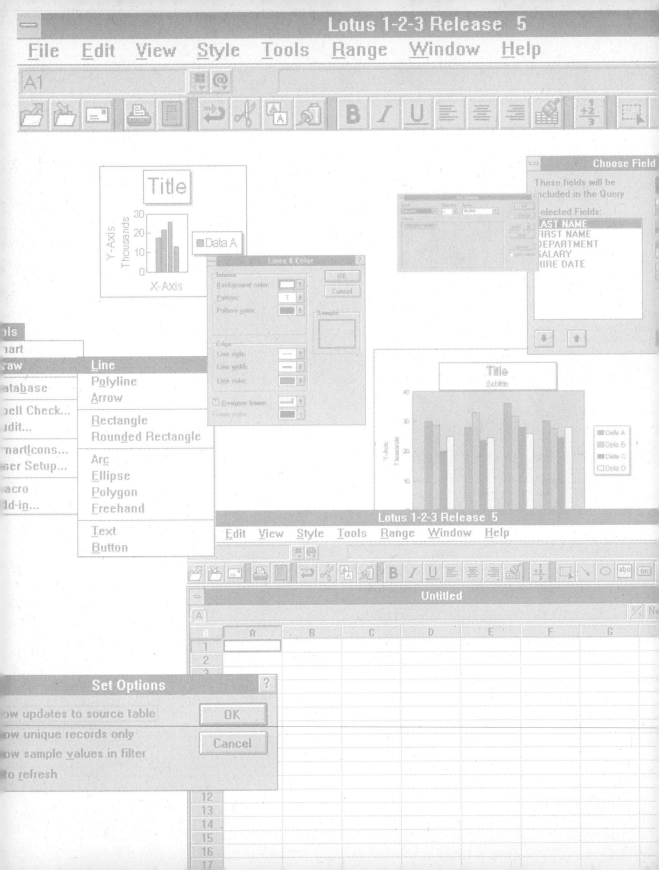

Chapter 1

Getting Around in 1-2-3 and Windows

If you are not familiar with Microsoft Windows or 1-2-3 for Windows, this chapter provides an introduction to using 1-2-3 in the Windows environment. You can use the ideas and concepts you learn here in all your 1-2-3 operations and, in fact, in all your Windows use.

You start 1-2-3 and become familiar with the screen elements. From there, you learn how to use the mouse or keyboard to choose menu commands, access the quick menu, make selections in dialog boxes, and access the 1-2-3 Help system. You also learn how to manipulate windows so that you can access and use multiple worksheet files at once.

In this chapter, you learn to do the following:

- Start and quit 1-2-3 for Windows

- Choose commands from the menu and make selections in dialog boxes

- Use the keyboard or mouse for 1-2-3 operations

- Work with windows

- Use the SmartIcon palette

- Get help

Using 1-2-3 in the Windows Environment

Microsoft Windows 3.1 is a powerful, easy-to-use extension to the MS-DOS operating system. If you are new to Windows 3.1, the following basic information should help you get started with Windows 3.1.

Windows 3.1 is a *graphical user interface* (GUI). A GUI combined with a PC that has an 80386, 80486, or Pentium processor offers new levels of power and ease of use compared to non-GUI operating environments (such as DOS).

A mouse is highly recommended although not specifically required. Using Windows 3.1 and 1-2-3 for Windows are much easier with a mouse.

Windows 3.1 can run DOS programs and Windows programs (in fact, programs such as 1-2-3 for Windows, Ami Pro, and PageMaker for Windows cannot run without Windows 3.1). Programs designed for Windows 3.1 have many advantages over non-Windows programs, including the capability to access much more memory than the 640K available to DOS-based programs.

One feature that makes Windows 3.1 programs easier to use is the nature of the GUI. Instead of typing commands to start and run a Windows 3.1 program, you can select the program's *application icon* (a small picture that represents the program). Figure 1.1 shows several typical Windows 3.1 application icons displayed in the Accessories group window.

Fig. 1.1

The Accessories group window and its application icons.

Application icons

Program group icons

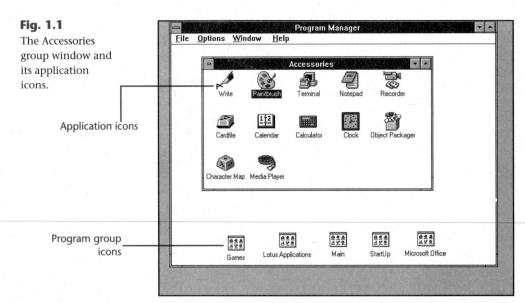

Since personal computers entered the business world over 10 years ago, Lotus 1-2-3 has been one of the most popular software packages for PCs. Over 20 million people use 1-2-3 to solve business problems, analyze financial transactions, perform statistical analysis in engineering and production environments, and so on. Lotus 1-2-3 offers users an electronic worksheet, a database manager, business graphics, and a presentation-level report generator—all in one package.

1-2-3 Release 5 for Windows is similar to other versions of 1-2-3 in its basic functions, although Release 5 has many impressive enhancements. 1-2-3 Release 5 for Windows can be used for simple applications or very complex financial planning. The program organizes data and includes typical database functions such as those that sort, extract, and find data within 1-2-3 databases (as well as external disk-based databases such as dBASE, Paradox, Informix, the IBM OS/2 Database Manager, and SQL Server). With 1-2-3 Release 5 for Windows, you can produce graphic representations of financial and scientific data and add those graphics directly to the worksheet to create presentation-quality reports.

1-2-3 for Windows extends a new level of capability and performance to the personal computer user by using Wysiwyg (what-you-see-is-what-you-get) capabilities and other advanced features that take full advantage of the Microsoft Windows operating environment (versions 3.0, 3.1, 3.11, and Windows for Workgroups 3.1 and 3.11).

In fact, 1-2-3 for Windows paved the way for a new operating standard for DOS versions of 1-2-3. Older DOS versions of 1-2-3, such as 2.2 and 3.1, were primarily character based, so the on-screen display and graphics capabilities were limited. Versions 2.4 and 3.4 have been modeled after 1-2-3 for Windows, so that they incorporate features similar to Windows, for example, use of the mouse and icon palettes. These GUI features create a powerful yet easy-to-use spreadsheet environment.

Windows gives you wide varieties of colors and fonts so that you can organize data in easily identifiable ways and create presentation-quality graphics. Full mouse support gives you direct manipulation of objects; for example, you can size and move Worksheet windows, select ranges, and execute commands with the mouse. A Wysiwyg display enables you to see data on-screen almost exactly as it appears when printed. Pull-down and cascade menus show where you are in the menu structure at all times.

Windows also gives 1-2-3 for Windows speed, power, and flexibility. The Windows multitasking capabilities enable you to print one worksheet, recalculate another, and graph another all at the same time. With Dynamic Data

Exchange (DDE) and Object Linking and Embedding (OLE), you can link and embed 1-2-3 for Windows worksheets with other Windows applications. The ability to open multiple windows and applications enables you to view several worksheets at the same time or display the Help window while you work.

Starting 1-2-3 for Windows

You can start 1-2-3 for Windows three different ways. The normal way to start 1-2-3 for Windows is from the Program Manager. You can also start 1-2-3 for Windows from the File Manager by opening the 1-2-3 for Windows executable file or a 1-2-3 for Windows worksheet file. The following sections describe these options.

> **Note**
>
> Need more information on using Windows? Que offers a variety of books for all levels of readers. Beginners should consult *Easy Windows 3.1* or *Windows 3.1 QuickStart*. Intermediate or less-experienced users may find *I Hate Windows* or *Windows VisiRef* (a visual reference guide to Windows) particularly helpful. For maximum detail in a reference format, try *Using Windows 3.1*, Special Edition. Advanced users with special needs should consider *Killer Windows Utilities*.

Starting 1-2-3 for Windows from the Program Manager

If you have installed 1-2-3 for Windows according to the directions in Appendix A, the 1-2-3 for Windows program is stored in the following drive and directory: C:\123R5W\PROGRAMS. The 1-2-3 for Windows icons may be in a separate group window, called Lotus Applications, or located in the Windows Applications group window. If you choose to install the 1-2-3 for Windows Dialog Editor, Macro Translator, Mapping, Lotus Guided Tour, or the View Product Updates, these application icons are located in the same group window as the program icon.

To start 1-2-3 for Windows, follow these steps:

1. If necessary, start Windows from the DOS prompt by typing **win** and pressing Enter.

2. Open or activate the group window that contains 1-2-3 for Windows. This is usually the Lotus Applications group. Figure 1.2 shows the Lotus

Applications group window open with the 1-2-3 for Windows program icon selected.

If the Lotus Applications group is minimized to an icon at the bottom of the screen, you can open the group by double-clicking the icon. If the Lotus Applications group is open on-screen, activate it by clicking in the title bar or pressing Ctrl+Tab until the window becomes active. The title bar will be highlighted when the window is active.

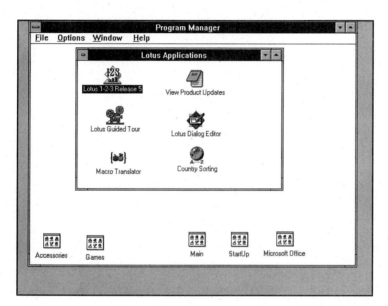

Fig. 1.2
Double-click the 1-2-3 for Windows program icon to start 1-2-3.

3. To use the mouse to start 1-2-3 for Windows, double-click the 1-2-3 for Windows program icon. To use the keyboard to start 1-2-3 for Windows, press the arrow keys until the 1-2-3 for Windows program icon is selected as shown in figure 1.2 and then press Enter.

Note

You can have 1-2-3 for Windows start automatically when you start up Windows by copying the 1-2-3 for Windows icon to the StartUp program group. To perform this copy, press Ctrl and drag the 1-2-3 application icon to the StartUp program group window.

Troubleshooting

I can't find the 1-2-3 for Windows application icon.

The 1-2-3 for Windows application icon is normally placed in the Lotus Applications program group. If you can't find it, it may be in a different program group, like the Windows Applications group. Open each of your program groups to look for the 1-2-3 application icon. If you still do not find it, you may have to set up 1-2-3 again by using the Windows Setup program in the Main program group.

Starting 1-2-3 for Windows from the File Manager

You can start 1-2-3 for Windows from the File Manager by double-clicking the 123W.EXE file in a File Manager window, as shown in figure 1.3.

Fig. 1.3
You can start
1-2-3 from the
File Manager.

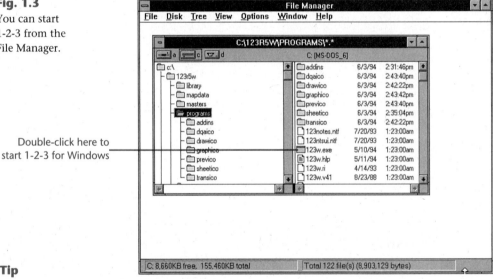

Double-click here to
start 1-2-3 for Windows

Tip
You can start
1-2-3 for Win-
dows and open
a specific work-
sheet file by
double-clicking
the worksheet
file's icon in the
File Manager.

If you have a worksheet file that you use every day, you can create an icon for that file in one of your program groups by dragging the file icon from the File Manager window to the desired program group window. This means that you must arrange your screen so that you can see the File Manager window and the program group window on-screen at once. Just think how convenient it would be to have an icon for your budget worksheet or expense report worksheet in one of your program groups!

Starting a New Worksheet or Using an Existing Sheet

When you open 1-2-3 for Windows, the Welcome to 1-2-3 dialog box shown in figure 1.4 appears. This box gives you the following choices:

■ *Create a new worksheet.* If you press Enter or click OK, you will be choosing Create a New Worksheet, because this is the default selection. When you create a new worksheet, you can create a plain worksheet or choose a predefined worksheet from a list of SmartMasters.

■ *Work on an existing worksheet.* If you click on this selection, you will see the Open File dialog box that enables you to select an existing worksheet from the disk. You will learn more about opening existing worksheets in Chapter 2.

■ *Start Tutorial.* This starts the on-line tutorial, which leads you through the basic functions of 1-2-3.

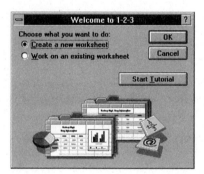

Fig. 1.4
You can choose to create a new worksheet or to work an existing worksheet from the Welcome to 1-2-3 dialog box.

When you choose Create a new worksheet, you see the New File dialog box shown in figure 1.5. Notice that **C**reate a plain worksheet is checked, so that if you press Enter or click OK at this point, you will be starting out with a blank worksheet. Use this when you wish to create your own worksheet from scratch.

The New File dialog box shows a list of SmartMasters. *SmartMasters* are worksheets that have been predesigned for many common applications. They contain text, formatting, and formulas, so that all you need to do is enter your specific information into the worksheet. These enable you to create a variety of spreadsheets with a minimum amount of work.

Fig. 1.5
Press Enter or
click OK to start a
plain worksheet
or choose a
SmartMaster
from the list.

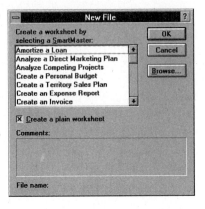

Tip
You can see a
description of a
SmartMaster by
clicking on the
SmartMaster
name in the
list.

Note

If you do not want to see the Welcome to 1-2-3 dialog box every time you enter
1-2-3, choose **T**ools **U**ser Setup and turn the S**k**ip New File and Welcome screens
check box off. This also turns off the New File dialog box that enables you to choose
a SmartMaster. However, if you do not plan to use the SmartMasters, you can save
time by turning these dialog boxes off.

Understanding the 1-2-3
for Windows Screen

1-2-3 for Windows, like other versions of 1-2-3, can be described as an *electronic accountant's pad* or an *electronic spreadsheet*. When you start 1-2-3 for
Windows, the computer screen displays a grid of columns and rows into
which you can enter text, numbers, or formulas as an accountant does on
one sheet of a columnar pad. 1-2-3 for Windows extends this analogy further
by offering true three-dimensional worksheets. You can easily page through
the worksheets by using the worksheet tabs, and you can view up to three
worksheets on-screen at a time.

In 1-2-3 for Windows, as in other versions of 1-2-3, the worksheet is the basis
of the whole product. Whether you work with a database application or create graphs, you create everything within the structure of the worksheet. All
commands and procedures are initiated from the 1-2-3 Release 5 for Windows
menu, the 1-2-3 Classic menu, or the SmartIcon palette. Release 5 also enables you to access frequently used commands with quick menus and a live
status bar. You create graphs from data entered in the worksheet and perform

database operations on data organized into the worksheet's column-and-row format.

Access to all of these features is accomplished via various screen elements. All Windows applications have some common screen elements. Once you learn how to work with the common features in all windows, you can learn new Windows applications easily. Figure 1.6 shows one way your screen might look when you start 1-2-3 for Windows and Table 1.1 describes standard windows screen elements.

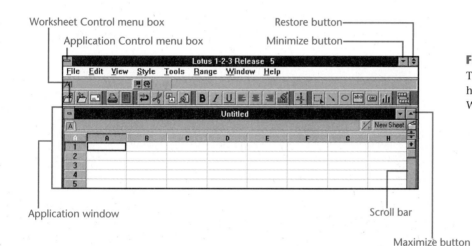

Worksheet Control menu box

Application Control menu box

Restore button

Minimize button

Application window

Scroll bar

Maximize button

Fig. 1.6
The 1-2-3 screen has many standard Windows features.

Everyday Worksheet Tasks

Table 1.1 Standard Windows Screen Elements	
Part	**Description**
Application window	The window within which 1-2-3 for Windows runs.
Application Control menu box	Opens a menu that enables you to control the application window using the keyboard.
Minimize button	A downward facing arrowhead, located at the upper right corner of all windows, which reduces the window to an icon at the bottom of the screen.
Maximize button	An upward facing arrowhead, located at the upper right corner of all windows before they are maximized, which enlarges the window to fill the available area. When you maximize an application, it fills the entire screen. When you maximize a Worksheet window, it fills up the entire application window.

(continues)

Table 1.1 Continued	
Part	**Description**
Restore button	Arrowheads pointing up and down. When you maximize a window, the Maximize button changes to a Restore button. Click this button to restore the window to its previous size.
Scroll bar	A gray horizontal or vertical bar that enables you to scroll the screen using the mouse. The scroll box in the bar shows the current position, relative to the entire worksheet.
Worksheet Control menu box	Opens a menu that enables you to control the Worksheet window.

Other parts of the screen are specific to the 1-2-3 for Windows program. The 1-2-3 for Windows screen display is divided into several parts: the control panel, work area (containing the SmartIcons and the Worksheet window or windows), and the status bar. Together, these parts enable you to work with and display worksheets and graphs. Figure 1.7 shows some of the screen elements that are specific to the 1-2-3 for Windows program and these screen parts are described in Table 1.2.

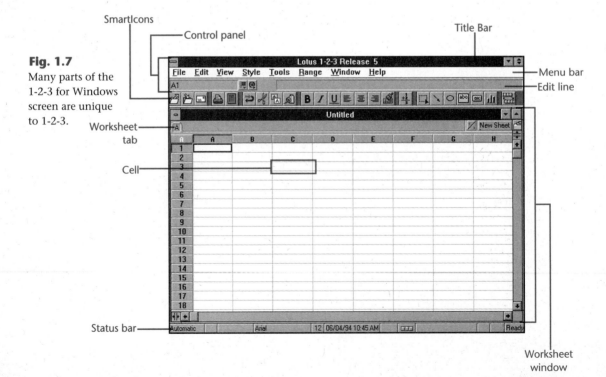

Fig. 1.7
Many parts of the 1-2-3 for Windows screen are unique to 1-2-3.

Table 1.2 1-2-3 for Windows Screen Elements

Part	Description
Worksheet window	A window within the 1-2-3 for Windows program that displays a specific worksheet file with rows and columns into which you enter data. There may be multiple worksheet files open on-screen at once.
Control panel	The top three lines of the program window, containing the title bar, menu bar, and edit line.
Work area	The section of the 1-2-3 window between the control panel and the status bar.
SmartIcons	A bar containing buttons or icons that provide quick access to many commands and tools available in 1-2-3 for Windows.
Worksheet tabs	Tabs to identify different worksheets within a 1-2-3 for Windows file. These provide a method of moving between multiple worksheets.
Cell	One location in the worksheet, the intersection of a column and row.
Status bar	A bar at the bottom of the screen that provides information and a means of quickly changing fonts, sizes, formatting, and icon palettes.

Each of these elements is described in more detail in the following sections.

Troubleshooting

My screen has different SmartIcons than Figure 1.4.

There are many SmartIcon palettes available in 1-2-3 for Windows. To make your screen look like the samples, click the symbol that looks like three buttons in the status bar. This displays a menu of SmartIcon palettes. Click Default Sheet to choose the palette shown in the figures.

My worksheet doesn't have a title bar.

Perhaps your Worksheet window is maximized inside the 1-2-3 for Windows program window. If you are familiar with the Restore button, click the lower Restore button (the Worksheet window's Restore button) at the upper right corner of the screen. If not, read the later section "Manipulating Windows."

The Control Panel

The control panel, which appears at the top of the program window, contains three segments:

- The *title bar*, which contains the program title, the Control menu box, and the Minimize, Maximize, or Restore buttons.

- The *menu bar*, which displays the 1-2-3 menus currently available.

- The *edit line*, which displays information about the active cell and enables you to edit data in the worksheet.

The Edit Line

▶ "Entering and Editing Data," p. 83

The edit line provides information about your worksheet and tools for entering data into the worksheet. Figure 1.8 shows each element of the edit line.

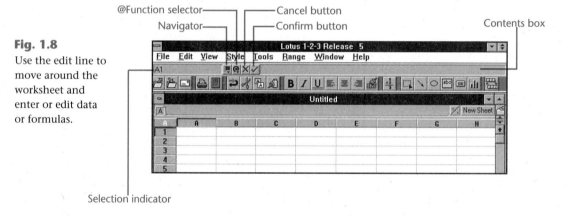

Fig. 1.8
Use the edit line to move around the worksheet and enter or edit data or formulas.

The edit line is made up of these items:

▶ "Understanding Worksheets and Files," p. 60

- *Selection indicator.* This indicator displays the address of the current selection (the selected cell or range). A *cell address* consists of the column letter and the row number of the cell in the worksheet. The address of the top left cell, for example, is A1. If you add another worksheet to your file, the worksheets are initially lettered A, B, etc. In this case, the cell address is made up of the worksheet letter, followed by a colon, the column letter, and the row number. So, the upper left corner of the first worksheet would be A:A1. For more information on multiple worksheets, see the section on "The Worksheet Window" later in this chapter. When you select a range, the contents box displays two addresses separated by two periods, which define opposite corners of the range.

■ *Navigator.* This is a pull-down list (click the navigator to see the list) that displays all named ranges and objects in the worksheet. If you choose a name from this list while you are entering data into a cell (that is, while you are working in Edit mode), 1-2-3 places the selected name in the formula that you are entering. Otherwise, choosing a name from the navigator list selects (or jumps to) the named range or item. If there are no named ranges, 1-2-3 displays an error dialog box when you click the Navigator. Just click OK to clear the dialog box.

■ *@Function selector.* This displays a list of functions available in 1-2-3. You can use this tool to insert functions into the formula you are currently typing or simply to remind yourself of functions available in 1-2-3.

■ *Cancel button, Confirm button.* These appear only when you are entering or editing data on the edit line. Click the Confirm button to enter the data or click the Cancel button to undo the entry and return the cell to its previous state.

▶ "Entering Data into the Worksheet," p. 84

■ *Contents box.* When you enter information into a 1-2-3 for Windows worksheet, the information appears both in the contents box and in the selected cell. When you highlight a cell, the cell's contents appear in the contents box. The difference between the information displayed in the contents box and the information displayed in the cell is that the cell displays the *result* of information that you enter. If you enter a formula, for example, the cell displays the result of the formula—not the formula itself. The contents box, on the other hand, displays the formula exactly as you entered it.

▶ "Entering Functions," p. 137

The SmartIcons

SmartIcons are tools that appear below the control panel in the Worksheet window. Some SmartIcons are shortcuts for menu commands. One icon executes the **F**ile **S**ave command; another adds an outline with a drop shadow. Another icon automatically totals data, providing a shortcut for entering a formula..

The SmartIcons you see at the top of the screen are only a few of the many icons available in 1-2-3 for Windows. You can customize the icon set or choose icons from other sets. The later section "SmartIcon Basics" describes in detail how to use this special 1-2-3 feature.

▶ "Customizing the SmartIcons," p. 982

Tip
The location of
the SmartIcons
palette can be
changed using
the **Tools**
SmartIcons
command.
Placing the
palette at the
top or bottom
of the screen
fits the maxi-
mum number
of icons.

1-2-3 for Windows usually displays the SmartIcons near the top of the screen, below the selection indicator and contents box.

The Worksheet Window

1-2-3 for Windows creates special files called *worksheet files*. Each application you create in 1-2-3 uses a worksheet file. When you open a worksheet file in 1-2-3, the file appears in a window called a *Worksheet window*. You can open and view several Worksheet windows at one time and even arrange them on-screen for convenience.

Figure 1.9 shows 1-2-3 with several Worksheet windows in view, including one minimized Worksheet window. Notice that all Worksheet windows appear inside the *1-2-3 window*, in the space below the SmartIcons.

Each worksheet has its own title bar, which contains a Control menu, Mini-mize button, and Maximize or Restore button. These are standard items in all windows. You can use them to move and size the individual Worksheet windows within the 1-2-3 program window. In figure 1.9, you can see two Worksheet windows that have been moved and sized, plus a third worksheet that has been minimized.

Fig. 1.9
1-2-3 for Windows
screen showing
multiple work-
sheets open and
a minimized
worksheet

Open worksheets

Minimized
worksheet

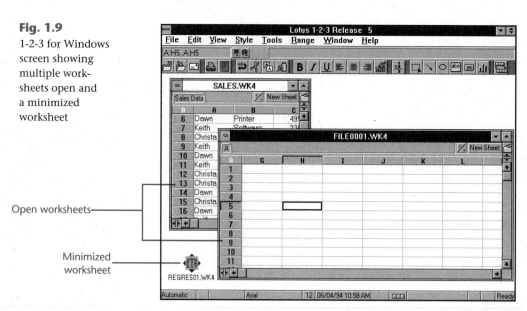

One file can contain up to 256 worksheets; each worksheet is made up of 256 columns (labeled A through IV) and 8,192 rows (numbered consecutively). Each worksheet is identified by a letter followed by a colon. A: is the first worksheet; B: is the second; C: is the third; and so on (up to IV:). 1-2-3 also uses worksheet tabs, which appear at the top of the worksheet, to identify each worksheet in the file. They are initially named A, B, C, and so on (up to IV). Figure 1.10 shows worksheet tabs and the New Sheet button that can be used to add worksheets to a file.

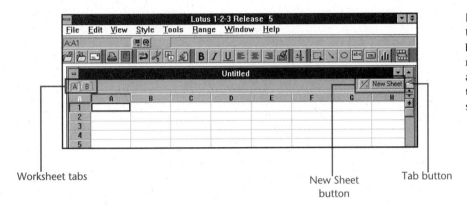

Worksheet tabs

New Sheet button

Tab button

Fig. 1.10
Use the New Sheet button to add multiple sheets to a file and the tabs to move from sheet to sheet.

I

Everyday Worksheet Tasks

Troubleshooting

My worksheet doesn't have any tabs, not even one for the first worksheet, which should be labeled A.

The Tab button (just above the vertical scroll bar on the right side of the window) turns the tab display on or off. Perhaps you clicked on this by accident. Just click the tab button again to see the worksheet tabs.

Tip
You can assign specific names to the worksheet tabs by double-clicking the tab and typing a new name.

The intersections of rows and columns in the worksheet form *cells*; you enter data in cells. Each cell is identified by an address that consists of a worksheet letter (or worksheet name), column letter, and row number. Potentially, you can fill over two million cells in one worksheet and include 256 worksheets in one file. Many users, however, never handle this much data—or do not have the necessary computer equipment.

▶ "Moving around the Worksheet" p. 66

The Status Bar

The *status bar* is the bottom line of the screen. This bar displays information about the attributes of the current cell, such as the font applied to the cell and the number of decimal places used. As you move from cell to cell in the worksheet, the status bar changes to reflect the attributes of each cell.

▶ "Enhancing the
Appearance of
Data," p. 343

The status bar also provides a quick method of changing cell attributes. Simply click any formatting attribute displayed in the status bar to display a list of options for that attribute.

The status bar displays other information in the special indicators described in the following section (see fig. 1.11). The status bar provides information and an easy way to change the format, font, and size of data in cells. The section between the SmartIcons selector and the mode indicator includes the status indicator and the Calc and circular-reference buttons.

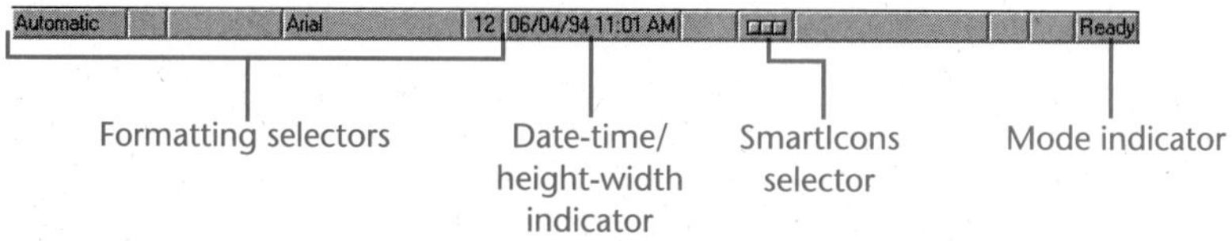

Fig. 1.11
The segments
of the status
bar display
much useful
information.

| Automatic | Arial | 12 | 06/04/94 11:01 AM | ⬚⬚⬚ | Ready |

Formatting selectors   Date-time/height-width indicator   SmartIcons selector   Mode indicator

Tip
You can re-
move the status
bar by using
the **V**iew Set
View **P**refer-
ences com-
mand and
deselecting the
Status **B**ar
option in the
Preferences
dialog box.

> **Note**
>
> If you highlight two or more cells that contain different attributes, the status bar is blank, indicating that several attributes apply to the selection. If you choose a new attribute for the selection, the attribute applies to all the selected cells.

The Mode Indicators

The *mode indicator* appears at the right end of the status bar. This indicator tells you what mode 1-2-3 for Windows is in and what you can do next. When 1-2-3 for Windows is waiting for your next action, the mode indicator is Ready. When you change the information in a cell, the mode indicator changes to Edit. Table 1.3 lists the mode indicators and their meanings.

Table 1.3   Mode Indicators

Mode	Description
Edit	You pressed F2 (Edit) to edit an entry, made an incorrect entry, or are positioned in a text box in a dialog box. 1-2-3 for Windows places you in Edit mode automatically if it does not understand what you entered.
Error	1-2-3 is displaying an error message. Press F1 (Help) to get Help, or press Esc or Enter to clear the error message.
Find	You chose Tools Database Find Records.
Label	You are entering a label.

Mode	Description
Menu	You pressed Alt, F10 (Menu) or the slash (/) key to choose a menu option. 1-2-3 is displaying a menu of commands.
Names	1-2-3 is displaying a list of range names, graph names, print-settings names, functions, macro commands, or external-table names.
Point	1-2-3 is prompting you to specify a range, or you are creating a formula by highlighting a range.
Ready	1-2-3 is ready for you to enter data or choose a command.
Value	You are entering a value.
Wait	1-2-3 is completing a command or process, such as saving a file.

The Status Indicators

Some of the status indicators just let you know that you pressed a certain key, for example End, or Alt F6 for Zoom; whereas others, such as Circ and Calc indicate potential errors or actions that you should take. Table 1.4 lists and explains these indicators.

▶ "Handling Circular References," p. 131

Table 1.4 Status Indicators	
Indicator	**Description**
Calc	You need to recalculate formulas by pressing F9 (Calc) or by clicking the Calc button in the status bar.
Circ	You entered a formula that contains a circular reference. Click the Circ button in the status bar to jump to the circular reference.
Cmd	1-2-3 is running a macro.
End	You pressed the End key to use it with a direction key.
Group	The current file is in Group mode.
Rec	You chose Tools Macro Record to record your actions as macro commands in the Transcript window. To stop recording, choose Tools Macro Stop Recording.
RO	The current file has read-only status, which means you cannot save changes to the file unless you get the file reservation. RO appears in the title bar of the Worksheet window, next to the file name.

(continues)

Everyday Worksheet Tasks

I

Table 1.4 Continued	
Indicator	**Description**
Step	You pressed Alt+F2 (Record) and chose Step to run a macro in Step mode.
Zoom	After using **V**iew **S**plit to create panes, you pressed Alt+F6 (Zoom) for a full-screen view of the current window.

The SmartIcon Selector

▶ "Using the Standard SmartIcon Palettes," p. 979

The status bar contains a special tool that helps you choose SmartIcon palettes. Just click the SmartIcon selector to view a list of palettes. Choose the desired palette from the list and the screen changes to reflect your selection. You can change back again at any time by repeating the procedure.

The Date-Time/Height-Width Indicator

The date-time/height-width indicator on the status bar shows you the current time and date according to the computer's internal clock. You can change the time and date using Windows Control Panel. If you click this indicator, the time and date display change to a row-height and column-width indicator. Click this indicator to switch between the two displays.

The Formatting Selectors

The left side of the status bar includes several formatting selectors. These buttons serve two purposes: first, they display information about the format of the active cell or block. (If the active block contains conflicting formats, the indicator displays nothing for that format.) For example, if you click cell A4, the font selector displays the font currently active in cell A4. The second function these selectors serve is that they let you change the formats of the selected cell or block. Click the selector you want to change to view a list of additional selections. Next, choose from the list to change the format.

Because of their dual purpose, these selectors are more than just feedback for the current selection; they let you control the formatting of your worksheet on the spot. For more information about worksheet formatting and these selectors, refer to Chapter 9.

Using the Mouse with 1-2-3 for Windows

One of the most exciting 1-2-3 for Windows features is its mouse capabilities. As with the keyboard, the mouse enables you to choose commands and manipulate objects on-screen. You can perform many tasks more quickly with the mouse, such as moving through windows, setting column widths, and moving around in dialog boxes. Some tasks in 1-2-3 for Windows can be performed *only* with a mouse—such as using SmartIcons, selecting individual elements in a chart, selecting collections of data, and selecting one or more drawn objects, and quick menus.

Most mouse devices have a left and a right button. You use the left button to select cells and ranges, use menus, and enter information in dialog boxes. When the mouse pointer highlights a SmartIcon, pressing the right mouse button displays the SmartIcon's description. If you select a range of cells or an object in a chart, clicking the right mouse button displays a context-sensitive quick menu. Table 1.5 describes the mouse terminology you need to know as you read this book.

Table 1.5 Mouse Terminology	
Term	**Meaning**
Point	Place the mouse pointer over the menu, cell, or data you want to select or move.
Click	Press and quickly release the left mouse button.
Double-click	Quickly press and release the left mouse button twice.
Drag	Press and hold down the left mouse button and then move the mouse. This action, which is also called "click-and-drag," is usually performed to highlight a range of cells or to move an object.
Select	To select a range of cells, click and drag the mouse pointer over the range. To select an object, click the mouse pointer on the object.

Usually, the mouse pointer is in the shape of an arrow. As you perform different tasks in 1-2-3 for Windows, the mouse pointer changes shape. In the Help window, for example, the mouse pointer becomes a hand with an extended index finger, indicating that you can select highlighted Help topics. Table 1.6 explains the various shapes of the mouse pointer.

Table 1.6 Mouse Pointers	
Shape	**Meaning**
	Normal operation; you are pointing to a cell, menu, icon, or other area of the screen that you can select by clicking.
	The pointer is over data in the contents box or a text box; if you click the box, you can edit or enter data.
	The pointer is over the lower right corner of a selected cell or range that you can drag to fill contiguous cells by example or drag to clear.
	The pointer is over a worksheet range; you can drag the current selection or a copy of the current selection.
	You can drag the current selection to a new location.
	You can drag a copy of the current selection to a new location.
	The pointer is in a row or column heading and close to a grid line; you can widen a column or heighten a row.
	You can select a worksheet range (using Range Selector in dialog box).
	1-2-3 for Windows is in the middle of an operation and you cannot do anything with the mouse.
	The pointer is over a highlighted Help topic or a macro button.
	You can position a new chart on the worksheet.
	You can position a drawn object.
	You can select drawn objects.
	You can use the pointer to create a freehand drawing.
	The pointer is on a window border; you can resize the window.
	You chose **S**ize or **M**ove from the Control menu, and the pointer is on a window border; you can resize the window by using the keyboard.

Using 1-2-3 for Windows Menus

Almost every task you perform in 1-2-3 for Windows is part of a *command*. Commands help you copy, move, and format data, create charts, open and close worksheet files, and customize worksheets with colors and fonts, and so on.

There are actually three different types of menus in 1-2-3 for Windows:

- *Main menu*. This is the menu bar across the top of the 1-2-3 for Windows screen, which includes selections that enable you to access the 1-2-3 commands. Unlike other versions of 1-2-3, the 1-2-3 for Windows menus always appear on-screen. The main menu changes from time to time, depending on your actions. For example, when you work with charts, the **R**ange menu changes to the **C**hart menu to provide you with commands specific to charting.

- *Quick menu*. This type of menu pops up onto the Worksheet window when you press the right mouse button. It consolidates commands from several of the 1-2-3 for Windows main menu selections onto one easy-to-use menu. The quick menus contain different commands, depending on what is selected in the worksheet.

- *Classic menu*. This is the classic 1-2-3 Release 3.1 menu and is available to make the transition to 1-2-3 for Windows easier for experienced users of 1-2-3 for DOS.

Understanding the Main Menu

All the commands on the 1-2-3 for Windows main menu lead to pull-down menus; many (but not all) pull-down menus lead to cascade menus, which appear beside the pull-down menu. Other menu options open dialog boxes (described later in this chapter).

Table 1.7 summarizes the selections in the 1-2-3 for Windows main menu.

Table 1.7 Menu Selections	
Selection	**Description**
File	**F**ile commands save, open, and manage files, as well as send electronic mail and print worksheets and charts.

(continues)

Table 1.7 Continued	
Selection	**Description**
Edit	**E**dit commands link cells from one worksheet to another, copy and move cells or their attributes, erase the contents of cells, undo your last action, change the arrangement of drawn objects, link to other Windows programs, and find or replace data.
View	**V**iew commands change the on-screen appearance of the worksheet by changing magnification, freezing the headings so that they are always visible, or splitting the Worksheet window to view multiple sections of the worksheet.
Style	**S**tyle commands change the format of values in the worksheet, including the font, color, and numeric format of data. This menu also has options for changing the height and width of cells, protecting cells from changes, hiding sections of the worksheet, inserting and deleting page breaks, and changing worksheet default settings.
Tools	**T**ools commands provide access to various 1-2-3 features such as charting, mapping, graphics, database management, spelling, auditing, SmartIcons, and macros.
Range	**R**ange commands access the Version Manager window and fill, manipulate, and analyze ranges of data. This includes sorting, parsing, naming, and transposing ranges.
Chart	**C**hart commands control the 1-2-3 for Windows charting feature. (The **C**hart menu replaces the **R**ange menu when a chart is selected.)
Window	**W**indow commands arrange Worksheet windows within the 1-2-3 window.
Help	**H**elp commands access on-line, context-sensitive help; use these commands to search for specific topics, learn 1-2-3 basics, and run a tutorial program.

Choosing Commands from the Menu

1-2-3 for Windows uses the standard Windows techniques for choosing commands from the menus. You can choose commands with the mouse, arrow keys, keystrokes, or shortcut keys. Many users mix the way they select commands based on a specific situation. If your hands are on the keyboard while you are initially entering data into a worksheet, you might want to select commands with keystrokes. However, if you are editing and revising a worksheet and your hand is on the mouse, use the mouse techniques to select commands.

To display a pull-down menu, you use one of these methods:

■ Use the mouse to click the command you want; 1-2-3 for Windows automatically activates the menu and displays the pull-down menu options.

■ Activate the main menu by pressing the Alt key or the F10 (Menu) key. Use the arrow keys to move the menu pointer to the name of the command and then press Enter or the down-arrow key to see the pull-down menu.

When you activate the main menu and press the right- or left-arrow key, the menu pointer moves across the menu bar and highlights commands. When you reach the first or last item in the main menu, pressing the right- or left-arrow key activates the Control menus for the 1-2-3 window and the Worksheet window.

■ Press and hold down the Alt key and type the underlined letter of the command. For example, to choose the **R**ange menu, hold down Alt and type **r**. The Alt key activates the menu, and **r** selects the **R**ange menu option.

> **Note**
>
> The underlined letter in a command or option is called a *hot key*. The hot key is often the first letter of a command or option, but not always.

Using Pull-Down and Cascade Menus

When you choose a command from the main menu, the resulting pull-down menu appears. Menu items in the pull-down menu can appear with a triangle, an *ellipsis* (...), or nothing beside them (see fig. 1.12). If the menu item has a triangle, the item results in a cascade menu when selected. If the menu item has an ellipsis, 1-2-3 for Windows needs more information to complete the command and displays a *dialog box* for you to complete. If the menu item has no marker, the item is usually the last selection in the command sequence: if you click the command (or highlight it and press Enter), 1-2-3 for Windows executes the selected command.

To choose a command from the pull-down or cascade menus, use one of these techniques:

■ Use the mouse to click the command you want. 1-2-3 for Windows performs the command and displays the cascade menu or a dialog box, depending on the situation.

Tip

If you have experience in other versions of 1-2-3, just press the slash key (/) and the 1-2-3 Classic menu (which includes 1-2-3 for DOS Release 3.1 commands) displays at the top of the screen.

■ Use the arrow keys to highlight the command and then press Enter.

■ Type the underlined letter of the command. For example, to choose **N**ame from the **R**ange menu, type **n**. The Range menu must already be open (pulled down).

Fig. 1.12
Arrowheads
indicate a cascade
menu, while an
ellipsis indicates
that a dialog box
appears.

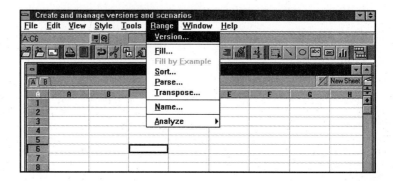

Note

You can explore command menus without actually executing the commands. Highlight a menu option on the main menu or a pull-down menu and read the command description in the title bar to find out more about the selected option. For more detailed information about a command, move the menu pointer to the command and press F1 (Help).

Troubleshooting

I pull down a menu and choose a gray option but nothing happens.

Grayed out menu selections are standard in all Windows applications. It means that the particular menu selection is not available or is not appropriate at this time. Many commands require you to select an area of the worksheet before you can issue a command. Another example is that **E**dit **P**aste may be gray if you have not copied anything.

Tip
If you pull down a
menu by mistake,
click the main
menu word
again. The menu
disappears.

Canceling a Command

If you make a mistake while choosing menu commands, press Esc to return to the preceding menu. If you press Esc at the main menu, you deactivate the menu and return to Ready mode.

If you execute a command accidentally, you usually can undo the action of that command. For example, if you erase a range by mistake, you can press Alt+Backspace (Undo), click the Undo SmartIcon, or use the **E**dit **U**ndo command to recover the erased range.

Saving Time with Quick Menus

A 1-2-3 for Windows quick menu combines commands from various menus to make them available in a single location as you work in the worksheet. Quick menus provide all the commands you are likely to require for the current activity and they appear right in the worksheet location, so that you don't have to move the mouse up to the top of the screen to choose commands.

▶ "Using the Undo Feature," p. 113

To access a quick menu, follow these steps:

1. Select a range of cells in the worksheet if you wish to perform a command on the range.

2. Click the right mouse button on the cell, range, column or row heading, or other worksheet or graphic element with which you are working.

The quick menu that appears is appropriate for the selected element. For example, figure 1.13 shows the quick menu that appears for a 1-2-3 for Windows chart.

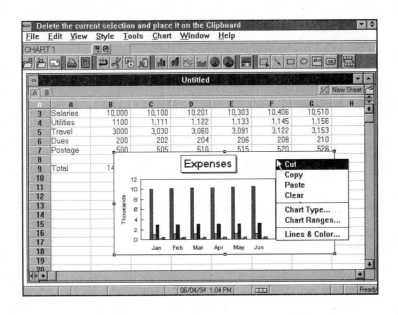

Fig. 1.13
When a chart is selected, the quick menu includes commands for working with the chart.

Working with Dialog Boxes

When 1-2-3 for Windows needs more information about a menu command, a *dialog box* is displayed. To execute the command, you must complete the dialog box and choose OK or press Enter. You can also cancel a command before it executes by choosing Cancel or pressing Esc to close the dialog box.

A dialog box contains many sections so that you can read and enter information easily. 1-2-3 for Windows uses many dialog boxes that contain different parts; but every dialog box has a *title bar* and *command buttons* (see fig. 1.14). The title bar displays the name of the dialog box. When one dialog box appears in front of another, the title bar of the active dialog box is highlighted.

Fig. 1.14
Click the command buttons to execute the command or cancel out of the dialog box.

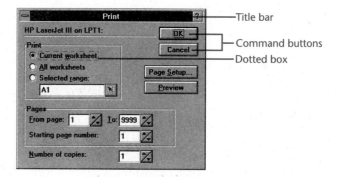

When you choose a command button, you execute or cancel a command. To confirm the selections in a dialog box and execute the command the dialog box controls, you choose OK. To cancel the command and close the dialog box, choose Cancel or press Esc or Ctrl+Break.

The names on some buttons are followed by an ellipsis to indicate that an additional dialog box appears if you select the button. Other buttons, such as OK and Cancel, execute a selection with no further action required.

A dialog box is composed primarily of *fields*; fields organize *options* (also called *choices*). Before you can specify an option, you first must select the field. The *dotted box* in a dialog box functions like the menu pointer: when an option is highlighted (shown in a dotted box) in a dialog box, you can select that option. When the dotted box appears in a command button, you can press Enter to execute the button.

Note

Not all fields have an underlined letter or can be surrounded by the dotted box. A field that has no underlined letter acts as a label for the choices below it. You do not have to worry about selecting these fields; you can bypass them and select the choices below them directly. When you select an option, the markers and the highlight move to show what you can select next.

You rarely need to fill in every field of a dialog box. For example, the dialog box shown in figure 1.15 has several options. To print multiple copies of a worksheet, increase the number in the **N**umber of copies text box and choose OK or press Enter to confirm the whole dialog box. You don't have to select specific pages, a page range, or Page Setup, if these items are set the way you want already.

Navigating Fields

If you use the mouse in a dialog box, you do not need to select a field before specifying the choice you want; just click on the choice to select it. Moving around in a dialog box often is easier with the mouse. Table 1.8 describes how the direction keys work in a dialog box.

Table 1.8	Dialog Box Keys
Key	**Action**
←	Moves to the preceding choice in a field
→	Moves to the next choice in a field
↑	Moves to the preceding choice in a field; in a list box, highlights the item one level up
↓	Moves to the next choice in a field; in a list box, highlights the item one level down
Ctrl+Break	Cancels a dialog box
Del	Deselects a check box; in a text box, deletes text to the right of the cursor
End	Moves to the last choice in a list box
Enter	Completes the command and closes the dialog box

(continues)

Table 1.8 Continued	
Key	**Action**
Esc	Closes the dialog box without completing the command; equivalent to choosing Cancel
Home	Moves to the first choice in a list box
PgDn	Scrolls down a list
PgUp	Scrolls up a list
Shift+Tab	Moves to the preceding field
Space bar	Toggles a selection in a check box
Tab	Moves to the next field
Alt+*letter*	Moves to and selects an option with the underlined *letter* you pressed
letter	In a text box, moves to and selects an option with the first letter you press
Alt+space bar	Opens the Control menu of a dialog box (the Control menu contains commands to move and close the dialog box)

Using Check Boxes and Option Buttons

Figure 1.15 shows the Page Setup dialog box with several different types of fields, including check boxes, option buttons, and text boxes.

Fig. 1.15
Click an option button or check box with the mouse to select (or deselect) the item.

Option buttons ⎯

Text boxes ⎯

Check boxes ⎯

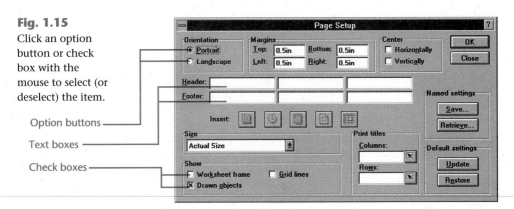

Check boxes turn choices on or off. If a choice is turned on, an x appears in the box. Several check boxes can be selected at once.

Option buttons (also called *radio buttons*) indicate choices within a field of mutually exclusive items. You can select only one option button at a time in a field.

To select or deselect a check box or option button with the keyboard, use one of these techniques:

- Press Alt and the underlined letter.

- Use the Tab key to move to the field and then use the direction keys to move through the choices. For a check box, press the space bar to select the choice and put an x in the check box. If the check box already contains an x, pressing the space bar makes the x disappear and turns off the choice (*deselects* it).

To select or deselect a check box or option button with the mouse, just click it.

Troubleshooting

Choices that I didn't make seem to be active. What's going on?

If you use the direction keys to move around in a dialog box, you might select option buttons or even list selections that you did not intend to select. Be sure to use Tab to move from field to field. Only use the direction keys to move to specific option buttons or text boxes. If you make a mistake like this, return to the field and select another option button; 1-2-3 for Windows deselects the option button you selected by accident because only one option button in a group can be selected at a time.

Entering Information in Text Boxes

A *text box* is a box in which you type information, such as worksheet ranges or file names. 1-2-3 for Windows includes several types of text boxes in which you can type and edit text. Text boxes can appear with or without *list boxes* or a *range selector* (described in the next section). When text boxes appear alone, you must enter information in the box.

Figure 1.15 shows text boxes with entries in them (the margin boxes) and text boxes with no entries (the header and footer boxes).

Use one of these techniques to enter information into a text box:

- If 1-2-3 for Windows fills in a text box with a suggested entry, press Enter to accept the suggestion.

- If the suggestion in the text box is highlighted, to erase the suggestion and type your own entry, begin typing; the suggested information is erased.

- To edit the text, press F2 (Edit) and then type the additional information or move the mouse pointer over the text and click at the location where you want to make changes. If the text box is empty, just click on it and type your entry.

Using Number Boxes or the Range Selector

Some text boxes contain numbers as shown in figure 1.16. You can type a new number directly into this type of box, or click the up or down arrow next to the box to increase or decrease the number.

Fig. 1.16
Use the arrows to change a number in a text box, or the range selector to select a range from the worksheet.

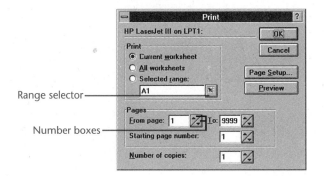

Range selector

Number boxes

Other text boxes have a range selector next to them, as shown in the Select range text box in figure 1.16. This means that you can either click in the text box and type a range from the worksheet (for example A1..Z20); or you can click the range selector to select a range from the worksheet with the mouse.

To use the range selector to fill in a text box, follow these steps:

1. Click the range selector. 1-2-3 for Windows switches temporarily to your worksheet.

2. Move the mouse pointer over the first cell in the range you want to select. Press and hold down the mouse button to drag over the range.

3. When you release the mouse button, 1-2-3 for Windows switches back to the dialog box and the range you selected is supplied in the chosen text box.

Selecting Items from List Boxes

List boxes display lists of choices. You can select only one choice from a list box.

To use the keyboard to select items from a list box, press a direction key to highlight the choice you want and then press Enter. With the mouse, just click your choice. A list box often has a text box on top that displays the choice highlighted in the list box. As you use the direction keys to highlight different choices, notice that the text box changes to reflect the new choice. Figure 1.17 shows the Open File dialog box. The list of files available on disk shows in the list box and the text box shows the highlighted file.

Text box with
List box

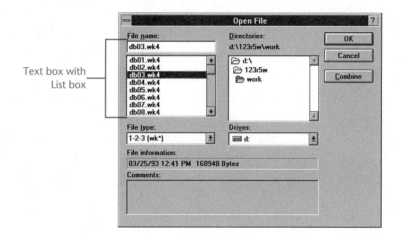

Fig. 1.17
You can make a selection in the list box or type your selection into the text box above it.

If a list box has more choices than it can display, you can scroll through the list box and see all the choices by using the direction keys and the PgUp, PgDn, Home, and End keys. If you use the mouse, click the *scroll arrows* (the up and down arrows) or drag the *scroll box* in the *scroll bar*, or click in the scroll bar to scroll the list.

Displaying Information

Information boxes display information about the current worksheet file. For example, in the Open File dialog box in figure 1.17, the information box called File Information tells you how many bytes of disk space the currently selected file occupies, as well as the date and time the file was created. You cannot type information in an information box.

Drop-Down Boxes

Drop-down boxes contain two or more choices. For example, the Drives drop-down box in the File Open dialog box contains a list of disk drives. You display the choices in a drop-down box by clicking the arrow at the right end of the drop-down box or by highlighting the drop-down box and pressing Alt+down arrow. To select an item from the drop-down box with the keyboard, press the first letter of the item or use the up- and down-arrow keys to move to the item. If you use a mouse, click the item.

Moving a Dialog Box

Occasionally, a dialog box covers worksheet data you need to see to complete the command. To see the worksheet data, you have to move the dialog box.

You can use the keyboard to move a dialog box by pressing Alt+- (hyphen) to open the Control menu for the dialog box and then selecting **M**ove (see fig. 1.18). A four-headed arrow appears in the dialog box; use the direction keys to move the box.

Fig. 1.18

Access the Control menu to move a dialog box with the keyboard or drag the title bar of the dialog box to a new location.

Dialog box ——
Control menu

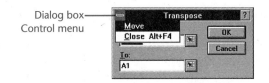

To move the dialog box with the mouse, move the mouse pointer to the dialog-box title bar, click the title bar by pressing and holding the left mouse button, and drag the dialog box to another location.

You do not need to move a dialog box in order to select cells from the worksheet. If you use the range selector to specify a range in a dialog box, 1-2-3 for Windows temporarily removes the dialog box from the screen so that you can see data and select cells freely.

SmartIcon Basics

SmartIcons are on-screen buttons that you can use to make many 1-2-3 for Windows tasks easier and more automatic. Instead of moving through several layers of menus to choose commands, you can click a SmartIcon to initiate the action. You need a mouse to use SmartIcons; they cannot be accessed from the keyboard.

1-2-3 for Windows provides nearly 200 SmartIcons, which duplicate common menu commands or perform tasks for which no menu command exists. SmartIcons are grouped together into palettes that you can display on-screen. The default palette (the one that appears at the top of the screen when you start 1-2-3) includes SmartIcons that perform a broad range of common tasks. You aren't limited, however, to the SmartIcons displayed in the default palette; you can create custom SmartIcons to execute the macros that you create.

Using SmartIcons To Perform Commands

To use a SmartIcon, follow these steps:

1. Depending on the purpose of the SmartIcon, select the data, rows, columns, or other worksheet element that you want to work on.

2. Place the mouse pointer on the SmartIcon.

3. Click the left mouse button once. This click invokes the SmartIcon's action.

Changing SmartIcon Palettes

There are eight SmartIcon palettes that come with 1-2-3 for Windows. You can view different palettes using any of these techniques:

■ Click the Select Next Palette SmartIcon at the right edge of the current SmartIcon palette (see figure 1.19).

■ Click the SmartIcon selector in the status bar and choose a different palette.

■ Choose **T**ools Smart**I**cons, then drop down the list of palettes at the very top of the dialog box and choose a different palette.

Many of the default icon palettes contain the same or repeated tools so that you do not have to move to a different palette to perform some standard operations. For example, the first icon in any of the standard palettes activates the Open File dialog box, in which you can select a worksheet file to open. To save your work, click the second SmartIcon (save the current file) in any of the standard palettes; this SmartIcon executes the **F**ile **S**ave command.

Tip

You can see a description of each SmartIcon by moving the mouse pointer over the icon and pausing or pressing the right mouse button. Appendix B contains a listing of all the SmartIcons.

▶ "Using the Standard SmartIcon Palettes," p. 979

Fig. 1.19

Click the Select Next Palette SmartIcon or the SmartIcons selector to choose a different palette

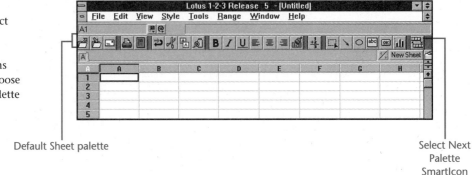

Default Sheet palette

Select Next Palette SmartIcon

Manipulating Windows

You use the 1-2-3 window to display and work with 1-2-3 for Windows worksheet files. You can change the size and position of the 1-2-3 window or a Worksheet window by using the mouse or the keyboard. You can enlarge a window to fill the entire screen, reduce the window to a smaller size, or shrink the window to an icon.

There are three ways you can manipulate windows: with the Control menu, with the mouse, or with the Windows menu.

Using the Control Menu

Every window has a Control menu in the upper left corner of the window. This menu is similar to the Control menu in all Windows 3.1 applications. The 1-2-3 Control menu enables you to manipulate the size and position of the 1-2-3 window, close 1-2-3 for Windows, and switch to other Windows 3.1 applications (see fig. 1.20).

Fig. 1.20

Use the 1-2-3 for Windows Control menu to manipulate the 1-2-3 for Windows window.

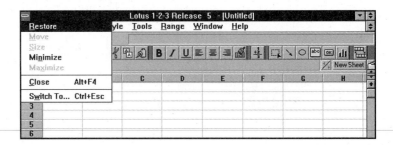

The menu shown in figure 1.20 has seven options, but **M**ove, **S**ize, and Maximize are *dimmed* (or *grayed*); this means that their functions are currently

unavailable. Because 1-2-3 for Windows is running as a full-screen application (that is, it is *maximized*) in this figure, the three grayed choices are inappropriate. If you are running 1-2-3 for Windows in a partial-screen window or have reduced it to an icon (that is, have *minimized* the window), different choices on this menu are dimmed, indicating that they are currently unavailable.

To access the 1-2-3 Control menu with the keyboard, follow these steps:

1. Press Alt and then the space bar.

2. Type the underlined letter of the command or, alternatively, use the arrow keys to highlight the command and then press Enter.

3. If you chose a command like **M**ove or **S**ize, use the direction keys to move or size the 1-2-3 window.

To access the 1-2-3 Control menu with the mouse, click the 1-2-3 Control menu box and then click the command you want to activate.

The *Worksheet Control menu* controls the size and position of the Worksheet window; it is accessed through the *Worksheet Control menu box* in the upper left corner of the Worksheet window. Although similar to the 1-2-3 Control menu, the Worksheet Control menu applies only to its own Worksheet window. The 1-2-3 Control menu's S**w**itch To option (which switches between active Windows 3.1 applications) is replaced on the Worksheet Control menu by the Nex**t** option (which switches between active 1-2-3 Worksheet windows). Figure 1.21 shows the Worksheet Control menu.

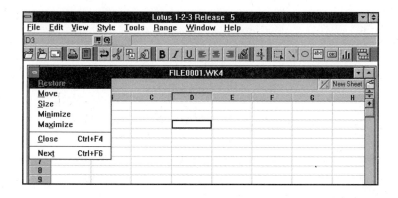

Fig. 1.21
Use the Worksheet Control menu to move and size a specific Worksheet window.

Tip
The 1-2-3 Control menu controls the 1-2-3 window; the Worksheet Control menu controls a single Worksheet window within the 1-2-3 window.

To access the Worksheet Control menu with the keyboard, press Alt+- (hyphen). To select a command, type the underlined letter of the command; alternatively, use the arrow keys to highlight the command and then press Enter.

To activate the Worksheet Control menu with the mouse, click the Worksheet Control menu box and then click the command you want to activate.

To close the Worksheet Control menu by using the keyboard, press Esc twice. To close the Worksheet Control menu with the mouse, click anywhere outside the menu.

Maximizing and Restoring Windows

When you *maximize* the 1-2-3 window, it fills the screen. When you maximize the Worksheet window and other windows within the 1-2-3 window, each window fills the work area of the 1-2-3 window.

The Control menu of each window has a Ma**x**imize command. To maximize a window with the keyboard, select the Ma**x**imize command from the appropriate Control menu. If you use the mouse to maximize a window, you don't need the Control menus. At the top right corner of the screen and of each window are a *Minimize button* and a *Maximize button* or a *Restore button*.

You click a window's Maximize button to enlarge that window. When you maximize the 1-2-3 window or a Worksheet window, the Maximize button changes to the Restore button (the Restore button appears only when a window is maximized). In figure 1.22, the Worksheet window is maximized; the Restore button appears instead of the Maximize button. (The 1-2-3 window in this figure is slightly reduced from the maximized size so that you can see the 1-2-3 window's Maximize button.)

Maximize button
Minimize button

Fig. 1. 22
Click the Maximize button to maximize a window and the Restore button to restore it to its former size.

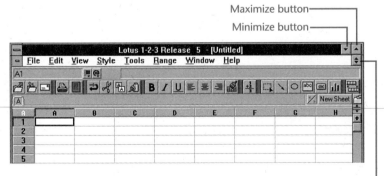

WorksheetRestore button

If you select the **R**estore command from the Control menu or click the Restore button, 1-2-3 for Windows restores the window to its previous size—that is, the size it was before it was last maximized.

Tip
Double-click the title bar to maximize or restore a window.

Minimizing Windows

To shrink the 1-2-3 window to an icon on the desktop, select the Minimize command from the 1-2-3 Control menu or click the Minimize button of the 1-2-3 window. If you are using another Windows application and want to run 1-2-3 for Windows in the background, you can minimize the 1-2-3 window or use Ctrl+Esc to open the Task List and switch to the other application. Minimizing Worksheet windows can be useful if you are working with several utilities or worksheet files. Each type of window is identified by its own icon. For example, the Transcript window icon has a movie camera; the Worksheet window icon has a grid. Figure 1.23 shows examples of these icons.

To open a minimized window, double-click the window icon with the mouse or click once on the minimized icon with the mouse to see the Control menu, then choose **R**estore.

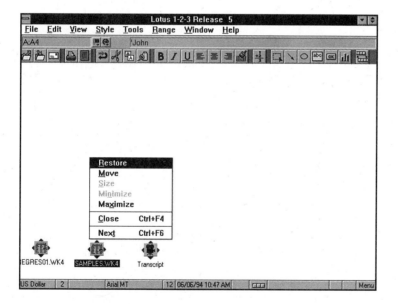

Fig. 1.23
The Minimize button reduces a window to its minimum size—an icon.

Everyday Worksheet Tasks

Troubleshooting

My Worksheet window suddenly disappeared—where did it go?

You might have accidentally minimized the window containing the worksheet and reduced it to an icon on-screen. Depending on what other worksheets are open you might not be able to see the minimized icon. The easiest way to find your worksheet again is to open the **W**indow menu and choose the worksheet from the list at the bottom of the menu.

Sizing Windows

To change the size of a window, use the **S**ize command from the window's Control menu and the direction keys; alternatively, use the mouse. You also can control the display of Worksheet windows by using the **W**indow **T**ile and **W**indow **C**ascade commands.

To size the 1-2-3 window or a Worksheet window with the keyboard, follow these steps:

1. Open the appropriate Control menu and choose **S**ize.

2. When the mouse pointer changes to a four-headed white arrow, use the direction keys to move the arrow and resize the window. As you resize the window, an outline shows the size and shape of the window. Press the left and right arrows to change the window horizontally; press the up and down arrows to change the window vertically.

3. Press Enter when you have sized the window as desired.

To size a window with the mouse, follow these steps:

1. Move the mouse pointer to the border you want to change.

2. When the mouse pointer changes to a thick white double arrow, press and hold the left mouse button and drag the border to its new location.

Moving Windows

With the keyboard or mouse, you can move a window or its icon. With the keyboard, choose the **M**ove command from the appropriate Control menu, use the direction keys to relocate the window or icon, and press Enter. An outline of the window or icon moves as you use the arrow keys. Moving a window is easier with the mouse: just click the title bar and drag the window to its new location. If the window is minimized, you can click the window's icon and drag it to a new position.

Closing Windows

Each window's Control menu has a **C**lose command that enables you to close the 1-2-3 window or a Worksheet window. To close the 1-2-3 window with the mouse, double-click the 1-2-3 Control menu box. To close a Worksheet window, double-click the Worksheet Control menu box.

If you have made any changes to a file in a window and haven't saved them before you select the **C**lose command, a dialog box prompts you to save any files before closing the window (see fig. 1.24).

Cascading Windows

Choose the **W**indow **C**ascade command or click the Cascade Windows SmartIcon to arrange open windows so that they appear on top of one another, with only their title bars and the left edges of the windows showing (see fig. 1.25). The active window always appears on top. To use the keyboard to switch between cascaded windows, press Ctrl+F6 (Next). To use the mouse, click the title bar or the edge of the window you want. You can change the size and location of the cascaded windows as described in the preceding sections.

Tip

To quickly close the 1-2-3 window (or any Windows 3.1 application window), press Alt+F4 (Exit). To close a Worksheet window (or any Windows 3.1 document window), press Ctrl+F4 (Close).

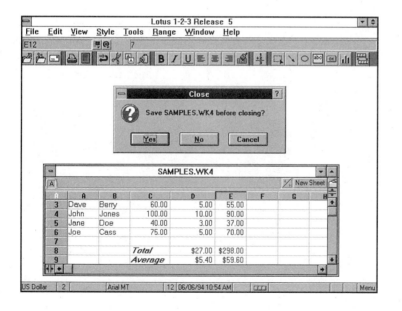

Fig. 1.24

If you close a window without saving the latest changes, 1-2-3 for Windows prompts you to save the file.

Fig. 1.25
Use **W**indow
Cascade to display
overlapping
windows.

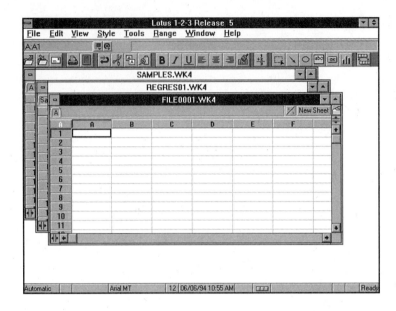

Tiling Windows

When you select **W**indow **T**ile or click the Tile Windows SmartIcon, 1-2-3 for Windows sizes and arranges all open windows side by side, like floor tiles (see fig. 1.26). The active window's title bar has a dark background. To use the keyboard to switch between tiled windows, press Ctrl+F6 (Next); to use the mouse, click the window you want. You can change the size and location of the tiled windows as described earlier in this chapter.

Fig. 1.26
Use **W**indow **T**ile
to see small parts
of each Worksheet
window on-screen.

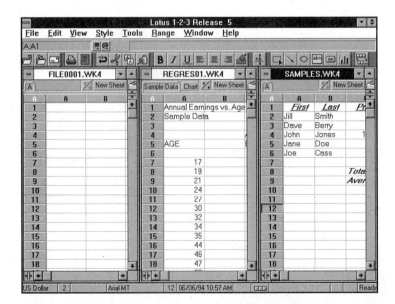

Choosing a Window Display Mode

In addition to the cascade and tile display-mode options described in the preceding sections, 1-2-3 for Windows offers other choices for displaying Worksheet windows. You can, for example, split a Worksheet window into two *panes* either vertically or horizontally and maximize a Worksheet window to fill the entire work area. In addition, if you have multiple sheets in your worksheet file, you can display a three-dimensional view of your worksheet. With all these choices, you may find it difficult to choose the best display mode for your needs. The following guidelines may help you select the best display mode for your worksheets:

■ Maximizing the window provides the largest visible work area.

■ Tiling the windows enables you to view portions of several files at the same time.

■ Cascading the windows provides a large visible work area for the current window (although not as large as a maximized window) and makes switching between files easy.

■ A worksheet can be displayed in only one window at a time. To display two views of the same worksheet, use **V**iew **S**plit **H**orizontal or **V**iew **S**plit **V**ertical.

■ If your worksheet contains multiple sheets, you can view three worksheets at the same time by using the **V**iew **S**plit **P**erspective command.

The **V**iew **S**et View Preferences command enables you to further control the display of a Worksheet window. Use this command to specify whether or not grid lines are displayed and to turn off the display of the edit line and status bar to maximize the 1-2-3 work area.

▶ "Customizing the 1-2-3 for Windows Screen," p. 965

▶ "Changing the Display of a Worksheet File," p. 486

Switching Windows

When you choose the **W**indow command from the Worksheet Control menu, 1-2-3 for Windows lists up to nine open windows at the bottom of the **W**indow menu; a check mark appears next to the active window's name. To make another window active, type the number displayed next to the window name, or click the number in the menu with the mouse. If you have more than nine open windows, you can display the names of the additional windows by using the **W**indow **M**ore Windows command (which appears only if more than nine windows are open).

Tip
Press Alt+Tab to switch from application to application. If the application you switch to is reduced to an icon, the icon restores to a window when you release the Alt key.

You can make another window active without using the **W**indow menu. To cycle through the open windows in the 1-2-3 window, activating each window in turn, press Ctrl+F6 (Next). You also can activate a window by clicking anywhere in that window.

Using the Task List

With the **S**witch To command on the 1-2-3 Control menu, you can switch to the *Task List*, a Windows Program Manager utility that manages multiple applications. You can, for example, use the Task List to switch to the Print Manager so that you can pause or resume printing and remove print jobs from the print queue. To switch to the Task List with the keyboard, press Ctrl+Esc. Figure 1.27 shows the Task List window. For more information about the Task List, refer to your Windows documentation.

Fig. 1.27
Use the Task List to switch to other windows applications.

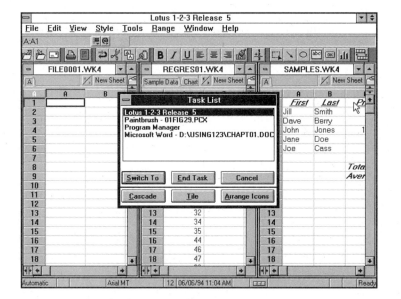

Getting Help

1-2-3 for Windows provides three different types of help to assist you as you work:

■ *Guided Tour*. The guided tour is an animated presentation that shows you the major features of 1-2-3. It is accessed as a separate application from the Lotus Applications program group. Just double-click the Guided Tour icon to see the presentation.

- *On-line Tutorial.* The on-line tutorial leads you through the major features of 1-2-3 for Windows. You perform the tasks with the guidance of the tutorial. Choose **H**elp **T**utorial to access this powerful help feature.

- *On-line Help.* This is the on-line, context-sensitive help that you can access at any time while using 1-2-3. You can be in the middle of any operation and press F1 (Help) to display one or more screens of explanations and advice on what to do next.

Using On-line Help

You can use the on-line help several ways. If you press F1 while in the Ready mode or choose **H**elp **C**ontents, you will see the contents window that enables you to access help on different topics. The Help contents appears in a window on the right side of the screen, as shown in figure 1.28, that you can move and size like any other window. The major categories of Help are represented as icons. Click one of the icons to get a window of topics for that icon. To move back and forth between your worksheet and the Help window, click in the window you want to work in or press Alt+Tab.

Tip

Keep the Help window on-screen while you work by choosing Always on **T**op from the **H**elp menu in the Help window.

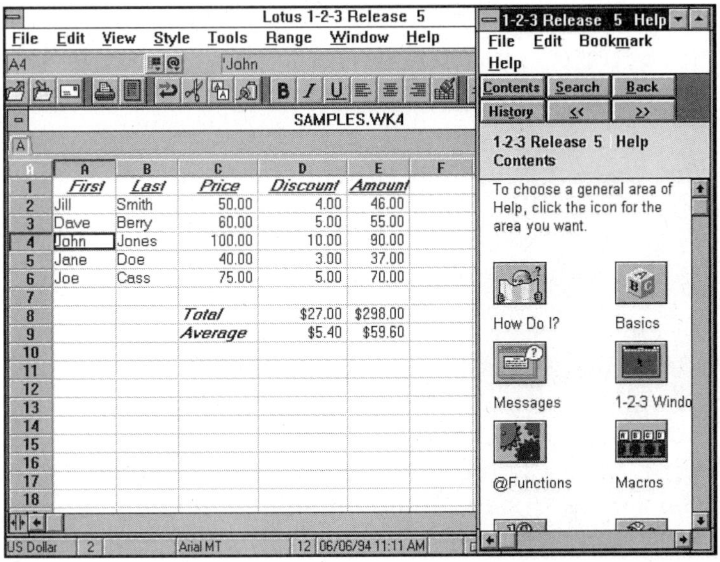

Fig. 1.28
Choose **H**elp **C**ontents or press F1 to see the table of contents for the help screens.

You can press Help (F1) at any time, even while you execute a command or edit a cell. The help that you receive always is context-sensitive. If, for example, you are executing the **R**ange commands and you press F1 (Help), 1-2-3 for Windows displays a Help window for the **R**ange commands.

All Windows help systems have a series of buttons across the top of the Help window that enable you to navigate in the Help screens. Choose a button by clicking it or pressing Alt+*letter*. These buttons are described in table 1.9.

Table 1.9 Help Buttons	
Button	**Action**
Contents	Shows the index or contents of the Help screens.
Search	Displays a dialog box with a text entry and a list of key words. You can type a term or choose a term for which you want help from the list.
Back	Returns to the preceding Help topic. This enables you to retrace your steps and choose different help topics.
His**t**ory	Shows a list of previously selected help topics. You can double-click a topic to jump directly to it or use the arrow keys to move to a topic and press Enter.
>>	Some help topics may have several screens of information. Click this button to move to the next screen.
<<	Choose this button to move to the previous screen (if applicable).

Jumping between Help Topics

Certain Help topics appear in a color or intensity different from the rest of the Help window. If you place the mouse pointer on a colored topic, the pointer changes from an arrow to a hand with a pointing index finger. To see more information about one of these topics, click that topic.

Tip
Get a hard copy of any help topic by choosing **File** **P**rint Topic from the help menu.

Some of the different color topics have a dashed underline. These are glossary terms. If you click one of these topics, a definition of the term appears.

Searching for a Topic in Help

One of the most useful features of the Windows help system is the ability to search for specific words or topics. To search for a specific topic in the help screens, follow these steps:

1. Open the **H**elp menu and choose **S**earch, or choose the **S**earch button once in help. The Search dialog box shown in figure 1.29 displays.

2. Type a word in the top text box, or use the mouse to scroll and select a word from the top list box.

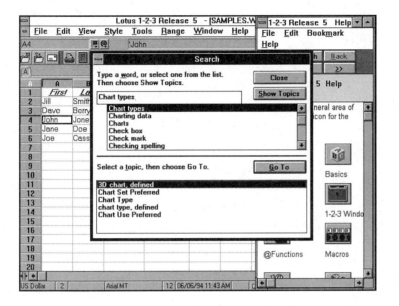

Fig. 1.29
Use the Search
dialog box to
search for help for
specific topics.

Everyday Worksheet Tasks

3. When you find the right topic in the top list box, choose **S**how Topics
   to see a specific list of topics. The bottom list box displays topics related
   to the selected word or phrase.

4. Select a topic from the bottom list box and choose **G**o To to jump to
   that topic, or double-click the topic in the bottom list to jump directly
   to it.

Closing the Help Window

Don't forget that Help opens a separate window on-screen. Close the Help
window when you are done with it by double-clicking the Control menu box
for the Help window, choosing **F**ile E**x**it from the help menu, pressing
Alt+F4, or pressing Esc.

Exiting from 1-2-3 for Windows

Windows 3.1 applications can open multiple document windows. You can,
for example, have several different worksheet files open at the same time.
1-2-3 for Windows enables you to close individual Worksheet windows or to
exit from 1-2-3 for Windows entirely, closing all open windows.

To exit from 1-2-3 for Windows and close all open windows at the same time,
use the **F**ile E**x**it command or click the End 1-2-3 Session SmartIcon.

To quit 1-2-3 for Windows with the keyboard, use the following procedure:

1. Open the **F**ile menu and choose E**x**it. If you have saved changes in active worksheet files, 1-2-3 closes. If you have not saved changes to active files, a confirmation box appears, prompting you to save your worksheets.

2. Select **Y**es to save the current worksheet file before exiting; select **N**o to exit without saving the file; choose Cancel or press Enter to cancel the exit command and return to 1-2-3 for Windows. If you have multiple Worksheet windows open, select **S**ave All to save all files before exiting.

You also can use the Windows 3.1 shortcut method of exiting 1-2-3 for Windows: Press Alt+F4 to make the Exit confirmation box appear. Make your selection as outlined in step 2.

▶ "Understanding Worksheets and Files," p. 60

To use the mouse to quit 1-2-3 for Windows, double-click the 1-2-3 Control menu box; the Exit confirmation box appears. Make your selection as outlined in step 2.

From Here...

You might now be ready to start creating a worksheet in 1-2-3 for Windows, or you might want to customize your screen and learn more about the screen display. The following chapters provide related information:

- Chapter 2, "Navigating and Selecting in 1-2-3 for Windows," covers how to open and work with multiple worksheets, move around in worksheets, and select cells and ranges.

- Chapter 3, "Entering and Editing Data," shows you how to create a new worksheet by entering data and using the Fill feature.

- Chapter 32, "Customizing the 1-2-3 for Windows Screen," discusses how to change the colors and screen display and how to set various preferences in 1-2-3 for Windows.

Chapter 2

Navigating and Selecting in 1-2-3 for Windows

This chapter introduces the basic skills you need to use 1-2-3 for Windows. All work in 1-2-3 for Windows is held in worksheets; one or more worksheets comprise a file. In this chapter, you learn how to create a new worksheet file and save it to and retrieve it from disk. You learn how to create files containing multiple worksheets.

To use 1-2-3 for Windows skillfully, you need to be able to maneuver from cell to cell and worksheet to worksheet with ease. In this chapter, you also learn a variety of methods for moving the cell pointer around in a file.

At various times when you are using 1-2-3 for Windows, you will need to refer to rectangular collections of cells, called ranges. You can define ranges by their cell addresses, as well as through a method called "naming ranges," assigning descriptive text like "Qtr4" or "Western Region" to represent these rectangular collections.

When you create worksheets, you will often find the need to enter a sequence of values or labels in adjacent cells. These sequences might be simple consecutive numbers (1, 2, 3), a sequence of dates (April 1, April 2, April 3), or a sequence of descriptions (Qtr 1, Qtr 2, Qtr 3). 1-2-3 for Windows gives you a tool for creating such sequences easily. You learn to use the **R**ange **F**ill and **R**ange Fill by **E**xample commands, as well as a technique involving dragging with the cursor to fill the range.

In this chapter you learn to do the following:

■ Open, view, and save worksheets

■ Move the cell pointer around a worksheet

■ Create and use multiple page worksheets

■ Define ranges, both by cell addresses and range names

Understanding Worksheets and Files

▶ "Saving Files,"
p. 283

You can think of a worksheet as the electronic version of one page of a large ledger pad or one piece of graph paper: it is a page containing boxes into which you can place information. When you start 1-2-3 for Windows, a blank worksheet (with the name Untitled) appears, together with the Welcome to 1-2-3 dialog box, discussed in Chapter 1 (see fig. 2.1).

Fig. 2.1
When you start 1-2-3 for Windows or open a new file, you see an un-named worksheet and the Welcome to 1-2-3 dialog box.

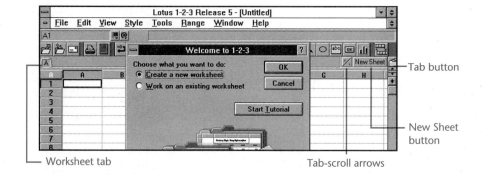

Notice that a *worksheet tab* containing the letter A appears at the top of the worksheet. You can add up to 255 more worksheets (also called *sheets*) to the worksheet file. Each additional worksheet is identified by a different letter. The identification scheme is similar to the scheme used for worksheet columns; columns are labeled A through Z, then AA through AZ, BA through BZ, and so on, out to column IV, 256 columns to the right. Similarly, the first worksheet is A; the second is B; the 27th is AA; and so on. The sequence continues to IV, the 256th worksheet in the file. Together, these 256 worksheets are considered to be a *worksheet file*. You can enter data into one or more worksheets in a worksheet file and then save the work in a file on disk under a single file name. After you save the worksheet file, the title bar displays the file name.

Figure 2.2 shows the worksheet file SALES.WK4, which contains two worksheets. Notice the two Worksheet Tabs, A and B.

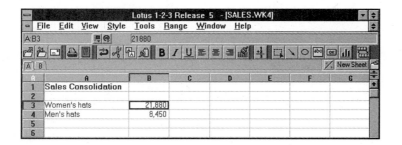

Fig. 2.2
The SALES.WK4 worksheet file, containing two worksheets.

Opening and Saving Worksheet Files

Although a blank worksheet appears each time you start 1-2-3, you will eventually need to open other (existing) files. You also may need to start a new file and save it for future use. In 1-2-3, you can open a worksheet file at any time and even view two or more separate files at the same time.

The following sections explain the procedures for opening and saving worksheet files.

Opening New and Existing Files

If, for example, you are beginning a new fiscal year, you might decide to start a new worksheet file, rather than add another worksheet to the existing file. To start a new, blank worksheet file, choose the **F**ile **N**ew command or click the Create File SmartIcon. 1-2-3 displays a new worksheet file without removing any existing files from the screen. The new worksheet file initially has only one worksheet. As explained in Chapter 1, you can rearrange individual worksheet files (windows) and even minimize them to accommodate multiple files in the 1-2-3 window.

◀ "Manipulating Windows," p. 46

You also can open worksheet files that you created and saved previously. To open an existing file, choose the **F**ile **O**pen command or click the Open File SmartIcon. The Open File dialog box appears (see fig. 2.3).

▶ "Opening Existing Files," p. 290

Use the Dri**v**es and **D**irectories lists to locate a file; its name appears in the File **N**ame list. Double-click the name to open the file. Alternatively, type the entire file name, including the directory path, in the File **N**ame entry box, and then click OK to open the file.

▶ "Saving Files," p. 283

Fig. 2.3
The Open File
dialog box.

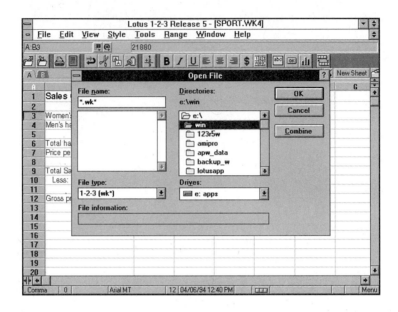

Saving Files

When you build a new worksheet file or make changes in an existing one, all the work exists only in the computer's memory. If you do not save new worksheets or changes before you quit 1-2-3 for Windows, you lose that work. (1-2-3 for Windows provides a warning, asking you whether you want to save the file before closing.)

When you *save* a file, you copy the file in memory to the disk and give the file a name. The file remains on disk after you quit 1-2-3 for Windows or turn off the computer.

To save changes in an existing file, choose **F**ile from the 1-2-3 for Windows main menu and then choose **S**ave from the pull-down menu, or click the Save File SmartIcon. 1-2-3 automatically updates the file to include whatever alterations you made. If you are saving a new worksheet, one that has never been saved to disk, 1-2-3 for Windows automatically assigns a name to the file. The file name is in the form of FILE*nnnn*.WK4, with *nnnn* representing a number (0001, 0002, and so on).

When you want to name a new file, or when you want to save an existing file under a new name while keeping the old file, use the **F**ile Save **A**s command. 1-2-3 for Windows displays the Save As dialog box that enables you to save the file and to assign a password (see fig. 2.4).

Tip

If you have a file already in memory and you try to open it a second time, you see a dialog box that reminds you that the file already exists in memory. You cannot open it a second time.

▶ "Saving Files," p. 283

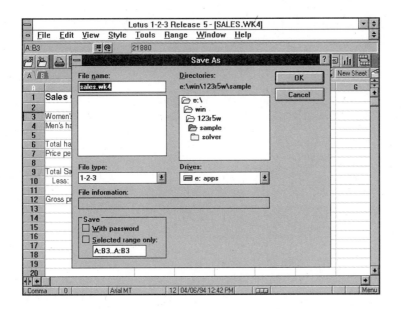

Fig. 2.4

The Save As dialog box.

Using Multiple Worksheets

Occasionally, you need only one worksheet to analyze and store data. At other times, however, you need to use multiple worksheets to organize your information effectively. Some applications are especially well-suited to multiple worksheets. First, multiple worksheets are ideal for consolidations. If you need a worksheet that tracks data for several departments, you can create a separate worksheet for each department and store all the worksheets as individual sheets in the same file. Each worksheet is smaller (and easier to understand and use) than a large worksheet containing all the data for all of the departments. You can enter into a cell in any worksheet a formula that refers to cells in the other worksheets.

Use multiple worksheets for any consolidations that contain separate parts, such as products, countries, or projects. Although you can accomplish many of these objectives by putting data in separate files, creating and maintaining separate files is more difficult than keeping all the data in a single multiple-worksheet file.

Another example of a multiple-worksheet file is a file in which each worksheet represents the activity for a month. Twelve worksheets contain the data for an entire year; and a 13th worksheet, placed before or after the others, represents a consolidation of data for all 12 months.

You also can use multiple worksheets to place separate sections of data in separate worksheets. You can, for example, place input areas, data ranges,

▶ "Linking Worksheets and Files with Formulas," p. 601

formulas, assumptions, constants, and macros in separate worksheets. You then can customize each worksheet for a particular purpose. This technique of organizing data includes using global formats and setting column widths and row heights, as described in Chapter 9.

Tip
If your file contains different types of information, separate the information on different worksheets, rather than placing them all on the same large, two-dimensional worksheet.

Breaking your large applications into separate worksheets of a worksheet file has other advantages. As long as Group mode is not activated, you can change one worksheet without accidentally changing the others. If all the data is in one worksheet, you could insert or delete a row or column in one area and destroy part of another area that shares the same row or column. If you use multiple worksheets, however, you can insert and delete rows and columns anywhere without affecting other parts of the file.

Another common accident is writing over formulas in input areas. When you use multiple worksheets, you can separate input areas and formulas so that this error is less likely to occur.

Commands related to multiple worksheets include the following:

■ Insert one or more worksheets before or after the current worksheet by opening the **E**dit menu and then choosing **I**nsert and **S**heet. A fast way to insert a worksheet after the current worksheet is to click the New Sheet button under the worksheet title bar or click the New Sheet SmartIcon.

■ Remove a worksheet by opening the **E**dit menu and then choosing **D**elete and **S**heet after activating the desired worksheet. You can delete selected worksheets quickly by clicking the Delete Sheet SmartIcon.

■ Move among the various worksheets by clicking their tabs.

■ Display up to three worksheets at one time by opening the **V**iew menu and then choosing **S**plit and **P**erspective or clicking the Perspective View SmartIcon. (Details about this command appear in the following section.)

■ Display or hide the worksheet tabs by clicking the Tab button on the far right side of the worksheet window (refer to fig. 2.1). You also can show or hide the tabs by opening the **V**iew menu and choosing Set View **P**references. Then select or deselect the Worksheet **T**abs option from the View Preferences dialog box.

▶ "Grouping
   Worksheets,"
   p. 277

■ Group several or all worksheets in a worksheet file so that some commands affect the whole group, not just the current worksheet, by using the **S**tyle **W**orksheet Defaults command and then specifying **G**roup Mode from the Worksheet Defaults dialog box that appears.

- Customize a worksheet's tab by double-clicking the tab and then typing the desired name. For example, you might name the sheets Jan, Feb, Mar, and so on. You can enter up to 255 characters, but it's best to use short, descriptive names.

Displaying Multiple Worksheets

You can use the **V**iew **S**plit **P**erspective command or the Perspective View SmartIcon to view up to three worksheets in perspective view. The default screen display is a window that shows part of one worksheet with other worksheets "behind" it, as indicated by their tabs (refer to fig. 2.2). The tabs, similar to tabs in a looseleaf notebook, represent worksheets behind the one currently appearing on the screen.

▶ "Changing the Display of a Worksheet File," p. 486

Figure 2.5 shows a perspective view of three worksheets. In this file, worksheet A is the consolidation worksheet; worksheet B contains data for Region 1; and worksheet C contains data for Region 2. (Worksheets D and E, which represent sales for regions 3 and 4, do not appear on-screen.)

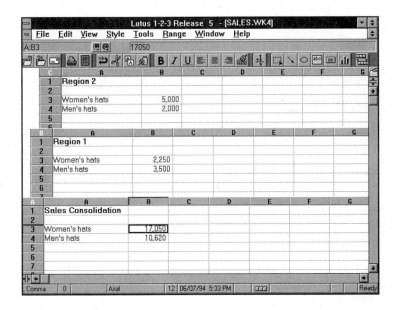

Fig. 2.5

A three-dimensional worksheet displayed with the **V**iew **S**plit **P**erspective command.

If you use **V**iew **S**plit **P**erspective to display more than one worksheet in a worksheet file, the *current worksheet* is the one that contains the cell pointer; the cell the cursor currently is in. You can determine the current worksheet in figure 2.5 in several ways. For example, the cell pointer is in worksheet A, and the cell address in the selection indicator begins with A:. In this figure, worksheet A is the current worksheet, and the *current cell* is A:B3. Notice also

Tip
If the worksheet tabs don't appear on-screen when you are viewing a single worksheet (that is, you're not viewing your worksheet in perspective view), click the Tab button to make them appear (refer to fig. 2.1). You can also make the tabs appear by selecting **V**iew Set View **P**references and clicking the Worksheet tabs check box.

in worksheet A that the B column heading at the top and the row designator 3 on the left both appear to be depressed. This, too, indicates both the current worksheet, as well as the current cell.

To return to a display of one worksheet, use the **V**iew C**l**ear Split command. If you prefer to toggle between displaying three worksheets at one time and displaying only one of the worksheets, use the key combination Alt+F6 (Zoom).

Moving around the Worksheet

You can enter data only at the location of the cell pointer. Because you can display only a small part of the worksheet at one time, you must know how to move the cell pointer to see other parts of the worksheet. The following sections focus on moving the cell pointer within a worksheet file and among worksheet files.

Using the Direction Keys

The four arrow keys that move the cell pointer are located in the numeric keypad (or in a separate keypad on an enhanced keyboard). The cell pointer moves in the direction of the arrow on the key. If you hold down the arrow key, the cell pointer continues to move in the direction of the arrow key. When the cell pointer reaches the edge of the screen, the worksheet continues to scroll in the direction of the arrow.

You can use several other direction keys to move around the current worksheet a screen at a time. Press the PgUp or PgDn key to move up or down one screen. Press the Tab key or Ctrl+right arrow to move one screen to the right; press Shift+Tab or Ctrl+left arrow to move one screen to the left. The size of one screen depends on the size of the worksheet window.

▶ "Changing the Display of a Worksheet File," p. 486

Pressing the Home key moves the cell pointer directly to the *home position* (usually, cell A1 of the current worksheet. In Chapter 15, you learn how to lock titles on-screen. Locked titles affect the location of the home position.) Pressing End and then Home moves the cell pointer to the last active cell in the current worksheet.

Two direction keys, PgUp and PgDn, are especially important for moving around a worksheet file. Ctrl+PgUp moves the cell pointer to the following worksheet, and Ctrl+PgDn moves the cell pointer to the preceding worksheet. These key combinations also cause the cell pointer to cross file boundaries if the cell pointer is positioned in the last or first worksheet of a file.

End Ctrl+Home moves the cell pointer to the end of the active area of the last worksheet in a file (similar to End+Home in a single worksheet).

End Ctrl+PgUp and End Ctrl+PgDn move the cell pointer up or down through the worksheets to the next cell that contains data (similar to End+up arrow and End+down arrow in a single worksheet).

Using the Scroll Lock Key

The Scroll Lock key toggles the scroll feature on and off. When you press Scroll Lock, you activate or deactivate the scroll feature. If you press Scroll Lock and then press an arrow key, the cell pointer stays in the current cell, and the entire worksheet moves in the direction of the arrow. If you continue to press the same arrow key when the cell pointer reaches the edge of the screen, the cell pointer remains next to the worksheet frame as the entire window scrolls. Scroll Lock does not affect the other direction keys.

To use the mouse to scroll the worksheet without moving the cell pointer, turn off Scroll Lock and then click one of the arrows in the scroll bars at the right and bottom edges of the worksheet. If you click an arrow one time, the worksheet scrolls one column or row in the direction of the arrow, and the cell pointer doesn't move. If you click an arrow and hold down the mouse button, the worksheet scrolls continuously in the direction of the arrow until you release the mouse button.

As you click on the left or right arrows, you will notice a small square, the scroll box, slide left and right along the scroll bar. You can also scroll from side to side by dragging this box along the scroll bar and releasing it in a new position. Finally, if you click on the scroll bar to the right or left of the scroll box, you will shift your view one full screen to the right or left. You can perform the analogous tasks on the vertical scroll bar, on the right side of the screen.

Note

If when you press an arrow key to move the cursor and your screen moves in an unexpected manner, you may have pressed the Scroll Lock key accidentally. Check to see if the Scroll Lock indicator on your keyboard is lit. If it is, press Scroll Lock once to deactivate this feature.

Using the End Key

When you press and release the End key, the End status indicator appears in the status bar. Suppose cells A5 through A50 *all* contain data. If your cursor is in cell A5 and you press the End key and then the down arrow key, the cursor will move to cell A50, the last cell containing data, just before a blank cell. If you then press End and the up arrow, you will move to cell A5, again the last cell containing data, just before a blank cell. If you start at A1 and press End and the down arrow, the cursor will move to cell A5, the first filled-in cell after blank cells. In general, the End key is used to move to the intersections of blank cells and cells that contain data.

▶ "Enhancing the Appearance of Data," p. 343

The End key works the same with the left- and up-arrow keys. In figure 2.6, pressing End and then the left-arrow key takes you to cell A4. From cell A4, pressing End and the up-arrow key takes you to cell A1 (the edge of the worksheet). After you press the End key, the End indicator stays on only until you press an arrow key or the End key again. If you press End by mistake, you can press End again to make the End status indicator disappear.

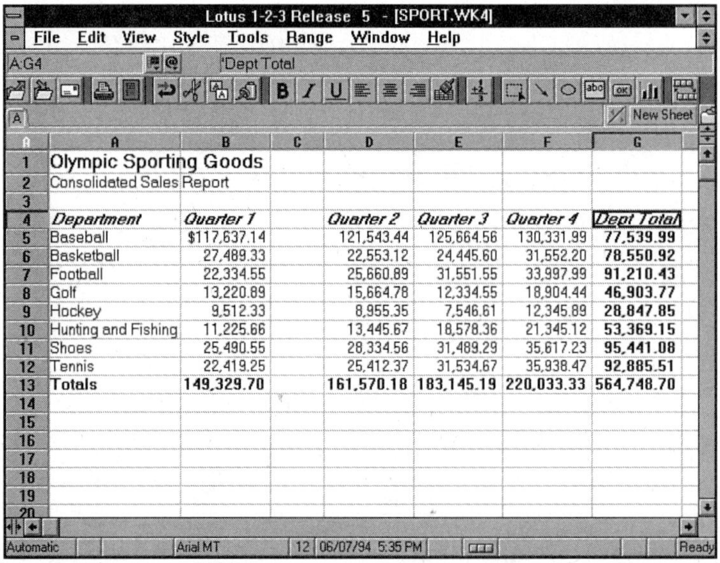

Fig. 2.6
The End key moves between blocks on the worksheet.

	A	B	C	D	E	F	G
1	Olympic Sporting Goods						
2	Consolidated Sales Report						
3							
4	Department	Quarter 1		Quarter 2	Quarter 3	Quarter 4	Dept Total
5	Baseball	$117,637.14		121,543.44	125,664.56	130,331.99	77,539.99
6	Basketball	27,489.33		22,553.12	24,445.60	31,552.20	78,550.92
7	Football	22,334.55		25,660.89	31,551.55	33,997.99	91,210.43
8	Golf	13,220.89		15,664.78	12,334.55	18,904.44	46,903.77
9	Hockey	9,512.33		8,955.35	7,546.61	12,345.89	28,847.85
10	Hunting and Fishing	11,225.66		13,445.67	18,578.36	21,345.12	53,369.15
11	Shoes	25,490.55		28,334.56	31,489.29	35,617.23	95,441.08
12	Tennis	22,419.25		25,412.37	31,534.67	35,938.47	92,885.51
13	Totals	149,329.70		161,570.18	183,145.19	220,033.33	564,748.70

Tip
Use the End and Home keys to find the end of the active area, perhaps to add a section to the worksheet without interfering with existing data, or to specify a print range.

If you press End and then Home, the cell pointer moves to the last cell that contains data in the worksheet or in the active area. The *active area* includes all rows and all columns that contain data or cell formats. (Cell formatting is discussed in Chapter 9.) If you press the End key and then the Home key in the worksheet shown in figure 2.6, the cell pointer moves to cell G28, the end of the active area (see fig. 2.7). Although blank, cell G28 is the end of the active area because entries appear in column G and row 28.

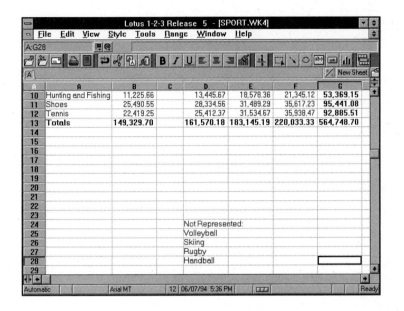

Fig. 2.7
Press End Home to move to the bottom right corner of the worksheet's active area.

Tables 2.1 and 2.2 contain lists of keys you can use to navigate around your worksheets and files.

Table 2.1   File Navigation Keys

Keys	Actions
Ctrl+End Home	Moves to the cell last highlighted in the first open file
Ctrl+End End	Moves to the cell last highlighted in the last open file
Ctrl+End, Ctrl+PgUp	Moves to the cell last highlighted in the next open file
Ctrl+End, Ctrl+PgDn	Moves to the cell last highlighted in the preceding open file
Ctrl+F6	Makes the next open worksheet, graph, or transcript window active

Table 2.2   Direction Keys

Keys	Actions
→ or ←	Moves right or left one column
↑ or ↓	Moves up or down one row

(continues)

Table 2.2 Continued

Keys	Actions
Ctrl + ←	Moves left one worksheet screen
Ctrl + → or Tab	Moves right one worksheet screen
Ctrl+Home	Moves to the home position (usually cell A:A1) in the current file
PgUp or PgDn	Moves up or down one worksheet screen
Home	Moves to the home position in the current worksheet (usually cell A1)
End Home	Moves to the bottom right corner of the worksheet's active area
Ctrl+PgUp	Moves to the following worksheet
Ctrl+PgDn	Moves to the preceding worksheet
End + →	Moves right to the next intersection between a blank cell and a cell that contains data
End + ←	Moves left to the next intersection between a blank cell and a cell that contains data
End + ↑	Moves up to a cell that contains data and is next to a blank cell.
End + ↓	Moves down to a cell that contains data and is next to a blank cell.
End Ctrl+Home	Moves to the bottom right corner of the current file's active area
End Ctrl+PgUp	Staying in the same row and column, moves back through worksheets to the next intersection between a blank cell and a cell that contains data
End Ctrl+PgDn	Staying in the same row and column, moves forward through worksheets to the next intersection between a blank cell and a cell that contains data

Using the Goto Feature

Tip
To move quickly to the desired range, double-click it in the list.

The Goto feature enables you to jump directly to cells in the current worksheet, to cells in other worksheets of the current worksheet file, or to any cell in any worksheet of any other open worksheet file. You can use *range names* with Goto so that you do not need to remember cell addresses. A *range*

is a rectangular group of cells and can be three dimensional, spanning
several worksheets in a file. A range name designates a cell address; for example, you can give cell H11 the range name TOT_POST_TAX. (For more
information about ranges and range names, see "Working with Ranges"
later in this chapter.)

You can access the Goto feature in two ways: press F5 (GoTo), or choose the
Edit **G**o To command. When you press F5 (GoTo) or choose **E**dit **G**o To, the
Go To dialog box appears (see fig. 2.8). In this dialog box, you specify in
the **T**ype of Item box what you want to find: a range, chart, drawn object, or
other item. The specified ranges for that type of item appear in the large list
box in the center of the dialog box; you can select from this list. If you are
moving to a range that you previously named with **R**ange **N**ame, simply
highlight the range name in the list box. When you choose OK, the cell
pointer moves directly to this address.

This box also contains the names of other open files; to move the cell pointer
to another file, choose the file name from the In **F**ile list. All previously
named ranges in the selected file appear in the Go To list box.

When you are in the Go To dialog box, to move to a specific cell in a specific
worksheet in the chosen file, you need to type the worksheet letter and cell
address. To move to cell B3 in worksheet C of the existing file, for example,
type **C:B3** in the Range text box and choose OK.

Working with Ranges

A range is a rectangular group of cells in a worksheet. A single cell can be
defined as a range. A column or row of adjacent cells can be defined as a
range. A block of cells spanning worksheets in a file can be defined as a range.

Tip
You can jump to a range quickly by using the navigator (see fig. 2.12) in the edit line. All defined range names appear when you click this button. Click the range name to jump to that range.

Fig. 2.8
The Go To dialog box.

Tip
An easier way to move to another worksheet file is to click the file (if the file is visible). If the file is hidden behind another window, press Ctrl+F6 repeatedly to cycle through the open windows until the file you want appears.

You define a range with the cell addresses of any two diagonally opposite corners of the range. When you specify a range address, you separate the cell addresses with one or two periods when typing, but two periods always appear when 1-2-3 for Windows displays the dimensions of a range. Notice in figure 2.9 that a range can be a single cell (E1..E1), part of a row (A1..C1), part of a column (G1..G5 and F14..F15), or a rectangle that spans multiple rows and columns (B4..E9 and A13..C15).

Fig. 2.9

Different types of ranges in one worksheet.

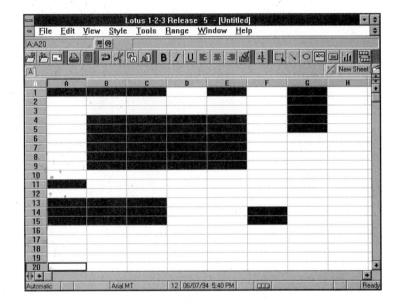

If you were to drag the cursor from A:A5 to A:B10, A:A5, the beginning cell of the range is called the *anchor cell*. A:B10, the end point of the range is called the *free cell*. Whenever you highlight a range, the cell diagonally opposite the *anchor cell* is the *free cell*.

A range can also be three-dimensional, spanning two or more worksheets. A three-dimensional range includes the corresponding cells in each worksheet. When you use a three-dimensional range, you must include the worksheet letters with the cell addresses. For example, if cells A3 through D3 are highlighted in worksheets A, B, and C, the address of this range is A:A3..C:D3. For more information on three-dimensional ranges, see the "Using Three-Dimensional Ranges" section later in this chapter.

Specifying Ranges

Many commands act on ranges. For example, the **R**ange **S**ort command prompts you for the range to be sorted. When 1-2-3 for Windows prompts you for a range, you can respond in one of three ways:

- ■ Type the cell addresses of two of the opposite corners of the range or of the cells in the ranges. Separate the two references with two dots (periods). For example, the range that includes cells A1, A2, B1, and B2 can be specified as A1..B2, B2..A1, A2..B1, or B1..A2.

- ■ Highlight the range with the keyboard or the mouse either before or after you select the command.

- ■ Type the range name or press F3 (Name), and select the range name if one has been assigned.

The following sections describe these options in detail.

Typing Range Addresses

The first method of specifying ranges, typing the address, is used the least because it is most prone to error. With this method, you type the addresses of any two cells in diagonally opposite corners of the range, separating the two addresses with one or two periods. (If you type only one period, 1-2-3 for Windows automatically inserts a second period to separate the addresses.) For example, to specify the range B4..E9, you can type B4..E9 or B4.E9, or E9..B4 or E9.B4. Or you can specify the other two corners: E4..B9 (E4.B9), or B9..E4 (B9.E4). No matter how you type the range, 1-2-3 for Windows stores it as B4..E9.

Pointing is faster and easier than typing range addresses. Because you can see the cells as you select them, you make fewer errors by pointing than by typing. The following sections describe pointing methods.

Highlighting a Range

You can highlight a range by clicking the mouse pointer on a cell and dragging to highlight a range. This action places you into Point mode (POINT appears as the mode indicator in the status bar) and is the most popular method of identifying the range. You can highlight ranges for commands and functions in the same way you point in a formula. You can highlight a range with the keyboard or the mouse either before or after you issue a command. Special considerations for highlighting ranges in functions are covered in Chapter 5, "Using Functions."

Everyday Worksheet Tasks

Tip
If you have a large
range of contigu-
ous cells contain-
ing data you want
to highlight, use
the End key along
with the Shift key.
Move to the
beginning of the
range (that is, its
upper left cell)
and press and
hold the Shift key.
Then press End,
the right arrow,
End again, and
the down arrow.
This technique
assumes that the
range is sur-
rounded by blank
cells and has
blank cells in
neither the top
row nor the last
column.

1-2-3 for Windows enables you to highlight cells before you issue a command. When you *preselect cells* and then issue a command, the address automatically appears in the dialog box. You need not reenter the address. One
exception exists; when you group worksheets together with Group mode, the
default range is the three-dimensional range that spans the whole group,
even if you have preselected a range in one worksheet only. To override the
default range in this case, you must type the range address.

To use the keyboard to preselect a range, press F4 and highlight the range by
using the arrow keys. When you finish specifying the range, press Enter. Using the Shift key can make the selection process even faster (this method also
works if you select the range after you issue the command). Just move to the
beginning of the range, press and hold the Shift key, and press the arrow keys
as necessary to highlight the rest of the range. When finished, release the
Shift key.

To highlight a range with the mouse, just click any corner of the range and
drag to the diagonally opposite corner. All cells between the corners are highlighted. You also can click a corner once, press and hold the Shift key, and
click the opposite corner once.

Highlighting Groups of Ranges

You can highlight a group of ranges, called a *collection*. Highlight the first
range using any method you like, and then press and hold the Ctrl key as you
highlight other ranges. All ranges are highlighted as a collection. (Refer to fig.
2.9 to see a collection of highlighted ranges.)

  When you press the Enter key, you move from cell to cell within the collection. Press Shift+Enter and you move backward within the collection. Also,
you may click the Next Range and Previous Range icons to move between
individual ranges within the existing collection. If you work with collections
often, you might consider creating a SmartIcon palette that includes these
two icons.

To specify a collection as a reference (such as when you want to sum
the numbers in A1..C1, E1, and G1..G5), you must separate each
distinct range reference with a semicolon. For example, you can enter
A1..C1;E1;G1..G5;B4..E9;A11;A13..C15;F14..F15 to specify the collection
shown in figure 2.9.

It is easier and more efficient to highlight a range before you issue a command, but if you forget to select a range beforehand, you can select one after
you issue the command. When the command leads to a dialog box, you can
type or point to the range within the dialog box.

To highlight a range after issuing a command, simply highlight the existing reference in the text box and then click and drag on the worksheet to highlight the desired range. You can move the dialog box aside to gain better access to the worksheet; move the dialog box by clicking its title bar and dragging. The reference of the range you highlight replaces the old reference.

Alternatively, you can use a range selector in a dialog box. If you click in the range selector area of a dialog box, this temporarily removes the dialog box while you select the desired range in the worksheet. The dialog box reappears when you finish selecting the range or press Enter.

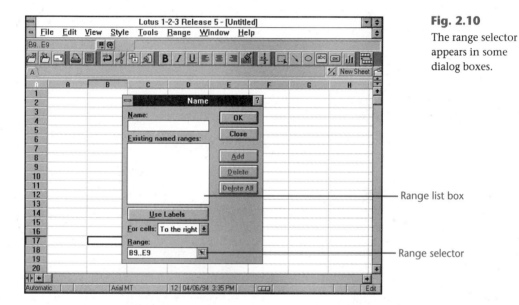

Fig. 2.10
The range selector appears in some dialog boxes.

Range list box

Range selector

Using Range Names

The third way to specify a range is to refer to the range by name. Range names, which should be descriptive, can include up to 15 characters and can be used in formulas, functions, and commands. You can apply a range name with the **R**ange **N**ame command or the Create/Delete Range Name SmartIcon; a list of existing range names can be viewed by using the navigator on the edit line.

Using range names has a number of advantages: range names are easier to remember than addresses. Using a range name is usually faster than pointing to a range in another part of the worksheet. You can, for example, remember more easily that the sales totals are in a range named TOTALS instead of in cells G5..G12. Also, if you highlight a named range by dragging across it, its name appears in the selection indicator, at the top of the screen.

Range names also make formulas easier to understand. For example, if you want to calculate a grand total from subtotals, you can give the range containing the subtotals a name and then use the range name in a formula that adds all the subtotals. As an example, you can enter into the contents box (on the edit line) the formula @SUM(TOTALS). Because this formula uses a range name, it is equivalent to but easier to understand than the formula @SUM(A:G5..A:G12).

Whenever 1-2-3 for Windows expects the address of a cell or range, you can specify a range name. Three ways to specify a range name are available. You can type the range name in the dialog box, press F3 (Name) to display existing range names, or click the navigator on the edit line. The navigator lists the range names in alphabetical order (see fig. 2.11). When you edit a formula and choose a range name from the navigator's range list, the range name is inserted into the formula.

Fig. 2.11
You can use the navigator to insert range names into a formula.

Range list   Navigator

▶ "Using Functions," p. 135

Because a single cell is considered a valid range, you can name a single cell as a range. If a command or action, such as F5 (GoTo), calls for a single-cell address, you can specify the cell by typing its range name. If you type a range name that refers to a multiple-cell range when 1-2-3 calls for a single-cell address, 1-2-3 for Windows uses the upper-left corner of the range.

Tip
Remember, you can prevent yourself from typing range names incorrectly by using the navigator to select from existing range names.

If you type a nonexistent range name, 1-2-3 for Windows displays an error message. Press Esc or Enter or choose OK to clear the error. Errors may occur when you use range names in formulas.

Naming Ranges with the Range Name Command

To create a range name, use the **R**ange **N**ame command to assign a name to a cell or range. Follow these steps:

- Select the cell or range you want to name.

- Choose **R**ange **N**ame or click the Create/Delete Range Name SmartIcon. The Name dialog box appears.

■ Type the new range name, and choose OK or press Enter. If you want, you can choose the range after selecting the **R**ange **N**ame command: Choose the command, click the range selector in the **R**ange text box, and highlight the range.

> **Caution**
>
> When you are in the Range Name dialog box, if you type an existing range name after you preselect a range different from the one previously assigned to that name, 1-2-3 for Windows changes the range name so it refers to your newly-designated cells. It does not warn you when it does so. If you have written formulas that contain this range name, the formulas automatically refer to the new addresses and will likely produce errors. To help prevent this problem, scan the navigator list before applying new range names.

A range name can include up to 15 characters. You can type or refer to the name by using any combination of uppercase and lowercase letters, but 1-2-3 for Windows stores all range names as uppercase letters. Note the following rules and precautions for naming ranges:

■ Do not use spaces, commas, semicolons, or the following characters: → + - * / & > < @ #

■ You can use numbers in range names, but don't start the name with a number. TOTAL1 is okay, but 1TOTAL is not.

■ Do not use range names that are also cell addresses, column letters, or row numbers (such as A2, IV, or 100), names of keys (such as GoTo), function names (such as @SUM), or macro commands (such as FORM).

▶ "Writing 1-2-3 for Windows Macros," p. 1033

> **Note**
>
> Lotus 1-2-3 does, in fact, allow you to begin range names with a number, for example, 1TABLE. However, you cannot use range names beginning with numbers in formulas. If you create the range named 1TABLE and attempt to use it in an @SUM function, for example @SUM(1TABLE), Lotus doesn't accept the entry. You should get in the habit of naming ranges with names beginning with a letter.

If you have named a range but later want to change the cells that the range name refers to, you can do so easily. Follow these steps to redefine a range name's address:

1. Open the **R**ange menu and choose **N**ame, or click the Create/Delete Range Name SmartIcon. The Name dialog box appears.

2. Locate the range name in the **E**xisting Named Ranges list. Click the name to insert it into the **N**ame text box.

3. Click the range selector at the bottom of the dialog box.

4. Use any method to select the new range on the worksheet.

5. Choose OK or press Enter to close the Name dialog box. The existing range name now refers to a new group of cells.

Creating Range Names from Labels

You can use the **R**ange **N**ame command to create range names from labels already typed into the worksheet. In figure 2.12, for example, you can use the labels in cells B5..B8 to name the cells with sales data in C5..C8.

By choosing the **U**se Labels button in the Name dialog box, you can automatically create range names using column and row labels in the highlighted range. With the **F**or Cells drop-down list in the Name dialog box, specify whether the cells to be named appear Above, Below, To the Right, or To the Left of the labels you want to use as range names.

Fig. 2.12

Labels can be used to name adjacent ranges.

	A	B	C	D	E	F	G	H
1								
2		Fourth Quarter Sales						
3								
4			Oct	Nov	Dec			
5		Dept 1	6654	7565	8123			
6		Dept 2	1200	1450	1215			
7		Dept 3	3325	3680	4123			
8		Dept 4	6635	6900	7500			
9								
10		Totals	17814	19595	20961			
11								
12								

Lotus 1-2-3 Release 5 - [Untitled]
File Edit View Style Tools Range Window Help
A:B12

Suppose that you want to name the cells to the right of the labels in figure 2.12. In other words, you want to assign the range name "Dept 1" to cell C5, "Dept 2" to cell C6, and so on. Select cells B5..B8. Select **R**ange **N**ame, click the **U**se Labels button in the Name dialog box, and select To the Right from the **F**or Cells list box. Then press Enter. You could also have selected the range after using the command but before choosing OK in the dialog box.

When you specify cells that contain labels you want to use as range names, only cells that contain labels are used. If you specified the range B2..B10 in the preceding example (refer to fig. 2.12), the blank cells in B3, B4, and B9 are ignored.

The first 15 characters of the label in B2 become the range name for C2 (the two words Fourth Quarter, the space between the words, and the space following the second word). If you specify cells that are blank or that include numbers or formulas, 1-2-3 ignores them when it uses labels to name ranges.

To delete an unwanted range name, use **R**ange **N**ame or the Create/Delete Range Name SmartIcon and then select the name from the list of existing range names. Then choose the **D**elete button. To delete all range names in a file, use the Delete All command button.

You can use the 1-2-3 Classic command **/R**ange Name **T**able to insert a table of range names and their respective range references into the worksheet at the cell-pointer location.

Using Three-Dimensional Ranges

Three-dimensional ranges are particularly useful when you build consolidation worksheets. Consolidations are worksheets that combine data from different files, each of which contains data from one department, region, product, and so on.

A three-dimensional range has the shape of a three-dimensional rectangle. The first two dimensions include the height (number of rows) and width (number of columns) in the range. The third dimension, the depth, occurs when you add worksheets to the range. A range can span multiple worksheets within a worksheet file, giving you a range that goes several levels "deep." However, you must use contiguous sheets. That is, you cannot skip sheets in your three-dimensional references.

For example, to create the range A:C4..C:E10 shown in figure 2.13, move the cell pointer to A:C4. Press and hold the Shift key (or press F4) to anchor the range. Press the down-arrow key six times and the right-arrow key twice to highlight A:C4..A:E10; then press Ctrl+PgUp twice to move to worksheet C. Release the Shift key. Alternatively, you can highlight the entire range by first highlighting A:C4..A:E10 on worksheet A and then hold the Shift key and click cell C:E10. The range A:C4..C:E10 is highlighted.

Fig. 2.13
A three-dimensional range that spans three worksheets (shown in perspective view).

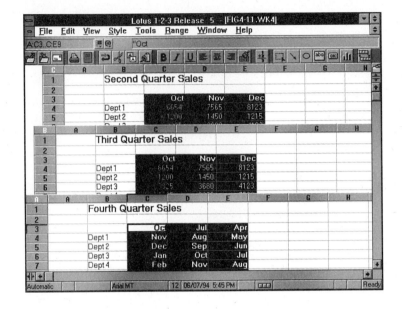

Still another way to select the range A:C4..C:E10 is available *provided* the worksheets are *not* in the perspective view which is shown in fig. 2.13. In that case, you can highlight A:C4..A:E10 and then select the corresponding cells on pages B and C by holding the Shift key and clicking the C worksheet tab.

▶ "Grouping
Worksheets,"
p. 277

You also can select three-dimensional ranges by first grouping worksheets together. When worksheets are grouped, range selections applied to one worksheet occur in all the worksheets simultaneously. Using this feature, you can avoid moving between worksheets and can use the mouse more easily.

Highlighting a three-dimensional range is much easier than typing the corner addresses. If you do type the addresses, make sure that you use the correct worksheet letters. The corners of a three-dimensional range are diagonally opposite; usually, this means the upper left corner cell in the first worksheet and the lower right corner cell in the last worksheet.

Entering Data in a Range

When you highlight a range in a worksheet, the cell pointer remains within that range as you type information into the cells. When you press Enter to complete an entry, the cell pointer moves to the next cell inside the highlighted range. Until you press an arrow key or click the mouse outside the range, pressing Enter simply moves the cell pointer within the highlighted area. This arrangement can be useful for entering numeric values down a column.

The order 1-2-3 uses in moving around in a highlighted range is as follows: 1-2-3 begins in the upper left corner cell of the range, moves down until the first column is completed, moves to the top of the next column to the right, completes that column, and so on. After the cell pointer reaches the bottom right corner of the highlighted range, 1-2-3 for Windows returns to the upper left corner of the range. The fill area is two-dimensional only; even if the specified range is three-dimensional, 1-2-3 for Windows fills only the specified range in the current worksheet.

Note

To make successive entries down a column, first highlight the column. The cell pointer is in the top cell. Type information into the first cell and press Enter. The column remains highlighted, but the cell pointer moves to the next cell in the range. You can continue to make entries in these cells by typing each entry and pressing Enter, rather than having to use the arrow keys.

Filling a Range with Values

1-2-3 includes a special feature for filling ranges with sequential values, such as numeric sequences or dates. The **R**ange **F**ill command (or the Fill Range SmartIcon) lets you generate sequences automatically by specifying the starting value, the ending value, and the desired increment.

The **R**ange Fill by **E**xample command (or the Fill Range by Example SmartIcon) continues a linear sequence you have started in a worksheet. Figure 2.14 shows some before and after sequences you can create by example.

Note

1-2-3 continues the sequence in any direction in which you have highlighted cells.

Fig. 2.14
The **R**ange Fill by **E**xample command creates sequences based on your example.

Tip
After you use **R**ange **F**ill or **R**ange Fill by **E**xample to fill a range of cells with a series of numbers, use the **S**tyle **A**lignment command to align the numbers.

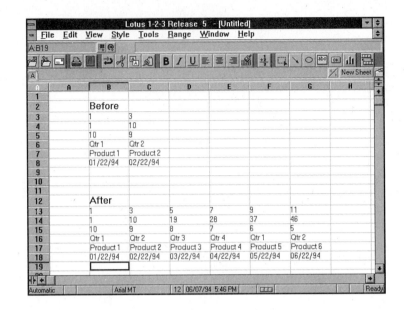

From Here...

Now that you have learned to create, save and retrieve files, and you have learned to maneuver around an open file, you may want to refer to the following chapters:

- Chapter 3, "Entering and Editing Data," covers topics related to entering and editing labels and values, using a variety of tools.

- Chapter 4, "Working with Formulas," discusses how to have 1-2-3 for Windows do calculations for you.

- Chapter 5, "Using Functions," discusses the over 200 mathematical functions built into 1-2-3 for Windows.

- Chapter 23, "Creating a Database," which introduces 1-2-3 for Windows database capabilities.

Chapter 3

Entering and Editing Data

This chapter presents the skills you need to start creating your own worksheet. You enter data into worksheet cells by typing the data or by using a Fill command to enter sequential numbers, month names, dates, and so on into the worksheet. Once you have entered data into a worksheet, you need to know how to edit the data, erase entries, and reorganize the worksheet by inserting or deleting rows and columns.

1-2-3 for Windows also has some features similar to your word processing program. You can check the spelling of data in a worksheet or use a find and replace command to search for specific data and replace it with new information.

In this chapter you learn how to

- ■ Enter text, numbers, and dates

- ■ Improve your data entry efficiency

- ■ Fill ranges with a series of numbers, dates, or text

- ■ Edit the contents of a cell

- ■ Find and replace text

- ■ Insert and delete cells, rows, and columns

- ■ Undo previous actions

- ■ Check the spelling of text in your worksheet

Entering Data into the Worksheet

The first way that you can enter data into a worksheet is to type the data. You can create two kinds of cell entries: labels and values. A *label* is a text entry, and a *value* is a number or formula. 1-2-3 for Windows determines the kind of cell entry from the first character you enter. When you type the first character, the mode indicator changes from Ready to Value or Label.

1-2-3 considers an entry to be a value (a number or formula) if the entry begins with one of the following characters:

0 1 2 3 4 5 6 7 8 9 + - (@ # . $

If the entry begins with any other character, 1-2-3 considers the entry to be a label.

To enter data into a worksheet, use these steps:

Tip

A quick way to type data into a worksheet is to type an entry and then press an arrow key to move to the next location for typing.

1. Move the cell pointer to the appropriate cell.

2. Type the entry.

   As you type, the entry appears in the contents box of the edit line and in the cell (see fig. 3.1). While the data is still on the edit line, you can press the Backspace key to back up and correct your typing, or you can press Esc or click the Cancel button to cancel your entry.

3. Press Enter or a direction key (for example, Tab, PgDn, or arrow key), or click the Confirm button. The entry now appears in the cell.

> **Caution**
>
> If you type data into a cell that already contains information, your typing replaces the old text.

Tip

Avoid starting your worksheet in cell A1. Leave an extra row or two at the top of the worksheet and an extra column at the left side to make your worksheets easier to read.

Another way to enter information into a cell is to double-click the cell. Double-clicking places the *cursor* (the flashing bar) in the cell, and you can begin typing.

Entering Labels

Labels, or text entries, make the numbers and formulas in your worksheets understandable by providing titles, row and column headings, and descriptive text. A label can be a string of up to 512 characters.

Cancel button — Confirm button   Text appears in the contents box

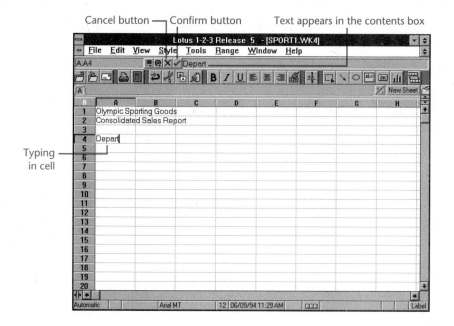

Typing in cell

Everyday Worksheet Tasks

Fig. 3.1
As you type an entry, it appears in the contents box on the edit line and in the cell.

When you enter a label, 1-2-3 for Windows adds a *label prefix* to the cell entry. 1-2-3 uses the label prefix to identify the entry as a label and to determine how to display and print the entry. By default, the program uses an apostrophe (') for a left-aligned label, meaning that labels are automatically lined up at the left edge of the cell. To place your label in the center or right edge of a cell, type one of the label prefixes shown in Table 3.1 as the first character of the label.

▶ "Setting View Preferences," p. 965

Table 3.1   Label Prefix (Alignment) Characters

Prefix	Description
'	Left-aligned (the default)
"	Right-aligned
^	Centered
\	Repeating (if you change the column width, 1-2-3 changes the length of a repeating label to fill the new column width)
|	Nonprinting (the contents of the cell don't print)

The label prefix is not visible in the worksheet but appears in the contents box (see fig. 3.2).

Label prefix

Fig. 3.2
The prefix
character shows in
the contents box,
not the worksheet
cell.

Repeated character

Centered label

Right-aligned label

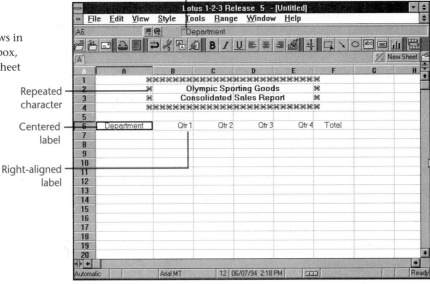

Tip
You can use
the alignment
SmartIcons to
align entries after
they are typed.
See Chapter 9
for more
information.

The following table gives examples of when you might use the different label prefix characters and figure 3.2 shows examples of these uses.

Typical Alignments	Usage
Left-aligned text	Use for normal text.
Right-aligned text	Column headings placed over numeric columns often look better right-aligned so that the labels line up over the numbers below.
Centered text	Use for column headings and other text you want centered.
Repeated text	Use this with special characters (try the Wingding font) to create borders and other interesting effects in a sheet.

In figure 3.2, cells A6 and F6 are centered, while cells B6 through E6 are right aligned. Because numbers and numeric formulas are always right-aligned, the headings above columns of numbers also are generally right-aligned. When an entry fills the cell width, the alignments do not make a difference in the appearance of that cell.

Cells B1..E1 and B4..E4 show the use of a repeated character. In this case, the character is a "wingding," a special font that consists entirely of symbols. By repeating the wingding character, a fancy border was created around an area of the worksheet.

Note

If you want a label prefix character to appear as the first character of a label, you first must type the label prefix and then type *another* label prefix as the first character of the label. If you type **\015** in a cell, for example, the 1-2-3 displays 015015015015015015 as a repeating label, rather than \015. You first must type another label prefix—here, an apostrophe ('). Therefore, you must type **'\015** to get \015 in the cell.

Typing Dates, Phone Numbers and Social Security Numbers

Some types of data may look like numbers, but should really be entered as labels. Dates, phone numbers, and Social Security numbers fall into this category. If the data you need to type contains numbers, but the entry really is not a number, you must type a label prefix before typing the entry. If you do not type a prefix, when you type the numeric character, 1-2-3 for Windows switches to Value mode and expects a valid number or formula to follow.

Let's look at some examples. If you type a telephone number such as **317-555-6100**, 1-2-3 evaluates the entry as a formula and subtracts the second two numbers from the first. Similarly, if you type **9-30-95** to refer to a date, 1-2-3 evaluates the entry as a formula and displays the result -116. 1-2-3 considers a date entry of **9/30/95**, however, to be valid, and the program stores that entry as a date serial number.

Note

If the entry contains any character that is not interpreted as an appropriate character in a value or formula, 1-2-3 does recognize the entry as a label. For example, if you type a phone number and place a space between the area code and the rest of the number, 1-2-3 enters the phone number as a label. When you type an address, like **123 Main St.**, 1-2-3 recognizes it as a label because it contains spaces and alphabetic characters.

Tip

Type dates with slashes (9/12/94), and 1-2-3 interprets them as a date.

▶ "Calendar Functions," p. 142

Tip

If you have many phone numbers to type, you can select a range and format it to contain labels using **S**tyle **N**umber Format **L**abel.

Typing Long Labels

If a label is longer than a cell's width, 1-2-3 displays the label across blank cells to the right of the cell. The data is not actually filling all these cells but is spilling across them. A long text entry may spill across several blank cells. This enables you to type headings in a worksheet across several cells (see fig. 3.3).

If the cells to the right of the label cell are not blank, 1-2-3 for Windows cuts off the display of the entry at the cell border. The program still stores the complete entry in the contents box, however, and displays the full entry when the cell is highlighted. Figure 3.3 shows an entry that was *truncated* in the worksheet, but the full entry shows in the contents box.

Fig. 3.3
Long entries
borrow space from
adjacent cells.
If an entry is
truncated the full
entry still shows in
the contents box.

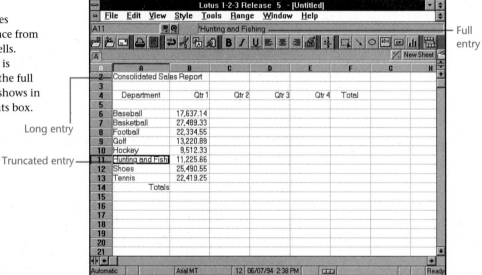

► "Enhancing the Appearance of Data," p. 343

► "Setting Column Widths," p. 312

Note

To display the entire label in the worksheet, you can insert blank columns to the right of the cell containing the long label, or you can widen the column. Widening the column is easy when you use the mouse; simply move the mouse pointer over the column border to the right of the column letter and drag the border to the desired width.

Troubleshooting

When I type a phone number with the area code in parentheses, 1-2-3 does not accept it.

You must tell 1-2-3 to expect a label, not a number, when you type a phone number as described. To do this, type a label prefix character before the number or format the cell for a label.

Help! My long entries are truncated when I type data in an adjacent column.

Don't worry, you didn't lose your entry. Just make the column wider to see your long entry.

Entering Numbers

To enter a valid number in a worksheet, you can type any of the 10 digits (0 through 9) and certain other characters, as shown in the following table. The results in the Displayed/Stored column of the table are based on the default column width (9) and the default font (12-point Arial MT).

Character	Example	Displayed/ Stored	Description
+ (plus)	+123	123	If the number is preceded by a plus sign, 1-2-3 for Windows doesn't store the plus sign.
– (minus)	–123	–123	If the number is preceded by a minus sign, 1-2-3 for Windows stores the number as a negative number.
( ) (parentheses)	(123)	–123	If the number is in parentheses, 1-2-3 for Windows stores the number as a negative number, displays the number preceded by a minus sign, and drops the parentheses.
$ (dollar sign)	$123	123	If the number is preceded by a dollar sign (unless the cell is formatted as Automatic or Currency), 1-2-3 for Windows doesn't store the dollar sign.
. (period)	.123	0.123	You can include one decimal point, which 1-2-3 for Windows stores with the number.

(continues)

Character	Example	Displayed/ Stored	Description
, (comma)	123,456	123456	Three digits must follow each comma; 1-2-3 for Windows doesn't store the commas unless you formatted the cell as Automatic or Comma.
% (percent)	123%	1.23	If the number is followed by a percent sign, 1-2-3 for Windows divides the number by 100 and drops the percent sign unless you formatted the cell as Automatic or Percent.

Note

▶ "Working with Number Formats," p. 326

If you type dollar signs, commas, or percent signs into numbers, 1-2-3 automatically formats the cell to have those characteristics. This is because 1-2-3 defaults to *automatic formatting*, which formats a cell based on the data first entered into it. Although this is a handy feature, it can create some problems for you. For example, if you type a percent into a cell (**10%**), the cell is automatically formatted as a percent and any number that you subsequently type into that cell is interpreted as a percent.

1-2-3 for Windows stores only 18 digits of any number. If you enter a number with more than 18 digits, 1-2-3 rounds the number after the 18th digit. When displaying numbers on-screen, the program stores the complete number (up to 18 digits) but displays only what fits in the cell. If the number is too long to display in the cell, 1-2-3 for Windows tries to display as much of the number as possible. If the cell uses the default General format and the integer part of the number fits into the cell, 1-2-3 rounds the decimal characters that don't fit. If the integer part of the number doesn't fit in the cell, the program displays the number in *scientific (exponential) notation*. If the cell uses a format other than General or the cell width is too narrow to display in scientific notation and the number cannot fit into the cell, 1-2-3 for Windows displays asterisks. Figure 3.4 shows a worksheet where some of the columns are not wide enough.

1-2-3 stores a number in scientific notation only if it contains more than 20 digits. If you enter a number with more than 18 digits, 1-2-3 rounds the number to end with one or more zeros. You can actually type a number by using scientific notation, but 1-2-3 still rounds to 18 digits.

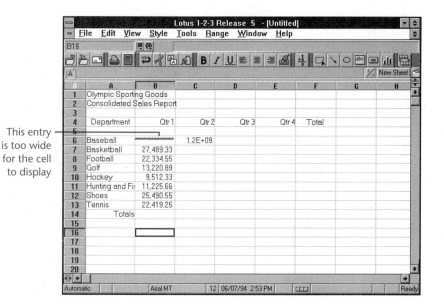

This entry
is too wide
for the cell
to display

Fig. 3.4
The number
appears in
scientific notation
or as asterisks (*)
when a column is
not wide enough
to display a
number or date.

Everyday Worksheet Tasks

The appearance of a number in the worksheet depends on the cell's format,
font, and column width. When you use the default font (12-point Arial MT)
and the default column width (9), 1-2-3 displays the number 1234567890 as
1.2E+09. If you use a column width of 11, however, 1-2-3 displays the number
as entered.

▶ "Setting
  Column
  Widths,"
  p. 312

▶ "Working
  with Number
  Formats,"
  p. 326

Troubleshooting

*I accidentally typed the date 8/30/94 into a cell and now when I type a number into that
cell, I get a strange date.*

The Automatic Format feature of 1-2-3 formats a cell for the type of data that you
initially enter into the cell. So, when you entered a date into the cell, the cell was
formatted as a date. Every number you type into that cell is then formatted as a date,
too. Click the format selector at the lower-left corner of the status bar and choose
another format to get rid of the date formatting. This same thing could happen if
you type a percent into a cell as well.

When I type a number into the cell, I get asterisks.

If the number you type has a dollar sign, comma, or percent sign and is too large to
fit in the cell, you will see asterisks displayed in the worksheet. You can make the
column wider or change the format.

Making Data Entry Easier

You can make the process of entering data (especially numbers) into a worksheet even easier if you like to use the number pad for typing your values. If you select the range into which you are going to enter data, you can type an entry and press Enter. 1-2-3 automatically moves to the next cell down in the selected range and, when appropriate, wraps around to the top of the next column, too! To use this technique for entering data, follow these steps:

1. Select the range that you are going to enter data in.

2. Type each entry and press Enter. You can correct an entry before you have entered it with the Backspace key, but do not use an arrow key or you deselect the range.

Figure 3.5 shows a range selected and data entry in progress.

Fig. 3.5
Select a range,
type an entry, and
press Enter to
move to the
next cell.

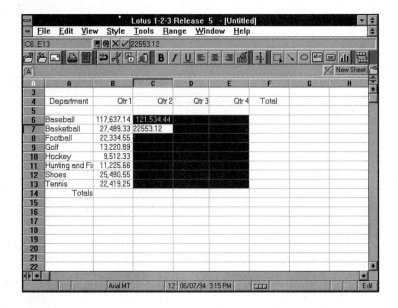

Filling Ranges

Two 1-2-3 for Windows commands—**R**ange **F**ill and **R**ange Fill By **E**xample—can make entering data easier. You can use these commands, for example, to fill a series of month names or dates into column headings in a worksheet or to fill sequential numbers or any type of number pattern. **R**ange **F**ill and **R**ange Fill By **E**xample fill a range of cells with a series of numbers (which can be in the form of numbers, formulas, or functions), dates, or times that increase or decrease by a specified increment.

The following table shows some examples of how you can use the fill by example function. Figure 3.6 shows some cells that were filled by using the **R**ange Fill by **E**xample.

You can accomplish a fill in 3 ways:

- Drag-and-Fill performs a Fill by example using only the mouse

- SmartIcons perform a Range Fill or Range Fill by Example

- Menu selections perform a **R**ange **F**ill or **R**ange Fill by **E**xample

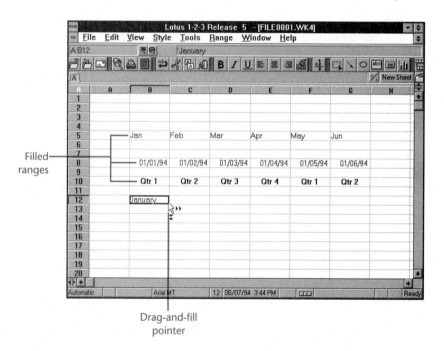

Filled ranges

Drag-and-fill pointer

Fig. 3.6
The Fill by Example fills a range based on an initial entry.

Using the Drag-and-Fill

The quickest and easiest way to fill a range is with the Drag-and-Fill technique, which enables you to accomplish the fill by just dragging the mouse. The critical part of using the fill by example in any form is entering the initial value (or values). The fill then uses the initial values as an example for filling a selected range with information. Follow these steps to use the Drag-and-Fill feature:

1. Type the first occurrence of the sequence that you want to fill into an area of your sheet. If you want to fill a range with an irregular pattern, type the first two or three entries to establish the pattern.

2. Select the cell or cells containing your initial value(s).

3. Move the mouse pointer over the lower right-hand corner of the selected cell or cells. The mouse pointer turns into the symbol that looks like arrows pointing to the right and down (refer to figure 3.6).

4. Click and drag the lower-right corner of your initial cell(s) into the range you want to fill. As you drag across the range, the mouse pointer changes to the pointer that displays anytime you select a range.

1st Entry	2nd Entry	Filled Entries
1	(none)	1, 2, 3, 4, 5...
1	3	1, 3, 5, 7, 9...
Jan	(none)	Jan, Feb, Mar, Apr...
January	(none)	January, February, March...
Jan	Apr	Jan, Apr, July, Oct, Jan...
1/1/94	(none)	1/1/94, 1/2/94, 1/3/94, 1/4/94...
1/1/94	1/8/94	1/1/94, 1/8/94, 1/15/94, 1/22/94...
Qtr 1	(none)	Qtr 1, Qtr 2, Qtr 3, Qtr 4, Qtr 1...
1994	(none)	1994, 1995, 1996...
Product 1	(none)	Product 1, Product 2, Product 3...

Notice that 1-2-3 recognizes date related entries and starts over at the end of a year. If 1-2-3 cannot recognize a pattern in your examples, the Drag-and-Fill just copies the original entries into the selected cells.

 The quickest and easiest way to use these commands is with the Fill Range by Example SmartIcon, which fills a range based on the selected data in a worksheet.

Using the Fill Range by Example SmartIcon or Range Fill By Example

The Fill Range by Example SmartIcon (or **R**ange Fill By **E**xample command) provides the same functions as the Drag-and-Fill, with a small difference in operation.

To use Fill by Example, follow these steps:

1. Type the first occurrence of the sequence that you want to fill into an area of your sheet. If you want to fill a range with an irregular pattern, type the first two or three entries to establish the pattern.

2. Select the cell containing the data you just typed and the range to be filled (these must be contiguous).

3. Click the Fill Range by Example SmartIcon, or open the **R**ange menu and choose Fill By **E**xample.

> **Note**
>
> The Range Fill by Example SmartIcon is not included on any of the standard icon palettes. If you would prefer to use the SmartIcon, rather than the Drag-and-Fill technique, you can add the icon to the Default Sheet palette or any of the other icon palettes. See "Customizing the SmartIcons" in Chapter 9 for information on how to add an icon to the icon palettes.

Using Range Fill for More Control

An alternative to using the Range Fill by Example SmartIcon is the **R**ange **F**ill command, which enables you to choose the type of fill and the starting, increment, and stop values for the fill. When you issue the **R**ange **F**ill command, 1-2-3 for Windows displays the Fill dialog box (see fig. 3.7).

The Fill dialog box has two advantages over using the Drag-and-Fill or Range Fill by Example:

■ *Interval Options.* The Fill dialog box provides a variety of options for the interval, so that you do not have to type examples to fill a range with weekly, monthly, or yearly dates.

■ *Stop Value.* The Stop value entry enables you to control the last value in the filled range. The Fill stops at the Stop value or the end of the range, whichever comes first. When you use Drag-and-Fill, you can only guess how large a range to select.

▶ "Calendar
Functions,"
p. 142

One example of when the Fill dialog box works better than a Drag-and-Fill or Fill by Example SmartIcon is when you want to create a calendar that ends with the last day of the year (or any other specific date). Just type the last desired date in the Stop value and select a range large enough to extend past the last date. Figure 3.7 shows a Fill dialog box with entries that start on 1/1/94 and continue until 12/31/94.

To fill a range with the **R**ange **F**ill command, use these steps:

1. Select the range to be filled.

2. Open the **R**ange menu and choose **F**ill. The Fill dialog box appears (see fig. 3.7).

Fig. 3.7
Use the Fill dialog box to choose the type of fill and the starting, increment, and stop values.

3. Choose an interval from the Interval area of the dialog box.

4. Choose the **S**tart text box, and type a starting value.

5. Choose the **I**ncrement text box (a quick way to move there is to press Tab), and type an increment.

6. If desired, choose the St**o**p text box and type an ending value. For many fill operations, you can leave this at the default of 8191.

7. Choose OK or press Enter to fill the range.

When a range that includes several columns and rows is selected as shown in figure 3.7, 1-2-3 fills down the column and then wraps around to the top of the next column in the range. The first cell is filled with the start value, and each subsequent cell is filled with the value in the preceding cell plus the increment. Filling stops when 1-2-3 for Windows reaches the stop value or the end of the fill range, whichever happens first.

Filling Ranges with Numbers

Most of the time, the easiest way to fill a range with numbers is to place the starting number in the worksheet and use the Fill by Example. However, anything that can be done with the Fill by Example can also be accomplished with a **R**ange **F**ill. Consider, for example, using year numbers as titles in a sales-forecast worksheet. Choose the range of cells to be filled, and then enter for the **S**tart value **1995**. The **I**ncrement value in this example is set at 1. The St**o**p value can be left at the default (8191).

You also can use the **R**ange **F**ill command to build a list of interest rates (see fig. 3.8). After you specify the fill range, enter the starting value as a decimal fraction (**0.05** for 5 percent, for example) and another decimal fraction (**0.01** for 1 percent) for the increment value. Leave the default ending value at 8191. The **R**ange **F**ill command fills only the specified range and doesn't fill cells beyond the end of the range.

Tip
After you use **R**ange **F**ill or **R**ange Fill By Example to fill a range of cells with a series of numbers, use the **S**tyle **A**lignment command to align the numbers.

Fig. 3.8
Type the **S**tart and **I**ncrement values to accomplish any type of numeric fill.

A third use for the **R**ange **F**ill command is in combination with **R**ange **S**ort or **Q**uery **S**ort. Suppose that you are going to sort a database, and you want to be able to restore the records to their original order if you make a mistake as you are sorting. All you need to do is add a field to the database and use **R**ange **F**ill to fill the field with consecutive numbers. Then sort the database, including the new field of numbers. If you find that the result of the sort is unacceptable, sort the database on the number field to return the database to its original order.

▶ "Restoring the Presort Order," p. 736

Note

The **R**ange **F**ill is not able to fill all types of series. For example, if you want to have a series of numbers that increase geometrically (1, 10, 100, 1000), the **R**ange **F**ill can't do it. You can still accomplish this by placing the starting value in a cell, for example, type **1** in cell A1. Then, enter a formula in the second cell (for example, **+A1*10**) and copy this formula to the range. See "Creating Formulas," in Chapter 4 for more information on formulas.

Filling Ranges with Dates or Times

Most numeric fills can be accomplished easily with the Drag-and-Fill. **R**ange **F**ill works well when you want to fill a worksheet range with a sequence of dates or times. You use the options listed in the Interval section of the Fill dialog box to specify the increase from one cell in the range to the next. Selecting **L**inear just increases by the number specified in the **I**ncrement text box; selecting **M**onth, **D**ay, Mi**n**ute, increases the next value by the same number, but measured in months, days, minutes, and so on.

When you use one of the time intervals to fill a range, 1-2-3 for Windows automatically formats the range with an appropriate date or time format. In addition, the program automatically supplies the current date or time as a default starting value (which you can change if necessary).

Figure 3.9 shows an example of the Fill dialog box set to fill a range with weekly values, with the result already shown in the worksheet.

Fig. 3.9

Type the starting value for your fill with the format you want for all the filled values.

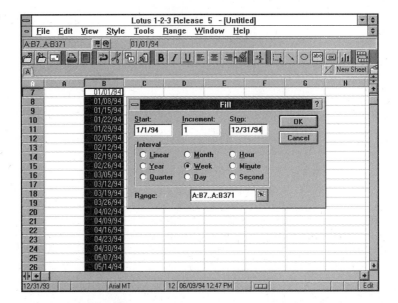

Note

Range **F**ill can fill only contiguous ranges, not collections.

Notice that when you fill a range with times, 1-2-3 for Windows may put in the last cell of the fill range a time slightly different from the stop value you specified. A slight loss of accuracy sometimes occurs when 1-2-3 for Windows converts between the binary numbers that it uses internally and the decimal numbers used for times. To avoid this problem, specify a stop value less than one increment larger than the desired stop value. If the increment is 10 minutes, for example, and you want the last cell in the range to contain 10:30, specify a stop value between 10:30 and 10:40, such as 10:35.

Caution

If you perform multiple fill operations in a single worksheet, the Fill dialog box contains the information from the last fill. Don't forget to enter new start, increment, and stop values if you want to perform a different type of fill.

Troubleshooting

*When I tried to use **R**ange **F**ill to add numbers to a range, only part of the range was filled. Why wasn't the entire range filled, as I expected?*

Range **F**ill fills the selected range until all the cells are filled or until the St**o**p value is reached. You may have forgotten to make the St**o**p value large enough to accommodate the entire range that you wanted to fill.

*Why did **R**ange Fill By **E**xample fill the entire range with the same label that I entered in the first cell of the range?*

If **R**ange Fill By **E**xample cannot recognize the correct pattern to use for incrementing labels, it copies the starting label to the entire range. Make certain that the starting label is one that **R**ange Fill By **E**xample can recognize (for example, Qtr 1 or January), or create a custom-fill sequence so that **R**ange Fill By **E**xample knows how you want to fill the range.

When I fill a range in my worksheet, I get dates or percents instead of the numbers I expected.

If the range you fill previously contained dates or percents, the cells are formatted that way. Change the range to a numeric format with the **S**tyle **N**umber Format command.

*I can't select "Fill by Example" in my **R**ange menu, since it is grayed out.*

If you do not have a range selected in your worksheet, the Fill by **E**xample menu selection is unavoidable. Select the range containing your example and the area to be filled, then you see Fill by **E**xample.

Creating Custom Fill Sequences

If you often enter the same set of labels in your worksheets, you may want to create your own custom fill sequences for use with the **R**ange Fill By **Ex**ample. Row 6 in figure 3.10, for example, shows a custom fill sequence that enters planet names. Other custom fill sequences that might be useful include region names, store locations, and sales representatives' names.

Fig. 3.10
Use the Notepad to create your own custom sequence to fill labels that you use frequently.

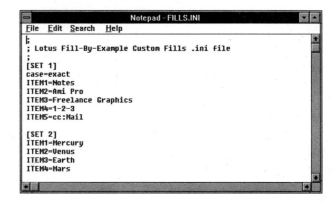

Custom fill sequences are stored in a text file, FILLS.INI, which usually is located in the \123R5W\PROGRAMS directory. You can edit this file with Windows Notepad, the MS-DOS Editor, or any other text editor that does not add special codes. (Most word processing programs add formatting information as special codes.)

Custom fill sequences are stored as numbered sets in FILLS.INI. Following is the custom fill sequence [SET 2], which enters planet names:

```
[SET 2]
ITEM1=Mercury
ITEM2=Venus
ITEM3=Earth
ITEM4=Mars
ITEM5=Jupiter
ITEM6=Saturn
ITEM7=Uranus
ITEM8=Neptune
ITEM9=Pluto
```

You can edit an existing custom fill sequence or create a new one, using the existing set as a model. Each custom fill sequence must follow certain rules:

- The first line of each set must consist of [SET, a space, and the set number].

■ You must list the items in order in lines that begin with ITEM#= (where # is the item number).

■ To make 1-2-3 for Windows enter the data in the same combination of upper- and lowercase letters that appear in the list, type **CASE=EXACT** on a separate line anywhere in the list. Otherwise, 1-2-3 for Windows determines case based on the label in the first cell of the range that you want to fill.

When you make all your additions or corrections, save the file. To add a special list of location names, for example, you could add the following text to FILLS.INI:

```
[SET 4]
CASE=EXACT
ITEM1=Reno
ITEM2=Prior Lake
ITEM3=Manteca
ITEM4=Hopkins
ITEM5=Fishers
```

You can create any custom fill sequence you need for values that you frequently use in your worksheets.

Editing Data in the Worksheet

After you enter data in a cell, you may want to change the data. Perhaps you misspelled a word in a label or created an incorrect formula, or you have more current information. You can change an existing entry in either of two ways:

■ *Type over*. You can replace the contents of a cell by typing a new entry into the cell.

■ *Edit*. You can change part of a cell's contents by editing the cell.

▶ "Hiding Worksheet Data," p. 498

Typing Over Existing Entries

The quickest way to make a change to a short entry is to just type over the old data using these steps:

1. Move the cell pointer to the cell you want to change.

2. Type the new data.

3. Press Enter.

Tip

If you accidentally type over a cell, use **E**dit, **U**ndo or the Undo SmartIcon to undo the typing.

Note

You can protect cells in a worksheet against accidental changes.

Editing Entries

If you need to make a correction to a long entry or a formula in the worksheet, you might want to edit the entry instead of typing over it. This enables you to add or delete characters in the entry, the same way you do in your word processing package.

There are four ways to enter Edit mode so that you can correct a cell. Use one of these techniques:

■ Move the cell pointer to the cell and press F2 (Edit).

■ Double-click the cell.

■ Move the mouse pointer to the contents box. When the shape of the pointer changes from an arrow to an I-beam, move the I-beam to the area you want to change and then click the mouse button to place an insertion point in the text.

■ 1-2-3 places you in Edit mode automatically when you type something that it does not understand; for example, if you type a phone number like (303) 444-3333 without typing a label prefix character first.

■ In this situation, 1-2-3 may not show Edit as the mode indicator. The mode indicator still shows Value, but the insertion point jumps to the location in the entry that 1-2-3 cannot understand. As soon as you move the insertion point, Edit shows as the mode indicator.

When 1-2-3 for Windows is in Edit mode, a cursor flashes in the cell. You can then use the keys shown in Table 3.2 to move around the entry and make changes to the entry. When you press Enter or move to another cell, the edited information is entered into the worksheet.

Table 3.2 Editing Keys	
Key	**Action**
← or →	Move to previous or next character.
Ctrl+←	Move to previous word.

Key	Action
Ctrl+→	Move to next word.
Home	Move to start of entry.
End	Move to end of entry.
Any character	Insert character at insertion point.
Del	Delete character to right of insertion point.
Backspace	Delete character to left of insertion point.
Insert	Switch to overtype mode to type over existing characters.
Enter	Enter the revised text permanently into the cell.
↑ or ↓	Enter revised text and move to next cell.
Esc	Escape without changing the cell entry.

Note

The Edit mode of 1-2-3 assumes that you are inserting characters into the entry. This means that if you move the insertion point in the entry and start typing, the characters you type are inserted into the entry and existing characters are moved to the right. If you wish to type over some existing characters, press the Insert key to switch to overtype mode, or select the characters to be replaced and then type the new characters.

If you press Esc while 1-2-3 for Windows is in Edit mode, the cell entry is blanked out. Press Esc or Enter at this point and the cell is returned to its original state.

Finding and Replacing Data

When you need to make the same change to several entries in a worksheet, use the **E**dit **F**ind & Replace command or the Find SmartIcon to find and replace characters in a range of labels and formulas. The command works much like the search-and-replace feature in many word processing programs. When you choose **E**dit **F**ind & Replace, the Find & Replace dialog box appears. You can specify what data to search for, what kind of data to search through, what characters to find or replace, and which range to search.

> **Caution**
>
> An incorrect search-and-replace operation can harm a file. You should first save the file before choosing **E**dit **F**ind & Replace, even though you can undo an incorrect search.

Suppose that you have a list of department names as labels (see fig. 3.11) and want to shorten the labels from Department to Dept.

Fig. 3.11
You can use the Find & Replace dialog box to replace Department with Dept.

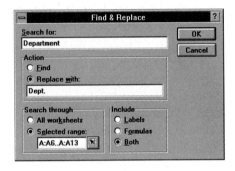

Tip
You can use the **E**dit **F**ind & Replace command to locate information in the spreadsheet without changing it. Just use the **F**ind option instead of the Replace **W**ith option in the Find & Replace dialog box.

The following steps explain how to search for and replace a label:

1. Highlight the range to search. (This step is optional; you can specify the range in the Find & Replace dialog box.)

2. Choose **E**dit **F**ind & Replace or click the Find SmartIcon. The Find & Replace dialog box appears.

3. Type the search string in the **S**earch For text box. In this example, you want to search for Department, so type **Department** in the **S**earch For text box.

4. If necessary, choose the type of search: **L**abels, **F**ormulas, or **B**oth. The default setting of **B**oth works for most situations, unless you specifically wish to restrict the search to labels or formulas.

Tip
When you type text in the Replace **W**ith text box, 1-2-3 automatically turns on the Replace **W**ith radio button.

5. Specify the action: **F**ind or Replace **W**ith. In this example, you want to do more than just find the word Department; you want to replace it with new text. Therefore, select Replace **W**ith.

6. Enter the replacement string in the Replace **W**ith text box. In this example, you want to replace every occurrence of Department with the text Dept. Type **Dept.** (and remember to include the period).

7. Choose OK or press Enter. When 1-2-3 finds the first occurrence of the text Department, the Replace dialog box shown in figure 3.12 appears.

8. In the Replace dialog box, choose **R**eplace, Replace **A**ll, Find **N**ext, or Close. Remember, you can move the dialog box out of the way if it covers up the text in your worksheet.

Fig. 3.12
Choose **R**eplace or Replace **A**ll to replace occurrences or Find **N**ext to skip an occurrence.

If you only want to replace certain occurrences, choose Find **N**ext and then choose **R**eplace for each appropriate occurrence.

If you choose Find **N**ext instead of Replace **A**ll as the search mode, the cell pointer moves to the first matching cell in the range. Choose Find **N**ext to find the next occurrence; alternatively, choose Close to cancel the search and return to Ready mode. If there are no more matching strings, 1-2-3 for Windows displays an error message and stops searching. At the end of a replace operation, the cell pointer remains at the beginning of the selected range.

Tip
Choose **R**eplace for the first occurrence to make sure the change is correct, and then choose Replace **A**ll to replace all occurrences quickly. If the replacement isn't correct, close the dialog box and try again.

> **Note**
>
> You can even use the **E**dit **F**ind & Replace to eliminate a word or text. For example, if you decided not to have the word "Department" at all in the worksheet, enter **Department** in the **S**earch For text box and do not enter anything in the Replace **W**ith text box. Just be sure to choose the Replace **W**ith radio button.

You also can use **E**dit **F**ind & Replace to modify formulas. If you have many formulas that round to two decimal places, such as @ROUND(A1*B1,2), you can change the formulas to round to four decimal places with a search string of ,2) and a replace string of ,4). See "Entering Formulas" in Chapter 4, and Entering 1-2-3 for Windows functions in Chapter 5 for information on entering formulas into your worksheet.

> **Caution**
>
> Be extremely careful when you replace numbers in formulas. If you just replace 2 with 4 in this example, the formula @ROUND(A2*B2,2) becomes @ROUND(A4*B4,4).

Erasing Cells and Ranges

As you correct and revise your worksheet, you probably need to erase or blank out cell entries. You can clear part or all of the worksheet in several ways. Any data you clear is removed from memory, but these changes don't affect the file on disk until you save the current version of the file to disk, as explained in Chapter 8, "Managing Files."

Any of the following techniques can be used to erase or clear cell entries:

- *Delete key.* Select the cell or cells and press the Delete key. This clears the contents of the cell but leaves the format (like dollar signs, commas, or percents). This is roughly equivalent to the 1-2-3 classic command **/R**ange **E**rase.

- *Delete SmartIcon.* Select the cell or cells and click the Delete SmartIcon to clear the contents of the cell.

- *Edit Clear.* Select the cell or cells and choose **E**dit Cl**e**ar from the main menu or Clear from the quick menu. This displays the clear dialog box that enables you to clear the cell contents and/or format. For example, if a cell previously contained a percent and you no longer want it to contain a percent, use **E**dit Cl**e**ar and clear the contents and format.

- *Edit Cut.* Select the cell or cells and choose **E**dit Cu**t** from the main menu or Cut from the quick menu. This places the data in the Windows Clipboard so that it could later be pasted back into the worksheet at a different location. Chapter 6 covers moving and copying data in more detail.

> ### Note
>
> You might think that an easy way to clear or blank out the contents of a cell is to move to the cell and type a space into the cell. This does appear to clear the cell, but the cell is not empty, it contains a space character. This is considered to be a filled cell and takes up memory and space on disk when you save the worksheet. It also can create problems in calculations. For example, the @AVG function ignores empty cells when it averages a range of values. But a cell with a space in it is counted as zero and makes the average invalid!

To clear the contents and/or formatting from a cell with the **E**dit Cl**e**ar command, follow these steps:

1. Select the cell or cells to be cleared.

2. Open the **E**dit menu and choose Cl**e**ar or click the right mouse button and choose Clear. The Clear dialog box appears (see fig. 3.13).

3. Select the command that describes what you want cleared.

4. Choose OK or press Enter.

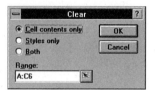

Fig. 3.13
Use the Clear dialog box to clear contents or styles (formats) from a cell.

If you accidentally clear a cell's contents, styles, or both, choose **E**dit **U**ndo or the Undo SmartIcon to restore the entry, styles, or both.

The **C**ell Contents Only option in the Clear dialog box clears just the data from the cell, so it has the same effect as using the Delete key to erase a cell. The **S**tyles Only option clears only the styles from the cell. Styles include any type of formatting or enhancements including numeric formats (dollar signs or percent signs), alignments (center or right), and enhancements (bold or italic).

Caution

Many users make the mistake of choosing **E**dit **D**elete instead of **E**dit Cl**e**ar when they want to clear a cell, cells, or even an entire row or column in the sheet. These commands perform very different functions. The **E**dit Cl**e**ar leaves cells in place and just clears the contents (or styles). The **E**dit **D**elete affects the structure of the worksheet. **E**dit **D**elete removes the selected cells from the worksheet, like pulling bricks out of a wall. Adjacent cells are moved up or in to fill in the void.

Tip
Use the Drag-and-Fill to fill blank, unformatted cells from an adjacent area over filled cells to clear them.

Inserting and Deleting Cells, Rows, and Columns

After you have created a worksheet, you may discover that you forgot an item. This is easily fixed by inserting cells, rows, or columns into the worksheet with the **E**dit **I**nsert command or Insert SmartIcons.

When you insert rows, all rows at and below the cell pointer move down. When you insert columns, all columns at and to the right of the cell pointer move to the right. You can even insert a cell or cells into the worksheet and move adjacent cells to the right or down. This is helpful when you forget a cell entry and enter data into the wrong cells.

Edit Insert and **Edit Delete** can also be used to insert or delete whole worksheets in a multiple worksheet file. See Chapter 7 for details on using multiple worksheets in a file.

Caution

If Group mode is activated and you insert columns or rows in one worksheet, those changes are reflected in every worksheet in the file.

Inserting Rows or Columns

The quickest way to insert a row(s) or column(s) is to select the entire row or column first. To insert rows or columns, take these steps:

1. Select the entire row(s) or column(s) at the location where you want the new row(s) or column(s) to appear by clicking the row or column header(s). Figure 3.14 shows a worksheet with an entire row selected.

Fig. 3.14
Click the column or the row header to select an entire column or row, then choose insert.

Tip
To insert multiple rows or columns, drag across several row or column headers with the white arrow mouse pointer.

Row header

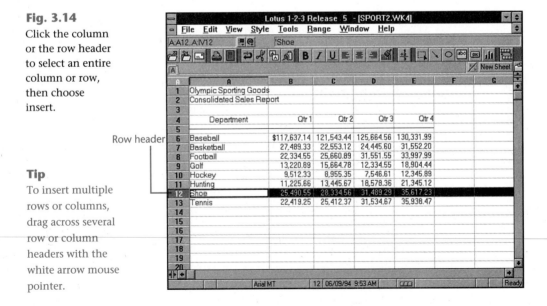

2. Open the **E**dit menu and choose **I**nsert, or use the quick menu to choose Insert, or press Ctrl+gray + to insert. A new blank row or column is inserted at the selected location and existing rows are moved down, existing columns are moved to the right.

> **Note**
>
> If you forget to select an entire row or column in step 1, the Insert dialog box displays and you can choose **R**ow or **C**olumn from this box to insert a row or column at the current location.
>
> You can save even more time when you use the quick menu to insert a row or column. You do not even need to preselect the row or column first, just click directly on the row or column header with the right mouse button to both select the row or column and access the quick menu.

You may worry that inserting rows or columns into a worksheet requires you to redo existing formulas. If you insert a row or column within the borders of a range, the range expands to accommodate the new rows or columns. For example, if you have the range A1..B4 referenced in a formula, and insert a row above row 3, the reference now reads A1..B5.

◄ "Understanding the 1-2-3 for Windows Screen," p. 20

► "Entering Functions," p. 137

Inserting Cells

Occasionally, you may want to insert an individual cell or range into the worksheet. This enables you to add new blank cells into the worksheet and push existing entries down or to the right. This is especially handy when you have missed an entry while typing a column or row of data. Just insert a new blank cell at the appropriate location and move the existing entries out or down.

To insert a cell or cells into the worksheet, use these steps:

1. Select the cell or cells at the location where you want the new cells inserted.

2. Open the **E**dit menu and choose **I**nsert. The Insert dialog box appears.

3. Mark the **I**nsert Selection check box to insert cells, and choose **R**ow to move existing cells down or **C**olumn to move existing cells to the right. Figure 3.15 shows the Insert dialog box filled in to insert a cell at B11 in the worksheet and move the two existing numbers down. Figure 3.16 shows the worksheet after the insertion.

4. Choose OK or press Enter.

Fig. 3.15

Choose **R**ow,
Column, or **I**nsert
Selection to
control what is
inserted.

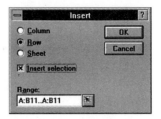

Fig. 3.16

A cell was inserted
and existing data
moved down.

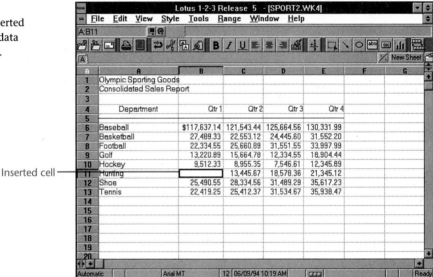

Inserting Cells with SmartIcons

You can use SmartIcons to insert ranges, rows or columns. Select a cell or cells
at the desired location and use the SmartIcons below to insert quickly:

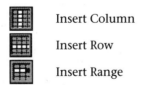

Insert Column

Insert Row

Insert Range

Deleting Cells, Rows, and Columns

When you erase cells with **E**dit Cle**a**r or **E**dit Cu**t**, the cells still exist in the
worksheet, but they are empty. In contrast, when you delete a cell, row, or
column, 1-2-3 for Windows removes the entire cell, row, or column and

moves others to fill the gap created by the deletion. 1-2-3 for Windows also updates addresses, including those in formulas.

To delete a cell, row, or column, follow these steps:

1. Select the row, column, or cells to be deleted.

2. Open the **E**dit menu and choose **D**elete, or press Ctrl+gray-. If you selected an entire row or column by clicking the row or column header, the selected row or column is deleted and existing rows moved up, existing columns moved in from the right.

3. If you did not select an entire row or column, 1-2-3 for Windows displays the Delete dialog box (see fig. 3.17). Choose **C**olumn, **R**ow, or **D**elete Selection, depending on what you want to delete.

Note

When you delete cells, pay attention to the **R**ow and **C**olumn selection. The default selection is **R**ow, meaning that when the cells are deleted, adjacent cells are moved up. If you want adjacent cells to move in from the right, change this selection to **C**olumn.

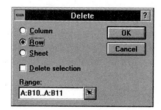

Fig. 3.17
Choose what you want to delete in the Delete dialog box.

Note

If you did not select the item to be deleted or were in the wrong location in the worksheet, you can use the **R**ange text box to specify the range to be deleted. You can type the address or highlight cells with the range selector.

When you delete a column, 1-2-3 for Windows moves subsequent columns to the left to fill the gap caused by the deletion. When you delete a row or worksheet, 1-2-3 for Windows moves up the remaining rows.

▶ "Correcting
Errors in
Formulas,"
p. 128

Range references in formulas are adjusted; for example, if you delete row 4, the formula +A3+A6 becomes +A3+A5. If a formula refers specifically to a deleted cell, however, the formula results in an error message (ERR).

Deleting Cells with SmartIcons

You can also use SmartIcons to delete ranges, rows, columns, or sheets. Just select cells at the desired location in the worksheet and then use one of the SmartIcons shown below:

 Delete Column

 Delete Row

 Delete Range

Caution

Deleting rows or columns usually affects only the current worksheet. If, however, you have grouped together several worksheets with Group mode and you delete (or add) rows or columns in one worksheet, you delete (or add) the same rows or columns in all the grouped worksheets.

Troubleshooting

I meant to insert an entire row into my worksheet, but only one cell was inserted and now some entries in my worksheet don't line up correctly.

You probably forgot to choose **R**ow in the Insert dialog box and only a single cell was inserted into the worksheet, shifting existing entries down. Use **E**dit **U**ndo to undo the insertion. If you can't undo the insertion, select the inserted cell and choose **E**dit **D**elete to delete the cell and return the worksheet to the way it was before. Then, select an entire row before choosing **E**dit **I**nsert again.

I deleted a row from my worksheet and now one of my formulas shows ERR.

Although 1-2-3 does its best to revise formulas to account for insertions and deletions, if you delete a cell that was specifically referenced in a formula, you lose your calculation and see ERR in the cell. You need to edit the formula to replace the ERR with a valid cell reference.

Using the Undo Feature

When you type an entry, edit a cell, or issue a command, you change the worksheet. If you change the worksheet in error, you can undo your last change using one of these techniques:

■ Press Alt+Backspace (Undo)

■ Choose the **E**dit **U**ndo command.

■ Click the Undo SmartIcon.

If you type over an existing entry, you can undo the new entry and restore the old one. The Undo feature undoes only the last action performed, whether that action was entering data, executing a command, or running a macro.

> **Note**
>
> When you use the Undo feature, 1-2-3 for Windows must remember the most recent action that changed the worksheet. This feature requires a great deal of computer memory; how much memory depends on the different actions involved. If you run low on memory, you can disable the Undo feature by using the **T**ools **U**ser Setup command and deselecting the **U**ndo option from the User Setup dialog box. If you run out of memory while 1-2-3 for Windows is undoing an action, 1-2-3 suspends the undo operation.

The Undo feature is powerful. Undo also is tricky, so you must use this command carefully. To use Undo properly, you must understand what 1-2-3 for Windows considers to be a change. A change occurs between the time 1-2-3 for Windows is in Ready mode and the next time 1-2-3 for Windows is in Ready mode.

Suppose that you press F2 (Edit) to go into Edit mode to change a cell. You can make changes in the cell and then press Enter to save the changes and return to Ready mode. If you press Undo at that point, 1-2-3 for Windows returns the worksheet to the condition the worksheet was in during the last Ready mode. The cell returns to the state it was in before you performed the edit.

You can change many cells at one time or even erase everything in memory with a single command. If you use Undo after a command, you cancel all the effects of the command.

Some commands and actions cannot be canceled, including the Undo command. If you press Alt+Backspace (Undo) at the wrong time and cancel an entry, you cannot recover the entry. Other commands and actions that cannot be canceled include the following:

- A previous use of Edit Undo

- All commands in the Control menus

- Changes to files on disk

- Actions that move the cell pointer or scroll the worksheet, including GoTo (F5) and Window (F6)

- Formula recalculations that result when you press F9 (Calc)

Checking Your Spelling

1-2-3 includes a spell check utility that reviews and helps you correct spelling throughout your worksheet files. The spell check utility checks the words in your worksheet against a dictionary and flags words that are not found. You then have the opportunity to replace the incorrect word with a suggested word or move on to the next spelling error.

Follow these steps to use the spelling checker:

1. Open the **T**ools menu and choose **S**pell Check or click the Check Spelling SmartIcon. The Spell Check dialog box appears (see fig. 3.18).

Fig. 3.18
Use the Spell Check dialog box to indicate whether you want to check the entire worksheet or part of the worksheet.

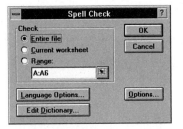

2. Select the area of the worksheet that you want to spell check by choosing **E**ntire file, **C**urrent worksheet, or a specific **R**ange. You can also change other **O**ptions at this point. When you're ready, choose OK to begin checking the selection.

3. If the spelling checker finds an unknown word, a dialog box like the one shown in figure 3.19 appears. Use the actions in this box, described in Table 3.3 to correct the mistake or otherwise deal with the item.

4. If you wish to stop the spell check, you can close the Spell Check dialog

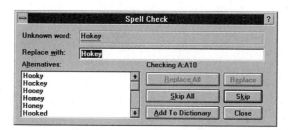

Fig. 3.19
Correct your spelling with the second Spell Check dialog box.

box by clicking the Close button or using the Control menu's **C**lose command. Otherwise, when the spell check is complete, you are notified with a dialog box and can choose OK to end the check.

Tip
You can move the dialog box, so that you can see the misspelled word in context.

Table 3.3 Spelling Actions	
Option	**Action**
R**e**place	Replace the incorrect word with the word in the Replace **W**ith box. You can type a word into this box, or choose one of the words in the A**l**ternatives list.
Replace All	Replace all occurrences of the misspelled word with the word in the Replace **W**ith box.
S**k**ip	Skip this word and proceed to the next misspelling.
Skip All	Skip all occurrences of this word.
Add to Dictionary	Add this word to the dictionary so that 1-2-3 will not flag it as misspelled again.

The spelling checker may flag some correctly spelled words as incorrect, simply because those words are not in the spelling checker's dictionary. You can add those words to the dictionary using the **A**dd to Dictionary button. By adding words to the dictionary, you begin to create your own personal dictionary for repeated use. If the word is flagged, but you don't want to add it to your dictionary, use the S**k**ip command to skip the word or the **S**kip All command to skip all occurrences of the word throughout this spell check session.

Tip
A quick way to select a replacement word is to double-click the desired alternative in the list.

Remember, the spell check only checks for spelling, not for usage. As long as a word is in the dictionary, the spell check program thinks that the word is correct. So, if you type "too" instead of "to," the spell check does not flag it. Or if you type "far" instead of "car," the spell check thinks it is correct. The bottom line is that you still need to proofread your worksheet!

Changing the Spelling Options

The **O**ptions button in the first Spell Check dialog box enables you to specify your preferences about how the spelling checker works and includes these choices:

- Check for **r**epeated words. When this is selected, the spell check flags repeated words.

- Check for words with **n**umbers. Turn this off if you do not want the spell check to flag words that contain numbers as incorrect.

- Check words with initial caps. Turn this off if you do not want the spell check to flag proper names as incorrect.

- Include **u**ser dictionary alternatives. Turn this on if you want the spell check to list words that you have added to the dictionary in the list of Alternatives.

- Include **m**acro/@function keywords, punctuation. Turn this on if you want the spell check to include a dictionary of special macro and @function words.

From Here...

This chapter introduced you to entering and editing your worksheet. For more information, you can review any or all of the following chapters:

- Chapter 2, "Navigating and Selecting in 1-2-3 for Windows." As you can see, in order to enter data you must be able to move around the worksheet efficiently. And, to edit your data, you need to be able to select rows, columns, and ranges with ease. See Chapter 2 for learning these skills.

- Chapter 4, "Working with Formulas." This is the next step if you are just learning how to use 1-2-3 for Windows. This chapter shows you how to enter formulas to add, subtract, multiply, or divide numbers in your worksheet.

- Chapter 5, "Using Functions." The special functions enable you to easily perform calculations such as sums and averages.

- Chapter 6, "Moving or Copying Data." In this chapter, you learn additional ways to modify and improve your worksheet by moving and copying data.

- Chapter 9, "Formatting Worksheets." In this chapter, you learn how to change the column width and formats of data in the worksheet.

Everyday Worksheet Tasks

Chapter 4

Working with Formulas

Probably the single most basic and important characteristic of 1-2-3 for Windows is that after you've created a worksheet by using formulas, when you change any number on the worksheet, all formulas that depend on that number change automatically.

To use 1-2-3 for Windows effectively, you must be able to create a variety of types of formulas to help you analyze the data on your worksheets. This chapter shows you a variety of methods for creating and editing formulas. You also explore techniques to deal with incorrectly written formulas.

On particularly complex worksheets or worksheets with a large number of complex formulas, 1-2-3 for Windows automatic recalculation feature can take some time to recalculate all formulas. While it is recalculating, you cannot continue to enter other data on your worksheet. You learn in this chapter how to turn off the automatic recalculation feature so that 1-2-3 for Windows only recalculates your worksheet when you tell it to do so.

In this chapter, you learn how to do the following:

- Enter formulas into a cell

- Use operators in numeric, string, and logical formulas

- Point at cells when creating a formula

- Edit formulas

- Modify the method 1-2-3 for Windows uses when recalculating a worksheet

- Identify, locate, and modify circular references

Creating Formulas

Because 1-2-3 for Windows is used primarily for financial and scientific applications, its capability to use formulas is one of its most sophisticated yet easy-to-use features. You can create a simple formula that adds the values in two cells on the same worksheet:

+A1+B1

This formula indicates that the value stored in cell A1 is to be added to the value stored in B1. The formula that adds the values in A1 and B1 is recalculated if you enter new data into either of those cells. For example, if A1 originally contains the value 4 and B1 contains the value 3, the formula results in the value 7. If you change the value in A1 to 5, the formula is recalculated to result in 8.

You create formulas with symbols called *operators: + (addition), – (subtraction), * (multiplication), and / (division)*. Logical formulas use logical operators: *< (less than), > (greater than), and = (equal to)*. You can also combine the operators to create *<= (less than or equal to), >= (greater than or equal to), and < > (not equal to)*. Operators tell 1-2-3 for Windows the relationship between numbers.

The power of 1-2-3 for Windows formulas, however, is best showcased by the program's capability to link data across worksheets and worksheet files. By referencing cells in other worksheets and worksheet files, formulas can calculate results from many worksheet applications. To create a formula that links data across worksheets, you first specify the worksheet in which the data is located (indicated by the letters A through IV or by a defined worksheet name), followed by a colon (:), and the cell address. The following example shows a formula that links data across three worksheets (A, B, and D):

+A:B3+B:C6+D:B4

If the formula links data across files, include the file name, surrounded by double-angle brackets. For example, the following formula adds the contents of cell C6 on worksheet A of the current file to the contents of cell C6 on worksheet A in the file named SALES1.WK4.

+A:C6+<<SALES1.WK4>>A:C6

Tip
If the files you want to link are open, click the cells you want to include in the formula. When you do this, 1-2-3 for Windows inserts the file name, worksheet name, and cell address for you.

Entering Formulas

The real power of 1-2-3 for Windows comes from the program's capability to calculate formulas. Formulas make 1-2-3 an electronic worksheet, not just a computerized way to assemble data. You enter the numbers and formulas into the worksheet, and 1-2-3 for Windows calculates the results of all the formulas. As you add or change data, you do not need to recalculate the worksheet to reflect the changes; 1-2-3 for Windows recalculates the data for you.

In the example shown in figure 4.1, if you change the value of Sales or Variable Costs, 1-2-3 for Windows recalculates Variable Margin.

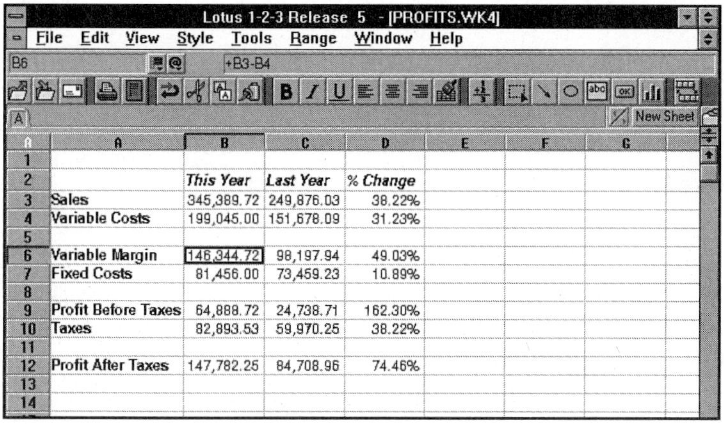

Fig. 4.1

Results in the Variable Margin row reflect changes in the value of Sales or Variable Costs.

You can enter formulas that perform calculations on numbers, labels, and other cells in the worksheet. As with a label, a formula can contain up to 512 characters. A formula can include numbers, text, operators, cell and range addresses, range names, and functions. A formula cannot include spaces except within a range name or a text string.

You can create four kinds of formulas: numeric, string, logical, and function. *Numeric formulas work with numbers, other numeric formulas, and numeric functions. String formulas work with labels, other string formulas, and string functions. Logical formulas are true-or-false tests for numeric or string values.*

Numeric and string formulas are covered primarily in this chapter.

Formulas can operate on numbers or on the contents of cells. The formula 8+26 uses 1-2-3 for Windows as a calculator. A more useful formula involves cell references in the calculation. In figure 4.2, the formula in cell F16 is

▶ "Using Functions," p. 135

+B16+C16+D16+E16. The contents box shows the formula, and the worksheet shows the result of the calculation: 183. The result in cell F16 changes when you change any number in the other cells. This automatic recalculation capability is the basis of the power of the 1-2-3 for Windows worksheet.

Fig. 4.2
The result, not the formula, appears in the worksheet. The formula appears in the contents box, near the top of the screen.

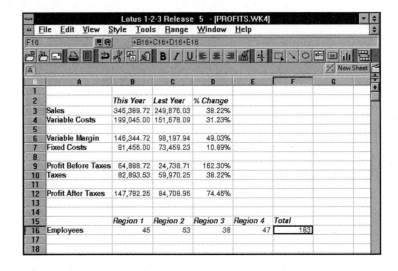

Notice that the formula begins with a plus sign (+). If the formula begins with B16, 1-2-3 for Windows assumes that you are entering a label and performs no calculations.

 You can add a row or column of values quickly by placing the cell pointer in the blank cell at the bottom of a column (or at the right end of a row) and then clicking the Sum SmartIcon to calculate the result.

A formula is an instruction to 1-2-3 for Windows to perform a calculation. All formulas begin with a number, a decimal point, +, –, @, $, #, or (.

Any entry that begins with any other character is treated as a label by 1-2-3 for Windows.

Caution

Be sure you begin formulas with one of the symbols shown in the preceding text. If you don't, 1-2-3 for Windows will treat what you type as text and enter it into a cell preceded by an apostrophe ('), a label prefix. To correct the entry so that it becomes a formula, you need either to retype the formula or to delete the apostrophe and replace it with one of the numeric indicators shown above.

You use operators in numeric, string, and logical formulas to specify the cal-culations to be performed, and in what order. Table 4.1 lists the operators in the order in which 1-2-3 for Windows uses them.

Table 4.1	Operators and Their Order of Precedence	
Operator	**Operation**	**Precedence**
^	Exponentiation	1
–, +	Negative, positive value	2
*, /	Multiplication, division	3
+, –	Addition, subtraction	4
=, <>	Equal to, not equal to	5
<, >	Less than, greater than	5
<=	Less than or equal to	5
>=	Greater than or equal to	5
#NOT#	Logical NOT	6
#AND#	Logical AND	7
#OR#	Logical OR	7
&	String formula	7

Using Operators in Numeric Formulas

You use numeric operators for addition, subtraction, multiplication, division, and *exponentiation* (raising a number to a power). The simplest kind of for-mula is a simple reference, such as the following:

    +C4

You can enter this formula into any cell except C4. It takes whatever is in C4 and reproduces it in the cell containing this formula. That way, if the content of C4 changes, the cell containing the formula also changes.

Another formula might be

    +C4+C5

This formula adds the values in two cells: C4 and C5.

You might include a constant value if needed, such as in the following example:

+C4+C5+100

In this formula, the value 100 is constant but the values in cells C4 and C5 are variable; those values depend on the numbers that currently appear in those cells.

If a formula uses all the operators shown in table 4.1, 1-2-3 for Windows calculates the exponentials first and then works down the list. If two operators are equal in precedence, 1-2-3 can calculate either first. The order of precedence affects the result of many formulas. To override the order of precedence, use parentheses; 1-2-3 always calculates operations within a set of parentheses first.

Table 4.2 shows how 1-2-3 for Windows uses parentheses and the order of precedence to evaluate complex formulas. The examples use numbers instead of cell references to make the calculations easier to follow.

Table 4.2   Evaluating Complex Formulas in 1-2-3 for Windows

Formula	Evaluation	Result
5+3*2	(5+(3*2))	11
(5+3)*2	(5+3)*2	16
–3^2*2	–(3^2)*2	–18
–3^(2*2)	–(3^(2*2))	–81
5+4*8/4–3	5+(4*(8/4))–3	10
5+4*8/(4–3)	5+((4*8)/(4–3))	37
(5+4)*8/(4–3)	(5+4)*8/(4–3)	72
(5+4)*8/4–3	(5+4)*(8/4)–3	15
5+3*4^2/6–2*3^4	5+(3*(4^2)/6)(2*(3^4))	–149

Troubleshooting

After pressing Enter to enter a formula, 1-2-3 for Windows beeps and doesn't enter the formula into a cell.

Although you begin the formula with a symbol 1-2-3 for Windows recognizes as a formula indicator, somewhere in the formula you have made an error, and the formula cannot be interpreted or evaluated. Common errors include neglecting to put in an operator where one is necessary (A1B1 rather than A1*B1), or typing a cell reference incorrectly (for example, 1A rather than A1). If you can easily spot the error, move the cursor to the location of the error and correct it. If you can't spot your error, the easiest solution is to press Escape until you return to READY mode (look for Ready at the right end of the status bar at the bottom of your screen) and reenter the formula, this time pointing at the cells with your cursor rather than typing in cell addresses.

When I type a complicated formula containing numerous parentheses and press Enter, 1-2-3 for Windows beeps and doesn't enter the formula into the cell.

You either have a different number of opening and closing parentheses, or you have placed a parenthesis in an incorrect position in the formula. Depending on the formula you entered, 1-2-3 for Windows may be able to guess where a parenthesis is missing and will move the cursor to the relevant function. You can then type in the missing symbol.

At other times, 1-2-3 for Windows may not be able to interpret where the symbol is missing. In that case, count the number of opening parentheses and the number of closing ones. If there is a difference between the two, you need to determine where to put the missing one. Once you have done so, use the left- and right-arrow keys to position the cursor correctly and insert the missing symbol.

Another approach involves using the @function selector, discussed in Chapter 5, "Using Functions."

Using Operators in String Formulas

The rules for string formulas are different from the rules for numeric formulas. A string is a label or a string formula. Only two string-formula operators exist, so you can perform only two operations with string formulas: repeat a string or concatenate (join) two or more strings.

The simplest string formula uses only the plus sign (+) to repeat the string in another cell:

+C4

In this example, cell C4 contains a text label, which is reproduced in the cell containing this formula.

The string-concatenation operator is the ampersand (&), and the following is an example:

+A4&B4

If, for example, cells A4 and B4 contain the text strings *New* and *York*, respectively, the result of the formula is the concatenated text string, *NewYork*, with no space between the words.

The first operator in a string formula must be a plus sign; all other operators in the formula must be ampersands. If you do not use the ampersand but use any of the numeric operators, 1-2-3 for Windows considers the formula to be a numeric formula and calculates the data in the cells as numeric values. A cell that contains a label is considered to have a numeric value of 0 (zero).

If you use an ampersand in a formula, 1-2-3 for Windows considers the formula to be a string formula. If you also use any numeric operators (after the plus sign at the beginning), the formula results in ERR. The formula +A3&B3+C3, for example, results in ERR.

In many string formulas, you need to put a space between the various parts of the formula. You can insert a space directly into a string formula by placing the space inside double quotation marks (" "). If cells A4 and B4 contain the text *New* and *York*, for example, you can enter the formula **+A4&" "&B4** to get the result *New York* instead of *NewYork*.

Note

You can insert text, as well as spaces between entries in a string formula. Suppose, for example, that cell A1 contains the name *Lynne Kay*, B1 contains *Berkeley*, and C1 contains *California*, and this formula is entered into D1:

+A1&" lives in the city of "&B1&" in the state of "&C1

The result is the following entry:

```
Lynne Kay lives in the city of Berkeley in the state of California
```

Note the spaces in the formula, including the one between the opening quotation mark and the word *lives*. If that space were not included in the formula, the result in the cell would, in part, look like this

```
    Lynne Kaylives in . . .
```

with no space between *Kay* and *lives*.

To write more complex string formulas, you can use string functions. For a detailed discussion of these functions, see Chapter 5, "Using Functions."

Using Operators in Logical Formulas

Logical formulas are true/false tests. A logical formula compares two values and returns 1 if the test is true or 0 if the test is false.

Pointing to Cell References

Formulas consist mainly of operators and cell references. The formula +C4+C5+C6+C7, for example, has four cell references. You can type each reference, but there is an easier way to enter them. When 1-2-3 for Windows expects a cell address, you can use the direction keys or the mouse to point to the cell or range. When you move the cell pointer, 1-2-3 for Windows changes to POINT mode, and the address of the cell pointer appears in the formula in the contents box.

To point to a cell when entering a formula, you can use the arrow keys to move the cell pointer to the correct cell, or you can click on the cell. If this location marks the end of the formula, press Enter. If the formula contains more terms (or parts of the equation), type the next operator and continue the process until you finish; then press Enter.

You can type some addresses and point to others. You cannot tell in a completed formula whether the cell references were entered by typing or pointing.

In formulas, you also can refer to cells in other worksheets in the worksheet file. To refer to a cell in another worksheet, include the worksheet letter (or custom tab label) in the cell address. To refer to cell C4 in worksheet b, for example, type **+B:C4.** To point to a cell in another worksheet, type + and then use the direction keys, including Ctrl+PgUp and Ctrl+PgDn. To move the cell pointer to other worksheets, you also can click on the Next Worksheet and Previous Worksheet SmartIcons.

Because typing an incorrect address in a formula is easy, pointing to a cell usually is faster and more accurate than typing the cell's address. The only time when typing an address is easier is when the cell reference is far from the current cell and you happen to remember the address. If you enter a formula in cell Z238 and want to refer to cell K23, typing **K23** may be faster than pointing to cell K23.

Tip

String formulas are the only formulas in which spaces are allowed and then only when the spaces are enclosed within quotation marks.

Everyday Worksheet Tasks

◄ "Working with Ranges," p. 71 You also can use range names instead of cell addresses in formulas. Experienced 1-2-3 for Windows users rarely type cell addresses and frequently use range names.

Correcting Errors in Formulas

◄ "Editing Data in the Worksheet," p. 101 If you accidentally enter a formula that 1-2-3 for Windows cannot evaluate, the program beeps, changes to EDIT mode, and then usually moves the cursor to the place in the formula where the program encountered an error. You cannot enter an invalid formula into a worksheet.

Common errors that make a formula invalid are extra or missing parentheses, misspelled function names, and incorrect arguments in functions. Following are a few examples of common errors:

Formula	Error
+A1(A2*A3)	Missing an operator between A1 and the product in parentheses
@SIM(A1..A3)	Misspelled @SUM function
@IF(A1>200,200)	Missing argument in function

If you cannot find, or do not know how to fix, the error in the formula, you can use the Help utility to check the format of the function. Before you can do anything else, you must clear the error. If you press Esc, you erase the entire entry. If you press Esc again, you return to Ready mode, but you lose the entire formula.

Since all labels are valid entries, instead of deleting the entire formula and starting over again, you can convert the formula to a label. This allows you to continue working until you have the time and/or information to determine the error in the formula. Once you have corrected the formula, you can delete the label prefix and change the entry back to a formula.

Follow these steps to convert a formula to a label, clear Edit mode, and return to Ready mode:

1. Press Home to move to the beginning of the formula.

2. Type an apostrophe (') as the label prefix. (1-2-3 for Windows accepts anything preceded by an apostrophe as a label.)

3. Press Enter.

You can use the Help utility again or look at another part of the worksheet that has a similar formula. When you find the error, correct the formula and remove the apostrophe.

> **Note**
>
> 1-2-3 for Windows will correct certain types of errors for you. For example, if you type **@SUM(A1..A5** and forget to close the parentheses before you press Enter, 1-2-3 for Windows closes the parentheses for you and enters the formula into the cell.

Recalculating a Worksheet

When a value in a cell changes, 1-2-3 for Windows recalculates every cell that depends on the changed value. This recalculation demonstrates the power of an electronic spreadsheet. Usually, 1-2-3 recalculates a worksheet automatically when a cell changes. If you prefer, you can tell 1-2-3 for Windows you want to recalculate manually.

Unless you specify otherwise, 1-2-3 for Windows recalculates only those formulas whose values have changed since the last recalculation. If you change the data in one cell and that cell is used in one formula, 1-2-3 for Windows recalculates only that formula.

Specifying the Recalculation Method

You can tell 1-2-3 for Windows not to recalculate the worksheet automatically by choosing **T**ools **U**ser Setup, choosing the Recalculation button in the User Setup dialog box, and selecting Manual in the Recalculation dialog box (see fig. 4.3). (If you followed along with this example, use the Tools User Setup Recalculation command again to reset 1-2-3 for Windows to Automatic recalculation.)

After recalculation is set to manual, you can use any of the following methods to recalculate the worksheet:

- Press F9 (Calc)

- Click on the Calc button in the status bar

- Click on the Recalculate SmartIcon

- Invoke recalculation in a macro with the CALC, RECALC, or RECALCOL macro command

Fig. 4.3
Use Tools User
Setup Recalcula-
tion to change to
and from manual
and automatic
recalculation.

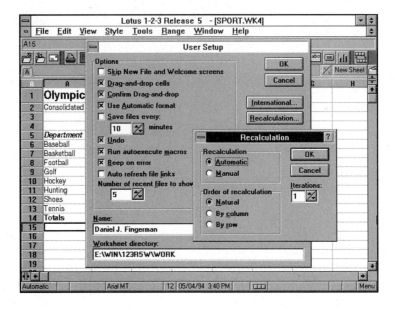

> **Note**
>
> Generally, manual recalculation is used only if you have a large file that contains a
> great number of complex formulas. In that case, 1-2-3 for Windows could take some
> time—seconds to perhaps minutes or more—to recalculate each time you enter a
> value into a cell. In cases like this, it is sensible to turn on manual recalculation, enter
> all of the values you want to change, and then use one of the techniques described
> earlier to recalculate all formulas.

Specifying the Recalculation Order

You can control the order in which 1-2-3 for Windows recalculates. By default, 1-2-3 for Windows recalculates in natural order. In natural order recalculation, 1-2-3 for Windows determines which formulas depend on which
cells and then sets up a recalculation order to produce the correct results.

If you prefer, you can tell 1-2-3 for Windows to recalculate By Row or By
Column. Row recalculation starts in cell A1 and continues across the cells in
row 1, then row 2, and so on. Columnar recalculation starts in cell A1 and
continues down the cells in column A, then column B, and so on.

To change the order of recalculation, select **T**ools **U**ser Setup Recalculation
and select either By column or By row, as shown in figure 4.3.

> ### Note
>
> Unless you have a specific reason for being sure one cell is calculated before another, let 1-2-3 for Windows recalculate in natural order. When calculating by row or by column, 1-2-3 for Windows must sweep through columns and rows several times to make sure that formulas produce correct results. Natural order is faster because 1-2-3 for Windows first determines which cells have changed and then recalculates them in one sweep.

If you specify By Row or By Column, you should tell 1-2-3 for Windows the number of iterations to perform (how many times to recalculate). Specify a number from 1 (the default) to 50 in the Iterations text box. If 1-2-3 for Windows is set to recalculate in natural order and no circular references exist, 1-2-3 for Windows may stop calculating before it reaches the number of iterations indicated.

Handling Circular References

The natural order of recalculation is not always accurate if a circular reference exists. A circular reference is a formula that depends, either directly or indirectly, on its own value. Whenever 1-2-3 for Windows performs a recalculation and finds a circular reference, the Circ indicator appears on the circular-reference button in the status bar. A circular reference is almost always an error, and you should correct it immediately. Figure 4.4 shows an erroneous circular reference in which the cell containing the @SUM function includes itself.

In some cases, a circular reference is deliberate. Figure 4.5 shows a worksheet with such a reference. In this example, a company has set aside 10 percent of its net profit for employee bonuses. The bonuses themselves, however, represent an expense that reduces net profit. The formula in cell C5 shows that the amount of bonuses is net profit (in cell D5) multiplied by 0.1 (10 percent). But net profit (the formula in cell D5) is profit after bonuses (B5 minus C5). The value of employee bonuses depends on the value of net profit, and the value of net profit depends on the value of employee bonuses. In figure 4.5, C5 depends on D5, and D5 depends on C5. This situation is a classic circular reference.

Tip

If Circ indicator still appears on the status bar, try auditing the formula by choosing **T**ools **A**udit and then selecting Circular References.

▶ "Auditing Worksheets," p. 617

Fig. 4.4
Notice how the
formula in B14
refers to itself: a
circular reference.

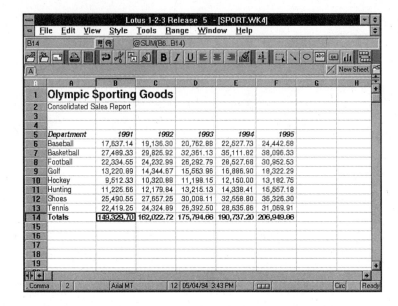

Fig. 4.5
A worksheet with
a deliberate
circular reference.

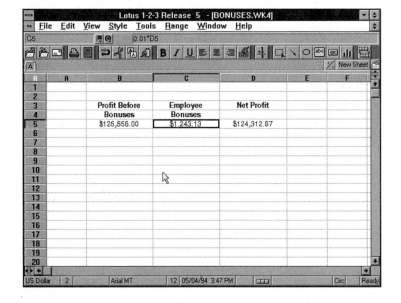

If a deliberate circular reference exists, each time you recalculate the
worksheet, the values change by a smaller amount. Eventually, the changes
become insignificant. This reduction is called *convergence*. Notice that the
erroneous circular reference in figure 4.4 never converges, and the @SUM
result is bigger every time you recalculate.

The worksheet in figure 4.5 needs three recalculations before the changes become less than one cent. After you establish this number, you can tell 1-2-3 for Windows to recalculate the worksheet five times every time it recalculates by specifying 5 in the Iterations text box in the Recalculation dialog box. In most cases, you can calculate a converging circular reference with a macro (see Part VIII, "Automating 1-2-3 for Windows with Macros," for details on using macros).

From Here...

Now that you have learned to create and edit formulas on 1-2-3 for Windows worksheet, you may want to refer to the following chapters:

- Chapter 5, "Using Functions," covers all of the @functions that are built in to 1-2-3 for Windows.

- Chapter 6, "Moving or Copying Data," shows you how to save time by duplicating formulas in other areas where they are appropriate.

- Chapter 9, "Formatting Worksheets," shows you how to enhance the appearance of your worksheets by changing fonts, type size, use of color and shading, and so on.

- Chapter 11, "Creating Charts," shows you how to take your data and represent it graphically.

Chapter 5

Using Functions

In addition to creating your own formulas in a worksheet, you can take advantage of 1-2-3 for Windows predefined formulas, or *functions*. Functions can perform math, text, and logical calculations as well as determine information about the worksheet.

By using a function rather than writing a formula, you speed your work and avoid typing errors. To find the average of the amounts in five cells, for example, you could enter the formula +(A3+B3+C3+D3+E3)/5. It is faster and simpler, however, to use the @AVG function, @AVG(A3..E3). You can enter a function by typing it in a cell or using the @function selector.

1-2-3 for Windows provides more than 220 built-in functions broken into the following 10 categories:

- Calendar

- Database

- Engineering

- Financial

- Information

- Logical

- Lookup

- Mathematical

- Statistical

- Text

This chapter describes the general steps you follow to use 1-2-3 for Windows functions and then provides discussions and examples of specific functions in each category.

In this chapter, you learn:

- Basic concepts about functions

- How to enter functions

- How to customize the @function-selector list

- The syntax and arguments for commonly used functions

Understanding 1-2-3 for Windows Functions

A function is a preprogrammed set of instructions that returns a value. You can use a function as an independent formula that shows results based on information in the function—for example, the @NOW function returns the value of the current date and time. You also can use a function as a component of another formula or function—for example, @IF(@NOW < @DATE(100,01,01),"This is still the 20th century","The 21st century"). In this formula, the text string that the @IF function returns depends on the values returned by the functions it contains: @NOW and @DATE.

Functions have a general format, which includes the following:

- The @ symbol, which tells 1-2-3 for Windows that what follows is a function.

- The name of the function. (There is no space between the @ symbol and the function name.)

- Arguments, which appear in parentheses.

Tip
If an argument is a text string, you must enclose the string in quotation marks (" "). Otherwise, 1-2-3 for Windows assumes that the text string is a range name.

Arguments are information that the function needs to complete its task. This information can be provided by you, when you enter the function, or by a formula or other function.

Some functions do not require arguments. Most functions require one or more arguments; many have optional arguments as well. If a function contains multiple arguments, the arguments are separated by commas.

> **Note**
>
> You also can use a period (.) or semicolon (;) to separate arguments, but the argument separator should never be the same as the decimal separator in the worksheet. This restriction rules out the period separator used in the United States. If the worksheet will be used internationally, the semicolon is the best separator to use.

Entering Functions

You can use any of three methods to enter functions in a worksheet. After you click the cell that should contain the function, you can:

- Use the @function selector to display the @Function List dialog box

- Type @ and then press the F3 (Name) key to display the @Function List dialog box

- Type the function in the cell

Whichever method you use, the function appears both in the current cell and in the contents box as you enter it. When you finish, press Enter or click the Confirm button to complete the entry.

Using the @Function Selector

The @function selector automates your entry of functions. To use the @function selector, follow these steps:

1. Click the @function selector, which is the second icon in the edit line. A short drop-down list of common functions appears, as shown in figure 5.1. This list includes at least two sections separated by a solid line.

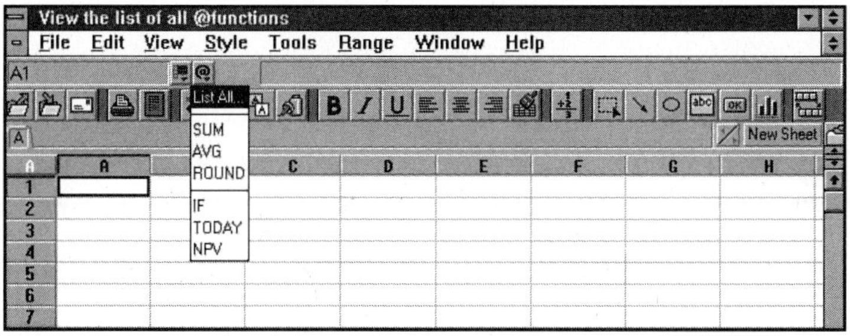

Fig. 5.1

When you click the @function selector, a short list of common functions appears.

2. If the function you need appears in the short list, you can select it. 1-2-3 for Windows enters the function, with the proper argument syntax, in the current cell and in the contents box. (Skip to step 6.)

   If the function you need is not in the short list, click the List All option at the top of the drop-down list. The @Function List dialog box appears, listing all the available functions (see fig. 5.2).

Fig. 5.2

The @ Function List dialog box lists all the functions.

3. You can look through the list of functions to find the function you want, or you can use the Category drop-down list to display only functions in a certain category—for example, the financial functions. When you select a category, only functions of that type appear in the functions list.

Tip

If you know the category of functions you want to see, you can select that category quickly by typing its first letter.

4. Scroll through the list, using the scroll bars, or type the first letter of the function name and then scroll through the functions that begin with that letter. As you highlight different functions in the list, the help box at the bottom of the dialog box displays the correct syntax and a brief description of the highlighted function.

> **Note**
>
> When you look for a function in the @Function List dialog box by typing its name, you cannot type the entire function name. If you type the second letter of the name, 1-2-3 for Windows moves the highlight to the function in the list that starts with this letter.

5. When you find the correct function, highlight it and choose OK, or simply double-click it. 1-2-3 for Windows closes the dialog box and enters the function, with the proper argument syntax, in the current cell and in the contents box (see fig. 5.3).

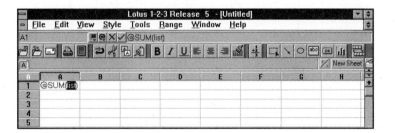

Fig. 5.3
1-2-3 for Windows places the function in the current cell and the contents box.

6. Replace the argument names in the function with the necessary information. Highlight the argument name and then type the specific information, or select the appropriate cells or ranges with the mouse. For example, the @SUM function appears as @SUM(*list*). Replace the *list* argument name with the list or range of cells that you want to sum.

7. When the function is complete, press Enter or click the Confirm button to complete the entry. 1-2-3 for Windows displays the result of the function in the cell.

Tip
If you point to a range that has been named, 1-2-3 for Windows uses the range name, rather than the cell addresses, in the function formula.

Using F3

If you have used previous versions of 1-2-3 for Windows, you may be in the habit of entering functions by typing @ and then pressing the F3 key. You can continue to use this method as you start entering functions in 1-2-3 for Windows.

When you type the @ symbol and then press F3, the @Functions List dialog box appears. For details about using this dialog box, see steps 3 through 7 in the preceding section.

Typing the Function

You can type the entire function, including its arguments. Save this method for simple functions that you use repeatedly (and thus remember their argument requirements). Typing a function may be the fastest method of entry, as long as you remember and use the proper syntax.

Troubleshooting

I have entered all of the required arguments for a function as well as the last optional argument. Why won't 1-2-3 accept the function formula?

If you are using optional arguments in a function, you must use them sequentially. That means that to use the last optional argument, you must also enter all previous optional arguments. (You can specify the default values for these previous arguments, which won't change your results.)

1-2-3 refuses to accept the function I have entered. It just beeps at me.

Check that you have used the proper syntax for the function and have included all required arguments. Also make sure that text arguments are enclosed in quotation marks and that all opening and closing parentheses are in place. If you are nesting functions, it is especially easy to forget an opening or closing parenthesis.

Customizing the @Function-Selector List

When you click the @function selector, a drop-down list of common functions appears. 1-2-3 for Windows lets you to customize this list so that it includes the functions you use most frequently. In addition to adding and removing functions, you can add and remove separator lines. These lines let you group the functions in the list in the way that's most useful to you.

To customize the @function-selector list, follow these steps:

1. Click the @function selector and select List All to display the @Function List dialog box.

2. Click the Menu button. The dialog box expands to include the Current Menu list and the Add, Remove, and Separator buttons (see fig. 5.4). The Current Menu list contains all the functions that currently appear in the @function-selector list.

3. To add a new function, highlight it in the @Functions list. In the Current Menu list, highlight the function that you want the new function to follow. Finally, click the Add button. 1-2-3 for Windows adds the new function after the highlighted function in the Current Menu list.

4. To add a separator, highlight the function in the Current Menu list that you want the separator to follow, and click the Separator button.

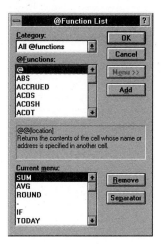

Fig. 5.4
You can customize
the @function-
selector list by
using the ex-
panded @Function
List dialog box.

5. To remove a function or a separator from the list, highlight it in the
   Current **M**enu list, and click the **R**emove button.

6. When you are satisfied with the Current Menu list, click OK.

1-2-3 for Windows Function Dictionary

1-2-3 for Windows's functions are divided into 10 categories:

- *Calendar functions* provide a set of conversion tools that let you perform
  date and time arithmetic. These functions are valuable for worksheets
  that use logic based on dates and times; they also are useful for calculations that show the number of days, months, or years between specific
  events.

- *Database functions* perform statistical calculations as well as queries in
  worksheets and external databases based on criteria that you specify.

- *Engineering functions* perform advanced mathematical operations,
  numeric-type conversions, and specific engineering calculations.

- *Financial functions* aid you in many business worksheets. With these
  functions, you can discount cash flow, calculate depreciation, and find
  the interest rate necessary for an annuity to grow to a future value. This
  set of functions provides great flexibility in investment analysis as well
  as cash-planning strategies.

■ *Information functions* provide a quick way to find the status of cells and ranges, the system, and errors in the worksheet.

■ *Logical functions* let you add decision-making capabilities to the worksheet. With logical functions, you can test whether a condition— one that you have defined in a worksheet or a 1-2-3 for Windows predefined condition—is true or false. Logical tests are important for formulas that need to make decisions.

■ *Lookup functions* find and return the contents of a cell. These functions are used primarily in conjunction with logical functions in macros to determine the information contained in a cell, making your worksheets more efficient and valuable.

■ *Mathematical functions* complement engineering functions. These tools are useful in complex and simple worksheets because they perform a variety of standard arithmetic operations, such as rounding values and calculating square roots.

■ *Statistical functions* let you perform all the standard statistical calculations on data in the worksheet or database. You can find minimum and maximum values, calculate averages, and compute standard deviations and variances.

■ *Text functions* provide a means to manipulate text. Text functions (also called *string functions*) are used to repeat characters; convert letters to uppercase, lowercase, or proper case; and change characters to numbers and numbers into text or strings. Text functions can be important when you are converting data for use by other programs, such as word processor mailing lists.

Tip
To get help on any function, open the @Function List dialog box, highlight the function in the @Function list, and press F1.

The following sections discuss each category and describe the most commonly used functions.

Calendar Functions

1-2-3 for Windows stores dates as serial numbers that represent a date between January 1, 1900 and December 31, 2099. For example, 1 is the serial number for January 1, 1900; and 33554 is the serial number for November 12, 1991. 1-2-3 for Windows stores times as serial numbers that range from .0 for 12:00:00 a.m. to .9999884 for 11:59:59. By using these date and time serial numbers, you can use dates and times in calculations such as elapsed time or days.

The 1-2-3 for Windows calendar functions let you convert dates and times to serial numbers so that you can use them in worksheet calculations.

Note

1-2-3 for Windows expresses time as a decimal fraction of a full day. For example, 0.5 is equal to 12 hours (or 12:00 p.m.). In addition, 1-2-3 for Windows works on international time: 10:00 p.m. in U.S. time is 22:00 in international time. Although the 1-2-3 for Windows timekeeping system may seem a little awkward at first, you will become used to it soon. Following are some guidelines to help you understand the system:

Time Increment	Serial-Number Equivalent
1 hour	0.0416666667
1 minute	0.0006944444
1 second	0.0000115741

These numeric equivalents are approximate; 1-2-3 for Windows actually calculates these numbers to 18 decimal places.

@DAYS360(*start_date,end_date*) and @D360(*start_date,end_date*)

@D360 returns the number of days between two dates, based on 12 months, each with 30 days—a 360-day year.

@DAYS360 is a more technical version of @D360. @DAYS360 has the same format as @D360; it, too, returns the difference between two dates based on a 360-day year. The @DAYS360 function, however, bases its calculations on the Security Industries Association's 1990 modifications to the 1986 edition of the *Standard Security Calculation Methods*. This is the standard in the securities industry for calculating the difference between two dates based on a 360-day year.

The two functions generally return different answers for the same data whenever the *start_date* or *end_date* arguments are the last day of the month. You should use @DAYS360 to calculate the number of days between two dates based on a 360-day year unless you must use calculations that are consistent with earlier worksheets in which the @D360 function was used.

Limits: Both date arguments must be expressed as valid serial numbers, or the function returns ERR. If the *end_date* occurs before the *start_date*, 1-2-3 for Windows returns a negative number.

Examples: @DAYS360(33554,B5) or @D360(33554,B5) returns 881, where 33554 is the serial number for 11/12/91 and cell B5 contains the date 4/23/94. There were 881 days between these two dates.

@DATE(*year,month,day*)

Tip

@DATE works with all algebraic symbols. For ex-ample, the syntax for adding a day to the @DATE function is @DATE(*year,month,day*)+1.

@DATE returns the serial number for the day specified by the arguments. You can enter numbers for the arguments or reference cells containing the values or formulas that calculate the values.

Limits: You must enter numbers that are valid to represent the year, month, and day. For example, the *day* argument for February cannot be 30 or 31.

1-2-3 for Windows returns serial numbers for dates between January 1, 1900 and December 31, 2099. Enter years from 1900 to 2099 either by entering all four digits or by entering from 00 (for 1900) to 199 (for 2099). Enter months from 1 to 12, and days from 1 to 31 (or the last day of the specified month).

Example: Both @DATE(51,04,06) and @DATE(51,4,6) return the date serial number for April 6, 1951: 18724. If the cell has a date format, the result appears in that date format. If the cell format is General, the serial number appears.

Note

Even though 1900 wasn't a leap year, 1-2-3 for Windows assigns the serial number 60 to the date February 29, 1900 (a date that never existed). Although this assignment should not be a problem, you may have difficulty if you transfer data between 1-2-3 for Windows and other programs. In that case, you must adjust for this error yourself.

Everyday Worksheet Tasks

@DATEVALUE(*date_string*)

@DATEVALUE computes the serial number for a date entered in one of the date formats that 1-2-3 for Windows recognizes. Click the Number Format button in the status bar, or open the **S**tyle menu and choose the **N**umber Format command to display the acceptable formats. If 1-2-3 for Windows does not recognize the format, @DATEVALUE results in ERR.

▶ "Date and Time Formats," p. 333

Be sure to enclose the date string in quotation marks when you specify the date as the *date_string* argument. Alternatively, you can specify a cell address of a cell that contains a date string as the *date_string* argument.

Limits: 1-2-3 for Windows returns serial numbers for dates between January 1, 1900 and December 31, 2099. Enter years from 1900 to 2099 either by entering all four digits or by entering from 00 (for 1900) to 199 (for 2099). Enter days from 1 to 31.

Examples: If cell A1 contains the formatted date 31-Dec-2099, you can use @DATEVALUE(A1) to return the serial number 73050. Alternatively, you can use @DATEVALUE ("31-Dec-2099") to return the same serial number.

Note

If you reset the default date format so that you can use international date formats, make sure that the *date_string* argument is in one of the date formats for the country you selected. To change the default date format, open the **T**ools menu and choose **U**ser Setup **I**nternational.

@DATESTRING(*date*)

@DATESTRING computes the date from the date serial number and displays it as a label using the default international date format. To change the default international date format, open the **T**ools menu and choose **U**ser Setup, click the **I**nternational button, and choose the date format that you would like.

Limits: The *date* argument must be expressed as valid serial number or the function returns ERR.

Example: @DATESTRING(32780) returns 09/29/89 when the default international date format is mm/dd/yy.

@DAY(*date_number*)

@DAY converts a serial number to a numeric day of the month. The function accepts a valid date serial number as its single argument and returns a number ranging from 1 to 31. You can use a cell reference or another function (such as @TODAY) to supply the value for the *date_number* argument.

Limits:	The serial number must range from 1 (January 1, 1900) to 73050 (December 31, 2099).
Examples:	@DAY(32780) returns 29 as the day of the month, because this serial number represents September 29, 1989. @DAY(B3) returns 29 when cell B3 contains the date 29-Sep-89.

@WEEKDAY(*date_number*)

@WEEKDAY converts a serial number to a numeric day of the week. The function accepts a valid date serial number as its single argument and returns a number ranging from 0 (for Monday) to 6 (for Sunday). You can use a cell reference or another function (such as @DATE) to supply the value for the *date_number* argument.

Limits:	The serial number must range from 1 (January 1, 1900) to 73050 (December 31, 2099).
Examples:	@WEEKDAY(32780) returns 4 (Friday) as the day of the month, because this serial number represents September 29, 1989. @WEEKDAY(B3) returns 4 (Friday) when cell B3 contains the date 29-Sep-89. @WEEKDAY(@DATE(89,9,29)) also returns 4 (Friday).

@MONTH(*date_number*)

@MONTH converts a serial number to a numeric month. The function accepts a valid date serial number as its single argument and returns a number ranging from 1 (January) to 12 (December). You can use a cell reference or another function (such as @DATE) to supply the value for the *date_number* argument.

Limits: The serial number must range from 1 (January 1, 1900) to 73050 (December 31, 2099).

Examples: @MONTH(32780) returns 9 (September) as the month, because this serial number represents September 29, 1989. @MONTH(B3) returns 9 (September) when cell B3 contains the date 29-Sep-89. @MONTH(@DATE(89,9,29)) also returns 9 (September).

@NEXTMONTH(*start_date,months,[day_of_month],[basis]*)

@NEXTMONTH returns the date serial number for a date that is the specified number of months before or after the specified start date.

The *start_date* argument is any valid date serial number. The *months* argument is a positive or negative integer; use a positive integer to specify the number of months after the start date and a negative integer to specify the number of months before the start date.

The optional *day_of_month* argument indicates which day of the month the results should fall on. Enter 0 for the same day of the month as that specified in the *start_date* argument, for example, the 15th of the month. Enter 1 for the first day of the month and 2 for the last day of the month. The default if the argument is omitted is 0.

The optional *basis* argument specifies the type of day-count basis that 1-2-3 should use. Enter 0 for a 30/360 day-count basis, 1 for actual/actual, 2 for actual/360, and 3 for actual/365. The default if the argument is omitted is 1 (actual/actual).

Limits: The serial number must range from 1 (January 1, 1990) to 73050 (December 31, 2099)

Examples: 32780 is the date serial number for 9/29/89. @NEXTMONTH(32780,2) returns 32841, the date serial number for 11/29/89, which is two months after the start date. @NEXTMONTH(32780,2,1) returns 32813, the date serial number for 11/01/89, which is the first day of the month two months after the start date.

@YEAR(*date_number*)

@YEAR converts a serial number to a numeric year. The function accepts a valid date serial number as its single argument and returns a number ranging from 0 (for 1900) to 199 (for 2099). You can use a cell reference or another function (such as @DATE or @NOW) to supply the value for the *date_number* argument.

Limits:	The serial number must range from 1 (January 1, 1900) to 73050 (December 31, 2099).
Examples:	@YEAR(32780) returns 89 as the year, because this serial number represents September 29, 1989. @YEAR(B3) returns 89 when cell B3 contains the date 29-Sep-89. @MONTH(@NOW) returns the current year.

@NOW

@NOW retrieves the current system date and time as date and time serial numbers. The integers to the left of the decimal point specify the date; those to the right of the decimal point specify the time.

@NOW is a convenient tool for recording the date and time when a worksheet is modified or printed. 1-2-3 for Windows recalculates @NOW every time you recalculate your work. If you selected automatic recalculation (open the **T**ools menu, choose the **U**ser Setup command, click the **R**ecalculation button, and select **A**utomatic), 1-2-3 for Windows recalculates @NOW every time it recalculates any value.

If you format the cell containing @NOW as a date, only the date portion of the result appears. If you format the cell as a time, only the time portion appears. To change formats, click the Number Format button in the status bar or open the **S**tyle menu and choose the **N**umber Format command.

Example:	On June 14, 1994, at 3:14:29 p.m., @NOW returns 34499.63502314. 34499 is the serial number for June 14, 1994, and 63502314 is the serial number for 3:14:29 p.m.

Note

Use the @INT function to calculate the date or time portion of the @NOW function. To extract the date portion of the @NOW function, use @INT(@NOW); the result is the same as the result of @TODAY. To extract the time portion, use @NOW-@INT(@NOW); the result is the same as the result of @NOW-@TODAY.

@TODAY

@TODAY retrieves the current system date (not the system time) as a serial number. This function is a convenient tool for recording the date when a worksheet is modified or printed. 1-2-3 for Windows recalculates @TODAY every time you recalculate your work. If you selected automatic recalculation (open the **T**ools menu, choose the **U**ser Setup command, click the **R**ecalculation button, and select **A**utomatic) 1-2-3 for Windows recalculates @TODAY every time it recalculates any value.

You can format the cell containing @TODAY as a date. To change formats, click the Number Format button in the status bar or open the **S**tyle menu and choose the **N**umber Format command.

> Example: On June 14, 1994, @NOW returns 34499, which is the serial number for that date.

@TIME(*hour,minute,seconds*)

@TIME returns the serial number for the time specified by the arguments. You can enter numbers for the arguments or reference cells containing the values or formulas that calculate the values. You can use @TIME to calculate the time period between events.

> Limits: Enter hours from 0 (for midnight) to 23 (for 11 p.m.), hours from 0 to 59, and seconds from 0 to 59.

> Example: @TIME(14,0,0) returns the time serial number for 2:00:00 p.m.: .583333. If the cell has a time format, the result appears in that time format. If the cell format is General, the serial number appears.

One way to produce a range of times is to use the **R**ange menu's **F**ill command. The following steps produce a table that can be used as an event calendar for the period 8:00 a.m. to 7:30 p.m., in 30-minute increments:

1. Select the range in which you want the times to appear. For this example, select the range A4..A19.

2. Open the **R**ange menu and choose the **F**ill command.

3. Choose the Mi**n**ute option in the Interval box.

4. Select the **S**tart text in the Start box; type **8:00**.

5. Select the **I**ncrement text in the Increment box; type **30**.

6. Select the Stop text in the Stop box; type **4:00pm**.

7. Click OK. 1-2-3 for Windows fills the range A4..A19 with time-conversion numbers.

8. 1-2-3 for Windows formats the range of cells with the default time format. To change the time format, open the **S**tyle menu and choose the **N**umber Format command. In the Number Format dialog box, select Time, and then select the time format 11:59AM and choose OK. 1-2-3 for Windows converts the cells in the selected range to this format.

9. Repeat steps 1 through 8 for the range F4..F12 to fill in the time from 4:00 to 8:00 p.m.

@TIMEVALUE(*time_string*)

Like @DATEVALUE and @DATE, @TIMEVALUE is a variation on @TIME. Like @TIME, @TIMEVALUE produces a serial number from the hour, minute, and second information you supply. Unlike @TIME, however, @TIMEVALUE uses string arguments rather than numeric arguments.

You must enter the time string in one of the time formats that 1-2-3 for Windows recognizes. To display the acceptable formats, click the Number Format button in the status bar or open the **S**tyle menu and choose the **N**umber Format command. If 1-2-3 for Windows does not recognize the format, @TIMEVALUE results in ERR.

Be sure to enclose the time string in quotation marks when you specify the time as the *time_string* argument. Alternatively, you can specify the cell address of a cell that contains a time string as the *time_string* argument.

Limits: Enter hours from 0 (for midnight) to 23 (for 11 p.m.), hours from 0 to 59, and seconds from 0 to 59.

Examples: If cell A1 contains the formatted date 02:00 pm, you can use @TIMEVALUE(A1) to return the serial number .583333. Alternatively, you can use @TIMEVALUE("02:00 pm") to return the same serial number. To display the time serial number for the current system date, enter **@TIMEVALUE(@NOW-@TODAY)**.

> **Note**
>
> If you reset the default time format so that you can use international time formats, make sure that the *time_string* argument is in one of the time formats for the country you selected. To change the default time format, open the **T**ools menu and choose the **U**ser Setup command; then choose the **I**nternational option.

@SECOND(*time_number*)

@SECOND extracts the seconds from a time serial number. The function accepts a valid time serial number as its single argument and returns a number ranging from 0 to 59. You can use a cell reference or another function (such as @TIME) to supply the value for the *time_number* argument.

Limits: The serial number must range from .000000 (for midnight) to .999988 (for 11:59:59 p.m.).

Examples: @SECOND(.590394) returns 10 as the seconds, because this serial number represents 02:10:10 p.m. @SECOND(B3) returns 10 when cell B3 contains the time 02:10:10. @SECOND(@TIME(02,10,10) also returns 10.

@MINUTE(*time_number*)

@MINUTE extracts the minutes from a time serial number. The function accepts a valid time serial number as its single argument and returns a number ranging from 0 to 59. You can use a cell reference or another function (such as @TIME) to supply the value for the *time_number* argument.

Limits: The serial number must range from .000000 (for midnight) to .999988 (for 11:59:59 p.m.).

Examples: @SECOND(.590394) returns 10 as the minutes, because this serial number represents 02:10:10 p.m. @SECOND(B3) returns 10 when cell B3 contains the time 02:10:10. @SECOND(@TIME(02,10,10) also returns 10.

@HOUR(*time_number*)

@HOUR extracts the hours from a time serial number. The function accepts a valid time serial number as its single argument and returns a number ranging from 0 to 23. You can use a cell reference or another function (such as @TIME) to supply the value for the *time_number* argument.

Everyday Worksheet Tasks

@HOUR is useful for calculations that involve hours, such as calculating hourly wages or elapsed hours.

Limits:	The serial number must range from .000000 (for midnight) to .999988 (for 11:59:59 p.m.).
Examples:	@HOUR(.590394) returns 14 (2:00 p.m.) as the hour because this serial number represents 02:10:10 p.m. @HOUR(B3) returns 14 when cell B3 contains the time 02:10:10. @HOUR(@TIME(02,10,10)) also returns 14.

@NETWORKDAYS(*start_date,end_date,[holiday_range],[weekends]*)
@NETWORKDAYS returns the number of days between two dates excluding holidays and weekends.

The *start_date* and *end_date* arguments are valid date serial numbers. You can use the @DATE function in either argument. The optional *holdiay_range* argument is the name or address of a range that contains the date serial numbers of the holidays that should be excluded from the calculations.

The optional *weekends* argument indicates which days of the week should be omitted as weekend days. The argument is text and as such should be enclosed in quotation marks. Enter from 0 (for Monday) to 6 (for Sunday). For example, enter "45" to indicate that Friday and Saturday should be used as weekend days. Enter 7 to specify no weekends. The default argument is "56."

Limits:	The serial number must range from 1 (January 1, 1990) to 73050 (December 31, 2099)
	The *weekend* argument must be enclosed in quotation marks.
	To use weekends without using holidays, specify a blank cell for the *holiday_range* argument.
Examples:	Suppose you want to determine the number of working days between December 1, 1994 and January 12, 1995, excluding the holidays listed in a range named HOLIDAYS and excluding Saturday and Sunday as the weekends (the default). Use @NETWORKDAYS(@DATE(94,12,1),@DATE(95,1,1),HOLIDAYS) to return the number or workdays, 22.

Database Functions

1-2-3 for Windows database functions manipulate database fields. Like other functions, the database functions perform—in one simple statement—calculations that otherwise would require a complex series of operations. The efficiency and ease of application make these functions excellent tools for examining database records in either worksheet databases or external database tables (see Part V, "Managing Databases," for details about working with databases).

Following is the general syntax of all database functions except @DQUERY:

@DSUM(*input,field,criteria*)

The *input* argument specifies the database or part of a database to be scanned; it can be the address or name of a single-worksheet range that contains a database table or the name of an external database table. You can use more than one *input* argument in a database function by separating the *input* arguments with commas. 1-2-3 for Windows reads database-function arguments from right to left, so it uses the last argument as the *criteria*, the next-to-last argument as the *field*, and the remaining arguments as *input*. You can use an unlimited number of *input* arguments, provided that you do not exceed 512 characters in the cell that contains the function. You do not need to identify an *input* (by opening the **T**ools menu, choosing Data**b**ase, and then choosing **N**ew Query) before you use it as an *input* argument in a database function.

The *criteria* argument specifies which records are to be selected. The *criteria* argument can be a criteria formula or a range address or a range name of a range containing a criteria formula.

The *field* argument is the field name from the database table, enclosed in quotation marks. If you use just one *input* argument, you can represent the *field* argument with an offset number. If you use more than one *input* argument, and the field name you want to use as the *field* argument appears in more than one of the input ranges, the *field* must be entered as the name of the *input*, followed by a period, and the *field* name, enclosed in quotation marks. For example, if you have two input ranges named SALES (A1..E20) and BUDGET (A22..E42), each of which has a field called DEPARTMENT, you can refer to the DEPARTMENT field in the SALES range this way:

"SALES.DEPARTMENT" or "A1..E20.DEPARTMENT"

Database functions are similar to statistical functions, but database functions process only data items that meet the criteria you specify. For example, if you have a list of employees, the departments where they work, and their annual salaries, you can use @AVG to calculate the average of all salaries. Use @DAVG to calculate the average salaries of any subgroup, such as the Sales department, without first extracting the Sales department records.

Figure 5.5 shows a few examples of common database functions.

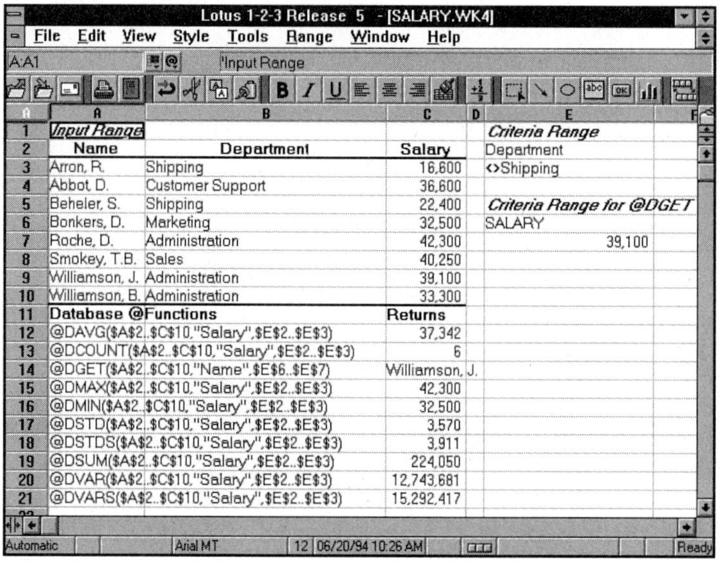

Fig. 5.5
Database functions manipulate database fields.

	Lotus 1-2-3 Release 5 - [SALARY.WK4]			
	A	B	C	D	E
1	*Input Range*				*Criteria Range*
2	Name	Department	Salary		Department
3	Arron, R.	Shipping	16,600		<>Shipping
4	Abbot, D.	Customer Support	36,600		
5	Beheler, S.	Shipping	22,400		*Criteria Range for @DGET*
6	Bonkers, D.	Marketing	32,500		SALARY
7	Roche, D.	Administration	42,300		39,100
8	Smokey, T.B.	Sales	40,250		
9	Williamson, J.	Administration	39,100		
10	Williamson, B.	Administration	33,300		
11	Database @Functions		Returns		
12	@DAVG($A$2..$C$10,"Salary",$E$2..$E$3)		37,342		
13	@DCOUNT($A$2..$C$10,"Salary",$E$2..$E$3)		6		
14	@DGET($A$2..$C$10,"Name",$E$6..$E$7)		Williamson, J.		
15	@DMAX($A$2..$C$10,"Salary",$E$2..$E$3)		42,300		
16	@DMIN($A$2..$C$10,"Salary",$E$2..$E$3)		32,500		
17	@DSTD($A$2..$C$10,"Salary",$E$2..$E$3)		3,570		
18	@DSTDS($A$2..$C$10,"Salary",$E$2..$E$3)		3,911		
19	@DSUM($A$2..$C$10,"Salary",$E$2..$E$3)		224,050		
20	@DVAR($A$2..$C$10,"Salary",$E$2..$E$3)		12,743,681		
21	@DVARS($A$2..$C$10,"Salary",$E$2..$E$3)		15,292,417		

@DAVG(*input,field,criteria*)

@DAVG calculates the average of the values in a field of the *input* argument for records that match the criteria.

Example: In figure 5.5, the average in the Salary field for records that match the non-Shipping department criteria is 37,342.

@DCOUNT(*input,field,criteria*)

@DCOUNT counts the *nonblank cells*—cells that contain data—in a field of the *input* argument for records that match the criteria.

Example: In figure 5.5, the number of cells containing data in the Salary field for records that match the non-Shipping department criteria is 6.

@DGET(*input,field,criteria*)

Although @DGET uses the same three arguments as most other database functions, @DGET performs a different function. @DGET returns the value of the *field* argument for the record that matches the condition set in the *criteria* argument. Because @DGET returns ERR if no records match or if more than one record matches the criteria, @DGET often requires a more selective *criteria* argument.

Example: In figure 5.5, the criteria used for @DGET specifies the single record where the Salary field value equals 39,100; the value returned for the Name field is Williamson, J.

@DMAX(*input,field,criteria*)

@DMAX finds the largest value in a field for records that match the criteria.

Example: In figure 5.5, the maximum in the Salary field for records that match the non-Shipping department criteria is 42,300.

@DMIN(*input,field,criteria*)

@DMIN finds the smallest value in a field for records that match the criteria.

Example: In figure 5.5, the minimum in the Salary field for records that match the non-Shipping department criteria is 32,500.

@DQUERY(*external_function,[external_argument]*)

@DQUERY performs a function similar to opening the **T**ools menu, choosing Data**b**ase, and then choosing **S**end. @DQUERY sends a command to an external database management program and uses the results of the command in a criteria range.

The argument *external_function* is the name of a command or function in the external database management program; the optional *external_arguments* are the values that the external program uses for that command or function.

Limits: @DQUERY cannot be used with another database function whose *input* argument contains more than one database table.

Example: Suppose that the external database management program contains a function, LIKE, that matches data phonetically. LIKE has one argument—the data you are matching—so LIKE("SMITH") matches the names *Smith*, *Smyth*, and *Smythe*.

Suppose that one of the field names in the external data base is "STREET," and you are interested in finding the "STREET" associated with the people with last names like "SMITH." In the criteria range of the worksheet you are looking from, you enter **+STREET=@DQUERY("LIKE","SMITH")**. The @DQUERY function uses the LIKE function from the external database management program and returns the data from the external database field "STREET."

@DSTD(*input,field,criteria*)

@DSTD calculates the population standard deviation of values in a field for records that match the criteria.

Example: In figure 5.5, the standard deviation of the Salary field for records that match the non-Shipping department criteria is 3,570.

@DSTDS(*input,field,criteria*)

@DSTDS calculates the sample standard deviation of values in a field for records that match the criteria.

Example: In figure 5.5, the standard deviation of a sample population of the Salary field for records that match the non-Shipping department criteria is 3,911.

@DSUM(*input,field,criteria*)

@DSUM totals the values in a field for records that match the criteria.

Example: In figure 5.5, the sum of the Salary field for records that match the non-Shipping department criteria is 224,050.

@DVAR(*input,field,criteria*)

@DVAR calculates the population variance of values in a field for records that match the criteria.

Example: In figure 5.5, the population variance of the Salary field for records that match the non-Shipping department criteria is 12,743,681.

@DVARS(*input,field,criteria*)

@DVARS calculates the variance of sample values in a field for records that match the criteria.

Example: In figure 5.5, the variance of sample values of the Salary field for records that match the non-Shipping department criteria is 15,292,417.

Engineering Functions

The engineering functions provide solutions for Bessel calculations, hex-to-decimal conversions, error-function calculations, and power-series summations.

Bessel Functions

Bessel functions are used in calculations dealing with cylindrical symmetry. You use these functions in conjunction with diffusion, elasticity, wave propagation, and fluid motion.

- @BESSELI(*x,n*) calculates the modified Bessel function of integer order $\ln(x)$. This function approximates to within $+/-5*10^{\wedge}-8$.

- @BESSELJ(*x,n*) calculates the Bessel function of integer order $Jn(x)$. This function approximates to within $+/-5*10^{\wedge}-8$.

- @BESSELK(*x,n*) calculates the modified Bessel function of integer order $Kn(x)$. This function approximates to within $+/-5*10^{\wedge}-8$.

- @BESSELY(*x,n*) calculates the Bessel function of integer order $Yn(x)$. This function sometimes is called the Neumann function. This function approximates to within $+/-5*10^{\wedge}-8$.

In each of these functions, the x argument is the value at which to evaluate the function; it can be any value. The n argument is the order of the function, which can be any positive integer or (for @BESSELI and @BESSELJ) 0.

@BETA(*z,w*)

@BETA calculates the Beta function to within at least six significant digits. The z and w arguments can be any value.

Example: @BETA(.5,.5) returns 3.141593.

@BETAI(*a,b,x*)

@BETAI calculates the incomplete Beta function to within at least six significant digits. The *a* and *b* arguments can be any value. The *x* argument must be
a value ranging from 0 through 1.

Example: @BETA(.5,.5,.668271) returns 0.050012.

@DECIMAL(*hexadecimal*)

@DECIMAL converts a hexadecimal value to its signed decimal equivalent.
The *hexadecimal* argument, which you enter as text, can be a value ranging
from 00000000 through FFFFFFFF. The value 0 and all positive hexadecimal
numbers are in the range 00000000 through 7FFFFFFF. Negative hexadecimal
numbers are in the range 80000000 through FFFFFFFF.

Limits: The argument can contain only valid hexadecimal dig-
                its and letters. Valid digits range from 0 through 9; valid
                letters range from A through F. The letters are not case-
                sensitive.

Example: @DECIMAL("1A") returns 26.

@ERF(*lower_limit,[upper_limit]*)

@ERF is an approximation function that calculates the error function integrated between the lower limit and the upper limit. The approximation is
within +/-1.2x10^7.

The *lower_limit* argument is the lower boundary for integrating @ERF; it
can be any value. The optional *upper_limit* argument specifies the upper
boundary for integrating @ERF; it can be any value greater than or equal to
the *lower_limit* value. If you omit the *upper_limit* argument, @ERF integrates
between 0 and *lower_limit*.

Examples: @ERF(.7) returns 0.677801, and @ERF(.8) returns
                0.742101. Notice that @ERF(.7,.8) returns 0.0643 and is
                the difference between the first two examples.

@ERFC(*x*)

@ERFC calculates the complementary error function integrated between the
argument and infinity. The @ERFC function is 1-@ERF(*x*), which approximates the complementary error function to within +/-3*10^-7. The *x* argument can be any error-function value.

Example: @ERFC(0.7) returns 0.322199.

@ERFD(*x*)

@ERFD calculates the derivative of the error function, using the formula (2/@SQRT(@PI))*@EXP(-*x*^2). The *x* argument can be an error-function value ranging from approximately -106.56 to 106.56. If the argument falls outside this range, 1-2-3 for Windows returns ERR. If the argument is outside the boundaries -15.102 to 15.102, 1-2-3 for Windows can calculate and store the value for use in other calculations, although it cannot display the value in the cell (a series of asterisks appears instead).

Example: @ERFD(0.7) returns 0.691275.

@GAMMA(*x*)

@GAMMA approximates the Gamma distribution accurately to within six significant figures. The *x* argument can be any positive value greater than 0.

Examples: @GAMMA(.5) returns 1.772454, and @GAMMA(3.6) returns 3.717024.

@GAMMAI(*a,x,[complement]*)

@GAMMAI calculates the incomplete Gamma function and is accurate to within six significant figures. The *a* argument can be any positive value. The *x* argument can be any positive value or 0.

The optional *complement* argument controls how 1-2-3 for Windows calculates @GAMMAI; you can set this value to 0 or 1. If you use 0, 1-2-3 for Windows calculates P(*a,x*). (This is the default if you omit the *complement* argument.) If you use 1, 1-2-3 for Windows calculates Q(*a,x*) or 1-P(*a,x*).

Example: The value of @GAMMA(7.5,12.4497,1) is 0.050024.

@GAMMALN(*x*)

@GAMMALN calculates the natural log of the gamma function to within six significant digits. The *x* argument can be any value greater than 0.

Example: @GAMMALN(0.5) returns 0.572365.

@HEX(*decimal*)

The @HEX function converts a decimal value to its signed hexadecimal equivalent. The *decimal* argument can be a value ranging from -2,147,483,648 through 2,147,483,647. Enter the argument as a value; if it is not an integer, 1-2-3 for Windows truncates it to an integer.

Example: @HEX(162) returns A2.

@SERIESSUM(*x,n,m,coefficients*)

@SERIESSUM calculates the sum of a power series. The *x* argument is the power series' input value. The *n* argument's value is the initial power to which to raise *x*. The *m* argument's value is the increment to increase *n* for each term in the series.

The *coefficients* argument is a range that contains the coefficients by which 1-2-3 for Windows multiplies each successive power of *x*. The number of terms in the series is determined by the number of cells in the *coefficients* argument. For example, if *coefficients* contains eight cells, the power series contains eight terms.

Example: Suppose that a range called INPUT contains the values 0.2, 0.7, and 1.3 for the *coefficients* argument. @SERIESSUM(3.5,2,1,INPUT) returns 227.5438.

Financial Functions

1-2-3 for Windows provides a series of financial functions that calculate discounted cash flow, loan amortization, depreciation, investment analysis, and annuities. The 1-2-3 for Windows financial functions are categorized into the following five groups, so that you can find the best type of function quickly:

- Annuities
- Bonds
- Capital-Budgeting Tools
- Depreciation
- Single-Sum Compounding

Annuity Functions

You use annuity functions as financial-analysis tools. These functions give you full-range capability to calculate current payments, future values, and interest rates. You can use this information to make prudent financial decisions.

@FV(*payments, interest, term*) and @FVAL(*payments, interest, term,[type],[present_value]*)

@FV calculates the future value of an investment based on a specific interest rate and a fixed number of regular investment payments. @FVAL calculates the future value of an investment based on a specific interest rate, a fixed number of regular payments, the optional position of the period in which the payments are made, and the optional starting amount of the investment. @FV and @FVAL are helpful for estimating the future balances of savings accounts, college funds, and investments.

The *payment* argument is the amount of each equal payment. The *interest* argument is the periodic interest rate. The *term* argument is the total number of payments.

For @FVAL, the optional *type* argument can be 0 or 1. A value of 0 causes 1-2-3 for Windows to calculate based on payments being made at the end of the period. This value is the default value if you omit the *type* argument. A value of 1 causes 1-2-3 for Windows to calculate based on payments being made at the beginning of the period.

For @FVAL, the optional *present_value* argument indicates the current value of the series of future payments. It can be any value. If you omit the *present_value* argument, 1-2-3 for Windows assumes a value of 0.

Tip

When payment is made at the end of the period, you are calculating an ordinary annuity. When payment is made at the beginning of the period, you are calculating an annuity due.

Limits: The interest argument must be greater than -1.

You must use the same period for the *payment, interest,* and *term* arguments. Therefore, if you are calculating a monthly payment, use monthly increments for *interest* and *term*. This means you need to divide the annual interest rate by 12 and multiply the number of years by 12. If you keep the *interest* and *term* arguments annual, increase the *payment* argument to a yearly amount by multiplying the monthly payment by 12.

Example: You start your 3-year-old's college-education fund with $2,000, and you plan monthly contributions of $200 at the end of the period. The annual interest rate is 6 percent, and the time period is 15 years. Use the function @FVAL(2400,0.06,15,0,2000) to calculate the result of your savings at the end of the term: $60,655.44.

Everyday Worksheet Tasks

> ### Note
>
> When entering optional arguments, you must enter all the optional arguments before the optional argument that you want to use. For example, for @FVAL(*payments, interest, term,[type],[present_value]*), to use the *present_value* argument, you first must enter a *type* argument.

@IPAYMT(*principal,interest,term,start_period,[end_period],[type], [future_value]*)
and
@PPAYMT(*principal,interest,term,start_period,[end_period],[type], [future_value]*)

Performing loan analysis can be very beneficial when you are looking for a loan. @IPAYMT and @PPAYMT are complementary functions: @IPAYMT calculates the interest on payments that you make on a loan, and @PPAYMT calculates the principal contributed to the loan you are paying off.

The *principal* argument is the amount of the loan. The *interest* argument is the periodic interest rate. The *term* argument is the number of payment periods for the loan (frequently, the number of months or years). The *start_period* argument is the point in the term when you want to begin calculating interest or principal.

The optional *end_period* argument is the point in the term when you want to stop calculating interest or principal. If you omit this argument, 1-2-3 for Windows assumes that the *start_period* and *end_period* arguments are the same.

The optional *type* argument can be 0 or 1. A value of 0 causes 1-2-3 for Windows to calculate based on payments being made at the end of the period. This value is the default value if you omit the *type* argument. A value of 1 causes 1-2-3 for Windows to calculate based on payments being made at the beginning of the period.

The optional *future_value* argument indicates the future value of the series of payments; it can be any value. If you omit the *future_value* argument, 1-2-3 for Windows assumes a value of 0.

Tip
You can enter interest rates in the function as a percentage. 1-2-3 for Windows converts the percentage to the decimal format it requires. If you enter **5%**, for example, 1-2-3 for Windows enters 0.05 in the function.

Limits: The *interest* argument must be greater than -1.

The *term* argument can be any value except 0.

The *start_period* argument can be any value greater than or equal to 1, but it cannot be greater than the *term* value.

You must use the same period for the *interest* and *term* arguments. Therefore, if you are calculating a monthly payment, use monthly increments for *interest* and *term*. This means you need to divide the annual interest rate by 12 and multiply the number of years by 12.

Example: You have a $5,000 loan at 10.25 percent, to be paid back in 2 years (24 months). To determine the interest amount for the 12th month, use @IPAYMT(5000,0.1025/12,24,12), which returns $24.21 (when rounded for Currency format). To determine the principal amount for the 12th month, use @PPAYMT(5000,0.1025/12,24,12), which returns $207.09 (when rounded for Currency format).

@IRATE(*term,payment,present_value,[type],[future_value],[guess]*)

@IRATE calculates the rate of interest necessary for an investment to grow to a specific future value. This function is useful for determining the interest rate necessary to maintain the principal amount of an investment while generating a specific amount in interest—for example, for a trust or retirement fund.

The *term* argument is the number of payments. The *payment* argument is the payment amount. The *present_value* argument is the starting amount of the investment.

The optional *type* argument can be 0 or 1. A value of 0 causes 1-2-3 for Windows to calculate based on payments being made at the end of the period. This value is the default value if you omit the *type* argument. A value of 1 causes 1-2-3 for Windows to calculate based on payments being made at the beginning of the period.

The optional *future_value* argument indicates the future value of the series of payments; it can be any value. If you omit the *future_value* argument, 1-2-3 for Windows assumes a value of 0.

The optional *guess* argument is your estimate of the interest rate; it can be a value between 0 and 1. If you omit this argument, 1-2-3 for Windows assumes a value of .1 (10%).

Limits: You must use the same period for the *term* and *payment* arguments. Therefore, to find an annual interest rate, enter the term in years and multiply the monthly payment by 12 to use a yearly payment figure.

Example: You have a $200,000 retirement fund, from which you want to withdraw $2,000 monthly for 25 years. Use @IRATE(25,24000,200000) to determine that your investment needs an interest rate of 11.15 percent.

@TERM(*payments,interest,future_value*) and @NPER(*payments,interest,future_value,[type],[present_value]*)

@TERM calculates the number of periods required to accumulate a specified future value by making equal payments into an interest-bearing account at the end of each period. The number of periods is the term for an ordinary annuity.

Tip
You can calculate the term necessary to pay back a loan by using a negative *future_value* argument with @TERM.

@NPER performs the same calculation, with a slight twist: it allows for optional *present_value* and *type* arguments. These arguments provide flexibility by adjusting the starting amount and the time of the period within the estimation.

The *payment* argument is the amount of each payment. The *interest* argument is the periodic interest rate. The *future_value* argument is the amount you want to have at the end of the payment schedule.

For @NPER, the optional *type* argument can be 0 or 1. A value of 0 causes 1-2-3 for Windows to calculate based on payments being made at the end of the period. This value is the default value if you omit the *type* argument. A value of 1 causes 1-2-3 for Windows to calculate based on payments being made at the beginning of the period.

For @NPER, the optional *present_value* argument indicates the current value (the starting balance); it can be any value. If you omit the *present_value* argument, 1-2-3 for Windows assumes a value of 0.

Limits: The *interest* argument must be greater than -1.

The *payment* argument can be any value except 0.

Examples: To determine how long it will take to accumulate $5,000 by making a monthly payment of $50 into an account that pays 8 percent annual interest compounded monthly (0.67 percent per month), use @TERM(50,0.0067,5000), which returns 76.80 (months).

If you have $200 saved and want to start with that amount, use @NPER(50,0.0067,5000,0,200), which returns 72.84 (months).

@PMT(*principal,interest,term*) and
@PAYMT(*principal,interest,term,*[*type*],[*future_value*])

@PMT and @PAYMT calculate the periodic payments necessary to pay the entire principal on an amortizing loan. @PMT assumes that the payments are made at the end of each period, whereas @PAYMT lets you specify that payments are made at the beginning or the end of each period. In addition, @PAYMT includes an optional argument for the future value.

The *principal* argument is the amount of the loan. The *interest* argument is the periodic interest rate. The *term* argument is the number of payment periods for the loan.

For @PAYMT, the optional *type* argument can be 0 or 1. A value of 0 causes 1-2-3 for Windows to calculate based on payments being made at the end of the period. This value is the default value if you omit the *type* argument. A value of 1 causes 1-2-3 for Windows to calculate based on payments being made at the beginning of the period.

For @PAYMT, the optional *future_value* argument indicates the future value of a series of payments; it can be any value. If you omit the *future_value* argument, 1-2-3 for Windows assumes a value of 0.

Tip
@PMTC is similar to @PMT, except that it supports Canadian mortgage conventions.

Everyday Worksheet Tasks

Limits: The *interest* argument must be greater than -1.

You must use the same period for the *interest* and *term* arguments. Therefore, if you are calculating a monthly payment, use monthly increments for *interest* and *term*. This means you need to divide the annual interest rate by 12 and multiply the number of years by 12.

Examples: To calculate the monthly payments on a $10,000 5-year loan with an interest rate of 9 percent and payments due on the last day of the month, use @PMT(10000,0.09/12,60), which returns a figure of $207.58 (when rounded for Currency format). If payment is due on the first day of the month, use @PAYMT(10000,0.09/12,60,1), which returns a figure of $206.04 (when rounded for Currency format).

> **Note**
>
> If you make monthly payments, enter the interest rate as the monthly interest rate (annual rate divided by 12) and the term as the number of months for which you make payments (number of years multiplied by 12). Alternatively, if you make annual payments, enter the interest rate as the annual interest rate and the term as the number of years for which you make payments.

@PV(*payments,interest,term*) and @PVAL(*payments,interest,term,[type],[future_value]*)

Tip

Use @PV in conjunction with @PMT to create an amortization table.

@PV and @PVAL calculate the present value of an investment made as a series of equal payments. Use @PV and @PVAL to compare different investments. For example, you can compare a single-payment investment with a pension fund that has multiple equal payments.

The *payment* argument is the amount of the payments. The *interest* argument is the periodic interest rate. The *term* argument is the number of payment periods for the investment.

For @PVAL, the optional *type* argument can be 0 or 1. A value of 0 causes 1-2-3 for Windows to calculate based on payments being made at the end of the period. This value is the default value if you omit the *type* argument. A value of 1 causes 1-2-3 for Windows to calculate based on payments being made at the beginning of the period.

For @PVAL, the optional *future_value* argument indicates the future value of the payments; it can be any value. If you omit the *future_value* argument, 1-2-3 for Windows assumes a value of 0.

Limits: The *interest* argument must be greater than -1.

You must use the same period for the *interest* and *term* arguments. Therefore, if you are calculating a monthly payment, use monthly increments for *interest* and *term*. This means you need to divide the annual interest rate by 12 and multiply the number of years by 12.

Examples: To calculate the present value of 20 yearly payments of $1,000 invested at 5 percent and paid at the end of each period, use @PV(1000,0.05,20), which returns a figure of $12,462.21 (when rounded for Currency format). If payments are made at the beginning of each period, use @PVAL(1000,0.05,20,1), which returns a figure of $13,085.32 (when rounded for Currency format).

Bonds Functions

Bond functions provide the tools you need to analyze investments. With these tools, you can make better investment judgments and (ideally) increase your scope of investments.

@ACCRUED(*settlement,issue,first_interest,coupon,[par],[frequency],[basis]*)

@ACCRUED calculates the accrued interest for securities that have periodic interest payments. You can use @ACCRUED for short, standard, and log coupon periods.

Following are this function's arguments and limits:

settlement   A date serial number that represents the settlement date, or date of ownership, for the security.

issue   The date serial number of the security's issue or dated date.

first_interest   The date serial number of the security's first interest date; it must be greater than or equal to the *issue* argument.

coupon   The annual coupon rate for the security; it can be any positive value or 0.

[par]   An optional argument that represents the value of the security's principal when paid at maturity. 1-2-3 for Windows assumes the value of 100 if this argument is omitted. If a value is included, it must be positive.

[frequency]   An optional argument that represents the number of coupon payments per year. This argument has four options:

Frequency	Representing
1	Annual
2	Semiannual (the default if you omit the argument)
4	Quarterly
12	Monthly

[*basis*]   An optional argument specifying the type of day count (*days_per_month/days_per_year*) to use. This argument has four options:

Basis	Days_per_Month/ Days_per_Year
0	30/360 (the default if you omit the argument)
1	Actual/Actual
2	Actual/360
3	Actual/365

Tip
Use @DATE to specify the date serial numbers within @AC-CRUED. @DATE converts the dates that you enter in a valid 1-2-3 for Windows date format to the date serial number that @ACCRUED requires.

Example: A bond has a settlement date of May 1, 1990, an issue date of January 1, 1990, and a first-interest date of April 1, 1990. The semiannual coupon rate is 6 percent, with 100 par value and a 30/360 day count (that is, the default for all optional arguments is appropriate). To calculate the accrued interest use @ACCRUED(@DATE(5,1,90),@DATE(1,1,90),@DATE(4,1,90),0.06), which returns 0.5.

@PRICE(*settlement,maturity,coupon,yield*,[*redemption*],[*frequency*],[*basis*])

@PRICE calculates the price per $100 face value on installments that have periodic interest payments and a maturity date.

Following are this function's arguments and limits:

settlement   A date serial number that represents the settlement date, or date of ownership, for the security.

maturity   The date serial number for the security's maturity date. The maturity date must be greater than the settlement date.

coupon   The annual coupon rate for the coupon; it must be a positive value or 0.

yield   The annual yield on the security; it must be a positive value.

[*redemption*]   An optional argument that specifies the redemption value of the security per $100 face value. If used, [*redemption*] must be a positive number; if [*redemption*] is omitted from the argument list, 1-2-3 for Windows assumes that the value is 100.

[*frequency*]   An optional argument that represents the number of coupon payments per year. This argument has four options:

Frequency	Representing
1	Annual
2	Semiannual (the default if you omit the argument)
4	Quarterly
12	Monthly

[*basis*]   An optional argument specifying the type of day count (*days_per_month/days_per_year*) to use. This argument has four options:

Basis	Days_per_Month/ Days_per_Year
0	30/360 (the default if you omit the argument)
1	Actual/Actual
2	Actual/360
3	Actual/365

Everyday Worksheet Tasks

Example: A bond has a settlement date of May 1, 1990 and a maturity date of December 1, 1995. The semiannual coupon rate is 6 percent and the annual yield is 6.11 percent, with a 30/360 day-count basis (that is, the default for all optional arguments is appropriate). To calculate the price, use @PRICE(@DATE(90,5,1),@DATE(95,12,1),0.06,0.0611), which returns 99.47989.

@YIELD(*settlement,maturity,coupon, price,[redemption],[frequency],[basis]*)

@YIELD calculates the price per $100 face value on instruments that have periodic interest payments and a maturity date.

Following are this function's arguments and limits:

settlement   A date serial number that represents the settlement date, or date of ownership, for the security.

maturity   The date serial number for the security's maturity date. The maturity date must be greater than the settlement date.

coupon   The annual coupon rate for the coupon; it must be a positive value or 0.

price   The price per $100 of face value; it must be a positive value.

[*redemption*]   An optional argument that specifies the redemption value of the security per $100 face value. If used, [*redemption*] must be a positive number; if [*redemption*] is omitted from the argument list, 1-2-3 for Windows assumes that the value is 100.

[*frequency*]   An optional argument that represents the number of coupon payments per year. This argument has four options:

Frequency	Value
1	Annual
2	Semiannual (he default if you omit the argument)
4	Quarterly
12	Monthly

[*basis*]   An optional argument specifying the type of day count (*days_per_month/days_per_year*) to use. This argument has four options:

Basis	Days_per_Month/ Days_per_Year
0	30/360 (the default if you omit the argument)
1	Actual/Actual
2	Actual/360
3	Actual/365

Example: A bond has a settlement date of May 1, 1990 and a maturity date of December 1, 1995. The semiannual coupon rate is 6 percent. The bond cost $99. It has a $100 redemption value and a 30/360 day-count basis (that is, the default for all optional arguments is appropriate). To calculate the price, use @YIELD(@DATE(90,5,1),@DATE(95,12,1),0.06,99), which returns 0.62133.

@DURATION(*settlement,maturity,coupon,yield,*[*frequency*],[*basis*]) and @MDURATION(*settlement,maturity,coupon,yield,*[*frequency*],[*basis*])

@DURATION returns the annual duration for a security that pays periodic interest, and @MDURATION returns the modified annual duration for a similar security.

Following are this function's arguments and limits:

settlement	A date serial number that represents the settlement date, or date of ownership, for the security.
maturity	The date serial number for the security's maturity date. The maturity date must be greater than the settlement date.
coupon	The annual coupon rate for the coupon. It must be a positive value or 0.
yield	The annual yield on the security. It must be a positive value or 0.
[frequency]	An optional argument that represents the number of coupon payments per year. There are four available options:

Frequency	Representing
1	Annual
2	Semiannual (assumed as the default if you omit the argument)
4	Quarterly
12	Monthly

[basis]	An optional argument specifying the type of *day count* (*days_per_month/days_per_year*) to use. There are four available options:

Basis	Days_per_Month/Days_per_Year
0	30/360 (assumed as the default if you omit the argument)
1	Actual/Actual
2	Actual/360
3	Actual/365

Example: A security has a settlement date of May 1, 1990 and a maturity date of December 1, 1995. The semiannual coupon rate is 6% and the annual yield is 6.11%, with a 30/360 day-count basis (that is, the default for all optional arguments is appropriate). To calculate the duration, use @DURATION(@DATE(90,5,1),@DATE(95,12,1),0.06,0.0611), which returns 4.706783. To calculate the modified duration, use @MDURATION(@DATE(90,5,1),@DATE(95,12,1),0.06,0.0611), which returns 4.567254.

Capital-Budgeting Tools Functions

These functions work with cash flows and rates of return.

@IRR(*guess,range*)

The @IRR function calculates the internal rate of return on an investment.

The *guess* argument typically should be an estimate of the internal rate of return. Because it is an interest rate (and, therefore, a percentage value), the *guess* argument should be a decimal between 0 (0%) and 1 (100%).

You should start the calculation with an estimated interest rate as close as possible to the internal rate of return on your investment. From this guess, 1-2-3 for Windows attempts to converge on a correct interest rate with .0000001 precision within 30 iterations. If the program cannot do so, the @IRR function returns ERR. When that happens, try again with another *guess* argument.

The *range* argument is the address or range name that contains the cash flows. Initial cash flow at time 0 is negative (because the cash flows out from you). Cash flows in the range after that may be negative (payments by you) or positive (payments to you). Cash flows occur at the end of equally spaced periods, with the initial payment by you being at time 0. 1-2-3 for Windows assigns the value of 0 to empty cells and labels in the range of cash flows. (Ranges can span more than one column, but remember about empty cells.)

Tip
If you calculate several rates, use @AVG to determine the internal rate of return.

Everyday Worksheet Tasks

Limits: The *guess* argument should be a decimal between
                     0 and 1.

Example: Figure 5.6 shows the @IRR function calculating the
                     internal rate of return on an investment with uneven
                     cash flows. Notice that during the same period, the
                     investor injected additional cash into the investment.
                     Notice also that multiplying the monthly amount by
                     12 converts the monthly internal rate of return to an
                     annual rate.

Fig. 5.6

Use the @IRR
function to
calculate the
internal rate of
return on an
investment.

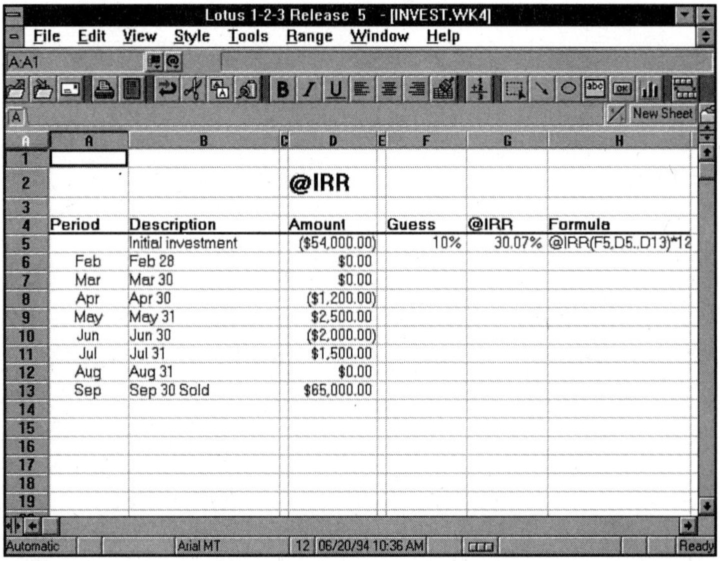

A Warning About the Internal Rate of Return Method

Although the internal-rate-of-return profit measure is widely used, you should be
aware that the formula has multiple detriments when used to analyze investments.
The problem is with the internal-rate-of-return method, not with 1-2-3 for Windows
@IRR function.

One problem is evident when you use the internal-rate-of-return measure for an
investment that has multiple internal rates of return. In theory, the formula for calculating the internal rate of return for an investment with cash flows over 10 years is a
10th-root polynomial equation with up to 10 correct solutions. In practice, an investment may have as many correct internal rates of return as sign changes in the cash
flows.

A *sign change* occurs when the cash flow changes from positive to negative (or vice versa) between periods. Accordingly, even if the @IRR function returns an internal rate of return with your first guess, try other guesses to see whether another correct internal-rate-of-return answer is evident; you probably should not use the measure when it delivers multiple solutions.

A serious problem with the @IRR method is that it tends to overestimate a positive rate of return from the investment and neglects to account for additional outside investments that must be injected into the investment over its life span. The overestimate on return occurs because the @IRR method assumes that positive cash flows are reinvested at the same rate of return earned by the total investment. Actually, a small return rarely can be reinvested at the same high rate as that of a large investment. This feature is especially true when you are analyzing large fixed assets and land investments.

@MIRR(*range,finance_rate,reinvest_rate,[type]*)

The @MIRR function calculates the modified internal rate of return from a range of cash-flow values in an investment. The internal rate of return is the percentage rate that equates to the present value of an expected future series of cash flows to the initial investment.

The *range* argument is the address or range name that contains the cash flows. Initial cash flow at time 0 is negative (because the cash flows out from you). Cash flows in the range after that may be negative (payments by you) or positive (payments to you). 1-2-3 assumes cash flows occur at regular equal intervals. 1-2-3 for Windows assigns the value as before and labels in the range of cash flows. (Ranges can span more than one column, but remember about empty cells.)

The *finance_rate* argument is the rate of interest paid on cash flows. The *reinvest_rate* argument is the interest rate you receive on cash flows as you reinvest them.

The optional *type* argument can be 0 or 1. A value of 0 causes 1-2-3 to calculate based on payments being made at the end of the period. A value of 1 causes 1-2-3 to calculate based on payments being made at the beginning of the period. This value is the default value if you omit the *type* argument.

Limit: The range must contain at least one positive and one negative value. *Finance_rate* and *reinvest_rate* can be any values.

Example: Figure 5.7 calculates the profit from a small used-car dealership, for which an initial payment of $100,000 was made. Over the next five years, the investor made a living from the sale of cars and logged the profits in a range called INCOME. The interest rate on the initial loan is 9.5 percent; because of the investor's skill, he or she has been earning 13.18 percent return on the profits.

Fig. 5.7
Use the @MIRR function to calculate the modified internal rate of return on an investment.

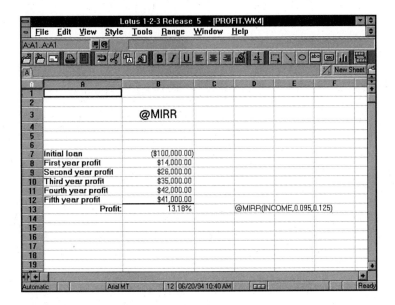

@NPV(*interest,range,[type]*)

@NPV is similar to @PV, except that @NPV can calculate the present value of a varying, or changing, range of cash flows. @NPV assumes that cash outflows occur at the same time in each subsequent period.

The *interest* argument is the interest rate. The *range* argument is the address or name of the range that contains the cash flows.

The optional *type* argument can be a 0 or 1. A value of 0 causes 1-2-3 to calculate based on payments being made at the end of the period. This value is the default value if you omit the *type* argument. A value of 1 causes 1-2-3 to calculate based on payments being made at the beginning of the period.

Limits: @NPV returns ERR if the *range* argument contains more than one row or column. The *interest* argument must be greater than -1.

Example: Figure 5.8 shows how you can use @NPV to calculate
the present value of a stream of varying cash flows with
cash outflows made at the end of the period. In the
figure, the range CASH is B10..B17.

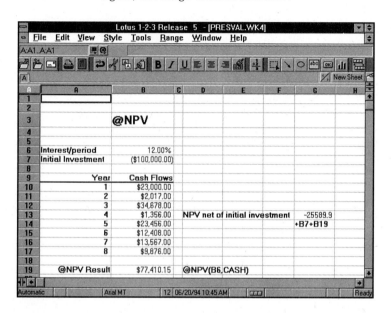

Fig. 5.8
Use the @NPV
function to
calculate the
present value of
varying cash flows.

Note

Accountants and financial analysts use the term *net present value* to refer to a measure of an investment's profitability by including the initial cash outlay for the investment. To calculate the actual profitability measure, or *net present value*, subtract the
initial investment from the result of @NPV. When you construct a formula that uses
@NPV in this way, you essentially test whether the investment meets, beats, or falls
short of the interest rate specified in @NPV. Such a formula can be the following:

    +INITL_AMOUNT+@NPV(interest,range)

The value in the cell named INITL_AMOUNT is negative because the amount is
money you paid out. The formula in G14 in figure 5.8 is:

    +B7+B19

If the calculated result of the preceding formula is a positive amount, the investment
produces an investment return that beats the interest rate specified in @NPV. If the
calculated result equals 0, the investment produces an investment return that equals
the interest rate specified in @NPV. If the calculated result is a negative amount, the
investment produces an investment return that falls short of the interest rate specified
in @NPV.

Depreciation Functions

Depreciation functions allow for asset management. The following functions let you calculate different methods of depreciation.

@DB(*cost,salvage,life,period*)

@DB calculates the depreciation allowance of an asset with an initial value of *cost*, an expected useful *life*, and a final *salvage* value for a specified *period* of time. @DB uses the fixed-declining-balance method.

The *cost* argument is the amount paid for the asset; it is a positive value. If *cost* is 0, the value of @DB also is 0. The *salvage* argument is the estimated value of the asset at the end of its useful life; it is a positive value. If *salvage* is larger than *cost*, the value of @DB is negative. The *life* argument is the number of periods the asset takes to depreciate to its salvage value. The *period* argument is the time period for which you want to find the depreciation allowance; it is a value greater than or equal to 1.

Limits: The *cost* and *salvage* arguments must be positive values or 0. The *life* and *period* arguments can be any value greater than or equal to 1. The *life* and *period* arguments must be in the same units of time, which usually is years.

Example: Figure 5.9 shows how you can use @DB to calculate the depreciation allowance, by year, for a $10,000 piece of equipment.

Fig. 5.9
Use the @DB function to calculate the depreciation allowance.

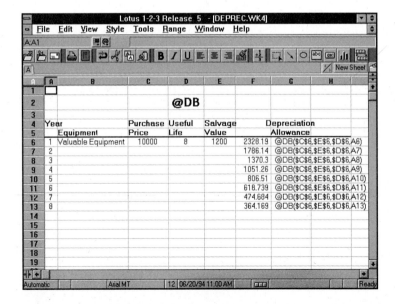

@DDB(*cost,salvage,life,period*)

@DDB calculates depreciation by using the double-declining-balance method, in which depreciation ceases when the book value reaches the salvage value. The double-declining-balance method accelerates depreciation so that greater depreciation expense occurs in the earlier periods instead of in the later ones. *Book value* in any period is the purchase price less the total depreciation in all preceding periods.

> **Note**
>
> Generally, the double-declining-balance depreciation in any period is
>
> *book_value**2/*n*
>
> In this formula, *book_value* is the book value in the period, and *n* is the depreciable life of the asset. 1-2-3 for Windows, however, adjusts the result of this formula in later periods to ensure that total depreciation does not exceed the purchase price less the salvage value.

The *cost* argument is the amount paid for the asset. The *salvage* argument is the estimated value of the asset at the end of its useful life. The *life* argument is the number of periods the asset takes to depreciate to its salvage value. The *period* argument is the time period for which you want to find the depreciation allowance.

Limit: *Cost* must be greater than or equal to the *salvage* value. *Salvage* can be any value. *Life* is any value greater than 2. *Period* is any value greater than or equal to 1.

Example: Figure 5.10 shows how the @DDB function can calculate depreciation on an asset purchased for $10,000, with a depreciable life of 8 years and an estimated salvage value of $1,200. Compare these results with those obtained with the @DB function shown in figure 5.9.

Everyday Worksheet Tasks

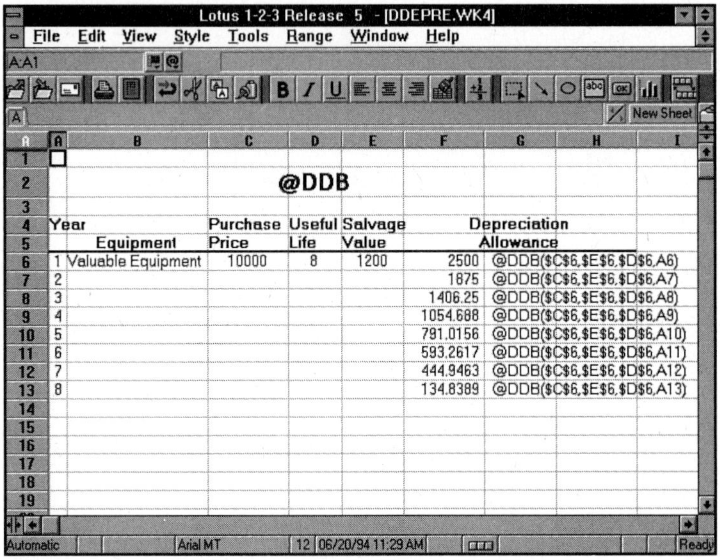

Fig. 5.10

Use the @DDB function to calculate double-declining-balance depreciation.

	A	B	C	D	E	F	G	H	I
2					@DDB				
4	Year		Purchase	Useful	Salvage	Depreciation			
5		Equipment	Price	Life	Value	Allowance			
6	1	Valuable Equipment	10000	8	1200	2500	@DDB($C$6,$E$6,$D$6,A6)		
7	2					1875	@DDB($C$6,$E$6,$D$6,A7)		
8	3					1406.25	@DDB($C$6,$E$6,$D$6,A8)		
9	4					1054.688	@DDB($C$6,$E$6,$D$6,A9)		
10	5					791.0156	@DDB($C$6,$E$6,$D$6,A10)		
11	6					593.2617	@DDB($C$6,$E$6,$D$6,A11)		
12	7					444.9463	@DDB($C$6,$E$6,$D$6,A12)		
13	8					134.8389	@DDB($C$6,$E$6,$D$6,A13)		

Note

Keep in mind that when you use the double-declining-balance depreciation method for an asset with a small salvage value, the asset does not fully depreciate in the final year. If this is the case with one of your assets, use the @VDB function (discussed later in this section).

@SLN(*cost,salvage,life*)

@SLN calculates straight-line depreciation for an asset, given the asset's cost, salvage value, and depreciable life. Straight-line depreciation divides the *depreciable cost* (the cost minus the salvage value) into equal periods (typically, years) for the useful life of the asset.

The *cost* argument is the amount paid for the asset. The *salvage* argument is the estimated value of the asset at the end of its useful life. The *life* argument is the number of periods the asset takes to depreciate to its salvage value.

Limits: *Cost* and *salvage* can be any value. *Life* can be any value except 0.

Example: Suppose that you purchased, for $10,000, a machine
                that has a useful life of 8 years and a salvage value
                estimated at 12 percent of the purchase price
                ($1,200) at the end of the machine's useful life. Use
                @SLN(10000,1200,8) to determine the straight-line
                depreciation for the machine, which is $1,100 per year.

@SYD(*cost,salvage,life,period*)

The @SYD function calculates depreciation by the sum-of-the-years'-digits
method. This method accelerates depreciation so that earlier periods of the
item's life reflect greater depreciation than later periods do.

The *cost* argument is the purchase cost of the asset. The *salvage* argument is
the estimated value of the asset at the end of its depreciable life. The *life* argument is the depreciable life of the asset. The *period* argument is the period for
which depreciation is to be computed.

Limits: *Cost* and *salvage* can be any value. *Life* and *period* can be
                any value greater than or equal to 1.

Example: Figure 5.11 shows how you can use @SYD to calculate
                depreciation for an asset that cost $10,000, with a de-
                preciable life of 8 years and an estimated salvage value
                of $1,200.

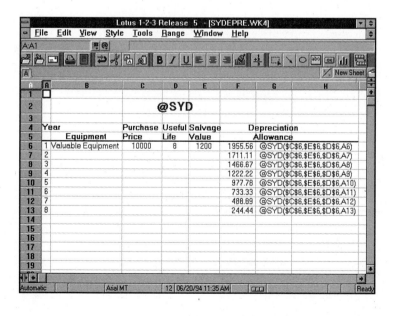

Fig. 5.11
Use the @SYD
function to
calculate sum-of-
the-years'-digits
depreciation.

Everyday Worksheet Tasks

> ### Note
>
> @SYD calculates depreciation with the following formula:
>
> $$\frac{(cost\text{-}salvage)*(life\text{-}period+1)}{life*(life+1)/2}$$
>
> The expression *(life-period+1)* in the numerator shows the life of the depreciation in the first period, decreased by 1 in each subsequent period. This expression reflects the declining pattern of depreciation over time. The expression in the denominator, *life*(life+1)/2*, is equal to the sum of the digits, as in the following expression:
>
> $$1 + 2 +...+ life$$
>
> The name *sum-of-the-years'-digits* originated from this expression.

@VDB(*cost,salvage,life,start_period,end_period,[depreciation_factor],[switch]*)

@VDB calculates depreciation by using a variable-rate declining-balance method. The variable-rate depreciation method provides accelerated depreciation during the early part of the term.

The *cost* argument is the purchase cost of the asset. The *salvage* argument is the estimated value of the asset at the end of its depreciable life. The *life* argument is the depreciable life of the asset.

The *start_period* and *end_period* arguments correspond to the beginning and end of the asset's life, relative to the fiscal period. For example, to find the first year's depreciation of an asset purchased at the beginning of the third quarter of the fiscal year, *start_period* is 0 and *end_period* is .50 (half the year).

The optional *depreciation_factor* argument is the percentage of straight-line that you want to use as the depreciation rate. If you omit the *depreciation_factor* argument, 1-2-3 for Windows uses 200 percent (the double-declining-balance rate).

Usually, @VDB switches from accelerated depreciation to straight-line depreciation when this switch is most advantageous—that is, when the straight-line calculation is greater than the declining-balance calculation. You can set the *switch* argument if you do not want the function to switch over to straight-line depreciation automatically. Set *switch* to 0 if you want 1-2-3 for Windows to switch to straight-line depreciation automatically. If you omit the *switch* argument, 1-2-3 for Windows assumes a value of 0. Set *switch* to 1 so that 1-2-3 for Windows never changes to straight-line depreciation.

Limits:	*Cost* must be greater than *salvage*. *Salvage* can be any value. *Life* can be any value greater than 0. *Start_period* can be any value greater than 0 but less than *life*. *End_period* must be greater than *start_period*. *Depreciation_factor* can be any value greater than or equal to 0. *Switch* can be 0 or 1.
Example:	Figure 5.12 shows how you can use @VDB to calculate depreciation on an asset purchased for $10,000, with a depreciable life of 5 years and an estimated salvage value of $1,200 when it is placed into service at the beginning of the third quarter of the fiscal year. The optional *depreciation_factor* argument is set to 150 percent.

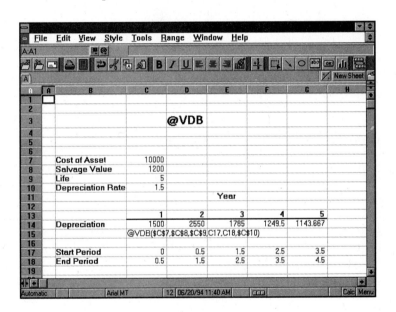

Fig. 5.12
Use the @VDB function to calculate the 150 percent declining-balance depreciation.

Single-Sum Compounding Functions

The single-sum compounding functions deal with growing your investment. Use these functions to monitor and work with future values.

@CTERM(*interest,future_value,present_value*)

> **Note**
>
> Use @TERM to calculate the number of periods needed for a series of payments to grow to a future value. Use @CTERM to calculate the number of periods needed for an initial amount (its *present_value*) to grow to a future value.

@CTERM calculates the number of periods required for an initial investment that earns a specified interest rate to grow to a specified future value.

The *interest* argument is the interest rate for the investment. The *future_value* argument is the value you want the investment to reach. The *present_value* argument is the amount of the investment.

Limits:	*Interest* can be any value greater than 1 except 0. Both *present_value* and *future_value* must be either positive or negative values.
Example:	To determine how many years it takes for $2,000 invested in an IRA at 10 percent interest to grow to $10,000, use @CTERM(0.1,10000,2000), which returns 16.89—just over 16 years and 10 months.

@RATE(*future_value,present_value,term*)

Tip

@RATE also is useful in forecasting applications that calculate the compound growth rate between current and projected future revenue, earnings, and so on.

@RATE calculates the compound growth rate for an initial investment hat grows to a specified future value over a specified number of periods. The rate calculated is the periodic interest rate; it is not necessarily an annual rate.

The *future_value* argument is the amount you want the investment to reach. The *present_value* argument is the amount of the investment. The *term* argument is the length of the investment.

Example:	You can use @RATE to determine the yield of a zero-coupon bond sold at a discount from its face value. Suppose that for $350, you purchase a zero-coupon bond with a $1,000 face value that matures in 10 years. Use @RATE(1000,350,10) to determine the implied annual interest rate: 11.07 percent.

Information Functions

The information functions return information about cells, ranges, the operating system, Version Manager, and Solver.

@CELL(*attribute,location*) and @CELLPOINTER(*attribute*)

@CELL and @CELLPOINTER provide an efficient way to determine the nature of a cell. These functions return information on one of 42 cell characteristics, such as a cell's number or value, color, or width.

Because you want to examine a cell's attributes, both functions have *attribute* as a string argument. @CELL, however, also requires the specification of a range as the *location* argument. If you specify a single cell, such as A6, 1-2-3 changes it to a range format (A6..A6) and returns the attribute of the single-cell range. If you define a larger range, 1-2-3 evaluates the cell in the top-left corner of the range.

@CELLPOINTER works with the current cell—the cell where the cell pointer was positioned the last time the worksheet was recalculated. The result remains the same as long as the current position of the cell pointer does not change and you do not recalculate the worksheet by entering a value or by pressing F9 (Calc).

The *attribute* argument is a text string and must be enclosed in quotation marks. If a range of cells is specified for the *location* argument in the @CELL function, the returned value refers to the top-left cell in the range.

Table 5.1 lists the full set of attributes that you can examine with @CELL and @CELLPOINTER.

Tip
Before you use @CELL or @CELLPOINTER, press F9 (Calc) to make sure that the results are correct.

Table 5.1 Attributes Used with @CELL and @CELLPOINTER	
Attribute	**What the Function Returns**
"across"	1 if data in the cell is aligned across columns; 0 if not
"backgroundcolor"	A number from 0 to 255 that indicates the background color from the color palette
"bold"	1 if the cell is formatted as bold; 0 if not
"bottomborder"	A number from 0 to 8 that indicates the line style from the list in the Style Lines & Color dialog box; 0 indicates no border
"bottombordercolor"	A number from 0 to 15 that indicates the line color from the list of line colors in the Style Lines & Color dialog box

Everyday Worksheet Tasks

(continues)

Table 5.1 Continued	
Attribute	**What the Function Returns**
"address"	The abbreviated absolute cell address
"col"	The number of the column, from 1 (A) to 256 (IV)
"color"	1 if negative numbers are formatted in color; 0 if not
"contents"	Contents of the cell
"coord"	The full cell address (abbreviated)
"datatype"	The type of data; b for a blank cell, V for a number or numeric formula, 1 for a label or text formula, e for ERR, n for NA
"filedata"	The date and time serial numbers that indicate the date and time the file with the cell was last saved.
"filename"	Name of the file containing the cell
"fontsize"	The cell's typeface setting
"fantasize"	The cell's point size setting
"format"	F0 to F15: Fixed decimal, 0 to 15 decimal places S0 to S15: Scientific, 0 to 15 decimal places C0 to C15: Currency, 0 to 15 decimal places ,0 to ,15: Comma, 0 to 15 decimal places G: General +: +/- P0 to P15: Percent, 0 to 15 decimal places D1 to D9: Date/Time format A: Automatic T: Text L: Label H: Hidden -: negative numbers displayed in color ( ): negative numbers displayed in parentheses
"formulatype"	The type of formula in the cells; b for blank, v for a number, 1 for a label, fv for numeric formula, f1 for a text formula, fe for a formula that evaluates to ERR, fn for a formula that evaluates to NA
"halign"	Cell's horizontal alignment; 0 for general (left-aligned labels, right-aligned values), 1 for left, 2 for center, 3 for right, 4 for evenly spaced
"height"	Row height in points
"italic"	1 if cell is formatted as bold; 0 if not
"leftborder"	A number from 0 to 8 that indicates the line color from the list of line colors in the Style Lines & Colors dialog box

Attribute	What the Function Returns
"leftbordercolor"	A number from 0 to 15 that indicates the line color from the list of line colors in the Style Lines & Colors dialog box
"orientation"	A number from 0 to 4 that indicates the orientation of rotated text
"parenthesis"	1 if negative numbers are displayed in parentheses; 0 if they are displayed without parentheses
"pattern"	A number from 0 to 63 that indicates the pattern from the list in the Style Lines & Colors dialog box
"patterncolor"	A number from 0 to 255 that indicates the pattern color from the color palette
"prefix"	Same as label prefixes; blank if no label
"protect"	1 if protected; 0 if not
"rightborder"	A number from 0 to 8 that indicates the line style from the list in the Style Lines & Colors dialog box
"rightbordercolor"	A number from 0 to 15 that indicates the line color from the list in the Style Lines & colors dialog box
"rotation"	From 0 to 90 degrees that indicates text's rotation angle
"row"	Row number, 1 to 8,192
"sheet"	Worksheet number, 1 (A) to 256 (IV)
"sheetname"	The worksheet name or, if unnamed, letter
"textcolor"	Color of data in the cell; 0 through 255 indicates a color in the color palette
"topborder"	A number from 0 to 8 that indicates the line style from the list in the Styles Lines & Colors dialog box
"topbordercolor"	A number from 0 to 15 that indicates the line color from the list in the Style Lines & Colors dialog box
"type"	b if blank; v if value; l if label
"underline"	Underline style; from 0 (no underline) to 3
"valign"	Cell's vertical alignment; 0 for bottom, 1 for center, 2 for top
"width"	Column width

Limit: You can address only one attribute at a time in any @CELL or @CELLPOINTER function. The *attribute* argument is a text string and must be enclosed in quotation marks.

Examples: If the range named SALES is C187..E187, use @CELL("address",sales) to find the address of the top-left cell in the range, $C$187. This function is particularly useful for listing ranges' addresses in the worksheet.

Use @CELL("format",A10) to find the format of cell A10. 1-2-3 returns a text string using the same notation as that used in the worksheet—for example, C2 for Currency format with two decimal places.

Note

You use @CELL and @CELLPOINTER primarily in macros and advanced macro-command programs (see Part VIII, "Automating 1-2-3 for Windows with Macros"). The @CELLPOINTER function works well in @IF statements to test whether data in a cell is numeric or text. @CELL and @CELLPOINTER frequently are used in macros to examine the current contents or format of cells. Macros that use IF then can use the results to change the worksheet accordingly.

@COLS(*range*), @ROWS(*range*), and @SHEETS(*range*)

@COLS, @ROWS, and @SHEETS describe the dimensions of ranges. These functions are useful in macros to determine the size of a range. After you determine the size of a range, you can use FOR loops to step the macro through all the cells in the range.

The *range* argument is a range address or range name. If you specify one cell (such as C3) as the argument, 1-2-3 changes the argument to range format (C3..C3), and the function returns the value 1.

Example: Suppose that you want to determine the number of columns in the range PRICE_TABLES, which has the cell coordinates A:D4..C:G50. You also want to display that value in the current cell. To determine the number of columns, use @COLS(PRICE_TABLES). Similarly, you can use @ROWS(PRICE_TABLES) to display the number of rows in the range and @SHEETS(PRICE_TABLES) to display the number of worksheets in the range.

@COORD(*worksheets,column,row,absolute*)

You use @COORD to create an absolute, relative, or mixed cell address. When you use @COORD, it returns the actual address, not a value.

The *worksheet* argument corresponds to the worksheet containing the referenced cell. The *column* and *row* arguments refer to the column and row that contain the cell address. The *absolute* argument refers to the exact type of reference (absolute, relative, or mixed) that you want the function to return. Table 5.2 lists values for the *absolute* argument.

Table 5.2   Values of the Absolute Argument

Value	Worksheet	Column	Row	Example
1	Absolute	Absolute	Absolute	$A:$A$1
2	Absolute	Relative	Absolute	$A:A$1
3	Absolute	Absolute	Relative	$A:$A1
4	Absolute	Relative	Relative	$A:A1
5	Relative	Absolute	Absolute	A:$A$1
6	Relative	Relative	Absolute	A:A$1
7	Relative	Absolute	Relative	A:$A1
8	Relative	Relative	Relative	A:A1

Limits: The *worksheet* argument is a number from 1 to 256. Use 1 for worksheet A, 2 for worksheet B, and so on up to 256 for worksheet IV. The *column* argument is a number from 1 to 256. Use 1 for column A, 2 for column B, and so on up to 256 for column IV. The *row* argument is a number from 1 to 8192. The *absolute* argument is a number from 1 to 8, as described in table 5.2.

Example: To change the cell address A:A1 to the mixed address A:A$1, use @COORD(1,1,1,6), which returns the address A:A$1.

@INFO(*attribute*)

Tip

Before using @INFO, you should recalculate your work to ensure accurate results.

@INFO lets you tap 30 types of system information for the current session.

The *attribute* argument is a text string and must be enclosed in quotation marks. Table 5.3 summarizes the attributes you can check with @INFO.

Table 5.3   Session Attributes

Attribute	Description
"author"	The name of the person who first saved the file
"creation-date"	The date serial number for the date when the file was first saved
"editing-time"	The time serial number for the amount of time the file has been open
"dbreturncode"	Returns the most recent error code from an external database driver
"dbdrivermessage"	Returns the most recent message from an external database driver
"dbrecordcount"	Returns the number of records processed in the most recent query to an external database
"directory"	Returns the current directory path
"last-revision-by"	The name of the person who last saved the file
"last-revision-date"	The date serial number for the date when the file was last saved
"macro-step"	Yes if Step mode is on; No if not
"macro-trace"	Yes if the Macro Trace window is open; No if not
"memavail"	Returns the amount of memory available, in bytes
"mode"	Returns a numeric code indicating one of the following modes:

	0	Wait
	1	Ready
	2	Label
	3	Menu
	4	Value
	5	Point
	6	Edit
	7	Error
	8	Find
	9	Files

Attribute	Description
	10 Help
	11 Stat
	13 Names
	99 All other modes (such as those set by the INDICATE command)
"numfile"	Returns the number of currently open files
"origin"	Returns the cell address of the first cell in the window containing the cell pointer
"osreturncode"	Returns the value returned by the most recent operating-system command
"osversion"	Returns the current operating system's description
"recalc"	Returns the current recalculation setting
"release"	Returns the 1-2-3 for Windows release number
"setup-user-name"	Your e-mail or network user name
"screen-height"	The screen height in pixels
"screen-width"	The screen width in pixels
"selection"	The address of the currently selected range or the name of the selected chart, drawn object, or query table
"selection-part"	The name of a selected part of a range or object
"selection-type"	The type of current selection; Range, Draw, Query, Chart
"system"	Returns the name of the operating system
"totmem"	Returns the total amount of memory, in bytes (used plus available)
"windir"	The path to the Windows directory
"worksheet-number"	The number of worksheets in the current file
"worksheet-size"	The size of the current file, in kilobytes

Also, the *attribute* argument can be any Info component. Info components store information about the 1-2-3 session, such as the current background color, the current data sort range, or the current state of Edit Undo. When you use an info component as the @INFO attribute argument, you can find out the value of that Info component.

The values returned by @INFO are useful in macros that monitor such things as application memory size, the current mode, and the current directory. After the macro obtains this information, it can warn users to make changes in their activities, upgrade their systems, and so on. When used in conjunction with @IF, this function can tell 1-2-3 for Windows what to do under specific conditions— for example, to close active files when memory is low.

@SOLVER(*query_string*)

Tip

The @SOLVER function does not recalculate when 1-2-3 for Windows recalculates. When you use @SOLVER in a macro, make sure that you use RECALC or RECALCCOL to recalculate the @SOLVER results.

@SOLVER lets you determine the status of the Solver utility. Usually, @SOLVER is run from a macro so that the macro first can start Solver and then monitor Solver's status, making changes or requesting information if necessary. Chapter 21, "Solving Problems with Solver and Backsolver," discusses the Solver utility.

The *query_string* argument can be one of the eight strings listed in table 5.4.

Table 5.4   String Arguments for @SOLVER

Query String	Value Returned	Description
"consistent" (Are constraints satisfied?)	1	All constraints are true (1)
	2	One or more constraints are false (0); not satisfied
	ERR	Solver not active or no answer
"done" (Is Solver done?)	1	Solver finished
	2	Still solving
	3	Solver active but not started
	ERR	Solver not active
"moreanswers" (Are there more answers?)	1	All answers found
	2	More answers may be found if you continue with Solver
"needguess" (Is a guess needed?)	1	No guess is needed
	2	Guess needed
	ERR	Solver inactive or no answer
"numanswers" (How many answers or attempts resulted?)	n	Number of answers found or number of Solver attempts
	ERR	Solver not active or still running

Query String	Value Returned	Description
"optimal" (What type of answer was found?)	1	Optimal answer found
	2	Best answer found
	3	Problem unbounded
	4	No answer or optimization not requested
	ERR	Solver inactive or not started
"progress" (What is Solver's progress in finding an answer?)	*n*	Percentage complete as a decimal
	ERR	Solver inactive or not started
"result" (What is the result?)	1	One or more answers found
	2	No valid answers found
	ERR	Solver inactive or no solution found yet

Limits: Notice that no spaces are used in the query string and that the string must be enclosed in quotation marks.

@ERR and @NA

@ERR and @NA let you flag errors in data entry or calculations. You rarely use these functions by themselves; instead, you can use them with @IF to return ERR or NA when a certain condition exists, such as an unacceptable entry in a cell.

Example: Suppose that you are developing a checkbook-balancing macro in which checks with values less than or equal to 0 are unacceptable. One way to indicate the unacceptability of such checks is to use @ERR to signal that fact. You can use the following version of the @IF function to check the value of the check and to invoke @ERR if the value is less than 0:

```
@IF(B9<=0,@ERR,B9) or @IF(B9<=0,@ERR,B9)
```

In plain English, this statement says, "If the amount in cell B9 is less than or equal to 0, display ERR on-screen; otherwise, use the amount." Another approach is to display a message to the operator that indicates the specific error, as in the following example:

```
@IF(B9<=0,"Enter positive amounts",B9)
```

Note

1-2-3 for Windows also uses ERR as a signal for unacceptable numbers—for example, if you divide by 0 or mistakenly delete cells. ERR often shows up temporarily when you reorganize the cells in a worksheet. If ERR persists, you may have to do some careful analysis to figure out why.

1-2-3 for Windows displays ERR (as it does NA) in any cells that depend on a cell with an ERR value. Sometimes, the ERR cascades through other dependent cells. To return the worksheet to the way it was before the change, open the **E**dit menu and choose **U**ndo, or press Alt+Backspace. For more information about the **U**ndo command, refer to Chapter 3, "Entering and Editing Data."

@SCENARIOINFO(*option,name,[creator]*) and @VERSIONINFO(*option,version_range,name,[creator]*)

@SCENARIOINFO returns information about a scenario and @VERSIONINFO returns information about a version.

The *option* argument is text that specifies what information should be returned. Table 5.5 lists the options for this argument.

Table 5.5   Option Argument Options

Arguments	Options
"creator"	The name of the person who created the scenario or version
"modifier"	The name of the person who last modified the scenario or version
"created"	The date and time serial numbers for when the scenario or version was created
"modified"	The date and time serial numbers for when the scenario or version was last modified
"comment"	The comment for the scenario or version, truncated after 512 single-byte characters
"hidden"	1 if the scenario or version is hidden; 0 if it is not hidden
"protected"	1 if the scenario or version is protected; 0 if it is not protected

The *name* argument is the name of the scenario or version. For @VERSIONINFO, the *version_range* argument is the name of the range containing the version.

The optional *creator* argument is the name of the person who created the scenario or version.

Limits:	If more than one scenario or version has the same name specified in the *name* argument, 1-2-3 uses the most recently created one.
	The *option, name,* and *creator* arguments are text arguments and as such must be enclosed in quotation marks.
	The *version_range* argument must be an existing range name.
Examples:	@SCENARIOINFO("creator","QTR1") returns the name of the person who created the latest QTR1 scenario. @VERSIONINFO("comment",SALES,"North") returns the comment for the latest North version in SALES.

@SCENARIOLAST(*file_name*)

@SCENARIOLAST returns the name of the last scenario displayed in the file during the 1-2-3 session. If no scenario has been displayed during the current 1-2-3 session, @SCENARIOLAST returns ERR.

The *file_name* argument is the full file name (including extension) of the file. If you do not include the full path, 1-2-3 looks for the file in the current directory.

Limits:	The *file_name* argument must be enclosed in quotation marks.
Example:	@SCENARIOLAST("c:\123r5w\sheets\q4budget.wk4") returns the name of the last displayed scenario in Q4BUDGET.WK4. This file is stored in C:\123R5W\SHEETS.

Logical Functions

The logical functions let you use Boolean logic within worksheets. Most logical functions test whether a condition is true or false. The test—and what the function returns based on the test—are built into the function. @ISSTRING is a good example because it tests whether the argument is a string and returns 1 if the test is true or 0 if the test is false. For one of the logical functions—@IF—you describe the test and what the function result should be, based on the test.

@IF(*condition,true_result,false_result*)

@IF tests a condition and returns one value or label if the test is true and another value or label if the test is false.

@IF is a powerful tool, one that you can use to manipulate text within worksheets and to affect calculations. Use this function to add decision-making logic to a worksheet. For example, you can use the @IF function to test the condition "Is the inventory on hand below 1,000 units?" and then return one value or string if the answer to the question is true and another value or string if the answer is false.

The *condition* argument is the condition that should be tested. The logical test can be based on string or numeric comparison.

The *true_result* and *false_result* arguments are what 1-2-3 for Windows should return when the condition is true or false, respectively. These arguments can be text enclosed in quotation marks or names of cells that contain values or labels.

You can use any of six operators when you use @IF to test conditions. Table 5.6 summarizes these operators.

Table 5.6 Logical Test Operators	
Operator	**Description**
<	Less than
<=	Less than or equal to
=	Equal to
>=	Greater than or equal to
>	Greater than
<>	Not equal to

You can expand the power of @IF by using compound tests. You also can perform complex conditional tests by using @IF with logical operators that let you test multiple conditions in one @IF function. Table 5.7 summarizes these complex operators.

Table 5.7 Complex Operators	
Operator	**Description**
#AND#	Used to test two conditions, both of which must be true for the entire test to be true
#NOT#	Used to test that a condition is *not* true
#OR#	Used to test two conditions; if either condition is true, the entire test condition is true

Examples: You can check whether cell A6 contains a value greater than 4 by using @IF(A6>4,"Valid","Not Valid"). If the A6 value is greater than 4, 1-2-3 for Windows returns Valid; otherwise, the program returns Not Valid.

A simple but valuable use for complex @IF functions is to test whether data entries are in the correct range of numbers. Consider the following formula:

```
@IF(A15=A12#OR#A15=A13,"Send a Card","There is Still Time")
```

This formula compares the contents of cell A15 with those of two other cells (A12 and A13). If the value in A15 is the same as the value in either A12 or A13, the string *Send a Card* is inserted into the current cell. If the value A15 does not equal either A12 or A13, the string *There is Still Time* appears in the current cell.

Note

Within @IF, you can use another @IF function as the *true_result* or *false_result* argument. Putting @IF functions inside other @IF functions is a common and important logical tool. This technique, called a *nested @IF*, lets you construct sophisticated logical tests and operations in your 1-2-3 for Windows worksheets.

@ISEMPTY(*location*)

@ISEMPTY tests a location for a blank cell and returns a 1 if the cell is empty and a 0 if it is not. 1-2-3 considers a cell blank if it contains no letters, numbers, spaces, or label prefix character (such as an apostrophe for a left-aligned label or a caret for a centered label).

The *location* argument is the name or address of a single cell. If you enter a name for a range as the *location* argument, 1-2-3 returns 0 (false).

Example: @ISEMPTY(B3) returns 1 if cell B3 is blank or 0 if cell B3 contains a number or label.

@ISERR(*cell_reference*) and @ISNA(*cell_reference*)

@ISERR tests whether the argument equals ERR. If the test is true, @ISERR returns the value 1; if the test is false, it returns the value 0.

@ISNA works in a similar way, testing whether the argument is equal to NA. If the test is true, @ISNA returns the value 1; if the test is false, it returns the value 0.

@ISERR and @ISNA are handy, because you can use them to trap errors produced in one location that may cause more drastic results in other locations.

The *cell_reference* argument can be any value, location, text, or condition. The argument can be as simple as a cell reference, or it can perform some simple arithmetic (such as divide two cells to determine whether an error exists before the actual division result is displayed in the cell).

Example: Figure 5.13 shows how to use @ISERR and @ISNA with @IF to trap a possible division-by-zero error or a serious data-entry error that can cause an error to appear on-screen or in the printout.

Fig. 5.13
Use @ISERR and @ISNA to test for errors.

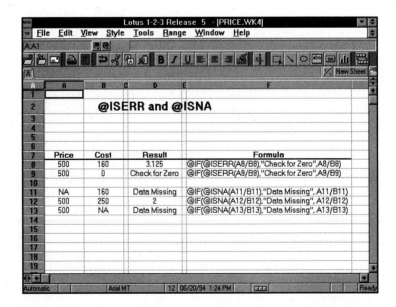

Price	Cost	Result	Formula
500	160	3.125	@IF(@ISERR(A8/B8),"Check for Zero",A8/B8)
500	0	Check for Zero	@IF(@ISERR(A9/B9),"Check for Zero",A9/B9)
NA	160	Data Missing	@IF(@ISNA(A11/B11),"Data Missing", A11/B11)
500	250	2	@IF(@ISNA(A12/B12),"Data Missing",A12/B12)
500	NA	Data Missing	@IF(@ISNA(A13/B13),"Data Missing", A13/B13)

@TRUE and @FALSE

Use the @TRUE and @FALSE functions to check for errors. Neither function requires arguments. These functions are useful for providing documentation for formulas and advanced macro commands. @TRUE returns the value 1, which is the Boolean logical value for true. @FALSE returns the value 0, which is the Boolean logical value for false.

@ISRANGE(*cell_reference*)

@ISRANGE checks whether the argument is a valid range. The range can be a valid cell address or a range name. If the argument is valid, @ISRANGE returns the value 1; otherwise, it returns the value 0.

The *cell_reference* argument can be a cell reference to a string or the string itself. The string need not be a text label; the string can be a cell reference containing a text label or a formula that returns a text label.

Example: One of the best uses of @ISRANGE is within macro programs that test for the existence of range names. The following statement from a print macro, for example, tests for the existence of the range name PRINTAREA:

```
{IF @ISRANGE(PRINTAREA)=1}{SUBPRINT}
```

Translated, this statement says that if the range name PRINTAREA exists, @ISRANGE returns the value 1 (making the IF statement true); the macro then executes the subroutine to print the PRINTAREA range. If PRINTAREA does not exist, @ISRANGE returns the value 0 (making the IF statement false); the macro continues without branching to the print subroutine.

@ISSTRING(*cell_reference*) and @ISNUMBER(*cell_reference*)

Two functions that help determine the type of value stored in a cell are @ISSTRING and @ISNUMBER. These functions often are used with @IF to check for data-entry errors—numbers entered in place of text or text entered in place of numbers.

For @ISNUMBER, if the *cell_reference* argument is a number, the function returns 1 (true). If the *cell_reference* argument is a string, including the null string " " (nothing), @ISNUMBER returns 0 (false).

For @ISSTRING, if the *cell_reference* argument is a string, the function returns 1 (true). If the *cell_reference* argument is a number or is blank, however, @ISSTRING returns 0 (false).

Example: Suppose that you want to test whether the value entered in cell B3 is a number. If the value is a number, you want to show the label *number* in the current cell; otherwise, you want to show the label *string*. Use the following statement to accomplish this goal:

```
@IF(@ISNUMBER(B3),"number","string")
```

With the example statement, you can be fairly certain that the appropriate label appears in the current cell. @ISNUMBER, however, returns 1 (true) after testing empty cells as well as cells that contain numbers. Obviously, the function is incomplete because it assigns the label number to the current cell if cell B3 is empty. For complete reliability, the statement must be modified to handle empty cells.

> **Note**
>
> Use @CELL to check whether a cell is empty or contains a numeric value. @CELL is explained in the "Information Functions" section earlier in this chapter.

The following example shows a complete test that determines whether cell B3 is blank, contains a numeric value, or contains a string value:

@IF(@CELL("type",B3)="b","blank",

@IF(@ISNUMBER(B3),"number","string"))

The first part of this formula uses @CELL to determine whether the cell type is "b" (which stands for blank). If this test is true, the formula results in the label blank. If this test is false, the next step is to use @ISNUMBER to test whether the cell contains a number. If the second test is true, the formula results in the label number. If the second test is false, the formula results in the label string.

You also can complete the formula with the help of @ISSTRING, as follows:

@IF(@CELL("type",B3)="b","blank",

@IF(@ISSTRING(B3),"string","number"))

The first part of this formula uses @CELL to determine whether the cell type is "b" (which stands for blank). If this test is true, the formula results in the label blank. If this test is false, the next step is to use @ISSTRING to test whether the cell contains a string. If the second test is true, the formula results in the label `string`. If the second test is false, the formula results in the label `number`.

Lookup Functions

1-2-3 for Windows provides a group of functions that service the contents of a cell or a group of cells. These functions are very useful in a variety of situations, from locating the contents of a cell in a macro to matching the contents of a cell.

@@(*location*)

@@ provides a way to reference one cell indirectly through the contents of another cell.

The *location* argument must be a cell reference for a cell that contains an address. This address is an *indirect address*. Similarly, the cell referenced in the *location* argument must contain a string value that evaluates to a cell reference. This cell can contain a label, a string formula, or a reference to another cell, as long as the resulting string value is a cell reference.

@@ is useful primarily when several formulas have the same argument and the argument must be changed from time to time during the course of the application. 1-2-3 for Windows lets you specify the argument of each formula through a common indirect address, as shown in figure 5.14.

Tip

If the location argument refers to a cell that contains a formula, press F9 (Calc) to update @@ after automatic recalculation; otherwise, @@ returns 0.

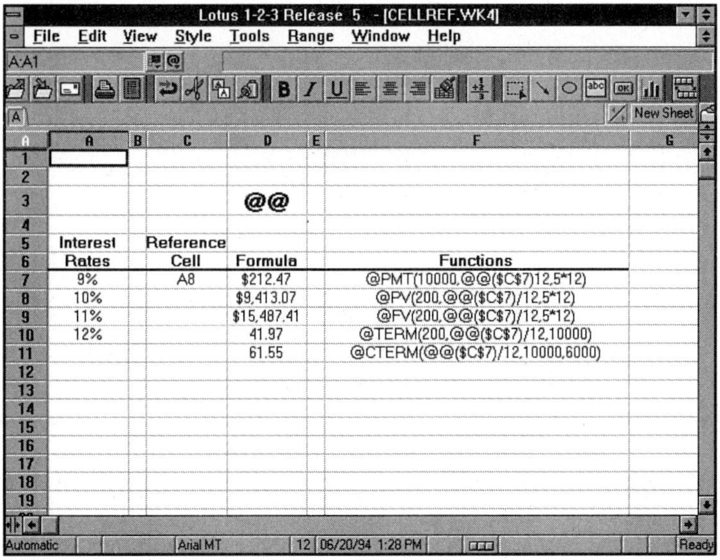

Fig. 5.14
Use @@ to reference one cell indirectly through another cell.

Examples: If cell A1 contains the label 'A2 and cell A2 contains the
                 number 5, the function @@(A1) returns the value 5. If
                 the label in cell A1 is changed to 'B10, and if cell B10
                 contains the label 'hi there, @@(A1) returns the string
                 value hi there.

In figure 5.14, column F contains a variety of financial functions, all of
which use @@ to indirectly reference one of seven interest rates in column A
through cell C7. When you are ready to change the cell being referenced,
you change only the label in cell C7 instead of editing all five formulas in
column F.

@CHOOSE(*offset_number,list*)

@CHOOSE selects an item from a list according to the item's position in the
list.

The *offset_number* argument indicates the position in the list whose value
should be returned. This argument can contain the position number or the
cell address of the cell that contains the position number.

The *list* argument is a group of values or labels or cell addresses of cells that
contain values or labels. The positions in the list are numbered starting with
0; the first position is 0, the second is 1, the third is 2; and so on.

Limits: If the *offset_number* argument is not an integer, 1-2-3 for
                 Windows ignores the decimal portion of the offset; an
                 offset of 3.9 is treated like an offset of 3.

Example: For @CHOOSE(1,"East","West","North","South"), 1-2-3
                 for Windows returns the value or label in position 1:
                 West.

@HLOOKUP(*key,range,row_offset*) and
@VLOOKUP(*key,range,column_offset*)

@HLOOKUP and @VLOOKUP retrieve a string or value from a table, based on
a specified key used to find the information. The operation and format of
the two functions are essentially the same, except that @HLOOKUP looks
through *horizontal* tables (hence, the H in the function's name) and
@VLOOKUP looks through *vertical* tables (the source of the V in its name).

The *key* argument is either a value or text, depending on what the first row/column of the lookup table includes. If the first row or column contains values, *key* can be any value equal to or greater than the first value in the range. If the first row or column contains labels, *key* can be text enclosed in quotation marks, a formula that returns text, or the address or name of a cell that contains a label or a formula that returns a label.

The *range* argument is the area that makes up the entire lookup table.

The *row_offset* or *column_offset* argument specifies which row or column contains the data you are looking up. This argument always is a number, ranging (in ascending order) from 0 to the greatest number of columns or rows in the lookup table. The offset number 0 marks the column or row that contains *key* data. The next column or row is 1, the next is 2, and so on. When you specify an offset number, the number cannot be negative or exceed the correct number of columns or rows.

Limits:
If the *key* argument is text, it must be enclosed in quotation marks. The *key* argument must match the contents of a cell in the first row/column of the range; text key arguments are case-sensitive. When you use numeric *key* arguments, make sure that the *key* values in the table range are in ascending order; otherwise, you may get an incorrect value. By contrast, if the *key* arguments are text strings, they can be listed in any order.

If the *range* argument specifies a 3-D range, 1-2-3 for Windows uses only the first worksheet in the range.

Example:
Suppose that you want to create a worksheet that figures out the state tax for all employees of your company. This seems straightforward except that for some reason, employees are continually changing their filing status. When the filing status changes, you must change the formula that computes the tax. Figure 5.15 shows a @VLOOKUP table that solves your problem. You can see how to use @VLOOKUP (or @HLOOKUP) to find any type of value that you may have to look up manually in a table, such as price changes in inventory items, tax rates, shipping zones, or interest charges.

Fig. 5.15
Use @VLOOKUP to
retrieve strings and
values from a
vertical lookup
table.

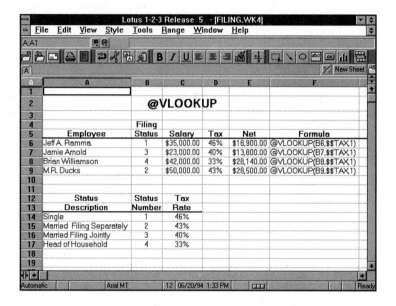

Employee	Filing Status	Salary	Tax	Net	Formula
Jeff A. Ramma	1	$35,000.00	46%	$18,900.00	@VLOOKUP(B6,$$TAX1)
Jamie Arnold	3	$23,000.00	40%	$13,800.00	@VLOOKUP(B7,$$TAX1)
Brian Williamson	4	$42,000.00	33%	$28,140.00	@VLOOKUP(B8,$$TAX1)
M.R. Ducks	2	$50,000.00	43%	$28,500.00	@VLOOKUP(B9,$$TAX1)

Status Description	Status Number	Tax Rate
Single	1	46%
Married Filing Separately	2	43%
Married Filing Jointly	3	40%
Head of Household	4	33%

Watch for These Three Common Errors when You Construct @HLOOKUP and @VLOOKUP Functions:

■ When you use a string as the *key* argument, the lookup function returns ERR if it cannot find the string in the lookup table. If @HLOOKUP or @VLOOKUP with a string *key* returns ERR, make sure that you didn't misspell the string in the function or in the lookup table.

■ If you fail to include the columns or rows that contain the *key* strings or values in the *range* argument for the lookup table, the result is ERR. The example shown in figure 5.15 uses cell addresses to define the lookup table so that you can understand the example easily; you probably will name your lookup tables instead. Be aware that naming lookup tables can make spotting missing rows or columns more difficult.

■ Do not place the *key* argument's strings or values in the wrong row or column. Remember that the *key* argument's strings or values belong in the first column or row of the lookup table; column and row numbering starts at 0 (at the row or column that contains the *key*). Accordingly, the first row or column offset is 0 (the row or column that contains the *key*); the second row or column is 1; the third is 2, and so on.

@INDEX(*range,column_offset,row_offset,*[*worksheet_offset*]) and @XINDEX(*range,column_heading,row_heading,*[*worksheet_heading*])

@INDEX and @XINDEX are data-management functions that are similar to the lookup functions described in the preceding section, but @INDEX and @XINDEX have some unique features. Like @HLOOKUP and @VLOOKUP, @INDEX and @XINDEX find a value within a table.

Unlike the lookup functions, however, @INDEX does not compare a key value with values in the first row or column of the table. Instead, @INDEX requires you to indicate the column offset, row offset, and (optionally) worksheet offset of the range from which you want to retrieve data. The function returns the value of the cell at the intersection of these offset locations. @XINDEX is more like @HLOOKUP and @VLOOKUP in that you specify the contents of the first column or row—that is, the headings—to indicate which column, row, and (optionally) worksheet 1-2-3 for Windows should look in.

The *range* argument is the range address or range name of the area that makes up the table.

For @INDEX, the offset arguments use number offsets to refer to the columns, rows, and worksheets; 0 corresponds to the first column/row/worksheet; 1 corresponds to the second column/row/worksheet; and so on. If you leave out the optional *worksheet_offset* argument, 1-2-3 for Windows assumes the first worksheet of the range. For example, using 3 for the *column_offset* argument and 2 for the *row_offset* argument indicates that you want an item from the fourth column, third row.

For @XINDEX, you can use number offset numbers or the value or text in the column and row headings and the first cell of the range (for the *worksheet_heading* argument).

Limits:	With both @INDEX and @XINDEX, you cannot use column, row, or worksheet numbers outside the specified range. Using negative numbers or numbers that are too large for the range causes 1-2-3 for Windows to return ERR.
Example:	Figure 5.16 shows an example of an @INDEX function that returns the employee's name (M.R. Ducks) in E13 and salary ($28,500.00) in E16.

Fig. 5.16

Use @INDEX to return the value of a cell specified by column, row, and worksheet offset numbers.

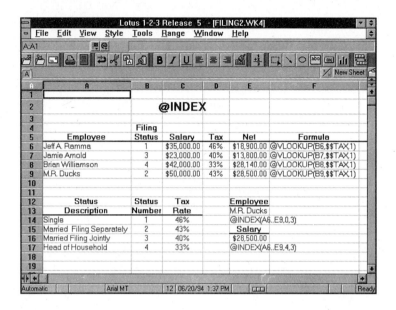

@MATCH(*cell_contents,range,*[*type*])

@MATCH returns the location of the cell whose contents match what you are searching for. You can search for either text or a number value.

@MATCH searches the rows of a column from top to bottom and the columns from left to right until it finds a match. @MATCH returns a numerical value that indicates the offset from the top-left cell of the range you are searching. (The cells in the range are numbered down the columns and then across the rows. In the range A1..D4—a 16-cell range—an offset of 4 refers to cell B1.)

The *cell_contents* argument is the value of the information for which you are searching. The value can be text (enclosed in quotation marks) or numeric. If the value is text, you can include wild cards to aid in your search.

The *range* argument is the range name or address of the data for which you are searching.

The optional *type* argument indicates how you want 1-2-3 for Windows to look for the data. *Type* can be 0, 1, or 2. A value of 0 indicates that 1-2-3 for Windows should return the first cell whose contents match the *cell_contents* argument. A value of 1 indicates that 1-2-3 for Windows should return the first cell whose contents are less than or equal to the *cell_contents* argument. If you omit the *type* argument, 1-2-3 assumes 1. A value of 2 indicates that 1-2-3 for Windows should return the first cell whose contents are greater than or equal to the *cell_contents* argument.

Example: Figure 5.17 shows how you can use @MATCH to locate data.

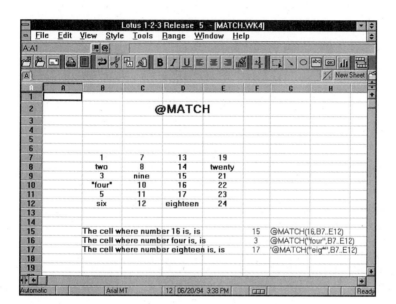

Fig. 5.17
Use @MATCH to locate values in a table.

Everyday Worksheet Tasks

@MAXLOOKUP(*range_list*) and @MINLOOKUP(*range_list*)

@MAXLOOKUP returns an absolute reference to the cell containing the largest value in a list of ranges, and @MINLOOKUP returns an absolute reference to the cell containing the smallest value in a list of ranges. The absolute reference includes the file name. When evaluating, 1-2-3 ignores any labels or blank cells in the specified list of ranges. If none of the cells in the specified ranges contains values, both functions return NA.

The *range_list* argument is one or more range names or addresses. Separate multiple range names or addresses with argument separators (such as commas or semicolons).

Example: Suppose you have four files, VENDOR1.WK4 throught VENDOR$.WK4, each containing pricing information from different vendors. In each, the total materials price is in a range named MATERIALS. To find the highest materials price, use @MAXLOOKUP(<<VENDOR1.WK4>>MATERIALS, <<VENDOR2.WK4>>MATERIALS,<<VENDOR3.WK4>>MATERIALS, <<VENDOR4.WK4>>MATERIALS). To find the lowest materials price, use@MINLOOKUP(<<VENDOR1.WK4>>MATERIALS, <<VENDOR2.WK4>>MATERIALS,<<VENDOR3.WK4>>MATERIALS, <<VENDOR4.WK4>>MATERIALS).

Mathematical Functions

1-2-3 for Windows provides mathematical functions that perform most of the common—and some of the more specialized—mathematical operations. To simplify calculations, 1-2-3 for Windows offers five general mathematical categories of functions: general, conversion, hyperbolic, rounding, and trigonometric. The following sections discuss some of the most commonly used mathematical functions.

General Mathematical Functions
@ABS(x)

@ABS calculates the absolute value of a number. The result of @ABS is the positive value of its argument. @ABS converts a negative value to a positive value. @ABS has no effect on positive values.

@ABS is useful for showing the difference between two values, regardless of whether the difference is positive or negative. @ABS can be helpful if used with @IF to determine whether two numbers are within a specific range, regardless of which number is greater. In data-entry macros, use @ABS to ensure that an entered number results in a positive or negative number, regardless of what the user typed. @ABS also can be helpful in some trigonometric calculations.

The *x* argument can be a numeric value or the cell reference of a numeric value.

Tip
To force the @ABS result to be negative, use -@ABS.

Examples: If A6 contains 9 and B6 contains -9, @ABS(A6) returns 9 and @ABS(B6) returns 9.

@EXP(*x*) and @EXP2(*x*)

@EXP calculates *e* (approximately 2.718282), raised to the power of the *x* argument. @EXP2 calculates *e* (approximately 2.718282), raised to the power (x^2).

Limits:	For @EXP, do not use an argument larger than 709. With @EXP, you can create very large numbers quickly. If the function's resulting value is too large to be displayed, 1-2-3 for Windows displays asterisks.
	For @EXP2, do not use an argument larger than approximately 106.57 or one smaller than -106.57; if you do, the calculation results in ERR.

@FACT(*x*)

@FACT calculates the factorial of a number. The *factorial* of a number is the product of all positive integers from 1 to that number (the *x* argument). The *x* argument can be any positive integer or 0.

Limits:	If *x* is greater than or equal to the integer 1755, the result is ERR because the result is too large for 1-2-3 for Windows to store. If *x* is greater than or equal to 70, 1-2-3 for Windows can calculate and store the result but cannot display it.
Examples:	@FACT(3) returns 6; @FACT(10) returns 3628800.

@FACTLN(*x*)

@FACTLN calculates the natural log of the factorial of a number. The *x* argument can be any positive integer or 0.

Example:	@FACTLN(3) returns 1.791759; @FACTLN(10) returns 15.10441.

@INT(*x*)

@INT converts a decimal number to an integer by truncating the decimal portion of a number. @INT is useful for computations in which the decimal portion of a number is irrelevant or insignificant.

The *x* argument can be a numeric value or the cell reference of a numeric value.

Examples: @INT(3.1) returns 3; @INT(4.5) returns 4; @INT(5.9) returns 5.

If you have $1,000 to invest in XYZ Company and shares of XYZ sell for $17 each, you divide 1,000 by 17 to compute the total number of shares that you can purchase. Because you cannot purchase a fractional share, you can use @INT to truncate the decimal portion.

> **Note**
>
> Do not confuse the @INT and @ROUND functions. @ROUND rounds decimal numbers to the nearest integer; @INT cuts off the decimal portion, leaving the integer.

@LARGE(*range,x*)

@LARGE finds the *x*th largest value in a range of values. The *range* argument is the range name or address of the range that contains values. The *x* argument is any positive integer.

Limit: If *x* is larger than the number of values in the range, @LARGE returns ERR.

Example: Suppose that you have a list of 7 test scores—56, 74, 89, 99, 75, 98, and 83—with the range name SCORE. To find the highest test score, use @LARGE(SCORE,1), which returns 99. To find the second-highest test score, use @LARGE(SCORE,2), which returns 98.

@LOG(*x*) and @LN(*x*)

@LOG computes the base-10 logarithm. @LN computes the natural, or base-*e*, logarithm. For both @LOG and @LN, the *x* argument is any value greater than 0.

Limit: If the *x* argument is negative, @LOG and @LN return ERR.

Examples: @LOG(5) returns 0.69897; @LN(5) returns 1.609438.

@MOD(*x,y*)

@MOD computes the remainder (or *modulus*) when two numbers are divided—that is, *x*/*y*.

Both the *x* and *y* arguments can be numeric values or cell references. The sign of the *x* argument (+ or -) determines the sign of the result.

Limit:	The *y* argument cannot be 0, or @MOD returns ERR.
Examples:	@MOD(11,5) returns 1; @MOD(11,3) returns 2.

@RAND

@RAND generates random numbers between 0 and 1, to 17 decimal places.

Examples: If you want a random number greater than 1, multiply the @RAND function by the maximum random number you want. For example, @RAND*10 generates numbers between 0 and 10.

If you want a random number in a range of numbers, use a formula similar to +10+@RAND*20, which generates numbers between 10 and 30.

You can enclose random-number calculations in an @INT function if you need random integers—for example, 10+@INT(@RAND*20) generates integers between 0 and 19.

Tip

@RAND generates new random numbers each time the worksheet is recalculated. To see the results from new random numbers, press F9 (Calc).

@SIGN(*x*)

@SIGN determines whether a value in a cell is positive, 0, or negative. If the value or cell reference is positive, @SIGN returns 1. If the value is 0, @SIGN returns 0. If the value is negative, @SIGN returns -1. The *x* argument can be any value or a cell reference.

Examples: @SIGN(A6) returns 1 if A6 contains 9 and -1 if A6 contains -9.

@SMALL(*range,x*)

@SMALL finds the *x*th-smallest value in a range of values. The range of values can be a range name or an address that contains values.

The *range* argument is the range name or address of the range that contains values. The *x* argument is any positive integer.

Limit:	If *x* is larger than the number of values in the range, @SMALL returns ERR.
Example:	Suppose that you have a list of 7 test scores—56, 74, 89, 99, 75, 98, and 83—with the range name SCORE. To find the lowest test score, use @SMALL(SCORE,1), which returns 56. To find the next-lowest test score, use @SMALL(SCORE,2), which returns 74.

@SQRT(*x*)

Tip

The @SQRT function is equivalent to using the ^ (exponentiation) operator with an exponent of 0.5. For example, @SQRT(25) and 25^0.5 both calculate the square root of 25, which is 5.

@SQRT calculates the square root of a positive number. The *x* argument must be a non-negative numeric value or a cell reference to such a value.

Limit:	If @SQRT is a negative value, it returns ERR.
Example:	@SQRT(20) returns 4.472136; @SQRT(25) returns 5.

Hyperbolic Functions

> **Note**
>
> @DEGTORAD and @RADTODEG convert angular measurements. @DEGTORAD converts degrees to radians, and @RADTODEG converts radians to degrees. You can use these functions to convert the values returned by hyperbolic functions.

@ACOSH(*angle*)

@ACOSH calculates the inverse (arc) hyperbolic cosine of an angle, using the hyperbolic cosine value of the angle being calculated. The function returns a result in radians.

Example:	If the value of the hyperbolic cosine of an angle is 3, @ACOSH(3) results in 1.762747 (radians).

@ACOTH(*angle*)

@ACOTH calculates the inverse (arc) hyperbolic cotangent of an angle, using the hyperbolic cotangent value of the angle being calculated. The function returns a result in radians.

Example: If the value of the hyperbolic cotangent of an angle is 3,
                @ACOTH(3) results in .346574 (radians).

@ACSCH(*angle*)

@ACSCH calculates the inverse (arc) hyperbolic cosecant of an angle, using
the hyperbolic cosecant value of the angle being calculated. The function
returns a result in radians.

Example: If the value of the hyperbolic cosecant of an angle is
                2.54, @ACSCH(2.54) results in .38418 (radians).

@ASECH(*angle*)

@ASECH calculates the inverse (arc) hyperbolic secant of an angle, using the
hyperbolic secant value of the angle being calculated. The function returns a
result in radians.

Example: If the value of the hyperbolic secant of an angle is .25,
                @ASECH(.25) results in 2.063437 (radians).

@ASINH(*angle*)

@ASINH calculates the inverse (arc) hyperbolic sine of an angle, using the
hyperbolic sine value of the angle being calculated. The function returns a
result in radians.

Example: If the value of the hyperbolic sine of an angle is 3,
                @ASINH(3) results in .1.818440 (radians).

@ATANH(*angle*)

@ATANH calculates the inverse (arc) hyperbolic tangent of an angle, using
the hyperbolic tangent value of the angle being calculated. The function
returns a result in radians.

Example: If the value of the hyperbolic tangent of an angle is
                .6223, @ATANH(.6223) results in .72875 (radians).

@COSH(*angle*)

@COSH calculates the hyperbolic cosine of an angle, measured in radians.
The function returns a result in radians. The result of @COSH is a value
greater than 1.

The *angle* argument (the value in the cell or the value of the cell reference) must be in radians instead of an angular measurement. The value in radians can be between -11355.1371 and 11355.1371, although it cannot be the value 0. Use @DEGTORAD to convert an angle to radians before using @COSH.

> Example: @COSH(@DEGTORAD(30)) returns 1.140238 (radians).

@COTH(*angle*)

@COTH calculates the hyperbolic cotangent of an angle. The function returns a result in radians.

The *angle* argument (the value in the cell or the value of the cell reference) must be in radians instead of an angular measurement. The value in radians can be between -11355.1371 and 11355.1371, although it cannot be the value 0. Use @DEGTORAD to convert an angle to radians before using @COTH.

> Example: @COTH(@DEGTORAD(30)) returns 2.081283 (radians).

@CSCH(*angle*)

@CSCH calculates the hyperbolic cosecant of an angle. The function returns a result in radians.

The *angle* argument (the value in the cell or the value of the cell reference) must be in radians instead of an angular measurement. The value in radians can be between -11355.1371 and 11355.1371, although it cannot be the value 0. Use @DEGTORAD to convert an angle to radians before using @.

> Example: @CSCH(@DEGTORAD(30)) returns 1.825306 (radians).

@SECH(*angle*)

@SECH calculates the hyperbolic secant of an angle. The function returns a result in radians.

The *angle* argument (the value in the cell or the value of the cell reference) must be in radians instead of an angular measurement. The value in radians can be between -11355.1371 and 11355.1371, although it cannot be the value 0. Use @DEGTORAD to convert an angle to radians before using @SECH.

> Example: @SECH(@DEGTORAD(30)) returns .87701 (radians).

@SINH(*angle*)

@SINH calculates the hyperbolic sine of an angle. The function returns a result in radians.

The *angle* argument (the value in the cell or the value of the cell reference) must be in radians instead of an angular measurement. The value in radians can be between -11355.1371 and 11355.1371, although it cannot be the value 0. Use @DEGTORAD to convert an angle to radians before using @SINH.

> Example: @SINH(@DEGTORAD(30)) returns `.547853` (radians).

@TANH(*angle*)

@TANH calculates the hyperbolic tangent of an angle. The function returns a result in radians.

The *angle* argument (the value in the cell or the value of the cell reference) must be in radians instead of an angular measurement. The value in radians can be between -11355.1371 and 11355.1371, although it cannot be the value 0. Use @DEGTORAD to convert an angle to radians before using @TANH.

> Example: @TANH(@DEGTORAD(30)) returns `.480473` (radians).

Rounding Functions

The rounding functions let the user control the scope of values. The functions do this by allowing the user to round up, round down, or truncate numerical values.

@ROUND(*number,precision*)

@ROUND rounds values to a precision that you specify. @ROUND rounds a number according to the old standard rule: numbers less than 0.5 are rounded down; numbers equal to or greater than 0.5 are rounded up. @ROUND is most useful for rounding a value used in other formulas or functions.

The *number* argument is the number you want to round or a cell reference to the cell that contains the number.

The *precision* argument determines the number of decimal places to which you round. This argument can be a numeric value between -100 and +100. Use positive *precision* values to specify places to the right of the decimal place;

use negative values to specify places to the left of the decimal place. A *precision* value of 0 rounds decimal values to the nearest integer.

Note

@ROUND and the **S**tyle menu's **N**umber Format command do different things. @ROUND actually changes the contents of a cell; the **N**umber Format command changes only how 1-2-3 for Windows displays the cell'. contents.

In 1-2-3 for Windows, the formatted number you see on-screen or in print may not be the number used in calculations. This difference can cause errors of thousands of dollars in worksheets such as mortgage tables. To prevent errors, use @ROUND to round formula results or the numbers feeding into formulas so that the numbers used in calculations are the same as those in the display.

Examples: @ROUND(123.456,2) returns 123.46;
              @ROUND(123.456,0) returns 123;
              @ROUND(123.456,-2) returns 100.

Note

If you want to round up to the nearest integer, you can do so by adding a number a little less than 0.5 to the number you want to round. If you work with numbers to two decimal places, add .49. If you work with numbers to four decimal places, add .4999.

@EVEN(*x*) and @ODD(*x*)

@EVEN rounds the value in the argument to the nearest even integer value away from 0. This means that positive values are made larger and negative values are made smaller.

@ODD rounds the value in the argument to the nearest odd integer value away from 0. This means that positive values are made larger and negative values are made smaller.

Examples: @EVEN(4.4) returns 6; @EVEN(5) returns 6; @ODD(4.4) returns 5; @ODD(3.1) returns 5.

@TRUNC(*x*,[*precision*])

Like other rounding functions, @TRUNC modifies the values in the worksheet by truncating the value to the number of decimal places specified by the *precision* argument.

The *x* argument is any value or a cell reference to a cell that contains the value.

The optional *precision* argument can be a value between -100 and +100. If the *precision* value is negative, the integer portion of *x* is rounded to the value of the decimal position, starting from the left of the decimal point. If you omit the *precision* argument, @TRUNC truncates to the nearest integer.

Examples: @TRUNC(5849.8204) returns 5849;

@TRUNC(5849.8204,2) returns 5849.82;

@TRUNC(5849.8204,-2) returns 5800;

@TRUNC(-5849.8204) returns -5849;

@TRUNC(-5849.8204,-3) returns 5000.

Note

Compare @TRUNC with @ROUND. @TRUNC(5849.8204) returns 5849, whereas @ROUND(5849.8204) returns 5850.

Trigonometric Functions

1-2-3 for Windows provides the standard trigonometric functions, which are described in this section.

@ACOS(*angle*), @ASIN(*angle*), @ATAN(*angle*), and @ATAN2(*x,y*)

@ACOS, @ASIN, @ATAN, and @ATAN2 calculate the arccosine, the arcsine, the arctangent, and the four-quadrant arctangent, respectively. @ACOS computes the inverse of cosine. @ASIN computes the inverse of sine, returning a radians angle between $-\pi/2$ and $\pi/2$ (-90 and +90 degrees). @ATAN computes the inverse of tangent, returning a radians angle between $-\pi/2$ and $\pi/2$ (-90 and +90 degrees). @ATAN2 calculates the four-quadrant arctangent, using the ratio of its two arguments.

Because all cosine and sine values lie between -1 and 1, @ACOS and @ASIN work only with values between -1 and 1. This means that the angular measurements in the argument will be in radians. Either function returns ERR if you use an argument outside this range. @ASIN returns angles between $-\pi/2$ and $+\pi/2$; @ACOS returns angles between 0 and $\pi/2$.

For @ATAN, the *angle* argument can be any number, and the function returns a value between $-\pi/2$ and $+\pi/2$.

Tip
To convert the values from radians to degrees, use @RADTODEG.

@ATAN2 computes the angle whose tangent is specified by the *x* and *y* arguments. At least one of the arguments must be a number other than 0. @ATAN2 returns radians angles between -π and +π.

@ACOT(*angle*), @ACSC(*angle*), and @ASEC(*angle*)

@ACOT, @ACSC, and @ASEC calculate the arccotangent, the arccosecant, and the arcsecant, respectively, of an angle. The results of the calculations are in radians. @ACOT computes the inverse of cotangent. @ASEC computes the inverse of secant, returning a radians angle between 0 and pi (0 and +180 degrees). @ACSC computes the inverse of cosecant, returning a radians angle between -π/2 and π/2 (Å90 and +90 degrees).

@COT(*angle*), @CSC(*angle*), and @SEC(*angle*)

Tip
Be sure to convert angle measurements to radians before you use @COT, @CSC, @SEC, @COS, @SIN, and @TAN. You can accomplish this task quickly by using the @DEGTORAD function described earlier in this chapter.

@COT, @CSC, and @SEC calculate the cotangent, cosecant, and secant, respectively, of an angle. For each function, the *angle* argument is measured in radians.

@COS(*angle*), @SIN(*angle*), and @TAN(*angle*)

@COS, @SIN, and @TAN calculate the cosine, sine, and tangent, respectively, of an angle. For each function, the *angle* argument is measured in radians.

@PI

@PI results in the value 3.14159265358979324. Use @PI in calculations for the area of circles and the volume of spheres. You also can use @PI to convert angle measurements in degrees to angle measurements in radians (if you prefer to make this calculation on your own instead of using @DEGTORAD).

Statistical Functions

1-2-3 for Windows provides five statistical function categories: forecasting, general, probability, ranking, and significance tests.

Many statistical functions use the *list* argument. This argument can contain individually specified values, cell addresses, a range of cells, multiple ranges of cells, or range names. For example, 1-2-3 for Windows considers each of the following formats to be a valid *list* argument:

```
@SUM(1,2,3,4)
@SUM(B1,B2,B3,B4)
@SUM(B1..B4)
@SUM(A1..B2,B3..E10)
@SUM(NAME)
```

Labels can be used as valid items within the group of cells in a range or range name. 1-2-3 for Windows assigns a 0 to the position occupied by the label in the group.

Caution

1-2-3 for Windows ignores blank cells imbedded within a range in calculations. If the blank cells in a list are referenced as specific items in the list, however, the function counts and uses them. For example, the @AVG function can use either of these two *list* formats: (A1..A3) or (A1,A2,A3). In both *list* formats, assume that cell A1 is blank (that is, it has nothing in it). The @AVG(A1..A3) function does not include cell A1 as a value or position and divides by 2. In @AVG(A1,A2,A3), cell A1 is counted and @AVG divides by 3.

Forecasting Functions

You can create forecasts by performing regression analysis. This section explores @REGRESSION.

@REGRESSION(*x_range,y_range,attribute,*[*compute*])

@REGRESSION performs multiple linear regression on ranges of values and returns the statistic.

Following are this function's arguments and limits:

x_range	Also known as the *independent variable,* the *x_range* argument can be a range name or an address that contains up to 75 columns and 8,192 rows.
y_range	Also known as the *dependent variable,*the *y_range* argument can be a range name or an address that has a single column and the same number of rows as the *x_range*.
attribute	Specifies which regression output value to calculate. Following are the available attributes:

Attribute	Calculation Performed
1	Constant
2	Standard error of Y estimate
3	R squared
4	Number of observations
5	Degrees of freedom
101 to 175	X coefficient (slope) for the independent variable specified by *attribute*
201 to 275	Standard error of coefficient for the independent variable specified by *attribute*

[*compute*]   An optional argument that specifies the Y-intercept. This argument has the following options:

Compute	1-2-3
0	Uses 0 as the Y-intercept
1	Calculates the Y-intercept and is the default if omitted from the argument

Tip

For the same data, @REGRESSION returns the same result as the **R**ange menu's **A**nalyze **R**egression command.

1-2-3 for Windows numbers the independent variables in the *x_range*, starting with the number 1, from top to bottom in a column, and in columns from left to right. If the *x_range* is A1..C10, you can find the X coefficient for the independent variable in A2 by using the attribute 102. Using the same *x_range*, you can find the standard error of coefficient for the independent variable in A5 by using the attribute 205.

General Statistical Functions

1-2-3's general statistical functions help you perform standard statistical analysis. The following sections describe some of the commonly used general statistical functions.

Tip

Essentially, @AVG produces the same result as if you divided @SUM(*list*) by @COUNT(*list*)— two functions described later in this section.

@AVG(*list*) and @PUREAVG(*list*)

To calculate the average of a set of values, you add all the values and then divide the sum by the number of values. @AVG calculates this arithmetic mean for a list of values. For @AVG, if a label is specified in the list as a cell value, 1-2-3 for Windows counts that cell in the @AVG calculation.

Like @AVG, @PUREAVG calculates the average of a set of values. @PUREAVG, however, has the added feature of ignoring cells in the list that are labels, rather than converting them to zero.

The *list* argument can be values, cell addresses, cell names, cell ranges, range names, or a combination of all these formats.

Examples: Suppose that cells A5 through A12 contain the values January, 5, 4, 5, February, 5, 6, and 4. @AVG(A5..A12) returns 3.625 because it adds the numbers (using 0 for the two labels January and February) and divides by 8. @PUREAVG(A5..A12) returns 4.833 because it ignores the labels, adds only the numbers, and divides by 6.

@CORREL(*range1,range2*)

@CORREL calculates the correlation coefficient for two ranges of values. @CORREL matches cell pairs in the two specified ranges to calculate the correlation coefficient. The function orders the cell pairs from top to bottom and left to right. If the ranges use multiple worksheets, the worksheets start at the first and progress to the last.

The result of the @CORREL function is a pure correlation value; there are no units.

The *range1* and *range2* arguments can be range names or addresses. Both range arguments must be the same size and shape, and the arguments must contain only values. If the ranges are not the same size and shape, @CORREL returns ERR. Blank cells in either of the ranges are ignored.

@COUNT(*list*) and @PURECOUNT

@COUNT totals the number of cells that contain nonblank entries of any kind, including labels, label-prefix characters, and the values ERR and NA. @PURECOUNT totals the number of cells that contain nonblank entries that are values only.

For both @COUNT and @PURECOUNT, the *list* argument can be values, cell addresses, cell names, cell ranges, range names, or a combination of these formats—including ERR and NA. @PURECOUNT, however, counts only the cells that contain values.

Everyday Worksheet Tasks

Limits: Include only ranges as the argument in @COUNT. If you specify an individual cell, 1-2-3 for Windows counts that cell as though it has an entry, even if the cell is empty. If you absolutely must specify a cell individually, but want that cell to be counted only if it actually contains an entry, use @PURECOUNT.

Note

1-2-3 for Windows considers ERR and NA to be values. Also, be aware that different situations call for the use of different functions. Use @COUNT to include all cells, no matter what is included in those cells; use @PURECOUNT to include only cells that contain values. Make sure that the result reflects what you are trying to accomplish.

@COV(*range1,range2,[type]*)

@COV calculates either the population covariance or a sample covariance of two ranges of numbers. *Covariance* is the average of the products of deviations of corresponding values. @COV matches cell pairs in the two specified ranges to calculate the correlation coefficient. The function orders the cell pairs from top to bottom and left to right. If the ranges use multiple worksheets, the worksheets start at the first and progress to the last.

The *range1* and *range2* arguments can be range names or addresses. Both range arguments must be the same size and shape, and the arguments must contain only values. If the ranges are not the same size and shape, @COV returns ERR. Also, if the range arguments have blank cells, contain labels, or have text formulas, the function returns ERR.

The optional *type* argument specifies the covariance you are calculating; it can be either 0 or 1. A value of 0 tells 1-2-3 for Windows to calculate a population covariance. 1-2-3 for Windows assumes 0 if you omit the *type* argument. A value of 1 tells 1-2-3 for Windows to calculate a sample covariance.

Note

@COV is similar to @CORREL in that both functions measure a relationship between two sets of values. @COV depends on the unit of measure between the ranges, which is not the case with @CORREL.

@DEVSQ(*list*)

@DEVSQ calculates the sum of squared deviations from the mean of the values in the argument.

The *list* argument can be values, cell addresses, cell names, cell ranges, range names, or a combination of all these formats.

Limits:
: A blank cell in the range of cells is not counted in the @DEVSQ calculation. A text label, however, is counted as the value 0 and can make a difference in the result.

Example:
: @DEVSQ(2,3,9,8,15,2,1) returns 159.4286. If you give the range that contains these values the name GENERIC, and you insert a blank cell into the middle of the range, the result is the same. If you enter any text or a 0 in the blank cell, however, the result changes to 188.00000.

@GEOMEAN(*list*)

@GEOMEAN calculates the geometric mean of a range of values.

The *list* argument must refer to cells that contain values; these cells cannot contain any elements less than or equal to 0. Blank cells are allowed but ignored in the calculation. @GEOMEAN returns ERR if the *list* argument does not contain at least one positive nonzero value or if values are not entered as values, cell addresses, cell names, cell ranges, range names, or a combination of all these formats.

Example:
: @GEOMEAN(2,3,9,8,15,2,1) returns 3.868254. If you give the range that contains these values the name GENERIC, and you insert a blank cell into the middle of the range, the result is the same. If you enter any text or a 0 in the blank cell, the result changes to ERR.

@GRANDTOTAL(*list*) and @SUBTOTAL(*list*)

@GRANDTOTAL calculates the sum of all cells that contain the @SUBTOTAL function. @SUBTOTAL adds a list of values and returns the sum. This function is a tool that lets you mark values—most commonly, for use with @GRANDTOTAL.

For @SUBTOTAL, the *list* argument can be numbers, numeric formulas, and range addresses or range names that contain numbers or formulas.

For @GRANDTOTAL, the *list* argument is a group or range of @SUBTOTAL formulas. Notice that if the range of cells for @GRANDTOTAL includes cells that contain @SUM formulas, 1-2-3 for Windows ignores the @SUM formulas.

Example: Figure 5.18 shows how @SUBTOTAL and @GRANDTOTAL can be used.

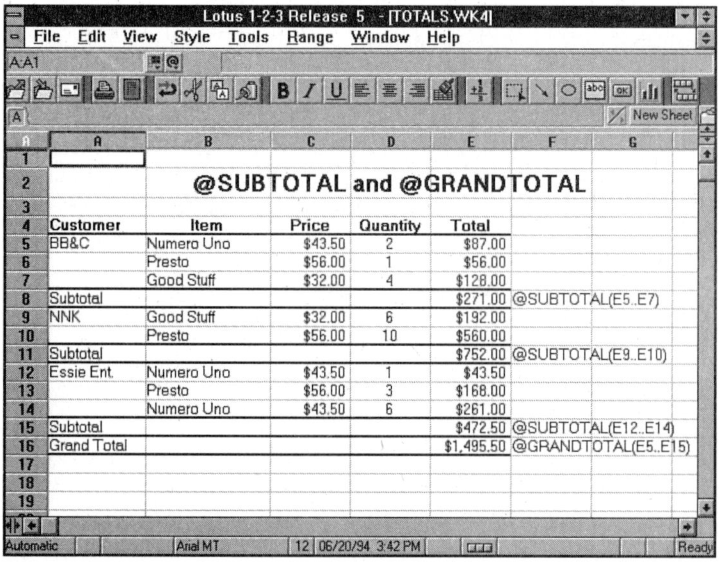

@SUBTOTAL and @GRANDTOTAL

Customer	Item	Price	Quantity	Total	
BB&C	Numero Uno	$43.50	2	$87.00	
	Presto	$56.00	1	$56.00	
	Good Stuff	$32.00	4	$128.00	
Subtotal				$271.00	@SUBTOTAL(E5..E7)
NNK	Good Stuff	$32.00	6	$192.00	
	Presto	$56.00	10	$560.00	
Subtotal				$752.00	@SUBTOTAL(E9..E10)
Essie Ent.	Numero Uno	$43.50	1	$43.50	
	Presto	$56.00	3	$168.00	
	Numero Uno	$43.50	6	$261.00	
Subtotal				$472.50	@SUBTOTAL(E12..E14)
Grand Total				$1,495.50	@GRANDTOTAL(E5..E15)

Fig. 5.18
Use @SUBTOTAL to mark values to be gathered into a grand total by @GRANDTOTAL.

Note

@SUBTOTAL and @SUM both sum a series of values and return the same results. If you want use @GRANDTOTAL to calculate a grand total, however, you must sum values with @SUBTOTAL, because @GRANDTOTAL ignores @SUM values.

@HARMEAN(*list*)

@HARMEAN calculates the reciprocal of the arithmetic mean of a range of values.

The *list* argument can be values, cell addresses, cell names, cell ranges, range names, or a combination of all these formats.

Limits: A blank cell in the range is not counted in the
              @HARMEAN calculation. Also, text labels are not al-
              lowed. The values in the list must be positive, nonzero
              values.

Example: @HARMEAN(2,3,9,8,15,2,1) returns 2.655427. If you
              give the range that contains these values the name
              GENERIC, and you insert a blank cell into the middle
              of the range, the result is the same. If you enter any text
              or a 0 in the blank cell, the result changes to ERR.

@KURTOSIS(*range*,[*type*])

@KURTOSIS measures the concentration of a distribution around the mean of
a range of values. A negative kurtosis indicates a relatively flat or stable distribution; a positive kurtosis is an indication of a peaked distribution.

The *range* argument is the name or address of a group of values. @KURTOSIS
requires a minimum of four values; otherwise, it returns NA. A blank cell in
the range of cells is not counted in the @KURTOSIS calculation. A text value
is allowed and is counted as a 0.

The optional *type* argument specifies whether to calculate for an entire population of values or a sample. The argument can be either 0 or 1. The value 0
tells 1-2-3 for Windows to calculate for a population covariance. 1-2-3 for
Windows assumes 0 if you omit the *type* argument. The value 1 tells 1-2-3 for
Windows to calculate for a sample.

Examples: Suppose that you have a range named GENERIC
              that contains the values 2, 3, 9, 8, 15, 2, and 1.
              @KURTOSIS(GENERIC) returns -0.65706, and
              @KURTOSIS(GENERIC,1) returns 0.223055. If you insert
              a blank cell into the middle of the range, the result is
              the same. If you enter any text or a 0 in any of the cells,
              the result calculates the kurtosis, treating the label as
              zero and ignoring the blanks. Thus, @KURTOSIS(3,9,8,0
              or label,15,2,1) returns .51684019.

@MAX(*list*), @MIN(*list*), @PUREMAX(*list*), and @PUREMIN(*list*)

@MAX finds the largest value in the *list* argument; @MIN finds the smallest
value in the *list* argument. Both functions assign a value of 0 to a label and
include the label in their evaluation. @PUREMAX and @PUREMIN also find
the largest and smallest value, respectively, in the *list* argument, but both

functions ignore cells that contain labels and do not include those cells in their evaluations.

The *list* argument can be numbers, numeric formulas, and range addresses or range names that contain numbers or formulas. Any blank cells are ignored. For @MAX and @MIN, any cell with a label is given the value 0. For @PUREMAX and @PUREMIN, any cell with a label is ignored.

Examples: Suppose that you have a range named PRICES that contains the entries 35, 43, unknown, 43, 55, and 23. @MAX(PRICES) and @PUREMAX(PRICES) return 55, the largest value. @MIN(PRICES) returns 0, because the label *unknown* is evaluated as 0. @PUREMIN(PRICES) returns 23 because it ignores the label *unknown*.

Note

If you are familiar with statistics, you may recognize that the @MAX and @MIN functions provide the two pieces of data you need to calculate a popular statistical measure: a range. A *range*—which is one measure of variability in a list of values—is the difference between the highest value and the lowest value in a list of values. (A range as a statistical measurement is not the same thing as a worksheet range, which is a rectangular block of cells.)

@MEDIAN(*list*)

@MEDIAN returns either the middle value in a list or the arithmetic average of the list. 1-2-3 for Windows looks at the number of values in a list; if the number of physical entries is odd, the result of @MEDIAN is the middle value of the list. If the number of physical entries is even, the result is the arithmetical average of the two middle values in the list.

The *list* argument can be values, cell addresses, cell names, cell ranges, range names, or a combination of all these formats. Blank cells are ignored.

Examples: Suppose that the GENERIC range contains the values 3, 3, a blank cell, 9, 8, 15, 2, and 1; the @MEDIAN value is 3. If you enter **5** in the blank cell, the @MEDIAN value is 4.

@PRODUCT(*list*)

@PRODUCT multiplies the values in the argument list. This function works exactly like a calculator, multiplying the values in the *list* argument to return the result. The key portion of the preceding sentence is *exactly like a calculator*. If you include a 0 or a label in the list, the result is 0.

The *list* argument can be values, cell addresses, cell names, cell ranges, range names, or a combination of all these formats. Blank cells are ignored.

@STD(*list*), @STDS(*list*), @PURESTD(*list*), and @PURESTDS(*list*)

@STD uses the *n*, or population, method of calculating standard deviation; the @STDS function uses the *n*-1, or sample population, method of calculating the standard deviation. Both functions assign a value of 0 to a label and include the label in their evaluations. @PURESTD and @PURESTDS also use the population and sample methods, respectively, of calculating the standard deviation, but both functions ignore cells that contain labels and do not include those cells in their evaluations.

The *list* argument can be values, cell addresses, cell names, cell ranges, range names, or a combination of all these formats. Blank cells are ignored. For @STD and @STDS, any cell that contains a label is given the value 0. For @PURESTD and @PURESTDS, any cell that contains a label is ignored.

Examples: Suppose that you have a range named PRICES that contains the entries 35, 43, unknown, 43, 55, and 23. @STD(PRICES) returns 17.68631, and @STDS returns 19.37438. The difference reflects the adjustment that @STDS makes, because that function assumes a sample of the population. @PURESTD(PRICES) returns 10.55272, and @PURESTDS(PRICES) returns 11.7983. The differences between these results and those of @STD and @STDS reflect the fact that the PURE functions ignore the label *unknown* rather than include it (as 0) in their calculations.

Everyday Worksheet Tasks

> **Note**
>
> Essentially, the standard deviation is a measure of how individual values vary from the mean or average of all of the values in the list. A smaller standard deviation indicates that values are grouped closely around the mean; a larger standard deviation indicates that values are widely dispersed from the mean. Perhaps not surprisingly, a standard deviation of 0 indicates no dispersion—that is, every value in the list of values is the same.
>
> To choose the correct function, you need to know whether you are dealing with the entire population or with a sample. If you are measuring, or including, every value in a calculation, you are working with a population. If you are measuring, or including, only a subset or a portion of the values in a calculation, you are working with a sample. @STDS and @PURESTDS use the *n*-1, or sample population, method to calculate standard deviation for sample populations. This method adjusts the standard deviation so that it is slightly higher to compensate for possible errors because the entire population was not used.

@SEMEAN(*list*)

@SEMEAN calculates the standard error of the sample mean of values.

The *list* argument can be values, cell addresses, cell names, cell ranges, range names, or a combination of all these formats. Blank cells are ignored. Cells containing labels are evaluated as 0.

| Example: | Suppose that you have a range of values named GENERIC that contains the values 2, 3, a blank cell, another blank cell, 9, 8, 15, 2, and 1. @SEMEAN(GENERIC) returns 1.948312. If you fill the blank cell with text or a 0, the result is 1.832251. |

@SKEWNESS(*range*,[*type*])

@SKEWNESS measures the symmetry of a distribution around the mean of a range of values. A negative skewness indicates a drawn-out tail to the right; a positive skewness indicates a drawn-out tail to the left.

The *range* argument is the name or address of a group of values. @SKEWNESS requires a minimum of three values; otherwise, it returns NA. A blank cell in the range of cells is not counted in the @SKEWNESS calculation. A text value is allowed and counted as a 0.

The optional *type* argument specifies whether to calculate for an entire population of values or a sample. The argument can be either 0 or 1. The value 0 tells 1-2-3 for Windows to calculate for a population covariance. 1-2-3 for Windows assumes 0 if you omit the *type* argument. The value 1 tells 1-2-3 for Windows to calculate for a sample.

Example:	Suppose that you have a range of values named GENERIC that contains the values 2, 3, 9, 8, 15, 2, and 1. @SKEWNESS(GENERIC) returns .81594, and @SKEWNESS(GENERIC,1) returns 1.057951. If you insert a blank cell into the middle of the range, the result is the same. Enter any text or a 0 in any of the cells, and the result of the first example changes to .921696; the result of the second example changes to 1.149556.

@SUM(*list*)

@SUM provides a convenient way to add a list of values. Of all the functions that 1-2-3 for Windows provides, @SUM is the one that you probably will use most often. You can calculate a total of cell values by typing a formula that uses the cell addresses, as follows:

+E5+E6+E7+E8+E9

This method, however, is inefficient and conducive to typing errors. A more efficient way to total the values is to use the following formula:

@SUM(E5..E9)

The *list* argument can be numbers, numeric formulas, and range addresses or range names that contain numbers or formulas.

Tip

Use the Sum icon to enter the @SUM function automatically. The list argument is the range address or name of cells containing values either above or to the left of the current cell.

Note

When you sum a range of cells and include the horizontal totaling line in the @SUM formula, you can insert cells into or delete cells from the range and keep the formula intact and working perfectly; you never have to adjust the range. If you include a *placeholder* (a blank or text-filled cell) at the top or bottom of the range of cells being summed, maintaining the worksheet is easier. The placeholder cell does not affect the total, because the cell is text and adds as 0.

@SUMPRODUCT(*list*)

@SUMNEGATIVE(*list*) and @SUMPOSITIVE(*list*)

@SUMNEGATIVE sums only the negative values in the speicfied list, and @SUMPOSITIVE sums only the positive values in the specified list.

The *list* argument can be numbers, numeric formulas, and range addresses or range names that contain numbers or formulas. Separate the elements of the list with argument separators (such as commas or semicolons).

> Example: @SUMNEGATIVE(3,-5,7,9,-10,1) returns -15.
> @SUMPOSITIVE(3,-5,7,9,-10,1) returns 20.

@SUMPRODUCT gets its name because it sums the products of corresponding cells in multiple ranges.

The *list* argument can be any combination of ranges that are the same size and shape. If the ranges are not the same size and shape, @SUMPRODUCT returns ERR. If the ranges in the list are rows, @SUMPRODUCT multiplies by columns. If the ranges are columns or span more than one column, @SUMPRODUCT multiplies by rows.

> Example: Figure 5.19 shows how you can use @SUMPRODUCT to calculate the total dollar value of inventory.

Fig. 5.19

Use @SUMPRODUCT to sum the products of corresponding cells in multiple ranges.

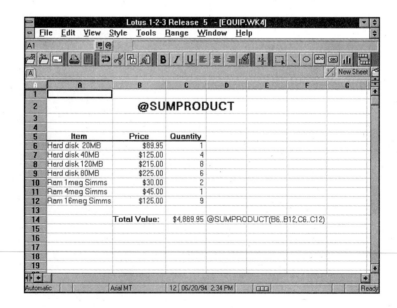

@VAR(*list*), @VARS(*list*), @PUREVAR(*list*), and @PUREVARS(*list*)

The *variance*, like the standard deviation, is a measure of how much the individual values within the measurement vary from the mean or average. @VAR calculates the variance by using the population, or *n*, method. @VARS calculates the variance by using the sample population, or *n*-1, method. Both functions give a label a value of 0 and include the label in their evaluations. @PUREVAR and @PUREVARS also use the population and sample methods, respectively, of calculating the variance, but both functions ignore cells that contain labels and do not include those cells in their evaluations.

The *list* argument can be values, cell addresses, cell names, cell ranges, range names, or a combination of all these formats. Blank cells are ignored. For @VAR and @VARS, any cell that contains a label is given the value 0. For @PUREVAR and @PUREVARS, any cell that contains a label is ignored.

Examples: Suppose that you have a range named PRICES that contains the entries 35, 43, unknown, 43, 55, and 23. @VAR(PRICES) returns 312.8056, and @VARS(PRICES) returns 375.3667. The difference reflects the adjustment that @VARS makes because it assumes a sample of the population. @PUREVAR(PRICES) returns 111.36, and @PUREVARS(PRICES) returns 139.2. The differences between these results and the @VAR and @VARS results reflect the fact that the PURE functions ignore the label *unknown* rather than include it (as 0) in their calculations.

@WEIGHTAVG(*range1,range2*)

@WEIGHTAVG calculates the weighted average of a list by multiplying the values in corresponding cells in multiple ranges, summing the products, and finally dividing by the number of values in the list.

The ranges in the arguments must be the same shape and size; if they are not, @WEIGHTAVG returns ERR. If the ranges are columns, @WEIGHTAVG multiplies by rows; otherwise, the function multiplies by columns. If each list spans more than one column, @WEIGHTAVG multiplies by rows.

Example: Suppose that you run a real estate office and want to calculate the weighted average of the sales commissions payable to an agent for a month's house sales. The data obtained from the computer gives you the following information:

SOLD	COMMIS
$25,000	.04
$34,580	.04
$77,325	.05

You can use @WEIGHTAVG(SOLD,COMMIS) to determine the agent's monthly commission amount: $48,072.69.

Probability Functions
@BINOMIAL(*trials,successes,probability,*[*type*])

@BINOMIAL calculates the binomial probability mass function or the cumulative binomial distribution. The function approximates the cumulative binomial distribution to within +/-3*10^-7.

Following are this function's arguments and limits:

trials	The number of independent trials. This value must be a positive nonzero integer. If *trials* is not entered as an integer, 1-2-3 for Windows truncates the value to an integer.
successes	The number of successes in *trials*. This value can be any positive integer or 0, but it must be less than or equal to *trials*. If *successes* is not entered as an integer, 1-2-3 for Windows truncates the value to an integer.
probability	The probability of success on each trial. This value must be any valid probability between 0 and 1.
[*type*]	This optional argument specifies whether 1-2-3 for Windows calculates the probability mass function or the cumulative binomial distribution. This argument has three switch options:

Type	Switch Value
0	The probability of the exact number of successes specified by the *successes* argument (the default if [*type*] is omitted)
1	The probability of at most the number of successes specified by the *successes* argument
2	The probability of at least the numbers of successes specified by the *successes* argument.

Examples:

Suppose that you want to know how many people prefer Cola A over Cola B in a blind taste test. You set up a polling booth at the local mall and call the local TV station. Ten random entrants appear; you hand each person two glasses of cola. There is no difference in the glasses except for the code on the bottom, which identifies which glass contains which cola. Because the people showed up at random, there should be a probability of 50 percent of the participants' liking either cola.

To determine the probability that *exactly* 7 of 10 will prefer Cola A, use @BINOMIAL(10,7,.5), which returns `0.117188`. To determine the probability that *at most* 7 of 10 will prefer Cola A, use @BINOMIAL(10,7,.5,1), which returns `0.945313`. To determine the probability that *at least* 7 of 10 will prefer Cola A, use @BINOMIAL(10,7,.5,2), which returns `0.171875`.

@CHIDIST(*x,degrees_of_freedom,*[*type*])

@CHIDIST calculates the chi-square distribution. The *chi-square distribution* is a continuous, single-parameter distribution derived as a special case of the gamma distribution. The chi-square distribution is approximated to within $+/-3*10^{-7}$; if the result is not approximated to within .0000001 after 100 attempts, @CHIDIST returns `ERR`.

Following are this function's arguments and limits:

x

The value at which to evaluate the chi-squared distribution. The value of *x* depends on the optional [*type*] argument. You have two choices for *x*:

0	This value is the upper boundary for the value of the chi-squared cumulative distribution random variable and is a value greater than or equal to 0 (the default if [*type*] is omitted).
1	A significance level, or probability, between 0 and 1.
degrees_of_freedom	The number of degrees of freedom for the sample. This argument is a positive integer. If the value is not entered as an integer, 1-2-3 for Windows truncates it to an integer.
[*type*]	This optional argument specifies how the @CHIDIST is calculated. You have two options:

Type	How Calculated
0	The significance level corresponding to *x* (the default if [*type*] is omitted)
1	The critical value that corresponds to the significance level

@COMBIN(*n,r*)

The binomial coefficient is the number of ways that *r* can be selected from *n*, without regard to order. @COMBIN approximates the binomial coefficient to within +/-3*10^-7.

Following are this function's arguments and limits:

n	The number of values. This argument can be any positive integer or 0.
r	The number of values in each combination. This argument can be any positive integer less than or equal to *n* and can be 0.
Example:	Suppose that a cup contains six pennies, each with a different date and mint mark. You pick two at random. As you pick a penny from the cup, you do not replace it. To determine the number of date combinations you could have, use @COMBIN(6,2), which returns 15.

@CRITBINOMIAL(*trials,probability,alpha*)

@CRITBINOMIAL returns the largest integer for which the cumulative binomial distribution is less than or equal to *alpha*. @CRITBINOMIAL approximates the cumulative binomial distribution to within +/-3*10^-7.

Following are this function's arguments and limits:

trials	The number of Bernoulli trials. This argument can be any positive integer or 0.
probability	The probability of success for a single Bernoulli trial. This argument can be a value between 0 and 1.
alpha	The criterion probability. This argument can be a value between 0 and 1.
Example:	Suppose that you manage a small plant that manufactures oil filters. The filters are manufactured in lots of 100, and there is an 85 percent chance that each filter is free from defects. A 100-filter lot is rejected if more than 90 percent of the filters are defective. Your task is to determine the largest number of defective filters that can come off the assembly line before you have to reject the lot.

In this situation, you can use the following facts to calculate the quantity of filters:

trials = 100

probability = 85% or .85

alpha = 90% or .9

Use @CRITBINOMIAL(100,.85,.9), which returns 89.

@FDIST(*x,degrees_of_freedom1,degrees_of_freedom2,[type]*)

@FDIST is a continuous distribution obtained from the ratio of two chi-squared distributions, each divided by its number of degrees of freedom. You can use @FDIST to determine how much two samples vary. @FDIST approximates the F-distribution to within +/-3*10^-7 by comparing the result of the calculation. If the approximation cannot be accomplished to within 0.0000001 after 100 iterations, 1-2-3 for Windows returns ERR.

Following are this function's arguments and limits:

x	The value at which to evaluate the F-distribution. The value of *x* depends on the optional [*type*] argument. You have three choices for *x*:

    0   The critical value or upper boundary for the value of the F-distribution cumulative distribution random variable. This argument can be a value greater than or equal to 0 (the default if you omit the [*type*] argument).

    1   A probability between 0 and 1.

    2   The value of the F-distribution random variable. This argument can be a value greater than or equal to 0.

degrees_of_freedom1	The number of degrees of freedom for the first sample. This value must be a positive integer. If the value is not entered as an integer, 1-2-3 for Windows truncates it to an integer.
degrees_of_freedom2	The number of degrees of freedom for the second sample. This value must be a positive integer. If the value is not entered as an integer, 1-2-3 for Windows truncates it to an integer.
[*type*]	This optional argument specifies how the @FDIST is calculated. You have two options:

Type	How Calculated
0	The significance level corresponding to *x* (the default if [*type*] is omitted)
1	The critical value that corresponds to the significance level

@FDIST(3.07,8,10) returns 0.050078, and @FDIST(0.05,8,10) returns 0.999865.

@NORMAL(*x*,[*mean*],[*std*],[*type*])

@NORMAL calculates the normal distribution factor for *x*.

Following are this function's arguments and limits:

x	The upper boundary for the value of the cumulative normal distribution. The value of *x* used in the calculation is the absolute value of the number used as the argument.
[*mean*]	This optional argument specifies the mean of the distribution. If used, [*mean*] must be a positive value; if [*mean*] is omitted, 1-2-3 for Windows defaults to 0.
[*std*]	This optional argument specifies the standard deviation of the distribution. If used, [*std*] must be positive or 0; if [*std*] is omitted, 1-2-3 for Windows defaults to 1.
[*type*]	This optional argument specifies the function you want @NORMAL to calculate. You have three options:

Type	What Is Calculated
0	Cumulative distribution function (the default if [*type*] is omitted)
1	Inverse cumulative distribution function
2	Probability density function

@PERMUT(*n,r*)

@PERMUT calculates the permutations of *r* selected from *n*.

The *n* and *r* arguments must be integers; otherwise, 1-2-3 for Windows truncates them to integers for the calculations. The *n* argument is any positive integer or 0. The *r* argument is any positive integer or 0; it cannot be greater than the *n* argument.

Example:	Suppose that meetings scheduled for 9:00, 10:00, and 11:00 are to be conducted by three of the five vice presidents of your company. To calculate the number of possible combinations (which vice president conducts which meeting), use @PERMUT(5,3), which returns 60.

@POISSON(*x,mean,*[*cumulative*])

@POISSON calculates the Poisson distribution by approximation. @POISSON approximates the Poisson distribution to within +/-3*10^-7. @POISSON is useful for predicting the number of events that occur during a specified period.

Following are this function's arguments and limits:

x	The number of observed events. This argument can be a positive integer or 0.
mean	The expected number of events. This argument can be a positive integer or 0.
[*cumulative*]	This optional argument specifies how @POISSON is calculated. You have two options:

Cumulative	Calculation
0	The probability of fewer than or exactly *x* events (the default if [*cumulative*] is omitted)
1	The probability of exactly *x* events

Examples: Suppose that you are expecting a number of strollers to pass through the gates of a local amusement park at a rate of 26 per hour. Being optimistic, you want to know the probability that at most 20 strollers will pass through the gates in an hour. To determine the percentage, use @POISSON(20,26), which returns `0.041849`.

If you want to know the probability that exactly 20 strollers will pass through the gates, use @POISSON(20,26,1) to determine the percentage: `0.13867`.

@TDIST(*x*,*degrees_of_freedom*,[*type*],[*tails*])

@TDIST calculates the student's T-distribution. The student's T-distribution is the distribution of the ratio of a standardized normal distribution to the square root of the quotient of a chi-squared distribution by the number of its degrees of freedom. The student's T-distribution is approximated to within $+/-3*10^{-7}$. If the result is not approximated to within .0000001 after 100 attempts, 1-2-3 for Windows returns ERR.

Following are this function's arguments and limits:

x	The value at which to evaluate the student's T-distribution. The value of *x* depends on the optional [*type*] argument. You have two choices for *x*:

0   The upper boundary for the value of the cumulative T-distribution random variable. This argument can be a value greater than or equal to 0 (the default if [*type*] is omitted).

1   A significance level, or probability, between 0 and 1.

degrees_of_freedom   The number of degrees of freedom for the sample; must be a positive integer. If the value is not an integer, it is truncated to an integer.

[*type*]   This optional argument specifies how the @TDIST is calculated. You have two options:

Type	How Calculated
0	The significance level corresponding to *x* (the default if [*type*] is omitted)
1	The critical value that corresponds to the significance level

[*tails*]   This optional argument specifies the direction of the T-test. You have two options:

Tails	How Calculated
1	One-tailed T-test
2	Two-tailed T-test (the default if [*tails*] is omitted)

Ranking Functions
@PERCENTILE(*x,range*)

@PERCENTILE calculates the *x*th sample percentile among the values in a range.

The x argument is the percentage you want to find; it can be a value from 0 to 1. The *range* argument is the range name or address of the values. In the range, blank cells are ignored and cells with labels are assigned the value of 0.

Example: Suppose that you have given a test and gathered the scores. The scores are entered in a range named SCORES in a worksheet and have the following values: 98, 80, 59, 77, 97, 88, 69, and 89. To determine the 95th percentile, use @PERCENTILE(.95,SCORES), which returns 97.65.

@PRANK(*x,range,[places]*)

@PRANK finds percentile of *x* among the values in a range.

The *x* argument is any value. The *range* argument is the range name or address of the values. In the range, blank cells are ignored and cells with labels are assigned the value of 0.

The optional *places* argument specifies the number of decimal places to round the result of @PRANK. This argument can be a value from 0 to 100. If you omit the *places* argument, 1-2-3 for Windows assumes 2.

Example: Suppose that you have given a test and gathered the scores. The scores are entered in a range named SCORES in a worksheet and have the following values: 98, 80, 59, 77, 97, 88, 69, and 89. To determine the percentile for a score of 88, use @PRANK(.88,SCORES), which returns 57.

@RANK(*item,range,[order]*)

@RANK calculates the relative size or position of a value in a range, relative to other values in the range. 1-2-3 for Windows assigns the same rank to duplicate numbers in the range, although duplicate numbers affect the rank of subsequent numbers in the range.

The *item* argument is the value whose rank you want to determine. The *range* argument is the range name or address of a group of values. The *item* argument must be part of the range.

The optional *order* argument specifies how to rank items. This value can be 0 or 1. The value 0 indicates descending order (9 to 1) of ranking. If you omit the *order* argument, 1-2-3 for Windows assumes 0. The value 1 indicates ascending order (1 to 9) of ranking.

Examples: Suppose that you have given a test and gathered the scores. The scores are entered in a range named SCORES in a worksheet and have the following values: 98, 80, 59, 77, 97, 88, 69, and 89. To determine the highest ranking of the score of 88, use @RANK(88,SCORES), which returns 4. To determine the lowest ranking of the score of 88, use @RANK(88,SCORES,1), which returns 5.

Significance Tests
@CHITEST(*range1,range2*)

@CHITEST performs a chi-square test.

The argument list contains two ranges of values that must be the same size and can contain only values. If the ranges are not the same size, @CHITEST returns ERR. If the ranges are blank, contain labels, or have text formulas, @CHITEST returns ERR.

@FTEST(*range1,range2*)

@FTEST performs an F-test on two ranges to determine whether two samples have different variances. The probability of @FTEST is approximated to within +/-3*10^-7. The range arguments contain the values for the test. The ranges do not have to be the same size.

@TTEST(*range1,range2,[type],[tails]*)

@TTEST performs a student's T-test on the data in two ranges and returns the associated probability.

Following are this function's arguments and limits:

range1	Contains values. If *range1* contains labels, text formulas, or blank cells, 1-2-3 for Windows returns ERR.
range2	Contains values. If *range2* contains labels, text formulas, or blank cells, 1-2-3 for Windows returns ERR.
[*type*]	This optional argument specifies what type of T-test to perform. You have three options:

Type	T-Test
0	A T-test for samples drawn from populations with the same variance (*homoscedastic* populations); *range1* and *range2* do not have to contain the same number of cells (the default if [*type*] is omitted)
1	A T-test for samples drawn from populations with unequal variances (*heteroscedastic* populations); *range1* and *range2* do not have to contain the same number of cells
2	A paired T-test; *range1* and *range2* must contain the same number of cells

[*tails*]   This optional argument specifies the direction of the T-test. You have two options:

Tails	How Calculated
1	One-tailed T-test
2	Two-tailed T-test (the default if *[tails]* is omitted)

Text Functions

1-2-3 for Windows offers a variety of functions that give you significant power to manipulate text strings. The program provides a few special functions for working with the 1-2-3 for Windows character set (the IBM PC Multilingual code page—code page 850). The complete character set, listed in Appendix B of this book, includes everything from the copyright symbol (©) to the lowercase *e* with a grave accent (è).

Strings are labels or portions of labels. More specifically, strings are data that consists of characters (alphabetical, numeric, blank, and special) enclosed in quotation marks—for example, "total." The functions specifically designated as string functions are not the only 1-2-3 for Windows functions that take advantage of the power and flexibility of strings; logical, error-trapping, and special functions also use strings as well as values. The string functions, however, are specifically designed to manipulate strings.

You can link strings to other strings by using the concatenation operator (&). The discussion of the individual string functions in this section shows several examples of the use of the concatenation operator. Keep in mind that you cannot link strings to cells that contain numeric values or that are empty. If you try, 1-2-3 for Windows returns ERR.

Avoid mixing data types in string functions. Some functions produce strings, but other functions produce numeric results. If a function's result is not the data type you need, use @STRING to convert a numeric value to a string; use @VALUE to convert a string to a numeric value.

The numbering scheme for positioning characters in a string begins with 0 and continues to the number that corresponds to the last character in the label. The label prefix (') is not counted for numeric positioning. In the label '*dog*, for example, *d* is position 0, *o* is position 1, and *g* is position 2. You cannot use negative position numbers.

@CHAR(*number*) and @CODE(*string*)

@CHAR takes a code-page number that specifies a character and returns that character. @CODE does the opposite; it takes an IBM multilingual character and returns a code-page number. Keep in mind that uppercase and lowercase characters have different codes.

Example: Figure 5.20 shows several examples of the use of @CHAR and @CODE.

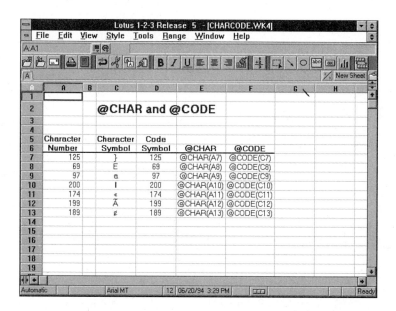

Fig. 5.20

Use @CHAR and @CODE to convert character and code-page equivalents.

Note

1-2-3 for Windows does not support some numerical-equivalent characters; these characters return a symbol that does not match the code-page symbol. Character number 200 in figure 5.20 shows a different character from the one presented in the code-page examples in your Lotus documentation.

@FIND(*search_string,string,start_number*)

@FIND locates the starting position of one string within another string. When @FIND cannot find a match, the result is ERR.

The *search_string* argument is the string you want to locate; it can be one or more characters long. The *string* argument is the string in which to locate the *search_string*. Both *search_string* and *string* can be text enclosed in quotation marks, a formula that returns text, or an address of a cell that contains text or a formula that returns text. @FIND's comparison of the search_string and the string arguments is case-sensitive. For example, @FIND will not find the search_string "j" in the string "Jim."

The *start_number* argument is the position number in *string* at which you want to start the search. Remember that the first character in the string is counted as 0, not 1.

Example: To determine the position of the blank space within the string "Jim Johnson," which appears in cell A6, use @FIND(" ",A6,0). Here, the search string is " " (a blank space enclosed in parentheses). The 0 indicates the search should begin at the first character of the string being searched. @FIND(" ",A6,0) returns the value 3.

Note

You can search for a second occurrence of *search_string* by adding 1 to the result of the first @FIND function and using that value as the *start_number* argument. This action starts the next @FIND operation at the character location after the blank space already found. The following formula searches for the character position of the second blank space for the string in cell A6:

@FIND(" ",A6,@FIND(" ",A6,1)+1)

@MID(*string,start_number,number*)

@MID extracts one string from another.

The *start_number* argument is a number that represents the character position in *string* at which you want to begin extracting characters. The *number* argument indicates the length of the string to be extracted; it is the number of characters to extract.

Example: To extract the first name from a label containing the full name "Mary Baggett," use @MID("Mary Baggett",0,4). This function extracts the string starting in position 0 (the first character) and continuing for four characters—through the string "Mary."

Extracting Names with @MID and @FIND

You can use the @MID and @FIND functions to extract the first and last names from a column of full names and to put the extracted names in separate columns. Use @FIND to locate the blank space between the first and last names; then use an @MID function to extract the first name and another @MID function to extract the last name.

If C6 contains the full name, use @MID(C6,0,@FIND(" ",C6,0)) to extract the first name. In this formula, @FIND returns the character-position number of the blank space between the first and last name and uses that number as the length of the string to extract for the @MID function. Thus, all characters up to the space (the first name) are extracted.

Then use @MID(C6,@FIND(" ",C6,0)+1,99) to extract the last name. Here, @FIND indicates that the *start_number* of the @MID function is one character beyond the blank space. The length of the string to be extracted is 99 characters (although 99 is more than you need, no ERR results from this excess). Thus, all characters after the space (the last name) are extracted.

If you use this type of formula to convert a long string in a database to shorter strings, convert the string formulas (first and last names) to values before using the database.

@LEFT(*string,number*) and @RIGHT(*string,number*)

The @LEFT and @RIGHT functions are variations of @MID; you use them to extract one string of characters from another, beginning at the leftmost and rightmost positions in the string.

The *string* argument is the string from which you want to extract characters. The *number* argument is the number of characters to be extracted.

> Example: If you want to extract the ZIP code from the string "Cincinnati, Ohio 45243," use @RIGHT("Cincinnati, Ohio 45243",5). To extract the city, use @LEFT("Cincinnati, Ohio 45243",10).

@REPLACE(*original_string,start_number,length, replacement_string*)

@REPLACE replaces one group of characters in a string with another group of characters. @REPLACE is a valuable tool for correcting a frequently incorrect text entry without retyping the entry.

Example: If you need to change to all phone numbers in a database that have area codes 301 to 407, you could use @REPLACE ("301",0,3,"407").

The *start_number* argument indicates the position at which 1-2-3 for Windows should begin removing characters from *original_string*. The *length* argument shows how many characters to remove. The *replacement_string* argument contains the new characters that will replace the removed ones. @REPLACE starts counting character positions in a string at 0 and continues to the end of the string (up to 511).

@LENGTH(*string*)

@LENGTH calculates the length of a string. @LENGTH frequently is used to calculate the length of a string being extracted from another string. You also can use this function to check for data-entry errors. @LENGTH returns ERR as the length of numeric values or formulas, empty cells, and null strings.

Example: @LENGTH("welcome back") returns 12.

@EXACT(*string1,string2*)

@EXACT compares two strings and returns 1 (true) if the strings are the same or 0 (false) if the strings are different. @EXACT checks for an exact match that distinguishes between uppercase and lowercase characters.

The *string1* and *string2* arguments can be text, the result of text formulas, or references to cells that contain text or text formulas.

> **Note**
>
> The @EXACT function's method of comparison is similar to the = operator in formulas (except that the = operator checks for a match regardless of uppercase and lowercase characters). If cell B7 holds the string "Wrench" and cell D7 holds the string "wrench," the logical value of B7=D7 is 1, because the two strings are an approximate match. The value of @EXACT(B7,D7), however, is 0, because the two functions are not an exact match; their cases are different.

@EXACT cannot compare nonstring arguments. In fact, if either argument is a nonstring value of any type (including numbers) or is blank, 1-2-3 for Windows returns ERR. (You can use the @S function, which is explained later in this chapter, to ensure that the arguments used within @EXACT have string values.) When you use = to compare a string with a number or a blank cell, the string is treated as the number 0, as is a blank cell. This means that if you use the = formula, any string is equal to a blank cell or to a cell that contains the number 0.

Example: Figure 5.21 demonstrates the use of @EXACT.

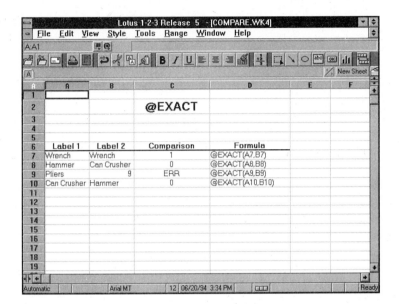

Fig. 5.21
Use @EXACT to
compare strings.

@LOWER(*string*), @UPPER(*string*), and @PROPER(*string*)

1-2-3 for Windows offers three functions for converting the case of a string value. @LOWER converts all letters in a string to lowercase, @UPPER converts all letters in a string to uppercase, and @PROPER capitalizes the first letter in each word of a label and the remaining letters in each word to lowercase. (Words are defined as groups of characters separated by blank spaces or nonletter characters.)

The *string* argument can be a string enclosed in quotation marks or a cell reference to a cell that contains a string. If a cell contains a number or a null string (" "), 1-2-3 for Windows returns ERR. (You can use the @S function, which is explained later in this chapter, to ensure that the arguments of these functions have string values.)

Examples: If cell A6 contains the string "welcome BACK,"
                 @UPPER(A6) returns WELCOME BACK, @LOWER(A6) returns
                 welcome back, and @PROPER(A6) returns Welcome Back.

> **Note**
>
> Use @LOWER, @UPPER, or @PROPER to modify the contents of a database so that all entries in a field have the same capitalization. This technique produces consistent reports. Capitalization also affects the sorting order: uppercase and lowercase letters do not sort together. To ensure that data with different capitalization sorts together, create a column (use one of the functions that references the data) and then sort on this new column.

@REPEAT(*string,number*)

@REPEAT repeats strings a specified number of times, much as the backslash (\) repeats strings to fill a cell. @REPEAT, however, has some distinct advantages over the backslash. With @REPEAT, you can repeat the string the precise number of times you want. If the result is wider than the cell width, the result is displayed in empty adjacent cells to the right.

The *string* argument is the string you want repeated. The *number* argument indicates the number of times you want to repeat *string* in the cell.

> Example: If you want to repeat the string "=**=" three times, use @REPEAT("==",3). The resulting string is "=**=**=**=".

@N(*range*) and @S(*range*)

@N and @S ensure that a cell contains numeric values or string values. These functions are important when you use other functions that operate on numeric values only or on string values only. When you are unsure whether a cell contains a numeric or text value, use @N or @S to force the contents to become a number or text.

@N forces the contents of a cell to be a number. If the cell contains a numeric value, @N returns that value. If the cell is blank or contains a label, @N returns the value 0. @N always returns a numeric value.

@S forces the contents of a cell to text. If the cell contains a string or a formula that evaluates to a string, @S returns that string. If the cell contains a number or is empty, @S returns the null string (" "). @S always returns a string value.

These functions prevent formulas from resulting in ERR when data in a cell is not of the expected type.

The *range* argument must be a range or a single-cell reference. If you use a single-cell reference, 1-2-3 for Windows adjusts the argument to range format and returns the numeric or string value of the single cell. If the *range* argument is a multiple cell range, @N or @S returns the numeric or string value of the top-left corner of the range.

@SETSTRING(*string,length,*[*alignment*])

@SETSTRING returns a label, specified by the *string* argument, that is the length specified by the *length* argument. @SETSTRING adds blank spaces to achieve the length and the alignment specified by the *alignment* argument. This function is particularly useful when working with the proportionally spaced fonts that are used with Windows.

The *string* argument is any text, enclosed in quotation marks. The *length* argument is any number from 1 to 512. If *length* is smaller than the number of characters in the *string* argument, 1-2-3 returns the *string* argument intact, ignoring *length*.

The optional *alignment* argument indicates how to align the label and where 1-2-3 should add the blank spaces. Its value is 0 to left-align the text and add all blank spaces to the right of the text. This is the default value if you omit the argument. Its value is 1 to center the text and add the blank spaces equally to both the left and right of the text. If there are an uneven number of spaces, 1-2-3 adds it to the left of the text. Its value is 2 to right-align the text and add the blank spaces to the left of the text.

Example: If each * represents a space, @SETSTRING
("Welcome back",18) returns `Welcome back******`,
@SETSTRING("Welcome back",18,1) returns `***Welcome back***`, and @SETSTRING("Welcome back",18,2) returns `******Welcome back`.

@STRING(*value,format*)

@STRING lets you convert a number to its text-string equivalent. @STRING formats this label as Fixed, Comma, Scientific, or General format, according to the *format* argument's value.

@STRING ignores all numeric formats placed on the cell you are converting and operates on just the numeric contents of the cell.

The *value* argument is any value. The *format* argument specifies how 1-2-3 should format the resulting label. The possible *format* arguments values are:

Value	Format
0 through 116	Fixed; with *value* decimal places
1000 through 1116	Comma; with *value*-1000 decimal places
-18 through -1	Scientific; with @ABS(*value*) digits
10001 through 10512	General; with up to *value*-1000 characters

Examples: If cell A6 contains 12345.678, @STRING(A6,2) returns
12345.68, @STRING(A6,1002) returns 12,345.68, and
@STRING(A6,-1) returns 1E+04.

@VALUE(*string*)

@VALUE converts a number that is a string to a numeric value that can be
used in calculations.

The *string* argument must be text or a label made up only of numbers and
numeric formatting characters, such as the comma, decimal point, and dollar
sign. The string cannot contain other alphabetical characters or an illegal
number format (such as 1,23.99); it can include leading or trailing spaces and
can begin with a currency symbol (such as $). Do not include spaces between
the currency symbol and the numbers in the string.

A nice feature of @VALUE is that it converts text fractions to decimal numbers. This function is useful, therefore, for converting stock data from databases or wire services to numbers that you can analyze and chart.

Example: If cell A6 contains the label 2 3/4, @VALUE(A6) returns
2.75.

@TRIM(*string*)

@TRIM eliminates unwanted blank spaces from the beginning, end, or middle
of a string. If a string contains multiple adjacent spaces, the function reduces
them to one space.

@TRIM is useful for trimming spaces from data as it is entered into a macro or
for trimming unwanted spaces from data in a database. Such spaces in a database can cause the sort order to be different from what you expect.

The *string* argument can be text enclosed in quotation marks, a formula that results in text, or a cell reference to a cell containing text or a formula resulting in text.

> Example: If cell A6 contains the string "welcome back,"
> @TRIM(A6) returns `welcome back`.

@CLEAN(*string*)

When you import text files with the **F**ile menu's **I**mport command, particularly files transmitted with a modem, the strings sometimes contain nonprintable characters. @CLEAN removes the nonprintable characters from the strings

The *string* argument can be text enclosed in quotation marks, a formula that results in text, or a cell reference to a cell containing text or a formula resulting in text. 1-2-3 for Windows cannot accept a cell entry that contains @CLEAN with a range argument specified.

From Here...

Now that you have learned how to create and use functions, you may want to refer to the following chapters:

- Chapter 18, *"Manipulating and Analyzing Data,"* In this chapter, you learn how to combine whole and partial units of text, use formulas that make decisions, analyze and obtain data from tables, and create what-if tables

- Chapter 37, *"Advanced Macro Techniques,"* introduces you to advanced macro commands, not by teaching programming theory and concepts but rather by describing the capabilities of programming with the macro commands.

Everyday Worksheet Tasks

Chapter 6

Moving or Copying Data

As you develop more and more sophisticated models on 1-2-3, you will need to duplicate or move data and/or formulas from one location to another. In this chapter, you learn a variety of techniques for handling these procedures. You also learn about absolute and relative cell references and the part they play in copying formulas.

In this chapter, you learn how to

- Move and copy data to a new location by using drag-and-drop

- Move and copy data to a new location by using the Windows Clipboard

- Move and copy a formula to a new location

- Move and copy a format to a new location

- Change a cell reference in a formula so that it is absolute or mixed

Moving Data

1-2-3 for Windows provides a number of ways to move data, including dragging the cell or range with the mouse, using commands or shortcut keys from the **E**dit menu, and using SmartIcons.

In a move operation, the data being moved is called the *source*; the location to which you are moving the data is called the target or *destination*. When you move data, the source data disappears from its original location and reappears at the target location.

The following sections describe all the available moving methods and discuss how 1-2-3 for Windows handles the movement of formulas or data used in formulas and the movement of formatting and style attributes.

Dragging a Range to a New Location

Tip
Remember that you can use the **E**dit **U**ndo command to correct a mistake in moving a range; press Ctrl+Z (Undo), or click the Undo SmartIcon.

Dragging the cell or range is the simplest way to move data. You can use this technique to move a single cell or a range of cells to another location on the same worksheet, to another worksheet in the same file, or even to a range in another file. You cannot drag a collection (two or more separate ranges) with the mouse.

To drag a range to another location in a worksheet, first highlight the range you want to move and position the mouse so the pointer is at one of the edges of the range—anywhere other than the bottom right corner of the cell or range. When you move the mouse pointer to the edge of a range or to the edge of a single cell containing the cursor, the pointer changes to a hand (see fig. 6.1).

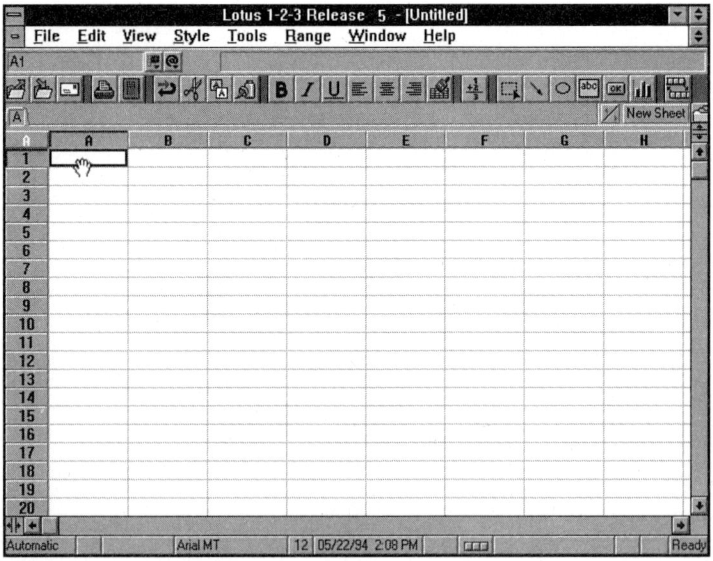

Fig. 6.1
When you move the mouse pointer to the edge—other than the bottom right corner—of a single cell containing the cursor or a range of cells, the mouse pointer changes to a hand.

Then click and hold down the left mouse button.

Tip
If you move the cursor to the bottom right corner of a selected range, the cursor changes shape to a 123ABC range fill by example shape.

When you click and hold down the left mouse button while the cursor is shaped like a hand, the cursor changes to a fist. This indicates that 1-2-3 is in drag mode. Drag the range to another location.

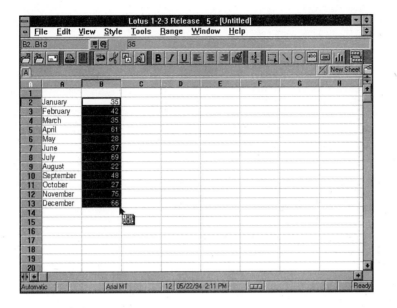

Fig. 6.2
When you move
the mouse pointer
to the lower right
corner of a
highlighted range
of cells, the mouse
pointer changes to
a 123ABC shape.

Often the new location will be on the same worksheet. If you want to drag
to another worksheet in the file, you can have the other worksheet visible on
the screen by using one of the **V**iew **S**plit options (refer to Chapter 15 for
more information on **V**iew **S**plit) and then drag the range, as before, to the
new worksheet.

If you have not split the screen you can still drag information to another
worksheet in the same file by dragging, as before, but when the cursor
changes into a fist, drag to the tab indicating the worksheet on which you
want the information placed. That worksheet will appear and you can position the cursor anywhere on that worksheet.

To drag information from one file to another, both files must be open and
visible on the screen. You can use either the **W**indow **T**ile or **W**indow **C**ascade options to have both files appear (refer to Chapter 1 for information on
the **W**indow **T**ile and **W**indow **C**ascade commands). When both files are
visible, you can drag a range from one file to the other, as discussed above.

Occasionally you may accidentally drag and drop a range onto another range
that already contains information. If you are about to do so, 1-2-3 warns you
by displaying the dialog box shown in figure 6.3.

Tip
When you move
a cell or a range
that contains one
or more formulas,
the formulas stay
intact. For ex-
ample, say you
have the formula
+A1+B1 in cell
C1. If you move
cell C1 to C5, the
formula in C5
will also be
+A1+B1. The
formula will not
change when
moved.

Fig. 6.3

The confirmation dialog box you will see if you attempt to drag and drop information onto a range that already contains information.

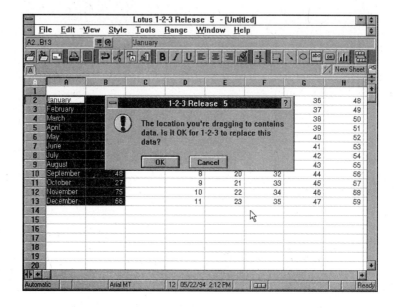

Troubleshooting

Nothing happens when I try to drag-and-drop. I don't even see the hand appear when I move the mouse pointer to the edge of a highlighted area.

Drag-and-drop may not be enabled. To check to see whether it is, select **T**ools **U**ser Setup. The first check box under Options, **D**rag-and-drop cells, must be checked.

I accidentally dragged-and-dropped one range on top of another, and the new one overwrote what was originally there. Is there a way to prevent this from happening in the future?

You can have 1-2-3 warn you if you are about to drag-and-drop information on top of other information. To do so, select **T**ools **U**ser Setup. In the User Setup dialog box, click the check box to the left of **C**onfirm Drag-and-drop. Click the OK button to make this warning mode the default.

Cutting and Pasting a Range

To move data by cutting and pasting, you cut the data from the worksheet to the Clipboard (a Windows holding area in memory). Then you paste the data from the Clipboard to a new location in the same worksheet, to a different worksheet in the same file, to a different file, or to a different Windows 3.x application. You can move entire columns, rows, or worksheets with this method, but you cannot use this technique to move a column so it becomes a row, a row so it becomes a column, or a worksheet or file so it becomes a column or row.

You can paste data many times if you want to copy the same information to many different locations. If you want to copy data to many different places, however, do not interrupt the pasting operation by cutting or copying other data to the Clipboard. Pasting makes a copy of whatever is on the Clipboard, and only the contents of the most recent copy or cut operation are stored on the Clipboard.

To cut and paste data, follow these steps:

1. Highlight the range or cell you want to move.

2. Choose **E**dit Cu**t**, press Shift+Del or Ctrl+X, or click the Cut SmartIcon.

3. Move the cell pointer to the first cell of the destination range.

4. Choose **E**dit **P**aste, press Shift+Ins or Ctrl+V, or click the Paste SmartIcon. You can also simply press Enter to paste the information in the new location.

5. To paste the data in another location also, move the cell pointer or select the target range and either press Shift+Ins or Ctrl+V, or click the Paste SmartIcon. Pressing Enter will not paste the information in the new location, as is the case immediately after you have cut or copied information to the Clipboard.

Troubleshooting

When I paste data, I don't get the correct information copied into the cells.

Be certain when you copy or cut information to the Clipboard that you immediately paste it into the destination cells. If you don't do so immediately, you may inadvertently copy additional data to the Clipboard, wiping out what you meant to copy.

When I pasted data onto my worksheet, it overwrote other information that was already there.

When you paste data onto your worksheet, it overwrites information already in that area. Be certain when you are pasting information onto your worksheet that there is adequate room into which to place the information. Otherwise, information will be overwritten. If necessary, insert extra columns or rows to make room for your information. For information on inserting rows and columns, see "Inserting Cells, Rows, and Columns," in Chapter 3.

> **Note**
>
> The Confirm Drag-and-drop warning discussed in the Troubleshooting note in the previous section *does not* apply to this paste/overwrite situation. Even if Confirm Drag-and-drop is checked, pasted data will still overwrite other information with no warning.

Moving a Formula

If you move one corner of a range used in a formula, the range expands or contracts and the formula is adjusted. Figure 6.4 shows a range of data that includes formulas. Figure 6.5 shows what happens after you move the range F2..H6 to G2. Notice that 1-2-3 for Windows adjusted the range in the @SUM formula (shown in the contents box of the edit line in both figures). In figure 6.4, the formula in cell G3 is @SUM(D3..F3). The move changed the formula (now in cell H3) to @SUM(D3..G3). The @SUM in both formulas starts with cell D3. Because this cell did not move, that portion of the range was not altered. But the @SUM range expanded to include D3..G3. A common use of this kind of range movement is to make room for a new row or column in the range of data.

Fig. 6.4
A worksheet before cells F2..H6 are moved to cell G2.

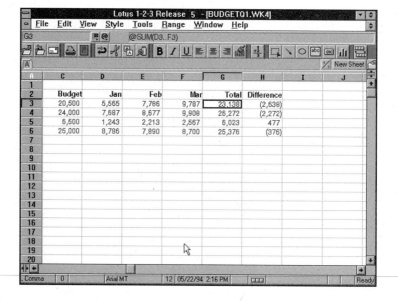

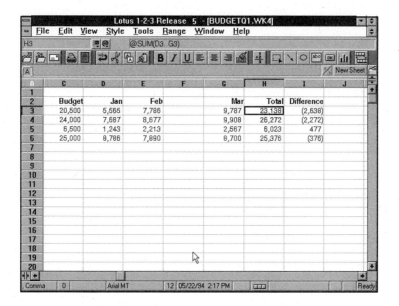

Fig. 6.5
Notice how the @SUM formula, now in cell H3, changes after cells F2..H6 are moved to G2.

If you move the range G2..I6 in figure 6.5 back to cell F2, the formula reverts to the one shown in figure 6.4. ERR does not appear even though part of the range is eliminated.

Caution

Be careful when moving cells that are referenced in formulas without also moving the formulas. If you move a portion of a range without its formula, the resulting formula might not be accurate.

Moving Formats and Data Types

If you want to move just the formatting and style attributes of a cell or range to another cell or range, select the **E**dit Paste **S**pecial command instead of the **E**dit **P**aste command. In the Paste Special dialog box, shown in figure 6.6, you have the following options:

- The **A**ll option pastes normally (like the **E**dit **P**aste command).

- **C**ell contents only pastes the contents of the cells without the styles.

- **S**tyles only pastes the styles from the selection.

- **F**ormulas as values converts formulas into values when pasting.

Fig. 6.6

The Paste Special dialog box enables you to move the format and style attributes of a cell or a range to another location.

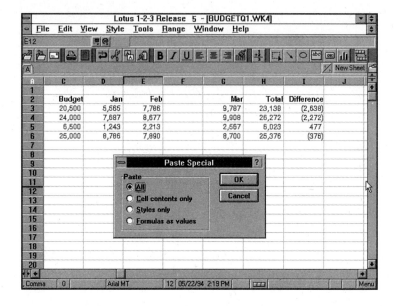

Copying Data

The copying methods provided by 1-2-3 for Windows are very much like the moving methods described in the preceding sections. You can drag the cell or range with the mouse, use commands or shortcut keys from the **E**dit menu, or use SmartIcons.

In a copy operation, just as in a move operation, the data being copied is called the *source*; the location to which you move the data is called the target or *destination*. When you copy data, 1-2-3 for Windows leaves the source data in its original location and places a copy of the data in the target location—in other words, the copied data appears in both places. Copied data includes the same labels and values—as well as the same formats, fonts, colors, protection status, and borders—as the original data. You do not, however, copy the column width or row height. You can use **E**dit Copy with **E**dit Paste **S**pecial to paste only some of the properties or types of data that were copied.

Tip

Remember that you can use the **E**dit **U**ndo command to correct a mistake in copying a range, press Ctrl+Z (Undo), or click the Undo SmartIcon.

Whenever you need to copy data, the drag-and-drop technique is probably the right choice. The **E**dit **C**opy command is primarily for copying data to and from other applications or when you want to copy the same data to a number of different locations. The **E**dit **C**opy command is also helpful when dragging would be tedious because you're copying data across large areas of the worksheet. Also, use **E**dit **C**opy when you need to copy information from one worksheet to another. You cannot drag-and-drop between worksheets.

Copying is one of the most frequently performed actions in 1-2-3, and the copy operation can be simple and straightforward or more subtle. The following sections begin with basic examples of copy procedures and progress to more complex ones.

Copying with Drag-and-Drop

Copying a cell or range by using drag-and-drop is very similar to moving data by using drag-and-drop. The only difference is that you press the Ctrl key as you drag to the new location in order to copy.

To copy a cell or range by using the drag-and-drop technique, follow these steps:

1. Highlight the cell or range you want to copy.

2. Move the mouse pointer to any edge of the selection, other than the bottom right corner, so the mouse pointer changes to a hand.

3. Press and hold the Ctrl key as you click and drag the selection to its new location.

4. When you reach the destination, release the mouse button and the Ctrl key. The data is copied to the new location without changing the original.

Copying with the Clipboard

You can use commands and SmartIcons to copy data. The **E**dit **C**opy command and the Copy SmartIcon use the Clipboard to copy data. No dialog box appears; 1-2-3 for Windows just copies the source data to the Clipboard. Notice that when you copy data to the Clipboard, 1-2-3 places the message `Select destination and press ENTER or choose Edit Paste`. To complete the copying action, you paste the source data with the **E**dit **P**aste command or the Paste SmartIcon or you can press Enter. You also can copy data from and to other Windows applications by using the **E**dit **C**opy and **E**dit **P**aste commands.

To copy data with commands or SmartIcons, follow these steps:

1. Highlight the range or cell you want to copy.

2. Choose **E**dit **C**opy, press Ctrl+Ins or Ctrl+C, or click the Copy SmartIcon.

Tip
If you have activated the **T**ools **U**ser Setup **C**onfirm Drag-and-drop option and your drag-and-drop copy process overwrites already existing information, you see the warning shown in figure 6.3 and are asked to confirm the process.

3. Move the cell pointer to the first cell of the destination range.

4. Press Enter, choose **E**dit Paste, press Shift+Ins or Ctrl+V, or click the Paste SmartIcon.

Copying Formulas

Tip
Pressing Enter to paste information in a new location only works *immediately* after you copy information to the Clipboard. If you perform *any* other task, the press Enter to paste information option becomes inoperative.

The real power of copying becomes evident when you copy formulas. When you copy a formula, 1-2-3 for Windows adjusts the new formula so that its cell references are in the same location relative to the original formula. *Relative addressing* is one of the most important concepts in 1-2-3 for Windows.

The best way to understand relative addressing is to understand how 1-2-3 for Windows stores addresses in formulas. The formula @SUM(A1..A5) means to add the contents of all the cells in the range from cell A1 to cell A5, but that's not the way 1-2-3 for Windows stores it. If this formula is in cell A6, for example, 1-2-3 for Windows reads the formula as "Add the contents of the five cells directly above this one," as illustrated in figure 6.7. When you copy this formula from cell A6 to cell B6, 1-2-3 for Windows uses the same relative formula but displays it as @SUM(B1..B5), as shown in figure 6.8.

Fig. 6.7

1-2-3 interprets the formula in cell A6 as "Add the contents of the five cells directly above this one."

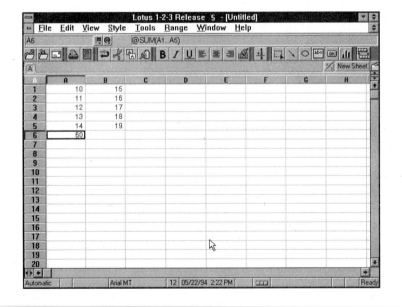

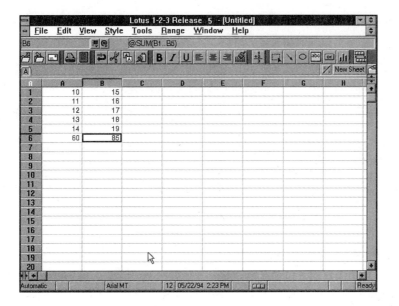

Fig. 6.8
When the formula
in cell A6 is copied
to cell B6, 1-2-3
maintains the
same relative
interpretation,
"Add the contents
of the five cells
directly above this
one."

In most cases, when you copy a formula, you want the addresses adjusted automatically. At times, however, you do not want some addresses to be adjusted, or you may want only part of an address to be adjusted. These cases are examined in the next sections.

Copying a Formula with Absolute Addressing

In figure 6.9, the formula in cell C9 is +C7/F7. This figure represents January's sales as a percent of the total. 1-2-3 interprets this formula as "Take the number two rows above this cell (C7), and divide it by the number two rows above and three columns to the right of this cell (F7)."

Suppose you want to figure out February's sales as a percent of the total sales. If you copy the formula in cell C9 to cell D9, the resulting formula is +D7/G7, which maintains the same relative interpretation as the original formula, as shown in figure 6.10. The D7 part of the formula, which represents the sales for February, is correct. The G7 portion (which refers to the difference between the budgeted amount and the actual amount), however, is incorrect, even though it is two rows above and three columns to the right of the cell containing the formula.

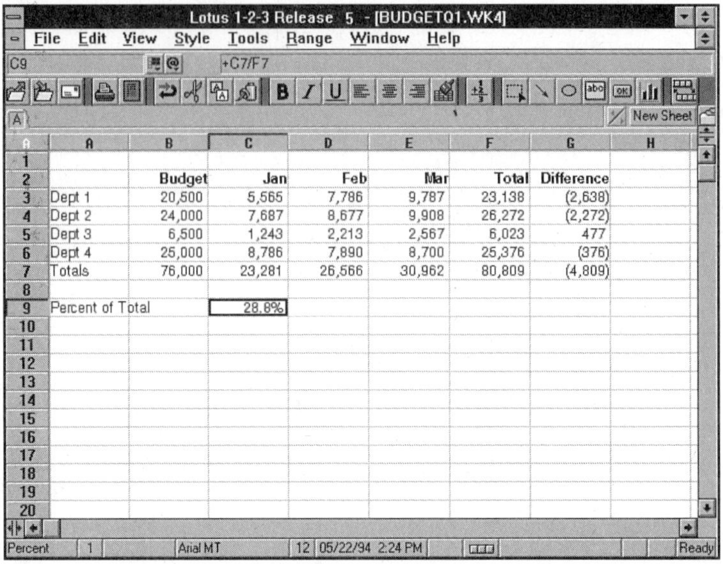

Fig. 6.9
A formula with a relative address.

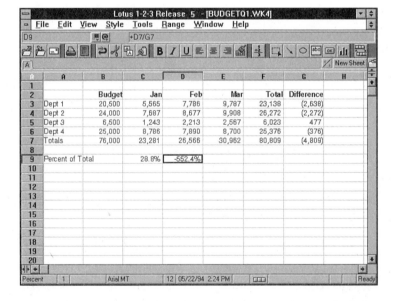

Fig. 6.10
When a formula containing relative references is copied, the relative relationships are maintained, even if they should not be.

To solve this problem, you must copy the F7 address (the total sales) as an absolute address when you copy the formula from cell C9 so that the F7 address (the total sales) doesn't change.

To specify an absolute address, type a dollar sign ($) before each part of the address (worksheet, column, and row) you want to remain absolutely the same. The formula in cell C9 should be +C7/$F$7. When you copy this formula to cell D9, the formula becomes +D7/$F$7.

You also can specify an absolute address without typing dollar signs. After you type (or point to) the address, press F4 (Abs); the address changes to absolute. After copying the absolute formula +C7/$F$7 in cell C9 to cells D9..F9, the worksheet appears as shown in figure 6.11.

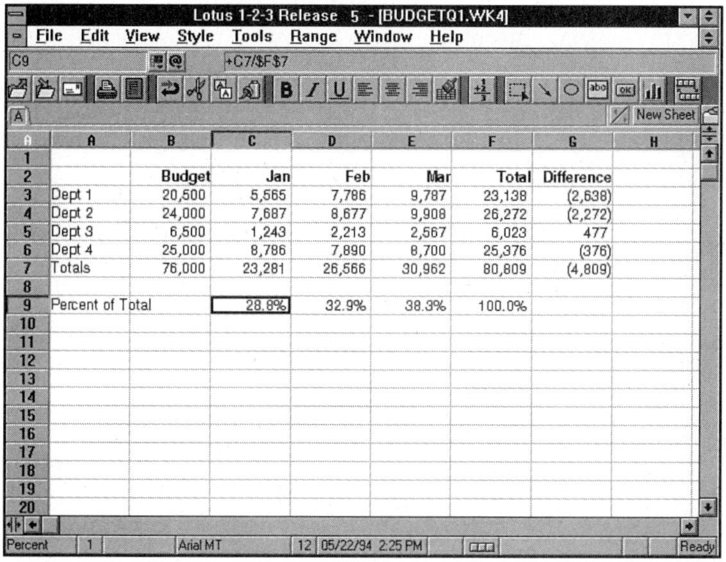

Fig. 6.11
The result after copying a formula with an absolute address.

Everyday Worksheet Tasks

If you want to change an absolute reference back to a relative reference, press F2 (Edit), move the cursor to the reference, and then press F4 (Abs) as many times as necessary until the address contains no dollar signs. Press Enter to reenter the formula. You can also edit a formula containing dollar signs by deleting the signs as you would any other character.

Copying a Formula with Mixed Addressing

In some cases, you must use formulas with a mix of absolute and relative references if you want the formula to copy correctly. The example presented in this section shows you how to keep a row reference absolute while letting the column reference change during the copy.

Tip
If you make an error and forget to make an address absolute, *be sure the cursor is in the correct cell and press F2 (Edit), move the cursor in the contents box to the address you want to make absolute, and press F4 (Abs).*

Figure 6.12 shows a price-forecasting worksheet with a different price increase percentage for each year. When you copy the formula in cell C3 down column C, you do not want the reference to cell C1 to change, but when you copy the formula across row 3, you want the reference to change for each column. The mixed reference is relative for the column and absolute for the row. The formula in cell C3 is +B3*(1+C$1). When you copy this formula down one row to cell C4, the formula becomes +B4*(1+C$1). The relative address B3 becomes B4, but the mixed address C$1 is unchanged. When you copy this formula to cell D3, the formula becomes +C3*(1+D$1). The relative address B3 becomes C3, and the mixed address C$1 becomes D$1. You can copy this mixed-address formula from cell C3 to C3..F10 for correct results throughout the worksheet.

Fig. 6.12
A formula with a mixed address.

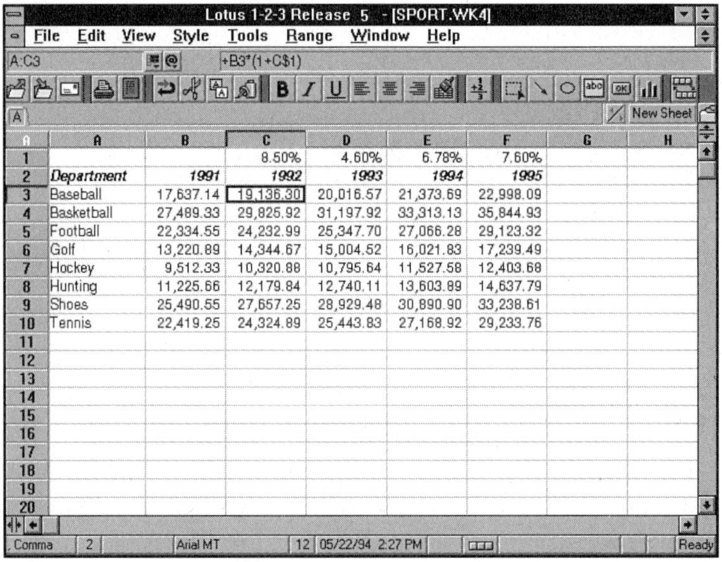

	A	B	C	D	E	F
1			8.50%	4.60%	6.78%	7.60%
2	*Department*	*1991*	*1992*	*1993*	*1994*	*1995*
3	Baseball	17,637.14	19,136.30	20,016.57	21,373.69	22,998.09
4	Basketball	27,489.33	29,825.92	31,197.92	33,313.13	35,844.93
5	Football	22,334.55	24,232.99	25,347.70	27,066.28	29,123.32
6	Golf	13,220.89	14,344.67	15,004.52	16,021.83	17,239.49
7	Hockey	9,512.33	10,320.88	10,795.64	11,527.58	12,403.68
8	Hunting	11,225.66	12,179.84	12,740.11	13,603.89	14,637.79
9	Shoes	25,490.55	27,657.25	28,929.48	30,890.90	33,238.61
10	Tennis	22,419.25	24,324.89	25,443.83	27,168.92	29,233.76

To make an address mixed without typing the dollar signs, use F4 (Abs). The first time you press F4, the address becomes absolute. If you continue to press F4, the address cycles through all the possible mixed addresses and returns to relative. The complete list of relative, absolute, and mixed addresses is found in table 6.1. To change the relative address C1 to the mixed address C$1 shown in figure 6.12, press F4 twice.

Table 6.1 Using F4 (Abs) To Change the Address Type	
Address	**Status**
$A:$D$1	Completely absolute
$A:D$1	Absolute worksheet and row
$A:$D1	Absolute worksheet and column
$A:D1	Absolute worksheet
A:$D$1	Absolute column and row
A:D$1	Absolute row
A:$D1	Absolute column
A:D1	Relative

When you work with multiple worksheets, be careful with absolute and mixed addresses. When you first press F4, the worksheet label is made absolute. In many cases, you do not want this effect. Consider the worksheet in figure 6.12. If you changed the formula in cell C3 to +B3*(1+$A:C$1), the absolute address of the worksheet identifier (the **$A:** part of the formula) would force the C$1 reference to remain in worksheet A. If you planned to expand this model to multiple worksheets, you would want each worksheet to reference the growth range for that worksheet. You would want the worksheet letter to change relative to its new worksheet; therefore, you would want the formula to use the mixed address A:C$1, not $A:C$1, so that the A: worksheet is not always referenced as you copy to other worksheets. In this case, the correct formula to place in cell C3 before copying it would be +B3*(1+A:C$1).

Copying One Cell to a Range

When copying and pasting, you can copy a single cell to a range of cells by highlighting the destination range before using the **E**dit **P**aste command.

You also can copy a single cell to larger ranges in multiple rows and columns. In the price-forecasting model in figure 6.13, the current prices are in column B. The formula in cell C3 increases the price by the percentage in cell B1. To copy this formula throughout the table in worksheet A, use **E**dit **C**opy to copy cell C3 to the Clipboard, select range C3..F10, and then choose **E**dit **P**aste to paste the Clipboard contents to the selected range. Figure 6.14 shows the result.

◄ "Working with Ranges," p. 71

Fig. 6.13
A formula in cell
C3 before being
copied.

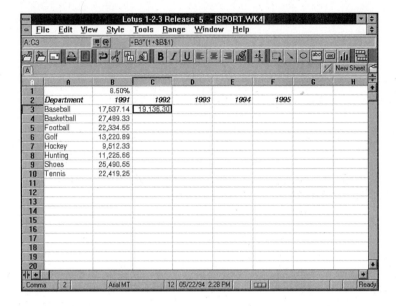

Fig. 6.14
The results of
copying cell C3 to
the range C3..F10.

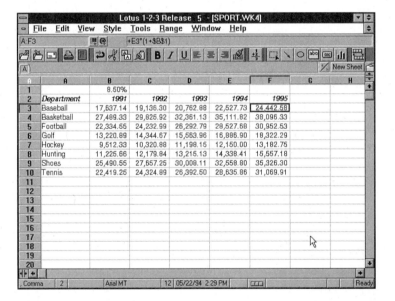

In addition, you can copy a cell to multiple rows and columns in different
worksheets. For example, if the same price-forecasting model for different
departments is found in different worksheets, you can fill in multiple
worksheets with one three-dimensional copy. Just copy the original cell, and
then select a three-dimensional range as the destination for the **Edit P**aste
command.

If you want to copy a cell across a row or down a column, you might find the **E**dit Copy **R**ight and **E**dit Copy Do**w**n commands useful. Just highlight the original cell and any blank cells to the right or below; then use the **E**dit Copy **R**ight or **E**dit Copy Do**w**n command to copy the cell into the blank area. You can also use the following SmartIcons for this purpose:

 Copy Row to Range (same as **E**dit Copy Do**w**n)

 Copy Column to Range (same as **E**dit Copy **R**ight)

 Copy Cell to Range (row or column)

Using Paste Special To Copy Styles

When you use the **E**dit **C**opy command, 1-2-3 for Windows copies all aspects of the cell or range, including the underlying values and the formats. If you want to paste only one aspect of the copied data, use the **E**dit Paste **S**pecial command instead of **E**dit **P**aste. The Paste **S**pecial command enables you to copy just the formatting of cells instead of data and formats. Formatting includes the following attributes: cell format, font, border (including lines and drop shadows), color, and shading.

You also can choose the **F**ormulas as Values option to convert formulas into their underlying values when pasting. This option can be useful when you need to reference the values elsewhere in the worksheet without the underlying formulas in place.

Caution

1-2-3 for Windows does not recalculate formulas before it converts the formulas to values. If recalculation is set to manual or if the Calc indicator appears in the status bar, press F9 (Calc), click the Calc button in the status bar, or click the Recalculate SmartIcon before you use the Formulas as Values option.

Troubleshooting

The Paste command is grayed out when I try to use it.

You haven't copied anything to the Clipboard. The **E**dit P**as**te command is only available if you previously used either the **E**dit **C**opy or the **E**dit Cu**t** commands (or their keyboard shortcuts or the corresponding SmartIcons) to place something on the Clipboard.

Transposing Ranges

The **R**ange **T**ranspose command and Transpose Data SmartIcon provide another way to copy data. This operation converts rows to columns or columns to rows and changes formulas to values at the same time. In figure 6.15, the range A1..H9 is to be transposed to the range A12..I19.

To perform the transposition,

1. Highlight the range from which you want to transpose data, in this case, A1..H9.

2. Select **R**ange **T**ranspose, or click the Transpose SmartIcon if it appears on the current SmartIcon palette.

3. The Range Transpose dialog box, shown in figure 6.15, appears. This dialog box provides the **F**rom and **T**o options.

4. In the **T**o text box of the dialog box, indicate the top left corner of the range where you want the transposed data placed. In this example, the location is cell A12.

5. The resulting transposed information is shown in figure 6.16; the rows and columns are transposed, and the formulas in row 9 become numbers in column I.

Fig. 6.15

The Transpose dialog box used to transpose the range A1.. H9 to A12.

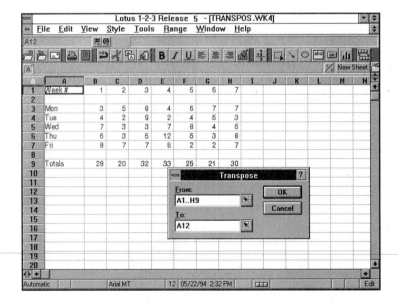

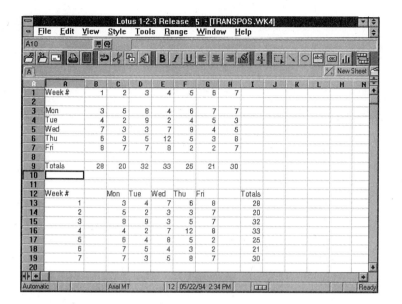

Fig. 6.16
The result of transposing A1..H9 to the range A12..I19. Only the top left corner of the To range (A12) needs to be specified.

The **R**ange **T**ranspose command copies formats, fonts, colors, and shading but does not copy shadow boxes or border lines.

Caution

Range Transpose doesn't recalculate the worksheet before transposing data. You can freeze incorrect values if you execute the command without recalculating. Always recalculate the worksheet before you transpose a range.

Caution

1-2-3 does not warn you if you transpose data to a range that already contains information. 1-2-3 will overwrite information already in the range when you do so. Be sure you have adequate blank space in the range to which you are transposing data so you don't inadvertently overwrite other information.

From Here...

Now that you have learned how to move and copy data and formulas in a 1-2-3 for Windows worksheet, you may want to refer to the following chapters:

- Chapter 7, "Reorganizing Worksheets," shows you how to work efficiently with multiple worksheets at one time.

- Chapter 9, "Formatting Worksheets," teaches you how to enhance the appearance of your worksheets by using a variety of style options.

- Chapter 19, "Linking and Consolidating Worksheets," shows you how to bring together data from multiple files for more efficient analysis.

Chapter 7

Reorganizing Worksheets

By default, a new file in 1-2-3 has a single worksheet. However, you can use the 1-2-3 for Windows multiple-worksheet feature to include up to 256 worksheets in a single worksheet file. With multiple-worksheet files, you can organize your data more efficiently than you would be able to using a single worksheet. For example, you can create a separate worksheet for each sales region, and then consolidate sales figures in a worksheet that calculates total sales for all regions. You might also create 12 separate worksheets to track company activity for each of the 12 months, and then create a 13th worksheet to consolidate those figures into a yearly report.

This chapter teaches you the basics of creating and managing multiple-worksheet files. In this chapter, you learn how to do the following:

- Insert worksheets

- Rename worksheets

- Delete worksheets

- Group worksheets

Inserting Worksheets

Just as you can insert columns and rows in a worksheet, you can use the Edit Insert command to insert additional worksheets anywhere in a worksheet file. When you select this command, the Insert dialog box appears. You can also press Ctrl+Gray Plus(+) to display the Insert dialog box.

From the Insert dialog box, select the **S**heet option button to display additional dialog box options (see fig. 7.1). Select the **B**efore option button to insert sheets before the current worksheet, or select the A**f**ter option button to insert sheets after the current worksheet. Use the up and down arrows under **Q**uantity to specify how many sheets to insert, or type a number in the **Q**uantity text box. For example, if worksheet B is the current worksheet, and you select A**f**ter and type **3** in the **Q**uantity text box, 1-2-3 for Windows inserts three new worksheets named C, D, and E.

Fig. 7.1
Use the Insert
dialog box to
insert more than
one worksheet at a
time.

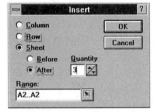

> **Note**
>
> The Insert dialog box is the only way to insert a worksheet or worksheets *before* the current worksheet.

 To insert one worksheet at a time *after* the current worksheet, use the New Sheet button at the top right of the worksheet window or the Insert Sheet SmartIcon.

◄ "Understanding
Worksheets
and Files,"
p. 60
When you insert a worksheet or worksheets, 1-2-3 assigns new worksheet letters to all the worksheets behind the worksheets you insert. For example, if you insert a new worksheet after worksheet A, and worksheet B already exists, the new worksheet becomes B, the former worksheet B becomes worksheet C, and so on. 1-2-3 also adjusts all addresses and formulas in the file automatically.

If you insert a worksheet within a range that spans worksheets, the range expands automatically to accommodate the new worksheet. Formulas referring to that range include the new cells. However, if you insert a worksheet after a range that spans worksheets A, B, and C, the new worksheet will not be considered part of the range unless you redefine the range.

Renaming Worksheets

By default, 1-2-3 for Windows names the worksheets you add to a file A, B, C, and so on. It includes these worksheet names on the worksheet tabs. However, you can give worksheets meaningful names to make it easier to navigate to different parts of a multiple-sheet file. For example, you might name the worksheet that includes first quarter sales totals *Quarter 1*, the worksheet for the second quarter *Quarter 2*, and so on. You might also name a fifth consolidation worksheet *FY 94* or *Yearly* (see fig. 7.2).

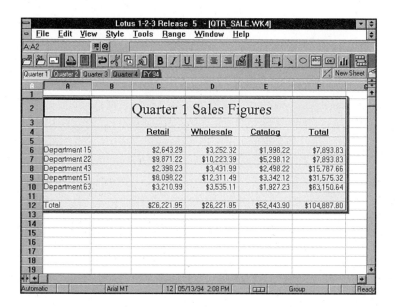

Fig. 7.2
A multiple worksheet file with descriptive worksheet names.

To rename a worksheet, double-click the worksheet tab and type the new name. A name can be up to 15 characters long, but it's best to use something short and descriptive so that you and any other users that share the file can navigate easily from worksheet to worksheet.

When you name a worksheet, remember these rules:

- Avoid ambiguous names, such as **C:**, because 1-2-3 does not distinguish between uppercase and lowercase letters in names and might confuse a worksheet of that name with the third worksheet in a file (worksheet C).

- Don't create worksheet names that resemble cell addresses, @function names, key names, or macro commands.

Tip
1-2-3 automatically names worksheets you insert before or after a worksheet whose name 1-2-3 recognizes as part of a fill sequence. For more information about fill sequences, see "Filling Ranges" in Chapter 3.

Tip
To restore the original letter name of the worksheet (for example, A), double-click the tab, press Delete or Backspace, and press Enter.

■ Don't start a worksheet name with an exclamation point (!), a dollar sign ($), or the at sign (@), and don't use any of the following characters in a worksheet name:

+ * - / & > ^ < @ # { ? (,) =

Deleting Worksheets

When you erase a range in a worksheet with **E**dit Cl**e**ar or **E**dit Cu**t,** the cells still exist in the worksheet, but they are empty. In contrast, when you delete a worksheet, 1-2-3 for Windows removes the entire worksheet and moves others to fill the gap created by the deletion. 1-2-3 for Windows also updates addresses, including those in formulas.

To delete a worksheet, use the **E**dit **D**elete command. After you choose this command, 1-2-3 for Windows displays the Delete dialog box (see fig. 7.3). Select the **S**heet option button, and then specify the range of worksheets to be deleted by using one of the following methods:

■ Preselect the range by using the mouse or the Shift+Ctrl+PgUp and Shift+Ctrl+PgDn key combinations to highlight multiple worksheets before choosing **E**dit **D**elete.

■ Type the range address into the R**a**nge text box in the Delete dialog box.

■ Click the range selector in the Delete dialog box, and then specify the range by using the mouse or keyboard.

Fig. 7.3
The Delete dialog box enables you to delete worksheets, as well as rows and columns.

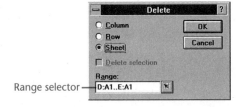

Range selector

After you have specified the range, click the OK button or press Enter to confirm the dialog box and delete the worksheets.

When you delete a worksheet, 1-2-3 for Windows moves up the remaining worksheets, and adjusts the range references in formulas. For example, if you delete worksheet A, the formula +B:A3+B:A6 becomes +A:A3+A:A5.

You can also use the Delete Sheet SmartIcon to delete worksheets. The Delete Sheet SmartIcon deletes the current worksheet or range of worksheets without first opening the Delete dialog box.

If you delete worksheets that are part of a named range, the named range becomes smaller. If you delete an entire named range, 1-2-3 for Windows deletes the range and its name so that formulas that refer to that range name result in an ERR message.

Tip
Use the Undo SmartIcon or choose **E**dit **U**ndo to reverse a worksheet deletion.

Troubleshooting

When I click the range selector in the Delete dialog box and then highlight the range of worksheets I want to delete, I can't seem to get the Delete dialog box to reappear so that I can complete the command.

When you use the range selector method to highlight a range in a 1-2-3 worksheet or worksheets, make sure to press Enter or click the Confirm button on the Edit line to return to the dialog box and complete the command.

When I delete a worksheet, some of the formulas in my other worksheets evaluate to ERR.

Before you delete a worksheet, make sure that none of the formulas in the remaining worksheets rely on values in the worksheet to be deleted.

Grouping Worksheets

With 1-2-3 for Windows, you can group together all the worksheets in a worksheet file so that formatting changes you make to one worksheet affect all the other worksheets.

To use Group mode, open the **S**tyle menu and choose **W**orksheet Defaults. In the Worksheet Defaults dialog box that appears, select the **G**roup Mode option. When you close the dialog box, the Group mode indicator appears in the status bar at the bottom of the screen (see fig. 7.4).

Fig. 7.4
Grouped
worksheets
displayed in
perspective view.

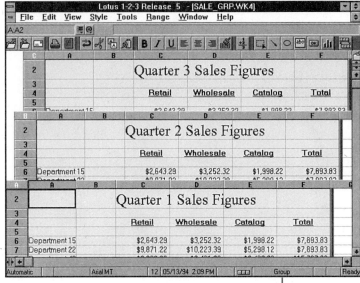

Group mode indicator

In figure 7.4, the **V**iew **S**plit **P**erspective command was used to show the worksheets in perspective view. When you scroll or move the cell pointer, these movements are synchronized within the group so that you always see the same part of each worksheet.

When you select a cell or range in one worksheet in a group, 1-2-3 for Windows selects the same area in all of the worksheets in that group, even though it does not indicate the selection with a highlight. When you format a cell or range in one worksheet, the corresponding cell or range is formatted in all of the other worksheets.

Similarly, if 1-2-3 for Windows is in Group mode, and you use a command that prompts you for a cell address or range, 1-2-3 for Windows does not need the address of the three-dimensional selection that spans the group—it just needs the range in one of the worksheets. When you complete the command, the effect takes place in all worksheets in the group, even though you only referred to cells in one of the worksheets.

If you add one or more new worksheets to a group using the **Edit Insert Sheet** command or the New Sheet button; the new worksheet takes on the formatting and attributes of the active worksheet. However, bear in mind that 1-2-3 for Windows does not copy any data from the active worksheet in a group to the other worksheets; it only copies cell formats and attributes. If Group mode has not been selected before you insert the new worksheets, 1-2-3 for Windows does not copy the current worksheet's formats and settings to the new worksheets.

Caution

If you have turned on Group mode and you delete (or add) rows or columns in one worksheet, you delete (or add) the same rows or columns in all the worksheets in the file.

Troubleshooting

When I type data into one of the worksheets in a grouped worksheet file, nothing appears in the other worksheets.

Groups do not duplicate data you enter—only formatting and style changes.

I want to reformat my consolidation worksheet so that the totals are more prominent. However, I want to keep the formatting of the other, monthly worksheets the same.

To reformat a single worksheet, you need to turn off Group mode so that the formatting changes apply to one worksheet only. To turn off Group mode, choose **S**tyle **W**orksheet Defaults, and deselect the **G**roup mode check box in the Worksheet Defaults dialog box.

From Here...

Now that you have learned how to add, delete, name, and group worksheets in a multiple-worksheet file, you're ready to learn how to work with multiple files and format the data in a file.

- Chapter 8, "Managing Files," teaches you how to manage 1-2-3 for Windows files, how to protect the information in files, and how to take advantage of 1-2-3's ability to have more than one file open in memory at the same time.

■ Chapter 9, "Formatting Worksheets," demonstrates how to enhance the appearance of your worksheets in order to present data efficiently and professionally.

■ Chapter 19, "Linking and Consolidating Worksheets," teaches you how to set up your 1-2-3 files to store and work with data more efficiently, how to create links between worksheet files, and how to consolidate worksheets to take advantage of the worksheet and file management features of 1-2-3 for Windows.

Chapter 8

Managing Files

The commands on the 1-2-3 for Windows **F**ile menu provide a wide range of capabilities for file management, modification, and protection. Some commands, such as **F**ile **O**pen, **F**ile **S**ave, and **F**ile Save **A**s, are similar to commands in other Windows applications. Other commands are related to specific 1-2-3 for Windows tasks and applications. This chapter discusses the **F**ile commands and good file-management techniques for 1-2-3 for Windows.

In this chapter, you learn how to do the following:

- Create new files

- Name files

- Save files

- Close files

- Open existing files

- Change file directories

- Enter and display file information

- Protect files

- Delete files

- Transfer files

- Translate files

- Send mail

Determining which File Type To Use

The type of file you create most often in 1-2-3 for Windows is a worksheet file. 1-2-3 for Windows files are stored in a single file format with the WK4 extension. This file format is used by both Release 4 and Release 5. A worksheet file saves all the data, formulas, and text you enter into a worksheet, as well as the format of cells (including Wysiwyg formatting), the alignment of text, range names, and settings for ranges that are protected. 1-2-3 for Windows can also read the following file formats:

- WKS files (1-2-3 Release 1A); WRK, WR1, and FMS files (Symphony). 1-2-3 creates a copy of the file in Release 5 format, and leaves the original file unchanged. You cannot save file changes in these formats.

- WK1, (1-2-3 Release 2); FMT, and ALL files (1-2-3 Releases 2.01, 2.2, 2.3, and 2.4).

- WK3 and FM3 files (1-2-3 Releases 3, 3.1, 3.1+, 3.4, 4.0, and 1-2-3 Release 1.1 for Windows).

- XLS, XLT, XLW files (Microsoft Excel Releases 2.0, 2.1, 2.2, 3.0, and 4.0). 1-2-3 creates a copy of the file in Release 5 format, and leaves the original file unchanged.

- DBF files (dBASE).

- DB files (Paradox).

- TXT files (text files).

- BAK files (backups of WK4, WK3, and WK1 files).

> **Note**
>
> 1-2-3 for Windows cannot read or write 1-2-3 for OS/2 files. However, you can share files between 1-2-3 for OS/2 and 1-2-3 Release 5 by saving them with the WK3 file extension.

If you use Lotus Notes, you also can open and save 1-2-3 Release 4 and 5 shared (NS4) files containing versions and scenarios created with the Version Manager. See Chapter 30, "Using 1-2-3 with Lotus Notes," and Chapter 22, "Managing Multiple Solutions with Version Manager," for more information on sharing 1-2-3 files with Lotus Notes and using the Version Manager.

Creating Files

When you start 1-2-3, the Welcome to 1-2-3 dialog box opens, asking you if you want to create a new file or work on an existing file. To create a new file, select **C**reate a New Worksheet. This opens the New File dialog box, where you can choose to create a file based on a SmartMaster or create a file with default worksheet settings.

◀ "Understanding Worksheets and Files," p. 60

To create a file based on a predefined template, select a SmartMaster and then click OK. For more information about SmartMasters, see Chapter 34, "Working with Templates and Creating Custom Dialog Boxes."

To create a file with default worksheet settings, mark the **C**reate a Plain Worksheet check box and then click OK.

If you want to create additional new files during the same work session, choose **F**ile **N**ew or click the Create File SmartIcon or the Quick New File SmartIcon. The **F**ile **N**ew command and the Create File SmartIcon open the New File dialog box. The Quick New File SmartIcon opens a new file with a blank worksheet in the current window. Any files that are open when you choose **F**ile **N**ew or click the Create File or Quick New File SmartIcon remain open. The new file becomes an open file and is listed on the **W**indow menu. 1-2-3 assigns temporary file names to new files you create, as described in the next section.

Saving Files

When you create a new worksheet file or when you make changes to an existing file, your work exists only in the computer's memory. If you don't save a new worksheet or the changes you make before you exit 1-2-3 for Windows, you lose your work. Saving a file copies the file from memory onto the disk.

To save your work, choose File **S**ave or File Save **A**s, or click the Save File SmartIcon. If you select **F**ile **S**ave or click the Save File SmartIcon and the file has been saved previously, 1-2-3 saves the file under the current file name without displaying a dialog box. If you select **F**ile Save **A**s (or if you are saving a new file for the first time and use **F**ile **S**ave or click the Save File SmartIcon), 1-2-3 for Windows displays the Save As dialog box shown in figure 8.1.

Fig. 8.1
The Save As dialog box is where you specify the file's name, drive, directory, and file type.

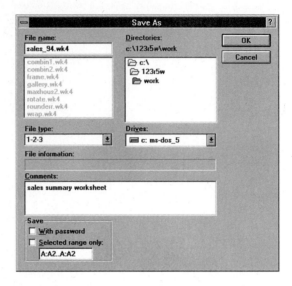

After you specify the save information, choose OK or press Enter. If an existing worksheet file already uses the file name you entered in the Save As dialog box, 1-2-3 displays a message saying that the file already exists. Choose **R**eplace to overwrite the existing file; choose **B**ackup if you want 1-2-3 to make a backup copy of the file; or choose **C**ancel to cancel the save operation.

> **Note**
>
> You also use the Save As dialog box to assign a password or to save only a selected range of cells in the current worksheet. These features are discussed later in this chapter.

Naming Files

When you create a new file, 1-2-3 automatically assigns the file a temporary file name, FILE*nnnn*.WK4, where *nnnn* is replaced with a number. The first temporary file name is FILE0001.WK4. If you create additional new files, 1-2-3 names these files FILE0002.WK4, FILE0003.WK4, and so on, incrementing the numeric portion of the file name with each new file (see fig. 8.2). You can save your work using the temporary file names 1-2-3 assigns, or you can choose a descriptive name.

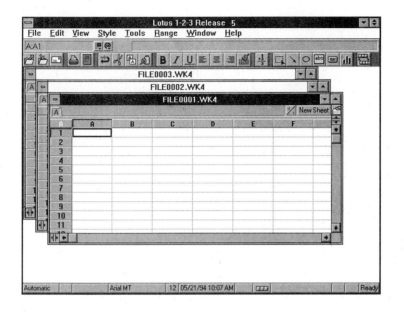

Fig. 8.2
New worksheets—
FILE0001.WK4,
FILE0002.WK4,
FILE0003.WK4—
created during one
work session

The maximum length of a file name is eight characters. A file name can contain any combination of letters, numbers, hyphens, and underscores. However, with the exception of a single period between the file name and the extension, you cannot use any other special characters, such as spaces, commas, backslashes, or periods. In addition, your computer's operating system, DOS, reserves some file names for its use. You cannot use the following as file names:

Tip
Give all your files
descriptive names.
Such names make
it easy to identify
the contents of the
file.

AUX	COM1	LPT1
CLOCK$	COM2	LPT2
CON	COM3	LPT3
NUL	COM4	PRN

The standard file extension for 1-2-3 for Windows worksheet files is WK4. When you open or save a file, type only the descriptive part of the name; 1-2-3 for Windows supplies the appropriate file extension for you. 1-2-3 for Windows uses the file extensions shown in table 8.1.

Table 8.1   File Extensions and Descriptions

Extension	Description
AL3	A file in which named page settings are saved
BAK	A backup copy of a worksheet file
FMB	A backup version of a format file (FM3 and FMT extensions). From earlier releases of 1-2-3, a *format file* is a file that stores a worksheet's style information only.
MAC	A macro for a customized icon
NS4	A 1-2-3 shared file (saved on a Lotus Notes server)
TXT	A text file
WK1	1-2-3 Release 2 worksheet files
WK3	1-2-3 for Windows Release 1 and 1-2-3 for DOS Release 3 files

You can override these standard extensions and type your own, but keep in mind that file extensions help identify the file type. If you use **F**ile **O**pen to open the file BUDGET.WK1, for example, you can tell by the file extension that the file is a 1-2-3 for DOS Release 2 file. If you rename the file to BUDGET.JAN, 1-2-3 for Windows can still identify and translate the file type, but you cannot readily identify the file as a 1-2-3 worksheet file.

 When you choose **F**ile **O**pen or click the Open File SmartIcon, 1-2-3 for Windows lists all the files with extensions beginning with WK. To open a file that has a different extension, you must type the complete file name and extension or use *wild cards* (see "Using Wild Cards to Open Files" later in this chapter).

Note

Sometimes you may want to save a file with a nonstandard extension so that the file does not automatically appear when the Open File dialog box lists files in the current directory. For example, you may want to assign a nonstandard extension to a file that is part of a macro-controlled system so that you don't accidentally open the file outside the macro. The nonstandard extension "hides" the file from the standard list of worksheet files.

Saving a Portion of a File

The **S**elected Range Only option in the Save As dialog box saves data from a cell, range, or worksheet to a new or existing worksheet file (refer to fig. 8.1). You might use this command to save part of a file before you change it, to break a large file into smaller files, to create a partial file for someone else to work on, or to send information to another file. For example, you may want to use this feature to break a large budget file into separate files, each one containing information about a single department's budget. This technique is useful when you need to work with portions of a worksheet's data in separate worksheet files.

The **S**elected Range Only option copies all settings associated with the copied cells, including styles, formats, protection status, range names, column widths, row heights, fonts, and font characteristics.

To save a selected range, follow these steps:

1. Open the worksheet that contains the range you want to save.

2. Select the range.

3. Choose the **F**ile Save **A**s option to display the Save As dialog box.

4. In the File **N**ame box, enter a name for the file in which you want to save the range.

5. Select the **S**elected Range Only check box in the Save As dialog box.

6. Choose OK. 1-2-3 displays the Save Range As dialog box (see fig. 8.3).

Fig. 8.3
The Save Range As dialog box.

7. Select either the F**o**rmulas and Values option or the Val**u**es Only option. When you save a range with the F**o**rmulas and Values option, 1-2-3 for Windows adjusts the addresses in formulas to reflect their new locations in the destination file. The Val**u**es Only option, on the other hand, saves all calculated cells as values.

> **Note**
>
> If you save a range that contains a formula, be certain to include all the cells that the formula refers to; otherwise, the formula does not calculate correctly. If the cells you are saving are part of a named range, you must select the entire range; otherwise, the range name does not refer to the correct cell addresses.

8. Choose OK or press Enter to complete the saving process. 1-2-3 saves the specified range in the specified file. 1-2-3 *doesn't* automatically open the file. To view the file, use the **F**ile **O**pen command to open the file.

Remember that 1-2-3 for Windows also enables you to copy and move data between worksheet files with the **E**dit Cu**t**, **E**dit **C**opy, **E**dit **P**aste, and **E**dit Paste **S**pecial commands. In some cases, using these commands may be just as easy as saving a range of cells. For more information about these commands, see Chapter 6, "Moving or Copying Data."

Saving Files in Other 1-2-3 Formats

▶ "Using the Clipboard for Basic Copying and Pasting," p. 815

1-2-3 Release 5 for Windows enables you to save Release 5 files in file formats used by previous releases of 1-2-3. This feature is useful if you need to send a file to someone who is using an earlier release of 1-2-3. To use this feature, open the **F**ile menu and choose Save **A**s to access the Save As dialog box. Then choose the appropriate file format from the File **T**ype drop-down list box. For example, you can save a 1-2-3 Release 5 worksheet file in a WK1 (1-2-3 for DOS Release 2) format by choosing the 1-2-3 (wk1) option. You can also save a file in the WK3 (1-2-3 for Windows Release 1 or 1-2-3 for DOS Release 3) format by choosing the 1-2-3 (wk3) option (see fig. 8.4). Choosing these options adds the WK1 or WK3 extension to the file name. If you prefer, you can simply type the file name with the WK1 or WK3 extension in the File **N**ame text box.

Although saving 1-2-3 for Windows files in 1-2-3 WK1 or WK3 format is possible, you lose some of the worksheet information in the conversion because 1-2-3 Release 5 supports features that some earlier releases of 1-2-3 do not support. When you save the file, 1-2-3 warns you that you may lose some worksheet information, such as the following:

■ For a WK1 file, versions and scenarios created with the Version Manager

■ Queries and query tables

- Drawn objects (not including charts)

- Embedded data from other Windows applications

- Worksheet settings (including tabs for a WK1 file, range names, default text, and cell background colors)

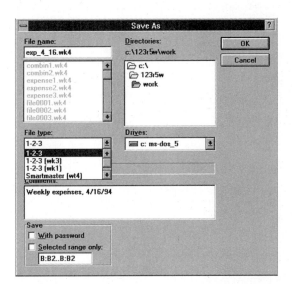

Fig. 8.4
The File **T**ype drop-down list box in the Save As dialog box.

You can also save a file as a SmartMaster template with a WT4 file extension. To do so, choose SmartMaster (WT4) from the File **T**ype drop-down list in the Save As dialog box. Then type a file name, and press Enter or click OK.

▶ "Creating a SmartMaster," p. 1011

Troubleshooting

I want to use 1-2-3 for Windows to rename a worksheet file without returning to the Windows File Manager, but can't find the command to rename a file.

Technically, you cannot rename the file from within 1-2-3. A command does not exist on the **F**ile menu for renaming files. However, you can save a copy of the file under a new name by using the **F**ile Save **A**s command. The old file still exists under its original name, but 1-2-3 also creates a copy of the file under the new name you specify. If you no longer need the original file, you can return to DOS or the Windows File Manager at your convenience to delete the file.

Closing Files

 Closing a file is not the same as saving a file. *Closing* a file removes the file from the screen and from memory without necessarily saving it. *Saving* a file saves the changes and keeps the file open. When you finish working with a file, choose **File Close** or click the Close Window SmartIcon to remove the current file from the screen and from the list of open files on the **W**indow menu. If you have made unsaved changes to the file when you select **File Close** or click the Close Window SmartIcon, 1-2-3 displays a warning that allows you to save the recent changes. Choose **Y**es to save changes, **N**o to close the file without saving changes, or **C**ancel to return to working on the file.

 You can use the **File Exit** command and the End 1-2-3 Session SmartIcon to exit the 1-2-3 program; these commands don't automatically close all open files, however. If you choose **File Exit** or click the End 1-2-3 Session SmartIcon while files are still open, 1-2-3 gives you the opportunity to save any open files that have been changed but not yet saved.

Tip

If you are working with many files at one time, close any files that you are finished with. Closing files frees up memory, enabling you to work more efficiently with the files that remain open.

Opening Existing Files

By using the **File Open** command, you can open an existing file without closing the current file. 1-2-3 displays the file you open in the current window. The file that was current before you opened the new file remains active, but the new file becomes the current file in the current window. If other worksheet files are open, they remain open and are unaffected by the file you open. (All open files are listed on the **W**indow menu.)

 To open a file, choose **File Open** or click the Open File SmartIcon to display the Open File dialog box (see fig. 8.5). The current directory name appears above the **D**irectories box. For example, in fig. 8.5, the current directory is c:\123R5W\work. Work is a subdirectory of 123R5W, and 123R5W is a directory on drive c. Each directory is indented under its parent directory and under drive c:\.

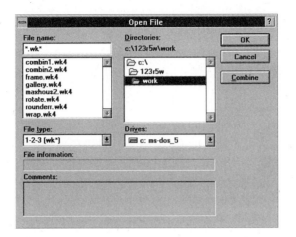

Fig. 8.5
The Open File
dialog box.

Everyday Worksheet Tasks

In the File **n**ame text box, 1-2-3 automatically enters `*.wk*` so that worksheet files are listed in the Files list box. Click the name of the file you want to open, or type the file name in the File **n**ame text box. Then click OK to open the file.

Opening Multiple Files at Once

You can also use the Open File dialog box to open multiple files at once—up to 32 at one time. Note, however, that the files must all be in the same directory.

To open multiple files, choose one of the following procedures:

- Type a series of file names in the File **N**ame text box, separating each name with a space.

- Click a file name to select it; then press and hold Ctrl and click any additional file names (up to 32).

- Click the first in a series of file names to select it; then press and hold Shift, and click the last file name in the series. 1-2-3 selects all the files between and including the two file names you selected.

- Drag the mouse over a list of file names to select them.

Once you have typed in or selected the names of the files you want to open, click OK to open the files. 1-2-3 opens multiple files alphabetically by file name.

▶ "Understanding the Guidelines for Creating Macros," p. 1042

Note

If more than one of the files you select to open has an autoexecute macro, 1-2-3 runs the autoexecute macro in the last file it opens.

Opening Files from Subdirectories and Other Drives

Often, the file you want to open is stored in a different directory, so the file name isn't currently shown in the Files list box. To list the file name in the Files list box, you must first select the correct directory name from the **D**irectories list box.

The directory where the file is stored could be a parent directory to the current directory, or it could be a subdirectory to the current directory. To select a parent directory, double-click any of the directory names listed *above* the current directory in the **D**irectories list box. (For instance, in fig. 8.5, you could double-click 123R5W, or you could double-click c:\ to list all directories on drive c.) To select a subdirectory, double-click the directory name listed *below* the current directory in the Directories list box. (In fig. 8.5, the work directory doesn't contain any subdirectories.)

When you have selected the correct directory by double-clicking it, 1-2-3 lists all files with a .wk* extension in that directory. (If necessary, use the scroll bar or arrow keys to display all entries.) To list *all* files in the current directory, replace the .wk* entry in the File **N**ame text box with *.*. Then click OK to update the list. Alternatively, you can display all files of a different file type by entering the correct file extension. Select the file you want to open, and then click OK.

If the file you want to open is stored on another drive, select the appropriate drive in the **D**rives drop-down list. When you select a different drive, 1-2-3 displays all files with a .wk* file extension in the last directory you used on that drive. To select a different directory, follow the guidelines in the previous paragraph. Remember that you can also list all files in the current directory by typing *.* in the File **N**ame text box and clicking OK. Select a file from the files list, and then choose OK.

Using Wild Cards to Open Files

In the Open File dialog box, you can include an asterisk (*) or a question mark (?) as *wild card characters* (often just called *wild cards*) in the File **N**ame box. Wild cards act as placeholders that match one character or any number of characters in sequence. The ? wild card matches any one character in the file name. The * matches any number of characters in sequence. When you use wild cards in a File **N**ame text box, 1-2-3 for Windows lists only the files whose names match the wild card. In fact, 1-2-3 uses the * wild card by default each time the Open File dialog box is displayed (refer to fig. 8.5).

The *.wk* in the File **N**ame box tells 1-2-3 to list all files with file extensions that begin with .WK followed by any number of other characters. Suppose that you type **????TREE.WK*** in the File **N**ame text box shown in figure 8.5. 1-2-3 for Windows lists all the file names that start with any four characters, followed by TREE and an extension beginning with WK; examples are AUDITREE.WK4, BACKTREE.WK3, SOLVTREE.WK1, and VIEWTREE.WK. If you type **BUDGET*.***, 1-2-3 for Windows lists all the file names that start with BUDGET, such as BUDGET.WK4, BUDGET1.TXT, and BUDGET99.WK3.

Opening a File Automatically When You Start 1-2-3

When you first start 1-2-3 for Windows, you can display a blank worksheet or a worksheet based on a SmartMaster, see the earlier section "Creating Files." However, if you usually begin a work session using the same worksheet file, you can tell 1-2-3 to automatically display that worksheet when the program starts. You do this by naming the file AUTO123.WK4 and placing it in the default directory.

Another way to open a specific worksheet in 1-2-3 is to use the Windows File Manager. Without starting 1-2-3, open the File Manager. In the File Manager window, select the 123R5W directory (or a subdirectory where the file is located) to display all the files in the directory (see fig. 8.6). Double-click the name of the file you want to open. Because worksheet files have a WK4 file extension, the file you select is associated with the 1-2-3 for Windows program. When you double-click the file name, the Windows File Manager starts 1-2-3 for Windows and opens the file.

Fig. 8.6

Double-click the name of a 1-2-3 for Windows file in the File Manager to start 1-2-3 for Windows and open the file in one step.

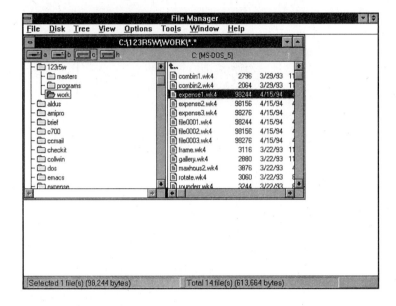

Opening Recently Used Files

1-2-3 provides a convenient feature that enables you to quickly open the files you used most recently. This feature saves you the trouble of selecting a file name from the Open File dialog box when you want to open a file. By default, 1-2-3 lists the five most recently read files at the bottom of the File menu. To open a recently read file, you click its name.

To change the number of files displayed, choose the **T**ools User **S**etup command. In the User Setup dialog box (shown in figure 8.7), enter a number between 0 and 5 in the Number of Recent **F**iles to Show box, and then click the OK button. 1-2-3 adds the names of the files (up to the number you specify) at the bottom of the **F**ile menu. To open a file, simply click the file name on the **F**ile menu.

Fig. 8.7
The User Setup
dialog box.

Opening Spreadsheet Files from Other Programs

1-2-3 Release 5 for Windows enables you to open files from previous releases
of 1-2-3, from Lotus Symphony, and from Microsoft Excel. Table 8.2 lists
these programs and their file extensions.

Table 8.2	Spreadsheet Programs and File Extensions
Extension	**Program**
WK3, FM3	1-2-3 for Windows Release 1; 1-2-3 for DOS Release 3
WKS	1-2-3 for DOS Release 1A
WK1, ALL, FMT	1-2-3 for DOS Release 2
WRK	Symphony Release 1.0 and 1.01
WR1, FMS	Symphony Release 1.1, 1.2, 2.0, 2.1, 2.2, and 3.0
XLS	Microsoft Excel version 2.1, 2.2, 3.0, and 4.0
DB	Paradox version 3.5 and 4.0
DBF	dBASE version III+ and dBASE IV version 1.5 or earlier and FoxPro 2.0.

To open any of these files, select the file from the correct directory in the Open File dialog box, and then click OK. You can save 1-2-3 and Symphony files in their original file formats, or you can save them as 1-2-3 Release 4 or 5 (WK4) files. Keep in mind, however, that if you add features to the file that are available only in 1-2-3 Release 4 or 5, these features are lost when you save the file in its original file format. See "Saving Files in Other 1-2-3 Formats" earlier in this chapter for more information.

Troubleshooting

I tried to open a 1-2-3 file from the Windows File Manager and got an error message No application is associated with this file.

You tried to open a file that 1-2-3 cannot open or display. You must choose a valid worksheet file with a WK4 file extension or other format that 1-2-3 understands. Try again, using the correct file type.

I tried to open a file by clicking the file name listed at the bottom of the File menu, but 1-2-3 says File does not exist. *What's wrong?*

The file is no longer available from the location in which you last opened it. It has been deleted, renamed, or moved to a different directory. If the file has not been deleted, open the file by using **F**ile **O**pen, and 1-2-3 will remember its new location the next time you select the file name from the **F**ile menu.

Changing Your Working Directory

As discussed earlier in this chapter in the section "Opening Existing Files," a hard disk is divided into a number of *directories* and *subdirectories* that store related data files. The list of directories that leads from the root directory (usually c:\) to the file you want is the *path* or *path name*.

If you installed 1-2-3 for Windows according to the instructions in Appendix A, your worksheet files are stored in the path C:\123R4W\WORK. This directory is called your *working directory*. Each time you choose **F**ile **O**pen, **F**ile **S**ave, or **F**ile Save **A**s, 1-2-3 automatically assumes you want to save files to open files in your working directory.

To organize your work, you may have created other directories and subdirectories under 123R5W. If so, you might want 1-2-3 to save files automatically to a different directory. You use the **T**ools **U**ser Setup command to specify a new working directory. In the User Setup dialog box (shown in figure 8.7), enter a new path name in the **W**orksheet directory text box, and then choose OK to change the working directory for the current and all future work sessions.

Entering and Viewing File Information

You can keep track of useful information about files using the Doc Info dialog box. To open the Doc Info dialog box, choose **F**ile **D**oc Info (see fig. 8.8).

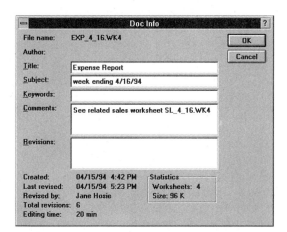

Fig. 8.8
The Doc Info dialog box.

The Doc Info dialog box also displays statistics about the file, including the file size and the number of worksheets. You also can use this dialog box to view information about revisions and total editing time. To update document information, type the desired changes in the text boxes, and click OK.

You can enter a title and a subject for your file in the Doc Info box, as well as comments about the file, which appear when you select the file name in the Open File or Save As dialog box. You can also enter a keyword or keywords to share file information with Lotus Notes. For more information about key-words, see Chapter 30, "Using 1-2-3 with Lotus Notes."

Protecting Files

1-2-3 for Windows offers two methods of protecting files. You can protect confidential worksheet files by assigning a *password* when you save the file, or you can *seal* a file to prevent unauthorized changes. When you save a file with a password, no one can open, copy, or print the file without first issuing the password. When you seal a file, no one can make changes to a file's reservation status or to the data and styles in the worksheet.

Assigning Passwords

You assign a password to a file by using the **F**ile Save **A**s dialog box, as explained in the following steps:

1. Open the file you want to protect.

2. Choose **F**ile Save **A**s to display the Save As dialog box (see fig. 8.9).

Fig. 8.9
The Save As dialog box with the **W**ith password check box selected.

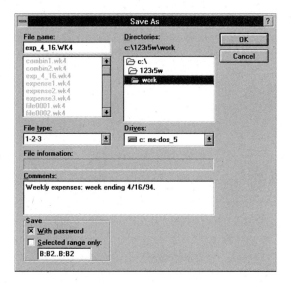

3. Type a new file name in the File **N**ame text box or leave the file name unchanged.

4. Select the **W**ith password check box, and then click OK. 1-2-3 for Windows displays the Set Password dialog box (see fig. 8.10).

5. In the **P**assword text box, type a password. For security, 1-2-3 displays an asterisk (*) for each character you type.

6. In the **V**erify text box, type the password again exactly as you typed it before. Again, 1-2-3 displays asterisks in place of the characters you type.

7. Select OK.

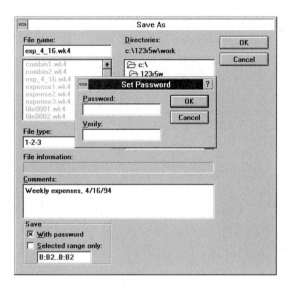

Fig. 8.10
The Set Password
dialog box.

Everyday Worksheet Tasks

If, in the File **N**ame box, you enter a file name that already exists, 1-2-3 for Windows asks whether you want to replace the existing file, back up the existing file, or cancel saving the file. You must select **R**eplace or **B**ackup to save the file with the password. If you select Cancel, 1-2-3 for Windows doesn't assign the password and returns to the Worksheet window. If the file doesn't already exist, the password is assigned automatically.

A password can contain any combination of uppercase or lowercase characters. It's best not to use obvious passwords such as your birth date, license plate number, children's or pet's names. Because longer passwords are more difficult for someone to guess, phrases with no spaces between words (such as **itrainsinapril**) work well. As you enter the password, 1-2-3 for Windows displays an asterisk for each character you type. Remember that passwords are case-sensitive; if you specify **JustForMe** as the password, typing **justforme** to open the file does not work.

Caution

Remember your password exactly as you type it. You cannot open the file again unless you enter the password in precisely the same way.

Opening a Password-Protected File

When you try to open a password-protected file by using **F**ile **O**pen, 1-2-3 for Windows prompts you for the password. You must enter the password exactly as you originally entered it, with the correct upper- and lowercase letters. If you make an error as you enter the password, an error message appears, saying that you entered an invalid password. Try opening the file again, using the correct password.

Changing and Deleting Passwords

You can change or delete a file's password at any time, provided you know the current password. To change a password, follow these steps:

1. Open the **F**ile menu and choose **O**pen or use the Open File SmartIcon to open the file.

2. Type the name of the current password in the Get Password dialog box and click OK. 1-2-3 opens the file.

3. Open the **F**ile menu and choose Save **A**s and make sure the With password check box is selected, and then click OK.

4. Type a new password in the **P**assword and **V**erify text boxes.

5. Click OK. 1-2-3 displays a message saying that the file already exists.

6. Choose **R**eplace or **B**ackup to save the file with the new password.

To remove a password from a file, follow these steps:

1. Open the **F**ile menu and choose **O**pen or use the Open File SmartIcon to open the file.

2. Type the name of the current password in the Get Password dialog box and click OK. 1-2-3 opens the file.

3. Open the **F**ile menu and choose Save **A**s, and then turn off the **W**ith password check box.

4. Click OK. 1-2-3 displays a message saying that the file already exists.

5. Choose **R**eplace or **B**ackup to save the file without a password.

Sealing a File to Prevent Changes

Sealing a file prevents a user from changing data, styles, or other settings used in the file. When a file is sealed, you cannot insert or delete columns, show hidden worksheets or columns, change, add, or delete range names, page breaks, frozen titles, or set new formats, column widths, row heights, or cell alignments.

You seal a file when you want other users to be able to open and read the file, but not change it. A sealed file is also password-protected. Although you can open and read the file without knowing the password, you must know the password to change the file in any way. The password protection on a sealed file allows you to give read access to a large group of users while giving only one or a few users the authority to change the file. (Without the password protection, only the user who creates the file can change it.)

To seal a file, follow these steps:

1. Choose the File **P**rotect command to display the Protect dialog box, shown in figure 8.11.

2. Choose the **S**eal File check box, and then click OK. 1-2-3 displays the Set Password dialog box, the same dialog box used to save a file with a password (refer to fig. 8.10).

3. Type the password in the **P**assword text box, and then type the password a second time in the **V**erify text box. Just like when you save a file with a password, you can use any combination of upper- and lowercase characters in the password.

4. Click OK to seal the file.

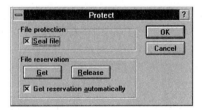

Fig. 8.11
The Protect dialog box.

Protecting Selected Cells or a Range

In some cases, you may want users to be able to change certain cells in a file, even though the file is sealed. You can leave certain cells unprotected by using the **S**tyle **P**rotection command *before* you seal the file. First, select the cells you want unprotected, and then choose **S**tyle **P**rotection to display the Protection dialog box, shown in figure 8.12.

Fig. 8.12

The Protection
dialog box.

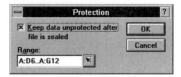

The Range box shows the range of cells you selected. Select the **K**eep data
unprotected after file is sealed option, and then ciick OK. Now that a range of
cells has been set as unprotected, you can seal the file using the steps outlined in the preceding section. When a sealed file contains unprotected cells,
the status bar displays Pr when the cell pointer is in a protected cell and U
when the cell pointer is in an unprotected cell.

Remember that sealing a file is different from protecting a file with a password. Saving a file with a password prevents *all* access to the file unless the
user knows the password. When the file is open, however, a user can change
it. When you seal a file, other users can open and read the file and make
changes to any unprotected cells. Without a password, however, they cannot
change data, styles, or other settings in protected cells.

Reserving Shared Files

If you use 1-2-3 for Windows on a network, two or more people can read the
same file at the same time. If more than one person can change a file at the
same time, the result can be inaccurate data or formulas. To avoid multiple
updates of the same shared file, 1-2-3 for Windows has a *reservation* system.
1-2-3 for Windows also enables you to hide and protect confidential data in a
shared file.

The **F**ile **P**rotect command displays the Protect dialog box, which enables you
to **G**et or **R**elease a file reservation or change a file reservation setting to automatic or manual (refer to fig. 8.11). By default, 1-2-3 for Windows gives you
the reservation when you open a shared file. If you try to open a shared file
that someone else is currently working on, 1-2-3 for Windows displays a message box that asks whether you want to open the file without having the
reservation. If you select **Y**es, you can read the file and change the data, but
you cannot save the changes to the same file name. You can, however, save
the file with another name so that your changes are preserved.

If you have the reservation for a file, you keep the reservation until you close
the file, or you can release the reservation by using **F**ile **P**rotect **R**elease. The
file is still open on your computer, but you cannot save the file under the
same name because you no longer have the reservation.

You can change the setting for a file so that a user must get the reservation manually instead of automatically. To change the default, deselect the **F**ile **P**rotect Get reservation **a**utomatically check box. Now, anyone who opens the file has read-only access until one user reserves the file using the **F**ile **P**rotect **G**et command.

You can seal a file's reservation setting after you change it so that no one else can change the setting. Select **F**ile **P**rotect and choose the **S**eal file option. When 1-2-3 displays the Set Password dialog box, enter a password in the **P**assword and **V**erify text boxes. (Passwords are case-sensitive.) Remember the password exactly as you type it. If you or someone else later tries to change the reservation setting, 1-2-3 for Windows prompts for the password.

Troubleshooting

I want to leave a range of cells in a sealed file unprotected, but the Protection command is unavailable (grayed) on the Style menu. How can I unprotect a cell range?

To leave a range of cells unprotected in a sealed file, you must use **S**tyle **P**rotection *before* you seal the file. Unseal the file, use **S**tyle **P**rotection, and then reseal the file.

How can I seal one worksheet in a file that contains multiple worksheets?

1-2-3 doesn't allow you to seal individual worksheets in a file. If you want only one worksheet sealed, copy or save that worksheet to its own file and seal that file.

I can't remember the password for a spreadsheet I created some time ago. How can I display a list of all the current passwords?

You can't. Passwords are intended to restrict *all* access to a file and, therefore, are not recorded anywhere except with the file itself. If you forget the password, you can't reopen the file; all you can do is re-create the spreadsheet.

I am trying to open an Excel file (XLS) in 1-2-3 Release 5 for Windows but can't open the file. What's wrong?

Check to see whether the Excel file is password protected. If so, remove the password from the Excel file before opening it in 1-2-3.

Deleting Files

When you create and save a file, the file occupies disk space. Eventually, you run out of disk space if you do not occasionally delete old, unneeded files from the disk. Even if you have disk space left, you have more difficulty finding the files you want to open if the disk contains many obsolete files.

Tip
Before you delete
old files, you may
want to save them
to a floppy disk in
case you need
them again.

1-2-3 for Windows does not have a command on the **F**ile menu for deleting unneeded files. You must use the Windows File Manager or a DOS command.

Transferring Files

1-2-3 for Windows provides a number of ways to pass data between, to, and from other programs. The simplest method is to save or print a file as a text file or an ASCII file. Most programs, including spreadsheets, word processors, and database management systems, can create and read text files. To create a text file in 1-2-3 for Windows, use **F**ile Save **A**s and choose the Text (txt) option in the File **T**ype drop-down list. For more information, refer to Part VI, "Integrating 1-2-3."

Translating Files

You may have worksheet or database files from other programs that you would like to use in 1-2-3 Release 4. Although you can't convert a file directly to Release 4 and 5 format, you can use the Translate utility to convert the file to Release 3 format first, and then save it in Release 4 and 5 format.

> **Note**
>
> The Translate utility does not ship with 1-2-3 Release 5 for Windows. To receive a copy of the Translate utility, you need to call Lotus Customer Service or download the utility from CompuServe.

If you need to use a 1-2-3 Release 3 file in another database or spreadsheet program, you can also use the Translate utility to convert files from 1-2-3 Release 3 format. The Translate utility supports the following programs when you are converting files from 1-2-3 Release 3 format:

Lotus 1-2-3 Release 1A

Lotus 1-2-3 Release 2

Lotus 1-2-3 Release 3

dBASE III and dBASE III+

DIF

Enable Version 2.0

Multiplan 4.2

SuperCalc4

Symphony 1 and 1.01

Symphony 1.1, 1.2, and 2

The Translate utility converts the following program files to 1-2-3 Release 3 format:

dBASE III and dBASE III+

DIF

Enable 2.0

Multiplan 4.2

SuperCalc4

The Translate utility runs outside of the 1-2-3 Release 5 for Windows program. You access it by clicking the Translate icon in the Lotus Applications group in the Program Manager.

The Translate Utility screen shows programs to translate *from* on the left and programs to translate *to* on the right. Instructions appear at the bottom of each screen throughout the translation process. To choose items in the From and To boxes, use the up- and down-arrow keys, and then press Enter.

Follow the instructions shown on-screen to translate a file or multiple files at once. The following steps briefly review those shown on-screen:

1. In the From list, use the up- and down-arrow keys to select a program or file format from which to translate, and then press Enter.

2. The Translate utility highlights the To list. Choose a program or file format to which to translate, and then press Enter. A screen appears explaining what the Translate utility does not translate.

3. Press Esc to clear the screen. The Translate utility displays the current directory name and lists files that have the file extension for the program (or file format) from which you are translating. If necessary, you can change to a different directory by editing the directory name currently shown.

4. Using the arrow keys, highlight the file you want to translate, and then press the space bar to select the file. Repeat this step to select and

Tip

For step-by-step instructions on using the Translate utility while the utility is open, press F1 at any time.

translate additional files. Press Enter when all files you want to translate are selected.

5. Enter the directory name to which you want to translate the selected files. Press Enter and follow the instructions as shown on-screen.

Sending Mail

 Electronic mail systems allow you to communicate with other users of electronic mail by sending and receiving files and messages via your computer. To use electronic mail, your computer must be connected to a computer network or have access to a computer network (for example, via a modem) running an electronic mail program. You can then use the Send **M**ail command on 1-2-3's **F**ile menu, the Send E-mail SmartIcon, or the {SEND-MAIL} macro command to send an entire file or a portion of a file (range, chart, or object) as an electronic mail message. (For more information about macro commands, see Part VIII, "Automating with Macros.")

You can send mail from 1-2-3 for Windows using Lotus Notes, cc:Mail for Windows, VIM mail applications, and Microsoft Mail.

Setting Up Windows to Launch Your Mail Program

You can set up 1-2-3 for Windows to launch your mail program when you choose **F**ile Send **M**ail, use the Send E-mail SmartIcon, or use the {SEND-MAIL} macro command by adding the following lines to your WIN.INI file. (In each of these examples, substitute your path to your mail program if different from the path in the example.

For Lotus Notes add these lines:

```
[LOTUSMAIL]
Application=Notes
Program=C:\notes\notes.exe
For cc:Mail for Windows, add these lines:
[LOTUSMAIL]
Application=wMail
Program=C:\ccmail\wmail.exe SendMail
For VIM mail applications, add these lines:
MAIL
SMI=1
For MicroSoft mail add these lines:
[MAIL]
MAPI-1
```

Sending a Mail Message

To send an electronic mail message, choose **F**ile Send **M**ail, click the Send E-Mail SmartIcon, or use the {SEND-MAIL} macro command. This opens the Send Mail dialog box (see fig. 8.13). You can use this dialog box to select the following mail options:

- Choose Message Only to send a message without attaching a 1-2-3 file. This option starts your mail application, if it is not already active, or switches you to your active mail application.

- Choose the Save and Attach File option to save a copy of the current file and attach it to a mail message. Then click OK. If you have not yet saved the file, 1-2-3 opens the Save As dialog box. After you name and save the file, a dialog box from your mail application opens. If you have saved the file and select this option, a dialog box from your mail application opens. For information about your mail application, see the documentation.

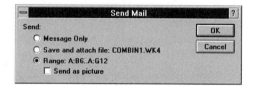

Fig. 8.13
Use the Send Mail dialog box to send a mail message only, a file, or a range.

Sending a Range in a Mail Message

You can choose to send a range in a mail message. When you do so, 1-2-3 attaches a file to the mail message that consists of a worksheet containing the range, a box for your comments, and command buttons for mailing the message. To send a range, follow these steps:

1. Highlight the range you want to send.

2. Open the **F**ile menu and choose Send **M**ail. The Send Mail dialog box opens.

3. Click OK to verify the range selection. The Send Range As dialog box appears.

4. Choose either the **F**ormulas and Values or the **V**alues Only option button and click OK. **F**ormulas and Values leaves the formulas in the range as is. **V**alues Only converts the formulas to values.

1-2-3 opens a file with a text box containing your name and today's date, **S**end and Cancel command buttons, and the range you specified.

5. Enter any additional text in the text box. You can also edit the range, or send it on as it is.

6. Click **S**end. The Send dialog box appears (see fig. 8.14).

Fig. 8.14
Use the Send dialog box to route your messages in a sequence or all at once.

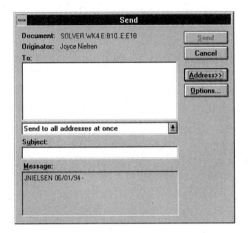

7. Enter the names of people you want to receive the range in the To list box by separating the names with commas or pressing Enter after each name.

8. From the drop-down list, choose either Route to Addresses in Sequence or Send to All Addresses at Once. If you choose to send the message to addresses in sequence, make sure you've entered the correct order of names in the To list box. You can use range routing to get a series of responses to the information in a range you send.

9. Enter a S**u**bject for your message. You can also choose to work with your mail program's name and address book and specify tracking options.

10. Choose OK. 1-2-3 sends the range to the addressees.

> **Note**
>
> You can click the cc:Mail SmartIcon to start cc:Mail, or the Lotus Notes SmartIcon to start Notes. However, clicking these SmartIcons doesn't open the Send Mail dialog box.

From Here...

Now that you have learned how to manage files, you are ready to learn how to enhance the data you present in files so that it is professional-looking, emphasizes important information, and is easy to read.

- Chapter 9, "Formatting Worksheets," demonstrates how to enhance the appearance of your worksheets. You learn about setting column widths and row heights, and defining styles and number formats to enhance the appearance of your data.

- Chapter 19, "Linking and Consolidating Worksheets," teaches you how to set up your 1-2-3 files to store and work with data more efficiently, how to create links between worksheet files, and how to consolidate worksheets to take advantage of the worksheet and file management features of 1-2-3 for Windows.

Chapter 9

Formatting Worksheets

Although you can create a perfectly acceptable worksheet for your personal use using a plain worksheet template with default font and color settings, 1-2-3 for Windows provides many features that let you format your worksheets so that they present your data in a professional, easy-to-read fashion (see fig. 9.1). When you first create a file by choosing File New, 1-2-3 gives you the option of choosing from the available SmartMasters, templates for common business tasks that pre-format your worksheets, charts, and forms for you. Once you assign a SmartMaster, you can use many of the Style commands, SmartIcons, and status bar buttons to customize your worksheet. You also can choose to create a plain worksheet when you start a new file, and then format your data as you enter it, also using commands on the Style menu, SmartIcons, and formatting buttons on the status bar.

	May Sales Figures			
	Retail	Wholesale	Catalog	Total
Department 15	$2,643.29	$3,252.32	$1,998.22	$7,893.83
Department 22	$9,871.22	$10,223.39	$5,298.12	$7,893.83
Department 43	$2,398.23	$3,431.99	$2,498.22	$15,787.66
Department 51	$8,098.22	$12,311.49	$3,342.12	$31,575.32
Department 63	$3,210.99	$3,535.11	$1,927.23	$63,150.64
Total	$26,221.95	$32,754.30	$15,063.91	$126,301.28

Fig. 9.1
A formatted, professional-looking worksheet.

This chapter discusses the many ways you can format your worksheets. You learn how to:

- Work with column widths and row heights

- Change column widths and row heights in Group mode

- Set global and worksheet style defaults

- Format text and numbers

▶ "Using the Standard SmartIcon Palettes," p. 979

▶ "Using Worksheet Templates," p. 995

▶ "Creating Your Own Templates," p. 1010

- Change colors and add borders to cells and ranges
- Work with styles

Setting Column Widths

When you start a new, plain worksheet (and do not assign a SmartMaster template), the default column width of all columns is nine characters. You may need to change the width of a column or the height of a row to display data properly. If columns are too narrow, asterisks appear instead of numbers in the cells, and labels are truncated if the cell to the right of a long label contains data. If columns are too wide, you may not be able to see enough data on-screen or print enough data on one page.

> **Note**
>
> 1-2-3 may display more or fewer characters than you expect in a cell. The column-width number approximates the number of characters that can be displayed. The actual display depends on the typeface and point size of the cell and the individual characters you have entered in the cell.

You can change the width of all the columns in the worksheet or the width of individual columns.

Whether a number can fit into a cell depends on both the column width and the format of the number. For example, some worksheets are formatted so that negative numbers appear with parentheses. This makes every negative number two extra characters long. If a number appears as a row of asterisks, you can change the column width, the format, or both to display the number itself.

Changing the Default Column Width

You can change the column width for the entire worksheet by using the **S**tyle **W**orksheet Defaults command. In the Worksheet Defaults dialog box (see fig. 9.2), specify the new column width, from 1 to 240 characters, in the Column **w**idth text box, and choose OK or press Enter. This new setting is applied as the default column width for the current worksheet; any columns you insert use the new width. 1-2-3 also immediately adjusts the widths of all columns in the worksheet not formatted locally (set earlier to specific individual widths).

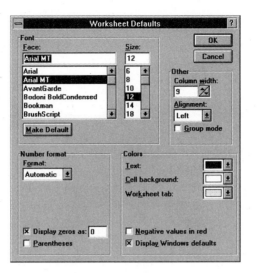

Fig. 9.2
The Column width
text box in the
Worksheet
Defaults dialog
box.

Everyday Worksheet Tasks

Note

Individual column-width settings override the global column width. If you change the global column width after changing the width of individual columns, the individual columns retain their previously adjusted widths.

Changing Individual Column Widths

You can change the width of one or more columns by using the keyboard and the **S**tyle **C**olumn Width command. Alternatively, you can use the mouse to change the width of one or more columns.

To change the width of an individual column or a range of columns, follow these steps:

1. Select a cell or range in the column you want to change.

2. Choose **S**tyle **C**olumn Width. The Column Width dialog box appears (see fig. 9.3).

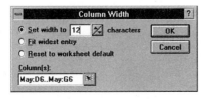

Fig. 9.3
The Column
Width dialog box.

3. Type the new column width, from 1 to 240 characters, in the Set Width To text box or use the scroll arrow to set the new value.

4. If you didn't preselect the column you want to change, you can specify the column or columns you want to change in the **C**olumn(s) text box.

5. Press Enter or click OK.

Fig. 9.4

The Date/Time/ Style indicator on the status bar, set to display the current column width and row height.

Date/Time/Style indicator

You can change the width of several columns by selecting a range that includes several columns before you issue the command. All columns represented in the range are affected when you use the **S**tyle **C**olumn Width command.

Tip

To display the width of the current column in a button on the status bar, click the Date/Time/Style indicator once to display the column width and row height instead of the date and time (see fig. 9.4). If several columns are selected and contain different widths, the indicator is blank.

To change the width of an individual column with the mouse, use these steps:

1. Move the mouse pointer to the column border (to the right of the column letter in the worksheet frame) until the mouse pointer changes to a double-arrow pointing horizontally.

2. Press and hold the left mouse button.

3. Drag the column border to the left or right to its new position and release the mouse button.

When you use the mouse to change the width of a column, 1-2-3 for Windows displays a solid vertical line that moves with the mouse pointer to show you the position of the new column border.

You can change several columns at once with the mouse by clicking the first column's heading (for example, the letter C for column C) and dragging to highlight additional columns (see fig. 9.5). Then adjust the width of any one of the highlighted columns, and the widths of all the columns change to match the width of the column whose border you drag.

Fig. 9.5

Change the width of several columns at once with the mouse.

Fitting the Column Width to the Data

You can set up a column in a 1-2-3 worksheet so that its width automatically conforms to the longest data entry in the column. Using this feature ensures that every column width will accommodate long entries. You can adjust the column width to fit the widest entry in the column by using one of three methods:

- Double-click the right border of the column heading.

- Choose **S**tyle **C**olumn Width, specify **F**it widest entry in the Column Width dialog box, specify the range in the **C**olumn text box (if you didn't preselect the range), and choose OK or press Enter.

- Place the cell pointer in any cell in the column and click the Size Column SmartIcon.

When you use any of these methods, 1-2-3 for Windows immediately adjusts the column width to match the widest entry in the column.

Restoring the Default Width

To reset an individual column width to the worksheet default, select a cell in the column and choose **R**eset to worksheet default from the **C**olumn Width dialog box. Alternatively, you can choose the **S**tyle **C**olumn Width command and then specify the column(s) you want to reset in the **C**olumn(s) text box.

Changing Column Widths in Group Mode

Individual column widths and global column widths can apply to several worksheets if you first group them together with Group mode. In Group mode, all the worksheets change column widths at the same time based on changes made to a single worksheet's column settings.

Use Group mode when you want all of the worksheets in a file to have the same format—for example, when each worksheet contains the same data for a different department or division. When you group worksheets together, any formatting change (such as setting column widths) made to one worksheet in the group affects all the worksheets in that group.

> **Caution**
>
> You cannot group a selected range of worksheets in a file (and exclude individual worksheets). When you select **G**roup mode in the Worksheet Defaults dialog box, any changes you make to one worksheet apply to all worksheets in the file. You should therefore exercise caution when selecting the **G**roup mode option.

◀ "Grouping Worksheets," p. 277

Tip

To restore a column's width to the global column width, choose **S**tyle **C**olumn Width and select the **R**eset to worksheet default option in the Column Width dialog box.

Everyday Worksheet Tasks

> **Troubleshooting**
>
> *I changed the global column width for the entire worksheet, but some columns did not change.*
>
> Any columns you have manually adjusted are not affected by the global column width changes. You can reset any column to the worksheet default by using the **S**tyle **C**olumn Width command and specifying **R**eset to Worksheet Default.
>
> *Do I have to expand a column's width just because text entries spill over the edge of the column?*
>
> No. Text can spill over the edge of a column without problems. However, if the next column contains data, that data will hide any data that doesn't fit in the current column width.
>
> *I want to adjust the widths of several nonadjacent columns at once.*
>
> Select nonadjacent columns by holding the Ctrl key as you click the column headings. Then adjust the width of any one column to affect them all.

Setting Row Heights

By adjusting row heights, you can make worksheet entries more attractive and easier to understand. The default row height, which depends on the default font, changes if you change the global font. For example, if the global font is 12-point Arial MT, the default row height is 14 points. If you change the global font to 14-point Arial MT, the default row height changes automatically to 17 points. A point is approximately 1/72 of an inch when printed; therefore, 12-point type is about one-sixth of an inch high when printed.

1-2-3 for Windows adjusts row height automatically to accommodate changes in point size. Occasionally, however, you may need to change a row's height—for example, to add more white space between rows of data. The following sections describe the process of changing row heights.

Setting the Default Row Height

You can change the row height for the entire worksheet by using the **S**tyle **R**ow Height command. In the Row Height dialog box (see fig. 9.6), enter the address A1..A8192 in the **R**ow(s) text box (or substitute a different worksheet letter or worksheet name for A). This address includes all rows in the worksheet. Type the new row height (in points) in the **S**et height to text box or click on the scroll arrows. Press Enter or choose OK.

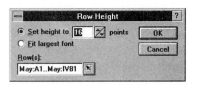

Fig. 9.6
The Row Height
dialog box.

Note that changing the default row height involves a different procedure than changing the default column width. Changing the default row height is a matter of selecting all rows and changing the height.

Setting Individual Row Heights

You can change the height of a single row by placing the cell pointer in that row, using the **S**tyle **R**ow Height command, and typing the desired height into the **S**et **H**eight To text box in the Row Height dialog box or use the scroll arrows to set the value. Press Enter or choose OK when finished.

You can change the height of several rows by selecting a range that includes all the rows you want to change before you issue the command. All rows represented in the range are affected when you use the **S**tyle **R**ow Height command.

To change the height of an individual row with the mouse, use these steps:

1. Move the mouse pointer to the row border (below the row number in the worksheet frame) until the mouse pointer changes to a double-arrow pointing vertically.

2. Press and hold the left mouse button.

3. Drag the row border up or down to its new position and release the mouse button.

When you use the mouse to change the height of a row, 1-2-3 for Windows displays a solid horizontal line that moves with the mouse pointer to show the position of the new row border. You can change several rows at once with the mouse by clicking the first row's number (for example, the number 1 for row 1) and dragging to highlight additional rows. Then adjust the height of any one of the highlighted rows. All highlighted rows comply with the changes made to the individual row.

Fitting the Row Height to the Font

You can automatically fit the row height to the largest font in the row by using the Fit largest font option in the Row Height dialog box (see fig. 9.7). With this option selected, 1-2-3 for Windows automatically locates the largest

Tip
1-2-3 shows the row height in the Date/Time/Style indicator in the status bar. If the indicator shows the date and time, click it once to display the column width and row height.

Tip
No command is available to hide a row (as there is to hide a column). Although you cannot change a row height to 0, you can set it to 1, which may accomplish your objective. Unless you use the Zoom feature to enlarge the display, rows with a height of 1 are barely visible.

font in the row and adjusts the row's height to fit that font. Since row heights automatically fit your font selections as you make them, the only time you would need to select this option is when you have changed the normal row height after setting the font.

Fig. 9.7
The Fit largest font option in the Row Height dialog box.

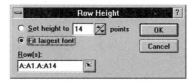

Changing Row Heights in Group Mode

Individual row heights can apply to several worksheets if you first group them together with Group mode. In Group mode, all the worksheets change row heights at the same time based on changes made to a single worksheet's row settings.

◄ "Grouping Worksheets," p. 277

Use Group mode when several worksheets have the same format—for example, when each worksheet contains the same data for a different department or division. When you group worksheets together, any formatting change (such as setting row heights) made to one worksheet in the group affects all the worksheets in that group. Therefore, you should be sure that you want to apply any formatting changes to all worksheets before you turn on Group mode.

Understanding Style

1-2-3 Release 5 for Windows groups all style commands under a menu called **S**tyle. The term *style* refers to virtually any type of formatting you can apply to data in a cell, such as currency symbols; commas and decimal places; a new font or point size; bold, underline, or italics; or the alignment of data in a cell. It also includes setting row heights and columns widths, as discussed earlier in this chapter.

The first four options on the **S**tyle menu allow you to change, delete, or add formatting to cell data. Figure 9.8 shows the **S**tyle menu.

When style characteristics are applied to a cell, the entry in the cell reflects those characteristics; indicators for certain of the style characteristics appear on the status bar. For example, in figure 9.9, the entry in cell C11 displays a formula result ($2,775) in currency format, complete with a dollar sign, comma, and zero decimal places—in a 12-point sans-serif font. The status bar displays the indicators US Dollar (the number format), 0 (the number of decimal places), Arial MT (the font), and 12 (the point size).

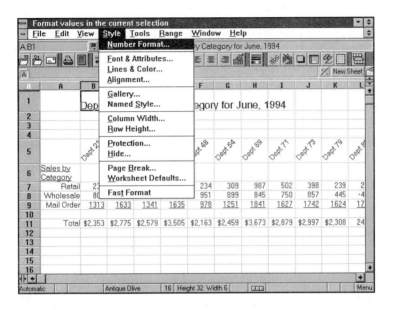

Fig. 9.8
The **S**tyle menu.

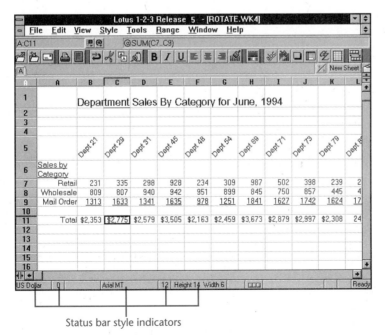

Fig. 9.9
Indicators for certain style characteristics appear on the status bar.

Status bar style indicators

To change the style characteristics of a cell or a range of cells, first select the cell or range and then choose any of the first four commands on the **S**tyle menu: **N**umber Format, **F**ont & Attributes, **L**ines & Color, or **A**lignment. Choose style options from the dialog box that appears.

◀ "Understanding the 1-2-3 for Windows Screen," p. 20

You also can use the status bar to change the number format, decimal places, font, and point size of a cell or range. At first glance, you may not realize that the boxes making up the status bar are actually buttons, or *selectors*. For example, if you click the font selector, 1-2-3 displays a pop-up list of other fonts (see fig. 9.10). The status bar selectors let you quickly change certain style characteristics for the selected cell or range without choosing menu and dialog-box options. (For a complete discussion of the status bar, see Chapter 1, "Getting Around in 1-2-3 and Windows.") Use the mouse or the arrow keys and the Enter key to choose an item from the pop-up list.

Fig. 9.10
Font pop-up list.

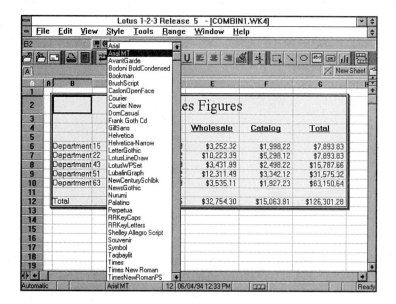

Setting Global Style Defaults

1-2-3 for Windows provides a number of default settings that determine how the program operates under most circumstances. When you choose the **T**ools **U**ser Setup command, you access the User Setup dialog box (see fig. 9.11). Use this dialog box to change many of the default settings that affect the display and behavior of 1-2-3 in the current session and all future sessions. Of the options in this dialog box, only two affect the formatting of data in the 1-2-3 worksheet:

■ The Use **A**utomatic format option affects the default format of numbers in 1-2-3 cells. When you deselect this option, 1-2-3 uses the General format instead of Automatic format as the default for all new worksheets. (Number formats are described later in this chapter.)

■ The **I**nternational button changes the display of certain date, time, currency, and punctuation defaults. (The International dialog box settings are discussed in the next few sections.)

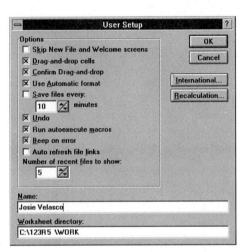

Fig. 9.11
User Setup dialog box.

Setting International Default Values: The Date

When you install 1-2-3 for Windows, the default international values are determined by the country you choose. At times, you may want to change some or all of the international settings. For example, if you work with international currency, you may want to change the currency symbol. You change international settings by clicking the **I**nternational button in the User Setup dialog box to access the International dialog box (see fig. 9.12).

The **D**ate option specifies how 1-2-3 for Windows displays dates in cells with a date format. The **D**ate drop-down box provides four possible formats, in which *MM*, *DD*, and *YY* stand for month, day, and year, respectively:

12/31/93 is an example of *MM/DD/YY* format

31/12/93 is an example of *DD/MM/YY* format

31.12.93 is an example of *DD.MM.YY* format

93-12-31 is an example of *YY-MM-DD* format

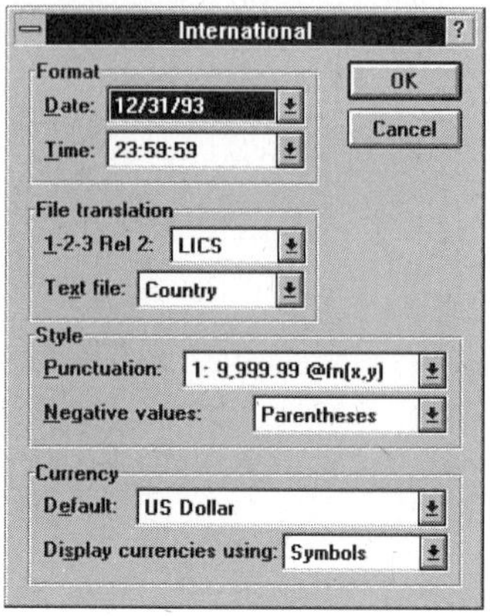

Fig. 9.12
International
dialog box.

Setting International Default Values: The Time

The **T**ime option in the International dialog box specifies how 1-2-3 for Windows displays times in cells with a Time format. The **T**ime drop-down box provides four possible formats, in which *HH*, *MM*, and *SS* stand for hour, minutes, and seconds, respectively:

23:59:59 is an example of *HH:MM:SS* format

23.59.59 is an example of *HH.MM.SS* format

23,59,59 is an example of *HH,MM,SS* format

23h59m59s is an example of *HHhMMmSSs* format

Setting International Default Values: Punctuation

With the **P**unctuation option, you control the display of numbers and the separators used between arguments in functions. The **P**unctuation drop-down box lists the possible combinations available (see fig. 9.13). The default setting uses a comma (,) as the thousands separator, the period (.) as the decimal point, and the comma (,) as the argument separator.

Use the **N**egative values option to specify how to display a negative number in a cell formatted as Currency or , Comma. The drop-down box has two choices:

■ *Parentheses* encloses a negative number in parentheses

■ *Sign* places a minus sign in front of the number

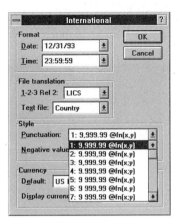

Everyday Worksheet Tasks

Fig. 9.13
The Punctuation
drop-down box.

Setting International Default Values: Currency

The **D**efault option in the International dialog box specifies the default currency (see fig. 9.14), based on the country you chose when you installed 1-2-3 for Windows. You can choose from among 43 international currencies (or specify the Other option).

Fig. 9.14
The Default option
in the International dialog box.

You can also choose to display either ISO or Symbols for currency by choosing ISO or Symbols from the Di**s**play currencies using list box.

After you change the International settings, press Enter or click OK to close the International dialog box and return to the User Setup dialog box. Press Enter or click OK to close the User Setup dialog box.

Setting Worksheet Style Defaults

In 1-2-3, you can set certain style characteristics for an entire worksheet or file before you begin entering data. Set styles for the entire worksheet when you want to specify the style characteristics used in most cells of the worksheet. For example, if you want the data in the worksheet to appear in a large typeface, you can specify a point size of 14 for the entire worksheet. If all the values in the worksheet represent dollars, you can apply the US Dollar number format to the entire worksheet. Later you can override the default format on a cell-by-cell basis.

To set style characteristics for the entire worksheet, use the **W**orksheet Defaults command on the **S**tyle menu to display the Worksheet Defaults dialog box (see fig. 9.15).

Fig. 9.15
The Worksheet
Defaults dialog
box.

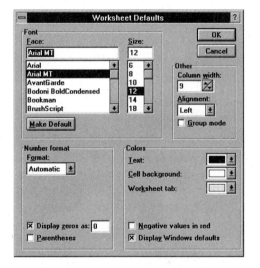

Using the Worksheet Defaults dialog box, you can specify the font, number format, colors, and other options for the entire worksheet. The options in this dialog box are the same as the options that you can specify for an individual cell or range (with the exception of the worksheet tab color specification). For detailed descriptions of these options, refer to "Working with Number Formats," "Changing Fonts and Attributes," and "Formatting Cells with Color and Borders," later in this chapter. If you intend to create multiple worksheets for the current file, you can apply the style characteristics to all worksheets in the file by selecting the **G**roup Mode check box.

> **Note**
>
> You can set the color of an individual worksheet tab by selecting a color from the Worksheet tab drop-down list box in the Worksheet Defaults dialog box (refer to fig. 9.15). To set the color for each worksheet tab in a file, you need to open the Worksheet Defaults dialog box for each worksheet.

After you specify the desired settings, choose OK or press Enter to close the Worksheet Defaults dialog box and save your changes.

The remainder of this chapter describes all the style characteristics you can apply to individual cells or to entire worksheets.

Understanding the Difference between Content and Format

Cell formatting changes the appearance of data—not its actual value. For example, some formats display a number as a rounded value. However, even when a number appears rounded in the cell, 1-2-3 for Windows stores the exact value of the number and uses the exact value in formulas and calculations. For example, if you format 1234.5 in Fixed format with 0 decimal places, the number appears as 1235, but 1-2-3 for Windows uses the exact value 1234.5 in formulas.

In figure 9.16, the sales total in cell C11 looks like an addition error. The formula in cell C9 is +B9*1.1, resulting in 95.7. Cell C9 displays 96, however, because it is formatted as Fixed with 0 decimal places. The result of a similar formula in cell C10 is 83.6, but the cell displays 84. The result of the formula in cell C11 is 179.3, but the cell displays 179. The formula appears to add as follows: 96+84=179, when the equation should result in 180. This apparent error is produced by rounding the displayed values without rounding the actual values.

To avoid rounding errors, round the *actual value* of the numbers used in formulas, not just their displayed value. To round values in a formula, use the @ROUND function. For example, to eliminate the rounding error in figure 9.16, change the formula in cell C9 to @ROUND((B9*1.1),0). Then copy the formula to cell C10. When you round the numbers in the formula with this technique, the @SUM function in cell C11 correctly results in 180. (For complete information on functions, see Chapter 5, "Using Functions.")

Fig. 9.16
The value in cell
C11 is the result of
a rounding error.

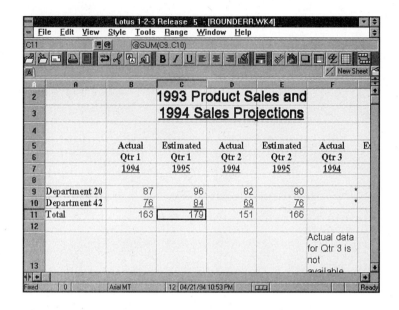

> **Note**
>
> 1-2-3 for Windows displays numbers with up to 15 decimal places. By default, negative numbers have a minus sign and decimal values have leading zeros.

Working with Number Formats

The first option on the 1-2-3 for Windows Style menu is **N**umber Format. You use this option to assign a specific number format to a cell or range of cells. Assigning a format to cells maintains consistency throughout the worksheet and saves you the effort of typing symbols (dollar signs, commas, parentheses, and so on) along with the cell value.

Number formats apply only to numeric data (numeric formulas and numbers). If you format a label as Fixed or Scientific, for example, the number format has no effect on how a label appears. One exception to this rule is the Hidden format, which can apply to both labels and string formulas.

Table 9.1 shows samples of the available cell formats and how each one changes the appearance of data. Date formats in this table assume that the current year is 1994. For a discussion of available currency formats, see "Changing the Currency Format" later in this chapter.

Table 9.1	Number Formats	
Format	**Entry**	**Displayed**
General	**1234**	1234
General	**1234.5**	1234.5
Fixed, 2 decimal places	**1234.5**	1234.50
Fixed, 0 decimal places	**1234.5**	1235
, Comma, 2 decimal places	**1234.5**	1,234.50
US Dollar, 2 decimal places	**1234.5**	$1,234.50
Percent, 1 decimal place	**0.364**	36.4%
Scientific, 4 decimal places	**1234.5**	1.2345E+03
+/-	**5**	+++++
31-Dec-94 (date format)	**2/14/94**	14-Feb-94
31-Dec (date format)	**2/14/94**	14-Feb
Dec-94 (date format)	**2/14/94**	Feb-94
12/31/94 (date format)	**2/14/94**	02/14/94
12/31 (date format)	**2/14/94**	02/14
11:59:59 AM (time format)	**10:15**	10:15:00 AM
11:59 AM (time format)	**10:15**	10:15 AM
23:59:59 (time format)	**10:15**	10:15:00
23:59 (time format)	**10:15**	10:15
Text	**+C6**	+C6
Hidden	**1234.5**	No display
Label	**57 Main St.**	57 Main St.
Automatic	**1234.5**	1234.5

Everyday Worksheet Tasks

Note

Automatic format is the default format that 1-2-3 uses whenever you create a new worksheet. The Automatic format "reads" the entries you type and applies the appropriate format. This format is discussed in detail later in this chapter.

If a column isn't wide enough to display a formatted numeric entry, asterisks fill the cell. If the numeric entry is unformatted and too long to fit in the cell, 1-2-3 for Windows converts the entry to scientific notation. To display the data, you must change the format or the column width. See "Setting Column Widths," earlier in this chapter, for instructions on changing column width.

> **Note**
>
> If you have a color monitor, you can display negative numbers in the worksheet in red. For details, see the section "Formatting Cells with Color and Borders" later in this chapter.

Handling Zeros

By default, 1-2-3 displays a zero (0) in any cell that contains an entry of zero or a formula that evaluates to zero. Using the Worksheet Defaults dialog box (refer to fig. 9.15), you can control how 1-2-3 displays zeros in your worksheet. You have the option of changing the Display zeros as setting so that 1-2-3 displays a blank cell or a label that you specify. (A *label* is defined as any entry that begins with a letter or a label-prefix character, such as ' for left-alignment or " for right-alignment.) To have 1-2-3 display a blank cell, delete the 0 from the Display zeros as text box and leave the text box blank. To have 1-2-3 display a label (such as the word "zero"), type the label in the Display zeros as text box.

Assigning Number Formats

To change the format of a cell or range use the **S**tyle **N**umber Format command to access the Number Format dialog box (see fig. 9.17). If you preselected a range, that range is listed in the **Ra**nge text box; if you did not preselect a range, specify one in the dialog box. Select one of the formats from the **F**ormat list box. You can select a format by typing the initial character of the format (such as **F** for Fixed) or by using the arrow keys or the mouse.

If you choose Fixed, Scientific, , Comma, Currency, or Percent, you can specify the number of decimal places or use the default number, 2, shown in the **D**ecimal places box. To change the number of decimal places, type another number between 0 and 15 or use the scroll arrows to change the number. For some formats like General, the **D**ecimal Places text box doesn't appear in the dialog box. When all settings are correct, select OK to close the Number Format dialog box and change the format of the selected range.

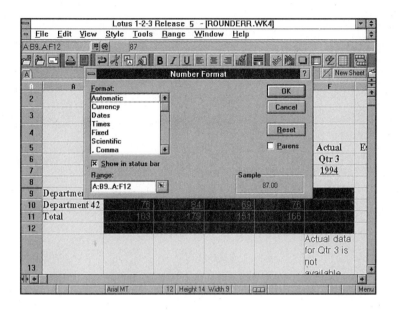

Fig. 9.17
The Number
Format dialog box.

I

Everyday Worksheet Tasks

The format button on the status bar displays the format of the current cell (see fig. 9.18). For example, Fixed appears on the format button when the current cell is formatted with the Fixed format. The number of decimal places for the current cell appears on the decimal button. In figure 9.16, the status bar shows Fixed on the format button and 0 on the decimal button. You can use the format button to select a number format for the highlighted cell or range.

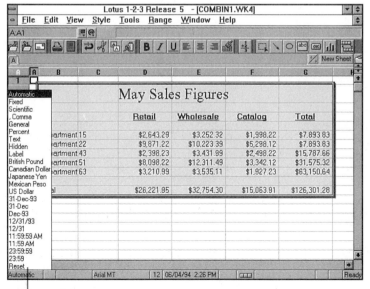

Format pop-up list

Fig. 9.18
The format pop-up
list.

◀ "Entering Data into the Worksheet," p. 84

The next section describes how to change the choices displayed on the format pop-up list. The following sections describe the formats available in the Number Format dialog box and from the format pop-up list on the status bar.

Automatic Format

As mentioned earlier in this chapter, *Automatic format* is the default setting for all 1-2-3 worksheet files (unless you turn it off by using the **T**ools **U**ser Setup command and deselecting the Use **A**utomatic Format option in the User Setup dialog box). When you enter data in a cell that uses Automatic format, 1-2-3 for Windows examines the entry and selects an appropriate format. For example, if you enter **$325**, 1-2-3 for Windows changes the Automatic format for that cell to US Dollar; if you enter **50%**, 1-2-3 changes the Automatic format to Percent. If you enter **325** or **50**, however, 1-2-3 makes no change to the format, and the cell remains formatted as Automatic.

Note

If you turn off Automatic format as a default setting (using the User Setup dialog box mentioned earlier in this chapter), it does not affect the current worksheet. All new worksheets you create, or new worksheets that you add to your current worksheet, however, will use the General format.

Table 9.2 lists examples of how entries are treated when you enter data into a cell formatted as Automatic. (The cell has a column width of 9; the default font is 12-point Arial MT.) The first column shows how the entry was typed. The second column shows the number format 1-2-3 assigns to the entry. The third column shows how the entry is stored in the worksheet; the fourth column shows how the data is displayed in the worksheet. Date examples in this table assume that the current year is 1994.

Table 9.2 Examples of Automatic Format			
Typed Entry Result	**Cell Format**	**Data Stored**	**Display**
57 Main	Automatic	57 Main	57 Main
258	Automatic	258	258
258.46	Automatic	258.46	258.46
258.00	Automatic	258	258

Typed Entry Result	Cell Format	Data Stored	Display
1,258	, Comma, 0	1258	1,258
87.00	, Comma, 2	87	87.00
$258.00	Currency, 2	258	$258.00
25%	Percent, 0	0.25	25%
2.50%	Percent, 2	0.025	2.50%
1.2e4	Scientific, 1	12000	1.2E+04
2.587e-16	Scientific, 3	2.587E-16	2.587E-16
25.87e-17	Scientific, 2	2.587E-16	2.59E-16
20-Oct-94	31-Dec-93	34627	20-Oct-94
20-Oct	31-Dec	34627*	20-Oct
Oct-94	Automatic	"Oct-94	Oct-94
10/20/94	12/31/93	34627	10/20/94
10/15	Automatic	0.666666666 66666666.7	0.666667
6:23:57 AM	11:59:59 AM	0.266631944 444444444	**************
6:23:57	23:59:59	0.266631944 444444444	06:23:57
6:23:57 PM	11:59:59 AM	0.766631944 444444444	**************
6:23 AM	11:59 AM	0.265972222 2222222222	06:23 AM
6:23	23:59	0.265972222 2222222222	06:23
6:23 PM	11:59 AM	0.765972222 2222222222	06:23 PM
18:23:57	23:59:59	0.766631944 444444445	18:23:57
18:23	23:59	0.765972222 222222222	18:23

After you enter a number into a cell and 1-2-3 for Windows applies a format, the format stays with the cell. The format does not change if a number with a different format is entered. For example, if you type **$250.00** into a cell formatted as Automatic, 1-2-3 for Windows assigns the US Dollar format with 0 decimal places to the cell. If you later type **25%** into the cell, instead of formatting the cell as a percent, 1-2-3 for Windows retains the Currency format and displays the number as $0 (though you can see 0.25 in the edit line). To change the format after using the Automatic format, select **S**tyle **N**umber Format or use the status bar.

If you type an invalid number in a cell formatted as Automatic, such as **57 Main Street**, 1-2-3 for Windows precedes the invalid entry with a label prefix and considers the entry a label.

If the number looks like one of the date or time formats, 1-2-3 for Windows uses that date or time format. However, in Automatic format, 1-2-3 for Windows does not recognize the date formats Dec-93 or 12/31; it stores Dec-93 as a label and 12/31 as a formula (12 divided by 31).

1-2-3 for Windows formats a cell automatically only when you enter a number or a label. If you enter a formula in a cell, the format remains Automatic. If you later enter a number or a label into the cell, 1-2-3 for Windows formats the cell appropriately. If the cell contains a formula and you convert the entry to a number with F2 (Edit) or F9 (Calc), 1-2-3 for Windows applies a format at that time.

Currency Format

1-2-3 for Windows provides 43 possible default currency formats. You select the default currency for the worksheet file in the International dialog box. Numbers formatted as any of the 43 currencies can have from 0 to 15 decimal places. Thousands are separated by a comma (or other specified international separator). Negative numbers appear with a minus sign or in parentheses—depending on the current setting in the International dialog box.

 1-2-3 for Windows also provides three SmartIcons to quickly format a number to the default currency symbol, the default thousands separator, and two decimal places (two for the pound and the dollar, zero for the year). First select the range to format and click the SmartIcon.

> **Note**
>
> If a SmartIcon does not appear in your SmartIcons set, choose Tools SmartIcons to add it to the icon set you work with. For more information about SmartIcons, see "Customizing the SmartIcons," in Chapter 33.

Table 9.3 shows several examples of currency formats in cells that have a column width of 9 and the default font of 12-point Arial MT. The examples include international currency symbols in addition to the dollar sign.

Table 9.3   Examples of Different Currency Formats

Typed Entry	Number of Decimal Places	Display Result
123	2	$123.00
123	2	¥123
123	2	£123.00
-123.124	0	($123) or -$123
1234.12	0	$1,234
1234567.12	2	**************

Date and Time Formats

All the formats discussed so far deal with regular numeric values. You use *date and time formats* when you work with date and time calculations or functions (see Chapter 5, "Using Functions"). For example, the Dec-93 format is used to format a date as Month-Year. 8/29/93, therefore, appears as Aug-93.

When you choose **S**tyle **N**umber Format, the Number Format dialog box displays a **F**ormat list box. If you scroll through the list box, you can see the five date formats and four time formats.

Date Formats. When you use date functions, 1-2-3 for Windows stores the date as a serial number representing the number of days since December 31, 1899. The date serial number for January 1, 1900 is 1. The date serial number for January 15, 1991 is 33253. The latest date 1-2-3 for Windows can display is December 31, 2099 (that date has the serial number 73050).

> **Caution**
>
> All the date serial numbers starting with March 1, 1900 are off by one day. The calendar inside 1-2-3 treats 1900 as a leap year; it isn't. A date serial number of 60 appears as 02/29/00—a date that never existed. Unless you compare dates before February 28, 1900 to dates after February 28, 1900, this error has no effect on the worksheets. Dates can be off by one day, however, if you export data to a database program.

If the number in a cell formatted with a date format is less than 1 or greater than 73050, the date appears as asterisks. Date formats ignore fractions; the value 34627.99 in a cell with the 12/31/93 date format appears as 10/20/94. The fraction represents the time—a fractional portion of a 24-hour clock.

To format a cell as a date, select **S**tyle **N**umber Format and select one of the date formats. To quickly choose a date format, click the format selector in the status bar and choose a format from the pop-up list.

Tip

Don't be concerned with which serial number refers to which date. Let 1-2-3 for Windows format the date serial number to appear as a textual date.

To enter a date, you do not have to know the serial number or the date and time functions. Type what looks like a date in any of the 1-2-3 date formats that begin with a number. That is, type an entry like 10/20/94 or 20-Oct-94 or 20-Oct. (If you enter a date without the year, 1-2-3 for Windows assumes you want the current year.) 1-2-3 for Windows converts the entry to a date serial number and, if you have not yet formatted the range with a date format, 1-2-3 for Windows changes the Automatic format to the appropriate date format. The contents box in the edit line displays the serial date, and the cell displays the formatted date. If you have already formatted the range, the date appears according to the format you specified.

> **Note**
>
> if you type an entry such as Oct-94, 1-2-3 does not automatically apply the Dec-93 format to the cell. Instead, 1-2-3 interprets the entry as a label and retains the Automatic format because the entry begins with a letter. To use the Dec-93 format, you must enter a date in a format that begins with a number (such as 10/20/94 or 10-20-94), then apply the Dec-93 format to the cell. 1-2-3 will convert the 10 to Oct.

Table 9.4 shows several examples of dates in cells that have a column width of 9 and the default font of 12-point Arial MT. In each case, the cell format shown was applied to the cell before the entry was typed. This table assumes that the current year is 1994.

Table 9.4   Examples of Date Formats

Typed Entry Result	Cell Format	Data Stored	Display
10/20	31-Dec-93	34627	20-Oct-94
10/20	31-Dec	34627	20-Oct
10/20	Dec-93	34627	Oct-94
10/20	12/31/93	34627	10/20/94
10/20	12/31	34627	10/20
20-Oct	31-Dec-93	34627	20-Oct-94

Time Formats. When you use a time function, such as @NOW, 1-2-3 for Windows stores the time as a *time fraction*. You can format a time fraction so that it looks like a time of day by choosing any of the time formats in the Number Format dialog box or by clicking the format selector in the status bar and choosing a time format.

When you enter a specific time, such as **3:00 AM**, **12:00 PM**, or **6:00 PM**, 1-2-3 applies the correct time format to the entry but stores the entry as a time fraction. For example, 3:00 AM is stored as 0.125, 12:00 PM is stored as 0.5, and 6:00 PM is stored as 0.75. If you type **6:23**, **6:23:00**, **6:23AM**, or **6:23:00 AM**, 1-2-3 for Windows converts the entry to the time fraction 0.265972... (to 18 decimal places). If you type **6:23:57** or **6:23:57 AM**, 1-2-3 for Windows converts the entry to the time fraction 0.26663194... (to 18 decimal places).

1-2-3 uses a 24-hour clock system; noon is regarded as 12:00 and midnight as 24:00. Times between midnight and 1:00 A.M. are displayed as 00:01, 00:02:00, and so on. You don't have to type **AM** for times before noon. For times after noon, however, type **PM** or type the hour using the numbers 12 to 23.

Tip
You can quickly enter today's date in the current cell by clicking the Insert Date icon. 1-2-3 automatically applies the 12/31/93 date format to the cell.

◄ "Calendar Functions," p. 142

Note

You can type the letters *AM* or *PM* in either uppercase or lowercase; it isn't necessary to type a space between the time and the AM or PM designator.

Table 9.5 shows several examples of time formats in cells that have a column width of 9 and the font of 10-point Arial MT. The Data Stored column displays only 10 of the 18 decimal places that 1-2-3 stores.

Table 9.5 Examples of Time Formats			
Typed Entry Result	**Cell Format**	**Data Stored**	**Display**
6:23:57	11:59:59 AM	0.2666319444	6:23:57 AM
6:23:57 PM	11:59:59 AM	0.7666319444	6:23:57 PM
6:23	11:59 AM	0.2659722222	06:23 AM
6:23:57	23:59:59	0.2666319444	06:23:57
6:23:57 PM	23:59:59	0.7666319444	18:23:57
6:23	23:59	0.2659722222	06:23
6:23 PM	23:59	0.7659722222	18:23

Fixed Format

You use *Fixed format* when you want to display numbers with a fixed number of decimal points. Table 9.6 shows several examples of Fixed format in cells that have a column width of 9 and the default font of 12-point Arial MT. In all cases, the full number in the cell is used in calculations, even though the displayed value may be rounded, or asterisks may appear.

Table 9.6 Examples of Fixed Format		
Typed Entry	**Number of Decimal Places**	**Display Result**
123.46	0	123
123.46	1	123.5
-123.46	2	-123.46
123.46	4	123.4600
1234567.89	4	**************
123456789	2	**************

Scientific Format

You use *Scientific format* to display very large or very small numbers. Such numbers usually have a few significant digits and many zeros as place holders to show how large or small the number is.

A number in scientific notation has two parts; a *mantissa* and an *exponent*. The mantissa is a number from 1 to 10 that contains the significant digits. The exponent tells you how many places to move the decimal point to get the actual value of the number.

1-2-3 for Windows displays numbers in Scientific format in powers of 10, with 0 to 15 decimal places, and an exponent from –99 to +99. If a number has more significant digits than the number you specify in the format, the number is rounded on the display, although 1-2-3 for Windows uses the full value for formulas and calculations.

1230000000000 appears as `1.23E+12` in Scientific format with 2 decimal places. E+12 signifies that you must move the decimal point 12 places to the right to get the actual number. 0.000000000237 appears as `2.4E-10` in Scientific format with 1 decimal place. E–10 means that you must move the decimal point 10 places to the left to get the actual number.

> **Note**
>
> A number too large to appear in a cell in General format appears in Scientific format.

Table 9.7 shows several examples of Scientific format in cells that have the default column width of 9 and the default font of 12-point Arial MT.

Table 9.7   Examples of Scientific Format

Typed Entry	Number of Decimal Places	Display Result
1632116750000	2	1.63E+12
16321167500000	2	1.63E+13
-1632116750000	1	-1.6E+12
-1632116750000	2	-1.63E+12
00000000012	2	1.20E+01
-.00000000012	0	-1E-10

Comma Format

Like the Fixed format, the **,** *Comma format* displays data with a fixed number of decimal places (from 0 to 15). The **,** Comma format separates the thousands with commas (or another symbol specified with **T**ools **U**ser Setup **In**ternational). Negative numbers appear with a minus sign or in parentheses—depending on the current setting in the International dialog box. Positive numbers less than 1,000 appear the same way in Fixed format and **,** Comma format.

Table 9.8 shows several examples of **,** Comma format in cells that have a column width of 9 and the default font of 12-point Arial MT.

Table 9.8 Examples of , Comma Format		
Typed Entry	**Number of Decimal Places**	**Display Result**
123.46	0	123
1234.6	2	1,234.60
-1234.6	0	(1,235) or -1,235
-12345678	2	**************

 To apply the default thousands separator (for example, comma) and zero decimal places to selected cells, click the Comma 0 SmartIcon.

General Format

Numbers in *General format* have no thousands separators and no trailing zeros to the right of the decimal point. Negative numbers are preceded by a minus sign; if the number contains decimal digits, it can contain a decimal point. If a number contains too many digits to the right of the decimal point to fit within the column width, the decimal portion is rounded. If a number has too many digits to the left of a decimal point, the number appears in Scientific format. For example, 123400000 appears as 1.2E+08.

Table 9.9 shows several examples of General format in cells that have a column width of 9 and the default font of 12-point Arial MT.

Table 9.9 Examples of General Format	
Typed Entry	**Display Result**
123.46	123.46
-123.36	-123.36
1.2345678912	1.234568
15000000000	1.5E+10
-.000000026378	-2.6E-08

+/– Format

The +/– *format* displays numbers as a series of plus signs (+), minus signs (–), or periods (.). The number of signs displayed is equal to the entry's value, rounded to the nearest whole number. A positive number appears as a row of plus signs; a negative number appears as a row of minus signs; a number between –1 and +1 appears as a period.

This format originally was devised to create imitation bar charts in early electronic spreadsheets that had no graphing capability. The format has limited use today.

Table 9.10 shows several examples of +/- format in cells that have a column width of 9 and the default font of 12-point Arial MT.

Table 9.10 Examples of +/- Format	
Typed Entry	**Display Result**
6	++++++
.5	.
4.9	++++
-3	―――
0	.
17.2	**************

Percent Format

You use *Percent format* to display percentages. A number formatted as a percentage can have from 0 to 15 decimal places. The number displayed is the value of the cell multiplied by 100, followed by a percent sign (%). Notice that the number of decimal places you specify is the number as a percent: for example, only 2 decimal places are needed to display .2456 as 24.56% in Percent format.

The number displayed is multiplied by 100, but the value of the cell is unchanged. To display 50% in a cell, type **.5** and use the Percent format. If you type **50** and use the Percent format with 0 decimal places, `5000%` appears. If you simply type **50%**, 1-2-3 automatically assigns the Percent format to the cell and displays 50%.

 To apply the percent format with two decimal places to selected cells, click the Percent 2 SmartIcon.

Table 9.11 shows several examples of Percent format in cells that have a column width of 9 and the default font of 12-point Arial MT.

Table 9.11 Examples of Percent Format		
Typed Entry	**Number of Decimal Places**	**Display Result**
2	2	200.00%
-.3528	2	-35.28%
30	0	3000%
300	4	**************

Text Format

You use *Text format* to display numeric and string formulas instead of their results. Numbers formatted as Text appear the same way as they do in General format. If a formula is too long to appear in the column width, the formula is truncated unless the cell to the immediate right is blank. In this case, the formula spills over and is displayed in full in the cell or cells to the right.

Text format is useful for criteria ranges (covered in Chapter 26, "Finding and Extracting Data"). You also can use Text format when you enter or debug complex formulas.

Hidden Format

A cell in *Hidden format* appears blank no matter what the cell contains. You use Hidden format for sensitive data or intermediate calculations you don't want to display. If a cell is unprotected, the contents of a hidden cell appear in the contents box of the edit line when you move the cell pointer to that cell. If the cell is protected, the data isn't visible in the cell or in the edit line.

◄ "Protecting Files," p. 297

► "Hiding Worksheet Data," p. 498

In figure 9.19, cell D7 appears to be blank but the edit line shows that the cell entry is 9871.22. Notice the Hidden indicator on the format selector in the status bar.

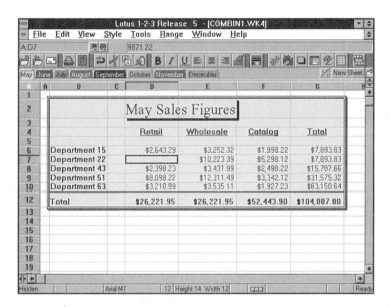

Fig. 9.19
The value of a cell with Hidden format appears in the edit line.

Label Format

You use *Label format* on blank cells to make numbers that are labels easier to enter. In Label format, all entries are considered labels; 1-2-3 for Windows precedes the entry with the default label prefix. You can easily enter a label that looks like a number or a formula—either of which begins with a numeric character.

In a worksheet in which cells are still formatted with the default Automatic format, suppose that you type the label **57 Main Street** and press Enter. Because the entry contains letters, 1-2-3 for Windows considers the entry a label and inserts a label prefix. The format type remains Automatic. Now suppose that you type the label **10/15** and press Enter. 1-2-3 considers 10/15 a formula (10 divided by 15), converts the entry to a number, and displays 0.666667.

In both preceding examples, if you format the range as Label before you type the entry, 1-2-3 for Windows precedes the entry with a label prefix, and the entry becomes a text label.

◀ "Entering Labels," p. 84

If you format numeric entries with the Label format, they do not become labels, even though the format is changed. For example, after the Label format is applied, the entry 0.666667 remains the same until you retype the entry **10/15**. At that point, the entry appears as the label 10/15 in the cell.

The Parentheses Option

The parentheses option is a style characteristic that is available in the Number Format dialog box. You choose the **P**arens check box when you want 1-2-3 to enclose negative numbers in parentheses. This option adds parentheses to negative numbers that use any of 1-2-3's number formats (labels are unaffected). When you want to use parentheses for every unformatted cell in the current worksheet, select the **P**arentheses option in the Worksheet Defaults dialog box. (Refer to the section "Setting Worksheet Style Defaults" earlier in this chapter.) To use parentheses with a specific cell or range, select the **P**arens option in the Number Format dialog box and specify the range and the number format.

The Parentheses option can produce confusing results, so use it with care. For example, if you apply the **P**arentheses option with the Automatic format to the number 456, the number appears in the cell as (456). If you apply parentheses to a negative number, the number still appears as negative—but with varying results depending on the number format used. With the General format, -1234 appears as (-1234); with the **,** Comma format, -1234 appears as ((1,234)); with the Currency format, -1234 appears as (($1,234)).

Troubleshooting

*If I turn off the Use **A**utomatic Format option in the User Setup dialog box, what format does 1-2-3 use for new worksheets?*

1-2-3 uses the General format in all new worksheets if you turn off the Use **A**utomatic Format default setting.

When I enter and format a date, why does 1-2-3 display the wrong date?

1-2-3 can format a date correctly only if you enter it in a format 1-2-3 recognizes. If the date you enter is in some other format, 1-2-3 interprets the entry as a label or a formula. If you enter **12-31-94**, for example, 1-2-3 recognizes the hyphens as minus signs and returns -113. However, if you enter **31-Dec-94**, 1-2-3 formats the entry correctly because 31-Dec-94 is a valid date format.

When I enter time and date serial numbers, why doesn't 1-2-3 display a recognizable time or date?

Unless the cell is already formatted with a date or time format, 1-2-3 uses the Automatic format and interprets the number as an integer.

How can I perform mathematical operations on dates and times?

You construct the formula just like you do for any other values in the worksheet. Remember that 1-2-3 stores dates and times as serial numbers and uses these numbers to perform the calculation you specify.

Enhancing the Appearance of Data

The **S**tyle menu provides options for enhancing the appearance of data in the worksheet. These enhancements include changes to the worksheet fonts; the addition of borders, lines, shading, and colors; and changes to the alignment of data in worksheet cells. You use the **F**ont & Attributes, **L**ines & Color, and **A**lignment options on the **S**tyle menu to change these characteristics for a cell or range of cells.

> **Note**
>
> You can specify a default set of worksheet styles (typeface, point size, default cell alignment, column width, default number format, and text and cell background colors) with the Worksheet Defaults dialog box. These settings apply to the current worksheet (or all the worksheets in the file if you specify **G**roup Mode). For more details, see "Setting Worksheet Style Defaults," earlier in this chapter.

Changing Fonts and Attributes

A typeface, or *face* (as 1-2-3 calls it), is a particular style of type, such as Arial MT or TimesNewRoman PS. Typefaces can have different *attributes*, such as weight (regular, bold, italic) and underline. Most typefaces are available in a number of point sizes. The *point size* describes the height of the characters (there are 72 points in an inch). The most commonly used point sizes for "standard" print are 10 point and 12 point. Titles and headings are often set in 14-point or 18-point type.

A typeface of a given point size with a given set of attributes is called a *font*. In practice, many people use the terms *typeface* and *font* interchangeably, although they have different meanings. In 1-2-3 for Windows, a *font* is a typeface of a given size.

To change the typeface, point size, and attributes for a cell or range, use one of the following methods:

- Choose **S**tyle **F**ont & Attributes or click the Font & Attributes SmartIcon to open the Font & Attributes dialog box (see fig. 9.20). Change the settings as desired. If you select **U**nderline, specify an underline style with the drop-down box. The Sample box shows how the font and other attributes you select will look in the worksheet. Select OK to close the dialog box and apply the font to the selected cell or range.

- To apply boldface, italics, or underline to a selected cell or range, click the Boldface, Italics, Single Underline, or Double Underline SmartIcon. You can apply several attributes by clicking more than one of these formatting SmartIcons.

- Select the cell or range to change and click the font selector or point-size selector in the status bar to reveal a pop-up list of choices. Select the font and point size from the list with the mouse or arrow keys.

Fig. 9.20
The Font &
Attributes dialog
box.

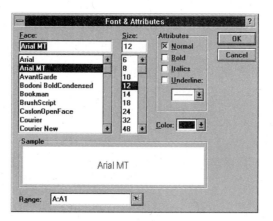

If necessary, 1-2-3 for Windows enlarges the row height to fit the selected fonts. However, 1-2-3 for Windows does not adjust column widths automatically. After you change a font, numeric data may no longer fit in the columns; numeric data may display as asterisks. Change the column widths as needed to correctly display the data (see "Setting Column Widths," earlier in this chapter).

You can restore the previous font and attributes to selected cells by choosing **E**dit **U**ndo immediately after applying a new font or attribute. If you have made other editing changes already, you can change the font using the Font & Attributes dialog box or by clicking the font selector in the status bar.

To remove boldface, underline, and italics all at once from selected cells, click the Normal Format SmartIcon. To remove these characteristics individually, click the appropriate SmartIcon.

Aligning Labels and Values

By default, 1-2-3 for Windows aligns labels to the left and values (numbers and formulas) to the right of the cell. You can change the default worksheet alignment of labels or values to the left, right, or center by choosing **S**tyle **W**orksheet Defaults. The Worksheet Defaults dialog box appears. Choose the desired alignment option and click OK. If the file contains multiple worksheets, be sure to click the **G**roup mode check box to change the default alignment in all the worksheets. Notice that changing the default alignment has no effect on existing worksheet entries. Any new entries you type into the worksheet, however, conform to the new default alignment style.

To change the alignment of existing entries, select the range and then use **S**tyle **A**lignment. The Alignment dialog box shown in figure 9.21 appears.

Tip

Use the Delete Style SmartIcon to delete all styles and formats from selected cells, while leaving the data intact.

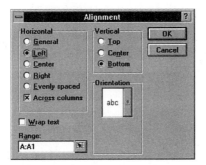

Fig. 9.21
The Alignment dialog box.

The following sections describe the options in the Alignment dialog box you can use to align text horizontally and vertically and to wrap, orient, and rotate text.

Aligning Labels Horizontally

Use the settings in the Horizontal section of the Alignment dialog box to align data. The **G**eneral option left-aligns all labels and right-aligns all numbers in the selected range. The **L**eft, **C**enter, and **R**ight options align data at the left of the cell, in the center of a cell, and at the right of a cell respectively. The **E**venly spaced option adds spaces, if necessary, between characters so that label entries fill the selected cell from edge to edge (like justifying text with a word processing program). The **E**venly Spaced option is ignored if the label ends with a period (.), colon(:), question mark (?), or exclamation point (!). This option has no effect on numbers.

> **Note**
>
> Any spaces that are included at the beginning or end of an entry are considered valid characters when 1-2-3 aligns the data. For instance, if you type the entry "Sales Projections " in a right-aligned cell and the entry includes two extra spaces at the end as shown, the entry will not appear to be properly right-aligned. (The same is true if extra spaces appear at the beginning of an entry in a left-aligned cell.) When extra spaces appear in an entry that is centered, the spaces also affect where 1-2-3 centers the entry in the cell. To ensure that data is properly aligned, remove all unnecessary spaces from cell entries.

When centering a long entry, 1-2-3 will allow the label to spill over and be displayed in the cells to the immediate right and immediate left of the current cell if those cells are blank. If the adjacent cells are not blank, 1-2-3 still centers the entry but the label is truncated where data appears in an adjacent cell.

 To align data quickly in a selected cell or range, click the Left Align, Center Align, Right Align, or Even Align SmartIcon.

You can also align data automatically when you type an entry by preceding the entry with a label prefix. Type an apostrophe (') to left-align an entry, type a quotation mark (") to right-align an entry, or type a caret (^) to center an entry.

Aligning Text Vertically

Use the options in the Vertical section of the Alignment dialog box (refer to fig. 9.21) to align cell data at the top, center, or bottom of a cell. This option is most useful when the row height has been extended or when a smaller-than-normal font has been used in a particular cell in a row. In either case, the row or cell contains extra vertical space within which the entry can be moved up or down. The **T**op option aligns data along the top boundary of the cell, the **B**ottom option aligns data along the lower boundary of the cell, and the Center option centers data between the top and bottom boundaries of the cell. By default, 1-2-3 uses bottom alignment in worksheet cells.

Aligning Labels across Multiple Columns

When you center or right-align a label, the alignment is relative to the column width of the cell. If you select the Across Columns option in the Alignment dialog box, the label is aligned relative to all selected columns. This option can be handy when you want to center a title over a worksheet. When you align across columns, you can specify whether the label should be aligned **L**eft, **C**enter, **R**ight, or **E**venly Spaced. You can also click the Center text across columns icon as a shortcut for opening the Alignment dialog box.

Wrapping Text in a Cell

Sometimes you need to include a large section of text in a worksheet but you don't want it to extend across columns. Instead, you want the text to continue line by line within that cell rather than across adjacent columns. In this case, you can use the **W**rap text option in the Alignment dialog box. 1-2-3 automatically wraps text at the right edge of the column and carries it to the next line in the cell. 1-2-3 also increases the cell height automatically, if necessary.

> **Note**
>
> As you type an entry in a cell formatted with the **W**rap Text option, the characters appear across the adjacent columns instead of wrapping. 1-2-3 wraps the text after you confirm the entry in the cell.

Changing the Text Orientation

You can alter the direction in which characters appear in a cell or range (the *orientation* of the text) by using the options in the Orientation section of the Alignment dialog box. This option can be useful for labeling a worksheet as shown in figure 9.22. In the figure, the labels in column A and rows 5 and 6 use a horizontal orientation. The year labels across row 7 use a diagonal orientation of 45 degrees. Choose the 45-degree angle option in the Orientation box, then use the Rotation box to specify the exact angle in degrees.

To quickly change data in a selected cell to a 45-degree orientation, click the Angle Text SmartIcon. Note that this SmartIcon will only set the text at 45 degrees whereas the Rotation option in the dialog box allows you to specify an exact number of degrees (between 1 and 90).

Fig. 9.22
A worksheet that
uses the 45-degree
angle orientation
option.

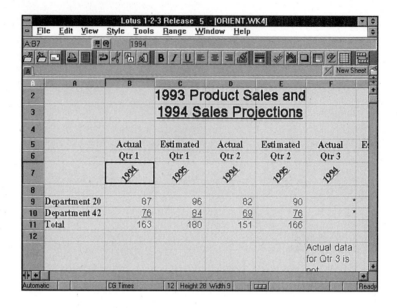

Formatting Cells with Color and Borders

The Lines & Color dialog box shown in figure 9.23 enables you to enhance
and emphasize data in a worksheet by choosing colors, specifying borders,
and adding frames. To access the dialog box, choose **S**tyle **L**ines & Color or
click the Lines & Color SmartIcon. Just under the **C**ancel button, the Sample
box shows how the choices you make in the Lines & Color dialog box will
appear in the worksheet. Refer to the Sample box as you experiment with
different colors, patterns, borders, and frames before actually applying them
to the selected range. When you are satisfied with the choices you have
made, click OK.

Before choosing the Lines & Color dialog box, select the cell or cell range
to which you want to apply these attributes. You can apply any of the attributes to all sheets in a file by including all sheets in the R**a**nge text box.
For instance, the range A:A1..D:F9 includes cells A1 through F9 in sheets A
through D.

◀ "Working with
Ranges," p. 71

Note

You must have a color printer to accurately print colors chosen in the Lines & Color
dialog box. However, if the colors and patterns you choose contain enough contrast,
many monochrome printers can substitute shades of gray for the different colors you
choose; patterns can be duplicated on the printer as closely as possible.

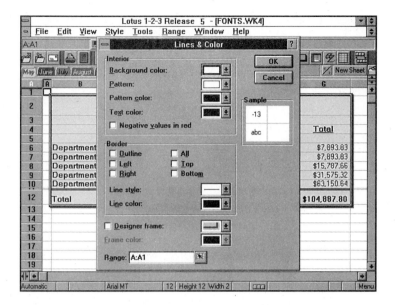

Fig. 9.23
The Lines & Color
dialog box.

Everyday Worksheet Tasks

The settings in the Interior section of the Lines & Color dialog box let you specify a **B**ackground color, **P**attern, Pattern **c**olor, and Te**x**t color for any cells or ranges in the worksheet. The background color is the color that fills the cell (white by default). If you choose a pattern, it appears in black unless you choose a pattern color. Text appears in black as well, unless you choose a text color.

▶ "Previewing Reports before Printing," p. 363

Use the settings in the Border section of the Lines & Color dialog box to draw lines above, below, on the sides of, and around cells in a range. To outline all cells in a selected range (as if they were one object), choose **O**utline or click the Add Border SmartIcon. To outline individual cells in the selected range, choose A**l**l. Choose a style and color for the border from the Line St**y**le and Li**n**e Color drop-down boxes.

You can add a drop shadow to a cell or selected range by clicking the Drop Shadow SmartIcon.

To further enhance borders, you can click the **D**esigner frame check box to choose from a collection of specially designed frames. After you choose a frame style, choose a color from the **F**rame Color drop-down list. Figure 9.24 shows an example of a designer frame used in a worksheet.

Fig. 9.24
An example of a
designer frame.

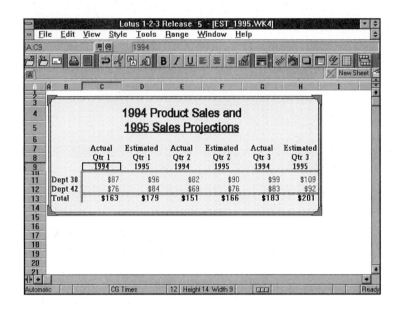

▶ "Developing
Business
Presentations,"
p. 517

Troubleshooting

How do I change the alignment of data in a cell by using the edit line?

1-2-3 uses label prefixes to identify the alignment of label entries. The label prefix is visible in the edit line but not in the cell itself. You can use the edit line to change the alignment of a label by erasing the old prefix and typing a new one just in front of the entry. Type an apostrophe (') for left alignment, a caret (^) for center alignment, and a quotation mark (") for right alignment. You must use a menu command or SmartIcon to evenly space an entry across a cell or range.

*I applied the **W**rap Text option to a cell containing a long text entry, but instead of filling the cell, the text begins near the bottom of the cell and fills the next three cells to the right. What did I do wrong?*

Check the Alignment dialog box to make sure that the Across Columns option isn't selected. The Across Columns option causes an entry to be displayed across adjacent columns, even though the **W**rap Text option is selected.

*I used the Del key to delete a long text entry from a cell formatted with the **W**rap Text option. I want the new entry to display into the next column, but it wraps, too. I know I can turn off the **W**rap Text option, but isn't there a better way to solve this problem?*

When you use the Del key to delete an entry, you delete only the contents of the cell, not the style. You can use **E**dit Cl**e**ar to display a dialog box that asks whether you want to delete the cell contents only, the style only, or both. If you select **B**oth, 1-2-3 clears the cell contents as well as the wrap-text style.

*When I deleted a long text entry from a cell that used the **W**rap Text option, the row height was not readjusted. Did I do something wrong?*

No. When you use the **W**rap Text option for a long text entry, 1-2-3 adjusts the row height to accommodate the entire entry. When you delete the cell contents, style, or both, 1-2-3 doesn't assume that you want the row height readjusted. You can readjust the row height quickly by choosing the **F**it Largest Font option in the Row Height dialog box.

Copying a Cell's Style

With the commands on the Style menu, you can select many different characteristics to modify the appearance of data in a worksheet. Applying style attributes to cells can be time-consuming, however, especially when you use multiple styles for different areas of a worksheet. Often, you apply several styles to a cell or range and then discover you want to apply the same style characteristics to another cell or range. You can save yourself the trouble of respecifying each attribute individually by simply copying the style you want to the new range. Select the cell with the style you want to copy and choose Edit Copy. Select the cells to which you want to copy the formats and choose Edit Paste Special. In the Paste Special dialog box, choose the Styles only option and click OK. If the target range you copy to contains data, the style attributes are applied immediately. If the range does not contain data, the attributes are applied when you enter data.

Tip
You can copy a cell's styles quickly by selecting the cell containing the styles you want to copy and then clicking on the Fast Format SmartIcon. The mouse pointer changes to a paint brush. Click on the cell to which you want to copy the formats (or click-and-drag across a cell range) and release the mouse button.

Using Named Styles

Another way to assign styles (groups of formats) is to name them. Using a *named style* is especially helpful when a cell or range has several style characteristics attached to it. You can assign names to up to 16 different sets of styles with the Named Style dialog box shown in figure 9.25. Use this dialog box to define styles as well as to apply a style to a selected cell or range. You access this dialog box by choosing **S**tyle Named **S**tyle or clicking the Named Style SmartIcon.

Fig. 9.25

The Named Style dialog box.

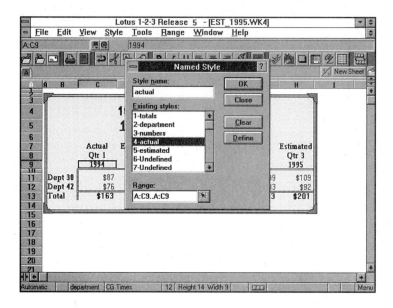

A named style includes all style characteristics (font, point size, number format, decimal places, color, border, and so on) to be assigned to the selected cell or range. To define a named style, do the following:

1. Select the cell or cell range that represents all the style characteristics you want to name.

2. Choose the **S**tyle Named **S**tyle command or click the Named Style SmartIcon. The Named Style dialog box appears (refer to fig. 9.25).

3. In the **E**xisting Styles list box, choose one of the 16 existing styles. (All undefined styles are identified as #-Undefined, where # is a number between 1 and 16.)

4. In the Style **n**ame text box, enter a name for the style (up to 15 characters).

5. Click the **D**efine button.

6. Select OK or press Enter.

When you define named styles, the third box from the left on the status bar becomes the style selector (see fig. 9.26). (This selector is inactive until you create named styles.) To apply a named style, select the cell or range to which you want to apply the style, then click the style selector. 1-2-3 pops up a list of all named styles. Click a style from the list to apply all attributes of the style to the selected range. You can also apply a named style to a cell or range by selecting the cells, then choosing a style from the **E**xisting Styles box.

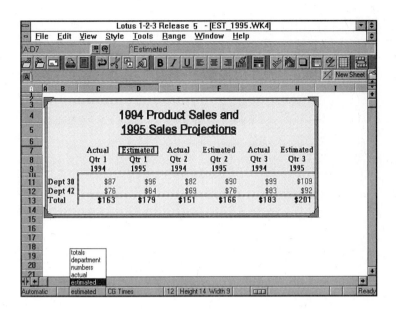

Fig. 9.26
The style selector
on the status bar.

I

To delete a named style from the list of named styles, follow these steps:

1. Choose the **S**tyle Named **S**tyle command or click the Named Style SmartIcon. The Named Style dialog box appears.

2. In the **E**xisting Styles list box, choose the style you want to delete.

3. Click the **C**lear button.

4. Click OK.

Using the Style Gallery

Like the named-style feature, the Style **G**allery command (or Style Gallery SmartIcon) allows you to apply styles quickly to a selected range of cells. The difference between the named-style feature and the Style Gallery is that the Style Gallery contains 14 predesigned style templates. Just choose a template from the list in the Gallery dialog box and all the style characteristics that make up the template are applied to the selected range.

To remove a template from the selected range, choose **E**dit Cl**e**ar **S**tyles Only or click the Delete Styles SmartIcon.

The Gallery dialog box is shown in figure 9.27. Refer to the Sample area in the dialog box to preview each template before applying it to the selected range. In the figure, the Note Pad template is shown in the Sample box. The worksheet underneath the dialog box is formatted with the Chisel1 template.

Tip

You can quickly remove all styles from a selected range of cells by clicking the Delete Styles SmartIcon. This removes styles only; the data in the cells remains intact.

Fig. 9.27
The Gallery dialog
box.

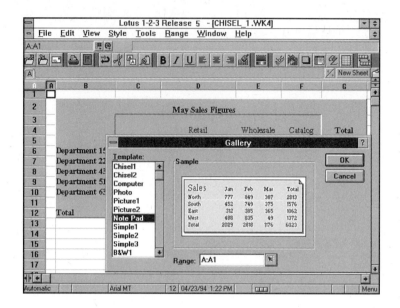

From Here...

Now that you have learned how to format your worksheets, you are ready to
learn how to preview and print them and, for added impact in presenting
your work, how to use graphics and business presentation pointers to
enhance the appearance of your data.

■ Chapter 10, "Printing Worksheets," teaches you how to preview and
  print professional reports. You learn how to hide data in a print range,
  how to specify titles, headers, and footers, how to set margins, and how
  to create and use named print settings.

■ Chapter 16, "Adding Graphics to Worksheets," teaches you how to use
  graphics (text boxes, lines, arrows, and rectangles, for example) to further enhance the appearance of your work and highlight important
  data.

■ Chapter 17, "Developing Business Presentations," teaches you to refine
  your worksheets even further so that they work well in presentations,
  and convey your message effectively.

Chapter 10

Printing Worksheets

1-2-3 for Windows gives you considerable control over the design of printed output—from one-page reports to longer reports that incorporate data from multiple worksheets and sophisticated graphs.

Many features you may associate with printing are actually part of the worksheet. For example, boldface, italics, and underlining are selected from the **S**tyle menu, not through a print command. When you are ready to print, these attributes automatically print on the report. With 1-2-3 for Windows, you are always in a Wysiwyg (what-you-see-is-what-you-get) environment— what you see on-screen closely resembles the printed output on paper.

This chapter shows you how to perform the following tasks:

- Preview reports

- Print a one-page or multiple-page report

- Print multiple ranges

- Compress a report to fit on one page

- Hide areas within a print range

- Set up report pages for printing

- Create and use named print settings

Enhancing Reports

Unless a report is for your eyes only, you will want to format it so that it is attractive, readable, and professional looking before you print it. 1-2-3 for Windows offers a number of features that let you enhance printed reports.

You can use different fonts; you can also add borders, drop shadows, and colors. These **S**tyle menu formatting options are for highlighting important areas of the worksheet and improving its readability. However, if you use too many formatting options, your audience may be overwhelmed: a report that's too busy may be difficult to read.

◄ "Using the Style Gallery," p. 353

To save yourself time when you format a report, use one of the templates included with 1-2-3 Release 5. Choose **S**tyle **G**allery and select one of the preformatted templates in the list. Figure 10.1 shows a printout of a worksheet formatted with the Photo template.

Fig. 10.1
This report was formatted with the Photo template from the Style Gallery.

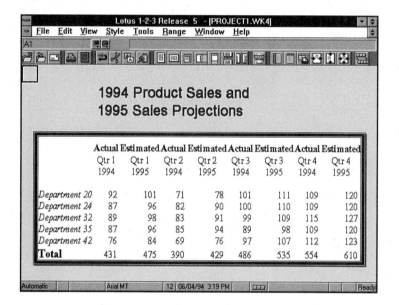

1994 Product Sales and 1995 Sales Projections

	Actual Qtr 1 1994	Estimated Qtr 1 1995	Actual Qtr 2 1994	Estimated Qtr 2 1995	Actual Qtr 3 1994	Estimated Qtr 3 1995	Actual Qtr 4 1994	Estimated Qtr 4 1995
Department 20	92	101	71	78	101	111	109	120
Department 24	87	96	82	90	100	110	109	120
Department 32	89	98	83	91	99	109	115	127
Department 35	87	96	85	94	89	98	109	120
Department 42	76	84	69	76	97	107	112	123
Total	431	475	390	429	486	535	554	610

Using the Windows Default Print Settings

In 1-2-3 for Windows, you use the **F**ile Prin**t**er Setup commands to set printer defaults. Because you are using Windows, many printer settings are already in place. The Windows environment retains basic information about the printer, such as resolution, paper size, and amount of memory. This information is available to all your Windows applications, including 1-2-3 for Windows.

By using the Windows Control Panel in the Main program group of the Program Manager, you can change the hardware-specific printer defaults. You can add or delete printer drivers and set other printer defaults (such as the kind of paper feed, orientation, and paper size). Refer to the Windows documentation for details on changing these defaults, or see *Using Windows, 3.1, Special Edition.*

Using the Printing SmartIcons

Many printing-related commands are available in the Printing SmartIcons set (see fig. 10.2). These SmartIcons offer a faster way to give printing commands. Most of the SmartIcons require you to select a range before clicking the SmartIcon. Many of the available Printing SmartIcons are discussed throughout the chapter, and the Printing SmartIcons set is displayed in all the figures in this chapter. To display this set, choose **T**ools Smart**I**cons (or click the SmartIcons button in the status bar) and then select Printing from the list of SmartIcon sets.

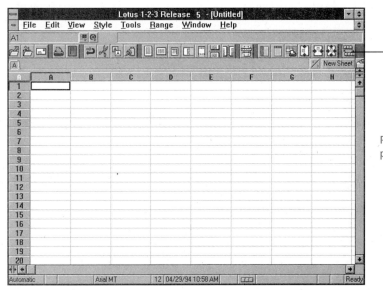

Fig. 10.2
The SmartIcons set displayed here is specifically for printing-related commands.

Printing SmartIcons palette

Understanding 1-2-3 Printing Commands

The 1-2-3 for Windows commands you use to print are similar to the **/P**rint and **:P**rint commands from DOS versions of 1-2-3 (the DOS versions of these commands also are offered in the 1-2-3 Classic menu). The 1-2-3 for Windows commands, however, offer more functionality and ease of use.

In 1-2-3 for Windows, printing is an easier task that involves a less complex menu structure than in DOS versions of 1-2-3.

In 1-2-3 for Windows, the **F**ile menu contains four different commands that you can use to control printed output: Print Preview, Page Setup, **P**rint, and Printer Setup. These commands are grouped together on the **F**ile menu (see fig. 10.3).

Fig. 10.3
The File menu contains the commands for printing.

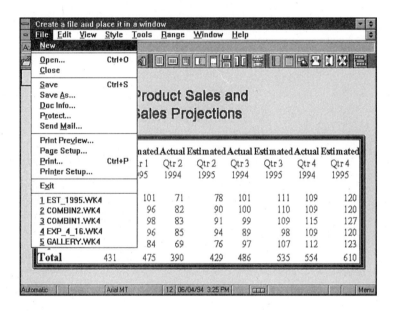

The following sections provide an overview of the purpose of each printing command and the dialog box each command opens. Later sections of this chapter explore the specific options in the dialog boxes and explain the relationship of each option to the printing process.

The File Page Setup Command

You select most printing options through the Page Setup dialog box, accessed by choosing Page Setup from the **F**ile menu or by clicking the Page Setup SmartIcon. You also can access this dialog box from the Print and Print Preview dialog boxes (displayed by selecting the **F**ile **P**rint and **F**ile Print Pre**v**iew commands, respectively).

As shown in figure 10.4, the Page Setup dialog box includes options for specifying orientation, margins, header and footer information, size, frame, grid lines, and print titles. You also can assign a name to a particular group of settings and later use these settings from any worksheet. You can designate the current settings as the default settings, or you can restore the default settings to replace the current settings.

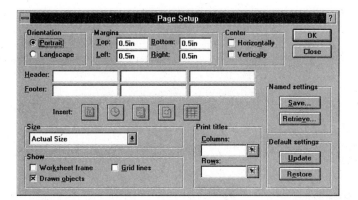

Fig. 10.4
The Page Setup dialog box.

Note

Although no direct correlation exists between the 1-2-3 Classic commands and the standard 1-2-3 for Windows printing commands, most printing options are located in the Page Setup dialog box. Some print commands that appear in the 1-2-3 Classic menu, such as printing cell formulas, have no corresponding command in the 1-2-3 for Windows menu.

The File Print Command

The **F**ile **P**rint command starts the printing process; you can select **F**ile **P**rint (or press Ctrl+P) to send data directly from 1-2-3 for Windows to the printer. You also can click the Print SmartIcon to begin printing.

When you choose **F**ile **P**rint, 1-2-3 for Windows displays the Print dialog box (see fig. 10.5). Use this dialog box to specify the pages you want to print, the number of copies you need, the range or ranges to print, and so on. The Page **S**etup button accesses the Page Setup dialog box (described in the preceding section); when you close the Page Setup dialog box, you return to the Print dialog box. The **P**review button displays a preview of the printed output; when you are done looking at the preview, you return to the worksheet.

Fig. 10.5
The Print
dialog box.

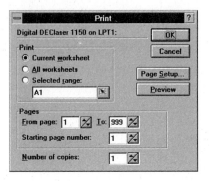

The File Printer Setup Command

The primary use of the **F**ile Prin**t**er Setup command is to select the printer to which you want to send the report if you have more than one printer. You can also use Prin**t**er Setup to specify additional print settings such as the orientation of the print job on the paper (portrait or landscape), scaling, paper size, paper source, and number of copies. You set these options by clicking the **S**etup button in the Printer Setup dialog box. This dialog box has additional settings you can change by clicking the **O**ptions button. The exact options available depend on the printer you select.

The File Print Preview Command

Tip

Use the Print Manager feature of Windows (accessible from 1-2-3 for Windows by pressing Ctrl+Esc and selecting Print Manager) to find information about print jobs in progress or in the print queue.

To get an idea of what your report looks like before you print it, you can preview each page on the screen with the **F**ile Print Pre**v**iew command. 1-2-3 displays the report in a special preview window so that you can determine whether the page breaks and margins are appropriate. If you like what you see, you can print the report while previewing it. Otherwise, you might want to alter your worksheet before printing.

Specifying the Print Range

Before you can print anything, you have to tell 1-2-3 what you want to print. You specify a print range in the same way you specify other ranges: You can select the print range before using a print command or SmartIcon, or you can specify the range from the Print or Print Preview dialog box.

Specifying a Single Print Range

To select a print range before you choose a print command, highlight the range with the mouse or keyboard:

If you forget to preselect the range you want to print, you can specify the range in the Selected **R**ange text box of the Print or Print Preview dialog box (see fig. 10.6). You can type the cell addresses, enter a range name, or high-light the range from this text box. To highlight the print range, first click the range selector and then select the range with the mouse or keyboard.

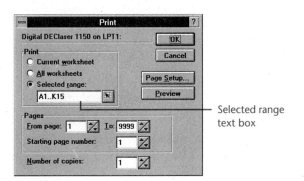

Fig. 10.6
A range indicated in the Selected range text box.

Selected range
text box

◄ "Working with Ranges," p. 71

Tip
To specify the entire worksheet as the print range, press Home, pe-riod, End Home.

For many reports, a *two-dimensional range*—that is, a rectangular area in a worksheet—is all you need to specify. The next section describes how to specify multiple ranges for a single print job.

Printing Multiple Ranges

Most reports require only a single print range. You can, however, specify that a single print job include a *collection*—that is, several ranges in one or more worksheets.

Specifying multiple print ranges is similar to specifying a single range in a single worksheet: preselect the range or specify the range address or range name in the Print dialog box. If you are typing several print ranges in the Selected **R**ange field, type a comma or semicolon between each range. If you want to highlight a range that spans multiple worksheets or highlight mul-tiple ranges in the same worksheet, you *must* preselect the ranges; the Print dialog box does not permit you to highlight multiple ranges. To preselect a three-dimensional range, highlight the range in the first worksheet and then hold Shift as you click the last worksheet tab you want to select; the same range is selected in the group of worksheets. You also can use Ctrl+PgUp and Ctrl+PgDn to move among worksheets. To preselect multiple ranges, hold Ctrl as you indicate each range (except the first) or click the worksheet tab to move to other worksheets.

> **Caution**
>
> If you forget to hold Ctrl when selecting ranges, all currently selected ranges are deselected.

▶ "Working with Templates and Creating Custom Dialog Boxes," p. 995

Figure 10.7 shows a worksheet with a three-dimensional print range selected; figure 10.8 shows the resulting report, printed on a DEClaser 1152. The worksheets in the file were formatted using the Expense Report SmartMaster template.

Fig. 10.7
Highlighting a 3-D range to be printed.

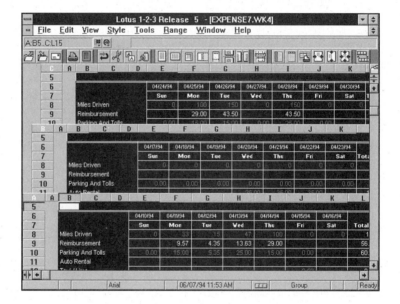

 The Range to Print SmartIcon in the Printing SmartIcon set specifies the selected range or ranges as the print range in the Print dialog box. You may find it handy to click this SmartIcon immediately after you select a collection of print ranges. You can then perform other worksheet tasks—or even open other files to cross-check information—before you issue the **File Print** command.

You can specify any combination of two-dimensional and three-dimensional print ranges. 1-2-3 for Windows prints the ranges in the order in which you enter the range addresses or select the ranges.

	04/10/94	04/11/94	04/12/94	04/13/94	04/14/94	04/15/94	04/16/94	
	Sun	Mon	Tue	Wed	Thu	Fri	Sat	Totals
Miles Driven	0	33	15	47	100	0	0	195
Reimbursement		9.57	4.35	13.63	29.00			56.55
Parking And Tolls	0.00	15.00	5.35	25.00	15.00	0.00		60.35
Auto Rental								
Taxi / Limo						9.50		9.50
Other (Rail Or Bus)								
Airfare								
Transportation Total		24.57	9.70	38.63	44.00	9.50		126.40

	04/17/94	04/18/94	04/19/94	04/20/94	04/21/94	04/22/94	04/23/94	
	Sun	Mon	Tue	Wed	Thu	Fri	Sat	Totals
Miles Driven	0	0	0	0	0	0	0	
Reimbursement								
Parking And Tolls	0.00	0.00	0.00	0.00	0.00	0.00	0.00	
Auto Rental				35.00	35.00	35.00		105.00
Taxi / Limo								
Other (Rail Or Bus)								
Airfare				375.00		375.00		750.00
Transportation Total				410.00	35.00	410.00		855.00

	04/24/94	04/25/94	04/26/94	04/27/94	04/28/94	04/29/94	04/30/94	
	Sun	Mon	Tue	Wed	Thu	Fri	Sat	Totals
Miles Driven	0	100	150	0	150	0	0	400
Reimbursement		29.00	43.50		43.50			116.00
Parking And Tolls	0.00	15.00	15.00	0.00	25.00	0.00		55.00
Auto Rental								
Taxi / Limo								
Other (Rail Or Bus)								
Airfare								
Transportation Total		44.00	58.50		68.50			171.00

	05/01/94	05/02/94	05/03/94	05/04/94	05/05/94	05/06/94	05/07/94	
	Sun	Mon	Tue	Wed	Thu	Fri	Sat	Totals
Miles Driven	0	33	15	47	100	0	0	195
Reimbursement		9.57	4.35	13.63	29.00			56.55
Parking And Tolls	0.00	15.00	5.35	25.00	15.00	0.00		60.35
Auto Rental								
Taxi / Limo						9.50		9.50
Other (Rail Or Bus)								
Airfare								
Transportation Total		24.57	9.70	38.63	44.00	9.50		126.40

Fig. 10.8
The printed version of the 3-D range.

Everyday Worksheet Tasks

Previewing Reports before Printing

Previewing a worksheet on-screen before sending it to the printer can save paper, printer ink (or toner or ribbon), and time. You can find and fix many minor errors before printing if you use the 1-2-3 Print Preview feature. With Print Preview, you can see how 1-2-3 for Windows breaks up a large print range over several pages, how multiple ranges fit on one or more pages, whether the specified margins are appropriate, and so on.

1-2-3 for Windows Release 5 also has a new feature that automatically determines whether you have a color or a black-and-white printer when you preview, and it displays a worksheet accordingly, translating colors into shades of gray for a black-and-white printer, and displaying the worksheet in color for a color printer.

Tip
When you print multiple ranges, always preview the report, as described in the next section.

To preview a print job, you can use any of the following methods:

- Open the **F**ile menu and choose Print Pre**v**iew.

- Open the **F**ile menu and choose **P**rint. From the resulting Print dialog box, choose the **P**review button.

- Click the Preview SmartIcon. This SmartIcon is available in the default set as well as the Printing set. After you select this SmartIcon, you see a preview of the current range selection; if no current range is selected, the last range you used in a print command is depicted in the preview.

All these methods access the Print Preview dialog box (see fig. 10.9). Use the Print Preview dialog box to specify whether you want to preview the current worksheet, all worksheets, a selected range, or a range of pages. Before accessing this dialog box, you can preselect a print range (as described in the preceding section); that range is automatically entered into the Selected **R**ange field in the dialog box.

Fig. 10.9
The Print Preview dialog box.

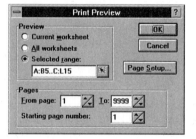

> ### Note
>
> By choosing the Page **S**etup button in the Print Preview dialog box, you can access the Page Setup dialog box (refer to fig. 10.4) and make changes to the setup before you see the preview. After making changes and choosing OK in the Page Setup dialog box, you return to the Print Preview dialog box.

After you finish specifying the options in the Print Preview dialog box, choose OK or press Enter to preview the worksheet. 1-2-3 for Windows displays the preview in a special preview window. Notice that the menu options are inactive and that the SmartIcon set changes (see fig. 10.10). The following sections describe how to use the preview window and its associated SmartIcons.

> **Note**
>
> 1-2-3 may require a few seconds to display the preview of the print job.

Browsing the Preview Report

As you preview a report, you may want to see more than just the first page. You can use the keyboard or the mouse to browse through the report. The first two SmartIcons in the Print Preview window SmartIcon set let you browse through the pages in a multiple-page report. Click the Preview Next Page SmartIcon (the first SmartIcon from the left) to display the next page; click the Preview Previous Page SmartIcon (the second SmartIcon) to display the previous page. To use the keyboard, press Enter to see the next page or PgUp to see the previous page. When you are zooming a report, you can also use the scroll bar and the up and down arrows to scroll up and down a previewed page.

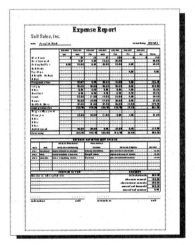

Fig. 10.10
The screen preview of an expense report.

Previewing Multiple Pages at a Time

You can use the icons at the top of the Print Preview window to preview more than one page at a time. Click the SmartIcon that displays two pages to view two pages of your report side by side. Click the four page SmartIcon to view four pages (see fig. 10.11). Click the four page SmartIcon a second time to view nine pages in the Preview window.

Fig. 10.11
Previewing all four
pages of the report
at once.

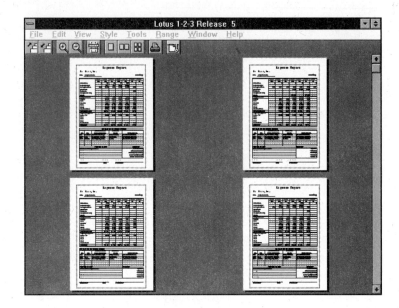

Zooming the Preview Report

  The two magnifying-glass SmartIcons in the Print Preview window enable you to zoom in and zoom out on the report so that you can read the worksheet text or see a miniature version of the entire worksheet. The Zoom-In SmartIcon has a plus sign; the Zoom-Out SmartIcon has a minus sign. Alternatively, you can press the plus key to zoom in.

You can zoom several times until you zoom to the appropriate level of magnification. Each time you zoom in or out, the screen display is magnified (when zooming in) or reduced (when zooming out) by 10 percent. Once you zoom in, use the arrow keys to move around the page. To zoom back out, click the Zoom-Out SmartIcon or press the minus key on the numeric keypad to decrease the display 10 percent at a time. Alternatively, you can press the asterisk (*) key to return to the original level of magnification.

Making Setup Changes while Previewing the Report

 As you preview a report, you may sometimes discover that the margins aren't quite right or that you forgot to specify headers or footers. For these types of changes, you can go directly to the Page Setup dialog box by clicking the Page Setup SmartIcon. After you make changes to the page setup, choose OK or press Enter; 1-2-3 returns to the preview screen and displays the report with the changes you made.

Closing the Preview Window

To clear the preview at any time, press Esc or click the Close Window SmartIcon. 1-2-3 returns to the worksheet.

If the report is fine as shown in the preview window, you can print it immediately by clicking the Print SmartIcon.

Troubleshooting

When I zoom in while previewing my report, nothing shows on-screen. What's happening?

The zoom-in command (a left mouse button click, the plus key, or the magnifying-glass SmartIcon that has the plus sign) magnifies the center of the page. If the report is short, you see nothing on the screen. Press the up-arrow key to see the top of the report. Use the arrow keys to see all parts of the page as you zoom.

Printing the Report

With the printing commands, you can print a simple or a very complex worksheet. To print a range quickly (for data that requires no special enhancements, such as headers, footers, or different margin settings) use the **F**ile **P**rint command or the Print SmartIcon.

This section shows you how to print reports quickly and efficiently. First, you learn how to print a short report (one page or less of data); then you learn how to print a multiple-page report. In subsequent sections of this chapter, you learn how to include headers and footers in reports, compress a report to fit on one page, add grid lines, column letters and row numbers, and repeat certain columns or rows (as column or row labels) on each page.

Printing a One-Page Report

For most one-page print jobs, once the defaults and the printer are set up, printing involves only the following steps:

1. Check that the printer is on-line and that the paper is properly positioned.

2. Select the print range.

3. Open the **F**ile menu and choose **P**rint, click the Print SmartIcon, or press Ctrl+P. The Print dialog box appears (refer to fig. 10.5).

4. Choose OK or press Enter to send the report to the printer.

Figure 10.12 shows the first worksheet in an expense report with range A:B16..A:L22 highlighted for printing. Figure 10.13 shows the range printed on a DECLaser 1152.

Fig. 10.12

The range A:B16..A:L22 highlighted in the expense report model.

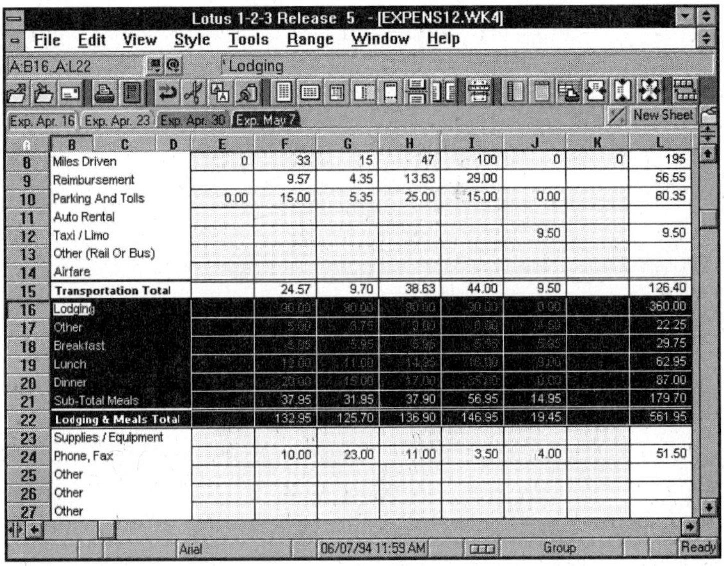

Fig. 10.13

The printout of the range A:B16..A:L22.

Transportation Total		24.57	9.70	38.63	44.00	9.50		126.40
Lodging		90.00	90.00	90.00	90.00	0.00		360.00
Other		5.00	3.75	9.00	0.00	4.50		22.25
Breakfast		5.95	5.95	5.95	5.95	5.95		29.75
Lunch		12.00	11.00	14.95	16.00	9.00		62.95
Dinner		20.00	15.00	17.00	35.00	0.00		87.00
Sub-Total Meals		37.95	31.95	37.90	56.95	14.95		179.70
Lodging & Meals Total		132.95	125.70	136.90	146.95	19.45		561.95

Printing a Multiple-Page Report

To print a multiple-page report, follow the steps for printing a one-page report (as described in the preceding section). If the print range contains more rows or columns than can fit on a page, 1-2-3 for Windows prints the report on multiple pages. Figure 10.14 shows how 1-2-3 for Windows indicates a split print range—the vertical and horizontal dashed lines show the page boundaries. The numbers of rows and columns that fit on a page depend on the global font, individual column widths and row heights, and whether or not you have chosen to compress the worksheet.

When you print a multiple-page report, you must pay attention to where 1-2-3 for Windows splits the worksheet between pages—vertically *and* horizontally. 1-2-3 for Windows can split pages at inappropriate locations, resulting in a report that is hard to read or understand. By previewing the report as described earlier in this chapter, you can see exactly how 1-2-3 for Windows prints a large range. You can then adjust the page breaks, change the page orientation, compress the worksheet, or make other changes to improve the look of the report. The next section describes the options for changing the format of the report.

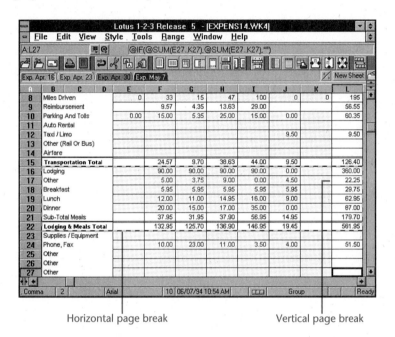

Horizontal page break   Vertical page break

Fig. 10.14
Dashed lines indicate where the page breaks will be when the worksheet is printed.

Changing the Page Contents

1-2-3 automatically sets up page breaks to fit a long worksheet onto several pages, but the page breaks may separate headings from explanatory text or columns of figures. Sometimes you may want to break the report into specific groups of data. And occasionally you may want to exclude some parts of the report from the printout, even though that text is included in the print range. The following sections explain how to make these types of changes.

Inserting Manual Page Breaks

If you are unhappy with the way 1-2-3 splits the data in a long report, you can manually insert horizontal and vertical page breaks. A horizontal page break controls a long worksheet; a vertical page break controls a wide worksheet. To insert a page break, move the cell pointer to where you want the page break to occur. Horizontal breaks are inserted *above* the cell pointer;

vertical breaks are inserted to the *left* of the cell pointer. When you insert manual page breaks, you see dotted lines that represent the placement of these breaks.

 To insert a horizontal page break just above the section of the Expense worksheet, for example, place the cell pointer in row 16 and choose **S**tyle **P**age Break or click the Horizontal Page Break SmartIcon. If you use the SmartIcon, 1-2-3 immediately displays a dotted line indicating the page break in the worksheet. The **S**tyle **P**age Break command, on the other hand, displays the Page Break dialog box, from which you can choose **C**olumn (for a vertical page break) or **R**ow (for a horizontal page break). Figure 10.15 shows the Page Break dialog box. After specifying the type of page break you want, choose OK or press Enter. A dotted line indicating the page break appears in the worksheet.

  The Printing SmartIcon set offers two page-break SmartIcons. The SmartIcon with a horizontal dotted line between two pages inserts a horizontal page break above the cell pointer. The SmartIcon with a vertical dotted line between two pages inserts a vertical page break to the left of the pointer.

To remove page breaks, choose **S**tyle **P**age Break and deselect the **C**olumn or **R**ow box.

Fig. 10.15
The Page Break
dialog box.

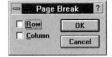

Hiding Segments in the Print Range

Sometimes data appears in a worksheet that you don't want to appear in a report. For example, you may have a column of data in the middle of the worksheet that is necessary for a calculation but not important to view on a report. 1-2-3 offers different ways to exclude data from a printout, depending on whether you want to hide a cell, a row, or a column.

Excluding Rows from a Print Range. 1-2-3 for Windows does not have a command to hide rows, although there is a way to exclude a row from a printout. To prevent a row from printing, type a vertical bar (|) in the row's leftmost cell within the print range. The vertical bar does not appear onscreen or on the printout; this character is a label-prefix that tells 1-2-3 for Windows not to print the contents of that row. A row marked in this way does not print, although the suppressed data remains in the worksheet and is used in all calculations.

Suppose that you want to print the breakdown of expenses from the Expense Report worksheet. Figure 10.16 shows a printout of the range A:B2..A:L29.

	04/10/94	04/11/94	04/12/94	04/13/94	04/14/94	04/15/94	04/16/94	
	Sun	Mon	Tue	Wed	Thu	Fri	Sat	Totals
Miles Driven	0	33	15	47	100	0	0	195
Reimbursement		9.57	4.35	13.63	29.00			56.55
Parking And Tolls	0.00	15.00	5.35	25.00	15.00	0.00		60.35
Auto Rental								
Taxi / Limo						9.50		9.50
Other (Rail Or Bus)								
Airfare								
Transportation Total		24.57	9.70	38.63	44.00	9.50		126.40
Lodging		90.00	90.00	90.00	90.00	0.00		360.00
Other		5.00	3.75	9.00	0.00	4.50		22.25
Breakfast		5.95	5.95	5.95	5.95	5.95		29.75
Lunch		12.00	11.00	14.95	16.00	9.00		62.95
Dinner		20.00	15.00	17.00	35.00	0.00		87.00
Sub-Total Meals		37.95	31.95	37.90	56.95	14.95		179.70
Lodging & Meals Total		132.95	125.70	136.90	146.95	19.45		561.95
Supplies / Equipment								
Phone, Fax		10.00	23.00	11.00	3.50	4.00		51.50
Other								
Other								
Other								
Entertainment		65.00	25.00	0.00	22.50	0.00		112.50
Total Per Day		232.52	183.40	186.53	216.95	32.95		852.35

Fig. 10.16
A printout of rows 2 through 29 of the Cash Flow worksheet.

Now suppose that you don't want the printout to show the expense details (rows 8 through 14; 16 through 21; and 23 through 28). Move the cell pointer to column A and insert a vertical bar in the leftmost cell of these rows. You can avoid editing each cell if you insert a new column (column A) at the left edge of the print range and narrow this column to a width of 1. Then type the vertical bar (|) in cell A8 and copy this entry to the other rows you don't want to print. Remember to include the new column in the print range, or the vertical bar (|) has no effect. Figure 10.17 shows the results of printing A:B2..A:L29 with the vertical bars in place for the detail rows.

To restore the worksheet after printing, use **E**dit **D**elete Column to delete the column that contains the vertical bars. If you didn't insert the vertical bars in their own column, you'll need to edit each cell and delete this symbol.

	04/10/94	04/11/94	04/12/94	04/13/94	04/14/94	04/15/94	04/16/94	
	Sun	Mon	Tue	Wed	Thu	Fri	Sat	Totals
Transportation Total		24.57	9.70	38.63	44.00	9.50		126.40
Lodging & Meals Total		132.95	125.70	136.90	146.95	19.45		561.95
Total Per Day		232.52	183.40	186.53	216.95	32.95		852.35

Fig. 10.17
A printout of rows 2 through 29, with the expense detail rows suppressed.

Excluding Columns from a Print Range. You can use the Style Hide command to indicate columns that you don't want displayed on-screen. If you include these hidden columns in a print range, the columns do not print.

Suppose that you are working with the Expense Report worksheet and you want to print the expense information for weekdays only. You want to hide the columns for Sunday and Saturday (columns E and K). Issue the **S**tyle **H**ide command for each of these two columns to suppress the data. Figure 10.18 shows the result of hiding columns E and K.

Fig. 10.18
Columns E and K are hidden to prevent them from printing.

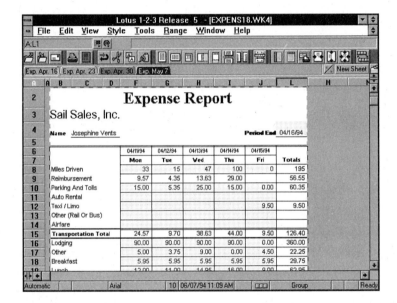

Another way to hide a column is to set its width to zero. To set the column width to 0, either select **S**tyle **C**olumn Width and enter **0** in the **S**et Width To field text box of the Column Width dialog box or drag the right border of the column so that it touches the left border.

To redisplay a column, use **S**tyle **H**ide, select the R**a**nge text box, and enter the address of one cell in the column you want to redisplay. After you click the Sho**w** button, the column reappears. Another way to unhide a column is to select the range by highlighting across the column to be unhidden. For example, to unhide column D, drag across columns C and E and click the Sho**w** button in the Hide dialog box.

Excluding Cells and Ranges from a Print Range. A worksheet may include information you want to save on disk but omit from a printed report. For example, you may want to omit the employee Name (in the cell named DATA_02) from a printout of the Expense Report. To hide only part of a row or column or an area that spans one or more rows and columns, use the **S**tyle **N**umber Format command and select Hidden from the **F**ormat list in the Number Format dialog box. For this example, select cell C4 (with the range name DATA_02), choose **S**tyle Number **F**ormat, and highlight Hidden in the **F**ormat list; then print the range A:B2..A:L29 (see fig. 10.19). Note that the employee Name is omitted from the report since it resides in the hidden cell.

Expense Report
Sail Sales, Inc.

Name _____   Period Ending 04/16/94

	04/11/94	04/12/94	04/13/94	04/14/94	04/15/94	
	Mon	Tue	Wed	Thu	Fri	Totals
Miles Driven	33	15	47	100	0	195
Reimbursement	9.57	4.35	13.63	29.00		56.55
Parking And Tolls	15.00	5.35	25.00	15.00	0.00	60.35
Auto Rental						
Taxi / Limo					9.50	9.50
Other (Rail Or Bus)						
Airfare						
Transportation Total	24.57	9.70	38.63	44.00	9.50	126.40
Lodging	90.00	90.00	90.00	90.00	0.00	360.00
Other	5.00	3.75	9.00	0.00	4.50	22.25
Breakfast	5.95	5.95	5.95	5.95	5.95	29.75
Lunch	12.00	11.00	14.95	16.00	9.00	62.95
Dinner	20.00	15.00	17.00	35.00	0.00	87.00
Sub-Total Meals	37.95	31.95	37.90	56.95	14.95	179.70
Lodging & Meals Total	132.95	125.70	136.90	146.95	19.45	561.95
Supplies / Equipment						
Phone, Fax	10.00	23.00	11.00	3.50	4.00	51.50
Other						
Other						
Other						
Entertainment	65.00	25.00	0.00	22.50	0.00	112.50
Total Per Day	232.52	183.40	186.53	216.95	32.95	852.35

Fig. 10.19
The printed output does not display the data contained in cell C4 (cell C4 is formatted as Hidden).

To restore the employee name after you finish printing, select **S**tyle **N**umber Format and click the **R**eset button. You can also click the Format button on the status bar and select Reset.

Tip
To hide a cell or a range of cells quickly, select the data you want to hide, click the Format button on the status bar, and select Hidden.

Tip
If you find your-
self repeating
certain print op-
erations, you can
save time by de-
veloping and
using print mac-
ros. For more
information on
using macros, see
Chapters 35
through 38.

Troubleshooting

I wanted to retrieve my named print settings, but the file wasn't there. What happened to it?

Unless you specify otherwise, print settings are stored in the current directory—the directory in which you last saved or opened a file. You are probably in a different directory from the one in which you saved the print settings. Navigate the Directories list, changing to the different directories you use in 1-2-3, until you locate the appropriate AL3 file.

I'm trying to point to multiple print ranges in the Print dialog box, but 1-2-3 won't let me. As soon as I define the first range, I return to the Print dialog box. What am I doing wrong?

Nothing. 1-2-3 won't let you point to multiple ranges when defining the print range from the Print dialog box. You must either type the ranges (separated by commas or semicolons) in the Selected **R**ange field or preselect the ranges before you give the print command.

I successfully hid a column I didn't want printed in my report. Now I want to display the column again but I can't get it to appear. In the Hide dialog box, I specify the column I want to unhide, but the column remains hidden.

After you specify a cell in the hidden column, you must click the Show button in the Hide dialog box. If you click OK, 1-2-3 thinks you are trying to hide the column again. The Show button is what tells 1-2-3 you want to unhide the column.

Enhancing Reports with Page Setup Options

A printed report that contains numbers without descriptive headings is diffi-cult, if not impossible, to interpret. You can make a report easier to under-stand by using 1-2-3 for Windows features that help you fit an entire report on a single page by changing the orientation. You can specify that specific data ranges print on each page of a multiple-page report (these ranges are called *row* or *column titles*). You also can print the worksheet frame (the row numbers and the column letters). The sections that follow show you how to create headers and footers, repeat row and column headings on succeeding pages, and print the worksheet frame and grid lines. You also learn how to set margins and save the print settings.

Remember, to access the Page Setup dialog box, you can use any of the following techniques:

- Open the File and choose Page Setup.

- Choose the Page Setup SmartIcon.

- In the Print dialog box, choose the Page Setup button.

- In the Print Preview dialog box, choose the Page Setup button.

- In the preview window, choose the Page Setup icon.

Switching the Page Orientation

One way to get a wide report to fit on a single page is to change the *orientation* (direction) of the printing. Normally you print in *portrait orientation*; that is, the text prints across the narrower part of the page. If you want to print horizontally on the page (across the longer width of the page), use *landscape orientation*.

To switch between portrait and landscape orientation, you can click the Portrait or Landscape SmartIcons. The SmartIcon showing a vertical page selects portrait orientation; the SmartIcon showing a horizontal page selects landscape orientation. You also can change the orientation in the Page Setup dialog box. To change the orientation with the dialog box, choose Portrait or Landscape to indicate the direction you want 1-2-3 to print.

Compressing and Expanding the Report

If your report doesn't fit on one page, you can have 1-2-3 automatically shrink the data using the Size option in the Page Setup dialog box. Five sizes are available:

- Actual Size

- Fit all to page

- Fit columns to page

- Fit rows to page

- Manually scale

With Actual Size (the default setting), 1-2-3 makes no attempt to alter the size of the printed output; that is, the data is not compressed at all. If you select Fit All to Page, 1-2-3 compresses the print range, in an attempt to fit the information on one page. The report can be compressed up to one-seventh of its original size. If the print range still does not fit, 1-2-3 prints the first page with the most compression possible and subsequent pages with the same compression. A new feature since Release 4 is the ability to compress just the columns (Fit columns to page) or just the rows (Fit rows to page).

You also may enter a specific percentage by choosing the Manually Scale option. (The report in Figure 10.11 was manually scaled to 90%.) If you select this option, the dialog box displays a text box in which you can enter a percentage; this number can be as low as 15 (representing 15 percent of normal size) or as high as 1000 (representing 1,000 percent, or 10 times the normal size). By manually scaling, you can compress or expand the worksheet.

The Printing SmartIcon set offers three SmartIcons for fitting the print range on a single page: Fit Rows to Page, Fit Columns to Page, and Fit All to Page.

◀ "Setting
Column
Widths,"
p. 312

There are several other ways to fit more of your worksheet on a printed page. One way is to narrow the column widths as much as possible, either globally or individually. You can also print the report in landscape orientation or set smaller margins. See "Switching the Page Orientation" in the previous section and "Setting Margins" later in this chapter for details.

Centering a Print Range

1-2-3 for Windows Release 5 has a new group box in the Page Setup dialog box that lets you center your report Horizontally, Vertically, or both on the page. Select the appropriate check box to center your report the way you want to.

Creating Headers and Footers

A *header* is a single line of text that prints at the top of every page in your report; a *footer* prints at the bottom of each page. You can use headers and footers to print page numbers, the worksheet file name, the report date and time, the report title, and so on. The header text, which is printed on the first line after the top margin, is followed by two blank header lines preceding the report (for spacing). The footer text is printed above the bottom margin and below two blank footer lines (again, for spacing).

You specify a header or footer in the Page Setup dialog box. A header or footer can have three parts: left-aligned, centered, and right-aligned text. There are boxes provided for each of these three parts in the Page Setup dialog box (see fig. 10.20). Whatever is entered in the first box is aligned at the left margin; the text in the second box is centered between the left and right margins; the text in the third box is aligned at the right margin. The header and footer text is printed in the worksheet's default typeface and size.

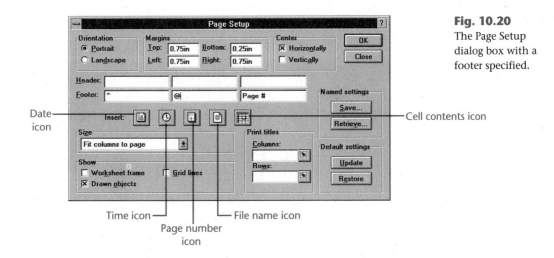

Fig. 10.20
The Page Setup
dialog box with a
footer specified.

In addition to any text you enter, the header or footer can include codes for
inserting page numbers, the date or time of printing, the file name, or the
contents of a cell. First, place the cursor in the appropriate box (left-aligned,
centered, or right-aligned) next to **H**eader or **F**ooter in the page Setup dialog
box. The insert icons immediately become active. Then specify the codes you
want to use from the following list:

- To number pages sequentially (starting with 1), enter a pound sign (**#**)
  or click the Page Number Insert icon (the center icon).

- To print the current date, enter an at sign (**@**) or click the Date Insert
  icon (the calendar).

- To print the time, enter a plus sign (**+**) or click the Time Insert icon
  (the clock).

- To insert the file name, type a caret symbol (**^**) or click the File Name
  Insert icon (the one that looks like a page).

- To use the contents of a cell as a header or footer, enter a backslash (****)
  or click the Cell Contents Insert icon (it looks like a worksheet grid).
  Then type the address or range name of the cell that contains the text
  you want to include in the header or footer. The specified cell address
  or range name can contain a formula. If you specify a range name, 1-2-3
  for Windows uses the contents of only the first cell in the range.

Figure 10.21 shows a printout with the footer specified in figure 10.20. This
footer has a left-aligned file name, a centered date, and a right-aligned page

number. You can see from this example how the file name, date, and page number are formatted.

Fig. 10.21
The footer produced by entering codes in the Footer field of the Page Setup dialog box.

Expense Report

Sail Sales, Inc.

| Name | Josephine Vents | | | | | | Period Ending | 04/16/94 |

	04/10/94	04/11/94	04/12/94	04/13/94	04/14/94	04/15/94	04/16/94	
	Sun	Mon	Tue	Wed	Thu	Fri	Sat	Totals
Miles Driven	0	33	15	47	100	0	0	195
Reimbursement		9.57	4.35	13.63	29.00			56.55
Parking And Tolls	0.00	15.00	5.35	25.00	15.00	0.00		60.35
Auto Rental								
Taxi / Limo						9.50		9.50
Other (Rail Or Bus)								
Airfare								
Transportation Total		24.57	9.70	38.63	44.00	9.50		126.40
Lodging		90.00	90.00	90.00	90.00	0.00		360.00
Other		5.00	3.75	9.00	0.00	4.50		22.25
Breakfast		5.95	5.95	5.95	5.95	5.95		29.75
Lunch		12.00	11.00	14.95	16.00	9.00		62.95
Dinner		20.00	15.00	17.00	35.00	0.00		87.00
Sub-Total Meals		37.95	31.95	37.90	56.95	14.95		179.70
Lodging & Meals Total		132.95	125.70	136.90	146.95	19.45		561.95
Supplies / Equipment								
Phone, Fax		10.00	23.00	11.00	3.50	4.00		51.50
Other								
Other								
Other								
Entertainment		65.00	25.00	0.00	22.50	0.00		112.50
Total Per Day		232.52	183.40	186.53	216.95	32.95		852.35

Printing Titles

To make a multiple-page printed report more understandable, you can add headings from row or column ranges by using the Print Titles options in the Page Setup dialog box. To specify row titles in the Ro**w**s box of the Page Setup dialog box, select one or more rows of labels to print above each print range and at the top of all pages. To specify column titles in the **C**olumns box of the Page Setup dialog box, designate one or more columns of labels to print to the left of every print range and at the left edge of all pages. Setting titles in a printout is similar to freezing titles in the worksheet. The Ro**w**s option produces a printed border similar to a frozen horizontal title display; the **C**olumns option produces a printed border similar to a frozen vertical title display.

▶ "Changing the Display of a Worksheet File," p. 486

SmartIcons for these commands are also available in the Printing SmartIcon set. To specify one or more columns to print at the left of each page, select the range of columns and then click the Set Columns as Print Titles SmartIcon. To specify rows to print at the top of each page, select the range of rows and then click the Set Rows as Print Titles SmartIcon.

Caution

If you include the print titles in the print range, 1-2-3 prints these elements twice. Be careful, therefore, not to include the range containing the print titles in the print range.

To cancel a print title, highlight the entry in the **C**olumns or Ro**w**s text box in the Page Setup dialog box. Press Del to clear the contents and then press Enter.

Printing the Worksheet Frame and Grid Lines

Printing the worksheet frame is particularly useful during worksheet development, when you want the printouts to show the location of data in a large worksheet. In the Show section of the Page Setup dialog box, you can make two selections to print the worksheet frame. The Wor**k**sheet Frame option prints column letters across the top of a worksheet and row numbers down the side of the worksheet. The **G**rid Lines option prints lines between all cells in the print range.

Figure 10.22 shows an example of a report with the worksheet frame and grid lines displayed.

A	A	B	C	D	E	F	G
1			Actual	Estimated	Actual	Estimated	Actual
2			Qtr 1	Qtr 1	Qtr 2	Qtr 2	Qtr 3
3			1994	1995	1994	1995	1994
4							
5		Department 20	92	101	71	78	101
6		Department 24	87	96	82	90	100
7		Department 32	89	98	83	91	99
8		Department 35	87	96	85	94	89
9		Department 42	76	84	69	76	97
10		Total	431	474	390	429	486
11							

Fig. 10.22
This report shows the worksheet frame and grid lines.

Setting Margins

The Page Setup dialog box enables you to change the margins of the report. Select **T**op, **B**ottom, **L**eft, or **R**ight, and enter the margin width in inches. The default settings are as follows:

Top	0.75in
Bottom	0.25in
Left	0.75in
Right	0.75in

Tip
You can also choose to print drawn objects by marking the Drawn **O**bject check box under Show.

If your report has a header, it appears *after* (not within) the top margin, and footer text appears above the bottom margin. If you didn't specify a header, the report begins printing immediately after the top margin.

Naming and Saving the Current Settings

When you have several worksheet reports with a similar layout, you may want to save the page setup so that you can retrieve the settings for other files. Saving the page setup options keeps you from having to specify the same settings over and over again. The Named Settings area in the Page Setup dialog box offers buttons for saving and retrieving page settings.

To assign a name to the current print settings, select the **S**ave button; you are prompted for a file name. The **S**ave button creates a file, with the AL3 extension, that you can use with other worksheets. When you want to use these named settings in another worksheet file, select the Retrie**v**e button from the Page Setup dialog box and then select the file name from the list of settings file names.

Tip

The page setup file is stored in the current directory, unless you specify otherwise. For organizational purposes, you may want to store all AL3 files in the same directory.

Troubleshooting

I want to print my report on legal-sized paper, but the Page Setup dialog box doesn't have an option for specifying the paper size.

You can print on legal-sized paper by choosing an option in a different dialog box. Choose **F**ile Prin**t**er Setup and make sure that the printer you want to use is selected. Then click the Setup button; from here, you can find the Paper Size option.

In Release 5, how do I create borders, columns, or rows that repeat on each page? There appears to be no such command.

In Release 5, borders are called *print titles*. The Columns and Rows print-title options are located in the Page Setup dialog box.

The header is not centered over my report, even though I entered the header text in the middle Header box in the Page Setup dialog box.

The text in the middle Header box is centered between the report's left and right margins. If your report is not very wide and doesn't extend to the right margin, the header can look off-center. The solution is to increase the left and right margins as much as possible.

Stopping and Suspending Printing

After starting one or more print jobs, you may find that you made a mistake in the worksheet data or print settings and that you need to correct an error before the report finishes printing. You can halt the current print job, clear the print queue, and temporarily suspend printing by accessing the Print Manager (press Ctrl+Esc and select Print Manager). To cancel the printing of a report, click the name of the file in the print queue and then click the **D**elete button. To temporarily suspend printing, click the **P**ause button. When you are ready to continue, choose the **R**esume button. See the Windows manual for more information on the Print Manager.

Printing a Text File to Disk

To create an ASCII text file that you can incorporate into a word processing document, you use no printing-related commands. This represents a deviation from DOS versions of 1-2-3; DOS versions of 1-2-3 use the **/P**rint **F**ile command to print a file to disk. In 1-2-3 for Windows, you create an ASCII file by selecting the **F**ile Save **A**s command and choosing the Text (txt) file type in the Save As dialog box. Enter a name in the File **N**ame field; if you don't type an extension, TXT is automatically assigned.

> **Note**
>
> If you want to incorporate your formatted worksheet in another Windows application, you can transfer the data via the Windows Clipboard. Select the worksheet range, and choose **E**dit **C**opy. Then switch to the application you want to copy the worksheet into and choose **E**dit **P**aste. For example, if you copy a worksheet range to an Ami Pro document, Ami Pro treats the range as an Ami Pro table.

Printing a PostScript File to Disk

You can also print a PostScript file to disk using the **F**ile Prin**t**er Setup command.

1. Choose the printer name from the Printers list.

2. Then click the **S**etup button.

3. In the dialog box for your printer, click the **O**ptions button.

◀ "Copying Data," p. 260

◀ "Saving Files," p. 283

4. Under Print To in the Options dialog box, select Encapsulated PostScript File and type the file name.

5. Click OK.

From Here...

The following chapters show you how to take full advantage of the powerful graphing capabilities in 1-2-3 for Windows. You learn how to create, view, and print graphs to give visual impact to worksheet data.

■ Part II, "Working with Charts," teaches you how to use graphics (text boxes, lines, arrows, and rectangles, for example) to further enhance the appearance of your work and highlight important data. You can then use the skills you learned in this chapter to print reports enhanced with graphics and charts.

■ Chapter 17, "Developing Business Presentations," teaches you to refine your worksheets even further so that they work well in presentations and convey your message effectively. You also learn how to print slides for your presentations.

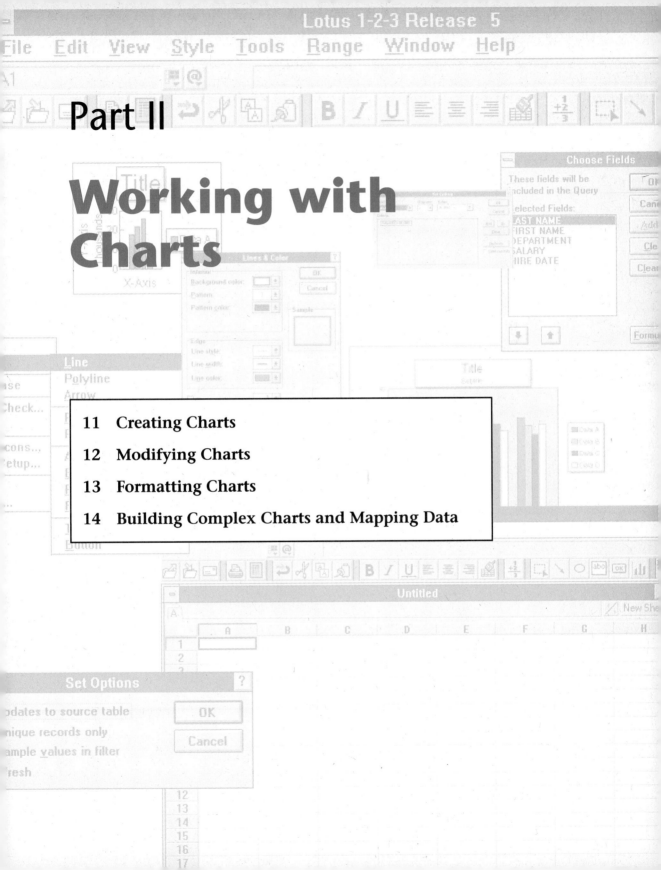

Part II

Working with Charts

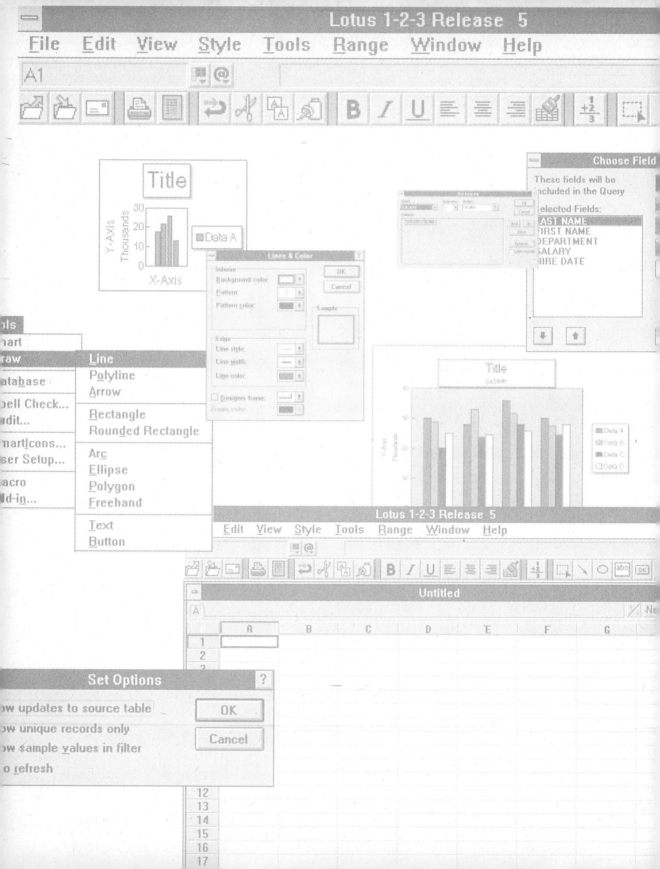

Chapter 11

Creating Charts

Even if 1-2-3 for Windows provided only worksheet capabilities, the program would be extremely powerful. Despite the importance of keeping detailed worksheets that show real or projected data, however, data that is difficult to understand can be worthless.

Drawing conclusions from countless rows of numeric data is often difficult. To make data more readily understandable, 1-2-3 for Windows offers graphics capabilities that enable you to display data graphically. The program offers several types of business charts and sophisticated options for enhancing the appearance of charts. The real strength of 1-2-3 for Windows graphics, however, lies in the graphics' integration with the worksheet. When you create a chart in the worksheet file, the chart is linked to the worksheet file. When you change data in the graphed range, the chart is automatically updated to reflect the change.

This chapter shows you how to accomplish the following tasks:

- Create charts automatically from data in a worksheet file

- Define a chart's data ranges manually

- Add charts to worksheet files

Understanding Common Chart Elements

When you create a chart, 1-2-3 for Windows includes several elements. Figure 11.1 shows a bar chart with these elements; the default chart type is a bar chart. Except for pie charts, all charts have a *y-axis* (a vertical left edge) and an *x-axis* (a horizontal bottom edge). In horizontally oriented charts, the y-axis is the bottom edge, and the x-axis is the left edge. 1-2-3 for Windows also enables you to use an optional second y-axis along the right side of a chart.

1-2-3 for Windows divides the axes with *tick marks* and scales the numbers on the y-axis based on the minimum and maximum numbers in the associated data range. The intersection of the y-axis and the x-axis is the *origin*. Although you can plot charts with a nonzero origin, using a zero origin makes a chart easier to compare and understand.

A chart is made up of one or more *data series,* each of which reflects a category of data. The first category of data is always series A, the second is series B, and so on. Some chart types use a limited number of data ranges; for example, pie charts use one data range, and XY charts use two. Other chart types, such as line and bar charts, can graph up to 23 data ranges. When a chart has more than one data series, a *legend* is necessary to describe each of the data series.

The main part of the chart is called the *plot.* The plot includes the axes and their labels and titles and all the data plotted on the axes. A pie chart's plot is the pie and data labels. The plot does not include the legend, titles, or footnotes.

Figure 11.1 shows the elements of a simple chart.

Fig. 11.1
Parts of a 1-2-3
chart.

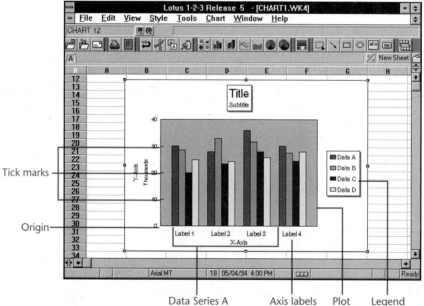

Tick marks

Origin

Data Series A   Axis labels   Plot   Legend

Selecting the Worksheet Cells To Be Charted

To create a chart, you first must open the worksheet file that contains the data you want to plot. The examples in this chapter are based on the quarterly sales report shown in figure 11.2.

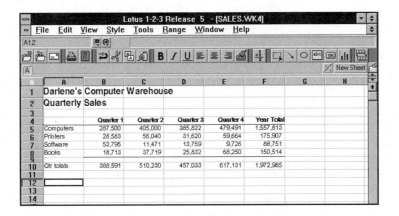

Fig. 11.2

The quarterly sales report worksheet.

To graph information from the sales report, you must know which data you want to plot and which data you want to use to label the chart. In figure 11.2, the labels in rows 1 and 2 are suitable for the chart titles. Time-period labels are listed across row 4; these labels will go on the x-axis. Category identifiers are located in column A; these labels will become part of the legend. The numeric entries in rows 5 through 8 contain four different data series.

Creating an Automatic Chart

If your worksheet is set up properly (as described in the section "Understanding the Rules for Automatic Charting," later in this chapter) creating an automatic chart is a very simple process:

1. Pull down the **T**ools menu and choose **C**hart; or click on the Create Chart SmartIcon. The Chart dialog box appears (see fig. 11.3). It shows and describes the steps to create the chart.

2. Click on the range selector in the Chart dialog box, then select the range of cells to be charted, including titles, legend labels, x-axis labels, and the numeric data. You can select the range with either the mouse (click and drag) or the keyboard (use the arrow keys to highlight the range, then press Enter). For example, you could select the range A1..E8 in figure 11.2.

Working with Charts

II

Fig. 11.3
The Chart dialog box coaches you through the automatic chart creation process.

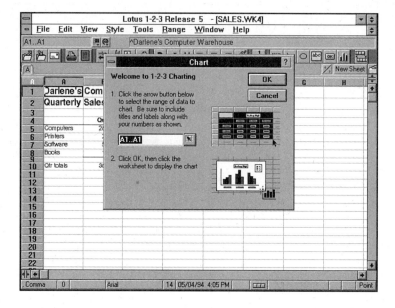

Tip
Preselect the range you want to chart before you click the Create Chart SmartIcon or select the **C**hart command from the **T**ools menu; this lets you create the chart without displaying the Chart dialog box.

▶ "Resizing the Entire Chart," p. 398

3. The range you selected appears in the Range dialog box. To create a chart with this range, click the OK button. The Chart dialog box disappears and the mouse pointer changes to the chart pointer, which looks like a bar chart. The message at the top of the window tells you to click and drag where you want to display the chart.

4. Indicate where you want to place the chart in the worksheet. For example, to create the chart in figure 11.4, you could click on cell C26.

There are two ways you can indicate placement of the chart. If you just click the chart pointer on the upper-left corner of where you want to place the chart, it will be inserted at a default size (about 4 by 2.5 inches). Alternatively, you can click and drag a box, indicating the size of your chart. Either way, the chart is inserted into the worksheet. There is no special graph window, unlike previous versions of the program, nor do you have to give a command to view the chart—it is always in the worksheet.

Looking at the Default Automatic Chart

Figure 11.4 shows the default automatic chart created for the worksheet range A1..E8. Notice that the default chart type is a bar chart. To change the type (for example, to a line or pie chart), use the **C**hart **T**ype command or the

Select Chart Type SmartIcon. Chart types are discussed in more detail in the next chapter.

When 1-2-3 creates the chart, it is automatically *selected*; that is, you can move, resize, and manipulate the chart in other ways. You can see that the chart is selected because it has *selection handles*—small black boxes that appear around the border of the chart (see fig. 11.4).

▶ "Changing the Chart Type and Style," p. 401

▶ "Building Complex Charts," p. 433

Selection handles

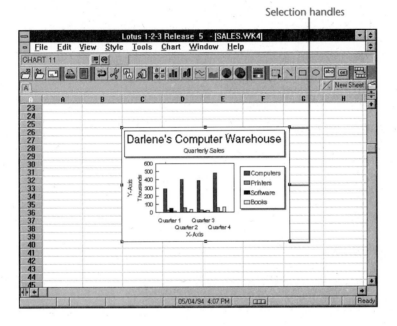

Fig. 11.4
A bar chart created from the range A1..E8.

Here are a few other things to notice about the default chart:

■ The title and subtitle are enclosed in a frame and are centered at the top of the chart.

■ The framed legend is located to the right of the plot.

■ The entire chart is framed.

■ Default axis titles (X-Axis and Y-Axis) are inserted.

Also notice that after you create a chart, a new option, **C**hart, replaces **R**ange in the menu bar. This option displays only if the chart, or an element in the chart, is selected. Chapters 12, 13, and 14 cover how to manipulate and change these chart elements.

II

Working with Charts

Caution

If you click a worksheet cell, the chart is no longer selected and the **C**hart menu option disappears. To access the **C**hart menu again, you must select an element on the chart by clicking it; you then see selection handles around the object, and the **C**hart menu returns.

Understanding the Rules for Automatic Charting

You learned previously that creating an automatic chart requires that the worksheet be properly set up. In other words, if you know the rules 1-2-3 uses to create a chart automatically, you can make sure that your worksheet is set up in such a way that the chart will look the way you want it to. Here are the rules 1-2-3 follows when it creates the chart:

Rule 1. If a title is anywhere in the first row of the selected range, it becomes the chart title.

Rule 2. If a title is anywhere in the second row, it becomes the chart's subtitle.

Rule 3. Blank rows and columns are ignored.

Rule 4. If more rows than columns are in your selected range, 1-2-3 plots the data by column. The first column becomes the x-axis labels, the second column becomes the first data series, the third column becomes the second data series, and so forth. The first row after any titles becomes the legend labels.

Rule 5. If more columns than rows are in the selected range, 1-2-3 plots the data by rows. The first row (after any titles or blank rows) becomes the x-axis labels, the second row becomes the first data series, the next row becomes the second data series, and so on. The first column becomes the legend labels.

Rule 6. If there are the same number of columns and rows in the selected range, 1-2-3 plots the data by column. (See rule 4.)

Rule 7. If you select only numeric data when you create a chart, 1-2-3 follows rules 4 and 5 to determine how to lay out the chart (by column or by row). 1-2-3 creates a default heading and legend, and default axis titles (see fig. 11.5); you can modify this default text by double-clicking the appropriate chart element. You then see the appropriate dialog box (Headings, X-Axis, Y-Axis, or Legend) in which you can change the text. These dialog boxes are discussed in Chapter 12, "Modifying Charts."

Although it may seem that there are a lot of rules for creating automatic charts, you do have quite a bit of flexibility. 1-2-3 is smart when it looks at your selected range. 1-2-3 ignores blank rows and columns and can determine whether a row contains a title for the heading, labels for the x-axis or legends, or numbers to be plotted. If you don't include the legend labels or x-axis labels in your chart range, 1-2-3 Release 5 for Windows does not use the first row or column of numeric values as your labels—it leaves the row or column blank so that you can specify the range later. The labels are undefined until you specify the range.

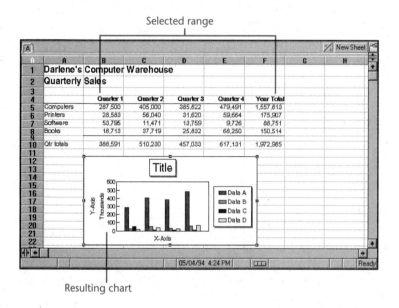

Selected range

Resulting chart

Fig. 11.5
1-2-3 creates default titles and legend labels when you have only values in the chart range.

II

Troubleshooting

*I created an automatic chart by preselecting the range and choosing **T**ools **C**hart. However, the chart isn't set up the way I want it. The legends and x-axis labels are switched. Is there a way to fix this?*

When 1-2-3 for Windows produces automatic charts, it looks at your preselected range and uses its rules for determining how to set up your chart ranges. To switch your legends and data labels, choose **C**hart **R**anges to display the **R**anges dialog box, then select By row or By column in the A**s**sign Ranges field. Unfortunately, this dialog box doesn't tell you what the current direction is; however, when you choose By row or By column, 1-2-3 does show you a sample layout. If you aren't sure which option

(continues)

(continued)

you want, choose one, and if the chart doesn't change, go back and try the other one.

Can I place a chart on a different sheet than the one the worksheet data appears in?

Yes. First, create the new sheet for the chart if it doesn't already exist (click the New Sheet button or select the **I**nsert command on the **E**dit menu). Then move to the sheet with the data and perform the steps to select the chart data ranges. When the mouse pointer changes to the chart pointer (a bar chart), click on the tab for the sheet on which you want to place the chart and click the cell in which you want the upper-left corner of the chart to begin, or click and drag to make the chart a size other than the default.

Creating a Chart Manually

As you learned in the previous section, when you preselect the range, 1-2-3 uses the data in your worksheet to produce a default chart. But that isn't the only way to create a chart. 1-2-3 provides a **C**hart menu so that you can define the elements of your chart (see fig. 11.6). You'll want to go to this menu if your worksheet isn't laid out in the prescribed fashion, if you must modify any of the ranges, or if you would just rather define the data series, titles, and legends yourself.

Fig. 11.6
The **C**hart menu.

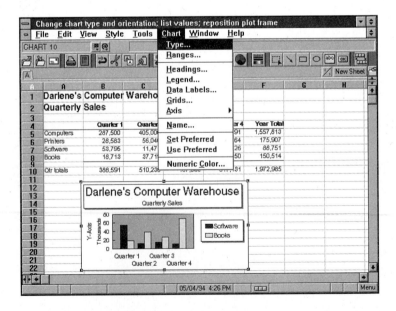

To create a chart from scratch, go directly to the **T**ools **C**hart option or click the Create Chart SmartIcon, without preselecting a range. The Chart dialog box will appear. Now you can either select one of the ranges for the chart (the A data series is best) or leave a single cell selected. Click OK, then indicate where you want the chart in the worksheet. When you are done, you'll see an empty frame.

Your next step is to define the ranges containing your x-axis labels and your data series. The **C**hart **R**anges command lets you define or modify your chart's x-axis labels and data series ranges. Figure 11.7 shows the Ranges dialog box. Another way to display this dialog box is to place the mouse pointer on the chart, press the right mouse button to display the quick menu, and choose Chart Ranges.

Fig. 11.7
You can define or modify chart ranges in the Ranges dialog box.

A chart can contain up to 23 data series, represented by the letters A through W in the Se**r**ies list box. If you have already created a chart and specified a legend, the legend labels appear next to each series letter (see fig. 11.7). As you click different series letters, the defined range (if any) appears in the Ra**n**ge text box. When a series range is undefined, `Empty` appears next to the series letter.

You can define your chart's ranges individually or as a group (choosing Individually, By row, or By column in the A**s**sign Ranges drop-down list). Defining them as a group is clearly the easiest way. If you choose By row in the A**s**sign Ranges drop-down list, 1-2-3 displays a sample grid, showing the proper worksheet layout for this choice (x-axis labels in the first row, legend labels in the first column). If you choose By column, the sample grid displays legend labels in the first row and x-axis labels in the first column. Figure 11.8 shows the Ranges dialog box when By column is selected in the A**s**sign

Tip
If the labels you want on the x-axis appear in a row, choose By row. If the x-axis labels appear in a column, choose By column.

II

Working with Charts

Ranges drop-down list. Notice that when either By row or By column is selected under Assign Ranges, the Series list box is replaced by the sample layout diagram. The Series list box disappears.

Fig. 11.8
A sample
worksheet grid
shows the way
1-2-3 assigns the
date series when
you choose By
Column for Assign
Ranges.

After you determine the layout that is appropriate (By Row or By Column), enter the appropriate range in the Range text box or use the range selector to select the range in the worksheet. When you choose OK, 1-2-3 creates a chart and places it in the worksheet range you defined earlier. If you redisplay the Ranges dialog box, the legend labels appear next to each series letter, assuming you included the labels in the range you defined. If you didn't include the legend labels, the generic names (Data A, Data B, and so on) appear in the legend and in the Ranges dialog box.

Defining the ranges individually requires more work but is sometimes the only way to define chart ranges. When you don't want to plot certain columns or rows that are in the middle of a range, you must define the series one at a time. For example, if you want to graph computer sales (see row 5 of fig. 11.2) versus software sales (see row 7 of fig. 11.2), you must define the series individually so that you don't plot the printer sales (see row 6 of fig. 11.2).

> **Note**
>
> If the ranges for the chart are not next to each other, you can still create the chart automatically by selecting the collection of ranges for the chart before you click on the Create Chart SmartIcon or select the **C**hart command from the **T**ools menu.
> To select a collection of ranges, press Ctrl while you select additional ranges for the collection.

Troubleshooting

*My worksheet is not set up to produce a chart automatically, so I want to create a chart manually. However, the **C**hart option does not appear in my menu bar. How do I create a chart manually?*

The **C**hart option appears in the menu bar only if a chart, or an element on a chart, is selected. Otherwise, **R**ange appears in the menu bar. To create a chart manually, you perform the same steps that you would if you could create the chart automatically, only instead of selecting all the ranges for the chart, select a single blank cell so that 1-2-3 creates an empty chart. Or you can select the A data series range to create the chart that plots that data series alone. In either case, once the chart appears in the worksheet, select it so that the **C**hart option appears in the menu bar, then select the **R**anges command from the **C**hart menu and, in the Ranges dialog box, specify all or the remaining data ranges individually.

Naming and Finding Charts

1-2-3 automatically names your charts as you create them (Chart 1, Chart 2, and so forth). The name of the selected chart (or the last one you selected) appears in the selection indicator on the edit line. To give your charts more descriptive names, use the **C**hart **N**ame command. Select the current chart name in the **E**xisting Charts list, type the new name in the **C**hart Name field, and then click on the **R**ename button.

To display the chart associated with a name, press F5 (GoTo) or choose **E**dit **G**o To to display the dialog box. In the **T**ype of Item field, choose Chart and then select the chart name from the list.

Creating Multiple Charts in a File

1-2-3 for Windows lets you create an unlimited number of charts in each worksheet file. You can define new charts and place them in different parts of the worksheet. For organizational purposes, you might want to place each chart in its own sheet; use the New Sheet button to insert a sheet after the current one.

From Here...

In this chapter, you learned how to create a chart automatically from data in a worksheet and how to define a chart manually. You also learned how to name and find charts. To learn how to modify charts and create more complex charts, refer to the following chapters:

- Chapter 12, "Modifying Charts," introduces the different types of charts you can create. This chapter also covers how to manipulate the elements in a chart, including resizing the whole chart or parts of the chart, adding and deleting elements, editing the titles and legends, and other tasks.

- Chapter 13, "Formatting Charts," covers how to change colors and patterns, number format, and text attributes, as well as how to annotate a chart. You also learn to preview and print charts.

- Chapter 14, "Building Complex Charts," shows how to create the most complicated chart types offered by 1-2-3 for Windows, as well as how to add graphics to a chart.

Chapter 12

Modifying Charts

In Chapter 11, you saw how easy it was to create a chart from worksheet data. Although the default bar chart may suit your needs perfectly, you may find that a different kind of chart would illustrate your data more effectively, or you may want to add titles or notes to make your chart's message more clear.

1-2-3 for Windows offers many different chart types and styles that you can select with the click of the mouse. You can also move and resize chart elements, add titles and notes, and exercise more advanced control over the way 1-2-3 for Windows graphs the data, such as changing the scale of the y-axis.

In this chapter, you learn to:

- Select chart objects

- Move and delete chart objects

- Select an appropriate chart type and style

- Change the default chart type and style

- Change a variety of other chart options, including orientation, legend, titles, axis titles, axis scale, and tick marks

- Add elements to a chart, including notes, a background grid, data labels, and a table of values

Manipulating Chart Elements

One nice aspect of 1-2-3's charts is how malleable they are. You can move individual elements on the chart, and then move, size, delete, or format them. It's this flexibility that makes it so easy to build charts in 1-2-3 for Windows.

Resizing the Entire Chart

The printed dimensions of a chart correspond to its size in the worksheet. However, you might discover that the default size or the size you initially made the chart does not meet your needs. Resizing a chart is straightforward. First, click the chart frame so that you see selection handles surrounding the chart. Next, drag one of the handles until the chart is the desired size. While you drag the handles, the mouse pointer changes to a four-headed arrow.

Options for Resizing

The way that 1-2-3 for Windows resizes depends on which handle you drag:

- If you drag a corner handle, you change both the height and width of the chart.

- By dragging a middle handle on the right or left side of the chart, you change just the width.

- If you drag a middle handle on the top or bottom of the chart, you adjust the height only.

- If you want to size the chart proportionally, hold down the Shift key as you drag.

Showing Units of Measurement in the Worksheet Frame

Tip

If a chart is too large to fit on-screen, select the Zoom **O**ut command on the **V**iew menu to show more of the worksheet.

▶ "Printing a Chart," p. 438

▶ "Previewing a Chart," p. 440

1-2-3 does not provide a way that you can directly define a chart's dimensions in inches. For instance, you can't go to a dialog box and specify a width of 5 and a height of 3 inches, although you can specify an option to print a full-page chart.

You can, however, measure your chart size by displaying a ruler in the worksheet frame. Open the **V**iew menu and choose the Set View **P**references command. Then, in the Set View **P**references dialog box, choose Inches from the Worksheet Frame drop-down list box. (You can also choose Characters, Metric, or Points/Picas.) Figure 12.1 shows the inch ruler displayed in the worksheet frame. When you finish using the ruler to measure your chart size, you'll want to go back to the standard worksheet frame (column letters and row numbers). To change the worksheet frame back to row numbers and column letters, select the Set View **P**references command from the **V**iew menu and change the setting for Worksheet Frame back to Standard.

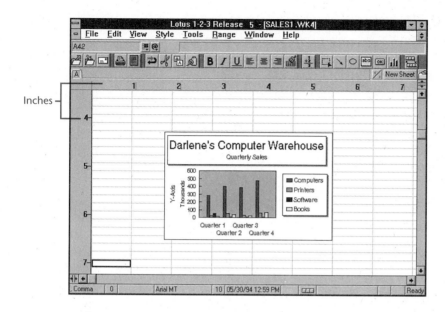

Fig. 12.1
To help you
measure the size
of your charts,
change the
worksheet frame
so that it displays
an inch ruler.

Selecting Chart Objects

Before you can copy, delete, rearrange, move, or otherwise mess with an object, you must select it. You can select one or several objects. When an object is selected, selection handles appear around the object.

To select an object, just click it. To select several objects with the mouse, click the Select Objects SmartIcon, which enables you to "lasso" the objects you want to select; after selecting the icon, drag the mouse until you surround all the objects. As you drag, you see a box with a dotted outline. When you release the mouse button, all the objects that were in this box will have selection handles.

Because a chart contains so many different elements, it can be difficult sometimes to determine whether the mouse pointer is actually on the object you want to select. To help you select objects, the mouse pointer reflects what you are pointing to. For example, when you point to text, the mouse pointer has a capital A underneath it. When you are pointing to a line, you see a diagonal line underneath the mouse pointer; when you are pointing to a bar, the pointer has a hollow rectangle underneath it. A circle underneath the mouse pointer indicates that you are pointing to a data point.

To deselect all selected items, position the mouse pointer anywhere on the worksheet outside the chart and click the mouse. To deselect one item when several items are selected, position the mouse pointer on the item, and then press and hold down Shift while you click the mouse.

Moving Objects

You can move objects in the chart by dragging them with the mouse or, in some cases, by selecting an available position from a dialog box. For example, the Legend dialog box has options for placing the legend to the right or below the plot, but you are not restricted to these two places. You can move the legend anywhere inside the chart frame. You can also move the plot, the titles, the footnotes, the entire chart, and any objects that you added by using the **D**raw commands on the **T**ools menu. (For more information about using dialog boxes to move the legend and titles, see "Specifying or Changing the Legend" and "Customizing the Chart Titles and Adding Notes" later in this chapter.)

Tip

To move the legend or titles and have 1-2-3 for Windows automatically adjust the positions of other objects, first try the positions offered in the dialog boxes that appear when you double-click the legend or titles.

To move an object, perform the following steps:

1. Select the object you want to move by clicking it; make sure selection handles are on the desired object or you might move the wrong thing.

2. Place the mouse pointer inside the object and begin dragging the object by moving the mouse. As you drag the object, the mouse pointer turns into a hand and a dotted box appears around the object and is moved to the new location. (A dotted line appears on lines and arrows.)

3. When you finish moving the object, release the mouse button. The dotted box disappears, and the object is moved to the new location.

Caution

If you move a chart object with the mouse, 1-2-3 for Windows does not automatically adjust the position of other chart objects. For example, if you move the legend to the left side of the chart, the legend will overlay the plot. You then must move the plot to the right.

Resizing Objects in the Chart

To change the size of an object, select it and then place the mouse pointer on one of the selection handles. Before dragging, make sure you see a four-headed arrow, which is the mouse pointer for sizing an object. To define the new size, drag the selection handle until the object is the desired size. Release the mouse button when you are done.

Resizing a frame that contains text, such as the titles or legend, works a little differently. As you drag a selection handle, both sides of the box expand or contract. For example, if you drag a right-hand handle to the right, the frame expands on the right and the left, keeping the text inside centered within the frame. This applies to title, footnote, and legend frames only.

Deleting Objects

If the chart contains an element you don't want, delete it by selecting the object and pressing the Del key. 1-2-3 lets you delete the title frame (along with its contents), the legend, axis titles, the footnote frame (and its contents), the unit indicator, individual data series, the entire chart, and any objects that you added by using the **D**raw commands on the **T**ools menu. You cannot delete the plot, x-axis labels, or the y-axis scale. Also, you cannot delete a frame's contents without deleting the entire frame.

If you accidentally delete an object, choose the **U**ndo command from the **E**dit menu, click the Undo SmartIcon, or press Ctrl+Z.

Tip
Another way to delete a chart object is to click the object, then press the right mouse button to display the quick menu, and then select Clear.

Troubleshooting

How can I tell whether the chart and the worksheet data it comes from will both fit on a page?

You can open the **F**ile menu and choose the Print Pre**v**iew command. Or you can open the **V**iew menu, the Set View **P**references command, and choose Inches from the Worksheet Frame drop-down list box to display inches in the worksheet frame.

I enlarged the title frame to accommodate the length of the chart title and now the title frame does not fit in the chart frame.

Enlarge the size of the entire chart until the title frame is completely displayed.

II

Working with Charts

Changing the Chart Type and Style

Although the default chart that 1-2-3 creates may suit your needs, you may need to change the chart to make it more appropriate for your report or presentation. Sometimes a different type of chart can present the data more effectively. This section describes the many chart types that are available in 1-2-3 for Windows, as well as how to change the chart type and select different styles for each chart type.

By default, 1-2-3 for Windows displays a bar chart when you create a chart. To change the type of chart that 1-2-3 for Windows displays, you can click one of the SmartIcons that directly selects a new chart type (such as the Line Chart SmartIcon or the 3D Pie SmartIcon). Or to select from all the types available in 1-2-3 for Windows, you can display the Type dialog box by performing one of the following steps:

- Click the Select Chart Type SmartIcon.

- Open the **C**hart menu and choose **T**ype.

- Select the chart, press the right mouse button to display the quick menu, and choose Chart Type.

- Double-click the plot.

In the Type dialog box (see fig. 12.2), you can choose from all chart types, select one of the styles available for the selected chart type, and change from vertical to horizontal orientation. When you choose the type of chart from the list on the left, 1-2-3 for Windows changes the display to reflect your choice. You also can include a table below the chart that shows the values used to graph each range.

Fig. 12.2
Experiment with different chart types to see which one best conveys your data by making selections in the Type dialog box.

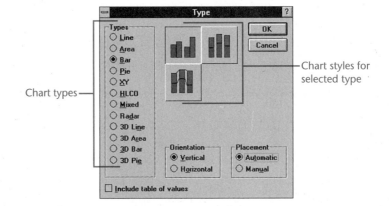

Selecting the Chart Style

Tip
If you want to return to the default style (standard bar), open the **C**hart menu and choose the **U**se Preferred command.

To the right of the Types field, the Type dialog box displays several large buttons showing the different styles for the current type of chart. In figure 12.2, three styles of bar charts are displayed. The upper left style button is used to select a standard bar chart. The button to the right produces a stacked bar chart. Stacked style charts show the individual data ranges and their totals. In a stacked bar chart, for example, the sections of a bar represent the individual data ranges and the top of the bar shows the total of the data ranges. The button on the bottom is a variation of a stacked bar chart.

To select one of the chart style buttons, click it with the mouse. Choose OK to accept your selection.

The SmartIcon palette that appears when a chart is selected is called the Default Chart SmartIcon palette. It contains a number of chart types and styles that you can select by clicking the appropriate SmartIcon. 1-2-3 for Windows includes several other SmartIcons that select other chart types and styles. If you find that you frequently use one or more of these other chart types, you can use the SmartIcons command on the **T**ools menu to add the appropriate SmartIcons to the Default Chart palette or create a palette of your own.

▶ "Customizing the SmartIcons," p. 982

Selecting the Chart Type

Choosing the best chart for a given application is often a matter of personal preference. 1-2-3 for Windows provides eight basic types of charts: line, area, bar, pie, XY, HLCO, mixed (bar and line), and radar. Four of them also are available with a three-dimensional effect: line, area, bar, and pie. Table 12.1 lists and briefly explains each chart type. The next sections discuss each chart type in more detail.

Table 12.1	Chart Types	
Type		**Description**
	Line	Shows the trend of numeric data over time.
	Area	Shows broad trends in data that occur over time.
	Bar	Compares related data at a certain time or shows the trend of numeric data over time.
	Pie	Graphs a single data range, showing what percentage of the total each data point contributes. Do not use this type of chart if the data contains negative numbers.
	XY	Shows the relationship between one independent variable and one or more dependent variables.
	HLCO (High-Low-Close-Open)	Shows fluctuations in data over time, such as the high, low, close, and open prices of a stock.
	Mixed	Shows a bar chart for the first three ranges and a line chart for three additional ranges.

(continues)

Working with Charts

Type	Description
Table 12.1 Continued	
Radar	Wraps a line chart around a central point, showing the symmetry or uniformity of data.
3D Line	Shows, in a three-dimensional line chart, the trend of numeric data over time.
3D Area	Shows, in a three-dimensional area chart, broad trends in data that occur over time.
3D Bar	Uses a three-dimensional bar chart to compare related data at a certain time or show the trend of numeric data over time.
3D Pie	Graphs, in a three-dimensional pie chart, a data range, showing what percentage of the total each data point contributes.

▶ "Creating Special Charts," p. 444

To select a chart type, select the type from the list on the left in the Type dialog box. The next sections describe the most common types of charts: **L**ine and 3D Li**n**e, **A**rea and 3D A**r**ea, **B**ar and **3**D Bar, **P**ie and 3D Pi**e**.

Line Charts

Line charts are ideal for displaying trends and changes in data over time. Figure 12.3 shows the styles available for line charts. The first style in the left column has lines with symbols at each data point, the next style down has lines with no symbols, and the last style has symbols only (no lines). The styles in the right-hand column are similar except that the data is *stacked*; in other words, the line closest to the x-axis is series A, the next line up is the total of series A and B, the next line up is the total of series A, B, and C, and so forth.

Fig. 12.3
The line chart styles are ideal for showing changes over time.

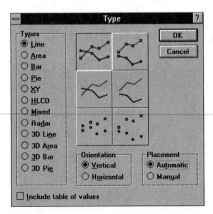

As figure 12.4. shows, the 3D **L**ine chart type offers two styles: standard and stacked. In 3D charts, the data series and plot frame show 3D effects.

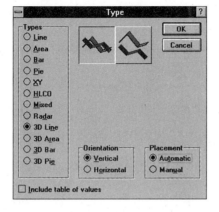

Fig. 12.4
3D Line chart styles.

Tip
Because the 3D lines are fairly thick, you shouldn't use a 3D chart type if your chart has many data series.

Area Charts

An **A**rea chart, which emphasizes broad trends, is similar to a stacked line chart except that the area between data ranges is filled with a different color or pattern. The two-dimensional **A**rea chart has only one basic style (see fig. 12.5).

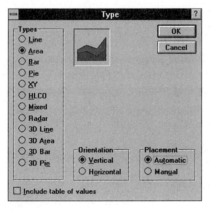

Fig. 12.5
Area charts resemble stacked-line charts and show not only the changes in each data series but also the total of all the data series.

The 3D **A**rea chart is available in two styles (see fig. 12.6). In the first style, the base of each data series begins at 0. In the second style, the series are stacked on top of one another.

II

Working with Charts

Fig. 12.6
3D Area charts are
available in two
different styles.

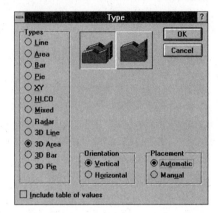

If you want to show the total of all series at each data point, use the standard area chart or the 3D stacked area chart. To compare the individual data series, use the 3D area chart that displays one data series behind another; however, in order to see all the data series, the data series in front need to have smaller values than the data series in the back.

Bar Charts

Although Standard **B**ar is the default chart type, you might want to make a trip to the Type dialog box to choose a different style of bar chart (for example, a stacked bar), to select a **3**D Bar type, or to change the chart's orientation.

The **B**ar chart type offers three styles, as shown in figure 12.7. The *standard bar chart*, the default, places the bars side by side. A *stacked bar chart* shows data as a series of bars piled on top of one another. The *comparison bar chart* is a stacked bar chart with dotted lines that connect the data points. These lines make it easier to see the differences between corresponding segments in each bar.

Stacked bar charts are useful for showing the portion that data series contribute to a whole and for comparing totals over time. Comparison bar charts serve the same purpose, as well as show trends between the portions.

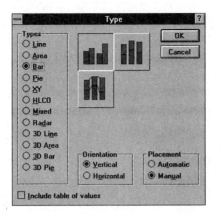

Fig. 12.7
The bar chart
styles.

Figure 12.8, figure 12.9, and figure 12.10 plot the same data, comparing the quarterly sales of each department. However, these three charts present different messages. The chart in figure 12.8 compares the relative sales in dollars of the departments. The chart in figure 12.9 compares each department's contribution to the combined sales. The chart in figure 12.10 is the same as figure 12.9, except that comparison lines help to show changes in the individual data series.

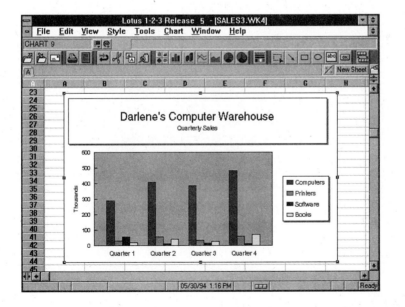

Fig. 12.8
A standard bar
chart of the sales
data worksheet
shows each
product category
for each quarter in
a single bar.

II

Working with Charts

Fig. 12.9
A stacked bar chart of the sales data worksheet shows each product category as a part of the total sales for the quarter.

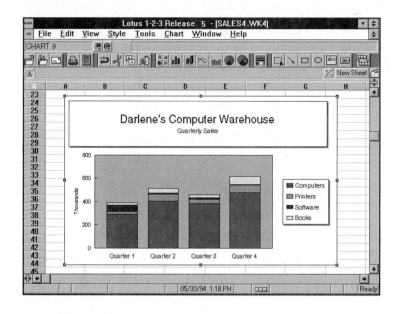

Fig. 12.10
The comparison lines show trends over time for the individual data series in a stacked bar chart.

Comparison lines illustrate changes

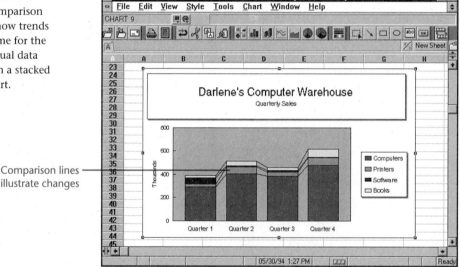

 Figure 12.11 shows the three styles that the **3**D Bar type offers. The first style has three-dimensional bars placed side-by-side. In the second style, the bars are placed behind one another. Stacked bars are the third **3**D Bar style.

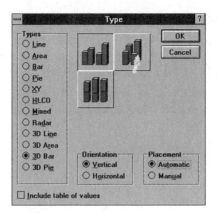

Fig. 12.11
The 3D Bar chart
styles are more
sophisticated
renderings of the
other 1-2-3 bar
chart styles.

Pie Charts

In a pie chart, each value determines the size of a pie slice and represents a percentage of the total. Unlike other chart types, pie charts can have only one data series (the A data range). If you select an adjacent row or column of labels, 1-2-3 for Windows uses it as the legend to identify the pie slices.

Suppose that you want to graph the percentage of computer equipment sales for each quarter using the data shown in figure 12.2. Use the range A4..E5 and specify **P**ie or 3D Pi**e** as the chart type; 1-2-3 for Windows assigns the values in row 5 to data series A and the pie slices and assigns the labels in row 4 to data series X and the legend.

When creating a pie chart, you can choose to plot the data counterclockwise, starting at the 3:00 position, or clockwise, starting at 12:00. Figure 12.12 shows the standard version of the pie chart, with the first slice starting at the 3:00 position and the others following in counterclockwise order. 1-2-3 for Windows automatically calculates and displays the percentages of the whole represented by each slice. Instead of percentages, you can display the actual values or other information (see "Showing the Values and Percentages of Pie Slices" later in this chapter).

The 3D pie chart styles are the same as the standard pie chart styles, except that they show three-dimensional effects. Figure 12.13 shows the 3D Pi**e** chart type, using the clockwise style with the slices beginning at the 12:00 position.

Tip
If you choose the
3D Bar chart style
that begins each
data series at 0,
specify the small-
est series first (as
series A) or the
shorter bars will
be hidden behind
the taller bars
in front.

II

Working with Charts

Fig. 12.12
A counterclockwise
Pie chart of
quarterly computer
sales; pie charts
show each data
series as a part of
the whole.

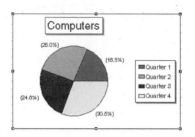

Fig. 12.13
The clockwise 3D
pie chart of
quarterly computer
sales.

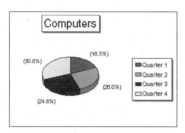

Changing the Orientation of a Chart

Another way to change the chart style is to change the orientation of the
chart. The chart types that are plotted on an x- and y-axis (**L**ine, **B**ar, **A**rea,
XY, and **H**LCO) offer an Orientation option in the Type dialog box. **V**ertical
is the standard orientation. If you choose **H**orizontal, the x- and y-axes are
swapped. Horizontal orientation is typically used in bar charts to show
progress or distance. For example, figure 12.14 shows progress toward a goal
in a charity drive.

Fig. 12.14
A horizontal
stacked bar chart
can show progress
toward a goal. The
x-axis is on the left
and the y-axis is
on the top.

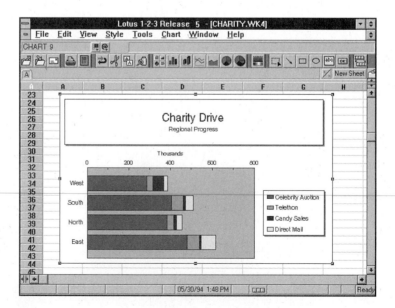

> **Note**
>
> 1-2-3 Release 5 includes SmartIcons for horizontal bar charts and horizontal stacked bar charts, but they do not appear on the default chart SmartIcon palette. If you find that you use these chart types frequently, you may want to add these SmartIcons to the chart SmartIcon palette. See Chapter 33.

Setting the Default Chart Type and Style

As was previously mentioned, the default chart type is a standard bar. If you use a different type or style more often, you can change the default type and style (the kind of chart 1-2-3 for Windows initially uses when you create a chart) by performing the following steps:

1. Create a chart with chart type and style you want to be the default.

2. From the **C**hart menu, choose the **S**et Preferred command.

Thereafter, any new charts you create will have that chart type and style by default.

> **Note**
>
> The default (or preferred) chart setting controls only the type (such as **L**ine or **3**D Line) and style (for instance, whether the line has symbols). It doesn't control other settings such as orientation, legend placement, or grid lines.

Troubleshooting

I no longer have a **C***hart option in my menu bar. Where did it go?*

The **C**hart option displays only if a chart or an element on a chart is selected. Otherwise, **R**ange displays in the menu bar. Just click anywhere on the chart to make the **C**hart option reappear.

I want to show expenditures for salaries and health benefits as parts of the whole compensation package for the past five years. I thought I wanted to use a pie chart, but I have more than one data series, so what kind of chart should I use?

You can use either an area chart or a stacked bar chart to show salaries and health benefits as parts of the whole compensation package. Make sure the years form the x data series so that the chart shows change over time.

Modifying Other Elements of a Chart

Once you select the type and style of chart that best illustrates your data, you can modify the chart in other ways so that it presents the data effectively and clearly points out information you want others to see. For example, you will probably want your chart to have a title. You may also want your chart to have a legend. In some cases, the layout of your data in the worksheet may make it necessary to enter the legend by hand, or you may want to change one of the legend labels. In some charts, you may want to change the default scale of the y-axis to make the values easier to read. The rest of this chapter explains how to control these and other attributes of charts in 1-2-3 for Windows.

Specifying or Changing the Legend

When you graph a data range, 1-2-3 for Windows uses colors, symbols, or patterns to identify data ranges. The *legend* shows which data range each color, symbol, or pattern represents. By default, 1-2-3 for Windows places legend labels in a frame to the right of the chart.

The Legend dialog box (see fig. 12.15) enables you to add or edit legend labels or change the position of the legend box. To access this dialog box, open the **C**hart menu and choose **L**egend. You can also display this dialog box by double-clicking existing legend or placing the mouse pointer on a legend, pressing the right mouse button, and choosing Legend from the quick menu that appears.

Fig. 12.15
The Legend dialog box lets you specify legend labels and control the position of the Legend box.

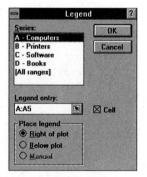

Entering the Legend Labels

To specify a legend label in the Legend dialog box, perform the following steps:

1. Click the appropriate data series letter.

2. Type the label in the **L**egend Entry text box. Or to use the contents of a cell as the legend label, select the Cell check box, and then enter the worksheet cell address that contains the label or use the range selector to point to the cell.

3. Repeat the process for each legend label you want to specify or change.

> ### Note
>
> If the labels you want to use for the legend appear in a range in the worksheet, you can use that range to assign the all the legend labels at once. Choose [All ranges] in the **S**eries field. Then, in the **L**egend entry text box, enter the worksheet range containing the legend labels or use the range selector to highlight it.

Selecting the Legend Position

In the Legend dialog box, you can also indicate where to place the legend: **R**ight of Plot, **B**elow Plot, or **M**anual. **R**ight of Plot stacks the labels vertically. **B**elow Plot creates a legend with a horizontal orientation; depending on how many labels there are, the legend may wrap onto several lines. You don't have to select the **M**anual option—it's automatically selected after you drag the legend and move it elsewhere within the chart frame.

> ### Caution
>
> When you manually position a legend, the chart does not automatically move to accommodate the legend. You may have to select the plot and drag it so that it doesn't overlap the legend.

Customizing Chart Titles and Adding Notes

The **H**eadings command on the **C**hart menu lets you create two titles and two footnotes for your chart. Figure 12.16 shows the Headings dialog box. You use the two Title text boxes to create the title and subtitle; the titles appear centered above the chart, with the first title in larger type above the second title. You use the Note text boxes to add footnotes that appear below the chart.

Fig. 12.16
The Headings
dialog box lets you
specify the title
and note text and
positions.

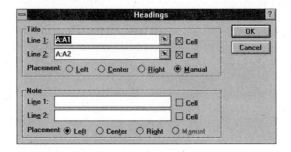

Entering Title and Note Text

To enter titles and notes, select the appropriate text box from the Headings
dialog box. You can type the text directly in the text box or select the Cell
check box and type the address of the cell that contains the label or number
to be used as the title or note. Alternatively, you can click the range selector
and point to the cell in the worksheet that contains the information you
want to use. In figure 12.16, the cells A:A1 and A:A2 are entered as the titles.

To edit a title or note, double-click the title or note in the chart to display
the Headings dialog box, or move the mouse pointer to the title or footnote,
press the right mouse button to display the quick menu, and choose
Headings. Replace existing text by highlighting the appropriate text box and
typing in the new text. To delete text, press Del while the text box is highlighted. Another way to delete a title or note is to select the text on the chart
and press Del.

Selecting Title and Note Positions

By default, titles are centered at the top of the chart and notes are left-aligned
at the bottom of the chart. You can left-align, right-align, or center-align
titles and notes by choosing an option from the appropriate Placement field
in the Headings dialog box. Another way to change the position of titles and
notes is to select the text you want to move by clicking it and then drag the
block anywhere inside the chart frame. After you manually move a title or
note, the Manual option in the related Placement field is automatically
selected.

Changing the Axis Titles

By default, 1-2-3 inserts X-Axis and Y-Axis as your axis titles. To change these
axis titles to something more descriptive, open the **C**hart menu and choose
the **A**xis command; then either **X**-Axis, **Y**-Axis, or **2**nd Y-Axis to open the
appropriate dialog box. You can also double-click an existing title to display

the appropriate Axis dialog box. This dialog box enables you to add titles for the **X**-Axis, **Y**-Axis, and **2**nd Y-Axis. Enter the titles you want in the appropriate text boxes.

The placement of axis titles depends on whether the chart is horizontally or vertically oriented. In a vertical chart (the default chart orientation), the y-axis title appears left of the y-axis; the x-axis title is centered below the x-axis; and the second y-axis title appears to the right of the second y-axis. In a horizontal chart, the y-axis title appears above y-axis; the x-axis title appears to the left of the x-axis; and the second y-axis title appears below the second y-axis.

Figure 12.17 shows the standard bar chart for the revenue worksheet after the x-axis title was deleted and the y-axis title was edited.

Tip

X-axis and y-axis titles are often unnecessary. To delete an axis title quickly, select it with the mouse and press Del.

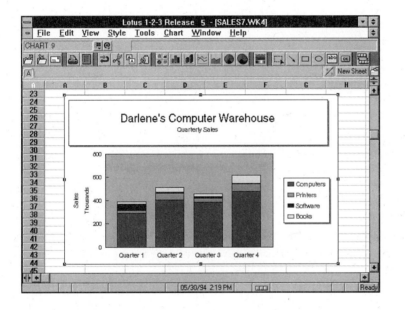

Fig. 12.17
A bar chart after the x-axis title was deleted and the y-axis title was edited.

Controlling the Axis Scale

When you create a chart, 1-2-3 for Windows automatically sets the *scale* (the minimum to maximum range) of the y-axis based on the smallest and largest numbers in the data range(s) plotted. This default also applies to the second y-axis when you use it. For **XY** charts, 1-2-3 for Windows also establishes the x-axis scale based on values in the X data range.

To modify an axis scale, open the **C**hart menu, choose **A**xis and then choose the command that corresponds to the axis whose scale you want to modify. For example, to change the y-axis scale, open the **C**hart menu, choose **A**xis, and then choose **Y**-Axis. The Y-Axis dialog box appears (see fig. 12.18). The

▶ "Adding a Second Y-Axis to a Chart," p. 452

II

Working with Charts

X-Axis and 2nd Y-Axis dialog boxes offer the same settings. Another way to display these dialog boxes is to double-click the axis labels or click the right mouse button on the labels and choose X-Axis or Y-Axis from the quick menu that appears.

Fig. 12.18
The Y-Axis dialog box lets you change the axis title and control the axis scale upper and lower limits and tick mark intervals and display.

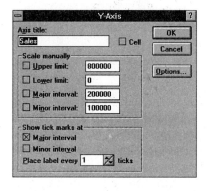

Setting the Minimum and Maximum Values

You can change the scale by selecting options in the Scale Manually fields in the appropriate Axis dialog box. These fields initially contain the values that 1-2-3 determines are appropriate for your data. You can change the scale by specifying different numbers in the **U**pper Limit and Lo**w**er Limit text boxes. Only data that falls between the Lo**w**er and **U**pper limit values is graphed.

Changing the Tick Marks

Use the **M**ajor Interval and Mi**n**or Interval text boxes under Scale Manually to specify the increments between tick marks. For example, the automatic scale may have increments of 100 on the y-axis (100, 200, 300, 400, and so on). If you want fewer increments, you can change the **M**ajor Interval setting to an increment such as 200; the major tick marks will then be labeled 200, 400, 600, and so on. You probably shouldn't change the Mi**n**or Interval value unless your chart has tick marks displayed at these intervals (they are turned off by default).

To control the display of tick marks, use the Show Tick Marks at sections; these options include check boxes for M**a**jor Interval and Minor Inter**v**al.

Returning to Automatic Scaling

To return to automatic scaling, deselect all the check boxes in the Scale Manually field—you don't have to clear out the values or return options to their original values.

Tip
To increase the distance between data points and reduce the white space at the top of the chart, make the **U**pper limit closer to the largest value in the chart.

Tip
If your chart does not contain enough tick marks to tell what values the data series represent, decrease the value in the **M**ajor interval field and/or display Minor inter**v**al tick marks.

Changing Other Scale Options

If you choose the **O**ptions button in the X-Axis, Y-Axis, or 2nd Y-Axis dialog box, you see additional axis settings in the Options dialog box (see fig. 12.19). This dialog box lets you change the type of scale, the units used in the scale, and the title identifying the units.

The Ty**p**e of Scale field determines whether a Standard (linear), Log (logarithmic), or 100% scale is used. On a logarithmic scale, each unit of distance represents 10 times the value of the preceding unit; the scale is labeled 1, 10, 100, 1000, and so forth.

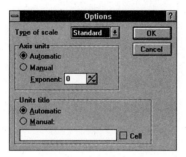

Fig. 12.19
Additional axis options include changing the scale type, axis units, and units title.

If your chart contains widely fluctuating data, use a logarithmic scale. For example, if the minimum value you are plotting is 1,000 and the maximum value is 10,000,000, the smaller data points are virtually invisible on a standard scale (they are relatively so close to zero that they lie on the x-axis). By using a logarithmic scale, you can show all the data points. Figure 12.20 shows a chart that has a standard scale, and figure 12.21 shows the same data plotted with a logarithmic scale.

A 100% scale is similar to a pie chart in that it shows the relative portion each series is of the total; the scale is labeled from 0 to 100 percent. A 100% scale is most appropriate for stacked bar charts, as shown in figure 12.22.

In the Axis Units Section, you can set the order of magnitude (power of 10) used to scale the values. Usually, 1-2-3 for Windows does this automatically. If you select Ma**n**ual, you can specify a value between –95 and +95 in the **E**xponent text box. If you enter a positive exponent, the decimal point moves to the left that number of places. A negative exponent moves the decimal point to the right (zeroes are added to the number). When you enter an exponent, 1-2-3 indicates this change in the units title next to the axis. For example, if you specify an exponent of 3, the units title will say Times 1E+03; this indicates to multiply each of the values on the scale by 10 to the third power (1,000). If this title is too cryptic, you can choose Manual in the Units Title Section and type your own title (or click the Cell check box and specify a cell containing the label you want to use as your units title).

Fig. 12.20
With a standard y-axis scale, some of the values are relatively so small that the data points lie on the x-axis.

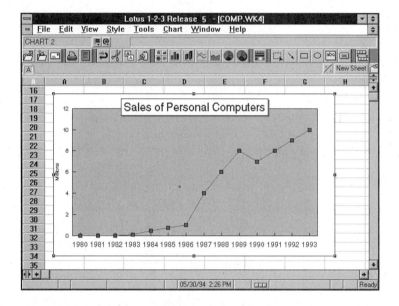

Fig. 12.21
With a logarithmic scale, you can clearly see all data points.

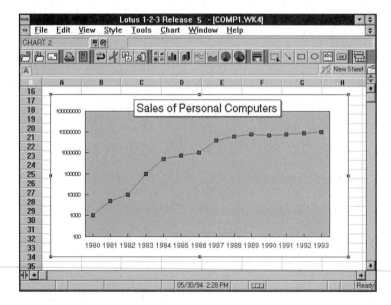

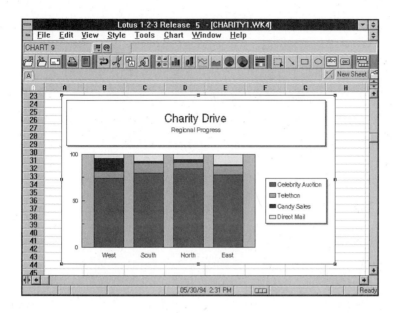

Fig. 12.22
A stacked bar chart
that has a 100%
scale.

In some cases, changing the exponent and units title can make the chart easier to interpret. For example, the automatic scale on your chart might range from 0 to 4000 and the automatic units title might read Thousands. In other words, 4000 actually represents 4,000,000. If you specify an **E**xponent value of 6, the scale would range from 0 to 4; with a Ma**n**ual units title that says Millions, the chart would be much easier to understand.

Sometimes 1-2-3 uses an exponent on your axis when you would rather show the exact values. For example, the scale might have the labels 1, 2, 3, 4,... with Thousands as the units title. If you would rather have the scale show 1000, 2000, 3000, 4000,..., choose Ma**n**ual for the axis units and enter **0** for the **E**xponent.

Adjusting the Display of Axis Labels

When your axis is crowded with many labels, you can use the **P**lace Label Every [__] Ticks field in the Y-Axis, X-Axis, or 2nd Y-Axis dialog box to determine how many axis labels appear. For example, if the value in this field is 2, every second label appears (see fig. 12.23).

Displaying a Background Grid

Grids often make it easier to interpret the data points in charts, especially if the data points are far from the x-axis and y-axis labels. The chart in figure 12.24, for example, uses horizontal grid lines to make the data easier to interpret.

Tip
You also can use the Units title field when you want to modify the title that 1-2-3 automatically generates. For example, you could change the title from Thousands to In Thousands.

Tip
Skip tick mark labels only if the axis contains values or units of time so that it's obvious what the missing labels are.

II

Working with Charts

Fig. 12.23
Every other label is
displayed on the
x-axis.

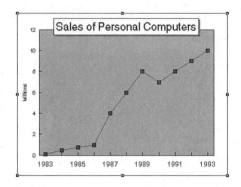

Fig. 12.24
A chart with y-
axis grid lines
added to make it
easier to deter-
mine the values
represented by the
bars.

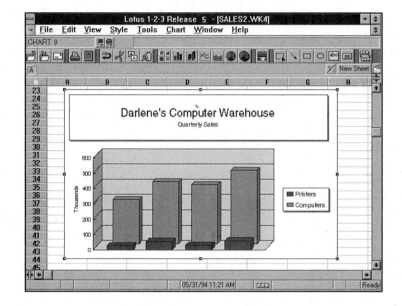

Tip
To create dotted
or dashed grid
lines, click the
right mouse
button on the
grid lines and
choose Lines &
Color from the
quick menu. You
can then select a
different line
style.

The **G**rids command on the **C**hart menu enables you to create horizontal and vertical grid lines for charts that have axes (**L**ine, **B**ar, **A**rea, **X**Y, **H**LCO, and **M**ixed charts). The x-axis grid lines extend from tick marks on the x-axis and are perpendicular to the x-axis. The y-axis grid lines extend from y-axis tick marks and are perpendicular to the y-axis. The second y-axis grid lines extend from the tick marks on the second y-axis.

To turn on grid lines, choose **G**rids from the **C**hart menu and then display the drop-down list for **X**-Axis, **Y**-Axis, or **2**nd Y-Axis, and choose the settings: Major Interval, Minor Interval, Both, or None. As described earlier, the intervals refer to the tick marks on the axis. The major intervals are those tick marks that are labeled; the minor intervals are the smaller tick marks in between major intervals. The Both setting draws grid lines for major *and* minor intervals, and the None setting eliminates grid lines.

Adding Data Labels

Knowing the exact value of a data range in a chart is sometimes helpful. To label data points in a chart with the corresponding value (called *data labels*), open the **C**hart menu and choose the **D**ata Labels command; figure 12.25 shows the resulting dialog box.

Fig. 12.25
The Data Labels dialog box lets you show the exact values represented by each bar, bar segment, or data point.

To specify a data label in the Data Labels dialog box, perform the following steps:

1. In the **S**eries list box, highlight the series (A, B, C, and so on) for which you want to create data labels.

2. Specify the range of labels in the R**a**nge of Labels field. You can either type the range or use the range selector to highlight the range.

3. Using the **P**lacement drop-down list, you can control whether the data label appears above, centered, below, or to the left of or to the right of the data point.

4. Repeat this process for each series.

When you close the dialog box, 1-2-3 for Windows displays in the chart the exact value of each data range. Figure 12.26 shows a chart with data labels.

Fig. 12.26
The chart after
adding data labels.

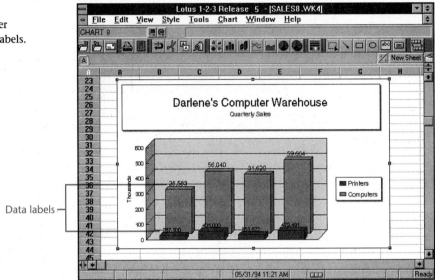

Data labels —

Including a Table of Values in the Chart

Data labels can be difficult to read and can clutter the chart. An alternative method of displaying the data values being graphed is to select the **I**nclude Table of Values check box in the Type dialog box (which you can open by clicking the Select Chart Type SmartIcon or selecting the **T**ype command from the **C**hart menu). If you select this option, a miniworksheet of the graphed data is displayed below the chart (see fig. 12.27). The x-axis labels appear in the top row of the table, and the data legend labels are placed in the left-side column. The **I**nclude Table of Values option is available only with certain chart types. **P**ie, **X**Y, **H**LCO, Ra**d**ar, and **3**D pie charts do not offer this option.

Showing the Values and Percentages of Pie Slices

If you create a pie chart, you can show the values and/or percentages corresponding to each pie slice by choosing **D**ata Labels from the **C**hart menu to access the Data Labels dialog box shown in figure 12.28. (Notice that this version of the dialog box varies from that shown in figure 12.25.)

Tip
To specify all your data labels at once, choose [All ranges] in the **S**eries list box in the Data Labels dialog box and then indicate the range in the **R**ange of labels text box by typing or pointing.

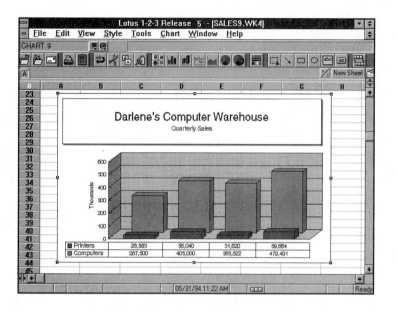

Fig. 12.27
A chart using a table of values rather than data labels.

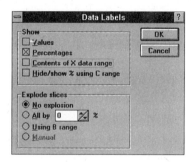

Fig. 12.28
The Data Labels dialog box for pie charts lets you specify what information the data labels include.

By default, 1-2-3 for Windows displays the percentages of the whole represented by each slice. You can also display the values of each slice. The pie in figure 12.29 shows values, percentages, and the slice labels. The legend has been removed from this chart because it is no longer necessary.

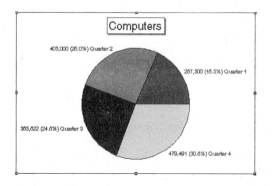

Fig. 12.29
A pie with values, percentages, and slice labels.

II

Working with Charts

Tip
Use the **H**ide/
Show % Using C
Range option to
direct attention to
a particular slice in
a pie chart by
hiding the labels
for the other
slices.

The final Show option in the Data Labels dialog box for pie charts is **H**ide/
Show % Using C Range. This option lets you show only selected labels. To use
this option, perform the following steps:

1. Create a range with one cell for each slice of the pie. Enter 0 in the
   cell(s) that correspond to each slice for which you do not want to show
   the value, percentage, or identifying label. Leave the other cells in the
   range blank.

2. Select the **R**anges command on the **C**hart menu to specify this range as
   the C Slice label settings data series.

3. Select the **D**ata Labels command from the chart menu to open the Data
   Labels dialog box. Then select **H**ide/Show % Using C Range under Show
   and select OK to accept the change.

▶ "Exploding Pie
Slices," p. 435

The chart will then display labels for all the slices for which the C data series
is blank and hide the labels for slices for which the C data series contains 0.

Troubleshooting

*My chart has only one data series, and 1-2-3 created a legend that I don't need. How
can I get rid of it?*

Select the legend and press Del.

*My pie slices aren't labeled, even though I indicated them as my x-axis range. How can I
get them to display?*

The Data Labels dialog box has check boxes for controlling the display of x-axis
labels, values, and percentages next to each slice. To display the x-axis labels, open
the **C**hart menu and choose the **D**ata Labels command and turn on the **C**ontents of
X data range setting in the Data Labels dialog box.

My chart has overlapping labels on the x-axis. Is there any way to relieve this crowding?

Open the X-Axis dialog box by double-clicking the x-axis labels or by opening the
Chart menu, selecting **A**xis, and then selecting **X**-Axis. Then enter a value greater
than in the **P**lace Label Every [__] Ticks field.

From Here...

By experimenting with the techniques presented in this chapter and in the
following chapters, you can create printed reports that effectively present the
data in tabular and graphical form.

■ Chapter 13, "Formatting Charts," covers how to change colors and patterns, number formats, and text attributes, as well as how to annotate a chart. You also learn how to preview and print charts.

■ Chapter 14, "Building Complex Charts and Mapping Data," shows how to create the more complicated chart types offered by 1-2-3 for Windows (2Y-axis, XY, Mixed, and HLCO), as well as how to import graphics into a chart. This chapter also shows how to illustrate data about geographical regions with charts.

■ Chapter 16, "Adding Graphics to Worksheets," covers how to add text boxes, lines, arrows, ellipses, and other graphic elements to a chart.

■ Chapter 17, "Developing Business Presentations," shows how to include charts in slide shows and computer presentations.

II

Working with Charts

Chapter 13

Formatting Charts

1-2-3 for Windows includes many ways to format and enhance charts. For example, in order to call attention to a particular data series, you might want to "explode" a pie slice (that is, move it slightly outward from the rest of the pie) or display it in a special color. With 1-2-3 for Windows, you can change the attributes and colors of chart text, lines, and areas the same way you format ranges in the worksheet. You can also add to your charts special effects such as design frames. These options help you create more attractive charts and communicate the message in the data more effectively.

In this chapter, you learn how to enhance charts in the following ways:

- Change the typeface, point size, and attributes of the titles and labels

- Change the color of any chart element

- Choose a pattern for a data series

- Change the style and width of the lines and outlines

- Add designer frames to your chart

- Explode pie slices

- Preview and print charts

Enhancing the Chart

Just as the Style menu in 1-2-3 for Windows lets you change the settings for many worksheet items—number formats, font attributes and size, colors, and line styles—it also gives you a wide range of flexibility in formatting charts. Figure 13.1 shows a chart with the following changes made from the Style menu: different typeface, size, and attributes of text, different colors of chart elements, new patterns for data series, different style and width of the lines. The chart also draws attention to one slice.

Fig. 13.1
A chart with a new title typeface, chart frame style, slice patterns, and with an exploded pie slice.

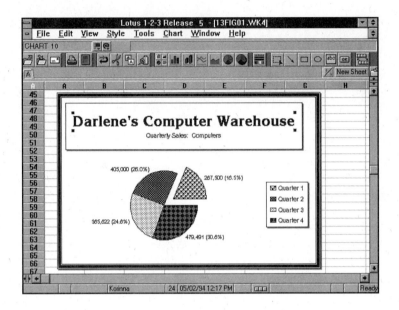

Changing the Format of Numbers

Tip
When the y-axis represents currency, you should change the number format for the y-axis scale to Currency.

By default, 1-2-3 for Windows displays numbers in a chart in General format, which is also the default format for worksheet values. You can display x-axis, y-axis, or the second y-axis labels, data labels, or pie labels in any of 1-2-3 for Windows' numeric formats.

To change the format of numbers in a chart, click one of the numbers you want to format, and the group of numbers is selected. Then choose **S**tyle, **N**umber Format and select the desired format from the list. Some formats require that you specify a number of decimal places, and date and time formats require that you specify format types for those entries.

◀ "Working with Number Formats," p. 326

Another way to display the Number Format dialog box is to click the right mouse button on the numbers and choose Number Format from the quick menu. You can also use the status bar number format indicators at the bottom of the screen to change the format of numbers in a chart.

Formatting Text Attributes

You can change the typeface, point size, color, and attributes (boldface, italics, and so on) of any text on a chart. You also can format the chart titles, legend text, data labels, and axis labels as well as text blocks you created with the **T**ools **D**raw **T**ext command or the Text Block SmartIcon.

Formatting chart text is not much different from formatting worksheet cells. First, select the text you want to change. If you are formatting a group of objects (such as all the data labels or the labels on the x-axis), click one of the labels and 1-2-3 automatically selects all related labels. Next, select **S**tyle, **F**ont & Attributes or click the Font & Attributes SmartIcon. The Font & Attributes dialog box appears. Notice that you use this same dialog box to format text in the worksheet.

An alternate way to display the Font & Attributes dialog box is to click the right mouse button on the labels and choose Font & Attributes from the Quick menu. You also can use the status bar font and text size indicators at the bottom of the screen to change the format of text and numbers in a chart.

Changing Data Series Colors and Patterns

With 1-2-3 for Windows, you can easily select colors for each of the data series on a chart. You can change the color and pattern of lines, bars, areas, and individual pie slices.

To change the color of a series, first click on any data point of that series. For example, if you are changing the color of a line, click the line or one of the data points on the line. If you are choosing a different color for one of the data series in a bar chart, click one of the bars. 1-2-3 then selects all the bars or bar segments in that series. Another way to change the color of a series is to click on the appropriate color box in the legend.

Once you have selected the data series you want to change, select **L**ines & Color from the **S**tyle menu to display the Lines & Color dialog box or click the Lines & Color SmartIcon. Another way to display the Lines & Color dialog box is to select a data series, click the right mouse button, and choose Lines & Color from the Quick menu.

The Lines & Color dialog box displays different options, depending on the selected chart type. These different options are described in the sections that follow.

Colors in Line Charts

Figure 13.2 shows the dialog box that appears when you select a data point or line in a line chart and choose **S**tyle, **L**ines & Color. To change the line color, click the down-arrow for **C**olor field. The color palette appears. The current color has a flashing outline around it. To select a different color, click the desired color box. (The St**y**le, **W**idth, and **S**ymbol options in this dialog box

Tip
When you resize the chart by dragging the frame, 1-2-3 for Windows does not automatically change the font sizes, so you may want to do so manually.

◄ "Enhancing the Appearance of Data," p. 343

Tip
Unless your printer can print in color, you may be better off using hatch (or line) patterns, shades of gray, or symbols to differentiate data ranges.

are covered in the "Formatting Lines and Outlines" section later in this chapter.)

Fig. 13.2
The Lines & Color dialog box for formatting lines.

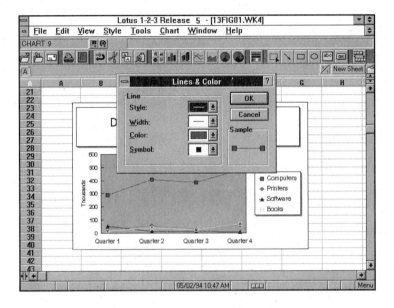

Colors in Bar, Area, Pie, and Radar Charts

Tip
When you intend to print the chart on a black and white printer, it is often a good idea to alternate light and dark colors or shades of gray for bars or pie slices that are next to each other.

When you select a bar, area, pie slice, or radar spiral, the Lines & Color dialog box looks like the one shown in figure 13.3. Here you can change the color of the interior of the object as well as its outline. You also can specify a pattern (see the next section, "Patterns in Bar, Area, Pie, and Radar Charts").

To choose a different color, move the pointer to the Interior options and click on the down-arrow to the right of the **B**ackground color field. Choose a new color from the displayed palette.

To change the color of the object's outline, move the pointer to the Edge options and choose **C**olor; then select the new color from the palette. By default, the outline is black. (Another way to change the colors in pie charts for individual data points within data series is described in the section, "Changing Colors and Patterns of Data Points and Pie Slices," later in this chapter.)

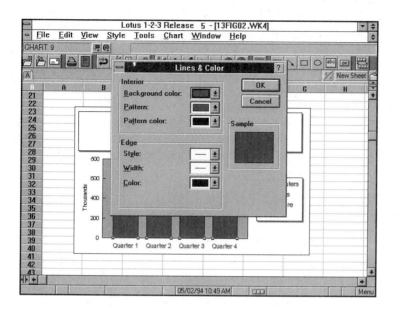

Fig. 13.3
The Lines & Color
dialog box for
objects that can be
filled.

Patterns in Bar, Area, Pie, and Radar Charts

You can also enhance the chart by filling an area with a pattern—this mixes
two colors you choose (the **B**ackground color and Pa**t**tern color) in a pattern
you specify. First, select the data series you want to change and select the
Style, **L**ines & Color command. Then click the **P**attern down-arrow in the
Interior section of the Lines & Color dialog box to display the pattern palette.
There are 61 different patterns available, including bricks, checkerboards,
stripes, dots, basketweaves, and cross-hatches. In addition to those patterns,
you can choose T(ransparent), solid white, or solid color, making a total of 64
options. After you choose a pattern, use the **B**ackground color and Pa**t**tern
color fields to select the two colors used in the pattern. Figure 13.4 shows a
stacked-bar chart with black-and-white patterns.

Tip
To create a
black-and-white
pattern, choose
black for the
background
color and white
for the pattern
color (or vice-
versa).

Caution

If the **B**ackground color and Pa**t**tern color in the Lines & Color dialog box are the
same, the **P**attern palette will not show any patterns. Make sure the two colors are
different before you click **P**attern.

Fig. 13.4
Stacked-bar chart
with black and
white patterns.

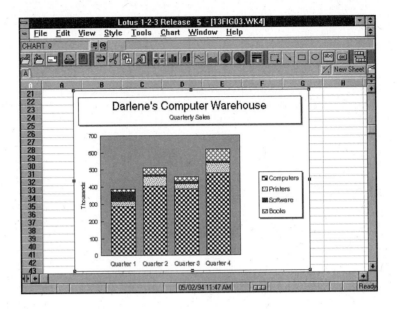

Changing Colors and Patterns of Data Points and Pie Slices

The previous sections explain how to use the Lines & Color dialog box to assign colors and patterns to each data *series*; in other words, if you change the color of a data series in a bar chart, all the bars in that series change to the same color. 1-2-3 for Windows offers a way to change the colors of individual data points (the individual bars or line segments and symbols that make up the data series): the Numeric **C**olor command on the **C**hart menu. You can also use this command to change the color (or pattern on monochrome monitors) of pie-chart slices. The command works by using values in a worksheet range to tell 1-2-3 what color to use for each data point or pie slice.

To change colors for data points within a data series, perform the following steps:

1. Set up a range in the worksheet that is the same size and shape as the worksheet data range for the data series you want to control. Enter a value between 0 and 15 in the cell that corresponds to each data point you want to change. Each number represents a different color or hatch pattern, except for 15, which hides the data point. The color values correspond to the colors in the top row of the color palette. (To display this palette, choose **S**tyle **L**ines & Color or click the Lines & Color SmartIcon, and click on any of the fields that refer to color.) With

Tip
In general, you should assign different colors to individual data points in a bar or line chart only when the chart has a single data series. Otherwise, the chart may be confusing.

pattern codes, the values 1 through 8 represent different hatch patterns and 9 through 14 represent shades of gray. If you want both colors and hatch patterns, set up two ranges. Figure 13.5 shows a color range setup for a pie chart.

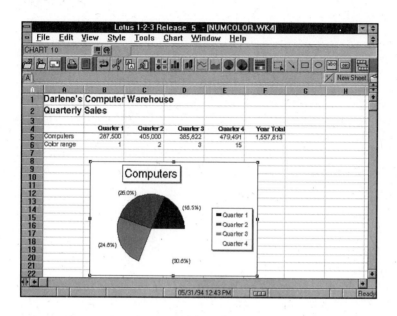

Fig. 13.5
Color range setup for a pie chart.

2. Next, select the chart to display the **C**hart option on the main menu.

3. Select **C**hart, Numeric **C**olor command. The Numeric color dialog box appears.

4. In the **S**eries area, select the data series you want to change.

5. Enter the range containing your color codes in the **R**ange of **c**olor values field, or use the range selector (the button to the right of the text box) to point to the range.

6. If applicable, specify the Range of **p**attern values.

7. If you wish, repeat steps 1 through 6 for other data series.

8. Click OK to return to the chart.

When you select OK, 1-2-3 for Windows changes the color and/or pattern of each line segment and symbol, bar or bar segment, or pie slice in the data series according to the values in the specified range(s).

Formatting Lines and Outlines

You can change the color, style, and width of any line on a chart, including the following:

- Lines in line, XY, HLCO, and radar charts

- Outlines of bars, areas, and pies

- Grid lines

- Objects created with the **T**ools **D**raw commands

Before you can change the style of a line or an outline, you must select the object. Then choose the **L**ines & Color command from the **C**hart menu, click the Lines & Color SmartIcon, or press the right mouse button and choose Lines & Color from the Quick menu. The Lines & Color dialog box appears.

In the Lines & Color dialog box, 1-2-3 offers six different line styles. In the St**y**le drop-down list, you can choose solid lines, long dashes, short dashes, a combination of long and short dashes, two dots between each dash, large dots, and small dots. Or, if you don't want a line, choose None. The **W**idth drop-down list offers eight different line widths.

Selecting Symbols for Line Charts

On line and XY charts, you can choose a different symbol shape for each data series. These symbols appear at each data point and in the legend. To select a symbol for a data series, select the line or a data point for the series, then choose **L**ines & Color from the **C**hart menu, click the Lines & Color SmartIcon, or press the right mouse button and choose Lines & Color from the Quick menu.

The **S**ymbol option in the Lines & Color dialog box offers a variety of symbol shapes, including boxes, squares, stars, triangles, diamonds, and circles. If you don't want any symbols at the data points, select None for the **S**ymbol op-tion or choose a line-only chart style in the Type dialog box.

Formatting a Frame

By default, the legend, heading, and chart itself are enclosed in *frames* (boxes). To change the format of a frame, select it and then choose the **L**ines & Color command from the **C**hart menu, click the Lines & Color SmartIcon, or press the right mouse button and choose Lines & Color from the Quick menu.

When you select a frame, the Lines & Color dialog box has two additional options: **D**esigner frame and **F**rame color. If you click on down-arrow for the **D**esigner frame, you see a palette of frame corners, shown in figure 13.6. After you select a frame, you can choose a color with the **F**rame color field.

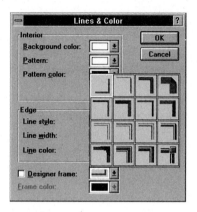

Fig. 13.6
The palette of designer frames.

Exploding Pie Slices

To emphasize one or more portions of a pie chart, you can *explode,* or pull out, slices of the pie. For example, in figure 13.7, a slice of the pie has been exploded for emphasis. 1-2-3 offers several ways to explode slices.

Probably the fastest way to explode a single slice is to select it and drag it the desired distance away from the pie. A selected pie slice has three selection handles on it. As you drag the slice, the mouse pointer is shaped like a hand (to indicate that you are moving something) and the slice has a dotted outline surrounding it. When the slice outline is where you want the slice to be, release the mouse button; the slice then moves to that position.

> **Note**
>
> Exploding a slice may reduce the size of the pie because of the extra space required to display the entire pie with the slice pulled out.

A second way to explode pie slices is to pull them all out by a certain percentage. To do so, choose **C**hart, **D**ata Labels. The Data Labels dialog box appears. Enter a value in the **A**ll by [__] % field. Figure 13.8 shows a pie whose slices are exploded 10 percent.

◀ "Changing Fonts and Attributes," p. 343

◀ "Formatting Cells with Color and Borders," p. 348

Tip
To make sure your pie chart is as effective as possible, explode only the one or two pie slices that deserve special attention.

II

Working with Charts

Fig. 13.7
A pie graph with an exploded slice.

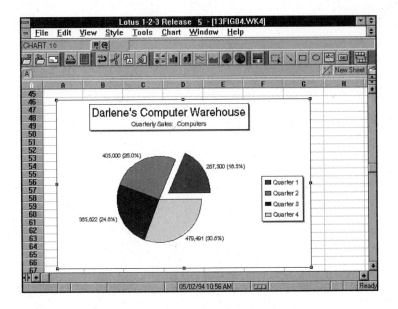

Fig. 13.8
All slices in this pie are exploded by 10 percent.

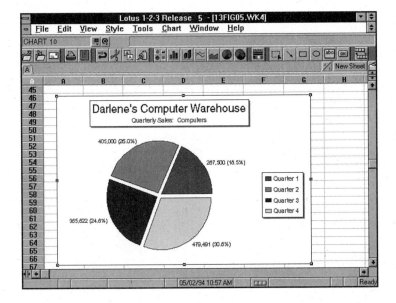

The third way to explode slices is to create a B range and then turn on the **U**sing B Range check box in the Data Labels dialog box. This method is described in the section, "Changing the Data Series Colors and Patterns," earlier in this chapter.

> **Note**
>
> If you change your mind after exploding one or more slices, you can eliminate the effect by choosing **N**o Explosion in the Data Labels dialog box.

Troubleshooting

My y-axis scale shows single digit numbers (1, 2, 3,...) with a unit indicator of Thousands, but I would prefer to see the actual numbers (1000, 2000, 3000,...). How can I do this?

Choose **C**hart, **A**xis and then select **Y**-Axis. In the Y-Axis dialog box, select the **O**ptions button. Then choose Ma**n**ual in the Axis units field and enter 0 for the **E**xponent.

I exploded a pie slice by manually dragging it out of the pie. Now I have decided that I don't want the slice to be exploded. How can I be sure to put it back in exactly the right place?

Select the **D**ata Labels command from the **C**hart menu, then select **N**o explosion under Explode Slices in the Data Labels dialog box.

How can I make it easier to tell the difference between the data series in a line chart?

Assign each data series a different line style and/or width and different symbols at the data points. To change the line style, width, and symbol for each data series individually, click one of the lines in the chart, and then display the Lines & Color dialog box by either clicking the Lines & Color SmartIcon, selecting Lines & Color from the Quick menu, or selecting **L**ines & Color from the **S**tyle menu. Then make selections from the St**y**le, **W**idth, and **S**ymbol drop-down lists. Repeat for each data series.

Even though the numbers in my worksheet are formatted for currency, the y-axis scale in the chart doesn't show the dollar sign.

1-2-3 for Windows does not automatically use worksheet formatting in charts. To change the number format of the y-axis scale to currency, select one of the numbers on the y-axis, and then display the Number Format dialog box by either choosing **N**umber Format from the **S**tyle menu or clicking the right mouse button on the numbers and choosing Number Format from the Quick menu.

Previewing and Printing Charts

You can easily view on-screen a chart you create in 1-2-3 for Windows (and so can anyone looking over your shoulder), but often you need to print copies of charts to share with coworkers. If you have used earlier versions of 1-2-3

II

Working with Charts

for DOS, you may notice a major change in the way charts are printed in 1-2-3 for Windows. Rather than using a separate PrintGraph program, you now can preview and print charts the way you print worksheets—by using the **P**rint command on the **F**ile menu.

Printing a Chart

Before printing a chart, select it—any element on the chart will suffice. Then choose **F**ile, **P**rint or click the Print SmartIcon. The Print dialog box shows the name of the selected chart in the Selected **c**hart field. Figure 13.9 shows the dialog box with the name CHART 1 as the Selected **c**hart. When you choose OK, the chart prints at the size it appears in the worksheet.

Fig. 13.9
The Print dialog box.

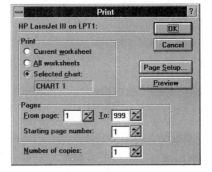

Printing a Chart Full Page

In some cases, you may want a chart to fill a printed page—such as when you are printing charts for a presentation. 1-2-3 for Windows provides a command that automatically enlarges a chart to fill a page, adjusting the size of all elements and the point size of text proportionally. To use this option, select the chart; then choose **F**ile, Pa**g**e Setup. (You can also display the Page Setup dialog box by clicking the Page **S**etup button in the Print or Print Preview dialog boxes.)

The Si**z**e option in the Page Setup dialog box has three settings for charts: Actual Size, Fill Page, and Fill Page But Keep Proportions.

Tip
The Size option Fill Page But Keep Proportions in the Page Setup dialog box is often more effective when you change the Orientation setting to Landscape.

- Actual Size is the default.

- If you choose Fill Page, the chart is enlarged or reduced until it fills the page.

- Because Fill Page may produce a distorted chart, a better choice is often Fill Page But Keep Proportions. This chart prints as large as possible without any distortion.

Printing Charts and Worksheet Data on the Same Page

You can print a chart and its supporting data on separate pages and then collate them to produce a report. However, printing a chart and its worksheet together on one page can sometimes be easier for your coworkers to read (see fig. 13.10). How you print this type of report depends on where the chart is located in the worksheet in relation to its supporting data.

- If the chart and data are placed exactly where you want them in the report, you can define a single print range: select the range of cells that includes the data and the chart. (Even though 1-2-3 for Windows highlights the cells behind the chart without appearing to select the chart, the chart is selected when you select *all* the cells behind it.)

- If the data is in one part of the worksheet and the chart is in another, you must define two print ranges. To define multiple ranges, type the ranges, separated by commas or semicolons. To point to the ranges, you must preselect them; remember to hold down the Ctrl key as you select the second and subsequent ranges.

Tip
To add white space between a worksheet data and chart, include blank rows as part of the range(s) to be printed.

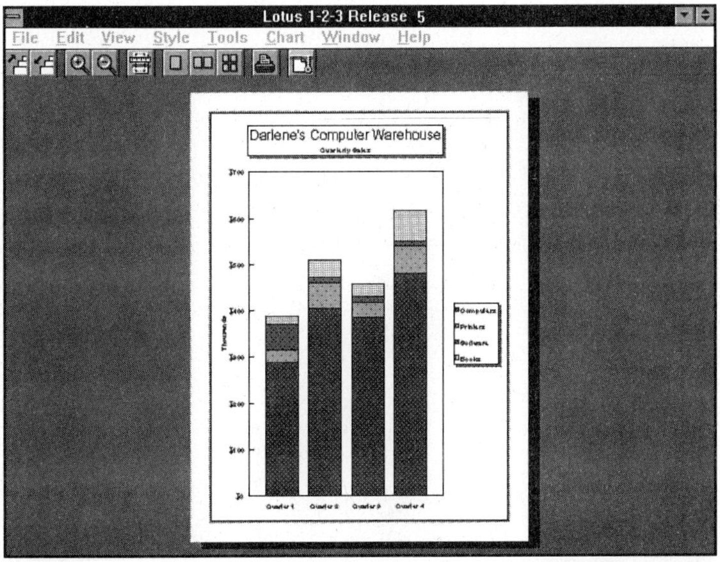

Fig. 13.10
A chart printed with its supporting data.

Working with Charts

Note

To select more than one chart to print on a page, you must select the worksheet cell range(s) behind the charts; you cannot select multiple charts by holding down Ctrl as you click them.

Selecting a Chart with Draw Objects

If you have used **T**ools, **D**raw to add any text or objects to your chart, they will not print if you simply select the chart name in the Print dialog box. To print the chart and objects you have added to it, you must use the Select Objects SmartIcon to "lasso" the chart. Then, when you display the Print dialog box, the word `Collection` appears in the Selected Drawn Object field. This means that 1-2-3 will print the chart with all the graphic elements you selected.

▶ "Annotating a Chart," p. 456

▶ "Working with Graphics," p. 508

Previewing a Chart

You can preview a chart before you print it. Previewing can save you time and paper, enabling you to make all necessary adjustments and changes before you print. To preview a chart, select the chart, and then choose **F**ile, Print Pre**v**iew or click the Preview SmartIcon. You also can select the **P**review button from the Print dialog box.

When you add a chart to a worksheet, you specify the size of the chart and the location at which it appears on the page. By previewing the report, you can determine how the chart fits on the printed page. You then can decide whether you should use one of the Si**z**e options described earlier in this chapter. Figure 13.11 shows a previewed chart in **P**ortrait orientation, with the Fill Page.

Fig. 13.11
A preview of a chart.

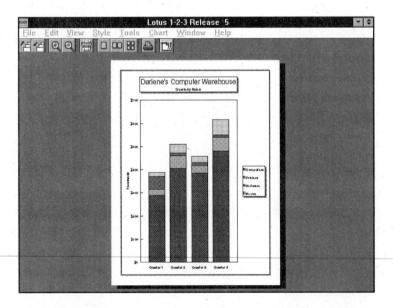

Printing Color Charts on a Black-and-White Printer

If you try to use a black-and-white printer to print a color chart, here's what happens:

- Colored text prints in black

- Colored lines print in black

- The background color of the plot area is ignored

- The interior colors of objects (bars, areas, and so on) are converted to shades of gray

For greater control over the way the chart appears in black and white, you can change the solid colors to shades of gray or black-and-white hatch patterns. (See the section, "Changing Data Series Colors and Patterns," earlier in this chapter.) Also, be sure to include symbols in your line charts to make the data series easier to distinguish.

Troubleshooting

When I printed my bar chart on a black and white printer, it was difficult to tell the difference between the data series, even though the colors on the screen made it perfectly obvious.

When printing a chart on a black and white printer, it is a good idea to do one of the following: change the data series colors to contrasting shades of gray or use a different pattern instead of different colors to represent each data series. In either case, you change each data series individually by clicking one of the bars in the chart, and then display the Lines & Color dialog box by clicking the Lines & Color SmartIcon, selecting Lines & Color from the Quick menu, or selecting **L**ines & Color from the **S**tyle menu. To change the data series colors to shades of gray (which will make the screen look more like the printed chart), display the **B**ackground color palette and then select one of the shades of gray from the far right column in the palette. Repeat for each data series, selecting alternating lighter and darker shades of gray. To change the pattern for each data series, use the **P**attern palette in the Lines & Color dialog box to select a pattern and use the **B**ackground color and **P**attern color palettes to select contrasting colors for the pattern (black and white are safest). Repeat this process for each data series.

I'm having trouble selecting the worksheet data and two charts that I want to print on one page.

Remember to press and hold the Ctrl key while you use the mouse to highlight the worksheet range and click on the charts.

◄ "Previewing Reports before Printing," p. 363

◄ "Printing the Report," p. 367

(continues)

II

Working with Charts

(continued)

I want to put some white space on the printed page between the worksheet data at the top of the page and a chart at the bottom. How do I do it?

If there are blank rows below the worksheet range, select those rows to provide the white space. If not, select the worksheet range, select another blank range in the worksheet for the white space, then select the chart.

From Here...

To learn how to create more complex charts and incorporate charts in business presentations, refer to the following chapters:

- Chapter 14, "Building Complex Charts and Mapping Data," shows how to create the most complicated chart types offered by 1-2-3 for Windows, as well as how to add graphics to a chart. This chapter also covers how to illustrate data for geographical regions in maps.

- Chapter 16, "Adding Graphics to Worksheets," covers how to add text boxes, lines, arrows, ellipses, and other graphic elements to a chart.

- Chapter 17, "Developing Business Presentations," shows how to include 1-2-3 graphs in slides shows and computer presentations.

Chapter 14

Building Complex Charts and Mapping Data

The previous chapters covered how to create, format, enhance, and print the most commonly used chart types. In most cases, these chart types and styles are sufficient to show trends, track changes, show relationships, and visually emphasize other information.

Some business and scientific purposes, however, require special charts to illustrate specific kinds of data. For example, stockbrokers often work with high-low-close-open charts to track stock prices, and scientists use XY charts to show the relationship between independent and dependent variables. 1-2-3 for Windows enables you to create these and other types of charts for special purposes as easily as you create basic line, bar, area, and pie charts. In addition, you can create charts that mix the basic chart types and plot data against a second y-axis.

You also might want to make a chart more complex by adding an arrow or another device to catch the reader's attention. You may want to add your company's logo or include clip art or graphics from another program. Ideally, these elements help convey the chart's message.

Another way that you can illustrate data in 1-2-3 for Windows is with maps. Suppose that you have sales figures for each state in the United States. In 1-2-3 for Windows Release 5, you can create a map that automatically assigns six colors to indicate the sales level in each state. You can create maps of the world or regions in many individual countries.

This chapter shows you how to do the following:

- Create XY charts, mixed charts, HLCO charts, radar charts, and second y-axis charts

- Annotate charts with graphics

- Use clip art with charts

- Illustrate data with maps

Creating Special Charts

The following sections cover when and how to create XY charts, mixed charts, HLCO charts, radar charts, and second y-axis charts. One thing that these charts have in common is that they use their data series in very specific ways, so you need to make sure that you set up the charts properly.

XY Charts

Tip

Some other kinds of relationships that would be well-illustrated by XY charts are population density versus number of crimes, luxury purchases versus age, or quantity of algae per water sample versus oxygen and nitrogen levels.

An XY chart, or *scatter chart*, is a variation on a line chart. Like a line chart, an XY chart has values plotted as points, but an XY chart uses numeric values rather than labels on its x-axis. XY charts are most useful for scientific or statistical data.

XY charts show the correlation between two or more sets of data. To use XY charts effectively, you must understand two terms: independent variables and dependent variables. One data range represents the *independent variable*, which is data that you can change or control. The other data ranges, the *dependent variables*, depend on the independent variable; you cannot control or change the dependent variables. For example, the worksheet shown in figure 14.1 has average daily temperatures in column A. Column B contains ice cream sales on days that had corresponding average daily temperatures. The temperature is the independent variable, and ice cream sales are the dependent variable. The XY chart beside the worksheet data in figure 14.1 illustrates the relationship between the temperature and ice cream sales. Each data point represents ice cream sales for a particular average daily temperature.

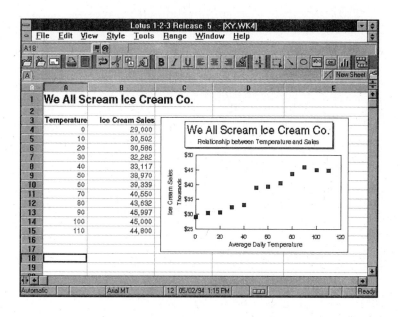

Fig. 14.1
An XY chart of
how average daily
temperature affects
ice cream sales.

Usually, the independent variable is plotted against the x-axis and the dependent variable(s) is plotted against the y-axis. You should not try to use 1-2-3 for Windows automatic chart feature when you create an XY chart; the X data series for an XY chart needs to contain values rather than labels, so the worksheet data cannot conform to the rules for automatic charts. You are better off creating a chart from scratch, following these basic steps:

1. Create an empty chart frame by selecting an empty cell and then opening the **T**ools menu and choosing the **C**hart command. The Chart dialog box appears. Choose OK to create the chart with the selected range; then click the worksheet where you want the chart to appear.

2. Open the **C**hart menu and choose the **R**anges command; or point to the empty plot, open the quick menu, and choose Chart Ranges. The Ranges dialog box appears.

3. Select the range that contains the independent variable (such as temperature or population density) to be used as the X data series. Unlike all other chart types, an XY chart uses an x-axis label range that contains values, not labels. To select the range, type the address in the **Ra**nge text box or use the range selector to point to the range.

4. Select the range that contains the first dependent variable (also values, such as ice cream sales or number of crimes) to be used as the A data series. To select the range, type the address in the **Ra**nge text box or use the range selector to point to the range.

Working with Charts

5. Repeat step 4 for additional data series (B, C, and so on). Select OK when done.

 6. Open the **C**hart menu and choose the **T**ype command to change the chart type to **X**Y. Then select the appropriate style (lines with symbols, lines with no symbols, or symbols only). Figure 14.2 shows the styles for the XY chart in the Type dialog box. The most common style for XY charts is unstacked, with symbols only.

Fig. 14.2
The XY chart styles.

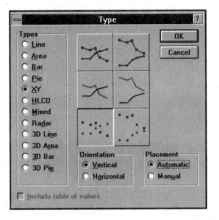

◀ "Changing the Axis Titles," p. 414

◀ "Controlling the Axis Scale," p. 415

◀ "Adjusting the Display of Axis Labels," p. 419

7. Open the **C**hart menu and choose the **A**xis command. You also can point to the x- or y-axis labels in the chart and choose the quick menu's X-Axis or Y-Axis command to perform this task.

> **Note**
>
> Legends are required only in XY charts that have more than two data series. For an XY chart with only X and A data series, use the x- and y-axis titles to identify the data, and delete the legend box.
>
> 1-2-3 Release 5 includes a SmartIcon for a vertical XY chart without lines, but it does not appear on the default chart SmartIcon palette. If you find that you use this chart type frequently, you may want to add it to the chart SmartIcon palette. See Chapter 33, "Creating Custom SmartIcon Palettes," for more information.

HLCO (High-Low-Close-Open) Charts

HLCO charts are specialized for stock-market information, but you can use them to track other kinds of data that have high and low values over time, such as daily temperatures and currency-exchange rates. Figure 14.3 shows the standard HLCO chart style, called *whisker* (referring to the tick marks on the left and right sides of the vertical lines, which resemble an animal's whiskers).

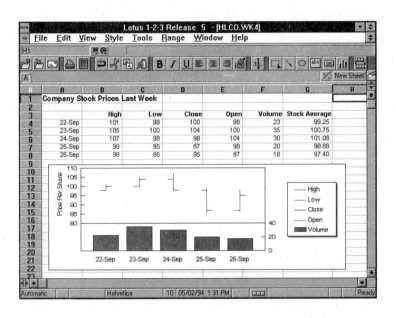

Fig. 14.3
Stock-price worksheet data and an HLCO chart using the whisker style.

An HLCO chart typically has four series, representing high, low, close, and open values. This data is represented on the chart as a vertical line; the line extends from the *low value* to the *high value*. A tick mark extending to the right of the line represents the *close value*, and a tick mark extending to the left represents the *open value*. The total number of lines in the chart depends on the number of time periods included. Following are the meanings of the four values:

High	The stock's highest price during the given period
Low	The stock's lowest price during the given period
Close	The stock's price at the end, or close, of the period
Open	The stock's price at the start, or open, of the period

An HLCO chart can include a set of bars below the HLCO section of the chart and one or more lines across the HLCO section. In the financial world, the bars often are used to represent the daily trading volume for the stock; the line can represent a changing stock-price average.

II

Working with Charts

You can use 1-2-3 for Windows automatic chart feature if your worksheet ranges are set up in the following order: the first four data series (A through D) represent the high, low, close, and open values, respectively. If you specify a fifth set of data, the E range appears as bars plotted against a second y-axis on the right side of the chart's frame. Any additional ranges appear as lines plotted against the y-axis.

Tip

If you want to emphasize the open and close values, use the candlestick style; otherwise, use the default whisker style.

1-2-3 for Windows offers a second style of HLCO chart, called *candlestick*. The only difference between the two styles is in the way that the open and close data is illustrated. Instead of using tick marks, the candlestick style has a bar that spans the range between the open and close value. The bar is empty if the close value is lower than the open value; otherwise, it is filled in.

Figure 14.4 shows an example of the candlestick style. The candlestick style places more emphasis on the open and close data; as you can see, the open/ close bars in figure 14.4 are much more prominent than the tiny tick marks of the whisker style shown in figure 14.3.

Fig. 14.4

A candlestick-style HLCO chart.

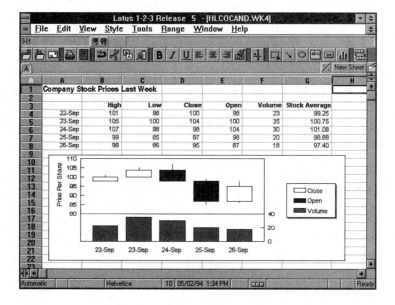

> **Note**
>
> Stock-market figures often are downloaded from on-line information services as text labels, in the format '45 3/8. To change these labels to values for use in an HLCO chart, use @VALUE, as described in Chapter 5, "Using Functions."

Mixed Charts

The mixed chart type enables you to use two or three different chart types in a single chart. When you choose the **M**ixed type in the Type dialog box, you can assign to each data series the appropriate type (line, area, or bar). Follow these steps:

1. If your worksheet data is laid out properly, create an automatic chart; otherwise, define your ranges individually.

2. Open the **C**hart menu and choose the **T**ype command; then choose **M**ixed in the Type dialog box.

3. The style buttons offer six combinations of **L**ine, **A**rea, and **B**ar styles. Choose the appropriate style. If your mixed chart will have lines, you can choose to have lines with or without symbols at the data points. If your mixed chart will have bars, indicate whether you want standard or stacked bars. Click OK to change the chart to the selected Mixed style.

4. Finally, decide which data series to display in which format. Open the **C**hart menu and choose the **R**anges command, or choose the quick menu's Chart Ranges command; the Ranges dialog box appears.

5. Click a series letter under **S**eries; then select Line, Area, or Bar in the **M**ixed type drop-down list.

6. Repeat step 5 for each series letter.

   Figure 14.5 shows the Ranges dialog box with a **M**ixed selection for the C data series.

II

Working with Charts

Fig. 14.5

The Ranges dialog box for a mixed chart with bars for data series A and B and a line for data series C.

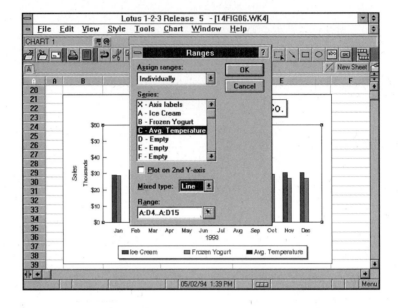

One common use for a mixed chart is to show an average or trend line in a bar chart. Suppose that you are plotting temperature levels over the past three decades. First, you could plot as bars the temperatures for the 1960s, 1970s, and 1980s; then you could plot the average temperature during the measured time span and display this series as a line. Mixed charts also are useful in charts that have a second y-axis.

Radar Charts

A radar chart plots data as a function of distance from a central point, with each spoke representing a set of data points. This chart type shows symmetry or uniformity of data. Figure 14.6 shows a radar chart.

The radar chart in figure 14.6 illustrates the basic characteristics of radar charts:

- The central point from which each value is measured from is 0,0 (unless you change the minimum value of the y-axis).

- All spokes that extend from the central point are labeled with what typically are used as x-axis labels. In figure 14.6, the spokes are labeled with months.

- The data points for each series are connected, forming a spiral around the central point.

■ For each major interval on the y-axis, 1-2-3 for Windows draws a dotted circle around the central point. Figure 14.6, for example, shows circles at 300, 500, and 700. These circles function like grid lines, helping readers interpret the values of the data points.

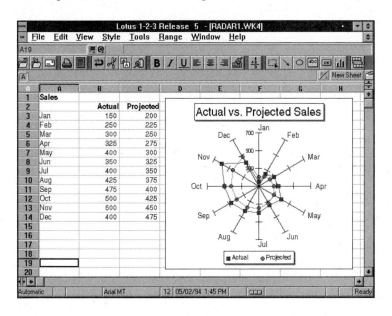

Fig. 14.6
A radar chart.

You can gather two pieces of information from a radar chart. First, you can compare the data series; the greater the distance between the data points in each spoke, the greater the difference between the series. Second, you can see how much the data fluctuates; a smooth spiral indicates a steady increase, and a jagged spiral indicates more variability. In figure 14.7, notice how smooth the spiral for the projected series is (a steady increase was predicted) and how the spiral for the actual series jumps around (sales increased during some months and decreased in others).

The Type dialog box offers two styles of radar charts. The first style is the one shown in figure 14.6. The second style stacks the series and fills in the area between spirals. Figure 14.7 shows a chart with the stacked-area style. This style is not appropriate for all types of data, because accumulating data doesn't always make sense. For example, adding projected and actual sales makes no sense.

II

Working with Charts

Fig. 14.7

A stacked-area-style radar chart.

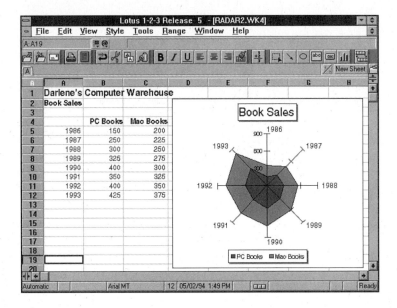

Adding a Second Y-Axis to a Chart

Sometimes you may want to chart two kinds of data in a single chart to show how the two are related. The worksheet shown in figure 14.8 shows sales data for an ice cream company. Notice that the worksheet also contains a column for average monthly temperatures.

Fig. 14.8

Data for ice cream sales and average temperatures each month.

	Ice Cream	Frozen Yogurt	Avg. Temperature
We All Scream Ice Cream Co.			
Jan	29,000	28,645	30
Feb	32,282	30,188	31
Mar	33,117	28,745	38
Apr	40,550	28,367	45
May	43,632	33,027	60
Jun	45,997	31,032	65
Jul	47,943	33,276	71
Aug	47,447	31,728	70
Sep	39,339	29,737	55
Oct	38,970	29,459	48
Nov	30,586	26,901	39
Dec	30,502	26,820	32

The company is interested in finding out whether there is a relationship between the temperature and sales. Figure 14.9 shows a line chart created with this data. Because temperature is a much smaller number than ice cream and frozen yogurt sales, the temperature line barely registers in the chart. Creating another scale to display the temperatures would be helpful. To create this scale, add a second y-axis to the chart.

Tip
You should use a second y-axis only to plot two different types of data in the same chart.

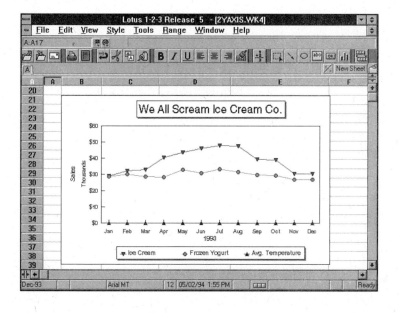

Fig. 14.9
Temperature and sales values are too different to be plotted against the same y-axis scale.

Figure 14.10 shows the same chart with a second y-axis scale on the right to plot the temperatures. Notice that the chart also is a mixed chart. Using a mixed chart to display a second y-axis scale helps to cue the reader that the chart contains two types of data.

To create a second y-axis chart, select the data series range or range(s) that you want to plot on a second y-axis, and then follow these steps:

1. Create a line, area, or bar chart.

2. Open the **C**hart menu and choose the **R**anges command, or choose the quick menu's Data Ranges command. The Range dialog box appears.

3. In the **S**eries list, select the series that you want to plot on the second y-axis.

II

Working with Charts

Fig. 14.10
A mixed chart with a second y-axis accurately plots both sales and temperature values.

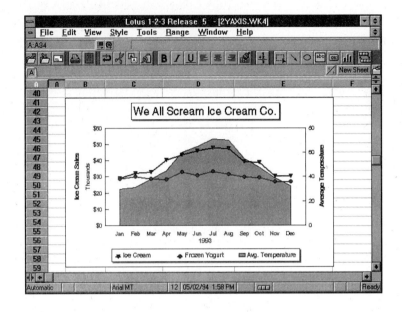

4. Choose the **P**lot on 2nd Y-axis option for the selected data series. Figure 14.11 shows this option selected for data series C.

5. If you want to create a mixed chart to display the second y-axis data, move to the Mixed type drop-down list and select the chart type you want to use for the data series. In figure 14.11, the C data range not only will be plotted against the second y-axis, but also will be displayed with an area chart, making this chart a mixed chart. (For more information about mixed charts, refer to "Mixed Charts" earlier in this chapter.)

6. Repeat steps 3, 4, and 5 for any other data series you want to plot on the second y-axis.

Tip
It is very important to use the y-axis and 2nd y-axis titles to indicate which data series are plotted against which y-axis.

After you add the second y-axis, you can treat it the way you treat a regular y-axis: you can give it a title, format the numbers, adjust the scale, and so on. To make any of these changes, open the Chart menu and choose the **A**xis command; then choose 2nd Y-Axis. (Alternatively, choose the quick menu's 2nd Y-Axis command.) The 2nd Y-Axis dialog box appears. This dialog box is exactly the same as the Y-Axis dialog box.

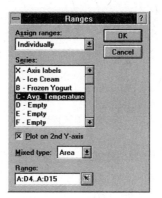

Fig. 14.11
Selections in the Ranges dialog box for a mixed chart with a second y-axis.

Troubleshooting

I'm having trouble creating an XY chart. I preselected the range and created an automatic chart, but the ranges are all wrong. 1-2-3 for Windows used the x-axis values as series A and the y-axis values as series B. How do I solve this problem?

Because of the rules that 1-2-3 for Windows follows when producing an automatic chart, you can't use this feature successfully when you create XY charts. 1-2-3 for Windows gets confused, because the x-axis labels in an XY chart must be values. The best way to create an XY chart is to create a chart from scratch and define the ranges yourself.

I chose the Mixed chart type, but all my data series display as bars. How can I get one of them to display as a line?

Open the **C**hart menu and choose the **R**anges command; click the series letter (A, B, C, and so on) that you want to be a line; and select Line in the **M**ixed type drop-down list.

◀ "Changing the
Axis Titles,"
p. 414

◀ "Controlling
the Axis Scale,"
p. 415

II

Working with Charts

Adding Graphics and Clip Art to Charts

You may want to use graphics to make your charts more attractive or to highlight specific data. In 1-2-3 for Windows, you can use the **D**raw command (**T**ools menu) and the various drawing SmartIcons to create graphics. You also can import graphics or clip art from other programs into your charts. The following sections explain how to accomplish these tasks.

Annotating a Chart

In 1-2-3 for Windows, you can add descriptive labels, lines, objects, and arrows to existing charts. For example, you might want to explain why a data point is particularly high or low, or to state a conclusion illustrated by the chart. Figure 14.12 shows a chart annotation created with the Text Block SmartIcon and the Draw Arrow SmartIcon. You create such an annotation by opening the **T**ools menu and choosing the **D**raw command.

Fig. 14.12
A chart annotated with the drawing commands.

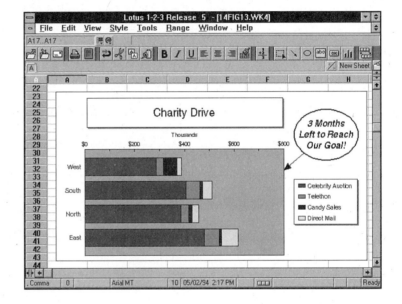

Adding Clip Art

◄ "Selecting a Chart with Draw Objects," p. 440

► "Adding Graphics to Worksheets," p. 503

You might want to enhance your charts and worksheets further by using *clip art*—graphics imported from other programs. Although 1-2-3 for Windows does not have a specific command for importing graphics files into a chart, you can bring in clip art easily by using the Windows Clipboard. To add a graphic to a 1-2-3 for Windows chart, perform the following steps:

1. Copy the graphic to the Windows Clipboard.

2. In 1-2-3 for Windows, select a range of cells in the worksheet; the graphic is pasted into this range.

3. In 1-2-3 for Windows, open the **E**dit menu and choose the **P**aste command to copy the graphic into the selected worksheet cells. (If you did not preselect a range, the graphic is pasted into a single cell.)

4. Drag the graphic into your chart.

5. Resize the graphic as necessary by dragging the selection handles.

> **Note**
>
> 1-2-3 for Windows automatically adds a visible frame around imported graphics. To remove the frame, open the Style menu and choose the **L**ines & Color command; then choose None as the Line St**y**le.

Figure 14.13 shows a chart that displays clip art—a drawing of a computer—next to the chart heading. The drawing was pasted into the worksheet and then moved into the chart.

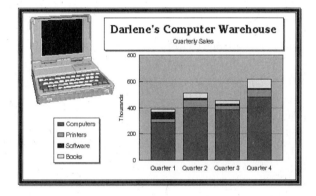

Fig. 14.13
The graphic was pasted into the worksheet and then moved into the chart.

Tip
Graphic elements in 1-2-3 for Windows are stacked on top of one another. 1-2-3 for Windows treats the entire chart as a single graphic element.

Where does clip art come from? Many drawing programs, such as CorelDRAW! and Lotus Freelance Graphics, come with a collection of images that you can use in other programs. You also can purchase packages of clip art from companies such as Masterclip Graphics, 3G Graphics, TMaker, and Image Club. Lotus Development Corporation offers its own clip-art package, called SmartPics. (The computer drawing shown in figure 14.13 came from SmartPics.) For more information on SmartPics for Windows, call Lotus Selects at 1-800-635-6887.

II

Working with Charts

Troubleshooting

When I try to copy a graphic from another program into my chart, 1-2-3 for Windows beeps.

You cannot copy a graphic directly into a chart. Copy the graphic to the worksheet and then drag it into the chart.

 I imported the company-logo graphic, but it appears in a box. How can I get rid of the box frame and the solid white fill inside the frame?

Select the graphic; then open the **S**tyle menu and choose the **L**ines & Color command. For the Line style, choose None. For the **P**attern, choose T(ransparent).

Illustrating Data with Maps

1-2-3 for Windows Release 5 offers a useful new feature: maps that illustrate data in the worksheet. Suppose that you have compiled sales figures for each U.S. state. Instead of trying to create a bar chart, you can link the data to colors in a map. As figure 14.14 shows, 1-2-3 for Windows evaluates the worksheet data and automatically assigns each state one of six colors, depending on the sales figure for the state. You also can illustrate a second kind of data with up to six patterns; in this case, the map shows sales volumes in colors and sales regions in patterns. You can create maps of this type for other countries and regions in the world as well.

Fig. 14.14
Map illustrating
United States sales
data.

Colors for sales ⎯

Patterns for regions ⎯

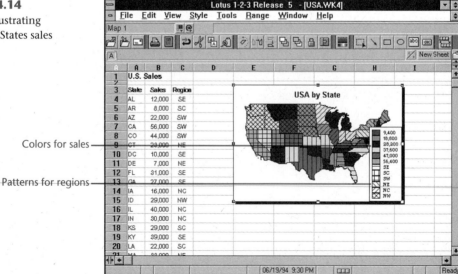

Setting Up the Map Data Ranges

Before you can create a map, you need to set up the data ranges in the way that 1-2-3 for Windows can interpret them to create a map. To do so, follow these rules:

■ In the first column, identify the geographic regions you want to illustrate in the map. The regions can be countries in the world, U.S. states, Canadian provinces, or other provincial regions throughout the world. To identify the regions, you can either enter the name of the country, state or province or use a two-letter map code. 1-2-3 for Windows recognizes as map codes the standard two-letter post office abbreviations for U.S. states, but you will probably have to look up the two-letter map codes for other regions or countries.

■ In the second and third columns, place the data that you want to illustrate with colors and patterns in the map. Make sure that each column contains the same kind of data, such as all values or all labels. The range of numeric values is unlimited, but you can only map six different labels. If you only want to map one set of data, place it in the second column, where 1-2-3 for Windows will use it to determine the colors. The way 1-2-3 for Windows determines how to illustrate the data is described in the next section, "Creating the Map."

> **Note**
>
> 1-2-3 for Windows also lets you point out exact locations in a geographic region, such as a city, by specifying the character you want to use to mark the site (called the pin character) and the latitude and longitude of the site. The pin character, latitude, longitude, and (optional) pin character color may be entered in the fourth, fifth, and sixth columns, respectively. This technique is covered in "Showing Pin Characters in a Map," later in this chapter.

■ In the third column, place the pattern values or labels; these are the values or labels that 1-2-3 for Windows uses to display regions in different patterns. You can use this column for a variety of purposes, such as dividing the total area in the map into regions or showing another set of values in the map. The range of values for patterns is unlimited; 1-2-3 for Windows always divides these values into six bins. You can use no more than six labels in the pattern column, however.

Tip

If you use labels instead of values to determine colors or patterns, each label can be as short as one or two characters or as long as you think looks all right in the legend.

II

Working with Charts

Fig. 14.15

Data ranges for a map.

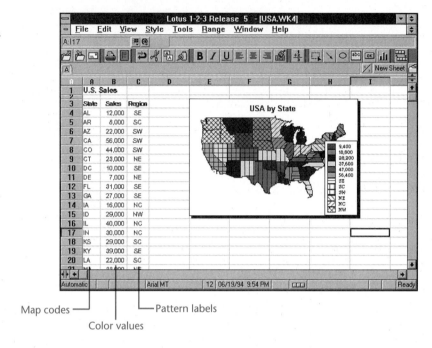

Map codes ——
Color values ——
Pattern labels ——

There are several ways to look up the names and two-letter map codes for the geographic regions. 1-2-3 for Windows includes one or more data files (with WKY extensions) for every available map in the \MAPDATA subdirectory of the 1-2-3 for Windows program directory. These files contain the map codes and region names, which you can copy from those files into your worksheet.

Another way to copy names and codes automatically is to use the Lotus Map Viewer. When you display a map in the Lotus Map Viewer, you can point to a state or country, then display the quick menu and select either Copy Region Name or Copy Region Code to copy the name or code to the Windows Clipboard. Then you can paste the copied data into the worksheet. Because you need to point to the map to copy the names and codes, this method is less useful when you are creating a map for the first time. (For more information about the Lotus Map Viewer, see "Using the Lotus Map Viewer" later in this chapter.)

Creating the Map

You can create a map as easily as you can create a chart: automatically, as long as you set up the map data ranges following the rules in the previous section, "Setting Up the Map Data Ranges." To create or edit a map, you open the **T**ools menu, then select Ma**p** to display the Ma**p** cascade menu (see fig. 14.16).

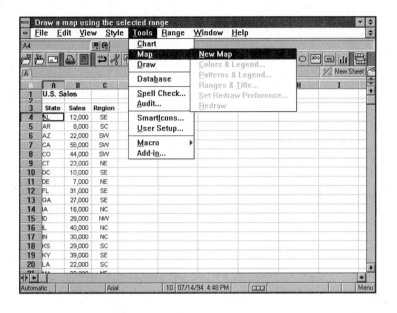

Fig. 14.16
The Ma**p** cascade menu.

To create a map automatically, perform the following steps:

1. Select the range that contains all the data ranges for the map: the map codes column, color column, and (optionally) pattern column. Alternatively, select a single cell in ranges of data you want to map; 1-2-3 for Windows will select all the contiguous cells with data during the map creation process.

2. Open the **T**ools menu and choose the Ma**p** command; the Ma**p** cascade menu appears. Choose the **N**ew Map command from this menu.

> **Note**
>
> If an empty cell is selected when you select the Insert Map Object command, 1-2-3 for Windows displays the Map Assistant dialog box, which prompts you to specify the map data ranges. You can type the range address or use the range selector to select the ranges. Then select OK to continue to create the map.

3. The mouse pointer changes to the map pointer (which looks like a small globe), and the title bar indicates that you should click the worksheet to insert the map. Click the worksheet where you want 1-2-3 to place the upper-left corner of the map.

▶ "Using OLE,"
    p. 819

It takes a moment for 1-2-3 for Windows to evaluate the data and develop the map. When this process is complete, 1-2-3 for Windows inserts the map in the default size. Figure 14.17 shows a map created from the data in figure 14.16. Notice that the map automatically includes a legend that identifies the colors and patterns; the values in the legend are the highest number in each bin. The default title is determined by the map. The selection handles around the map frame indicate that the map is selected.

Notice that the edit line identifies the map as Map 1. Each map that you create with 1-2-3 for Windows is a single embedded OLE object. The sections that follow tell you how you can change the title and control other aspects of the map.

Fig. 14.17
Map created from
U.S. sales data.

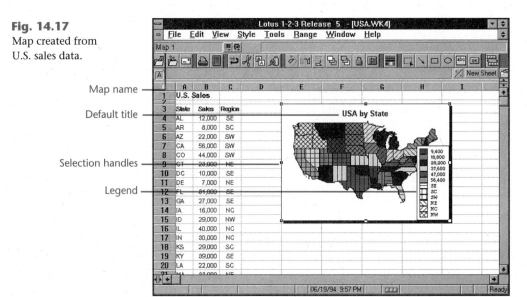

The following list explains how 1-2-3 for Windows handles the data when it creates the map:

■ 1-2-3 for Windows evaluates the map codes to determine which map to use.

■ 1-2-3 for Windows uses the first column containing numeric data to determine the color of each geographic region. Because a map is limited to six colors, 1-2-3 for Windows usually has to divide the range of data into six *bins*. For example, if the numbers range from 0 to 60, the bins might be 0–10, 11–20, 21–30, 31–40, 41–50, and 51–60. In figure 14.17, the numbers range from 7,000 to 56,000, so 1-2-3 created the bins 0–9,400, 9,401–18,800, and so on. (For information on changing the bins, see "Changing the Bin Definitions," later in this chapter.)

■ The other column will be illustrated with up to six patterns. If this column also contains numeric data, 1-2-3 for Windows divides the range of values into six bins. Alternatively, if this column contains labels, 1-2-3 for Windows evaluates how many different labels there are to determine how many patterns to use in the map; the limit is six. If neither of the columns contains numeric data, 1-2-3 for Windows uses the first column for colors and the second column for patterns. (For information on changing the color and pattern ranges, see "Modifying a Map," later in this chapter.)

■ If you have entered pin characters, the latitude and longitude of the sites for the characters, and (optional) pin character color in the fourth, fifth, and sixth columns, respectively, 1-2-3 for Windows calculates the locations for the pin characters. (In most cases, you will add pin characters to an existing map. For more information about this option, see "Adding Pin Characters to a Map," later in this chapter.)

■ Finally, 1-2-3 for Windows draws the map, assigning each state, province, or country in the map code column a color and (optionally) a pattern. The legend shows the colors and patterns and their associated bin value upper limit and/or label. The pin characters (if any) appear at the specified locations on the map.

Dealing with New or Incorrect Geographic Codes

During the map creation process, if 1-2-3 for Windows encounters geographic codes that do not belong in the same map or a code that it does not recognize (one that does not match any of the geographic codes in the system), it gives you a chance to select the map type you want and to correct the error and complete the map creation process.

Suppose, for example, that you are creating a map of the United States, which misspelled the code for Connecticut (CT) as CQ. You select the map data ranges, open the **T**ools menu, select the Ma**p** command, and then select the **I**nsert Map Object command from the Ma**p** cascade menu. 1-2-3 for Windows begins to develop the map, but encounters the geographic code CQ in cell A:A8; this code is not part of the U.S. map.

If there are many codes that 1-2-3 for Windows does not recognize, the Map Type dialog box appears, which prompts you to select the map you intend to create (see fig. 14.18). Select map from the Select a Map list box, then select OK.

Fig. 14.18
Select the map type you want in the Map Type dialog box.

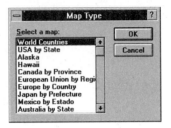

If there are few misspellings, or after you select the map type, 1-2-3 for Windows displays the Region Check dialog box to let you correct the misspelling (see fig. 14.19). Notice that the cell and the incorrect code are displayed in the top two fields of the Region Check dialog box.

Fig. 14.19
The Region Check dialog box lets you correct a misspelled name or code or create a custom name for a region.

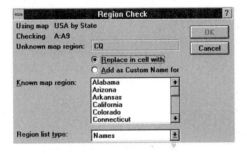

If the entry is a misspelling that you want to correct in the worksheet so that you can create the map, perform the following steps to change the entry in the cell and continue to create the map with the correct map region:

1. Select the **R**eplace in cell with button.

2. In the Region list **t**ype drop-down list, select Codes if you need to correct a two-letter map code, or select Names if you need to correct the name of a state, country, or region. The **K**nown map region list box will display either all the map codes or region names, depending on your choice. If you want to replace the entry in the cell with a previously created custom name, select Custom Names from the Region list **t**ype drop-down list.

3. Select the correct map code, name, or custom name in the **K**nown map region list box. To scroll through the list quickly, type the first letter of the code or name.

4. Click OK to change the cell entry to your selection and continue to create the map with the corrected information.

Sometimes you may want to use a region name or map code that you supply instead of the one that 1-2-3 for Windows recognizes. For example, you may want to use Deutschland instead of Germany. To create a custom name or alias for a specific region, perform the following steps.

1. Select the **A**dd as Custom Name for button.

2. In the Region list **t**ype drop-down list, select Codes if you want to create a new map code alias or Names if you want to create a new name alias. The **K**nown map region list box will display either all the region map codes or names, depending on your choice.

3. Select the map code or name in the **K**nown map region list box for which you want to create the alias. To scroll through the list quickly, type the first letter of the code or name.

4. Click OK to add the cell entry to the list of custom names. Thereafter, whenever you create a map, 1-2-3 recognizes either the correct code or the new alias for this region.

Moving and Resizing the Map

You can move the entire map the way you move a chart or other graphic object in a worksheet. Click the map so that the selection handles appear around it; then drag the map to the new position.

To resize the entire map, click it to select it. Point to one of the selection handles; the mouse pointer should change to a four-headed arrow. Then drag the selection handle in the direction in which you want to change the size. If you want to maintain the map's current proportions, drag a corner handle.

> **Caution**
>
> Be careful when you resize maps. It is easy to distort the proportions. Use the corner handles to maintain the proportions.

Modifying a Map

1-2-3 uses default colors and patterns, which you can change. You can also edit the legend labels, change the bin definitions, and supply a new title for the map. All of these elements are controlled with the commands on the Ma**p** cascade menu and are described in the following sections.

Changing the Title

By default, a map's title comes from the graphic that 1-2-3 for Windows used to create the map. To change the title, select the map object; then open **T**ools menu, choose the Ma**p** command, then select the Ranges & **T**itle command from the Ma**p** cascade menu. The Ranges and Title dialog box appears (see fig. 14.20). Type a new title in the Title text box. Alternatively, use the contents of a cell as the title by choosing the Cell option and using the range selector to indicate the appropriate cell. Select OK to make the change to the map title.

Fig. 14.20

The Ranges & Title dialog box lets you control the ranges for the map and the map title.

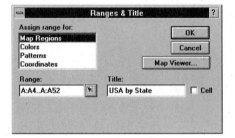

Changing the Data Ranges

You can change the ranges that define the map. You may want to add additional items at the bottom of the list, for example, or to change the map so that it shows only some of the regions. Select the map object; then open **T**ools menu, choose the Ma**p** command, then select the Ranges & **T**itle command from the Ma**p** cascade menu. The Ranges & Title dialog box appears. Next, choose the appropriate Assign range for option. To select the map code column, choose Map Regions; to select the color column, choose Colors; to select the pattern column, choose Patterns. Then you can either type the new range or select the range with the range selector. When you choose OK, 1-2-3 redraws the map. (The Coordinates option controls the pin characters. This feature is described in "Adding Pin Characters to a Map," later in this chapter.)

The Map Viewer button in the Ranges & Titles dialog box opens the Map Viewer, in which you can make a variety of other changes to the map. This option is covered in "Using the Lotus Map Viewer" later in this chapter.

Choosing Other Colors and Patterns

You may want to use different colors or patterns in a map, perhaps to provide better contrast when the map is printed on a black-and-white printer. Or you may want to modify the bin definitions to divide the values in to bins that are more relevant to the way you view the data. To control the colors and patterns and how they are assigned, select the map object; then open **T**ools menu, choose the Ma**p** command, then either:

- Choose **C**olors & Legend from the Ma**p** cascade menu to change the colors; the Colors & Legend dialog box appears (see fig. 14.21).

- Choose **P**atterns & Legend from the Ma**p** cascade menu to change the patterns; the Patterns & Legend dialog box appears (see fig. 14.22).

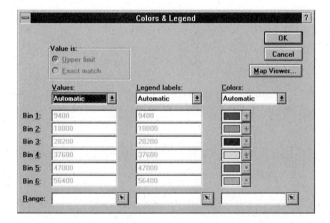

Fig. 14.21
The Colors &
Legend dialog box.

Fig. 14.22
The Patterns &
Legend dialog box.

Working with Charts

As you can see in figures 14.21 and 14.22, changing the colors and patterns is essentially the same. These figures show the default settings for the map shown in figure 14.17. Notice that the values, legend labels, colors, and patterns are automatically assigned by default.

Changing the Bin Definitions

Sometimes, you may want to define the bin values instead of using the ones that 1-2-3 for Windows creates. You may know that the lowest numbers in the color range are exceptions, for example, and want to group them with higher numbers, or you may want the bins to be defined by round numbers (10,000, 20,000, 30,000, and so on).

To change the bin definitions, display either the Colors & Legend or Patterns & Legend dialog boxes, and then do one of the following things.

■ To enter your own bin values, select Manual from the **V**alues drop-down list, and type the bin values in the text boxes for bins 1 through 6.

■ To use a worksheet range to define the bin values, select From Range from the **V**alues drop-down list; then use the range selector to indicate the range in the worksheet that contains the bin values.

■ To let 1-2-3 for Windows determine the bin values automatically, select Automatic from the **V**alues drop-down list.

Figure 14.23 shows manually entered bin values and figure 14.24 shows the map that resulted from those values. Notice that the legend automatically changed to reflect the new values.

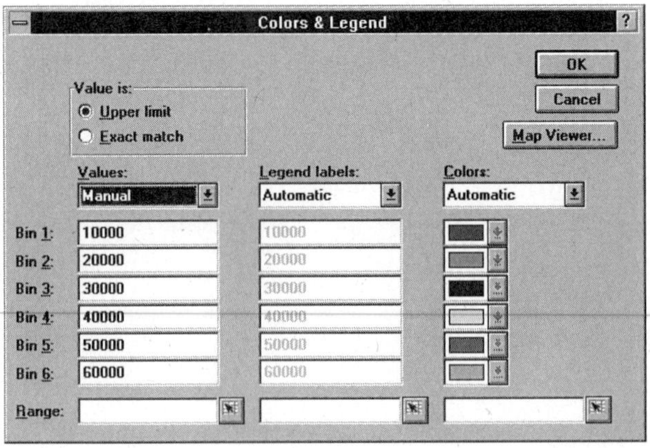

Fig. 14.23
Manually entered
bin values.

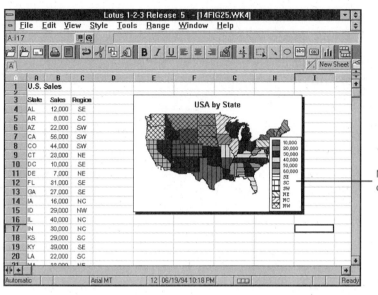

Fig. 14.24
Map with
manually entered
bin definitions.

New bin
definitions

The Value Is section at the top of the Colors & Legend and Patterns & Legend dialog boxes controls the way 1-2-3 for Windows uses the bin values. By default, the bin values are upper limits, as in the Colors & Legend dialog box shown in figure 14.21. You can, however, tell 1-2-3 for Windows to use exact matches to color the states or countries by choosing the Exact Match under Value Is. When this option is selected, 1-2-3 for Windows colors only those states or countries whose values match the value in any of the bin text boxes.

If the color or pattern column contains labels instead of values, however, 1-2-3 for Windows matches the labels by default, as shown in the Value Is section of the Pattern Settings dialog box in figure 14.22. This is the best setting for labels.

Tip
The Exact Match option under Value is should only be used if there are no more than six possible options in the color or pattern data column.

Changing the Legend Labels

By default, 1-2-3 automatically uses the values in the bin text boxes as the legend labels, whether these values are determined automatically, manually, or from a range. If you want to edit or change these labels, you can do one of the following things in either the Colors & Legend or the Patterns & Legend dialog box:

- Select Manual from the **L**egend labels drop-down list, and then type new labels in the text boxes. You can either enter entirely new labels, or add text or currency symbols to the automatically generated labels.

II

Working with Charts

- Select From Range from the **L**egend labels drop-down list, and then use the range selector to indicate the range in the worksheet that contains the labels.

- Select Automatic from the **L**egend labels drop-down list to use values or labels in the **V**alues text boxes as the legend labels.

Selecting Other Colors

Tip

For greater control of the way the map appears printed in black and white, change the map colors to shades of gray.

You can control the colors in the map individually. To select other colors, pull down the **T**ools menu, choose the Ma**p** command, then select **C**olors & Legend from the Ma**p** cascade menu. Then, in the Colors & Legend dialog box, you can use one of the following methods to change one or more colors in the map:

- Select Manual from the **C**olors drop-down list, then click the drop-down arrow for the first color you want to change. From the palette of 256 colors that appears, select the new color for the bin. Repeat this process to change other bin colors.

◄ "Changing Colors and Patterns of Data Points and Pie Slices," p. 432

- Select From Range from the **C**olors drop-down list, and then use the range selector to indicate the range in the worksheet that contains the color values. 1-2-3 for Windows associates numbers with the colors in the color palette; for example, the numbers 0 through 15 represent the colors in the top row of the color palette from left to right.

- Select Automatic from the **C**olors drop-down list to have 1-2-3 for Windows select the colors automatically.

Selecting Other Patterns

Only six patterns are available in 1-2-3 for Windows maps. To change the patterns in the map, open the **T**ools menu and choose the Ma**p P**attern command. In the Patterns & Legend dialog box, you can change the patterns in one of the following ways:

- Select Manual from the **P**atterns drop-down list, and then click the drop-down arrow for the first pattern you want to change. In the palette of six patterns that appears, select the new pattern for the bin. Repeat this process to change other bin colors.

- Select From Range from the **P**atterns drop-down list, and then use the range selector to indicate the range in the worksheet that contains the pattern values. The pattern values can be a number from 1 to 6, representing the six available patterns.

■ Select Automatic from the **P**atterns drop-down list to have 1-2-3 for Windows select the patterns automatically.

Changing the Redraw Preference

By default, 1-2-3 automatically redraws the map whenever you make changes in a map dialog box or in the data ranges that define the map. However, if you are making several changes, you may not want 1-2-3 for Windows to redraw the map after each change. You can change 1-2-3 for Windows redraw preference from automatic to manual. Open the **T**ools menu and choose the Ma**p** command; then choose the **S**et Redraw Preference command from the Ma**p** cascade menu. In the Set Redraw Preference dialog box, select **M**anual, then select OK. The next time you want to redraw the map, open the **T**ools menu and choose the Ma**p** command, then choose **R**edraw from the Ma**p** cascade menu.

Editing the Map Graphic

Unlike a chart, in which you can select and manipulate elements individually, 1-2-3 for Windows considers a map to be one object. You cannot, for example, move the map title in the map directly in the worksheet. But 1-2-3 for Windows includes a feature in which you can edit the map graphic: the Lotus Map Viewer. This section covers how to use the Lotus Map Viewer to change the font sizes, move the legend and title, show only part of the map, and overlay other maps.

Using the Lotus Map Viewer

To edit the map graphic, you must display it in the Lotus Map Viewer. To do so, double-click anywhere in the map. The Lotus Map Viewer opens, displaying the map (see fig. 14.25). Notice that the title bar lists the name of the worksheet file in which the map appears. Other ways to open the Lotus Map Viewer include selecting Edit Object from the quick menu when the map is selected, or selecting the **M**ap Viewer command from either the Color Settings, Pattern Settings, or Ranges & Title dialog box.

As you see in figure 14.25, the Lotus Map Viewer displays the map as you see it in the worksheet. Notice also that you can identify the states and/or countries in the map by pointing to them; in the status bar, the Lotus Map Viewer displays the state or country two-letter map code.

Fig. 14.25
The Lotus Map
Viewer.

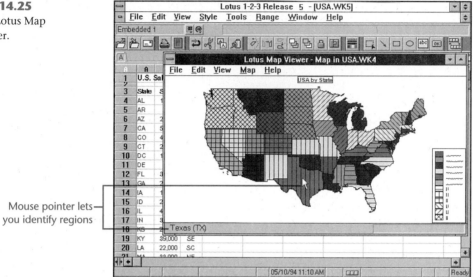

Mouse pointer lets
you identify regions

The Lotus Map Viewer appears in its own window, which you can resize by dragging the window frame. The Map viewer will automatically resize the map within the frame. However, this will not have any effect on the size or shape of the map in the worksheet. To change the size and shape of the map in the worksheet, you must change the size and shape of the map frame embedded in the worksheet.

After you make the changes you want, they are automatically transferred to the map embedded in the worksheet when you do one of the following:

- Open the **F**ile menu and choose the E**x**it & Return to Lotus 1-2-3 command to close the Lotus Map Viewer and display the updated map in the worksheet.

- Open the **F**ile menu and choose the **U**pdate Lotus 1-2-3 command to up-date the map in the worksheet without closing the Lotus Map Viewer so that you can continue to make other changes, choose E**x**it and press Enter.

Changing the Text Attributes

The two map elements that contain text are the title and the legend. In the Lotus Map Viewer, you can change the size, font, and attributes of this text. To change the actual text of the title or the legend labels, you use the commands or the **T**ools Ma**p** menu. (Refer to "Changing the Title" and "Changing the Legend Labels" earlier in this chapter.)

◀ "Enhancing the Appearance of Data," p. 343

To change the font and attributes of the title or legend labels, select the appropriate element in the Lotus Map Viewer window; then, open the **E**dit menu and choose the **F**ont & Attributes command. Alternatively, select Font & Attributes from the quick menu. The Font dialog box appears, as shown in figure 14.26. This dialog box works the same way as the 1-2-3 for Windows Font & Attributes dialog box, enabling you to change the typeface, style, size, and other attributes of the text. When you finish making changes, choose OK.

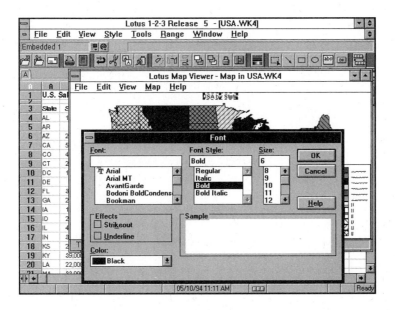

Fig. 14.26
The Font dialog box in the Lotus Map Viewer.

Moving or Deleting the Title and Legend

The Lotus Map Viewer enables you to drag the map title and legend to other positions within the map frame. To change the sizes of these items, however, you can change the font sizes (refer to the preceding section), or you can use the mouse to click and drag the selection handles to create the new size.

To delete the title or legend, you can use a number of methods. The simplest way is to select the title or legend in the Lotus Map Viewer, then press the delete key. Alternatively, you can select Clear from the quick menu to delete the selected object.

Another way to remove the title or legend is to open the **V**iew menu and select the Set View **P**references command; the Set View Preferences dialog box appears. The Show in Map section of the dialog box lets you turn on and off the display of the title and the two parts of the legend—the part that identifies the colors and the part that identifies the patterns. To remove the title from the map, for example, you select **T**itle to remove the X from the **T**itle check box, then select OK.

II

Working with Charts

> **Note**
>
> The Set View Preferences dialog box also lets you turn on and off the display of the Lotus Map Viewer status bar.

Resizing the Map

You can change the size of the map itself (as separate from the frame, title, and labels) by zooming in and out in the Lotus Map Viewer. To make the map a little smaller (as it appears in fig. 14.27), open the **V**iew command and choose the Zoom **O**ut command. The map becomes a little smaller within the frame, but the title and legend do not change. You can repeat this command several times to make the map even smaller.

Fig. 14.27
Use the View menu's Zoom Out command to make the map smaller.

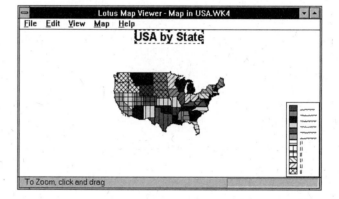

You may want to show only part of the map that 1-2-3 for Windows draws—perhaps to show only the New England region of figure 14.27. You can zoom in on part of the map in two ways:

- Open the **V**iew menu and choose the **Z**oom In command. The Lotus Map Viewer makes the map larger in the frame. When the map becomes too big to fit in the frame, you see only the part that fits. You can repeat this command several times to make the map larger in the frame.

Tip
Use the mouse to zoom in on South America, Europe, or Asia to create maps of these regions alone.

- The one disadvantage of the **V**iew menu's **Z**oom In command is that you cannot control which part of the map remains in the frame when you make the map larger. To select a specific part of the map to zoom in on, point to a corner of the area you want to enlarge, press the Ctrl key, and then click and drag to outline the area you want to zoom in on. When you release the mouse button, the area becomes large enough to fill the frame. This method was used to create the map of the New England region shown in figure 14.28.

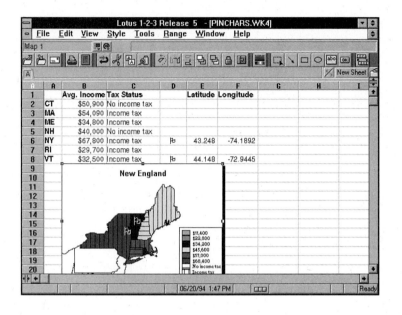

Fig. 14.28
Zoom in on part of the map to show particular regions.

Sometimes when you zoom the map to the size you want, the part of the map you want to see is not centered in the frame. For example, Ohio might appear in the middle of the New England map in figure 14.28 instead of Connecticut. To center the map on the part you want, move the mouse pointer to the spot that you want to be the new center point, then select the Recenter command from the quick menu.

To return the map to its original size, open the **V**iew menu and choose the **R**eset command.

Adding an Overlay

Sometimes, you may want to show adjacent maps for which you are not actually illustrating data. You can achieve this effect by *adding an overlay*— placing another map over the map graphic.

To add a map overlay, open the **M**ap menu in the Lotus Map Viewer and choose the **A**dd Overlay command. The **A**dd Overlay dialog box appears, which displays the available map files in the MAPDATA subdirectory of the program directory for 1-2-3 for Windows Release 5. Select one of the map overlays (which have TV extensions), such as CANADA.TV, USA.TV, or WORLD.TV. Then choose OK. The Lotus Map Viewer adds the overlay to the map. The overlay appears as an outline without color because there is no data to color it.

> **Note**
>
> To remove an overlay, open the **M**ap menu and choose the **R**emove Overlay command. Then, in the Remove Overlay dialog box, select the overlay you want to remove and select OK.

Adding Pin Characters to a Map

Suppose that you want to show the location of capital cities in the U.S. or flag the countries in which you have recently opened sales offices. On a paper map on a wall, you would use push pins to show the specific sites. In a 1-2-3 for Windows map, you can use pin characters—characters that you add to a map by telling 1-2-3 for Windows what character to use, the latitude and longitude of the site, and (optionally) the color you want the pin character to be.

Setting Up the Coordinates Data

Before you can add the pin characters, you need to set up the data ranges. You need to set up consecutive columns to contain the data; the first three columns are required; the fourth is optional:

■ The first column contains the character or label you want to display in the map. You create the characters by formatting letters with symbol fonts such as Wingdings, ZapfChancery, or Symbol. You can use a different character for each site or use the same character for each site you flag in the map.

■ The second column contains the latitude of the pin character site.

■ The third column contains the longitude of the pin character site.

■ 1-2-3 for Windows automatically selects a color that contrasts with the background color of the region in which the pin character is placed. If you want to select a different specific color, enter a number from 0 to 255 in the fourth column. 1-2-3 for Windows associates numbers with the colors in the color palette; for example, the numbers 0 through 15 represent the colors in the top row of the color palette from left to right.

Fortunately, you do not need to know the latitude and longitude of each site. You can use 1-2-3 for Windows commands to generate the correct coordinates automatically. To copy coordinates of a site into worksheet cells, perform the following steps:

1. Display the map in the Lotus Map Viewer.

2. With the mouse, point to the site where you want to put a pin character.

3. Press the right mouse button to display the quick menu, then choose the Copy Coordinates command. The Lotus Map Viewer copies the latitude and longitude of the site to the Windows Clipboard and displays the coordinates in the right-hand side of the status bar.

4. Return to the 1-2-3 for Windows worksheet. Click the cell in which you want to place the latitude and paste the coordinates in the worksheet by either opening the **E**dit menu and selecting the **P**aste command or selecting the Paste command from quick menu. 1-2-3 for Windows will paste the latitude in the selected cell and the longitude in the next cell to the right.

Where in the worksheet you set up the pin character data ranges depends on where and how many pin characters you want. If there will only be one pin character per geographic region, such as state capitals, it is probably easiest to place the pin character data in the columns immediately to the right of the map data so that each pin character site is in the same row as the region in which it falls. You do not need to include a pin character in every region.

Suppose that you want to mark the site of each international sales office and you have more than one office in some countries. In a situation like this, it would be easier to place the pin character data in a separate part of the worksheet; the pin character data does not need to line up in rows with the map regions. The character and coordinates for each pin character need only be in consecutive rows and columns.

Adding the Coordinates to the Map Definition

Note

If you know the pin character coordinates before you create a map, you can include the pin character, latitude, longitude, and optional pin character color columns as the fourth through seventh columns in the map data ranges when you create the map. (See "Creating a Map" earlier in this chapter.)

After you set up the pin characters data ranges, you need to add them to the definition of the map ranges. Perform the following steps:

1. Select the map.

2. Open the **T**ools menu and choose the Ma**p** command; then select the Ranges & **T**itles command from the Ma**p** cascade menu. The Ranges and Title dialog box appears.

3. From the Assign Range For list box, choose Coordinates.

4. Either type the range that includes the pin character, latitude, longitude, and optional pin character columns in the Range text box or select the range with the range selector.

5. Choose OK to redraw the map with the pin characters in it.

Changing and Deleting Pin Characters

To change the pin character displayed at a sight to a different character or label, enter a new character or label in the worksheet cell containing the pin character you want to change; when 1-2-3 for Windows redraws the map, it will display the new character or label.

To delete a pin character, delete the pin character, latitude, and longitude from the worksheet cell; when 1-2-3 for Windows redraws the map, it will no longer appear.

Enhancing the Map with Other Text and Graphics

◄ "Formatting a Frame," p. 434

► "Working with Graphics," p. 508

Just as you can enhance worksheets and charts by adding text blocks and graphics (such as lines and arrows), you can add these elements to enhance a map and make its meaning clearer. For example, you may want to add a title to the legend or change the map frame. The map shown in figure 14.29 is a map of the world in which the legend has been moved to the other side.

To add graphic elements to the map, you can use the following 1-2-3 for Windows features:

■ To add a text block, open the **T**ools menu and choose the **D**raw command.

■ To add an arrow, open the **T**ools menu and choose the **D**raw command. (This command also enables you to add rectangles, ellipses, circles, and other elements.)

■ To change the background color of the map graphic and/or the frame style and color, open the **S**tyle menu and choose the Lines & Color command.

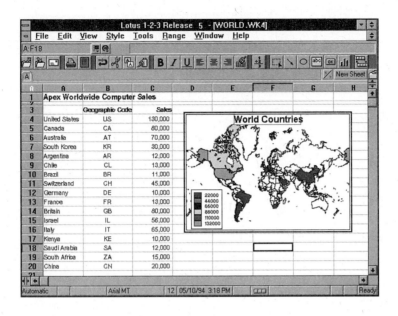

Fig. 14.29
Map of the world.

Previewing a Map

Before you print a map, you can preview it. Previewing can save you time and paper, enabling you to make all necessary adjustments and changes before you print. To preview a chart, select the chart, and then open the **F**ile menu and choose the Print Pre**v**iew command. You also can click the **P**review button in the Print dialog box.

◄ "Previewing Reports before Printing," p. 363

◄ "Previewing and Printing Charts," p. 437

► "Working with Graphics" p. 508

Printing a Map

You can preview and print maps the way you print worksheets and charts: by opening the **F**ile menu and choosing the **P**rint command.

Before printing a map, select it; then open the **F**ile menu and choose the **P**rint command. When a map is selected, the Print dialog box displays the map name (such as Map 1) in the Selected **D**rawn Object field (see fig. 14.30). When you choose OK, the map prints at the size it appears in the worksheet.

You have the same options for printing maps as for printing charts. You can do any of the following things:

■ Print it full-page. Select the chart; then open the **F**ile menu and choose the Pa**g**e Setup command. The Si**z**e option in the Page Setup dialog box has three settings for maps and charts: Actual Size, Fill Page, and Fill Page But Keep Proportions.

Fig. 14.30
The Print dialog
box.

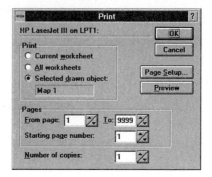

Tip
To add white
space between a
worksheet data
and chart, include
blank rows as part
of the range(s) to
be printed.

■ Print the map and its worksheet data together on one page. If the map
and data are placed exactly where you want them to appear in the report, you can define a single print range: select the range of cells that
includes the data and the map. If the data is in one part of the worksheet and the map is in another, you must define two print ranges. To
define multiple ranges, type the ranges, separated by commas or semicolons. To point to the ranges, you must preselect them; remember to
hold down the Ctrl key as you select the second and subsequent ranges.

■ If you used the **T**ools menu's **D**raw command to add any text or objects
to your map, those elements will not print if you simply click the map
in the worksheet to select it. To print the map and added objects, you
must click the Select Objects SmartIcon to "lasso" the map. Then, when
you display the Print dialog box, Collection appears in the Selected
Drawn Object field.

Troubleshooting

I want to create a map of the world, but I don't know the mapcode for each country.

You can look up the codes in the Help system by searching for the name of the map,
such as Countries of the World or USA by State. You also can look in the Lotus 1-2-3
for Windows Release 5 *User's Guide.*

How can I add commas and currency symbols to the color legend labels?

Select the map; open the **T**ools menu and choose the Ma**p** command; then select
the **C**olors & Legend command from the Ma**p** cascade menu. In the Colors &
Legend dialog box, you can edit the numbers that appear under Legend labels.

When I created my map, it did not include patterns. Now I want to add them.

Create a range in the worksheet that contains the pattern values or labels. Make sure that there is one pattern value or label for each map region code. Select the map; then open the **T**ools menu and choose the Ma**p** Ranges & **T**itle command to open the Ranges & Title dialog box. Select Patterns in the Assign range for list, and use the range selector to highlight the range you set up. When you choose OK, 1-2-3 for Windows will add patterns to the map.

◀ "Printing the Report," p. 367

From Here...

In this chapter, you learned how to work with more complex chart types, add graphics to charts, and use maps to illustrate certain types of data. To learn how to create graphics in 1-2-3 for Windows and how to incorporate charts into business presentations, refer to the following chapters:

- Chapter 16, "Adding Graphics to Sheets," explains how to add text boxes, lines, arrows, ellipses, and other graphic elements to a chart.

- Chapter 17, "Developing Business Presentations," shows you how to include graphs in slide shows and computer presentations.

Working with Charts

Part III

Optimizing 1-2-3

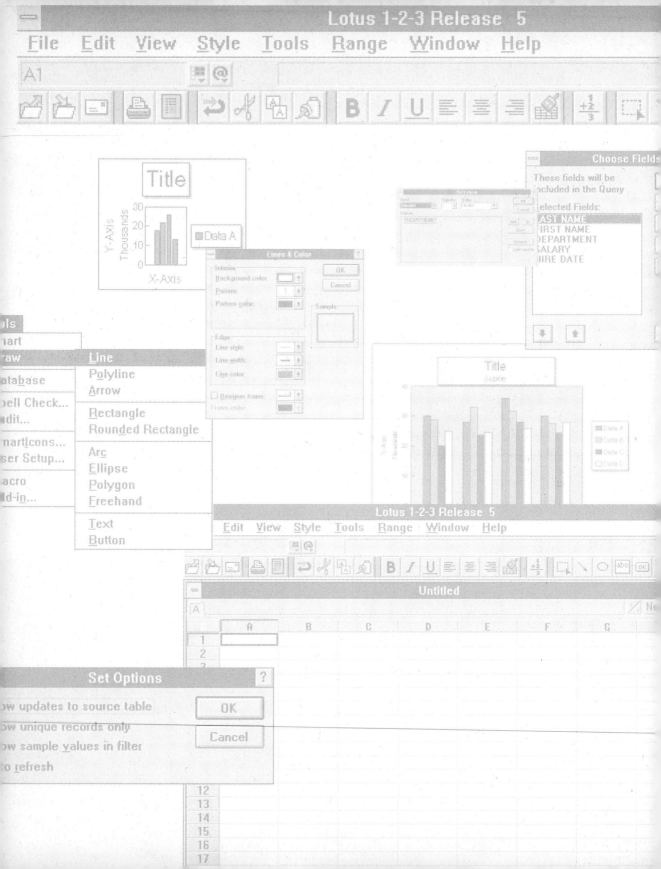

Chapter 15

Managing the Worksheet Display

Each 1-2-3 for Windows worksheet file appears in a Worksheet window within the 1-2-3 window. You can change the way you view an individual file by choosing different view preferences—such as the way the worksheet frame is displayed, whether a grid is used to separate cells, and whether scroll bars are included along the right and bottom edges of the Worksheet window. Additionally, you can freeze titles on-screen, split a worksheet window, display the worksheet in perspective view, or reduce or enlarge the displayed worksheet.

You also can change the way 1-2-3 for Windows displays multiple Worksheet windows for those occasions when, for example, you need to compare data in two or more worksheet files or open utility windows within a worksheet or chart. You can view parts of up to three worksheets in a single file at the same time.

In this chapter, you learn how to:

- ■ Choose worksheet display preferences
- ■ Freeze worksheet titles
- ■ Split and scroll worksheet windows
- ■ Display perspective view
- ■ Magnify and restore worksheet display
- ■ Hide worksheet columns, rows, and ranges

Changing the Display of a Worksheet File

Tip
Use **V**iew Set
View **P**references
to hide or display
screen elements.

The 1-2-3 worksheet provides you with a number of options you can change to customize the way your worksheet appears. You may want to change the frame surrounding the worksheet, remove gridlines or change their color, or hide the scroll bars. You control all of these options—as well as a few others—by using the **V**iew Set View **P**references command to display the Set View Preferences dialog box shown in figure 15.1.

Fig. 15.1
Use Set View
Preferences to
change the way
worksheet items
appear on-screen.

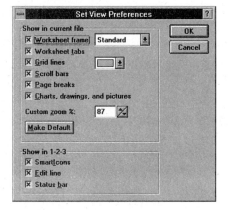

Choosing a Different Worksheet Frame

Depending on the type of worksheet you're creating, you may want to change the frame that surrounds the worksheet area. 1-2-3 allows you to choose from the Standard frame, which displays the default letter column labels and numeric row labels, Characters, Inches, Metric, or Points/Picas. If you are creating a worksheet that needs to fit within a specific area, being able to change the frame—for example, to inches—means that you can accurately control the size and width of the worksheet while you are creating it. To choose a different frame, click on the down-arrow beside the **W**orksheet frame box, then select your choice from the displayed list. Figure 15.2 shows the worksheet after *Inches* has been selected from the Worksheet frame setting.

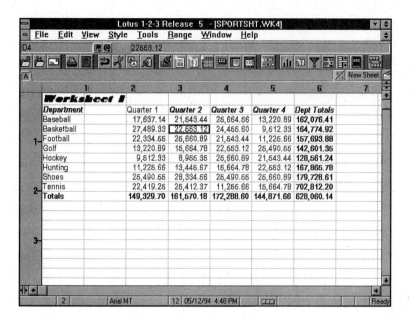

Fig. 15.2
The Worksheet
displayed with an
Inches frame.

Removing and Recoloring Gridlines

In some cases, such as when you are creating a data-entry form or a report,
you may want to remove the gridlines that divide your worksheet into individual cells. 1-2-3 displays the gridlines by default, but you can remove them
by selecting the **V**iew Set View **P**references and clicking **G**rid lines to remove
the X in the checkbox. This method displays your worksheet without
gridlines (see fig. 15.3). Select OK to close the dialog box. To redisplay the
gridlines, display the Set View Preferences dialog box again and click the **G**rid
lines checkbox. Select OK to close the dialog box**.**

You also can change the color of the gridlines on the worksheet. To do so,
click on the down-arrow beside the Grid lines color box. A palette appears,
displaying a wide range of color choices. Click on the color you want; then
click on OK to close the Set View Preferences dialog box and return to the
worksheet.

Tip
Add a customized
frame to selected
cells by choosing
Style **L**ines &
Color, and select-
ing **D**esigner
frame.

III

Optimizing 1-2-3

Fig. 15.3
You can remove gridlines to help display data more clearly.

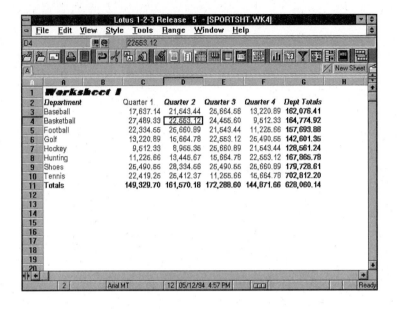

Hiding and Redisplaying Scroll Bars

The scroll bars along the right and bottom edges of the Worksheet window appear by default when you create a worksheet file. You can hide the scroll bars, if you like, in case you're working with a small spreadsheet that doesn't require scrolling. You want to display more of a large worksheet on-screen, or you want to keep other users from accessing information in a later portion of the file.

To hide the scroll bars in your Worksheet window, follow these steps:

1. Open the **V**iew menu.

2. Choose the Set View **P**references command.

3. Click on the **S**croll bars checkbox to deselect it.

4. Choose OK.

When the worksheet redisplays, the scroll bars are hidden. This change affects the current file as well as any other files in a grouped set.

To return the scroll bars, choose **V**iew Set View **P**references again and select the **S**croll bars checkbox; then click on OK.

At the bottom of the Set View **P**references dialog box, you see the Show in 1-2-3 settings, offering three choices: SmartIcons, Edit line, and Status bar. All three of these options are checked, which means that all of the items are displayed by default in every 1-2-3 worksheet. You can suppress the display of any or all of those items by clicking in the desired box to remove the X. After you click on OK, any items you deselected are hidden from the 1-2-3 view.

If you want to suppress the display of screen elements temporarily, use the Hide Worksheet Elements SmartIcon. (This SmartIcon is available in the Goodies palette.) When you click on this SmartIcon once, the scroll bars, edit line, row and column labels, and status bar all disapear. When you click on the SmartIcon a second time, the elements are redisplayed.

You can save the settings you enter in the Set View **P**references dialog box as the default settings for every 1-2-3 worksheet you create. To do this, click on the Make the default button, just beneath the Custom zoom option. 1-2-3 then records the settings you've entered and applies them to subsequent worksheets you create.

Freezing Worksheet Titles

Most worksheets are much larger than can be displayed on-screen at one time. As you move the cell pointer, you scroll the display. New data appears at one edge of the display as the data at the other edge scrolls out of sight. Data can be hard to understand when titles at the top of the worksheet and descriptions at the left scroll off-screen. Without the titles to refer to, you may have trouble remembering what the data means.

To prevent titles from scrolling off-screen, move the cell pointer to the row and/or column that marks the top-left cell of the "working area" of the worksheet. In other words, everything above and/or to the left of the cell pointer will be frozen. Next, use the **V**iew **F**reeze **T**itles command to lock titles on-screen. When you select this command, the Freeze Titles dialog box appears (see fig. 15.4).

Tip

Freeze titles to keep them on-screen when you scroll the worksheet file.

III

Optimizing 1-2-3

Fig. 15.4
With two simple clicks, you can freeze titles on-screen.

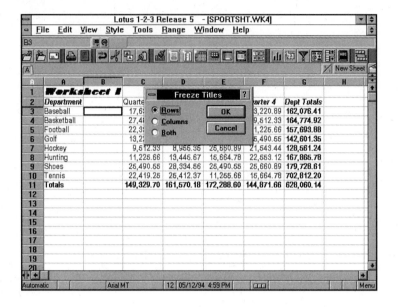

Caution

If you don't position the pointer correctly, your titles may not freeze. Place the pointer below the row you want to freeze or to the right of the column you want to freeze.

◄ "Reorganizing Worksheets," p. 273

You can freeze the top rows of the worksheet with the **R**ows option, the leftmost columns with **C**olumns, or both rows and columns with **B**oth. To unfreeze the titles, select **V**iew **C**lear **T**itles. To change the locked area, choose **V**iew Cle**a**r Titles and then specify the new titles area.

If you use Group mode, freezing titles affects all worksheets in the group. When you clear the titles, the titles of all worksheets are released.

To freeze titles in both the top rows and the leftmost columns, follow these steps:

1. Position the worksheet so that the titles you want to lock are at the top and to the left of the display.

2. Move the cell pointer to the cell in the first row below the titles and the first column to the right of the titles.

3. Choose **V**iew Freeze **T**itles **B**oth to lock both horizontal and vertical titles.

These steps freeze the titles along the top of the worksheet and the titles in column A. When you move the pointer downward through the file, as shown in figure 15.5, the top titles remain in place. If you move the pointer off-screen to the right, the titles in column A remain frozen in place.

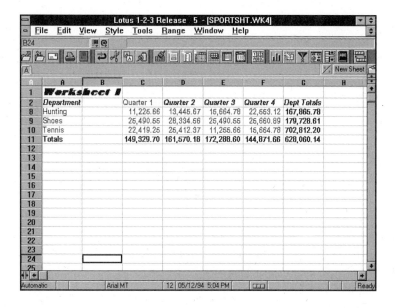

Fig. 15.5
Those titles aren't going anywhere.

If you press Home when titles are locked, the cell pointer moves to the position below and to the right of the titles rather than to cell A1. When you move the mouse pointer into the titles area, you cannot select any cells. Moreover, you cannot use the direction keys to move into the titles area, although you can use F5 (GoTo).

Tip
In a split window, locking titles affects only the current pane.

When you use GoTo to move to a cell in the titles area, the title rows and columns appear twice. Clear the duplicate display by using the direction keys (for example, pressing Tab and PgDn to put the cell pointer well beyond the titles area) and then pressing Home to return to the home position next to the locked titles.

III

Optimizing 1-2-3

Troubleshooting

I don't want to change the color of all the gridlines; I just want to change the outline color of a single cell.

The command you want is in the menu—choose **S**tyle **L**ines & Color. When the Lines & Color dialog box appears, click **O**utline in the Borders area and choose the color you want in the Li**n**e color box.

My frozen titles appear duplicated on the worksheet.

Press PgDn or Tab to move the cell pointer outside the titles area. The display should correct itself.

When I froze the titles in my worksheet, scrolled the display, and then pressed Home to move back to the upper left corner of the worksheet, I found rows 2 and 3 repeated several times.

This, again, is one of those freezing problems. Press PgDn or Tab to use the arrow keys to move the pointer back up in the worksheet until the worksheet display is returned to normal.

Splitting the Worksheet Window

When you need to compare two different portions of the same worksheet—or even simple sections of different worksheets—you can split the worksheet display and move through the sections independently or together.

In a split window, you can change data in one pane and see how the change affects data in the other pane. This capability is quite useful for what-if analysis. A split window also is useful when you write macros. You can write the macro in one pane and see the data that the macro is working on in the other pane.

Suppose that you want to see how a change in data affects totals, located in an area of the worksheet off-screen. You can split the window to see the data and the totals at the same time. If the worksheet is designed so that totals are in a column to the right, split the window vertically (see fig. 15.6). If the worksheet displays totals in a row at the bottom, split the window horizontally.

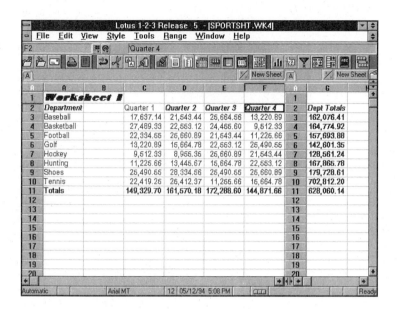

Fig. 15.6
Split windows.

Understanding Split Options

1-2-3 gives you three different ways to split a window. You can divide the window horizontally so that one window appears in the top half of the Worksheet window and the other window appears in the bottom half. If you split a window vertically, you have one window on the left side of the display and another on the right. If you choose perspective view, 1-2-3 displays the same cell ranges for each of three worksheets. (See "Displaying Worksheets in Perspective View," later in this chapter).

Tip
Be sure to position the pointer at the point you want to split the window before you choose View Split.

Splitting the Window with View Split

The first step in splitting your worksheet display involves positioning the pointer. Click on a cell in the row or column where you want the window to be split. If you want to split the window horizontally, click on the row at which you want the window to be divided. If you are splitting the window vertically, click on the column that will act as the dividing line.

Next, use the **V**iew **S**plit command. The Split dialog box appears (see fig. 15.7). Choose whether you want to split the window horizontally or vertically. Then click on OK. The window is divided at the pointer location.

III

Optimizing 1-2-3

Fig. 15.7
Splitting windows
with the Split
dialog box.

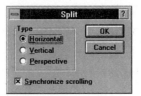

Using Splitters To Divide the Window

Right there on the worksheet, 1-2-3 provides tools you can use to split the window at any time without using **V**iew **S**plit, if you choose. In the upper right corner and the lower left corners of the Worksheet window, you see small buttons called *splitters*. To use a splitter to divide the window, position the pointer and then drag the splitter—use the lower left splitter to split the window vertically and the upper right splitter to split the window horizontally. Figure 15.8 shows a splitter used to divide the window horizontally.

Fig. 15.8
Using the splitter
to divide the
window.

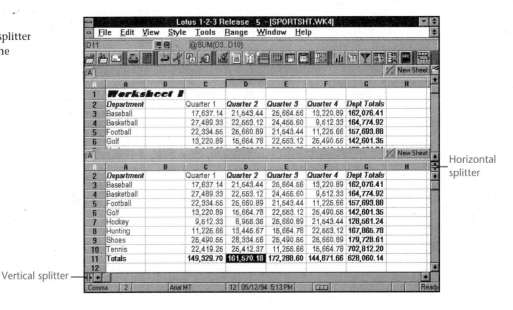

Scrolling Split Windows

Note

When scrolling is synchronized, both panes move together as you scroll the worksheet.

At times, you may want to see two unrelated views of the same worksheet. For example, you may want to see data in one pane and macros in the other pane. In this case, you want the two panes to scroll separately. Use the **V**iew **S**plit command and deselect **S**ynchronize scrolling in the Split dialog box to make scrolling unsynchronized; select the **S**ynchronize scrolling option if you want to restore synchronized scrolling.

To move between panes, press the F6 (Pane) key or click in the other window with the mouse.

Clearing Split Windows

To clear a split window and return to a single pane, use **V**iew Clear **S**plit. No matter which pane the cell pointer is in when you choose this command, the cell pointer moves to the left pane (in a vertically split window) or to the upper pane (in a horizontally split window) when you clear a split window.

Tip
Because a split window displays two frames, you cannot display quite as much data at one time as you can with a full window. To remove the frames, choose **V**iew Set View **P**references and deselect the **W**orksheet Frame option in the Set View Preferences dialog box.

Troubleshooting

I displayed the Split dialog box and clicked on Vertical, but my screen didn't split.

The pointer determines the boundary at which the screen is divided. Try positioning the pointer in the center of your worksheet and try splitting the worksheet again.

I divided the worksheet, but the column I wanted ended up on the wrong side of the split.

Position the mouse on the vertical splitter; then drag it to the desired location.

I split the worksheet into two windows, but I need to compare data with yet another worksheet.

Use perspective view to see three similar ranges of different worksheets.

Displaying Worksheets in Perspective View

1-2-3 lets you display your multiple-worksheet files in three separate windows in *perspective view*. When you've got more than one worksheet in a file, you may want to compare similar ranges in multiple files. Perspective view displays up to three worksheets in a layered fashion (see fig. 15.9).

Fig. 15.9
Worksheets in
perspective view.

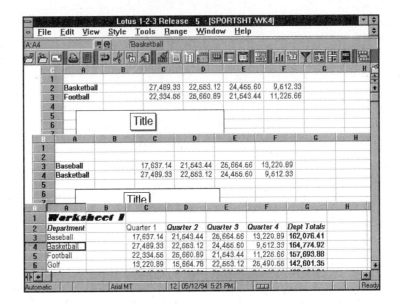

 To show a file in perspective view, choose **View Split** and select the **Perspective** option in the Split dialog box, or click on the Perspective View SmartIcon.

> **Note**
>
> You can have a split window or a perspective view, but not both at the same time.

  To move among the worksheets in a perspective view, press Ctrl+PgUp or Ctrl+PgDn, or click on the Next Worksheet and Previous Worksheet SmartIcons. If you have more than three sheets in the file, they will cycle through the perspective view—so you can see any three consecutive sheets at one time.

Zooming the Display

One of the limitations of a monitor's size is that often you cannot see very much of the worksheet on-screen. The preceding sections explained how to split a window to view data from widely separate parts of the worksheet and how to lock specific data on-screen to provide references as you scroll through a large worksheet. Sometimes, however, you want to see the layout of the worksheet, not the actual data.

By using the **V**iew Set View **P**references command and changing the Custom **Z**oom % setting in the Set View Preferences dialog box, you can specify a percentage (anywhere from 400 to 25) by which to enlarge or shrink the worksheet display. Select 400 to make the worksheet four times larger; select 25 to make the display shrink to one-fourth its normal size. If you reduce the display, the resulting image is barely readable, but it gives you a view of many cells. In figure 15.10, where 25-percent reduction was used, the screen shows about 80 rows and about 300 characters across a row. The readability of these settings varies from monitor to monitor.

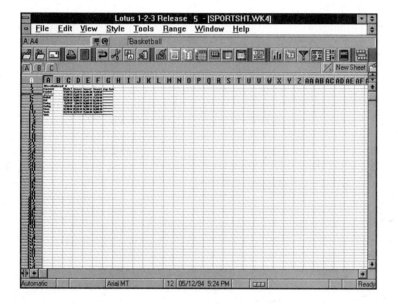

Fig. 15.10
The worksheet reduced to 25 percent its normal size.

You can also use the three commands (**Z**oom In, Zoom **O**ut, and **C**ustom) in the **V**iew menu or the Zoom In and Zoom Out SmartIcons to switch among different zoom percentages. Each time you choose **Z**oom In or Zoom **O**ut, the display increases or decreases, respectively, by a factor of 10 percent to a maximum of 400 percent or a minimum of 25 percent of the default size specified in the Set View Preferences dialog box.

To return the display to the default size, click on the Default Size SmartIcon or enter **87** as the default zoom percentage in the Set View Preferences dialog box.

III

Optimizing 1-2-3

> **Note**
>
> There is no relationship between the size of the worksheet as displayed on the screen and the size you get when printing. To enlarge or reduce the printed worksheet, use the **F**ile Pa**g**e Setup command with the Size options. Refer to Chapter 10, "Printing Worksheets" for more information.

Hiding Worksheet Data

Some worksheets you create may include sensitive information, data not meant for inquiring minds. On other worksheets—particularly those to be used by other people—you may want to protect certain formulas, labels, or data values so they cannot be changed. This section shows you how to suppress or hide the display of various items in your worksheet.

Hiding Cells and Ranges

◄ "Working with Number Formats," p. 326

Sometimes you want to do more than just stop someone from changing data or formulas; you want to prevent other users from even seeing the information. To hide a cell or range, use **S**tyle **N**umber Format and select Hidden from the **F**ormat list. A hidden cell appears as a blank cell in the worksheet (see fig. 15.11). To redisplay the cell contents in the worksheet, choose any other number format as usual or display the Number Format dialog box and click on the Reset button.

Fig. 15.11

A hidden cell appears blank.

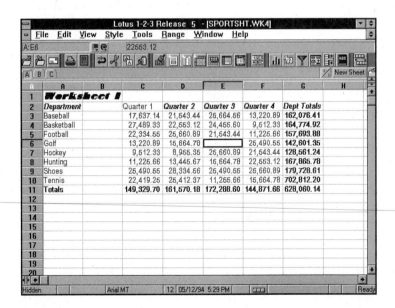

Caution

You can hide data so that it's not easily visible, but you cannot prevent someone from seeing hidden data if that person knows how to use 1-2-3 for Windows. The only way to keep data truly confidential is to save the file with a password (see Chapter 8, "Managing Files").

You cannot use the Hidden format to hide data completely. If you move the cell pointer to that cell, you can see the contents of the cell in the contents box. And remember that all you have to do to redisplay the contents of the cell is to change the number format for that cell. If the file is sealed, however, you cannot change the format or view the contents of the cell in the edit line.

◀ "Protecting Files," p. 297

Note

When you print a range containing hidden cells, columns, or worksheets, the hidden text does not appear in the printout.

Caution

Hidden cells appear empty; protect the cells and seal the file to prevent users from accidentally typing over the contents of hidden cells or reformatting the cells.

Hiding Worksheets, Columns, and Rows

When you hide worksheets, columns, and rows, they retain their letters and numbers, but 1-2-3 for Windows skips them in the display. For example, if you hide columns B and C, 1-2-3 for Windows displays in the column border columns A, D, E, and so on.

Hiding Worksheets

To hide a worksheet, move the cell pointer to the worksheet you want to hide, use **S**tyle **H**ide, and select the **S**heet option from the Hide dialog box. Select OK to close the dialog box. 1-2-3 for Windows removes the worksheet from the screen, and the cell pointer moves to the next worksheet.

To display a hidden worksheet, use **S**tyle **H**ide, type the hidden worksheet's letter in the **R**ange text box, along with a cell address (for example, A:A1), and click on the Sho**w** button.

Tip

Make hidden data less obvious by eliminating the frame. To do so, select **V**iew, Set View **P**references, and click on the **W**orksheet frame checkbox to deselect it. Then click on OK.

III

Optimizing 1-2-3

Although a hidden worksheet does not appear on-screen, formulas that refer to the worksheet remain valid and intact. For example, if you hide worksheet A, and worksheet B includes a reference to worksheet A in a formula, the formula is not affected. The worksheet is actually still part of the file—it's just invisible.

Hiding Columns

To hide a column, move the cell pointer to a cell in the column you want to hide. Then use **S**tyle **H**ide and select Column. If you don't preselect one or more columns, you can type a column address in the **Ra**nge text box of the Hide dialog box. To redisplay hidden columns, choose **S**tyle **H**ide, specify a range that includes cells in the hidden columns, and click on Sho**w**.

A hidden column does not appear in the worksheet, but the column letter is retained. Formulas that refer to cells in hidden columns are calculated correctly, and 1-2-3 for Windows continues to store the full value of hidden data.

Figure 15.12 shows a worksheet after columns are hidden. Notice that in the worksheet frame, column letters C and D are missing. The columns are still there, but they do not appear and you cannot move the cell pointer to them. When you print a range that contains hidden columns, the hidden columns do not print.

Fig. 15.12
Hiding worksheet columns.

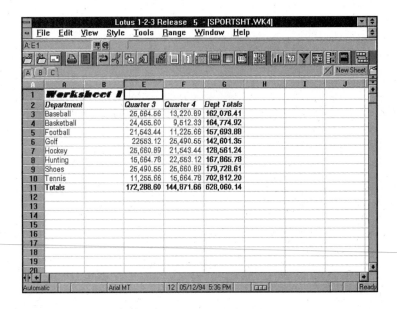

Hiding Rows

No specific command to hide a row is available, but you can use the **S**tyle **R**ow Height command to set a row's height to 1, making it nearly invisible. You also can use a mouse to point to the border between the current row's number and the next row's number in the worksheet frame and then click and drag the mouse up or down to shrink or expand the height of the row.

Use the **S**tyle **R**ow Height command or the mouse to make the row visible again by making its height greater than 1. When you print a range that contains hidden rows, the hidden rows do not print. If data appears in the reduced row, however, your printout may display dots and dashes where the row was located.

Tip

Hide rows by using the **S**tyle **R**ow Height command.

Troubleshooting

I have three files open, but only one file appears in perspective view.

Perspective view doesn't display three different worksheet files. Rather, perspective view shows three different worksheets that are included in the same file. In other words, only grouped worksheets can be layered three at once in perspective view.

*I chose a different custom zoom and now that number is displayed in the **V**iew menu.*

Whenever you change the Custom **z**oom % in the Set View Preferences dialog box, the new setting is displayed in the **C**ustom option of the **V**iew menu. To change back to the default setting, click the Default size SmartIcon or enter **87** as the value for the Custom **z**oom.

I hid sensitive data, but the frame is still there.

Use the **V**iew Set View **P**references command and deselect the **W**orksheet Frame option to remove the frame around hidden data.

III

Optimizing 1-2-3

From Here...

For information directly related to the way your worksheets are displayed, you may want to review the following chapters of this book:

- Chapter 7, "Reorganizing Worksheets." Find out how to manage your worksheet files—and not just their display—in this chapter on adding, renaming, deleting, and grouping worksheets.

- Chapter 9, "Formatting Worksheets." Need a refresher on how to control the display of your data? This chapter explains all the basic procedures—and then some—for controlling and customizing how your worksheet looks.

- Chapter 17, "Developing Business Presentations." Learn another way of displaying the information on-screen: create a business presentation. This chapter shows you how to create and print slides, add charts, and work with color effectively.

- Chapter 19, "Linking and Consolidating Worksheets." Learn how to put important worksheets together and create links that help you move easily from one displayed worksheet to another.

Chapter 16

Adding Graphics to Worksheets

Included with 1-2-3 for Windows is a set of basic drawing tools that you can use to enhance your worksheets and charts. There are tools for drawing shapes (such as ellipses, rectangles, and polygons), lines, arrows, and arcs. There is also a tool that enables you to type text anywhere on the chart.

You can use the drawing tools to add lines and arrows that point out specific items in your chart, add a rectangle to a selected cell range in a worksheet to call attention to important data, draw a simple logo, or add note text to charts. Figure 16.1 shows a rectangle and arrow used to point out the data to which a chart refers.

In this chapter, you learn how to:

- Add and modify graphics text
- Draw lines and arrows
- Add shapes
- Draw freehand graphics
- Arrange objects

Displaying the Drawing Tools

To display the drawing tools, open the **T**ools menu and choose **D**raw. A cascade menu appears that contains the drawing tools (see fig. 16.2).

Fig. 16.1
Two drawn objects—a rectangle and an arrow—used in a spreadsheet.

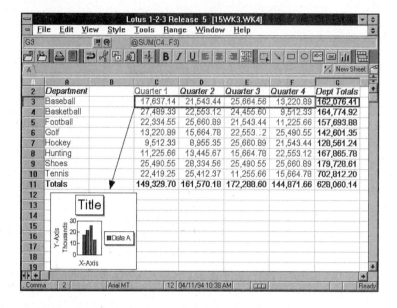

Fig. 16.2
Displaying the drawing tools.

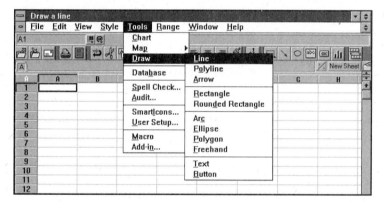

Tip
Create a SmartIcon set just for drawing tools if you use these tools often. For more information, see "Understanding SmartIcon Basics," in Chapter 1.

You can also use one of the many drawing SmartIcons to add graphics to your worksheets and charts. Table 16.1 shows you the different SmartIcons and provides a description of each.

Table 16.1   The Drawing SmartIcons

SmartIcon	Name	Description
	Line	Draws a line
	Line segment	Draws a segmented line

SmartIcon	Name	Description
	Draw arrow	Draws a forward-pointing arrow
	Double-headed arrow	Draws a double-headed arrow
	Rectangle	Draws a rectangle or square
	Rounded Rectangle	Draws a rounded rectangle
	Arc	Draws an arc
	Ellipse	Draws an ellipsis or circle
	Polygon	Draws a polygon
	Freehand	Lets you draw freehand shapes
	Text block	Allows you to add graphics text

Working with Graphics Text

Graphics text may be one of the first additions you make to your worksheets. You might want to add a note, for example, to clarify a chart you've added on the worksheet.

When you choose **T**ools **D**raw **T**ext or click the Text Block SmartIcon, you are ready to click and drag a text block. A *text block* is the container for your descriptive text.

To add graphics text, take the following steps:

1. Choose Text **D**raw **T**ext or click on the TextBlock SmartIcon.

2. Place the mouse pointer on the chart or worksheet in which you want the text to go.

3. Click on a corner of where you want the text block to be and drag to create a text block the approximate height and width that you want.

Tip
To enter mul-
tiple lines of
text, you can
either let the
text wrap or
press Enter after
each line.

Don't worry too much about the size and placement because it's easy enough to move and resize the text block later.

4. Release the mouse button. A flashing text cursor appears in the box.

5. After drawing the box, type the text.

Figure 16.3 shows a worksheet after graphics text has been added.

Fig. 16.3
Graphics text
added to the
worksheet.

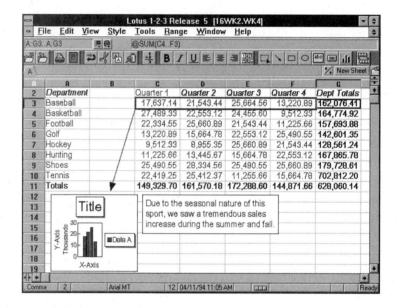

 By default, the text block is surrounded by a frame with a white background. To change the interior color or to format the frame, use the **S**tyle **L**ines & Color command, the Lines & Color SmartIcon, or press the right mouse button when the mouse pointer is positioned on the text block and choose Lines & Color from the quick menu (see fig. 16.4). The Lines & Color dialog box appears.

If you are adding a block of text to a chart, for example, you might want to change the interior color of the text block so that it has the same background color as the plot. To do this, select the block (you'll see selection handles around the frame), display the Lines & Color dialog box, and, in the palette for **B**ackground color, choose the same color as your plot background.

◀ "Enhancing the
Chart," p. 427
To eliminate the frame from a text block, click on the down arrow beside the Line St**y**le box and choose None.

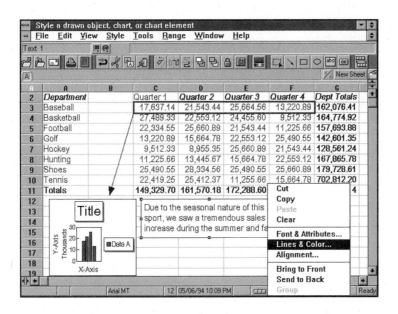

Fig. 16.4
Click the right
button on an
object to display
the quick menu.

Editing Graphics Text

To edit the text later, double-click the text block. A cursor then appears at the
beginning of the text. Use the mouse or arrow keys to position the cursor and
make your corrections.

To change the typeface, point size, and attributes of the text, select the text
block (make sure that selection handles are around the text block). Then
choose the **S**tyle **F**ont & Attributes command, the Font & Attributes
SmartIcon, or press the right mouse button and choose Font & Attributes
from the quick menu. The Font & Attributes dialog box appears. Note that
you cannot format individual characters inside the block; it's all or nothing.

◄ "Enhancing the
Appearance of
Data," p. 343

Formatting Graphics Text

The **S**tyle **A**lignment command enables you to align the text within its frame.
For instance, for a multiple-line text block, you might want to center the
lines inside the block. This command is for horizontal alignment only; you
cannot align text vertically in a text block. You can also left-align or justify
text. Another way to display the Alignment dialog box is to select the frame,
press the right mouse button, and choose Alignment from the quick menu.

Tip

You can
place
text diagonally
on the work-
sheet or chart
by using the
Angle Text
SmartIcon. Just
select the text
block by click-
ing on it and
then click on
the Angle Text
SmartIcon.

III

Optimizing 1-2-3

Troubleshooting

I was entering text when the characters I had typed disappeared.

If you don't make your text block long enough, your text may scroll out of view after you type another line. If this happens, you must lengthen the block by dragging the center handle at the bottom of the selected text block.

I want to change the style of my text, but the commands in the menu are dimmed.

Before you make any changes to text, you need to tell 1-2-3 what text you want to work with. Select the text block by clicking it before you open the menu.

Working with Graphics

If you've ever used a simple graphics program—like Windows Paintbrush— you may be familiar with the way graphics tools work. You click the tool and draw the shape on-screen. 1-2-3 for Windows includes a number of graphics tools you can use to add shapes and freehand drawings to your worksheets and charts.

Drawing Lines and Arrows

To emphasize specific areas in a chart or worksheet, you can add lines and arrows with **T**ools **D**raw **L**ine and **T**ools **D**raw **A**rrow; or select the Draw Line, Draw Arrow, or Draw Double-Headed Arrow SmartIcons.

Note

Only the Draw Arrow icon is displayed in the default chart palette.

To create the line or arrow, take these steps:

1. Click the Line or Arrow tool. 1-2-3 prompts you to click and drag to draw the line or arrow.

2. Place the cross at the location of the first data point you want to highlight, and then click and drag in the direction you want to draw the line or arrow.

3. When you reach the end of the line, release the mouse button.

> **Note**
>
> If you are creating an arrow, the final data point displays an arrowhead. If you are creating the double-headed arrow, arrowheads appear on both ends of the line.

1-2-3 for Windows displays a line or arrow on the chart or worksheet, with selection handles to indicate that the line or arrow is selected. While selected, the line or arrow can be moved or changed. Notice also that the Default SmartIcon palette is replaced with a new palette—this one is called the Default Arrange palette. The SmartIcons in the new palette provide you with tools you need in order to edit and arrange the lines and shapes you draw (see fig. 16.5).

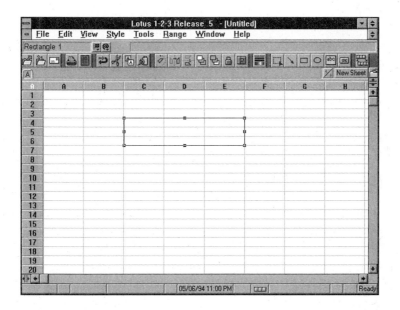

Fig. 16.5
The Default Arrange SmartIcon palette appears after you draw a line or shape.

Connecting Lines

To connect two or more line segments, use the **T**ools **D**raw **P**olyline command or the Draw Segmented Line SmartIcon. Click at the beginning of the first line, and then click at the end of the line. The next segment automatically begins at the end of the first line. Each time you click, one segment ends and the next begins (see fig. 16.6). When you are finished, double-click.

III

Optimizing 1-2-3

Fig. 16.6
Using the polyline
tool.

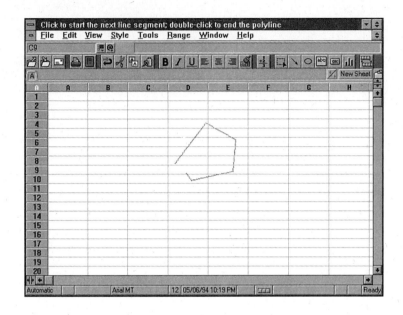

Tip

To draw a
horizontal,
vertical, or
diagonal line,
hold down
Shift as you
draw. The Shift
key restricts the
line to incre-
ments of 45
degrees.

Editing Lines

To change the style, width, and color of the line, you can use the **S**tyle **L**ines
& Color command, the Lines & Color SmartIcon, or press the right mouse
button and choose Lines & Color from the quick menu. The Lines & Color
dialog box appears.

◄ "Resizing
Objects,"
p. 400

You can use the **A**rrowhead option to move the arrowhead to the opposite
end of the line, to place arrowheads at both ends of the line, and to add or
remove the arrowhead. You can use the mouse to change the size and direction of a line or arrow.

Drawing Arcs

An arc is simply a curved line and, in fact, drawing an arc is just like creating
a line except you use a different tool. To create an arc, use the **T**ools **D**raw
Ar**c** command or the Draw Arc SmartIcon. Then click and drag in the direction you want the arc to curve. The shape of the arc is controlled by the way
you move the mouse. When the arc is the size and shape you want, release
the mouse button.

Tip

To draw a
perfect circle or
square, press
and hold Shift
while drawing
the shape.

Drawing Shapes

1-2-3 has four tools for drawing enclosed shapes: Ellipse, Rectangle, Rounded
Rectangle, and Polygon.

Ellipse

To draw an ellipse, choose **T**ools **D**raw **E**llipse (or choose the Draw Ellipse SmartIcon), and then click in the upper left corner of the area you want the ellipse to fill and drag the mouse down until the ellipse is the desired size and shape. Then release the mouse button. To create a perfect circle, hold down Shift as you drag.

You might use an ellipse or a circle to highlight information or add a special design element to your page.

Rectangle

The procedure for drawing a rectangle or rounded rectangle (a rectangle with rounded corners) is similar. First, choose **T**ools **D**raw **R**ectangle (or Roun**d**ed Rectangle) or click the Draw Rectangle or Draw Rounded Rectangle SmartIcon. Then you click in the upper left corner of the rectangle and drag the mouse down until the rectangle is the desired size and release the mouse button by holding down Shift as you drag, creating a square.

You might use a square or rectangle to highlight worksheet cells, call attention to a specific portion of a chart, draw a background shaded box for text or other graphics, or provide a customized legend or shaded area for selected cells.

Polygon

A polygon is a multisided object. The object can have as many connecting lines as you want.

To create a polygon, follow these steps:

1. Open the **T**ools menu, select **D**raw, and then choose **P**olygon; or click the Draw Polygon SmartIcon.

2. Place the mouse pointer where you want the first point of the polygon to be and click the mouse button.

3. Move the pointer to the opposite end of the first line and click again.

4. Continue clicking at each point of the polygon, and double-click when you are finished.

You don't need to concern yourself with connecting the last point with the first because 1-2-3 automatically connects these points for you when you double-click.

Tip
Holding down Shift as you create a polygon restricts the angle to increments of 45 degrees.

III

Optimizing 1-2-3

Changing Shape Color and Style

The object's interior is white; to change the color (for example, to the color of the plot background), use the **S**tyle **L**ines & Color command. You can also use the Lines & Color dialog box, shown in figure 16.7, to change the style, color, or width of the object's outline.

Fig. 16.7
Changing the color and style of shapes.

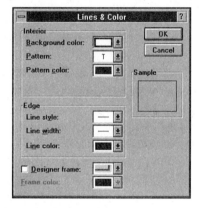

To change the shape color and style, first click the object and then choose **S**tyle **L**ines & Color. When the Lines & Color dialog box appears, use the Interior settings to change the color and pattern inside the shape and the Edge settings to change the look of the line surrounding the shape. Click OK after you make your changes.

Drawing Freehand

When you use the Freehand tool, it's as if someone gave you a pencil and let you draw on the screen. However, unless you have some artistic ability, freehand drawing looks more like freehand scribbling.

 To activate this tool, choose **T**ools **D**raw **F**reehand; or select the Freehand Drawing SmartIcon. The mouse pointer then turns into a pencil. Place the pencil where you want to begin and click and drag to draw. Release the mouse button when you are finished drawing.

Troubleshooting

I created a polygon but don't like the way it looks.

You can instantly remove any shape you just added by choosing **E**dit **U**ndo.

I drew a line with a single arrow, but I meant to draw a double-headed arrow.

Click the line, choose **S**tyle **L**ines & Color, and use the Arrowhead option to change the arrowhead style.

I added a rectangle but it blocks out half my chart.

Objects on your chart are displayed on different layers. The chart is behind the rectangle you added. Click the chart, and then click the Bring to Front SmartIcon.

Rearranging Graphic Objects

A finished worksheet may include many different items—numbers in cells, charts, shapes, graphics text, and so on. The more you add, the more crowded things get. To control how items are displayed—which item is placed on top of another item, which box goes behind a chart, and so on— you need to be able to work with the different layers on your worksheet. You also need to be able to move the graphics you create: 1-2-3 for Windows lets you flip graphics horizontally or vertically. Finally, you can put all the objects you create together into a group and lock them in place to prevent accidental changes. You'll find all these options in the **E**dit **A**rrange cascade menu. Table 16.2 explains the different rearranging options.

Table 16.2 Rearranging Graphics	
Option	**Description**
Bring to Front	Moves selected object in front of other objects
Send to Back	Moves selected object in back of other objects
Flip Left-Right	Flips the selected object horizontally
Flip Top-Bottom	Flips the selected object vertically
Rotate	Rotates the selected object
Group	Joins a number of selected objects into a single group
Lock	Locks the grouped objects in place to avoid changes
Fasten to Cells	Attaches the selected object to specific cells on the worksheet

III

Optimizing 1-2-3

Understanding Layering

All objects you create are stacked on top of one another, in the order you create them. If your chart is on the bottom layer, for example, any objects you draw or text blocks you create are layered on top of the chart. If you draw an object on top of a text block, the text in the text block is hidden unless you change the stacking order.

Changing the Stacking Order

  You can change the stacking order of objects in your command by using the Bring to Front SmartIcon and the Send to Back SmartIcon or by using the **E**dit **A**rrange command.

To change the order in which objects are displayed, follow these steps:

1. Click the object.

2. Open the **E**dit menu and choose **A**rrange. A cascade menu appears (see fig. 16.8).

3. Click **B**ring to Front or **S**end to Back, depending on the direction in the stacking order you want to move the object.

Fig. 16.8
Changing the stacking order.

Tip
Change the stacking order quickly by positioning the mouse pointer on the selected object, pressing the right mouse button, and choosing **B**ring to Front or **S**end to Back from the quick menu.

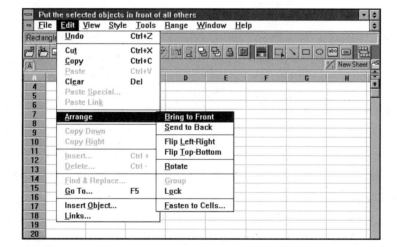

These commands send an object all the way to the back or bring it all the way to the front; there is no way to move an object forward or backward one layer.

Flipping Graphics Objects

If you want to flip an object you've created, click the object to select it; then choose **E**dit **A**rrange. When the cascade menu appears, choose Flip **L**eft-Right if you want to flip the graphic horizontally and choose Flip **T**op-Bottom to flip the object vertically. If you prefer, you can use the Flip Horizontal SmartIcon or Flip Vertical SmartIcon to make the change.

Grouping and Locking Graphics Objects

Grouping allows you to select multiple objects and put them all together in one group. This is helpful, for example, when you've created a logo out of several different shapes. Whenever you move the logo, if the items are not grouped, you have to move each shape individually. Once you group the objects, you can move, resize, cut, and paste the group as a single graphic.

Tip
To select multiple items to group, press Shift while clicking each object desired.

To group items, follow these steps:

1. Click the items you want to group.

2. Open the **E**dit menu and choose **A**rrange.

3. From the cascade menu, choose **G**roup.

The handles on the individual items disappear and the objects are treated as a single object. Later, you can ungroup the objects by choosing **E**dit **A**rrange **U**ngroup.

Once you put the objects together as a group, you may want to lock the image to keep it from accidentally being altered. Choose **E**dit **A**rrange **Lo**ck.

From Here...

For information directly related adding graphics to your worksheet, you may want to review the following chapter in this book:

■ Chapter 14, "Building Complex Charts," shows you how to add bells, whistles, and clip art to your charts.

■ Chapter 17, "Developing Business Presentations," demonstrates how a few simple graphic items can enhance and call attention to the message you're displaying on-screen.

III

Optimizing 1-2-3

Developing Business Presentations

You can use the graphic and printing capabilities of 1-2-3 for Windows in many creative ways in addition to charting and reporting worksheet data. This chapter discusses using 1-2-3 for Windows to create high-quality presentation slides, overheads, and screen shows.

In this chapter, you learn how to do the following:

- Set up your worksheet for presentations

- Organize presentation layout

- Use color to emphasize main points

- Add charts and graphics to your presentation

- Print your presentation

Presentation Possibilities

The way in which you present your information will have some effect on the type of presentation you create. If you are creating handouts and transparencies, you can move through the pages as quickly or slowly as you like, allowing plenty of time for audience questions. If you are working with an on-screen presentation, called a *screen show*, you can design your presentation to advance pages automatically or to advance only when you click the mouse or press Enter on the keyboard. The following paragraphs describe different presentation options.

■ *Producing transparencies.* You can print slides and graphics, using black-and-white or color printers supported by 1-2-3 for Windows. With a color printer, you can print directly on transparent overhead-projector film, resulting in colorful and persuasive overhead presentations. If you don't have a color printer, you can print the presentation to a file and send the file to a slide-generating service.

If you are presenting the transparencies to a large group (20 to 100 people), you may want to buy or rent a display device called an *LCD projection panel*, which fits on top of the overhead projector and displays your magnified transparency on a movie screen. Because this device is relatively inexpensive and easy to set up and use, it is your best bet for presenting to a large audience.

■ *Presenting a screen show.* You also can use your computer to display presentation pages on-screen. This technique is often called a *computer screen show*. Screen-show capabilities are available in many presentation graphics packages, such as Lotus' Freelance Graphics for Windows, but 1-2-3 for Windows provides many of the same capabilities and can create a visually interesting screen show.

You can display a slide show from your computer screen directly to an audience in several ways. The method you choose depends on the size of the audience and your budget. The easiest way to make a presentation to a moderate-size group (10 to 15 people) is to use a very large computer monitor.

If you are presenting to a large group (50 or more people), you may want to use a video projector. This type of projector is very expensive to rent, however, and may be difficult to set up; but it looks better than an LCD projection panel, and it is quieter, so you can be heard by your audience.

Setting Up Your Worksheet for Presentations

An important first step in using 1-2-3 for Windows for a presentation is setting up the work area for the presentation. The following sections describe how you can use 1-2-3 for Windows to create presentations and then provide many tips for projecting the presentation from the PC or printing it on overhead transparencies.

Creating a Slide Layout

Creating slides in 1-2-3 for Windows is as easy as typing the text in worksheet cells. Depending on the nature and length of your presentation, you may want to set up one basic slide format that you use repeatedly; or you may want to create a few different formats that you use depending on the information on the slides.

Choosing Slide Type

What kind of slides do you need? Table 17.1 lists the four basic presentation slide types.

Table 17.1	Presentation Slide Types	
Slide	**Description**	**Use For**
Title slide	Shows title and subtitle of presentation	First slide of presentation; parts slides between presentation sections
Bullet slide	Displays slide title and bulleted list of information	Slides in which you introduce a series or steps, options, or ideas
Chart slide	Shows slide title and a 1-2-3 for Windows chart	Slides that require a large display of charted information
Text and graphics slide	Shows slide title, text, and clip art or custom graphics	Text slides that need illustration (or chart)

When you decide which slide type you want to start with, you can create a basic layout for that type, setting up the column widths for, say, a bullet slide. Then you can copy the basic settings from slide to slide for other bullet slides as necessary.

Setting Up Column Widths

The key to creating the slide layout is setting up the appropriate column widths for text, bullets, and graphics. Organizing the columns in this manner enables you to indent bullets and other text easily. Figure 17.1 shows how you can use 1-2-3 for Windows to set up a template for a bullet slide.

◄ "Setting Column Widths," p. 312

III

Optimizing 1-2-3

Fig. 17.1
A template for
a bullet page
in 1-2-3 for
Windows.

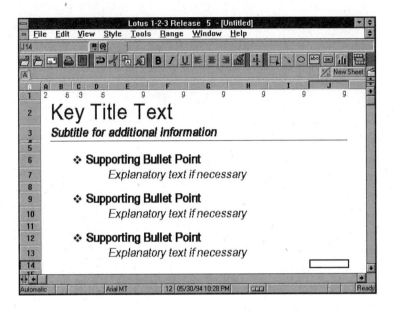

Tip
After you set the
column width,
you can get a
better idea of how
the slide will look
by choosing **V**iew
Set View **P**refer-
ences **G**rid Lines.

In this example, the column widths appear in the first row of the worksheet. The differences in the column widths help you align the title, subtitle, bullets, and bullet text. You can simply press Tab to move from one column to the next, rather than use the space bar to get characters to line up.

Here's how the columns in figure 17.1 were set up:

Column	Width	Description
A	2	Space to separate the overall slide contents from the slide frame
B	5	Indentation for subtitles below the leader
C	3	Space for the bullet characters
D	5	Indentation for text below bullet items

Tip
Skip a row between
bullet points to
leave space be-
tween lines of text.

Adding Text to Slides

To add text, highlight the appropriate cell and type the new information. Long labels will appear across the adjacent columns. Press the arrow keys as necessary to move the cell pointer.

After you add the text, you can use the **S**tyle commands, the status bar, the quick menus (displayed when you click the right mouse button), and the SmartIcons to make the text more readable.

Creating the Presentation Display

Although the standard 1-2-3 for Windows screen looks nothing like a presentation, giving 1-2-3 for Windows the appearance of a presentation-graphics screen show is easy. How do you turn a worksheet screen into a presentation screen?

Open the **V**iew menu and choose the Set View **P**references command to change the way 1-2-3 for Windows elements are displayed on-screen. (Later in this chapter, in "A Macro for Preparing the Presentation Display," you'll create a macro that takes care of the display changes for you.) To change the display of the 1-2-3 for Windows screen, follow these steps:

1. Open the **V**iew menu and choose the Set View **P**references command to display the Set View Preferences dialog box.

2. Uncheck the **W**orksheet Frame, **G**rid Lines, and **S**croll Bars check boxes. These settings are saved for each worksheet file.

3. Uncheck the **E**dit Line, Smart**I**cons, and Status **B**ar check boxes. These settings apply at the 1-2-3 for Windows level. Figure 17.2 shows the appropriate settings for the Set View Preferences dialog box.

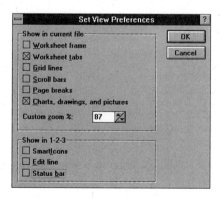

Tip

Larger typefaces and other attributes, such as bold, italics, and lines, make the information clearer for your audience.

Fig. 17.2
The Set View Preferences dialog box with settings for slide shows checked.

III

Optimizing 1-2-3

4. Click the OK button to apply the settings to the current worksheet.

5. Open the **F**ile menu and choose the **S**ave command to save the settings in the worksheet file.

Developing Multiple-Page Presentations

Tip
Keep Worksheet **T**abs displayed so you have an easy way to move from slide to slide.

Most presentations take up more than one page or worksheet screen; 1-2-3 for Windows can accommodate presentations of almost any length. Although you create individual slides one to a page, you can put the slides together as a group the way you would a series of worksheet files. You then can move among the slides by clicking the tabs at the top of the slides. Simply click the tab you want and that slide is displayed. Figure 17.3 shows a presentation using the worksheet tabs.

Fig. 17.3
Using the 1-2-3 for Windows worksheet tabs to organize slides on multiple pages.

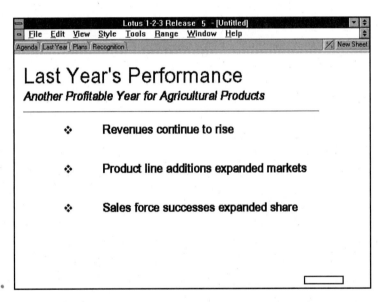

Tip
Set the font colors and other formats on one slide and then enable Group mode. This procedure copies the same format settings to any new worksheets you create in that group. Disable Group mode to alter the format settings of individual worksheets.

The Group mode feature enables you to use the format of one worksheet to format all the pages in multiple worksheets. The formats applied across the worksheets include column widths and Wysiwyg spreadsheet publishing formats. To enable Group mode, open the **S**tyle menu and choose the **W**orksheet Defaults command.

Troubleshooting

I turned on Group mode so I could preserve the same column widths from slide to slide, but when I click File New, a separate worksheet is added.

After you set your format, open the **S**tyle menu and choose **W**orksheet Defaults. Next, select **G**roup Mode to enable group mode, and add a new worksheet by clicking the New Sheet button, not by using **F**ile **N**ew.

I used a few standard text formats for my first slide. Is there an easy way to apply these formats to other slides in my presentation?

You can create named styles that contain all the style information you need. Place the cell pointer in the cell from which you want to define the named style. Open the **S**tyle menu and choose the Named **S**tyle command; type a Style **N**ame; and choose **D**efine. You now can use the style by opening the **S**tyle menu and choosing the Named **S**tyle command or by clicking the style selector in the status bar.

I want to change the indents in all my slides. Do I have to do this for every slide individually?

No. If you followed the guidelines described in this chapter, you indented your bullets by using varying column widths. You can change the column width in every slide by selecting a three-dimensional range of columns. The easiest way to do this is to place the cell pointer in the appropriate column in the first worksheet, hold down the Shift key, and click the worksheet tab for the last worksheet you want to format. You have selected that column in every worksheet. Now open the **S**tyle menu and choose the **C**olumn Width command, select the new column width, and click the OK button.

Using 1-2-3 for Windows To Convey a Message

Although 1-2-3 for Windows provides many features that enable you to format printed pages and screen layouts, be careful about the features you choose. You can create clear, persuasive, and successful presentations by following some simple style and format rules. Because an audience reads presentations from a distance, slides must be clear, in large type, and contain as few words as possible.

◀ "Understanding Style," p. 318

Guidelines for Presenting Text

You can create persuasive slides by following some basic guidelines. 1-2-3 for Windows provides great flexibility in text size and font, colors, lines, and shading. The key to a successful presentation, however, is using these elements in moderation. By following a few guidelines, you can create impressive and effective presentations.

III

Optimizing 1-2-3

Use Large Point Sizes for Text

Use fonts that can be read from a distance. For titles, use a 24-point font or larger. Never make text smaller than 14 points.

Reduce Point Size for Subtitles and Bullets

Use type size to indicate the relative importance of text in a slide. To draw attention to the slide's key message, use the largest text for titles. Choose smaller typefaces for subtitles and bullets.

Limit the Number of Fonts in a Slide

Tip

Be consistent with text style and size. Use the same size and style for titles, the same size for bullets, and so on.

Although 1-2-3 for Windows enables you to use up to eight different fonts on a page, the best slides use only one or two typefaces in up to three different point sizes. Too many type styles make the slide difficult to read and reduce the impact of the slide's message.

Use a Sans-Serif Typeface

Format slide text in a sans-serif typeface such as Arial. Serif typefaces such as Times New Roman may be appropriate with longer lines of text, but sans-serif text is easier to read, particularly if the audience is far from the projected slide.

Tip

Show the screen show to friends or coworkers before you present it to make sure that the text is readable and understandable.

Use Italics for Subtitles

A subtitle message usually supports or expands on the title message. Differentiate the subtitle from the title by using a smaller point size and italics.

Use Boldface for Titles and Bullets

For all titles, subtitles and bullets, use boldface, which makes slide text much easier to read. Be sure, however, to apply the boldfacing consistently.

Emphasize the Title of the Slide

Slides convey information better when the title is easy to locate and read. You can use a solid line below the title to separate the title from the body of the slide, as shown in figure 17.4. Use the **S**tyle menu's **L**ines & Color command to place a solid line under the slide title.

Dotted lines also can separate the title from the rest of the slide effectively (see fig. 17.5). Dotted lines can be less jarring than a solid line and can give a softer tone to the slide. You can create a dotted line as a series of periods separated by spaces. To create a dotted line that spans the width of the screen, you need approximately 38 periods and spaces formatted with a 24-point Arial font.

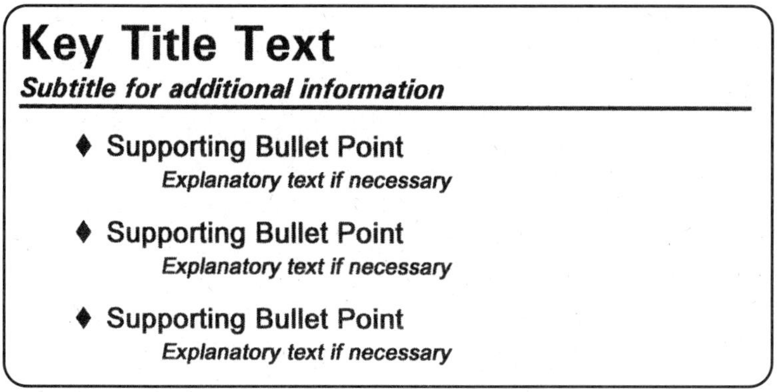

Key Title Text
Subtitle for additional information
_____

◆ **Supporting Bullet Point**
        Explanatory text if necessary

◆ **Supporting Bullet Point**
        Explanatory text if necessary

◆ **Supporting Bullet Point**
        Explanatory text if necessary

Fig. 17.4
A solid line
emphasizing the
slide title.

Key Title Text
Subtitle for additional information
. . . .

◆ **Supporting Bullet Point**
        Explanatory text if necessary

◆ **Supporting Bullet Point**
        Explanatory text if necessary

◆ **Supporting Bullet Point**
        Explanatory text if necessary

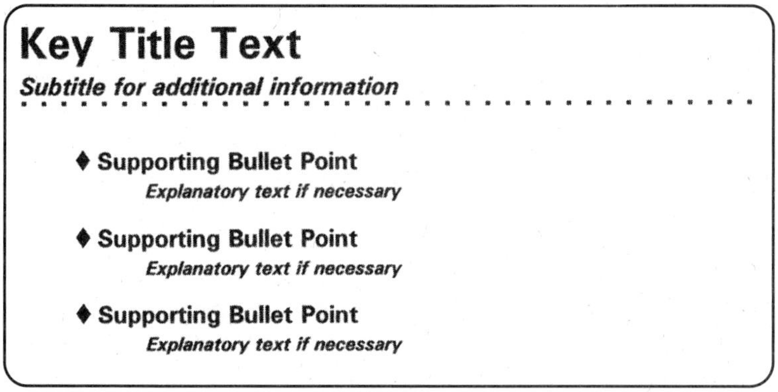

Fig. 17.5
A dotted line
emphasizing the
slide title.

You also can emphasize a title by enclosing the text in a colored box. Figure 17.6 shows slide text with a shaded title box. In addition, you can use one of the designer frames to emphasize the title. Highlight the range, and then open the **S**tyle menu and choose the **L**ines & Color command.

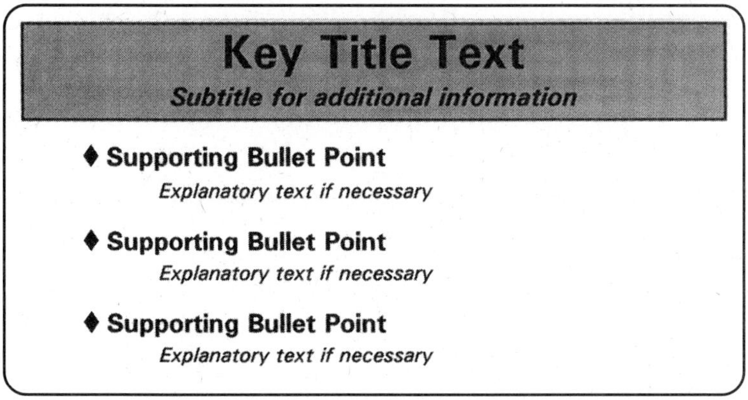

◀ "Formatting
    Cells with
    Color and
    Borders," p. 348

Key Title Text
Subtitle for additional information

◆ **Supporting Bullet Point**
        Explanatory text if necessary

◆ **Supporting Bullet Point**
        Explanatory text if necessary

◆ **Supporting Bullet Point**
        Explanatory text if necessary

Fig. 17.6
A shaded box and
designer frame
emphasizing the
slide title.

III

Optimizing 1-2-3

Keep Slide Text to a Minimum

Tip
Adding another
slide is always
better than
crowding too
much informa-
tion into a single
slide.

Slides should not be narratives of the entire presentation. Use the titles, sub-titles, and bullet items to present the essential points clearly. Rely on the spoken presentation to explain and elaborate on the basic information that the slides present. You also can print handouts or create collaborative materials so that viewers can read your presentation later.

Limit the Number of Bullet Items

Effective slides contain a title and no more than four or five bullet points. If the bullets require sub-bullets, make sure that the slide contains no more than three main bullets. Limit the sub-bullets to two or three lines.

Use Parallel Grammatical Structure

Use the same grammatical construction for all bullets in a slide. Bullets can start with a noun or a verb of any tense, but all the bullets should use the same structure. The slide shown in figure 17.7 shows bullet items that use parallel structure. Compare this slide with the one shown in figure 17.8, which does not use parallel structure. A parallel construction creates a tighter presentation and conveys information more clearly.

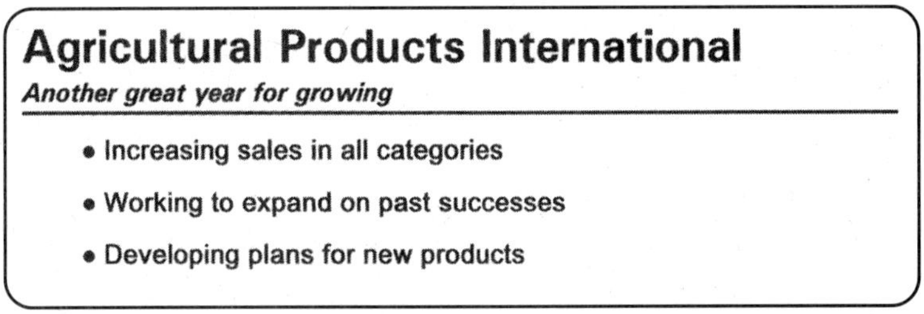

Fig. 17.7
Bullets that are
parallel.

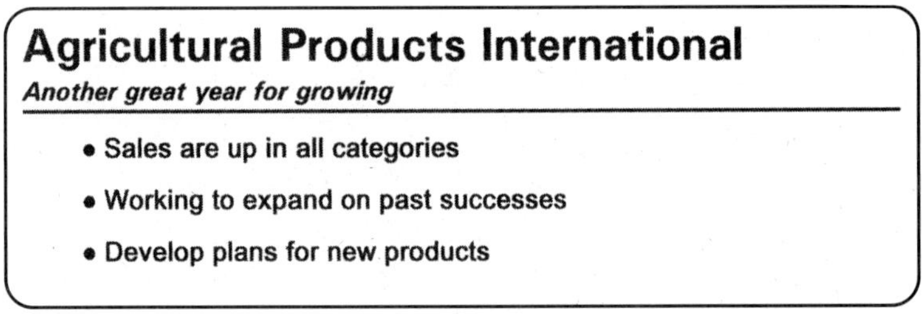

Agricultural Products International
Another great year for growing

- Increasing sales in all categories
- Working to expand on past successes
- Developing plans for new products

Fig. 17.8
Bullets that aren't
parallel.

Agricultural Products International
Another great year for growing

- Sales are up in all categories
- Working to expand on past successes
- Develop plans for new products

Guidelines for Presenting Graphics

To make presentation slides more effective and persuasive, you can use graphics images. Like text, graphics are more effective when you follow certain guidelines.

Use Graphics To Explain the Key Point

A graphic can draw attention to the key point of the slide. You can use the **T**ools menu's **C**hart and **D**raw commands to add charts and drawings to a worksheet. Do not try to encompass too many concepts, however, and do not present detailed information in a single graphic. The best graphics are clear, easy-to-read presentations of a single key point.

Use Text To Introduce and Explain the Graphic

Effective graphics have a clear purpose. Use titles to introduce the key message and to establish the context for the graphic. You can use bullets in your graphics to clarify or emphasize the points made by the text; however, do not overload the page with information, and make sure that you balance the elements of the overall layout.

In figure 17.9, the information is poorly organized and the slide is unbalanced. Figure 17.10 presents the same information clearly.

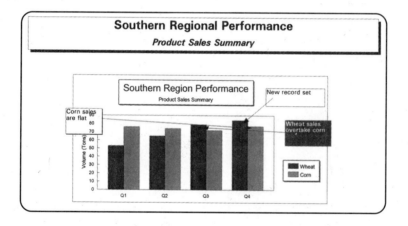

Fig. 17.9
An unbalanced presentation of graphics.

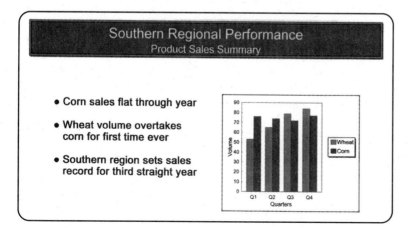

Fig. 17.10
Bullets explaining the chart and balancing it in the slide.

III

Optimizing 1-2-3

Position the Graphic To Balance the Page

Graphics add substance to a slide. You need, however, to position a graphic to balance the page. Center a graphic if the slide contains little text; otherwise, position the graphic to the right or left to offset the weight of the other slide elements (refer to fig. 17.10).

Use a Single Graphic Per Slide

In most cases, effective slides contain only a single graphic. The key to an effective slide presentation is to present the key points with clear, simple illustrations.

Add Visual Interest with Clip Art

◄ "Adding Clip Art," p. 456

You can use commercially available clip art to make the presentation more interesting. You can paste clip art in Windows metafile format directly into the 1-2-3 for Windows worksheet. Choose images that support your presentation's theme and are appropriate to the setting (see fig. 17.11).

Fig. 17.11
Clip art used to enliven a presentation.

Welcome to the
Annual Sales
Meeting

Use Graphics To Represent Concepts

Tip
Make sure that your graphics fit your message.

Use graphics of common objects to convey new ideas. Look at your environment for metaphors that effectively communicate your message. Building blocks, for example, can show the addition of new products over time. Pie charts can show that a combination of various parts make a whole (see fig. 17.12). A bridge can represent the joining of two separate entities.

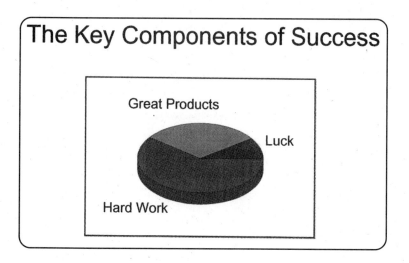

Fig. 17.12
A pie chart representing proportions.

Present Key Trends or Relationships

Use 1-2-3 for Windows charts to illustrate key trends in data or to show the relationship among items. (The chart in figure 17.10, for example, clearly shows the trends in product sales.) Keep the chart simple by limiting the amount of information it contains.

Tables of formatted data also can make great illustrations. You can draw attention to the trends and relationships among data items by using lines and arrows, added with the **T**ools menu's **D**raw command (see fig. 17.13).

Tip
A table can help you present information in a new way.

Fig. 17.13
Drawings that point out key information in a worksheet table.

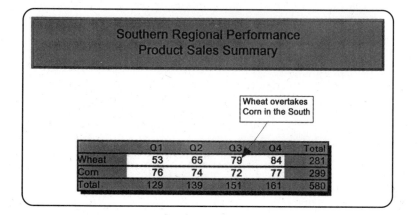

III

Optimizing 1-2-3

Using the Color Capabilities of 1-2-3 for Windows

In addition to graphics, color enhances presentations. Color can add interest to the slides and highlight key data. Some colors, such as green and red, can add impact to the information that is being presented.

> **Note**
>
> To present in color, you must be able to print to a color printer or use a computer to give the presentation as a screen show. On black-and-white printers, colors print as different shades of gray, which also can create a useful effect.

◀ "Formatting Cells with Color and Borders," p. 348

1-2-3 for Windows allows you to choose the color of cell backgrounds, text, lines, and drawing objects from 256 color choices. By using the color capabilities, you can create appropriately colorful presentations.

Using Color To Highlight Presentation Elements

In a presentation, you can use colors in several ways. The most obvious method of adding color is using a different color for the main point in the presentation. Yet you can choose among several other common ways to use color.

Tip
Keep your colors consistent to help viewers understand what they represent.

Color can enhance the organizational structure of the presentation. Using a standard color layout makes the slides easy to understand and more interesting to read. Choose consistent colors for the different regions of the slide, such as blue text for the titles, red for the bullet symbols, and black for the bullet text. You also can use different background colors for different sections of the slide (see fig. 17.14).

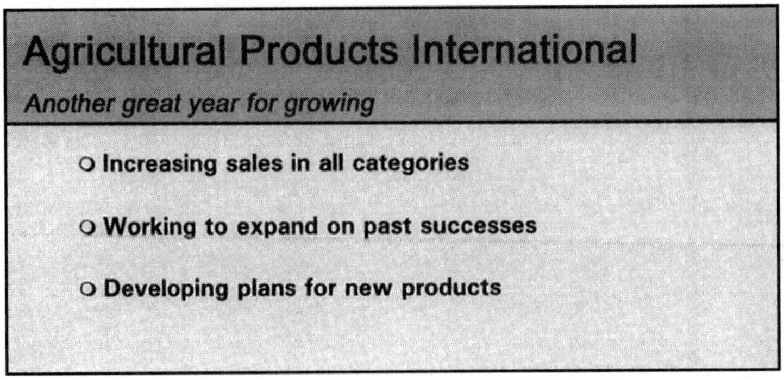

Fig. 17.14
Using color to organize the slide layout.

Agricultural Products International
Another great year for growing

    ○ **Increasing sales in all categories**

    ○ **Working to expand on past successes**

    ○ **Developing plans for new products**

Conveying Information with Selected Colors

Because many colors have common connotations, you can use color to convey meaning in a presentation. In business, for example, red represents a monetary loss or negative number, and black represents a profit or positive number.

Figure 17.15 shows a slide that easily could contain color. If the third bullet of the slide in this figure were red, for example, the viewer would immediately know that excessive expenses would result in a loss for the company.

Agricultural Products International
Review last year's performance

○ Revenues continue to increase

○ Expenses still hard to control

○ Loss in Q3 a great concern!

Fig. 17.15
A slide that can use red to convey monetary loss.

Red also can suggest danger. Blue, generally considered to be a peaceful and even soothing color, can imply tranquillity or coolness. Green—the color of U.S. currency and the stoplight color for GO—often implies profit or advancement. Yellow often means caution, a message that also comes from traffic lights and road signs.

Tip
Choose colors that show up well, even at a distance.

Selecting Colors for Black-and-White Printing

With most printers, 1-2-3 for Windows prints different colors in different shades of gray. However, you also can directly select shades of gray with the **S**tyle menu's **L**ines & Colors command. The color drop-down box in this dialog box includes gray shades on the far right side.

Selecting Colors for Background, Text, and Graphics

With 1-2-3 for Windows, you can select the color of the cell background and the cell contents. This feature enables you to emphasize text or areas of the presentation file. Open the **S**tyle menu and choose the **L**ines & Color command to set the background color and shading of the cells. To set the color of text, open the **S**tyle menu and choose the **F**ont & Attributes command.

Tip
Set the background color before setting the text color.

Using Color To Guide the Audience

◄ "Changing Fonts and Attributes," p. 343

Most presentations start with an agenda. You can tie a presentation together by repeating the agenda slide before switching to the next topic. This method is more effective if you also highlight the topic that follows. One way to highlight the topic is to use color.

Figure 17.16 shows the slide you might use to introduce the second topic (*Define plan for upcoming growing season*). In this example, the first and third bullets are shaded gray with the grayscale choices in the Font & Attributes dialog box.

Fig. 17.16
Introducing the next topic by emphasizing a bullet item.

Emphasizing Text or Graphic Elements

1-2-3 for Windows provides extensive options for formatting worksheets. You can use these capabilities to emphasize text and charts and to make the content of the slide easier to read.

Selecting the Appropriate Font

◄ "Changing Fonts and Attributes," p. 343

The beginning of this chapter discusses several guidelines for choosing fonts. Although they are not hard-and-fast rules, these guidelines are important to consider as you design a slide page.

You must use point sizes that are readable from a distance and typefaces that work together, and you must balance the images on-screen. Figure 17.17 shows a slide with effective font selections. Figure 17.18, on the other hand, contains too many typefaces and type styles. The viewer is distracted by a multitude of fonts and loses focus on the slide's message.

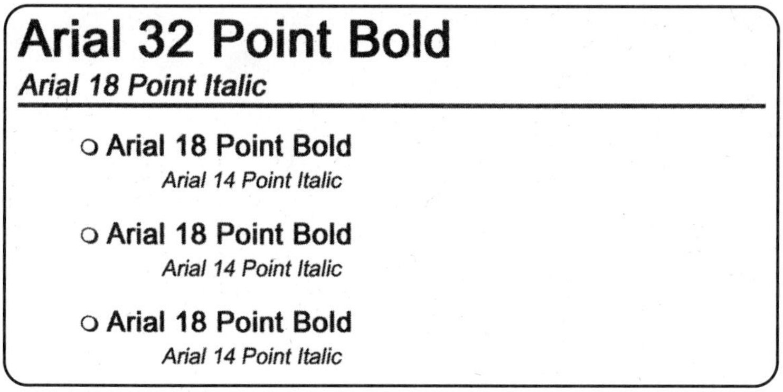

Arial 32 Point Bold
Arial 18 Point Italic

　○ **Arial 18 Point Bold**
　　Arial 14 Point Italic

　○ **Arial 18 Point Bold**
　　Arial 14 Point Italic

　○ **Arial 18 Point Bold**
　　Arial 14 Point Italic

Fig. 17.17
Fonts that work together for clarity of presentation.

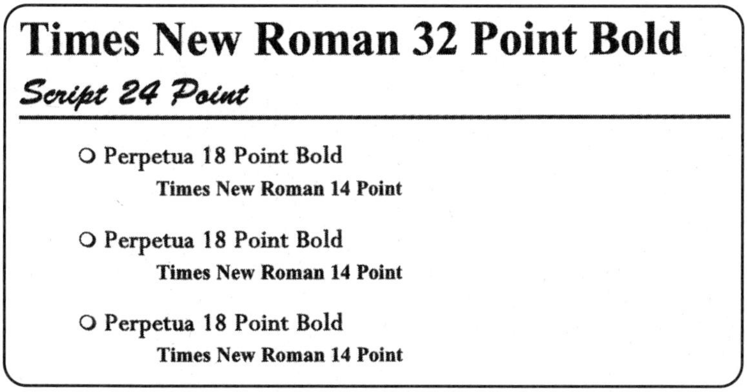

Times New Roman 32 Point Bold
Script 24 Point

　○ **Perpetua 18 Point Bold**
　　Times New Roman 14 Point

　○ **Perpetua 18 Point Bold**
　　Times New Roman 14 Point

　○ **Perpetua 18 Point Bold**
　　Times New Roman 14 Point

Fig. 17.18
Fonts that make the slide hard to read and understand.

Using Bullets

You can precede text items with bullet symbols, such as diamonds or arrows. These symbols are available in the Windows Wingdings, Monotype Sorts, Zapf Dingbats, and Symbols typefaces. You can create a check mark symbol, for example, by placing the appropriate character (4) in a cell and formatting the character with the Monotype Sorts font. Choose a symbol-font point size that corresponds to the adjacent text. Figure 17.19 shows the bullets on-screen. For example, if the bullet text is set to 18-point type, make sure the bullet is 18 points also.

Tip
Depending on the bullet character you choose, you may need to make it one or two point sizes larger than the accompanying text to make the character easy to see.

III

Fig. 17.19
Check mark symbols formatted with the Monotype Sorts font.

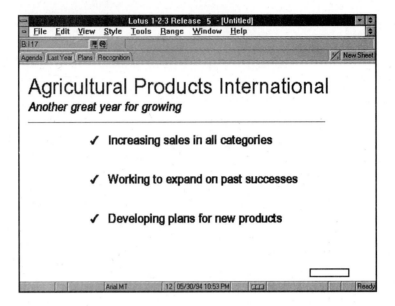

Using the Character Map

The Windows accessory Character Map provides an easy way to add special characters to Windows applications. To add special characters with the Windows Character Map, follow these steps:

1. Launch the Character Map from the Accessories group.

2. Select the Symbols or Wingdings font in the **F**ont drop-down list. The bottom-right corner of the dialog box displays the keystroke for the highlighted item.

3. Highlight the symbol you want to use (press the arrow keys to move to the symbol, or click the symbol). Then double-click the symbol, press Enter, or choose **S**elect. The character appears in the Characters to Copy text box. Repeat this process until the Characters to Copy text box contains all the characters you want to use.

4. Choose the **C**opy button to copy the characters to the Clipboard.

5. Switch back to 1-2-3 for Windows, and place the cell pointer in the appropriate cell.

6. Set the font to Symbols or Wingdings; then open the **E**dit menu and choose the **P**aste command to add the character(s) to your worksheet. You also can record the keystroke for the character displayed in the Character Map window and then type it in a cell in 1-2-3 for Windows.

Using Boldface and Italics

Most audiences view slides from a distance. Because plain type tends to fade into the projection screen and become unreadable, use boldface for most title and subtitle text.

You also can use boldface to outline the structure of the slide; for example, you can reinforce the slide's structure by formatting symbols in boldface and leaving explanatory subtext plain. Figures 17.20 and 17.21 show a slide before and after boldface was added to the text.

Agricultural Products International
Year End Performance Review
_____

Agenda

○ Review last year's performance

○ Define plan for upcoming growing season

○ Recognize contributions of top performers

Fig. 17.20
An organized slide with no boldface.

Agricultural Products International
Year End Performance Review
_____

Agenda

○ **Review last year's performance**

○ **Define plan for upcoming growing season**

○ **Recognize contributions of top performers**

Fig. 17.21
The same slide with the addition of boldface.

You also can use italics to separate the parts of the slide and to show that text has special meaning. Italics is effective for emphasizing direct or indirect quotations, for example.

Figures 17.22 and 17.23 show different ways of using bold and italics to add emphasis and clarity to slides.

Tip
Use bold italic to make italicized text stand out.

III

Optimizing 1-2-3

Agricultural Products International
Year End Performance Review

Agenda

● Review last year's performance
   Profits are up but at risk

● Define plan for upcoming growing season
   It's never too early to plant the seeds for success

● Recognize contributions of top performers
   Individual performance is still key to our success

Our Service is the Best in the Industry
Agricultural Products gets Rave Reviews

Important Foreign Customer:

"I never thought they could do it, but every order I placed was delivered on time and in top condition."

Key Grain Supplier:

"I've had problems getting paid by just about every other company I've dealt with. Agricultural Products really treats me like a partner."

Agricultural Industry Journal:

"Agricultural Products International continues to set the standard for customer service."

Using Lines, Boxes, Frames, and Shading

◄ "Drawing
Shapes," p. 510

Effective use of lines, boxes, frames, and shading can add structure and emphasis to a slide. By using these elements, you emphasize important text. You can use lines to emphasize slide titles, as described earlier, and to organize the slide.

You can use text boxes and designer frames to emphasize other text in the slide and to organize tables. Figure 17.24 shows a slide with a corporate-mission statement set off from the worksheet by a designer frame.

Agricultural Products International
Corporate Mission Statement

Our corporate mission is to provide the
best service at the best price and to
continue to lead the industry into
new and emerging markets.

Fig. 17.24
Using a designer
frame to empha-
size key slide text.

The use of lines, boxes, frames, and shading is essential to creating clear,
organized slides. When used judiciously, these elements greatly enhance the
effectiveness of any presentation.

Adding Tables

The row-and-column structure of 1-2-3 for Windows worksheets enables you
to include tables in presentations. Simple rows and columns of numbers and
labels can be very hard to read, but you can add lines, borders, and shading
to a table to increase the clarity of those numbers and labels.

◄ "Formatting
Cells with
Color and
Borders,"
p. 348

In addition to providing all the capabilities necessary to format a table, 1-2-3
for Windows provides a gallery of 14 predefined table formats. These table
formats are a quick way to create an easy-to-read worksheet table.

Figure 17.25 shows an example of a table with little formatting; figure 17.26
shows a table formatted with the Chisel2 table format, obtained by opening
the **S**tyle menu and choosing the **G**allery command.

◄ "Using the Style
Gallery," p. 353

Using the Tools-Menu Commands To Add Impact

Graphic images can make slide presentations come alive. The **T**ools menu's
Chart and **D**raw commands provide a vast array of capabilities for adding
1-2-3 for Windows charts, clip art, and freehand drawings to presentations.
Charts and graphics images can make slides easier to understand by presenting the information in pictures, relating the text to common images, or providing visually interesting breaks in the presentation.

III

Optimizing 1-2-3

Fig. 17.25
A table with basic formatting.

Regional Performance Summary
Products Sold by Geographic Region

		Products		
Region	Wheat	Corn	Oats	Barley
U.S. North	405.1	408.8	412.4	416.1
U.S. South	405.7	409.4	NA	NA
U.S. Mid West	406.3	410.0	NA	NA
U.S. Far West	406.9	410.6	414.3	417.9
Europe	407.6	411.2	414.9	418.6
New Markets	408.2	411.8	NA	NA
Total	2439.8	2461.8	1241.6	1252.6

Fig. 17.26
A table formatted with a table format from the Gallery.

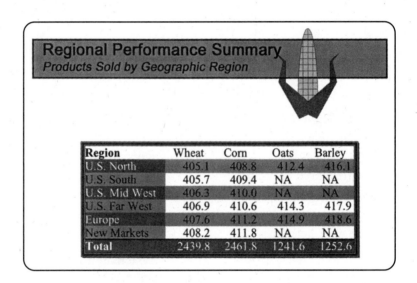

Regional Performance Summary
Products Sold by Geographic Region

Region	Wheat	Corn	Oats	Barley
U.S. North	405.1	408.8	412.4	416.1
U.S. South	405.7	409.4	NA	NA
U.S. Mid West	406.3	410.0	NA	NA
U.S. Far West	406.9	410.6	414.3	417.9
Europe	407.6	411.2	414.9	418.6
New Markets	408.2	411.8	NA	NA
Total	2439.8	2461.8	1241.6	1252.6

Adding 1-2-3 for Windows Charts

◄ "Creating Charts," p. 385

Long tables of data are seldom effective in slide presentations and, in most cases, should be supplemented or replaced by charts. When you must include a table in your presentation, like the one shown in figure 17.27, use it to provide the information for a chart that illustrates the data graphically like the chart shown in figure 17.28.

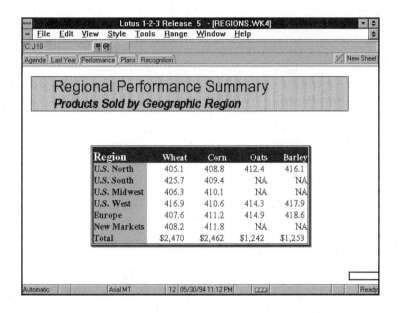

Fig. 17.27
Worksheet data with charts presented in a slide.

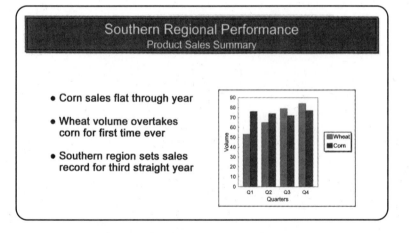

Fig. 17.28
A 1-2-3 for Windows chart added to a slide.

Adding Graphic Drawings to the Worksheet

You can add graphics drawings anywhere in the 1-2-3 for Windows worksheet area. Use the **T**ools menu's **D**raw command or the drawing SmartIcons to draw in the worksheet. You can use the draw layer to explain difficult concepts or to illustrate key points presented in the slide. Figure 17.29 shows an example of an organizational chart created by adding rectangles to the draw layer.

◄ "Working with Graphics," p. 508

III

Optimizing 1-2-3

Fig. 17.29
An organizational
chart drawn in the
worksheet draw
layer.

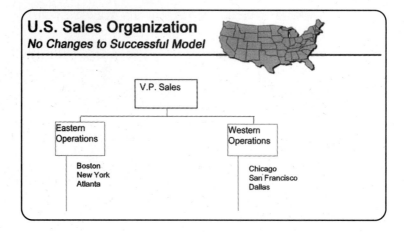

Using Clip Art

Virtually any image seems to be available as clip art in the Windows Metafile
format. Clip art adds interest to a slide presentation and often communicates
key concepts. After you add clip art to the worksheet, you can use the **T**ools
menu's **D**raw command to adapt the image to the specific presentation.
Figure 17.30 illustrates clip art used in a slide.

Fig. 17.30
Adding clip art to a
presentation.

Creating Effective Background Presentations

A distinctive background color can greatly enhance a slide's readability. You
can change the default worksheet background colors through the Windows
Control Panel. Use the following steps to change the background color:

1. Launch the Control Panel from the Main Windows applications group.

2. Double-click the Color icon, and then click the Color **P**alette button.

3. Select Window Background in the Screen **E**lement drop-down list, and choose the desired background color.

4. Click the OK button to accept the change and make this color the default window background.

Note

Changing the background in the Control Panel has no effect on the way the slides print.

You also can use the **S**tyle menu's **W**orksheet Defaults command to select a background color for each worksheet page. When you use this method, each slide can be a different color. Different-color slides can become distracting during the presentation, yet if you use different colors judiciously, you can create a striking impression.

Unlike a changed default background color, the shaded background prints with the slide. When you select the color for a background, make sure that the text and graphic colors offer enough contrast to be readable from a distance. Follow these steps to change the color of a worksheet:

1. Open the **S**tyle menu and choose the **W**orksheet Defaults command.

2. In the Color section of the dialog box, drop down the **C**ell Background Color list and select a background color for the worksheet.

3. Click OK.

Repeat these steps to change the background colors of other worksheets.

Using Designer Frames for Slide Borders

You can frame a slide on a page or a printout with a border. To frame a slide with a border, open the **S**tyle menu and choose the **L**ines & Color command to display the Lines & Color dialog box. Choose **D**esigner Frame to display the pop-up list of frame choices. You can choose among 16 frame styles, and you can make the frame any color with the **F**rame Color control. Figure 17.31 shows a designer frame used as a page border.

◀ "Formatting Cells with Color and Borders," p. 348

III

Optimizing 1-2-3

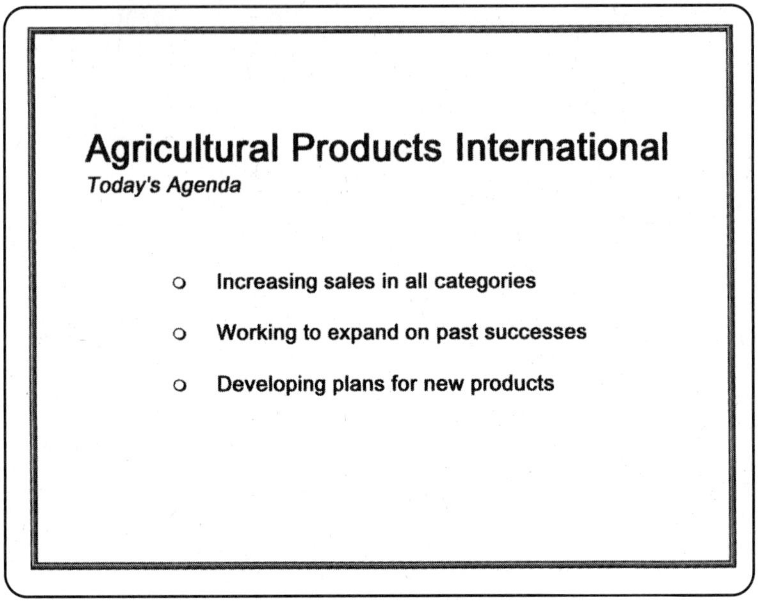

Fig. 17.31
A slide framed by
a designer frame.

Troubleshooting

I added a clip-art image to my worksheet, but I want the cells under the Windows metafile to show through.

The default background for a metafile is opaque. You can choose to allow cell information to display through the clip-art image. Select the clip-art image; then click the right mouse button and choose the Lines & Color command. Click the **P**attern option to display the Patterns drop-down list. Select pattern T (for transparent), and click the OK button.

I added some drawing objects to my slide, but when I insert columns or change widths, my drawings move around.

By default, the top-left and bottom-right corners of objects are fastened to the cells behind them. You can, however, fasten only the top-left corner of an object. Open the **E**dit menu and choose the **A**rrange command; then choose **F**asten to Cells. Choose the **T**op Left Cell Only button to fasten the object only in the top-left corner.

I want to show a general growth trend in a chart, but I don't have any real data. Do I have to draw the entire chart with the draw tools?

You can draw the chart if you want, but you may find it easier to create dummy data from which to draw the chart. Type a starting value, such as 10, in a cell. If you want 10 percent growth, type in the cell next to it a formula that multiplies the first cell by 1.1. Copy the formula to the right for as many cells as you need in your chart; then create a chart from this range.

I've been trying to put borders in my slides with the designer frames, but they turn out looking really dark and uninteresting. What am I doing wrong?

You probably are using black as the frame color. Display the Lines & Color dialog box by opening the **S**tyle menu and choosing the **L**ines & Color command. Select gray or some other light color from the **F**rame drop-down list to give more contrast to your frame.

Printing Slides from 1-2-3 for Windows

Most presentations ultimately are printed for distribution or duplication on overhead transparencies. You can use the 1-2-3 for Windows print commands to print slides created on-screen.

You usually design slides to fit landscape orientation. If you have a printer that is capable of printing landscape, open the **F**ile menu and choose the Pa**g**e Setup command to select the correct orientation.

You can use the **S**tyle menu's Page **B**reak command to insert page breaks between slides. Choosing **R**ow inserts a horizontal page break into the worksheet. Place this break at the bottom of each slide. The page breaks appear on-screen.

If you arranged your slides on multiple worksheets, you can place a page break at the bottom of each page. Follow these steps:

1. Place the cell pointer in the appropriate row of the first worksheet.

2. Press and hold down the Shift key, and then click the last worksheet tab for the presentation.

3. Open the **S**tyle menu and choose the Page **B**reak command to set the page breaks in the selected range.

Tip

If the slides look fine in Print Preview, click the Quick Print Smart-Icon to print.

A slide formatted to fit the screen does not fill a printed page. You can enlarge the slide, however. Open the **F**ile menu and choose the Pa**g**e Setup command; choose Si**z**e, and select Manually Scale in the drop-down list. A ratio of 125 percent enlarges the image to fit an 8 1/2-by-11-inch page.

Before printing, use Print Preview to verify that the slides fit correctly on the page.

III

Optimizing 1-2-3

Using Macros for Computer Presentations

Although many users print presentations created in 1-2-3 for Windows, more and more users are delivering presentations directly from the computer. Delivering presentations directly from the computer enables you to use color and to create a "live" presentation environment.

1-2-3 for Windows macros can make computer slide shows easier to present and more interesting to view. With macros, for example, you can move automatically from slide to slide or simulate screen animation. You can use the macros described in the following sections to automate and animate your 1-2-3 for Windows slide shows.

A Macro for Preparing the Presentation Display

Tip
To run this macro each time you load the worksheet file, name the macro \0 (backslash zero). You can also add a macro button to the worksheet and attach this macro to the button.

Although most of these settings are saved in the worksheet file, make sure that the edit line, scroll bars, and status line are turned off each time you run a screen show from 1-2-3 for Windows. The following macro will choose these settings.

```
{SET "WINDOW-DISPLAY-EDIT-LINE","NO"}
{SET "WINDOW-DISPLAY-SMARTICONS","NO"}
{SET "WINDOW-DISPLAY-STATUS-BAR","NO"}
```

To redisplay these window attributes, create a second macro replacing NO with YES. Use the **E**dit **C**opy command to duplicate the preceding macro, and then use **E**dit **F**ind & Replace to change NO to YES. Name this macro \r so you can easily reset these display settings.

Using Macro Buttons for Slide Changes

1-2-3 for Windows enables you to place macro buttons in the worksheet. These buttons can provide an easy way to change between slide pages. Follow these steps to create a button:

1. Open the **T**ools menu and choose **D**raw and then **B**utton or click the Macro Button SmartIcon and specify the desired button location. (The lower right corner of the screen is usually the best place for the button.)

2. The Assign to Button dialog box appears. Click the **E**nter Macro Here box and type the macro command **{NEXTSHEET}** into the text box.

3. Click in the **B**utton text box and type **NEXT** or some other appropriate text to describe the action (see fig. 17.32).

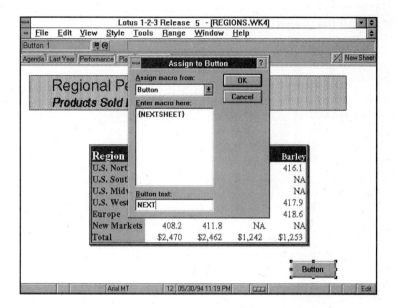

Fig. 17.32
Creating a macro button to move between slides.

Should you need to reverse through the slides, create another button to move to the previous sheet. Follow the steps above but input the macro command **{PREVSHEET}** and appropriate text in the button name text field. Figure 17.33 shows a slide with buttons you use to move to the next or the previous worksheets.

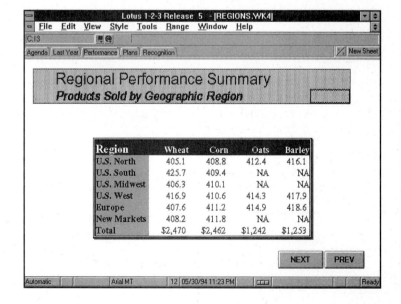

Fig. 17.33
Macro buttons that move between slides.

Tip
Use **Edit Copy** and **Edit Paste** to copy these buttons to other sheets.

III

Optimizing 1-2-3

A Macro for Changing Slides with the Enter Key

The simplest screen show macro pauses until you press the Enter key and then uses the GOTO macro command to move to the next slide. To specify the worksheet letter as the range to go to, you type the worksheet letter followed by a colon for each slide. You can also specify the tab name followed by a colon (:). Figure 17.34 shows the macro in the worksheet.

Fig. 17.34
A slide show macro.

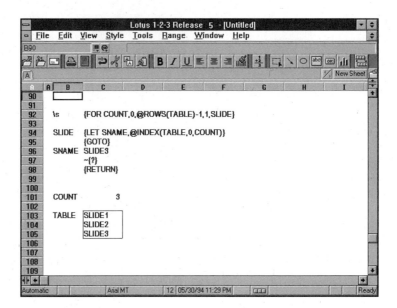

The \s macro works for any number of slides. Build the table of slide names and use **R**ange **N**ame command or the Create/Delete Range Name SmartIcon to name the range TABLE.

  You can use the **E**dit **C**opy and **E**dit **P**aste commands (or the Copy and Paste SmartIcons) to arrange the slides in the range TABLE without having to re-type all the names.

A Macro for Timing the Slide Changes

▶ "Planning, Invoking, and Debugging Macro Command Programs," p. 1083

This macro enhances the preceding slide show macro by establishing a predetermined delay before the screen moves to the next slide. In this macro, the number of seconds of delay is entered in the column to the right of the slide name (see fig. 17.35). The range name TABLE must include both columns (columns F and G, in this example). If you press any key, the show moves to the next slide before the time elapses.

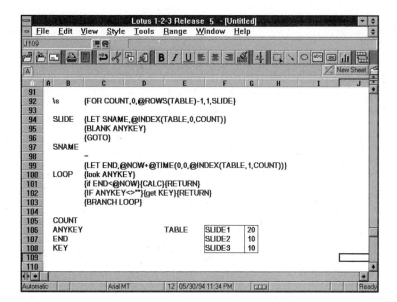

Fig. 17.35
An automatic
screen show
macro.

From Here...

For information directly related to the tasks involved in creating slides, you may want to review the following sections of this book:

- Chapter 9, "Formatting Worksheets," provides a brush-up on the basics of formatting cells, ranges, and entire worksheets. You also learn to choose number formats, change data appearance, and use the Style Gallery.

- Chapter 14, "Building Complex Charts and Mapping Data." In this chapter, you learn to create attention-getting charts you can add to the slides in your presentation. You also find out about selecting and adding clip art to your slides.

- Chapter 16, "Adding Graphics to Worksheets." In this chapter, you learn how to draw shapes and freehand graphics to include in your presentations.

- Chapter 35, "Writing 1-2-3 for Windows Macros." Learn more about using 1-2-3 for Windows' macro language and try writing a few macros of your own.

III

Optimizing 1-2-3

Part IV

Analyzing the Worksheet

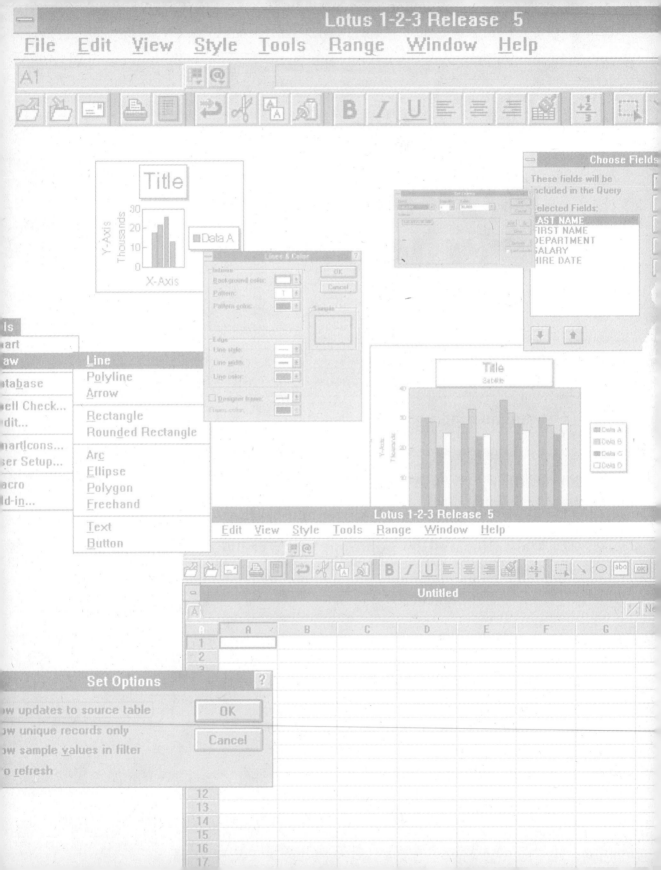

Chapter 18

Manipulating and Analyzing Data

In this chapter, you learn key skills for manipulating and analyzing data to develop answers that you and your business want. Businesses have and need large bodies of data that are best organized in tables—for example, information on your company's employees such as names, addresses, years of service, and salary rates and data on its customers, such as names, addresses, phone numbers, recent purchases, dates of last sales calls, and amounts they owe.

But the practical use and value of such data depends on the ability to quickly and efficiently obtain the answers that are needed, when they are needed. Typically such data is text or mainly text with some values. For data of this kind, 1-2-3 for Windows offers powerful methods for manipulation and analysis to find answers fast. You learn some of these methods in this chapter.

Some very important business data is purely values that are mathematically related to each other. Among the most important are the finances of the business and its parts—your product line, a proposed investment, and your whole division or company. The mathematical nature of such data enables extremely powerful and valuable analyses, such as exploring future financial effects of various combinations of what-ifs for prices, sales, various expenses, and other business factors. 1-2-3 for Windows offers you vast powers for applying such analyses very quickly and easily. In this chapter, you learn skills of the highest value for such analyses.

In this chapter, you learn to:

- Combine whole and partial units of text
- Use formulas that make decisions

■ Analyze and obtain data from tables

■ Create what-if tables

> **Note**
>
> Keep in mind which groups of data are *values* and which are text. With 1-2-3 for Windows you can apply powerful manipulations and analyses to both—but vastly more to values.

Manipulating Text

You can combine units of text from different sources by using text formulas. By applying this skill together with knowledge of text functions from Chapter 5, you can perform powerful manipulations of text data such as combining selected parts of text units from different sources. From a table with last and first names in separate columns, for example, you can combine the last name and first initial in a single cell.

Combining Text Units

Tip

With text formulas, you can add text units from different sources—that is, "glue" a text unit to the end of another.

In a single worksheet cell, you can combine units of text from two or more sources by following three rules:

■ Begin the cell entry with a + (plus sign). In 1-2-3 for Windows, a combined text unit is a formula (a text formula). The plus sign makes the cell a formula cell.

■ Between consecutive units of text to be combined, use & (an ampersand).

■ Enclose in " " (double quotes) any unit of text you type into the cell entry. For a copy of the text in another cell, enter the cell address without quotes.

Figure 18.1 shows, in rows 10, 12, and 14, three examples of combining units of text. For each example, column B shows the result of combining text units, and column C shows what was entered in column B to get the result. (Cells E18 and F18 are source cells, containing units of text to be combined in column-B cells.)

Fig. 18.1
Use text formulas to combine text from different sources.

Cell C10 shows what was entered in cell B10:

    +E18

This is an example of the simplest kind of text formula: a cell address preceded by a plus sign. You use it to copy the contents of a cell containing text, just the same as you do to copy the contents of a cell containing a value. You have to start with a plus sign so that 1-2-3 for Windows knows what follows is a formula. If in cell B10 you typed E18 without the starting plus sign, B10 would contain E18, instead of E18's cell contents. But with the starting plus sign, B10 contains the contents of cell E18.

Cell C12 shows what was entered in cell B12:

    +E18&F18

The + that begins the entry makes it a formula. The rest of the entry, addresses of two text-containing cells combined with &, makes the formula combine the texts of cells E18 and F18. The combination appears in cell B12.

Of course, for readability you want the first and last names separated by a space—a comma followed by a space is even better. You achieve this result by entering **+E18&", "&F18** in B14.

After the first & the next unit of text added is a comma followed by a space, enclosed in double-quotes. This is followed by & and the second cell address, F18. The result is the last name (from E18), a comma and space, and then the first name (from F18). The combination is displayed in cell B14.

Tip
For formulas that combine text units, the "addition sign" or "glue" is the ampersand: &.

Tip
You can combine
several text units,
some from other
cells and others
typed in.

This third text-combining entry, in row 14, shows in a concise example all the keys you need for applying text formulas to combine multiple text units.

■ Start with +

■ Between consecutive text units enter &

■ For each text unit from another cell, just enter the cell address, but for each typed-in text unit use enclosing double-quotes

Changing and Combining Text Units

Along with cell contents and direct entries, text formulas can also include *text functions*. (You learn about text functions in Chapter 5.) With the combination of text formulas and text functions, you can make a cell entry that chooses parts of texts in other cells, modifies those parts, and combines them, along with text you type in directly.

In figure 18.2, row 8 repeats the last text-formula entry from the preceding figure 18.1, which produced the combined text BARTH, SUE. Rows 10, 12, and 14 have three examples of using text functions in text formulas to refine the combined text. As in the preceding figure 18.1, for each example column B shows the result and column C shows what was entered in B to get its result. (Again, E and F cells at lower right are source cells.)

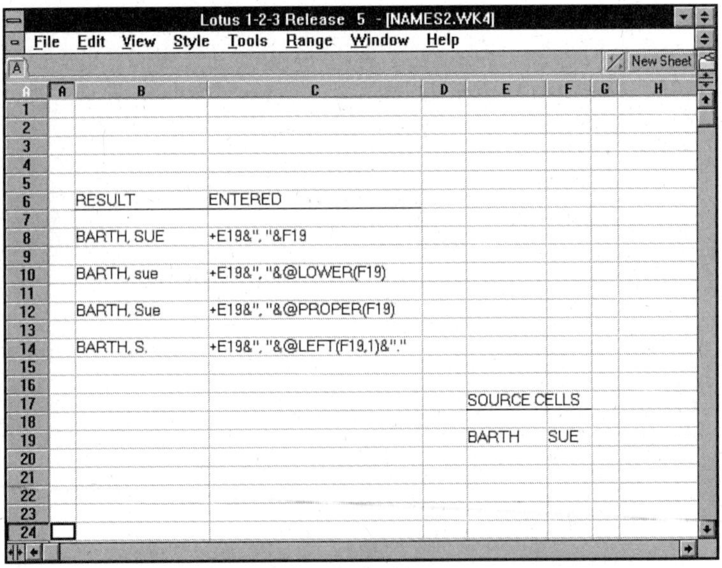

Fig. 18.2
With text formulas
that include text
functions, you can
modify texts and
combine them
with texts from
other sources.

	A	B	C	D	E	F	G	H
6		RESULT	ENTERED					
8		BARTH, SUE	+E19&", "&F19					
10		BARTH, sue	+E19&", "&@LOWER(F19)					
12		BARTH, Sue	+E19&", "&@PROPER(F19)					
14		BARTH, S.	+E19&", "&@LEFT(F19,1)&"."					
17					SOURCE CELLS			
19					BARTH	SUE		

Lotus 1-2-3 Release 5 - [NAMES2.WK4]
File Edit View Style Tools Range Window Help
New Sheet

In row 10, the part of the text formula referring to cell F19 is the text function @LOWER, which delivers text in all lowercase. After the last &, instead of just F19, the last part of the formula is

    @LOWER(F19)

as shown in cell C10. The result of this formula, including the function, is the same as in row 8 except that sue is all lowercase.

Row 12 shows a similar use of another text function, @PROPER, within a text formula. @PROPER returns text with the first letters capitalized and the rest lowercase. To make the text copied from cell F19 appear this way, the appropriate formula is

    @PROPER(F19)

The result, Sue, appears in B12.

Row 14 demonstrates the use of another kind of text function, @LEFT. This is a function that returns a part of a text unit (see Chapter 5). The @LEFT text function returns part of a text starting at the text's left. The function has two arguments: The first argument specifies the text; the second argument indicates how many characters of the text to return, starting at its left. If you want just the first letter from cell F19 (an initial), enter **@LEFT(F19,1)**.

You can add a period after the initial by ending the formula with another & and then "." (a period in double quotes). Cell C14 shows the entire formula, and cell B14 shows the result.

Note

Here are some text functions you can use in text formulas:

Purpose	Functions
Return parts of text	@LEFT, @MID, @RIGHT
Control uppercase and lowercase	@UPPER, @PROPER, @LOWER
Remove unprintables or blanks	@CLEAN, @TRIM
Change part of text	@REPLACE
Convert value to text	@STRING

To learn more about these text functions, see Chapter 5.

Multiplying Your Text-Manipulation Power

The preceding examples illustrate the two kinds of text-manipulation power that 1-2-3 for Windows gives you: text formulas and text functions. In text manipulation and every other area of application, this is the number one key to full use of the power of 1-2-3 for Windows: combine individual powers for the job you want to do.

The last example can be used to illustrate combining powers. Your friend might look at the text formula that produced BARTH, S. and ask, "Wouldn't it be simpler to just type it in?" If this were the only name you wanted, it is certainly easier to just type it in. But business data typically includes tables of tens, hundreds, or thousands of employees or customers. Under BARTH and SUE there may be very long lists of other last and first names. Typing the last name and first initial for every one could take you days, and to be sure they are all correct, you'd have to proof every one. How do you get it done much faster, error-free?

The answer is that the text formula you've entered in row 14 can. If you simply copy it to other rows, this formula combines the last name and first initial from any or every row in the table.

Since your entry has relative cell references, it works with any pair of text cells that have the same relative locations that E19 and F19 have to B14. So if you copy the formula in cell B14 down row B, row B automatically displays the last name and first initial for every pair of last and first name cells in the table (see fig. 18.3).

Fig. 18.3

To combine selected text units for every row of a table, beside the top row enter one text formula containing a text function with relative cell references and copy it down the column to the table's bottom row.

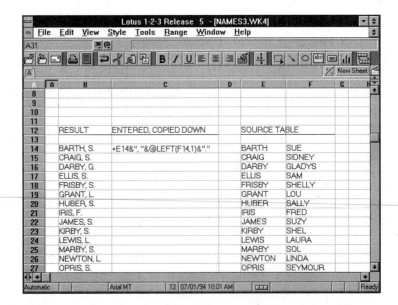

	B	C	D	E	F	G
8						
9						
10						
11						
12	RESULT	ENTERED, COPIED DOWN		SOURCE TABLE		
13						
14	BARTH, S.	+E14&", "&@LEFT(F14,1)&"."		BARTH	SUE	
15	CRAIG, S.			CRAIG	SIDNEY	
16	DARBY, G.			DARBY	GLADYS	
17	ELLIS, S.			ELLIS	SAM	
18	FRISBY, S.			FRISBY	SHELLY	
19	GRANT, L.			GRANT	LOU	
20	HUBER, S.			HUBER	SALLY	
21	IRIS, F.			IRIS	FRED	
22	JAMES, S.			JAMES	SUZY	
23	KIRBY, S.			KIRBY	SHEL	
24	LEWIS, L.			LEWIS	LAURA	
25	MARBY, S.			MARBY	SOL	
26	NEWTON, L.			NEWTON	LINDA	
27	OPRIS, S.			OPRIS	SEYMOUR	

By combining *three* powers of 1-2-3, you eliminate a giant day-long typing-and-proofing job. You enter in one cell a text formula that includes a text function and then copy it down the worksheet beside the table. Easy as 1-2-3. By spending more time studying this book and thinking not only of the individual features but of creative ways to combine them to meet your goals, you can save time, improve accuracy, and do things you thought impossible.

Troubleshooting

I want a cell to display a sentence saying what profit is, getting the current profit number from the financial reports part of my worksheet. The profit number is in cell C12, so in the cell for the sentence I entered +"Profit is "&C12&".". But the cell shows ERR. What is wrong?

A text formula cannot include a value. It can contain items from other cells only if they are text.

Can I incorporate a number from a value cell in a text formula? If so, how?

Yes, you can. The key is to use the @STRING function, which converts a value to text.

Instead of just entering the address of the value cell, enter **@STRING** with that cell's address as its first argument, and a second argument for the number of decimal places you want shown.

In the example, if you want the profit number with no decimal places, instead of just entering C12, you enter **@STRING(C12,0)**. Your entire entry is

```
+"Profit is "&@STRING(C12,0)&"."
```

This entry delivers the result you want. If the profit figure in your financial reports is 300, your text-formula cell displays Profit is 300. If next week the financial reports have profit of 400, the text-formula cell displays Profit is 400.

For more on @STRING and other text functions, see Chapter 5.

Using Formulas That Make Decisions

With the @IF function, you can create formulas that apply tests to parts of the worksheet and then "decide" what to do next based on the test results.

The @IF function has three arguments:

◀ "Logical Functions," p. 195

- A *condition*, to be tested as true or false

- An *if-true_result*, to be delivered if the test result is true

- An *if-false_result*, to be delivered if the test result is false

1-2-3 for Windows executes the @IF function by first determining whether the *condition* is true or false. If the *condition* is true, the *if-true_result* is delivered; otherwise, the *if-false_result* is delivered.

To express conditions in @IF functions, you can use any one or more of the logical operators summarized below.

Operator	Description
<	Less than
<=	Less than or equal to
=	Equal to
>=	Greater than or equal to
>	Greater than
<>	Not equal to
#AND#	Used to test two conditions, both of which must be true for the entire test to be true
#OR#	Used to test two conditions; if either condition is true, the entire test condition is true
#NOT#	Used to test that a condition is *not* true

This single function, @IF, provides power that can be used in a very wide variety of ways and can be of critical value in many major applications. Of all the individual powers that 1-2-3 for Windows offers, the @IF function is one of the most valuable to learn well, so as you face tasks that require creative approaches, keep @IF in your mind as a potential key to your solution.

Following are examples of use of @IF for two very different kinds of applications: analysis and extraction of text data from tables and structuring complex aspects of quantitative what-if business planning analyses. You can use these examples as models for your work, and more broadly, from these examples you can see how powerful and flexible @IF is to build your capabilities for applying it creatively for analyses very different from these.

Using @IF for Manipulating Text and Analyzing Tables of Data

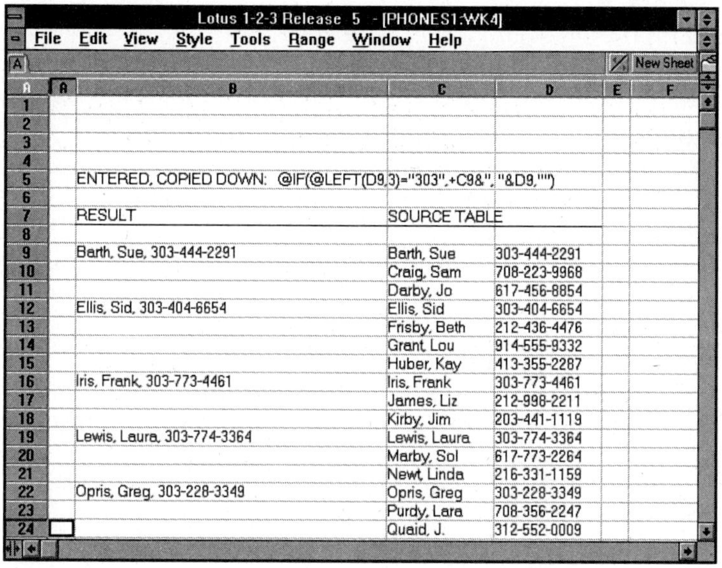

IV

Analyzing the Worksheet

Fig. 18.4
Use @IF with another function to find people with a particular area code.

```
Lotus 1-2-3 Release 5  - [PHONES1.WK4]
File  Edit  View  Style  Tools  Range  Window  Help
```

	B	C	D	E	F
5	ENTERED, COPIED DOWN: @IF(@LEFT(D9,3)="303",+C9&", "&D9,"")				
7	RESULT	SOURCE TABLE			
9	Barth, Sue, 303-444-2291	Barth, Sue	303-444-2291		
10		Craig, Sam	708-223-9968		
11		Darby, Jo	617-456-8854		
12	Ellis, Sid, 303-404-6654	Ellis, Sid	303-404-6654		
13		Frisby, Beth	212-436-4476		
14		Grant, Lou	914-555-9332		
15		Huber, Kay	413-355-2287		
16	Iris, Frank, 303-773-4461	Iris, Frank	303-773-4461		
17		James, Liz	212-998-2211		
18		Kirby, Jim	203-441-1119		
19	Lewis, Laura, 303-774-3364	Lewis, Laura	303-774-3364		
20		Marby, Sol	617-773-2264		
21		Newt, Linda	216-331-1159		
22	Opris, Greg, 303-228-3349	Opris, Greg	303-228-3349		
23		Purdy, Lara	708-356-2247		
24		Quaid, J.	312-552-0009		

Suppose that the names and phone numbers at right in figure 18.4 are the top of a very long table of customers, and the vice president of sales has suddenly decided to take the whole sales team skiing. To have them develop sales from the lodge, she wants you to find everybody on the list in Colorado area code 303.

In cell B9, enter **@IF(@LEFT(D9,3)="303",+C9&", "&D9,"")**—this formula also appears in row 5.

Within the parentheses for the @IF function's arguments, the first argument is the test, the condition to be judged true or false. @LEFT(D9,3) defines the first three characters in the row's phone-number cell, the area code; and the rest of the test condition is ="303". So if the area code is 303, the result is true; if not, the result is false. The second argument, which specifies what to do if true, combines and delivers the contents of the name and phone-number cells separated by comma and space. The third and final argument, specifying what to do if the test result is false, returns nothing.

When you enter this @IF function in B9, 1-2-3 for Windows applies the test on that row, and upon finding a true result displays the name and phone number. For example, in figure 18.4, cell D9 has the area code 303, which is a

Tip
Multiply @IF power and flexibility by nesting other functions in its arguments. Anywhere in an @IF argument where you can place a value, you can instead place a function that delivers a value.

true result. So, cell B9 displays the combination of cell C9 and D9, Barth, Sue, 303-444-2291.

To complete the analysis for the entire table, copy cell B9 down column B all the way to the bottom of the table. Since the @IF function's cell references are relative, each row's copy has references to the cells on its row. Immediately, 1-2-3 for Windows executes the function on every row. In column B, on every row with a 303 area code the name and phone number appear, and on every other row nothing appears, as shown in column B of figure 18.4.

In similar ways, you can use the @IF function with @RIGHT or @MID nested inside to have 1-2-3 for Windows identify various categories of data from tables. For example, figure 18.5 has at its right a table of names and phone numbers similar to the table in figure 18.4 with an additional column of addresses including zip codes.

Fig. 18.5
Using the @IF function with other functions nested inside, you can manipulate and analyze data from tables in many creative ways.

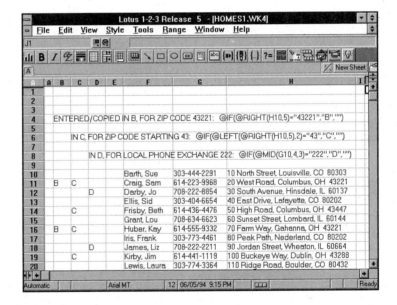

To display a B on the rows of all the people in Columbus zip code 43221, enter in cell B10 **@IF(@RIGHT(H10,5)="43221","B","")** and then copy downward.

If this function finds that the five rightmost characters cell H10 are 43221, a B is displayed in B10.

If you wanted to cast a bigger net and display a C on the row of every person with zip code beginning 43, in column C you enter a similar @IF function with a test condition that uses both @LEFT and @RIGHT, one nested within the other.

```
@IF(@LEFT(@RIGHT(H10,5),2)="43","C","")
```

In this @IF function, the @RIGHT function returns the five-character zip code; the @LEFT function, which contains the @RIGHT, returns its first two characters; and the @IF, which contains them both, tests whether or not their result is 43; and if true, displays C.

If you have a list with people in greater Chicago and you want to display a D on each row with a person with the local phone exchange 222, enter **@IF(@MID(G10,4,3)="222","D","")**.

The @MID function goes to column G, skips to the fourth character, and starting there obtains three characters. Then the @IF function containing @MID tests whether or not the three characters are 222. If the test is true, D is displayed.

As these examples show, with the @IF function, as with other functions, you can multiply flexibility and power to do what you want by *nesting*—using one function within another. In these cases, using the @IF function with @LEFT, @RIGHT, and @MID nested within its test condition enables you to make the @IF base its selection of data on any part of a text cell's contents.

Using @IF in Quantitative Decision Analysis

Suppose that you're part of a team planning the launch of a new product. In the plan, the sales price is $20, the unit cost is $10, and fixed costs are $3,000, but fixed costs jump to $5,000 when monthly unit sales pass 400. You predict that unit sales will grow 100 per month. But everybody on the team knows that monthly unit sales growth could be much higher—or much lower. So you develop a financial plan (see fig. 18.6).

To test various what-ifs for Units Growth/month, you want the financial plan to be set up so that whenever you change the Units Growth/month number in C4, everything else changes as it should to reflect your change.

For everything except Fixed Costs, you can make the entries with simple algebra. For each month, Units Sold is Units Growth/month (C4) plus the preceding month's Units Sold; Sales is the product of Unit Price (C5) and the current month's Units Sold; Variable Costs is the product of Unit Cost (C6) and the current month's Units Sold; and Profit is current month's Unit Sales minus current month's Variable Costs and Fixed Costs. For the first month, in column C, make these entries:

Units Sold (row 13)	+B13+$C4
Sales (row 15)	+C13*$C5
Variable Costs (row 16)	+C13*$C6
PROFIT (row 19)	+C15-C16-C17

Fig. 18.6
Use @IF in what-if business plans to make fixed costs jump when they should.

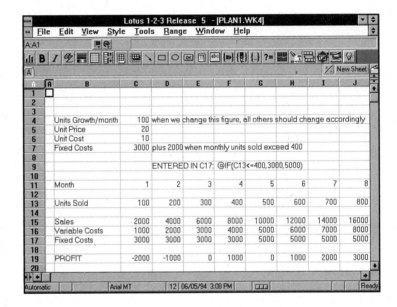

Copy these entries across to the right for the following months. (Since all the cell references that do not have $ before column-letter are relative as to column, when you copy these formulas to the right, each one adjusts correctly for its month. For example, in the month in column D, the entry for sales changes to D13*$C5, *that* month's units sold times price.)

Now, whenever you change the Units Growth/month number in cell C4, all the numbers for every month change to correctly reflect results with your new number—except that Fixed Costs are not yet entered, and Profit is not yet correct because it is affected by Fixed Costs. For Fixed Costs entries, you will use @IF as described next.

Using @IF for Discontinuities in Business Plans

But what about Fixed Costs? The plan is that as Units Sold grow, Fixed Costs stay at 3,000 until monthly Units Sold passes 400, when Fixed Costs jump to 5,000 and stay at that level as Monthly Units Sold keeps growing. If Units

Growth/month is high, Units Sold may pass 400 and cause the Fixed Costs to jump in an earlier month; or if Units Growth/month is lower, the Fixed Costs jump in a later month. The team doesn't know how to put this in the worksheet with algebra.

Here is a place where you can use the @IF function for an easy answer to an important need. For each month, in the Fixed Costs cell, what you want is an entry that says:

> "If it's true that this month's Units Sold are 400 or less, enter 3000, and if it's false enter 5000."

For the first month of Fixed Cost's row 17, in column C, you enter

> **@IF(C13<=400,3000,5000)**

which means "if it's true C13 is less than or equal to 400, deliver 3000, if it's false deliver 5000".

Copy this formula across the Fixed Costs row so that it applies to every month. (Since the C13 is relative, the letter keeps changing so that in each column it refers to that month's Units-Sold figure.)

Now, whenever you change the Units Growth/month figure in C4, Fixed Costs remains at 3000 until units sold passes 400, and thereafter are 5000.

Now, with the right entries in the Fixed Costs row, the Profit row has the numbers it needs to produce the right results. The financial plan provides the what-if tool you want. For whatever number you enter for Units Growth/ month growth in C4, all the other numbers change as required to reflect the plan with that Units Growth/month number.

Using @IF for Analyzing and Predicting Taxes

You can also use the @IF function for income tax in business-financial what-if plans. When you visit the CPA for advice on income tax rate for the plan, she may tell you that the tax rate is about 25% of profit, but it isn't that simple. As the venture moves from losses to rising profits, there are different tax calculations in these four phases:

Losses: No income tax

Profit, but cumulative prior losses are larger: Still no tax

Profit, exceeding cumulative prior losses: Tax on difference

Profit, no prior losses left to subtract: Tax on full profit

By using nested @IF functions, you can make your financial plan apply to this set of rules to calculate Tax and all profit figures correctly for any Units Growth/month number you enter (see fig. 18.7).

Fig. 18.7
Use @IF in what-if business plans to reflect income-tax rules.

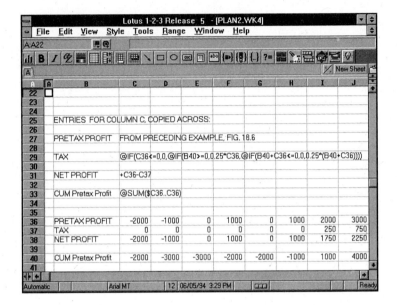

In figure 18.7 the Pretax Profit numbers in row 36 come from the plan in figure 18.6; this row has been moved down on the worksheet to provide space for showing and explaining the profit and tax entries. For each month, the entry for Net Profit is Pretax Profit minus tax, and Cum Pretax Profit is the net sum of all Pretax Profits through current month. For these two rows, in column C for the first month, you make the entries shown at upper left in figure 18.6:

Net Profit (row 38) +C36-C37

Cum Pretax Profit (row 40) @SUM($C36..C36)

Then you copy these entries across to right for subsequent months, completing the entries for all rows except Tax.

Diagramming Uses of Nested @IF Functions
A goal that's complex enough to require nested what-ifs can appear challenging, but if you approach it systematically, you can clarify it and develop an answer that works. First, determine the number of @IF functions you need to use together. To determine the answer note that you need one fewer @IF

function than the number of situations you need the @IFs to handle, because you can handle one situation with no @IFs and each @IF adds the ability to handle one more. For the Tax part of your financial plan, which requires different handling of four different situations, you need a nested unit of three @IF functions.

Then, to think out how the rest of @IF functions should work for what you are analyzing, diagram it. Sketch a diagram that looks like a tree with branches, or a road with forks, to show how @IF functions can split what you are analyzing into its different situations and handle each differently. For the financial-plan Tax row, a diagram of this type is shown in figure 18.8.

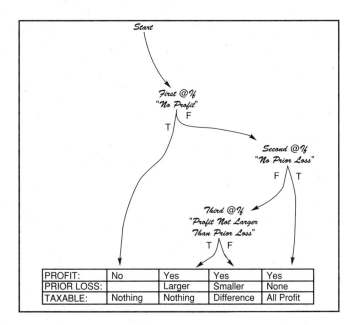

Fig. 18.8
With tree or road-fork diagrams, you can clarify complex analyses that require nested @IF functions.

In figure 18.8, the top of the diagram is where you start, and across the bottom are the four situations that you want the @IF nest to handle differently. For another analysis you can put Start at the left and the different situations at right; but for the financial plan's Tax, putting the situations across the bottom has the extra advantage of making them show, left-to-right, the four profit-development phases that the venture hopes to pass through as the months pass.

Start the road down from the top, and draw a first fork, representing the first @IF function's test. For that @IF fork, define a test condition so that its being true represents the road to one of the situations, and the @IF function can deliver the right result for that situation; if false, the other road goes to the next @IF fork. In figure 18.8, the first @IF test-condition is "No Profit." If the result is true, the road goes to this first situation, and the @IF can return the right result for this first situation: Tax zero. If the first @IF condition is false, the road continues to the second @IF fork.

Along the false road from the first @IF fork, repeat the same procedure: draw the second @IF fork, and then define its test so that its true road can go to and deliver the right result for another situation and its false road can proceed to another @IF fork. In figure 18.8, the second @IF fork is reached only if the current month is profitable; and the second @IF fork's test condition is "No Prior Loss." So its true road goes to the fourth situation, profit and no losses to subtract, and can deliver the right result for that fourth situation, tax on the entire current profit. The false road goes to a third @IF fork.

When there are only two remaining situations, one more @IF fork can provide roads to both. Define its @IF test so that if true it can deliver the right result for one of those situations and if false for the other. In figure 18.8, the third and final @IF is reached only if there is current-month profit and also prior losses to subtract. Its test condition is "Profit Not Larger Than Prior Loss." Its true road goes to and delivers the right result for the second situation: profit but not exceeding prior loss, therefore, no tax. And its false road goes to and delivers the right result for the third situation: current profit and smaller prior loss, therefore, tax on the excess of the current profit over the prior loss.

With this kind of diagramming, you can think out uses of nested @IF functions to handle very complex analyses. You can also use this kind of diagramming to develop clear understanding of complex @IF nests created by others, and to explain complex @IF nests to other people whether or not you created them.

Once you've sketched out the structure of a set of @IF forks and tests that can deliver the right results for each of the situations, the remaining step is to enter a nest of @IF functions that work as your diagram shows. For the financial plan's Tax row, you enter an @IF function containing a second @IF that in turn contains a third @IF, like this:

```
@IF(C36<=0,0,@IF(B40>=0,0.25*C36,@IF(B40+C36<=0,0,0.25*(B40+C36))))
```

(This entry is written for column C, the first month's column. It is written with relative cell references so that when copied to the right it works correctly for every month.)

This nested set of @IF functions works as follows:

- The first @IF determines Tax for months before the venture becomes profitable, and passes other situations on to the second @IF. This first @IF determines whether the current month is or is not profitable. If the month is not profitable, Tax is zero; otherwise, the function continues to the second @IF.

- The second @IF determines Tax for months after the venture is profitable and has made enough profit so that there are no more past losses to subtract in figuring Tax and passes remaining situations on to the third @IF. This second @IF gets applied only if the first @IF determines that the current month is profitable. For each such month, if the second @IF determines that cumulative past profits are non-negative (no past losses to subtract), Tax is 25% of the month's profit; otherwise, the function continues to the third @IF.

- The third @IF determines Tax for the two remaining situations, where there is profit this month but cumulative past loss to subtract. This third @IF gets applied only in these situations, after the first @IF has determined the current month profitable and the second @IF has determined there are cumulative losses to subtract. If the third @IF determines that cumulative past losses exceed current month's profit, Tax is zero; otherwise, Tax is applied to the excess of current profit above cumulative past losses.

Caution

Whenever you create a complex @IF function, test it, for each combination of true and false test-condition results.

For each situation the @IF function should handle differently, define tests for which you can think out the right answers or figure them out easily. Then see if the @IF delivers the right answer for each case.

As you build nested @IF functions, they quickly become challenging to proofread, as the @IF example for income tax demonstrates. But any mistake, even a single typo, can result in wrong answers that you and others may not know are wrong. And depending on the purpose of the worksheet, wrong answers can lead to very costly planning and decision mistakes. In the venture example above, a typo in the @IF function could lead the venture team to underestimate cash needs to finance the venture to self-sufficiency, and later when the venture runs out of cash, raising more cash may be far more costly or not possible—a very costly typo.

After making this entry in the Tax row of column C, you copy it to the right for subsequent months. With its relative cell references, each month's copy works correctly for that month, using the Pretax Profit figure for its month and the Cum Pretax Profit figure from its prior month.

Now the entries for the profit and Tax rows shown in figure 18.7 are completed. These rows are at the bottom of your venture plan, shown earlier in figure 18.6. The Pretax Profit numbers for which they calculate Tax and Net Profit are those of your venture plan. So now, whenever you enter a new test number in the plan's cell C4 for Units Growth/month (refer to fig. 18.6) these rows show resulting month-by-month profit-and-tax figures for your venture with the new Units Growth/month number you just entered.

Troubleshooting

I have situations requiring one decision based on multiple tests, such as "if A and B or if C do thing 1, otherwise do thing 2." Can I do this with @IF?

Yes. By using @IF with nesting and/or complex operators such as #AND#, you can define complex tests and often have several ways of expressing them.

To illustrate, here are three ways of expressing the test you stated:

@IF(A,@IF(B,1,@IF(C,1,2)),@IF(C,1,2))	Done with nesting
@IF(A#AND#B#OR#C,1,2)	Done with complex operators
@IF(A#AND#B,1,@IF(C,1,2))	Done with combination

The first says: If A is true, then if B is true do 1, and otherwise if C is true do 1 and otherwise do 2; if A is false, then if C is true do 1 and otherwise do 2.

The second says: If A and B are true or C is true do 1, otherwise do 2.

The third says: If A and B are true do 1; otherwise, if C is true do 1 and otherwise do 2.

They all say the same thing in different ways. In this case, the second is clearest. All three are presented to illustrate alternative approaches that may fit other situations better, and to give you examples so that for each situation you can use whatever approach you find easiest to think out.

Using Functions To Find and Analyze Data in Tables

From the descriptions of all functions in Chapter 5, you can see that in the lookup and database function categories, 1-2-3 for Windows offers you an extensive set of tools for obtaining and analyzing data in tables. With these functions you can obtain data contained in data tables and develop from data tables valuable *new* information that the data tables do not display, through the data-*analysis* powers of these functions.

◄ "Lookup Functions," p. 201

◄ "Database Functions," p. 153

As with other tools, you can multiply the powers and value of these functions by using them in combination with other tools and powers of 1-2-3 for Windows. For example, from a giant sales-department data table with many columns of data on sales to every customer, you can extract a concise table of regional sales totals by product line and turn it into a bar graph.

To make effective use of these functions—and also to make your data tables themselves as clear as possible when you and others look at them—you should first make sure that the data table has meaningful headings for both the columns and the rows. Figure 18.9 shows, in its lower two-thirds, a table similar to that in figure 18.5, with columns of data added, but now it is revised to show meaningful headings for both the columns and the rows.

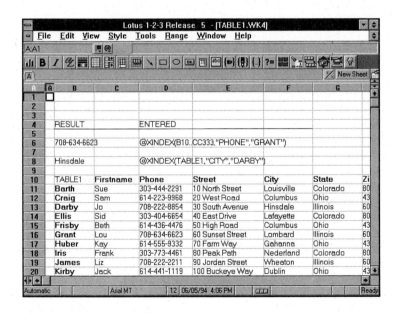

Fig. 18.9
Use the @XINDEX function to get the data from any column and row.

Now, if you say what column and row you want data from, such as "the data from the Grant row of the phone column," it's clear to you and other people what you're after. And when you get the unit of data, it is clear to you and other people what it is: it is Grant's phone number. At the same time, your column and row headings enable you to make full use of the data-getting and data-analysis powers of lookup and database functions.

Using Functions To Find Data in Tables

Tip

For most users, the best lookup function for getting data from a column and row is @XINDEX.

Chapter 5 shows you that, for the specific purpose of getting the data in a specified column-and-row of a table, 1-2-3 for Windows offers you four lookup functions: @HLOOKUP, @VLOOKUP, @INDEX, and @XINDEX. But unless you have specific reasons for doing otherwise, the most practical approach is to learn and use @XINDEX and ignore the others. Compared to all the others, @XINDEX has the very important advantage of permitting you to specify both column and row in whatever headings are most meaningful to you. And compared to @HLOOKUP and @VLOOKUP, @XINDEX also has the advantage of applicability for three-dimensional multi-worksheet tables.

Using @XINDEX To Find Data from a Specified Column and Row

Say the table in figure 18.9 is huge, with hundreds of rows of names all the way to worksheet row 333 and scores of columns with data for each row all the way to worksheet row CC. If you want Grant's phone number, in a blank cell you make an @XINDEX entry like this

@XINDEX(B10..CC333,"PHONE","GRANT")

This @XINDEX function entry delivers the contents of a cell in the row titled GRANT and the column titled PHONE in range B10..CC333. In the cell where you make this entry, Grant's phone number appears. See figure 18.9, row 6. The @INDEX was entered in cell B6 and Grant's phone number appears there. The @INDEX entry is shown to its right.

You can make it easier to use functions with data tables by giving each data table's range (its rectangle of worksheet cells) a range name. Instead of having to determine and type in the table's upper left and lower right cell addresses, such as B10..CC333, each time you use a function with the table, you can just enter the table's range name. In figure 18.9, row 6 shows this more convenient approach. The table's range has been named TABLE1. Now, to get the data for what city Darby lives in, you enter

@XINDEX(TABLE1,"CITY","DARBY")

In B8, 1-2-3 for Windows displays Darby's city, Hinsdale. See figure 18.9. The @XINDEX shown at right was entered in B8 and Hinsdale appears there.

You may deal with data tables in which the column headings correspond to the column *numbers*—1 for first column, 2 for the second, 3 for the third, and so on. Or the row headings may match row *numbers*. This may be true for both the columns and the rows. Figure 18.10 shows a table of price-discount percentages for a fastener company in which both the column headings and the row headings correspond to the columns' and rows' numbers.

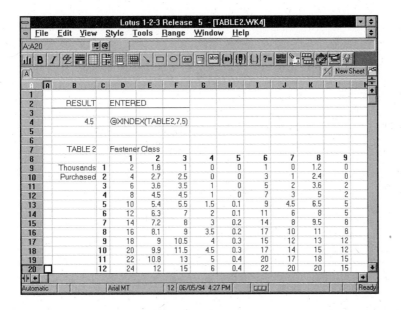

Fig. 18.10
Get data from a column and row with @XINDEX when the columns and rows are numbered 1, 2, 3, and so on.

When you have a set of data that you could organize in a data table so that the most meaningful headings for the columns or rows are the column or row numbers, it's helpful to do so. If your data is grouped by product class, name the product classes with numbers so that their row or column headings are the rows' or columns' numbers, like the column headings for numbered fastener classes in figure 18.10. If the columns or rows represent values that can be defined with numbers that correspond to the column or row numbers, do so. In figure 18.10, each row actually represents $1,000 more than the preceding row, but in such a case you can make the row headings match the row numbers by defining the overall label for what each row's number represents, such as thousands of dollars in the fastener-company table in figure 18.10.

For columns or rows in which the headings match the column or row numbers, 1-2-3 and so on, when you use @XINDEX, you can specify such numbered column or row headings without the double-quotes. To obtain the data in column 7 and row 5 of the fastener company's data table in figure 18.10, you can use @XINDEX with column and row headings without the double-quotes.

```
@XINDEX(TABLE2,7,5)
```

If you make this @XINDEX entry in cell B4, in that cell the contents of the table's column 7 and row 5 appear (refer to fig. 18.10).

When you use @XINDEX this way, specifying column or row by number without quotes, it's important to understand and keep in mind how @XINDEX uses these numbers. When numbers without double-quotes are entered for column and row, @XINDEX does not actually pay any attention to your headings, instead it interprets the number as a *value*, and uses it to *count* its way out to the column or row. These numbers are called *offset numbers*, and what they mean is how many columns or rows to go from the upper left cell of the table's range, where the column and row headings meet, which is considered zero for both column and row.

So if your headings deviate in any way from consecutive numbers starting with 1, the column or row from which @XINDEX gets the data may not be the column headed by the number you entered in the @XINDEX argument. On the other hand, the fact that @XINDEX treats these argument numbers as values instead of text opens possibilities for expressing them through formulas based on other value data anywhere in the worksheet—even in other worksheets or files.

Using Functions with Criteria Arguments To Find Data

You can also get data items from data tables with the three database functions @DGET, @DMIN, and @DMAX. Chapter 5 describes the three-argument system that is common to these and other database functions—range, field, and criteria—providing you a description, use, and example for each of the functions.

With these database functions, along with others addressed later in this chapter that analyze data tables to produce new information, the key power is *criteria*.

In use of @XINDEX (or other lookup functions), the arguments you specify are range (table), column, and row. With @DGET, @DMIN, and @DMAX, and with other database functions, the first two arguments are also range (table) and column (which database functions call field). But the third argument is not row—it is *criteria*, which you can define as a test of the contents of any cell in any column of rows, and in which you can use logical operators.

Figure 18.11 shows a corner of a huge table in which a company maintains extensive current sales-related records. As a first step toward analysis of data in this table using functions, you give this table's range a range name, such as TABLE1.

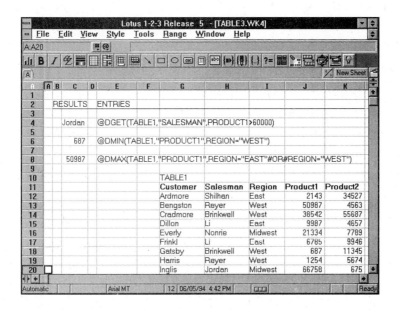

Fig. 18.11
Get data from data table cells with functions using criteria.

Rows 4, 6, and 8 of figure 18.11 show the entries and results for @DGET, @DMIN, and @DMAX. In these examples, and in database functions generally, the number-one key to what you can do is the criteria argument.

Imagine that the vice president of sales just heard that somebody has sold over $60,000 of product 1, and he wants to know who, right away. Using @DGET, enter **@DGET(TABLE1,"SALESMAN",PRODUCT1>60000)**. In the @DGET function you enter the first two arguments specifying the table you want a cell's contents from and specifying that you want it from the Salesman row. Then, to make the salesman the row that has Product1 sales of over $60,000 enter **PRODUCT1>60000** for the criteria argument.

The cell where you enter this @DGET function displays the name of the salesman with Product1 sales over $60,000 (see cell C4 of fig. 18.11).

This @DGET example is a basic illustration of the power of database function criteria that you can apply very quickly and easily. You can define the row from which you want the salesman-column contents in terms of a test of content of the rows of *another* column. To define the test for the contents of rows of the other column, you can use *logical operators*, such as > (greater-than).

In the @DMIN function, the *function itself* is a criterion of whatever cells the arguments define, this function delivers the one with the smallest value. So the criteria argument does not have to be narrow enough to designate a single cell. In the @DMIN function in row 6 of figure 18.11, the first argument defines the table, Table1; the second defines the column (field), the Product1 column; and the criteria argument defines a subset of the table's rows—all those in which the region is West. In figure 18.11, you enter this function in cell C6; and then, of all the values in the cells defined by the three arguments—Table1's Product1 column in West rows—this function delivers the smallest of these values.

Similarly, the @DMAX function delivers the largest value in the set of cells defined by its arguments.

In the @DMAX example in figure 18.11 row 8, the criteria argument has two tests joined by the complex operator `#OR#`. The criteria argument is:

```
REGION="EAST"#OR#REGION="WEST"
```

(Note that the test on each side of the `#OR#` has to be expressed *completely*, on its own. If you hope the first `REGION=` applies to both sides of the `#OR#`, and entered **REGION="EAST"#OR#"WEST"**, it would not work.)

This criterion includes items from all the rows where either of these two tests is met—in this case, it includes data from both East rows and West rows. When enter this @DMAX function, the cell where you make the entry (C8) shows the result, the highest value in the Product1 column where the region is either East or West. This result appears in figure 18.11's cell C8.

Through full and creative use of criteria, you can develop very powerful abilities to extract data from data tables. You learn more about use of criteria, and see more examples, in the material on analyzing data tables that comes next.

Using Functions To Analyze Data in Tables

With the database functions that 1-2-3 for Windows provides, you can very quickly and easily perform analyses of the contents of entire columns of data tables. (For basic information on these functions and their common trio of arguments—range, field, criteria—see Chapter 5.) For a data table column (field), you can use these functions to determine or analyze the following:

Number of items	@DCOUNT delivers total item-count.
	@DPURECOUNT counts the values.
Total of values	@DSUM delivers total of values.

You can complete Analysis Table B with the same steps, using the @DAVG function entry shown in figure 18.12's upper right in row 6. In Analysis Table B, make this entry in cell C13. Copy this entry down the Product1 column, and in each row edit the third argument to specify that row's salesman. Then copy the Product1 column entries to the Product2 column, and edit each Product2 column entry's second argument to make it specify Product2. That completes Analysis Table B—this table will now also show the correct result in every cell, as shown in figure 18.12's lower left.

With the full set of database functions provided by 1-2-3 for Windows, from big tables of raw data you can quickly and easily develop full sets of analysis tables that deliver high business information value very concisely.

Using Criteria Power Fully

The preceding examples illustrate a powerful and valuable data-table analysis capability that the criteria argument gives to database functions. In a column include only items in rows where another column has particular contents. For example, in summing values in the Product1 field, include only values on rows where the Region column says East or where the Salesman column says Shilhan.

But this is just the beginning of the power and value that the criteria argument gives to the database functions offered for analysis of data tables. In expressing criteria for the analyses to be performed by these functions, you can use the same logic-test operators that you can use with the @IF function, summarized earlier in this chapter. You can use the comparison operators, such as < (less-than) and > (greater-than). You can also use the complex operators expressed in words enclosed in ## (pound signs), such as #AND#, which enables you to set multiple criteria for any of the analyses. With these powers that the criteria argument provides, the database functions offer you opportunities to apply your creativity to achieve nearly unlimited capability to analyze data tables and develop maximum business-information value from data table contents, far beyond what the raw data in the big data tables themselves actually show.

Figure 18.13 shows two examples of use of logic operators in criteria of database analysis functions. In the entry numbered 1, the function calls for a sum of values in the Product2 field on rows in which the `PRODUCT2>10000` criterion is met.

Fig. 18.13

Use logical operators in database-function criteria for increased data table analysis power.

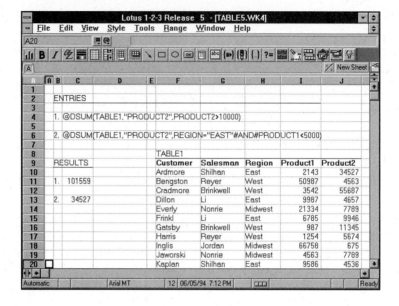

When you enter the @DSUM function entry with this criterion argument in cell C11, 1-2-3 for Windows sums all values in the Product2 column that exceed 10,000 and delivers the result, shown in that cell in figure 18.13. (For this example, all the values that meet the criteria have been located in the part of the table shown in the figure so you can check the results.)

In the entry numbered 2, shown on row 6 and to be entered in cell C13 in figure 18.13, the function again calls for a sum of values in the Product2 field, this time including the values on rows in which two criteria are both met.

```
REGION="EAST"#AND#PRODUCT1<5000
```

When you enter the @SUM function with this criteria argument in cell C13, 1-2-3 for Windows sums all values in the Product2 field in rows where both conditions are met—the region is East and the Product1 value is less than 5,000—and delivers the result, as shown in that cell in figure 18.13.

Obtaining Information Value from Data Tables

With modern computer capacities and powers, businesses have or can have almost infinite amounts of data and almost infinite power to process it all. But delivering maximum business information value depends on effective communication to people of the information that can help them most. This requires accessing the right raw data, then sifting, selecting, manipulating, analyzing, and boiling down the data so that what counts most isn't hidden in floods of less important data—and effective communication so that people grasp and remember the information that can help them most.

For turning data into business-information value, 1-2-3 for Windows provides you a marvelously broad combination of powerful tools. And for obtaining business information value from data tables, functions described or mentioned in this chapter are some of the best. But as with other individual features of 1-2-3 for Windows, the number one key to achieving highest business-information value is to apply combinations of these tools and powers.

From data tables, you can go a long way in developing business-information value by using functions to develop concise data-analysis tables along the lines suggested by the preceding examples—or perhaps very differently from these examples, depending on what you and your audience need. By combined use of these functions together with other 1-2-3 powers, you can make these analyses more valuable. For example, by going from the data table to Analysis Table A, as was shown in figure 18.12, and then using 1-2-3 for Windows chart capabilities to turn the analyses into vivid visual communication, you can make the information value you developed with the functions more clear, appealing, and memorable to the managers.

Figure 18.14 illustrates this process: from big data table, to concise analysis developed with functions, to visual communication of the analysis with a graph. At the lower right is a table of raw data, and at the upper left is Analysis Table A developed from the data table using functions, all as described

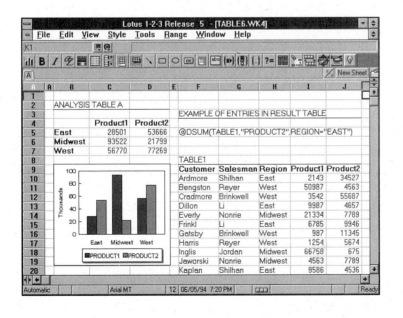

Fig. 18.14
Going from a table of raw data to most-effective delivery of business information value, using the database functions together with the charting capabilities of 1-2-3 for Windows.

previously and shown earlier in figure 18.12. In figure 18.14 these items are shown together with a graph of the values in the analysis table.

Once you have developed the analysis table, you can use charting powers of 1-2-3 for Windows to create and refine a graphic picture of your analysis in minutes. See Part II, "Working with Charts."

Creating What-If Tables

Of all the powers offered by 1-2-3 for Windows and all the things it enables or helps you do, the greatest potential value to businesses is what-if analysis to explore future possibilities. By using formulas that calculate key results (such as profit and cash flow) for various combinations of things a business decides (such as a marketing plan) and things the business predicts (such as resulting sales), and then changing numbers to explore what-ifs, a business can do better at choosing the key decisions that promise the best for the future and at preparing for what the results may be.

You can use the same powers and methods in major personal decisions, such as home and auto purchase and financing, stock and other investments, and overall financial planning.

Tip

To create what-if tables faster, while building far more valuable worksheet skills, ignore the What-if Table dialog box. See the section headed "Creating What-If Tables with Worksheet Skills" further on in this chapter.

For summarizing maximum what-if power most consisely and clearly, the most valuable of all the powers offered by 1-2-3 for Windows is the what-if table. In a what-if table, you can see the effects on one or more goal-results (such as profit and cash flow) of numerous possibilities for one key factor (such as sales); or you can see effects on one goal-result (such as profit) of many possible combinations of two or three key factors (such as sales, cost-per-unit, and advertising expense).

With 1-2-3 for Windows, you can create what-if tables in either of two ways. You can use the What-if Table dialog box, which you reach from the menu via **R**ange **A**nalyze **W**hat-if Table, after setting up your worksheet according to rules for use of this approach, as described next. Or you can set up what-if tables without the dialog box through use of basic universal worksheet powers, as described further on in this chapter.

Either way, for exploring what-if tables and their creation, it's a good idea to start with what-if tables for loans, using simple round numbers. For loans, you can create meaningful tables for one, two, and three variables—amounts of loans, interest rates, and numbers of months or years—and you can use simple formulas or functions. With round numbers, you can see clearly and easily how the results in the table reflect the various what-ifs.

Creating What-If Tables Using the What-if Table Dialog Box

To follow the rules for setting up the worksheet for use of the What-if Table dialog box, you need to understand some terms and concepts.

Understanding Terms and Concepts

A *what-if table* is an on-screen view of information in column format with the field names at the top and contains the results from use of the What-if Table dialog box plus some or all the information used to generate the results.

A *what-if table range* is a worksheet range that contains a what-if table.

A *variable* is a formula component whose value can change.

An *input cell* is a worksheet cell used by 1-2-3 for Windows for temporary storage during calculation of a what-if table set up with the What-if Table dialog box. For this approach, one input cell is required for each variable in the what-if table formula. The cell addresses of the formula variables are the same as the input cells.

An *input value* is a specific value that 1-2-3 for Windows uses for a variable during the what-if table calculations.

The *results area* is the portion of a what-if table in which the calculation results are placed. One result is generated for each combination of input values. The results area of a what-if table must be unprotected, as described in "Protecting and Hiding Worksheet Data," in Chapter 4.

The formulas used in what-if tables can contain values, strings, cell addresses, and functions. You should not use logical formulas because this type of formula always evaluates to either 0 or 1. Although the use of a logical formula in a what-if table does not cause an error, the results generally are meaningless.

Understanding the Three Types of What-If Tables

With the What-if Table dialog box, there are three types of what-if tables that 1-2-3 for Windows can generate. The three table types differ in the numbers of formulas and variables they can reflect. Descriptions of the table types follow:

1 variable	For various values of one variable, shows resulting values of one or more formulas.
2 variables	For various combinations of values of two variables, shows resulting values of one formula.

3 variables | For various combinations of values of three variables, shows resulting values of one formula.

Creating a 1-Variable What-If Table

Tip

In a 1-variable what-if table, the formulas for adjacent columns can be entirely different—such as one for sales, another for profit, a third for cash flow.

A what-if table created with the What-if Table dialog box and specifying 1 variable shows how changing one variable affects the results of one or more formulas.

Suppose that you plan to purchase a house with a 30-year mortgage in the $100,000 to $115,000 range and a 10-percent or 11-percent interest rate. For each interest rate, you want to determine the resulting monthly payment for each price.

Figure 18.15 shows a visual summary of how you set up the table you want. Figure 18.16 shows the result of the setup: for each formula (written for a specific interest rate); figure 18.16 shows a monthly payment for each of the four loan sizes.

Fig. 18.15

Set up a 1-variable what-if table by making worksheet entries and using the What-if Table dialog box.

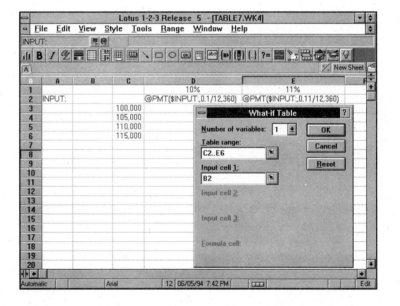

You can set up the kind of table shown in these figures using the What-if Table dialog box by following rules and procedures described next.

Before using the What-if Table dialog box, you must set up the what-if table range and a single input cell.

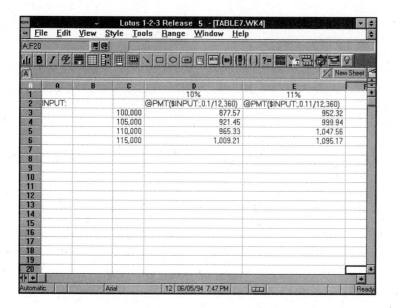

Fig. 18.16
View a 1-variable
what-if table
created through
use of the What-if
Table dialog box

IV

Analyzing the Worksheet

The input cell can be a blank cell anywhere in the worksheet. The best practice is to identify the input cell by entering an appropriate label either above or to the left of the input cell.

The what-if table range is a rectangular worksheet area that can be placed in any empty worksheet location. The size of the what-if table range can be calculated as follows:

- The range has one more column than the number of formulas being evaluated.

- The range has one more row than the number of input values being evaluated.

The general structure of a 1-variable what-if table range is as follows:

- The top left cell in the what-if table range is empty.

- The formulas to be evaluated are entered across the first row. Each formula must refer to the input cell.

- The input values to be plugged into the formulas are entered down the first column.

- After the what-if table is calculated, each cell in the results range contains the result obtained by evaluating the formula at the top of that column with the input value at the left of that row.

For the loan example shown in figures 18.15 and 18.16, use cell B2 as the input cell; identify it with a label in cell A2. You need one formula for each interest rate: The @PMT function can give you the payment information you want, so use it to enter **@PMT($B$2,0.1/12,360)** for the 10-percent interest rate in cell D2.

In cell E2, enter the following formula for the 11-percent interest rate:

    @PMT($B$2,0.11/12,360)

Because payments are monthly, each annual interest rate is divided by 12 to get the monthly interest rate. The 360 is the term of the 30-year loan in months.

Then enter the four possible prices of the house in cells C3 through C6. Select **R**ange **A**nalyze **W**hat-if Table to display the What-if Table dialog box. Specify **1** in the **N**umber of Variables drop-down list box; specify **C2..E6** as the **T**able Range; enter **B2** in the Input Cell **1** text box (see figure 18.15).

Click OK or press Enter to generate the table. The resulting table, which calculates the mortgage payments on four different amounts at two different interest rates, is shown in figure 18.16. Cells D2 and E2 have been formatted as text so that you can see the formulas they contain. Worksheet cells containing numbers have been formatted with appropriate numeric formats, as well.

Creating a 2-Variable What-if Table

A 2-variable what-if table enables you to evaluate a single formula based on changes in two variables.

Suppose that you want to create a what-if table that shows the monthly payments on a $12,000 loan at four interest rates (9, 10, 11, and 12 percent) and three loan periods (24, 36, and 48 months).

Figure 18.17 shows the worksheet entries you make to create a table of these results using the What-if Table dialog box and also shows the results after you have used the dialog box.

To create such a table with the What-if Table dialog box, you carry out the following steps.

To use a 2-variable what-if table, you need two blank input cells—one for each variable. They can be located anywhere in the worksheet and need not be adjacent to each other. The input cells commonly are identified with an appropriate label in a cell next to or above each input cell.

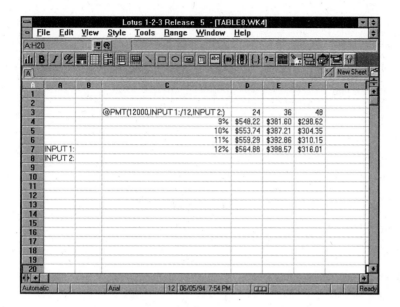

Fig. 18.17
Setting up the worksheet and seeing the results for a 2-variable what-if table created with the What-if Table dialog box.

The size of the what-if table range depends on the number of values of each variable you want to evaluate. The range is one column wider than the number of values of one variable and one row longer than the number of values of the other variable.

When you use the What-if Table dialog box, a major difference between a 1-variable and a 2-variable what-if table is the location of the formula to be evaluated. In a 1-variable table, the formulas are placed along the top row of the table, and the upper left corner is blank. In a 2-variable what-if table, the upper left cell of the what-if table range contains the single formula to be evaluated. This formula must refer to the input cells.

The cells below the formula contain the various input values for one variable. The cells these values occupy are what you specify in the Input Cell **1** text box in the What-if Table dialog box. The cells to the right of the formula contain the various input values for the second variable. The cells these values occupy are what you specify in the Input Cell **2** text box. Be sure that the formula refers correctly to the two input cells so that the proper input values are plugged into the correct part of the formula.

After the what-if table is calculated, each cell in the table range contains the result obtained by evaluating the formula with the input values in that cell's row and column.

To set up a 2-variable what-if table as shown in figure 18.17, first decide on a location for the two input cells. You can use cells B7 and B8. Put identifying labels in the adjacent cells, A7 and A8.

Because you have three values of one variable and four values of the other, the what-if table range is four cells wide by five cells tall in size. Use the range C3..F7 for the table range. Enter the formula **@PMT(12000,B7/12,B8)** in cell C3.

This formula uses the @PMT function to calculate the monthly payment on a $12,000 loan. For the interest-rate argument, the formula uses the annual interest rate supplied in cell B7 and divides it by 12 to get a monthly rate. For the period argument, the formula uses the number of months supplied in cell B8.

Enter the values in the what-if table range. Enter the four interest rates (**9%**, **10%**, **11%**, and **12%**) in the range C4..C7; enter the three loan terms (**24**, **36**, and **48**) in D3..F3. Select **R**ange **A**nalyze **W**hat-if Table; in the What-if Table dialog box, specify **2** as the number of variables; specify **C3..F7** as the table range; enter **B7** as input cell 1; enter **B8** as input cell 2. 1-2-3 for Windows calculates the what-if table (refer to fig. 18.17).

Creating a 3-Variable What-If Table

A 3-variable what-if table shows the effects of changing three variables in a single formula. The three dimensions of a 3-variable what-if table are represented by a three-dimensional worksheet range: the table spans two or more worksheets.

Calculating loan payments is a perfect application for a 3-variable what-if table because the relevant formula uses three variables: principal, interest rate, and term. You can create a what-if table that calculates monthly payments for three or more principal amounts, three or more interest rates, and three or more loan periods.

Worksheet setup for your creation of such a table with the What-if Table dialog box is shown in figure 18.18. The table that results after you use the What-if Table dialog box is shown in figure 18.19.

You can set up a 3-variable what-if table using the What-if Table dialog box with the steps that follow.

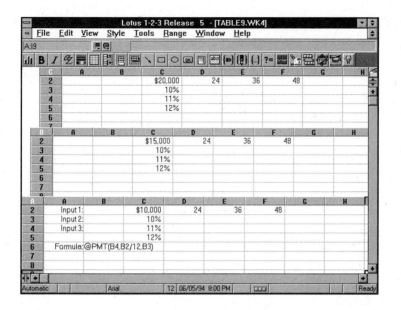

Fig. 18.18
Setting up worksheets for creating a three-dimensional 3-variable what-if table using the What-if Table dialog box.

IV

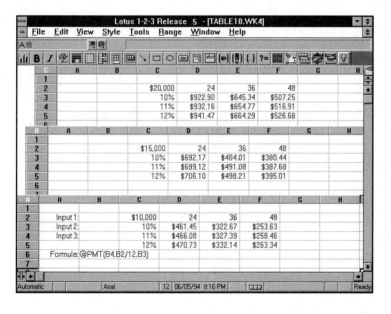

Fig. 18.19
Seeing results in three dimensions in a 3-variable what-if table created with the What-if Table dialog box.

The structure of a 3-variable what-if table is an extension of the 2-variable what-if table structure. The different values of variables 1 and 2 are represented by different rows and columns. The new variable (the third one) is located in the upper left corner of the what-if table range; the different values of the third variable are represented by different worksheets.

A 3-variable what-if table range spans a three-dimensional region. The size of the region is determined as follows:

Number of rows = (values of variable 1) + 1

Number of columns = (values of variable 2) + 1

Number of worksheets = (values of variable 3)

You also need three input cells. These cells can be located anywhere in any worksheet but are often grouped together for convenience. You should identify the input cells with labels in adjacent cells.

The formula evaluated in a 3-variable what-if table must correctly refer to all three input cells. When you fill out the What-if Table dialog box, the Input Cell **1** text box refers to the values in the first column of the what-if table range. Input Cell **2** refers to the values in the first row of the what-if table range. Input Cell **3** refers to the values in the upper left corner of the what-if table range in each worksheet.

To establish a 3-variable what-if table range as shown in figures 18.18 and 18.19, follow these steps:

1. Insert the additional two worksheets you need for this application by selecting **E**dit **I**nsert **S**heet A**f**ter and entering **2** in the Quantity text box. Press Enter or click OK. Then select **V**iew **S**plit **P**erspective, and click OK or press Enter to view all three active worksheets.

2. Refer to the size guidelines for a 3-variable what-if table, given earlier in this section. Use them to decide on an empty worksheet region for the what-if table.

   For this example, you need a what-if table range four rows high, four columns wide, and three worksheets deep. Use the range A:C2..C:F5 to define the table range.

3. In the top worksheet in the first column of the range, enter the values for variable 1 in the second through last cells.

   In this example, the interest rate is variable 1. Enter the three values for the interest rate (**10%**, **11%**, and **12%**) in cells A:C3..A:C5 respectively.

4. In the same worksheet, enter the values for variable 2 in the second through last cells of the first row in the range.

   In this example, the term of the loan is variable 2. Enter the three values for term (**24**, **36**, and **48** months) in cells A:D2..A:F2.

5. Copy the values for variables 1 and 2 to the two other worksheets in the range.

   In this example, copy **A:C2..A:F5** to **B:C2..C:C2**.

6. In the upper left cells of the what-if table range, enter the values for variable 3. Enter a different value in the corresponding cell in each worksheet.

   In this example, the principal is variable 3. Enter the three values for principal (**10000**, **15000**, and **20000**) in cells A:C2, B:C2, and C:C2.

   The range for the what-if table is now established.

7. Select the input cells. Use cells A:B2..A:B4 for input cells 1, 2, and 3. Remember to put identifying labels in cells A:A2..A:A4.

8. Enter the payment formula in any cell outside the what-if table range— for example, in cell A:B6. Use the following 1-2-3 for Windows function for calculating loan payments:

   ```
   @PMT(A:B4,A:B2/12,A:B3)
   ```

   Because payment periods are expressed in months, you divide the annual interest rate by 12 to obtain the monthly interest rate. (Note that when you enter the @PMT function in B6, you see ERR because there are no values in the input cells A:B2..A:B4. Format the cell containing the formula with the Text format to display the formula rather than ERR.) The worksheet now appears as shown in figure 18.18.

9. Select **R**ange **A**nalyze **W**hat-if Table. In the What-if Table dialog box, specify **3** as the number of variables, **A:C2..C:F5** as the table range, **A:B6** as the formula cell, **A:B2** as input cell 1, **A:B3** as input cell 2, and **A:B4** as input cell 3. Click OK or press Enter.

   Format the resulting data table using the Currency format. The results are as shown in figure 18.19.

Caution

When you use the What-if Table dialog box to create 3-variable what-if tables, even the simplest table can take many times the amount of disk space you might expect. For example, the file for the what-if table shown in figure 18.19 takes over 200,000 bytes on disk.

(continues)

(continued)

If you try to save a file that can't fit on your hard disk, serious problems can result, such as your computer's refusing to let you delete any files from the overloaded disk.

This is another reason to use the alternative approach described in the next section for creating what-if tables. Created that way, they take up only a tiny fraction of the same disk space. For example, the file for the 3-variable what-if table presented in the next section, shown in figure 18.21, takes less than 3% of the disk space of the example in figure 18.19.

Creating What-if Tables Using Worksheet Skills

By skipping the What-if Table dialog box and, instead, applying basic powers of the 1-2-3 for Windows worksheet, you can create what-if tables faster and more easily, without taking extra space for input cells and formulas. And in doing so, you develop your abilities to apply worksheet powers that have vastly wider applicability and are, therefore, much more valuable to learn and practice.

Creating a 1-Variable What-If Table

To create a 1-variable what-if table, simply list the various values of the variable in one column; then in the first row of the next column, enter the formula for the result, referring to the cell to its left for the variable, and then copy the formula down beside the variable-values column.

Figure 18.20 shows, in its upper half, an example of creation of such a table for calculation of monthly dollar interest on $10,000 at various interest rates. You list the interest rates in column B, in rows 3-7. In C3, enter **1000*B3/12**. (B3 contains the interest rate for that row.)

Copy this formula down column C beside the other interest rates. The table displays the desired answers, as shown in column C of the upper table.

If you want to see the effects of the various interest rates on more than one result, simply add another column and repeat there, for the second result, what you just did in column C for the first result. To see results of the various interest rates on something else, such as total annual interest, enter its formula in cell D3, again referring to interest rate as cell B3, and copy that formula entry down column D.

The upper half of figure 18.20 shows an example of per-year dollar interest in column D. In the top cell of column D, enter the formula for the annual dollar interest on $10,000 (the same as column C's formula for monthly dollar interest without the /12). Again, express the interest rate by referring to B3. The formula for D3 is shown in figure 18.20 beside the upper table in row 5.

```
10000*B3
```

Copy the formula down column D.

The table displays the answers as shown in column D of figure 18.21's upper table.

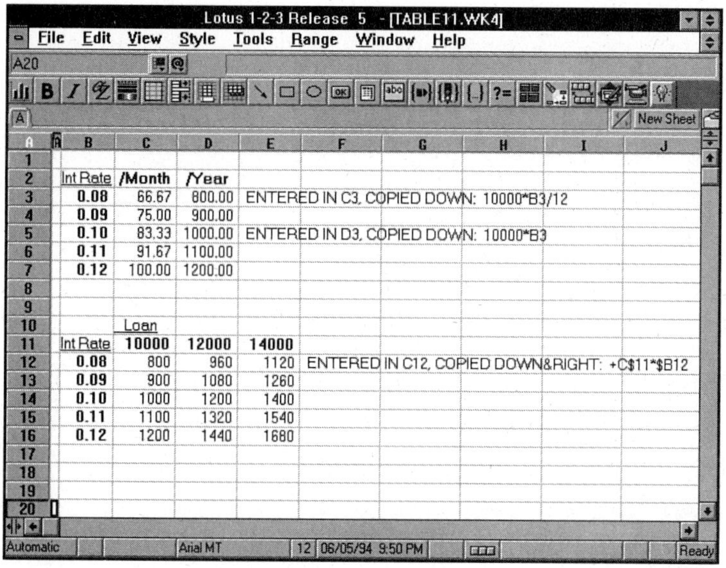

	B	C	D	E	F	G	H	I	J
1									
2	Int Rate	/Month	/Year						
3	0.08	66.67	800.00	ENTERED IN C3, COPIED DOWN: 10000*B3/12					
4	0.09	75.00	900.00						
5	0.10	83.33	1000.00	ENTERED IN D3, COPIED DOWN: 10000*B3					
6	0.11	91.67	1100.00						
7	0.12	100.00	1200.00						
8									
9									
10		Loan							
11	Int Rate	10000	12000	14000					
12	0.08	800	960	1120	ENTERED IN C12, COPIED DOWN&RIGHT: +C$11*$B12				
13	0.09	900	1080	1260					
14	0.10	1000	1200	1400					
15	0.11	1100	1320	1540					
16	0.12	1200	1440	1680					
17									
18									
19									
20									

Fig. 18.20
Creating 1-variable and 2-variable what-if tables through multipurpose worksheet skills.

Creating a 2-Variable What-If Table

For a 2-variable what-if table (for a single result-goal), you can do the setup even faster, by applying relative and absolute cell references.

For example, the lower half of figure 18.20 is a 3 x 5 table of annual dollar interest at various combinations of loan amount and interest rate. To create this table, first set up the framework of the two variables as the row and column headings: list the interest rate values in column B as you did for the upper table, this time in rows 12-16; and in column-heading row 11, starting in column C, enter the various loan amounts, as shown in the lower table in figure 18.20.

Next, to provide a single formula that works for all the answers, in the first answer cell (the upper left, in this case C12), enter **+C$11*$B12**, which is the formula for the annual-dollar-interest result.

This formula expresses annual dollar interest as the loan amount directly above the formula's cell in C11 times the interest rate directly to left in B12. Note the use of $ for absolute references:

■ In the first cell-reference, for loan amount, the column-letter C does not have a preceding $, so as you copy the formula to the right, the letter keeps changing to refer to the loan amount directly above in its own column. But the row-number 11 does have a preceding $ for absolute, so if you copy it down, it keeps referring to row 11 where all the loan amounts are.

■ In the second cell-reference, for interest rate, the use of $ is analogous but reversed, so it applies to column instead of row. The column-letter B does have a preceding $ for absolute reference, so as you copy the formula to the right, it keeps referring to column B where all the interest rates are located. But the row-number 12 does not have a preceding $, so as you copy it downward it keeps changing its row to refer to the interest rate directly to its left.

Now, by simply copying this cell to all other results cells—first copy it downward in row C and then copy row C rightward to D and E—you can complete the entire two-variable what-if table.

The answers appear in all columns and rows as shown in the lower table in figure 18.20.

Creating a 3-Variable What-If Table

With almost no additional work—still just one formula—you can create a 3-variable what-if table in three dimensions on three worksheets (see fig. 18.21).

Figure 18.21 contains the worksheet A showing the same two-variable table as the preceding figure 18.20, but figure 18.21 adds the use of multiple worksheets to show effects of a third variable, number of years.

First, add blank worksheets B and C and position them on the display (see fig. 18.21). From the Edit menu, choose **I**nsert, and in the Insert dialog box, choose **S**heet and a**f**ter and for Quantity enter 2, to add two worksheets, B and C. Then from the **V**iew menu, choose **S**plit, and in the Split dialog box choose **P**erspective, so the three worksheets are positioned on-screen as in figure 18.21.

Tip
Use what-if tables like these to compare alternatives in your personal finances: home and auto purchase/loan/ lease, investments in stock, and other investments.

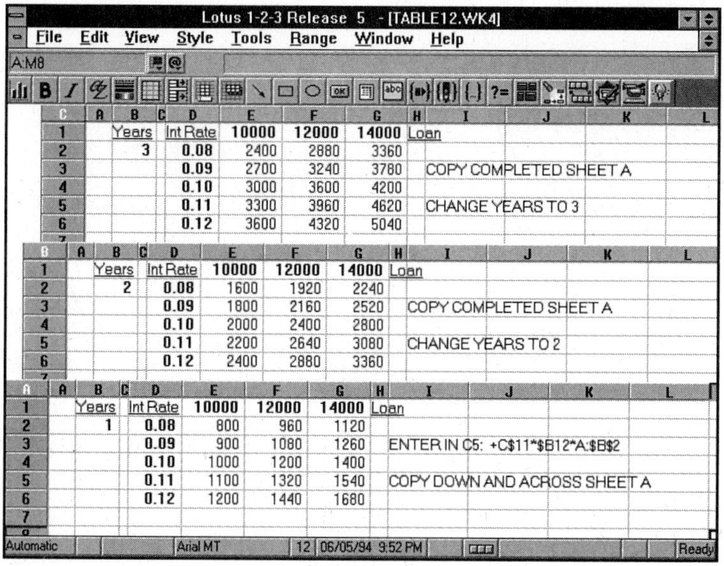

Fig. 18.21
Create a 3-variable
what-if table
through multipur-
pose worksheet
skills.

Tip
If you are con-
cerned with plan-
ning or analysis of
budgets, profits,
or investments,
put what-if tables
at the top of your
list of worksheet
skills to become
an expert on.

For a 3-variable what-if table, setup is so similar to that of a 2-variable table
that if you set up the 2-variable table in the lower half of figure 18.20, you
can do almost all the setup for figure 18.21 by copying. Start by setting up
the table for worksheet A, which you then copy to worksheets B and C.
Locate the table at the very top of worksheet A, with the loan-amounts row
across the very top so that you can see as much as possible of all three tables
when the worksheets are displayed together. Locate the interest-rate column
in D so that you have space to the left for specification of the third variable,
the number of years, which is used in the formula and also serves to label the
three worksheets.

The column and row headings for worksheet A are exactly the same as in
figure 18.20, interest rates down the left and loan amounts across the top,
and the formula is very similar, so you can just copy into the new worksheet
A the entire lower table from figure 18.21, locating it so that interest rates are
in D2 to D6 and loan amounts are in E1 to G1, as in worksheet A in figure
18.21.

In the upper left result cell of the table in worksheet A, cell E2, you want to
enter the formula incorporating $ for absolute cell references in such ways
that when copied, this single formula returns the correct result in every result
cell of all three worksheet tables. The formula shown in lower right in figure
18.21 does it:

    +E$2*$D3*A:$B$2

This is exactly the same formula that you entered for the 2-variable what-if table in figure 18.21, with the same selective use of $ for column and row references, but it multiplies each column-and-row product (loan times interest rate) by A:$B$2. What this new part of the formula does is multiply by the number of years shown in this worksheet's cell B2. This cell reference has $ before column-letter and also before row-number, making the column-and-row parts of the years cell reference absolute, so as you copy the formula down and across this worksheet, it keeps referring to this worksheet's cell B2 where number of years is located. But the years-cell reference does not have a $ before the A: for worksheet, so when you copy the whole table to worksheets B and C, those tables use whatever years numbers you enter in their B2 cells.

Now you copy this formula to all the rest of the result cells in the table in worksheet A—copy the formula in E2 down worksheet A's E column, and then copy the column-E cells rightward to columns F and G. In worksheet A, the table returns all the results, just like those in the 2-variable table, as shown in the bottom third of figure 18.21.

To enter the tables for worksheets B and C that add the effects of a third variable, copy the table in worksheet A to worksheets B and C, and then change number of years to 2 in worksheet B's cell B2 and to 3 in worksheet C's cell B2. As soon as you do this, you've completed the 3-variable what-if table. Worksheets B and C show complete table results for two and three years respectively, corresponding to worksheet A's table of results for one year, as shown in figure 18.21.

The Key to Creating What-if Tables

1-2-3 for Windows provides you with an extensive set of fundamental, universal tools that can be applied and combined to do an extremely wide range of things just as you want them done—for example, relative and absolute cell references. 1-2-3 for Windows also has special-purpose tools to do particular things you could do faster and more flexibly with its universal tools. For example, the What-if Table dialog box.

Whenever you can, it is far better to do the job with the universal tools. Generally, this way you have more power to tailor the results to just what you want, and you are building your expertise with far more valuable skills that you can use for many other tasks and purposes.

Compared to using the What-if Table dialog box, with the universal-worksheet-skills approach you avoid a whole series of special procedures and steps that have no other application, and replace them with a single step, an entry in one cell:

In the top left result cell of the first-worksheet table, enter the formula with selective use of $ in the cell-references to the variables so that when copied to the other result cells, the formula returns the right answer for every cell.

(For one-variable tables with multiple formula rows, do this in the top result cell of each column.)

Here are the rules for use of $ in the formula's cell-references to each of the variables:

Location of Values for the Variable	Example in Figure 18.21	Use of $ in References to the Variable
Listed down side	Interest rate	Before column-letter
Listed across top	Loan amount	Before row-number
Different on each worksheet	Number of years	Before column-letter and row-number

Not only is this manual approach of creating what-if tables much simpler, faster, and more compact in your worksheets, use of it builds your expertise in use of relative and absolute cell references in formulas. This is an essential and critically valuable skill for almost every use of 1-2-3 for Windows with numbers: budgets, sales plans, business projections and predictions, profit plans, and so on.

From Here...

For more information related to manipulating and analyzing data with 1-2-3 for Windows, see the following chapters and sections of this book.

On manipulating and analyzing data tables:

- Chapter 5, "Using Functions"—especially the sections on "Lookup Functions" and on "Database Functions."

- Chapters 25 on "Sorting Data," 26 on "Finding and Extracting Data," and 27 on "Understanding Advanced Data Management."

On analyzing quantitative data:

- Chapter 21, "Solving Problems with Solver and Backsolver."

- Chapter 22, "Managing Multiple Solutions With the Version Manager."

On presenting results of data manipulations and analyses:

- Chapters 11-14 in Part II, "Working with Charts."

- Chapters 16 on "Adding Graphics to Worksheets" and 17 on "Developing Business Presentations."

Chapter 19

Linking and Consolidating Worksheets

In essentially the same way that you can relate data in different cells in a worksheet, you can relate data in cells of different worksheets, not only within a file but also in worksheets of different files. In this way, you can increase your worksheet dimensions from two to three.

In this chapter, you learn to do the following:

- Use multiple worksheets and files

- Enter formulas that link worksheets and files

- Combine and consolidate worksheets

What Do Multiple Worksheets and Files Offer?

For any worksheet application except the smallest, you can multiply your worksheet power by using multiple worksheets and files.

Because computer displays and software-manual pages are two-dimensional, they are good at showing the power of the single 2-D worksheet, but they are not as good at showing how the third dimension of multiple worksheets and files multiplies worksheet power. By going beyond the standard 2-D view, thinking of your worksheets and your projects in 3-D, you can improve every quality of your spreadsheet work, from data organization to analysis to management and information control.

◀ "Reorganizing
Worksheets,"
p. 273

◀ "Managing
Files," p. 281

The top two sketches in figure 19.1 show how worksheet value is multiplied by the *second* dimension. With a single dimension (columns), spreadsheet use is limited; adding the second dimension (rows) truly multiplies spreadsheet value. The third sketch shows that with multiple worksheets and files you add a *third* dimension to multiply power and value again. For your work on larger data systems and analyses, going from two dimensions to three can be as valuable as going from one to two.

Fig. 19.1
Envisioning
multiplied 3-D
power from the
use of multiple
worksheets and
files.

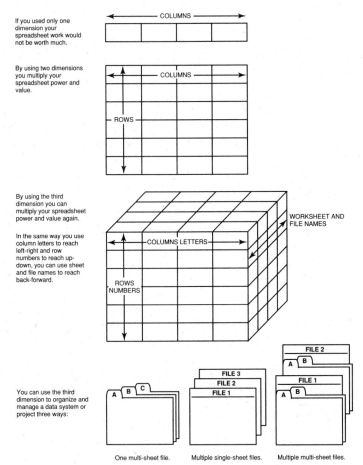

The third sketch in figure 19.1 also shows how you can increase the dimensions of your work from two to three. To use the most important capability of worksheets—relating items of data through formulas—in a single 2-D worksheet you use cell references to *reach* left to right and up and down to locate a data item. You reach left and right with column letters, and up and down with row numbers. In the same way, by including worksheet and file specifications in references to data items, you can extend your reach from two dimensions to three.

In addition, for any project or body of information, the third dimension of multiple worksheets and files gives you powers of organization and management that single-worksheet columns and rows do not provide. As the three sketches at the bottom of figure 19.1 show, when you use the third dimension, you can organize and control the project or information by creating separate worksheet files, a 3-D set of worksheets in a single file, or multiple 3-D sets of worksheets grouped in separate files.

When Should You Use Multiple Worksheets and Files?

Types of work in which you can gain major benefits by using multiple worksheets include the following:

- *Multiple similar reports*. If you are dealing with numerous identical-format reports, such as reports for several products or divisions of a company or reports for a sequence of months, using a separate worksheet for each report enables you to organize and handle the reports easily. For example, you can give each report item the same address in every report worksheet, such as C3 for each product's sales. You can display and manipulate multiple reports easily and clearly by using perspective for worksheets within a file or by tiling or cascading the file windows, using worksheet tabs or file-window title bars for clear report-by-report labeling (see fig. 19.2).

- *Complex analysis*. If you are developing a complex analysis, you can use multiple worksheets to organize the analysis and output for other people. For a complex what-if analysis, you can use one or more worksheets for the output that managers will see; you can use other worksheets to keep your underlying analysis organized—for example, using one worksheet for input plans and assumptions, another for output goal measures, a third for the formulas and other entries that translate inputs into outputs, and a fourth for tables of data used in the calculations (such as tax rates).

Tip

For fullest display of multiple worksheets and files, choose **V**iew Set View **P**references and eliminate unneeded screen items. (For display of linked files, however, keep the status bar. See "Updating and Recalculating File Links" later in this chapter.)

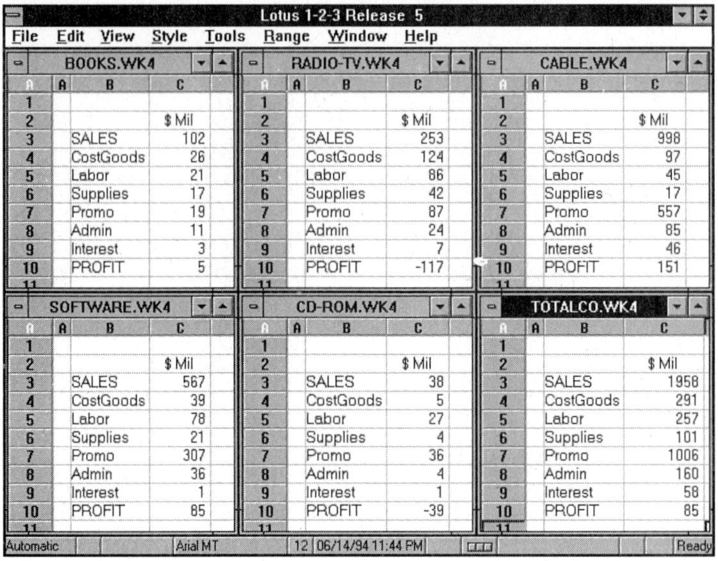

Fig. 19.2

For reports on several divisions or months, with multiple worksheets you can give each item the same cell in every report, and use worksheet tabs or file title bars for report names.

	A	B	C		A	B	C		A	B	C
		BOOKS.WK4				RADIO-TV.WK4				CABLE.WK4	
1											
2			$ Mil				$ Mil				$ Mil
3		SALES	102			SALES	253			SALES	998
4		CostGoods	26			CostGoods	124			CostGoods	97
5		Labor	21			Labor	86			Labor	45
6		Supplies	17			Supplies	42			Supplies	17
7		Promo	19			Promo	87			Promo	557
8		Admin	11			Admin	24			Admin	85
9		Interest	3			Interest	7			Interest	46
10		PROFIT	5			PROFIT	-117			PROFIT	151
		SOFTWARE.WK4				CD-ROM.WK4				TOTALCO.WK4	
1											
2			$ Mil				$ Mil				$ Mil
3		SALES	567			SALES	38			SALES	1958
4		CostGoods	39			CostGoods	5			CostGoods	291
5		Labor	78			Labor	27			Labor	257
6		Supplies	21			Supplies	4			Supplies	101
7		Promo	307			Promo	36			Promo	1006
8		Admin	36			Admin	4			Admin	160
9		Interest	1			Interest	1			Interest	58
10		PROFIT	85			PROFIT	-39			PROFIT	85

Tip

Make it your policy to use multiple worksheets for each project that you may refer to later. A single worksheet encourages hard-to-follow entry structure, whereas multiple worksheets encourage clear organization and structure.

Compared with a single giant worksheet analysis, smaller modules are easier to design, understand, and test. By keeping assumptions that you and others may want to change in a worksheet separate from formulas that calculate results, you can eliminate or reduce the risk of accidental damage to the formulas. If you lay out an analysis in different worksheets, you have more flexibility to make each worksheet's column widths right for its contents. By entering names in the worksheet file tabs, you can organize the project in seconds.

■ *Multiple contributors.* If different people are responsible for different parts of the whole, each person can work in his or her worksheet without disturbing work that the other people are doing.

There are further advantages in using separate worksheets in separate files, including the following:

■ *Separate locations.* If different parts of the data system are developed or managed at different locations, each location can use its file without using up disk space for the other locations and without changing the other files.

■ *Protection.* If parts of the project are confidential, you can keep those parts private. Besides ensuring privacy, providing each group a file that contains only nonconfidential data eliminates accidental changes of that data.

■ *Large worksheet projects*. For any project with large computer-memory requirements, use of multiple files can be beneficial. For multiple users of various parts, you can give each user a smaller file that contains just the parts that they need. Even if you are the only user, your use of multiple files may be the key to your handling a large amount of data and analysis on a small computer.

For almost every worksheet project of any size, it is worthwhile to consider these factors and to think about using multiple worksheets and possibly multiple files.

IV

Analyzing the Worksheet

Tip

For maximum ability to display multiple worksheets, use separate files. With separate file windows, you can display more than the single-file maximum of three worksheets, and you have much more control of the display.

> **Caution**
>
> If you work on *combining* or *consolidating* financial or accounting reports of parts of a business, beware of the loose use of these two words in spreadsheet Help systems, manuals, and books. Writers of spreadsheet materials use these two words interchangeably, without any rigorous definition of either term, as though they meant the same thing. In the language of accounting and financial reports, however, these words have precise meanings that have a critical difference. Briefly, in accounting and finance, when you *combine* financial reports and figures for parts of a business, you simply add them. When you *consolidate* reports and figures for parts of a business, however, you first net out transactions between the parts and then add them, so that the result represents all the parts of the business as a unit relative to the whole business's dealings with other parties.

Linking Worksheets and Files with Formulas

To use multiple 1-2-3 for Windows files, the essential skill to learn is using formulas that link files. These formulas are so similar to those that link worksheets that you should think of all multiple-worksheet linkings—single file and multiple files—as a single technique applied in two slightly different ways.

Figures 19.3 and 19.4 show identical formulas for identical uses of identical data in other worksheets, for multiple worksheets within the *same* file (fig. 19.3) and in *different* files (fig. 19.4).

◄ "Entering Formulas," p. 121

Fig. 19.3
In formulas, you
can refer to cells of
other worksheets
by preceding each
cell address with
the worksheet
name or letter and
a colon.

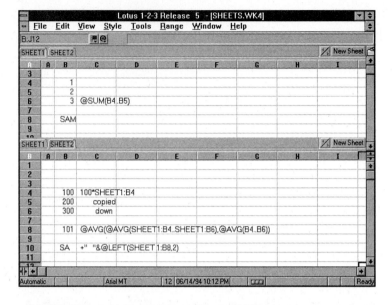

Fig. 19.4
In formulas,
you can refer to
worksheet cells in
other files by
beginning each
worksheet cell
with its file path
and name enclosed
in double angle-
brackets.

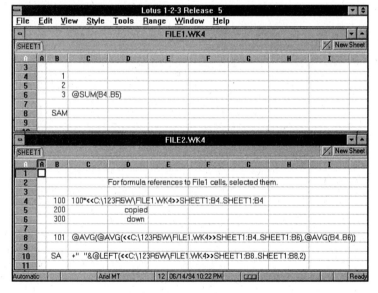

These two figures also show that in formulas, you refer to cells in other
worksheets and files in essentially the same way that you refer to cells in the
same worksheet. Compared with the way you make the cell references for
these figures' examples when all the cells are in the same worksheet, the only
difference is:

- In figure 19.3's references to cells in another worksheet within the same file, each SHEET2 reference to a cell in SHEET1 precedes the cell address with SHEET1: (worksheet name, followed by colon) to specify which worksheet contains the cells.

- In figure 19.4's references to cells in another worksheet in another file, each FILE2 reference to a cell in FILE1 precedes the worksheet name and cell/range reference with <<C:\123R4W\FILE1>> (the file path and name inside double angle-brackets) to specify which file contains the worksheet with the cell or range.

Caution

For linked files, make sure that you understand how 1-2-3 for Windows updates file links and recalculates data-change effects (see "Updating and Recalculating File Links" later in this chapter).

When you work with linked files, 1-2-3 for Windows may stop calculating the effects of your data changes. If you are not aware of how this can occur, you may rely on data that you think has been updated but in fact has not.

The best way for you to enter formula references to another file is to display the file that contains what you want to reference and then select the cell or range that contains that data. When you do this, 1-2-3 for Windows enters the complete, correct other-file reference in the formula: file path and name in double angle-brackets, worksheet name or letter with colon wherever required, and the address of the cell or range you selected.

This method of entering references is much faster and easier than other methods, and it eliminates the likelihood of typos or omitted reference elements.

Figures 19.3 and 19.4 illustrate that you can do all the following things:

- *In a formula, include references to other-worksheet cells in the same file or another file*, the same as with references to cells within a single worksheet.

  In each figure, cell B4 of the bottom worksheet contains a formula (shown to the right of the cell) that says, "100 times a cell in the other worksheet."

IV

Analyzing the Worksheet

Tip
Whenever you type the worksheet-specification part of a reference to another worksheet, even if the worksheet has a name, you can type only the letter that appears in its top-left corner. This method is fast and reduces the chances of typos.

■ *Copy formulas that contain references to other-worksheet cells in the same or another file*, taking advantage of relative references, the same as with references to cells within a single worksheet.

In each figure, cells B5 and B6 of the bottom worksheet contain copies of the formula entered in B4, which contains a relative reference to B4 in the top worksheet. In each figure, the copy of the formula in row 5 of the bottom worksheet refers to the cell in row 5 of the top worksheet, and the copy of the formula in row 6 of the bottom worksheet refers to the cell in row 6 of the top worksheet, as the results in cells B5 and B6 of the bottom worksheet show.

■ *In more complex formulas (such as functions), include references to other-worksheet cells and ranges in the same file or another file*, the same as with references to cells within a single worksheet.

In each figure, cell B8 of the bottom worksheet contains a more complex formula that contains references to top-worksheet cell ranges within functions (shown to the right of B8). In each figure, this B8 entry delivers the correct result, as shown in that cell.

■ *In text formulas and text functions, include references to other-worksheet text cells in the same file or another file*, the same as with references to cells within a single worksheet.

In each figure, cell B10 of the bottom worksheet contains a text formula with a text function that refers to a text cell in the top worksheet. In each figure, this entry delivers the correct result, as shown in B10.

The formulas and formula results shown in figures 19.3 and 19.4 illustrate how you can use formulas that link worksheets and files: wherever you can refer to a cell or range of cells in the same worksheet, you can refer to a cell or range in another worksheet within the same file or in another file.

The formulas in these two figures also illustrate the following rules for entering references to cells and ranges in other worksheets in the same file or another file:

■ *Other worksheet, same file.* In every reference to a cell in another worksheet within the same file, precede the cell address with the worksheet name (in its tab) or letter (in its tab or upper left corner) and a colon, as illustrated in figure 19.3 by the SHEET1: entry preceding each SHEET2 reference to a SHEET1 cell. In each reference, instead of entering **SHEET1:**, you can enter the worksheet's letter, **A:**, shown in its upper left corner.

■ *Other worksheet, other file.* In every reference to a cell or range in another worksheet in another file, precede the sheet name and cell-or-range reference with the file path and name enclosed in double angle brackets, as illustrated in figure 19.4 by the <<C:123R4W\FILE1>> entry preceding each FILE2 reference to a FILE1 cell or range.

Tip

Make your worksheets use not only other worksheets and 1-2-3 files, but also other software products. For ideas, see "Embedding a Freelance Presentation in a 1-2-3 Worksheet" in Chapter 29.

IV

Analyzing the Worksheet

Troubleshooting

For a reference to range B4 to B6 in another worksheet named SHEET1, I entered **SHEET1:B4..B6,** *but it didn't work right. What's wrong?*

When you refer to a range in another worksheet by specifying the range's beginning and ending cell addresses, you should precede each of the two cell addresses with the worksheet name and a colon. If you enter **SHEET1:B4..SHEET1:B6** (with the worksheet name before B6 as well as B4), the reference works.

When I enter the starting and ending cell to refer to a range in a worksheet in another file, do I have to enter the file path and name before each cell, too?

No. When you specify another file's range by its first and last cells, you need only one entry for the file, at the start of the entire range reference.

Notice this difference in figure 19.4, in the range reference in row 8 of FILE2. In this reference, each of the two cell addresses used to specify the range—B4 and B6—begins with SHEET1:, which is the name of the worksheet that contains the range. To specify the file, only one entry—<<C:\123R4W\FILE1>>—appears at the start of the entire range reference.

The figure 19.4 reference cited in this example is the entry that 1-2-3 for Windows makes when you select the referenced range with the mouse instead of typing it. Therefore, this reference appears exactly the way that 1-2-3 for Windows wants references to appear.

Updating and Recalculating File Links

When you use a *user* file with links to a *source* file, you generally want the user file data to reflect the source file's current data. To ensure such currency, unless you have strong reasons for doing otherwise, you should use the following two User Setup settings:

■ In the User Setup dialog box, the Refresh File **L**inks Automatically check box should be marked.

■ In the Recalculation dialog box, the **A**utomatic option button should be marked.

To mark these settings, do the following:

1. Open the **T**ools menu and choose the **U**ser Setup command.

2. The User Setup dialog box appears (see fig. 19.5). Mark Refresh File **L**inks Automatically.

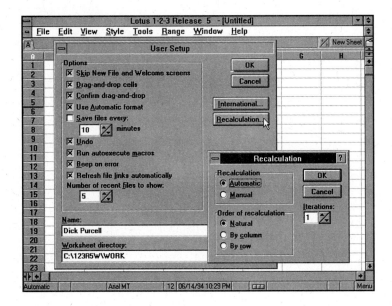

3. In the User Setup dialog box, click the **R**ecalculation button.

4. The Recalculation dialog box appears (see fig. 19.5). Mark **A**utomatic.

5. Click OK in the Recalculation dialog box. Then click OK again in the User Setup dialog box.

If you maintain these settings, a file with links to source files will always use current data from any source file that is either open or on disk in the computer (assuming correct file links).

If you don't want to mark the Refresh File **L**inks Automatically check box, after you open a user file with links to a source file that is on disk but not open, follow these steps to ensure that the user file is using current data from the source file.

1. Open the **E**dit menu and choose the **L**inks command.

2. The Links dialog box appears (see fig. 19.6). Choose File Links from the Link Type drop-down list box, and then click the Update **A**ll button.

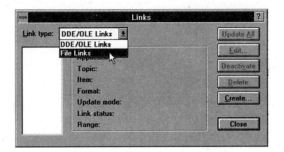

Fig. 19.6
Choosing File
Links in the
Links dialog box
activates the
Update **A**ll button.

▶ "Customizing
the 1-2-3 for
Windows
Screen,"
p. 965

◀ "Recalculating a
Worksheet,"
p. 129

IV

Analyzing the Worksheet

If you want Recalculation set to **M**anual instead of **A**utomatic, make sure that the status bar is displayed. Keep an eye on the status bar's Calc button (see fig. 19.7). Whenever the word `Calc` appears in this button, for current data click Calc button or the Recalculation SmartIcon, or press F9 (Calc).

> **Note**
>
> If the status bar is not displayed, open the **V**iew menu and choose the Set View **P**references command. The User Preferences dialog box appears. Click Status Bar.

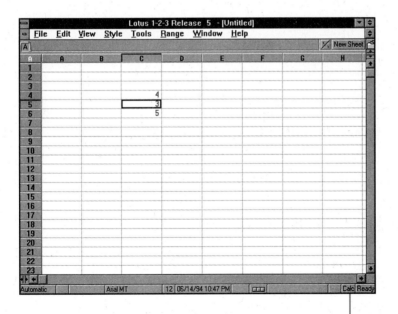

Calc button

Fig. 19.7
If any open files
have Manual
recalculation,
the need for a
recalculation
is signaled by
the word *Calc*
appearing in the
Calc button.

> **Caution**
>
> Each file contains a Recalculation setting, either Automatic or Manual, and whenever multiple files are open, 1-2-3 for Windows applies the Recalculation setting of the most recently opened file to all open files. For example, if you open file A, which has Automatic recalculation, and then open file B, which has Manual recalculation, if you change data in file A, file A will not recalculate the effects of the data change until you issue a Calc command.
>
> So whenever you are using multiple open files, if any of the files have Manual recalculation, keep the status bar displayed and watch the Calc button so that you know when a Calc command is needed to make all cells reflect current data.

Using the Combine 1-2-3 File Dialog Box

In working with a file in which you want to use data from other files, you may find it convenient to use the Combine 1-2-3 File dialog box. This dialog box enables you to do three things that you can do as well or better with formula file links or the Edit menu's Copy and Paste commands. Sometimes, however, the dialog box procedure is the most convenient.

> **Caution**
>
> Before each use of the Combine 1-2-3 File dialog box, save the current file. If you make a mistake, the result is likely to be an undesired effect on your current file that will take considerable time to repair—or that cannot be repaired.

Before going to the Combine 1-2-3 File dialog box, you may want to open the source file from which you want to get data and display it beside the current file in which you want to place the data. With the source file open, you can determine or check the data range that you want the current file to receive. Then place the cell pointer in the current-file cell where you want the incoming range of data to start (where you want its upper left corner to be).

Next, open the **F**ile menu and choose the **O**pen command to display the Open File dialog box. Select the file from which you want to bring in data, and then click the **C**ombine button. The Combine 1-2-3 File dialog box appears (see fig. 19.8).

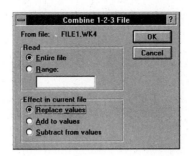

Fig. 19.8
For certain current-file uses of data from other files on disk, you may find the Combine 1-2-3 File dialog box convenient.

In the Read section of this dialog box, indicate what data in the source cell you want 1-2-3 for Windows to read and use to affect the current file: the contents of the source file (**E**ntire File) or only a range (**R**ange). (In the latter case, you must specify the range.)

In the Effect in Current File area, choose one of three effects on the chosen source-file data in the current file:

- *Replace **V**alues*. For this effect, the word *values* is misleading. If you choose this option, what comes in from the source file *replaces* anything in the corresponding part of the current file, starting in the cell where you left the cell pointer. But values aren't the only elements that come in; *all* types of source-file cell contents come into current-file cells, including entered numbers, formulas, and text. (If any incoming cells are blank, however, they do not replace the contents of the corresponding destination cells.)

- ***A**dd to Values*. For this effect, too, the word *values* is misleading; a better name would be Add Values to Numbers. This option adds source-cell data only to current-file cells that contain numbers (excluding cells that display numbers but contain formulas). Any current-file cell that contains either a formula or text is unaffected. In each destination-file cell that contains a number, if the corresponding cell of the source file contains a *value* (either a number or a formula that results in the display of a number), the source-file cell's number is added to the number that already appears in the current-file cell.

  For example, if a source-file cell contains a formula that results in the display of 300, and if you typed 400 in the corresponding current-file cell, 1-2-3 for Windows will add the 300 from the source-cell formula to the 400 in the current cell, changing the current-cell number to 700.

  But if the source-file cell contains the typed 300 and the current-file cell contains the formula that displays 400, there is no effect because the

Add to Values option does not add to values; it adds only to one kind of value (numbers) and not to the other kind (formulas that display numbers).

■ *Subtract from Values*. The third option works just like the second, except that in every current-file cell where it has effect, the incoming source-file number is subtracted from the number that already appears in the current-file cell. You should think of the **S**ubtract from Values option with a revised name: Subtract Values from Numbers. A source-file cell's number can be subtracted if that cell contains a value—either a number or a formula that displays a number—but that value will be subtracted only if the current cell contains a number, not a formula that displays a number.

Troubleshooting

When I display the source file for a combine operation and make revisions to it, the Combine 1-2-3 File dialog box keeps ignoring my revisions.

The dialog box gets the source-file data from the disk version of the source file, not from your display of the source file.

If you make revisions in the source file when you display it to find its range for use in the Combine 1-2-3 File dialog box, you should save the revised source file to disk before opening the dialog box.

When I use the Combine 1-2-3 File dialog box to combine results from separate files for several company divisions or several months, I often lose track of which source files I have added in and which I haven't. Does 1-2-3 for Windows provide any record of what I have combined?

No. That is one reason why it may be better to use formula file linking to combine files (see the following section).

Is there a good system that I can set up to keep track of the source files I have added in?

Pick a cell that is blank in all the files but is easy to include in the combine ranges. Use this cell to number the source files.

To make the numbers easy to interpret, you could give each source file's number one zero more than the preceding one. Number the first source file 1, the second 20, the third 300, and so on.

With this system, by looking at the number in the current file, you can tell which source files have been added in and which have not. For example, if the number in the current file is 7604341, you added in source file 2 twice and skipped source file 5.

Combining and Consolidating Files: An Example

Consider an example of using multiple files that's defined so that it fits the rigid capabilities of the Combine 1-2-3 File dialog box, so you can use it to see application of the Combine 1-2-3 File dialog box as well as formula file links.

Say that every month, financial reports with figures for every individual day come in from six divisions to headquarters where you work. The reports are in 1-2-3 for Windows files on disks, and one of your jobs is to put them together into reports for the whole company. Say that rules have been set up so that all the reports are laid out with the same item numbers in the same cells—first-day sales in C3 and so on. For every report, all the numbers are in the range C3 to AH54, and you already have a monthly whole-company worksheet with the column and row headings, ready to receive the divisions' numbers.

Combining

First, you consider how you would combine the six divisions' numbers using each of two methods: the Combine 1-2-3 File dialog box and formula file linking. Then you consider which method will be best.

Combining Division Figures with the Combine Box

If you use the Combine 1-2-3 File dialog box, each month you carry out these steps:

1. Put the six division files on your hard disk.

2. Open your whole-company worksheet.

3. Place the cell pointer in whole-company worksheet cell C3.

4. Open the **F**ile menu and choose **O**pen. Then select a division's file.

5. Click the File Open dialog box's **C**ombine button.

6. In the upper rectangle of the Combine 1-2-3 File dialog box, choose **R**ange and enter **C3..AH54**.

7. In the lower rectangle of the Combine box, choose **A**dd to Values. The Combine 1-2-3 File dialog box now appears as shown in figure 19.9.

Fig. 19.9
Using the
Combine 1-2-3 File
dialog box for the
combine-divisions
example described
in the text.

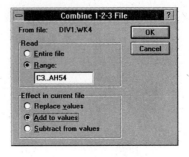

8. Click OK.

9–33. Repeat steps 4-8 for each of divisions 2 through 6.

Combining Division Figures with Formula File Linking

If you use formula file linking, before the first month enter this formula in your total-company worksheet's cell C3:

> **+<<C:\DIV1.WK4>>A:C3..A:AH54+<<C:DIV2.WK4>>A:C3..AH54**
> **+<<C:\DIV3.WK4>>A:C3..A:AH54+<<C:DIV4.WK4>>A:C3..AH54**
> **+<<C:\DIV5.WK4>>A:C3..A:AH54+<<C:DIV6.WK4>>A:C3..AH54**

To make entry of this formula as easy as possible, and to ensure that it has no typos in the references, you save six blank worksheet files with the six division file names, and then for the long references in the formula, you use the mouse to point to cell C3 in each of these files. All you have to type in is the six plus signs. Copy this formula down and right to all cells in the numbers range of your total-company worksheet, C3 to AH54.

For each month you take these steps:

1. Put the six division files on your hard disk under the names DIV1.WK4 through DIV6.WK4.

2. Open your whole-company worksheet file.

3. Open the **E**dit menu and choose **L**inks.

4. In the Links dialog box, choose File Links from the **L**inks Type drop-down list.

5. Click the Update **A**ll button.

Comparing the Methods

Even though this task of combining division figures was chosen to fit the relatively narrow and inflexible capabilities of the Combine 1-2-3 File dialog box, formula file linking is better for this task in three ways:

- *Monthly work much quicker and simpler.* In the lists of steps above, using the Combine 1-2-3 File dialog box, you have 33 steps to carry out each month, and using formula file linking you have 5. While these lists' definitions of what constitutes a separate step are somewhat arbitrary, it is certainly true that each month, using formula file linking will take you less than one-fifth the time and effort of using the Combine 1-2-3 File dialog box.

- *Verifiably correct results.* This is a very important advantage of using formula file linking. Using the Combine 1-2-3 File dialog box in every single combine, you risk making a mistake in moving data to correct range from correct range. If you make a mistake in either cell pointer location in the total-company file or the range you enter in the Combine 1-2-3 File dialog box for the division file, you will make all the numbers in your total-company worksheet wrong. If in any of the six combines for each month, you click **S**ubtract from Values instead of **A**dd to Values, all your total-company numbers for that month will certainly be wrong. And when you use the Combine 1-2-3 File dialog box, your worksheet provides you no record of how your total-company numbers have been calculated. After you've done your combining, neither you nor anyone else can find worksheet verification of how the total-company worksheet calculated the numbers it contains.

  By contrast, when you use formula file linking, in your total-company worksheet every cell contains the formula showing how the worksheet calculated its number. Of course, even with this approach it's possible to make a mistake. For example, in any month you might make a typo in the file name you give a division's file as you put it on your hard disk; in which case, the formulas can't find that file's numbers for their update. But compared to using the Combine 1-2-3 File dialog box, the risk of your making such mistakes in updating your formula file links is vastly less because the steps are far fewer and simpler. And there are better safeguards: if you type a division's file name wrong so the file-link formulas cannot find that file, your total-company worksheet's cells will not show you incorrect numbers. Instead, every cell will show ERR.

■ *Building far more valuable skills.* When you use the Combine 1-2-3 File dialog box, what you are practicing can be used only for the three specific things that dialog box does. But when you enter and use formula file linking, you are developing and practicing universally applicable skills that are valuable for working on, organizing, and managing almost every larger project or data system.

> **Note**
>
> You can use file links to de-combine as well as to combine—to move data from central out to branches. You can maintain a central data bank from which your files and other people's files can draw data with file linking formulas.

Consolidating

To turn the figures from the divisions into correct financial numbers for the whole company, each month you have to subtract out effects of interdivisional transactions, making your report for the whole company consolidated, so it represents the whole company as a unit in its dealings with the outside world. (If a company could count interdivisional sales and resulting divisional profits in its totals, it would have its divisions keep selling the same things back and forth, marking them up each time, and report incredibly high sales and profits.)

Say that each month the six divisions each provide you a second file with the interdivisonal figures to subtract out and lay out the worksheets in these files so each figure to subtract is in the right cell relative to the first set of files. Then you can use the Combine 1-2-3 File dialog box to produce the consolidated report by using its **A**dd to Values for the first set of files and its **S**ubtract from Values for the second set of files.

You follow the same steps described in the preceding section on combining, with twelve divisional files to put on your hard disk instead of six; but you have to carry out steps 4–8 a second time for each division, choosing that division's second file with interdivisional transactions and then in the Combine 1-2-3 File dialog box choosing **S**ubtract from Values. That raises your monthly steps from 33 to 63.

If instead you use formula file linking for the monthly consolidations, in advance of the first month you double the formula in C3. You add references for the second set of files, preceded by minus signs to subtract those files' contents. To distinguish each divisions' second file from its first, you add an I for interdivisional to the file name in the formula references:

```
+<<C:\DIV1.WK4>>A:C3..A:AH54+<<C:DIV2.WK4>>A:C3..AH54
+<<C:\DIV3.WK4>>A:C3..A:AH54+<<C:DIV4.WK4>>A:C3..AH54
+<<C:\DIV5.WK4>>A:C3..A:AH54+<<C:DIV6.WK4>>A:C3..AH54
-<<C:\DIV1I.WK4>>A:C3..A:AH54-<<C:DIV2I.WK4>>A:C3..AH54
-<<C:\DIV3I.WK4>>A:C3..A:AH54-<<C:DIV4I.WK4>>A:C3..AH54
-<<C:\DIV5I.WK4>>A:C3..A:AH54-<<C:DIV6I.WK4>>A:C3..AH54
```

As you did for the combine formula, you copy this formula to all of your worksheet's cells C3 to AH54.

Each month you carry out the same five steps as outlined above in the "Combining" section. With this formula file linking approach, your only additional monthly work for this consolidating, compared to combining, is that before you use the Links dialog box for the file links update and put twelve files on your hard disk instead of six.

> **Tip**
> You can enter in a cell formulas even longer than the one shown in six lines in the text. That formula is 324 characters. The limit is 512.

For this consolidating, the advantages of using formula file linking instead of the Combine 1-2-3 File dialog box are at least double what they are for the combining task. Your monthly steps are 5 instead of 66. And compared to each month depending on figures from twelve uses of the Combine 1-2-3 File dialog box in which it's easy to make a mistake, with your worksheet providing no verifiable evidence of how it calculated each total-company figure, the formulas in all your worksheet cells showing how the worksheet calculated every number is extremely valuable, for you and for anybody who may want to audit the figures.

From Here...

For more information related to use of multiple worksheets and files, see the following chapters:

- Chapter 7, "Reorganizing Worksheets," explains the basics of working with worksheets.

- Chapter 8, "Managing Files," explains the basics of working with worksheets and files.

- Chapter 20, "Auditing Worksheets." The Audit feature explained in this chapter includes an Audit tool you can use to see which of a worksheet's cells contain links to other files.

- Chapter 22, "Managing Multiple Solutions with Version Manager." Version Manager is a powerful and convenient system for managing and sharing multiple versions of worksheets.

Chapter 20

Auditing Worksheets

Using the audit feature of 1-2-3 for Windows, you can quickly and easily identify, trace, and clarify relationships among worksheet cells. You can see which cells affect or are affected by others through formulas.

In this chapter, you learn how to use the audit feature to find the following:

- All formulas in a worksheet

- Formulas affected by data in a selected range

- The cells that a formula references

- Formulas with circular references

- Cells that contain links to other files

Why Should You Use the Audit Feature?

Formulas can be located virtually anywhere, affecting or being affected by formulas and other entries almost anywhere else. Formulas themselves can be very hard to comprehend. Both of these conditions can make it very difficult to trace and correct errors. Worse still, these conditions can prevent users from even becoming aware of errors, which can be as tiny as a typo but lead to extremely costly mistakes. Additionally, these conditions can make even understanding worksheets very difficult.

For coping with these problems, the audit feature offers great value for a very wide range of uses, from error tracing to original worksheet setup:

Tip
The best time to use the audit feature is during worksheet development to help you build worksheet structures and layouts that you and others can understand.

■ *Error tracing.* This is the most obvious use of the audit feature. If something about the worksheet is not working or is producing answers you know are wrong, use audit tools to help trace the problem back to its source.

■ *Error discovery or worksheet checking.* The greater danger is that the worksheet has errors and is producing wrong answers without your being aware of it. Use audit tools to review your worksheets and help you find and correct hidden errors.

■ *Understanding worksheets prepared by others.* When you become responsible for using, revising, or building upon worksheets prepared by others, you are likely to find it very difficult to see and fully understand the worksheet structure. What is affecting what and how? What is affected by what and how? Use the audit feature to trace, see, and understand the worksheet relationship structure.

■ *Understanding your own worksheets.* It's very common for the developer of a worksheet to come back to it later and find it impossible to figure out. When you come back to worksheets you developed, use the audit feature to reacquaint yourself with your earlier work.

■ *Original worksheet development.* This is where audit tools are used least, but where they can be of their greatest value. The best time for minimizing all the problems cited earlier is as you develop the worksheet—and even before that, when you are planning the worksheet. For example, if you are developing a business planning worksheet, such as a budget, that will be used for what-if analysis, start by laying it out with three clearly labeled areas:

The *inputs* for which you test various numbers (such as next-year sales)

The *outputs* for which you want to see results (such as resulting next-year profit)

The *inputs-to-outputs relationships*—all the rest of the worksheet that translates the varying inputs into the resulting outputs.

Then as you develop the worksheet, sketch and maintain diagrams that show how it works—what affects what, what is affected by what, and how. Put major emphasis on making and keeping the worksheet layout and structure as logical and understandable as you can. As you develop the worksheet, use the audit feature frequently to help you build the relationships from inputs to outputs in the most clear, logical, and traceable way. Also use the audit tools to revise the worksheet whenever you can see ways to make it easier to understand.

What Can You Do with the Audit Feature?

1-2-3 for Windows provides six audit tools. Three are basic and universal, useful for seeing relationships in almost every worksheet with formulas. The other three are for more specialized or advanced worksheets or problems: for tracing circular references and for tracing links to other files of 1-2-3 for windows or other software products.

For a better understanding of what each of these tools does, you need more than the tool names. So the best way to think of these tools is in terms of a statement of what each does. You can then attach the name of the tool to the statement. See table 20.1 for a list of the audit tools and their functions.

Table 20.1 The Audit Tools	
Tool	**Description**
All Formulas	See what cells contain formulas (therefore, the ones likely to be affected by other cells)
Formula **P**recedents	For any cell (or range) containing formula(s), see what cells affect it (such as cells it refers to)
Cell **D**ependents	For any cell (or range), see what cells it affects (such as cells with formulas that refer to it)
Circular References	See what cells are involved in any circular reference (an error that prevents solutions)
File Links	See what cells contain links to other files (formulas with references to other files, which make cells affected by contents of other files)
DD**E** Links	See what cells contain formulas with DDE links to other Windows application software products, which make cells dependent on the contents of other software files

Understanding the Audit Process

The process of using audit tools has three major parts. For use of any of the six audit tools, the first part ends with the Audit dialog box. But if you want to see what a particular cell (or range) affects or is affected by—the second and third types of audit in table 20.1, Formula **p**recedents and Cell **d**ependents—then before you get the Audit dialog box you select that cell (or range). Then, for use of any of the six Audit tools, to get the Audit dialog box, from the menu you select **T**ools **A**udit.

Figure 20.1 shows the Audit dialog box. The second part of the process in using audit tools is to select the tool you want, from the six choices in the rectangle labeled Audit inside the Audit dialog box (see fig. 20.1).

Fig. 20.1
The Audit dialog box is where you can decide what audit tool to use.

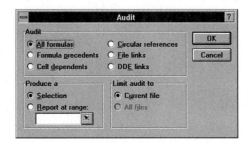

The third part of the process is to select how you want the audit results displayed, from the two choices in the box labeled Produce a at lower left inside the Audit dialog box as shown in figure 20.1, and to complete any options that result from this selection. If you choose **S**election you will have no further choices. But if you choose **R**eport at Range, you will have to specify the range where you want the audit report; and you will have the option of selecting All files in the Audit dialog box's rectangle labeled Limit Audit to, which will produce an audit of all active (open) files. To decide which way to have the audit displayed, see the following paragraphs on what you get with audit tools.

Displaying the Audit Results

Figures 20.2 and 20.3 show the two ways you can have an audit result displayed. The two are for the same School Candy Sales worksheet, and both display results of the same type of audit: **A**ll Formulas.

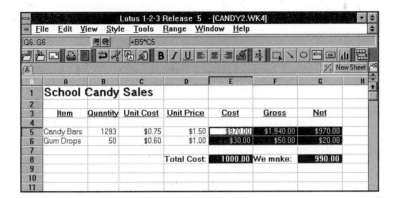

Fig. 20.2
If you choose
Selection, the
audit result is
displayed by
highlighting cells.

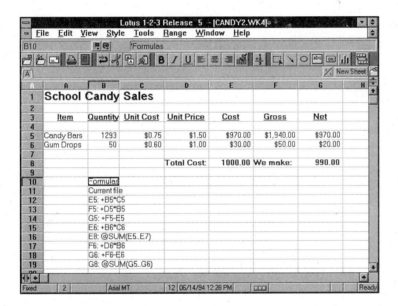

Fig. 20.3
If you choose
Report at Range,
the audit result is
displayed as a
separate listing in
the range you
choose.

Displaying Audit Results with Cell Highlighting

If you choose **S**election as the way to display the audit result, the audit result is displayed as shown in figure 20.2: 1-2-3 for Windows selects all the cells that meet the criteria of the type of audit you chose—in this example, **A**ll Formulas. The result is that all the cells containing formulas are highlighted.

Tip

When you get an
audit result dis-
played by high-
lighted cells, the
cell containing the
cell pointer is part
of the highlighted
cell's answer.

If you choose **S**election, the next time you select any cell the highlighting disappears, so the audit result is gone. But you can move among the highlighted cells while they are still highlighted. To move forward to the next highlighted cell, press Ctrl+Enter. To move back, press Ctrl+Shift+Enter.

When you choose **S**election, you cannot audit other files, just the current file.

Displaying Audit Results in a Separate Listing

If you choose **R**eport at Range as the way to display the audit result (and then specify the report should start at cell B10), the audit result is displayed as shown in figure 20.3. You get a separate listing, with a heading, starting at B10, of all the formula-containing cells—their addresses and their formulas.

When you choose **R**eport at Range, you have to specify the range where you want the report displayed in the worksheet. If you specify a range rectangle, the report items are listed down that range's first column, then second column, and so on; if there is more to report than fits in the specified range, the rest is not displayed. You can instead specify the cell where you want the report to start, declaring no ending. Unless you have a good sense of what the audit report's size will be and a good reason to place it in a particular range, it's a good idea to specify just the report's starting cell and to locate that cell below or to the right of all cells with contents, so that there is enough horizontal space for the report to show every formula fully—no matter how long.

Choosing **R**eport at Range gives you the option of auditing All Files (which means all active or open files), which you cannot do if you choose **S**election for a highlighted-cells result.

Choosing an Audit Display Method

In choosing how to display audit results, consider these differences:

- **R**eport at Range gives you the option of auditing all active (open) files, while the **S**election choice only enables you to audit only the current file.

- A highlighted-cell's audit result disappears as soon as you select any cell for further work, but an audit-result range stays where it was placed. If you want to keep the audit result for later use, choose **R**eport at Range. On the other hand, to check somebody else's worksheet without making any changes in it or for using audits to check current worksheet structure at various points while you are developing the worksheet, the temporary nature of the highlighted result is advantageous.

■ The cell-highlight method of displaying an audit result has a great advantage in communicating audit results to you visually. In all aspects of worksheet usage, from original development to error correction to review of completed worksheets, location is a key part of worksheet structure and a key factor in people's ability to understand the structure. While an audit report lists addresses of cells, highlighting shows their locations, which most people find much more helpful in grasping worksheet structure.

Understanding the Audit SmartIcons

1-2-3 for Windows offers a set of five icons for quick access to the audit tools, named the Sheet Auditing set of SmartIcons. Note that there is one for each type of audit except circular reference. (For each of these icons, the name is the word "find" followed by what it finds—for example, one is named Find Cell Dependents.)

Clicking any one of these SmartIcons is equivalent to doing all the following: choosing **T**ools **A**udit, the type of audit the SmartIcon represents, and **S**election as the audit report.

To get an audit returned as a separate report that you can keep during further worksheet use, via **R**eport at Range, and for multifile audits that this choice enables, you cannot use these SmartIcons; you must instead use the Audit dialog box. But for use of audit tools for cell-highlight audits to help you develop and review worksheet structure, the Sheet Auditing SmartIcon set is convenient.

To display the auditing SmartIcons, choose **T**ools **S**mart**I**cons; the SmartIcons dialog box appears. Select Sheet Auditing. (For more help in getting this SmartIcon set or more on getting other SmartIcons see Chapter 33.)

Tip

The Sheet Auditing set of SmartIcons can help you use audit tools conveniently during worksheet development and review.

Caution

While using the SmartIcons dialog box to choose icon sets, do not click the **D**elete Set button, which does not just delete icon sets from your current display. It deletes icon sets from your menu of icon sets for future choice. If you delete a set, you do not reduce the number of individual icons available, but you eliminate your ability to choose that predefined set.

You can also add to your SmartIcon row the Audit Cells SmartIcon. Clicking this SmartIcon is equivalent to choosing **T**ools **A**udit from the menu. To add the Audit Cells SmartIcon to the icon row on your display, from the SmartIcons dialog box, drag the Audit Cells icon in the Icons Available list box to the Current Icon list box. Click OK.

Using Individual Audit Tools

The following sections describe each of the auditing options available in the Audit dialog box. The figures and some of the audit-result descriptions assume you chose the **S**election option button, but in every case, you can choose **R**eport at Range and get a separate listing for the same cells.

Finding All Formulas

Use the **A**ll Formulas option when you want to check a worksheet's formulas for accuracy or understand the formulas in a worksheet that is new or unfamiliar to you. If you use the **S**election option, 1-2-3 for Windows highlights each formula it finds, as shown earlier in figure 20.2. If you choose the **R**eport at Range option, 1-2-3 for Windows lists the address of each cell it finds and displays the formula, as shown in figure 20.3.

 If you have added the Sheet Auditing icon set to your SmartIcons, to instantly highlight all cells with formulas in the active worksheet, simply click the Find Formulas SmartIcon.

Finding Formula Precedents

 Formula precedents are all the cells referenced by a formula, either directly or indirectly. In the School Candy Sales worksheet, for example, the formula precedents for cell E5 are B5 and C5 because these two cells are directly referenced by the formula in cell E5. The formula precedents for cell E8, however, include cells E5 and E6, which are referenced directly, as well as cells B5, B6, C5, and C6, which are referenced indirectly by the formula in cell E8 (see fig. 20.4).

To find a formula's precedents, first select the cell in the worksheet, and then choose **T**ools **A**udit or click the Audit Cells SmartIcon. 1-2-3 for Windows finds the precedents for the currently selected cell. If the cell you select does not contain a formula, 1-2-3 for Windows displays an error message.

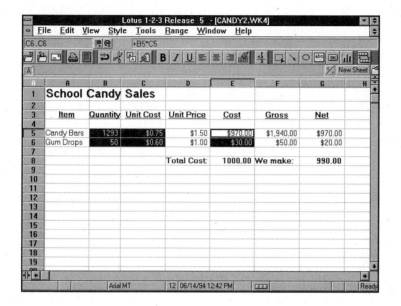

Fig. 20.4

Seeing all the cells that a particular formula cell is affected by, use the Formula **P**recedents audit tool.

Finding Cell Dependents

In the Audit dialog box, the Cell **D**ependents option tells you which formulas depend on a cell or on cells in a particular range. (This option is roughly the reverse of the Formula **P**recedents option.) In the School Candy Sales worksheet, for example, if you select cells B5 and B6 and choose the Cell **D**ependents option in the Audit dialog box, 1-2-3 finds cells E5 through G6 and cells E8 and G8 (see fig. 20.5). Cells E5..F6 refer to cells B5 or B6 directly; E8, G5, G6, and G8 refer to cells B5 or B6 indirectly.

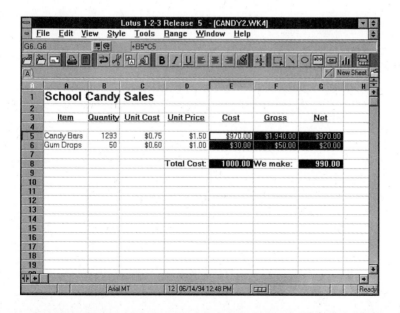

Fig. 20.5

Seeing all cells a particular cell affects, using the Cell **D**ependents audit tool.

To quickly find a cell's dependents, select that cell, and then click the Find Cell Dependents SmartIcon.

Finding Circular References

A circular reference is a formula that contains a direct or indirect reference to itself. In the School Candy Sales worksheet, for example, you have cells named Cost, Gross, and Net. If the Gross cell contains the formula +COST+NET, and the Net cell contains the formula +GROSS–COST, you cannot calculate the Net value because the value of Cost is unknown, and you cannot calculate the Cost value because the value of Net is unknown. If you use **T**ools **A**udit to find circular references in the School Candy Sales worksheet, 1-2-3 highlights cells F5 and G5 (see fig. 20.6).

Caution

If your worksheet contains a circular reference, it may display incorrect answers. The only sign of the problem may be the appearance of the `Circ` indicator in the status bar. Whenever `Circ` appears in the status bar, take steps to correct the problem immediately.

Fig. 20.6

Seeing all cells in a circular reference, using the **C**ircular References audit tool.

	A	B	C	D	E	F	G
1	**School Candy Sales**						
2							
3	Item	Quantity	Unit Cost	Unit Price	Cost	Gross	Net
4							
5	Candy Bars	1293	$0.75	$1.50	$970.00	+COST+NET	+GROSS–COST
6	Gum Drops	50	$0.60	$1.00	$30.00	$50.00	$20.00
7							
8				Total Cost:	1000.00	We make:	20.00

Lotus 1-2-3 Release 5 - [CANDY2.WK4]
File Edit View Style Tools Range Window Help
F5..G5 +COST+NET
New Sheet
US Dollar 2 Arial MT 12 06/14/94 12:56 PM Ready

If a worksheet has more than one circular reference, 1-2-3 displays the Multiple Circular References dialog box. This dialog box lists the first cell in each circular reference. In the Choose box, click the cell representing the circular reference you want to audit and then click OK. In the worksheet, 1-2-3 highlights the cells in the circular reference or lists them in the range you specify. After you solve the problem with the first circular reference, if you want to audit another circular reference you start the audit process again, choose **C**ircular References again, and this time in the dialog box choose the next circular reference.

Troubleshooting

My status bar says Circ. *What kind of problem do I have?*

A Circ (circular reference) is two (or more) cells that each depend on the result in the other. Neither can deliver its result because it needs the other's result first, like two people at a doorway each saying "You first."

For example, in an income statement the expenses may include management compensation of 5% of profit, and profit may be sales minus all expenses including management compensation. To calculate management compensation, the worksheet needs profit first, and to calculate profit, the calculation needs all expenses including management compensation first.

If I have two cells with such a Circ, *how do I see exactly what the problem is?*

Use audit tools. In the Audit dialog box, choose **C**ircular References and **S**election (or, if you prefer, choose **R**eport at Range). Click OK. 1-2-3 for Windows highlights the cells involved in the circular reference. Study the contents of these cells to see how their formulas make each need the result from the other.

After I understand the problem with Circ, *how do I solve it?*

You have to change one or more of the circular-reference cells so that the worksheet can calculate the result for each cell ("A") without requiring the result for any other cell ("B") that requires that cell A's result.

For example, in the circular-reference example described previously, you might handle management compensation the way income tax is handled. Take management compensation out of the listing of expenses, and enter a line labeled Profit before management compensation. Calculate Profit as Sales minus all expenses; however, don't include Management Compensation as an expense. On the next line, enter Management Compensation calculated as 5% of the Profit, and under that line, enter a final line for Net Profit calculated as the Profit minus Management Compensation.

Finding File Links and DDE Links

A **F**ile Links audit targets cells with formulas that refer to data in other files. This kind of reference occurs often in "roll-up" or summary worksheets. For example, you might track monthly sales figures for each department on individual worksheets and summarize the monthly figures of all departments on a separate worksheet. The summary worksheet includes file links to each of the department worksheets.

A DD**E** Links audit targets cells with formulas that refer to data in other Windows software products using the Windows Dynamic Data Exchange.

To find file links or DDE links in a worksheet, choose **T**ools **A**udit. The Audit dialog box appears. Choose the **F**ile links or DD**E** Links option. If you choose **S**election, 1-2-3 for Windows highlights all cells in the worksheet that contain file links or DDE links. If you choose **R**eport at Range, 1-2-3 for Windows lists all cells that contain file links or DDE links.

 To quickly select all cells in a worksheet that contain file links or DDE links, click the Find 1-2-3 links or Find DDE Links SmartIcon.

From Here...

For more information related to the contents of this chapter, see the following chapters:

- Chapter 33, "Creating Custom SmartIcon Palettes." For your 1-2-3 display, you can choose from over 150 1-2-3 SmartIcons. Reviewing the available SmartIcons is a good way to become aware of more 1-2-3 features, and choosing the SmartIcons most useful for you can help you work more efficiently.

- Chapter 22, "Managing Multiple Solutions with Version Manager." For the kinds of worksheet applications in which Audit tools are most useful, quantitative analyses such as business plans, take a look at this chapter.

Chapter 21

Solving Problems with Solver and Backsolver

For business planning and decision analysis, and for other applications of quantitative analysis, Backsolver and Solver are among the most valuable of 1-2-3 for Windows special tools:

- With *Backsolver*, you can specify the number you want for a result and see what some other number or range of numbers have to be to produce that result.

- With *Solver*, you can define a set of criteria for your plan and see one or more variations of your plan that meet the criteria, including one that optimizes the number in one key cell.

Of course, for all quantitative analysis, the most valuable tools of 1-2-3 for Windows are the fundamental universal powers of the worksheets themselves: the combination of columns and rows of cells, formulas that can refer to any cells with relative and absolute references, the library of functions, and so on. Backsolver and Solver are, by contrast, among the more specialized worksheet-application tools that 1-2-3 for Windows offers. But they provide such valuable worksheet applications that, if you are at all concerned with business planning and decision analysis or other quantitative analysis, you can gain greatly from learning and applying these tools. In addition to benefiting the immediate task, you can learn better ways to use the worksheet from using these tools.

In this chapter, you learn how to do the following:

- Identify ways to meet a goal

- Prepare goal-focused decision analyses

■ Find plans that meet sets of conditions

■ Find optimum plans for sets of conditions

Using Backsolver To Find Values That Meet Goals

Tip

On your list of 1-2-3's special tools for business plans and analyses, put Backsolver at the top. Other more complex tools get more help/ manual space, but in value, Backsolver is tops.

What you can do with Backsolver is what you might think of as solving an analysis backwards. You specify the result you want, and Backsolver shows you a way to get that result.

Understanding How Backsolver Works

For example, say that for a product you know costs will be $80, but you don't know what sales the company can achieve or what profit will result. Compare standard worksheet use with what you can do with Backsolver:

■ In standard worksheet use, after entering a formula for profit, you enter a prediction for sales (say $100), and let 1-2-3 for Windows tell you the resulting profit (in this case, $20).

■ With Backsolver, you can enter a goal for profit (say $40), and let Backsolver use the worksheet to tell you what sales have to be to meet your profit goal (in this case, sales of $120).

What you can do with Backsolver is that simple. The Backsolver is extremely valuable for almost every project in business planning and decision analysis (and personal financial planning). For a business plan, you can enter the profit goal and see what is required to meet it. For a decision such as a company investment, you can enter the company's minimum acceptable return-on-investment rate and see what any number in the investment plan has to be to meet that standard. If you are building a nest egg for Alexandra's college years or for retirement, you can enter the amount of nest egg you want to build and see what you have to add each year to build the desired sum.

Using Backsolver To Change a Single Cell

Once you've entered a plan or analysis, using Backsolver with the plan is as easy as saving the plan. For example, use the following steps to use Backsolver with the simple $80 product example introduced previously.

The first step is to enter or open a plan or analysis that you can use Backsolver for. You can use Backsolver with any plan or analysis that has these two components:

■ *Input numbers.* One or more cells containing numbers (not formulas) that are used to calculate results in one or more other cells with formulas. In business planning, these input numbers are often called *assumptions*.

■ *Output formulas.* One or more cells containing formulas that use one or more of the input numbers to calculate results.

Say that for the product mentioned on the preceding page, for sales you enter the number **100** in cell C& and for costs you enter **80** is C8, and then in C10 you enter a formula for profit: **+C7–C8**. Your worksheet now has the requirements for use of Backsolver: input number(s) and formula(s) that refer to them.

Since these are the two basic elements of all spreadsheet what-if analysis and virtually every worksheet business plan or decision analysis has them, you can use Backsolver with practically every business plan or decision analysis you already have.

Caution

Before using Backsolver, save your plan. When Backsolver acts, it replaces an input number (or range of input numbers) in your plan. And when it does so, the worksheet recalculates all cells with formulas dependent on what Backsolver changed.

Once you have your plan or analysis in the worksheet

1. Open the **R**ange menu and choose **A**nalyze and then **B**acksolver. The Backsolver dialog box appears (see fig. 21.1).

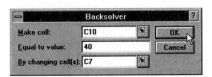

Fig. 21.1
You can learn to use Backsolver in minutes to double your what-if power.

2. In the **M**ake Cell text box, enter the address of the goal's output formula cell. For this example, the goal is a PROFIT goal and the PROFIT value cell is C10, so you enter **C10**.

IV

Analyzing the Worksheet

3. In the **E**qual to Value text box, enter the result that you want for that goal. For this example, enter the desired PROFIT result, **40**.

4. In the **B**y Changing Cell(s) text box, enter the cell address of the input number that you want Backsolver to change so that your goal is met. In this example, you want the input number for SALES changed to meet your profit goal, so enter its cell address, **C7**. Click OK, and the Backsolver goes to work.

5. Click OK.

Backsolver figures out and enters the input number required so that the output formula returns the result you want. In this example, for PROFIT to be 40, SALES must be 120. So Backsolver enters 120 for SALES, and that makes the formula return 40 for PROFIT.

Troubleshooting

*I have a worksheet in which my cash flow goal cell has a formula, and this formula refers to the profit cell which has another formula. According to 1-2-3 Help, in Backsolver's **B**y Changing Cell(s) text box I should enter a "value," and a "value" is either an entered number or a formula that calculates a number. But when in **B**y Changing Cell(s) I enter the profit cell, Backsolver will not work. What is wrong?*

1-2-3 Help does not use the word "value" consistently. In **B**y Changing Cell(s), Backsolver requires cells with entered numbers, not formulas.

Is there a way for me to get Backsolver to find how I can meet a cash flow goal by changing the profit number?

Yes. Save your worksheet, to preserve it with the profit formula, which you are going to temporarily replace. Then in the profit cell, enter the number the profit formula calculated and displayed for profit. In the Backsolver dialog box, enter the profit cell in the **B**y Changing Cell(s) text box.

Using Backsolver To Change a Range

In the Backsolver dialog box, note that **B**y Changing Cell(s) is plural. You can tell Backsolver to change an entire range when finding a solution for your goal. If you do, Backsolver changes all numbers in the range by the same percentage. In other words, Backsolver figures out the percentage change that, when applied to every number in the range, makes the result formula return the goal you entered. Backsolver then changes all numbers in the range by that percentage.

Changing Entries in a One-Dimensional Range

Figure 21.2 shows an example of using Backsolver to meet a goal by changing a range of input numbers, and figure 21.3 shows Backsolver's answer. The goal is a NET PROFIT of 2000 for the entire year (cell G19), so enter **G19** in the **M**ake Cell text box and **2000** in the **E**qual to Value text box. You want to see what changes are required in all four quarters' sales (all changed same percent) to meet this goal. So in Backsolver's **B**y Changing Cell(s) text box, enter the range of the four quarterly SALES numbers, **C4..F4**.

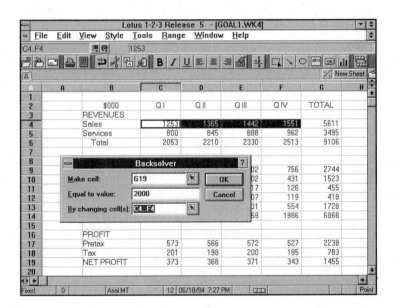

Fig. 21.2
Use Backsolver to meet a goal by changing an entire row of numbers in the plan.

When you click OK, Backsolver returns the result shown in figure 21.3: all four quarterly sales figures changed by a percentage that makes NET PROFIT for the entire year 2000.

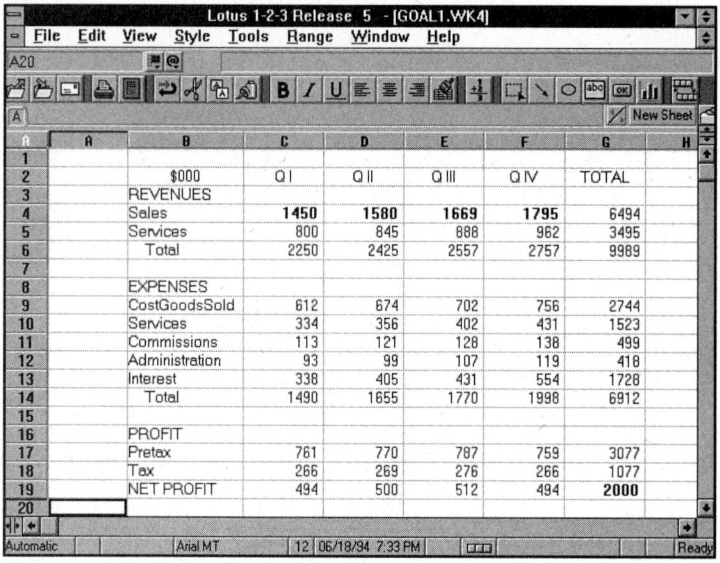

Fig. 21.3
Backsolver finds how to meet the goal by changing a row of input numbers—all by the same percent.

Changing Entries in a Two-Dimensional Range

With Backsolver you can also see how to meet a goal by changing all input numbers in a two-dimensional range. The example in figures 21.4 and 21.5 use the same example of NET PROFIT of 2000.

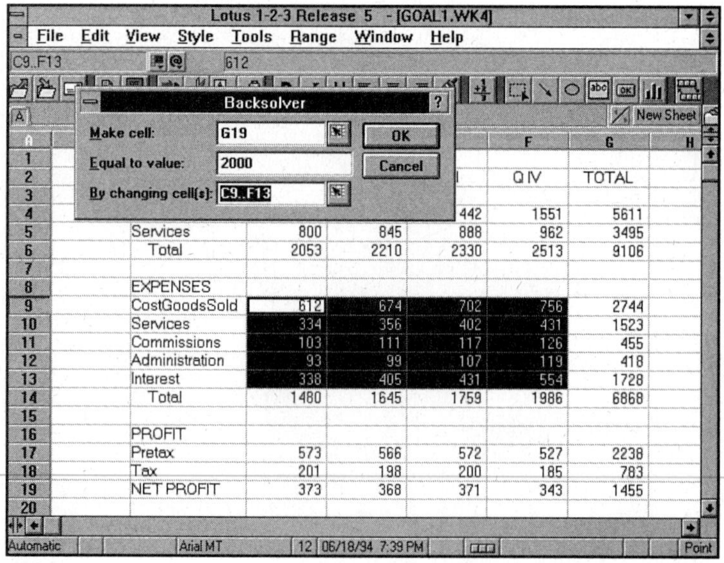

Fig. 21.4
Use Backsolver to meet a goal by changing an entire 2-D range of numbers by the same percent.

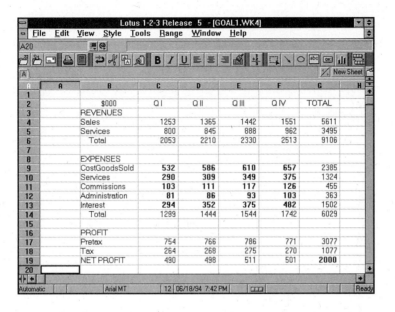

Fig. 21.5
Backsolver shows
how to meet the
goal by changing a
2-D range of input
numbers—all by
the same percent.

In figure 21.4, you want to see what changes are required in all expenses for all four quarters (all changed same percent) to meet the goal of a total-year NET PROFIT of 2000. So in the **B**y Changing Cell(s) text box, enter **C9..F13**. (Since the goal is the same as in the preceding example, leave the **M**ake Cell and **E**qual to Value text boxes as before: **G19** and **2000**).

Backsolver does what you want, illustrating that it can show ways to meet a goal by changing entire two-dimensional ranges just as well as by changing a single cell or a one-dimensional range. When you click OK, all expense numbers change by the same percentage, and all other cells dependent on these numbers show new numbers from new calculations, including total-year NET PROFIT at the target you entered, 2000 (see fig. 21.5).

Revealing Backsolver Percent Change

When you use Backsolver to meet a goal by changing a multicell range, the best way to summarize the route to the goal that Backsolver has found is the percent by which it has changed all the cells to meet the goal. Compared to all the number changes in all the individual cells, it is much easier for people to grasp, compare, and remember alternative ways to meet a goal when each is stated as a single percent change, such as "reduce all expenses by 13%."

Unfortunately, when Backsolver changes a multicell range by some percent to meet a goal, it does not display the percent change it applies to all the cells. But you can very easily make each of your Backsolver-result worksheets

Tip
To enter values into the **M**ake Cell and **B**y Changing Cell(s) text boxes quickly and correctly, click the target text box. In the worksheet, select the cell or range. This approach is shown in figures 21.2 and 21.4.

display the percent change that Backsolver found and applied to a range of cells to meet the goal. An illustration of how you can do so is shown in figure 21.6.

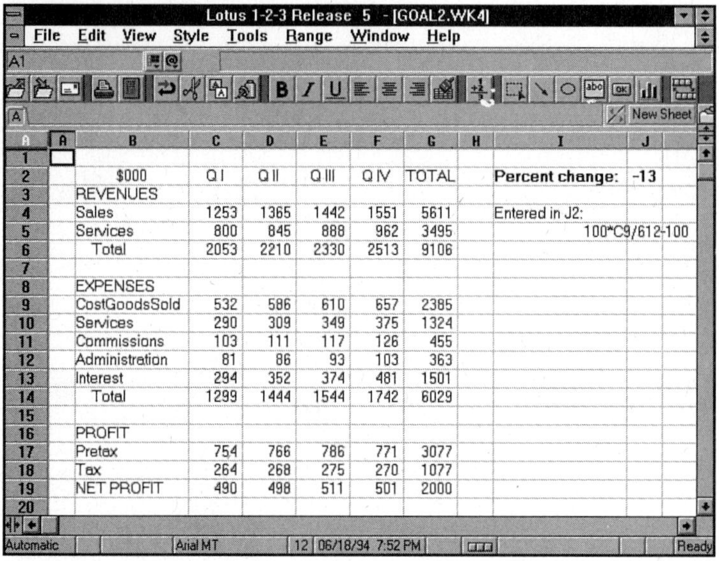

	A	B	C	D	E	F	G	H	I	J
1										
2		$000	Q I	Q II	Q III	Q IV	TOTAL		Percent change:	-13
3		REVENUES								
4		Sales	1253	1365	1442	1551	5611		Entered in J2:	
5		Services	800	845	888	962	3495		100*C9/612-100	
6		Total	2053	2210	2330	2513	9106			
7										
8		EXPENSES								
9		CostGoodsSold	532	586	610	657	2385			
10		Services	290	309	349	375	1324			
11		Commissions	103	111	117	126	455			
12		Administration	81	86	93	103	363			
13		Interest	294	352	374	481	1501			
14		Total	1299	1444	1544	1742	6029			
15										
16		PROFIT								
17		Pretax	754	766	786	771	3077			
18		Tax	264	268	275	270	1077			
19		NET PROFIT	490	498	511	501	2000			
20										

Fig. 21.6
By entering a simple formula, you can make a worksheet display the percent change Backsolver applied to all cells in a range to meet your goal.

Pick two cells: a cell in the **B**y Changing Cell(s) range to use as the percent change *monitor* cell and a blank cell outside the range to use as the percent change *display* cell. In the percent change display cell, make an entry that uses references to the monitor cell to calculate and show the percent change Backsolver makes in the monitor cell's number.

Figure 21.6 shows how you apply this approach for the Backsolver application you saw in figures 21.4 and 21.5—meeting the goal of 2000 for total-year NET PROFIT by changing all expenses. For the monitor cell, you could pick any of the By Changing Cell(s), any cell from C9 to F13. Say you pick C9, in which the pre-Backsolver number is `612`. In your blank percent-change display cell, J13, you enter:

+100*C9/612-100

This formula calculates the percent difference between the current number in C9 and its pre-Backsolver number of 612.

Before you use Backsolver, this percent change display cell displays `0`. After you use Backsolver, this cell displays the percent change Backsolver applied to cell C9.

Figure 21.6 shows what your display cell J13 displays after you use Backsolver to meet the profit goal by changing numbers for all expenses of every quarter: -13. Since Backsolver solves by applying the same percent change to all cells in the By Changing Cell(s) range, this percent-change number reports the percent change Backsolver applied to all cells in the entire range, all expenses, to meet your goal.

Making Backsolver Apply Multiple Percent Changes

If you want Backsolver to show you ways to meet your goals by changing some parts of a range by smaller percentages than other parts, you can do so in a very fast and clear way. For any category within the range that you want Backsolver to change by a lower percentage than the rest of the range, divide that category into two rows or columns, with a fraction of the category's numbers in each row or column, and include only one of the category's two rows or columns in the By Changing Cell(s) range.

Say that for the same plan in figures 21.2 through 21.6, you want to see how to meet the profit goal by changing all expenses, but with INTEREST changed only one-third the percentage that other expenses are changed. Figure 21.7 shows how you can do so with Backsolver.

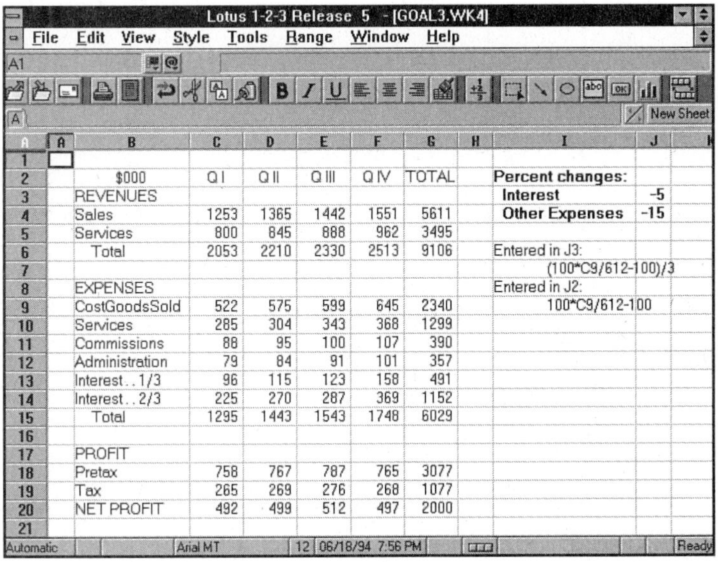

	B	C	D	E	F	G	I	J
1								
2	$000	Q I	Q II	Q III	Q IV	TOTAL	**Percent changes:**	
3	REVENUES						**Interest**	**-5**
4	Sales	1253	1365	1442	1551	5611	**Other Expenses**	**-15**
5	Services	800	845	888	962	3495		
6	Total	2053	2210	2330	2513	9106	Entered in J3:	
7							(100*C9/612-100)/3	
8	EXPENSES						Entered in J2:	
9	CostGoodsSold	522	575	599	645	2340	100*C9/612-100	
10	Services	285	304	343	368	1299		
11	Commissions	88	95	100	107	390		
12	Administration	79	84	91	101	357		
13	Interest . . 1/3	96	115	123	158	491		
14	Interest . . 2/3	225	270	287	369	1152		
15	Total	1295	1443	1543	1748	6029		
16								
17	PROFIT							
18	Pretax	758	767	787	765	3077		
19	Tax	265	269	276	268	1077		
20	NET PROFIT	492	499	512	497	2000		
21								

Fig. 21.7
Making Backsolver meet a goal by applying different percent changes to different parts of the plan.

You split INTEREST into two rows, with one-third of INTEREST in the upper row, just below the other expenses, and the other two-thirds of INTEREST in the lower row. See rows 13 and 14 in figure 21.7. When you use Backsolver, in the By Changing Cell(s) range you will include the upper INTEREST row but exclude the lower row.

To make the worksheet display the percent changes it will apply to INTEREST and to other expenses, use the formulas shown on the right in figure 21.7. For other expenses, you use the same formula you used for percent change in figure 21.6. For INTEREST, modify the formula with a "divide-by-three."

Now when you use Backsolver to meet your PROFIT goal of 2000, in the By Changing Cell(s) text box, the range you specify includes the four quarters for all other expenses, plus the upper INTEREST row, but not the lower INTEREST row. Enter **C9..F13**.

Tip

For a Backsolver goal cell, use the Audit feature's Formula Precedents tool to identify potential By Changing cells.

When you click OK, Backsolver delivers the results shown in figure 21.7: total-year NET PROFIT is 2000. To meet your goal, Backsolver changed by a single percentage all numbers for all other expenses and one-third of INTEREST. The percent-change formulas you entered at figure 21.7's upper right deliver the most valuable numbers in Backsolver's analysis: to meet your profit goal while changing INTEREST by one-third the percent-change of other expenses, Backsolver reduced INTEREST by 5% and all other expenses by 15%.

Summarizing Alternative Routes to the Goal

With percent-change added in your Backsolver result worksheets, you can prepare a very clear and concise summary of alternative routes to a business goal.

If you were analyzing the company plan in figures 21.2 through 21.7, you could prepare a report of alternative routes to the NET PROFIT goal as shown in figure 21.8. This report is focused on the company goal, NET PROFIT of 2000, and it spotlights three clearly defined alternative routes for raising NET PROFIT to meet the goal:

- Increase SALES 16%

- Reduce all expenses 13%

- Reduce INTEREST 5% and all other expenses 15%

In a typical business you could have several more routes to the goal.

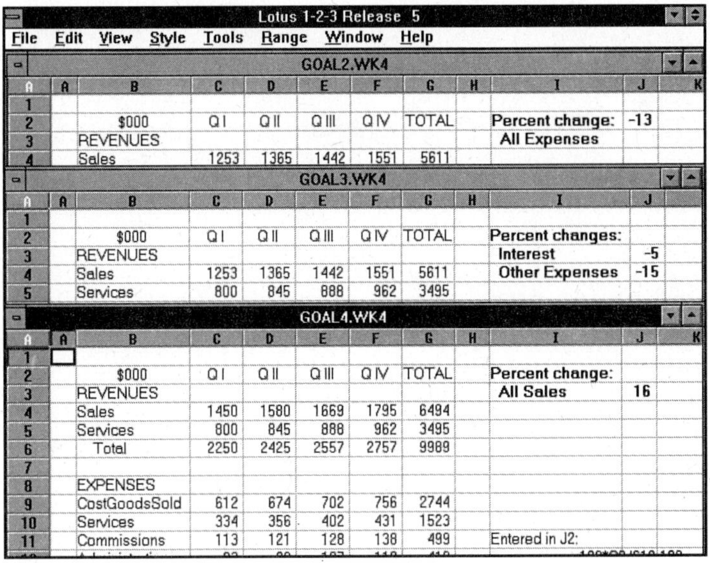

Fig. 21.8
With worksheets
that display
Backsolver percent
change, you can
clarify alternative
routes to the goal.

These worksheets have all the detailed numbers, for anyone who wants to dig into them—but they also deliver very concise summaries of the alternatives that are much easier for busy management teams to instantly grasp, evaluate, and remember.

Using Backsolver to Assess Risk

In most uses of Backsolver, you are seeking ways to meet a goal that you want to meet—this is called *goalseeking*. But you can also use Backsolver to see what changes or misses of plan would cause a result you want to avoid, to help you avoid that result. You could call this use of Backsolver *disasterseeking*—it's another very valuable use of Backsolver.

For example, say that you and other investors are planning to invest in a yacht that you will rent out, and your financial projection for the investment is as shown in the worksheet in figure 21.9. If you meet plan, the most cash you will ever be out over the life of the investment will be 133.75 (in $000), as shown in cell C6 labeled MAX CASH OUT. But you may fear that the RENT you receive will be less than plan (in the worksheet, C14 shows RENT as percent of plan). And it may be that if MAX CASH OUT reaches or exceeds $150,000, you and the other investors will run short of cash. You want to avoid this disaster, and if the investment will involve significant risk of this disaster, you want to avoid the investment.

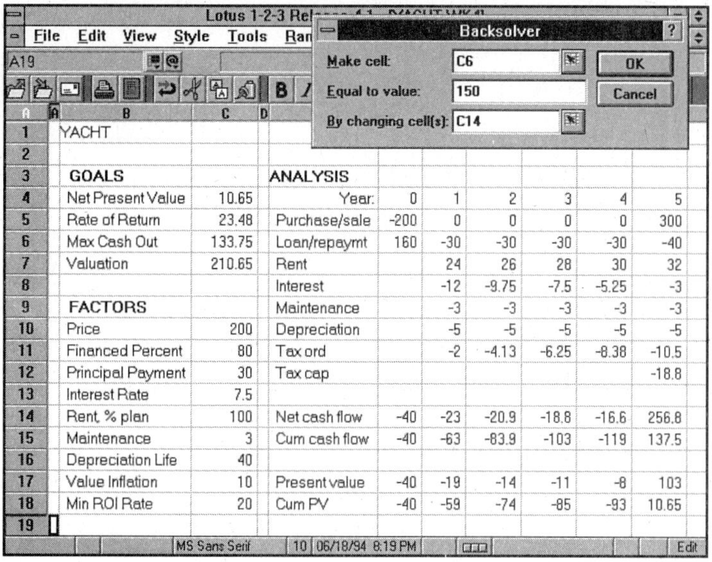

Fig. 21.9
Using Backsolver
to pinpoint
investment risk—
to see what
shortfall in rental
income would
cause a cash
problem.

Backsolver dialog box:
- Make cell: C6
- Equal to value: 150
- By changing cell(s): C14

	B	C		E					
1	YACHT								
2									
3	GOALS			ANALYSIS					
4	Net Present Value	10.65		Year:	0	1	2	3	4	5
5	Rate of Return	23.48		Purchase/sale	-200	0	0	0	0	300
6	Max Cash Out	133.75		Loan/repaymt	160	-30	-30	-30	-30	-40
7	Valuation	210.65		Rent		24	26	28	30	32
8				Interest		-12	-9.75	-7.5	-5.25	-3
9	FACTORS			Maintenance		-3	-3	-3	-3	-3
10	Price	200		Depreciation		-5	-5	-5	-5	-5
11	Financed Percent	80		Tax ord		-2	-4.13	-6.25	-8.38	-10.5
12	Principal Payment	30		Tax cap						-18.8
13	Interest Rate	7.5								
14	Rent, % plan	100		Net cash flow	-40	-23	-20.9	-18.8	-16.6	256.8
15	Maintenance	3		Cum cash flow	-40	-63	-83.9	-103	-119	137.5
16	Depreciation Life	40								
17	Value Inflation	10		Present value	-40	-19	-14	-11	-8	103
18	Min ROI Rate	20		Cum PV	-40	-59	-74	-85	-93	10.65
19										

To see what shortfall in RENT would cause MAX CASH OUT to be $150,000 or more, you could use Backsolver as shown in the Backsolver dialog box at upper right in figure 21.9. In Backsolver's **M**ake Cell and **E**qual To text boxes, enter the MAX CASH OUT cell (**C6**) and the result you want to avoid (**150**), and make the **B**y Changing Cell(s) the RENT cell (**C14**). Figure 21.10 shows Backsolver's result: if RENT is as low as 76.786 percent of plan, MAX CASH OUT will be 150 ($000).

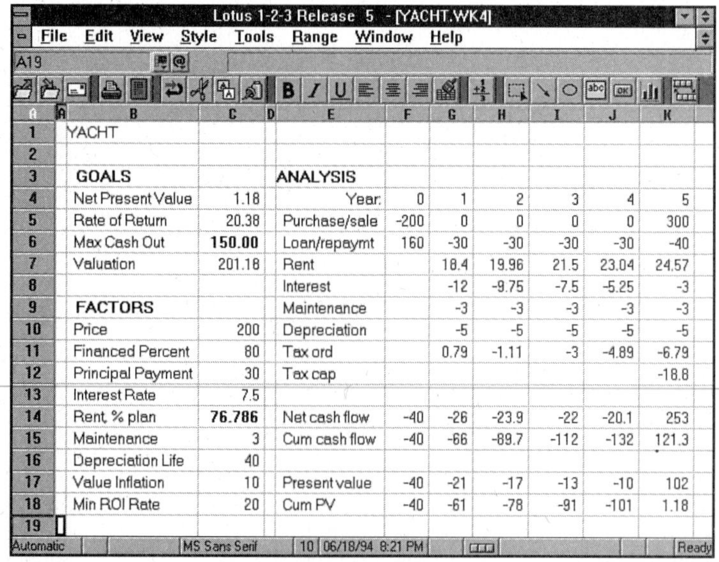

Fig. 21.10
Backsolver
pinpoints a risk.
It shows what
shortfall in rent
would make the
investment's cash
requirement too
high.

	B	C		E					
1	YACHT								
2									
3	GOALS			ANALYSIS					
4	Net Present Value	1.18		Year:	0	1	2	3	4	5
5	Rate of Return	20.38		Purchase/sale	-200	0	0	0	0	300
6	Max Cash Out	150.00		Loan/repaymt	160	-30	-30	-30	-30	-40
7	Valuation	201.18		Rent		18.4	19.96	21.5	23.04	24.57
8				Interest		-12	-9.75	-7.5	-5.25	-3
9	FACTORS			Maintenance		-3	-3	-3	-3	-3
10	Price	200		Depreciation		-5	-5	-5	-5	-5
11	Financed Percent	80		Tax ord		0.79	-1.11	-3	-4.89	-6.79
12	Principal Payment	30		Tax cap						-18.8
13	Interest Rate	7.5								
14	Rent, % plan	76.786		Net cash flow	-40	-26	-23.9	-22	-20.1	253
15	Maintenance	3		Cum cash flow	-40	-66	-89.7	-112	-132	121.3
16	Depreciation Life	40								
17	Value Inflation	10		Present value	-40	-21	-17	-13	-10	102
18	Min ROI Rate	20		Cum PV	-40	-61	-78	-91	-101	1.18
19										

With this Backsolver result, you assess the likelihood of RENT being this far below plan and if the risk is too high you avoid the investment. If you proceed with the investment, you know that if RENT may drop below 77% of plan, you should take action immediately to meet coming cash needs, before the crisis arrives.

Using Solver to Find Optimal Answers

In some ways Solver is similar to Backsolver, but Solver is more intricate and its best use is for more specialized analyses. The two most fundamental ways in which Solver differs from Backsolver are Solver's use of *constraints* and Solver's finding an *optimal* answer within the constraints.

In use of Solver, a *constraint* is a limit that you want Solver's answer to meet. For example, if you are seeking a plan to finance an auto purchase, you may want the down payment to be no more than $7,000. In preparing to use Solver, you enter constraints in worksheet cells using logical formulas. If down payment is in cell C3, in another cell that is blank you enter a down payment constraint formula: **+C3<=7000**.

An *optimal* Solver answer is the answer that makes the value in a particular cell as high as possible—or, if you choose, as low as possible—within constraints. For example, in your auto purchase plan you might want to know the highest car price you can meet, within your constraint of a down payment no more than $7,000. After making worksheet entries for auto purchase financing, including appropriate numbers and formulas for items such as interest rate and loan period and also making worksheet entries for your down-payment constraint, you can ask Solver to find the answer that reveals the highest car price you can meet.

Tip

Organize sets of Backsolver routes to a goal in Version Manager. At the worksheet get Version Manager, get Backsolver answers, and save them as versions.

Tip

To make Backsolver applications that are very easy for others to use, use the BACKSOLVE macro and macro buttons.

IV

Analyzing the Worksheet

Caution

1-2-3 product literature and Help describe Solver as useful for obtaining two types of results for a problem with constraints: finding an *optimal* answer, and finding *multiple* answers. But for finding multiple answers, Solver is not dependable: it commonly reports that it can find no more answers when there are other answers, which can mislead you into thinking the other answers do not exist. This flaw is described and illustrated in "Avoiding Solver's Weakness" later in this chapter.

Unless you have strong reasons for doing otherwise, it is generally best to apply Solver to a problem only to find the optimal answer.

Finding an Optimal Answer in Finance

1-2-3 has a series of Solver application examples in the file SOLVER.WK5, located in the \123R5W\SAMPLE\SOLVER directory. Three of these examples are especially good for illustrating use of Solver to find optimal answers to business problems in finance, production, and marketing. This section and the next two sections use and explain these three examples. If you want to see and explore these examples on your computer as you read these sections, and need help to do so, see "Exploring 1-2-3's Solver Examples" further on in this chapter. The example immediately below illustrates use of Solver to find the maximum auto price you can meet within certain constraints, using 1-2-3's Car Loan example.

Steps to an Optimal Solver Answer

To use Solver to find an optimal answer for any problem, you carry out the steps that are outlined below for the auto example.

1. Enter numbers and formulas in the worksheet. Solver will need at least one cell containing an entered number, which it will change in seeking the optimal answer. You will also want to enter one or more formulas in other cells, to calculate results from the entered numbers.

   To prepare for using Solver to find the highest auto price you can meet within your constraints, you might enter numbers and formulas in column D in the worksheet shown in figure 21.11. In cells D10 through D14 and in D16, numbers are entered for several items, as labeled in column C—Years to Pay and so on. Cells D19 through D21 contain formulas that use numbers in cells above to calculate results, as labeled in column C—Down-Payment and so on.

2. Also in the worksheet, enter constraints. In figure 21.11, cells F10 through F13 contain logical formulas expressing constraints on your auto payments, as displayed to the right of each of these cells. These constraints say Monthly Payment cannot exceed its maximum ($700 in cell D13) and cannot be negative, and Down-Payment cannot exceed its maximum ($3000 in cell D14) and cannot be negative.

> **Note**
>
> In logical formulas for Solver constraints, you can use five logical operators: =, <, >, <=, >=. You cannot use <>, **#AND#**, **#OR#**, or **#NOT#**.

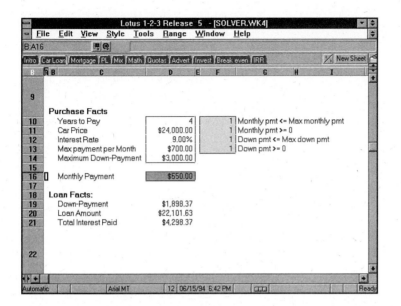

IV

Analyzing the Worksheet

Fig. 21.11
Making worksheet entries for an auto purchase financing plan, in preparation for using Solver to find the highest auto price you can meet.

3. Open the **R**ange menu and choose **A**nalyze and then **S**olver. This choice displays the Solver Definition dialog box, shown in figure 21.12.

   For frequent use of Solver, add the Solver SmartIcon to your SmartIcon palette. Clicking the Solver SmartIcon is equivalent to opening the **R**ange menu and choosing **A**nalyze and then **S**olver.

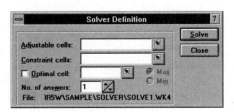

Fig. 21.12
With the Solver Definition dialog box, you can tell Solver to maximixe or minimize one cell's value by changing numbers in some cells while meeting constraints in other cells.

4. In Solver's **A**djustable Cells text box, specify the cells with entered numbers that you want Solver to be able to change in its search for the optimal answer. In the auto worksheet, there are only two such cells— D11 for Car Price and D16 for Monthly Payment. (Years To Pay and Interest Rate are set by the bank; the Max Payment per Month and Maximum Down-Payment numbers in D13 and D14 are your limits in ability to pay; and Down-Payment cell D19 is a formula cell, whose value will be calculated from numbers entered in other cells.) So in the **A**djustable Cells text box you enter **D11,D16**, as shown in figure 21.13.

(Note that in this text box your entry is not limited to a single range— you can enter two or more cells or ranges separated by commas.)

Fig. 21.13
Ready for Solver to solve. Solver will change numbers in D11 and D16 to find the answer with the maximum value for D11 within the constraints in F10..F13.

5. In the **C**onstraint Cells text box, specify the cells containing the constraints you want Solver's answer to meet. For the auto example, the constraints are in cells F10 through F13, so in this text box you enter **F10..F13** as shown in figure 21.13.

6. Click the **O**ptimal Cell check box; in the **O**ptimal cell text box, enter the cell for which you want Solver to find an optimal value, and choose either Ma**x** or Mi**n**. In the auto example, the answer you want Solver to find is the highest Car Price you can meet, so in the **O**ptimal Cell text box you enter the Car Price cell, **D11**. The default selection is Ma**x** rather than Mi**n,** so you do not have to click it. When you have completed this step, the Optimal Cell option of the Solver Definition dialog box appears as shown in figure 21.13.

(If you are using the 1-2-3 file for the Car Loan example on your computer, you will find that in the 1-2-3 Car Loan example the Solver Definition dialog box entries are set for not asking for an optimal answer. But what Solver does well is find an optimal answer, and what this example does best is illustrate Solver's finding an optimal answer. In the example on your computer, make changes in the Optimal Cell option of the Solver Definition dialog box to conform to figure 21.13.)

7. Enter **1** in the No. of Answers text box. Since you want the optimal answer, you have no need for other answers.

8. Click the **S**olve button.

Solver Delivery of an Optimal Answer

When you click the **S**olve button, Solver starts its search for the answer that, within your constraints, has the highest Car Price. While Solver is seeking the answer, it displays the Solver Progress dialog box showing information on its progress. When Solver has found the answer, it displays the Solver Answer dialog box, and in the worksheet, numbers in cells change to reflect the optimal answer Solver has found (see fig. 21.14).

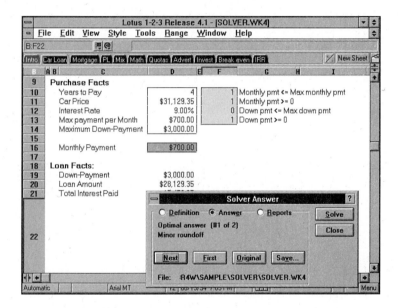

Notice that in the answer worksheet in figure 21.14, Monthly Payment and Down-Payment are both at the maximum values your constraints permit, $700 and $3000 respectively, and Car Price is $31,129.35—well above the $24,000 that was displayed in this cell before Solver found the optimal answer. The Car Price that Solver has displayed, $31,129.35, is the highest car price you can meet within your payment constraints.

Finding an Optimal Answer in Production

Figure 21.15 shows worksheet entries for use of Solver to find the most profitable mix of products to be produced at a bakery. (This is 1-2-3's Mix example.)

Tip
When Solver finds the optimal answer you asked for and other answers too, it presents the optimal answer first as Answer #1.

Fig. 21.14
Solver delivers an optimal answer. The Solver Answer dialog box appears, and worksheet numbers change to reflect the optimal answer, in this case the highest affordable Car Price.

Tip
A Roundoff error means that the answer meets the constraints but that worksheet calculation makes the answer appear as if it violates a constraint. A Minor means roundoff error is six or more places to the right of the decimal point.

Fig. 21.15
Worksheet entries for use of Solver to find most profitable product mix. Constraints are entered with logical formulas in B21..B24 and displayed in column C.

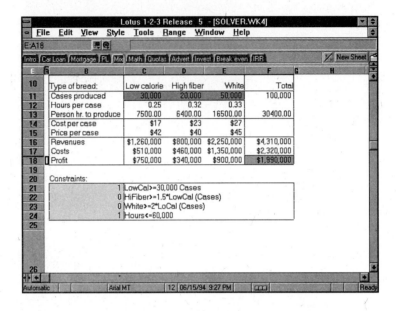

Cells C11 through Ell, Cases Produced for the three types of bread, are the only cells with entered numbers for Solver to change. The Hours Per Case, Cost Per Case, and Price Per Case rows have numbers that represent fixed conditions which the bakery has to deal with, so you don't want Solver changing numbers in these cells. All other cells showing numbers in rows 11 through 18 have formula entries for calculating results, based on numbers entered including those in the cells for Cases Produced for the three bread types.

The range B21..B24 holds the constraints for this example. The first three contraints are related to the number of Cases Produced: there must be at least 30,000 cases of Low Calorie, there must be 1.5 times as many cases of High Fiber as Low Calorie, and there must be double the number of cases of White as Low Calorie. The final constraint mandates that no more than 60,000 Hours be worked.

Tip
In each constraint cell, when the constraint is met the cell shows 1, and when the constraint is not met, the cell shows 0. Enter labels beside constraint cells and watch their 1s and 0s.

After completing these worksheet entries, you open the **R**ange menu and choose **A**nalyze and then **S**olver. The Solver Definition dialog box appears. Figure 21.16 shows the entries you make in this dialog box to assign Solver the mission of finding the most profitable product mix.

In the **A**djustable Cells text box, you enter the range containing the Cases Produced numbers for the three bread types: **C11..E11**. In the **C**onstraint Cells text box, you enter the range containing the logical formulas expressing the four constraints: **B21..B24**. Click the **O**ptimal Cell check box; in the

Optimal Cell text box, enter the cell containing the formula for Total Profit, **F18**; and leave the Ma**x** option button selected. Set or leave No. of Ans**w**ers at **1**. Click the **S**olve button.

Fig. 21.16
Solver seeks highest profit for F18 by changing production figures in C11..E11 while obeying constraints in B21..B24.

After a few seconds, Solver finds the optimal answer and displays the Solver Answer dialog box, and worksheet numbers change to reflect the optimal answer. The most profitable plan is to produce 43,165 cases of Low Calorie, 64,748 of High Fiber, and 86,331 of White, as shown in row 11 of the figure 21.17 worksheet. This product mix will produce Profit of $3,733,813 as shown in cell F18.

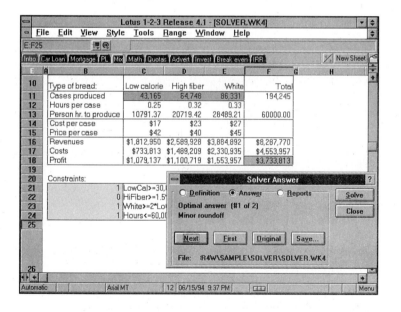

Fig. 21.17
Solver delivers the answer: optimal product mix (row 11) for maximal profit (F18).

Finding an Optimal Answer in Marketing

Some areas of business spending that offer "diminishing returns"—the more you spend, the less you get per dollar of additional spending. You spend the first X dollars on the program offering highest results per dollar, the next Y dollars on the second best program, and so on. Since you choose the best

Tip
After getting an optimal Solver answer, try to see why that answer is optimal. Seeing why can give you insights of practical value.

programs first, each additional amount you spend is a little lower in payoff per dollar.

Figure 21.18 shows worksheet entries for using of Solver to find the best plan for an advertising program that involves diminishing returns. (This example is based on the 1-2-3 Solver example named Advert.)

Fig. 21.18
Worksheet for using Solver to find best advertising media mix. The goal is highest total projected exposure number in G15.

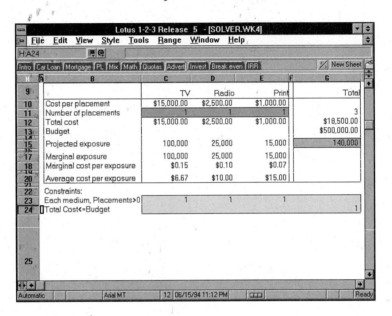

In this problem, the question is what combination of Number of Placements figures for the three media (in C11..E11) will produce the highest Total Projected Exposure (advertising results) in cell G15, within the $500,000 Budget in cell G13. The Cost per Placement figures in row 10 are cost factors the business has to deal with, which you do not want Solver to change. All the other cells showing numbers in the table have formulas to calculate results based on the Number of Placements figures for the three media.

The diminishing returns are expressed in the formulas in the two Exposure rows. The formulas in these rows indicate that for each of the media, every additional placement provides a little less exposure than the prior one.

The logical formulas for the constraints are entered in the range from C23 to G24, and summaries of the constraints are displayed in cells B23 and B24. In row 23, the cell for each of the media has a logical formula saying that medium's Number of Placements must be 1 or more. Cell G24 has the most important constraint: Total Cost for all three media cannot exceed the Budget figure in G13, $500,000.

After opening the **R**ange menu and choosing **A**nalyze and then **S**olver, in the Solver Definition dialog box, you make the entries shown in figure 21.19. For **A**djustable Cells you enter the three media's Number of Placements cells, **C11..E11**. For **C**onstraint Cells you enter the range containing the logical formulas for the constraints, **C23..G24**. In the dialog box **O**ptimal Cell row, after clicking the check box, enter the cell for Total Projected Exposure, which you want to maximize, **G15**, and leave the Max option button selected. Set or leave No. of Ans**w**ers at **1**. With these steps taken, the Solver Definition dialog box appears as in figure 21.19, and you click the **S**olve button.

Fig. 21.19
Ready to solve for best ad media mix. Solver changes the Number of Placements in row 11 to get the highest total projected exposure in G15 within the constraints in rows 23 and 24.

Note

If Solver is sure it has found the optimal answer, it calls the answer *optimal*. Otherwise it calls the answer *best*, which means the best answer Solver could find, but there may be better.

After a few seconds, Solver displays the Solver Answer dialog box, and, in the worksheet, numbers change to reflect the best answer, as shown in figure 21.20. With Number of Placements at 24 for TV, 42 for Radio, and 40 for Print, Total Cost equals the Budget of $500,000 and Total Projected Exposure is at the best Solver could find within the constraints, 678,413.

Avoiding Solver's Weakness

1-2-3 product literature and Help describe Solver as a key tool not only for finding an optimal answer to a problem, but also for finding *multiple* answers to a problem. But as noted in a Caution at the start of this chapter's section on Solver, for finding multiple answers to a problem, Solver is not a dependable tool, and you should not rely on it for this purpose.

If you use Solver to seek multiple answers to a problem, Solver will commonly fail to find answers that are valid and that Solver should find. Then, if you ask Solver to try again to seek more answers to the problem, Solver tries again and tells you it cannot find any more answers, implying that there are no more answers—when there may be more answers.

Fig. 21.20
The Number of
Placements in row
11 deliver the
highest total
projected exposure
in G15 within the
budget and other
constraints in rows
23 and 24.

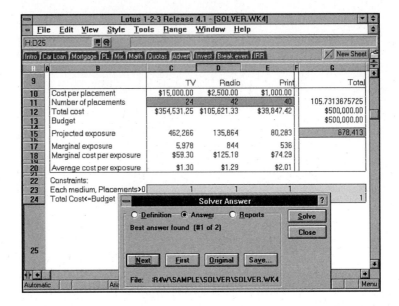

To see an example of this failure, consider asking Solver to find five pairs of
numbers that each equal 4. You know there are five easy answers: 4+0, 0+4,
3+1, 1+3, 2+2.

For this problem, figure 21.21 shows entries in the worksheet and the Solver
Definition dialog box. An answer requires changing the two 1s entered in B3
and B4 to meet the constraint in B7, which requires that B5's total of the two
numbers be 4; and Solver is asked to find five such answers.

Fig. 21.21
The Solver
Definition dialog
box is ready to ask
Solver for five
answers to a
simple problem:
find two numbers
that total 4.

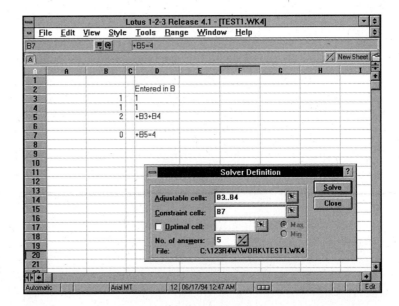

When you click the **S**olve button, Solver finds only one of the five requested answers that you know exist, 3+1 (see fig. 21.22). Note that in the Solver Answer dialog box, Solver displays a message indicating that the answer it is now showing is Answer (#1 of 1).

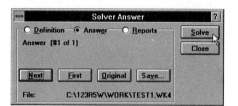

Fig. 21.22
Solver fails the multiple-answer test. For a simple problem with five simple answers, Solver finds only one.

Click the **S**olve button again, which is a request to Solver to make another search for more answers. When you do so, Solver displays a message box saying Cannot find any more answers.

This is the complete failure of Solver to perform its find-multiple-answers function, for a simple problem.

For this problem, even though Solver found only one answer, you can see that there are other answers. But what makes Solver's failure to find other answers most dangerous is that for realistic uses, which of course involve much more complex problems, you cannot so easily see that answers Solver failed to find do exist. So if you expect Solver to perform well in finding multiple answers, its failure to do so and its Cannot find any more answers message are likely to lead you to believe that no more answers exist, when they do exist but Solver has failed to find them.

Using Functions with Solver

In the formula cells that you tell Solver to focus on—constraint cells and optimal cells—there are limits on what functions you can use. Functions in these cells must be value functions—functions that deliver numbers, not text, times, or dates. Functions that deliver 1 for true or 0 for false are acceptable because these results are considered value numbers. Functions you can use in cells that Solver focuses on are listed in Table 21.1.

Other parts of your worksheet can contain any functions.

Table 21.1	Functions You Can Use in Solver Problem Cells		
@ABS	@FVAL	@PI	@SIN
@ACOS	@GRANDTOTAL	@PMT	@SLN
@ASIN	@HLOOKUP	@PUREAVG	@SQRT
@ATAN	@IF	@PURECOUNT	@STD
@ATAN2	@INDEX	@PUREMAX	@STDS
@AVG	@INT	@PUREMIN	@SUBTOTAL
@CHOOSE	@IRR	@PURESTD	@SUM
@COLS	@ISNUMBER	@PURESTDS	@SUMPRODUCT
@COS	@LN	@PUREVAR	@SYD
@COUNT	@LOG	@PUREVARS	@TAN
@CTERM	@MAX	@PV	@TERM
@DB	@MIN	@PVAL	@TRUE
@DDB	@MOD	@RATE	@VAR
@EXP	@NPER	@ROUND	@@VARS
@FALSE	@NPV	@ROWS	@VDB
@FV	@PAYMT	@SHEETS	@VLOOKUP

Using Solver Dialog Boxes

Solver has three principal dialog boxes: the Solver Definition, Solver Answer, and Solver Reports dialog boxes. Each of these three has, just under its title bar, a trio of option buttons for toggling among the three boxes (see fig. 21.22). While using these dialog boxes, you may encounter other Solver dialog boxes.

Solver Definition Dialog Box

The Solver Definition dialog box is shown in figure 21.12 and its use is illustrated in the preceding Solver examples and related figures 21.13, 21.16, 21.19, and 21.21.

Solver Answer and Related Dialog Boxes

The Solver Answer dialog box is shown and its use is illustrated in figures 21.14, 21.17, 21.20, and 21.22 and described in the texts on the examples these figures illustrate.

> **Caution**
>
> If in a worksheet showing one of Solver's answers, you enter changes, you can lose
> the entire set of Solver answers. Before editing any Solver answer worksheet, save all
> answers you want to keep.
>
> To see worksheet parts obstructed by a Solver dialog box, move the dialog box. Until
> you know Solver well, moving is better than closing the dialog box. Closing the box
> enables worksheet editing which can destroy all current Solver answers.

In the Solver Answer dialog box, across the bottom there are four buttons:
Next, **F**irst, **O**riginal, and Sa**v**e (see fig. 21.22). Assuming you have used
Solver to obtain only a single optimal answer, the **O**riginal and **F**irst buttons
toggle the worksheet back and forth between pre-solve values and the values
of Solver's optimal answer. Clicking **O**riginal changes the worksheet values
back to what they were before Solver carried out its solve, and clicking **F**irst
makes the worksheet display the first answer Solver found. If you asked
Solver to find multiple answers—or if you requested one answer but Solver
found more than one anyway—repeated clicking of **N**ext advances the
worksheet from one answer to the next through all the answers Solver found.

The Solver Answer dialog box Sa**v**e button displays the Save as Scenario dialog box, which is for saving the current answer as a scenario in Version Manager (see fig. 21.23). In the Save As Scenario dialog box, in the **S**cenario Name
text box enter the name with which you want Version Manager to save the
worksheet; in the **N**ote text box enter whatever notes you want Version
Manager to save with the worksheet. Click Sa**v**e.

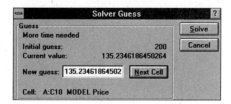

Fig. 21.23
Save a current
answer as scenario
in Version
Manager.

Tip
When Solver deliv-
ers an attempt
instead of an an-
swer, what it deliv-
ers violates one or
more constraints
but Solver has
delivered this
result anyway.

If Solver cannot find an answer, it may display the Solver Answer dialog box
with a message saying Guesses required and the **S**olve button that is usually
at its upper right replaced by a Guess button. If you click the Guess button,
the Solver Guess dialog box appears (see fig. 21.24). At its bottom this dialog
box names an Adjustable Cell, and just above this specification of the cell it
has a New **G**uess text box in which you can enter your guess for the right
value for that cell in the answer you want Solver to find. To the right of the

New Guess text box is a **N**ext Cell button for advancing to the next Adjustable Cell. To help Solver find the answer, in the Solver Guess dialog box click the **N**ext Cell button to advance one by one through all the Adjustable Cells, and at each Adjustable Cell for which you have a guess that may help Solver find the answer, enter that value in the New **G**uess text box. When you have entered your guesses for all Adjustable Cells for which you have guesses that you think may help Solver, click the **S**olve button. Solver makes a new attempt to find the answer with the help of your guesses.

Fig. 21.24

The Solver Guess dialog box. Click **N**ext Cell to advance through cells and at each, enter a value guess, to help Solver find an answer.

Solver Reports and Related Dialog Boxes

The Solver Reports dialog box is the third of the trio of principal Solver dialog boxes, among which you can toggle with the trio of option buttons under their dialog box title bars. The Solver Reports dialog box is shown in figure 21.25.

Fig. 21.25

Select a Re**p**ort Type, and then click **T**able or (if available) **C**ell.

At left in this dialog box, under the heading Re**p**ort Type, is a scrollable list of seven types of reports available on Solver answers. These seven report types are described in the next section, "Using Solver Reports."

To the right of this list are two buttons: **C**ell and **T**able. After choosing one of the report types, to get that report you click one of these two buttons. The **T**able button is available for any of the seven report types, including the How Solved Report which is the most valuable of the seven for reporting on an optimal answer. (See the next section on "Using Solver Reports.") When you click the **T**able button, the report type you selected is displayed in the format of one or more tables (see fig. 21.26).

The **C**ell button is available for only some of the report types, and is not available for the How Solved Report. If you select a report type for which the **C**ell button is available and then click the **C**ell button, in the current-answer worksheet a cell relevant to the problem is highlighted, and in front of the worksheet the Solver Cell Report dialog box appears with information on the highlighted cell. This dialog box has a **N**ext button, and by repeated clicking of that button you can move the highlight from one problem-relevant worksheet cell to the next, and at each cell the dialog box shows information on that cell.

If in the Solver Reports dialog box you select the Differences Report, the Solver Report Differences dialog box appears. Under the heading **C**ompare Answers, this dialog box has two small text boxes in which you enter the numbers of the two Solver answers you want compared, such as 1 and 2. If in the comparison you want to see only cell-value differences between the answers of some minimal amount or greater, such as 1000 or more, enter that minimal amount in the text box labeled **F**or Differences. For the Differences Report, click **R**eport.

Using Solver Reports

As described in the preceding section, the Solver Reports dialog box (shown in figure 21.25) contains a scrollable list of seven report types, and for an optimal answer, which is the kind of answer Solver finds dependably, the best of the seven report types is the How Solved Report. Figure 21.26 shows a How Solved Report for the optimal answer for the problem described earlier in this chapter in "Finding an Optimal Answer in Finance." (If you are using the 1-2-3 SOLVER.WK5 file on your computer, you can get this report in the Car Loan example.)

The How Solved Report

For the current answer (the one shown in the worksheet when you use the Solver Report dialog box), the How Solved report contains a text summary of what the answer represents and tables of data on that answer's Optimal cell (if an optimal answer), Adjustable cells, Binding constraints, and Nonbinding constraints. In each of these four tables, this report shows a row for each relevant cell, in which the first two columns provide cell addresses and (if any) cell range names. In the Optimal and Adjustable cell tables, the third column shows value for current answer. In the Binding and Nonbinding Constraints tables, the third column shows the constraint formula, and in the Nonbinding Constraint table there is a fourth column showing a modification of each nonbinding formula that would make it binding for the current answer (see fig. 21.26).

Fig. 21.26

For the most complete report on Solver's optimal answer use the How Solved Report.

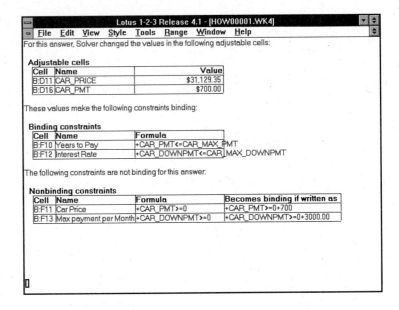

The Other Reports

Following are descriptions of the other six Solver report types, in the Table format in which all seven reports are available.

- *The Answer Table Report.* This report is a summary of all answers Solver found. Vertically it has three sections: at top, Optimal cell (if you specified one); center, Adjustable cells (a row for each); and bottom, Constraint cells (a row for each). In columns from left to right, it shows for each cell the cell's worksheet address; name (if any); lowest value in any answer; highest value in any answer; and then a column for each answer, showing cell values for that answer.

- *The Differences Report.* This report compares any two answers in cell-by-cell number differences. It shows a row for every cell whose number is affected by changes in Adjustable cells. For each cell, the first two columns provide address and name; the next two columns show number for each of the two answers being compared, and two more columns show the difference of the second answer values from those of the first in absolute number and in percent. In the Differences Report table, the percent difference figures compare first answer to second in percent difference—not ratio. For example, 12 is 200% as big as 6, but its difference from 6 is 100% of 6. This table reports the latter.

- *The What-if Limits Report.* This report is also answer-specific. It shows, for each Adjustable cell, two value ranges. For each Adjustable cell, the first two columns specify cell address and name (if any); the next two columns specify, for each adjustable cell, the lowest and highest values Solver used in all its answers; and two more columns show, for each adjustable cell, the highest or lowest its value could be for the current answer without violating any constraint—assuming no other adjustable cell's value in the answer is changed.

- *The Nonbinding Constraints Report.* This report is essentially the last section of the How Solved report. For the current answer, it shows for each nonbinding constraint the cell address, name if any, formula, and what change in formula would make the constraint binding for the current answer. See the Nonbinding Constraints table in figure 21.26.

- *The Inconsistent Constraints Report.* If you have one or more constraints that conflict with other constraints, this report provides information on the conflicts. For a conflicting constraint, it specifies cell, name if any, formula, and a modification of formula that would eliminate the conflict.

- *The Cells Used Report.* This report simply lists by address and name (if any) every cell Solver looked at in its search for the current answers—that is, exactly the cells you entered in the Solver Definition box when you defined the mission for Solver: optimal cell (if any), adjustable cells, and constraint cells.

Troubleshooting

My Solver report tables are not as clear and concise as the report shown in figure 21.26. What can I do to make my tables more comprehensible and useful?

First, select all columns with numbers, using the column letters across the top to select entire columns; choose **S**tyle **N**umber Format, set the format at Fixed, and set an appropriate number of decimal places to display, such as 0 or 2. Solver works with numbers carried way out in decimal places—but with 2 or 0 decimal places the reports are much easier to read.

Second, while the same columns are still selected, use **S**tyle **C**olumn Width to squeeze out unneeded column widths. Try to make the entire table less wide than the display so you can see it all, without making any column too narrow for its contents or heading. To do so, you may want to set individual columns at different widths.

(continues)

Analyzing the Worksheet

(continued)

Third, select key rows that contain report name and table headings, using row numbers down the left to select entire rows, and use **S**tyle **F**ont & Attributes to change these rows to Bold so they stand out.

Look at figure 21.25 to see how these steps help make the reports more clear and concise compared to Solver's standard report tables format.

If you are going to use the report again, save it now to retain your format improvements.

Exploring 1-2-3's Solver Examples

Tip

If SOLVER.WK5 is not on your disk, you can add it quickly with 1-2-3 custom install. This file is under 60K. If disk space is tight, after learning from it, delete it.

In the file SOLVER.WK5, located in the 123R5W\SAMPLE\SOLVER directory, 1-2-3 has eleven Solver application examples, including three on which Solver examples in this chapter are based. This section is a guide for your use of these examples on your computer.

When you open the Solver examples file, your display shows a series of eleven worksheet tabs (see fig. 21.26). All but the far left Intro tab are names of examples. (The Math tab has two examples, so the ten tabs contain eleven examples.)

Below the tabs, the initial display is the Intro, which presents some basic instructions for use of the examples. (In figure 21.27, you have already moved beyond the Intro to the Car Loan example by clicking that example's tab.) The Intro explains that at each example, there is an Example button set up so that if you click it, the Solver Definition box appears with the entries already made for the Solve you are expected to see.

Tip

Notice that the Solver examples use macro buttons to enter information into the Solver Definition dialog box. With this approach you can make Solver applications easier for others to use.

In the Solver examples, you do not have to just click the Example button and watch. In each example, you can move around, do things, and change things just as you could if you had set up the example yourself, and by doing so you can learn more from the examples. In the examples, you can

■ Move around on the worksheet.

■ As you move cell to cell, at each cell look at the edit line to see what is entered in the cell.

■ Change numbers—but hesitate before changing formula entries, most of which are just the right mathematics for the examples.

■ To get the Solver box, open the **R**ange menu and choose **A**nalyze and then **S**olver.

- Make your own Solver box entries.

- After Solver delivers an answer, click **R**eports option button in the Solver Answer dialog box, and then from the Solver Reports dialog box choose various Solver reports.

- Use the 1-2-3 menu to make adjustments in display appearance, such as removing parts of the 1-2-3 window to see more of a Solver report table.

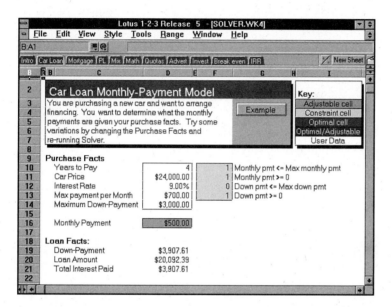

Fig. 21.27
An example from the 1-2-3 SOLVER.WK5 file. To get to this example, click the Car Loan tab.

Following is a summary guide to use of the better individual examples in the Solver file:

- First, use the Car Loan, Mix, and Advert examples, referring to the sections earlier in this chapter that are based on these three examples. These are the best examples of the use of Solver to find optimal answers in finance, production, and marketing.

- Second, look at the PL and Math examples. PL is another good example of using Solver to find optimal product mix. Math has two good examples, of which the second one (below the first) is better because it is more fully presented.

- Third, look at the Invest example. For this example, change the formula for Total Return in F21 so that it measures *after-tax* return. With this correction, you may want to adapt and use this example for your personal investment portfolio.

From Here...

For further information and ideas to increase value of answers you can obtain with Backsolver and Solver, see the following chapters in this book.

- Chapter 20, "Auditing Worksheets." In this chapter, you can learn how to use tools to identify formula cells, for which Backsolver can find ways to meet a goal and Solver can find optimal answers, and to identify the cells upon which these formula cells are dependent.

- Chapter 22, "Managing Multiple Solutions with Version Manager." In this chapter, you can learn a powerful way to organize answers produced with Solver or Backsolver.

- Chapters 35 and 36, respectively "Writing 1-2-3 for Windows Macros" and "Recording and Modifying Macros." In these chapters you can learn to set up Solver and Backsolver applications with macro buttons like those in the 1-2-3 Solver examples, making your Solver and Backsolver applications easier for others to use.

Chapter 22

Managing Multiple Solutions with Version Manager

Version Manager is a powerful system for managing multiple versions of worksheets, such as business plans, predictions, and decision analyses. For work you do by yourself, Version Manager can be valuable. For work that involves contributions from several people, such as developing a business plan that includes budgets and predictions from various departments, Version Manager offers tremendous value.

In this chapter, you learn to do the following:

- Create a system of data versions

- Combine versions into scenarios

- Manage versions and scenarios

- Create version and scenario reports

- Merge versions file to file

Managing Business Planning

For business planning, the principal value of Version Manager is in managing multiple what-ifs—multiple variations of a business plan that have specific differences, such as different sales predictions, but are otherwise alike. With Version Manager, for a business plan you can efficiently create and use two levels of what-ifs:

- *Versions*. These are multiple sets of numbers for particular parts of the plan, such as Fred's and Veronica's predictions for the sales row or for the production-overhead row.

- *Scenarios*. These are combinations of versions of various parts of the plan, such as one plan with Veronica's sales numbers and Fred's production-overhead numbers and another plan that is all Veronica's versions.

You set up the structure of the plan only once. The *structure* is the formulas that translate the numbers in versions and scenarios into results such as profit and cash flow and whatever you want to make the resulting reports as clear as possible, such as formatting the reports and charting the results. Then with Version Manager, you can create and manage various versions and scenarios and see and compare the reports and charts for each.

Finding Better Plans More Systematically

Managing multiple spreadsheet versions is critical to getting the most from worksheets for business plans and decisions.

Almost every plan or key decision has many possibilities. Worksheets are a marvelous tool for capturing all the possibilities, including each person's expertise, and seeing results for all alternatives in multiple worksheets. To go from more numbers to better plans and decisions, you need a system for keeping track of the worksheets, comparing alternatives in a uniform framework, and integrating parts from different experts into the overall plan. You need a *worksheet version management* system.

Version Manager is such a system. With Version Manager, you can give your planning and decision analysis the following key strengths:

- *Compare and integrate many predictions and other inputs in one planning framework.* As described earlier, with Version Manager you can set up one framework of formulas and reports and then insert and integrate various inputs into various versions.

- *Keep full track of all versions.* Version Manager automatically keeps a record of author (licensed user) and entry date and time for each version. It also provides a convenient system for labeling and annotating each version: what it represents, who contributed it, assumptions and reasoning behind this prediction, and other notes.

- *Sort and reorganize plan versions.* With Version Manager you can sort plan versions and scenarios according to various criteria, such as when created or by whom created.

- *Share integrated planning among coworkers, departments, and divisions.* Version Manager provides a powerful merge utility that combines versions and scenarios from one file into another file. If you use Lotus Notes, with Version Manager you can save your files as Notes databases and enable various people to enter versions into a file at the same time.

Entering Two Versions in Five Quick Steps

Say you have a plan for sales, expenses, and profit, and two managers named Fred and Veronica have different predictions for sales. To create two versions of the plan reflecting the two sales predictions, you take these five steps:

1. Enter or display the plan in the worksheet, with the number entered for one of the two sales predictions.

2. To get Version Manager, open the **R**ange menu and choose **V**ersion. The Version Manager window appears. (Initially it appears less "tall" than shown. To make it taller, which enables you to see its central area where comments on versions will be shown, drag the window's bottom border down.)

Fig. 22.1
The Version Manager window (behind the Create Version dialog box). Its bottom border has been dragged down to make it "taller."

3. In the worksheet, highlight the range containing the numbers you want to make a version, in this case the cell with the sales number, and then in Version Manager click the Create button. In front of Version Manager, a similar but larger Create Version dialog box appears (see fig. 22.2).

Fig. 22.2

The Create Version dialog box. It shows the proposed name SALES for the selected worksheet range, and the proposed name Version 1 for the current contents of that range.

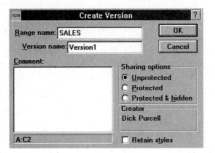

The Create Version dialog box assumes that you may want to create a version of the currently selected worksheet range, in this case the cell with the sales number. To have versions, a range must have a range name. The dialog box searches to the right of the selected range, and if you have entered SALES in the cell to the right of the sales number, the dialog box finds this name and displays it as a proposed **R**ange name. (See top text box in the Create Version dialog box in fig. 22.2)

4. In the Version name text box in the Create Version dialog box, enter whatever name you want to give the current sales version. The dialog box has proposed the name Version 1, but you may prefer a more informative name. If the current sales number is Fred's prediction, for **Ver**sion name you might enter FRED.

   Then if you wish, in the larger white comment area of the dialog box, enter any notes you want to record with this sales version, such as a brief explanation of why Fred predicts this number for sales.

   Then click the dialog box OK button. The Create Version dialog box disappears, making the Version Manager window visible again. For the sales range there is now a version named FRED.

5. To create a second SALES range version, use a similar procedure. In the worksheet, change the sales number to what Veronica predicts; with this range selected, in Version Manager click the Create button; in the dialog box, for **V**ersion name enter VERONICA, and enter any notes on this version in the Comment area, then click OK.

Viewing and Using Version Manager Results

Now Version Manager has two versions of the sales range of your plan, each with associated notes and each affecting dependent cells in the rest of your plan, and enables you to switch instantly from one version to the other.

In its Named range text box, Version Manager shows SALES, and in its With version(s) text box, it shows the name of the current sales range (which you have left as the VERONICA version). Names of all versions of the current range, SALES, are listed in the With version(s) dropdown box: FRED and VERONICA. To switch to either of these versions, select it in this dropdown list.

When you choose either version, in the worksheet the sales range number changes to show that version; the rest of the worksheet changes to reflect effects of that version—for example, if there is a profit formula that refers to the sales number, it recalculates to show the profit figure reflecting that version's number; and the center area in Version Manager shows the notes you entered in the Command area for that version. When you choose version FRED, sales and the rest of your plan reflect Fred's sales prediction and Version Manager shows your notes on Fred's sales prediction, and when you choose the VERONICA version your worksheet plan and the Version Manager central area showing Comment entries change to reflect her version. In sum, Version Manager provides you a very efficient way to manage multiple versions of the plan.

If you experiment a bit with the Version Manager, you can see the following:

- If you move the cell pointer to a cell containing an entered number that has a name in a cell to its left, when you click the **C**reate button, the Version Manager window uses the name for your highlighted cell. For example, when you clicked Version Manager's Create button with a range highlighted that has the label SALES to its left, the Create Version dialgo box proposed the **R**ange name SALES, as shown in figure 22.2.

- If you click the **I**nfo button at the bottom of the Version Manager window, you can revise the contents of the notes for the current version. At the lower right in the Version Manager window, you can see the name of the author (authorized or licensed user) and the date and time of entry of this version.

- If you click Version Manager's **T**o Index icon, the Version Manager window is replaced by the similar but more powerful Version Manager Index window.

Tip
To experiment with version and scenario examples, open the **H**elp menu, choose **T**utorial, and then choose Lesson 8, "Using Version Manager."
Or open the file \123R5W\SAMPLE \GLOBAL.WK4.

Maximizing Your Use of Version Manager

The sections that follow show you how to do the following:

- Understand how to use Version Manager to manage and share data

- Create and display different versions of data in a named range

- Group versions together into scenarios

- Use the Index to display information about versions and scenarios

- Create reports about the data in the versions

- Merge versions and scenarios from one file into another file

Understanding Version Manager Basics

Tip

If you want to manage multiple versions of a range larger than the 2,000-cell limit for a version, you can divide it into two or more named ranges and join versions of them as scenarios.

To apply Version Manager power, you have to fully understand the terms and windows described in this section.

When using Version Manager, the three key terms are as follows:

- *Named range.* You can create different sets of data only for named ranges. A *range* is a single cell or a 2-D or 3-D block of adjoining cells. A *named range* is a range to which you have assigned a name.

  You can use Version Manager to simultaneously assign a name to a range and create a version of that named range; alternatively, you can use **R**ange **N**ame Add to assign a name to a range and then use Version Manager to create a version of the range.

- *Version.* When you create different sets of data for a single named range, you assign each set a name, such as HIGH SALES or LOW SALES. Each named set of data for a named range is called a *version* of that range. When you create a version of a named range, Version Manager stores the current contents of the range as well as other information including your name, the date, and the time you created the version and an optional comment.

  For example, in a range named REVENUES, you can enter the values 500, 400, 300, and 200 and then use Version Manager to create a version with the name HIGH SALES. You then can enter the values 50, 40, 30, and 20 in the same named range and create a second version with the name LOW SALES. Both versions of the named range are stored in memory; you can use Version Manager to display either version. When you save the file, 1-2-3 for Windows saves both versions of the named range as part of the worksheet file.

You can create versions for any named range in a file. For example, if you want to compare different combinations of revenues and expenses, you can create several different versions of the range named EXPENSES and use Version Manager to display the different combinations.

■ *Scenario*. After you create versions, you can treat selected versions of different named ranges as a group. A named group of versions is called a *scenario*. For example, you can group the HIGH SALES version of the REVENUES range with the LOW EXPENSES version of the EXPENSES range to create a scenario named BEST CASE. You also can create a WORST CASE scenario that contains the LOW SALES version of REVENUES and the HIGH EXPENSES version of EXPENSES.

Tip
A version's range can contain anything you can enter in a cell: values, labels, formulas, functions, and even macros.

For full use of Version Manager, the two key windows are the Version Manager window, which you have already seen in figure 22.1; and the Version Manager Index window (see fig. 22.3).

Fig. 22.3
The Version Manager Index window is similar to the Version Manager window but offering more buttons and more powers.

Each of these windows has an icon for moving to the other. The Version Manager window enables you to create, display, modify, and delete versions. The Version Manager Index window enables you to do everything the Version Manager window enables, and also to create and manage scenarios, create reports, and merge versions and scenarios from one file into another.

The Version Manager window enables you to perform simple actions on one version at a time. To open the Version Manager window, open the **R**ange menu and choose **V**ersion or click the Version Manager SmartIcon. The Version Manager window appears.

The Version Manager Index window gives you information about many versions in one place. You can sort the information in the Version Manager Index window by range name, version name, scenario name, date, or contributor name. In addition, the Version Manager Index window enables you to perform actions that may affect more than one version, such as creating and modifying scenarios. To use the Version Manager Index window, choose the **T**o Index button located at the lower right in the Version Manager window. To go from the Version Manager Index window back to the Version Manager window, choose the **T**o Manager button at the lower right in the Version Manager Index window.

In the following sections, *Manager* means the Version Manager window, and *Index* means the Version Manager Index window.

Using the Manager

You use the Manager to create, display, update, modify, and delete versions. In this section, you learn how to use the Manager to create versions of named ranges in a revenue plan worksheet.

Understanding the Version Manager Window

The Version Manager window is similar to a dialog box; unlike a dialog box, however, you can leave the Version Manager window open while you work so that you can move back and forth between the worksheet and the Version Manager window. For example, you can use Version Manager to create a version of a range; move to the worksheet to enter new data in the range; and then return to the Version Manager window to create another version of the range. To move to the worksheet, click the worksheet or press Alt+F6 (Zoom Pane). To move to the Version Manager window, click the Version Manager window, press Alt+F6, or choose **R**ange **V**ersion.

> **Note**
>
> To see a description of what each of the Version Manager windows buttons does, point to the button, hold down the right mouse button, and read the button description that appears in the title bar at the very top of the 1-2-3 window. For more information about the buttons or about other parts of the Manager window, press **F1** or click the Help button in the right corner of the Manager window title bar. On the resulting help screen, click any part of the picture of the Manager window to get more information about that part.

You can move, resize, maximize, and minimize the Version Manager window just as you do any other window. When you close the Version Manager window (by clicking the **Cl**ose button), 1-2-3 keeps track of the window's size, position, and state (Manager or Index); the next time you open the **R**ange menu and choose **V**ersion, 1-2-3 opens the Version Manager in that size, position, and state.

The Manager window has two drop-down list boxes: Named **R**ange and With **V**ersion(s). The Named **R**ange drop-down list box contains a list of all named ranges that have versions in the current file. The With **V**ersion(s) drop-down list box contains a list of all versions for the named range selected in the Named **R**ange drop-down list box.

Below the drop-down list boxes is a row of buttons labeled **C**reate, **U**pdate, **I**nfo, **D**elete, C**l**ose, and **T**o Index. The four buttons on the left enable you to create, modify, and delete versions. The two buttons on the right enable you to close the Version Manager or go to the Index window.

At the bottom of the Manager window is another row of buttons. The button on the left displays the name of the current file; clicking it toggles between displaying just the file name and displaying the full path. The buttons on the right control the interaction between Version Manager and the worksheet.

Caution

To close the Version Manager window, choose C**l**ose or press Alt+L. Do not use the Windows accelerator sequence Alt+F4; it's very easy to close 1-2-3 accidentally instead of just closing the Version Manager.

Creating Versions

Figure 22.4 shows the 1995 Revenue Forecast worksheet for Resorts International. The chart at the bottom of the worksheet compares Lodging revenue to the total revenues from Transportation, Food, and Entertainment. Resorts International hopes to diversify its revenue sources by increasing total nonlodging revenues in 1995. You can use Version Manager to explore the results of different strategies for reaching this goal.

The first step in creating a version of a range is to enter the data for the version. If the range already contains data you want to preserve, begin by creating a version that contains the data currently stored in the range. This action saves that data so that you don't lose the original data when you enter different sets of data for the range.

Fig. 22.4
A worksheet plan well-suited for use of Version Manager: ranges in which you can enter various versions and scenarios and charts that show results for each.

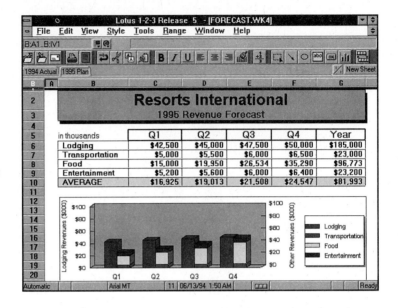

For example, to explore different assumptions about Lodging revenues, begin by creating a version that contains the data currently stored in the range B:C6..B:F6. If the Version Manager window is not already open, open it by opening the **R**ange menu and choosing **V**ersion, or by clicking the Version Manager SmartIcon. If necessary, switch from the Index to the Manager by choosing **T**o Manager. You're ready to create a version of the Lodging revenue data.

You can create versions only of named ranges. To assign a name to the Lodging range, select that range; then open the **R**ange menu and choose **N**ame; then in the Name dialog box, enter the name in the **N**ame text box, click the **A**dd button, click the OK button. Then to create a version of the range, choose **C**reate from the Version Manager window. You also can do it all in one step: the Create Version dialog box enables you to name a range as you create the first version of the range.

Caution

Avoid assigning more than one name to a range for which you have already created versions. When 1-2-3 for Windows finds more than one name for the same range, it uses the name that occurs earliest in the alphabet. This can cause problems for Version Manager because Version Manager uses the name that existed at the time you created the first version of the range.

To create the first version of a range, begin by selecting the range (in this case, the Lodging range in B:C6..B:F6). Then choose **C**reate from the Version Manager window. The Create Version dialog box appears as shown in figure 22.5.

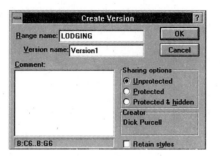

Fig. 22.5

When you click Version Manager's **C**reate button, your screen displays the Create Version dialog box, in which you can change range name or version name and add version comments.

The Version Manager suggests names for the range name and the version name. For the Range Name, Version Manager suggests a name based on the label in the worksheet (in this example, Version manager suggests Lodging as the range name) or proposes a default name such as RANGE1. For the Version Name, Version Manager suggests a default version name such as Version1. You can accept or change either of the suggested names.

Range names can be up to 15 characters long, should not contain spaces or special characters, and are not case-sensitive. Version names can be up to 32 characters long, can contain spaces or special characters, and are case-sensitive.

You can create more than one version with the same name. Because Version Manager also records the date and time when you create a version, it can distinguish the BEST CASE version of the SALES range created by one person at 2:30 p.m. on June 12 from the Best Case version of the SALES range created by the same person at 2:30 p.m. on June 13.

In the Create Version dialog box, you also can enter a comment for the version, select a sharing option, and choose whether to save styles as well as data with the version.

Version comments help you keep track of the assumptions behind the data in each version. In the **C**omment text box, enter a comment that helps you remember why you entered the data in this version. For this example, you can enter a comment identifying the data in the Lodging range as being the original revenue plan, based on actual 1994 results.

Sharing options are most useful when you use Version Manager to share data with other users. **U**nprotected is the default sharing option. Choose the

Protected option button to protect versions so that other users can't change them; choose the Protected & **H**idden button to hide versions so that other users can't display them.

The Creator information box shows the creator of the new version. 1-2-3 gets this information from your e-mail name, network log-in name, or the name you entered when you installed 1-2-3. If 1-2-3 for Windows gets the name from an *authenticated* source (that is, if a password is associated with the name, as there would be for a network log-in name), then you cannot change the name. If 1-2-3 cannot find an authenticated source, it uses the name you entered when you installed 1-2-3 for Windows, and you can change the name in the Tools User Setup dialog box.

You can save styles with versions (with the Retain S**t**yles check box) to give visual cues in the worksheet. For example, you can give all optimistic versions light-blue backgrounds. By default, 1-2-3 for Windows does not save styles with versions.

When you complete the Create Version dialog box, click the OK button to create the version and return to the Version Manager window.

Figure 22.6 shows the Create Version dialog box filled out to create the Plan version of the Lodging range.

Fig. 22.6

The Create Version dialog box after you enter version name and comments for the Plan version of the Lodging range.

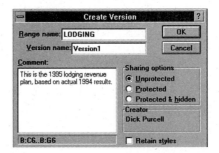

After you create a version of a range, the name of the range appears in the Named **R**ange drop-down box list of the Manager window; the name of the version appears in the With **V**ersion(s) drop-down list box. A check mark appears next to the version name, indicating that this version is currently displayed in the worksheet.

To create a second version of a range, begin by entering the data for the new version into the worksheet. As soon as you enter new data in the range, the check mark next to the version name in the Manager window changes to a crossed check mark; the version name appears in italics; and the **U**pdate button becomes available (see fig. 22.7).

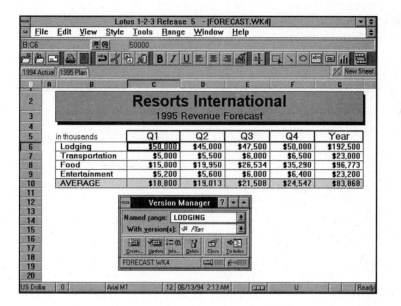

Fig. 22.7
The crossed check mark at the left of version name in the Manager indicates that data in that version's range changed since you last displayed this version.

These changes indicate that the data in the worksheet are not the data associated with the version last displayed in the range. In other words, the data in the worksheet have not been "saved" in a version.

> **Caution**
>
> Avoid creating versions for ranges that overlap. For example, the ranges A:A1..A:D2 and A:B2..A:C15 both contain the cells A:B2 and A:C2. If you do create versions for overlapping ranges, one of the ranges always appears with a crossed check mark next to its version name. If you create a scenario that includes versions in overlapping ranges, only one version's data appears in the cells that overlap. For example, if RANGE1 were A:A1..A:D2, and RANGE2 were A:B2..A:C15, and you created a scenario that included the best case version of RANGE1 and the worst case version of RANGE2, only the values from one of those versions could appear in cells A:B2 and A:C2.

For example, if the Plan version of the Lodging range is currently displayed in the worksheet (that contains the value 42,500 in cell B:C6 as shown in figure 22.4), and you then enter the value 50,000 in cell B:C6 (as shown in fig. 22.7), the data in the worksheet differs from the data in the Plan version. The crossed check mark is usually an indication that you should either create a new version (if you want to preserve both values for cell B:C6) or update the current version (if you want to replace the data in the current version with the data in the worksheet).

After you enter the data for the new version, click **C**reate in the Version Manager window to create another version as just described.

Displaying Versions

After you create several versions of a range, you can display the versions in the worksheet. To display a version of a range in the worksheet, select the desired range from the Named **R**ange drop-down list box, and then select the version from the With **V**ersion(s) drop-down list box. As soon as you select the version from the With **V**ersion(s) drop-down list box, 1-2-3 for Windows places the data for that version of the range into the worksheet, replacing any data already there.

When you request Version Manager to display a version, any data in that version's range that has not been made a version is lost. To help you guard against unintentional loss of such data, if you request display of a version in a range that contains non-version data, Version Manager displays a Show Version dialog box, warning that if you proceed with the version display the non-version data now in the range will be lost, and giving you an opportunity to confirm or cancel your version-display request. If you want to preserve the non-version data currently in the requested version's range, in this dialog box click Cancel, and create a version for the current data before displaying any other version for that range.

Caution

When a crossed check mark appears next to a version name, the current data in the range has not been saved in a version. Displaying a different version in that range destroys the current data in the range. Choose **C**reate to create a new version that includes the current data, or choose **U**pdate to update the current version with the data in the range.

In the Resorts International example, you can create several versions of the Lodging range, the Transportation range, the Food range, and the Entertainment range. Then you can use Version Manager to display the versions in the worksheet in different combinations and examine the effects of the revenue mix.

If you're creating a version of a range already named and you want to change the range name, first display the version in the worksheet and then enter the new name in the **R**ange Name text box in the Create Version dialog box.

Modifying and Updating Versions

After you create a version, you can change it in two ways: by changing the data (and styles, if you selected Retain St**y**les in the Create Version dialog box) for the version or by changing the comment and other settings for the version.

To change the data in a version, first display the version in the worksheet. Then enter the new data for the version (the crossed check mark appears next to the version name in the Manager window when you enter the new data). Then choose the **U**pdate button in the Version Manager window. The Update Version dialog box appears. To confirm that you want to update the version with the new data in the worksheet, choose the OK button.

Tip
To quickly display each version of a range in the worksheet, select the range from the Named **R**ange drop-down list box; press Alt+V to move to the With **V**ersion(s) drop-down list box; and then use the direction keys to cycle through the versions.

> **Caution**
>
> When you update a version, you replace the original data stored in the version with the data currently in the worksheet.

To change a version's comment, sharing options, and style-retention setting, display the version in the worksheet and then choose **I**nfo from the Version Manager window. The Version Info dialog box appears, as shown in figure 22.8.

Fig. 22.8
Use the Version Info dialog box to change a version's comments, sharing options, and style-retention setting.

Use the Version Info dialog box to edit the Comment text box and change the other settings for the version. The Version Info dialog box looks just like the Create Version dialog box, but you can't change the version name.

Tip

To change a version's name, create a second version with the same data, comment, and settings, but with the new name; then delete the original version.

Note

To change a range's name without creating a new version of the range, select an existing version of that range, choose **I**nfo, enter the new name in the **R**ange Name text box in the Version Info dialog box, and choose OK.

Note

To change sharing options or the style-retention setting for several versions at once, move to the Index window; use Shift+click or Ctrl+click to select all the versions you want to modify; and then choose **I**nfo to display the Versions Info dialog box. This dialog box enables you to change the sharing options or style-retention settings for all the versions you selected.

Troubleshooting

Version Manager always says the source of each version or version-modification is me. I want to let others enter versions or modify them on my computer and have Version Manager identify others as the sources of versions or modifications they enter. Can I do this? How?

Version Manager may be getting your name from what you entered during installation. If so, you can change the name it is showing as source of a version or modification by opening the **T**ools menu, choosing **U**ser setup, and changing the name entered near the bottom of the User setup dialog box.

If Version Manager is using an *authenticated* name—a name requiring a password on a network or in a system using Lotus Notes or cc:Mail—you cannot change it. In that case, the best answer is to have each person enter versions and modifications on their own computers. If this is not feasible or practical, the best answer is to show the name of the source of each version or modification in the version name itself or in the version's **C**omment space.

*In my Version Manager, the **U**pdate button is grayed and does not respond when I click it. Why?*

Version Manager makes buttons unavailable by graying them to prevent you from selecting things that are not relevant or do nothing in the current situation. The **U**pdate button is activated only when a range with one or more versions contains new data that have not yet been saved in a version.

Using Highlighting and Tracking

After you spend some time using Version Manager to create and manage different versions of worksheet data, you may find that some worksheets contain many named ranges with versions—and you may forget which ranges contain versions. The Highlighting and Tracking features of Version Manager can help you keep track of which ranges contain versions.

As figure 22.9 shows, the two buttons in the lower right corner of the Version Manager window are the Tracking and Highlighting toggle buttons.

Of these two buttons, the one on the left, with a picture of a flashlight pointed at a worksheet grid, is the Highlighting button. Use the Highlighting feature to see which ranges in a worksheet contain versions. When Highlighting is on, 1-2-3 for Windows displays a border around each range in the worksheet that contains versions. Figure 22.9 shows the Highlighting feature active; notice that the ranges C6..F6, C7..F7, C9..F9, and B10..G10 all have a border to indicate that these ranges have associated versions. Click the Highlighting button to turn Highlighting on and off.

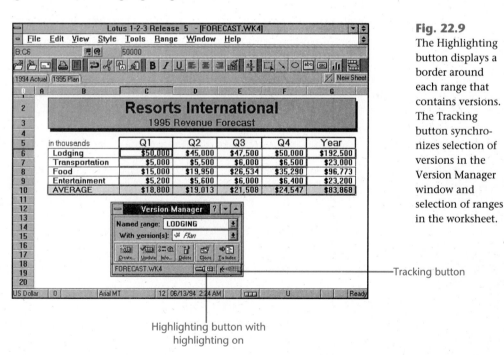

Fig. 22.9
The Highlighting button displays a border around each range that contains versions. The Tracking button synchronizes selection of versions in the Version Manager window and selection of ranges in the worksheet.

Highlighting button with highlighting on

Tracking button

The right button at the bottom of the Version Manager window, with the picture of a radar antenna pointed at a worksheet grid, is the Tracking button. Use the Tracking feature to navigate quickly to ranges that contain versions.

When Tracking is on, 1-2-3 for Windows synchronizes the selection in the worksheet with the selection in the Version Manager window. For example, with Tracking on selecting a named range in the Named **R**ange drop-down list box navigates to and selects that range in the worksheet. Selecting a cell in a named range in the worksheet selects that range in the Named **R**ange drop-down list box in the Version Manager window.

> **Note**
>
> If you work in a large worksheet with ranges that contain versions in different parts of the worksheet, turn Tracking off to prevent 1-2-3 for Windows from navigating around the worksheet (and repainting the screen) each time you select a range in the Version Manager window.
>
> To see the effects of different versions on a chart, turn Tracking off and then scroll to the chart. With Tracking off, you can keep the chart on-screen while you use the Manager to display different versions in the worksheet.

Displaying Version Comments in the Manager

To display the comments for the current version, drag the bottom border of the Manager window down to make the Manager window larger. The comment appears in a scrolling text box above the buttons (see fig. 22.10).

Fig. 22.10
When you vertically expand the Manager, you can see comments for versions.

Although the expanded Manager displays the comments, it doesn't let you edit them. To edit a version's comments, select the version and choose **I**nfo. The Version Info dialog box appears in which you can change the version comments, sharing options, and style-retention setting.

Using the Index

The Index is more powerful and flexible than the Manager. It shows information about all your versions in one place. The Index also enables you to group versions together into scenarios, making it easier to work with particular groups of versions. The Index gives you access to advanced features such as version reporting and merging. Using the Index has one disadvantage: it takes up more of the screen than the Manager. However, you can minimize the Index to an icon while you work in the worksheet, and then restore it when you want to work in the Index.

To display the Index, choose **T**o Index from the Manager window. As figure 22.11 shows. the main feature of the Index is the object list that occupies the center of the window. This list contains information about the versions and scenarios in the current file.

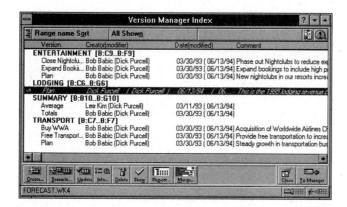

Fig. 22.11

In the Index window, you can see information about all the versions and scenarios in the current file, and you have access to more buttons than the Manager window offers.

Below the object list is a row of buttons. The **C**reate, **U**pdate, **I**nfo, De**l**ete, **C**lose, and **T**o Manager buttons are the same as the corresponding buttons in the Manager window, except that the Info and Delete buttons in the Index window also operate on scenarios. The **S**cenario, Sho**w**, Re**p**ort, and **M**erge buttons appear only in the Index window. The three buttons at the bottom of the window (the file-name indicator and the Highlighting and Tracking buttons) are identical to the corresponding buttons in the Manager window.

Another row of buttons appears above the object list. These buttons act on the list itself, enabling you to change the way the list is displayed or the information it contains. The leftmost button collapses and expands the object list as shown in figure 22.12. The next button, called the Sort selector, changes the way items in the object list are displayed. The Show selector button applies filters to the object list. The button with a picture of a clipboard copies the information in the object list to the Clipboard. The last button splits the object list into two panes and displays version and scenario comments in the right pane as shown in figure 22.13.

Fig. 22.12
When you click the leftmost button above the Index list, with horizontal stripes, the list collapses into summary form. A second click expands it.

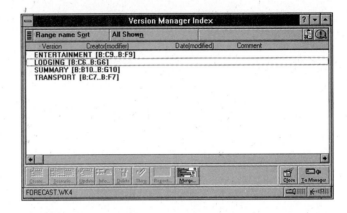

Fig. 22.13
When you click the rightmost button above the Index list, with a cartoon balloon, the list area shrinks to left, and the space to right shows version and scenario comments.

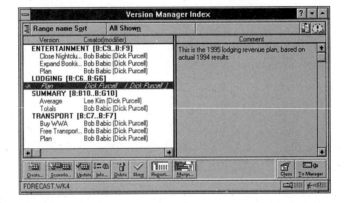

> **Note**
>
> To see a description of what each button does, click it with the right mouse button. For more information about the buttons or about other parts of the Index window, press F1 or click the Help button in the upper right corner of the Index window. On the resulting help screen, click any part of the picture of the Index window to get more information.

Exploring the Index

To get the most out of the Index, you must understand the object list and how to work with it. Remember that the row of buttons above the list operates on the list itself.

Two of the buttons, the **S**ort selector and the Show**n** selector, are similar to the selector buttons in the status bar at the bottom of the 1-2-3 for Windows window. Clicking the button displays a list of options; 1-2-3 for Windows displays the option you select on the button. For example, the first time you open the Index, the text on the Range Name Sort selector button is Range Name Sort, indicating that the list is sorted by range name (see fig. 22.11).

You can sort the object list by version name, scenario name, date, and user name in addition to the default range-name sort. 1-2-3 for Windows arranges the list in a hierarchy based on the sort you select. For example, in a range-name sort, the list displays each range name in boldface, followed by the versions for that range. For each version, the list displays the version name, creator, last modifier (if any), creation and modification date, and comment.

In a version-name sort, the list displays each version name in boldface, followed by the names of the ranges that contain a version with that name. Figure 22.14 shows a version sort. In it are three versions named Plan: one each for the ranges LODGING, TRANSPORT, and ENTERTAINMENT. The date sort and user-name sort are similar to the range-name and version-name sorts: they display versions sorted by date and by user, respectively. However, these two sorts display version names as range-version pairs, in the form RANGE. Version. For example, the Plan version of the TRANSPORT range appears in the date sort as TRANSPORT.Plan.

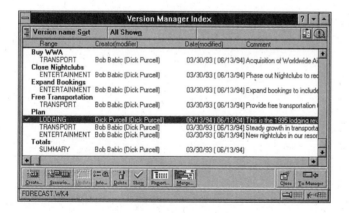

Fig. 22.14
In the Index window, you can sort versions and scenarios in various ways. Here, it's a sort by version name.

The scenario-name sort differs from the other sorts because it is the only sort that displays scenarios. In a scenario-name sort, the list displays each scenario name in boldface, followed by the names of the versions included in the scenario. The version names are displayed as range-version pairs. Figure 22.15 shows the Index window with a scenario-name sort that has two scenarios: the Big on Entertainment scenario and the Big on Transport scenario, each with its versions of the LODGING, TRANSPORT, and ENTERTAINMENT ranges.

Fig. 22.15
When you sort scenarios (by scenario-name), the Index list shows each scenario together with the versions it includes.

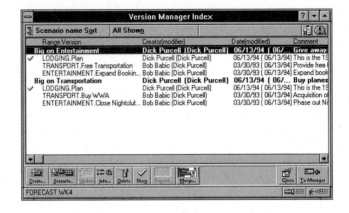

The Shown selector button, which contains the text All Show**n** the first time you open the Index window, enables you to control which versions (and scenarios, in a scenario-name sort) 1-2-3 for Windows includes in the list. You can show All Current Versions (versions currently displayed in the worksheet, as shown in fig. 22.16), New Only (versions created in the current work session), Hidden Only (so that you can select hidden versions to unhide them), and Protected Only (so that you can quickly see which versions are protected).

Fig. 22.16
With the Show**n** selector button, you can control which versions and scenarios are included or shown in a sort. Here, the sort includes only current versions.

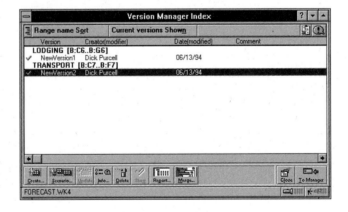

Selecting and Displaying Versions in the Index Window

In the Manager window, you can select only a single version; selecting a version displays that version in the worksheet. In the Index window, you can select multiple versions; selecting a version does not display it.

Versions currently displayed in the worksheet appear in the object list in blue text with a check mark. Versions currently selected in the Index window appear in white text on a blue background. When you first open the Index window, all currently displayed versions are also selected. Figure 22.17 shows the Index window with multiple versions selected.

Fig. 22.17
In the Index window list, you can select multiple versions.

Being able to select multiple versions is useful because you can then perform actions on several versions at once. With multiple versions selected, you can choose any of the following buttons from the bottom of the Index window:

- The **S**cenario button to group the versions together into a scenario

- The **I**nfo button to change sharing options and style-retention settings for the versions

- The **D**elete button to delete the versions

- The Sho**w** button to display the versions

To select multiple versions, click the first version and then use Ctrl+click to select additional versions. To select a group of adjacent versions, click the first version and drag the mouse pointer over the other versions you want to select.

To display a single version in the worksheet when you're using the Index window, double-click it in the object list. To display multiple versions, select the versions and then choose Sho**w**.

> **Note**
>
> To avoid confusion, don't select more than one version for a range and then choose Sho**w** or **S**cenario. 1-2-3 for Windows can show at one time only one version for a range, and only one version for each range in a scenario.

Creating, Displaying, and Modifying Scenarios

A scenario is a named group of versions. Use scenarios when you want to group a particular set of versions together. You may want to display all the Plan versions in the worksheet and then display all the versions that contain your most optimistic estimates. To do this easily, you can create a scenario named Plan that includes all the versions named Plan; create a second scenario named Optimistic that contains those versions with the most optimistic projections.

To create a scenario, click the **S**cenario button in the Index window. The Create Scenario dialog box appears as shown in figure 22.18.

Fig. 22.18
With the Index window's **S**cenario button, you can get the Create Scenario dialog box, in which you can select versions to include in the scenario, enter scenario name and comments, and choose sharing options.

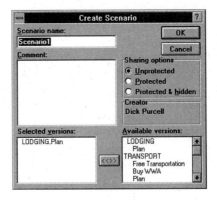

This dialog box is similar to the Create Version dialog box: you can enter a name for the scenario, add a comment, and choose sharing options.

Two list boxes appear at the bottom of the dialog box: Selected **V**ersions and **A**vailable Versions. Use these list boxes to choose the versions to include in the scenario. The **A**vailable Versions list box contains a list of all versions in the current file, sorted by range name. The Selected **V**ersions list box lists the versions you select to include in the current scenario.

To add a version to the Selected **V**ersions list box, select the version from the **A**vailable Versions list box and then choose <<; alternatively, double-click the version in the **A**vailable Versions list box. To remove a version from the Selected **V**ersions list box, select the version and choose >>, or double-click the version. When the Selected **V**ersions list box contains the versions you want to include in the scenario, choose OK to create the scenario. Figure 22.19 shows the completed Create Scenario dialog box for a scenario named Big on Transportation, consisting of the Buy WWA version of TRANSPORT, the Close Nightclubs version of ENTERTAINMENT, and the Plan version of LODGING.

Fig. 22.19
A Scenario dialog box completed for creation of a scenario. Versions included are selected, and scenario name and comments are entered.

A scenario can contain only one version of any named range. For example, you cannot create a scenario that contains two versions of the SALES range because you can only display one version of the range at a time.

When you create a scenario, the Index window automatically changes to Scenario Name S**o**rt (see fig. 22.15).

To display a scenario in the worksheet, make sure that the Index window is in Scenario Name S**o**rt. (If it is not in this sort order, choose the S**o**rt selector button and select Scenario name from the list of options.) From the list of scenarios in the Index window, double-click the scenario you want to display or select it, and choose Sho**w**.

When you request the Index to display a scenario, any data in that scenario's version ranges that has not been made a version is lost. To help you guard against unintentional loss of such data, if you request display of a scenario containing any versions in ranges that contain non-version data, the Index displays a Show Scenario dialog box, warning that if you proceed with the scenario display the non-version data now in any of the scenario's version ranges will be lost, and giving you an opportunity to confirm or cancel your scenario-display request. If you want to preserve the non-version data currently in the requested scenario's version ranges, in this dialog box click Cancel; then create versions for the current data before displaying the scenario you had requested.

To edit a scenario's comment, change its sharing options, or change the versions included in the scenario, select the scenario name from the Index-window list and choose **I**nfo. The Scenario Info dialog box appears (see fig. 22.20). This dialog box is exactly like the Create Scenario dialog box, except that it shows the last modification date, and you cannot change the scenario name.

To change sharing options for several scenarios at once, select all the scenarios from the Index-window list and choose **I**nfo to display the Scenarios Info dialog box. This dialog box enables you to change the sharing options for all the scenarios you selected.

Just as you can select multiple versions in the other sorts, you can select multiple scenarios in a scenario-name sort. However, if you select multiple scenarios and then choose Sho**w**, Version Manager can only show one version in any named range.

> ### Note
>
> If your worksheet contains versions of many named ranges, you may find it easier to preselect the versions you want to include in a scenario than to select them in the Create Scenario dialog box.
>
> One way to easily preselect versions for a scenario is to use the Manager window to display in the worksheet the versions you want to include in the scenario. Then choose **T**o Index to move to the Index window. When you move from the Manager to the Index, the current versions (the versions currently displayed in the worksheet) are automatically selected in the Index window. Choose **S**cenario to display the Create Scenario dialog box. The selected versions appear in the Selected **V**ersions list box.
>
> To include in the object list only the versions currently in the worksheet, choose the Show**n** selector button and select Current Versions. Then use the mouse to select all the current versions and choose **S**cenario.
>
> Another way to preselect versions for a scenario is to use a sort to collate the versions. For example, to create a Best Case scenario that includes all versions named Best Case, choose the S**o**rt selector and select Version Name to sort the Index window by version name. Then select all the Best Case versions and choose **S**cenario.

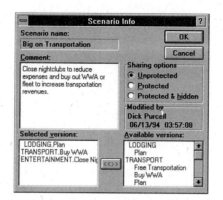

Fig. 22.20
With the Index window's **I**nfo button (with a scenario selected) you can get the Scenario Info dialog box, in which you can change the scenario's versions, comments, and sharing options.

Creating Reports

In addition to displaying versions and scenarios in the worksheet, you may want to create reports that show the data in different versions of a range or the effects of different versions on formulas in the worksheet.

To create a report showing the data and audit information for versions of a range—as well as the effects of the versions on formulas in the worksheet—choose the Re**p**ort button from the Index window. The Version Report dialog box appears (see fig. 22.21).

Fig. 22.21
With the Index window's Re**p**ort button you can get the Version Report dialog box, through which you can get a report on a named range with options you select, including versions and results for a range of worksheet formulas.

In the **R**eport on Named Range drop-down list box, select the named range for which you want to create a report. Then select one or more versions of the range from the **V**ersions list box.

If you want the report to include the effects of the different versions on a range of formulas in the worksheet, specify the range in the Include Results for **F**ormulas from This Range text box. In the example shown in figure 22.21, the report is to include the result of the formula located in cell G10 of the "1995 Plan" worksheet (the total revenue for the year). You can use point mode to select this range.

In the Include section of the dialog box, select Version **D**ata to include in the report the data in each version; select Audit **I**nformation to include the name of the creator or modifier, date, and time. The default setting selects both these options. In the Arrange Data area of the dialog box, select By **C**olumns or By Ro**w**s to choose the orientation of data in the report.

When you choose OK, 1-2-3 for Windows creates the report in a new worksheet file, makes that the active file, and minimizes the Version Manager window. Figure 22.22 shows the report that results from the selections shown in the Version Report dialog box in figure 22.21.

Fig. 22.22
With the Version Report dialog box, you can get reports like this. This report results from the Version Report dialog box selections shown in figure 22.21.

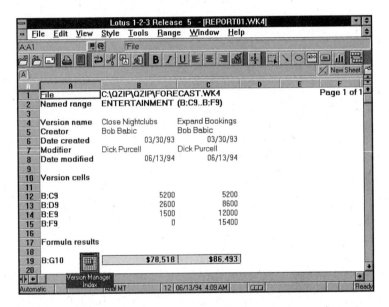

Caution

When you use the Version Report dialog box, and you specify a range in the Include Results for **F**ormulas From This Range text box, 1-2-3 for Windows recalculates formulas in all active files once for each version you include in the report. If you have several 1-2-3 for Windows files open, or if your file takes a long time to recalculate, you may want to create reports at a time when you don't need to use the computer for something else.

Merging Versions and Scenarios

If you use Version Manager to share data with other 1-2-3 for Windows users, you may want to combine the versions and scenarios from one copy of a worksheet file into another copy of the file. The Merge Versions and Scenarios feature copies versions and scenarios from a source file into a destination file.

For example, you can give copies of the Revenue Forecast worksheet file to two members of your staff and ask them to create versions containing their projections for the different types of revenue. You can then use the Merge Versions & Scenarios dialog box to combine their versions and scenarios into your master copy of the file.

For this feature to work, both files must contain named ranges with the same names and the same dimensions. Suppose that both files contain ranges named FOOD and TRANSPORT; the FOOD range is four columns by one row in both files, but the TRANSPORT range is four columns by one row in the source file and four columns by two rows in the destination file. Versions of FOOD are copied from the source file to the destination file, but versions of TRANSPORT are not.

In addition, 1-2-3 for Windows does not copy the following situations:

- Versions into ranges in the destination file that contain protected cells if the file is sealed

- Versions hidden in the source file

- Versions identical to versions in the destination file

- Scenarios hidden in the source file

- Scenarios containing one or more versions that could not be merged

To copy versions and scenarios from a source file (containing the versions and scenarios you want to copy) into a destination file (which must be the current file), begin by opening both files and making the destination file the current file. Then choose **M**erge from the Index window. The Merge Versions & Scenarios dialog box appears (see fig. 22.23).

Fig. 22.23
With the Index window's **M**erge button, you can use the Merge Versions & Scenarios dialog box for merging versions and scenarios into the current file from other files.

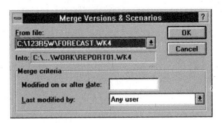

In the **F**rom File drop-down list, select the source file. To merge only the versions and scenarios last modified on or after a particular date, enter the date in the Modified On or After **D**ate text box. (Enter the date in a format 1-2-3 for Windows can recognize.)

To merge only the versions and scenarios last modified by a particular person, select the person's name from the **L**ast Modified By drop-down list box.

When you choose OK, 1-2-3 for Windows begins copying the versions and scenarios from the source file to the destination file. If 1-2-3 for Windows cannot merge any versions and scenarios from the source file that meet the criteria entered in the Merge Versions & Scenarios dialog box, the Merge Results dialog box appears, listing each item and the reason it cannot be merged (see fig. 22.24).

Fig. 22.24
If some versions or scenarios you attempt to merge from other files cannot be merged, the Merge Results dialog box lists which were not merged and why.

If 1-2-3 for Windows successfully merges all versions and scenarios from the source file that meet the criteria, the Merge Versions & Scenarios dialog box closes, and the Index window reappears.

Note

To find out which versions were merged, remember to open the **F**ile menu and choose **S**ave to save the destination file before you do the merge. After the merge is complete, choose the Show**n** selector button at the top of the Index window and select New Only. 1-2-3 for Windows displays in the object list only the versions added to the file in the current session. To find out which scenarios were merged, choose the **S**ort selector button and select Scenario Name.

Note

To save information reported in the Merge Results dialog box, use the mouse to highlight the information you want to save. Click the **C**opy button on the Merge Results dialog box or press Ctrl+C or Ctrl+Ins to copy the information to the Clipboard. Next use the **E**dit **P**aste command in the 1-2-3 for Windows menu or press Ctrl+V or Shift+Ins to paste the information into the worksheet.

Troubleshooting

When I merged versions and scenarios, the Merge Results dialog box did not appear. Why?

The purpose of the Merge Results dialog box is to report any versions and scenarios in other files that you requested be merged but that were not merged, and for each the reason why. If Version Manager Index can achieve all merges you request, it does not display the Merge Results dialog box.

When I chose merge, nothing was merged—and still the Merge Results dialog box did not appear. Why?

Based on both the contents of the source file and the criteria you specified for what to merge, Version Manager Index found nothing to merge or try to merge.

The source file may not contain any versions or scenarios. Or in the Modified On or After **D**ate text box, the date you entered may have eliminated all versions and scenarios to merge.

◀ "Saving Files,"
   p. 283

◀ "Opening Exist-
   ing Files,"
   p. 290

Using Version Manager To Share Data

In addition to enabling you to create and maintain different versions of data in your own worksheets, Version Manager makes it easier than ever to share data with other 1-2-3 for Windows users. Several users can enter versions in the same file without writing over each other's data. Version Manager provides audit information so that you always know who entered which version.

If you have a local area network, you can share data by keeping a file on a network file server. Users can add versions to the same file along with comments explaining the thinking behind each version. For example, different people can enter revenue forecasts based on their individual expertise. Coworkers can review each other's versions, use the comments section to add suggestions or ask questions, and perhaps create new versions based on someone else's ideas.

If you don't have access to a network, you can still use Version Manager to share data. One way is to pass around a single copy of a worksheet file, letting each person add versions to it. Another way is to distribute a copy of the file to each person who needs to use it. Then use the Merge Versions & Scenarios dialog box to combine all the versions and scenarios from the various copies of the file into a single master copy.

Any time you share a file, whether on a network or not, you may want to unprotect the ranges in which you want others to create versions and then seal the file with a password. This arrangement prevents other people from rearranging the file but lets them create versions in the unprotected ranges. Sealing the file also prevents other users from changing protected versions or from seeing hidden versions.

If you use Lotus Notes network communication software, you can create special files called shared files that are actually 1-2-3 worksheet files saved as Notes databases. Shared files enable multiple users to have concurrent access to a single worksheet file. Several people can create versions and scenarios in a single copy of the file, at the same time, without writing over or damaging each other's work.

Looking at Application Examples

You may now have an application in mind that would benefit from Version Manager features. Or you may need some additional ideas for how to put Version Manager to use in your environment. The following sections give you some ideas for ways to use Version Manager.

What-If Analysis

One of the most obvious uses for Version Manager is in *what-if analysis*. Suppose that your child is considering several colleges and financial aid packages;

you can create named ranges for Tuition and Financial Aid and then create versions in each range for all the options.

Another example is if you manage a cafeteria-style benefits plan where employees choose from different options in each benefit category; you can create versions for each benefit category that contain different selections of options.

Applications Requiring Frequent Updates or Iterations

Many spreadsheet applications go through several updates or iterations before being published as finished reports. For example, departmental expense budgets can go through several rounds of review and update before being approved and consolidated into the company budget. You can use Version Manager to save each round of updates without losing earlier data. You also can create customized reports to measure the effects of the changes by comparing the results of placing different versions in the worksheet.

Applications with Several Contributors

Some applications require contributions from several people. For example, a marketing forecast may require input from several product-line and marketing managers. Version Manager supports this kind of application by tracking all changes you and your coworkers make to a worksheet. You can manage this process by using a single copy of a worksheet that you pass from one person to the next or by making a copy for each person and then merging all the contributions into a single copy.

Reporting and Presentation Applications

You can use Version Manager to help deliver information concisely for maximum impact in a live presentation. For example, instead of creating a chart for last year's quarterly sales and a different chart for this year's quarterly sales, you can store last year's amounts and this year's amounts as different versions of the same range and then create one chart that refers to that range. Then use Version Manager to switch versions to change the data in the chart. Instead of moving from one chart to another, you use a single chart and change the data in the chart at the touch of a button.

Instead of storing expense totals, percent of sales, and percent change since last year in different columns of an income statement worksheet, store them as different versions of a range.

From Here...

For information on other features of 1-2-3 for Windows that you can use for worksheets you manage with Version Manager, see the following chapters of this book:

- Chapter 18, "Manipulating and Analyzing Data," especially the section titled "Using Formulas That Make Decisions," describes use of the @IF function to reflect worksheet complexities such as discontinuities in fixed costs or tax rules.

- Chapter 19, "Linking and Consolidating Worksheets," shows you other methods for managing plans and analyses with multiple worksheets and files.

- Chapter 20, "Auditing Worksheets," describes tools that can help you structure your worksheets and diagnose worksheets prepared by others.

- Chapter 21, "Solving Problems with Solver and Backsolver," explains how you use special features for finding worksheet answers.

- Chapter 17, "Developing Business Presentations." For worksheets you manage and share with Version Manager, you can obtain ideas and skills from this chapter to make Version Manager worksheets deliver key results with maximum clarity and impact.

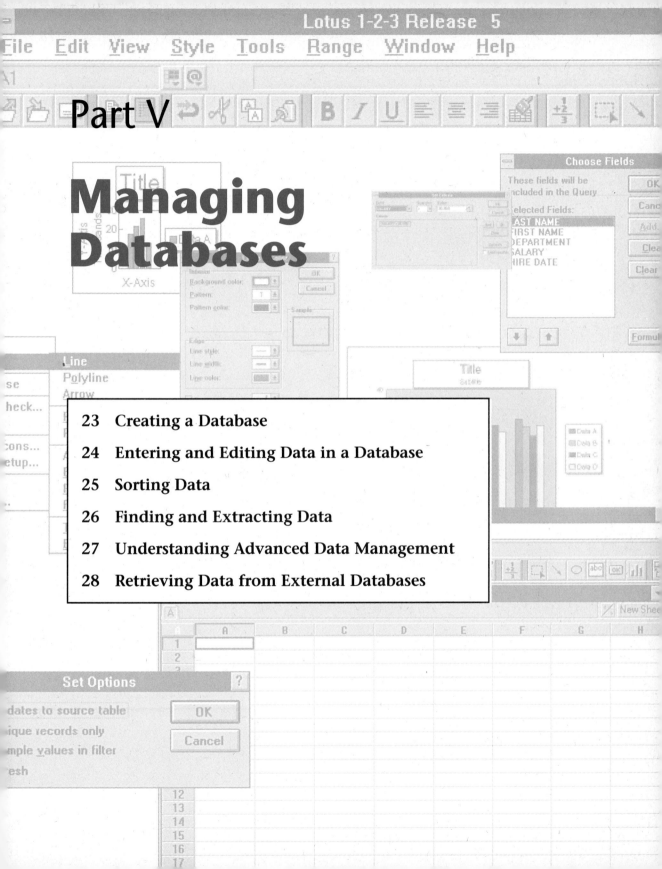

Part V

Managing Databases

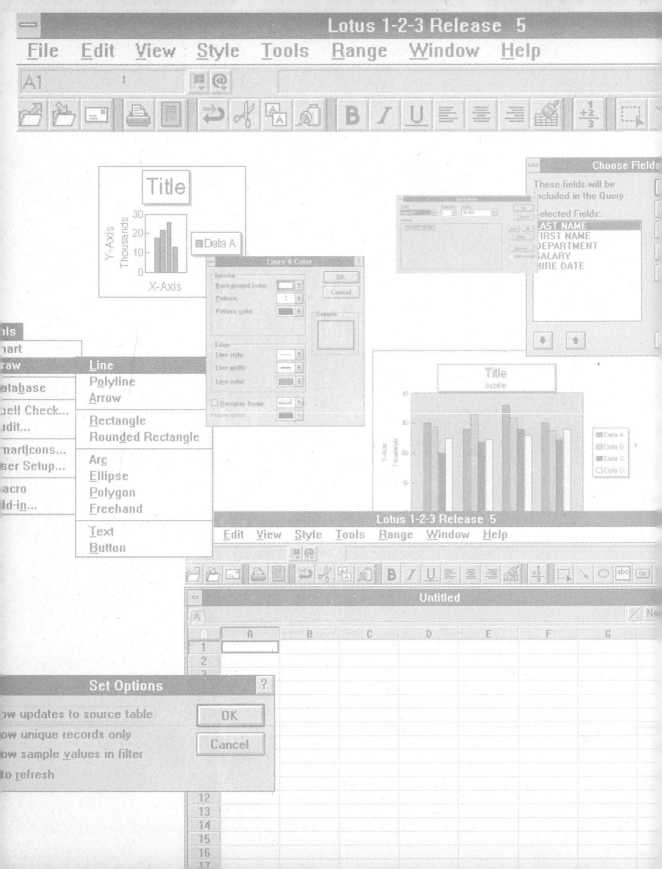

Chapter 23

Creating a Database

A *database* is a collection of related information—data organized so that you can list, sort, or search it. The list of data may contain any kind of information, from addresses to tax-deductible expenditures. Telephone books, rolodexes, and checkbooks are common examples of databases. Most businesses have databases to keep track of their employees, customers, inventory, and vendors. Figure 23.1 shows an example of an employee database built in 1-2-3 for Windows.

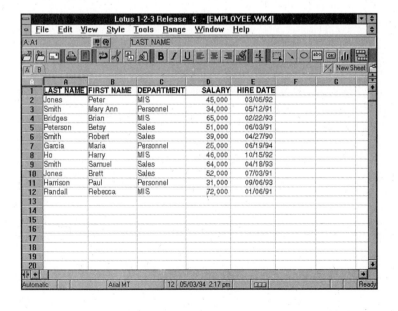

Fig. 23.1
This is an example of a database you can create in 1-2-3 for Windows.

The key advantage to computerizing a database is the ease and speed of data retrieval. Suppose you would like to know which customers purchased more than $30,000 of products from you last year. If you had to manually go through a cabinet full of customer files, it could take you days to compile this data. With a computerized database, you could locate this information in seconds. In this chapter, you learn about the following:

■ Database terminology

■ The capabilities of 1-2-3's database feature

■ How to plan or structure a database

■ How to build a database

■ How to enter data into a database

Understanding 1-2-3 Database Capabilities

1-2-3 provides true database management commands and functions so that you can sort, query, extract, and perform analysis on data and even access and manipulate data from an external database. One important advantage of 1-2-3 for Windows database functionality over independent database products is that 1-2-3's database commands are similar to the other commands used in the 1-2-3 program. As a result, you have a running start on using the 1-2-3 database manager.

After you build a database table (which is really no different than building any other worksheet application), you can perform a variety of functions on it. You accomplish some of these tasks by using standard 1-2-3 commands. For example, you can add a record to the database with the **Edit Insert Row** command. Editing the contents of a database record is as easy as editing any other cell: you move the cell pointer to that location and type.

When you need to manipulate the records in a database table, whether to find certain records or perform statistical analyses on the records, you define a *query*. Release 5 provides the Data Query Assistant to guide you through the process of building criteria. The Data Query Assistant presents a graphical approach to extracting information from a database, relying on a dialog box to guide you through the process.

In previous versions of 1-2-3, you had to set up a special spreadsheet range for entering your criteria and then you had to enter unintuitive formulas for specifying your criteria. For example, to search for employees whose salary is greater than $30,000, you would have to type **SALARY** in one cell and **+D2>30000** in the cell below it. Using Release 4's Data Query Assistant, you can quickly and easily build the criteria (SALARY>30000) by choosing options in the Set Criteria dialog box (see figure 23.2).

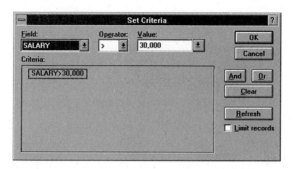

Fig. 23.2

Specifying criteria is easy when using Release 5's Set Criteria dialog box.

Although Release 5 has made it easier to query a database, you still have a wide range of options in defining criteria. Criteria can include complex formulas as well as simple numbers and text entries. You can join sets of criteria and change the relationship between one criteria and another with the AND and OR operators. You also can include wild-card characters to search for records that match certain characters in a field. This can all be done in the Set Criteria dialog box.

You can sort the data in a database as well as perform various kinds of analysis on the data. You can, for example, count the number of records in a database that match a specific criteria; compute the mean, variance, or standard deviation; and find the minimum and maximum values in a range. The capability to perform statistical analysis on a database is an advanced feature for database management systems on any microcomputer. 1-2-3 also has a special set of statistical functions that operate only on information stored in a database. Like the **Q**uery commands, the statistical functions use criteria to determine the records on which they are to operate.

1-2-3's capability to access external databases makes it a product well worth trying out. You can import records from another database, such as Paradox, into a 1-2-3 worksheet. If the right driver file exists and you establish a

V

Managing Databases

connection or link between 1-2-3 and an external database, you can perform several tasks: You can find and manipulate data in the external database and then work with that data in a worksheet; you can use formulas and database functions to perform calculations on the data in the external database; and you can create a new external database that contains data from the worksheet or from an existing external database.

Defining a Database

In 1-2-3 for Windows, the word *database* means a range of cells that spans at least one column and more than one row. Because a database is actually a list, the manner in which database data is organized sets it apart from data in ordinary cells. Just as a list must be organized to be useful, a database must be organized to permit access to the information that it contains.

Databases generally are organized in three ways:

- *A single database contained in a single worksheet*. This organization method is used in most of the examples in this chapter, as well as in most real-world applications.

- *Multiple databases in a single worksheet*. Each database occupies a different portion of the worksheet.

- *Multiple databases in two or more worksheet levels*. Be aware, however, that a single database table cannot span different worksheet levels. As you learn in Chapter 27, "Understanding Advanced Data Management," you can relate databases that are on different worksheet levels and thus produce a more efficient overall database structure.

Remember that a 1-2-3 for Windows database is similar to any other group of cells. This knowledge may help you as you learn about the different database commands covered in this chapter. In many instances, you can use these commands in what you may consider to be nondatabase applications. For example, you can use the **R**ange **S**ort command to sort any range, not just a database range.

Databases are made up of fields and records. A *field*, or single data item, is the smallest unit in a database. To develop a database of companies with which you do business, for example, you can include the following fields for each company:

Name

Address

City

State

ZIP code

Phone number

A *record* is a set of associated fields. In the above example, the accumulation of all data about one company forms one record. The six fields in the preceding paragraph represent one record on one company.

In 1-2-3 for Windows, a field is a single cell, and a record is a row of cells within a database.

A database must be set up so that you can access the information it contains. Retrieval of information usually involves key fields. A database *key field* is any field on which you base a list, sort, or search operation. For example, you can use ZIP code as a key field to sort the data in the company database and to assign contact representatives to specific geographic areas.

Working with a 1-2-3 for Windows Database

A 1-2-3 for Windows database resides in the worksheet's row-and-column format. Figure 23.2 shows the general organization of a 1-2-3 for Windows database. Labels, or *field names*, that describe the data items appear as column headings in row 1. Information about each specific data item (field) is entered in a cell in the appropriate column. In figure 23.3, cell B5 represents data (*3500 Bacon Ct.*) for the second field (ADDRESS) in the database's fourth record, which is in row 5.

Fig. 23.3

Organization of a
1-2-3 for Windows
database.

Field names ——

Record ——

Field ——

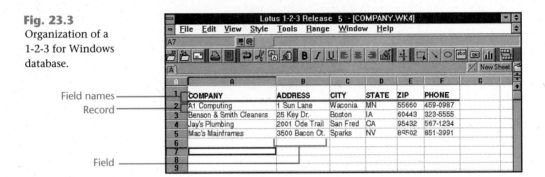

Theoretically, the maximum number of records you can have in a 1-2-3 for Windows database corresponds to the maximum number of rows in the worksheet (8,192 rows, minus 1 row for the field names). Realistically, however, the number of records in a specific database is limited by the amount of available memory: internal memory (RAM) plus disk storage for virtual memory.

When you estimate the maximum database size for your computer equipment, be sure to include enough blank rows to accommodate the maximum output you expect from extract operations. You also may be able to split a large 1-2-3 for Windows database into separate database tables on different worksheet levels if all the data does not have to be sorted or searched as a unit. You may, for example, be able to separate a telephone-list database by name (A through M in one file; N through Z in another) or area code.

> **Note**
>
> The size limits for 1-2-3 for Windows databases do not apply to external database files accessed with the 1-2-3 for Windows DataLens drivers (discussed in Chapter 28). External database files can hold any number of records and are limited only by available disk space.

You access the **T**ools Data**b**ase and the **Q**uery menu commands from the 1-2-3 for Windows main menu (the **Q**uery menu appears in place of the **R**ange menu when a *query table*—a workspace where you can manipulate database information—is selected). Because all the options in the main menu work in databases as they do in worksheets, the power of 1-2-3 for Windows is at your fingertips.

You also can use 1-2-3 for Windows' file-translation capabilities or the **T**ools Data**b**ase **C**onnect to External command (covered in Chapter 28) to access database files created with dBASE and with the @BASE add-in for earlier versions of 1-2-3 and for Symphony, IBM Database Manager, Informix, Paradox, and SQL Server. This feature enables you to take advantage of 1-2-3 for Windows data and chart commands.

▶ "Working with External Databases," p. 793

Figure 23.4 shows the options in the **T**ools Data**b**ase menu. Figure 23.5 shows the options in the **Q**uery menu.

You use both the **T**ools Data**b**ase and **Q**uery menu commands as you work with 1-2-3 for Windows databases. The **T**ools Data**b**ase commands create new query tables, access records in a database, and control connections to external database files. The **Q**uery commands enable you to manipulate data in query tables and to update information in the database.

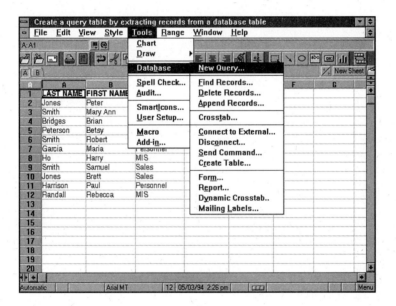

Fig. 23.4

The **T**ools Database menu contains options for basic database operations such as finding, deleting, and appending records.

V

Managing Databases

Fig. 23.5

The **Query** menu contains options pertaining to query tables: setting criteria, choosing fields, sorting, and updating.

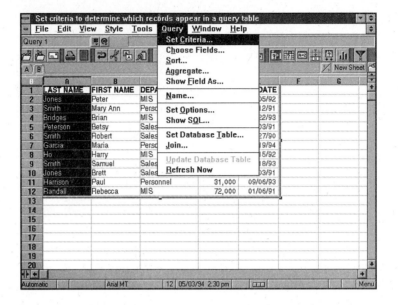

Choosing an Area for Your Database

You can create a database as a new worksheet file or as part of an existing file. If you decide to build a database in an existing worksheet, choose an area of the worksheet that you do not need for any other purpose. This area should be large enough to accommodate the number of records that you plan to enter during the current session and in the future.

Tip

Take advantage of 1-2-3 for Windows' 3-D capabilities by placing the different database elements in their own worksheets.

A better idea, however, is to add another worksheet to the current file so that the database and the existing worksheet don't interfere with each other. To add another worksheet for the new database, click the New Sheet button or use the **E**dit **I**nsert **S**heet command.

In addition, you may want to create a separate worksheet to hold a query table so that the query table doesn't overwrite existing data. You may want to add names to the worksheet tabs to make it easy to remember which worksheet holds the database and which holds the query table.

After you decide which area of the worksheet to use, you create a database by specifying field names across a row and entering data in cells, as you would for any other 1-2-3 for Windows application. The mechanics of entering database contents are simple; the most critical step in creating a useful database is defining the fields properly.

Planning Your Database

In locating and retrieving database information, 1-2-3 for Windows relies on field names. You may want to write down the output you expect from the database before you create the fields; writing this information down helps you determine what fields you need. You also need to consider whether any existing documents (such as order forms or customer information cards) contain information that you can use in your database (for example, names, addresses, and phone numbers).

When you are setting up the database, you must assign each field a name. 1-2-3 for Windows is not strict when it comes to your field names. The names can be up to 512 characters long (the maximum number of characters that can be entered in a cell) and can contain special symbols and spaces. However, the field names must be labels, even if they are numeric labels ('1, '2, and so on). Of course, field names must be unique—you can't have two fields with the same name. One restriction is that a field name must be entered in a single cell, and all field names must be entered into the same row. For example, if you have a field called *First Name*, do not enter **First** in one cell and **Name** in another.

> **Note**
>
> While 1-2-3 doesn't allow you to enter field names on multiple rows, you can achieve this look by turning on the **W**rap text option in the Alignment dialog box (to get there, choose **S**tyle **A**lignment). You can then increase the height of the row to display several lines of text in a single row.

A common error in setting up databases is choosing field names (and entering data) without thinking about the output you want from that field. For example, if you create an address field that contains the city, state, and ZIP code, you are likely to run into problems. You will not be able to sort by ZIP code, nor will you be able to search for a certain state. A similar problem can crop up if you create a single field for a person's name. If you enter a name as **John Smith**, you will not be able to sort the last names in alphabetical order. While there is a way to search for *Smith* in this example, the procedure is much more complicated than if you had separate fields for first and last name.

Tip
If you enter database contents from a standard form, you can increase the speed of data entry by setting up the field names in the order in which the data items appear in the form.

V

Managing Databases

Tip
When in doubt, separate your data into different fields; you will appreciate the flexibility later as you perform queries and sorts.

◀ "Working with
Number
Formats,"
p. 326

While creating your database, you may also want to preformat some of the fields. Your numeric fields should be formatted appropriately (Fixed, Comma, Currency, Percent, and so forth). Label fields do not need to be preformatted unless the data begins with a numeric character. Suppose you are entering social security numbers, telephone numbers, or part codes that begin with a number. You'll probably find it helpful to format these fields with Label format so that you do not have to type a label prefix before entering the data. Date fields should be formatted with the particular date format that you prefer; for example, 31-Dec-94, 12/31/94, or 12/31.

> **Note**
>
> If Automatic is the default for numeric formats, it is quite easy to enter dates into your database. Just type the date with slashes between the numbers (for example, **12/31/94**). The date will automatically be formatted and entered as a numeric date that can be sorted properly. You will also be able to perform math-based searches for all dates within a specified period or before a certain date.

◀ "Setting Column Widths,"
p. 312

While setting up your database, it's helpful to set an appropriate column width for each field. Try to guess what will be the longest piece of data that will go in a field, and set the column width to accommodate this data. Probably the easiest way to set the width is to drag the column borders. Keep in mind that numeric fields may require extra space for punctuation and decimal places, depending on the format you have selected for a field.

Rather than setting a different column width, some people space out their data by putting a blank column between fields. This is not a good idea because it can interfere with database queries. It is also an inefficient use of space.

Another consideration when defining the database is alignment. If you like, you can preformat the fields to be center- , left-, or right-aligned. By default, labels are left-aligned and numbers and dates are right-aligned.

Building a 1-2-3 Database

After you plan the database, you can build it. To understand how the process works, create a Company database as a new database in a blank worksheet (in READY mode). Enter the field names across a single row (A:A1..A:F1, as shown in fig. 23.3).

> **Caution**
>
> Do not leave a blank row between the field names and the first record. If you do, your query operations may not work correctly. Instead of a blank row, you can separate the field names from the records by increasing the height of the row containing the first record and/or formatting the field names differently (bold, italic, bottom border).

Entering Data

After you enter field names, you can add records to the database. To enter the first record, move the cursor to the row directly below the field-name row and then enter the data across the row. To enter the first record shown in figure 23.3, for example, type the following entries in the cells shown:

A:A2:	**A1 Computing**
A:B2:	**'1 Sun Lane**
A:C2:	**Waconia**
A:D2:	**MN**
A:E2:	**'55660**
A:F2:	**'459-0987**

Notice that you enter the contents of the ADDRESS, PHONE, and ZIP fields by typing an apostrophe (') label character. An easier method, however, is simply formatting these fields with Label format.

◄ "Entering Data into the Worksheet," p. 84

The sample Company database is used periodically throughout this section of the book to demonstrate the effects of various database commands. In this example, the fields are shown in a single screen. In real-life applications, however, you track many more data items. You can maintain 256 fields (the number of columns available) in a single 1-2-3 for Windows database. As previously mentioned, the number of records in a specific database is limited by the amount of available memory: internal memory (RAM) plus disk storage for virtual memory.

Assigning a Range Name to the Database

After you have entered all the records into the database, it's a good time to assign a range name to the database. Why bother naming the database range? There are several reasons. If you want to print the database, you won't need

◄ "Working with Ranges," p. 71

V

Managing Databases

to highlight the range—you can just specify the range name as your print range. Secondly, 1-2-3's database queries and functions require you to specify the database range; with a range name, it's very easy to do this. In the example used above, the **R**ange **N**ame command was used to assign the name COMPANY_DB to the range A1..F5.

Troubleshooting

The leading zero for some of the ZIP codes in my database are not displaying. For example, I typed **06987** *but the cell displays 6987.*

You are losing the leading zero because you have entered the ZIP codes as numbers instead of labels. Either enter a label prefix (such as the apostrophe) before typing each ZIP code or preformat the ZIP code field to Label format.

My database has more records and fields than can fit on-screen at one time. Therefore, it's difficult to enter data when the field names and the data in the first column of the database scroll off of the screen.

You need to freeze the field names and the first column so that these cells don't scroll off-screen. Place the cell pointer underneath the field names and to the right of the first column, then use the **V**iew Freeze **T**itles **B**oth command.

From Here...

Once you have created a database, you'll want to explore the following chapters:

- Chapter 24, "Entering and Editing Data in a Database," shows you how to insert and delete records in an existing database and modify the database structure.

- Chapter 25, "Sorting Data," shows you how to sort your data in alphabetical, numerical, or chronological order.

- Chapter 26, "Finding and Extracting Data," shows you how to locate certain records in a database as well as to extract information into reports.

Chapter 24

Entering and Editing Data in a Database

After you have created a database, you can easily modify its contents and structure. You can add new records, delete old or duplicate records, and edit the fields in any record. You can modify the structure of the database by inserting, deleting, and moving fields. You can even make significant changes such as dividing one field into two or combining two fields into one.

In this chapter, you will learn the following topics:

- ■ Adding and deleting records
- ■ Editing records
- ■ Inserting and deleting fields
- ■ Moving a field
- ■ Dividing and combining fields

Adding Records to a Database

You can take several approaches to add records to your database. One way is to type the new record in the first empty row at the bottom of the database. Use this technique, discussed in Chapter 23, "Creating a Database," when you are initially entering the records.

If you add new records to the bottom of a database, however, they won't automatically be included in the database range name. (As mentioned in Chapter 23, it's wise to assign a range name to your database to save time when printing and using database queries and functions.) You must use the

Range Name command to expand the database range name to include the new records. If you forget to adjust the database range, any commands or formulas that refer to the database name will not include the new records. Also, because you cannot simply add a row to an external database file, this method does not work with external databases.

You can use two methods to avoid having to manually adjust the database range name when adding records to a named database: you can insert them or append them.

Tip
If you are going to modify your database often, you may want to display the Editing SmartIcon palette.

Inserting Records

The simplest way to add records to a named database range is to insert the new records in the middle of the database; that way, the range name will automatically expand to include the new records. The inserted row can be anywhere within the database range. For example, you can insert the row above the first record, above the last record, or anywhere in between. This method does require that you issue a command to insert a row for each new record, however. You can insert a row four ways:

- Click the Insert Row SmartIcon.

- Click on the row number to select the entire row. Press the right mouse button to display the Quick menu and choose Insert. This technique is shown in figure 24.1.

◀ "Inserting Cells, Rows, and Columns," p. 108

▶ "Writing 1-2-3 for Windows Macros," p. 1033

- Click the row number to select the entire row, then choose **E**dit **I**nsert or press Ctrl+ + (grey + on key pad).

- Create a macro to insert a row. For example, you can create a macro so that a row is inserted above the cell pointer when you press Ctrl+I.

There are two disadvantages to inserting records in the middle of the range. First, the inserted rows may disrupt data to the right of the database. If you have any data to the right of the database, you'll want to move it to another worksheet before inserting records in your database. The second disadvantage to this technique is that you aren't putting new records in the most logical place—at the bottom of the database. If this bothers you, add records by using the technique described in the next section.

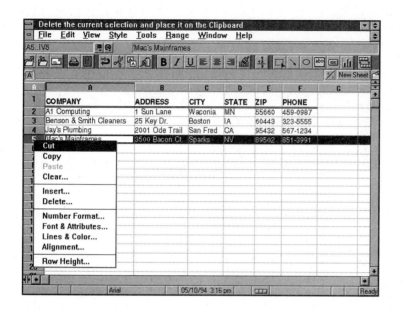

Fig. 24.1
Pressing the right mouse button displays the Quick menu; this menu offers a quick way to insert a row for a new database record.

Appending Records

With the final method of adding database records, you enter each new record into an entry form on another worksheet and then issue the **T**ools Data**b**ase **A**ppend Records command. This method works with databases in worksheet ranges and with external databases.

Before you use this method, you must do the following preparations:

1. If you have not already assigned a range name to the database, use the **R**ange **N**ame command to name the database range (cells A:A1..F5 in fig. 24.1). For this exercise, use the range name **COMPANY_DB**.

2. Double-click the worksheet tab and enter the name **Database**. This step is optional, but it makes using the database easier.

3. Click the New Sheet button (or use the **E**dit **I**nsert **S**heet command) to add a new worksheet for the data-entry form. Double-click the worksheet tab and name this new worksheet **Entry Form**.

4. Copy the field names from Database:A1..F1 to Entry Form:A1. The Entry Form should look like figure 24.2.

Fig. 24.2

The entry form is placed in another worksheet.

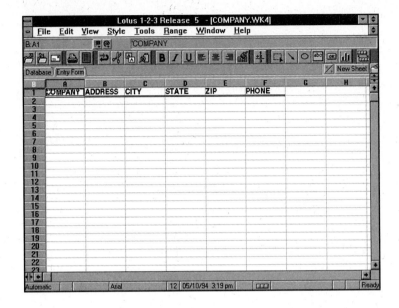

You need to do steps 1 through 4 only once. When you are ready to enter new records, follow these steps:

1. Go to the Entry Form worksheet and place the cell pointer in the first cell under the field names (cell A2 in this example).

2. Enter the data for the new record. In this example, make the following entries in the indicated cells:

    A2: **Ralph's Bar**
    B2: **'10 Lilac**
    C2: **Carmel**
    D2: **CA**
    E2: **'95309**
    G2: **'369-2468**

3. Type any other records in consecutive rows underneath the first record. For example, enter the next record beginning in cell A3.

4. When you finish entering records, highlight the field names and all records in the entry form. For example, in figure 24.3 you would highlight A1..F2.

5. Open the **T**ools menu and choose Data**b**ase **A**ppend Records to display the Append Records dialog box (see fig. 24.4).

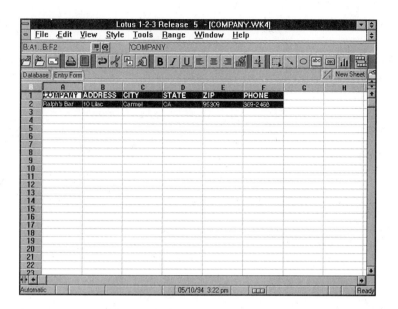

Fig. 24.3
Before appending the records, you must highlight the field names and all records entered into the entry form.

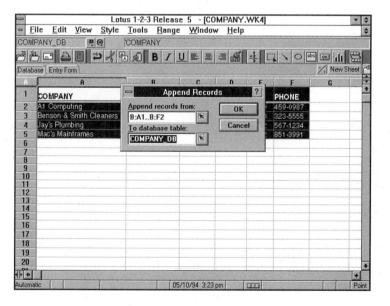

Fig. 24.4
In the Append Records dialog box, you indicate the range name of the database to which you want the highlighted records appended.

6. In the **T**o Database Table text box, enter the database range name, **COMPANY_DB**. You can type the name or address, point to the database range, or press F3 (Name) to display a list of named ranges.

7. Click OK or press Enter to add the record(s) to the database.

8. 1-2-3 returns you to the Database sheet and you will see that the new record(s) have been appended to the original database. 1-2-3 for Windows automatically adjusts the database range name to include the new record(s).

Troubleshooting

I added new records to my database but when I tell 1-2-3 to print the database range (which I had named DATABASE) the new records don't print. What am I doing wrong?

When you add new records to a previously-named database, the new rows aren't automatically included in the range name. There are several ways to solve this problem. You can manually lengthen the range associated with the name DATABASE, insert new records in the middle of the database so that they are automatically included in the range name, or use the Tools Database Append Records command.

When I try to append records to my database using the Tools Database Append Records command, I get the error message "Invalid field name." Why won't my records append to the database?

There are two possibilities. First, double-check the spelling of the field names in the append from and to ranges and make sure they are identical. If you used the Edit Copy command to copy the names, you can be certain the field names are identical in both ranges. Second, be sure to include the field names in the append from and to ranges. If you highlight only the new records (and not the field names) for the append from range, you will get the error message you mentioned.

I used the Tools Database Append Records command last week to add some new records to my database. When I went back to the Entry Form sheet to add more records, I noticed that the last records I had appended were still on the entry form. Do I leave these records there, type over them, or delete them?

Do not leave the old records on the entry form because they will be added to the database with your next batch of appended records (and you will end up with duplicates). You could type over them, but this can potentially create confusion. It's best to erase or delete the existing records on the entry form before you enter new records. (But make sure they have been appended before you delete them!)

Modifying Records in a Database

1-2-3 for Windows makes maintaining the accuracy of the database contents easy.

To delete records, select the rows that you want to delete and then choose the **E**dit **D**elete **R**ow command or click on the Delete Row SmartIcon. You can also press the right mouse button to display the quick menu and then choose Delete. You also can press Ctrl+– (grey – on keypad).

If **T**ools **U**ser Setup **U**ndo is not selected, be extremely careful when you specify the records to be deleted. **E**dit **U**ndo (Ctrl+Z) or the Undo SmartIcon can reverse an **E**dit **D**elete **R**ow command if it was the last command executed. If you want to remove only inactive records, consider first using the **T**ools Data**b**ase **N**ew Query command to store the extracted inactive records in a separate query table. (See Chapter 26 "Finding and Extracting Data" for information on using **T**ools Data**b**ase **D**elete Records to remove database records.)

You modify fields in a database the same way that you modify the contents of cells. As explained in Chapter 3, you change cell contents either by retyping the cell entry or by pressing the F2 (Edit) key and then editing the entry.

Modifying the Structure of a Database

You can modify the database structure just as easily as the database contents. The database *structure* refers to the set of fields in your database. After you use your database for awhile, you may discover that it needs additional fields or that one of the fields is obsolete. You also may find that you prefer the fields to be ordered differently.

Inserting a New Field

To add a new field to a database, place the cell pointer anywhere in the column and then issue the **E**dit **I**nsert **C**olumn command or click the Insert Column SmartIcon; the new column is inserted to the right of the cell pointer. You then can fill the field with the appropriate values for each record. To insert a CONTACT field between the ZIP and PHONE fields, for example, position the cell pointer on any cell in the PHONE column, issue the **E**dit **I**nsert **C**olumn command, and then type the new field name (**CONTACT**) in cell A:F1 (see fig. 24.5).

Tip

If the database is contained in a multiple-worksheet file, be sure that the **S**tyle **W**orksheet Defaults **G**roup Mode check box is not selected. This option prevents column-width settings and row or column insertions (or deletions) in one worksheet from applying to the other worksheet.

V

Managing Databases

Fig. 24.5

A column inserted
for a new database
field.

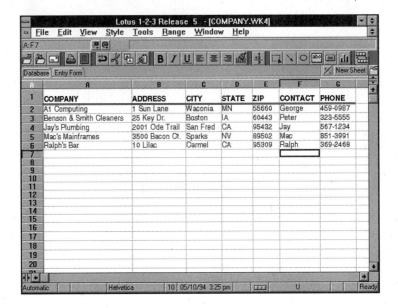

◄ "Inserting Cells,
Rows, and
Columns,"
p. 108

As you modify the structure of the database, you must think about possible effects on the range associated with the database range name. If you insert a field in the middle of the database, the range will automatically expand to accommodate the change. You will run into problems, however, when you insert a field before the first field or after the last field—the new field will not be part of the database range. In this case, you will need to respecify the range with the **R**ange **N**ame command so that the new field is included.

Deleting a Field

To delete a field, position the cell pointer anywhere in the column that you want to remove and then choose the **E**dit **D**elete **C**olumn command or use the Delete Column SmartIcon. You can also delete a column by selecting the column, pressing the right mouse button to display the quick menu, and then choosing Delete.

◄ "Deleting Cells,
Rows, and
Columns,"
p. 110

When you delete fields, you don't need to be concerned about the database range name. The range will automatically contract when you delete any fields—first, last, or middle fields.

Moving a Field

Moving a field is not just a simple cut-and-paste operation. When you move data in 1-2-3 for Windows, you must make sure the destination range is empty because any existing data in the destination will be overwritten.

Furthermore, after you move a field, you will be left with an empty column where the data originally was. Let's say you want to move the CONTACT field after the COMPANY field so that the database looks like figure 24.6. To do so, take the following steps:

1. Open the **E**dit menu and choose **I**nsert to insert a column where you want the moved field to go (between columns A and B in fig. 24.5).

2. Select the name and data to be moved (G1..G6). Then open the **E**dit menu and choose the Cu**t** command.

3. Place the cell pointer in the field header row of the column you inserted in step 1 (B1). Open the **E**dit menu and choose the **P**aste command.

4. Select the column that previously contained the data that is now empty (column G). Open the **E**dit menu and choose the **D**elete command.

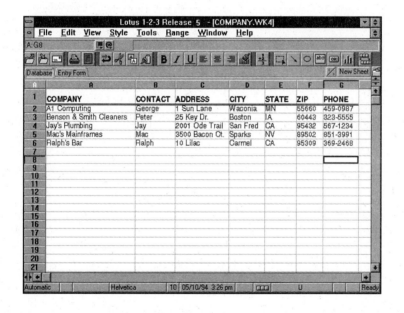

Fig. 24.6
The CONTACT field is moved after the COMPANY field.

Alternatively, you can move a field with the drag-and-drop method, as follows:

1. Open the **E**dit menu and choose the **I**nsert command to insert a column where you want the moved field to go (between columns A and B in figure 24.5).

2. Select the name and data (G1..G6) to be moved.

3. Place the mouse pointer near the border of the selected range and when you see a hand, press the left mouse button and drag the data to the destination.

4. Select the column that previously contained the data that is now empty (column G). Open the **E**dit menu and choose the **D**elete command.

◄ "Dragging a Range to a New Location," p. 254

◄ "Cutting and Pasting a Range," p. 256

Note that with the drag-and-drop method you still need to do the preparation and clean-up work that was necessary with the cut-and-paste technique.

> **Caution**
>
> If you move the first or last field in the database, the range associated with the database name will get scrambled. After moving these fields, make sure you redefine the range with the **R**ange **N**ame command.

Dividing One Field into Two

Chapter 23 advised you to separate your data into different fields as much as possible so that you have greater flexibility when performing queries and sorts. For example, instead of creating a single NAME field, it's best to create a FIRST NAME and a LAST NAME field. But what if you inherited a database created by another person who didn't follow this rule? Text functions can come to the rescue here.

Text functions, as explained in Chapter 6, allow you to manipulate your labels. With these functions, you can locate a particular string of text in a database field and then extract it and place it in a separate cell. The text functions that will help in field subdivision are @FIND, @LENGTH, @LEFT, @MID, and @RIGHT.

To begin, notice that in figure 24.7, the database currently has a field called NAME. Now, suppose you want to extract the first name from the NAME field and place it in the FIRST NAME field, and place the last name in the LAST NAME field. Without text functions, you would have to do this tedious work manually. With text functions, the restructuring takes a matter of minutes— no matter how many records are in your database.

The formula in B2 reads as follows:

@LEFT(A2,@FIND(" ",A2,0))

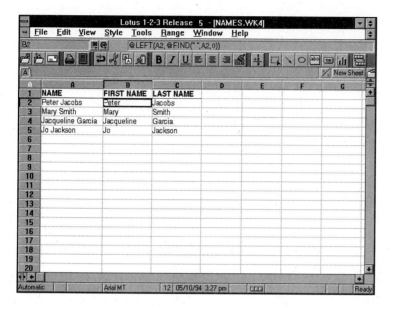

Fig. 24.7
The FIRST NAME
and LAST NAME
fields were created
with text functions.

This formula extracts the first name. It looks for the space between the first and last name and then extracts the text from the beginning of the cell up to (but not including) the space.

The formula in C2 is:

@MID(A2,@FIND(" ",A2,0)+1,@LENGTH(A2))

This formula extracts the last name. Like the previous formula, it locates the space. In this case, however, it extracts text in the middle of the cell.

◄ "Using Text
Functions,"
p. 242

As you may have already guessed, these formulas will not work if the name contains a middle initial or name. If all the names contain middle initials, you can modify the formulas to extract this information (though the formulas will be more complicated). If, however, some names have middle initials and some don't, you will need to do some manual editing.

After you have entered the formulas for the first record, you can copy them down to the other records. You now have two choices. You can consider your job done and leave the NAME, FIRST NAME, and LAST NAME fields just as they are. Alternatively, you can delete the NAME field.

V

Managing Databases

> **Caution**
>
> If you decide to delete the original data, do not immediately delete the column. If you do, you'll end up with ERRs in the FIRST NAME and LAST NAME fields. This is because the formulas refer to cells that no longer exist. Before deleting the NAME column, you'll need to convert the formulas to values.

Here are the steps for converting the formulas to values:

1. Select the cells containing the text functions (B2..C5 in figure 24.7).

2. Open the **E**dit menu and choose the **C**opy command to copy the formulas to the Clipboard.

3. With the same cells selected, open the **E**dit menu and choose the Paste **S**pecial command.

4. Choose the **F**ormulas as values option and click OK.

To see the difference in cell contents after this operation, look at the edit line in B2. The cell contents are now simply *Peter* instead of the long text function. The NAME field can now be safely deleted without disturbing the FIRST NAME and fields.

Combining Two Fields into One

For reporting purposes, you may want to combine two fields into one. Suppose you have divided the first and last names into two different fields so that you can easily sort and query the data, but in your report you would like to see the first and last name separated by a space. Figure 24.8 shows this example. The formula in cell C2 is:

+A2&" "&B2

◀ "Using Text Functions," p. 242

This formula simply "adds" the first name (in A2), a space, and the last name (in B2). The ampersand, called the *concatenation operator*, is what links each text string. This formula can be copied to the other records.

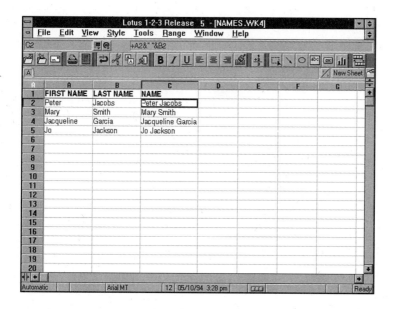

Fig. 24.8
The FIRST and
LAST NAME fields
were combined
into a single field
by creating a
formula with the
concatenation
operator (&).

From Here...

To learn more about database commands, turn to the following chapters:

- Chapter 25, "Sorting Data," shows you how to sort your data in alphabetical, numerical, or chronological order.

- Chapter 26, "Finding and Extracting Data," shows you how to locate certain records in a database as well as to extract information into reports.

Chapter 25

Sorting Data

1-2-3 for Windows enables you to change the order of records by sorting them according to the contents of the fields. Sorting a database can provide you with more meaningful information. Frequently, when a database contains people's names or company names, you will want to sort the list in alphabetical order. This reorganization makes it easier to locate information. In a database that contains addresses, you may want to sort by ZIP code to take advantage of bulk mailing rates.

By sorting numerical data, you can answer the following types of questions: Which customers purchased the most from you last year? Who has the highest salary in the marketing department? Which salespeople made the most sales last quarter? In which month were expenses the lowest?

You also can sort dates in chronological order, assuming the dates were entered as numerical dates, not labels. By sorting dates in your database, you quickly can see which employees have worked for the company the longest or which invoices are the oldest.

1-2-3 for Windows offers two ways to sort a database: using the **R**ange **S**ort command directly on the database range or using the **Q**uery **S**ort command on a query table.

In this chapter, you will learn to do the following:

- ◼ Sort a range by using a single sort key
- ◼ Sort a range by using multiple sort keys

■ Create a query table

■ Use a query table to sort records

Sorting a Range

The **R**ange **S**ort command sorts any range, not just a database range. Before issuing this command, select the range to be sorted. In figure 25.1, the sort range for the employee database is A2..E12. This range must include all the records to be sorted as well as all the fields in the database.

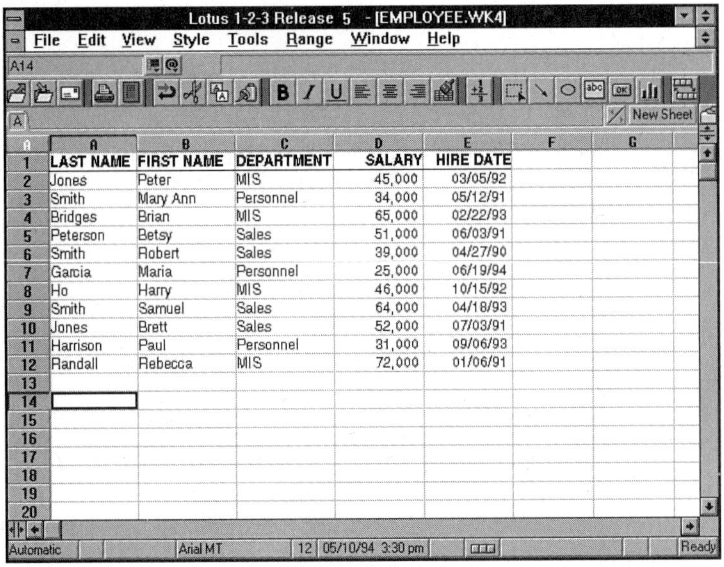

Fig. 25.1
The sort range for the employee database is A2..E12.

	LAST NAME	FIRST NAME	DEPARTMENT	SALARY	HIRE DATE		
1	LAST NAME	FIRST NAME	DEPARTMENT	SALARY	HIRE DATE		
2	Jones	Peter	MIS	45,000	03/05/92		
3	Smith	Mary Ann	Personnel	34,000	05/12/91		
4	Bridges	Brian	MIS	65,000	02/22/93		
5	Peterson	Betsy	Sales	51,000	06/03/91		
6	Smith	Robert	Sales	39,000	04/27/90		
7	Garcia	Maria	Personnel	25,000	06/19/94		
8	Ho	Harry	MIS	46,000	10/15/92		
9	Smith	Samuel	Sales	64,000	04/18/93		
10	Jones	Brett	Sales	52,000	07/03/91		
11	Harrison	Paul	Personnel	31,000	09/06/93		
12	Randall	Rebecca	MIS	72,000	01/06/91		

Tip
Do not include the field names in the sort range, though. If you do, they will be sorted within the records and will no longer be at the top of each column.

Caution

If you do not include all fields when sorting, you destroy the integrity of your database because parts of one record will end up with parts of other records. It's easy to think, "I want to sort the last names in alphabetical order so I'll select this column for the sort range." Don't do this! If you do, your names will indeed be in alphabetical order, but the data corresponding to each name will no longer be accurate.

Note that the sort range does not necessarily have to include all records in the database. If part of the database already has the organization you want, or if you do not want to sort all the records, you can sort only a portion of the database.

After selecting the sort range, issue the **R**ange **S**ort command. You will then see the Sort dialog box shown in figure 25.2. Because you preselected the range, the **R**ange field at the bottom of the dialog box is already filled in. What you need to indicate here are your *sort keys*. The sort key is one cell in the column you want to sort—it doesn't matter which cell you indicate. In figure 25.1, to sort the last names, you specify any cell in column A (A2, A3, and so on). You can even select a cell outside of the sort range (such as A1 or A6). Or, if you wanted to sort the salaries, you could specify any cell in column D.

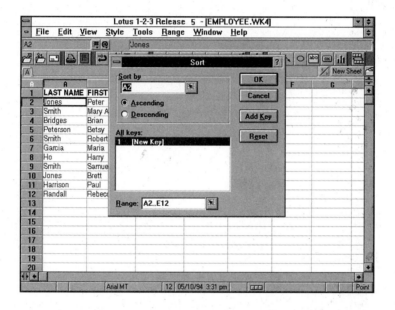

Fig. 25.2
In the **S**ort by field of the Sort dialog box, specify one cell (any cell) in the column you want to sort.

You can sort the column in **A**scending or **D**escending order. Ascending order sorts labels from A to Z, values from lowest to highest, and dates from earliest to latest. Descending order sorts labels from Z to A, values from highest to lowest, and dates from latest to earliest. If you don't specify a sort order, ascending is the default.

After the sort key is defined, you can click the OK button to sort the data. Figure 25.3 shows the employee database with the last names sorted in alphabetical order. Cell A2 was specified in the **S**ort by field and **A**scending order was selected.

◀ "Filling Ranges,"
p. 92

> **Note**
>
> To ensure that you can restore the original record order after sorting the database, you can add a Record Number field to the database before sorting. You then can restore the original order by re-sorting on the Record Number field. You can use the **R**ange **F**ill command to enter record numbers quickly.

Fig. 25.3

The database is sorted alphabetically by last name.

	A	B	C	D	E	F	G
1	LAST NAME	FIRST NAME	DEPARTMENT	SALARY	HIRE DATE		
2	Bridges	Brian	MIS	65,000	02/22/93		
3	Garcia	Maria	Personnel	25,000	06/19/94		
4	Harrison	Paul	Personnel	31,000	09/06/93		
5	Ho	Harry	MIS	46,000	10/15/92		
6	Jones	Brett	Sales	52,000	07/03/91		
7	Jones	Peter	MIS	45,000	03/05/92		
8	Peterson	Betsy	Sales	51,000	06/03/91		
9	Randall	Rebecca	MIS	72,000	01/06/91		
10	Smith	Mary Ann	Personnel	34,000	05/12/91		
11	Smith	Samuel	Sales	64,000	04/18/93		
12	Smith	Robert	Sales	39,000	04/27/90		

Using the Sort SmartIcons

Tip

Because the Sort SmartIcons are not on any of the palettes, you may want to use the **T**ools SmartIcons command to add the icons to the palette(s) you use.

1-2-3 for Windows offers two SmartIcons for sorting ranges; one for sorting in ascending order, and the other for sorting in descending order. Both icons are very simple to use. Just place the cell pointer on any cell in the column you want to sort and then click the Ascending Sort or Descending Sort SmartIcon. Note that you do not need to define the sort range—the SmartIcons automatically sort all adjacent columns and rows. These SmartIcons are truly smart in that they know to leave the column headings alone (that is, the headings are not sorted).

The SmartIcons are probably the fastest way to sort a range, but they are limiting because you cannot specify multiple sort keys, nor can you sort certain records.

Using Multiple Sort Keys

A single sort key works fine if there aren't any duplicate entries in the field you are sorting. But what if you are sorting by last names and there are five Smiths in the database? Or what if you are sorting by city and there are 20 companies in the same city? In these two examples, you would want to use a secondary sort key to serve as a tie-breaker. In the first scenario, the primary key would be the LAST NAME field and the secondary key (the tie-breaker) would be the FIRST NAME field. In the second scenario, the city field would be the primary key and the company name would be the secondary key.

While it is unlikely you would need to go beyond two or three sort keys, 1-2-3 for Windows allows you to define up to 255. To define multiple sort keys, follow these steps:

1. Select the sort range.

2. Open the **R**ange menu and choose the **S**ort command.

3. In the **S**ort by field, indicate your primary key—one cell in the column you want to sort.

4. Choose **A**scending or **D**escending order.

5. Click the Add **K**ey button. This sort key will appear in the All keys list.

6. In the **S**ort by field, indicate your secondary key.

7. Choose **A**scending or **D**escending order.

8. Click the Add **K**ey button.

9. Continue adding keys, as described above.

10. Press Enter or click OK to perform the sort.

Figure 25.4 shows the Sort dialog box with the Last Name field (A2) as the primary key and the First Name field (B2) as the secondary key. Ascending order is specified for both keys. After sorting, the range would look like figure 25.5.

V

Managing Databases

Fig. 25.4
The All keys field lists the sort keys.

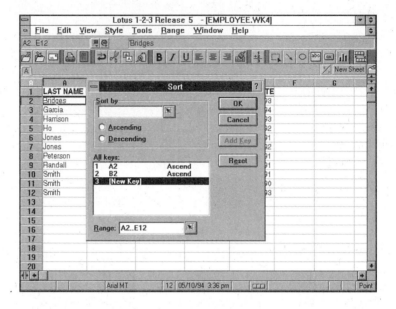

Fig. 25.5
This range was sorted with Last Name (A2) as the primary key and First Name (B2) as the secondary key.

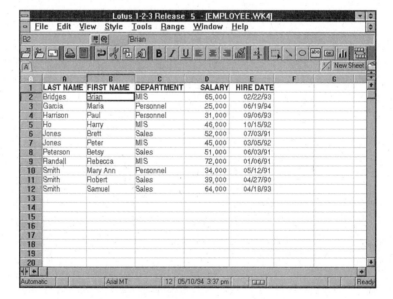

Performing Additional Sorts

You can sort a range as many different ways and as many different times as you like. Sometimes you may want the list sorted by last names. Other times you may want the list sorted by department with the last names sorted alphabetically within each department. Or perhaps you need a report in which you can easily determine who is making the most money in each department.

1-2-3 for Windows makes it easy to perform additional sorts. There are just two things to remember. First, each time you perform a sort, you must redefine the sort range—1-2-3 does not remember the range you defined for the previous sort. Second, 1-2-3 keeps track of the sort keys you previously specified. This feature is convenient when you have added more records to your database and you now want to sort them in the same order as the previously-entered records. If you want to sort by different columns, however, eliminate the old sort keys. You can easily clear out these sort keys by choosing the R**e**set button in the Sort dialog box. This command will clear the keys listed in the A**l**l keys field.

In figure 25.6, the employee database is sorted by department names, and within each department the last names are alphabetized. The following steps re-sort the database in this order:

1. Select the range A2..E12.

2. Open the R**a**nge menu and choose the **S**ort command.

3. Click the R**e**set button to clear old sort keys.

4. In the **S**ort by field, specify **C2** and click the Add **K**ey button.

5. In the **S**ort by field, specify **A2** and click the Add **K**ey button.

6. Press Enter or click OK. The database should now look like figure 25.6.

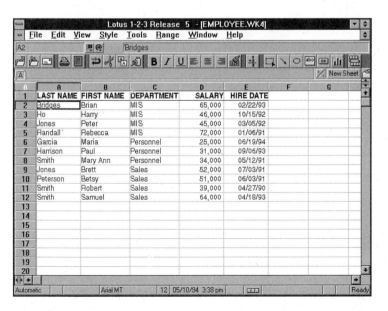

Fig. 25.6
The employee database is sorted by department and within each department the last names are alphabetized.

Using a Query Table to Sort Records

1-2-3 for Windows offers another way to sort a database: using a query table. *Query tables* are special workspaces in a worksheet that simplify selecting, sorting, and updating database records. In this chapter, you'll see how a query table can be used to sort a database; in Chapter 26, you'll learn how to select and update records by using a query table.

Sorting with a query table offers several advantages compared with directly sorting the records in a worksheet database range. First, you don't need to select the sort range because 1-2-3 automatically sorts all the fields and records in the query table. You therefore don't need to worry about defining the range incorrectly and inadvertently making scrambled eggs out of your database. Second, you can sort the records by selecting the field name from a list. Indicating that you want to sort the Last Name field is more intuitive than specifying cell A2. Third, you can try several different sort orders without affecting the original database. If you find a sort order that you like, you can apply the new order to the database. If you decide not to apply the changes, the database remains untouched and in the order in which records were initially entered.

Creating a Query Table

To create a new query table, follow the steps below. Refer to figure 25.7 for the example database.

1. Highlight the database range—in this case, A1..G6. Then open the **T**ools menu and choose Data**b**ase **N**ew Query, or click the Query Table SmartIcon. The New Query dialog box appears (see fig. 25.8).

Tip
Because query tables can overwrite existing worksheet data, it's wise to create a new worksheet for each query table you use. Add a new worksheet before you create the query table.

2. In the Select Location for New **Q**uery Table box, select a location for the query table. The best location is another worksheet, such as the Query Table sheet. You only need to specify a starting cell—you don't need to specify the complete range, although you can if you like. For this example, type **Query Table:A1** or **B:A1**.

3. Choose OK to confirm your dialog-box choices and create the query table (see fig. 25.9).

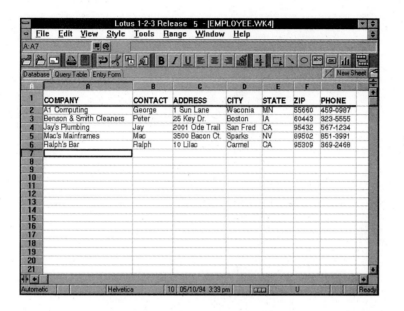

Fig. 25.7

The original database for which a query table will be created.

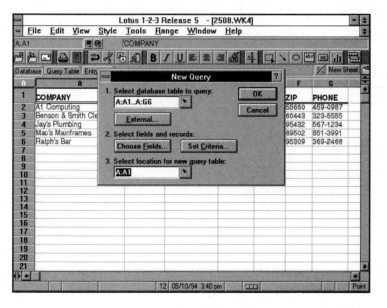

Fig. 25.8

The New Query dialog box.

Fig. 25.9
The query table.
(Column widths
have been adjusted
in this figure.)

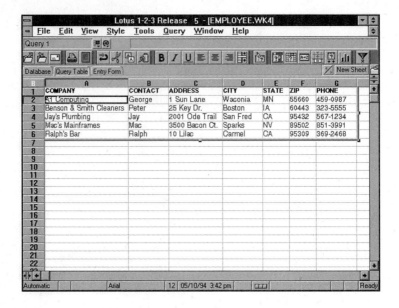

Notice in figure 25.9 that both the 1-2-3 for Windows menu bar and the SmartIcon set change when a query table is selected (click a cell within the query table to select the table). The **R**ange menu is replaced by the **Q**uery menu (fig. 25.10), and several standard SmartIcons are replaced by SmartIcons that pertain specifically to query tables. These changes make using a query table even easier.

Fig. 25.10
The **Q**uery menu
replaces the **R**ange
menu when a
query table is
selected.

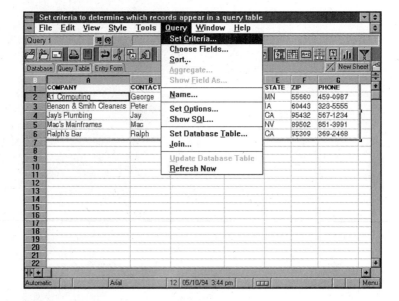

> **Note**
>
> When there isn't enough room to display all the records in the query table, the bottom border of the table displays with a dotted line. You can display the rest of the data by clicking the Show All Query Table Records SmartIcon. You also can resize the query table by clicking the query table border and dragging the handles.

Sorting the Query Table

Choosing **Q**uery **S**ort displays the Sort dialog box (see fig. 25.11). This dialog box is similar to the one displayed with the **R**ange **S**ort command, with two exceptions. First, the **S**ort by field displays a list of field names when you click it. Second, there is no field for the sort range because 1-2-3 automatically knows what data to sort (everything in the query table except for the field names).

To sort the records, you must specify the key(s) for the sort. As with the **R**ange **S**ort command, **Q**uery **S**ort can use up to 255 keys in a sort, but only the first key is required.

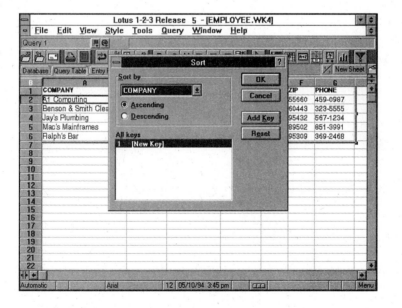

Fig. 25.11
This Sort dialog box is displayed with the **Q**uery **S**ort command.

Using a One-Key Sort

To specify a single sort key, follow these steps:

1. Click any cell in the query table.

2. Open the **Q**uery menu and choose **S**ort to display the Sort dialog box, or click the Sort Query Table SmartIcon.

3. In the drop-down **S**ort By list, select a field name. For this exercise, select STATE to sort the records by the values in the STATE field.

4. Choose either **A**scending or **D**escending sort order, depending on how you want to sort the records. For this exercise, choose **A**scending order.

5. Press Enter or click OK.

Figure 25.12 shows the query table sorted in **A**scending order by state.

Fig. 25.12

The query table sorted by STATE.

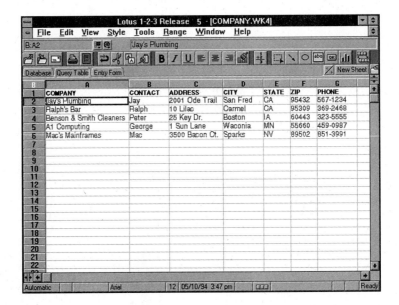

Using a Multiple-Key Sort

Sometimes, sorting on a single key does not sort the records in exactly the order you may need. In such a case, you can use multiple sort keys to specify additional sorting conditions.

A multiple-key sort uses more than one key to sort the records. In the telephone book's yellow pages, for example, records are sorted first according to business type (the first key) and then by business name (the second key). In the white pages, records are first sorted by last name and then by first name.

To specify additional sort keys, follow these steps:

1. Click any cell in the query table.

2. Open the **Query** menu and choose the **S**ort command to display the Sort dialog box.

3. After specifying each sort key and order (**A**scending or **D**escending), click the Add K**e**y button. For this example, STATE should already be listed as the first key. For the second sort key, select CITY in the **S**ort By drop-down list.

4. Press Enter or click OK.

Figure 25.13 shows the result of the multiple-key sort. Ralph's Bar, in Carmel, California, now appears before Jay's Plumbing, in San Fred, California. Because the first key remained STATE, none of the other records moved.

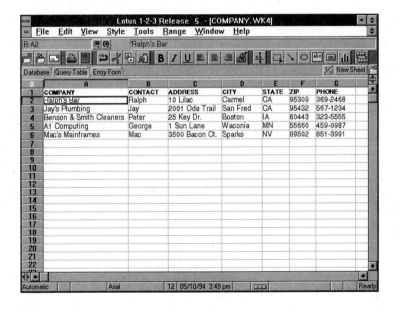

Fig. 25.13
The query table sorted by STATE (first key) and CITY (second key).

V

Managing Databases

Determining the Sort Order

When you sort in ascending order, here is the order in which data in the field is sorted:

Blank cells

Labels beginning with a space

Labels beginning with numbers

Labels beginning with letters (lowercase letters before uppercase letters)

Other characters

Values

When you sort in descending order, this sequence is reversed. These sorting rules apply to sorts performed with the **R**ange **S**ort command as well as with **Q**uery **S**ort.

Note

When you install 1-2-3, you can choose from three different sort orders. Numbers First, as previously described, is the default. The Numbers Last order is identical to Numbers First except that labels beginning with numbers come after labels beginning with letters. The ASCII order sorts blank cells first, then labels in LMBCS (Lotus Multibyte Character Set) code order, and then values.

Restoring the Presort Order

One of the advantages of sorting the query table, as opposed to sorting the original database, is that it does not change the original record order in the database (unless you use the **Q**uery **U**pdate Database Table command).

Note

If the **U**pdate Database Table command is dimmed on the **Q**uery menu, you will need to change one of the query table options. To make this change, choose **Q**uery Set **O**ptions and turn on **A**llow Updates to Source Table. The **U**pdate Database Table command will then become available on the **Q**uery menu.

Troubleshooting

My part number field is not sorting properly. For example, part 1234-AB is sorted before part 456-AB, even though I sorted in ascending order.

Because the part numbers are entered as labels, they are not sorted in numerical order. 1-2-3 reads the characters from left to right and determines that 1 is less than 4; it doesn't consider that 456 is less than 1234. A solution is to add enough leading zeros (0) to ensure that all the labels have the same length. For example, specify 0456-AB as the part number.

My dates are not sorting properly. For example, 03-05-94 comes before 12-15-93 even though I sorted in ascending order.

When dates are entered as labels, 1-2-3 reads the characters from left to right and sorts by month without regard to the year. You could avoid this problem by entering the year first (**'94-03-05**) but this is a non-standard format. A better solution is to enter the dates as values. This is done automatically when you enter your dates with slashes (**3/5/94**) and when the Automatic format is selected as your default. You can then sort dates in chronological order without a problem.

I have a Name field that contains a first name followed by a last name (for example, Peter Smith). When I sort this field, the first names are alphabetized, not the last names. Is there any way to sort the last names in alphabetical order?

No, not without restructuring the database. See Chapter 24 for an explanation on how you can divide one field into two. The problem you are having is a good lesson on the importance of dividing your data into separate fields as much as possible.

From Here...

Now that you have seen a little of what query tables can do, you'll probably want to explore it further.

- Chapter 26, "Finding and Extracting Data," shows you how to use query tables to locate certain records in a database, to extract information into reports, and to update the original database.

V

Managing Databases

Chapter 26

Finding and Extracting Data

One of the main advantages to computerizing a database is the ease and speed in which information can be retrieved. Even in a database containing hundreds or thousands of records, 1-2-3 can locate a particular record in a matter of seconds. Extracting meaningful information from a sea of data is another important capability. A list of 2,000 records with 15 fields each is too overwhelming to convey anything of importance. But if you were to narrow the list down to a subset of the database, such as a list of all the customers who have invoices over 60 days past due, you now have *information*, not just *raw data*.

Beginning with 1-2-3 Release 4 for Windows, querying the database has become straightforward and intuitive. Instead of entering formulas in a worksheet (as was required in previous versions), you select fields and matching conditions in a dialog box. This chapter shows you how to use this easy-to-use technique for selecting records. The sample database used throughout this chapter is shown in figure 26.1.

In this chapter, you will learn to do the following:

- Choose fields to appear in a query table

- Create computed fields in a query table

- Specify record-selection criteria

- Find records

- Delete specified records

Fig. 26.1

The employee database is used as an example throughout this chapter.

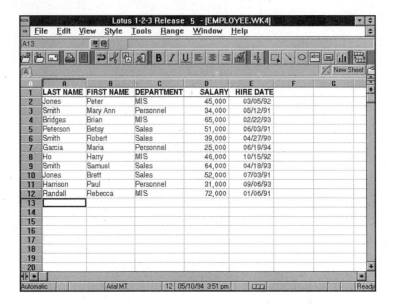

Using a Query Table

◀ "Sorting Data," p. 723

As explained in Chapter 25, *query tables* are special workspaces in a worksheet that simplify selecting, sorting, and updating database records. Query tables work with any database that 1-2-3 for Windows can use—a database in a worksheet, or a database contained in external files accessed through DataLens drivers (see Chapter 28).

Creating a Query Table

Chapter 25 covered how to create a query table, but the steps are repeated here for review and easy reference.

To create a new query table, follow these steps:

1. Use the New Sheet button to insert a sheet for the query table. This step is not mandatory, but keeping your database and query table in separate sheets helps keep your ranges organized.

2. Highlight the database range (all the fields and records). Then open the **T**ools menu and choose Data**b**ase **N**ew Query, or click the Query Table SmartIcon. The New Query dialog box appears (see fig. 26.2).

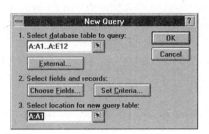

Fig. 26.2
The New Query
dialog box.

3. In the Select Location for New **Q**uery Table box, select a location for the query table. You only need to specify a starting cell—you don't need to specify the complete range, although you can if you want. Be sure to specify the sheet letter or name before the cell coordinate (for example, B:A1).

4. Choose OK to confirm your dialog-box choices and create the query table. A sample query table is shown in figure 26.3.

Notice in figure 26.3 that both the 1-2-3 for Windows menu bar and the SmartIcon set change when a query table is selected (click a cell within the query table to select the table). The **R**ange menu is replaced by the **Q**uery menu, and several standard SmartIcons are replaced by SmartIcons that pertain specifically to query tables. These changes make using a query table even easier.

Tip
If you have inserted a new sheet for the query table, you can click on the tab for that sheet.

V

Managing Databases

Lotus 1-2-3 Release 5 - [EMPLOYEE.WK4]

	A	B	C	D	E	F	G	H
1	LAST NAME	FIRST NAME	DEPARTMENT	SALARY	HIRE DATE			
2	Jones	Peter	MIS	45,000	03/05/92			
3	Smith	Mary Ann	Personnel	34,000	05/12/91			
4	Bridges	Brian	MIS	65,000	02/22/93			
5	Peterson	Betsy	Sales	51,000	06/03/91			
6	Smith	Robert	Sales	39,000	04/27/90			
7	Garcia	Maria	Personnel	25,000	06/19/94			
8	Ho	Harry	MIS	46,000	10/15/92			
9	Smith	Samuel	Sales	64,000	04/18/93			
10	Jones	Brett	Sales	52,000	07/03/91			
11	Harrison	Paul	Personnel	31,000	09/06/93			
12	Randall	Rebecca	MIS	72,000	01/06/91			

Fig. 26.3
A sample query
table in its own
worksheet.

Setting Query Table Options

Four options enable you to control the way a query table functions. To access these options, use the **Q**uery Set **O**ptions command to display the Set Options dialog box (see fig. 26.4).

Fig. 26.4

The Set Options dialog box enables you to control query table settings.

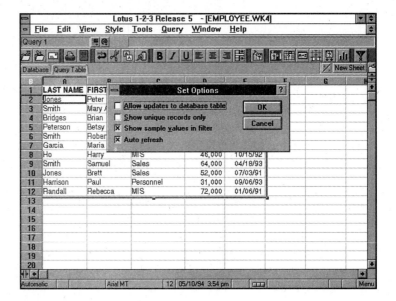

Choose the first option, **A**llow Updates to Source Table, to give yourself the option of updating the database after you make changes in the query table. For instance, if you edit a cell in the query table, you may want to update the corresponding cell in the database. However, you cannot select any other Query menu options while "Allow Updates" is selected. When **A**llow Updates is turned off, you cannot update the database table.

Note

Even when the **A**llow Updates to Source Table option is turned on, updates happen only when you issue the **Q**uery Update Database Table command.

Choose the second option, **S**how Unique Records Only, if you want to create a set of unique values. You can use this option a couple of ways. First, with this option turned on, the query table will not display duplicate records; you can use this option to help you cleanse your database of redundant data. Second, you can use this option to list the unique values in a particular field. For example, if you create a query table that includes only the ZIP field, you can create one record for each unique ZIP value. You may find such a list to be helpful for mailing purposes.

Choose the third option, Show Sample **V**alues in Filter, to make it easier to define criteria. When this option is selected, the **V**alue box in the Set Criteria dialog box displays a list of each unique value in a field.

The fourth option, Auto **R**efresh, ensures that when you make changes in any criteria, sort settings, field names, or aggregate settings, 1-2-3 for Windows updates your query table. If your database is large, you may find that database operations are slightly faster when this option is not selected. If you don't choose the Auto **R**efresh option, you can use the **Q**uery **R**efresh Now command or click the Update Query Table SmartIcon to update the query table as necessary.

Choosing Fields

Unless you specify otherwise, the query table contains all the fields in your database, in the exact order they appear in the database. You can, however, display a subset of the database fields, or change their order, by selecting Choose **F**ields in the New Query dialog box. Or, if you forget to do this while you are creating the query, you can issue the **Q**uery **Ch**oose Fields command or click the Choose Fields SmartIcon when a query table is selected. You will then see the Choose Fields dialog box shown in figure 26.5.

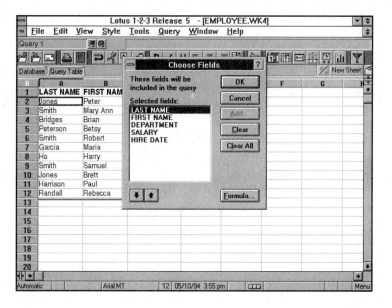

Fig. 26.5

Use the Choose Fields dialog box to select the fields to be included in the query table.

As you can see, all fields are chosen by default. To unselect a field, click it and choose **C**lear. Or, to unselect all fields (so that you can start choosing from scratch), choose C**l**ear All. To insert a field, use the **A**dd button. You can then select the field name from a list and choose whether to insert the field **B**efore Current Field or **A**fter Last Field.

> **Note**
>
> If the **A**dd button is dimmed (unavailable), then all fields are already selected. You will need to use the **C**lear button to unselect a field before the **A**dd option is available.

To move a field to another position in the query table, display the Choose Fields dialog box and highlight the field you want to move. Then click the up or down arrows at the bottom of the dialog box until the field is in the desired position.

Creating Computed Fields

In the Choose Fields dialog box, you can build formulas to create new fields in the query table. For example, in an employee database, you can create a BONUS field that multiplies the SALARY field by 10%. You can even create a field that combines two label fields. For instance, you can create a NAME field that displays the FIRST NAME followed by the LAST NAME. The easiest way to understand how to build field formulas is to look at some examples.

+SALARY*0.1	Creates a BONUS field by multiplying the SALARY field by 10%
+FIRST NAME&" "&LAST NAME	Creates a NAME field by combining the FIRST NAME and LAST NAME fields
(@NOW-HIRE DATE)/365	Creates a YEARS EMPLOYED field by subtracting the HIRE DATE field from today's date and then dividing by 365 days.

Notice that just like cell formulas, field formulas begin with a value such as +, @, or (. Also, fields are referenced by their names (which makes it easy to build these formulas). When you "add" two labels, use the ampersand (&),

◄ "Text Functions," p. 242

and place quotation marks around any text you want to include. (In the second example, there are quotation marks around a space.) Figure 26.6 shows the results of these field formulas in the employee database.

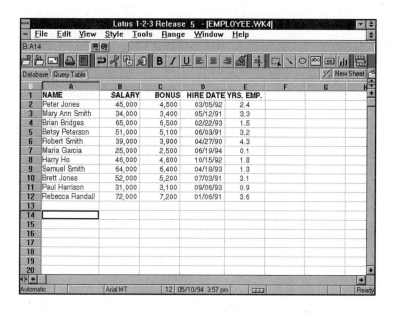

Fig. 26.6
The NAME, BONUS, and YRS. EMP. fields in this query table are new fields calculated with formulas.

Caution

If the **A**llow Updates to Source Table option (in the Set Options dialog box) is turned on, 1-2-3 for Windows will not let you create computed fields. (This makes sense since the original database doesn't contain the new fields.) To turn off **A**llow Updates, use the **Q**uery Set **O**ptions command.

Here are the steps for creating a field formula:

1. Position the pointer on the FIELD NAME list in the Choose Fields dialog box—the new field will be inserted above the highlighted field, or optionally, you can replace the highlighted field with the field formula.

2. Click the **F**ormula button. The Formula dialog box appears, as shown in figure 26.7. The name of the highlighted field automatically appears in the **E**nter Formula box. For example, if the SALARY field were highlighted, the **E**nter Formula box would display +*SALARY*.

Fig. 26.7
Enter field
formulas in the
Formula dialog
box.

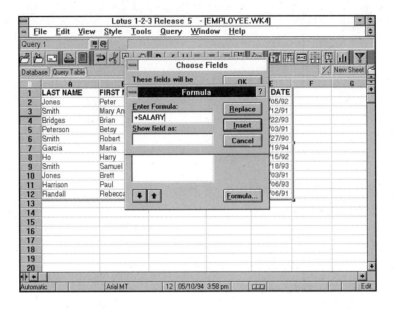

3. Enter the field formula, deleting the contents of the **E**nter Formula box if necessary.

4. In the **S**how Field As box, type a field name that describes the new field. For example, **BONUS** is an appropriate name for a formula that multiplies the SALARY field by 10%.

5. Choose **I**nsert to insert the new field above the previously-highlighted field or **R**eplace to clear the highlighted field and insert the new field in its place.

You can use the **Q**uery Show **F**ield As command or the Rename Field SmartIcon to change the name of a field in the query table. You must first click the field name to select the entire field before this command can be invoked.

Note that the fields you choose and create affect only the query table, not the database itself.

Troubleshooting

After entering a field formula in the Formula dialog box, I got the message Ambiguous
field reference in query. *Talk about ambiguous! What does this error message
mean?*

Most likely, you misspelled the field name. For example, you typed **LASTNAME** (one
word) instead of **LAST NAME** (two words). Another possibility is that you were
concatenating fields and you forgot to enter the concatenation operator (&). For
example, perhaps you typed +**FIRST NAME**" "&**LAST NAME** instead of +**FIRST
NAME**&" "&**LAST NAME**.

*In my query table, the column heading for my calculated field has the formula
(SALARY*0.1) instead of a field name (such as BONUS). How can I change this?*

When you were defining the formula in the Formula dialog box, you could
have entered BONUS in the **S**how Field As box. Because you forgot to do
this, you can define the field name after the query table is created by using the **Q**uery
Show **F**ield As command or the Rename Field SmartIcon.

Specifying Record-Selection Criteria

The Choose **F**ields button in the New Query dialog box lets you narrow
down the fields that are displayed in the query table. The Set **C**riteria button
lets you choose which records are displayed. A *criteria* is a condition that
must be satisfied in order for a record to be displayed in a query table. For
example, you may want the query table to list all the employees who make
more than $50,000 a year. In this case, your criteria would look like this:
SALARY>50000.

You can specify selection criteria when you use the **T**ools Data**b**ase **N**ew
Query command to create a new query table. Or, to define a selection criteria
after the query table is created, you use the **Q**uery Set **C**riteria command or
click the Set Criteria SmartIcon. The Set Criteria dialog box appears (see
fig. 26.8).

The basic steps for specifying a criterion are as follows:

1. In the Set Criteria dialog box, display the **F**ield drop-down list and
   select the field name you want to query.

V

Managing Databases

2. Display the **O**perator drop-down list and select the appropriate operator (see "Using Operators in Selection Criteria" in the next section).

3. Enter the text or value you are looking for in the **V**alue box. You also can click the arrow to display a list of all the different values entered in the field and then select the value from the list. (The list displays only if the Show Sample **V**alues in Filter option is turned on in the Set Options dialog box.)

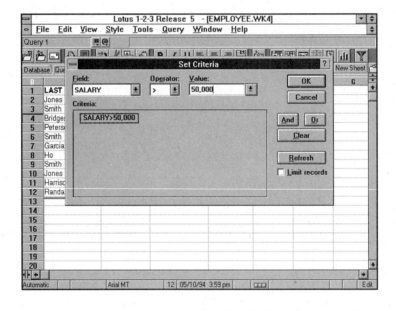

To list the employees in the database who are in the MIS department, for example, you can use a search operation to find any records with *MIS* as the value in the DEPARTMENT field. To set the criteria for this type of record selection, select **DEPARTMENT** in the **F**ield list, = in the O**p**erator list, and **MIS** in the **V**alue list. Click OK or press Enter to confirm your selection. The query table now contains only the records that match the selection criteria, as shown in figure 26.9.

After you locate the information that you want, you can use the query table to create a report. You also can copy or cut the information from the query table and place that information in a separate section of the worksheet.

In addition to searching for an exact match of a single label field, 1-2-3 for Windows enables you to conduct a wide variety of record searches: exact matches of numeric fields; partial matches of field contents; a range of values;

fields that meet all of several conditions; and fields that meet either one condition or another. Consider first some variations of queries on single fields.

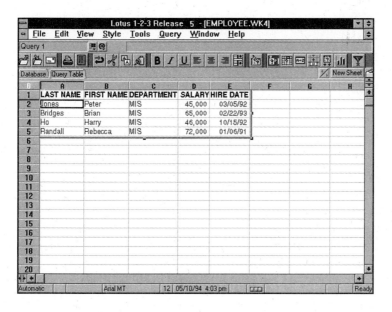

Fig. 26.9

The query table, showing only records that match specified criteria.

Using Operators in Selection Criteria

To set up criteria that query numeric or label fields in the database, you can use the following relational operators (in the Operator box of the Set Criteria dialog box):

>	Greater than
>=	Greater than or equal to
<	Less than
<=	Less than or equal to
=	Equal to
<>	Not equal to

You create a condition that describes the values of the field entries to be selected. 1-2-3 for Windows tests the condition on each record in the database. Here are some examples of valid conditions:

DEPARTMENT<>SALES   Excludes records in which the DEPART-
                                              MENT field is not SALES

LAST NAME=SMITH	All records in which the LAST NAME field contains SMITH
SALARY>=50000	All records in which the SALARY field is greater than or equal to 50,000
LAST NAME>L	All records in which the LAST NAME field begins with the letters M through Z
HIRE DATE<1/1/92	All records in which the HIRE DATE field contains a date before 1/1/92 (in other words, those who were hired before 1992)

Using Wild Cards to Match Similar Labels

You can use 1-2-3 for Windows' wild cards to match similar labels in database operations. Two characters—the question mark (?) and the asterisk (*)—have special meaning when used in criteria. The ? character instructs 1-2-3 for Windows to accept any character in that specific position; each ? represents one character and can be used only to locate fields of the same length. The * character tells 1-2-3 for Windows to accept any number of characters in that position.

Table 26.1 shows how you can use wild cards in search operations.

Table 26.1   Using Wild Cards in Search Operations

Enter	To Find
N?	Any two-character label starting with the letter N (NC, NJ, NY, and so on)
BO?L?	A five-character label (BOWLE) but not a shorter label (BOWL)
BO?L*	A four-or-more-character label (BOWLE, BOWL, BOLLESON, BOELING, and so on)
J??NSON	A label that starts with the letter J followed by any two characters, followed by the letters NSON (JOHNSON not JENSON)
SAN*	A three-or-more-character label starting with SAN and followed by any number of characters (SANTA BARBARA and SAN FRANCISCO)
SAN *	A four-or-more-character label starting with SAN, followed by a space, and then followed by any number of characters (SAN FRANCISCO, but not SANTA BARBARA)

Use the ? and * wild-card characters when you are unsure of the spelling or when you need to match several slightly different records.

Note

The * wild-card character can only go at the end of the search string. You cannot, for instance, use ***CA*** to locate all entries that have "CA" somewhere in the middle of the field.

Troubleshooting

I entered the criterion LAST NAME=SMITH but my query table didn't display one of the Smiths I know is in my database. What's going on?

Try changing your criterion to LAST NAME=SMITH*. If the elusive Smith appears in this query table, the cell probably has a space after *Smith*. To see whether this is the problem, go to this field in the database, and press F2 (Edit). If you see extra space after *Smith*, then press Backspace to eliminate the space.

Some of my records in my mailing list database are missing ZIP codes. I would like to list these records in a query table so that I can easily fill in this information. How can I specify a criterion that will locate all records with an empty ZIP CODE field?

The criterion you need is ZIP CODE="". The two sets of quotation marks, which indicate a blank cell, do not have a space between them.

*I am trying to locate last names that end in the letters "son". When I enter the criterion LAST NAME=*SON, the query table lists all records. What am I doing wrong?*

The * wildcard can be used only at the end of the character string; it can't be used at the beginning or in the middle. When 1-2-3 for Windows sees the asterisk, it ignores anything that comes after it. Thus, to 1-2-3, *SON* is the same as *—that's why all records are listed. Although 1-2-3 for Windows does not offer a way to perform this type of query in a query table, you do have an alternative. You can use the **E**dit **F**ind & Replace command to locate the characters *son*.

Specifying Multiple Criteria

You have seen how to base a selection on only one criterion. In this section, you learn how to use multiple criteria for your queries. You can set up multiple criteria as AND conditions (in which *all* the criteria must be met) or as

OR conditions (in which any *one* criterion must be met). For example, searching a music department's library for sheet music requiring drums AND trumpets is likely to produce fewer selections than searching for music appropriate for drums OR trumpets.

> **Note**
>
> Deciding on whether to use AND or OR can be a little tricky sometimes. For example, suppose you want a list of all companies in California and Nevada. While it may seem logical that you would use the AND connector in this example, OR is the appropriate connector. This is because a single field (STATE in this case) can only contain one value or another. In other words, in a single record the STATE field could not possibly contain two values (CA and NV).

Setting Up *AND* Conditions

You indicate two or more criteria, *all* of which must be met, by specifying the first condition in the Set Criteria dialog box, choosing the **A**nd button, and then specifying the second condition.

Suppose that you want to retrieve only those records for employees in the Sales department who make $50,000 or more a year. To specify those conditions, follow these steps:

1. If you want to create a new query table, open the **T**ools menu and choose Data**b**ase **N**ew Query Set **C**riteria. Or, to use an existing query table, choose **Q**uery Set **C**riteria. Either command displays the Set Criteria dialog box.

2. Select **DEPARTMENT** in the **F**ield list, = in the Op**e**rator list, and **Sales** in the **V**alue list.

3. Choose the **A**nd button.

4. Select **SALARY** in the **F**ield list and **>=** in the Op**e**rator list, and type **50000** in the **V**alue box.

   Figure 26.10 shows how the two conditions appear in the Criteria box.

5. Click OK or press Enter. The query table shows the results of performing this query; three records are displayed (see fig. 26.10).

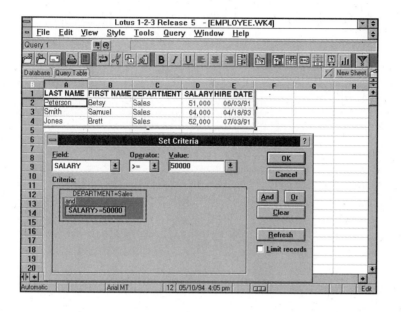

Fig. 26.10
Using AND to combine two criteria.

Setting Up OR Conditions

To retrieve records that meet either one condition or another, you combine the conditions by using Or instead of And. 1-2-3 for Windows retrieves the records that match either condition. The OR connector is frequently used to search for two possible values in a field, such as DEPARTMENT=MIS OR DEPARTMENT=Personnel. In figure 26.11, the two criteria connected with OR result in a list of everyone in the MIS or Personnel department.

To set up selection criteria for records containing either *MIS* or *Personnel* in the DEPARTMENT field, follow these steps:

1. Open the **Q**uery menu and choose Set **C**riteria to display the Set Criteria dialog box.

2. Choose the **C**lear button to clear the previous query.

3. Select **DEPARTMENT** in the **F**ield list, = in the Op**e**rator list, and **MIS** in the **V**alue list.

4. Choose the **O**r button.

5. Select **DEPARTMENT** in the **F**ield list and = in the Op**e**rator list, and choose **Personnel** in the **V**alue box.

6. Click OK or press Enter.

Figure 26.11 shows the completed Set Criteria dialog box and the result of the new set of criteria in the query table. Only one condition or the other had to be met in order for the record to be selected.

Fig. 26.11

Using OR to combine two criteria.

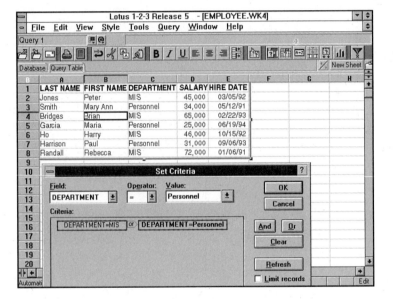

Changing Condition Types

Sometimes, you may find that you combined a set of criteria incorrectly. Suppose that you created the criteria set shown in figure 26.12 but later realized that combining the criteria with AND was a mistake. You really wanted to combine the criteria with OR, as shown in figure 26.11. You could choose the **C**lear button to remove the criteria and start over, but 1-2-3 for Windows provides an easier method.

As shown in figures 26.11 and 26.12, the Criteria box displays AND conditions in a single box vertically and OR conditions in two boxes horizontally. To change condition types, you can use the mouse to drag a criteria from one position to another. To change the AND condition shown in figure 26.12 to the OR condition shown in figure 26.11, for example, select the DEPARTMENT=Personnel criterion and drag it to the right of the

DEPARTMENT=MIS criterion. To change an OR condition to an AND condition, select one criterion and drag it on top of the other criterion.

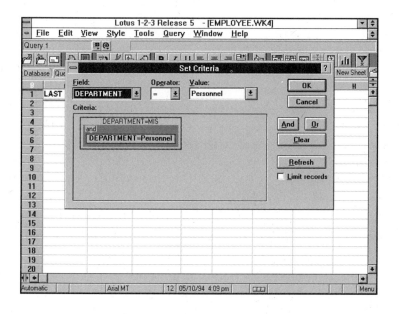

Fig. 26.12
When you improperly choose AND instead of OR (as was done in this example), you can simply drag the condition to the right; this action changes the AND condition into an OR.

You can add as many AND and OR criteria as necessary to select the desired
set of records. You may have a little trouble determining the correct set of
conditions for very complex selection requirements, but 1-2-3 for Windows
enables you to correct and adjust the criteria until they are perfect.

> **Note**
>
> If you are having difficulty narrowing down record selection to a precise set in com-
> plex situations, try extracting records in stages. First, extract a group that contains all
> the records you want—and also some that you don't want. Then, using the extracted
> records as the source, create another query table and extract a more precise set of
> records. If necessary, repeat the process until you have only the records that you
> need.

Finding Records

When you need to quickly look up information in a database, you may want
to use the **T**ools Data**b**ase **F**ind Records command instead of using a query
table. This command, unlike the Query operations, requires no set-up work.

You can issue the command, indicate what record you want to find, and then 1-2-3 for Windows highlights each matching record in the database.

Suppose your boss asks you on what date Betsy Peterson was hired. (Of course in a small database you could easily locate this information by looking on-screen, but assume the database has several hundred records.) You can quickly bring up this information using the **F**ind Records command. Another time when the **F**ind Records command comes in handy is when you need to update the information in a record. If Harry Ho were to get a raise, you could find his record, go to the SALARY field, and enter the new value.

When you issue the **T**ools Data**b**ase **F**ind Records command, 1-2-3 highlights each record in the database that meets the specified conditions. If the criterion is LAST NAME=SMITH, for example, the three employees named Smith are highlighted (see fig. 26.13).

Fig. 26.13
The **T**ools Data**b**ase **F**ind Records command highlights each record that meets the specified conditions.

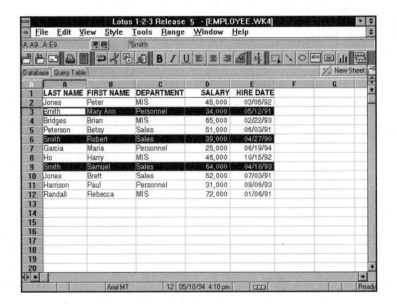

When you use the **T**ools Data**b**ase **F**ind Records command, you will see the Find Records dialog box shown in figure 26.14. First, specify the database range next to Find Records in **D**atabase Table. If you have assigned a range name to the database (which is always a good idea), you can press F3 (Name) and select the database name from a list of range names.

After you have selected the database range, the Find Records dialog box becomes customized to your database (compare fig. 26.15 with fig. 26.14). The Field drop-down list displays all the field names in your database and the

Value drop-down list displays all the different entries contained in the selected field. For example, if DEPARTMENT were selected for **F**ield, the **V**alue list would offer the choices MIS, Personnel, and Sales.

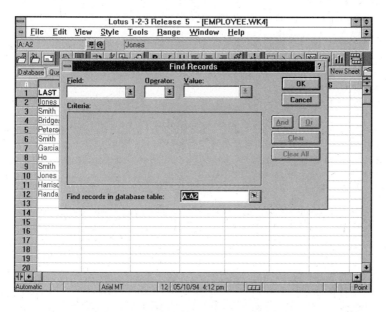

Fig. 26.14
The first step to filling in the Find Records dialog box is to specify the database range.

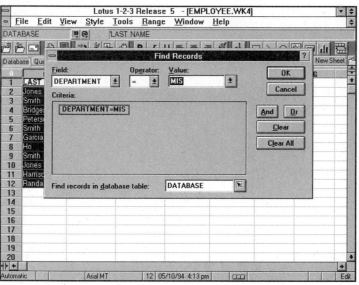

Fig. 26.15
After the database range is specified, the Find Records dialog box is customized to your database.

Note that you use the same techniques for creating and modifying selection criteria that you used in earlier examples in this chapter. Specifically, you would define a selection condition by choosing the **F**ield, **O**perator, and **V**alue. To string together multiple conditions, use **A**nd or **O**r. When you finish entering selection criteria, press Enter or click OK.

The matching records are then highlighted so you easily can scroll through them and edit them if necessary. Use the following keys to move between fields and records in the highlighted records:

Press	To Move to the
Enter	Next field
Shift+Enter	Previous field
Ctrl+Enter	Next record
Ctrl+Shift+Enter	Previous record

◄ "Entering and Editing Data," p. 83

To edit a cell, press F2 (Edit) and make your corrections. When you finish editing a cell, press Enter. To remove the highlighting from the selected records, press Esc.

Except in the scroll bar, don't use the mouse pointer to move to different highlighted cells. If you do, the highlighting will be removed from the selected records and you will need to issue the **F**ind Records command again.

> **Note**
>
> Another way to find data is with the **E**dit **F**ind & Replace command. This command looks for the character string you specify. It is more limiting than the **F**ind Records command because you don't have the flexibility of entering different operators, searching for values, using wildcards, or specifying multiple conditions. In certain circumstances, however, you can use **F**ind & Replace to update information in your database. For example, if an employee gets married and changes her name, you can search for her maiden name and replace it with her married name. See Chapter 3, "Finding and Replacing Data," for more information.

◄ "Modifying Records in a Database," p. 715

Deleting Specified Records

As mentioned in Chapter 24, one way to remove records from a database is with the **E**dit **D**elete **R**ow command. A fast alternative to this method is to use the **T**ools Data**b**ase **D**elete Records command to remove unwanted records from your database files.

> **Caution**
>
> Before you issue the **T**ools Data**b**ase **D**elete Records command, use **T**ools Data**b**ase **F**ind Records or **T**ools Data**b**ase **N**ew Query to make certain that the criterion you specify selects the correct group of records. The **T**ools Data**b**ase **D**elete Records command does not prompt for confirmation before deleting records.

Suppose that you want to remove all records with the HIRE DATE on or after 1/1/94. Follow these steps:

1. Select the database range (A1..E12 in the employee database).

2. Open the **T**ools menu and choose Data**b**ase **D**elete Records. The Delete Records dialog box appears.

3. Specify the criterion as **HIRE DATE>=1/1/94**.

4. Click OK or press Enter.

If you compare the query table in figure 26.16 to the original database in figure 26.1, you can see that the record for Maria Garcia was deleted. 1-2-3 for Windows packs the remaining records together and automatically adjusts the database range.

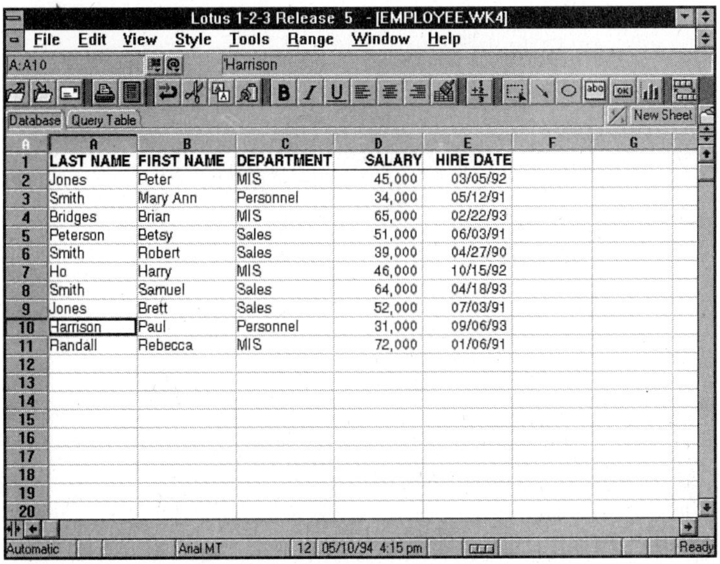

Tip
If you delete records in error, choose **E**dit **U**ndo (Ctrl+Z) immediately to restore the records.

V

Managing Databases

Fig. 26.16
The Tools Database Delete Records command removes unwanted records.

Modifying Records

In addition to finding and deleting database records, you probably will want to modify records. In worksheet databases, you can modify records directly in the database range, but using a query table is safer because the original database stays intact until you tell 1-2-3 that you want to update the database. The query-table procedure also enables you to modify records in external databases.

To use a query table to modify records, first specify the appropriate criteria for the group of records that you want to modify. Your query table should contain just the records you want to modify.

Caution

Before you make any modifications, use the **Q**uery Set **O**ptions command to make sure the **A**llow Updates to Source Table option is turned on. This is very important! If you turn it on after you have edited the query table, you will lose these changes.

You can edit the records directly in the query table, either by making the changes manually or by using **E**dit **F**ind & Replace. When you complete your changes, choose **Q**uery **U**pdate Database Table.

If **Q**uery **U**pdate Database Table is dimmed, the **A**llow Updates to Source Table option is not turned on. You can use the **Q**uery Set **O**ptions command to turn it on, but you will lose any changes you have made to the query table.

From Here...

If you want to do more sophisticated manipulations with your database, read the following chapters:

- Chapter 27, "Advanced Data Management," shows you how to join databases together, evaluate data with cross tabulations and aggregates, create frequency distributions, perform regression analysis, and work with matrices.

- Chapter 28, "Retrieving Data from External Databases," shows you how to work with external databases as well as import data from other programs.

Chapter 27

Understanding Advanced Data Management

This chapter builds on the basic database commands introduced in the preceding chapter and covers more advanced data-management techniques. You learn how to join databases to take advantage of relationships between them and how to use advanced analysis tools to analyze your data.

After you enter data in a worksheet, it is important to be able to analyze the data. 1-2-3 for Windows provides several powerful tools to assist you in analyzing data including the ability to cross tabulate and aggregate data, create frequency distributions (great for analyzing survey results), and perform regression analysis to analyze trends. By mastering these techniques, you can take advantage of some of the most advanced and useful features available to computer users.

In this chapter you learn to do the following:

- ■ Use related data contained in multiple databases

- ■ Create a cross tabulation of data

- ■ Analyze survey results with a frequency distribution

- ■ Project a trend line from data with regression analysis

- ■ Solve a linear programming problem with matrix inversion and multiplication

Joining Multiple Databases

A powerful feature of 1-2-3 for Windows is its capability to create a query table that contains fields or calculated columns based on records contained in two or more databases. To *join* databases, you relate two or more databases that have one or more key fields in common.

You may wonder why you should keep two or more databases of related information instead of keeping all the information together in one large database. One reason is to increase efficiency. Suppose that you had several business contacts at each of the companies listed in a company database, such as the one shown in figure 27.1. You could add a NAME field to the database and place each contact in a separate record. If you had three contacts at Jay's Plumbing, for example, you could type three complete records, one for each contact person. Of course, when Jay's Plumbing moves to a larger building, you have to change the addresses for all three records. On the other hand, if you have one database with the company information and another listing the contact persons with cross-references to their companies, you only have to update one company record to update the addresses for all the contacts you have with that company.

Fig. 27.1

A sample company database has one record for each company.

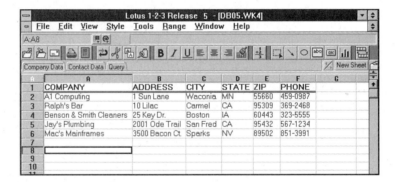

The examples that follow use the sample company data, sample contact data, and a query table. If you want to follow along with the examples in this chapter, just perform these steps:

1. Insert two new worksheets in the file that contains the sample company data. If you do not already have the sample COMPANY database from Chapter 26, enter the data as shown in figure 27.1. You can use the New Sheet button or the **E**dit **I**nsert **S**heet command to add the worksheets.

2. Name the three worksheets Company Data, Contact Data, and Query as shown on the worksheet tabs in figure 27.1.

3. Move the cell pointer to the Contact Data worksheet and enter the information shown in figure 27.2 to create the CONTACTS database. You can type the company name or read the upcoming section "Understanding the Key Field" for some tips on entering the company name.

4. Use the **R**ange **N**ame command or click the Create/Delete Range Name SmartIcon to name the two database ranges COMPANIES (A:A1..A:F6) and CONTACTS (B:A1..B:B10).

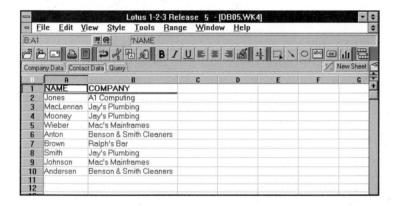

Fig. 27.2

A sample contacts database contains multiple contacts for each company.

Understanding the Key Field

A *key field* is one whose content is unique for each record in the database. In the sample company database, for example, COMPANY is a key field because every company has a different name. STATE is not a key field because two companies may be in the same state.

Because COMPANY is the key field that will be used to join or "match" information from the contacts and company database, it is important that you enter the company name exactly the same way every time. For example, if one entry says *Mac's Mainframe* and another says *Macs Mainframe*, then the join will not work correctly. Enter the company names in the contacts database exactly the same way they appear in the company database.

One way to ensure that the entries are exactly the same is to copy them from the company database to the contacts database. Another way is to create a lookup table that contains a shortcut code for the company and the full company name. (This also makes entering the data easier because you can just enter a shortcut code instead of having to type the full name.) Then place a

◄ "Lookup
Functions,"
p. 201

formula in your worksheet to look up the company name based on the code. Figure 27.3 shows an example of the company table with a shortcut code added for the company. Figure 27.4 shows the contact database using the shortcut and a formula for the @VLOOKUP.

Fig. 27.3
Add a shortcut code field to your company table and use this field to look up the company name.

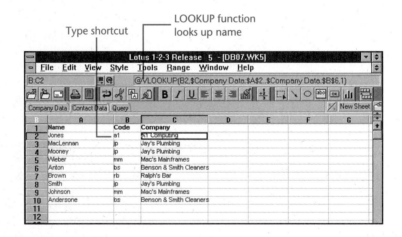

Shortcut code

Type shortcut

LOOKUP function
looks up name

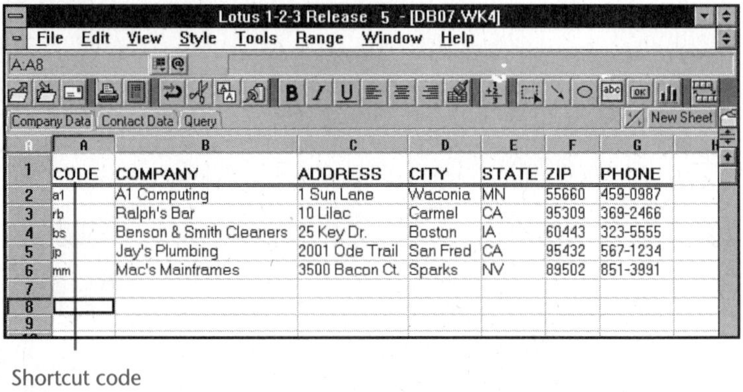

Fig. 27.4
Just key the shortcut code for each company into the contacts database and look up the company name.

Understanding Database Relationships

Related database tables can have several different types of relationships. Understanding these types of relationships makes it easier to create related databases so that you can join them in a meaningful manner. There are three possible relationships:

■ *One-to-one* relationship. For every record in one database, only one record from another database is related to it. In a one-to-one relationship, there is no real advantage to having multiple databases.

- *Many-to-one* relationship. Many records in the master database are related to one value in the second database. For example, the contacts database lists employees at each of the businesses found in the company database. Several employees can work at the same business, so many records in the contacts database point to the same value in the company database. A many-to-one relationship between databases is efficient because one record in the second database contains related information for many records in the master database.

- *One-to-many* relationship, one record in the master database is related to many records in the second database. For example, if the company database were the master database, its relationship with the contacts database would be a one-to-many relationship. A single record in the company database can point to several records in the contacts database. A one-to-many relationship does not let you easily select unique records from the second database, and offers no real advantage in most cases.

When you join databases in 1-2-3 for Windows, you usually want to determine which method of joining databases produces a many-to-one relationship, such as that between the contacts and company databases. This kind of relationship results in the highest efficiency. If you create databases with this advantage in mind, you find that you need to enter less data, your databases require less disk space and system memory, and you have higher performance.

Tip

Use the many-to-one relationship for best results when joining databases.

Performing the Join

Joining databases in 1-2-3 for Windows is quite simple. You start by creating a new query table (as explained in Chapter 26). Then you specify the name of the master database. Then you specify the related fields in the databases. Finally, you select the fields to display in the joined query table.

◀ "Building a 1-2-3 Database," p. 706

For example, you may want to create a phone list that contains the contact name, company name, and phone number for each contact. This requires you to combine information from the contacts and company databases. Use the following steps to join two databases. In this case, you will be joining the contacts and company databases to create the phone list.

◀ "Using a Query Table," p. 740

1. Select the master database by highlighting its range. In this example, highlight the contacts database (cells B:A1..B10).

2. Open the **T**ools menu and choose Data**b**ase **N**ew Query; or click the Query Table SmartIcon.

3. In the Select Location for New **Q**uery Table box, specify a blank location, probably in a new blank worksheet. In this case, choose **C:A1** (the top-left cell on the Query worksheet).

4. Click OK or press Enter to create the query table.

5. If necessary, adjust column widths, fonts, and point sizes to display the query table as you prefer. Figure 27.5 shows the query table, which displays the information from the contacts database.

6. Open the **Q**uery menu and choose Set Database **T**able to display the Set Database Table dialog box.

7. In the **D**atabase table box, specify the database that contains the "many" records. Remember, you are creating a "many to use" relationship. The contacts data has several records for each company, so in this case, specify **CONTACTS** as the master database (see fig. 27.6).

> **Note**
>
> Even if the correct cells are specified in this drawing box, you must type the range name of the database for this to work correctly.

Fig. 27.5
The query table initially displays only information from the contacts database.

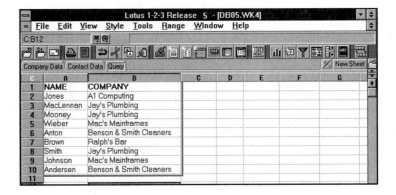

8. Click OK or press Enter.

9. Open the **Q**uery menu and choose **J**oin to display the Join dialog box (see fig. 27.7). This dialog box specifies the relationship between the databases.

   In this case, 1-2-3 for Windows has correctly determined that the COMPANY field in the contacts database holds the information that links it to the COMPANY field in the company database. The Join Criteria box shows the join formula: CONTACTS.COMPANY=COMPANIES.COMPANY. If the relationship determined by 1-2-3 for Windows is incorrect, use the options in this dialog box to specify the correct relationship.

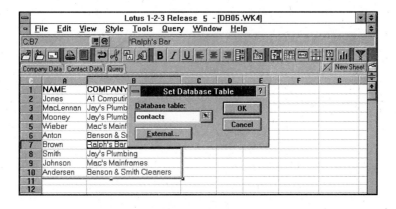

Fig. 27.6
Use the Set Database Table dialog box to specify the master database.

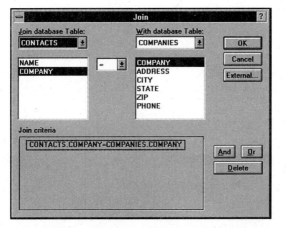

Fig. 27.7
Use the Join dialog box to specify the relationship between databases.

Note

1-2-3 specifies a field within a database using dot notation, as in COMPANIES.COMPANY. This notation specifies the COMPANY field in the COMPANIES database. Therefore, the join formula, CONTACTS.COMPANY=COMPANIES.COMPANY, means that the data in the COMPANY field of the Contacts database is related to the data in the COMPANY field of the Company database.

V

Managing Databases

10. Click OK or press Enter to display the Choose Fields dialog box (see fig. 27.8). Use this dialog box to specify the fields from the joined databases to display in the query table.

Fig. 27.8

Use the Choose Fields dialog box to specify the fields to display. Use the up or down arrows to rearrange the field order.

Tip

To select more than one field you want to exclude, hold down Ctrl as you click additional fields.

11. Select the fields you *do not* want to include in the query table by highlighting the field and choosing **C**lear. By default, the query table includes every field from both of the joined databases, including two copies of the field used to join the databases (one copy from each database). For example, select these fields to exclude: COMPANIES.COMPANY, ADDRESS, CITY, STATE, and ZIP. To select more than one field, hold down the Ctrl key as you select additional fields.

12. Choose the **C**lear button to remove the selected fields.

13. Click OK or press Enter to display the joined query table (see fig. 27.9).

Fig. 27.9

The joined query table displays information from both databases.

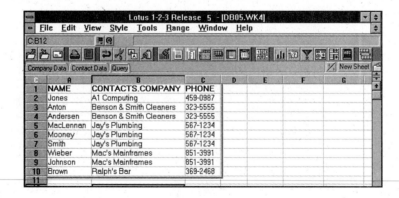

> **Note**
>
> If your database includes fields whose values you want to use in calculations, you can use the **F**ormula button in the Choose Fields dialog box to create a calculated field. For example, you may create a calculated field that budgets next month's sales as 10 percent higher than last month's sales.

This example shows how you can join databases that contain related information so that you can have more complete information than what is contained in either database alone. The resulting query table is similar to a single database query table, but is much more useful.

In the next chapter, you learn how to use external database files. The technique of joining databases is even more useful with external databases than it is with worksheet databases, because external databases often hold much larger collections of data. By applying the efficiencies gained through joining related databases, you make better use of disk space and memory.

Troubleshooting

When I try to join my databases, I get a message that says `Cannot join tables to a query that has an unnamed database table or a database table not in memory`.

When you issue the **Q**uery Set Database **T**able command, you must indicate the table by using its range name, not its cell range. Type the range name (in this case, **CONTACTS**) into the text box.

When I join two databases, no records show in the query table.

The most likely problem is that the databases are joined incorrectly. The fields used to join the databases must contain related information. That is, if one database refers to *Ralph's Bar* and the other to *Ralph's Cafe*, 1-2-3 for Windows cannot find a match. Make certain that the values in the join fields match.

When I join two databases, the query table contains too many records. Instead of supplying unique values, the query table contains several sets of values. What can I do to correct this?

Make certain that a many-to-one relationship exists between the master database and the matching database.

(continues)

(continued)

The query table correctly joined my databases, but why does it show two copies of the join field?

By default, a joined query table displays every field from the joined databases. Because both databases contain a copy of the field used to join the databases, the query table includes two copies of this field. Use **Q**uery **Ch**oose Fields to display a list of the fields, highlight the fields you want to remove, and choose **C**lear. Press Enter or click OK to return to the query table.

Evaluating Data with Cross Tabulations and Aggregates

One of the most useful ways to analyze data is to use a *cross-tabulation table* (or *crosstab*). Cross tabulations summarize data by showing how two factors influence a third factor. For example, the database shown in figure 27.10 tracks the amount of each sale for three different salespersons selling three different categories of products. A cross tabulation shows summary information you can use to analyze how well each salesperson is doing.

An *aggregate* is a variation of a cross tabulation. Instead of being placed in a separate cross-tabulation table, the data in an aggregate analysis is placed in a column of a query table.

Fig. 27.10
A sales database ready to be analyzed using a cross tabulation.

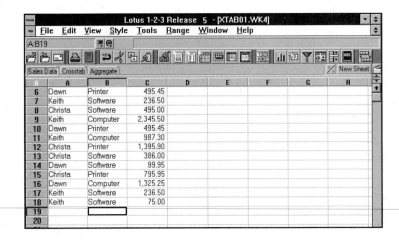

Creating a Cross Tabulation

To create a cross-tabulation table that summarizes the sales data shown in figure 27.10, follow these steps:

1. Select the database range you want to analyze. This range *must* include at least three columns and two rows. For example, select A:A1..C18.

2. Open the **T**ools menu and choose Data**b**ase Cross**T**ab; or click the Crosstab SmartIcon to display the Crosstab dialog box (see fig. 27.11).

3. Click the Continue button to display the Crosstab Heading Options dialog box (see fig. 27.12). In this dialog box, specify which database field contains the values you want to display down the left side of the cross-tabulation table (these values are the row headings) and which database field contains the values you want to display across the top of the cross-tabulation table (these values are the column headings).

   For example, the values in the NAME field are to be displayed along the left edge of the cross-tabulation table, and the values in the ITEM field are to be displayed along the top of the cross-tabulation table.

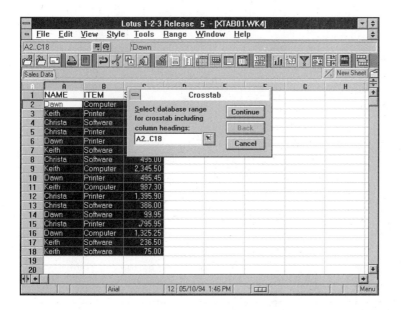

Fig. 27.11
Indicate the database range containing the data you want to cross tabulate in the first Crosstab dialog box.

V

Managing Databases

Fig. 27.12
Use the Crosstab
Heading Options
dialog box to
indicate which
values are to be
included in the
row headings and
in the column
headings.

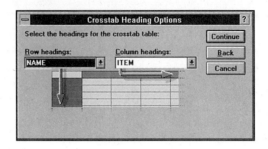

4. Click the Continue button to display the Crosstab Data Options dialog box (see fig. 27.13). In this dialog box, specify which database field you want to summarize as well as the type of calculation you want to perform.

   For example, if you wanted to summarize the values in the SALE field by showing their totals, you would select the **S**um type of calculation. You also can select **A**verage, **C**ount, **M**inimum, or Ma**x**imum, depending on which type of calculation provides the best analysis of your data.

Fig. 27.13
Choose the type of
calculation to
perform in the
Crosstab Data
Options dialog
box.

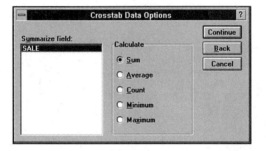

5. Click the Continue button. 1-2-3 for Windows calculates the cross-tabulation table and places it on a new worksheet following the current worksheet. Figure 27.14 shows the completed cross-tabulation table. You can double-click on the tab to name the new worksheet Crosstab.

You can enhance the presentation of cross-tabulation data by using any of the **S**tyle options. You also can graph the cross-tabulated data to show the analysis graphically. Figure 27.15 shows one example of how you can quickly graph the cross-tabulated data.

Fig. 27.14

The cross-tabulation results summarize the data into a concise table.

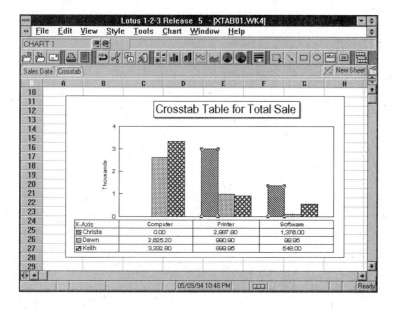

Fig. 27.15

A chart of the cross-tabulated results makes the data even easier to view.

Tip

Choose your chart type from the **C**hart menu and use the **I**nclude Table of Values option to display the cross-tabulation table below the chart.

V

Managing Databases

Creating an Aggregate

The **T**ools Data**b**ase Cross**t**ab command creates a new table of cross-tabulated data; the **Q**uery **A**ggregate command produces a similar summary in a single column of an existing query table.

To create a data summary of the numeric data in a query table, use the following steps. In this case, you will summarize the sales figures in the data (shown originally in fig. 27.10).

1. If you have not already created a query table, open the **T**ools menu and choose Data**b**ase **N**ew Query; or click the Query Table SmartIcon to create a query table starting at cell C:A1 (see fig. 27.16). Specify A:A1..C18 as the database range.

2. Click SALE to select the SALE column. This action indicates the column for which you want to produce an aggregate analysis.

Caution

If you select an alphabetic column, the aggregate command tries to calculate the column, resulting in all zeroes.

---

3. Open the **Q**uery menu and choose **A**ggregate; or click the Query Aggregate SmartIcon to display the Aggregate dialog box. Select **S**um as the analysis to perform (see fig. 27.17). 1-2-3 automatically places the word "Total" along with the original field name in the Show fiel**d** as box.

4. Click OK or press Enter. The query table now shows the summary values in the Total SALE column (see fig. 27.18).

Compare the results shown in figures 27.13 and 27.18 you can see that both the **T**ools Data**b**ase Cros**t**ab command and the **Q**uery **A**ggregate command produce the same values. Choose the command that best suits your data-analysis needs.

Fig. 27.16

Create a new query table for aggregate analysis.

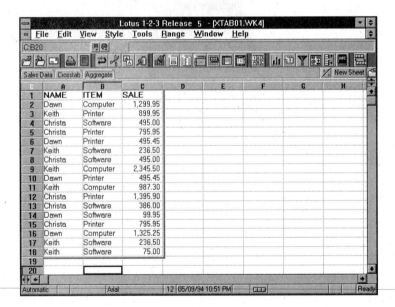

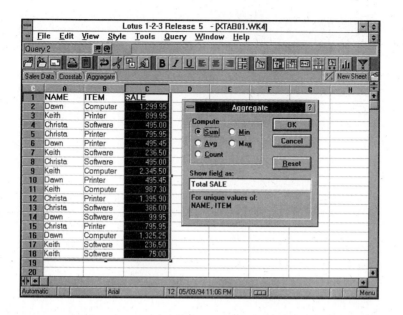

Fig. 27.17
Choose the type of calculation in the Aggregate dialog box.

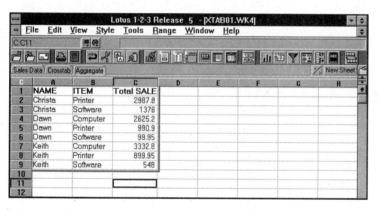

Fig. 27.18
The results of the **Query Aggregate** command summarize the information in the query table.

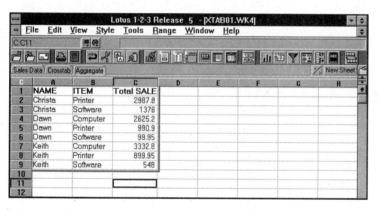

V

Managing Databases

Troubleshooting

Why does my cross-tabulation table only contain errors (ERR)?

A cross tabulation requires three columns of data. If your data only contains two columns, 1-2-3 for Windows generates a cross-tabulation table, but fills it with ERR.

(continues)

(continued)

*When I select **Q**uery, the **A**ggregate command is grayed out.*

You must select the column you want to calculate for the aggregate by clicking the field name at the top of the column. In addition, you can create an aggregate column in a query table only if no other aggregate column exists in the current query table. If you want to create another aggregate column, you must create another query table.

◄ "Creating What-
If Tables,"
p. 508

Note

You can achieve similar results without a query table by using the special Database @functions. This requires you to name your database range and create a criteria range. The @DSUM and @DAVG enable you to sum or average all or part of a database based on the criteria in the criteria range. By making the @DSUM or @DAVG the calculation for the **R**ange **A**nalysis **W**hat-If commands, you can produce exactly the same output as the **Q**uery **A**ggregate.

Analyzing Data with Frequency Distributions

When you collect certain types of data, such as performance data or survey results, you can analyze it using a frequency distribution. This analysis enables you to see how many people, widgets, or orders per day fit into certain categories that you create. A *frequency distribution* describes the relationship between a set of classes or categories and the number of members in each class. A consumer list that contains product preference demonstrates the use of the **R**ange **A**nalyze **D**istribution command to produce a frequency distribution (see fig. 27.19).

For example, figure 27.19 shows a list of customers identified as customer A through P in column A, and their feelings about the upcoming product line expressed in a zero to ten scale in column B. You must define the categories or *bins* you want to create. This has been done in column D of figure 27.19, and verbal descriptions of the bins have been placed in column F. Column E has intentionally been left blank in this example, because the results of the distribution analysis are automatically placed in the column immediately to the right of the bins.

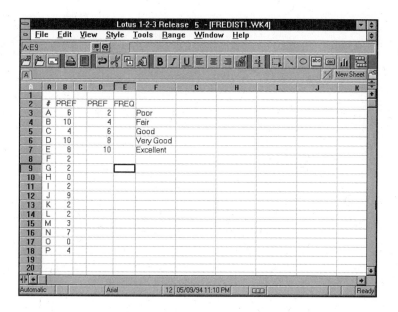

Fig. 27.19
Type in the data
and the bins in
order to perform a
frequency
distribution.

Performing the Frequency Distribution

To create a frequency distribution with the **R**ange **A**nalyze **D**istribution command, follow these steps:

1. Enter the data you want to analyze, one row per entry. In this example, the data is shown in figure 27.19.

2. Decide the range of intervals or bins that you want to use to group or summarize the data and enter this information. Figure 27.19 shows this information in column D.

Tip
If you have
evenly spaced
intervals, use
the **R**ange **F**ill
command to
enter the values
for the bin
range.

> **Caution**
>
> If there is data to the right of the bins, it is overlayed when you complete the **R**ange **A**nalyze **D**istribution command.
>
> Also, if the values in the bins are not in ascending order, you will get invalid results.

3. Select the range containing the initial values (A3..B18) in this example.

4. Open the **R**ange menu and choose **A**nalyze **D**istribution. The range selected in step 3 automatically appears in the **R**ange of Values text box. Use the range selector tool to select the range containing the bins (D3..D7, in this case). Figure 27.20 shows the completed dialog box for this example.

V

Managing Databases

Fig. 27.20

Specify the Range of Values and the bin range in the Distribution dialog box.

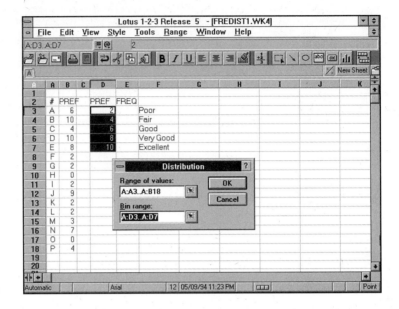

5. Press Enter or choose OK. 1-2-3 for Windows creates the results column (E3..E8) to the right of the bin range (D3..D7). The results column, which shows the frequency distribution, is always in the column to the right of the bin range and extends one row below the bin range.

The values in the results column represent the frequency of distribution of the numbers in the range of values for each interval. The first interval in the bin range in this example is for values greater than 0 and less than or equal to 2; the second interval is for values greater than 2 and less than or equal to 4, and so on. The last value in the results column, in cell E8 of this example, shows the frequency of leftover numbers (the frequency of numbers that do not fit into an interval classification).

Charting the Distribution Analysis

The **R**ange **A**nalyze **D**istribution command can help you create understandable results from a series of numbers. You can chart the results easily, as shown in figure 27.21. A manufacturer looking at this chart would probably realize that this product probably won't be next summer's big seller! Chapters 11-14 cover all aspects of creating charts in 1-2-3 for Windows.

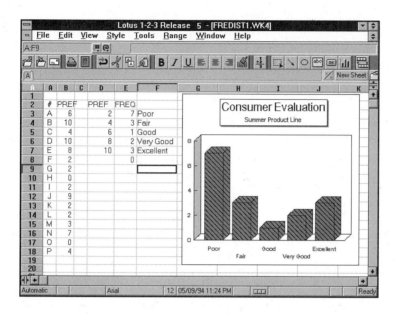

Fig. 27.21
Chart the frequency distribution for a clear picture of the results.

Note

To create a graph like the one shown in figure 27.21, select the frequency results in F3..F7 as the range of data to be graphed. Use the **C**hart **R**anges command to choose the descriptions of the categories in F3..F7 for the X-range of data.

◄ "Creating a Chart Manually," p. 392

Troubleshooting

I get zeroes as a result of my frequency distribution.

If you forget to highlight a range that contains values, the results of the frequency distribution will be zeroes. Or, if the data in your bin range is typed as lables instead of values, the results will be all zeroes.

Analyzing Trends with Regression Analysis

The **R**ange **A**nalyze **R**egression command gives you a multiple linear regression analysis package within 1-2-3 for Windows. Although most people don't have a need for this advanced feature, if you need to use it, 1-2-3 for

V

Managing Databases

Windows will save you the cost and inconvenience of buying a stand-alone statistical package for performing regression analysis.

Use **R**ange **A**nalyze **R**egression when you want to determine the relationship between one set of values (the *dependent variable*) and one or more other sets of values (the *independent variables*). Regression analysis has a number of uses in a business setting, including relating sales to price, promotions, and other market factors; relating stock prices to earnings and interest rates; and relating production costs to production levels.

Think of linear regression as a way of determining the best line through a series of data points. Multiple regression does this for several variables simultaneously, determining the best line relating the dependent variable to the set of independent variables. Consider, for example, a data sample showing Annual Earnings versus Age. Figure 27.22 shows the data; figure 27.23 shows the data plotted as an XY graph (using A7..A20 for the X-graph range and C7..C20 for the A-graph range).

Fig. 27.22
You can use Regression Analysis to calculate a line that relates the Annual Earnings versus Age data in this worksheet.

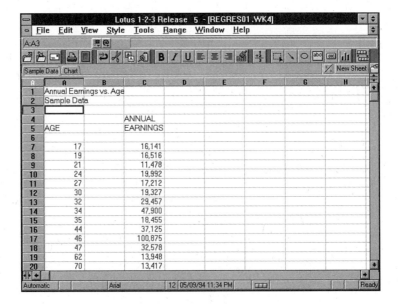

Performing a Regression Analysis

The **R**ange **A**nalyze **R**egression command can simultaneously determine how to draw a line through these data points and how well the line fits the data.

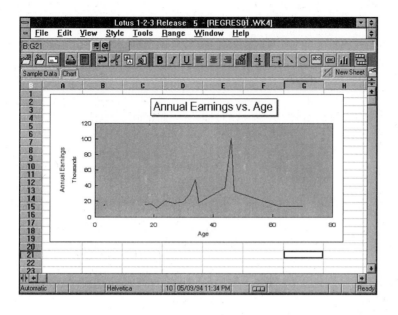

Fig. 27.23
Use the charting capabilities to create a graph of the Annual Earnings versus Age data.

To perform a regression analysis, use these steps:

1. Type in the data to be analyzed, similar to the example in figure 27.22.

2. Select the independent variable data. For example, select A7..A20.

3. Open the **R**ange menu and choose **A**nalyze **R**egression to display the Regression dialog box shown in figure 27.24.

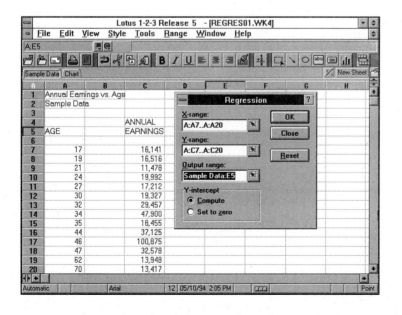

Fig. 27.24
Indicate the independent variable (X-range), dependent variable (Y-range), and output range in the Regression dialog box.

4. Use the **X**-range option to select one or more independent variables for the regression. The **R**ange **A**nalyze **R**egression command can use as many as 75 independent variables. In this example, the **X**-range is specified as **A7..A20**. If you selected this range in step 2, it automatically appears in the dialog box.

5. Type the Y-range or use the range selector tool to select the **Y**-range or dependent variable data. The **Y**-range must be a single column. (In this example, **C7..C20** is the **Y**-range.)

6. Indicate the upper-left corner of the range where you want the results placed in the **O**utput range box. (In this example, E5 is specified as the output range.)

> **Caution**
>
> This output range must be an unused section of the worksheet because the output is written over any existing cell contents.

7. Press Enter or choose OK to calculate the regression information. The information is placed in the worksheet at the specified location as shown in figure 27.25.

Fig. 27.25

The results of the regression are placed in the worksheet and can be used to calculate a trend or best-fit line.

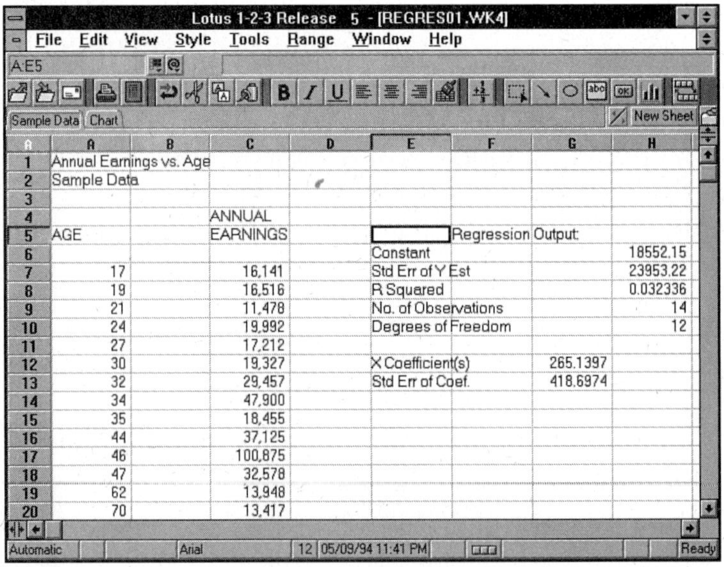

The Y-intercept options in the Regression dialog box enable you to specify whether or not you want the regression to calculate a constant value. Calculating the constant is the default; in some applications, however, you may need to exclude a constant.

Figure 27.25 shows the results of using the **R**ange **A**nalyze **R**egression command in the Annual Earnings versus Age example. The results (in cells E5..H13) include the value of the constant and the coefficient of the single independent variable that was specified with the **X**-range option. The results also include a number of regression statistics that describe how well the regression line fits the data. In this case, the R-Squared value and the standard errors of the constant and the regression coefficient all indicate that the regression line does not explain much of the variation in the dependent variable.

Using the Regression Information to Calculate a Trend Line

You can use the results of the regression analysis to calculate points on the "best fit" or trend line. The formula for this line is $y=mx+b$, where m is the X coefficient from the regression results (cell G12) and b is the constant from the results (cell H6). The formula for the regression line in this example, would then be:

$$+\$G\$12*A7+\$H\$6$$

The absolute references are necessary because the X coefficient and constant are always located in cells G12 and H6.

◄ "Copying a Formula with Mixed Addressing," p. 265

To calculate the regression line, perform the following steps:

1. Move to a blank location in the sheet (in this case, cell D7).

2. Type the regression formula, using the pattern $mx+b$, (in this case, **$G$12*A7+$H$6**).

3. Use the **S**tyle **N**umber Format, (Comma) 0 command to format the result, if desired.

4. Copy the formula down to all applicable rows. For this example, copy D7 to D8..D20. The results are shown in figure 27.26.

V

Managing Databases

Formula for Line

Fig. 27.26
Use a formula to
calculate a trend
line.

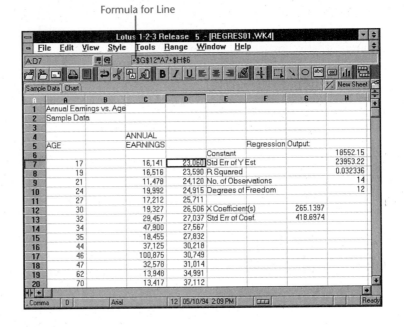

5. Create a chart with the original data and the newly calculated regression line. In this case A7..A20 would be the X-range, C7..C20 would be the X-range of data, and D7..D20 would be the B-range. (See figure 27.27.)

Fig. 27.27
Add the regression
line to a chart of
the Annual
Earnings versus
Age data to see
the trend.

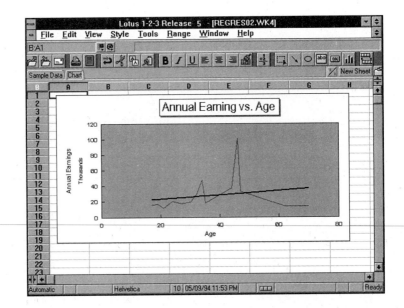

Taking the Analysis One Step Further: A Multiple Regression

The regression line calculated earlier does not give a valid indication of what is happening to the Annual Earnings versus Age data. The result of the single regression is a straight line that appears to be increasing with age. The large increase in earnings at age 46 makes the line appear to increase, when in reality, the income appears to rise with age until about age 50; then income begins to decline.

You can use the **R**ange **A**nalyze **R**egression command to fit a line that better describes the relationship between Annual Earnings and Age by performing a *multiple regression*. This means that the regression information will be calculated using two independent variables instead of one. In figure 27.28, a column of data has been added to column B, containing the square of the age in column A.

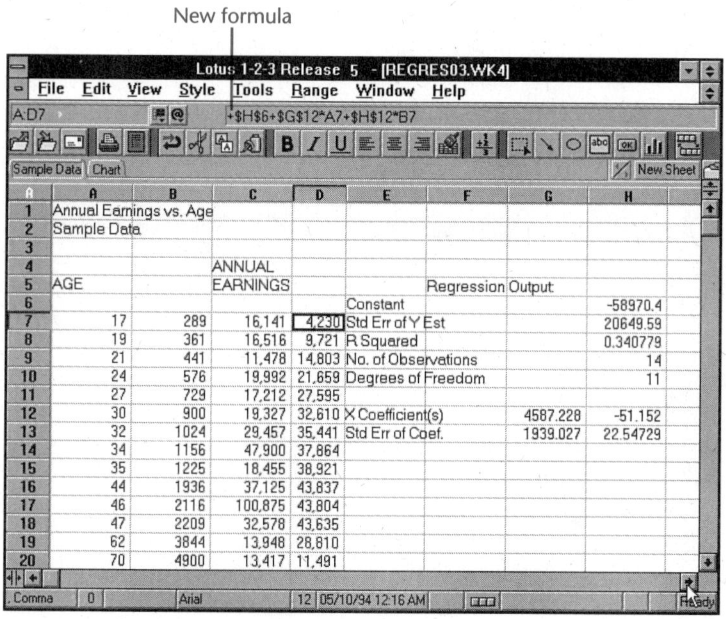

New formula

Fig. 27.28
Add the square of the Age to column B and use A7..B20 for the X-range to generate multiple regression.

V

Managing Databases

You can use the **R**ange **A**nalyze **R**egression command to fit a line that better describes the relationship between Annual Earnings and Age by performing a *multiple regression*. This means that the regression information will be calculated using two independent variables instead of one. Figure 27.28 shows the results of a completed multiple regression for this set of data. The following changes have been made:

- A column of data has been added to column B, containing the square of the age in column A.

- The **R**ange **A**nalyze **R**egression command was chosen and the data in columns A and B A7..B20) was specified as the **X**-Range.

  - This resulted in the new regression data as shown in figure 27.28 starting in E5.

  - The formula in column D was changed to:

    +$H$6+$G$12*A7+$H$12*B7

    - This formula was copied from cell D7 to D8..D20.

Notice that the regression statistics are much improved over the original regression of Annual Earnings versus Age. This fact means that the new line fits the data more closely than the old one. (However, the regression statistics indicate that the regression only explains about one-third of the dependent variable variation.) The chart of the new regression line, shown in figure 27.29, is now a parabola that rises until age 45 and then declines. The regression line generated by a multiple regression may or may not be a straight line, depending on the independent variables you use.

Fig. 27.29
The chart of the new line shows it fits the data better.

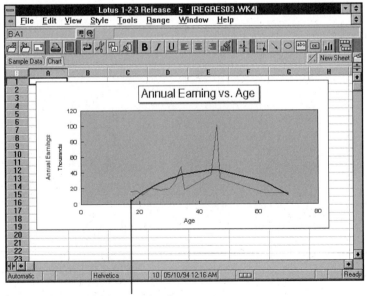

Multiple regression line

Using the Range Analyze Matrix Commands

The **R**ange **A**nalyze **I**nvert Matrix and **R**ange **A**nalyze **M**ultiply Matrix commands are specialized mathematical commands that enable you to solve systems of simultaneous linear equations and manipulate the resulting solutions. These commands are powerful but have limited applications in a business setting. If you are using 1-2-3 for Windows for certain types of economic analysis or for scientific or engineering calculations, you may find these commands valuable.

The **R**ange **A**nalyze **I**nvert Matrix command enables you to invert a nonsingular square matrix of up to 80 rows and columns. The **R**ange **A**nalyze **M**ultiply Matrix command enables you to multiply two rectangular matrices together in accordance with the rules of matrix algebra. The number of columns in the first matrix must equal the number of rows in the second matrix. The result matrix has the same number of rows as the first matrix, and the same number of columns as the second.

Figure 27.30 shows a sample problem that uses matrix inversion and multiplication to determine an airplane's air speed and the speed of the headwind or tailwind. In this problem, the distance between the two points (cell B1), the time required to travel from point 1 to point 2 (cell B2), the time required to travel from point 2 to point 1 (cell B3), and the relative wind speeds (cells B5 and B6) are known. Matrix inversion and multiplication make finding the actual air speed of the plane and the actual speed of the wind a simple task.

To solve this problem using matrix inversion and multiplication, follow these steps:

1. Enter the labels in column A, the data shown in column B, and the formulas in columns D and E (as indicated in columns F and G). The inversion output matrix and the result matrix will be calculated, and should be left blank.

2. Open the **R**ange menu and choose **A**nalyze **I**nvert Matrix to display the Invert Matrix dialog box (see fig. 27.31). Specify **D4..E5** as the **F**rom matrix and **D8** as the **T**o matrix. Click OK or press Enter.

3. Open the **R**ange menu and choose **A**nalyze **M**ultiply Matrix to display the Multiply Matrix dialog box (see fig. 27.32). Specify **D8..E9** as the **F**irst Matrix, **D12..D13** as the **S**econd Matrix, and **D16** as the **R**esulting Matrix. Click OK or press Enter.

Fig. 27.30

A problem that uses matrix inversion and multiplication to calculate speeds.

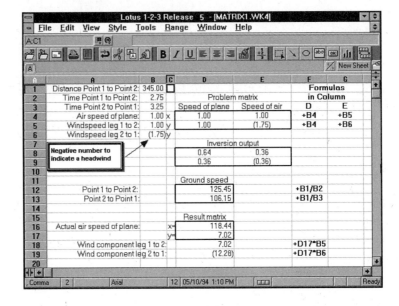

Fig. 27.31

Specify the range containing the original matrix in the **F**rom text box and the location for the new matrix in the **T**o text box.

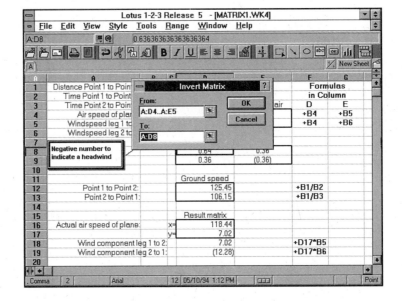

This problem shows an example of using matrix inversion and multiplication to solve a set of linear equations. The problem matrix (D4..E5) is used to define the equations. When you use **R**ange **A**nalyze **I**nvert Matrix to display the Invert Matrix dialog box, the problem matrix is called the *From matrix*. When this matrix is inverted, the *To matrix*, (D8..E9) holds its inverse.

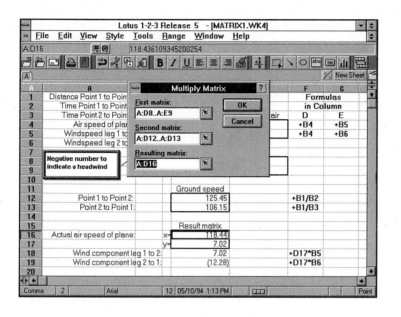

Fig. 27.32
Multiply two
matrices by
specifying the
location of the
first matrix, the
location of the
second matrix,
and the location
for the resulting
matrix.

After you perform the matrix inversion, the To matrix becomes the First matrix for the matrix multiplication, and is multiplied by the Second matrix (D12..D13), which contains the ground speed calculations, to produce the Resulting matrix (D16). The Resulting matrix displays the results of solving for the two variables, X (air speed) and Y (wind speed).

Tip
When data
in a problem
changes,
remember to
select **R**ange
Analyze **I**nvert
Matrix and
Range **A**nalyze
Multiply Matrix
again to calcu-
late updated
results.

> **Caution**
>
> Matrix inversions and multiplications can be time consuming, especially when you are dealing with large matrices or your system lacks a numeric coprocessor. The 80486DX processor has a built-in numeric coprocessor, but the 80486SX, as well as all 80386 and 80286 processors, do not.

From Here...

You can build on the skills learned in this chapter by reading the following chapters:

- Chapter 28, "Retrieving Data from External Databases." This chapter incorporates the techniques used to join database information with using and joining information in external databases.

- Chapter 35, "Writing 1-2-3 for Windows Macros." This chapter shows you how to automate repetitive tasks by writing macros. Creating multiple Query Tables, Frequency Distributions, or Aggregates would be likely candidates for macros.

Chapter 28

Retrieving Data from External Databases

The database tools discussed in Chapters 23 through 27 enable you to create, sort, and query data in 1-2-3. In addition, if you (or other people in your company) use database programs such as Paradox or dBASE for data management, you can create queries in 1-2-3 that read the files from Paradox, dBASE, and other databases and bring the data into a worksheet. Databases created in Paradox, dBASE, or other database programs are called "external databases."

This chapter shows you three ways to work with external data.

First, you can directly open a Paradox or dBASE file in 1-2-3. The information displays in rows and columns, just like a worksheet. You can update existing data and add new data. When you save the file, you have the choice of saving it back to Paradox or dBASE format or saving it as a 1-2-3 worksheet.

Second, you can access data in external databases from within 1-2-3 for Windows by using the database commands from Chapters 26 and 27. An *external database* is a file created and maintained by a database program other than 1-2-3 for Windows, such as dBASE or Paradox. Once a connection is established between your 1-2-3 for Windows worksheet and the external database, you can query, update, calculate, or append information to the external database from 1-2-3. You can even create a database in dBASE or Paradox by entering the data into 1-2-3 initially!

The third way to work with external data is to import into a 1-2-3 worksheet text created in another program. Depending on how the data in the text file was created, you might then need to "parse" the data, or break it up into columns of information, to use it effectively in 1-2-3 for Windows.

V

Managing Databases

In this chapter, you will learn how to do the following:

- Open a Paradox or dBASE file and work with it in 1-2-3

- Create a query table from data in an external database

- Update or add data to an external table from 1-2-3

- Create a new external table

- Import data from other programs to a 1-2-3 worksheet and parse it into columns

Using a Paradox or dBASE File

Data management in 1-2-3 for Windows is powerful and flexible because of 1-2-3 for Windows ability to access data from other sources. If you are a Paradox or dBASE user, 1-2-3 makes it especially easy to work with data you have created in those programs. All you need to do is open the Paradox or dBASE file directly into 1-2-3! After you have opened the file into a worksheet, you can edit, insert, or delete records or add new records to the data. When you save, you have the option of saving back to the original format, or saving the data as a 1-2-3 worksheet.

Opening a Paradox or dBASE File

You can open a Paradox or dBASE file directly into 1-2-3, using these steps:

1. Choose **F**ile, **O**pen, or click the Open SmartIcon.

2. In the Open File dialog box, drop down the list for File **t**ype and choose dBASE or Paradox. The File **n**ame dialog box then shows the list of database files.

3. Choose the desired file from the File **n**ame list and choose OK.

Editing Your Paradox or dBASE File from 1-2-3

Now that you have opened a dBASE or Paradox file into 1-2-3, you can use any editing techniques you know to edit the file, including any or all of the following:

- Type over existing entries, or edit them with the mouse, or use the F2 key.

- Insert new rows in the data or delete existing rows.

■ Insert new columns or delete columns.

■ Add new rows of data to the bottom of the worksheet. However, if you do this, use the **R**ange **N**ame command to expand the range DATA-BASE1 to include all of the data in your worksheet. Then when you save the file, the new data will be saved back into the dBASE or Paradox database.

Saving the dBASE or Paradox Data

You have two choices when you save data that originally came from dBASE or Paradox: You can use a normal **F**ile **S**ave command to save the data back to the original database, or you can use **F**ile Save **A**s to save the data as a 1-2-3 worksheet (or into some other format). Just remember to use the File type drop-down list in the Save As dialog box to choose the format for the file before you save it.

Working with External Databases

Opening a dBASE or Paradox file directly into 1-2-3 works well when you are dealing with small databases. However, dBASE and Paradox databases often contain many more records than you really need to use. A practical approach for large Paradox or dBASE databases is to create queries in 1-2-3 that retrieve specific records from the external database into your worksheet. Before you begin working with this feature, you should be familiar with several terms.

A *DataLens driver* is a program that serves as an interface between 1-2-3 for Windows and an external database so that 1-2-3 for Windows can transfer data to and from the external database. A separate database driver is required for each external database format you use.

An *external database* is simply the path in which the external database files reside.

Since many database programs are "relational," enabling users to access data from several files at once, an "external database" can contain multiple files or "tables" of information. In many cases, these tables are stored in a directory on disk; in the case of SQL, a database is comprised of multiple tables. So, when 1-2-3 prompts for an "external database or directory," it is prompting for the name of the SQL database or the name of the directory in which your dBASE or Paradox tables are stored.

A *table name* identifies the specific external table of information with which you want to work. When you use commands that access an external database, 1-2-3 leads you through a series of dialog boxes for each piece of information in the full path or name of the table. So, the full table name consists of three or four parts in the following order:

- The name of the database driver

- The name of the external database (its path)

- An owner name or user ID, if required by the external database program

- The name of the database or a 1-2-3 for Windows range name assigned to the database. For example, to connect to a Paradox database named *Company* in the C:\123W\DB directory, use the following:

    PARADOX C:\123W\DB COMPANY"

A *table-creation* string contains information used by a database driver to create an external database. When you create an external database from within 1-2-3 for Windows, you may have to specify a table-creation string, depending on the specific database driver in use. The Paradox driver, for example, enables you to use a table-creation string to specify a sort order for the database. When in doubt, refer to the database driver documentation.

A *table definition* is a six-column worksheet range that contains information about a new external database. Information in a table definition always includes field names, data types, and field widths, and may include column labels, table-creation strings, and field descriptions.

Connecting to an Existing External Database

Before you can work with an existing external database, you must create a connection, or link, to the database. This requires the DataLens drivers to be installed on your computer.

Tip
You can connect to an external database at the same time you create a new query using the database.

You should also know which drive and directory contain the external database and what the name of the database is. Follow these steps to connect to an external database:

1. Select **T**ools Data**b**ase **N**ew Query **E**xternal or **T**ools Data**b**ase **C**onnect to External to connect to an existing external database. The dialog box shown in figure 28.1 appears.

2. If more than one driver name is shown in the **S**elect a Driver box, highlight the name of the driver you want to use and then select **C**ontinue.

The following examples use the Paradox driver, but the procedures for using the other drivers are similar.

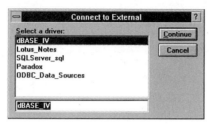

Fig. 28.1
Use the Connect to External dialog box to specify a connection to an external database.

3. If the selected DataLens driver accepts a password, the Driver Password dialog box shown in figure 28.2 appears. If a user ID and password are needed on your system, enter the information in the appropriate boxes and click on OK or press Enter. If your system does not require this information, simply click on OK or press Enter to continue.

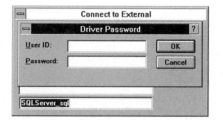

Fig. 28.2
Some drivers display the Driver Password dialog box.

> **Note**
>
> Networks and database programs used on networks usually include controls that limit access to database files. These same controls apply when you use 1-2-3 for Windows to access external database files. If you encounter problems, see your network administrator.

Tip
Add a different directory to the list of directories shown in the Connect to External dialog box by clicking the text box at the bottom of the dialog box and typing the new directory name. The existing directory name is replaced.

4. The text-box prompt in the Connect to External dialog box changes to **S**elect a database or directory, as shown in figure 28.3. Select the database or directory containing the tables you wish to access and then select **C**ontinue.

5. Once again, the text-box prompt changes—this time to **S**elect a table (see fig. 28.4). The *table* is the name of the database file you want to use. Select the table and press **C**ontinue. The text-box prompt changes to Refer To As (see fig. 28.5). Assigning a range name to the external database table enables you to use **Q**uery commands to access the external table.

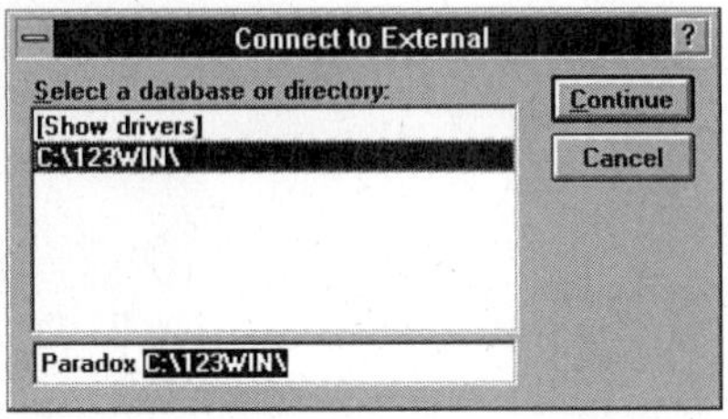

Fig. 28.3

Select the directory containing your database from the second Connect to External dialog box.

```
┌──────────────────────────────────────────────┐
│ ═          Connect to External            [?] │
│ Select a database or directory:    ┌─────────┐│
│ [Show drivers]                     │Continue ││
│ C:\123WIN\                         └─────────┘│
│                                    ┌─────────┐│
│                                    │ Cancel  ││
│                                    └─────────┘│
│                                               │
│ ┌──────────────────────────────┐              │
│ │Paradox C:\123WIN\            │              │
│ └──────────────────────────────┘              │
└──────────────────────────────────────────────┘
```

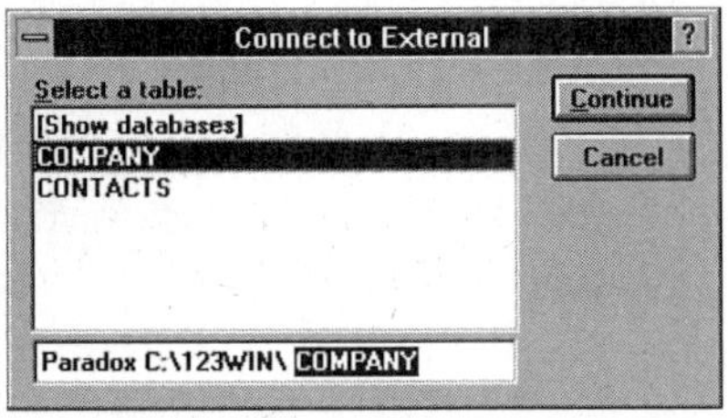

Fig. 28.4

Select an external database file from the third Connect to External dialog box.

```
┌──────────────────────────────────────────────┐
│ ═          Connect to External            [?] │
│ Select a table:                    ┌─────────┐│
│ [Show databases]                   │Continue ││
│ COMPANY                            └─────────┘│
│ CONTACTS                           ┌─────────┐│
│                                    │ Cancel  ││
│                                    └─────────┘│
│ ┌──────────────────────────────┐              │
│ │Paradox C:\123WIN\ COMPANY    │              │
│ └──────────────────────────────┘              │
└──────────────────────────────────────────────┘
```

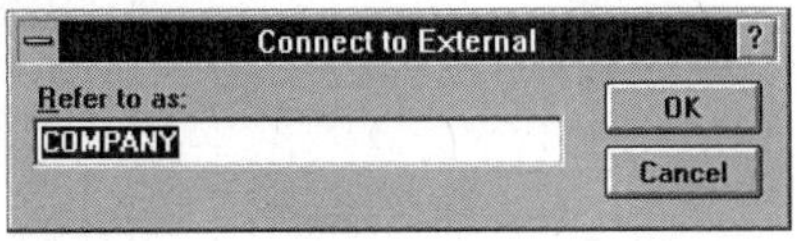

Fig. 28.5

Specify a range name for the external database in the final Connect to External dialog box.

```
┌──────────────────────────────────────────────┐
│ ═          Connect to External            [?] │
│ Refer to as:                       ┌─────────┐│
│ COMPANY                            │   OK    ││
│                                    └─────────┘│
│                                    ┌─────────┐│
│                                    │ Cancel  ││
│                                    └─────────┘│
└──────────────────────────────────────────────┘
```

Tip

If the Refer To As text box is blank, the external database's file name is already being used as a 1-2-3 for Windows range name. Specify a different name for the range name you want to assign to the external database file.

6. Press Enter or select OK. If you are using the **T**ools Data**b**ase **N**ew Query command, complete the selections in the New Query dialog box and press Enter or select OK again.

Figure 28.6 shows a new query table that displays the information in the COMPANY.DB Paradox database file. The column widths were adjusted in this figure for a clearer display.

┌──┐
│ **Troubleshooting**   │
├──┤
│ *No drivers are listed or the driver I want is not listed when I choose Tools Database New* │
│ *Query External.*   │
│   │
│ DataLens drivers are normally installed when you perform a standard installation. │
│ However, if no drivers show, perhaps they were not installed, or the driver you now │
│ want was not installed. If you run the install program again and choose "Custom │
└──┘

Installation," you will see a dialog box that lets you choose which DataLens drivers to install. Refer to your Lotus 1-2-3 documentation for more information on installing DataLens drivers.

When I try to open a Paradox database, why does 1-2-3 for Windows prompt me for a password? I'm not on a network, and no one else uses my PC.

Some databases (including Paradox) employ user IDs and passwords. If you don't use this information on your system, simply press Enter to bypass the dialog box.

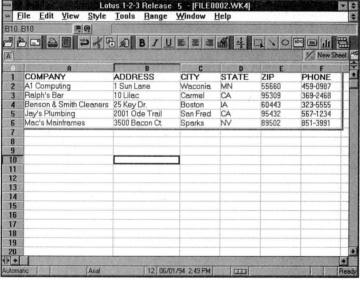

Fig. 28.6
A new query table displaying information from an external database file.

Managing Databases

V

Using an Existing External Database

Using the data in an external database is not much different than using a worksheet database. The major difference is that you need to establish a connection to the external database before you can use it; you also must break the connection when you are finished with the external database.

By using the range name assigned to the database, you can treat the external database as a worksheet database and perform the following tasks:

- Use formulas and database functions in the worksheet that reference data in the external database, such as

    @DCOUNT(COMPANY,"STATE",+STATE="CA")

- Copy some or all records from the external database to the worksheet with **T**ools Data**b**ase **N**ew Query

- Use **T**ools Data**b**ase **A**ppend Records to copy new records from the worksheet to the external database

- Modify records in the external database with **Q**uery **U**pdate Database Table

- Use **T**ools Data**b**ase **S**end Command to perform special database functions not available in 1-2-3 for Windows

- Terminate the connection to the external table with **T**ools Data**b**ase Dis**c**onnect

---

Caution

When you break the connection to an external database (as described later in this chapter), the range name assigned to it is lost. Formulas and functions that reference that range name become undefined when the connection is broken. You must respecify the range name whenever you re-establish the connection. Be sure to use the same range name each time if the worksheet contains formulas or functions that reference the external database range.

Creating a New External Table

◀ "Using a Query Table," p. 740

◀ "Adding Records to a Database," p. 709

◀ "Modifying Records in a Database," p. 715

You can actually create an external database from 1-2-3 for Windows that other users can analyze and update with their database programs. This enables all users in your company to work with the package most comfortable and productive for them!

To create an external table in 1-2-3 for Windows, follow these steps:

1. Type the information into a 1-2-3 for Windows worksheet, just as you would type any information that you want to use with Database commands. Figure 28.7 shows a new employee worksheet that will be used to create a Paradox database.

2. Choose **T**ools Data**b**ase **C**reate Table command. When you select this command, the Create Table dialog box appears (see fig. 28.8). The first step in creating an external table is to specify the name of the external database driver.

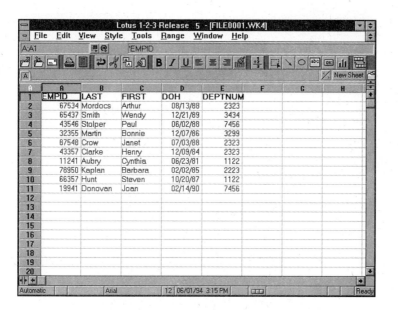

Fig. 28.7

Enter database information as the first step in creating an external database.

Fig. 28.8

Use the Create Table dialog box to choose the type of external database you want to create.

3. After you select the driver, you see the Create Table, Select a database or directory dialog box, similar to the dialog box in figure 28.3. Select the database or directory and choose **C**ontinue.

4. The final Create Table dialog box requires you to indicate the location of the model table, and, if necessary, enter a creation command (see fig. 28.9). The *model table* is a worksheet range or the range name of an external database file you want to use as a template for the new table.

5. Then the Create Table, Enter table name dialog box, similar to the dialog box you used to choose an existing table in figure 28.4, appears. However, this time 1-2-3 expects you to type a new name for your table. Type the new name and choose **C**ontinue.

6. Leave the **I**nsert records from model table check box checked if you want to have the data from your worksheet added to the new external

V

Managing Databases

database. If this box is not checked, a new database is created in the chosen database program, but no records are added to it.

7. When you have filled out the dialog box in figure 28.9, press Enter or click OK to create the new external database file. If you use an existing database as a template, the new database is either an exact copy containing all the same fields (with the same field names, field lengths, data types, and so on) but no records, or an exact copy containing all the same fields with copies of all records.

Fig. 28.9
Specify a **M**odel
Table to create an
external table with
the same data as
your worksheet.

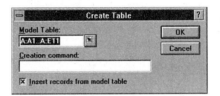

Whether or not a creation command is supported or required depends on the DataLens driver for the database you are using. See your database program's documentation for more information on table-creation commands.

Creating an External Database with a Definition

If you use the techniques described in the preceding sections to create an external database from a model in 1-2-3, the data types are determined using default values for the selected DataLens driver. For example, the Paradox DataLens driver only creates alphanumeric, number, and date fields in the new database. If you want to create other types of fields, or if you want to specify index fields, you must create a table definition range by using the **/D**ata **E**xternal **C**reate command (on the 1-2-3 Classic menu).

The *table definition range* is the area in the worksheet used to define the external table's structure. To create an external table, 1-2-3 for Windows needs to know the number, order, data types, and names of the fields in the new table. This information is provided in a table definition.

A table definition range always includes six columns, although not all DataLens drivers use every column of information. In addition, the range includes one row for each field in the database. The six columns (from left to right) specify the following information:

- Field name

- Data type

- Field width

- Column labels

- Field descriptions

- Field-creation strings

The allowable values are determined by the specified DataLens driver. Refer to the DataLens driver documentation to determine the allowable values. Figure 28.10 shows a table definition range used to create a Paradox database.

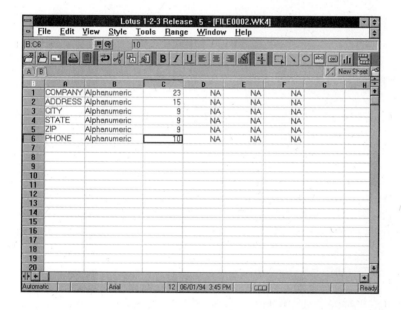

Fig. 28.10
Create a table definition range like this and use the /DEC classic command to create a Paradox database.

To create an external database from a definition, follow these steps:

1. Type the definition for the table into a worksheet using the guidelines for the specific DataLens driver. Figure 28.10 shows a sample used to create a Paradox database.

2. Select the /Data External Create Name command using the 1-2-3 Classic menu. A series of prompts appear, asking for all the necessary information:

   - When you are prompted to Enter name of table to create:, choose the DataLens driver from the list.

   - When the list of directories displays, choose the desired directory.

- When the list of existing databases displays, type a new name for your new database.

- When you are prompted to `Enter range name for table:`, type a new range name for your table.

- And finally, when you are prompted to `Enter table creation string`, type the string or press Enter to skip this step.

3. Select **D**efinition (still in the **/D**ata **E**xternal **C**reate menu) and select **U**se-Definition, and select the range containing the database definition.

4. Select **G**o from the menu to create the external database from the specified definition.

> **Note**
>
> You can use a sample worksheet to create a definition, and then edit it to change the field definitions or length. Use the **/D**ata **E**xternal **C**reate **D**efinition **C**reate Definition to create a definition from your model in a worksheet. Or, use **/D**ata **E**xternal **L**ist **F**ields (if the existing database is an external database) to create the definition. Modify the table definition by adding or changing field names, changing data types or field widths, and adding field-creation strings (if used). If the database driver you are using does not require a certain piece of information, the corresponding location in the table description contains NA.

Deleting an External Table

The **T**ools Data**b**ase and **Q**uery menus do not provide a way to delete an external database table. You must use the 1-2-3 Classic **/D**ata **E**xternal **D**elete command to delete external tables from the external database. Specify the database driver and database name and then highlight the external table to be deleted. Select **Y**es to delete the table and **Q**uit to return to Ready mode.

Using Tools Database Send Command

You use **T**ools Data**b**ase **S**end Command to send commands to a database management program so that you can perform database manipulations not possible with 1-2-3 for Windows alone. To use this command, 1-2-3 for Windows must be connected to an external table.

The capabilities of the commands you issue with the **T**ools Data**b**ase **S**end Command (as well as the command syntax) depend on the external database management program—the commands have no relationship to the 1-2-3 for Windows database management commands. You must be familiar with the commands of the database program to which you want to send a command.

When you choose **T**ools Data**b**ase **S**end, you will first be prompted for the driver, then the directory. Then the Send Command dialog box appears.

The database command is entered as a string in the Enter **D**atabase Command text box of the Send Command dialog box. 1-2-3 for Windows sends the command when you select OK and then returns to Ready mode.

Using the Query Show SQL Command

If you use an external database that understands SQL (Structured Query Language), 1-2-3 for Windows can show you the SQL command used to create a query table. The Query Show SQL command displays the Show SQL dialog box (see fig. 28.11). When this dialog box is displayed, you can select **C**opy to copy the displayed command to the Clipboard. This command can then be pasted into the worksheet or the Enter **D**atabase Command text box of the Send Command dialog box.

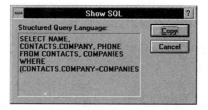

Fig. 28.11
The **Q**uery Show SQL command displays the SQL command used to create a query table.

Disconnecting 1-2-3 for Windows from the External Table

The **T**ools Data**b**ase Dis**c**onnect command severs the connection between 1-2-3 for Windows and an external table. You must specify the range name of the specific table whose connection you want to break.

After you break the connection, the range name of the table becomes undefined. Any worksheet formulas or queries that use that range name may produce errors.

Tip
Generate a table of SQL commands for different types of queries by using **Q**uery Show S**Q**L. Document the purpose of each command so that you can easily select the correct command for later use.

Troubleshooting

Why did several formulas in my worksheet change to ERR when I disconnected from an external database file?

1-2-3 for Windows uses range names to refer to external database files. If you use those range names in formulas, the formulas change to ERR because they refer to range names that are no longer defined once the external database is disconnected. To correct the problem, reconnect to the external database file and specify the same range name to refer to the file.

Importing Data from Other Programs

Lotus provides several means of importing data from other applications. The Translate utility (described in Chapter 8) has options that convert data directly to 1-2-3 for Windows worksheets from DIF, dBASE files, and other file formats. You then can access the data by using the **File O**pen command from the current worksheet.

The type of data that can be imported using the techniques in this section could be information that you printed to a file from another package or information that was downloaded from a mainframe or minicomputer. This is usually created with one of two formats:

- *Formatted Data.* This data is organized into records (or rows of data) and fields. The fields are uniquely identifiable because the alphabetic fields are enclosed in quotation marks and the numeric data is separated by commas or blanks.

- *Unformatted Data.* Although each record is on a unique line or row, there is no way to identify the individual fields, so when you import this information into 1-2-3, it comes in as one long label in column A. You then must disassemble these labels into the appropriate data values or fields by using functions or the **R**ange **P**arse command.

Importing Formatted or Unformatted Data

You use the same basic steps to import formatted or unformatted data. But, if the data is unformatted, you will have to parse it (discussed in the next section). Follow these steps to import the data into a 1-2-3 for Windows worksheet.

1. Select **F**ile **O**pen command or click on the Open File SmartIcon to read into a current worksheet the data stored on disk as a text file.

2. Select Text (`txt; prn; csv; dat; out; asc`) from the File **T**ype list box (see fig. 28.12) in the Open File dialog box.

3. Select Text **O**ptions to display the Text Options dialog box shown in figure 28.13. The following choices enable you to tell 1-2-3 how to separate the data in the text file into unique columns of data in the worksheet.

    Separator - Choose the character used to separate the fields in the text file.

    Layout of File - This breaks the data into columns based on the vertically aligned data in the file.

    Put everything in one column - Puts all the text into the first column. You need to use the parse commands to split it up into separate columns.

4. Choose OK to open the text file as a new worksheet or choose **C**ombine to bring the data from the text file into the current cell in the current worksheet.

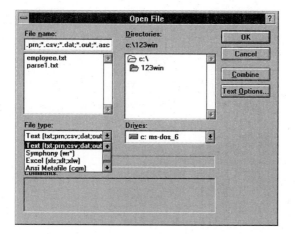

V

Managing Databases

Fig. 28.12
Specify Text in the
File **T**ype list box
to open a text file.

The **R**ange **P**arse command is a flexible and easy method of extracting numeric, string, and date data from long labels and placing it in separate columns. Suppose that you printed a report containing inventory data to a disk file, and now you want to load the ASCII file in 1-2-3 for Windows. After you load the file by using the **F**ile **O**pen command, you must reformat the data with the **R**ange **P**arse command.

Fig. 28.13

Choose a method
for dividing the
data into columns.

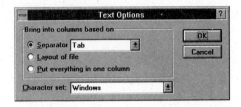

> **Note**
>
> Although the **R**ange **P**arse command does not require, for proper operation, the use
> of a fixed-space font such as Courier New, the examples of the **R**ange **P**arse com-
> mand shown in this chapter use Courier New for clarity. 1-2-3 for Windows can
> create a format line and parse data properly regardless of the font used, but the
> examples are easier to understand when a proportional font (such as the default
> Arial) is not used.

The **F**ile **O**pen command loads the inventory data into the range A1..A9 (see
fig. 28.14). Although the data seems to be formatted in a typical worksheet
range (A1..G9 in the example), the display is misleading. The current cell-
pointer location is A5; look at the contents box to see that the entire row
exists in cell A3 as a long label—and not in separate cells as you might
assume.

Fig. 28.14

The results
of a **F**ile **O**pen
command when
the data is
unformatted and
placed in the
column.

	Lotus 1-2-3 Release 5 - [FILE0002.WK4]						
	A	B	C	D	E	F	G	H
1	Inventory records						
2							
3	DESCRIPTION			QUANTITY	UNIT	COST	P.O.DATE
4							
5	HAMMER			10	EA	6.75	7/4/95
6	SCREWDRIVER			17	EA	8.75	
7	WRENCH			100	EA	15.75	7/24/95
8	HAMMER			10	EA	6.75	7/4/95
9	SCREWDRIVER			17	EA	8.75	

A:A5   'HAMMER   10   EA   6.75 7/4/95

To break the long-label columns into fields, use these steps:

1. Select the first range of data to be parsed (in this example, cell A3) and select **R**ange **P**arse. The Parse dialog box appears.

2. Click the **C**reate command button to create a new entry in the **F**ormat Line text box (see fig. 28.15). The **F**ormat Line specifies the pattern or patterns 1-2-3 is to use to split the long labels into numbers, labels, and dates.

3. If the **F**ormat line does not accurately reflect how the data should be divided, edit the line using the symbols described in table 28.1. Use the format line to mark the column positions and the type of data in those positions.

4. Choose **O**utput range and indicate in the upper-left corner of the range where you want the reorganized data to be placed (a blank area of the worksheet). In this example, choose A12.

> **Caution**
>
> Make sure that there are enough empty cells to the right and below that cell to hold the newly parsed data or you might overwrite existing data in the worksheet. The output data has as many rows as there are long labels; the number of columns depends on the format line. Also, because the **P**arse command adds the format line to the worksheet and moves everything else down, make sure that you account for this extra row in positioning your output range.

5. Press Enter or choose OK to parse the data. A suggested format line is inserted in the data at A3—moving the remaining worksheet contents down one line. The newly formatted data appears in the output range (now A13).

6. If the data to be parsed contains heading data along with text as this example does, repeat Steps 1 through 5, using the actual data (A6..A10 in this example) as the **I**nput Column and a blank cell below the previously parsed headings (A14 in this case) as the **O**utput Range.

7. Choose OK to perform the parse based on the specified **I**nput Column, **F**ormat Line, and **O**utput Range.

Tip
The **R**eset command button clears the previously set **I**nput Column and **O**utput Range text boxes, so that you can perform more than one parsing operation in a worksheet.

V

Managing Databases

Fig. 28.15
Choose **C**reate to
have 1-2-3 create a
format line for
you, and then edit
it if necessary.

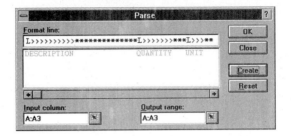

Troubleshooting

When I parse my data, my numeric values are turned into labels.

In many real-world situations, you will need to parse the column headings (cell A3 in
this example) by using one format line; then parse the data (cells A5..A9) with another format line and output range. Different format lines are necessary because all
the headings are labels, but the data is a mixture of label, numeric, and date data.

Using the Format Line to Control the Parse

You use combinations of certain letters and special characters in format lines
to control how the data is parsed. The letters denote the beginning position
and the type of data; special symbols define the length of a field and the
spacing. Table 28.1 explains the letters and symbols typically used in format
lines.

Table 28.1 Letters/Symbols Used in Format Lines	
Letter/Symbol	**Purpose**
D	Marks the beginning of a **D**ate field
L	Marks the beginning of a **L**abel field
S	Marks the beginning of a **S**kip position, which instructs 1-2-3 to ignore the data in this position
T	Marks the beginning of a **T**ime field
V	Marks the beginning of a **V**alue field
>	Defines the continuation of a field. Use one > for each position in the field (excluding the first position)
*	Defines blank spaces (in the data below the format line) that may be part of the block of data

Add as many format lines as you need in the data you want to parse. In the inventory example, two separate parse operations were performed because the headings in row 3 had a different format than the data in rows 5 through 9.

After parsing is complete, the data displayed in individual cells may not be exactly what you want. You can make a few changes in the format and column width, as shown in figure 28.16, and add or delete information to make the newly parsed data more usable. These enhancements are not part of the **R**ange **P**arse command, but they usually are necessary after importing any parsed data.

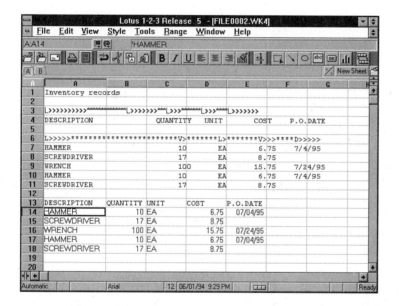

Fig. 28.16
The format lines are added to the worksheet by the parse command.

Using Caution when Parsing Data

If you want to parse a value that continues past the end of the field, you should know that 1-2-3 parses the data until it encounters a blank or until the value runs into the next field in the format line. This means that if you parse labels, make sure that the field widths in the format line are wide enough so that you avoid losing data because of blanks. If you parse values, the field widths are less critical.

Experiment on small amounts of data until you are comfortable using the **R**ange **P**arse command. After you understand how this important command works, you may find many more applications for it. Every time you develop a new application, consider whether existing data created with another software program can be imported and then changed to 1-2-3 for Windows format by using the **R**ange **P**arse command.

From Here...

Tip
You often can use the **Edit P**aste command as a shortcut to import and parse data from another Windows application. Try copying the data to the Clipboard in the other application and then using **E**dit **P**aste in 1-2-3 for Windows. You may find that this approach automatically places the data into separate worksheet cells, eliminating the need to use **R**ange **P**arse.

The chapters in this section described all the various ways that you can manipulate databases in 1-2-3 for Windows. There are two other related topics that enable you to enhance your ability to work with databases and external information.

■ Chapter 37, "Advanced Macro Techniques." This section covers macro commands that enable you to read and write an ASCII sequential file from within a 1-2-3 for Windows macro.

■ Chapter 5, "Using Functions." Special text @ functions help you parse and manipulate data that you import from other sources.

◀ "Editing Data in the Worksheet," p. 101

Part VI

Integrating 1-2-3

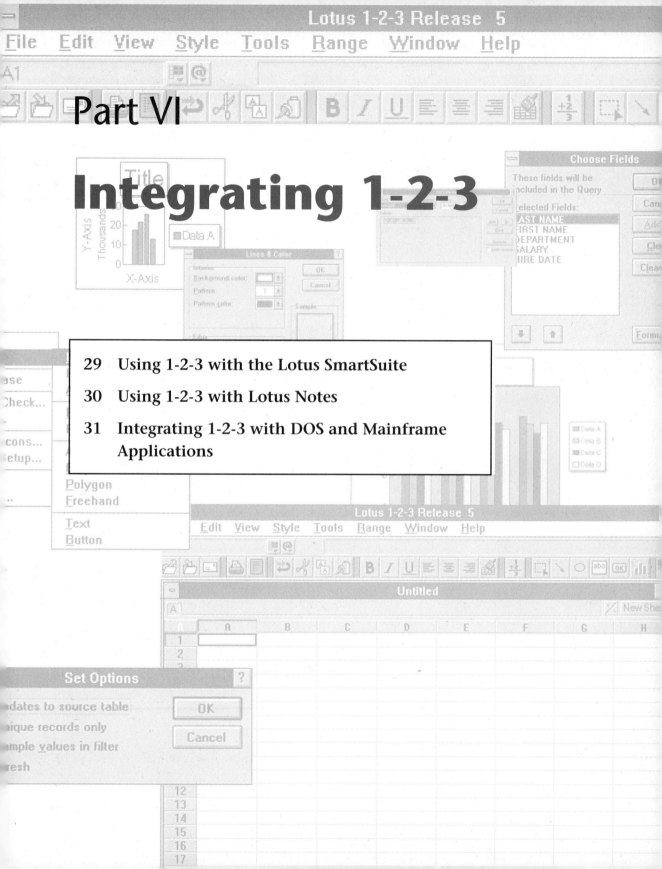

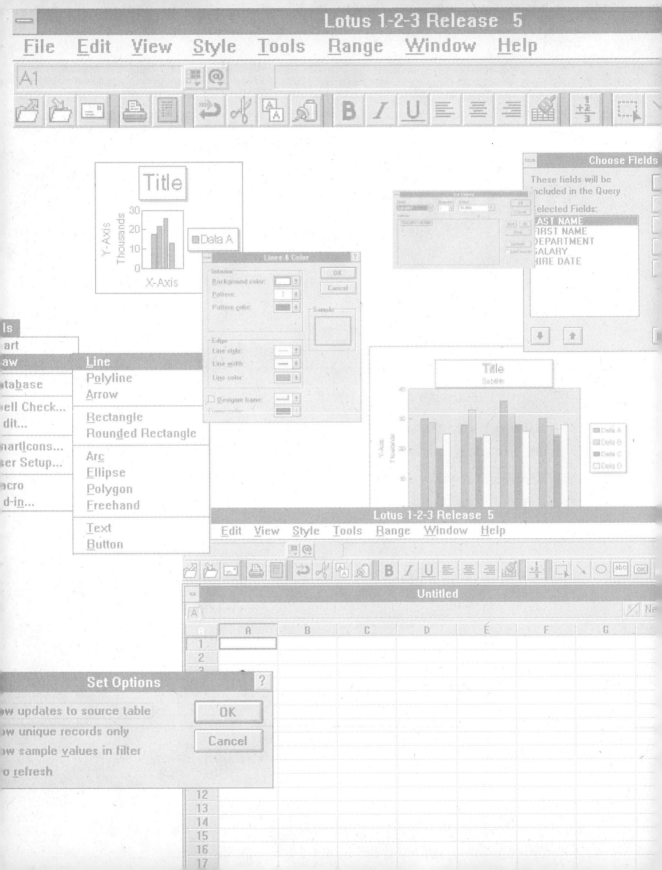

Chapter 29

Using 1-2-3 with the Lotus SmartSuite

Back when most programs ran on DOS without the benefit of Windows, getting work from one program to another was difficult, if not impossible. Even when a transfer was conceivable, you often had to export work to a file, convert the file with a second program, and then import the converted work to the final-destination software. To use a simple worksheet of numbers in a report created in a word processing program, for example, you had to export the numbers as an ASCII print file, convert the space-separated columns to tab-separated columns, and then import the ASCII file into a document.

Among all the other benefits that Windows provides, easy communication among applications makes it possible to create work in one application and then freely use that work in another application. You can create a logo in a graphics program and quickly transfer it to a word processing or spreadsheet program. You also can use the numbers in a worksheet to create a graph for incorporation into a printed report.

Passing work among applications easily is only the beginning; Windows enables you to set up and maintain active links between the work in the original application and the copies that you transfer to other applications. These links communicate any changes you make, so that the work is updated automatically in every application to which it has been copied. The result is an integrated system that lets you stay within the domain of each application, but that still combines the output of several applications to accomplish a task. You can use the data-analysis powers of a spreadsheet program, the visual-representation capabilities of a graphics program, and the presentation powers of a word processing program to create a monthly report.

Linking applications provides several other benefits. First, you can revise work in its native application, knowing that the revision will appear in every copy; you need not find the work everywhere it appears and make the same update over and over. Second, you can be confident that the original and its copies remain synchronized. Third, you virtually eliminate any chance of human error that can cause discrepancies in data; nobody needs to retype the numbers from a spreadsheet program into a word processing program, for example.

This chapter describes how you can combine the best features of 1-2-3 Release 5 for Windows with the strengths of the other Lotus Windows applications in the SmartSuite bundle. SmartSuite contains 1-2-3 for Windows, the presentation-graphics program Freelance Graphics for Windows 2.0, the Windows word processing program Ami Pro 3.01, the relational-database application Approach for Windows 2.1, and the electronic-mail package cc:Mail for Windows 2.0. The chapter describes the technical features of Windows that make such tight integration possible and offers real-world examples of how you can use the Lotus SmartSuite applications together.

> **Note**
>
> The general techniques you learn in this chapter work for other Lotus Windows applications (such as Lotus Improv) and Windows applications from other software makers (such as Excel, Word for Windows, and Paradox for Windows) that support OLE. Consult the user manual for the application to see if it is OLE-compatible.

In this chapter, you learn how to:

- Use the Clipboard to copy and paste information
- Use object linking and embedding (OLE) between the Lotus SmartSuite applications
- Link 1-2-3 data and charts to the other SmartSuites
- Exchange graphics and logos
- Send and receive cc:Mail

Understanding the Techniques

To transfer data from one Windows application to another, you can perform a simple copy-and-paste operation, or you can use the more sophisticated commands of *object linking and embedding* (OLE). The following sections describe these techniques.

Using the Clipboard for Basic Copying and Pasting

All Windows applications share a Clipboard that can transfer virtually anything from one Windows application to another. In this book, you have learned how to use the Windows Clipboard to copy and paste 1-2-3 data between cells or between worksheets. The same principle enables you to copy and paste information between different applications. You can copy a range of cells from 1-2-3 to an Ami Pro document, for example, or you can copy a corporate logo created in Freelance Graphics for Windows to a 1-2-3 worksheet so that the logo appears in a worksheet printout.

When you use the Clipboard to copy and paste work from one application to another, you end up with two unrelated objects: the original, in the application in which it was made; and the duplicate, in another application, with no ties that link it to the original. If you modify the original, the duplicate remains unchanged. Often, this arrangement is perfectly satisfactory. Your corporate logo, for example, may not have changed in years, and no changes are anticipated for many more years. After you create the logo in Freelance Graphics for Windows, you copy and paste it to a worksheet to be printed, examined one time, and then filed. In this case, setting up a link between the original in Freelance and the copy in 1-2-3 would be wasted effort. You have no need to ensure that any changes to the corporate logo are updated in the worksheet.

To perform a simple copy-and-paste operation of this sort, you select the item to be copied in the first application and use the **E**dit menu's **C**opy command to copy the item to the Windows Clipboard. Then you switch to the second application, in which you open the **E**dit menu and choose the **P**aste command to retrieve the item from the Windows Clipboard.

To copy a table of numbers from a 1-2-3 worksheet to an Ami Pro letter, for example, follow these steps:

1. In 1-2-3, select the range of cells to copy to the document that you have open in an Ami Pro window (see fig. 29.1).

VI

Integrating 1-2-3

Fig. 29.1
Selecting a range
of cells to copy in
1-2-3.

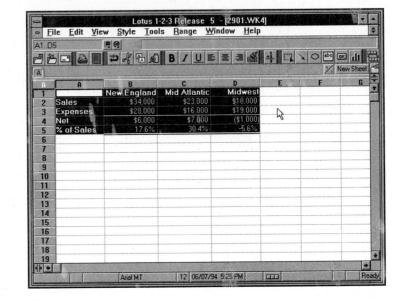

◀ "Manipulating
Windows,"
p. 46

2. In 1-2-3, open the **E**dit menu and choose the **C**opy command, or press Ctrl+C or Ctrl+Ins.

3. Switch to Ami Pro by pressing Alt+Tab or Ctrl+Esc.

4. Click the Ami Pro document where you want the table to appear.

5. In Ami Pro, open the **E**dit menu and choose the **P**aste command, or press Ctrl+V or Shift+Ins. The range of numbers appears in an Ami Pro table, as shown in figure 29.2.

Fig. 29.2
The table of
numbers pasted
into Ami Pro.

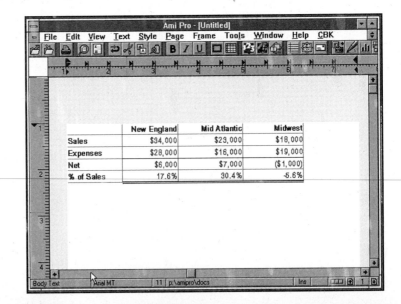

Here's another example of a simple copy-and-paste operation. In this example, you copy a logo created in Freelance Graphics for Windows to a 1-2-3 worksheet. Follow these steps:

1. In Freelance, select the logo you want to copy to a worksheet that is open in a 1-2-3 window (see fig. 29.3). If the logo is composed of a number of objects, you may want to group the objects before selecting the group; select the objects, and then open the **A**rrange menu and choose the **G**roup command.

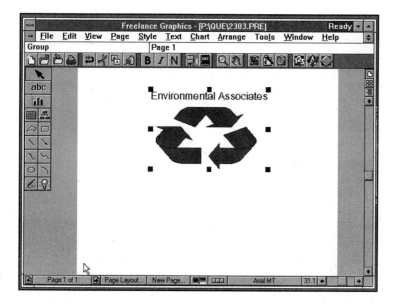

Fig. 29.3
The logo selected in Freelance Graphics for Windows.

2. In Freelance, open the **E**dit menu and choose the **C**opy command, or press Ctrl+C or Ctrl+Ins.

3. Switch to 1-2-3 for Windows by pressing Alt+Tab or Ctrl+Esc.

4. Click a cell that marks the upper-left corner of the location for the logo.

5. Open the **E**dit menu and choose the **P**aste command, or press Ctrl+V or Shift+Ins. The logo appears in the selected cell in the 1-2-3 worksheet, as shown in figure 29.4.

VI

Integrating 1-2-3

Fig. 29.4

The Freelance logo pasted into a 1-2-3 worksheet.

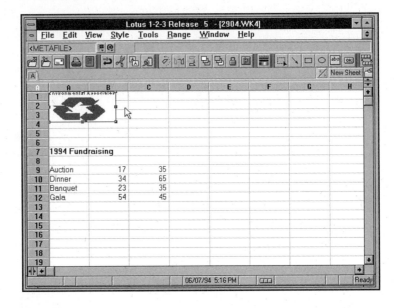

6. Position the mouse pointer on a corner handle of the logo, and drag diagonally out from the center to increase the size of the logo. Figure 29.5 shows how to resize the logo to fit properly on the page.

Fig. 29.5

Dragging a corner handle of the logo to size it properly.

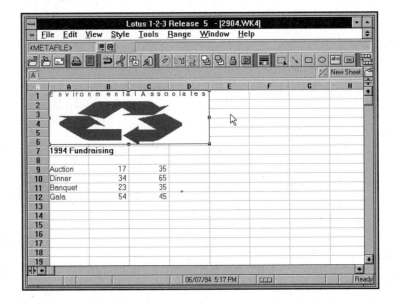

Using OLE

Using the **E**dit menu's **C**opy and **P**aste commands to transfer data from one Windows application to another does not set up a link between the original and the copy. Without a link, you can change either version without affecting the other. To establish a link, you must use a special capability of Windows applications called object linking and embedding (OLE). The entire suite of Lotus Windows applications can take full advantage of OLE.

Caution

Lotus recommends that you include in the PATH statement of your computer's AUTOEXEC.BAT file the full paths to the applications you use when linking and embedding data. If you have 1-2-3 for Windows, Ami Pro, and Freelance Graphics for Windows, for example, consider adding the following to the end of the existing PATH statement:

```
C:\123R5W\PROGRAMS;C:\AMIPRO;C:\FLW
```

Understanding the Difference between Linking and Embedding

Object linking and object embedding are two related techniques that seem to accomplish similar goals. The difference between the two can be confusing. Both techniques enable you to create work in one application and use a copy of the work in another application. You can create a graphic in Freelance Graphics and use it in Ami Pro and 1-2-3, for example.

When you use object linking to copy an object, the object appears in the second application, but the data for the object resides in the file in which it was created. If you use object linking to copy a table of numbers from 1-2-3 to Ami Pro, for example, the data remains in 1-2-3, but the table also appears in Ami Pro. To change the table in Ami Pro, you return to 1-2-3 and change the original numbers. Because a Dynamic Data Exchange (DDE) link has been set up between the two applications, any changes to the data in 1-2-3 change the table in Ami Pro.

Windows makes switching between applications easy. To return to the application in which an object was created, simply double-click the object. To return to 1-2-3 after linking the 1-2-3 data to Ami Pro, you double-click the 1-2-3 data in Ami Pro. If 1-2-3 is not running, Windows will start it for you. After you change the data in the original application, the change flows through to the other application through the DDE link.

VI

Integrating 1-2-3

When you use object embedding to copy an object, the data for the object is copied to the destination application. Because the data resides in both the original application and the destination application, you can move the file that contains the embedded data to another computer. When you take a file with embedded data to a different computer, you don't have to take all the files in which the original data is stored (as you would with object linking). As long as the computer to which you move the file has a copy of the application you used to create the embedded data, you can use that application to edit the embedded data.

When an object is embedded in another application, any edits you make to the object in the original application are not reflected in the embedded copy.

With object embedding, you can create an object in an application and then embed it in another application. You also can temporarily switch to another application to create an object you need. When you return to the first application, the object you created is embedded in the first application's work area: You switched to the second application only long enough to create an object before returning to the first application. The object appears in the application you started in—and its data is stored in the starting application, too.

As you type an Ami Pro report, for example, you may realize that you need a 1-2-3 table of numbers and a Freelance graph. Using AmiPro's **E**dit menu and selecting the **I**nsert New **O**bject command, you visit Freelance only long enough to create the graph you need and then return to Ami Pro. The graph appears in Ami Pro, and its data is stored in the Ami Pro document. Using the **I**nsert New **O**bject command again, you dip into 1-2-3 long enough to create a 1-2-3 table of numbers and then return to Ami Pro, where the table is stored and used.

Whether you use object linking or object embedding depends on several factors. If you have to give someone else a document that contains objects from several applications, embed the objects. Only if the objects are embedded is their data stored in the file you give someone else. If you create an Ami Pro report that includes 1-2-3 numbers and a Freelance graph, for example, and you intend to distribute the report to other offices, use object embedding. The 1-2-3 numbers and Freelance graph are stored in the Ami Pro file. The result is a larger file than if you had used object linking, but having the data available in the file is well worth the cost in disk space. If the document is to remain on your PC, however, and your concern is setting up a system that automatically updates copies of objects if you update the originals, object linking does that job.

Linking Data

You can link an object from one application to another in several ways, but the easiest way is to follow these steps:

1. Create the object.

2. Copy it to the Windows Clipboard.

3. Switch to the second application.

4. Open the **E**dit menu and choose the Paste **L**ink command to copy the object into the second application.

Here is the procedure in detail: First, create the object you need. (In Freelance Graphics, create a design or a graph. In Ami Pro, create a block of text. In 1-2-3, create a range of numbers.) Be sure to save the file before continuing. An object to be linked must be saved as a file in its original application. Even if you modify the object after you save the file, the modified object will be linked properly.

Select the object to be linked by clicking it. If the object is a range of numbers in 1-2-3, for example, select the range. Open the application's **E**dit menu and choose **C**opy to place a copy of the object in the Windows Clipboard.

To carry out the second half of object linking, switch to the second application. Position the pointer where the linked object should appear in that application. (In 1-2-3, move the cell pointer to the cell that the object should fill. In Ami Pro, move the insertion point to the place in the document where the object should appear. In Freelance, turn to the presentation page on which the object should appear.)

Open the **E**dit menu of the second application and choose the Paste **L**ink command. Figure 29.6 shows the Paste Lin**k** command in the Ami Pro **E**dit menu.

Tip
To see an object in the Clipboard, open Clipboard Viewer, located in the Accessories group of the Windows Program Manager.

> **Note**
>
> In Freelance Graphics for Windows, you choose P**a**ste Special, choose the Clipboard format you need, and then click **L**ink.

Caution

While you are still in the application you use to create an object, you m st save the object in a file before y can link it to another application. Othe wise, the Paste **L**ink ommand is not ava ab,e when you switch to the second application.

VI

Integrating 1-2-3

Fig. 29.6
The Paste **L**ink
command in
Ami Pro.

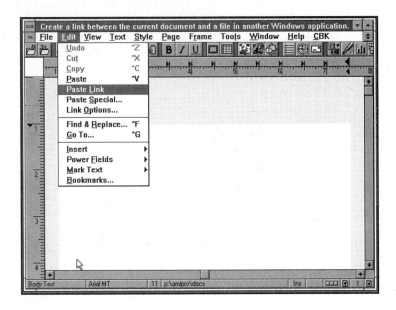

After you link an object, you can switch to the original application, make a change to the object, and see the revision appear in the second application, too.

To edit an object that has been linked, you do not need to manually switch to the application that created the object and then load and edit the object; you can simply double-click the object in the application to which it is linked. If you linked a table of numbers from 1-2-3 to an Ami Pro file, for example, you can double-click the table in Ami Pro.

> **Note**
>
> If you paste the data into an Ami Pro table, double-clicking the table doesn't bring up 1-2-3. It selects an item in the table.

When you double-click a linked object, Windows automatically opens the application used to create the object and loads the file with the data for the object. Because Windows tracks the origin of each linked object, you do not have to worry about where an object came from when it needs revision; you can simply double-click the object and let Windows retrieve the object in its original application. If the creator application is not installed, you cannot edit the object.

> **Note**
>
> You cannot create a DDE or OLE link between two 1-2-3 worksheets or files.
> You must use formulas to link worksheets.

Embedding an Object

You can embed an object from one application into another in several ways.
One way is to use an application's Insert **O**bject command. Follow these
steps:

1. Position the mouse pointer in the application where the object should
appear.

2. Open the **E**dit menu and choose the Insert **O**bject command. A dialog
box appears, listing all the available object types (see fig. 29.7). The
types listed are determined by the applications in your system that can
provide objects for embedding. The more applications you have, the
more object types you see in the list.

> **Note**
>
> In Ami Pro, open the **E**dit menu and choose the **I**nsert command; then choose
> New **O**bject.

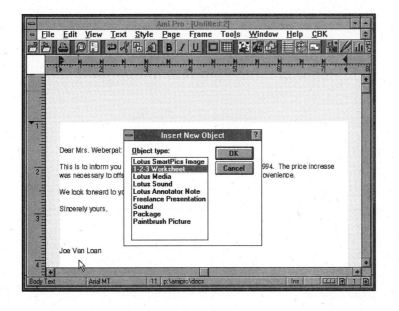

Fig. 29.7
The Insert New
Object dialog box.

VI

Integrating 1-2-3

3. From the list of object types, select a type. The application that creates objects of that type opens so that you can make the object you need.

4. Create the object, using the tools of the second application.

5. When you finish, open the **F**ile menu and choose the E**x**it & Return command. The second application closes, and you return to the original application, with the newly created object in place.

With this method of embedding, you visit a second application just long enough to create an object expressly for use in the first application. The data for the object is stored in the first application, along with information about which application created the object.

You can use a second method to embed an object by following these steps:

1. Create the object in an application.

2. Save the file.

3. Select the object.

4. Copy it to the Windows Clipboard.

5. Switch to a second application.

6. Open the **E**dit menu and choose the Paste **S**pecial command. The Paste Special dialog box appears, as shown in figure 29.8.

Fig. 29.8
The Paste Special dialog box.

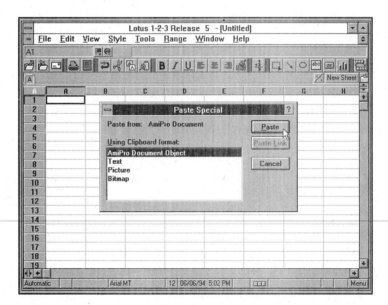

7. Select the object you just created from the list of available formats in the Clipboard. (When you copy something to the Clipboard, it is stored there in several different representations so that the destination application can automatically select the format it needs.) In this case, you must specify the format manually by selecting the item referred to as an "object."

8. Click the **P**aste button.

This second method is the method to use when you want to embed an object created in another application. The result of both methods is the same, however.

Caution

While you are still in the application you use to create an object, you must save the object in a file before you can embed it in another application.

The remainder of this chapter describes the specific steps you use to copy and paste, link, or embed work between particular pairs of Lotus Windows applications.

Using a Table of Data from 1-2-3 in an Ami Pro Document

◄ "Copying Data," p. 260

Ami Pro's table features are sophisticated and easy to use; they enable you to enter text and numbers and format a table quickly. But if you already have entered and calculated a set of data in the cells of a 1-2-3 worksheet, there's no need to manually reproduce that work in Ami Pro. You can easily transfer a range of cells from a 1-2-3 worksheet to an Ami Pro document.

The fastest way to copy a range of data from 1-2-3 is to select the range, **C**opy the data to the Clipboard, switch to Ami Pro, and **P**aste the data there. The labels and values in the 1-2-3 range appear in a neatly formatted Ami Pro table. You can use all the table-formatting commands in the Ami Pro Table menu to change the appearance of the table. If you formatted the range in 1-2-3, that formatting is transferred to Ami Pro along with the data. Even formatting applied by using the 1-2-3 **S**tyle menu **G**allery template transfers properly to Ami Pro.

Using the **E**dit menu's **C**opy and **P**aste commands to transfer a range from 1-2-3 to Ami Pro copies only the results of any formulas in the range; the formulas themselves are not copied to Ami Pro. Therefore, you cannot recalculate any of the data in the Ami Pro table unless you use Ami Pro formulas.

To create a table in Ami Pro that you can update if you revise any of the numbers in 1-2-3, you must either link or embed the data.

Linking the Data

Using object linking to copy a range from 1-2-3 to Ami Pro sets up a connection between the original range in the worksheet and the data in Ami Pro. Changes to the range in 1-2-3 update the Ami Pro data, too.

Tip
Use linking if you want changes to the 1-2-3 data to update in Ami Pro. Use embedding if you plan to move the Ami Pro document among PCs. The 1-2-3 data will be embedded in the Ami Pro file.

You have several options for object linking. The option you choose depends on how you want the data to appear in Ami Pro. To have the data appear with Ami Pro formatting in an Ami Pro table that is linked to the original data, you can set up a standard paste link. To have the 1-2-3 range appear in Ami Pro as it is formatted in 1-2-3, set up an OLE link.

Setting Up a Standard Paste Link

The easiest way to set up a standard paste link is to select the data in 1-2-3, copy it to the Windows Clipboard, switch to Ami Pro, and then use the **E**dit menu's Paste **L**ink command to paste the data into Ami Pro. To use this procedure, follow these steps:

1. In a 1-2-3 for Windows worksheet, enter the data and formulas you need.

2. Select the range you want to link to Ami Pro. Figure 29.9 shows a sample selected range.

3. Open the **E**dit menu and choose the **C**opy command.

4. Switch to Ami Pro by pressing Alt+Tab or Ctrl+Esc.

5. Position the insertion point in the Ami Pro document where you want the table of numbers to appear.

6. Open the **E**dit menu and choose the Paste **L**ink command. The range appears as an Ami Pro table.

The text and numbers in the range take on the default formatting characteristics of the Ami Pro table. If you formatted the range in 1-2-3, the 1-2-3 styling is transferred to Ami Pro along with the data.

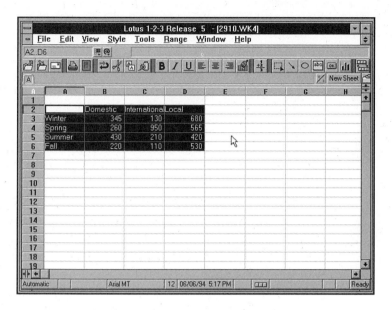

Fig. 29.9
A selected range
in 1-2-3.

Figure 29.10 shows a range formatted in 1-2-3; figure 29.11 shows the same range as it appears in an Ami Pro table. Notice that the title, which spills into adjacent cells in 1-2-3, is word-wrapped within a cell of the Ami Pro table. You may want to pull the title from the cell and then center it outside and above the table.

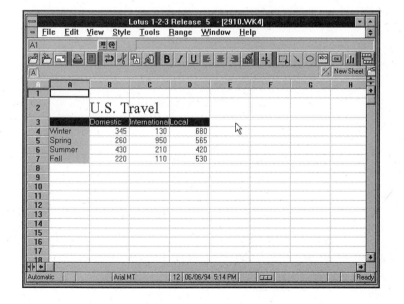

Fig. 29.10
A formatted
1-2-3 range.

VI

Integrating 1-2-3

Fig. 29.11
The same
formatted 1-2-3
range as it appears
in Ami Pro.

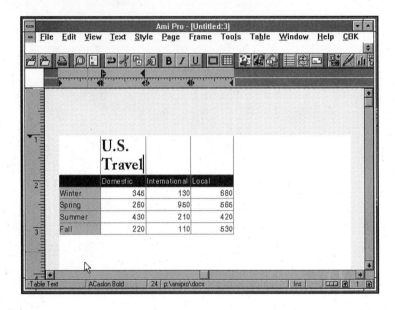

Another method you can use to create the same kind of link between 1-2-3 data and an Ami Pro document is to use the Paste **S**pecial command in Ami Pro and then select a DDE link. A *DDE link* is the kind of link that is set up when you use the Paste **L**ink command. The result is the same as that of the preceding method; only the procedure is different.

To use the Paste **S**pecial command to create a standard link, follow these steps:

1. In a 1-2-3 worksheet, enter the data and formulas you need.

2. Select the range you want to link to Ami Pro.

3. Open the **E**dit menu and choose the **C**opy command.

4. Switch to Ami Pro by pressing Alt+Tab or Ctrl+Esc.

5. Position the insertion point in the Ami Pro document where you want the table of numbers to appear.

6. Open the **E**dit menu and choose the Paste **S**pecial command. The Paste Special dialog box appears (see fig. 29.12).

7. From the list of formats, select DDE Link.

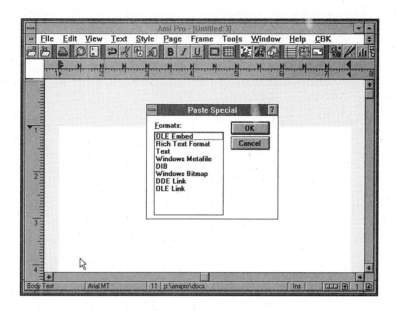

Fig. 29.12
The Paste Special
dialog box.

After you link a 1-2-3 range with an Ami Pro table, you can select individual cells of the table in Ami Pro and edit them just as you could if you created the table in Ami Pro. You even can edit the text and numbers in the table. But if you make any changes to the original data in 1-2-3, the changes in Ami Pro are overwritten when the link is updated.

Every time you open a saved Ami Pro file that contains a DDE link to a table of 1-2-3 data, Ami Pro opens a message box that asks whether you want to update the DDE links in the document. If you click Yes, Ami Pro reads the 1-2-3 worksheet file and reflects any changes in the data that it finds. If you click No, Ami Pro opens the document and displays the version of the 1-2-3 data from the last time the document was saved.

Troubleshooting

Why isn't the Paste **L***ink command available in the* **E***dit menu? Also, after selecting Paste* **S***pecial from the* **E***dit menu, why isn't DDE Link one of the available formats?*

You probably have not saved the object in a file in the source application. You must save the data in a file before you can create a link.

Why must the data file in the source application be saved to be able to link data between two applications?

(continues)

(continued)

Linked data must be stored in a file created by the application that was used to originate the data. The file name for the data is part of the information that is transferred to the destination application via the Windows Clipboard. This lets the destination application maintain a link with the data file even if the source application is not running, or even if that application is not installed on the system.

OLE Linking 1-2-3

Another approach to linking 1-2-3 and Ami Pro data is creating an OLE link between 1-2-3 and Ami Pro. This method copies an image of the 1-2-3 data and its formatting to Ami Pro. The method you learned about in the preceding section—creating a DDE link—copies the data to Ami Pro, where it takes on Ami Pro formatting. When you set up an OLE link, the result is a tabular arrangement of data in Ami Pro that looks just as the data did in 1-2-3. The picture fits in an Ami Pro frame, which can have standard frame formatting (such as a line surrounding the frame, a shadow, and rounded or square corners). Figure 29.13 shows how the same range of data used in an earlier example appears in an Ami Pro document when it is linked with an OLE link. Notice the shadow frame with rounded edges.

Fig. 29.13
1-2-3 data copied to Ami Pro with an OLE link.

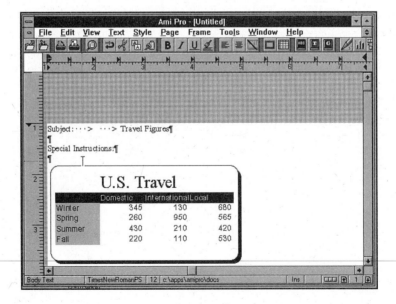

To copy data from 1-2-3 to Ami Pro with an OLE link, follow the procedure for creating a DDE link (refer to the preceding section), but first create an Ami Pro frame by opening the **F**rame menu and choosing the **C**reate Frame command. Then open the **E**dit menu and choose the Paste **S**pecial command. In the Paste Special dialog box, choose OLE Link rather than DDE Link.

You cannot directly edit data copied to Ami Pro with an OLE link. Instead, you must double-click the picture of the data to reopen a 1-2-3 window and see the original range of data. Any changes made to the 1-2-3 range are reflected in the Ami Pro document immediately.

Updating the Data in 1-2-3

To update data that has been copied to Ami Pro and linked, you should return to the original data in 1-2-3 and make edits there. If you created a DDE link, any edits you make to the data in Ami Pro will be overwritten when the link is updated. Therefore, you should edit the data in 1-2-3. If you created an OLE link, you must return to 1-2-3 to edit the data.

If you used Paste **L**ink to copy a range of 1-2-3 data into an Ami Pro table, you must switch to 1-2-3 manually (press Alt+Tab or Ctrl+Esc). If you used Paste **S**pecial and then chose OLE Link to copy 1-2-3 data into Ami Pro, you can double-click the picture of the data (or single-click and then press Enter). This action opens the 1-2-3 window.

If the file that contains the range is not open in 1-2-3, you must open the file, make changes to the data, and then switch back to Ami Pro. The changes do not appear in Ami Pro until you manually update the link or save the file and then reopen it. When you reopen the file, Ami Pro recognizes that the document contains links and asks whether you want to update them. Click Yes to update the links.

> **Note**
>
> This is only true if, when you opened the Ami document, you said no to the "update links" question.

To manually update a link in Ami Pro, follow these steps:

1. Select the frame that contains the linked data.

2. Open the **E**dit menu and choose the Link **O**ptions command. The Link Options dialog box appears (see fig. 29.14), listing all the links in the document.

Tip

If you arrange the 1-2-3 and Ami Pro windows side by side, you can see the data update in the Ami Pro window as soon as you change it in the 1-2-3 window.

3. Select the link you want to update, and then click Update.

Fig. 29.14
The Link Options
dialog box.

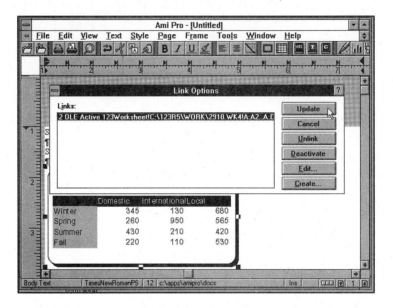

Each row of the list in the Link Options dialog box contains a complete set of information about a link. The items within the rows are separated by exclamation marks. The first item identifies the link as Text (a standard link) or OLE (an OLE link). The next item identifies whether the link is active or inactive. (An active link automatically updates whenever the 1-2-3 data changes.) The next item identifies the application that provided the data (123W or 123Worksheet, in this case, represents 1-2-3 for Windows). The last two items identify the file name of the worksheet and the range address of the data in 1-2-3. To see the application name, file name, and range address of a link more clearly, click the link and then click **E**dit. The Application, Topic (path and file name), and Item (range address) appear in text boxes in a Link dialog box. Figure 29.15 shows a Link dialog box.

Editing the Link

Selecting a link in the Link Options dialog box and then clicking **E**dit also is the way to redirect the link. You can make the link point to different data in a different part of the 1-2-3 worksheet or even to a different range in a different worksheet. After you click **E**dit, modify the entries in the **T**opic and **I**tem text boxes of the Link dialog box to link a different range to the Ami Pro document. Be sure to include the full path and file name in the **T**opic text box.

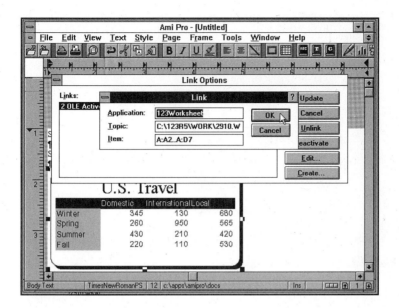

Fig. 29.15
A Link dialog box.

Removing the Link

To stop a link, select the link in the Link Options dialog box and then click **U**nlink. This action removes the link between the original data in 1-2-3 and the copy in Ami Pro. Any changes you make to the 1-2-3 data no longer are reflected in Ami Pro, but the data remains in Ami Pro, so you can have just the data without the complications of the link. After you remove a link, you cannot update the link, but you can re-create the link.

Deactivating the Link

To temporarily deactivate a link, select the link in the Link Options dialog box and then click **D**eactivate. This action stops Ami Pro from updating the link every time the data changes in 1-2-3. You might want to do this if a document should contain a historical picture of the data as it existed at a specific time. To reactivate the link, select the link and then click Update. Deactivating a link preserves memory in Windows and can make your work in Ami Pro faster.

Troubleshooting

Changing the data in the source application does not change it in the destination application, even though the data in two applications is linked.

(continues)

> (continued)
>
> The link may have been deactivated. To reactivate a link, open the **E**dit menu and then choose the **L**inks or Link **O**ptions command. Click the link in the list, and then click Update.
>
> *Every time a file with a link opens in a Lotus SmartSuite application, the application asks whether to update the DDE links. How can I eliminate this message?*
>
> Unlink the data. Unlinking leaves the data in the destination application, but removes the link between the data in the original application and the data in the destination application. The drawback is that the data in the destination application no longer will automatically change if the source data changes.

Embedding the Data

The alternative to pasting a link into Ami Pro is embedding 1-2-3 data in an Ami Pro file. In Ami Pro, the embedded 1-2-3 data appears as a picture of the data just the way it looked in 1-2-3. The embedded data automatically goes into an Ami Pro frame.

The advantage to embedded 1-2-3 data is that the data is contained in the Ami Pro file rather than in the original 1-2-3 worksheet. You can transport the Ami Pro file to another computer without also having to transport the 1-2-3 worksheet file. When you need to edit the 1-2-3 data, double-click it; Ami Pro uses the facilities of 1-2-3 on the current computer to edit the data.

You can embed 1-2-3 data in an Ami Pro file in two ways:

- In Ami Pro, open the **E**dit menu and choose the **I**nsert command; then choose New **O**bject to temporarily visit 1-2-3 and create the object you need. This procedure works best when you need to create a new 1-2-3 table while working in Ami Pro.

- In Ami Pro, open the **E**dit menu and choose the Paste **S**pecial command; then choose OLE Embed to paste the 1-2-3 data into Ami Pro. This procedure works best when you need to embed existing 1-2-3 data in an Ami Pro document.

Creating an Embedded Object While Working in Ami Pro

To create a 1-2-3 table and embed it in an Ami Pro document, follow these steps:

1. Position the insertion point in the Ami Pro document where you want the table to appear.

2. Open the **E**dit menu and choose the **I**nsert command.

3. From the Insert menu, choose New **O**bject. The Insert New Object
dialog box appears (see fig. 29.16).

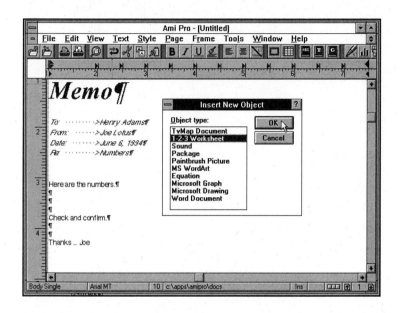

Fig. 29.16
The Insert New
Object dialog box.

4. Select 1-2-3 Worksheet in the list of object types. A frame for the embedded worksheet appears in the Ami Pro document, and the 1-2-3
window opens. If necessary, Windows starts the 1-2-3 application.
The 1-2-3 range will be resized to fit the frame.

5. Create the worksheet. Figure 29.17 shows a sample worksheet created in
1-2-3, ready to be embedded in Ami Pro.

6. In 1-2-3, open the **F**ile menu and choose the **U**pdate command. (You
can skip this step and proceed to step 7. After step 7, 1-2-3 asks whether
you want to update the link. Click Yes to proceed.)

7. Open the **F**ile menu and choose the E**x**it & Return command. The
worksheet appears in the frame in the Ami Pro document. You can
stretch the frame by dragging the right, bottom, or bottom-right
handle.

Figure 29.18 shows the frame sized properly in an Ami Pro page.

VI

Integrating 1-2-3

Fig. 29.17
A worksheet
created in 1-2-3.

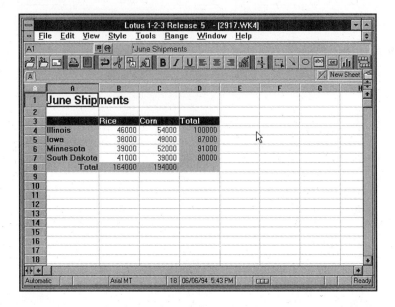

Fig. 29.18
The embedded
worksheet in the
Ami Pro page.

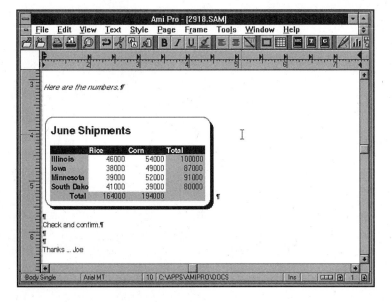

To edit the worksheet in 1-2-3, double-click the frame or select the frame and then press Enter. The 1-2-3 window reopens, showing the 1-2-3 worksheet. After you edit the 1-2-3 worksheet, open the **F**ile menu and choose the **U**pdate command; then, from the same menu, choose E**x**it & Return.

Embedding an Existing Object in an Ami Pro Document

If the 1-2-3 worksheet that you want to embed in Ami Pro already exists, follow these steps:

1. Open the worksheet in 1-2-3.

2. Select the range you want to embed in the Ami Pro document.

3. Open the **E**dit menu and choose the **C**opy command.

4. Switch to Ami Pro by pressing Alt+Tab or Ctrl+Esc.

5. Position the insertion point in the Ami Pro document where you want to place the embedded copy of the worksheet data.

6. Open the **E**dit menu and choose the Paste **S**pecial command. The Paste Special dialog box appears (see fig. 29.19).

Tip

While in 1-2-3, you can open the **F**ile menu and choose Save Copy **A**s File to save the worksheet you created as a separate file. This procedure enables you to use the worksheet outside Ami Pro later.

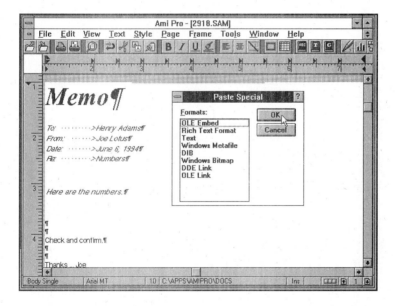

Fig. 29.19
The Paste Special dialog box.

7. From the list of formats, select OLE Embed. The worksheet range appears in an Ami Pro frame that can be resized and reformatted. Use the commands in the **F**rame menu to change the appearance of the frame.

To edit the 1-2-3 worksheet data, double-click the frame in Ami Pro or select the frame and press Enter. A 1-2-3 window opens, and the data is loaded automatically. After you make your changes, open the **F**ile menu and choose the **U**pdate command; then, from the same menu, choose the E**x**it & Return command to return to Ami Pro.

VI

Integrating 1-2-3

◀ "Using the Style Gallery," p. 353

Using a 1-2-3 Chart in an Ami Pro Document

Although Ami Pro's charting capabilities enable you to create a simple chart, you may want to make use of the superior charting capabilities of a program that is dedicated to chart making. If you have the entire Lotus SmartSuite of Windows applications, you can create sophisticated graphs in Freelance Graphics and copy them into Ami Pro documents. You even can link 1-2-3 data to a Freelance graph and then link the Freelance graph to an Ami Pro document. But if you do not have access to Freelance Graphics, you still can create professional-looking charts in 1-2-3 for Windows and use them in Ami Pro.

Tip

When you copy a chart from 1-2-3 for Windows to Ami Pro, any annotations that you drew in the chart with 1-2-3's drawing tools also are copied to Ami Pro. These objects or chart annotations must be grouped by using the **E**dit menu and selecting **A**rrange Group.

As usual, you can copy the charts from 1-2-3 to Ami Pro in one of three ways. The easiest is to perform a straight copy-and-paste operation by selecting the chart in 1-2-3, copying it to the Windows Clipboard, switching to Ami Pro, and then pasting the chart into the document. This method creates no link between the original 1-2-3 data and the chart in Ami Pro. To create a link, you must use either linking or embedding.

Linking a Chart

Use linking to copy a chart from 1-2-3 to Ami Pro when you want the Ami Pro file to remain on the current system, where it always has access to the 1-2-3 file in which you created the chart. When you link a chart from 1-2-3 to Ami Pro, the data remains in its original 1-2-3 worksheet file; only an image of the chart is copied to the Ami Pro file. To modify the chart, you must return to 1-2-3; any modifications to the 1-2-3 data automatically update the chart in Ami Pro, too.

To link a 1-2-3 chart to Ami Pro, follow these steps:

1. In 1-2-3, create and format the chart.

2. Save the worksheet file. This step is mandatory—you cannot link a chart if you have not saved it in a 1-2-3 worksheet file.

3. Click the chart's frame to select it, as shown in figure 29.20.

4. Open the **E**dit menu and choose the **C**opy command.

5. Switch to Ami Pro by pressing Alt+Tab or Ctrl+Esc.

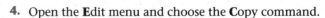

6. Position the insertion point in the Ami Pro document where you want the chart to appear.

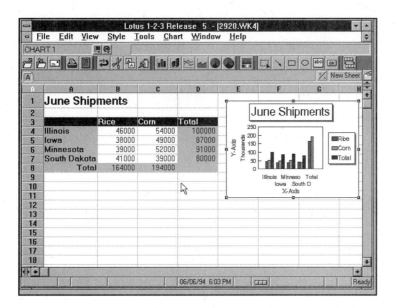

Fig. 29.20
A chart selected
in 1-2-3 for
Windows.

7. Open the **F**rame menu and choose the **C**reate Frame command to create a frame for the chart. The frame must remain selected. The DDE link will only work if the frame is selected.

8. Open the **E**dit menu and choose the Paste **L**ink command. The chart appears in the Ami Pro document, as shown in figure 29.21.

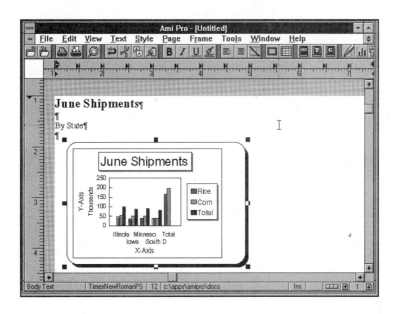

Fig. 29.21
A linked chart in
an Ami Pro
document.

Another way to link a chart is to create the chart in 1-2-3; select and copy it to the Windows Clipboard; switch to Ami Pro; and then open the **E**dit menu and choose the Paste **S**pecial command. When the Paste Special dialog box appears, select DDE Link or OLE Link from the list of formats. The DDE Link option copies the chart from 1-2-3 to Ami Pro and sets up an active link between the original and the copy. The OLE Link option performs the same action, but places the chart in an Ami Pro frame. You then can format the frame with the commands in the Ami Pro F**r**ame menu.

To edit the chart, you can manually switch to the 1-2-3 window and then modify the data, or you can double-click the chart in Ami Pro to switch back to 1-2-3 automatically.

When you save an Ami Pro document that contains a link to a 1-2-3 chart, the link information is saved in the Ami Pro document, but the data is saved in the 1-2-3 worksheet file. The next time you open the Ami Pro document, a message box asks whether you want to update the DDE links in the document. Click **Y**es to have Ami Pro read and reflect any changes to the data in the 1-2-3 worksheet file saved on disk. These updates will occur whether you created a DDE or OLE link. 1-2-3 does not have to be running (or even installed) for this update to occur, but the 1-2-3 worksheet file with the changes must be on your system. Click **N**o to have Ami Pro open the document and display the data as it existed the last time the Ami Pro document was saved. To update the link, open the **E**dit menu and choose the Link **O**ptions command, select the link in the Link Options dialog box, and then click **U**pdate.

Troubleshooting

*After I choose Paste **S**pecial to embed an object copied in another Windows application, why do so many formats appear in the list?*

When you copy an object to the Windows Clipboard, several different ways of representing the data are copied to the Clipboard simultaneously to ensure that the destination application will find a form of data in the Clipboard that it can accept. For example, when you copy a 1-2-3 table to the Clipboard, the numbers are copied to the Clipboard as text, as Rich Text in a table, and as a picture of the original 1-2-3 formatted table. If the destination application does not have the capability to edit numbers in a table, it can use the plain text or the picture of the 1-2-3 table instead.

Why did I get a `Cannot establish DDE link` *error message when linking a chart?*

You will receive a `Cannot establish DDE link, acceptable DDE format isn't available` message if you do not create and select a frame before choosing **E**dit Paste **L**ink.

Embedding a Chart

If you plan to transport the Ami Pro document to another computer (perhaps to copy it to a portable computer), you may want to embed a 1-2-3 chart in the document rather than link it. Embedding has the advantage of incorporating the chart data in the Ami Pro file so that you do not need access to the data in the original worksheet if the chart must be updated. You do need access to 1-2-3 on the destination computer to make any changes to the chart, however.

Think of embedding this way: Embedding places the chart data in Ami Pro, along with the information that the chart was created in 1-2-3. As long as 1-2-3 is available on the system, you can edit the chart. Double-clicking the chart transfers the data to the copy of 1-2-3 on the current system only long enough for you to use 1-2-3's commands to modify the data. Then the data and revised chart return to Ami Pro, where the chart is displayed.

You can embed a 1-2-3 chart in Ami Pro in either of two ways.

If you have created the chart in 1-2-3 and saved it in a worksheet file, follow these steps:

1. In 1-2-3, click the chart's frame to select it.

2. Open the **E**dit menu and choose the **C**opy command.

3. Switch to Ami Pro by pressing Alt+Tab or Ctrl+Esc.

4. Position the insertion point in the Ami Pro document where you want the chart to appear.

5. Open the **E**dit menu and choose the Paste **S**pecial command. The Paste Special dialog box appears (see fig. 29.22).

6. From the list of formats, select OLE Embed. The chart appears in a frame in the Ami Pro document.

To edit the chart, double-click the frame, or select the frame and then press Enter. The 1-2-3 window opens, displaying the data for the chart. Edit the data; open the **F**ile menu and choose the **U**pdate command to update the chart in Ami Pro; then open the **F**ile menu and choose the E**x**it & Return command to leave 1-2-3 and return to Ami Pro.

VI

Integrating 1-2-3

Fig. 29.22
The Paste Special
dialog box in
Ami Pro.

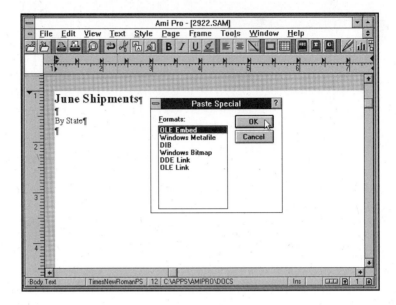

If you have not created the chart and want to create it on the fly, follow these
steps:

1. In 1-2-3, open the **E**dit menu and choose the **I**nsert command.

2. From the pop-out menu, choose New **O**bject.

3. Select 1-2-3 Worksheet from the list of object types that appears.

4. When the 1-2-3 window opens, enter the data you need and create
the chart.

5. Open the **F**ile menu and choose the **U**pdate command.

6. Open the **F**ile menu and choose the E**x**it & Return command to
return to Ami Pro.

When you use this method, a snapshot of the 1-2-3 worksheet is embedded
in Ami Pro, including both the data you entered and the chart you created.
By arranging the data and the chart in the 1-2-3 worksheet before you return
to Ami Pro, you can get an attractive display of both the 1-2-3 chart and the
data that it portrays.

Embedding an Ami Pro Document in a 1-2-3 Worksheet

◀ "Creating Charts," p. 385

With object linking, you can link selected text from an Ami Pro document to a 1-2-3 cell so that any changes to the text are reflected in the 1-2-3 file automatically. But copying and pasting selected text from Ami Pro to 1-2-3 probably is just as helpful. Text in an Ami Pro document is less likely to be updated regularly (unlike a table of numbers in 1-2-3, which may be updated frequently—perhaps even hourly or daily).

You may find it more useful to embed, rather than link, an entire Ami Pro document in a 1-2-3 worksheet file. The document can provide a report on a particular aspect of the data in the 1-2-3 worksheet or add background information that can help another user interpret the worksheet.

When you embed an Ami Pro document in a 1-2-3 file, an Ami Pro icon (the same icon that you double-click in the Windows Program Manager to start Ami Pro) appears in a worksheet cell. Double-clicking the Ami Pro icon in a 1-2-3 file opens Ami Pro so that you can read or print the Ami Pro document information embedded in the 1-2-3 file. To use the embedded Ami Pro information, you do not need the original Ami Pro document file on the system; you do need Ami Pro, however, so that you can use the document information embedded in the worksheet.

To embed an Ami Pro document, you can copy an existing document to 1-2-3 and use the **E**dit menu's Paste **S**pecial command, or you can use the Ami Pro **E**dit menu's **I**nsert New **O**bject command to temporarily use Ami Pro to create an embedded object. Either way, an Ami Pro icon appears in the worksheet. Double-clicking the icon loads the document in Ami Pro.

Embedding an Existing Ami Pro Document in 1-2-3

To embed an existing Ami Pro document in a 1-2-3 worksheet, follow these steps:

1. Make sure that the document is saved in an Ami Pro file.

2. Select any portion of the document. (You can select as little as a single character.) Figure 29.23 shows a document with a small portion of text selected.

Fig. 29.23
A portion of text selected in an Ami Pro document.

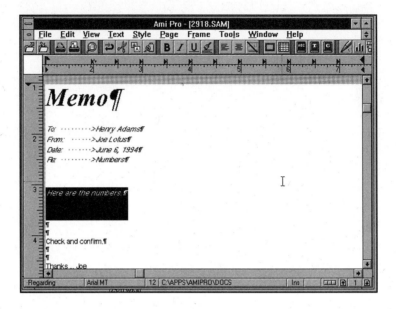

3. Open the **E**dit menu and choose the **C**opy command.

4. Switch to 1-2-3 for Windows by pressing Alt+Tab or Ctrl+Esc.

5. Position the cell pointer near the data you want to document with the Ami Pro text.

6. Open the **E**dit menu and choose the Paste **S**pecial command. The Paste Special dialog box appears.

7. From the list of Clipboard formats, select Ami Pro Document Object.

8. Click the **P**aste button to embed the Ami Pro document object. An Ami Pro icon appears in the 1-2-3 worksheet, as shown in figure 29.24.

The Ami Pro icon appears at a fairly large size and in a designer frame. You can reduce the size of the icon by dragging a corner handle toward the center of the icon. You also can remove the designer frame by following these steps:

1. In 1-2-3, select the icon.

2. Open the **S**tyle menu and choose the **L**ines & Color command.

3. In the Lines & Color dialog box, click the **D**esigner Frame check box to turn off the frame.

4. Click OK.

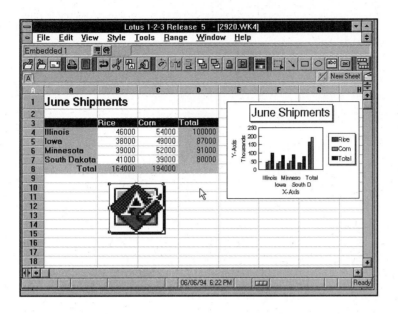

Fig. 29.24
An Ami Pro icon
embedded in a
1-2-3 worksheet
appears in a
shadowed
designer frame.

A simple icon without a designer frame appears in the worksheet, as shown in figure 29.25. The icon in this figure also has been manually sized to make it smaller.

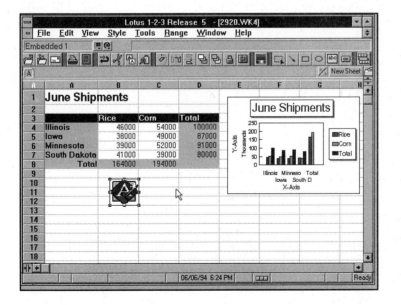

Fig. 29.25
A small icon
without a designer
frame.

Creating and Embedding an Ami Pro Document from within 1-2-3

The second method of embedding Ami Pro documents in 1-2-3 worksheets is to create a new Ami Pro document on the fly, so that the document is embedded in the 1-2-3 worksheet you are working on.

In the following exercise, you create a small 1-2-3 worksheet that tracks the profits for a business over four quarters. Unfortunately, expenses seem to be rising at a faster rate than sales, and profits have slipped. This phenomenon has been ably explained in an Ami Pro report. Before you send the 1-2-3 worksheet containing the numbers to the members of the board, you decide to embed the explanatory Ami Pro letter, so that the board members can read it after seeing the apparently gloomy picture depicted by the data.

To begin, follow these steps:

1. Create the small worksheet shown in figure 29.26. Type the labels and values in the cells, create the formulas that subtract expenses from sales, and then open the **S**tyle menu and choose the **G**allery command. When the Gallery dialog box appears, select the B&W3 template.

Fig. 29.26
The 1-2-3 worksheet, showing falling profits.

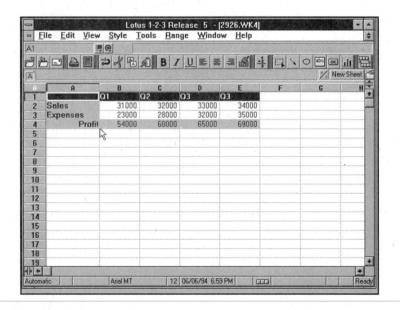

2. Type **Note:** in cell A6 to help the reader understand that the icon you will place next to the word Note: leads to a written explanation of something in the worksheet. Your next task is to use Ami Pro to create the explanatory letter.

3. Switch to Ami Pro by pressing Alt+Tab or Ctrl+Esc.

4. Create a new document, and then type the following explanatory text:

> **The opening of 17 new branch locations contributed heavily to our expenses during the past year.**

For this example, leave the simple message at that. But you also could enter a multipage, detailed report on the expenses incurred for the 17 new branch offices. Although the sample message is much shorter than such a report, the result is the same.

5. Save the Ami Pro file.

6. Select any of the text in the file, as shown in figure 29.27. You can select as little as a single character, but at least some (if not all) text must be selected.

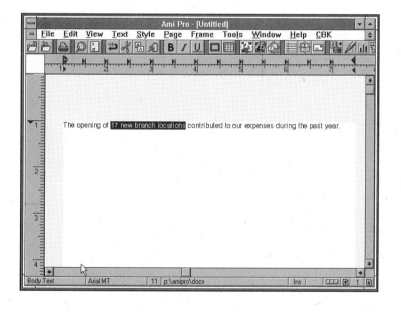

Fig. 29.27
Selecting text in the Ami Pro document.

7. Open the **E**dit menu and choose the **C**opy command.

8. Switch to 1-2-3 for Windows by pressing Alt+Tab or Ctrl+Esc.

9. Position the cell pointer in cell B6.

10. Open the **E**dit menu and choose the Paste **S**pecial command.

11. From the list of Clipboard formats in the Paste Special dialog box, select Ami Pro Document Object.

12. Click the **P**aste button. A large Ami Pro icon appears, as shown in figure 29.28.

Fig. 29.28
The Ami Pro icon that appears in 1-2-3 for Windows.

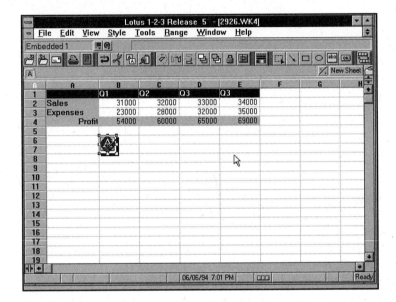

13. Use the icon's handles to reduce the icon's size; then drag the icon to position it next to Note: in cell A6. (You also can remove the designer frame from the icon, as you learned in the preceding section.)

To access the note from within 1-2-3, double-click the Ami Pro icon. The Ami Pro window reopens, with the note text loaded. After you read the text, open the **F**ile menu and choose the E**x**it & Return command to close the Ami Pro window. Then switch back to the 1-2-3 window manually.

 The alternative to using the **C**opy and Paste **S**pecial commands to embed an Ami Pro document in a 1-2-3 worksheet is to create the worksheet in 1-2-3 and then open the **E**dit menu and choose the Insert **O**bject command. When the Insert Object dialog box appears, select Ami Pro Document as the **O**bject Type and then click OK. The Ami Pro window opens. Type the note you want to embed in 1-2-3, and then open the **F**ile menu and choose the **U**pdate command. To finish and return to 1-2-3, open the **F**ile menu and choose the E**x**it & Return command. You return to the 1-2-3 window, where an Ami Pro icon representing the embedded document is in place.

Incorporating a Freelance Graphics Logo into a 1-2-3 Worksheet

Freelance Graphics for Windows, also from Lotus Development Corporation, is an easy-to-use but full-featured presentation-graphics application. Freelance makes creating professional-looking presentation handouts, overheads, transparencies, and slides simple and straightforward. In a single file, you can create a series of presentation pages, some with text and some with graphics, organization, and table charts.

Although Freelance excels at creating entire presentations, it also offers a comprehensive set of drawing tools and clip-art pictures you can use to create diagrams, designs, and logos. These tools surpass 1-2-3 for Windows basic drawing tools. Because Freelance is a Windows application, you easily can transfer a logo drawn in Freelance to a 1-2-3 worksheet. In addition to copying a drawn object to 1-2-3, you even can embed an entire Freelance presentation in a worksheet (a topic covered later in this chapter).

To transfer a logo drawn in Freelance to a 1-2-3 worksheet, complete the logo in Freelance, select the logo, and then open the **E**dit menu and choose the **C**opy command. After you switch to 1-2-3, place the cell pointer where you want to insert the logo, and then open the **E**dit menu and choose the **P**aste command. You can move and resize the logo and print it just as it appears in the worksheet.

> **Note**
>
> In Freelance, you cannot create an OLE link between a Freelance logo and a 1-2-3 worksheet; you can only copy and paste the logo. That's because Freelance does not permit you to select only certain items in a presentation page to link or embed to other applications. You must link the entire presentation page to another application.

Copying and Pasting the Freelance Logo into 1-2-3 for Windows

Following are the steps for transferring a logo from Freelance Graphics to 1-2-3:

1. Create the logo in Freelance. You do not have to save the file, because you do not create an OLE link.

2. Select the logo. Use the **Arrange Group** menu command to group the drawing objects that comprise the logo into one object. (A grouped object is easier to select.) Figure 29.29 shows a selected logo in Freelance.

Fig. 29.29
A logo selected in Freelance.

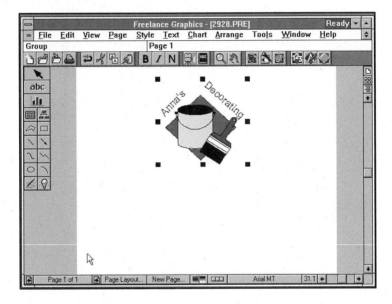

3. Open the **Edit** menu and choose the **Copy** command.

4. Switch to 1-2-3 for Windows by pressing Alt+Tab or Ctrl+Esc.

5. Place the cell pointer where you want to insert the logo.

6. Open the **Edit** menu and choose the **Paste** command. The logo appears in a worksheet cell.

Tip
You can resize the logo proportionally (change its size without changing its shape) by holding down the Shift key as you drag a corner handle.

To resize the logo, click a corner handle and drag diagonally. To reposition the logo, drag it to a new position. After it is resized, the logo appears as shown in figure 29.30.

The logo may appear in a 1-2-3 frame. To remove the frame, select the frame, and then open the **Style** menu and choose the **Lines & Color** command. To remove the frame, set the Edge Line Style to None. The logo appears as a free-floating object in the 1-2-3 worksheet.

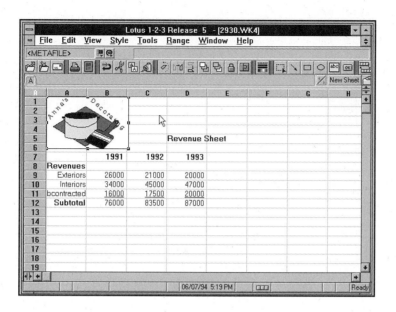

Fig. 29.30
The logo placed
and resized in a
1-2-3 worksheet.

The following exercise creates a simple logo in Freelance Graphics and copies it to a 1-2-3 worksheet. In this exercise, you create the logo for Lola's Pet Care and place it next to the title of a small worksheet that analyzes Lola's breakdown of revenue by animal type.

1. Open Freelance Graphics for Windows.

   In the Welcome to Freelance Graphics dialog box, select Create a New Presentation and click OK. The Choose a Look for Your Presentation dialog box appears.

2. Check the SmartMaster with Blank Background check box (this action selects a clear background design for the page), and then click OK. The Choose Page Layout dialog box appears.

3. Select [None] from the list of page layouts to get a clear page (a page without Click Here blocks). Click OK to continue.

4. In the toolbox at the left edge of the window, choose the Symbol tool (a light bulb). The Add Symbol to Page dialog box appears. From the list of symbol categories, select ANIMALS.SYM. Click the symbol of a reclining lion, and then click OK to transfer the symbol to the page. The symbol appears as shown in figure 29.31.

Fig. 29.31

The symbol placed on the page.

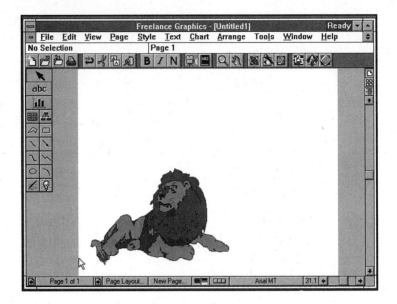

5. In the toolbox, click the Text tool (the letters *abc*). Click the page just above the lion, and type **Lola's Pet Care, Inc.** Click the OK button that is part of the text-entry box. The text appears on the page.

6. Open the **T**ext menu and choose the **F**ont command. The Font dialog box appears. Select Arial MT as the face and 48 as the point size; select **B**old as an attribute. Click OK to see the changes in the text on the page.

7. To complete the logo, open the **T**ext menu and choose the Cur**v**ed Text command. Select the first shape at the upper-left corner (this shape starts the text at the 9 o'clock position), and then click OK.

8. Select and drag the curved text to surround the lion's head, as shown in figure 29.32.

Now you can select both drawing objects that make up the logo and copy them to the Windows Clipboard. Follow these steps:

1. Click the text, press and hold down the Shift key, and click the lion symbol. Both drawing objects should be selected.

2. (Optional) Open the **A**rrange menu and choose the **G**roup command to group the two drawing objects as one object.

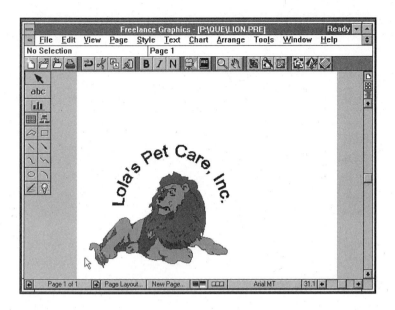

Fig. 29.32
The completed
logo.

3. Open the **E**dit menu and choose the **C**opy command to copy the
objects to the Windows Clipboard.

If you plan to use Lola's logo again, save it in a Freelance file; if not, close or
minimize the Freelance window. Open a 1-2-3 window so that you can finish
this exercise by following these steps:

1. In the 1-2-3 window, reproduce the small worksheet shown in
figure 29.33.

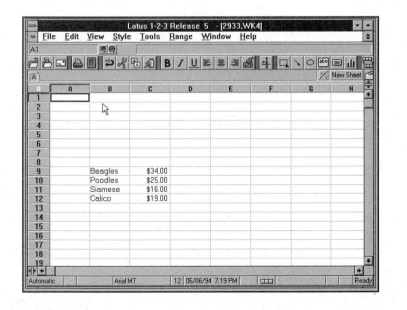

Fig. 29.33
The revenue-
breakdown
worksheet for
Lola's Pet Care.

VI

Integrating 1-2-3

2. Place the cell pointer in cell A1.

3. Open the **E**dit menu and choose the **P**aste command. The logo appears in cell A1 of the 1-2-3 worksheet.

4. Drag the lower-right handle of the frame surrounding the logo to resize the logo. Figure 29.34 shows the result.

Fig. 29.34
The logo copied
to the 1-2-3
worksheet.

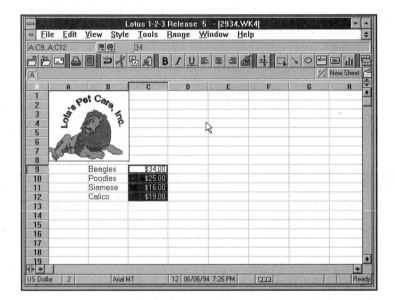

◀ "Formatting
Worksheets,"
p. 311

Embedding a Freelance Presentation in a 1-2-3 Worksheet

By copying and pasting a logo from Freelance to 1-2-3, you can transfer a single graphic image. But you also can embed an entire Freelance presentation as an object in a 1-2-3 worksheet file. Using this technique, you can embed a series of pages, containing a mix of text and graphics, that can explain the results shown in a worksheet file. While working in 1-2-3, you can double-click the presentation object to open Freelance and view the presentation.

To embed a Freelance presentation, you can create the Freelance presentation and then use the 1-2-3 **E**dit menu's Paste **S**pecial command to paste the presentation into 1-2-3 as an embedded object. Alternatively, you can open the 1-2-3 **E**dit menu's Insert **O**bject command to create an embedded presentation. Use the first method to embed an existing presentation in a 1-2-3 worksheet; use the second method to create and embed a Freelance presentation on the fly, as you work in 1-2-3.

Embedding an Existing Presentation

To embed an existing Freelance presentation, follow these steps:

1. Create the presentation in Freelance, and save it as a file.

2. Click the Page Sorter icon at the right edge of the Freelance window, or select **V**iew **P**age Sorter from the menu to view the presentation in Page Sorter view. You must use Page Sorter view to select the single page to be displayed in 1-2-3, even though the entire presentation will be embedded in 1-2-3.

3. Select the page you want to appear in 1-2-3. (The data for the entire presentation also is copied to 1-2-3.) Figure 29.35 shows a presentation in Page Sorter view with the title page selected.

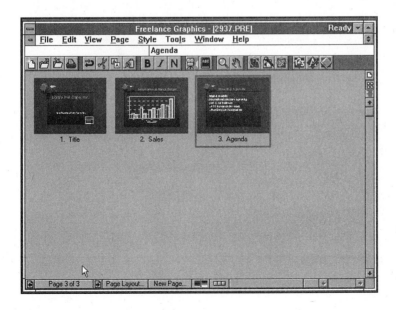

Fig. 29.35
A Freelance presentation in Page Sorter view.

4. Open the **E**dit menu and choose the **C**opy command.

5. Switch to 1-2-3 for Windows by pressing Alt+Tab or Ctrl+Esc.

6. Place the cell pointer in the cell where the presentation object should appear.

7. Open the **E**dit menu and choose the Paste **S**pecial command. The Paste Special dialog box appears.

8. Select Freelance Presentation Object, and then click the **P**aste button. The selected page of the presentation appears in the worksheet, as shown in figure 29.36. Use the handles to resize and reposition the page.

Fig. 29.36

The presentation embedded in 1-2-3.

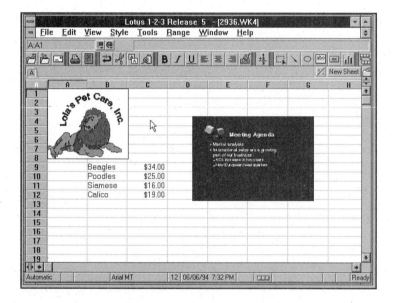

To open the Freelance window and view the presentation at any time, double-click the presentation page in the 1-2-3 worksheet.

Caution

Because all the Freelance presentation data is embedded in the 1-2-3 worksheet file, the worksheet file grows considerably larger. The advantage of embedding the presentation is that you can transfer the worksheet to another computer and view the presentation there (as long as Freelance Graphics for Windows exists on the other computer) without also transporting the Freelance presentation file.

Creating an Embedded Freelance Presentation from within 1-2-3

While working in a 1-2-3 worksheet, you can temporarily switch to Freelance Graphics long enough to create a presentation. When you return to 1-2-3, the Freelance presentation and its data are embedded in the worksheet. From within 1-2-3, you can view the Freelance presentation—complete with charts, tables, graphics, sound, and animation—by double-clicking the presentation page that appears in 1-2-3.

Preparing the Worksheet

To create an embedded Freelance presentation from within a 1-2-3 worksheet, follow these steps:

1. Position the cell pointer in the 1-2-3 worksheet where you want the presentation object to appear. (The embedded presentation will be represented by the display of a page from the presentation.)

2. Open the **E**dit menu and choose the Insert **O**bject command. The Insert Object dialog box appears.

3. Select Freelance Presentation as the **O**bject Type, and then click OK.

4. When the Freelance window opens, create the presentation pages as you normally would.

5. Open the **F**ile menu and choose the **U**pdate 123W command.

6. Open the **F**ile menu and choose the E**x**it & Return to 123W command to return to 1-2-3 and embed the completed presentation.

Creating a Presentation

The following example gives you the chance to embed a Freelance presentation in a 1-2-3 worksheet. Although you create a presentation of only two pages, the same procedure works if the presentation is dozens of pages long. To begin, open Freelance and follow these steps:

1. In the Welcome to Freelance Graphics dialog box, select **C**reate a New Presentation, and then click OK. The Choose a Look for Your Presentation dialog box appears.

2. Select the BLOCKS.MAS SmartMaster set, and then click OK. The Choose Page Layout dialog box appears.

3. Select the Title page layout, and then click OK.

4. Click the Click Here To Type Presentation Title block and type **Lola's Expansion Plans**.

5. Press the down-arrow key to move to the next Click Here block.

6. Type **1994 and Beyond**, and then click OK. Because you don't add a symbol to the title page, you can ignore the Click Here To Add Symbol block, which will appear in Freelance while you create the presentation but not when you view the presentation later. Figure 29.37 shows the completed title page.

Fig. 29.37

The completed title page.

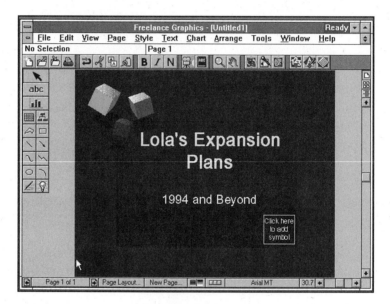

To create a second presentation page, follow these steps:

1. Click the New Page button at the bottom of the Freelance window. The New Page dialog box appears.

2. Select the Bulleted List page layout, and then click OK.

3. Click the Click Here To Type Page Title block, and type **Expansion Plans**.

4. Press the down-arrow key to move to the first bullet point.

5. Type the following list of bulleted text points, pressing Enter after each; click OK to complete the list:

> **Pet grooming service**
>
> **Pet sitting service**
>
> **Chain of retail pet supply stores**

Figure 29.38 shows the completed bulleted list page.

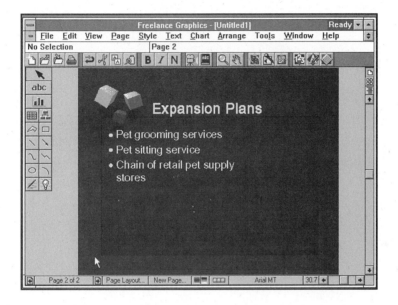

Fig. 29.38
The completed
bulleted-list page.

6. Click the Page Sorter icon at the right edge of the Freelance window to switch to Page Sorter view.

7. Select the title page by clicking it. The selected page is the one that displays when the presentation object is embedded in 1-2-3. To see the second page when you view the presentation, click the title page that appears in 1-2-3. Figure 29.39 shows the presentation with the title page selected in Page Sorter view.

Fig. 29.39
The presentation
with the title page
selected in Page
Sorter view.

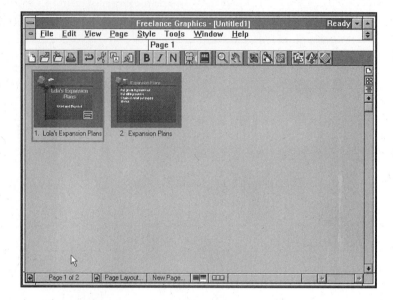

8. Open the **E**dit menu and choose the **C**opy command to copy the presentation to the Windows Clipboard.

9. Switch to 1-2-3 for Windows by pressing Alt+Tab or Ctrl+Esc.

Embedding the Presentation

In 1-2-3, you embed the presentation in the Windows Clipboard into a worksheet. Begin by following these steps:

1. Create the small sample worksheet shown in figure 29.40.

2. Position the cell pointer in a blank cell to the right of the worksheet title.

3. Open the **E**dit menu and choose the Paste **S**pecial command. The Paste Special dialog box appears.

4. Select Freelance Presentation Object, and then click the **P**aste button. The title page of the Freelance presentation appears in the 1-2-3 worksheet (see fig. 29.41). You can resize and reposition the page by dragging its handles.

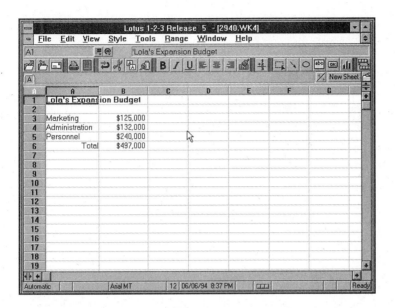

Fig. 29.40
The sample 1-2-3
worksheet.

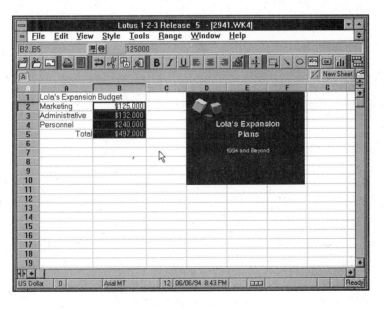

Fig. 29.41
The Lola presenta-
tion embedded in
a 1-2-3 worksheet.

To view the presentation from within 1-2-3, double-click the presentation
page in the 1-2-3 window. The Freelance Graphics window opens, with the
presentation loaded. Page through the presentation, using the page arrow
keys in the bottom status bar. To return to 1-2-3, open the File menu and
choose the Exit & Return to 123W command.

VI

Integrating 1-2-3

Troubleshooting

How do I embed a single object or group of objects from a Freelance page in 1-2-3?

You must embed an entire presentation. To transfer a single object, you can use the **E**dit menu's **C**opy and **P**aste commands to transfer the object, or you can link the object to 1-2-3.

When I create a logo in Freelance that I will use often in 1-2-3 worksheets, is there a way to save the logo in a readily accessible place?

In Freelance, you can copy the logo to the Windows Clipboard and then save the Clipboard contents as a CLP file on disk (by starting the Clipboard Accessory and then using the **F**ile menu's Save **A**s command). To get the logo, start the Clipboard from the Windows Program Manager and use the **F**ile menu's **O**pen command to retrieve the logo to the Clipboard; then you can switch to 1-2-3 and paste the logo into the worksheet. You may find it easier and faster to retrieve the logo from the Windows Clipboard than to open Freelance. In addition, you can copy the CLP file to any computer, whether or not Freelance is installed on it, and use the logo in Windows applications.

Using 1-2-3 Data in a Freelance Graphics Chart

The graphing capabilities of 1-2-3 for Windows are sophisticated enough that you may feel no need to use a separate graphics program like Freelance Graphics. But you may want to incorporate data from a 1-2-3 for Windows worksheet into a presentation you are preparing in Freelance. If so, you will find it easy to transport the data from 1-2-3 to Freelance and easy to set up an OLE link between the two programs.

If you need to copy data from a worksheet to a Freelance chart and have no concern about whether the chart is updated if the 1-2-3 data changes, a straightforward copy-and-paste operation through the Windows Clipboard can do the job. After selecting the range of data in 1-2-3, **C**opy the range to the Windows Clipboard, and then switch to the Chart Data & Titles window of a Freelance chart. There, use **P**aste to retrieve the data from the Windows Clipboard. This procedure performs a one-time-only transfer of the data and does not set up a link.

When you use the copy-and-paste method, the data in 1-2-3 must be arranged the same way you want it to appear in the Chart Data & Titles window. The data sets that you represent with lines or sets of bars must be arranged in columns, rather than rows, in the worksheet. Figure 29.42 shows a worksheet range that can be copied to Freelance easily, because the numbers for each town are arranged in a column. Figure 29.43 shows the same worksheet with the numbers for each town arranged in rows. In this worksheet, you must perform an additional procedure to transpose the rows and columns.

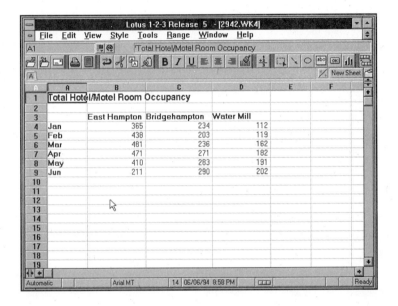

Fig. 29.42

An easily imported worksheet, with sequences of data arranged in columns.

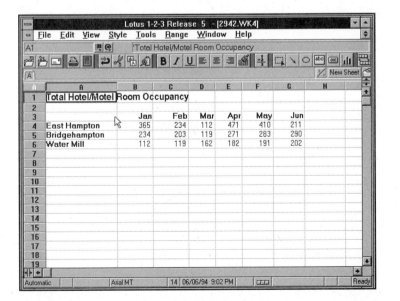

Fig. 29.43

The same sequences of data arranged in worksheet rows.

Copying 1-2-3 Data to a Freelance Chart

When data sets are arranged in worksheet columns and you do not need to create a link, follow this procedure to use 1-2-3 data in a Freelance chart:

1. Open the 1-2-3 worksheet that contains the data.

2. Select the range of data you want to copy to a Freelance Graphics chart, such as range A3..D9 in figure 29.44. Include the column and row headers in the selected range.

Fig. 29.44

A selected 1-2-3 range to copy to Freelance.

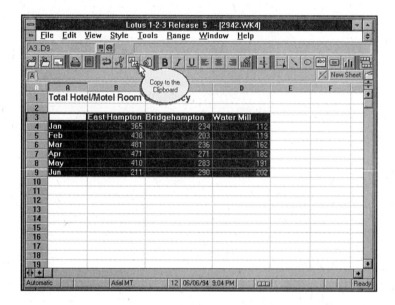

3. Open the **E**dit menu and choose the **C**opy command.

4. Switch to Freelance Graphics for Windows by pressing Alt+Tab or Ctrl+Esc.

5. Start a chart by clicking a Click Here To Create Chart block or by clicking the Chart icon in the toolbox. After you select a chart type and style, the Chart Data & Titles window opens (see fig. 29.45).

6. Position the mouse pointer in the Chart Data & Titles window where you want the data to appear. If you have selected the column and row headings in 1-2-3, place the pointer in the gray cell at the top of the Axis Labels column and at the left end of the Legend row (just outside the upper-left corner of the white data area, as shown in fig. 29.45). If you have selected only the data, without selecting the column and row headings, place the mouse pointer in the first blank cell.

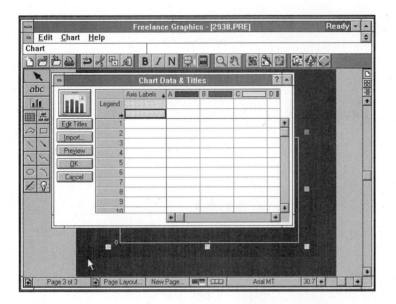

Fig. 29.45
The Chart Data &
Titles window for
a Freelance chart.

7. Open the **E**dit menu and choose the **P**aste command. Figure 29.46
   shows the data pasted in the Chart Data & Titles window.

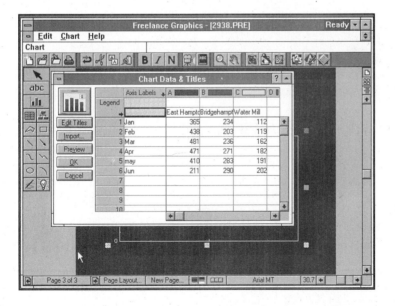

Fig. 29.46
The 1-2-3 data
pasted in the
Chart Data &
Titles window.

8. Click the E**d**it Titles button to add titles to the chart; click and hold the Pre**v**iew button to preview the chart; or click OK to place the chart in the presentation page. Figure 29.47 shows a stacked bar chart created from the data in the Chart Data & Titles window.

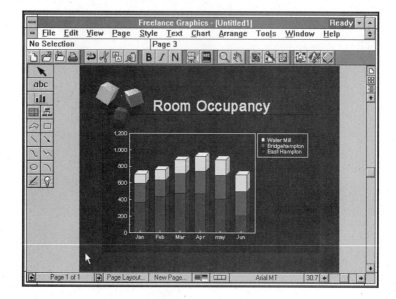

Fig. 29.47

A stacked bar created from the 1-2-3 data pasted in the Chart Data & Titles window.

Linking or Transposing 1-2-3 Data for a Freelance Chart

If you have to transpose the rows and columns of data in 1-2-3 before you can use them in the Freelance graph, or if you want to link the 1-2-3 and Freelance data, you must use the Freelance E**d**it menu's P**a**ste Special command to retrieve the data from the Windows Clipboard. Verify that the 1-2-3 data is coming from a normal (not untitled) file, otherwise Paste Special will not work.

After selecting a range in 1-2-3 and copying it to the Windows Clipboard with 1-2-3's **C**opy command, switch to an open Chart Data & Titles window in Freelance; then open the **E**dit menu and choose the P**a**ste Special command. The Edit Paste Special window opens, as shown in figure 29.48.

Freelance recognizes that the data in the Windows Clipboard is a range of data from 1-2-3 for Windows; in the Edit Paste Special dialog box, Freelance presents options for importing the data.

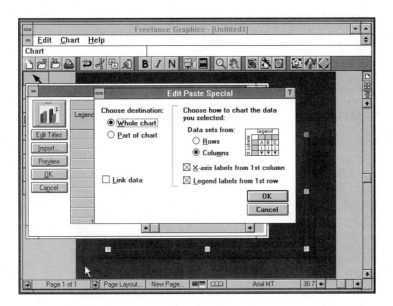

Fig. 29.48
The Edit Paste
Special window in
Freelance.

If the selected 1-2-3 range is the complete set of data for the chart, choose **W**hole Chart. A set of options at the right of the dialog box enables you to specify whether the data sets in the 1-2-3 data are arranged in rows or columns. If the data sets are arranged in columns, Freelance imports them as they are to the Chart Data & Titles window. If the data sets are arranged in rows, Freelance transposes the rows and columns before importing them.

Two check boxes in the Edit Paste Special dialog box enable you to indicate whether you included the column and row headings in the 1-2-3 range and whether you want to include them as x-axis labels or legend entries in the Freelance Chart Data & Titles window. To create a link between the 1-2-3 data and the Freelance chart, click the **L**ink Data check box. If a link exists, the 1-2-3 data in the Freelance chart is updated automatically.

If you select a 1-2-3 range that contains only part of the data for a chart—perhaps a single data set—choose **P**art of Chart in the Edit Paste Special dialog box. The dialog box displays a list of chart parts. Select one of these parts to specify where the 1-2-3 range goes in the Chart Data & Titles window. If you want to copy a data set with the **P**art of Chart option, you must type the legend or axis-label data; only the **W**hole Chart option automatically imports x-axis titles and legend entries. Figure 29.49 shows the Edit Paste Special dialog box when you choose **P**art of Chart.

VI

Integrating 1-2-3

Fig. 29.49
The Edit Paste
Special dialog box
when **P**art of
Chart is selected.

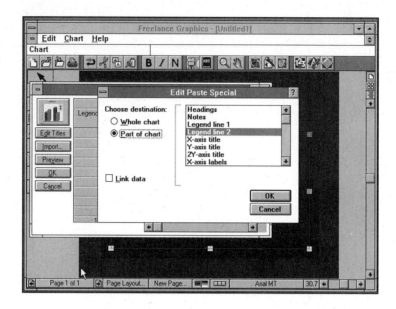

You can use the **P**art of Chart option when you want to import only a portion of a 1-2-3 worksheet. You can select a single series of numbers in 1-2-3
and then select a data set from the list in the Edit Paste Special dialog box.
The set of numbers is imported to that data set. You also can import only axis
titles, legend entries, and chart headings and notes by selecting them in 1-2-3
and then choosing the appropriate chart part from the list.

> **Note**
>
> Because the **P**art of Chart option enables you to pull selected data into a selected
> portion of a chart, you can use the option to consolidate sets of numbers from vari-
> ous 1-2-3 worksheets. You can select a range in one worksheet and then use **P**art of
> Chart to paste it into data set A. Then you can select a range in a different worksheet
> and use **P**art of Chart to paste it into data set B, and so on.

When you use the **P**art of Chart option, you can click the **L**ink Data check
box to set a link between the range in 1-2-3 and the selected part of the chart.
In one chart, therefore, you can have active links to several different ranges
in several different worksheets. Changes to any of the worksheets are reflected in the Freelance chart.

Linking Data from Several 1-2-3 Worksheets

In this exercise, you import a range from a 1-2-3 worksheet into a Freelance
chart. Then you add a range from a different worksheet and set up links between the data in 1-2-3 and the Freelance chart.

Begin by creating the small 1-2-3 worksheet shown in figure 29.50, and save it in a file. Then select the column and row headings, as well as the numeric data in range A6..D9 (see fig. 29.51). Do not include the cells at the bottom of the worksheet that contain calculations.

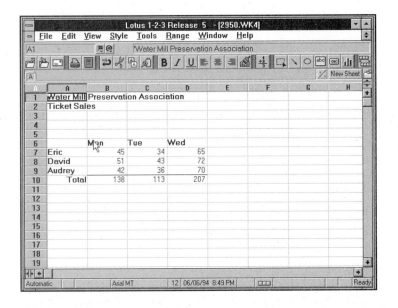

Fig. 29.50
The sample worksheet with data to be graphed in Freelance.

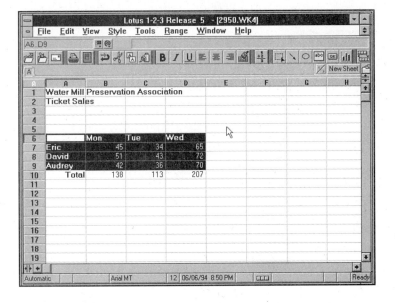

Fig. 29.51
The data selected in the 1-2-3 worksheet.

Open the **E**dit menu and choose the **C**opy command to copy the range to the Windows Clipboard. Then switch to Freelance Graphics and create a chart by following these steps:

1. In the Welcome to Freelance Graphics window that opens when you start Freelance, choose **C**reate a New Presentation, and then click OK. The Choose a Look for Your Presentation dialog box appears.

2. Select the 3LINE.MAS SmartMaster set, and then click OK. The Choose Page Layout dialog box appears.

3. Select the 1 Chart page layout, and then click OK.

4. Click the Click Here To Create Chart block. The New Chart Gallery dialog box appears.

5. Select **3**D Bar, and then click OK. (Do not change the selected chart style.) The Chart Data & Titles window opens.

6. Place the cursor in the lower of the two gray cells at the upper-left corner of the data area.

Now you use the **Pa**ste Special command to import the data from 1-2-3 and create a link. Because each individual's numbers are arranged in a row in the 1-2-3 data, you use the controls in the Edit Paste Special dialog box to transpose the data so that each row of numbers in 1-2-3 appears in a column in the Freelance Chart Data & Titles window. As a result, each set of numbers is represented by a set of bars of the same color. The legend indicates which person is represented by each color. To use **Pa**ste Special, follow these steps:

1. Open the **E**dit menu and choose the **Pa**ste Special command. The Edit Paste Special dialog box appears.

2. Select **W**hole Chart to tell Freelance to import all the data in the Windows Clipboard as a complete set of data for a chart.

3. Select **R**ows to specify that the data in 1-2-3 is arranged in rows.

4. Make sure that the **X**-Axis Labels From 1st Row and **L**egend Labels From 1st Column check boxes are checked, so that the row and column headings in the 1-2-3 data will be imported into the Legend and Axis Label cells of the Chart Data & Titles window.

5. Click the **L**ink Data check box to set up a DDE link between the 1-2-3 data and the Freelance chart.

6. Click OK. The data is imported into the Chart Data & Titles window. Notice that the rows and columns have been transposed, as shown in

figure 29.52. The blue underlines in the Chart Data & Titles window indicate that it contains linked data.

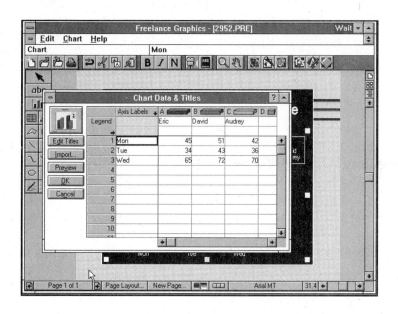

Fig. 29.52
The data after importing.

To see the chart that results from this data, click and hold the Pre**v**iew button. After you see the chart, release the Pre**v**iew button to return to the Chart Data & Titles window.

To complete the chart, you need to add one more person's information. That person's data is kept in a different worksheet. Switch to the 1-2-3 window, take a moment to create a new 1-2-3 worksheet, and enter the data shown in figure 29.53.

Select only the numbers (do not include the row heading in cell A3); then open the **E**dit menu and choose the **C**opy command to copy the selected range to the Windows Clipboard. Switch back to Freelance, and follow these steps:

1. Open the **E**dit menu and choose the P**a**ste Special command. The Edit Paste Special dialog box appears.

2. Choose **P**art of Chart, and then select Data Set D from the list of chart parts.

3. Make sure that the **L**ink Data check box is checked.

4. Click OK.

Fig. 29.53

The data for one last person.

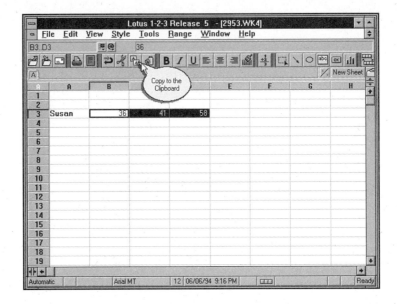

To complete the chart, type the name **Susan** in the Legend cell at the top of Data Set D (in the cell to the right of Audrey). To see the chart that results from this addition, click OK. Figure 29.54 shows the finished chart.

Fig. 29.54

The completed Freelance chart.

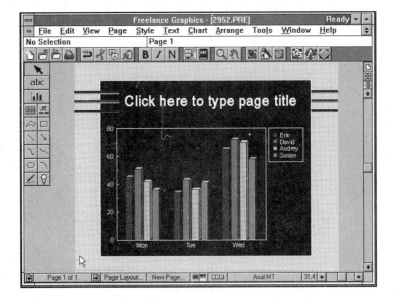

Using 1-2-3 with Approach

Approach for Windows 2.1, the newest member of the Lotus SmartSuite, is an easy-to-use, full-featured database management application. Approach is a relational database application that promotes versatility and end-user friendliness. With Approach, you can design data-entry forms, create reports, and maintain various views of important data.

Approach does not work directly in a database file; instead, the program uses a view file to create a *picture* of the data. Approach supports a variety of different database file formats so that you can exchange data freely. The easiest way to take advantage of this is simply to open database files created in other database applications, such as Paradox and dBASE. Approach supports object linking and formatting. You can add graphics, charts, and text created in other applications to your Approach forms, reports, and views. These object elements remain linked to their server applications so that they are updated whenever the source document changes.

Importing Approach Data into 1-2-3

Approach is a unique database product in that it can create views of another file format but cannot create its own file format. Because Approach does not use a proprietary file format, 1-2-3's Open File dialog box does not include an Approach file format in the File **T**ype drop-down list. You can open a desired database file in Approach and then save the file in a format that 1-2-3 can open (WK3, Paradox, dBASE, and so on.).

To import an Approach file into 1-2-3, follow these steps:

1. Using the **F**ile **O**pen menu, open sample DEALERS.VEW view file in Approach, as shown in figure 29.55. The DEALERS.VEW opens in Browse mode (**V**iew **B**rowse) ready for data entry. See figure 29.56.

2. Open the **F**ile menu and choose the **E**xport Data command. The Export Data dialog box appears, as displayed in figure 29.57.

3. In the List Files of **T**ype drop-down list, select Lotus 1-2-3(WK*).

4. Map the desired fields to export to 1-2-3 by selecting each field in the Database **F**ields list box and then clicking **A**dd to place each selected field in the Fields to **E**xport list box (see fig. 29.58).

Tip

Try using a 1-2-3 DataLens Driver to open a database directly from within 1-2-3. If the required 1-2-3 DataLens driver is not available, open the file by using Approach and its list of available file formats.

◀ "Creating a Database," p. 697

◀ "Understanding Advanced Data Management," p. 761

VI

Integrating 1-2-3

Fig. 29.55
Opening the
DEALERS.VEW file
in Approach.

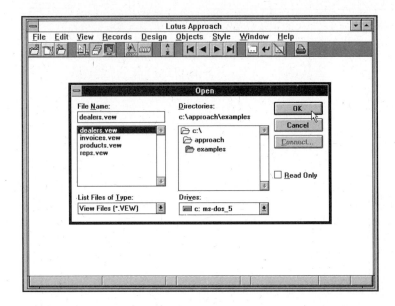

Fig. 29.56
The Approach
sample
DEALERS.VEW
file in Browse.

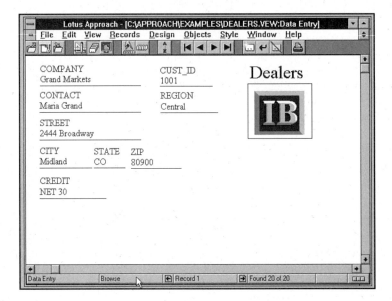

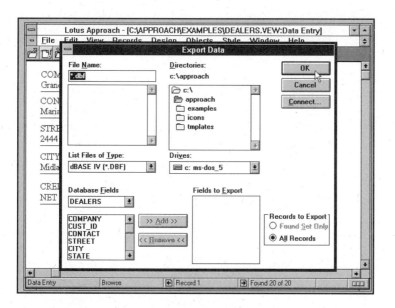

Fig. 29.57
The Export Data
dialog box in
Approach.

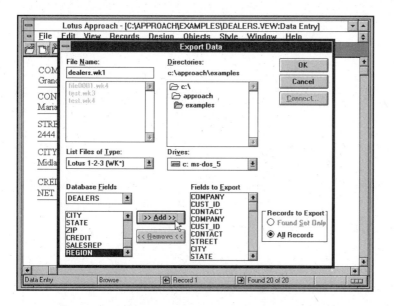

Fig. 29.58
Adding field to the
Fields Export List
Box.

Note

Approach exports fields into the same order as you add them to the Fields Export list.
Also, when using the Lotus 1-2-3 (WK*) file type, Approach automatically uses the
WK1 file extension.

5. Select the drive and directory, name the file and extensions, and click OK.

6. Switch to 1-2-3.

7. Open the named file in 1-2-3. Notice that the records are in row-and-column format.

Instead of saving the Approach file in WK4 file format, you can save the file in ASCII Text file format. Approach will prompt you to select a desired delimiter. You then can open the exported ASCII file in 1-2-3. The file will look identical to figure 29.59.

Fig. 29.59

The exported DEALERS file in 1-2-3.

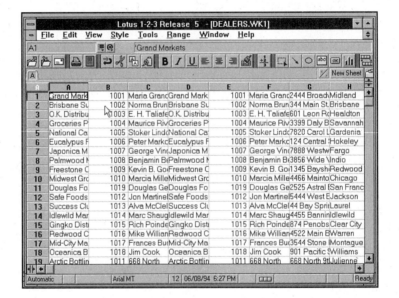

Exporting 1-2-3 Data to Approach

Approach has the capability to open a database file directly. In most cases, you do not need to import data to be able to use it in Approach; you can simply open an existing database file directly and begin working. If you want to use data in a 1-2-3 spreadsheet or text file format, however, you first must create a new database file and then import the spreadsheet or text file into the new file. This procedure is necessary because Approach does not use a proprietary file format and cannot read a WK* file format directly.

The initial step in importing 1-2-3 data is to select the type of file you want to import. Then select the file to be imported, and map the fields in the import file to those in the current Approach database file. Field mapping associates fields in the Approach View file with fields in an underlying database file. The Field Mapping dialog box opens automatically when you try to open a view file that contains fields that need mapping.

To import a 1-2-3 worksheet into a database file, follow these steps:

1. Open the 1-2-3 worksheet that you want to import. The example uses the sample 1-2-3 file EMPLOYEE.WK3 as shown in figure 29.60. The EMPLOYEE.WK3 file is in the 123R5/SAMPLE/DBASE subdirectory.

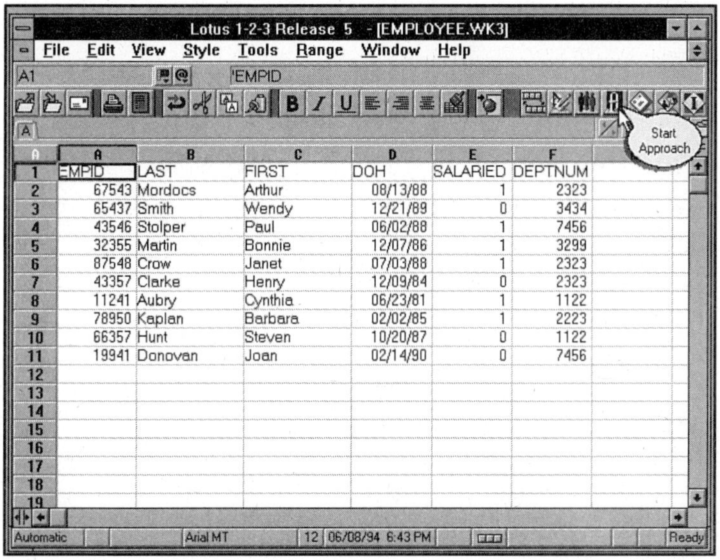

Tip
If the fields in the 1-2-3 file match the fields in the new Approach file, Approach maps them to each other for you.

Fig. 29.60
The 1-2-3 sample worksheet file EMPLOYEE.WK3.

2. Switch to Approach by using the SmartIcon or **A**lt+Tab.

3. Using the **F**ile **N**ew menu, create a **N**ew Approach view file. In the New dialog box type EMPLOYEE.DBF in the File **N**ame box and select dBASE IV(*.DBF) in the List Files of **T**ype list box. See figure 29.61.

4. Click OK. The Field Definition dialog box appears as shown in figure 29.62.

5. Add the fields to be mapped to the 1-2-3 worksheet file. Enter the field name in the **N**ame edit box, select the Type of field in the Type list box, and enter the length in the **L**ength edit box. Then click **A**dd after each field entry. The field mapping on this example should look identical to figure 29.63.

6. Click OK. Approach will create a database form as displayed in figure 29.64.

Fig. 29.61

The New dialog
box in Approach.

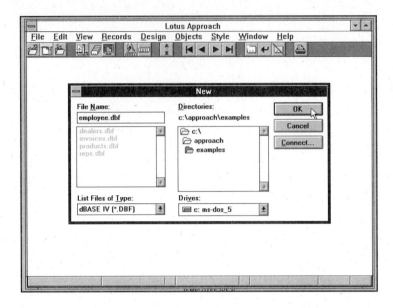

Fig. 29.62

The Field Defini-
tion dialog box.

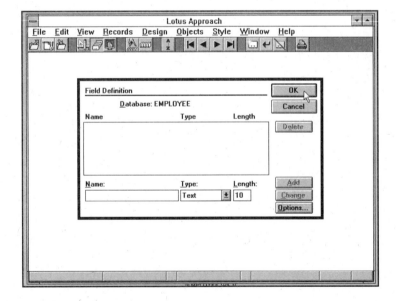

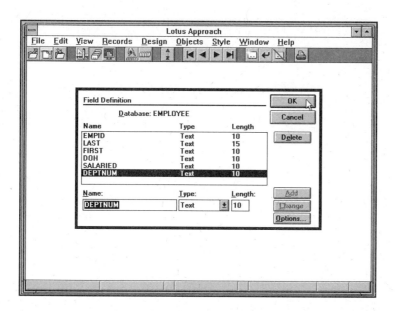

Fig. 29.63
Adding the fields to
EMPLOYEE.DBF.

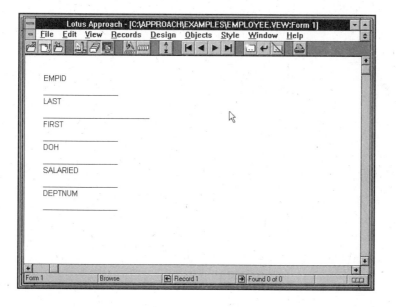

Fig. 29.64
The created form
displaying the
Mapped Fields.

VI

Integrating 1-2-3

7. Open the **F**ile menu and choose the **I**mport Data command.
    The Import Data dialog box appears. See figure 29.65.

Fig. 29.65
The Import Data
dialog box in
Approach.

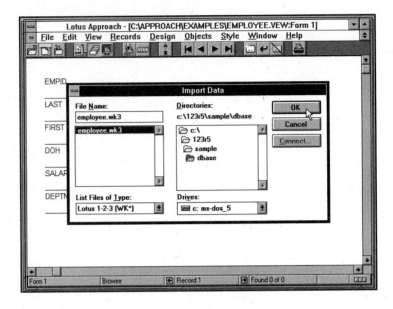

Tip
Another way to
export 1-2-3 data
to Approach is to
first save the 1-2-3
file as an ASCII
text file and then
open the text file
in Approach.

8. Select the desired 1-2-3 worksheet file, and then click OK. The Field Mapping dialog box appears.

9. Next, you need to map the fields from the 1-2-3 worksheet file to be imported to those in the Approach form. In the Fields to map list box, select a field to map, then in the Unmapped fields list box, select a field to map to, then select Map. The mapped field will appear in the Mapping list box. Map all of the fields to be imported. It should appear like figure 29.66. Click OK. The 1-2-3 worksheet data is imported into the Approach database file (see fig. 29.67).

Caution

If a field in the import file is not mapped to a field in the current database file, Approach ignores the field. Approach also ignores any fields in the current database that are not mapped.

Note

Approach imports the 1-2-3 file, adding the new records to the end of the file. If you import the same file twice, you will get duplicate records. The first record on the view will be the labels or column headings from the 1-2-3 worksheet.

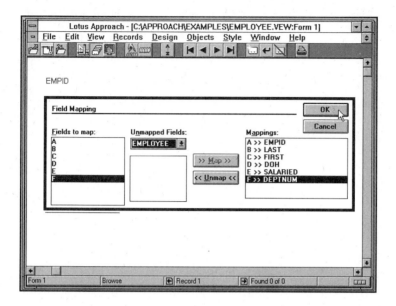

Fig. 29.66
Mapping the 1-2-3 fields (columns) to the fields in the Approach database.

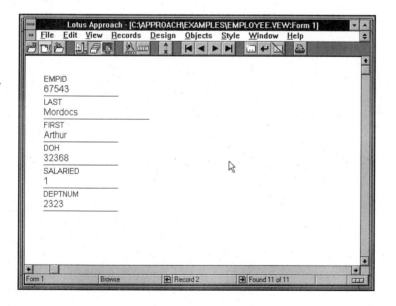

Fig. 29.67
The imported 1-2-3 EMPLOYEE.WK3 data in the Approach view.

Understanding OLE Objects in Approach

Approach enables you to include a variety of information in your database, such as graphics, charts, and text from 1-2-3. Depending on the server application, you will see the actual object (such as a Lotus 1-2-3 graph) or an icon that represents the object (such as an Ami Pro icon).

If you link a 1-2-3 object to Approach, the object remains in its server application, with a link to the Approach field. You must have 1-2-3 installed to edit the object. Any changes you make to the object automatically update the original.

Tip
You must use the **C**opy command to place the OLE object in the Clipboard, not the Cu**t** command. Also, most server applications require you to save the source file before you create an object.

If you embed an OLE object, the entire object is stored in the field. You can place OLE objects in a PicturePlus field in Approach's **V**iew Browse mode or directly in a form, report, or letter in Approach's **V**iew Design mode. If you place the object directly in a **D**esign view, the OLE object appears as a design element. Unless you want the OLE object to appear in every record of a database file, you most often will place an OLE object in a PicturePlus field in **B**rowse mode.

Linking 1-2-3 OLE Objects in Approach

You can place a linked object as a design element in every record or in a PicturePlus field in a single record. The object appears in the record. Any changes you make to the linked object from within Approach update the original object. Before linking, you must create the object in 1-2-3 and copy it to the Clipboard.

To insert a linked object from 1-2-3 into Approach, follow these steps:

1. In 1-2-3, create the object you want to link to by selecting the chart, graphic, or range of data, and then copy it to the Clipboard, as shown in figure 29.68.

Fig. 29.68
A 1-2-3 OLE object to be linked.

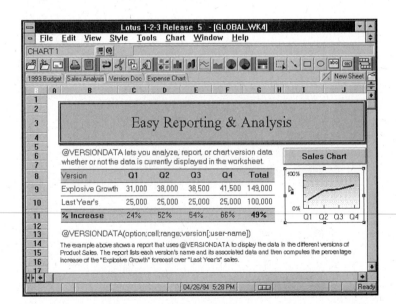

2. Prepare an Approach view file to receive the linked object. Open the view file into which you want to insert the object, and then switch to the form, report, or other view you want to use.

To paste the 1-2-3 OLE object as a design element, change to Design view; open the **V**iew menu, and choose the **D**esign command (see fig. 29.69). Then click where you want the object to appear.

If you are placing the linked object in a PicturePlus field, change to **B**rowse mode, go to the record, and select the field.

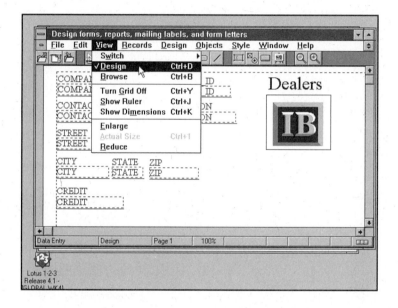

Fig. 29.69
Design mode in an Approach view.

3. Open the **E**dit menu and choose the Paste **S**pecial command. The Paste Special dialog box appears, as shown in figure 29.70.

4. Choose the 1-2-3 worksheet object format. Click Paste **L**ink. Approach displays the object in the current view. The object may appear as an object or icon, depending on the server application; a 1-2-3 OLE object appears as an object, as displayed in figure 29.71.

VI

Integrating 1-2-3

Fig. 29.70
The Paste Special
dialog box in
Approach.

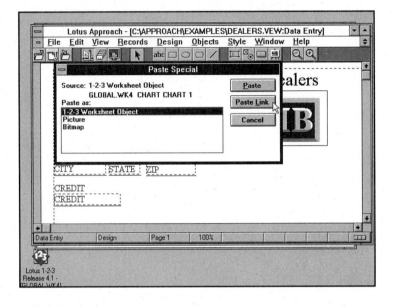

Fig. 29.71
The 1-2-3 OLE
linked object in
Approach.

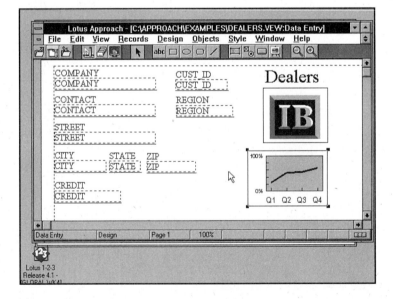

Note

To delete a linked object, select the object; then open the **E**dit menu and choose the
Cu**t** command. You also can press the Del key or select **E**dit Cle**a**r to remove the
object.

Editing a Linked Object

To edit a linked 1-2-3 object, follow these steps:

1. Select the 1-2-3 object. Next, open the **O**bjects menu and choose **L**inks.

2. Choose Au**t**omatic and Click OK to continue.

3. Double-click the 1-2-3 object to open the source document. Edit the object.

4. Switch to Approach by using Act+Tab or the Approach SmartIcon.

5. Notice that the object shows your changes.

> **Caution**
>
> When editing a 1-2-3 linked object in Approach, the normal functionality of a linked object disappears. The update capabilities under **F**ile **U**pdate disappear as does the **F**ile E**x**it & Return command.

Modifying the Link in Approach

To modify a 1-2-3 link in Approach, follow these steps:

1. Open the Approach view file that contains the linked object. If the object is a design element, open the View in design mode by using the View **D**esign menu. If the object is in a PicturePlus field, go to the record that contains the object and select the PicturePlus field.

2. Open the **O**bjects menu and choose the **L**inks command. The Links dialog box appears, as shown in figure 29.72.

3. Select the link you want to modify, and make the necessary changes. You can specify when the object is updated by selecting Au**t**omatic or **M**anual. Manual updating means that the object is updated only when you specifically update it. Automatic updating means that the object is updated whenever the source object changes. To manually update the link, click **U**pdate now.

> **Caution**
>
> When you cancel a link, the object remains in the current view, but you no longer can open 1-2-3 or the server application.

Fig. 29.72
The Links dialog
box in Approach.

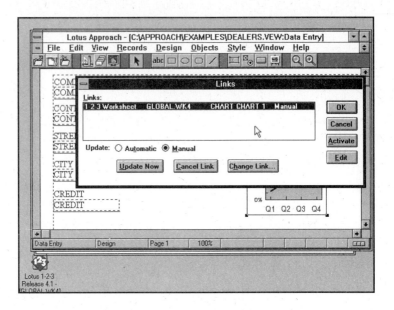

Embedding 1-2-3 Data in Approach

Embedding a 1-2-3 OLE object in an Approach view file creates a link to 1-2-3 the same way that linking to an object does. The difference between linking and embedding is that an embedded object is the only version of the object, whereas a linked object refers to and can update the original source object.

When you embed an object, you simply paste it into an Approach view. You can embed an object as a design element in a report or every record of a form, or in a PicturePlus field in a single record. You can embed an object by first creating it in 1-2-3, or you can embed an object that already exists. Either way, an embedded OLE object is easy to edit and update in an Approach view file.

Embedding an Object in Approach

To embed an existing 1-2-3 OLE object, follow these steps:

1. Create the 1-2-3 OLE object by selecting the graphic, range of data, or text, and then copy it to the Clipboard. In this example, the range A6..C117 is selected (see fig. 29.73).

2. Using the File **N**ew menu, create a new Approach view file by naming the file and using the Field definition dialog box to design new fields. You can prepare an Approach view file by switching to the form, report, or other view that has been previously defined.

3. Open the **E**dit menu and choose the Paste **S**pecial command. The Edit Paste Special dialog box appears, as shown in figure 29.74.

4. Select a format for the object—for this example, 1-2-3 Worksheet Object.

5. Choose the **P**aste command. The 1-2-3 data appears as an object, as displayed in figure 29.75.

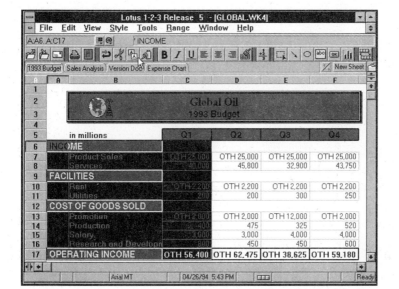

Fig. 29.73
The selected 1-2-3 OLE embedded object.

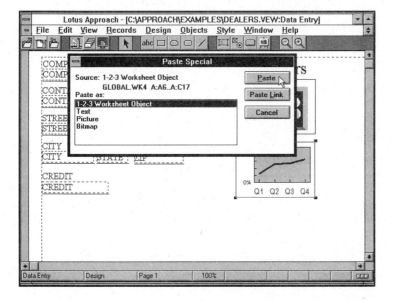

Fig. 29.74
The Paste Special dialog box in Approach.

Fig. 29.75
The 1-2-3 OLE
embedded object
in Approach.

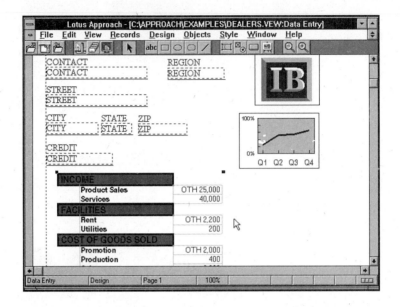

Embedding a Blank Object in Approach

You can embed an OLE object without creating the object first. You can embed first and create the object later by double-clicking the embedded object.

To embed a new 1-2-3 object in Approach, follow these steps:

1. Prepare an Approach view file by switching to the form, report, or other view you want to use.

2. Open the **O**bjects menu and choose the **I**nsert Object command. The Insert New Object dialog box appears, listing all formats that the server application can create, as displayed in figure 29.76. Select 1-2-3 worksheet in the Object **T**ype list box.

3. Select an object type. Approach opens in a new, blank, or untitled window.

4. Create the object in 1-2-3.

5. Open the **F**ile menu and choose the **U**pdate Approach command.

6. Close the 1-2-3 window or open the **F**ile Exit & Return command to return to Approach.

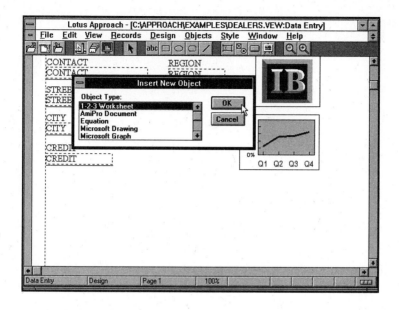

Fig. 29.76
The Insert New
Object dialog box.

Editing an Embedded Object in Approach

To edit a 1-2-3 OLE embedded object in Approach, follow these steps:

1. In Design view, select the object you want to edit.

2. Double-click the object.

3. Make the desired changes in the embedded object.

4. Open the **F**ile menu and choose the **U**pdate command.

5. Open the **F**ile menu and choose the E**x**it & Return command to return to Approach.

Tip
In a PicturePlus
field, you can
right-click the
object and then
choose Edit Object
from the pop-up
menu.

Using cc:Mail from within 1-2-3

Using cc:Mail is an easy way to send data and files to other users for work with the other SmartSuite applications. You can use the **F**ile menu's Send **M**ail command to send an attached file, a specified range, chart, or drawing as an electronic-mail message. To do this, you need cc:Mail for Windows Release 1.11 or later.

VI

Integrating 1-2-3

Note

You also can use the Send **M**ail command with other mail applications that use the Vendor-Independent Messaging Interface (VIM), with Microsoft Mail running under Windows for Workgroups Version 3.1, and with Lotus Notes Release 2.1 for Windows. The following sections will apply to your mail-messaging application.

▶ "Using 1-2-3 with Lotus Notes," p. 901

Sending a cc:Mail Message from 1-2-3

To send a cc:Mail message from within 1-2-3, follow these steps:

1. Open the **F**ile menu and choose the Send **M**ail command or select the Mail SmartIcon. If you are not currently logged into cc:Mail, a login dialog box appears and prompts for a password. The Send Mail dialog box appears as shown in figure 29.77.

Fig. 29.77
The Send Mail dialog box.

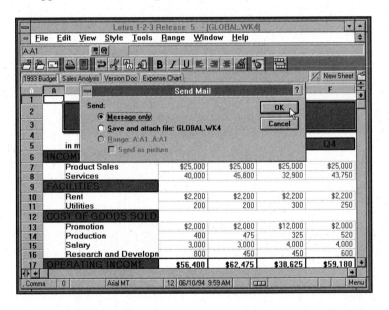

2. Choose the **M**essage only option.

3. Click OK to send a mail message. A dialog box for sending mail from cc:Mail or your mail application appears. After you use the dialog box to send a mail message, you return to 1-2-3.

Note

If you are using cc:Mail or Lotus Notes, 1-2-3 opens your mail application if it's not already open.

Attaching a File to a cc:Mail Message

When you use 1-2-3 to send a worksheet file, 1-2-3 reacts differently to the status of the current file. If a file has been saved, 1-2-3 automatically saves the file, and the cc:Mail dialog box appears; otherwise, untitled worksheets force the Save As dialog box to appear, prompting you to save the file.

To attach a title or named file to a cc:Mail message, follow these steps:

1. Make the file you want to attach the current file.

2. Open the **F**ile menu and choose the Send **M**ail command. The Send **M**ail dialog box appears as displayed in figure 29.78.

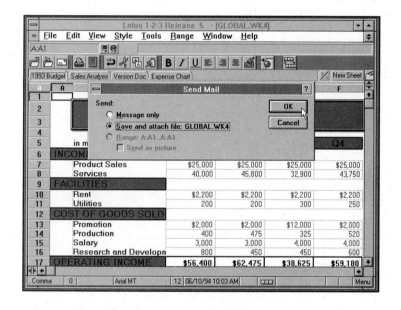

Fig. 29.78
The Send Mail dialog box with the **S**ave and Attach file option.

3. Choose the **S**ave and attach file option (or choose **A**ttach file, if the file has been saved).

4. Choose OK. A cc:Mail dialog box appears. After using the dialog box to send a mail message, you return to 1-2-3.

To attach an untitled or modified file to a cc:Mail message, follow these steps:

1. Open the **F**ile menu and choose the Send **M**ail command.

2. Choose the **S**ave and attach file option.

3. Choose OK. The Save As dialog box appears.

4. Name and save the file. A cc:Mail dialog box appears. After you use the dialog box to send a mail message, you return to 1-2-3.

Inserting a Selection into a cc:Mail Message

To insert a selection into a cc:Mail message, follow these steps:

1. Select the range, drawing, or chart to be included in the cc:Mail mail message.

2. Open the **F**ile menu and choose the Send **M**ail command.

3. If you are inserting a range, choose the S**e**nd as Picture check box below the **R**ange option (see fig. 29.79).

Fig. 29.79
Sending a selected
range or object.

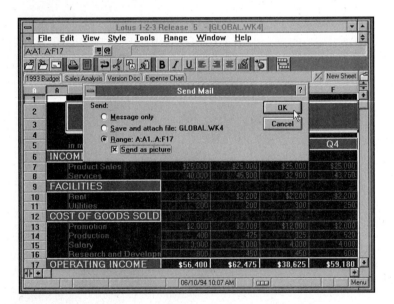

4. Click OK. The dialog box for sending cc:Mail appears. After you use the dialog box to send a mail message, you return to 1-2-3.

Sending and Routing a Range with a cc:Mail Message

Range Routing allows you to delegate or distribute work on a worksheet model to other uses for review purposes or a request for data. You can send a range of worksheet data to other cc:Mail-enabled 1-2-3 Release 5 users. When you send a range, 1-2-3 attaches a 1-2-3 file to the cc:Mail message. The file contains a worksheet with the selected range, boxes for comments and notes, and buttons to send the file. You can send the range to all recipients at once or route it from one recipient to the next.

> **Note**
>
> Range Routing also uses Notes or any VIM/MAPI mail system to allow users to distribute ranges.

Suppose that you need to finalize your organization's budget and must collect the numbers from several departments. You decide to route the budget worksheet to all those departments. You tell 1-2-3 who the recipients will be and the order in which you want to route the transmission; then you place your name at the end of the routing list. The recipients work with the data, entering their estimates and figures to the template. 1-2-3 automatically routes the worksheet to the next person on the list. When the worksheet returns to you, you can incorporate the updated changes into your original worksheet.

To send and route a range of worksheet data to a list of recipients, take the following steps:

1. Select the 1-2-3 range to be included in the message.

2. Open the **F**ile menu and choose the Send **M**ail command. The Send Mail dialog box appears.

3. Choose the **R**ange option as displayed in figure 29.80. In this example, do not select Send as Picture because you want recipients to work with the data. Click OK. The Send Range As dialog box appears as shown in figure 29.81.

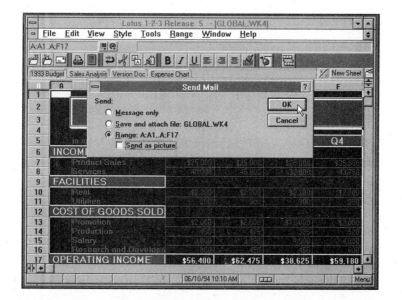

Fig. 29.80
Sending a selected range or object.

Integrating 1-2-3

Fig. 29.81
The Send Range As
dialog box.

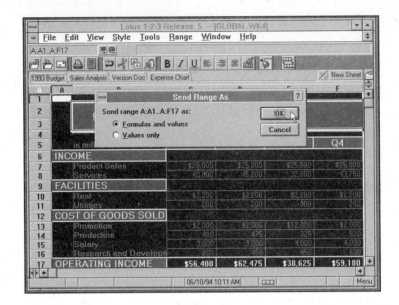

4. Select the **F**ormulas and Values or **V**alues Only option. If you want other recipients to work with the data, you should select **F**ormulas and values so they can review your assumptions.

5. Choose OK. The 1-2-3 Mail File appears as shown in figure 29.82.

    A 1-2-3 mail file is the 1-2-3 file that 1-2-3 attaches to a mail message when you send or receive a range. A 1-2-3 mail file contains a range of worksheet data, text blocks displaying names and documents. Depending on how the file is sent, the 1-2-3 mail file will display a button for sending, routing, replying, or merging the range.

6. 1-2-3 displays the range you are sending and lets you enter a message to the recipients of the range. 1-2-3 automatically displays your name and the date in the text block. In the text block, add a message or note to the recipients (see fig. 29.83). The message appears in the mail message the recipients get in their mail applications.

Note

A text block is a drawn object, shaped as a rectangle or square, that contains text. Text blocks can be moved, sized, and copied.

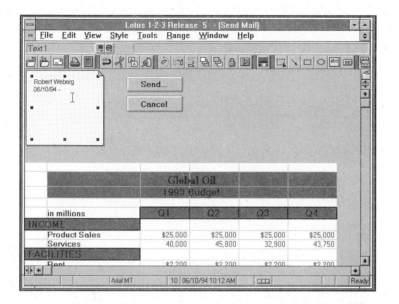

Fig. 29.82

The 1-2-3 Send Mail file.

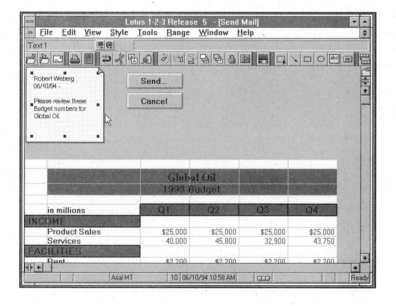

Fig. 29.83

Adding a message to the text block of the 1-2-3 Send Mail File.

VI

Integrating 1-2-3

7. Click the Send button. If you are not currently logged into cc:Mail, a Mail Login dialog box appears that requires you to show your password, as shown in figure 29.84. The Send dialog box appears, as shown in figure 29.85.

Fig. 29.84
The Mail Login
dialog box.

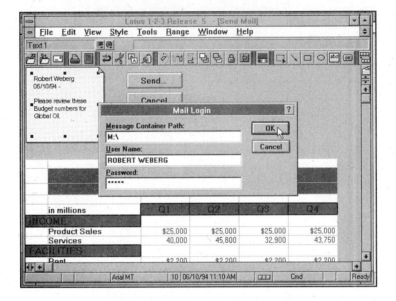

Fig. 29.85
The Send dialog
box.

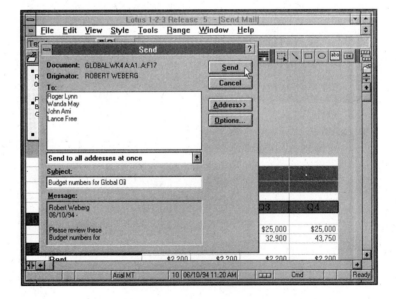

8. The Send dialog box lets you specify to whom and in what order you want to send the range. Enter the names of the recipients in the To: list box. You can separate names of the recipients by pressing Enter after each name or use commas.

Note

When routing the range from one recipient to the next, make sure that you enter the names in the order you want them to recieve it.

9. Select an option from the drop-down list box:

   ■ *Send to all addresses at once* sends the range to all the recipients at the same time.

   ■ *Route to addresses in sequence* converts your list to a numbered route list (see fig. 29.86). 1-2-3 routes the range to the first person on the list, then automatically routes it to the second person on the list when the second person clicks the Route button. This step is repeated as each user reads and routes the range.

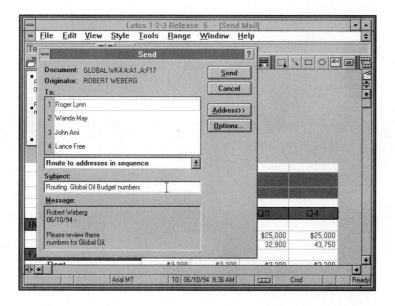

Fig. 29.86
Using the Route to addresses in sequence option.

10. Enter a subject in the S**u**bject text box. The Subject text appears in the mail message the recipients get in their mail applications. The subject will also appear in the title bar of the 1-2-3 mail file.

11. You can choose the **A**ddress button to display the list of people or groups in your mail application's address book. The names and/or groups can be added to your To: text list box.

12. You can also choose Options to select delivery and tracking options for ranges sent from 1-2-3 and define the **D**elivery priority for the range message, as shown in figure 29.87. Select one or both of the following check boxes:

■ *Return to **o**riginator* adds your name to the end of the list of recipients after you send the mail. When the range returns to you, 1-2-3 adds a Merge button that, when selected, allows you to incorporate other users' changes into the original range. If you are sending the range to all recipients simultaneously, 1-2-3 adds a Reply button to the worksheet.

■ ***R**eturn receipt and copy originator* sends a confirmation to each sender in a route list when the next person in the list opens their mail, and sends a copy of the file to the originator. This feature can help you track the current location of a routed range.

Fig. 29.87
The Options
dialog box in
Send.

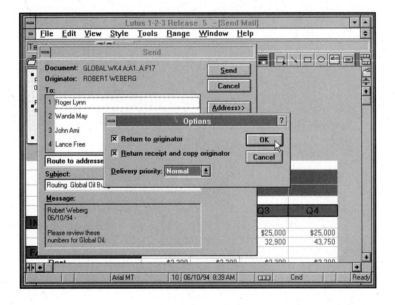

13. Click Send to send the range to the recipients.

Receiving Notification of a cc:Mail Message

If you use cc:Mail or another mail-messaging application and the application is open, 1-2-3 notifies you when you get new mail by beeping and displaying an envelope in the status bar. Click the envelope to switch to your mail application, as shown in figure 29.88.

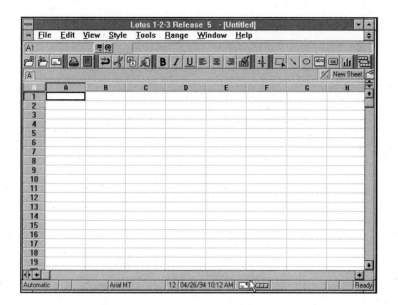

Fig. 29.88
Envelope in
status bar.

From Here...

In this chapter, you learned how to combine the presentation powers of Freelance, the document-preparation prowess of Ami Pro, and the data-analysis and storage capabilities of 1-2-3 to create a powerful, integrated system that excels at managing text, images, and numeric data. 1-2-3 also has the capability to use these techniques with a powerful new workgroup application called Lotus Notes. For more information about integrating 1-2-3 for Windows with Lotus Notes and other applications, read the following chapters:

■ Chapter 30, "Using 1-2-3 with Lotus Notes."

■ Chapter 31, "Using 1-2-3 with DOS and Mainframe Applications."

VI

Integrating 1-2-3

Using 1-2-3 with Lotus Notes

Lotus Notes is a "groupware" application that manages data and information for many users, enabling them to work together more efficiently. Imagine a container of information that everyone in the organization can access. The container is a Notes database, which is just a collection of documents. In the past, people worked independently and had to exchange data through floppy disks and company pouch mail; now, PCs are linked by local area networks (LANs). Notes enables you to collect and share information—1-2-3 worksheets, text, and graphics, for example—with other users through an exchange forum.

Workgroup members can use Notes to share documents created in other applications, collaborate on ideas, issue reports, track clients, monitor projects, and customize workgroup processes and reports.

In this chapter, you learn to do the following:

- Create a Notes Shared file in 1-2-3 for Windows

- Import a 1-2-3 worksheet into a Notes view

- Export a Notes view to 1-2-3 for Windows

- Create a 1-2-3 for Windows linked object in Notes

- Create a 1-2-3 for Windows embedded object in Notes

- Use Application Field Exchange with 1-2-3 for Windows

VI

Integrating 1-2-3

Creating a Lotus Notes Shared File in 1-2-3 for Windows

The unique combination of 1-2-3 for Windows and Lotus Notes provides users capabilities that far outweigh the benefits of each application in a stand-alone environment. These capabilities include simultaneously adding, modifying, and deleting information in a 1-2-3 for Windows file; maintaining security and access control; and providing database replication. Database replication allows you to store copies of a Notes database on multiple Notes Series and guarantees that they remain identical and in synchronization.

See figure 30.1 for a preview of a Notes workspace or desktop. The three major elements of the Notes screen are the title bar across the top of the window, the menu bar that lists the major commands, and the workspace—the rest of the window.

Fig. 30.1

Lotus Notes Workspace.

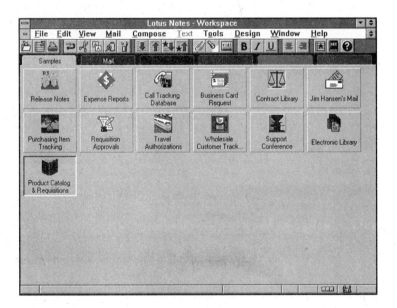

1-2-3 for Windows works with Notes to provide an environment in which workgroups can share 1-2-3 worksheets. 1-2-3 files stored as Notes databases have the NS4 extension; these files are referred to as *shared files*. More than one person can create, delete, update, and display versions and scenarios in the shared file without overwriting another person's work. In Version Manager, a version is a named set of data and styles for a named range. While a scenario is a named group of one or more versions, each version in a scenario must be associated with a normal range.

To create a shared NS4 file, follow these steps:

1. Open the **F**ile menu and choose the **O**pen command to open the 1-2-3 file you want to share. In this example, use the sample worksheet GLOBAL.WK4, as displayed in figure 30.2.

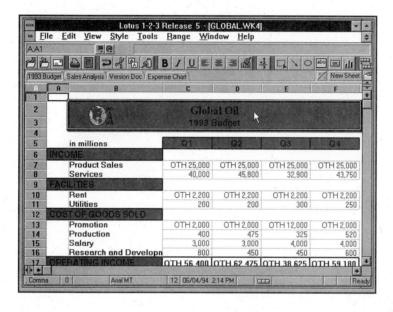

Fig. 30.2
The sample worksheet GLOBAL.WK4.

2. Highlight a range of 1-2-3 data. In the Name dialog box, open the **R**ange menu and choose **N**ame. Type a 15-character-or-less name in the **N**ame edit box. Choose **A**dd to add the named range to the list of **E**xisting named ranges for which you want other users to create versions.

3. Open the **S**tyle menu and choose the **P**rotection command to prevent changes to styles in the range. This step will allow you to change cell contents in the current selection or named range, but not to styles. Use **S**tyle **P**rotection, for example, if you want users to be able to enter data on a worksheet used as an entry form.

4. Open the **F**ile menu and choose the Save **A**s command to display the Save As dialog box.

5. In the File **T**ype list, select the file type Shared (NS4). The Dri**v**es drop-down list becomes the Notes Ser**v**ers drop-down list, displaying the available Lotus Notes servers to which you are connected (see fig. 30.3).

◀ "Managing Multiple Solutions with Version Manager," p. 661

VI

Integrating 1-2-3

Fig. 30.3
Saving a 1-2-3 file
in NS4 format.

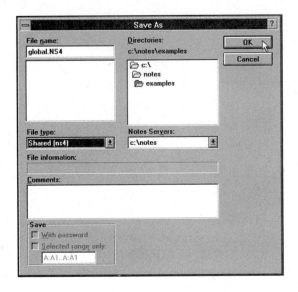

6. Choose a Notes server, and save the file. The File Seal Password dialog box appears (see fig. 30.4). Notes servers are similar to network drives but are usually given logical names like SERVER1 or SERVER2. Consult with your Notes systems administrator for more information about your company's Notes servers. You can also save a Notes database to a local or network drive.

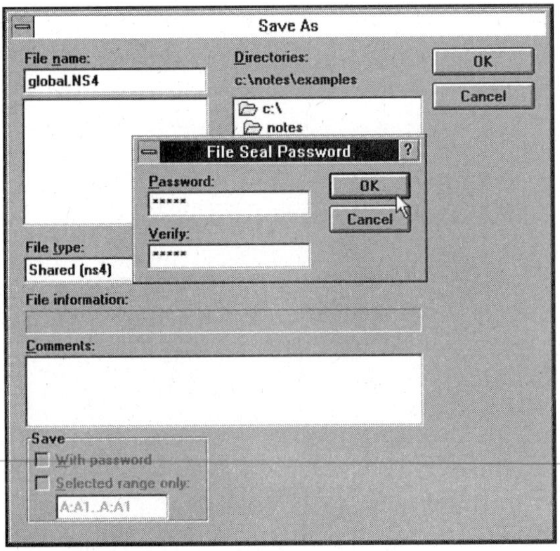

Fig. 30.4
The File Seal
Password dialog
box.

7. In the **P**assword and **V**erify text boxes, enter identical passwords for the shared file. The password letters you type will appear as asterisks to prevent others from seeing your password.

8. Click OK.

Caution

When you follow the preceding steps by using a file with no versions, you will get a warning dialog box telling you that the file contains no unprotected named ranges that contain versions. Select **Y**es if you want to continue saving the shared file. Select **N**o to change the file to contain versions with unprotected normal ranges. In order to share data in a shared file, the file must contain unprotected named ranges that contain versions.

You can use the Notes **F**ile menu's **O**pen Database command to place the 1-2-3 worksheet database icon on the Notes desktop, as shown in figure 30.5.

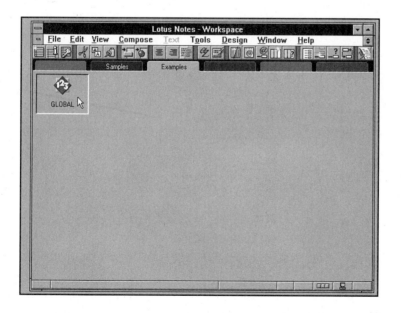

Fig. 30.5
GLOBAL.NS4 shared file added to the Notes Workspace.

You can open the shared file (Notes database) from within Notes by double-clicking on the Global Notes icon. This step will provide a view that is similar to the 1-2-3 Version Manager view (see fig. 30.6). Although you cannot read worksheet data in Notes view (this can be done only in 1-2-3), you can monitor who is contributing to a specific worksheet. You can select various views to see the document by opening the View menu (see fig. 30.7). By double-clicking on one of the Notes documents, you can view more specific information about the version (see fig. 30.8). Multiple users now can access and contribute to the worksheet file concurrently through 1-2-3. Also, the source file is saved as a file attachment in the first Notes document, enabling users to launch or detach the file from within Notes.

Fig. 30.6
The main view in the GLOBAL.NS4 database.

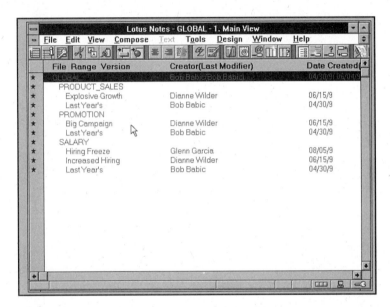

Fig. 30.7
The available views for the Global database.

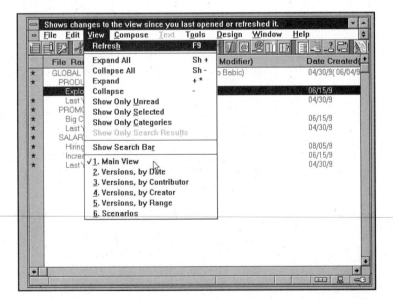

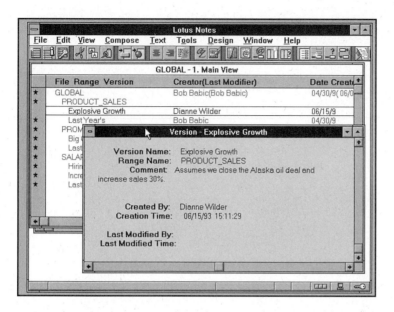

Fig. 30.8
More specific
information about
the Version
Manager.

> **Note**
>
> Although the worksheet is saved on a Notes server, 1-2-3 for Windows users still can access the file through the Open File dialog box in 1-2-3. Notes users actually input data and create versions by using the Version Manager dialog box in 1-2-3. Also, the shared file is password-protected; only designated unprotected ranges can be changed.

In a shared file, multiple users can enter versions and scenarios simultaneously. If another user is adding a version or scenario in a shared file at the same time you are using the file, the Refresh button will make those versions and scenarios available to you. Clicking the Refresh button, the fourth button from the right in the Version Manager Index, enables you to see new versions and scenarios that other users have added to your shared file. The Version Manager Index displays and lists versions and scenarios in the worksheet. You can also sort, create, update, and delete versions and scenarios; change settings; create reports on versions; and merge versions and scenarios from other files by using the Version Manager Index (see fig. 30.9). 1-2-3 for Windows beeps if another user creates versions or scenarios in a shared file while you are using the file, and displays the message New versions have been posted in the title bar of the Version Manager window (if it is open) or in the title bar of the 1-2-3 window.

VI

Integrating 1-2-3

> **Note**
>
> The Refresh button appears only if Notes is installed on your computer. The button is grayed and unavailable when no new versions or scenarios exist for the shared file or when the current file is not a shared file.

Fig. 30.9

The 1-2-3 for Windows Version Manager Index.

You also can mark as read versions and scenarios that other users entered. The Mark Read button, the third button from the right with the black star, removes the unread indicator from all versions in the shared file (see fig. 30.10).

Fig. 30.10

Marking versions as read.

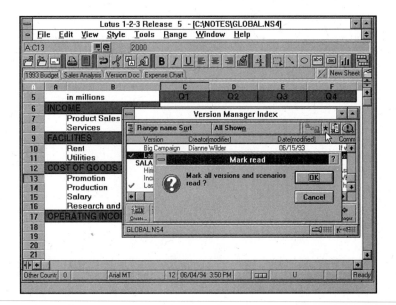

Version Manager for Lotus Notes benefits users in many ways, providing the following features:

■ *Concurrent access.* Multiple users can access and contribute to a worksheet at the same time by using versions, which enable people to contribute to a worksheet model without overwriting one another's data.

■ *Access control.* Users can create access lists to control certain users' privileges (editing, deleting, reading, and so on).

■ *User notification.* 1-2-3 notifies users if changes are posted to a shared file during a 1-2-3 session.

■ *Replication.* Database replication enables users on remote servers to access and contribute to a worksheet. This feature also enables users who occasionally are disconnected from a server (such as field personnel and laptop users) to participate in the sharing process.

■ *Unread flags.* This feature marks as unread any version changes since the last time you viewed a worksheet file.

■ *Summarized views.* Users can summarize different views of the same data.

Using DDE/OLE Between 1-2-3 for Windows and Lotus Notes

Dynamic data exchange (DDE) and object linking and embedding (OLE) are techniques for incorporating data from other programs into 1-2-3, and vice versa. DDE and OLE enable you to paste information created in one Windows application into another Windows application. The distinct advantage of DDE and OLE over normal copy-and-paste procedures is that you can edit the linked or embedded object in its source application without leaving the file that contains the object.

To use DDE and OLE, both Windows applications must support the current technology. An application that can be a source of objects is called an *OLE server;* an application that can be a recipient of objects is called an *OLE client.*

◀ "Using 1-2-3 with the Lotus SmartSuite," p. 813

> **Caution**
>
> 1-2-3 can act as an OLE client and OLE server, but Notes can act only as an OLE client. Therefore, you can place 1-2-3 objects in Notes documents, but you cannot place Notes objects in 1-2-3 worksheets.

VI

Integrating 1-2-3

Creating a Linked 1-2-3 for Windows Object in Lotus Notes

A *linked object* is a reference within a DDE/OLE client application file (Notes) to a file in a DDE/OLE server application (1-2-3). When an object is linked with DDE or OLE, the object maintains a relationship with the original source data. If you change or modify the source data, the linked object changes. For example, if you link an object or range created in a 1-2-3 worksheet to a Notes document, and then change the data in the 1-2-3 worksheet, the linked 1-2-3 object in the Notes document reflects those changes.

You should link 1-2-3 information under the following circumstances:

- You want to store 1-2-3 data in a central location.

- The 1-2-3 source file is permanent and will not be moved (i.e., a corporate logo).

◀ "Using 1-2-3 with the Lotus SmartSuite," p. 813

- The users who need to edit the data have access to the 1-2-3 file and the 1-2-3 application.

To create a 1-2-3 DDE link in Lotus Notes, follow these steps:

1. Open the source worksheet in 1-2-3. Figures 30.11 through 30.13 display using the sample GLOBAL.WK4 worksheet.

2. Select the information you want to use in the object—a range of data, a graph, text, and so on.

3. Open the **E**dit menu and choose the **C**opy command to place the information in the Clipboard (see fig. 30.11).

4. Switch to Notes by using Alt+Tab or clicking on the Notes SmartIcon, and start the application if it is not running already.

5. Open the Notes database and document that will contain the inserted link.

6. Place the document in edit mode, and then place the insertion point in a Rich Text Field (RTF).

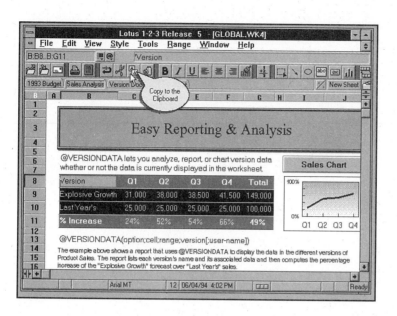

Fig. 30.11
Copying a 1-2-3
range to the
Clipboard.

Note

Most fields, but not all, are surrounded by tiny brackets or corners, which help you identify the location and size of fields in a document. Rich Text Fields enable you to enter words and sentences, but also enable you to make use of different sizes and styles of characters, as well as colors, tables, graphics, pictures, and objects.

Caution

Embedded and linked objects need to be inserted into Rich Text Fields in Notes documents because plain text fields cannot distinguish formatting and object information.

---

7. Open the **E**dit menu and choose the Paste **S**pecial command. The Paste Special dialog box appears.

8. In the **D**isplay As list, select the Clipboard format you want to display. The options are determined by the DDE server application (1-2-3). For this example, select Rich Text Format, as displayed in figure 30.12.

9. Choose **L**ink. The Clipboard data is pasted and linked into the Notes document. Page down by using the vertical scroll bar if necessary, because Notes may shift information in the document (see fig. 30.13).

Tip
Experiment with the various types in the **D**isplay As list to find the format you want to use in the Notes document.

Fig. 30.12
Paste Special
dialog box and
Selecting **L**ink.

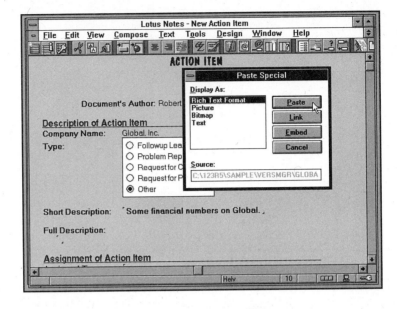

Fig. 30.13
Linked object in
Notes document.

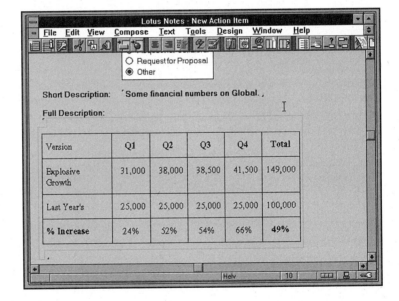

Troubleshooting

The text in my 1-2-3 object in Notes is enlarged and causing wordwrapping.

The text in 1-2-3 objects linked to Notes may appear enlarged, depending on the font and text size used in the source 1-2-3 file. You may need to widen columns or decrease font sizes in the source file to prevent cell word-wrapping in the linked object.

My 1-2-3 linked object is not updating properly.

You must save a document before creating a link. If the linked object is not updating properly, make sure that the source file has been saved.

Embedding a 1-2-3 Object in Lotus Notes

Embedding a 1-2-3 object differs from linking a 1-2-3 object, in that the object is not connected to the original worksheet. When a 1-2-3 object is embedded, the client application copies the object, and the connection to 1-2-3 is lost. Therefore, updating the worksheet in 1-2-3 does not update the embedded object within Notes. Instead, you must use OLE to activate 1-2-3 (double-click the 1-2-3 object) and directly edit the embedded copy of the object.

You should use object embedding under the following circumstances:

- You want to use 1-2-3 rather than Notes to edit the copy of the embedded 1-2-3 data in the document. (You must have access to the 1-2-3 for Windows application.)

- The document is going to be mailed, in which case any file link would be lost.

- Notes users wouldn't have access to the original 1-2-3 file.

Creating an embedded 1-2-3 object in a Notes document involves the following four steps. To demonstrate the difference between linked and embedded objects, use the worksheet data from the exercise in the preceding section. Follow these steps:

1. Open the source worksheet in 1-2-3.

2. Select the information you want to use in the object.

3. Open the **E**dit menu and choose the **C**opy command to place the information in the Windows Clipboard.

4. Switch to Notes. If the application is not running already, start it.

5. Open or create a Notes document to contain the 1-2-3 OLE object.

6. Place the insertion point in a Rich Text Field.

7. Open the **E**dit menu and choose the Paste **S**pecial command. The Paste Special dialog box appears.

8. In the **D**isplay As list, select the Clipboard format you want to display. The options are determined by the OLE server application (1-2-3).

9. Choose **E**mbed (see fig. 30.14). The 1-2-3 object is inserted into the Notes document, as shown in figure 30.15.

Fig. 30.14

The Paste Special dialog box and Selecting **E**mbed.

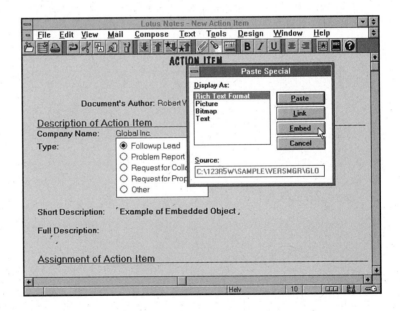

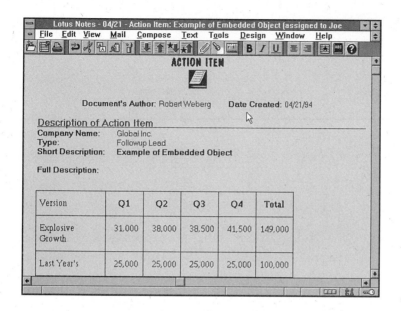

Fig. 30.15
Embedded object in Notes document.

Examining the Linked and Embedded Objects

Linked and embedded 1-2-3 objects behave in different ways. You can see the difference when you modify or edit the linked and embedded objects.

You can modify a 1-2-3 DDE-linked document in Notes in either of two ways:

- Double-click the DDE range of data within Notes to restart the link.

- Open 1-2-3, and edit the 1-2-3 source worksheet. When you open the Notes document that contains the linked object, it reflects the changes you made in the 1-2-3 worksheet.

A 1-2-3 embedded object in Notes does not maintain a relationship with the source worksheet, but you still can edit the object in its source application by double-clicking the object. This action opens the source application with a *copy or template of the embedded object versus the source document itself.*

To examine the difference between a linked and embedded 1-2-3 object in Notes, complete the following steps in your example Notes documents containing the linked and embedded objects:

1. Switch to 1-2-3, and make a change in the source worksheet.

2. Open the **F**ile menu and choose the **S**ave command to save the changes. You must save your changes for the changes to be reflected in the linked object.

VI

Integrating 1-2-3

3. Switch to Notes, and open the example documents with the linked DDE object and the embedded object. The document that contains the linked object will prompt you to refresh the link (see fig. 30.16).

Fig. 30.16
Embedded object in Notes document prompting you to refresh links to external objects.

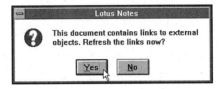

4. Click **Y**es to open the document and refresh the link.

Notice that the linked object reflects the modifications and edits made in 1-2-3, but the embedded object does not. To modify the embedded object, double-click it; the source application loads the object as a template in 1-2-3. Edit the file. Then open the **F**ile menu and choose the E**x**it & Return to Lotus Notes command. Selecting E**x**it & Return will apply your changes to the worksheet, update the embedded object in the Notes document, and return you to Notes.

Importing and Exporting 1-2-3 Data with Notes

You can import many types of worksheets, word processing, graphics, and text files into Notes documents and views. Because Notes is a Lotus product, it imports 1-2-3 worksheets easily. You also can export Notes views and documents to 1-2-3 files. These capabilities enable you to share your work with others in your organization more effectively.

You should import 1-2-3 files into Notes rather than use application-sharing tools such as DDE or OLE when faced with the following:

- The 1-2-3 data file is available to you, but you or other users who need the data do not have access to the 1-2-3 for Windows application.

- You want to edit the data in Notes rather than 1-2-3 (for example, you cannot edit graphics in Notes; you can only size them).

- The data file is too large for the Clipboard.

Importing a 1-2-3 Worksheet into a Notes Document

One of the most popular uses of Notes and 1-2-3 is to make 1-2-3 worksheets available to an entire organization by means of Notes. When the worksheet file is imported into a document, you can edit and format the text. The imported data is not linked to the original file, so changes made in Notes do not affect the original file.

To bring 1-2-3 worksheet data into a document, input the worksheet in a Rich Text Field. A Rich Text Field is so called because you can enter text and formatting information. You can change color, type style, justification and line spacing, and add tables and graphics to a Notes RTF. The body of a memo is an example of a Rich Text field. To input the worksheet in a Rich Text Field, follow these steps:

Caution

Objects and data imported from 1-2-3 worksheets, Ami Pro documents, and Freelance Graphics must be placed in a Rich Text Field because plain text fields in Notes cannot distinguish formatting and object information.

---

1. In Notes, select or compose a document.

2. Open the **E**dit menu and choose the **E**dit Document command.

3. Place the insertion point in the Rich Text Field where you want the imported file to begin.

4. Open the **F**ile menu and choose the **I**mport command. The Import dialog box appears as displayed in figure 30.17.

5. In the List Files of **T**ype drop-down list, select 1-2-3 Worksheet.

6. Select the desired 1-2-3 file. (Specify the drive and directory, if necessary.)

7. Click I**m**port. The 123/Symphony Worksheet Import dialog box appears (see fig. 30.18).

8. Choose **E**ntire Worksheet or **N**amed Range.

   If you choose **N**amed Range, type the range name in the **R**ange Name text box.

9. Click OK. Notes imports the worksheet into the selected Rich Text Field in the document, as shown in figure 30.19.

Fig. 30.17
The Import dialog
box in Notes.

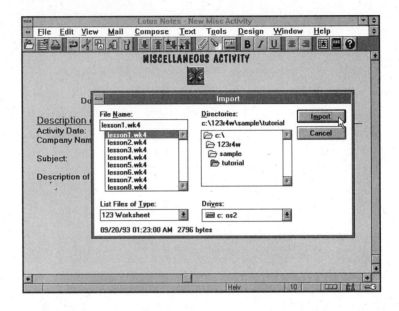

Fig. 30.18
123/Symphony
Worksheet Import
dialog box.

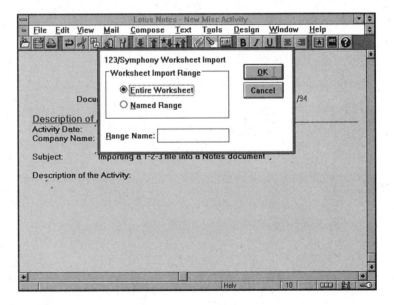

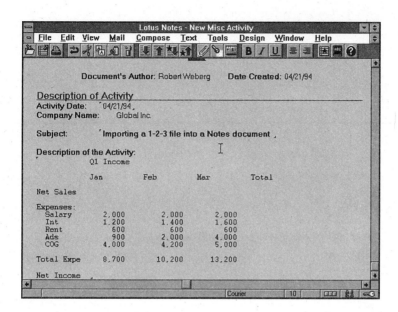

Fig. 30.19
The imported
1-2-3 worksheet.

You now have the capability to edit the data within Notes. You may need to edit the alignment and spacing of the imported worksheet, but the changes will not affect the original 1-2-3 source file.

> **Note**
>
> To import 1-2-3 data as a database, import it into a Notes view (see "Importing a 1-2-3 Worksheet into a Notes View" later in this chapter). Each worksheet row becomes a document, and each column becomes a field whose contents are the original cell contents.

Importing a 1-2-3 Graphics File into a Notes Document

Importing a 1-2-3 graphics file or chart into Notes is easy. Sharing 1-2-3 charts and graphs with Notes enables you to distribute important presentations and even use Notes as a storage facility for important business graphics. To import a 1-2-3 graphics file into a Notes document, take the following steps:

1. Open the 1-2-3 worksheet that contains the graphic you want to use in Notes.

2. Select the graphic or chart, as displayed in figure 30.20.

VI

Integrating 1-2-3

Fig. 30.20
The selected 1-2-3
graphic.

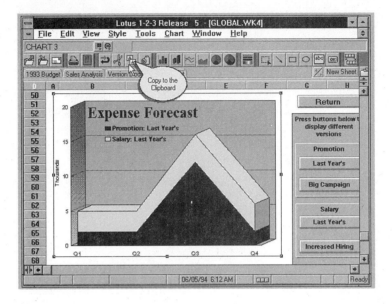

3. Open the **E**dit menu and choose the **C**opy command to copy the
   graphic to the Clipboard.

4. Switch to Notes; open a database and the desired document you want
   to paste the selected graphic into.

5. Place the insertion point in a Rich Text Field.

6. Open the **E**dit menu and choose the **P**aste command. The selected
   graphic is pasted into the Notes document as shown in figure 30.21.

Fig. 30.21
The imported
1-2-3 graphic in
Notes.

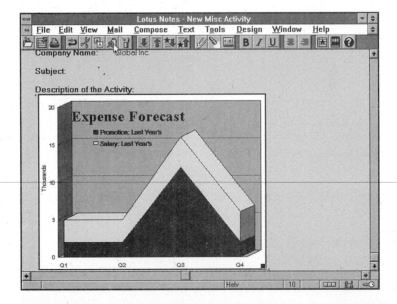

When you import a graphics file, you can size but cannot edit the graphic. To size the graphic, drag the handle in the lower-right corner of the imported graphics box.

Tip
You can use the **E**dit menu's Paste **S**pecial command and the Picture Format option to insert the graphic as an embedded or linked object that you can edit.

Importing a 1-2-3 Worksheet into a Notes View

You can import many worksheet, database, and tabular text files into a Notes view. When you import a 1-2-3 worksheet into a Notes view, each row becomes a separate document, and each column becomes a field that contains the original cell contents. To import at the view level, you must create a form and view that match the format of the worksheet you are importing. In other words, use the view to specify which fields you want to import from 1-2-3.

To import a 1-2-3 worksheet into a Notes view, you must design a form in a Notes database with fields that can accommodate and match the format of the 1-2-3 data. To import 1-2-3 data into Notes, follow these steps:

1. Create a 1-2-3 worksheet called TEST.WK4, using the data shown in figure 30.22.

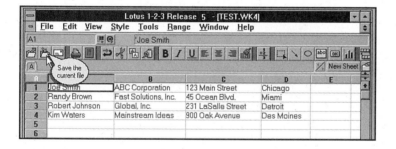

Fig. 30.22

A simple 1-2-3 worksheet named TEST.WK4

2. Create a Notes database called CLIENTS.NSF. Then create a new Notes form in the Clients database, similar to the one shown in figure 30.23 called Clients.

3. Create a new view in the Clients database.

   Make sure that you include the field names from the form. Figure 30.24 shows the designing of the Clients View and the Design Column Definition dialog box that defines the name column in this view. The text name in the Formula text box matches the name field in the clients form to this column in the view.

Fig. 30.23
A Notes form
called Clients.

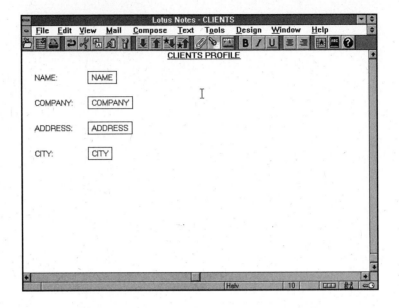

Fig. 30.24
The Design
Column Defini-
tion dialog box.

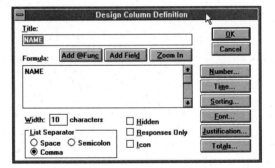

4. Open the Clients database, and switch to the Clients view.

5. Open the **F**ile menu and choose the **I**mport command. The Import dialog box appears as shown in figure 30.25.

Fig. 30.25
The File Import
dialog box.

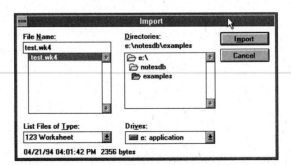

6. Select 123 Worksheet as the file format and then select the 1-2-3 worksheet TEST.WK4, which you created in step 1. Click I**m**port. The Worksheet Import Settings dialog box appears, as shown in figure 30.26.

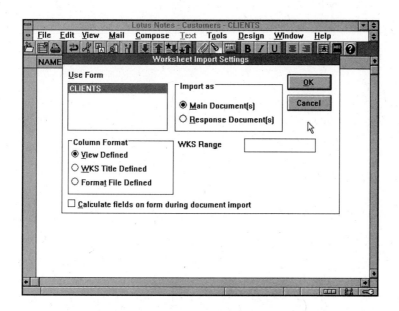

Fig. 30.26
The Worksheet
Import Settings
dialog box.

7. In the **U**se Form list, select the Clients form. In the Column Format box, choose **V**iew Defined.

These options are available in the Column Format area:

- **V**iew Defined. Choose this option if the format of the worksheet columns matches the format of the columns in the view. The column names and widths must be identical.

- **W**KS Title Defined. Choose this option if the cells in the first row of the worksheet file are to be column headers and fields. These cells must be labels. Field names will be created from the column titles for use in the database forms.

- Forma**t** File Defined. Choose this option in all other importing cases, when the relationship of the data to view is more complete. You must then write a COL file to define exactly how data is imported from the worksheet into the view. Consult your Notes documentation on how to define these complex Column Format Description files.

VI

Integrating 1-2-3

Note

If you are not sure how you want to structure the database, use the Worksheet Title Defined option in the Worksheet Import Settings dialog box. This option maps the existing worksheet column titles and contents to the fields in a Notes document.

Tip

You also can enter a named range in the WKS Range list box if you are importing a named range from the worksheet file.

Note

Choose the **C**alculate Fields on Form During Document Import option if you want to calculate some of the data. Notes will calculate any computed fields in the form during the import process.

8. In the Import As box, choose **R**esponse Document(s) or **M**ain Document(s). For this example, choose **M**ain document(s) to insert the imported data into Main documents.

9. Click OK to begin importing. The resulting documents are listed in the Clients view, because Notes imports each row of the 1-2-3 worksheet data into a Clients form (see fig. 30.27).

Fig. 30.27
The imported data in Notes documents.

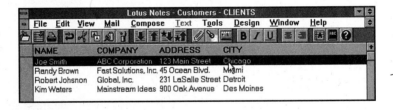

Tip

Before importing an entire worksheet, consider importing a named range of several rows and columns for test purposes.

Note

Only the current worksheet or range in the current worksheet is imported. The name of a range to be imported cannot span multiple worksheets. Also, Notes does not wrap lines of an imported worksheet. The maximum text width is 22.75 inches; any remaining text is truncated.

Exporting Lotus Notes Views and Documents to 1-2-3

You can export Notes data so that it can be used in 1-2-3 and other applications. Notes can export a Notes view to a 1-2-3 worksheet file and a Notes document in text-file format. For example, you might want to export view information to 1-2-3, where you can analyze or format the data in ways that you cannot in Notes.

> **Note**
>
> No link exists between the exported file and the original Notes view or document, so changes in one file are not reflected in the other.

To export a Notes view to a 1-2-3 file, follow these steps:

1. Open the Contact List by Contact Name view in the sample Notes Wholesale Customer Tracking database, as shown in figure 30.28.

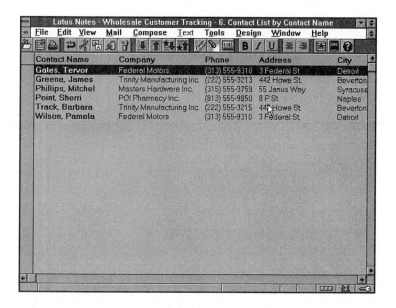

Fig. 30.28
Contact List by Contact Name view.

2. Open the File menu and choose the Export command. The Export dialog box appears, as shown in figure 30.29.

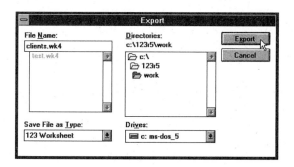

Fig. 30.29
The Export dialog box.

VI

Integrating 1-2-3

3. In the Save File As **T**ype drop-down list, select 123 Worksheet. Type the file name and directory in which you want the file stored and exported.

4. Choose Export. In the File **N**ame box, type a name for the exported file.

5. The Worksheet Export Settings dialog box appears as displayed in figure 30.30.

Fig. 30.30
The Worksheet
Export Settings
dialog box.

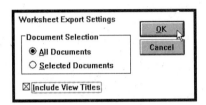

6. Choose **A**ll Documents to export all documents in the view; choose **S**elected Documents to export only certain documents. In this example, choose **A**ll documents. Select the check box Include view titles to include the view titles in the export procedure.

7. Click OK to export all the documents in the view to a 1-2-3 worksheet file.

8. Open and review the exported Notes file in 1-2-3 (see fig. 30.31).

Fig. 30.31
The exported
Notes view in
1-2-3.

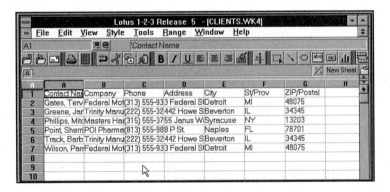

Note

When you export Notes views to 1-2-3 format, column headings become labels in the first row of the worksheet, and each row in the view becomes a row in the worksheet. Exporting a view to a 1-2-3 worksheet file may be useful if you want to create a graph or chart based on the data in that Notes document.

You can export Notes documents in many different formats. Text or ASCII format is the most common file format that 1-2-3 can read. The process is the same as exporting a Notes view to 1-2-3, except that you must export to ASCII text-file format and then open the file in 1-2-3 as a text file. Follow these steps:

1. Open the Wholesale Customer Tracking database, and open any document (see fig. 30.32).

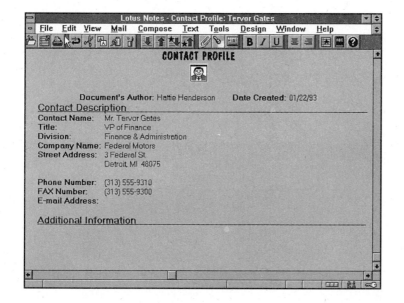

Fig. 30.32
A Notes document.

2. Open the **F**ile menu and choose the **E**xport command to open the Export dialog box, as shown in figure 30.33.

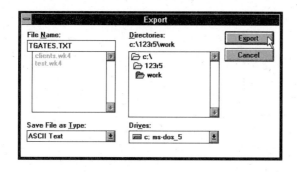

Fig. 30.33
The Export dialog box.

VI

Integrating 1-2-3

3. In the Save File As **T**ype list, select ASCII Text.

4. In the File **N**ame box, type a name for the file, and specify the directory in which you want the file to be stored and exported. Select E**x**port.

5. The Text File Export dialog box appears. Specify the number of characters that will make a new line or word wrap. The default is 75 characters per line (see fig. 30.34).

Fig. 30.34
The Text File
Export dialog box.

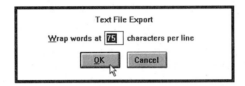

6. Open and review the exported, unformatted ASCII text file in 1-2-3 (see fig. 30.35).

Fig. 30.35
The exported
Notes document
in 1-2-3.

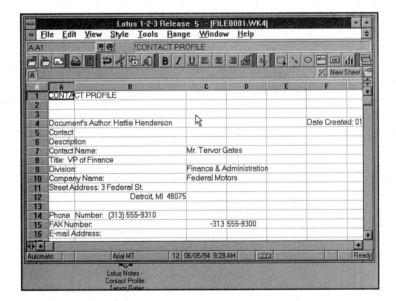

Using Notes Mail from 1-2-3 for Windows

◀ "Using 1-2-3
with the Lotus
SmartSuite,"
p. 813

Notes Mail enables you to send information directly to another user from 1-2-3. This feature is a convenient way to send a worksheet or range of data to another user without leaving 1-2-3.

If you are using Notes Mail, follow these steps to send a 1-2-3 file or range of data to another user:

1. Open the 1-2-3 file that you want to send or copy text from.

2. If you intend to send the entire worksheet, skip to step 3. If you intend to send a range of data, select that data.

3. Open the **F**ile menu and choose the Send **M**ail command. The Send Mail dialog box appears, as displayed in figure 30.36.

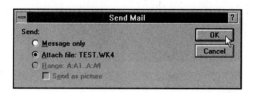

Fig. 30.36
The Send Mail dialog box selecting Attach.

4. 1-2-3 checks whether the file you are sending has been saved since it was last modified. If the file has been saved since it was last modified, choose the **A**ttach option to attach the file to your message.

   If the file has not been saved since it was last modified, choose the **S**ave and Attach option to save the file and attach it to your message (see fig. 30.37).

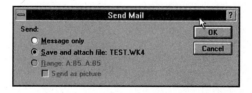

Fig. 30.37
The Send Mail dialog box selecting Save and Attach.

Caution

If the file is empty, the dialog box displays a greyed out **A**ttach File option because you cannot mail an empty 1-2-3 file.

---

5. Click OK. If Notes is active, the Lotus Notes dialog box appears. If Notes is not active, you are prompted to enter your password.

6. Your message or memo form appears. After addressing and writing your message, choose **S**end to mail the message and attached file. The message is mailed, and the dialog box closes.

Note

If a 1-2-3-format file exists for your worksheet, that file is attached to your message along with the worksheet. You should tell the recipient of the message to extract both files.

Troubleshooting

*My Send **M**ail command doesn't appear in the **F**ile menu.*

Make sure that you installed the appropriate release of each product. You can send mail from 1-2-3 with Lotus Notes, cc:Mail for Windows, Microsoft Mail, and other VIM mail applications. To use Lotus Notes Mail, verify that the following lines have been added to your WIN.INI file:

```
[LOTUSMAIL]
Application=Notes
Program=C:\notes\notes.exe
```

Substitute your path to Notes for c:\notes, if it is different. 1-2-3 will launch Lotus Notes when you use the **F**ile menu's Send **M**ail command.

Why does the envelope or letter icon display in the 1-2-3 status bar?

The envelope or Mail SmartIcon displayed in the status bar indicates that you have received mail from another end-user. Click on this SmartIcon button to activate your mail application.

Using Application Field Exchange

The latest releases of Lotus Notes, 1-2-3, Ami Pro, Freelance, and Improv include a powerful new technology called Notes Field Exchange. This new and powerful technology enhances the integration features of the Lotus SmartSuites with Lotus Notes. Notes/FX enables embedded objects in a Notes document to send data to Notes fields, and vice versa.

Notes/FX allows businesses to create applications that enable multiple users to create worksheets by using the same 1-2-3 worksheet. Users then can save, categorize, and view these worksheets in a Notes database. The Notes/FX feature promotes a many-to-many relationship versus a one-to-many or many-to-one relationship, in which many users have access to the many various files stored in the database.

You could create a Notes form for an expense report and embed a 1-2-3 worksheet object in the form. Notes can be programmed to launch 1-2-3 automatically whenever anyone uses the form to compose a new budget report, so that new expense-report data is entered in a 1-2-3 template. After the user completes the expense-report worksheet and closes 1-2-3, the expense worksheet is embedded in the Notes document. This expense information now can be used to create Notes views that enable the organization to view the data in various ways.

How Does Notes/FX Exchange Data?

Notes/FX uses OLE objects to exchange information with fields in a Notes form. If you use OLE to embed a 1-2-3 worksheet in a Notes database, 1-2-3 will make available to Notes data in cells and ranges, as well as some document information. Notes can use these fields in views and calculations, and exchange them with the 1-2-3 worksheet. For Notes/FX to exchange data with 1-2-3 (or any other OLE-enabled server application), the field names in the OLE embedded file created in 1-2-3 (the server) must match the field names in the Notes form being used.

You can use Notes/FX to change two type of data: 1-2-3 document information and 1-2-3 worksheet data. *Document information* is descriptive data about the specific embedded worksheet object, such as the file size, number of worksheets, date and time last revised, and worksheet name. Document information travels in only one direction: from 1-2-3 to Notes. *Worksheet data* is text and numbers in worksheet cells, or named ranges within the embedded object. 1-2-3 data can travel in both directions—that is, from 1-2-3 to Notes and from Notes to 1-2-3.

Setting Up Application Field Exchange

Before using Notes/FX with 1-2-3, you need the following system components:

- Notes 3.0

- 1-2-3 for Windows Release 5

- Windows 3.1

- SHARE.EXE (DOS share program)

Note

To load the DOS SHARE.EXE program on the workstation, follow these steps:

1. Exit Windows.

2. Start SHARE.EXE from the DOS directory (C:\DOS\SHARE).

3. Return to Windows.

You can start SHARE.EXE before every Windows session by adding the following line to your AUTOEXEC.BAT file:

    C:\DOS\SHARE

Using Application Field Exchange with 1-2-3 for Windows

1-2-3 includes a sample Notes Database file—EXPENSE.NSF—that demonstrates Application Field Exchange. To use the sample file, copy EXPENSE.NSF to your LOCAL Notes directory, and then add the database to your Notes desktop (see fig. 30.38). If EXPENSE.NSF is not in your Release 5 directory, check your Release 4 sample directory for this sample file.

Fig. 30.38
The sample Notes expense-report database.

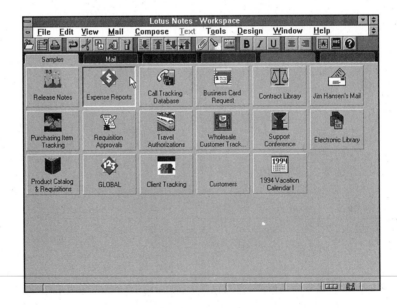

To preview how Application Field Exchange works, use the Notes Expense database to create an expense report. Follow these steps:

1. Open the **C**ompose menu and choose the **E**xpense Report command (see fig. 30.39). This action executes 1-2-3 and loads the expense-report template.

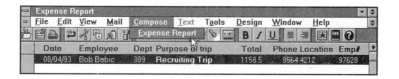

Fig. 30.39
Selecting an **E**xpense **R**eport from the Notes Compose menu in the Expense Reports database.

2. Edit the 1-2-3 expense template in 1-2-3 (see fig. 30.40).

3. Open the **F**ile menu and choose **U**pdate Lotus Notes or E**x**it & Return to Lotus Notes.

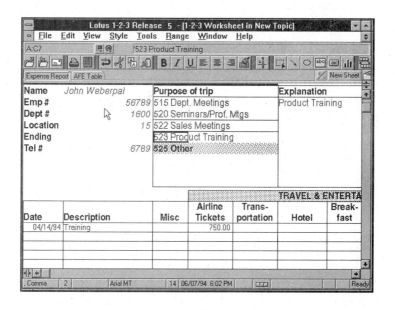

Fig. 30.40
Edit the expense-report object in 1-2-3.

4. Switch to Notes if you selected Update and not E**x**it & Return. Your new document appears in the view, including the new data entered in the 1-2-3 expense-report template (see fig. 30.41).

Fig. 30.41
The new document and data in Notes.

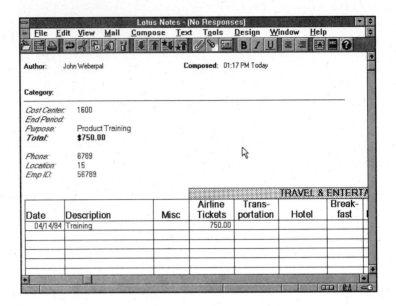

This procedure simplifies the process of creating expense reports—and also the process of reviewing the reports. In the old days, "Sneaker-Net" was used to distribute templates via floppy disk.

Establishing Application Field Exchange between 1-2-3 and Notes is an easy process. All you have to do is identify and match Note field names with 1-2-3 range names or cell addresses. The data in Notes field names and the 1-2-3 range names is exchanged through OLE, embedding the 1-2-3 worksheet as an object in the Notes form or document. To exchange data between 1-2-3 and Notes, you must embed a 1-2-3 worksheet object in a Notes form. In the worksheet object, you need to create a two-column table of the data you want to exchange.

To create the Notes form, follow these steps:

1. In Notes, select or create a new database.

2. Open the **D**esign menu and choose the **F**orms command. The Design Forms dialog box appears, as shown in figure 30.42.

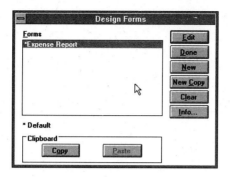

Fig. 30.42
The Design Forms
dialog box.

3. Choose **N**ew to create a form or **E**dit to edit an existing form.

4. Create and name the fields that will contain text and numbers from the 1-2-3 worksheet object. To create a field in a Notes form, open the **D**esign menu and select **N**ew Field. The Design New field dialog box appears. Select Create Field to be used only within this form radio button and then OK. The Field Definition dialog box will appear (see fig. 30.43). You will need to create fields on the form for all the 1-2-3 fields you want to exchange. For more information on creating forms in Notes, consult your Notes documentation.

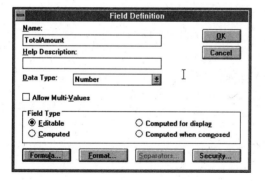

Fig. 30.43
Using the Field
Definition dialog
box to create fields
in a Notes form.

5. Close and save the form.

To create and embed the 1-2-3 worksheet, follow these steps:

1. Open the desired 1-2-3 worksheet, or create a new file.

2. Create a two-column table in the worksheet. The first column should contain field names (in Notes form) that will receive and send 1-2-3 data. The second column should contain cell addresses or range names of the data in the 1-2-3 worksheet.

3. Highlight the two-column table. Open the **R**ange menu and choose **N**ame. In the Name edit box, type **NOTES FIELDS** then select **A**dd to name the two-column table NOTES FIELDS (see fig. 30.44).

Fig. 30.44
Naming the Notes Fields range in 1-2-3.

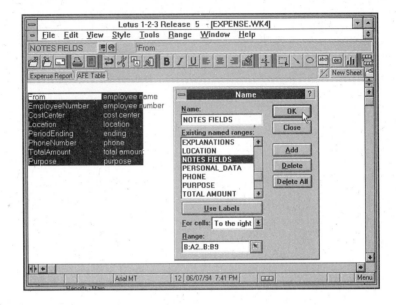

4. Open the **E**dit menu and choose the **C**opy command to copy part of the worksheet that you want to display in the Notes form (see fig. 30.45). The selected range doesn't have to display the information you want to exchange.

Fig. 30.45
Copy a range of data to display in Notes.

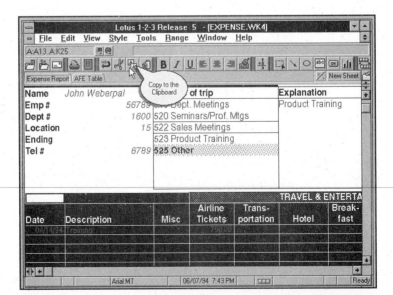

5. Open the **E**dit menu and choose the Paste **S**pecial command to display the Paste Special dialog box.

6. Choose **E**mbed to embed the 1-2-3 worksheet object in the form.

7. In the **D**isplay As list, select Picture or Bitmap.

> **Note**
>
> To have Notes automatically open the worksheet object when composing a new document, choose **D**esign Form **A**ttributes and then choose O**bj**ect Activation and then check **C**omposing a new document with this form; otherwise, Notes opens an embedded object only when you double-click the object.

8. Close and save the Notes form.

You can now create a new Notes document by using the form you just created. To do so, follow these steps:

1. Open the **C**ompose menu, and select the name of the form that you created. If you select Object Activation, Notes creates a new document that contains the embedded object and switches you into 1-2-3; otherwise, you will have to double-click the object to activate 1-2-3 and open the object.

2. Edit the data in the 1-2-3 object.

3. Open the **F**ile menu and choose the **U**pdate Lotus Notes command to update the worksheet object.

4. Open the **F**ile menu and choose the Exit & Return to Lotus Notes command to close 1-2-3 and return to Notes. Alternatively, choose **C**lose to close the worksheet object without exiting 1-2-3. The fields in the Notes document that match the 1-2-3 data are updated.

5. Switch to Notes. Your new document appears in the view, including the new data that was entered in the 1-2-3 expense report template.

The following procedure is useful if you want your updates in the Notes document to take effect in the 1-2-3 worksheet object. To update an existing Notes document, follow these steps:

1. Open a Notes document.

2. Open the **E**dit menu and choose the **E**dit Document command.

3. Edit the Notes field in the document whose value you want to update. In this example, the cost center number (which is the label for the Department number field in 1-2-3) has been modified from 1600 to 1805 (see fig. 30.46).

Fig. 30.46
Editing a Notes field in the Notes document.

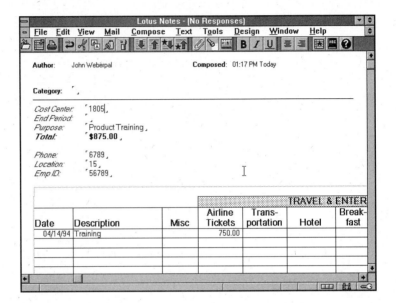

Caution

Not all Notes fields support two-way exchange of data. You cannot send data to 1-2-3 cells that contain formulas or those that are in protected cells, and you cannot send data to 1-2-3 from Notes computed fields.

4. Double-click the 1-2-3 worksheet object to activate and update the fields that you changed in Notes. Notice that the Department number has been updated to 1805, as shown in figure 30.47.

5. In the 1-2-3 object, edit the data that you want to change in the Notes document.

6. Open the **F**ile menu and choose the **U**pdate command to update the worksheet object.

7. Open the **F**ile menu and choose E**x**it & Return or **C**lose to close the worksheet object. The fields that you modified in 1-2-3 now are reflected in Notes.

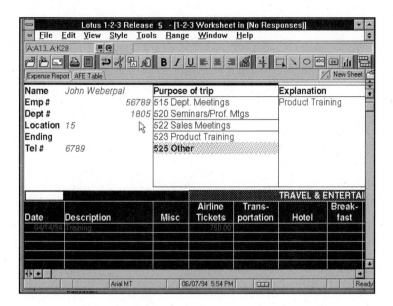

Fig. 30.47
The updated Notes
field in the 1-2-3
object.

This method is a powerful, easy way to integrate Notes and 1-2-3 so that users can create, store, disseminate, and locate a variety of data types. Businesses can dramatically improve customer service and internal workflow by making information accessible.

From Here...

The tools described in this chapter enable users in an organization to work together effectively by storing information and data in a central location. To learn more about integrating 1-2-3 with other applications, review the following chapters:

- Chapter 22, "Managing Multiple Solutions with the Version Manager." Learn how to create versions and scenarios by using Version Manager to use in what-if analysis.

- Chapter 29, "Using 1-2-3 with the Lotus SmartSuite." Explains how to integrate 1-2-3 with the other Lotus applications to increase your productivity and to learn more about object linking and embedding.

- Chapter 31, "Integrating 1-2-3 with DOS and Mainframe Applications." Explains what to do when you need to integrate 1-2-3 for Windows with DOS and mainframe applications.

VI

Integrating 1-2-3

Integrating 1-2-3 with DOS and Mainframe Applications

Sharing information with 1-2-3 Release 5 is easy if you use DOS applications such as dBASE, Microsoft Word, Paradox, and WordPerfect. 1-2-3 also allows for the simple transfer and exchange of ASCII (text) files with mainframe computers.

1-2-3 Release 5 opens, saves, and translates many file formats such as dBASE, Excel, SuperCalc, and previous 1-2-3 releases file formats. 1-2-3 also loads and creates text files for data transfer with applications that do not use one of the common formats as an interchange.

In this chapter, you learn how to do the following:

- Copy and paste information between 1-2-3 and DOS applications

- Save 1-2-3 worksheets in file formats readable by other applications.

- Open files created by other applications and then save the data in 1-2-3 format

- Use text files to transfer data to and from 1-2-3 and DOS or mainframe applications

VI

Integrating 1-2-3

> **Note**
>
> Most popular DOS programs are also available in Windows versions. If you use Excel, Word for Windows, WordPerfect for Windows, or any other Windows version of an application mentioned in this chapter, use the methods discussed in Chapter 29, "Using 1-2-3 with the Lotus SmartSuite," to share data. The instructions in this chapter relate to DOS applications only.

Understanding How Windows Runs DOS Applications

Microsoft Windows allows you to run more than one program at a time. The way the programs run—whether they continue processing information when another program is currently being used or stop processing until they are reselected—depends on the type of computer you have and the mode in which Windows is running. Windows can operate in 386 Enhanced mode or Standard mode. If you are running Windows on a 386-based computer with at least 2M of memory, Windows operates in 386 Enhanced mode. In 386 Enhanced mode, DOS applications continue to run even when the applications are in the background. On a computer with a 286-based processor, Windows runs in Standard mode. By default, all DOS applications do not run in the background. To specify how resources are allocated to non-windows DOS applications, you need to set the Foreground and Background priorities for these applications in the program's PIF file.

> **Note**
>
> 1-2-3 Release 5 for Windows requires an IBM-compatible 386 PC or higher and a minimum of 4M of RAM.

◄ "Manipulating Windows," p. 46

If you are using 386 Enhanced mode, you can display DOS applications full-screen or in a window (see fig. 31.1). To switch a running DOS application between a full-screen display and a window, press Alt+Enter.

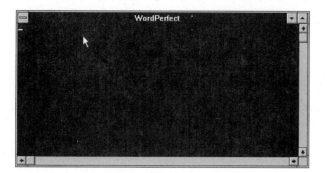

Fig. 31.1
WordPerfect, a
DOS application,
running in a
window.

Copying and Pasting between Applications

Tip
Display the
contents of the
Clipboard by
double-clicking the
Clipboard Viewer
in the Main group
window.

The item you use to transfer information between 1-2-3 and DOS applications is called the *Clipboard* (see fig. 31.2). You can use the Windows Clipboard in Standard or 386 Enhanced mode.

Clipboard —
Viewer

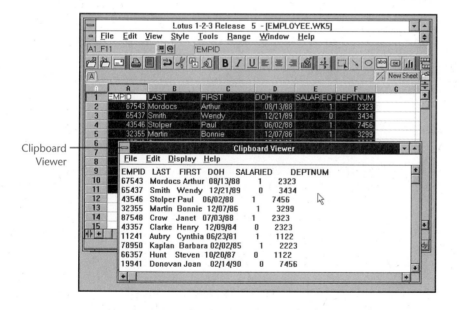

Fig. 31.2
The Clipboard
Viewer in
Windows.

Copying and Pasting in Standard Mode

DOS applications must run full-screen when you're running Windows in Standard mode. This means that you must copy an entire screen of text from the DOS program to paste into 1-2-3 for Windows. Generally, pasting an entire screen of data from a DOS application to 1-2-3 is impractical, especially

◀ "Using 1-2-3 with the Lotus SmartSuite," p. 813

if you want only a small portion of the information. You can paste the screen from the DOS application into a text editor, such as Windows Notepad, and then select and paste only the information you need.

> **Note**
>
> If you need to transfer more than one screen of data between 1-2-3 and a DOS application, try saving the data in a file format that both applications have in common or use a text file to transfer the information. Both transfer methods are covered later in this chapter.

Tip
If pressing PrtSc does not copy the screen to the Clipboard, you may have an unenhanced keyboard or an older ROM BIOS. Try pressing Alt+PrtSc or Shift+PrtSc.

To copy and paste into 1-2-3 the contents of a full-screen DOS application running in Standard mode, perform the following steps:

1. Start the DOS application and make sure the information you want to copy is displayed on the screen.

2. Press PrtSc to copy the DOS application's screen to the Windows Clipboard.

3. Start 1-2-3 if not currently open. If 1-2-3 is already running, switch to 1-2-3 by pressing Ctrl+Esc, and then select 1-2-3 Release 5 in the Windows Task List (see fig. 31.3). You can also utilize Alt+Tab to switch between running applications.

Fig. 31.3
Choosing 1-2-3 from the Windows Task List.

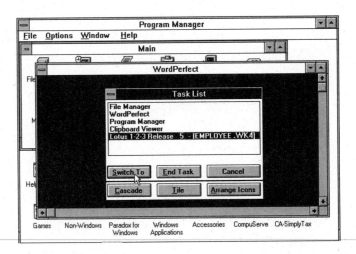

4. Open the 1-2-3 worksheet where you want to paste the data from the Clipboard.

5. Select the cell in which you want the first line of the data to be pasted.

6. Open the **E**dit menu and choose **P**aste, or click the Paste SmartIcon.

1-2-3 places each line data into separate cells below the selected cell. Each line from the DOS application's screen goes into a single cell. Text and numbers within that line are not separated into individual cells. To separate lines of data into individual cells, you need to parse the data.

To copy a cell or range of selected data from 1-2-3 and paste the data into a DOS application, complete the following steps:

◄ "Retrieving Data from External Databases," p. 791

1. Select the cell or range in 1-2-3.

2. Open the **E**dit menu and choose **C**opy, or click the Copy SmartIcon (see fig. 31.4).

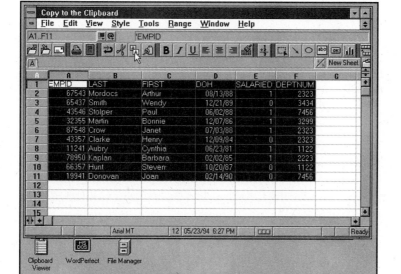

Fig. 31.4
Copying a range of 1-2-3 data.

3. Switch to the DOS application using the Task List or Alt+Tab.

4. Position the DOS application's cursor where you want to paste the 1-2-3 data.

5. Reduce the DOS application to a minimized icon by pressing Alt+Esc.

VI

Integrating 1-2-3

6. Select the DOS application's icon (press Alt+Esc to select it, if necessary), press Alt+space bar to display the icon's Control menu, and then open the **E**dit menu and choose **P**aste (see fig. 31.5). Switch back to the DOS application and notice that the data is pasted at the insertion point chosen in Step 4.

Fig. 31.5
Pasting in Standard mode by using a DOS program's Control menu.

Tip
You may need to minimize, move, or resize the 1-2-3 window or other application windows to find the DOS application's icon.

Tip
Transferring data to 1-2-3 for DOS is easier if you save the 1-2-3 for Windows worksheet in a file format that 1-2-3 for DOS can read and write (such as WK1 or WK3).

Pasted lines of data end with a carriage return (the character code produced when you press the Enter key). Most DOS applications move the cursor to a new line or cell when they receive a carriage return, so multiple lines of data pasted from 1-2-3 retain their formatting as separate lines.

Not all programs move the cursor to a new cell or line when they encounter a carriage return, however. For example, 1-2-3 for DOS pastes multiple lines of data into the selected cell or line, and all line breaks are lost. In this case, you would paste the 1-2-3 data one cell at a time, in order to preserve the data format.

Copying and Pasting in 386 Enhanced Mode

When Windows is running in 386 Enhanced Mode, you can run DOS applications full-screen or in a window. DOS programs running in a window act just like Windows programs, but you can use the same commands and work with the same display you used when running the DOS program from DOS.

When you run DOS applications in a window, you can copy selected information, the entire desktop, or a single window onto the Clipboard and then switch to another DOS or Windows application to paste the selection.

To copy and paste from a DOS application into 1-2-3, follow these steps:

1. Press Alt+Enter to toggle the DOS application from full-screen to a window.

2. Press Alt+space bar. Then open the **E**dit menu and choose Mar**k** (see fig. 31.6). Mar**k** allows you to use a keyboard or mouse to select text to move onto the Clipboard. Select the data you want copied by dragging across the data with the mouse. If you are using a keyboard, press the arrow keys to move to one corner of the data you want to select, and then press Shift+arrow keys to select the data.

Fig. 31.6
Using **E**dit Mar**k** to copy data.

3. Press Alt+space bar. Open Control menu and choose **E**dit and then Cop**y** Enter to copy the selected data into the Windows Clipboard (see fig. 31.7).

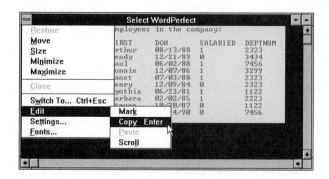

Fig. 31.7
Copying information from WordPerfect, a DOS application, in Enhanced mode.

VI

Integrating 1-2-3

> **Note**
>
> You cannot run a DOS application while in Mark mode (see Step 2). To return to the DOS application without copying any data to the Windows Clipboard, press Esc to leave the Control menu.

4. If 1-2-3 is running, use the Task List to switch it; otherwise, start 1-2-3 now.

5. Select the spreadsheet and cell where you want to paste the data.

6. Open the **E**dit menu and choose **P**aste, or click the Paste SmartIcon (see fig. 31.8).

Fig. 31.8
Clipboard data
pasted into 1-2-3.

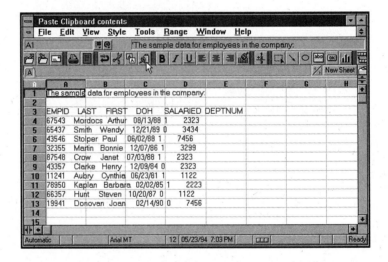

When you copy numbers from a DOS application into 1-2-3, you can copy a single number or a column of numbers. The numbers or column of numbers are pasted into a single cell or a column of cells. If you copy entire lines, the numbers are not pasted into individual cells in the row. To separate lines of numbers or data into individual cells, you need to parse the data.

◀ "Retrieving Data
from External
Databases,"
p. 791

To copy data from 1-2-3 and paste it into a DOS application, complete the following steps:

1. Select the cell or range in 1-2-3 that you want to copy.

2. Open the **E**dit menu and choose **C**opy, or click the Copy SmartIcon.

3. Use Ctrl+Esc to switch to the DOS application, if it is already running; otherwise, start it now.

4. Position the cursor in the application where you want to insert the data.

5. Press Alt+space bar to access the Control menu. Choose **E**dit and then **P**aste. If your application was running full-screen, selecting **E**dit **P**aste from the Control menu switches your application into a window mode (see fig. 31.9).

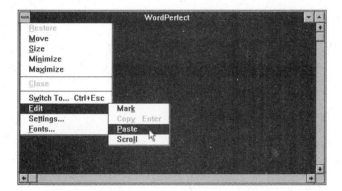

Fig. 31.9
Pasting 1-2-3 data into a DOS application.

The data is inserted into the DOS application just as though you typed it there. 1-2-3 places a tab between the contents of each cell, which makes tables of data easy to align once you paste them into a word processor. You need only to set tabs and align the columns of 1-2-3 data.

Exporting Data

Exporting data is an easy and efficient way to exchange data between 1-2-3 and DOS or mainframe applications. Why not use the Clipboard to exchange all of your data? The Clipboard is ideally suited for exchanging small blocks of text or data, while exporting allows you to exchange larger blocks of text in one step.

1-2-3 can share data and charts with other applications. To transfer information between a DOS application and 1-2-3, either export or translate data from 1-2-3 to a file format that the DOS application can read or import data from the DOS application into a file format that 1-2-3 can read, depending on which direction the data is going.

VI

Integrating 1-2-3

Understanding File Formats

1-2-3 Release 5 includes support for several different file types. This compatibility provides you with a number of ways to import and export data between DOS and mainframe applications. If no specific file format is available for 1-2-3 to transfer data directly, you can create a text file format that transfers text and numbers. 1-2-3 provides an enhanced method of opening ASCII text files. This new capability enables 1-2-3 to automatically parse text files into spreadsheet cells when selecting the File Open command.

Caution

By saving a 1-2-3 worksheet to text file format you will only save the text and numbers. The formatting (i.e., bold, underline, italics), formulas, charts, and drawn objects will be lost. 1-2-3 will leave blank lines in the text file where the chart or drawn objects would have appeared.

Table 31.1   DOS File Formats Read and Written by 1-2-3

File Extension	Description
WK1	1-2-3 for DOS Release 2 or earlier
WK3	1-2-3 for DOS Release 3
TXT	Text, ASCII, and Delimited files
Paradox	Paradox table files
dBASE	dBASE DBF files

Most DOS programs—including database management programs, spreadsheets, and word processors—can create and read text files. If you have a worksheet or database file from another program that you would like to use in 1-2-3, you can use the Translate utility to convert files to 1-2-3 Release 3 format (WK3). Once the file is in WK3 file format, you can open and save it in Release 4 format.

◄ "Managing Files," p. 281

Note

The Translate Utility is not shipping with 5. It is available only through Lotus Customer Service (1-800-343-5414) or CompuServe.

Caution

You can't convert a file directly to Release 4 format. You must convert a file to Release 3 format first, and then save it in Release 4 format.

Saving 1-2-3 Worksheets in a Different Format

The ability to save 1-2-3 Release 5 worksheets into a different file format can be very useful. For instance, coworkers may need to see your worksheet but they use an earlier DOS release of 1-2-3 requiring you to save the file in WK3 or WK1 file format. Maybe a manager or business client needs your customer address listing to import into Paradox for DOS. The capability to save 1-2-3 worksheets to different file formats allows you to transfer information with other applications easily.

To save 1-2-3 worksheets in a different format, perform the following steps:

1. Open the **F**ile menu and choose Save **A**s. The Save As dialog box appears (see fig. 31.10).

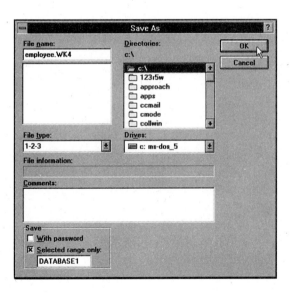

Fig. 31.10

The Save As dialog box.

2. Type a file name in the text box (do not add a file extension) and do not press Enter.

3. From the File **T**ype list box, select the format in which you want to save these files, and select from the Dri**v**es and **D**irectories list the desired drive and directory on which you want to save the file. Refer back to Table 31.1 for descriptions of the various file formats.

4. Choose the OK button.

> **Note**
>
> If you need to export a file to a format not shown in the Save As File **T**ype list box or in the Translate utility, read your DOS program's manual to find information on the program's capability to read 1-2-3 file formats. Some database management systems and word processing programs, such as Paradox and WordPerfect, can read data directly from 1-2-3 worksheets. This is easier for you because you eliminate the need to save to the proper file format.

Saving 1-2-3 Data to Paradox for DOS

There are two efficient ways to save and import 1-2-3 data into a Paradox for DOS file. The first method is to use **F**ile Save **A**s in 1-2-3 for Windows and specify the Paradox file type. The second method is to save your 1-2-3 Release 5 worksheet in WK1 format and then import the data using the Paradox menu commands. The first method is easier because it saves steps and time.

To save a 1-2-3 worksheet as a Paradox for DOS file using the 1-2-3 for Windows File Save As dialog box, complete the following steps:

1. Select **F**ile Save **A**s in 1-2-3 for Windows. The File Save As dialog box appears.

2. Specify Paradox in the File **T**ype list box (see fig. 31.11).

3. Select the drives and directories where you want the file saved, and then press OK.

To save a 1-2-3 worksheet as Paradox for DOS file, by first saving the worksheet into WK1 format, complete the following steps:

1. Save your 1-2-3 Release 5 worksheet in WK1 format.

2. Switch to Paradox if it is already running; otherwise, start it now.

3. Choose **T**ools **E**xportImport **I**mport **1**-2-3, and then select **2**)1-2-3 Release 2 to import a .WK1 file format.

4. Type the path and file name.

5. When Paradox asks you to name the new table, type a name of up to 8 characters and press Enter.

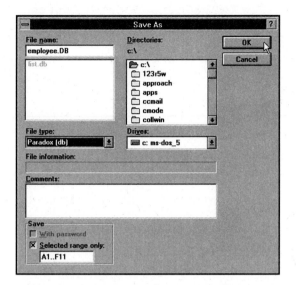

Fig. 31.11
Saving a 1-2-3 file
into Paradox for
DOS file format.

Note

Except for delimited ASCII files, data files from other programs can be imported only into new Paradox tables, not into existing tables.

Caution

Paradox automatically defines the structure of the new table. Only data values, not the formulas, are imported.

Saving 1-2-3 Data to WordPerfect 6.0 for DOS

To save and import 1-2-3 data into a WordPerfect 6.0 file, complete the following steps:

1. Save your 1-2-3 worksheet in 1-2-3 WK3 or WK1 format using the steps detailed in the previous section "Saving 1-2-3 Worksheets in a Different Format."

2. Use the Task List or Ctrl+Esc to switch to WordPerfect, if it is already running; otherwise, start it now.

3. Open the WordPerfect file in which you want to insert the 1-2-3 data and then position the cursor where you want the 1-2-3 data to appear.

VI

Integrating 1-2-3

4. Choose the **T**ools command, or press Alt+F7; then choose **S**preadsheet **I**mport. The Spreadsheet Import dialog box appears.

Tip
You can use WordPerfect's File List or Quicklist to find the file you need.

5. Choose **F**ilename, type the full path name, and then press Enter.

6. Choose **R**ange, and enter the data range or range name. If you don't specify a data range or range name, the entire worksheet is imported.

7. Choose the **T**ype command, and select Import as Table or Import as Text. You may need to reformat fonts and columns in tables to fit the data on the page.

8. Choose the Import command. WordPerfect inserts the data.

Importing Data

1-2-3 is used by many companies to analyze information and data stored in other applications and file formats. In the past, the only way to import data from another application was to save the application files as text files. Because most applications can work with text files, this format was and still is useful for transfers between vastly different systems. However, Lotus has improved its technologies to import and read other file formats.

◀ "Retrieving Data from External Databases," p. 791

1-2-3 for Windows allows you to open files saved in another file format by using the File Open dialog box. Plus, if you want to automate your system or create direct links between 1-2-3 and an external database, you should investigate the use of Lotus DataLens drivers. Lotus DataLens drivers allow you to connect to external database tables like Paradox and dBASE. During your connection to the external database you can read and send data directly to that external database. This is important because any changes or updates you make to the database take effect immediately. Plus, if you were working with these files on a network, other users also see the changes. Still, importing data from a different file format is very useful if you need to modify, change, format, or analyze data without having your changes affect the source data in the original file.

Opening Files Saved in Another File Format

The easiest way to import data into 1-2-3 is to import the data in one of the file formats 1-2-3 can read, and then resave the data in WK4 format. The DOS file formats 1-2-3 can read are listed in Table 31.1, shown earlier in this chapter.

To open a non-1-2-3 file, follow these steps:

1. Open the **F**ile menu and choose **O**pen, or click the Open File
   SmartIcon. The Open File dialog box appears (see fig. 31.12).

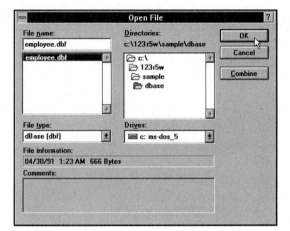

Fig. 31.12
The Open File
dialog box
showing the File
Type list box.

2. Select the file format desired in the File **T**ype list box.

3. Select the file you want to import in the File **N**ame list box. Locate the
   file using **D**irectories and Dri**v**es lists to switch the directory and drive,
   if necessary.

4. Choose the OK button. 1-2-3 imports the file. Generally, 1-2-3 reads
   and opens the file. In some instances, if you are opening a dBASE or
   Paradox file, 1-2-3 displays `Connecting dbase c:\path`. After processing
   and opening, 1-2-3 displays the file name in the title bar.

When 1-2-3 loads a non-1-2-3 file, 1-2-3 remembers the original file format.
When you save the file, 1-2-3 displays the Save As dialog box. To save the file
in its original non-1-2-3 format, choose the OK button. 1-2-3 prompts you to
confirm replacing the original file.

> **Caution**
>
> Saving to a non-1-2-3 format can result in the loss of formulas, functions, special
> features, and formatting that are unique to 1-2-3. Consult your non-1-2-3
> application's manual for differences before you save the file.

VI

Integrating 1-2-3

Importing Data from Mainframe Computers

If the database management system (DBMS) of the mainframe from which you want to import data supports Structured Query Language (SQL) and is connected to your computer via a network, you may be able to retrieve data easily and quickly from the mainframe database. Lotus DataLens is capable of accessing data in a variety of mainframe and personal computer database formats.

If the mainframe database management system is not available to your computer through a network, or if the mainframe database uses a format 1-2-3 cannot read, you must use a text file to import the data into 1-2-3.

Many corporations download text files from their mainframes into text file format. *Downloading* is the reception and storage of a data file or program from a distant computer via data communication links. 1-2-3 can separate text lines up to 255 characters long into individual cells in a worksheet.

Importing a Delimited Text File

A *delimited text file* is a file in ASCII format that contains rows of data separated by characters called *delimiters*. A delimiter is a , (comma), space, : (colon), or ; (semicolon) entered between numbers and text in each row. Each row must end with a carriage return.

All labels must be enclosed in quotation marks. For example, `"Jones","Chicago",24,"Engineer",32000` is a line from a delimited text file.

 To import data from a delimited text file into 1-2-3 worksheet format, use **F**ile **O**pen or click the Open File SmartIcon. In the File **T**ype list box, select Text as the file type to open. Next, select the desired text file in the file list box. 1-2-3 automatically separates the data into columns in the worksheet according to the delimiters.

Tip
Change the file type to Text in the Open File Dialog box before selecting OK. Doing this ensures that 1-2-3 recognizes that you are dealing or opening a text file.

Text Options is a feature in 1-2-3 for Windows that allows you to specify further information about how you want 1-2-3 to open a text file and parse it. To open a text file using Text Options do the following:

1. Choose Text **O**ptions in the Open File dialog box (see fig. 31.13).

Note

The Text **O**ptions button appears when you select Text as the file type in the File type list box.

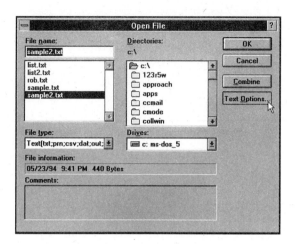

Fig. 31.13
Using Text
Options to open
a text file.

2. In the Text Options dialog box, choose an option from the Bring Into Columns Based On section (see fig. 31.14).

   ■ **S**eparator specifies the type of separator you want 1-2-3 to use for breaking the text into columns in the worksheet. You can specify Other Character(s) and then enter the separator character in the text box.

   ■ **L**ayout of File specifies that you are allowing 1-2-3 to autoparse the text file by determining the breaks and columns.

   ■ **P**ut Everything into One Column.

3. In the **C**haracter Set text box, specify the code page you want 1-2-3 to use for interpreting the data in the text file. Generally, you use the Windows (ANSI) or DOS code pages.

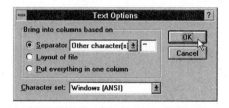

VI

Fig. 31.14
Specifying the text
options to open a
text file.

Integrating 1-2-3

4. Select OK to save your text options.

5. Select OK to import and open the text file.

Using File Open Combine to Import a Text File

When you open or import a text file, the file is entered into a new 1-2-3 worksheet. There may be situations when you need to combine or append data to a current worksheet. You can use 1-2-3 for Windows Combine feature to import and open a text file into a current worksheet. This method is easier and faster than importing a text file into it's own worksheet and then copying and pasting the information into another worksheet.

To import a file using the **C**ombine feature:

1. Open the **F**ile menu and choose **O**pen, or click the Open File SmartIcon. The Open File dialog box appears.

2. Select Text in the File **T**ype list box.

3. Choose **C**ombine (see fig. 31.15).

   The text file is added to your current worksheet (see fig. 31.16).

Fig. 31.15
Using **C**ombine to
import a file into a
current worksheet.

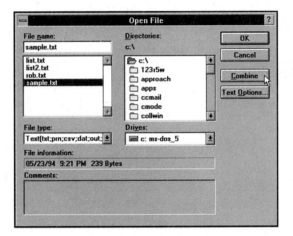

Parsing Text into Columns

Occasionally, you may import a text file that is not properly delimited or is improperly formatted with fixed length records. A fixed length record contains data combined into one line of text. If you are working with a text file that consists of fixed length records, you need to import the file as a single column of data. However, your goal is to separate each fixed length record in the imported text file into fields or columns so that you can attain a database in 1-2-3 that consists of rows (records) and columns (fields).

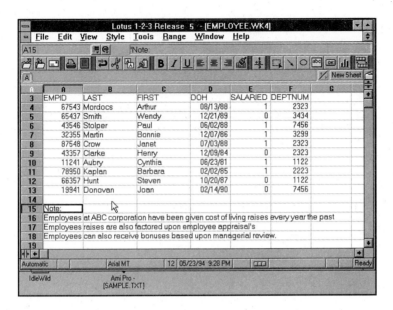

Fig. 31.16
The text file
combined or
added to the
current worksheet.

When you import a fixed length text file, each line of the text file is placed in a separate cell, and all cells form a single column. None of the data is separated into individual columns or cells. To separate the long lines into cells, you must parse, or separate, each line into its individual parts.

◄ "Using Caution when Parsing Data," p. 809

To parse a text file in 1-2-3, you need to use the Range Parse feature. Range Parse converts long labels from an imported text file into separate columns of data of one or more types of data (values, dates, time, and labels).

Follow these steps to parse a text file:

1. Open the text file in 1-2-3 via the Open File Dialog box.

2. Select the range that contains the long labels or records that you want to parse.

3. Open the **R**ange menu and choose **P**arse. The Parse dialog box appears (see fig. 31.17).

> **Note**
>
> If the first cell of the input column already contains a format line, this format line appears in the **F**ormat Line text box, where this can be edited. A format line is a line that contains the headings of your field names. 1-2-3 saves over the original format line if you edited the format line and chose OK. 1-2-3 creates only one format line for each **I**nput Column.

VI

Integrating 1-2-3

Fig. 31.17
The Format Line
in the Parse dialog
box.

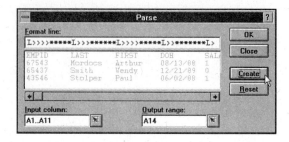

4. Select **C**reate. 1-2-3 enters the format line in the **F**ormat Line text box and displays up to five lines of long labels from the text file below it. The symbols in the format line represent the type of data and the width of each block of data in the first cell of the **I**nput Column.

The format line instructs 1-2-3 how to parse, or separate, data and enter it in a worksheet. When 1-2-3 creates the format line in Range Parse, it enters a symbol in the format line for each data block in the first line of the input column. Table 31.2 has a listing of available symbols to use in the format line when parsing a range.

Table 31.2	Symbols Used in Range Parse
Symbol	**Description**
L	Represents the beginning of a label block
V	Represents the beginning of a value block
D	Represents the beginning of a date block
T	Represents the beginning of a time block
S	Tells 1-2-3 to ignore the data block below the S when it parses the data. Enter this symbol when you edit a format line.
>	Represents any character in a data block after the first character
*	Represents a blank space that becomes part of a data block if that block requires extra characters

Note

When 1-2-3 parses dates, it enters dates as numbers in the worksheet. Format the date values using Style Number Format to display the dates in date format.

5. Compare the format line to the data by using the scroll bar to view any differences. If the format line does not accurately represent the type of data or length of entries in a data block located in the lines below it, edit the format line.

6. Specify the destination range for the parsed data in the **O**utput Range text box. You can specify the entire range or just the first cell in the range. 1-2-3 writes over any existing data in the output range, so verify that there is no data that you want to lose in the range.

◄ "Using Caution when Parsing Data," p. 809

7. Choose OK.

1-2-3 inserts a row, and then enters the **F**ormat Line in the worksheet above the **I**nput Column. The parsed data is entered in the designated **O**utput Range (see figure 31.18).

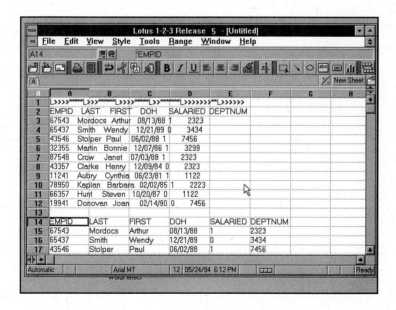

Fig. 31.18
The original data range and the parsed output range in 1-2-3.

From Here...

Learning how to use 1-2-3 with your existing DOS applications, or with downloaded files from mainframe applications, offers several advantages. Most businesses maintain corporate sales, marketing, and financial data on their large mainframe computers and then download the data as text files to 1-2-3 for analysis, charting, and report generation. For more information about accessing data from other sources, read the following chapters:

- Chapter 8, "Managing Files." Learn about File Commands and good file management techniques.

- Chapter 28, "Retrieving Data from External Databases." Learn how to use Lotus DataLens to connect to and import external database information into your 1-2-3 worksheets.

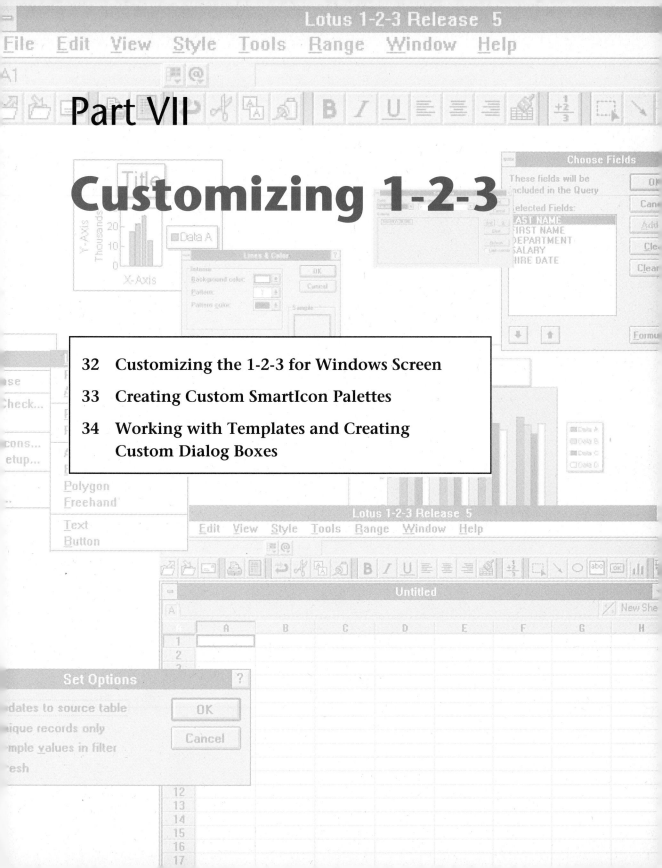

Part VII

Customizing 1-2-3

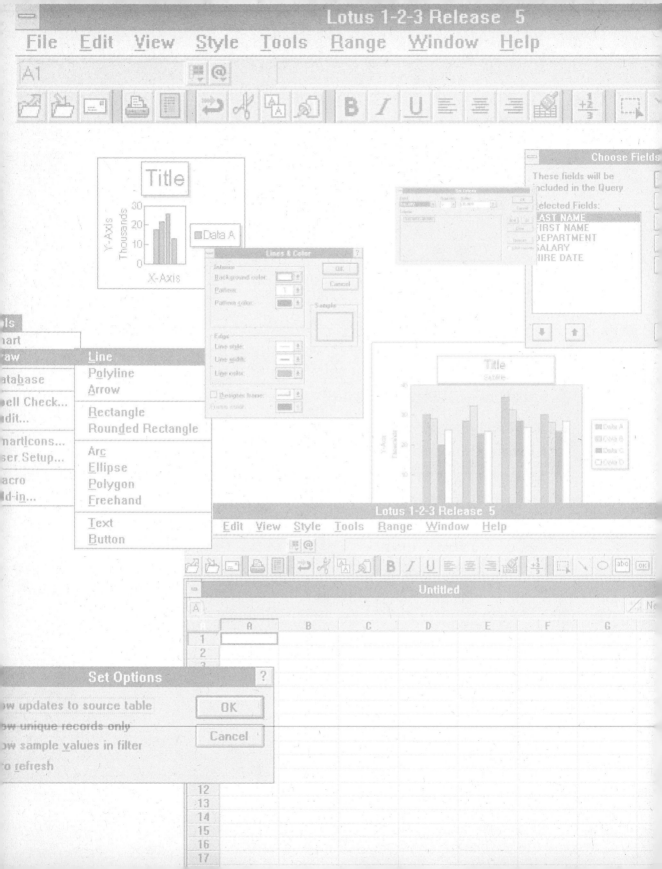

Chapter 32

Customizing the 1-2-3 for Windows Screen

The Windows environment invites customization of the screen so that you can accomplish your tasks as easily as possible. As a Windows application, 1-2-3 works with the Windows customization features and adds some of its own. Although there are many ways to customize your work with 1-2-3, this chapter focuses on two tools that control the appearance of the 1-2-3 screen: the 1-2-3 View Preferences dialog box and the Windows Control Panel.

In this chapter, you learn how to do the following:

■ Control which elements appear on the 1-2-3 screen

■ Control the appearance of the worksheet frame and grid

■ Change the screen's color scheme

■ Modify the desktop

■ Control the way the mouse works

Setting View Preferences

The 1-2-3 screen contains many different elements: SmartIcons, the status bar, the scroll bars, the worksheet grid and tabs, and so on. You can use the View Preferences dialog box to control the appearance of these elements. To display the View Preferences dialog box (shown in fig. 32.1), open the **V**iew menu and choose the Set View **P**references command.

Fig. 32.1
Use the View
Preferences dialog
box to control the
appearance of
1-2-3 screen
elements.

Turning Screen Elements Off and On

The check boxes in the View Preferences dialog box enable you to select the elements that you want to see on-screen. The choices you make here can determine how much of the worksheet you can see at one time. Your work habits will help you determine which elements you need to see and which you can hide. If you never use the scroll bars, for example, you can turn them off.

To turn different screen elements off or on, follow these steps:

1. Open the View menu and choose the Set View Preferences command. The View Preferences dialog box appears.

2. Select the check boxes for the elements you want to display, and deselect the check boxes for the elements you want to hide. The options in the Show in Current File section of the dialog box apply only to the current worksheet (unless you choose to make them the default by using the Make Default button). The options in the Show in 1-2-3 section of the dialog box apply to the current and subsequent 1-2-3 sessions.

Tip
Click the
SmartIcons button
in the status bar
and choose Hide/
Show SmartIcons
from the list as a
shortcut for the
SmartIcons op-
tion in the View
Preferences dialog
box.

3. Choose OK.

Use the Tab button near the upper-right corner of the worksheet (to the right of the New Sheet button) as a shortcut for the Worksheet **T**abs option in the View Preferences dialog box (see fig. 32.2).

To see as much of a worksheet as possible, turn off the SmartIcons, scroll bars, edit line, status bar, worksheet tabs, and worksheet frame. You then can turn off the grid to make the worksheet display less cluttered. Turning off the display of options also is useful if you need to create on-screen presentations.

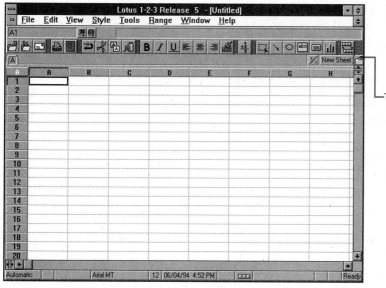

Fig. 32.2

The Tab button lets you quickly hide or show the worksheet tabs.

Tab button

Changing the Labels in the Worksheet Frame

You can change the labels in the worksheet frame to display units of measure rather than the standard column letters and row numbers. You can use characters, inches, metric, or points and picas.

Changing the labels in the worksheet frame does not change any cell or range addresses; it merely lets you see the worksheet according to the unit of measure you select. This procedure is especially useful if you want to create columns of a certain width and rows of a certain height.

Also, if you change the frame labels and then print the worksheet and its frame, 1-2-3 prints the column letters and row numbers. The units of measure are for screen-display purposes only.

To change the labels in the worksheet frame, follow these steps:

1. Open the **V**iew menu and choose the Set View **P**references command. The View Preferences dialog box appears.

2. Click the **W**orksheet Frame drop-down arrow, and select the unit of measure you want to use.

3. Choose OK. 1-2-3 changes the frame labels to reflect the unit of measure you chose (see fig. 32.3).

◄ "Setting Column Widths," p. 312

◄ "Setting Row Heights," p. 316

◄ "Enhancing Reports with Page Setup Options," p. 374

Fig. 32.3
Change the frame
labels to display
units of measure,
such as inches,
rather than
column letters and
row numbers.

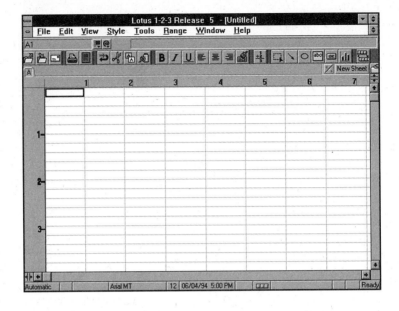

Changing the Color of the Worksheet Grid

By default, the worksheet grid is gray. You can change it to any of the
available 255 colors.

To change the color of the worksheet grid, follow these steps:

1. Open the View menu and choose the Set View **P**references command.
   The View Preferences dialog box appears.

2. Click the **G**rid Lines drop-down arrow, and select the color you want
   from the palette that appears.

3. Choose OK. The worksheet grid lines appear in the new color.

> **Note**
>
> Changing the color of the grid lines can affect the lightness or darkness of the
> grid lines when you print the worksheet on a black-and-white printer. A lighter
> color produces a lighter shade of gray; a darker color results in black grid lines.
> If you are printing grid lines when you print the worksheet, you should experi-
> ment with the grid-line color.

Changing the View Preferences Defaults

Although the Show in Current File section of the View **P**references dialog box changes the appearance of the current worksheet only, you may decide that this is the way you want all new worksheets to look. By choosing the **M**ake Default button in the dialog box, you tell 1-2-3 that the new settings should become your worksheet defaults. Then, any worksheet you subsequently create (except those using SmartMasters) will reflect the new defaults.

To change the View Preferences defaults, take these steps:

1. Open the **V**iew menu and choose the Set View **P**references command. The View Preferences dialog box appears.

2. Change the options in the Show in Current File section of the dialog box so that they reflect how you want your worksheets to look.

3. Click **M**ake Default.

4. Click OK. The next time you create a new worksheet (without using a SmartMaster), it will reflect the new default settings.

Applying Different Colors to the Worksheet Tabs

If you work with multipage worksheets, you may find it useful to color code the worksheet tabs. Not only does this make the worksheet more appealing visually, it can speed up your work. For example, if all your worksheets use red tabs for information about the North sales region, yellow for the South, green for the East, and purple for the West, you will use those visual clues as you work (see fig. 32.4).

To apply a different color to a worksheet tab:

1. Click the worksheet tab whose color you want to change so that it is the current worksheet.

2. Open the **S**tyle menu and choose **W**orksheet Default. The Worksheet Default dialog box appears.

3. Under the Color section, click the drop-down arrow for Wor**k**sheet Tab. The palette of possible colors appears.

4. Choose the color you want for the worksheet tab.

5. Click OK. The current worksheet's tab reflects the color you chose.

Fig. 32.4
Changing the
color of worksheet
tabs can give you
visual clues to your
worksheet's
organization.

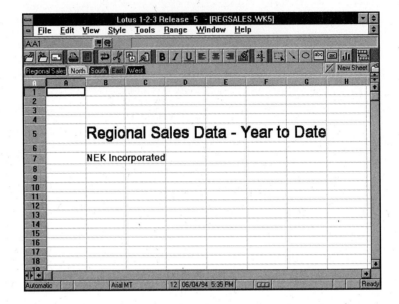

Customizing 1-2-3 with the Windows Control Panel

Like any product running under Windows, 1-2-3 reflects many of the changes you make in the Windows Control Panel. The Control Panel icon generally appears in the Main group window of the Program Manager. You can use the Control Panel to change Windows' color schemes, control the operation of your mouse, set the computer's date and time, configure your printers and ports, and so on.

To view the Control Panel, follow these steps:

1. Switch to the Program Manager, if necessary. Press Ctrl+Esc to display the Task List and then double-click Program Manager, or press Alt+Tab until the Program Manager window appears.

2. Make the Main group window the current window, if necessary, by clicking it (if it is already open), choosing it from the Windows menu, or double-clicking its icon.

3. Double-click the Control Panel icon to open it. Figure 32.5 shows the Control Panel.

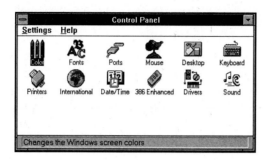

Fig. 32.5

The Windows Control Panel can help you customize the 1-2-3 screen.

VII

Customizing 1-2-3

The Control Panel contains icons for the different ways in which you can control your system's configuration and the Windows environment. Depending on your system's configuration, different icons may appear. If your computer is connected to a network, for example, a Network icon appears in the Control Panel.

Changing Color Schemes

Windows applications have common elements such as title bars, highlighting, and active and inactive windows. The colors used in these different elements reflect the currently selected Windows color scheme. You can choose a predefined color scheme, modify a predefined color scheme, or create a new color scheme; the screen elements in 1-2-3 will reflect your choice. If you choose a color scheme that specifies green for a highlight, for example, any highlighting in 1-2-3 will be green.

You switch between color schemes and create your own color schemes by using the Color icon in the Control Panel.

To change to another predefined color scheme, follow these steps:

1. In the Control Panel, double-click the Color icon. The Color dialog box appears (see fig. 32.6).

2. Click the drop-down arrow under Color **S**chemes, and select a color scheme. The sample windows in the dialog box change to reflect your selection.

3. Experiment with different color schemes by pressing the up- and down-arrow keys to select each scheme in turn.

Fig. 32.6
Use the Color
dialog box to
choose a different
color scheme.

Using a color scheme that includes only solid colors, such as the Windows Default color scheme, can speed screen-refresh time.

4. When you find a color scheme that suits you, choose OK to accept the change.

> **Note**
>
> If you are using a plasma or LCD screen adapter, you should choose one of the special color schemes designed for these screens. The Plasma Power Saver color scheme uses dark colors, which save power. By choosing the right LCD color scheme, you can prevent colors from appearing in reverse video.

To modify an existing color scheme or create your own color scheme, follow these steps:

1. In the Control Panel, double-click the Color icon. The Color dialog box appears.

2. Click the Color **P**alette button. The Color dialog box expands (see fig. 32.7).

3. Click the Screen **E**lement drop-down arrow to display a list of the screen elements for which you can change color.

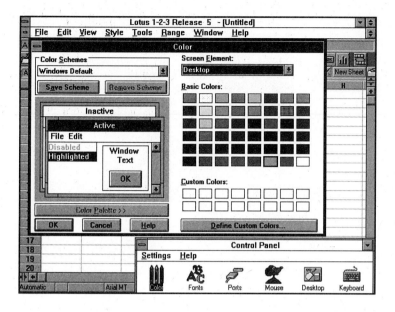

Fig. 32.7
Use the expanded
Color dialog box
to customize color
schemes.

VII

Customizing 1-2-3

4. Select the element whose color you want to change. Windows outlines (in black) the current color of the selected element in the **B**asic Colors or **C**ustom Colors palette.

5. Select a new color for the element. The sample windows in the dialog box reflect your change.

6. Repeat steps 4 and 5 for any screen element you want to change.

7. When you are satisfied with the color scheme, choose OK.

> **Note**
>
> After you change a color scheme, Windows uses the new scheme for every Windows session until you change it again. If you want to save a color scheme so that you can switch back to it after making other changes, click the S**a**ve Scheme button in the Color dialog box.

Modifying the Desktop

All applications and utilities that run under Windows, including Windows utilities themselves, sit on a desktop. This desktop appears as a solid color behind any windows you have open. You do not see the desktop when a window is maximized, but if you minimize windows to icons or restore them to a smaller size, the desktop appears.

One way to change the appearance of the screen is to modify the desktop that appears in the background. You can do this by selecting a two-color pattern and/or a wallpaper picture to appear in the background.

To add a pattern and/or wallpaper, follow these steps:

1. In the Control Panel, double-click the Desktop icon. The Desktop dialog box appears (see fig. 32.8).

Fig. 32.8

You can use the Desktop dialog box to select a desktop pattern or wallpaper.

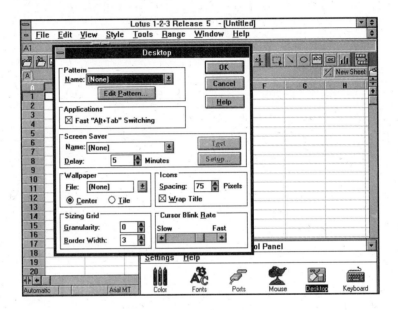

Tip

Because you can use any bitmap file as wallpaper, you can create your own wallpaper with Windows Paintbrush or any graphics program that can save a bitmap file. Simply save the image's bitmap file in the Windows directory.

2. To add a pattern, click the Pattern **N**ame drop-down arrow and select a pattern from the list. You can edit the pattern by clicking the Edit **Pat**tern button and editing the pattern, pixel by pixel, in the Edit Pattern dialog box.

3. To add wallpaper, click the Wallpaper **F**ile drop-down arrow and select a bitmap (BMP) file from the list. *Wallpapers* are bitmap files stored in the Windows directory. If the wallpaper file is a large graphic, click the **C**enter radio button to center the wallpaper on-screen. If the wallpaper file is a small graphic, click the **T**ile radio button to make the graphic repeat until it fills the screen.

4. Choose OK to accept the changes.

Controlling the Mouse

You can use the Control Panel to control the way the mouse buttons work, the double-click speed, and the rate of motion of the mouse (*tracking speed*). If you are left-handed, swapping the functions of the left and right mouse buttons may help you work more comfortably. Customizing mouse tracking and double-click speeds also can make your work with 1-2-3 and other Windows applications easier. For example, a beginner might like slower tracking and double-click speeds.

To customize the way the mouse works, follow these steps:

1. In the Control Panel, double-click the mouse icon. The Mouse dialog box appears (see fig. 32.9). The dialog box you see might look different depending on the type of mouse driver you have installed.

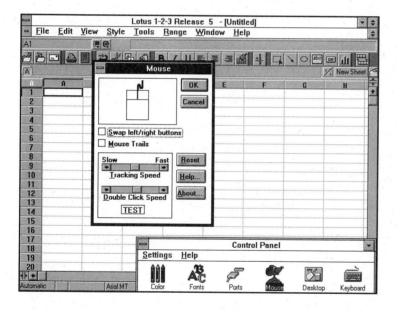

Fig. 32.9
You can use the Mouse dialog box to customize the operation of the mouse.

2. To switch the mouse-button functions, click the **S**wap Left/Right Buttons check box.

3. To control the mouse's rate of motion, drag the scroll box in the **T**racking Speed scroll bar. The faster you set this speed, the farther the mouse pointer will travel when you move the mouse.

4. To control the double-click speed, drag the scroll box in the **D**ouble-Click Speed scroll bar. The faster you set this speed, the quicker you will have to double-click for the double-click to be accepted. You can test

the double-click rate by double-clicking the TEST rectangle, which changes color when the double-click is accepted.

> **Note**
>
> It may be easier for beginning users to set a slow tracking and double-click speed. However, remember that you become accustomed to the speeds you use. If you start with slow rates, you will have to readjust if you speed the rates up later. It may be better to maintain medium rates rather than make the change.

5. Choose OK to accept the changes.

Using Other Customization Features

This chapter explores methods of customizing the 1-2-3 screen. Many other customization features, however, let you control 1-2-3 operations and worksheet appearance. You may want to review the following features and topics:

- *Zooming in and out to see less or more of the worksheet.* Open the **V**iew menu, and choose the **Z**oom In command to focus on a smaller area of the worksheet or the Zoom **O**ut command to step back and display more of the worksheet. Chapter 15, "Managing the Worksheet Display," explores these features.

- *Freezing titles.* Open the **V**iew menu and choose the Freeze **T**itles command to lock row and column labels—*titles*—in place. Chapter 15, "Managing the Worksheet Display," discusses how to freeze titles.

- *Hiding data.* Open the **S**tyle menu and choose the **H**ide command to hide entire worksheets or specific columns from view. Chapter 15, "Managing the Worksheet Display," covers hiding data.

- *Customizing the SmartIcons set.* You can change SmartIcons sets, add different icons to a set, create your own sets, and create your own icons. Chapter 33, "Creating Custom SmartIcon Palettes," discusses the different levels of customization for SmartIcons.

- *Creating templates.* You can create templates that specify worksheet formats, colors, and so on. Chapter 34, "Working with Templates and Creating Custom Dialog Boxes," explains how to create custom templates.

- *Creating custom dialog boxes.* Use the Lotus Dialog Box Editor to create custom dialog boxes; then use the dialog boxes to retrieve information from users and as part of custom 1-2-3 applications. Chapter 34, "Working with Templates and Creating Custom Dialog Boxes," explores this process.

- *Loading worksheets automatically.* Chapter 34, "Working with Templates and Creating Custom Dialog Boxes," explains how to load worksheets automatically.

From Here...

1-2-3 includes many more features that enable you to customize 1-2-3 operations and your worksheets. To learn more about customizing 1-2-3, examine the following chapters:

- Chapter 9, "Formatting Worksheets." This chapter explores how to change row and column size, set global styles, change number formats, change fonts and attributes, align entries, and use named styles.

- Chapter 15, "Managing the Worksheet Display." This chapter discusses splitting and zooming the worksheet window, as well as protecting and hiding data.

- Chapter 17, "Developing Business Presentations." In this chapter, you learn how to manipulate 1-2-3 to create business presentations. The chapter includes directions for optimizing the 1-2-3 screen for such presentations.

- Chapter 33, "Creating Custom SmartIcon Palettes." This chapter explores how to customize SmartIcons palettes, as well as how to create custom icons.

- Chapter 34, "Working with Templates and Creating Custom Dialog Boxes." This chapter explains how to create your own templates for use with multiple files, how to autoload files, and how to create custom dialog boxes for use with custom 1-2-3 applications.

Chapter 33

Creating Custom SmartIcon Palettes

1-2-3 for Windows provides nearly 200 SmartIcons, which provide single-click access to 1-2-3 commands and tasks. In addition, 1-2-3 ships with 11 predefined palettes, which group together common SmartIcons into a single palette. You aren't limited, however, to the SmartIcons displayed in the standard palettes; you can create custom SmartIcons to execute the macros that you create and you can create your own palettes that contain SmartIcons you use regularly.

This chapter shows you how to customize 1-2-3's SmartIcons. Specifically, the chapter covers the following topics:

◀ "SmartIcon Basics," p. 44

- Switching SmartIcon palettes

- Hiding and displaying SmartIcons

- Moving and rearranging SmartIcons

- Creating custom SmartIcon palettes

- Creating custom SmartIcons

Using the Standard SmartIcon Palettes

As you work in 1-2-3, you will notice that the SmartIcon palette changes from time to time, depending on your actions. Actually, 1-2-3 switches among four SmartIcon palettes. When you are working with ranges, the Default Sheet palette appears (see fig. 33.1). When you are working with a chart, the Default Chart palette appears (see fig. 33.2). When you are working with drawn objects in the worksheet, the Default Arrange palette appears (see fig. 33.3). When you are working with a query table, the Default Table palette appears (see fig. 33.4).

Fig. 33.1

The Default Sheet SmartIcon palette displays commonly used features.

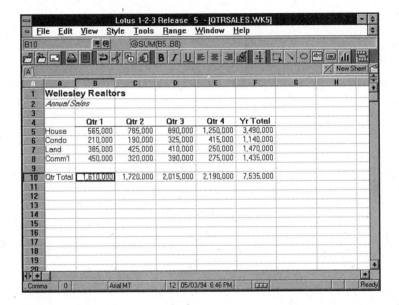

Fig. 33.2

The Default Chart SmartIcon palette displays SmartIcons for working with charts.

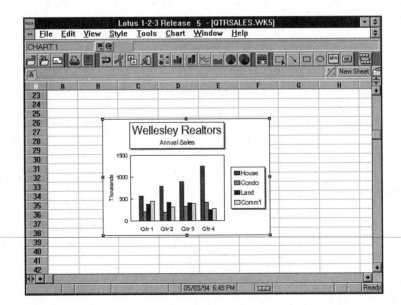

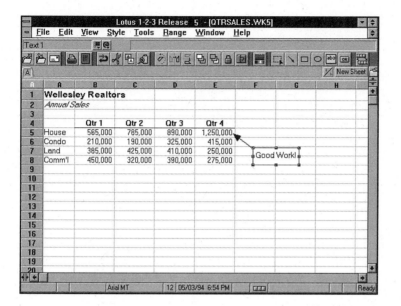

Fig. 33.3
The Default
Arrange SmartIcon
palette contains
SmartIcons for
manipulating
drawn objects.

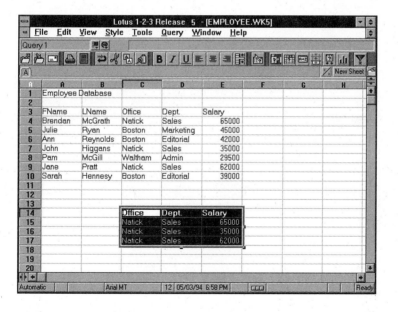

Fig. 33.4
The Default Table
SmartIcon palette
includes
SmartIcons
for accessing
1-2-3 database
commands.

1-2-3 automatically switches among these SmartIcon palettes when the appropriate object is selected in the worksheet. As soon as you select a chart, for example, the Default Chart palette replaces the current palette. When you select a range or cell, the Default Sheet palette appears again.

◀ "Working with
Ranges," p. 71

◀ "Manipulating
Chart
Elements,"
p. 397

Customizing the SmartIcons

Because 1-2-3 for Windows includes a large collection of SmartIcons, you may find that the SmartIcon you want already exists but isn't displayed in any of the standard palettes. Or you might want to combine several SmartIcons from different palettes into a single palette for convenience. 1-2-3 for Windows gives you several options for customizing the SmartIcon palette. You can add or remove SmartIcons, create your own named palettes, and even create your own SmartIcons.

The following sections describe the many ways in which you can customize the 1-2-3 for Windows SmartIcons to meet your needs.

Switching SmartIcon Palettes

Besides the standard palettes, 1-2-3 provides optional SmartIcon palettes. You can switch among the optional palettes in several ways. First, you can click the SmartIcons selector in the status bar at the bottom of the screen. When you click on this button, a list of optional palettes appears, which includes any custom palettes that you have created (see fig. 33.5).

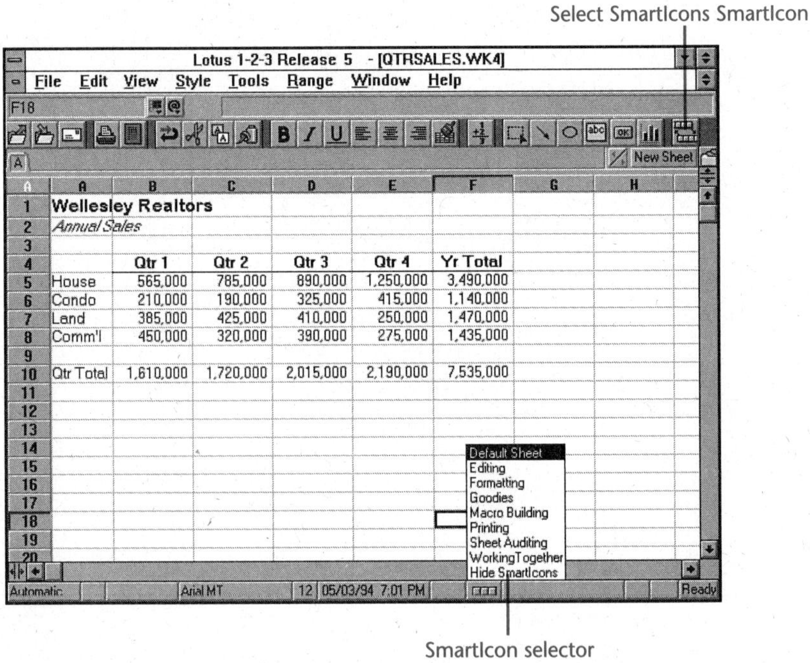

Fig. 33.5
Select the SmartIcon palette to display from the SmartIcon list.

Select SmartIcons SmartIcon

SmartIcon selector

Select the desired palette from this list, and 1-2-3 immediately replaces the current palette with the one you selected. You can switch among these palettes at any time.

> **Note**
>
> If you are using any of the standard palettes, such as the Default Chart palette, you cannot use the palette list to switch to another standard palette.

The second way to switch among SmartIcon palettes is to click on the Select SmartIcons SmartIcon, which appears at the far right end of each palette (see fig. 33.5). Clicking this SmartIcon cycles through the SmartIcon sets in the palette list.

The third way to switch among SmartIcon palettes is to use the **T**ools Smart**I**cons command. The Rearrange SmartIcon provides single click access to this command, however it is not displayed in any of the SmartIcon palettes. To add the Rearrange SmartIcon to a palette, refer to "Adding and Removing SmartIcons later in this chapter. Follow these steps:

1. Choose the **T**ools Smart**I**cons command to access the SmartIcons dialog box (see fig. 33.6).

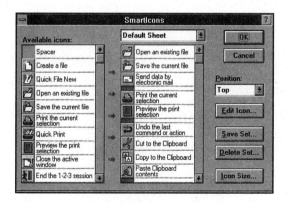

Fig. 33.6
In the SmartIcons dialog box, select the palette to display.

2. Click on the drop-down list at the top of the dialog box. This list contains the names of all SmartIcon palettes.

3. Select the desired palette.

4. Click on OK or press Enter.

Changing the Position of the Palette

Initially, the SmartIcon palette is displayed at the top of the Worksheet window. You can move the SmartIcon palette around the screen if you don't like its position. You can position the palette on any side of the screen or make it "float" within the program window.

To move the palette, follow these steps:

1. Choose the **T**ools Smart**I**cons command to access the SmartIcons dialog box.

2. Click on the **P**osition drop-down list to display a list of positions (Floating, Left, Top, Right, and Bottom).

3. Select the desired position.

4. Click on OK or press Enter.

If you choose the Floating option, you can click on any area of the palette and drag the palette around the screen. You also can change the size and shape of the palette by dragging its borders. If you want to close a floating palette, click on its Control menu (the box in the upper left corner of the palette window) and the palette disappears. Figure 33.7 shows the Default Sheet palette in a floating SmartIcon palette.

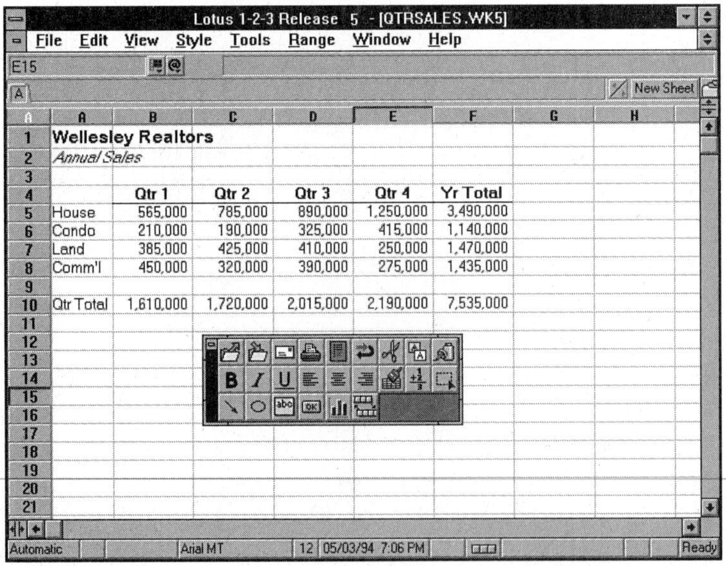

Fig. 33.7
Here the
SmartIcons are
displayed in a
floating palette.

Even with the Worksheet window expanded to the maximum size, the floating SmartIcon palette overlays the window and hides some data. One great advantage of using a floating palette, however, is that you can expand it to accommodate any number of SmartIcons—more than the default palette.

The Left and Right options provide less space for SmartIcons. Even the default SmartIcon palette is too large, and some SmartIcons at the end of the palette are not displayed.

Hiding the Palette

One of the options in the palette list (the list that appears when you click on the SmartIcon selector in the status bar) is Hide SmartIcons. This option removes the SmartIcon palette from the screen. You may want to hide the palette when you require maximum screen space for a worksheet.

After hiding the palette, you can show it again by choosing the Show SmartIcons option from the same list. You also can hide the SmartIcon palette by using the **V**iew Set View **P**references **S**martIcons command.

◀ "Setting View Preferences," p. 965

Rearranging SmartIcons in a Palette

If you don't like the arrangement of SmartIcons in a palette, you can rearrange them to suit your needs. Rearranging SmartIcons is simple: hold down the Ctrl key as you click a SmartIcon in the palette, drag the SmartIcon to a new position, and then release both the mouse button and the Ctrl key. Figure 33.8 shows a SmartIcon being moved in the palette at the top of the Worksheet window.

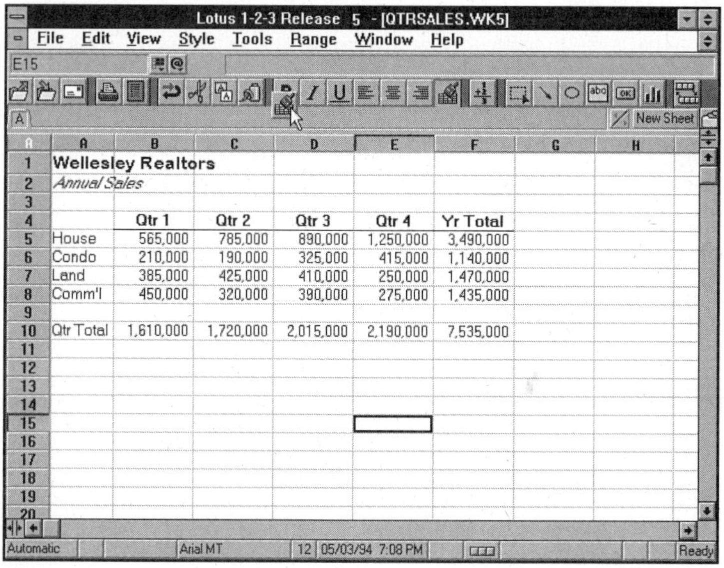

Fig. 33.8
Moving a SmartIcon in the current palette with Ctrl+click and drag.

Tip
If you press Ctrl+click and drag the SmartIcon off the palette, 1-2-3 moves the SmartIcon to the end of the palette.

Adding and Removing SmartIcons

In addition to rearranging the SmartIcons in a SmartIcon palette, you can also add new SmartIcons to a palette or remove SmartIcons that you do not use from a palette.

To add or remove a SmartIcon in a SmartIcon palette, follow these steps:

1. Choose the **T**ools Smart**I**cons command to access the SmartIcons dialog box (refer to fig. 33.6).

2. In the drop-down list at the top of the dialog box, select the SmartIcon palette that you want to modify. The SmartIcons in the selected palette appear below the name of the palette.

3. Use the scroll bars to set the position of the current palette in which you will add a SmartIcon.

4. In the Available Icons list box, locate the SmartIcon that you want to add.

5. Click on the SmartIcon, drag it across to the palette list box, and then release the mouse button. The SmartIcon appears in the palette where you dropped it. If you drop a SmartIcon into a position that already contains a SmartIcon, the new SmartIcon appears as the current SmartIcon.

> **Note**
>
> You can add as many SmartIcons as you wish to a palette, but only those that can be displayed in any one position on the screen. If the SmartIcons you have added to a palette are not displayed, change the position of the palette on the screen or use the Floating pallette position.

To remove a SmartIcon from a palette, drag it out of the palette list box.

Figure 33.9 shows a SmartIcon being moved into the blank position in list box for the Default Sheet palette. (You can change the order of the SmartIcons by dragging them in the palette list box.)

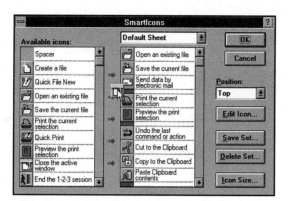

Fig. 33.9
Click and drag a
SmartIcon to add
it to the current
palette.

6. Click on OK to save the changes made to the current palette. When you
   return to the worksheet, the changes you made are reflected in the
   palette.

Tip
Use the Spacer
SmartIcon (at the
top of the Avail-
able Icons list box)
to separate
SmartIcons into
groups within a
palette. You can
use as many spac-
ers as you want.

Caution

When you modify an existing SmartIcon palette, the changes you make cannot be
undone. If you will be making substantial changes to an existing palette, use the Save
Set command to save the palette under a new name. See "Creating a New Palette"
in the next section for more information.

Creating a New Palette

Creating a new SmartIcon palette is a simple variation on the procedure described in the preceding section. Use the SmartIcons dialog box to group the
desired SmartIcons into the current set (you can start with any set). Add and
remove SmartIcons from that set as desired. Then use the **S**ave Set command
button to provide a new set name and file name for the palette.

To save the changes you made in a set of SmartIcons and create a new set,
follow these steps:

1. Click on **S**ave Set in the SmartIcons dialog box. 1-2-3 for Windows
   displays the Save Set of SmartIcons dialog box (see fig 33.10).

2. Type a name for the SmartIcon set in the **N**ame of Set text box.

3. Type a new file name for the SmartIcon set in the **F**ile Name text box.
   (Each SmartIcon set is stored on disk under a file name with the extension SMI.)

Fig. 33.10
Enter a name and
file name for the
new SmartIcon set.

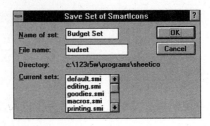

4. Click OK to close the Save Set of SmartIcons dialog box. You return to the SmartIcons dialog box.

5. Click on OK to close the SmartIcons dialog box and return to the worksheet.

The new palette appears in the palette list along with the others.

> **Note**
>
> You can delete SmartIcon palettes by using the **D**elete Set button in the SmartIcons dialog box. This button deletes the set that currently is selected in the list. Use care however, when deleting SmartIcon sets. 1-2-3 will not prompt you for confirmation.

Changing the Size of SmartIcons

You can display SmartIcons in two sizes: medium and large. By default, 1-2-3 for Windows displays medium SmartIcons. To display large SmartIcons, follow these steps:

1. Choose the **T**ools SmartIcons command to access the SmartIcons dialog box.

2. Click on the **I**con Size button to access the Icon Size dialog box.

3. Click on **L**arge.

4. Click on OK to close the Icon Size dialog box. You return to the SmartIcons dialog box.

5. Click on OK to close the dialog box and return to the worksheet.

> **Note**
>
> To return to medium size, repeat the preceding steps, but click on **M**edium in step 3.

Figure 33.11 shows the Default Sheet SmartIcons in a large floating palette. Notice that some SmartIcons change when you display them in a larger size; the pictures become more detailed. Large SmartIcons are usually best on super VGA monitors, but can be useful in other situations.

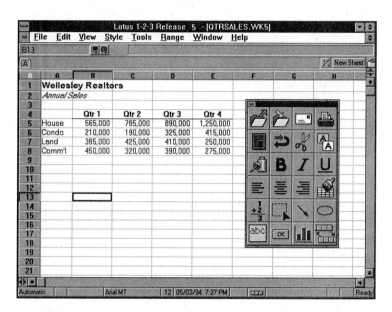

Fig. 33.11
The Default Sheet palette with large SmartIcons.

Troubleshooting

After choosing a SmartIcon, nothing happens.

Many of the SmartIcons require that you first select a range or perform some other action before activating the SmartIcon. For example, before you can use the Copy SmartIcon, you must first select the range of cells that you want to copy.

Some of the SmartIcons I added to the palette are not appearing on-screen. What should I do?

If you added more SmartIcons than the palette can display across the top of the screen (or along the side), 1-2-3 truncates the palette. To display all your SmartIcons, choose **T**ools SmartIcons **P**osition Floating. Click and drag the borders to resize the palette if necessary.

Creating SmartIcons

▶ "Defining a
Macro,"
p. 1034

Although nearly 200 SmartIcons are supplied with 1-2-3 for Windows, the most interesting feature of SmartIcons is the ability to create your own. You can assign to a SmartIcon any 1-2-3 for Windows task that can be performed by a macro—for example, placing your name and address in a worksheet. Another SmartIcon could perform a more complex task, such as combining data from several files and printing a report that includes the latest sales figures and a chart. The possibilities are endless.

One good use for custom SmartIcons is to automate a worksheet application that you create and distribute to other users in your company. Instead of a standard SmartIcon, such as one that prints a range, your application can have a SmartIcon that prints all the ranges of a standard company report. You can create another SmartIcon that uses the FORM macro command to automate data input.

Understanding Custom SmartIcons

Unlike the standard SmartIcons provided with 1-2-3 for Windows, custom SmartIcons can be modified. You can control their appearance and actions.

Custom SmartIcons are made up of two parts: a Windows 3.x bit-map file, which contains the image you see on the icon, and a text file, which contains the macro actions to be performed when the custom SmartIcon is selected. Both files have the same name, but the bit-map file uses a BMP extension and the text file uses a MAC extension.

When you install 1-2-3 for Windows, special directories are created under the \123R4W\PROGRAMS directory. Many of these directories contain the various SmartIcon files required for SmartIcon palettes, including the MAC files, the BMP files, and the SMI files.

When you create a custom SmartIcon, the MAC and BMP files are stored in the subdirectory containing the SmartIcon palette in which they were created. However, you can add a custom SmartIcon to any of the palettes, regardless of the palette in which it was created. Details for adding SmartIcon files are covered in the next few sections.

Creating SmartIcon Images

A Windows 3.x bit-map file is a special type of image file used by many Windows 3.x programs. Windows Paintbrush (a standard accessory provided with

VII

Customizing 1-2-3

Windows 3.x) uses the Windows 3.x bit-map image format by default. You can use Paintbrush or any other Windows bit-map paint package to create or edit SmartIcon files, but in this section, you learn how to use 1-2-3's icon editor.

To create the SmartIcon image file, follow these steps:

1. Choose the **T**ools Smart**I**cons command to display the SmartIcons dialog box.

2. Choose **E**dit Icon. The Edit Icon dialog box appears.

3. Choose the **N**ew Icon button to start a new icon from scratch. You are presented with a Save dialog box where you can enter a name for the new icon.

4. Type a name for the new icon. After you specify the name, a blank edit screen appears along with a blank icon in the Available Icons list box (see fig. 33.12).

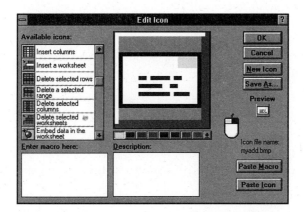

Fig. 33.12
Create an image for the custom SmartIcon in the icon editor.

5. Click on the arrow beside the color palette to view more colors for your drawing. Click on any color to select it. The selected color appears in the mouse icon to the right of the color palette to confirm your selection.

6. Use the mouse to draw in the edit area using the color you selected. You can erase parts of your image by selecting the background color and drawing over existing colors.

> **Note**
>
> You can access two colors as you are drawing the image. The color that appears in the left mouse button is used when you click the left mouse button; the color displayed in the right mouse button is used when you click the right mouse button.

Tip

You can create new icons by using existing icon images as a starting point. Select the image in the Available Icons list box, enter a name for the new image, and then use the edit area to change the original.

When you finish editing the image, you're ready to add a description and macro to the SmartIcon. The following section explains this procedure. If you are following along in 1-2-3, keep the Edit Icon dialog box open for the next procedure.

Attaching a Macro to a Custom SmartIcon

Before you assign a macro to a custom SmartIcon, create and test the macro in a 1-2-3 for Windows worksheet. When your macro is complete, ensure that it runs properly by using the **T**ools **M**acro **R**un command. When you edit the SmartIcon image, you can apply the macro to the icon using one of three methods.

First, you can type the macro commands directly into the **E**nter Macro Here text box in the Edit Icon dialog box. Type the macro exactly as it appeared in the worksheet when you tested it. Be sure to type a description into the **D**escription text box before you return to the worksheet.

▶ "Defining a Macro," p. 1034

▶ "Planning, Invoking, and Debugging Macro Command Programs," p. 1083

Another way to attach macros to your icons is to refer to macros in your worksheets. This is useful when your macros are long or complex. Enter the macro command {BRANCH *macroname*} into the **E**nter Macro Here text box, where *macroname* is a reference to the macro in the worksheet. The worksheet containing the macro you reference must be active when you click this icon in the future.

A final way to attach a macro to your custom icon is to copy it from the worksheet. Follow these steps to complete this procedure:

1. Highlight the entire macro, and then choose the **E**dit **C**opy command.

2. Select **T**ools SmartIcons, and choose **E**dit Icon to return to the Edit Icon dialog box.

3. Select the new icon from the Available Icons list box. Any icon you created appears in this list.

4. Place the mouse pointer (cursor) into the **E**nter Macro Here text box and click once.

5. Press Ctrl+V or choose Paste **M**acro to paste the macro into place.

6. Type a description for the macro into the **D**escription text box.

Figure 33.13 shows a sample macro that enters a name and address in the worksheet, formats the new text as bold, and moves the cell pointer. Although this macro is relatively simple, the macros that you assign to custom SmartIcons do not have to be simple.

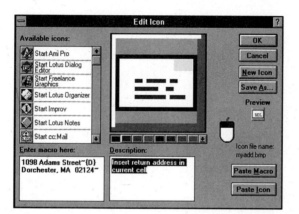

Fig. 33.13
A sample macro to be assigned to a custom SmartIcon.

> **Note**
>
> You are limited to 512 characters in the Enter Macro Here text box. If your macro requires more space, use the {BRANCH *macroname*} command to access a macro stored on a worksheet.

When you finish editing the image and entering the macro and description, click OK to save the SmartIcon. The SmartIcons dialog box is displayed and you can now add the custom SmartIcon to any palette, as described previously.

Distributing Custom Icon Files

SmartIcons are stored in palettes; each palette is stored as a file on disk with the SMI extension. Application developers can distribute copies of these files with their applications to control which SmartIcons are displayed.

Tip
You can view the macro associated with a custom SmartIcon (and even copy the macro) by selecting the SmartIcon in the Edit Icon dialog box.

If you distribute copies of SMI files, be certain to copy them into the C:\123R4W\PROGRAMS\SHEETICO directory of the destination computer. The copy of 1-2-3 running on that computer will use the SmartIcons that you distributed.

Troubleshooting

The macro I assigned to the icon doesn't run when I click the icon. What's wrong?

You may have used the {BRANCH *macroname*} command incorrectly. Check that your macro is properly referenced by name, including the worksheet name if the macro appears on a different sheet. Also, if the macro appears on a different sheet, that worksheet must be active when you click the icon. For this reason, it's best to branch to macros that exist on the worksheet that will be using the icon you developed.

Can I use existing artwork for my icon images?

Yes. The best way is to open one of the BMP icon files into a paint program (such as PaintBrush), and then copy existing artwork into the existing image. This gives you the proper size and proportions for your image. You can save the new BMP file directly into one of the SmartIcon directories inside the 123R4W\PROGRAMS directory to specify on which palette it belongs.

From Here...

In this chapter, you learned how to use and customize 1-2-3's SmartIcons. For additional information on customizing 1-2-3, refer to the following chapters:

■ Chapter 35, "Writing 1-2-3 for Windows Macros," introduces you to the task of automating 1-2-3 for Windows with macros.

■ Chapter 36, "Recording and Modifying Macros," shows you how to record 1-2-3 for Windows tasks.

■ Chapter 37, "Using Advanced Macro Techniques," presents the 1-2-3 for Windows macro language.

Chapter 34

Working with Templates and Creating Custom Dialog Boxes

In addition to customizing the 1-2-3 for Windows workspace and SmartIcons palettes, you also can create customized worksheet templates as well as design custom dialog boxes for use with 1-2-3 macros. 1-2-3 also provides a set of worksheet templates called SmartMasters that you can use to quickly create worksheets. You can use these SmartMasters as is or you can customize them to suit your needs.

In this chapter, you'll learn how to do the following:

■ Use the SmartMaster templates

■ Design custom templates

■ Create autoloading worksheets

■ Design custom dialog boxes for use with 1-2-3 macros

Using Worksheet Templates

Using worksheet *templates* is common practice in most business environ-ments. A template is a worksheet that contains predefined settings and data you use routinely in your worksheets. These templates can include budget worksheets, financial reports, and automated data input forms. The biggest benefit of working with worksheet templates lies in the fact that you create the template once but use it many times to create other worksheets.

1-2-3 for Windows provides predefined templates, called *SmartMasters*, which contain data, formulas, macros, and formatting for common business documents. Because each SmartMaster already contains the data and formulas you need, you can quickly get to work as you don't need to spend time re-creating complicated formulas and worksheet formatting.

Furthermore, each SmartMaster is automated with 1-2-3 macros so you only need click buttons to perform actions such as printing and switching to different areas of the worksheet.

The SmartMasters supplied by 1-2-3 for Windows range in functionality from business worksheets such as expense reports, balance sheets, and cash flow statements to personal finance models such as household budgets and mortgage amortization schedules. In addition to using the SmartMasters provided with 1-2-3, you can customize them to suit your needs as well as create and design your own templates.

Using the 1-2-3 SmartMasters

When you start 1-2-3 for Windows a Welcome screen is displayed where you can choose to create a new worksheet or work on an existing worksheet. When you choose the Create a New Worksheet option, the New File dialog box is displayed, which lists a series of SmartMaster templates (see fig. 34.1). Likewise, when you choose the File New command to create a new worksheet, 1-2-3 displays the same dialog box and list of SmartMasters.

To use a SmartMaster, you select the name of the SmartMaster you want to use and click OK. When you select a SmartMaster, a description of the SmartMaster appears in the Comments section of the dialog box. For a complete description of the SmartMasters provided by 1-2-3, refer to table 34.1. If you want to create a new blank worksheet, just select the Create a blank worksheet checkbox and click OK.

Fig. 34.1
Choose a SmartMaster template from the New File dialog box.

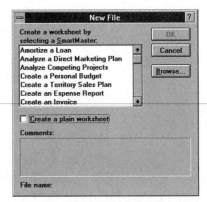

Once you have selected a SmartMaster, 1-2-3 for Windows creates a new untitled worksheet and displays the information provided by the SmartMaster. To use the SmartMaster, you simply fill in the input cells with your own data. In each SmartMaster, input cells appear shaded. Figure 34.2 displays the worksheet provided by the Budget SmartMaster.

> **Caution**
>
> Only enter data in the shaded cells. If you enter data in any other cells you may corrupt worksheet formulas.

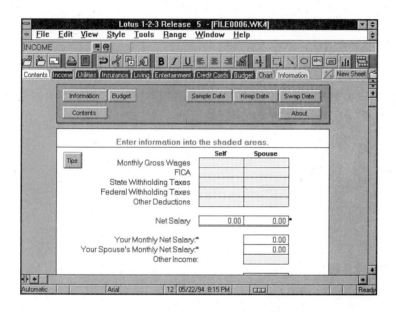

Fig. 34.2
Input cells appear shaded in each worksheet provided by the SmartMaster.

When you enter data in these shaded cells, formulas that exist in other cells in the worksheet are calculated by using the data you supplied. Once you have entered the appropriate data in each of the input cells, the worksheet is complete and then you can print the worksheet.

Table 34.1 1-2-3 SmartMasters	
SmartMaster	**Description**
Analyze a Direct Marketing Plan	Collection of worksheets for analyzing direct mail campaigns. Templates include gross margin, costs, and break-even analysis.

(continues)

Table 34.1 Continued	
SmartMaster	**Description**
Analyze Competing Projects	Decide between two investments based on analysis of each.
Create an Invoice	Invoice goods and services. Tracks associated costs.
Create an Expense Report	Worksheet for tracking weekly expenses.
Generate Financial Statements	Collection of financial statements, including balance sheet, income statement, and cash flow statement. Also includes charts for assets and income.
Amortize a Loan	Calculate monthly mortgage payments. Provides first year monthly schedule as well as summary schedule.
Create a Personal Budget	Worksheet for tracking monthly expenses.
Generate a Purchase Order	Purchase order form.
Track Sales and Associated Costs	Collection of models for the salesperson tracking expenses, mileage, and actual sales. Also provides summary reports.
Use Shell to Create a SmartMaster	Blank SmartMaster for creating your own SmartMaster.
Create a Territory Sales Plan	Sales forecast worksheet.
Fill out a Time Sheet	Track time spent, including billable hours.

Understanding the Contents of SmartMasters

In addition to the worksheet template, each SmartMaster also contains a Contents sheet which contains a description of the sheets contained in the SmartMaster (see fig. 34.3) and an Information sheet which provides instructions on how to work with the SmartMaster (see fig. 34.4).

You move to the other sheets in the worksheet by clicking the worksheet tab at the top of the worksheet window or by clicking the appropriate button.

The Information sheet also displays a series of macro buttons that you can use to access additional information for working in the SmartMaster. The How To button provides instructions on how to use the SmartMaster; the Tips button supplies a series of tips for working with the SmartMaster; the Steps button enables you to view the steps necessary to complete the worksheet. The Notes/FX-enabled fields button provides information on how to exchange data with Lotus Notes; the Macros button displays the worksheet that contains the macros used in the worksheet; and the About button provides information about the author of the SmartMaster.

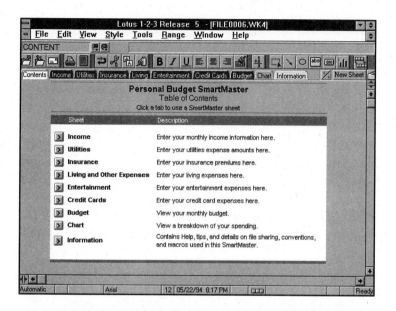

Fig. 34.3
The Contents sheet displays a description of each sheet in the worksheet template.

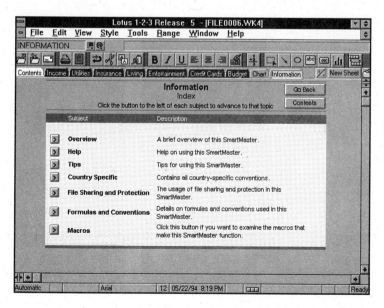

Fig. 34.4
The Information sheet provides instructions on how to work with the SmartMaster.

VII

Customizing 1-2-3

Each worksheet model contains macro buttons that enable you to work with the worksheet model (see fig. 34.5). For example, to print the worksheet you only need to click the Print button. Table 34.2 shows the macro buttons that are common to all SmartMasters.

Fig. 34.5
Macro buttons appear along the top of the worksheet template and provide quick access to commands for working with the template.

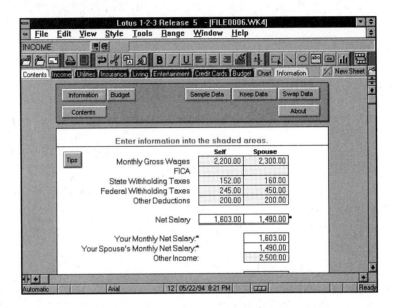

Table 34.2 SmartMaster Macro Buttons

Button	Action
Info	Displays the Information sheet
Zoom	Zooms in and out of the worksheet display
Print	Prints the worksheet
Sample Data	Inserts sample data in the model to illustrate how the model works
Keep Data	Enables you to save a set of values for the template
Swap Data	Enables you to switch among saved sets of data

The Create an Expense Report SmartMaster

Perhaps one of the most common business forms in any business environment is the Expense Report. The Create an Expense Report SmartMaster provides an easy-to-use form that you can use to keep track of your expenses.

To use the Expense Report, choose **F**ile **N**ew, select Expense Report, and click OK. You can then either click the sheet tab labeled Expense Report or you can click the Expense Report macro button on the Contents page (see fig. 34.6).

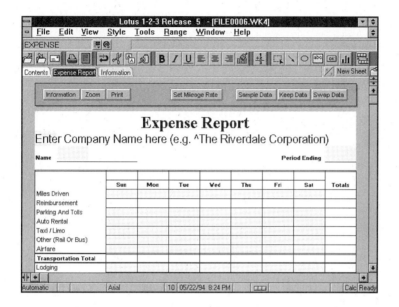

Fig. 34.6
The Create an Expense Report SmartMaster enables you to track weekly expenses.

The next step is to set the mileage reimbursement rate offered by your company. Click the Set Mileage Rate button to display the Set Rate dialog box (see fig. 34.7). Enter the mileage rate and click OK.

Fig. 34.7
Set the mileage reimbursement rate in the Set Rate dialog box.

Enter your name in the Name input cell followed by the Period Ending date. When you enter the date, formulas in the worksheet automatically fill in the appropriate dates and weekday names of the period (see fig. 34.8).

Fill in the rest of the information for the expense report in each of the shaded cells. As you enter data, formulas in the worksheet calculate the amounts (see fig. 34.9).

Fig. 34.8
Formulas automatically supply the dates of the expense period.

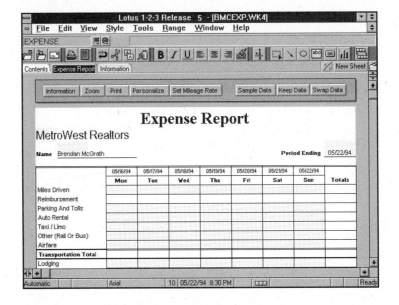

Fig. 34.9
The completed expense report.

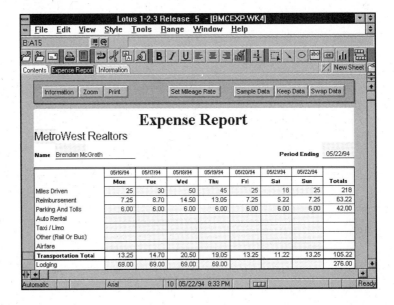

When you have completed the expense report, click the Print button to print the worksheet. To save the expense report, choose **F**ile **S**ave, enter a name for the worksheet, and click OK.

The Amortize a Loan SmartMaster

The Amortize a Loan SmartMaster enables you to track your own mortgage payments as well as provides an analysis tool for calculating the results of different loan amounts, interest rates, and terms. If you want to see how a lower interest rate could affect your mortgage payments or if you simply want to calculate whether or not you have the funds to purchase a home or car, use the Amortize a Loan SmartMaster. Figure 34.10 shows the Amortize a Loan SmartMaster.

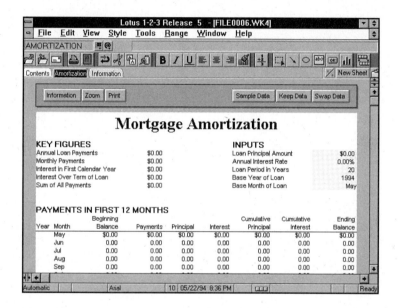

Fig. 34.10
The Amortize a Loan SmartMaster allows you to test the effects of interest rates, loan amounts, and terms.

To use the Amortize a Loan SmartMaster, choose **F**ile **N**ew, select Amortize a Loan from the list of SmartMasters, and click OK.

The inputs required by the Amortize a Loan SmartMaster include the loan amount, the annual percentage rate, the loan period in years, the first year of the loan, and the first month of the loan.

To begin, enter the loan amount, say $100,000, in the Loan Principal Amount input cell. Enter an annual percentage rate of 8%, the loan period of 30 years, and enter the current year and current month of the loan. When you enter this information, formulas in the key figures area automatically tally the totals (see fig. 34.11)

To test the effects of varying interest rates and loan amounts, click the Keep Data button to save the current input cells as a version. This macro takes advantage of the Version Manager feature of 1-2-3 for Windows. This feature

◀ "Understanding Version Man-ager Basics," p. 665

enables you to perform what-if analysis by saving iterations of data as a separate set of data. You can then switch among the various sets to see the end result.

Fig. 34.11
When you enter data in the Input Cells, formulas in the Key Figures section calculate the mortgage payment.

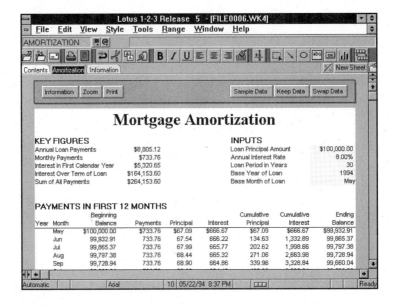

Click the Keep Data button to save this set of figures. The Keep Data dialog box is displayed where you are prompted to enter a name for the data set (see fig. 34.12). For this scenario, enter the name Current Rate and click OK.

Fig. 34.12
Enter a name for the Input Cells to save the set of data.

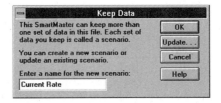

Enter a new set of data for the next scenario. For example, enter 8.5% to calculate the loan payments with a higher interest rate. Then, click Keep Data to save this set of values.

To switch back to the initial set of input values, click Swap Data. In the Swap Data dialog box, select Current Rate and click OK (see fig. 34.13). The initial set of values is redisplayed in the input cells and the formulas are recalculated to reflect the data.

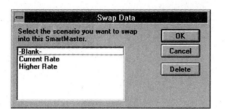

Fig. 34.13
Switch between saved sets of data in the Swap Data dialog box.

The Amortize a Loan SmartMaster provides two schedules: the payments made in the first twelve months of the loan and the payments made over the life of the loan. In addition, the schedules break down each payment to show the amount that is paid towards the principal of the loan and the amount that pays interest.

The Create a Personal Budget SmartMaster

For anyone who has ever wondered where his or her money goes, the Create a Personal Budget SmartMaster can help you keep track. The Personal Budget is broken down in five categories: Income, Utilities, Insurance, Living and Other Expenses, Entertainment, and Credit Cards. After supplying your monthly income, and the expenses in each category, you can view your expenses in the budget worksheet or view a graphical representation of where all your money is going each month.

To use the Personal Budget, choose File New, select Create a Personal Budget, and click OK. When the Contents sheet is displayed, click the sheet tab labeled Income or click the Income button (see fig. 34.14).

The first step is to enter your monthly income. The Income sheet provides input cells for yourself and your significant other. After entering your monthly income, formulas calculate your net salary and total monthly income (see fig. 34.15).

Once you've entered your income, proceed to each expense category and enter your monthly expenses. For example, to enter your monthly utility bills, click the Utilities tab to switch to that worksheet. Continue entering your monthly expenses in each of the supplied categories.

Fig. 34.14
Use the
Personal Budget
SmartMaster to
keep spending in
tow.

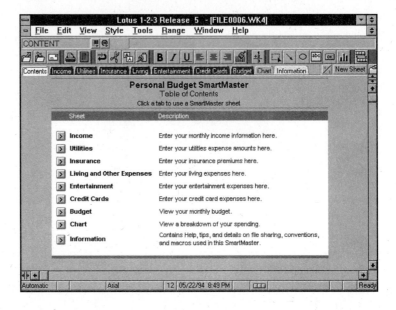

Fig. 34.15
Enter monthly
income and
deductions to
calculate your net
salary and total
monthly income.

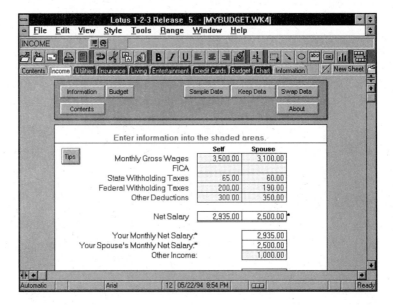

After completing the entries for each expense category, move to the Budget
worksheet to display the consolidated budget (see fig. 34.16). The Budget
worksheet displays your total monthly expenses using both a contingency
(you're bound to spend a little more than you anticipated) and using the
amount you specified. Each month, print the worksheet so that you have

a record of your spending. After you've completed the budget for a few months, you may just discover where all of your hard-earned money is going.

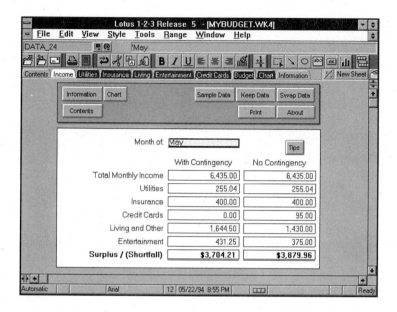

Fig. 34.16
The Budget Worksheet displays a summary of your spending for the month.

In addition to viewing your budget in numeric format, you can also view your spending in graphical form. To do so, click the Chart tab. The Personal Budget SmartMaster displays a pie chart illustrating the percentage of spending by category (see fig. 34.17).

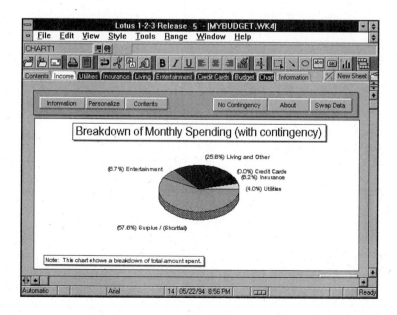

Fig. 34.17
View your budget in chart form for a graphical view of spending.

The Generate a Purchase Order SmartMaster

The Generate a Purchase Order SmartMaster offers a quick and easy way to generate purchase orders. Figure 34.18 displays the Purchase Order template and the information that is required when you fill one out.

Fig. 34.18
Place orders with the Purchase Order template.

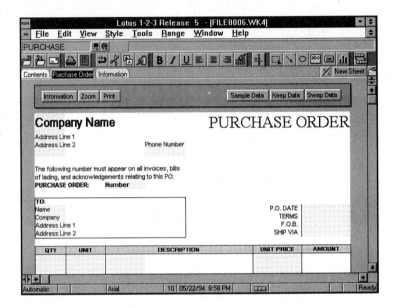

To use the Generate a Purchase Order SmartMaster, choose **F**ile **N**ew, select Generate a Purchase Order, and click OK. Then click the Purchase Order tab to display the worksheet and begin data entry.

Enter your company information and address and shipping information. To enter order items, position the cell pointer in the first line of the order area and enter the supplied information. Formulas in the Amount column calculate the totals based on quantity and unit price. A grand total is also calculated based on the information you enter (see fig. 34.19).

Creating Your Own Templates

A template is nothing more than a worksheet file that contains predefined data. Worksheet templates consist of explanatory labels, formulas, and formatting and can also include macros. Once you create a template, you can use it repeatedly to create additional worksheet files.

When you create a template, you use the same basic procedure you use to create any worksheet file. The main difference is that you include all of the common information, such as text entries, formulas, and worksheet formatting, so that you need to fill in only the appropriate data in order to complete the worksheet file.

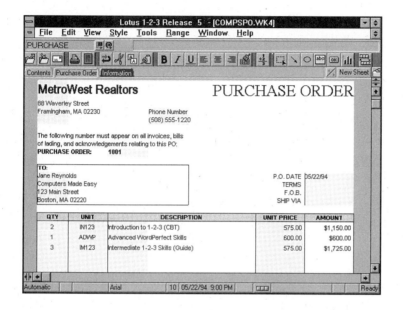

Fig. 34.19
A completed purchase order form.

1-2-3 for Windows includes many commands and features that help you design worksheet templates. The following list gives you a few tips for creating and working with templates:

- Use 1-2-3's multiple worksheet capability to organize distinct categories of data. For example, use one worksheet for user input, another worksheet for reports, and a third worksheet to store macro commands. This design not only protects macros from harm, but also provides a scheme that helps other users understand the template.

  ◀ "Reorganizing Worksheets," p. 273

- Protect cells and worksheet ranges with the **S**tyle **P**rotection command to prevent other users from changing worksheet data. Use the **F**ile **P**rotect command to restrict access to potentially destructive menu commands. Doing so maintains the integrity of the worksheet and also ensures that standard worksheet data remains the same.

  ◀ "Managing Worksheet Files," p. 281

- Hide worksheets that contain information—such as macros or data used in calculations—by using the **S**tyle **H**ide command. This prevents users from accessing the hidden information.

  ◀ "Managing the Worksheet Display," p. 485

- Assign worksheet display preferences with the **V**iew Set View **P**references command. See Chapter 15, "Managing the Worksheet Display," and Chapter 32, "Customizing the 1-2-3 for Windows Screen," for additional information.

◀ "Printing
Worksheets,"
p. 355

■ Define page settings such as margins, headers and footers, and print titles by using the **F**ile Pa**g**e Setup command. When you define this information within the template file, other people who use the worksheet need only to print the worksheet; they do not have to worry about additional print settings.

◀ "Navigating
and Selecting
in 1-2-3 for
Windows,"
p. 59

■ Use the **R**ange **N**ame command to assign range names to cells used by formulas or to worksheet ranges that will be manipulated with 1-2-3 commands.

■ Provide ample notes and documentation explaining the worksheet template and information on tasks the user may need to perform. You may want to store this explanatory information in a separate worksheet and assign a name such as Help or Notes so that the user can find the information immediately.

Creating a SmartMaster

Once you have created the worksheet template, you can save the worksheet as a SmartMaster. Before you do, however, you may want to use the **F**ile **D**oc Info command to supply the worksheet template with a worksheet title and description. When you do, this information is displayed when the SmartMaster template is selected in the File New dialog box.

To add a worksheet title and description with the Doc Info command, follow these steps:

1. Choose the **F**ile **D**oc Info command. The Doc Info dialog box is displayed (see fig. 34.20).

2. Type a title for the worksheet in the **T**itle text box.

3. Type a description of the template in the **C**omments text box.

4. Click OK.

To save the worksheet as a SmartMaster, follow these steps:

1. Choose the **F**ile **S**ave command or press Ctrl+S. The Save As dialog box is displayed (see fig. 34.21).

2. Enter a name for the template in the File name text box.

3. Select SmartMaster (WT4) from the File **t**ype drop-down list.

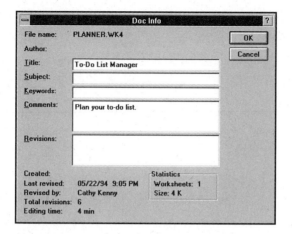

Fig. 34.20
Enter a title and description of the worksheet template in the Doc Info dialog box.

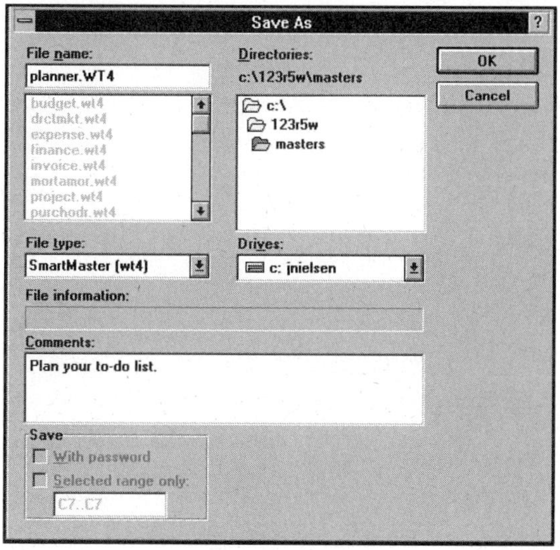

Fig. 34.21
Enter a file name for the SmartMaster in the Save As dialog box.

4. Specify the 1234\MASTERS subdirectory in the **D**irectories box.

5. Click OK.

Autoloading Worksheets

You can create a worksheet file that loads automatically when you start 1-2-3. The file can be any 1-2-3 worksheet you use on a daily basis. For example, you can create a to-do list worksheet and have that file appear automatically every time you start 1-2-3. Or you could create a worksheet that contains no data at all, but instead consists of standard worksheet settings, such as numeric formats, column widths, and display preferences.

The process of creating an autoloading worksheet is really quite simple: You create the worksheet and specify the default settings for that worksheet. Then you use the **File Save** command and assign the name AUTO123.WK4 to the worksheet file and save it in the default 1-2-3 directory (see fig. 34.22). The next time you start 1-2-3, the worksheet file is automatically opened and displayed in the worksheet window (see fig. 34.23).

Fig. 34.22
Assign the name AUTO123.WK4 to the worksheet and save it in the default directory to create an autoloading worksheet.

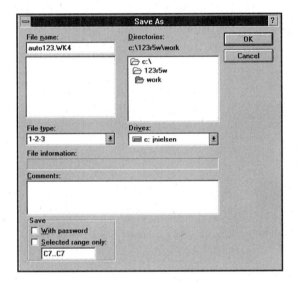

Fig. 34.23
The file named AUTO123.WK4 automatically appears in the Worksheet window when you start 1-2-3.

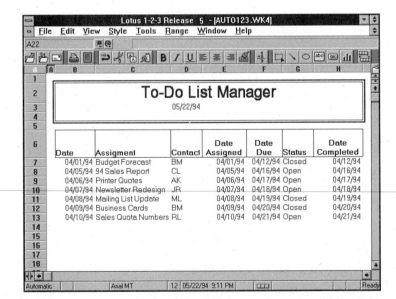

Using the Lotus Dialog Editor

The Lotus Dialog Editor enables you to create custom dialog boxes that are accessed through 1-2-3 for Windows macros. You can use custom dialog boxes to display messages, to prompt the user for input, or to present an entire series of options in a complex application.

> ### Note
>
> The Lotus Dialog Editor is a separate program, usually installed when you install 1-2-3 for Windows. If you chose not to install the Lotus Dialog Editor when you installed 1-2-3 for Windows, refer to your Lotus 1-2-3 Release 4.1 documentation for more information on installing the program.

Custom dialog boxes are dialog boxes you create for use with 1-2-3 macros. You use the DIALOG macro command to display a custom dialog box. 1-2-3 stores in the worksheet any response the user provides so that macro programs can examine and use the stored information. You learn to create custom dialog boxes later in this chapter.

▶ "Advanced Macro Techniques," p. 1077

In many ways, custom dialog boxes are similar to the standard dialog boxes displayed in 1-2-3 or other Windows programs. They can include the same elements, such as buttons, check boxes, and list boxes. Custom dialog boxes even look like standard dialog boxes. The primary difference is that you create custom dialog boxes to meet your special needs.

Understanding Dialog Box Controls

The dialog box elements, or *controls*, you include in your custom dialog box allow users to select program settings and choose options. You can add push buttons, radio buttons, check boxes, edit boxes, list boxes, static text, combo boxes, or group boxes to custom dialog boxes. Table 34.3 describes each of these controls.

Table 34.3   Dialog Box Controls

Control	Description
Push button	Closes a dialog box
Default push button	A push button that is automatically selected when the dialog box is displayed
Radio button	Allows user to select one option at a time

(continues)

Table 34.3 Continued	
Control	**Description**
Check box	Allows user to select multiple options that are not mutually exclusive
Edit box	Allows user to enter up to 511 characters
List box	Allows user to pick one item from a list of items
Static text	Provides explanatory information
Combo box	Combines list boxes and edit boxes in a single control
Group box	Groups and labels related controls
Bitmap button	Create a button with an image on it
Static bitmap	Place a bitmapped image in the dialog box

Creating a Custom Dialog Box

Creating a custom dialog box using the Lotus Dialog Editor is a fairly simple process, but one that requires a little planning if you want the dialog box to be useful.

Before you begin creating a custom dialog box, decide what type of output you expect. If the dialog box is intended to select program options, you want to present the user with a predetermined list of options—perhaps using radio buttons or list boxes. On the other hand, if the dialog box is intended to solicit user input, you need to provide an edit box (also known as a text box) in which the user can type variable information.

You also should decide whether a custom dialog box is really the proper approach to take. Although it may be tempting to create your own variations on standard dialog boxes (such as the File Open dialog box), consider whether this approach may confuse, rather than help, your application's users. Remember that you can use 1-2-3's built-in dialog boxes in your applications without having to worry about making sure that they work correctly!

Finally, consider the layout of the objects in custom dialog boxes. You may want to sketch out the dialog box on paper before you begin to create it in the dialog editor. If the objects in the dialog boxes don't line up, the appearance is anything but professional. Consider, too, the order of the objects in the dialog box. If possible, place edit boxes and other controls in a logical order so that the user can move easily from one object to the next.

> **Note**
>
> The Lotus Dialog Editor Help system contains information on conventions and standards you should follow when creating dialog boxes. To access the information, choose **H**elp **C**ontents and click Following Lotus Conventions and Standards.

Creating a New Dialog Box

To begin creating a custom dialog box, start the Lotus Dialog Editor by double-clicking on the Lotus Dialog Editor icon in the Windows Program Manager. If you are already working in 1-2-3 for Windows, click the Lotus Dialog Editor SmartIcon. Figure 34.24 shows the Lotus Dialog Editor program window.

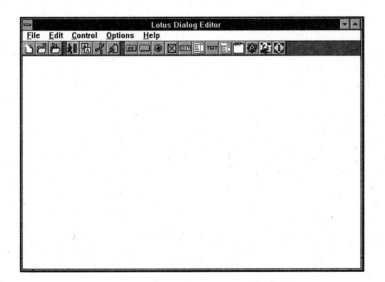

Fig. 34.24
Create custom dialog boxes in the Lotus Dialog Editor window.

You use this window to create and edit custom dialog boxes. The Lotus Dialog Editor window looks similar to any Windows program. The menu bar contains five drop-down menus: **F**ile, **E**dit, **C**ontrol, **O**ptions, and **H**elp.

Use the **F**ile menu commands to create, save, and open dialog box files and to exit the Lotus Dialog Editor. The **E**dit menu commands enable you to copy dialog box descriptions to and from 1-2-3; cut, copy, and paste dialog box objects (controls); and change the appearance of dialog box objects. The **C**ontrol menu enables you to select objects you want to include in a dialog box. The **O**ptions menu offers basic commands for how you use the Lotus Dialog Editor itself.

To start a custom dialog box, follow these steps:

1. Choose the **File New** command. The New dialog box appears (see fig. 34.25).

2. Type a name for the dialog box in the Dialog Box **N**ame text box; in this case, type **Persdata**. You use this name in macros when you want to refer to the custom dialog box.

3. Type a title for the dialog box in the Dialog Box **T**itle text box; in this case, type Personal Data. If you do not include a title, the title bar does not appear on your custom dialog box. If you include a title, it should describe the dialog box's purpose.

4. Select the type of title bar to use in the dialog box: Select Title **b**ar to display just the title; select Title bar with **s**ystem menu to display the title and include a system menu (also known as the Control menu) in the dialog box title bar. Select **P**lain to omit both the title bar and system menu. In this case, select Title **b**ar.

> **Note**
>
> Although the Help Icon option is available in other Lotus programs, like Ami Pro, it is not supported by 1-2-3 for Windows.

5. Choose OK or press Enter.

6. Position the mouse pointer anywhere in the Lotus Dialog Editor window and click the mouse button to create the basic dialog box in the default size (see fig. 34.26). If necessary, you can change the size of the dialog box by dragging the selection handles to the correct size.

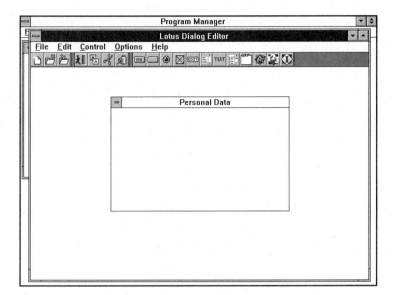

Fig. 34.26
A new, empty
dialog box is
created.

Adding Dialog Box Objects

You add objects to the dialog box by selecting the objects you want from the
Control menu or by clicking on the appropriate SmartIcon and then clicking
the location where you want to add the object.

After the object has been added to the dialog box, you double-click the object
and enter the appropriate controls. For example, when you add a static text
object, the object is initially labeled "Text." To enter the text that you wish to
use you double-click the object and then enter the label in the Modify Static
Text dialog box. When you click OK, the text you entered is displayed.

To add a static text object, follow these steps:

1. Choose the **C**ontrol **S**tatic Text command.

2. Position the mouse pointer in the location you want the static text to
   appear and click the left mouse button. The Static Text object is added
   to the dialog box (see fig. 34.27).

3. Double-click the object to display the Static Text dialog box
   (see fig. 34.28).

4. Type the text to appear in the Static Text object in the **T**ext edit box.

5. In the Styles section of the dialog box, select the label alignment and
   outline to apply to the object.

Fig. 34.27

A static text object is added to the dialog box.

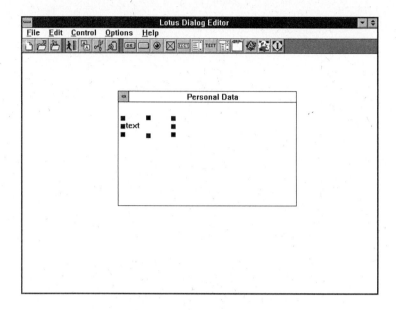

Fig. 34.28

Use the Modify Static Text dialog box to enter the attributes for the text object.

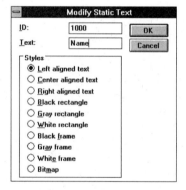

6. Click OK. The new label appears in the text object (see fig 34.29).

To create an edit box, follow these steps:

1. Choose the **C**ontrol **E**dit Box command.

2. Position the mouse pointer in the location you want the edit box to appear and click the left mouse button. The Edit Box object is added to the dialog box (see fig. 34.30).

3. Double-click the object to display the Modify Edit Box dialog box (see fig. 34.31).

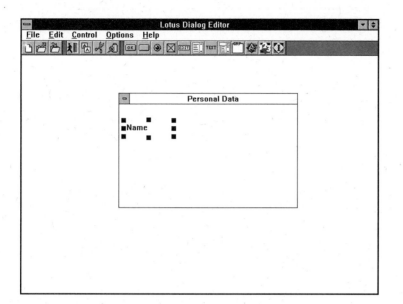

Fig. 34.29
The modified text object appears in the dialog box.

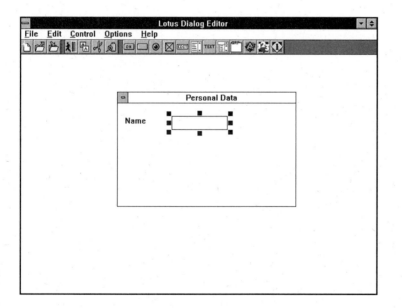

Fig. 34.30
An edit box object is added to the dialog box.

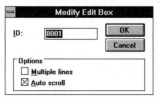

Fig. 34.31
Use the Modify Edit Box dialog box to select the attributes for the edit box object.

4. Select Multiple Lines to allow the user to enter multiple lines of text in the edit box. Select Auto scroll to have the edit box automatically scroll when users enter multiple lines of text.

5. Click OK.

To add a push button control to the dialog box, follow these steps:

1. Choose the **C**ontrol **P**ush Button command.

2. Position the mouse pointer in the location you want the push button to appear and click the left mouse button. The Push Button object is added to the dialog box (see fig. 34.32).

Fig. 34.32

A push button object is added to the dialog box.

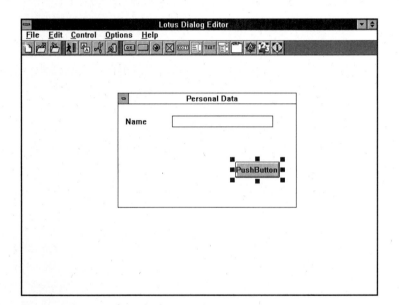

3. Double-click the object to display the Modify Button dialog box (see fig. 34.33).

4. Type the text to appear in the Push Button object in the Button **T**ext edit box.

5. In the Button Type section of the dialog box select the type of button you wish to create. Choose **D**efault push button to create a button that is selected by default when the dialog box is displayed. For example, in most dialog boxes, the OK button is selected by default.

6. Click OK. The push button appears in the dialog box (see fig 34.34).

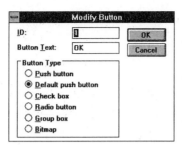

Fig. 34.33
Use the Modify
Button dialog box
to select the type
of push button to
create.

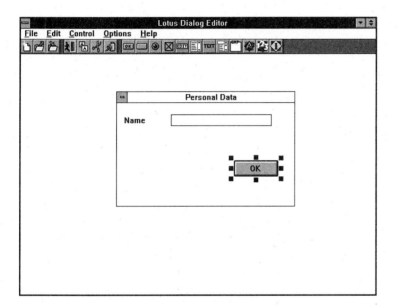

Fig. 34.34
Here, we created
an OK button.

To resize an object, click on the object to select it and drag the selection handles.

The following table shows the applicable SmartIcons and their corresponding Control menu options.

Tip
To make your
dialog box look
professional,
carefully align all
dialog box objects.

Table 34.4 Dialog Editor SmartIcons	
SmartIcon	**Control Menu Option**
	Push Button
	Default Push Button

(continues)

Table 34.4 Continued	
SmartIcon	**Control Menu Option**
 ⊚	Radio Button
 ⊠	Check Box
EDIT	Edit Box
 ▤	List Box
 TEXT	Static Text
 ▤	Combo Box
 GRP	Group Box

To complete the sample dialog box, add the four edit boxes, four static-text objects, the default push button (OK), and the push button (Cancel) shown in figure 34.35.

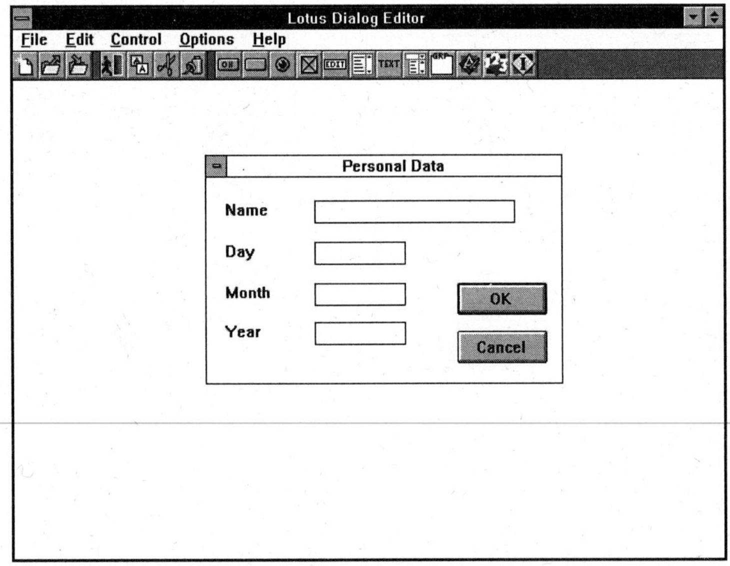

Fig. 34.35
A new dialog box
with added objects

Saving the Dialog Box

The sample dialog box is now ready to test—but first you should save it. Choose the **F**ile **S**ave command and specify a name you can remember, such as **MYDIALOG.DLG** (see fig. 34.36).

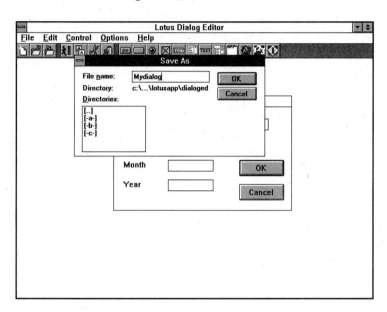

Fig. 34.36
Enter a file name for the custom dialog box.

Copying a Dialog Box to 1-2-3

You transfer a custom dialog box from the Lotus Dialog Editor to 1-2-3 for Windows by copying the dialog box to the Clipboard and then pasting it into 1-2-3. You do not paste the actual dialog box into 1-2-3, however. Instead, you paste a *dialog-description table* (information used by 1-2-3 to duplicate the dialog box). 1-2-3 does not use the dialog box file you saved in the Lotus Dialog Editor.

To copy the dialog box to 1-2-3, follow these steps (starting in the Lotus Dialog Editor):

1. Make certain that none of the individual dialog box objects is selected. Although you can select the entire dialog box, this is not necessary.

2. Select the **E**dit **C**opy command.

3. Press Ctrl+Esc or Alt+Tab to return to 1-2-3 for Windows. If you have not already started 1-2-3 for Windows, choose the **O**ptions **1**23 command to start 1-2-3 for Windows.

Tip
Create a separate worksheet for dialog-description tables to keep from overwriting existing data.

4. Position the cell pointer in the top-left corner of any empty area in your worksheet. (When you paste the dialog box contents, 1-2-3 will over-write any existing data.)

5. Choose the **E**dit **P**aste command. The data used to create the dialog box is pasted in table form, beginning at the pointer position. Figure 34.37 shows the dialog-description table for the sample dialog box in figure 34.35 (in this figure, column widths were adjusted to show all columns in the table on one screen).

Fig. 34.37
The dialog-description table for the example dialog box.

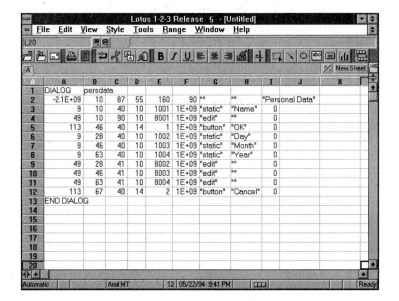

Don't worry if your dialog-description table doesn't match the figure. The dialog-description table lists the dialog box objects in the order they were created, so yours may be different. Also, if the objects you create are a different size or are positioned differently, their description lines will vary from the figure, as well.

Testing the Dialog Box
The next step is to test the dialog box to make certain that it works correctly. You use the DIALOG macro command to display a custom dialog box; you use the same command to test the dialog box.

First, create a range name for the dialog-description table. To do so, move to cell B1, choose **R**ange **N**ame, choose To the left from the **F**or Cells list, and click **U**se Labels to apply the name in cell B1, PERSDATA, to the upper-left corner of the dialog-description table.

Then create a macro that contains the following single command:

```
{DIALOG PERSDATA}
```

Name this macro \d and then run the macro by holding down the Ctrl key and pressing D. 1-2-3 displays the custom dialog box as shown in figure 34.38.

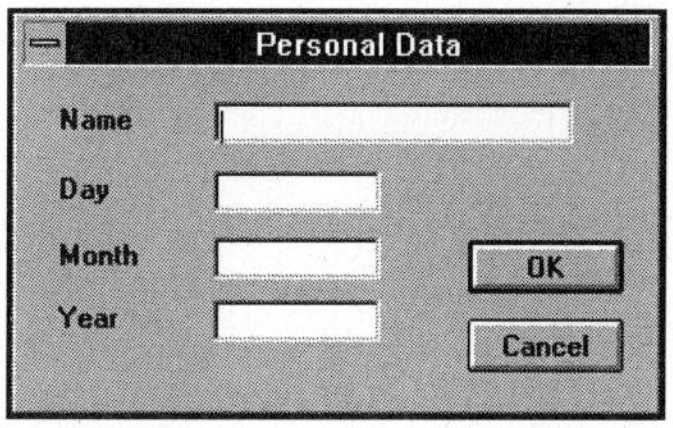

Fig. 34.38
The custom dialog box is displayed for user input.

To test the dialog box, add text to the edit boxes and then select OK or Cancel to close the dialog box and end the macro. When the macro ends, the dialog box is cleared from the screen. If the dialog box does not appear when you run the macro, make certain that the macro refers to the correct range (the dialog-description table). In particular, make certain that the name of the dialog box is assigned to the first cell in the dialog-description table (the cell containing the DIALOG label).

Using Custom Dialog Boxes

Although the sample dialog box appears to work, it is not very useful without a method to access the results. For example, after the user closes the dialog box, you need to know what information was typed in the edit boxes. You also need to know whether OK or Cancel was selected.

The key to accessing dialog box results is understanding where 1-2-3 stores those results. Once you know the location of the data, you can use the information in worksheet formulas or macro commands.

Understanding the Dialog-Description Table

The dialog-description table contains information required by the DIALOG macro command. It contains a description of each of the objects contained in the custom dialog box. Figure 34.39 shows the dialog-description table generated by the custom dialog box.

Fig. 34.39

1-2-3 uses the information supplied in the dialog-description table to display the dialog box.

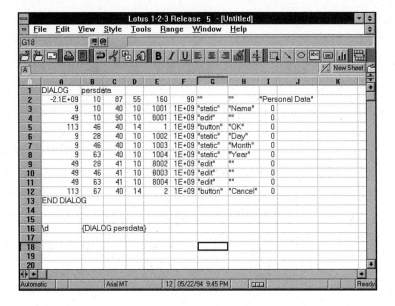

In the first row of the first column, the dialog-description table must contain the label DIALOG. This label tells 1-2-3 that this is the beginning of a dialog-description table.

In the last row of the first column, the dialog-description table must contain the label END DIALOG, to mark the end of the table.

The second row of the dialog-description table begins the description of the dialog box table. Column 9 (in our example, Column I) of the second row contains the dialog box title. The rows below the second row describe the dialog box objects.

The first nine columns of the dialog-description table hold the information 1-2-3 needs to display the dialog box and any objects it contains. The information in these columns is generated automatically when you paste the dialog box into 1-2-3 and should not be changed. Column 7 (column G) describes each object's type; column 8 (column H) shows the text (if any) displayed on the object.

Column 10 (here column J) of the dialog-description table is called the *input column*. Values in this column describe the initial state of dialog box objects. For example, if you add text to column 10 of a row that describes an edit box, the text you enter is displayed as a default value in the edit box. For the sample dialog box shown in figure 34.38, typing **Brian** in cell J4 displays

Brian as the default value in the Name edit box. If you add **@NA** to a cell in column J, the associated dialog box object appears dimmed and is unavailable. Typing **@NA** in cell J12 dims the Cancel button. If the object is a list box, the input column should contain the range name or address of a single-column range that holds the list of items to display in the list box.

Column 11 (in our example column K) of the dialog-description table is called the *output column*. 1-2-3 stores the results from the dialog box in column K. 1-2-3 stores the number of the push button used to close the dialog box in row 2, column 11 (here column K) of the dialog-description table. If a radio button or check box is selected, 1-2-3 stores 1 in the output column of that object's row. If the object is a list box, 1-2-3 stores the offset number of the selected item (from the input range) in the output column. For example, if the list box shows five items, and the first item is selected, the output column shows a 0. If the second item is selected, the output column shows a 1, and so on. Figure 34.40 shows the data entered in the dialog box in column K.

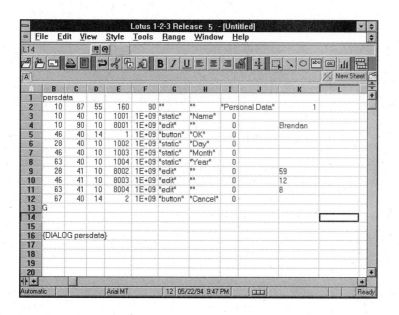

Fig. 34.40
Column K displays the data entered in the dialog box.

Using Dialog box Results

One of the best ways to use dialog box results is to name the cells in the output column (column 11 of the dialog-description table).

Write your macro so that it tests the results when the macro continues after the user selects one of the dialog box push buttons. For example, you can apply the range name USER_NAME to cell K4 in the sample dialog-description table. Then use the values the user enters to perform calculations or determine how the macro program should continue. For example, the macro shown in Figure 34.41 uses the {IF} macro command to test the results of user input. Here, if the user enters **Brian** the macro ends. If the user enters a different name, the dialog box is redisplayed and the user must enter another name. This is only a simple example of how the results of entries made with a custom dialog box can be manipulated by 1-2-3.

Fig. 34.41
This simple macro tests the results of user input with the {IF} macro command.

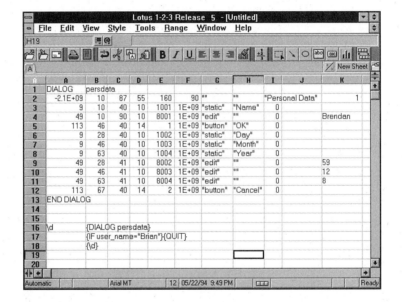

Custom dialog boxes are easy to create and easy to use. You will find that, with a little practice, you can customize your macro programs with your own dialog boxes and create a more professional appearance for your applications.

From Here...

Now that you have learned how to create custom worksheet templates and dialog boxes, you may want to explore the following chapters for additional information on 1-2-3 features that enable you to customize your 1-2-3 session.

- Chapter 15, "Managing the Worksheet Display," shows you how to change 1-2-3's display.

- Chapter 32, "Customizing the 1-2-3 for Windows Screen," provides additional information on customizing the 1-2-3 for Windows workspace.

- Chapter 35, "Writing 1-2-3 for Windows Macros," teaches you how to automate 1-2-3 techniques with macros.

VII

Customizing 1-2-3

Part VIII

Automating with Macros

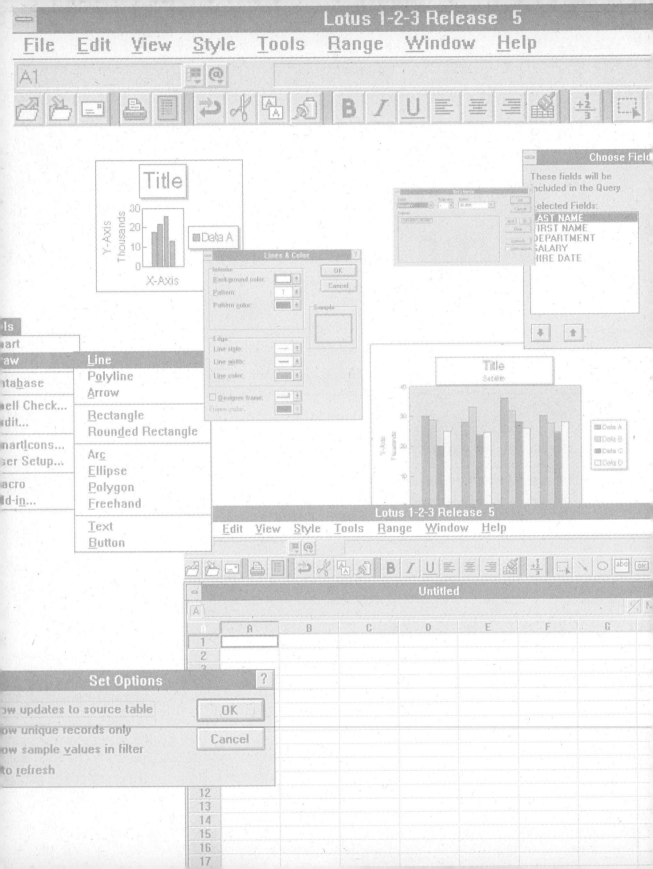

Writing 1-2-3 for Windows Macros

Although the basic worksheet, database, and graphics features of 1-2-3 Release 5 for Windows are very powerful, you can greatly enhance their utility by creating and using *macros*: small programs that automate 1-2-3 for Windows. Simple macros can duplicate the tasks that you perform repeatedly, such as printing worksheets, changing fonts, and entering the same data in several locations.

More advanced macros provide even more capabilities. You can construct sophisticated business applications that function the same as applications written in such programming languages as BASIC, C, and FORTRAN. Fortunately, creating advanced macro programs is much easier than creating programs in most other programming languages.

This chapter covers the following topics:

■ Defining macros

■ Developing and writing macros

■ Planning the layout of macros

■ Formatting macros

■ Naming and running macros

■ Documenting macros

■ Testing and debugging macros

■ Protecting macros

Chapters 36, 37, and 38 introduce more advanced macro techniques, including the use of the Transcript window for recording macros (Chapter 36) and the use of *macro commands*: a powerful set of programming tools that enable you to enhance macros (Chapter 37). Chapter 37 also helps you learn the functions and applications of those commands. Chapter 38, "Exploring a Corporate Macro Example," applies many of the macro concepts presented in previous chapters.

Defining a Macro

The simplest type of macro is nothing more than a short collection of keystrokes that 1-2-3 for Windows enters in a worksheet for you. Because the program stores this keystroke collection as text in a cell, you can treat the text as you would any label. Consider the number of times you save and retrieve worksheet files, print reports, and set and reset worksheet formats. In each case, you perform the operation by typing a series of keystrokes—sometimes, a rather long series. By running a macro, however, you can reduce any number of keystrokes to a two-keystroke abbreviation.

Consider a simple yet effective macro that enters text. Suppose that your company's name is Darlene's Computer Warehouse—an entry that requires quite a few keystrokes. You want to place this name at various points in worksheets. You can type the entry's many keystrokes every time you want to place the entry in the worksheet, or you can store all the keystrokes in a macro. When you want the company's name to appear in a worksheet, you can use just two keystrokes: the Ctrl key and a designated letter of the alphabet. Such a macro is called a Ctrl+*letter* macro. In a later section, you learn to create such a macro.

> **Note**
>
> Most macros created in earlier versions of 1-2-3 for Windows must be translated before use. Some very simple keystroke macros, such as this example, may work in 1-2-3 Release 5 for Windows, but most macros from earlier versions of 1-2-3 for Windows will not. For more information, see "Translating 1-2-3 Release 1 for Windows Macros" in Chapter 36.

You name a Ctrl+*letter* macro by using the backslash key (\) and a single letter of the alphabet. DOS versions of 1-2-3 called these macros Alt+*letter* macros, and the Alt key was termed the *macro key*. Windows applications, however, usually reserve the Alt key for invoking the window menu bar.

In 1-2-3 for Windows, therefore, Lotus changed its conventions for invoking macros named by a backslash and a single letter. You now start these macros in 1-2-3 for Windows by holding down the Ctrl key and pressing the respective alphabet-letter key.

The Ctrl+*letter* method is not the only way to name a macro. You learn about other methods later in this chapter.

Developing Your Own Macros

The steps for creating any macro are basic. Following is an outline of these steps; later sections of this chapter expand on the major steps.

Perform the following steps to create a macro:

1. *Plan what you want the macro to do.*

    Write down all the tasks you want the macro to perform; then arrange those tasks in the order in which they should be completed.

2. *Identify the keystrokes or commands that the macro should use.*

    Keep in mind that macros can be as simple as labels (text) that duplicate the keystrokes you want to replay.

3. *Find an area of the worksheet in which you can enter macros.*

    When you choose the worksheet area, consider the fact that executed macros read text from cells, starting with the top cell and working down through lower cells. Macros end when they encounter a blank cell, a cell that contains a numeric value, or a command that stops macro execution. Therefore, enter macros as labels in successive cells in the same column.

4. *Use the correct syntax to enter the keystrokes and macro commands in a cell or cells. Use the Help system to double-check whether macro command arguments have been entered correctly.*

5. *Name the macro.*

    You can name a macro in one of three ways:

    - Assign the macro a Ctrl+*letter* name. This type of name consists of a backslash (\) followed by an alphabetic character (for example, \a).

■ Choose a descriptive name, such as PRINT_BUDGET, for a macro. Macro names, like other 1-2-3 range names, can contain up to 15 characters.

■ Give the name \0 (zero) to a macro if you want that macro to run automatically when the file is loaded. The User Setup dialog box enables you to disable and re-enable the auto-execute feature of macros named \0. The Run Autoexecute **M**acros check box in this dialog box acts like a toggle switch: when the check box is selected, a macro named \0 executes automatically when a file that contains the macro is opened.

6. *Document the macro.*

   To facilitate the editing and debugging process, you can document a macro in several ways:

   ■ Use a descriptive macro name, and consistently use range names instead of cell addresses in macros. Addresses entered in the text of a macro are not updated when changes are made to the worksheet. A macro does not work properly with incorrect addresses, which can result from moving, inserting, or deleting ranges. Range names in a macro *are* updated when the worksheet changes.

   ■ Use the **/R**ange **N**ame **N**ote feature in the 1-2-3 Classic menu to attach notes to a range name.

   ■ Include comments in a separate column to the right of the actual macro within the worksheet.

   ■ Retain all the paperwork you used to design and construct the macro for later reference.

7. *Test and debug the macro.*

   Always test your macros for proper operation before giving them to a user. Make certain that the macros work correctly before you trust them to process important data.

When your macros become more complex as your expertise increases, continue to use these basic steps to create a macro. Remember that good planning and documentation are important for making macros run smoothly and efficiently.

Writing Your First Macros

The next two sections show you how to write two simple macros. The first macro enters text in a cell; the second macro enters commands specified in the macro.

Writing a Macro That Enters Text

In this section, you create a macro that enters a company name—Darlene's Computer Warehouse—in various locations in worksheets. This simple example introduces the basic concepts required to create macros in 1-2-3 for Windows. Later, you learn to use more advanced macro programming commands and techniques to make macros execute faster and more efficiently.

Before you begin creating a macro, plan what you want the macro to do, and identify the keystrokes the macro should enter. In the case of the macro that enters a company name in a worksheet, you want the macro to enter the letters, spaces, and punctuation that comprise the company's name. Then, as with any label, you want the macro to complete the entry by performing the equivalent of pressing the Enter key.

You begin building the macro by storing the keystrokes as text in a worksheet cell. After entering the letters that make up the company's name, you enter a tilde (~). In a macro, the tilde represents the Enter key.

Cell B3 in figure 35.1 contains the keystrokes you want 1-2-3 for Windows to type:

    Darlene's Computer Warehouse~

The tilde (~) is included at the end of the line. Remember that the tilde represents the press of the Enter key—an important step in ensuring that this macro executes correctly.

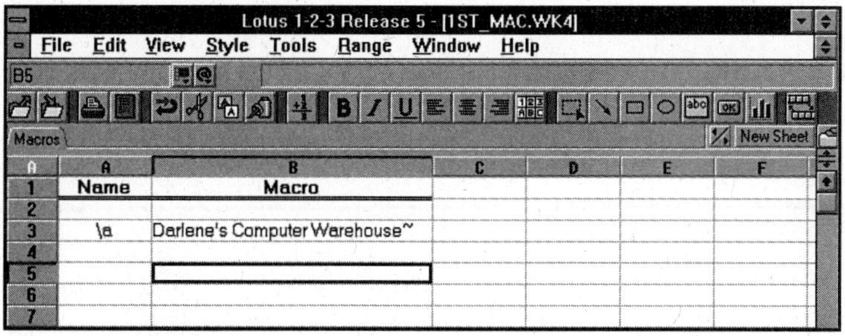

Fig. 35.1
A simple macro for entering a company name.

> **Note**
>
> You can adjust the width of column B to display all the macro's keystrokes. Move the mouse to the right edge of column B, directly above row 1, and double-click the boundary between columns B and C. Then drag the column boundary to the right to widen column B. The macro works, however, no matter how wide the column containing its instructions.

The next step in writing the macro is naming this sequence of keystrokes as a macro. This step is optional in 1-2-3 for Windows because you can use the Macro Run dialog box to run macros that have no name. Naming macros, however, has a few advantages, even in 1-2-3 for Windows. First, naming macros gives you a convenient form of self-documentation; second, you can start named macros more quickly.

You can name macros in several ways. This section describes one macro-naming technique; later sections of this chapter describe the others.

The following procedure is particularly convenient for naming a macro when the name is located to the left of the macro keystrokes, as is the name \a shown in figure 35.1. Follow these steps:

1. Move the cell pointer to cell A3.

2. Open the **R**ange menu and choose the **N**ame command. The Name dialog box appears (see fig. 35.2).

Fig. 35.2
The Name dialog box, used for naming a macro.

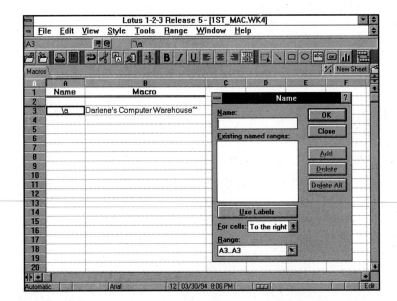

3. In the **F**or Cells list box, select To the Right as the direction of the adjacent cell to which you want 1-2-3 for Windows to apply the name.

4. Click the **U**se Labels command button. This action assigns the name in cell A3 (\a) to cell B3.

5. Choose OK.

By placing the macro's name one cell to the left of the first cell in the macro, you can document the macro's name easily. This technique helps you remember the macro name for later use.

To *execute* (run) this macro, move the cell pointer to the cell in which you want the company name to appear, hold down the Ctrl key, and then press **A**. 1-2-3 for Windows enters the sequence of characters identified as the macro \a.

Figure 35.3 shows the result of moving the cell pointer to cell B10 and then running the \a macro. To save this macro for future use, save the file in which the macro is located.

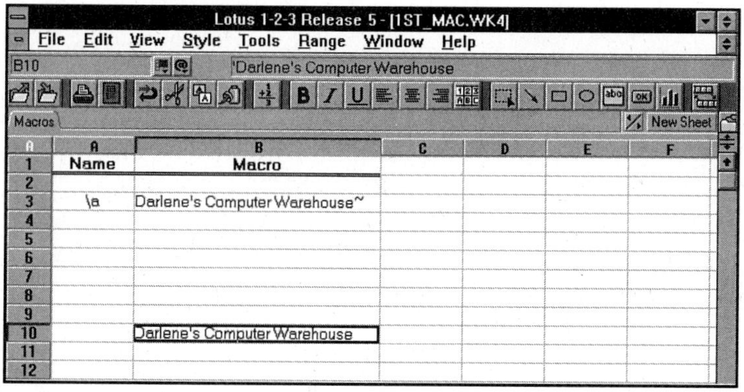

Fig. 35.3
The result of moving the cell pointer to cell B10 and running the \a macro.

Writing a Simple Command Macro

In addition to writing macros that repeat text, you can write macros that enter commands. If you follow the same procedure each time, macro writing should become second nature to you.

1-2-3 Release 5 for Windows command macros, however, do not simply duplicate the keystrokes you use to enter a command. Instead, command macros use a simple *command language*: a set of terms that replace keystroke representations with easy-to-read words. Macros that use the 1-2-3 Release 5 for Windows macro-command language not only are easier to read, but also function more efficiently than collections of keystrokes; therefore, macros written in this language execute more quickly. Don't worry if you don't know the 1-2-3 Release 5 for Windows macro-command language; as this example shows, the macro-command language is easy to learn and understand.

> **Note**
>
> An easy way to identify the commands for a task is to display the Transcript window while you manually perform the steps to complete the task. As you work, the Transcript window displays the macro commands that correspond to what you are doing. For more information on recording macros with the Transcript window, see Chapter 36, "Recording and Modifying Macros."

As described earlier in this chapter, the first step is to decide what you want the command macro to do. Then you need to identify each step necessary to complete the task. Suppose that you want to create a simple macro that enters commands, such as the commands for naming a macro (as you did in the preceding section). To perform this task manually, you normally complete the following steps:

1. Move the cell pointer to the cell containing the label you want to use as a range name—in this case, cell A3.

2. Press the Alt key to access the 1-2-3 for Windows menu.

3. Open the **R**ange menu and choose the **N**ame command. 1-2-3 for Windows displays the Name dialog box.

4. Make certain that the **F**or Cells list box displays To the Right as the direction of the adjacent cell to which you want to apply the name. If this is not the case, make the proper selection in the list box.

5. Click the **U**se Labels command button.

6. Choose OK to confirm your selection and close the dialog box.

These steps tell 1-2-3 for Windows to use labels contained in worksheet cells to create range names for the cells to the right of the labels. You can use the 1-2-3 Release 5 for Windows command language to create a macro that performs the same procedure. Following is the equivalent macro command:

```
{RANGE-NAME-LABEL-CREATE "right"}
```

Cell B5 in figure 35.4 shows the macro command entered in the worksheet.

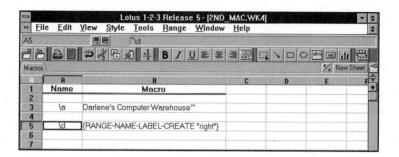

Fig. 35.4
The range-naming macro entered in cell B5.

> **Note**
>
> Instead of copying keystrokes, 1-2-3 Release 5 for Windows substitutes easy-to-read commands such as the RANGE-NAME-LABEL-CREATE command, which replaces the six steps shown earlier. Chapter 37, "Advanced Macro Techniques," includes a complete reference to the macro-command language.

For the purpose of this example, the intention is to name the macro \d. In this case, however, you cannot launch the macro in the typical Ctrl+*letter* fashion, because the name is not yet assigned. You can press Alt+F3 (Run) or open the **T**ools menu and choose the **M**acro **R**un command to display the Macro Run dialog box and run the macro even before it is named (see fig. 35.5).

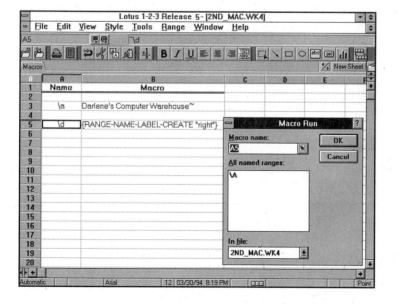

Fig. 35.5
The Macro Run dialog box, used to run an unnamed macro.

In figure 35.5, the cell pointer rests in cell A:A5, one cell to the left of the macro's first line. The **M**acro Name text box displays A:A5 (the current cell-pointer location—and the location of the label you want to use to name the macro). Before you can execute the macro, you must change the **M**acro Name text box to display the address of the first cell in the macro (in this case, A:B5). You can either type **A:B5** or click cell A:B5 in the worksheet. When you choose OK, the macro in cell A:B5 executes and names itself \d.

After you name the \d macro and assign the name to cell A:B5, you easily can use this macro to name other macros. Remember to start by positioning the cell pointer one cell to the left of a macro's first cell (that is, in the cell that contains the name you intend to assign to the macro). Then press the keystroke combination Ctrl+D.

Chapter 37, "Advanced Macro Techniques," includes a comprehensive list of 1-2-3 Release 5 for Windows macro commands.

Understanding the Guidelines for Creating Macros

In the preceding sections of this chapter, you learned to write simple macros. You learned the importance of planning the macro and identifying the tasks the macro should perform. The following sections elaborate on the major elements of successful macro creation and execution. These elements include planning the layout of the macro, formatting the macro, naming and running the macro, documenting the macro, and testing and debugging the macro.

Whether your macros simply duplicate keystrokes or use the 1-2-3 Release 5 for Windows command language, macros are easier to create and maintain if you follow the guidelines presented in the following sections.

Planning the Layout of Macros

Note

An easy way to break a macro into parts is to divide it in terms of small tasks. You can limit each cell to a single task (or a few tasks). When you limit the content of each cell, you find it easier to debug, modify, and document macros. Using multiple cells to store the macro makes the macro easier to read and understand.

Although you can enter as many as 512 characters in one cell, you should divide a long macro into smaller, more readable pieces. Break apart a macro by placing each part of the macro in consecutive cells down a column.

Figure 35.6 shows two macros that execute an identical sequence of keystrokes. The \m macro performs the same sequence of tasks as the Print_Macros macro, but it is difficult to read and understand because it is contained in a single cell. (In this figure, cell B3 was selected and is being edited so that the complete text of the macro appears in the contents box.)

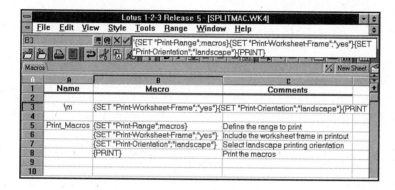

Fig. 35.6
Using multiple cells to store the macro.

VIII

Automating with Macros

Although both macros in figure 35.6 include the same set of macro commands, the Print_Macros macro has several advantages over the \m macro. For example, if you decide to change the range printed by the macro, the Print_Macros macro is much easier to modify. In addition, because the Print_Macros macro fits into a single column, you can easily read the macro commands it contains. Finally, the Print_Macros macro is much easier to document; you can enter comments in the column to the right of the macro commands.

The Print_Macros macro works whether you name the macro using just cell B5 or the entire range B5..B8. Remember that the commands execute starting at the top-left-corner cell of the range. After the commands in cell B5 are executed, the macro processor moves down one cell and executes any commands in cell B6. After completing those commands, the processor again moves down one cell. The macro processor continues to move down and execute commands until it encounters one of the following situations:

- An empty cell

- A cell that contains a numeric value, ERR, or NA

- A cell that contains a macro command that explicitly stops a macro (discussed in Chapter 37, "Advanced Macro Techniques")

The macros you create will be easier to read and understand later if you logically separate macro commands into separate cells. When you use macro instructions that include braces, such as {SET} and {PRINT}, however, you must keep the entire macro command in the same cell. Splitting the macro command {PRINT} into two cells—{PR in one cell, and INT} in the cell that follows—doesn't work.

Because macro commands must be labels, the macro processor ignores the label prefix (', ", or ^) in the macro cell when the keystrokes are executed. It does not matter which label prefix you use; the macros run regardless of which you choose.

1-2-3 for Windows enables you to repeat certain macro commands by including a *repetition factor*, which tells 1-2-3 for Windows that you want a command repeated the number of times you specify. The \a and \d macros in figure 35.7 perform the same keystrokes. The \a macro uses four {DOWN} commands to move the cell pointer down four rows. The \d macro uses a repetition factor, {DOWN 4}, to repeat the {DOWN} macro command four times. Both macros accomplish the same task, but the \d macro is more efficient. When you use a repetition factor, leave a space between the macro command and the number. See Chapter 37, "Advanced Macro Techniques," for more information on macro commands that can use a repetition factor.

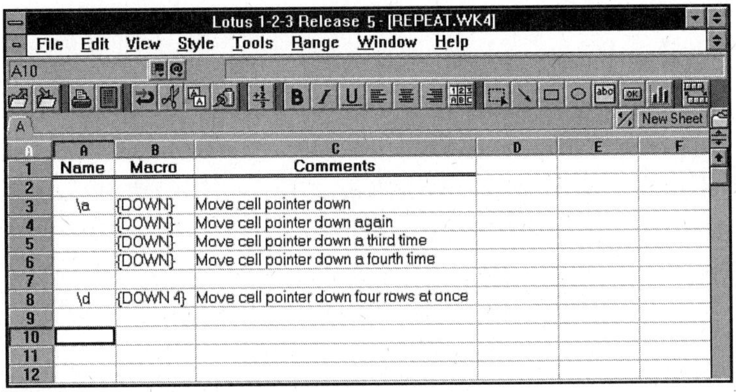

Fig. 35.7
A repetition factor used in the \d macro to repeat a macro command.

Formatting Macros

Certain formatting features are necessary to ensure the successful operation of 1-2-3 for Windows macros. Other conventions simplify the tasks of reading and analyzing macros. These tasks are particularly important when you need to debug or edit a macro by changing or adding an operation. The following sections present certain rules you should follow so that your macros run properly.

Enter Macro Cells as Text or String Formulas

When you type a macro in the worksheet, you must enter each cell of the macro as text or as a string formula. Certain keystrokes, such as numbers, cause 1-2-3 for Windows to change from Ready mode to Value mode; other keystrokes, such as the slash key (/), change 1-2-3 for Windows to Menu mode. Therefore, you must place an apostrophe (') before any of the following characters if that character is to be the first character in a macro cell:

A number from 0 to 9

/ + – @ # $. < (\

The apostrophe (') switches 1-2-3 for Windows to Label mode from Ready mode, especially if you are entering a macro that contains a number of lines that 1-2-3 does not recognize as labels. Using an apostrophe before any of the preceding characters and numbers ensures that 1-2-3 for Windows does not misinterpret your text entry. If any character *not* in this list is the first keystroke in the cell, 1-2-3 for Windows switches to Label mode and prefixes the entry with an apostrophe (') when you press Enter.

Use Braces with Macro Commands

Enter macro commands as described in Chapter 37, "Advanced Macro Techniques." Be sure to use curly braces ({ }) to enclose macro commands.

Use Correct Syntax for Macro Commands

The syntax of macro commands must be correct. For the correct syntax of the macro commands used in 1-2-3 Release 5 for Windows, see Chapter 37, "Advanced Macro Techniques." You must place each macro command within one cell; you cannot write a macro command so that the beginning brace is on one line and the closing brace is on another line.

Tip
Open the **S**tyle menu and choose the **N**umber Format command to apply Label format to cells in which you intend to enter macro commands. 1-2-3 for Windows automatically prefixes entries in Label-formatted cells with an apostrophe (').

VIII

Automating with Macros

> **Note**
>
> To quickly check the syntax of a macro command, type the left brace ({) and the macro command name in the cell; while you still are in Label mode, press F1 to invoke a context-sensitive help screen that describes the proper syntax.
>
> Pressing F3 after entering a left brace invokes the Macro Keywords dialog box, which contains a list of macro commands that you can view either alphabetically or by command category. Selecting a command from this list enters the command in the cell and highlights any command arguments that you must supply.

When you use 1-2-3 for Windows macro commands, you must keep the entire macro command in the same cell. For example, you cannot split the command {BLANK} into two cells; {BL in one cell and ANK} in another does not work. You also should be careful not to mix curly braces with parentheses or square brackets; avoid such constructions as {BLANK) and [BLANK}.

Use the Tilde To Represent the Enter Key

You use the tilde (~) in a macro to represent the action of pressing the Enter key. Most 1-2-3 Release 5 for Windows command-language macros do not require a tilde, but macros that duplicate keystrokes instead of using command-language statements usually do require the tilde.

Use Repetition Factors

Use repetition factors in macros whenever possible. Instead of typing **{LEFT}** three times, you can type **{LEFT 3}** or **{L 3}**. When you use repetition factors, be sure to place one space between the actual macro command and the number of repetitions. For more information on macro commands that can use a repetition factor, see Chapter 37, "Advanced Macro Techniques."

Naming and Running Macros

You can start macros in several ways, depending on how the macros are named. Consider the following examples:

- Execute a macro named with the backslash (\) and a letter by holding down the Ctrl key and pressing the designated letter of the alphabet. Alternatively, you can use the Macro Run dialog box. You invoke this dialog box by pressing Alt+F3 (Run) or opening the **T**ools menu and choosing the **M**acro **R**un command.

- Execute a macro with a descriptive name of up to 15 characters by using the Macro Run dialog box.

- You can launch an *auto-execute macro* (one with the name \0) in two ways. If you checked the Run Autoexecute **M**acros check box in the User Setup dialog box, such a macro will start when a file containing the \0 macro is loaded. You also can initiate an auto-execute macro by using the Macro Run dialog box.

- Execute any macro, even if it has no name, by using the Macro Run dialog box. Specify the macro's first cell as the address in the **M**acro Name text box, and then choose OK.

Earlier in this chapter, you learned how to name and run a macro with the Ctrl+*letter* combination. In the second method of naming and running macros, you assign a descriptive name to the first cell in the macro and then execute the macro from the Macro Run dialog box. In the third method, you create a macro named \0 that executes when you load the file. In the fourth method, you execute *any* macro by using the Macro Run dialog box. Invoking a macro in 1-2-3 for Windows with the Macro Run dialog box is a more user-friendly approach than the Alt+*letter* method available in previous versions of 1-2-3. Users of 1-2-3 for DOS versions before Release 2.2 could use only Alt+*letter* range names to start macros from the keyboard.

When you click the Run Macro SmartIcon, press Alt+F3 (Run), or open the **T**ools menu and choose the **M**acro **R**un command, the Macro Run dialog box appears; you can select a macro from the list of macro names. You also can type the cell address of the macro you want to run; you do not have to specify a range name.

Although you use the \0 name only if you want 1-2-3 for Windows to invoke a macro as soon as the file is retrieved, you can use the Ctrl+*letter* or descriptive name for any other macro. Both types of names have advantages. When you invoke a macro with a Ctrl+*letter* name, you use fewer keystrokes than when you invoke a macro with a descriptive name. The disadvantage of using a Ctrl+*letter* macro name, however, is that you may have difficulty remembering a macro's specific purpose, particularly when you have many macros. Your chance of selecting the correct macro is greater when you use descriptive names.

The following sections describe all three approaches to creating, naming, and running macros. Figure 35.8 shows three macros that demonstrate the rules and conventions for naming and running macros. Although these macros are intended only to demonstrate the three ways to name and run a macro, each is a fully functioning 1-2-3 Release 5 for Windows command-language macro. The comments included in column C for each macro explain the function of each line of the macro.

Ctrl+*letter* Macros

You can name a macro by using the backslash key (\) and a letter. This method is the Ctrl+*letter* method of naming a macro. Versions of 1-2-3 before 1-2-3 for Windows called these macros Alt+*letter* macros. In 1-2-3 for Windows, however, the Alt key is reserved for invoking the 1-2-3 for Windows menu. In 1-2-3 for Windows, therefore, macros named with a backslash and a letter of the alphabet are called Ctrl+*letter* macros. You start these macros in 1-2-3 for Windows by holding down the Ctrl key and pressing the appropriate alphabet-letter key.

Fig. 35.8

Three macros that show naming conventions.

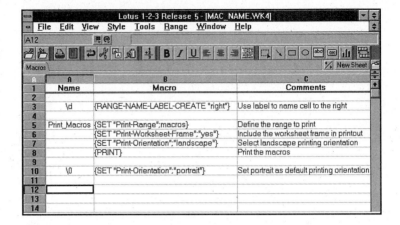

The \d macro shown in figure 35.8 demonstrates the Ctrl+*letter* approach to naming a macro. The function of the \d macro is one way to automate the naming of macros. You can use uppercase or lowercase characters to name a macro; 1-2-3 for Windows does not differentiate between uppercase and lowercase letters for range names. Accordingly, \a, \A, and \m are valid names for Ctrl+*letter* macros.

> **Note**
>
> 1-2-3 for Windows assigns keyboard shortcuts to several Ctrl+*letter* combinations (such as Ctrl+B for changing selected text and numbers to boldface). If you use the same Ctrl+*letter* combination to name a macro, the macro executes in place of the keyboard shortcut. To prevent conflicts with keyboard shortcuts, avoid using the letters B, C, E, I, L, N, O, P, R, S, U, V, X, and Z when naming Ctrl+*letter* macros.

To run a macro named with the backslash (\) and a letter, hold down the Ctrl key and press the character key that identifies the macro. To run the first macro shown in figure 35.8, for example, press Ctrl+D.

Macros with Descriptive Names

Because you can use up to 15 characters to name a range in 1-2-3 for Windows, you can use descriptive names for macros. One way to document macros is to give them longer, descriptive names. Another way is to retain hard-copy documentation for macros, including printouts of the macro code. The Print_Macros macro shown in figure 35.8 automates the preparation of these printouts.

When naming macros with descriptive names, however, do not use range names that also are macro-command names. For a list of command names, see Chapter 37, "Advanced Macro Techniques."

You can use the Macro Run dialog box to start macros that have descriptive names. To access this dialog box, click the Run Macro SmartIcon, press Alt+F3 (Run), or open the **T**ools menu and choose the **M**acro **R**un command. Figure 35.9 shows how the screen appears after this dialog box is invoked for the sample macros shown in figure 35.8.

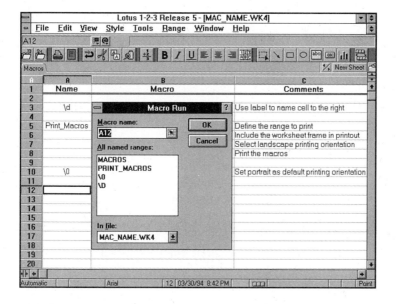

Fig. 35.9

The Macro Run dialog box displays a list of range names in the current file.

VIII

Automating with Macros

To start a macro from the current file, move to the **M**acro Name text box (refer to fig. 35.9) and type the range name of the macro you want to run; then choose OK.

When you access the Macro Run dialog box, 1-2-3 for Windows displays all the range names in the current file, including range names that are not macro names. If other 1-2-3 for Windows worksheet files are active in memory, 1-2-3 for Windows lists all these file names after the range names of the currently selected file.

To run a macro in a file that is not currently selected, double-click that file's name in the In **F**ile list box. The Macro Run dialog box lists the range names in the selected file. Then, in the **M**acro Name text box, type the range name of the macro you want to run.

You can start a macro in another file without selecting the file; simply precede the macro's name in the **M**acro Name text box with the name of the file in which it is located. Enclose the file name in double angle brackets (<< >>) and then type the macro name, as in the following example:

```
<<BUDGET.WK4>>Print_Macro
```

To run a macro from the keyboard, follow these steps:

1. Press Alt+F3 (Run) or open the **T**ools menu and choose the **M**acro **R**un command to access the Macro Run dialog box.

2. Press Tab to move from the **M**acro Name text box to the **A**ll Named Ranges list below it.

3. Use the arrow keys to highlight the desired entry, and then press Enter.

You can use any of the following procedures to designate and run a macro from the Macro Run dialog box:

- Type the name of the macro or the address of its first cell in the **M**acro Name text box; then choose OK. If you type the address without identifying the file, 1-2-3 for Windows assumes that you mean the current file. If you type an address that does not include the worksheet letter, 1-2-3 for Windows assumes that you mean the current worksheet. If you type a range name without identifying the file, 1-2-3 for Windows assumes that you mean a macro in the current file.

- Highlight one of the macro range names in the **A**ll Named Ranges list for the active file; then choose OK. To see the range names for one of the other active files, highlight the name of that file and press Enter (alternatively, double-click the name of the file); 1-2-3 for Windows displays the range names for that file. After the **M**acro Name text box displays the correct name for the macro you want to run, choose OK.

- Point to the first cell of the macro you want to run. With the highlight in the **M**acro Name text box, you can use the arrow keys or the mouse to point to the first cell of the macro you want to run. You also can click the range selector beside the **M**acro Name text box to remove the dialog box and point to the first cell of the macro; then choose OK.

Although you can use the method that best suits your needs, you may find the first method most useful when you want to invoke a macro located in another worksheet file. The second method generally is the easiest and least error-prone, and the third method is best when you want to see the actual contents of a macro before you execute it.

Auto-Execute Macros

You may want some macros to run automatically when you retrieve the worksheets that contain them. Use \0 to name the macro that you want to run as soon as the worksheet loads; such a macro is called an auto-execute macro. Each worksheet file can contain only one auto-execute macro.

Suppose that you print some worksheets in landscape orientation and others in portrait orientation. To ensure that the printing orientation is set properly for a worksheet that requires portrait orientation, you can include in that worksheet the \0 auto-execute macro shown in figure 35.8. By changing the argument from "portrait" to "landscape," you can create a similar auto-execute macro for worksheets that use landscape orientation.

Any task you want to perform automatically whenever a worksheet loads is a good candidate for an auto-execute macro. For example, if you create your own menus for a worksheet model, you may want to use an auto-execute macro to display the menu whenever the worksheet is loaded. You also may want to use an auto-execute macro to automatically move the cell pointer to a specific cell or to the end of a list of entries. In fact, you may have a whole series of tasks that should be performed whenever the worksheet is loaded. If so, simply include the correct commands in the auto-execute macro.

Troubleshooting

After entering \0, a string of zeros is repeated.

Be sure to precede the \0 with a single quote, so that it is entered as a label.

An auto-execute macro will not run when a worksheet is loaded.

Make certain that the Run Autoexecute **M**acros check box is selected in the User Setup dialog box. To access this dialog box, open the **T**ools menu and choose the **U**ser Setup command.

Documenting Macros

As with other parts of a 1-2-3 for Windows worksheet, you need to document the macros you write. You can document macros by using many of the same techniques you use to document worksheets, as follows:

- Use descriptive names as macro names.

- Include comments in the worksheet.

- Save any design notes that you've created on paper.

VIII

Automating with Macros

> **Note**
>
> In addition to placing macro comments in a worksheet, you can save comments with a file. When you save a file for the first time, or when you open the **F**ile menu and choose the Save **A**s command, you see a dialog box that contains a section for comments. Any comments that you save with the file appear when the file name is highlighted in the Open dialog box.

Use Descriptive Names

You have seen how you can use the backslash and an alphabetic character to name a macro. You then can use the Ctrl+*letter* combination to execute the macro. Although a Ctrl+*letter* macro is easy to execute, its name does not describe the macro's purpose. A better naming convention is to use range names as macro names. You can execute such macros by pressing Alt+F3 (Run) or by opening the **T**ools menu and choosing the **M**acro **R**un command.

Include Comments in the Worksheet

A description of the macro's function appears to the right of each of the three macros shown in figure 35.10. With these simple macros, you can identify the tasks that the macros perform just by reading the macro code—if you are familiar with the menu structure that the macros reference. The addition of the documentation provides a ready reference.

Fig. 35.10
Three macros,
shown with
documentation.

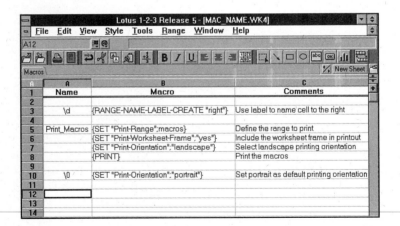

With longer, more complex macros, you probably will find such internal documentation helpful. Later, when you want to make changes in the macro, you can refer to these internal comments about the macro's purpose and intended action.

You may discover that you do not need to comment on each individual macro line, especially when you create simple macros. The following guidelines may be helpful when you document macros:

- Document the overall purpose of a macro or subroutine.

- Document individual macro lines when specific operations are unclear.

- If possible, avoid spending too much time and memory documenting simple macros.

Keep External Design Notes

Be sure to retain any paperwork you created as part of designing and constructing the macro. In addition to keeping any notes on keystrokes or commands that you incorporated into the macro, you should keep printed copies of all the range names and formulas in each worksheet.

Don't underestimate the value of this documentation, which will considerably ease the burden of modifying a macro later. The more people who use a macro, and the more important a macro is, the more critical external documentation becomes.

The most important piece of external documentation—which you never should neglect—is a printout of the macro. Other types of external documentation that may be particularly valuable are notes on who requested a macro, why the macro was requested, who created and tested the macro, the underlying assumptions that determined the overall design, and any diagrams or outlines of macro operations or structure.

If you used reference materials to develop the worksheet, consider including a bibliography and page references in the documentation. Any information that you supply in external documentation simplifies any maintenance of, or modifications to, the worksheet.

Tip
To create documentation on all formulas in a worksheet, open the **T**ools menu and choose the **A**udit command.

VIII

Automating with Macros

◄ "Auditing Worksheets," p. 617

Using Single Step and Trace To Test Macros

Macro writers soon recognize that even a well-designed macro program can contain *bugs* (errors that prevent the macro from functioning correctly). Because 1-2-3 for Windows executes macro instructions in rapid sequence, you often cannot determine why a macro is failing. This section introduces some methods that help you find and correct errors in macros.

No matter how carefully you construct a macro, it may not run flawlessly the first time. By taking a series of precautions, however, you can minimize your efforts to get macros to work correctly.

Before you create a macro, always invest the time to design the macro carefully. Just as a carpenter never starts construction of a house without blueprints, you should not start construction of a macro without a carefully conceived, well-documented design. Take time to plan the detailed steps a macro is to perform, create good documentation of the macro's purpose and actions, and write descriptions of any range names used in the macro.

Even if you have a good design and thorough documentation, plan to test and debug your macro. Testing enables you to verify that a macro works precisely the way you want. 1-2-3 for Windows provides two valuable tools that help you verify a macro's operation and locate macro errors: Single Step and Trace modes. *Single Step mode* enables you to execute the macro one keystroke at a time. This mode gives you a chance to see, one instruction at a time, exactly what the macro does. *Trace mode* opens a small window that shows the macro instruction being executed and the cell location of that instruction.

Single Step and Trace are independent features, but they work well together. You can watch and analyze the macro action within the worksheet by using Single Step mode; the Macro Trace window indicates which macro instruction is being executed. Without these tools, macros often execute too rapidly for you to see the problem areas.

Suppose that you want to use the Single Step and Trace features to test a macro that you created. Follow these steps:

1. Open the **T**ools menu and choose the Macro **T**race command. The Macro Trace window appears.

2. Open the **T**ools menu and choose the **M**acro Single Step command. This action causes 1-2-3 for Windows to execute macros one instruction at a time.

Tip
Press Alt+F2 (Step) to toggle Single Step mode on or off.

Figure 35.11 shows the Macro Trace window in the lower-right corner of the worksheet. Notice the Step indicator displayed below the worksheet. The \a macro in this worksheet contains a deliberate spelling error in a macro command in cell B4. When the macro is executed, 1-2-3 for Windows displays an error message.

3. Start the macro you want to step through one keystroke at a time. After the macro starts, 1-2-3 for Windows replaces the <Location> and <Instructions> place markers in the Macro Trace window with cell addresses and macro code, respectively.

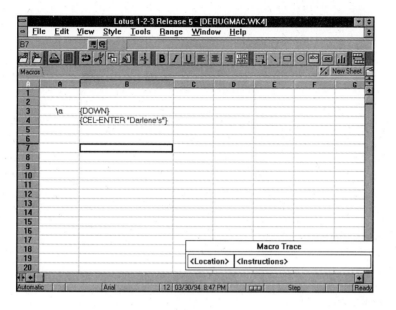

Fig. 35.11
The Macro Trace window and the Step indicator.

VIII

Automating with Macros

4. Start the macro by pressing any key. 1-2-3 for Windows executes the first keystroke or macro command in the macro. At the same time, the Macro Trace window highlights the macro instruction that is being executed and identifies the cell that contains that instruction (see fig. 35.12).

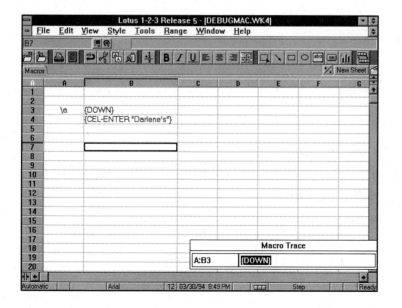

Fig. 35.12
The Macro Trace window shows each instruction as it is executed.

5. Execute each step in sequence by pressing any key after each subsequent step. Pressing a key tells 1-2-3 for Windows to perform the next step of the macro.

6. When you find an error, terminate the macro by pressing Ctrl+Break; then press Esc or Enter. Edit the macro to correct the error. Then repeat the test procedure in case the macro contains other errors (as often is the case in complex macros). Figure 35.13 shows the type of error message 1-2-3 for Windows displays when it encounters a macro error.

Fig. 35.13

1-2-3 for Windows displays a message when it encounters a macro error.

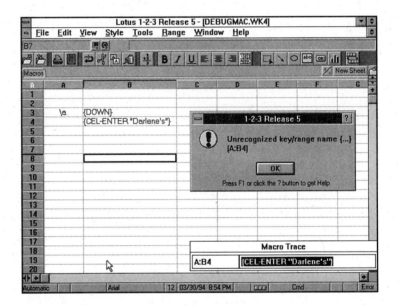

Edit a macro cell as you would any label. Move the cell pointer to the cell containing the label you want to edit (in this case, the macro line), press F2 (Edit) or double-click the cell to go into Edit mode, and then make your changes If you need additional help understanding the error message, press F1 or click the ? (Help) button while the error message is displayed. Figure 35.14 shows the help text that appears when you click the Help button for the error message displayed in figure 35.13.

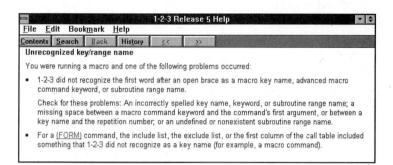

Fig. 35.14
Press F1 or click
the Help button to
display a detailed
message about the
error.

Protecting Macros

If you create worksheet applications that other people will use, secure the macros to prevent accidental erasure or alteration. Most programs (such as database management systems) separate data and programs into individual files. 1-2-3 for Windows, however, puts data and programs (macros) in the same files, making access to the macros easy—sometimes, too easy.

Even if you place all macros in separate files, the files still are 1-2-3 for Windows worksheet files; they can be changed by anyone who knows 1-2-3 for Windows well enough. You may want to consider saving macros in separate, sealed worksheet files. Macros saved in sealed worksheet files can be used by anyone who has access to the file, but they can be modified only by someone who knows the correct password to unseal the file.

Most users store macros that are customized for particular applications in the files that contain the applications. In these cases, group the macros outside the area occupied by the main model. Storing the macros together makes it easier to find a macro and also helps prevent accidental overwriting or erasure of part of a macro as you work with the model.

Tip
Store macros in
their own work-
sheet within a file.
Name the work-
sheet Macros by
double-clicking
the worksheet
tab and typing
Macros.

If you store macros in separate worksheets, you can avoid some common problems. Suppose that you want to use 1-2-3 for Windows commands to insert or delete columns or rows. When you use these commands—manually or within macros—the macros may become corrupted as rows are inserted or deleted (as can happen if the macros are in the same worksheet as the data being manipulated).

Inserting or deleting columns or rows also can cause problems with cell addresses used in macros, because changes in cell references that may occur as a result of an insertion or deletion are not reflected in the macros. Accordingly, use range names instead of cell addresses in macros.

From Here...

For information related to creating, editing, and saving macros, refer to the following chapters:

- Chapter 1, "Getting Around in 1-2-3 and Windows," describes the use of 1-2-3's menu commands including Tools and Range.

- Chapter 3, "Entering and Editing Data," teaches you how to enter data into cells.

- Chapter 8, "Managing Files," covers such things as creating, saving, closing, opening, protecting, deleting, and transferring files.

Chapter 36

Recording and Modifying Macros

1-2-3 for Windows provides tools that make macro creation and execution more convenient. Using the Transcript window to record the steps of a task simplifies the process of creating a macro; you can paste the recorded steps from the Transcript window to a worksheet range and give those steps a macro name. After creating the macro, you can assign it to a button; clicking the button will execute the macro.

This chapter covers the following topics:

- Recording macros with the Transcript window

- Adding macro buttons to a worksheet

- Translating 1-2-3 Release 1 for Windows macros

The next chapter introduces *macro commands*: a powerful set of programming tools that enable you to enhance macros. Chapter 37 also helps you learn the functions and applications of those commands.

Recording Macros with the Transcript Window

Macros can simplify your work with 1-2-3 for Windows. A powerful feature of 1-2-3 for Windows is the Transcript window, which can record keystrokes and mouse movements as macro commands. You can copy these recorded macros as labels into worksheet cells so that you can use or edit the macros.

Open the **T**ools menu and choose **M**acro Show Tra**n**script to display the Transcript window as it records commands (see fig. 36.1). Notice that when you display the Transcript window, 1-2-3 for Windows reduces the worksheet and displays a menu bar and SmartIcon palette appropriate for work in the Transcript window.

Fig. 36.1
The Transcript window records macro commands.

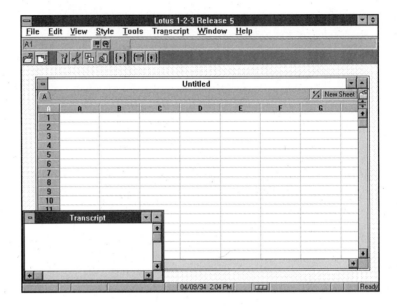

The Transcript window holds a fairly large number of characters. Each time you press a key or use the mouse, the action is recorded in the buffer. The *buffer* is, essentially, the Transcript window. Some actions use one character; others can use several.

 To begin recording a macro in the Transcript window, open the **T**ools menu and choose **M**acro Re**c**ord. Then press the keys you want to include in the macro. For example, if you press Alt+F1 and then type **y-**, the symbol for the Japanese yen (¥) appears in the worksheet. When you press Enter, the Transcript window records your actions as the following macro command:

```
{CELL-ENTER ¥}
```

The Transcript window also translates mouse actions into their command equivalents. This feature is particularly convenient when you work with dialog boxes, which are more mouse-friendly than keyboard-friendly. Recording mouse actions also enables users who are upgrading from earlier versions of 1-2-3 to have 1-2-3 for Windows write detailed instructions on how to perform basic tasks. For example, figure 36.2 shows the Transcript window after text was entered in the worksheet, the size of the type was modified, a background pattern and border were added, and a Japanese-yen symbol was inserted.

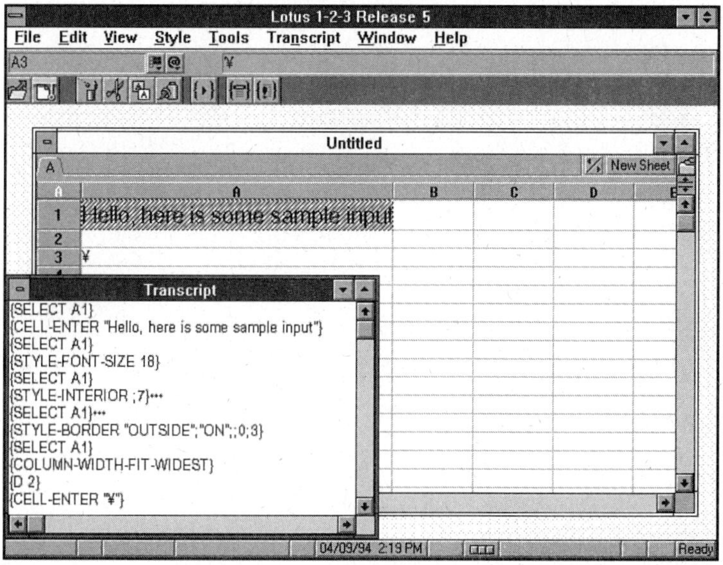

Fig. 36.2
Macro commands recorded in the Transcript window.

When the Transcript-window buffer is filled, 1-2-3 for Windows discards the oldest commands to make room for the newest ones. Save commands that you do not want to lose before they are discarded from the Transcript window. You can save commands from the Transcript window at any time before they are discarded.

You can copy keystrokes from the Transcript window; you also can play back the keystrokes from the Transcript window, clear the Transcript window, and copy information into the Transcript window. The following sections describe in detail the steps for using the Transcript window to create macros and to play back recorded commands.

Creating Macros with the Transcript Window

Suppose that you want to create a macro that sets the default format for a selected range to Label. The Label format enables you to enter text that begins with numbers (or other characters that indicate numeric or formula entries) as labels without first entering a label prefix. Such a macro can be very useful for creating other macros and for entering data, such as street addresses, that 1-2-3 for Windows might otherwise interpret as being incorrectly entered numbers.

Before you begin recording the macro, clear any existing entries from the Transcript window. Although this step is not absolutely necessary, it is less confusing if the Transcript window contains only the desired macro text. To clear the Transcript window, follow these steps:

1. Open the **T**ools menu and choose **M**acros Show Tra**n**script.

2. Open the **E**dit menu and choose the Clea**r** All command. (If the **E**dit menu does not include the Clea**r** All command, make sure that the Transcript window is the active window.)

3. Return to the worksheet by clicking it or pressing Ctrl+F6.

You can make the Transcript window the active window at any time. You also can resize the worksheet and Transcript window so that both are visible. Use any of the following four methods to make the Transcript window active:

■ Click the Transcript Window SmartIcon.

■ Press Ctrl+F6.

■ Click anywhere inside the Transcript window.

■ Use macro commands to activate the Transcript window.

You can use the same techniques to go back to the worksheet from the Transcript window. For example, you can click anywhere in the worksheet to make it active again.

To begin recording commands in the Transcript window, open the **T**ools menu and choose **M**acro Re**c**ord. (When macro recording starts, this command changes to **M**acro Stop Re**c**ording.)

Now type the keystrokes you want the macro to execute. For this example, open the **S**tyle menu and choose the **N**umber Format from command. Then highlight Label in the **F**ormat list box and click OK. Stop recording the macro by opening the **T**ools menu and choosing **M**acro Stop Re**c**ording. Press Ctrl+F6 to return to the Transcript window (see fig. 36.3).

You enter recorded commands in the worksheet by copying them from the Transcript window to the Clipboard and then pasting them into the worksheet. You then can assign a range name to the cell or range containing the keystrokes, as explained in the following sections. You can attach the recorded commands to macro buttons that you create in the worksheet; the Make Button in Transcript SmartIcon automates this process (see "Adding Macro Buttons to a Worksheet" later in this chapter). You also can attach recorded commands to custom SmartIcons (see Chapter 33, "Creating Custom SmartIcon Palettes").

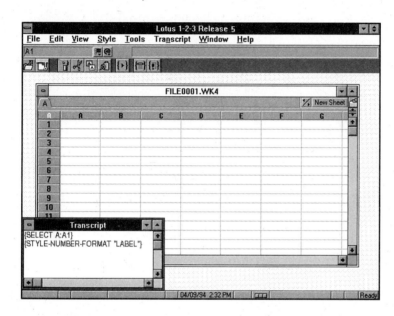

Fig. 36.3
The label macro recorded in the Transcript window.

VIII

Automating with Macros

Macros recorded in the Transcript window include cell addresses rather than cell-pointer movements. This makes the cell addresses easy to recognize but may not always produce the desired results. For example, the macro shown in figure 36.3 applies the Label format to cell A:A1, but you probably want a more general macro that applies the Label format to any selected range. Fortunately, you can modify the recorded macro to make it more general. The following sections explain how to make this type of modification.

Copying and Pasting the Recorded Keystrokes

To copy the keystrokes from the Transcript window to the worksheet, reactivate the Transcript window, as explained in the preceding section. The commands that you recorded appear in the window (refer to fig. 36.3).

Identify the commands you want to copy by following these steps:

1. Move the cell pointer to the first or last character of the command sequence that you want to copy to the worksheet.

2. Highlight the characters you want to copy.

For this example, copy the second command line (which applies the desired format) but not the first line (which selects cell A1):

`{STYLE-NUMBER-FORMAT "LABEL";;;A1}`

Figure 36.4 shows these keystrokes highlighted.

Fig. 36.4
The highlighted keystrokes in the Transcript window.

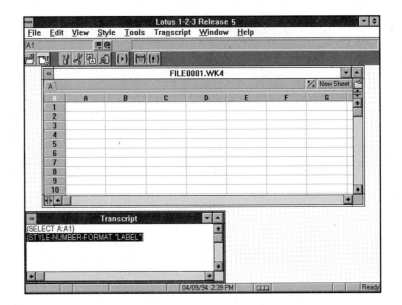

3. Press and release the Alt key to activate the Transcript-window menu bar. Then open the **E**dit menu and choose the **C**opy command. Alternatively, press Ctrl+Ins or Ctrl+C to copy the highlighted characters to the Clipboard.

4. Activate the worksheet window by clicking it or pressing Ctrl+F6.

5. Move the cell pointer to the cell in which you want to place the macro (such as cell B3).

6. Open the **E**dit menu and choose the **P**aste command to paste the macro into the current cell location (see fig. 36.5). Alternatively, press Shift+Ins or Ctrl+V to perform the paste operation.

Note

After the macro commands were pasted into the worksheet, the width of column B and the cell-pointer location were adjusted in figure 36.5 for clarity.

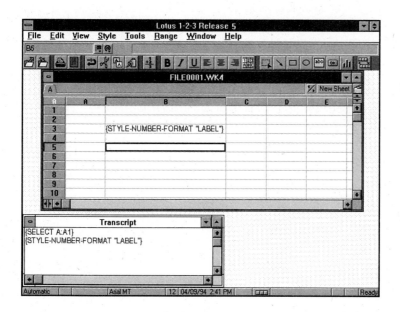

Fig. 36.5
A recorded macro copied to the worksheet from the Transcript window through the Clipboard.

VIII

Automating with Macros

Editing the Recorded Macro

Although the recorded macro can be run as it appears in figure 36.5, it has one distinct disadvantage: it always applies the Label format to cell A1. A simple modification, however, can convert the macro into a more general macro that applies the Label format to a selected range.

Like many other 1-2-3 for Windows macro commands, the STYLE-NUMBER-FORMAT macro command has several optional arguments: *format*, *decimals*, *parentheses*, and *range*. If you omit the optional *range* argument, the STYLE-NUMBER-FORMAT macro command applies the specified format to the currently selected range. In the preceding example, the recorded macro includes A1 as the optional *range* argument:

    {STYLE-NUMBER-FORMAT "LABEL";;;A1}

Note

You must enter macro-command arguments in a specific order. If you omit an argument but include a later argument, you must include placeholders (semicolons) for each argument that you omitted, for example {Macro command arg1;arg2;arg3}. However, if you want to skip the second argument, you enter {Macro command arg1;;arg3}. Chapter 37 covers macro-command arguments in more detail.

To convert this macro command to a more general form, edit the command to remove the optional arguments, as follows:

```
{STYLE-NUMBER-FORMAT "LABEL"}
```

Because no range is specified in the new version of the macro command, this generalized macro command applies the Label format to any range selected before the command is executed.

Running the Recorded Macro

To run the macro in cell B3 directly from the keyboard with a Ctrl+*letter* combination, you must name the macro. Type the label '\f in cell A3. With the cell pointer still in cell A3, open the **R**ange menu and choose **N**ame **U**se Labels; then choose OK. The label '\f is the range name assigned to the macro in cell B3. You then can press Ctrl+F to start the macro. Before running the macro, remember to highlight the range that you want to format with the Label format.

Creating More Complex Macros

The macros described in the preceding sections are simple. You can use the same procedures, however, to create complex, lengthy macros. When you are building larger or more complex macros with the Transcript window, keep the following information in mind:

- Because some keys on the keyboard do not have character equivalents, you may need to use several characters to represent a keystroke. The macro command GOTO, for example, represents the F5 key.

- The Transcript window does not record certain keystrokes. These keystrokes include keys that do not have character symbols or macro commands (such as Caps Lock, Num Lock, Print Screen, and Scroll Lock). The Transcript window does not record the key sequence for Compose (Alt+F1); it does, however, record the composed character.

- If you execute a Ctrl+*letter* macro as you are recording a macro, the Transcript window records the name of the macro instead of the macro's individual keystrokes. For example, if you execute a macro named \f as you are recording another macro, the Transcript window shows the command as {\F}. If 1-2-3 for Windows encounters {\F} while executing a different macro, the program executes the \f macro and then continues executing the macro in which {\F} is a step.

■ You can specify one row or many rows for the range to which you want to copy the characters from the Transcript window. 1-2-3 for Windows uses as many rows as necessary for the characters you select, copying characters down one column. The program does not split macro commands such as GOTO among cells, because doing so creates a macro error.

Playing Back Keystrokes

Another option available with the Transcript window is the capability to run keystrokes as a macro. This means that you can play back keystrokes without copying them into the worksheet. The steps for playing back your keystrokes (or a portion of them) parallel the steps for creating a macro. You can play back a sequence of keystrokes as many times as you want.

The playback feature is helpful when you want to repeat a sequence of keystrokes but do not want to create an actual macro for those keystrokes.

Before you play back keystrokes, position the cell pointer in the specific location of the worksheet where you want to repeat the keystrokes. To play back the keystrokes, follow these steps:

1. Activate the Transcript window by clicking it or pressing Ctrl+F6.

2. Highlight the commands you want 1-2-3 for Windows to perform. If you want 1-2-3 for Windows to perform all the commands in the Transcript window, highlight all the commands.

3. Open the Transcript menu and choose the **P**layback command. 1-2-3 for Windows repeats the commands that you highlighted until they are completed, an error occurs, or you press Ctrl+Break. Remember that you can edit the contents of the Transcript window before highlighting and running the commands.

Adding Macro Buttons to a Worksheet

A *macro button* is a button that you click to execute a macro associated with it. Adding a macro button to a worksheet makes it easy to perform certain tasks that you have automated with macros.

Macro buttons always appear in the same location in a worksheet (unless you move a button, as explained later in this chapter). After you create a macro

VIII

Automating with Macros

button, it scrolls along with the cells that it covers. If you create a macro button that covers cells A:B3..C4, for example, the button scrolls off the screen when you move the cell pointer to A:C50 or to B:B3.

This characteristic makes macro buttons ideal for executing macros that depend on the user's completing certain tasks. For example, you can create a macro button to run a macro that performs a set of calculations on newly entered data. When the user finishes entering the data, he or she can click the macro button to run the macro.

Macro buttons are an example of *event-driven programming*. That is, the macro program associated with a macro button runs when an *event*—a mouse click—is detected. When the macro button is clicked, the macro executes.

Creating a Macro Button

Regardless of the type of macro you attach to a macro button, the process of creating the macro button is the same. The example in this section shows you how to create a macro button that enters a company name in the currently selected cell. Follow these steps:

 1. Click the Macro Button SmartIcon. The mouse pointer changes from an arrow to a cross.

2. Point to the worksheet location where you want to place the macro button.

3. To create a button of the default size, click the left mouse button.

   To create a macro button of a different size (perhaps to allow room for more text on the button's face), drag the mouse pointer until the dotted button box is the desired size.

   The Assign to Button dialog box appears (see fig. 36.6).

4. If the macro you want to assign to the button is fairly short, enter the macro text in the **E**nter Macro Here text box.

   For example, enter the following in the **E**nter Macro Here text box:

   {CELL-ENTER "Darlene's Computer Warehouse"}

   To enter the address of a range containing a macro that already exists, drop down the **A**ssign Macro From list and select Range. The dialog box changes as shown in figure 36.7.

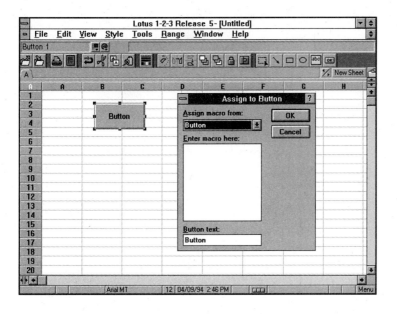

Fig. 36.6
The Assign to
Button dialog box.

Or enter the address of the existing macro in the **R**ange text box, or
select the name of the macro in the Existing **N**amed Ranges list box.

5. Change the text on the face of the button to show the button's purpose
   by typing the new description in the **B**utton Text box. For example,
   type **Add Name**.

6. Choose OK to return to the worksheet.

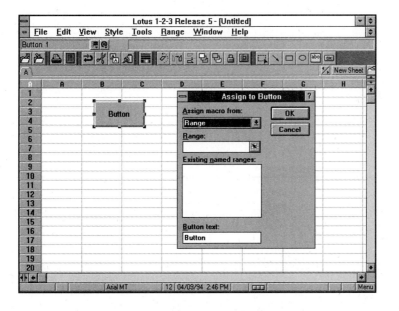

Fig. 36.7
The Assign to
Button dialog box
changes when you
select Range.

VIII

Automating with Macros

To test the macro button, move the cell pointer to an empty cell and then click the macro button. Figure 36.8 shows the effect of moving the cell pointer to cell A:C9 and clicking the Add Name macro button.

Fig. 36.8
The effect of
clicking the Add
Name macro
button with the
cell pointer in
A:C9.

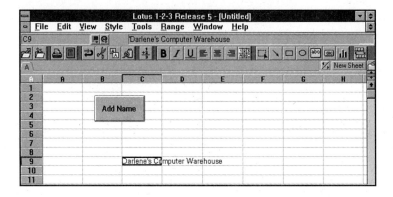

Changing a Macro Button

A macro button remains locked in the same location in the worksheet unless you move it. You cannot simply click and drag the button to a new location, however, because you execute the associated macro when you click the button. To move or resize a macro button—or to modify its actions—you first must select the button by holding down either the Shift or Ctrl key before clicking the macro button. When you select a macro button, handles appear around it.

You can change a selected macro button in the following ways:

- To resize the button, drag one of the handles until the button is the correct size.

- To move the button, drag it to the new location.

- To edit the button's text or to change the macro assigned to the button, double-click the button; then use the options in the Assign to Button dialog box to make the desired changes.

Troubleshooting

It is not possible to select a macro button to change the macro associated with it, because selecting the button causes the macro to run.

Be sure that you hold down either the Shift or Ctrl key before you click the macro button.

I upgraded a worksheet by adding macro buttons, but they weren't there when I reopened the worksheet.

Make certain that you save the worksheet in 1-2-3 Release 5 for Windows format (WK4). If you save the file as a WK3 file, you lose the Release 5 enhancements.

Avoiding Common Macro Errors

When you begin building your own macros, you will discover that editing is a regular part of macro creation, particularly when macros are fairly complex. In macros, as in computer programs, errors are called *bugs*. *Debugging* is the process of editing or eliminating bugs or errors from macros.

If 1-2-3 for Windows cannot execute the macro as written, the program displays an error message and the cell address where the error is located. Usually, this message points you to the error. Occasionally, however, the real error—the place where 1-2-3 for Windows stops executing keystrokes the way you want—precedes the error identified in the error message.

If you see a message about an unrecognized macro command or range name that is followed by a cell address, check the macro commands and range names to be certain that they are spelled correctly. In addition, verify that you are using braces ({ and }) rather than parentheses (( )) or brackets ([ ]); that arguments are correctly specified; and that no extra spaces appear in the macro, especially inside the braces.

Following are some simple guidelines for preventing typical errors in the process of creating macros:

■ *Check the syntax and spelling.* Incorrect grammar and spelling are common problems in macro commands, range names, and file names used in macros. All macro syntax and spelling must be exact.

■ *List all command steps.* If your macro uses any 1-2-3 for Windows menu commands, the macro must include each individual step required for the menu commands to run correctly.

■ *Erase the cell below the macro.* Even if 1-2-3 for Windows works all the way through a macro without a problem, the program may end with an error message or a beep. Remember that 1-2-3 for Windows continues executing macro commands until it encounters an empty cell, a cell that contains a numeric value, or one of the commands that stops macros. If 1-2-3 for Windows encounters data in the cell directly below the last line of the macro, the program may interpret that cell as being part of the macro. Always empty the cell below the last line of the macro by opening the **E**dit menu and choosing the Cl**e**ar command or by pressing the Del key. If you discover that the cell is not empty, you may have identified one of the macro's problems.

■ *Use braces correctly.* Remember that macro commands must be enclosed in braces rather than brackets or parentheses. Symbols and words within braces are used to represent all the special keys on the keyboard. In every case, the key's name, such as {RIGHT} for the right-arrow key or {CALC} for the function key F9, must be enclosed in braces, not in parentheses or square brackets. Macro commands also must be enclosed in braces within a macro.

■ *Use descriptive range names when possible.* Beginning macro users often forget that 1-2-3 for Windows macros are not like 1-2-3 for Windows formulas; cell references are *always* absolute in macros. The cell addresses in macros do not change automatically when you move data used by the macro. 1-2-3 for Windows does not update label cells; in fact, macros *are* label cells.

The absolute nature of cell references within macros is a strong argument in favor of using range names in worksheets. You should assign range names to all the cells and ranges in the worksheet that the macros use, and then use these range names in your macros. If you later move the ranges or insert or delete rows and columns, 1-2-3 adjusts the range names, and the macro continues to refer to the correct cells and ranges.

■ *Use unique range names.* Do not use range names or subroutine names that duplicate macro-command names. Never assign a name such as CALC, LOOK, or QUIT to a range or a subroutine.

- *Use valid cell references.* Cell references included in a macro must refer to cells that exist. Make sure that macros and formulas refer only to existing cells or ranges. Avoid incorrect cell references, such as +ZZ1..ZZ28. Remember that you can avoid such problems by using range names instead of cell addresses.

- *Define all names.* You must define all macro names, subroutine names, and range names used in macros. For example, do not use the range name TOTAL in a macro if you did not use the **R**ange menu's **N**ame command to define that range name.

- *Use the backslash in Ctrl+letter macro names.* When you use Ctrl+*letter* macros, remember that the macro's name must be exactly two characters. The first character always is a backslash (\); never use a regular slash (/). The second character is any letter from A to Z.

- *Use file references correctly.* If a macro refers to a file, enclose the file's name in double angle brackets, such as <<FINANCE>>, if the file extension is WK4. If the extension is not WK4, also list the file extension, such as <<SCREEN.TXT>>. Remember that 1-2-3 for Windows is *not* case-sensitive. When a macro refers to a file that is not active (that is, a file that is not open), give 1-2-3 for Windows the necessary information for locating the file. This information may include the drive and path, file name, and extension (if the extension is not WK4).

  If a macro refers to the file <<FINANCE>> and the file FINANCE.WK4 is not open, 1-2-3 for Windows looks for FINANCE.WK4 in the current subdirectory of the current drive. If the file is not in the current directory, you must specify the path to the file in the following manner:

      <<C:\BUDGET\FINANCE>>

Translating 1-2-3 Release 1 for Windows Macros

1-2-3 Release 5 for Windows macros use macro commands instead of menu-selection keystrokes. These commands result in macros that are more efficient than the older-style macros that used keystrokes. Macros that use macro commands not only execute faster but also are easier to read, and they continue to function even if a menu is modified.

Before you can use 1-2-3 Release 1 for Windows macros in 1-2-3 Release 5 for Windows, the macros must be translated to the new command format. When you install 1-2-3 Release 5 for Windows, the 1-2-3 Macro Translator is installed as well. You use this tool to perform a one-time translation of the macros in existing worksheets.

The 1-2-3 Macro Translator is installed in the same Windows program group as 1-2-3 Release 5 for Windows. You run the 1-2-3 Macro Translator as a separate program. To translate the macros in your existing worksheets, double-click the 1-2-3 Macro Translator icon in the Windows Program Manager. This action starts the 1-2-3 Macro Translator (see fig. 36.9).

Fig. 36.9
Use the 1-2-3
Macro Translator
to translate 1-2-3
Release 1 for
Windows macros.

1-2-3 Macro
Translator icon

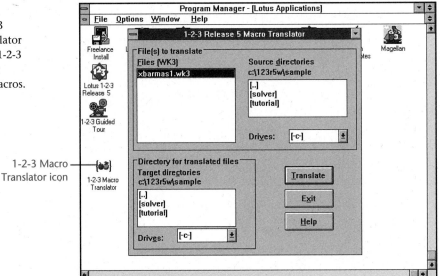

At the top of the Macro Translator dialog box, use the **D**irectories, Dri**v**es, and **F**iles (WK3) boxes to select the 1-2-3 Release 1 for Windows worksheet files that contain the macros you want to translate. You can select any number of files in a single directory to translate at one time.

Use the Dire**c**tories box at the bottom of the dialog box to select a different destination directory for the translated files. If you do not select a new destination directory, the 1-2-3 Macro Translator places the translated files in the same directory as the original files and renames the original files with a BK3 extension.

> ## Caution
>
> If you use the 1-2-3 Macro Translator more than once, specify the same files to translate, and specify the same directories, 1-2-3 for Windows overwrites the original files.

When you finish selecting the files to translate, choose the **T**ranslate button. If you do not select a new destination directory, the 1-2-3 Macro Translator warns you that it will back up the originals; choose **Y**es to continue. After the files are translated, the 1-2-3 Macro Translator informs you of the number of files it translated. Choose OK to return to the program. After you translate all the files you want to translate, chose E**x**it to leave the Translator.

Figure 36.10 shows some typical 1-2-3 Release 1 for Windows macros and how the 1-2-3 Macro Translator changed them for Release 5. Some commands, such as those in rows 5, 6, 9, 10, 13, 14, and 15, are unchanged. Other commands, such as those in rows 7 and 8, are considerably changed.

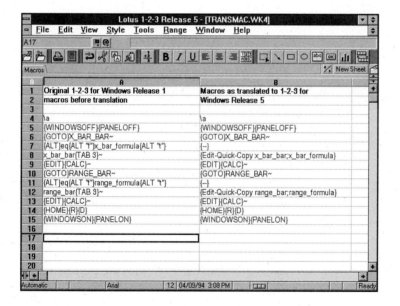

Fig. 36.10
Comparing macros before and after translation.

Often, a single Release 5 command (row 8) replaces several rows of Release 1 commands. Because the 1-2-3 Macro Translator retains the same macro layout as the original macro in the translated file, it places a {-} comment line in the translated macro. When the macro executes, comment lines are ignored.

Troubleshooting

After I upgraded from 1-2-3 Release 1 for Windows, my macro programs don't work as expected.

Remember to translate the macros by using the 1-2-3 Macro Translator. 1-2-3 Release 1 for Windows macros must be translated before they run correctly in Release 5.

Even after I translated 1-2-3 Release 1 for Windows worksheet macros with the 1-2-3 Macro Translator, the macros run incorrectly.

Be sure that you're using the translated worksheets. If you specified a new destination directory, the source directory still contains the original, untranslated worksheet files.

From Here...

This chapter showed you how to use the 1-2-3 for Windows Transcript window to create macros, how to create macro buttons, how to avoid common macro errors, and how to translate 1-2-3 Release 1 for Windows macros. For more information related to these topics, refer to the following chapters:

■ Chapter 16, "Adding Graphics to Worksheets," describes how to resize and move graphical elements like macro buttons.

■ Chapter 37, "Using Advanced Macro Techniques," Refer to this chapter for more detailed information on macro commands.

Chapter 37

Advanced Macro Techniques

In addition to providing keystroke macro capabilities, 1-2-3 for Windows provides a powerful set of macro commands that offer many options available with a full-featured programming language. Although the 1-2-3 Release 5 for Windows macro command language is probably not as powerful as a dedicated programming language like C, the macro language is much easier to learn. The 1-2-3 macro language can perform high-level programming functions such as looping and transferring the flow of the macro to a separate macro routine, and testing for conditions and branching to different routines based on the results.

The preceding chapter introduced you to the process of automating 1-2-3 for Windows by using macros. By using macros to automate repetitive tasks, to perform menu keystrokes quickly, or to type a long label into a cell, you can greatly decrease the time you spend building or working with a spreadsheet. A *macro command* is a macro instruction that tells 1-2-3 for Windows to perform one of the built-in programming functions. This chapter introduces you to these commands, not by teaching programming theory and concepts but rather by describing the capabilities of programming with the macro commands.

In this chapter, you learn about macro commands that enable you to perform tasks such as the following:

- Create menu-driven spreadsheet/database models

- Accept and control input from a user and make intelligent decisions based on user input

- Capture and process a user's keystrokes

- Manipulate data within 1-2-3 for Windows and between 1-2-3 for Windows and other Windows applications

- Change the contents of a cell in the middle of a program

- Execute tasks a predetermined number of times

- Control program flow

- Create a data-entry form that prompts the user for specific information, checks the responses, and enters the data in the worksheet

- Launch other Windows applications based on decisions made within a 1-2-3 for Windows worksheet

Why Use Macro Commands?

Programs created with macro commands give you added control and flexibility in the use of 1-2-3 for Windows worksheets, especially in the Windows environment. With these commands, you can construct, customize, and control worksheet applications created in 1-2-3 for Windows. You also can use the commands to weave together data from worksheets created in 1-2-3 for Windows and other Windows applications. The macro commands enable you to prompt a user for input, create your own menus, loop a specific number of times through a series of commands, launch another Windows application, and link data between 1-2-3 for Windows and other Windows applications. As you become more experienced with the macro commands, you can take full advantage of their power to develop a complete business system application—from order entry to inventory control to accounting.

> **Note**
>
> Although macros are powerful, sometimes nonmacro approaches are better. Don't start looking for macro solutions to every new problem you face. Macros are but one spreadsheet solution; don't forget the other tools in your 1-2-3 toolbox.

Understanding the Macro Command Categories

The 1-2-3 for Windows macro commands are a rich set of commands and keystroke equivalents you use to create macro programs. This chapter examines the macro command categories and includes examples of how to use some of the macro commands. The macro commands fit into 17 categories:

- Chart
- Data manipulation
- Database
- DDE and OLE
- Edit
- File
- Flow-of-control
- Keystroke equivalents
- Navigation
- Range
- Solver
- Style
- Text file manipulation
- Tools
- User environment
- Version Manager
- Window and screen display

Each macro command category includes closely related commands. For example, the chart commands include those that control the many aspects of 1-2-3 for Windows graphs, such as data ranges, colors, and chart types. Each of the 1-2-3 Release 5 for Windows macro command categories and the macro commands contained in each category are described in later sections of this chapter.

Although the macro command descriptions in this chapter are organized by category, typical macro programs may use commands from many different categories. In fact, there is no limit to the number or type of macro commands you can include in a single program.

For example, you might create a 1-2-3 for Windows application that uses window and screen display commands to control what the user sees as the macro executes. The same program might use database commands to retrieve information from an external database file on a network server, and chart commands to display that information. Finally, the program might use style and file commands to prepare and print a report containing the retrieved data.

Using the Correct Syntax for Macro Commands

All 1-2-3 for Windows macro commands are enclosed in braces ({}). The braces tell 1-2-3 for Windows where a macro command begins and ends. Some macro commands are a single command enclosed in braces. For example, to quit a macro, you use the following command, without arguments:

    {QUIT}

Many other macro commands, however, require arguments within the braces. The arguments, or parameters, that follow commands adhere to a syntax similar to that used in 1-2-3 for Windows functions. The following is the general syntax of commands that require arguments:

    {COMMAND *argument1;argument2;...;argumentN*}

The *command name,* or *key word* (represented in the example by the word *COMMAND*), is the part of the command that tells 1-2-3 for Windows what action to perform. The *arguments* supply the information 1-2-3 for Windows needs to complete the command.

For example, in the following command, BLANK tells 1-2-3 for Windows to erase the contents of a cell or range (a range in this example), and the argument A:A1..A:D10 tells the command what cell or range to erase:

    {BLANK A:A1..A:D10}

An argument can consist of numbers, strings, cell addresses, range names, formulas, or functions. Some commands, such as BLANK, only accept one argument. Other commands, such as LET or PUT, require multiple arguments.

The command and the first argument are always separated by a space. For most commands, multiple arguments are separated by semicolons (;) with no spaces between the arguments.

One common type of argument is a *Boolean argument.* A Boolean argument is one that is either true or false. You can use either yes, true, or on for true, and no, false, or off for false. Boolean arguments are always enclosed in quotation marks.

For a command to execute, its syntax must be correct, so following the conventions for spacing and punctuation is vitally important. When you use the BLANK command to erase the contents from a cell or from a range, the command {BLANK} must be followed by one space and then by a cell address or a range name. If you type a bracket ([) rather than a brace, the macro doesn't execute; the command is treated as if it were a label.

Use correct spelling as well as syntax. If you misspell the command or range name or if you type an invalid cell address (such as ABA12), the macro produces an error when it tries to execute the command.

The following are some basic rules of syntax to remember:

- Start the command with an open brace ({) and end the command with a close brace (}).

- Immediately after the open brace, type the command name. You can type the command name in upper- or lowercase letters.

- If the command requires arguments, separate the command name from the first argument with one space. If the command includes two or more arguments, separate the arguments from one another with semicolons. The only space in the command syntax occurs between the command name and the first argument. Do not include any other spaces in the command unless they are part of a text argument (for example, the prompt in a GET-LABEL command can include spaces between the words in the prompt). If the command takes no arguments, the command should include no spaces.

- If the command has several optional arguments and you skip one of them but include a subsequent one, enter an argument separator as a placeholder for the skipped argument. For example, if you skip the optional *width* argument in a CONTENTS command but include the optional *format* argument, use the following format:

    {CONTENTS *target;source;;format*}

The extra semicolon between the *source* and *format* arguments is a placeholder for the missing *width* argument.

- You can include any combination of macro commands in the same cell as long as the total number of characters does not exceed 512.

Troubleshooting

When I use commas as argument separators, syntax errors occur.

1-2-3 Release 5 for Windows can use commas and semicolons, or periods and semicolons as argument separators. You may have your system configured to use periods and semicolons as argument separators. Use the **T**ools **U**ser Setup **I**nternational **P**unctuation command to select your choice. Incidentally, you may want to make it a habit to always use semicolons as macro command argument separators—that way your macros can be used regardless of the **T**ools **U**ser Setup **I**nternational **P**unctuation setting.

Some macros don't work correctly; instead of using the literal argument that is specified, they seem to be using information from the worksheet as arguments.

Literal arguments should be enclosed in quotes. If you forget to enclose a literal argument in quotes, 1-2-3 first tries to use the argument as the name of a range in the worksheet and then uses the contents of that range as the argument.

Entering a Macro Command

 When you want to enter a macro command in the worksheet or quickly check the syntax of a macro command, you can obtain a list of all the valid macro commands by clicking the Select Macro Command SmartIcon or by pressing F3 (Name) after you enter an open brace ({). To enter the macro command, select the desired macro command from the **M**acro Keywords list box in the Macro Keywords dialog box. You can also press the first letter of the command name to move the highlight directly to the first command name that begins with that letter. If the macro command you are looking for is not the first one, use the down-arrow key to find the command you need. For example, if you press the letter T, the highlight moves to the first command that begins with T, which is TAB. To obtain additional help information on the highlighted command, press F1 or click the question mark in the upper right corner of the Macro Keywords dialog box.

Planning, Invoking, and Debugging Macro Command Programs

To ensure that your macro command programs are efficient and error-free, you begin by defining which actions you want the program to perform. Next, you determine the sequence of those actions. Then you develop the program, test it, debug it, and cross-check its results for all possible operations.

If you have not experimented with 1-2-3 for Windows macros, take some time to review the simple macros in Chapter 35 before you try to develop macro command programs. If you have some practice with simple macros, you will be better prepared to learn and apply the macro commands described in this chapter. Also, you might want to review Chapter 35's discussions of creating, using, and debugging macros; you also use those concepts in your more advanced macro command programs.

Planning and Documenting Macro Command Programs

You should plan macro programs carefully, not only for what they will accomplish but for where they will be positioned in the worksheet. If part of your macro is in row 10 of worksheet A and one of the instructions in the macro is to delete row 10 in worksheet A, you delete part of your macro.

Placing macro programs in a separate worksheet or file is the best practice. Take advantage of 1-2-3 for Windows multiple worksheet files and place your macros in their own worksheet. Double-click the macro worksheet tab and name the worksheet Macros so you can always easily identify which worksheet holds your macros. For example, figure 37.1 shows a macro that is stored in the worksheet named Macros; the data area and work area are in a worksheet named Data Input.

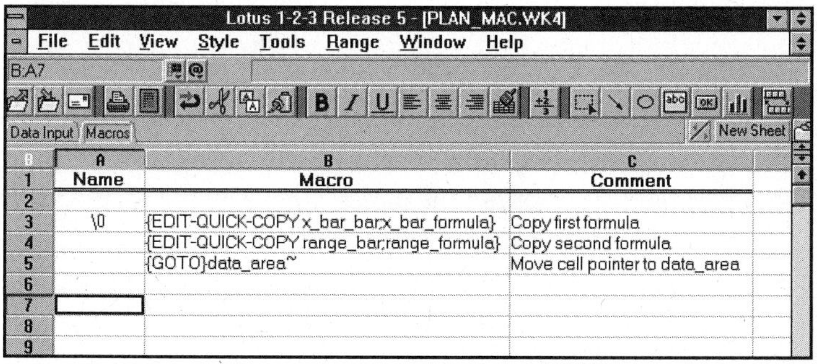

VIII

Automating with Macros

Fig. 37.1

Use a separate worksheet for your macros

You can also place macros in a separate file that you must open in addition to any worksheet file that uses those macros. Remember, though, that 1-2-3 for Windows always searches for macros in the current file first. To run a macro in another file that has the same name as a macro in the current file, you must specify in the Macro Run dialog box the file name that contains the macro. For example:

```
<<MACROS.WK4>>Print_Macro
```

You enter macro commands as lines of text in the worksheet. Remember to use a label prefix to start any line that begins with a nontext character (such as / or <) so that the commands are entered as a line of text in your macro rather than executed by 1-2-3 for Windows. After you decide where to place the program and begin entering program lines, remember to document macro command programs. Because macro command programs may be complex, documentation is essential for debugging and modifying the macro. In figure 37.1, note that the macro is documented.

Invoking Macro Command Programs

As Chapter 35 described, you can invoke macros in several ways:

- Ctrl+*letter* macros

  To invoke macros that you name by using the backslash key and a character (Ctrl+*letter* macros), press and hold down the Ctrl key while you press the appropriate character key. For example, you invoke a macro named \a by pressing Ctrl+A.

- Alt+F3 (Run)

  To invoke Ctrl+*letter* macros or macros that you name by using descriptive range names, press Alt+F3 (Run). The Macro Run dialog box appears (see fig. 37.2). From this dialog box, you have several options for invoking a macro.

  First, you can type the macro name or select the name from the **A**ll Named Ranges list box.

  Second, you can choose a macro name by using Point mode. Click the first cell of the macro, or use the direction keys to move the cell pointer to the first cell of the macro and press Enter. You also can click the range selector beside the **M**acro Name text box to remove the dialog box and point to the first cell of the macro. Then press Enter.

  Third, you can type the cell address in the **M**acro Name text box.

Fig. 37.2
The Macro Run
dialog box.

■ The **T**ools **M**acro **R**un command

You can invoke any macro by opening the **T**ools menu and choosing **M**acro and then **R**un. The Macro Run dialog box appears. This dialog box is the same one that appears when you press Alt+F3 (Run). At this point, you have the same three options for invoking a macro: type or select the macro name from the list, go into Point mode and start the macro from the worksheet, or type the cell address.

■ The Run Macro SmartIcon

You also can click the Run Macro SmartIcon to display the Macro Run dialog box and run the macro.

■ Macro Buttons

By creating macro buttons in the worksheet, you can make it easy for other users to run your macros. Users simply click a button to start the macro.

■ Autoexecute macros

If you check the Run Autoexecute **M**acros box in the User Setup dialog box, autoexecute (\0) macros execute when you load or open a file.

Debugging Macro Command Programs

After you develop and run a macro program, you might have to debug the program. All macro programs are subject to such problems as misspelled command and range names, improper syntax, and cell address changes.

One key to eliminating such problems is the practice of using range names in place of cell addresses whenever possible. Remember that a reference to a cell location is absolute and does not change when the worksheet structure changes. Range names, however, change location when the worksheet

structure changes. Suppose that cell D50 is named TOTAL. Because range names change with the worksheet, if you insert a row above cell D50, the range name TOTAL moves down a row but stays associated to the originally named cell (D51 now). If the LET statement is

```
{LET D50;@SUM(SALARIES)}
```

and you insert a row above row 50, the LET statement still places the sum of the salaries into cell D50. You can solve this problem by using range names in place of cell addresses, as in the following example:

```
{LET TOTAL;@SUM(SALARIES)}
```

Macros, however, can have problems other than absolute cell references. Debugging a macro involves finding out which macro instructions are causing the problem and editing the instructions. The easiest way to debug a macro is to use 1-2-3 for Windows Single Step and Trace debugging utilities, as discussed in Chapter 35.

Troubleshooting

A macro command program I developed in an earlier version of 1-2-3 does not execute.

Because the macro command language has been greatly updated, you must use the 1-2-3 Macro Translator to convert your older version macros before using them in 1-2-3 Release 5 for Windows. While a few simple macros may still work without translation, it only takes a few minutes to translate your macros. Then you can be certain that your macros function correctly. See Chapter 36 for more information on the 1-2-3 Macro Translator.

My Alt+letter macros do not work.

Don't forget that 1-2-3 Release 5 for Windows uses the Ctrl key, not the Alt key to start macros. Just press Ctrl and the *letter* to run your macros.

Using Variable Information in Macros

To be useful, macros must be flexible. For example, a macro that can apply the label format to any selected range is much more useful than one that can apply the label format only to cell A:A1.

Specifying Arguments

Many 1-2-3 for Windows macro commands accept *arguments*—variable information that helps determine how the macro functions. The three types of arguments for macro commands are numbers, text, and ranges and are used as follows:

■ To enter a numeric argument, use a number, a numeric formula, or the range name or address of a cell that contains a number or numeric formula, for example, 2, +A5/2, or NUMBER_OF_DAYS.

■ To enter a text argument, use any text enclosed in quotation marks, a text formula, or the range name or address of a cell that contains a label or text formula, for example, "Reno," +A5, or STORE_NAME.

■ To enter a range argument, use a range name or address, or any formula that evaluates to a range name or address, for example, STORE_NAME or @@A5.

For some text arguments, you can specify any text you want 1-2-3 for Windows to use literally—exactly as you specify it. For some other types of text arguments, you must use specific text. For example, when you use the OPEN command and you specify the type of file access, you must select R, W, M, or A (read, write, modify, or append).

One of the best ways to make your macros adaptable is to use named ranges to hold variable information and then specify the named range as the macro command argument. For example, in figure 37.3, the \a and \d macros both use the FILE-OPEN command to open a text file—in this case, FILE1.TXT. Suppose, however, that you want to open a file other than FILE1.TXT. Because the \d macro uses FILE_NAME, a named range, to specify the value for the argument specifying which file to open, you simply place a different file name in cell B7, the FILE_NAME range. When you run the \d macro, the file specified in the named range is opened. Modifying the file named in the \a macro is much more difficult.

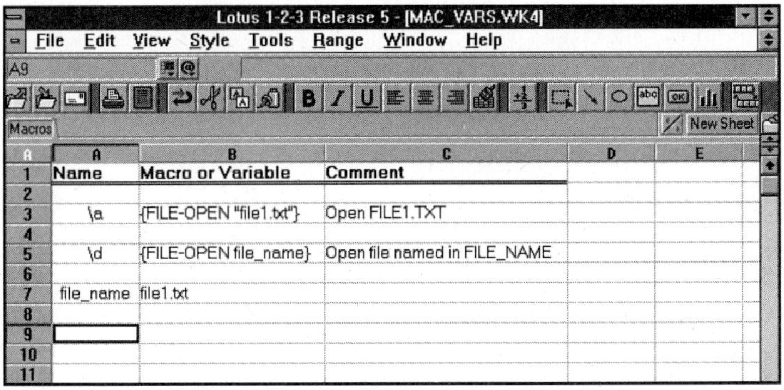

Fig. 37.3
Use named ranges to supply variable information in macros.

Avoiding Self-Modifying Macros

Because you enter macros as labels, a common technique in past versions of
1-2-3 has been to use string formulas—also called *concatenation formulas*—to
create macros that accept variable arguments. For example, another way to
duplicate the functionality of the \d macro in figure 37.3 is to use the following string formula:

```
+"{FILE-OPEN "&FILE_NAME&"}"
```

If FILE_NAME contains the text `file1.txt`, the string formula results in a
macro command identical to the \a macro.

Although this technique can be useful in limited instances, you should avoid
using it in 1-2-3 Release 5 for Windows. Self-modifying macros can be difficult to understand and are often likely to result in an error. Self-modifying
macros might not function quite as you expect, especially if you use macro
commands that modify worksheet data but do not cause the worksheet to
recalculate. Finding and correcting this type of macro program error is
difficult.

Instead of using string formulas to create self-modifying macros, supply variable information to macro commands by specifying named ranges that store
the variables. Not only are your macros easier to read, they are also less likely
to result in difficult-to-find errors.

Troubleshooting

A macro I previously tested enters data in the wrong cells and generally causes problems.

One of the most difficult problems to overcome is a macro which uses cell addresses
that do not correctly adjust when the worksheet is rearranged. Make certain your
macros always use range names—never cell addresses.

If your macros use range names exclusively, but are still having problems, did you
remember to create a separate worksheet for your macros? If your macros are on the
same worksheet as the data, they can be destroyed or modified inadvertently when
rows or columns are inserted or deleted. Other common operations, such as database queries, can also overwrite macros in the current worksheet.

The macros in a 1-2-3 worksheet application, which work pretty well, appear to change.

In the past, some macro programmers used string formulas to create "self-
modifying" macros that changed depending on values stored in worksheet cells.
These types of macros are not only difficult to read, they can be deceptive because
they may change while a macro is running. If you need to create macros which use
variable information, store the variable information in named ranges, and use those
named ranges as macro command arguments.

Categorizing the Macro Commands

The following sections group macro commands into categories that reflect the command's functions: chart, data manipulation, database, DDE and OLE, edit, file, flow-of-control, keystroke equivalents, navigation, range, Solver, style, text file manipulation, tools, user environment, Version Manager, and window and screen display.

> **Note**
>
> For compatibility with macros created in earlier releases, 1-2-3 Release 5 for Windows includes many macro commands that have more powerful replacements. For example, in Release 4, the GET-LABEL command replaces GETLABEL. The GET-LABEL command can accept new arguments to specify a default response and a dialog box title. If a more powerful 1-2-3 Release 5 for Windows macro command replaces an older macro command, the command tables refer you to the new command.

Commands That Manipulate Charts

The commands listed in table 37.1 create and control charts in 1-2-3 for Windows. You use these commands to graph data, to modify the settings for charts, and to control the default type of charts.

Table 37.1   Commands That Manipulate Charts

Command	Action
CHART-ASSIGN-RANGE	Assigns all data ranges for the current chart
CHART-AXIS-INTERVALS	Changes the intervals between x-axis, y-axis, or the second y-axis' tick marks in the current chart
CHART-AXIS-LIMITS	Creates a scale for the x-axis, y-axis, or the second y-axis that displays only the data that falls between an upper and lower limit
CHART-AXIS-SCALE-TYPE	Specifies the type of scale to use for an axis
CHART-AXIS-TICKS	Specifies major and minor tick marks for an axis
CHART-AXIS-TITLE	Changes an axis title
CHART-AXIS-UNITS	Changes the magnitude of the axis units and the axis-unit titles

(continues)

VIII

Automating with Macros

Table 37.1 Continued	
Command	**Action**
CHART-COLOR-RANGE	Sets the color for each value in a data series by using values in the color range
CHART-DATA-LABELS	Creates labels for data points or bars by using data in the label range as the labels
CHART-FOOTNOTE	Adds footnotes to a chart
CHART-GRID	Displays or hides grid lines for an axis
CHART-LEGEND	Creates legend labels that identify the colors, symbols, or patterns of the data range
CHART-NEW	Draws a chart by using data from the currently selected range
CHART-PATTERN-RANGE	Sets the pattern for each value in a data series by using values in the pattern range
CHART-PIE-LABELS	Creates labels for a pie chart
CHART-PIE-SLICE-EXPLOSION	Explodes slices in a pie chart
CHART-RANGE	Sets the data range, series type, and the second y-axis' flag for a data series
CHART-RANGE-DELETE	Deletes a data series
CHART-RENAME	Renames a chart
CHART-SET-PREFERRED	Defines the current chart's settings as the preferred chart
CHART-TITLE	Adds chart titles
CHART-TYPE	Sets the type of chart
CHART-USE-PREFERRED	Applies the preferred chart settings to the current chart

Figure 37.4 shows how you can use several chart macro commands to create a new chart and modify its settings. This macro example creates a new line chart, controls the display of grid lines, adds a footnote, and sets the colors used to display the data.

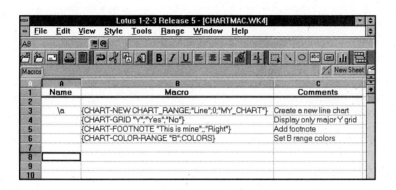

Fig. 37.4
Chart macro
commands create a
new chart and
modify its settings.

Commands That Manipulate Data

The commands described in table 37.2 enable you to place data precisely within worksheet files, edit existing entries, erase entries, and recalculate formulas.

Table 37.2   Commands That Manipulate Data

Command	Action
APPENDBELOW	Copies the contents from a source range to the rows immediately below a target range
APPENDRIGHT	Copies the contents from a source range to the columns immediately to the right of a target range
BLANK	Erases the contents of a range
CONTENTS	Copies the contents from a source range to a target range as a label
LET	Enters a number or left-aligned label in a range
PUT	Enters a number or left-aligned label in a cell within a range
RECALC	Recalculates the values in a range, proceeding row by row
RECALCCOL	Recalculates the values in a range, proceeding column by column

Commands That Manipulate Databases

The database commands enable you to create and use databases, both in a 1-2-3 for Windows worksheet and in separate database files. By combining these commands with the DataLens drivers, you can use data contained in almost any type of database file. Table 37.3 describes the 1-2-3 for Windows database commands.

Table 37.3 Commands That Manipulate Databases	
Command	**Action**
COMMIT	Completes pending external database transactions
CROSSTAB	Creates a cross-tabulation table
DATA-EXTERNAL-CONNECT	Use DATABASE-CONNECT
DATA-EXTERNAL-CREATE-TABLE	Use DATABASE-CREATE-TABLE
DATA-EXTERNAL-DISCONNECT	Use DATABASE-DISCONNECT
DATA-EXTERNAL-SEND-COMMAND	Use DATABASE-SEND-COMMAND
DATABASE-APPEND	Adds new records to a database
DATABASE-CONNECT	Establishes a connection to an external database
DATABASE-CREATE-TABLE	Creates and connects to an external database table
DATABASE-DELETE	Deletes specified records from a database
DATABASE-DISCONNECT	Disconnects from an external database
DATABASE-FIND	Locates and selects records in a database
DATABASE-SEND-COMMAND	Sends a command to an external database
QUERY-ADD-FIELD	Adds a field to the currently selected query table
QUERY-AGGREGATE	Performs calculations on groups of data from a query table
QUERY-CHOOSE-FIELDS	Specifies the fields to appear in a query table
QUERY-COPY-SQL	Copies to the Clipboard the SQL command equivalent of the current query
QUERY-CRITERIA	Specifies record selection criteria to determine which records appear in a query table

Command	Action
QUERY-DATABASE-TABLE	Changes the database for the current query table
QUERY-JOIN	Joins multiple databases that contain a common field
QUERY-NAME	Assigns a new name to the current query table
QUERY-NEW	Creates a new query table
QUERY-OPTIONS	Specifies options for the current query table
QUERY-REFRESH	Updates records in the current query table to reflect changes made to the database, query options, criteria, aggregates, or field names
QUERY-REMOVE-FIELD	Removes a field from the current query table
QUERY-SHOW-FIELD	Specifies an alias field name for a field in the current query table
QUERY-SORT	Arranges data in the current query table
QUERY-SORT-KEY-DEFINE	Defines a sort key to be used in a subsequent QUERY-SORT command
QUERY-SORT-RESET	Clears all sort keys for the current query table
QUERY-UPDATE	Applies changes to records in the current query table to the corresponding database
QUERY-UPGRADE	Upgrades a query from a previous version of 1-2-3 so that it works with the Query commands in 1-2-3 Release 5
ROLLBACK	Cancels pending external database transactions
SEND-SQL	Sends an SQL command to an external database driver

VIII

Automating with Macros

Figure 37.5 shows an example of how you can use several of the database macro commands to create a query that uses an external database file.

Fig. 37.5
The database
macro commands
manipulate
databases.

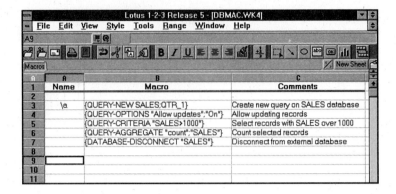

Commands That Transfer Data between Windows Applications

Some of the most useful Windows features available with 1-2-3 for Windows are its Dynamic Data Exchange (DDE) and Object Linking and Embedding (OLE) capabilities. DDE and OLE enable several different Windows applications to link and share data. The 1-2-3 for Windows macro language has many DDE and OLE commands, which table 37.4 lists. The macro language DDE and OLE commands, like the LINK commands, often work with one another.

Table 37.4   Commands That Transfer Data between Windows Applications

Command	Action
DDE-ADVISE	Specifies the macro executed when data changes in the server application
DDE-CLOSE	Terminates all current conversation with a Windows application
DDE-EXECUTE	Sends a command to an application
DDE-OPEN	Initiates a conversation with a Windows application
DDE-POKE	Sends a range of data to a server application
DDE-REQUEST	Transfers data from a Windows application to 1-2-3 for Windows
DDE-TABLE	Creates a table of conversations associated with all active files that were created with {DDE} commands
DDE-UNADVISE	Ends a DDE-ADVISE command

Command	Action
DDE-USE	Makes a specific conversation between 1-2-3 for Windows and another Windows application the current one
EDIT-OBJECT	Executes either the primary or secondary verb for the currently selected OLE embedded object
INSERT-OBJECT	Creates and places in the worksheet an OLE embedded object
LINK-ASSIGN	Specifies a range to link to a destination range
LINK-CREATE	Creates a link between the current worksheet file or a file created with another Windows application
LINK-DEACTIVATE	Deactivates a link in the current worksheet but leaves the link intact
LINK-DELETE	Erases a link in the current worksheet but leaves the values obtained through the link in the worksheet
LINK-REMOVE	Removes the currently used destination range for a link
LINK-TABLE	Creates a table of all links associated with the current file
LINK-UPDATE	Updates a link when the link update mode is Manual
UPDATE-OBJECT	Updates a 1-2-3 OLE object embedded in another application file

VIII

Automating with Macros

Figure 37.6 shows an example of using DDE commands to create a link and transfer data between 1-2-3 for Windows and Word for Windows. The LINK commands function in a similar manner.

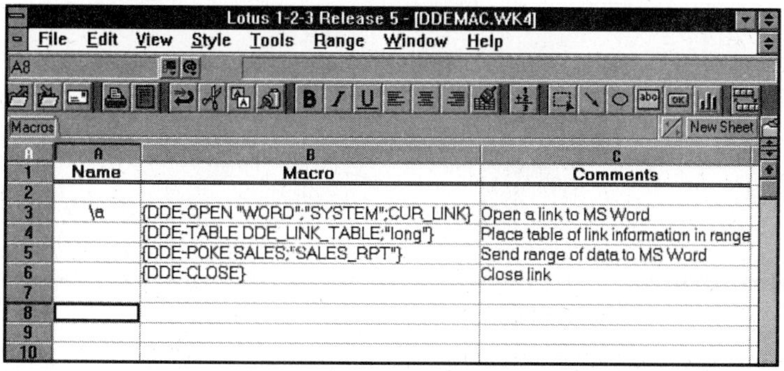

Fig. 37.6
The DDE and OLE macro commands link and transfer data between Windows applications.

Commands That Edit Worksheets

The commands described in table 37.5 provide the worksheet editing functions found on the 1-2-3 for Windows **E**dit menu. These commands enable macro programs to copy and paste data as well as rearrange worksheet layout.

Table 37.5 Commands That Edit Worksheets	
Command	**Action**
DELETE-COLUMNS	Deletes partial or complete columns in a range
DELETE-ROWS	Deletes partial or complete rows in a range
DELETE-SHEETS	Deletes each worksheet in a range
EDIT-CLEAR	Deletes data and formatting without using the Clipboard
EDIT-COPY	Copies data and formatting to the Clipboard
EDIT-COPY-FILL	Copies to a range the contents of a row, column, or worksheet
EDIT-COPY-GRAPH	Use EDIT-COPY
EDIT-CUT	Deletes data and formatting, and copies both to the Clipboard
EDIT-FIND	Finds specified characters in labels, formulas, or both
EDIT-FIND?	Displays the Edit Find & Replace dialog box
EDIT-PASTE	Copies data and formatting from the Clipboard
EDIT-PASTE-LINK	Creates a link between a 1-2-3 for Windows worksheet file and the file referenced on the Clipboard
EDIT-PASTE-SPECIAL	Use EDIT-PASTE
EDIT-QUICK-COPY	Copies data and formatting without using the Clipboard
EDIT-QUICK-MOVE	Moves data and formatting without using the Clipboard
EDIT-REPLACE	Finds and replaces specified characters in labels, formulas, or both
EDIT-REPLACE-ALL	Finds and replaces all instances of specified characters in labels, formulas, or both
INSERT-COLUMNS	Inserts complete or partial blank columns
INSERT-ROWS	Inserts complete or partial blank rows
INSERT-SHEETS	Inserts blank worksheets

Figure 37.7 provides some examples of using macro commands that edit the worksheet and its data.

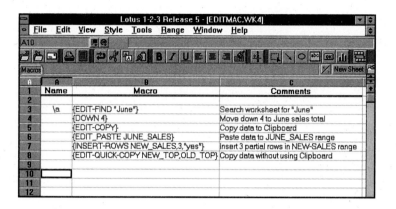

Fig. 37.7
Macro commands that edit the worksheet.

Commands That Manipulate Files

The commands described in table 37.6 provide the functions contained in the 1-2-3 for Windows File menu. These commands open and close files, print worksheets, and control network settings.

Table 37.6 Commands That Manipulate Files	
Command	**Action**
FILE-CLOSE	Closes the current file
FILE-COMBINE	Combines data and number formats from a 1-2-3 worksheet file on disk into the current file
FILE-EXIT	Ends the 1-2-3 session
FILE-EXTRACT	Saves a range to another file
FILE-GET-RESERVATION	Gets the network reservation for the current file
FILE-IMPORT	Combines data from a text file into the current file
FILE-NEW	Creates a new blank worksheet
FILE-OPEN	Reads a file into memory
FILE-OPEN?	Displays the File Open dialog box
FILE-PRINT?	Uses PRINT?

(continues)

Table 37.6 Continued

Command	Action
FILE-PRINT-NAME-ADD	Uses PRINT-NAME-ADD
FILE-PRINT-NAME-USE	Uses PRINT-NAME-USE
FILE-PRINT-RESET	Uses PRINT-RESET
FILE-RELEASE-RESERVATION	Releases the network reservation for the current file
FILE-RETRIEVE	Replaces the current file in memory with a file from disk
FILE-SAVE	Saves the current file
FILE-SAVE-ALL	Saves all active files
FILE-SAVE-AS?	Displays the File Save As dialog box
FILE-SEAL	Controls the reservation for the current file and seals the file
FILE-SEAL-NETWORK-RESERVATION	Seals only the network reservation setting of the current file
FILE-UNSEAL	Unseals the current file and releases its network reservation setting
FILE-UPDATE-LINKS	Recalculates formulas in the current file that contain links to other files
PRINT	Prints the current file, using the current settings
PRINT?	Displays the File Print dialog box
PRINT-NAME-ADD	Saves the current print settings in a file
PRINT-NAME-USE	Selects a saved print-settings file
PRINT-RESET	Replaces the currently selected Margins, Print Titles, Header, Footer, Options, Compression, and Orientation settings with their defaults
SEND-MAIL	Sends a mail message by using your mail application
SEND-RANGE	Sends a range of worksheet data to other 1-2-3 Release 5 users who have electronic mail
SEND-RANGE-LOGIN	Automatically logs in to your mail application

Figure 37.8 demonstrates the use of several macro commands that manipulate files. This macro first obtains the network reservation so no other user
can modify the original while the macro is executing. Next it combines sales
data from the R1SALES file, selects a named print setting, and prints five
copies of the SALES_REPORT range. The combined file is then saved and
finally, closed.

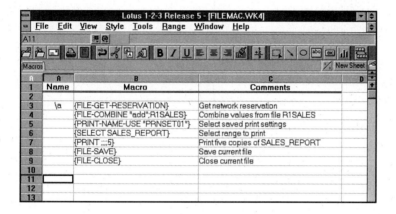

Fig. 37.8
Several macro
commands that
manipulate files.

VIII

Automating with Macros

Commands That Control Programs

The commands listed in table 37.7 provide varying degrees of control in 1-2-3
for Windows programs. Used alone or with decision-making commands,
these commands give the macro programmer precise control of program
flow.

Table 37.7   Commands That Control Programs

Command	Action
{subroutine}	Performs a call to a subroutine before continuing to the next line of a macro
BRANCH	Continues program execution at the specified location
DEFINE	Specifies cells for subroutine arguments
DISPATCH	Branches indirectly, through the specified location
FOR	Creates a FOR loop, which repeatedly performs a subroutine call to subroutine
FORBREAK	Cancels a FOR loop created by a FOR command

(continues)

Table 37.7 Continued	
Command	**Action**
IF	Evaluates condition as true or false and branches the program
LAUNCH	Starts and optionally switches to a Windows application
ONERROR	Traps and handles errors that occur while a macro is running
QUIT	Ends a macro immediately
RESTART	Clears the subroutine stack, ending the macro when the current subroutine ends
RETURN	Returns macro control from a subroutine to the calling macro
SET	Sets a specified Info component to a specified value
SYSTEM	Temporarily suspends the 1-2-3 session and executes the specified operating-system command

Commands That Duplicate Keystrokes

Table 37.8 describes the 1-2-3 for Windows commands that duplicate keystrokes. You can use these commands when a macro program must perform tasks that require pressing specified keys.

Table 37.8 Keystroke Equivalents	
Command	**Equivalent Keystrokes**
{	Enters left brace
}	Enters right brace
~	Enters tilde
ABS	F4
ALT	F10
ANCHOR	F4 (in Ready mode)
APP1	Alt+F7
APP2	Alt+F8

Command	Equivalent Keystrokes
APP3	Alt+F9
BACKSPACE or BS	Backspace
BACKTAB or BIGLEFT	Ctrl+←
BIGRIGHT	Ctrl+→
CALC	F9
DELETE or DEL	Del
DOWN or D	↓
EDIT	F2
END	End
ESCAPE or ESC	Esc
FILE	Ctrl+End
FIRSTCELL or FC	Ctrl+Home
FIRSTFILE or FF	Ctrl+End Home
GOTO	F5
HELP	F1
HOME	Home
INSERT or INS	Ins
LASTCELL or LC	End Ctrl+Home
LASTFILE or LF	Ctrl+End End
LEFT or L	←
MENU	/
NAME	F3
NEXTFILE or NF	Ctrl+End Ctrl+PgUp
NEXTSHEET or NS	Ctrl+PgUp
PGDN	PgDn
PGUP	PgUp

(continues)

VIII

Automating with Macros

Table 37.8 Continued

Command	Equivalent Keystrokes
PREVFILE or PF	Ctrl+End Ctrl+PgDn
PREVSHEET or PS	Ctrl+PgDn
QUERY	F7
RIGHT or R	→
SELECT-BIGLEFT	Shift+Ctrl+←
SELECT-BIGRIGHT	Shift+Ctrl+→
SELECT-DOWN	Shift+↓
SELECT-FIRSTCELL	Shift+Ctrl+Home
SELECT-HOME	Shift+Home
SELECT-LASTCELL	Shift+End Ctrl+Home
SELECT-LEFT	Shift+←
SELECT-NEXTSHEET	Shift+Ctrl+PgUp
SELECT-PGDN	Shift+PgDn
SELECT-PGUP	Shift+PgUp
SELECT-PREVSHEET	Shift+Ctrl+PgDn
SELECT-RIGHT	Shift+→
SELECT-UP	Shift+↑
TAB	Tab
TABLE	F8
UP or U	↑
WINDOW	F6
ZOOM	Alt+F6

Commands That Navigate the Worksheet

The commands listed in table 37.9 move around the worksheet, select worksheet areas, and enter data in specified locations.

Table 37.9 Commands That Navigate the Worksheet	
Command	**Action**
CELL-ENTER	Enters data in a specified location
EDIT-GOTO	Selects all or part of a range, query table, chart, or other drawn object and then scrolls to it
SCROLL-COLUMNS	Scrolls horizontally in the current worksheet
SCROLL-ROWS	Scrolls vertically in the current worksheet
SCROLL-TO-CELL	Scrolls in the current worksheet so that the first cell of a specified location is in the top left corner of the worksheet window
SCROLL-TO-COLUMN	Scrolls left or right in the current worksheet so that the leftmost column of a specified location is the leftmost column of the worksheet window
SCROLL-TO-OBJECT	Scrolls to but does not select a range, query table, chart, or other drawn object in the current worksheet
SCROLL-TO-ROW	Scrolls up or down in the current worksheet so that the top row of a specified location is the top row in the worksheet window
SELECT	Selects all or part of a range, chart, query table, or other drawn object without scrolling to it
SELECT-ALL	Selects the active area of the current worksheet, all charts or drawn objects in the current worksheet, or all worksheets in the current file
SELECT-APPEND	Selects all or part of a range, chart, or other drawn object without deselecting the current item selected
SELECT-REMOVE	Removes a range, chart, or other drawn object from the currently selected collection
SELECT-REPLACE	Replaces an item in a collection or group of items

Figure 37.9 demonstrates the use of macro commands that navigate in the worksheet.

Fig. 37.9
Worksheet
navigation
macros.

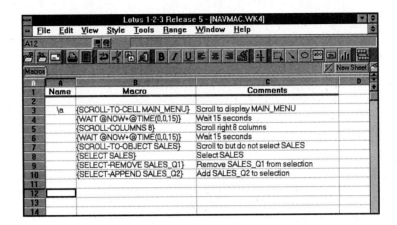

Commands That Manipulate Ranges

Table 37.10 describes macro commands that manipulate ranges. These commands enable macro programs to create and delete range names, create data tables, sort ranges, and perform advanced mathematics.

Table 37.10	Commands That Manipulate Ranges
Command	**Action**
DATA-DISTRIBUTION	Uses DISTRIBUTION
DATA-FILL	Uses FILL
DATA-MATRIX-INVERT	Uses MATRIX-INVERT
DATA-MATRIX-MULTIPLY	Uses MATRIX-MULTIPLY
DATA-PARSE	Uses PARSE
DATA-REGRESSION	Uses REGRESSION
DATA-REGRESSION-RESET	Uses REGRESSION
DATA-TABLE-1	Substitutes values for one variable in one or more formulas and enters the results in a specified output range
DATA-TABLE-2	Substitutes values for two variables in one formula and enters the results in a specified output-range
DATA-TABLE-3	Substitutes values for three variables in one formula and enters the results in a specified output range
DATA-TABLE-RESET	Clears the ranges and input-cell settings for all what-if tables in the current file

Command	Action
DISTRIBUTION	Creates a frequency distribution that counts how many values in a range fall within each numeric interval specified by another range
FILL	Enters a sequence of values in a specified range
FILL-BY-EXAMPLE	Fills a range with a sequence of data that is determined by the data already in the range
MATRIX-INVERT	Inverts a square matrix
MATRIX-MULTIPLY	Multiplies one matrix by another to create an output matrix
PARSE	Converts long labels from an imported text file into separate columns of data
RANGE-NAME-CREATE	Assigns a name to a range address
RANGE-NAME-DELETE	Deletes a range name
RANGE-NAME-DELETE-ALL	Deletes all range names in the current file
RANGE-NAME-LABEL-CREATE	Assigns an existing label as the range name for a single cell
RANGE-NAME-TABLE	Creates a two-column table of all defined ranges
RANGE-TRANSPOSE	Transposes data while copying
REGRESSION	Performs multiple-linear-regression analysis and calculates the slope of the line that best illustrates the data
SHEET-NAME	Names a 1-2-3 worksheet in the current file
SHEET-NAME-DELETE	Deletes a worksheet name in the current file
SORT	Sorts data in the order that you specify
SORT-KEY-DEFINE	Defines a sort key
SORT-RESET	Clears all sort keys and ranges

Commands That Seek Solutions

The commands described in table 37.11 use the Solver and Backsolver tools to seek solutions to complex problems.

Table 37.11 Commands That Seek Solutions	
Command	**Action**
BACKSOLVE	Finds values for one or more cells to produce a specified formula result
SOLVER-ANSWER	Displays Solver answers or attempts
SOLVER-ANSWER-SAVE	Saves the current answer or attempt as a scenario
SOLVER-DEFINE	Analyzes data in a worksheet and returns possible answers to a problem
SOLVER-DEFINE?	Displays the Solver Definition dialog box
SOLVER-REPORT	Creates a new file containing a report based on the current answer

Commands That Manipulate Worksheet Styles

The commands described in table 37.12 adjust the appearance of 1-2-3 for Windows worksheets.

Table 37.12 Commands That Manipulate Worksheet Styles	
Command	**Action**
COLUMN-WIDTH	Adjusts columns to a specified width
COLUMN-WIDTH-FIT-WIDEST	Adjusts columns to fit their widest entries
COLUMN-WIDTH-RESET	Returns columns to the default width
HIDE-COLUMNS	Hides all columns in a range
HIDE-SHEETS	Hides all worksheets in a range
NAMED-STYLE-USE	Applies a named style to a range or query table
PAGE-BREAK-COLUMN	Inserts or deletes a vertical page break
PAGE-BREAK-ROW	Inserts or deletes a horizontal page break
PROTECT	Protects a range
RANGE-PROTECT	Use PROTECT
RANGE-UNPROTECT	Use UNPROTECT
ROW-HEIGHT	Adjusts rows to a specified height

Command	Action
ROW-HEIGHT-FIT-LARGEST	Adjusts rows to the height of the largest font
ROW-HEIGHT-RESET	Returns rows to the default height
SHOW-COLUMNS	Redisplays hidden columns
SHOW-SHEETS	Redisplays hidden worksheets
STYLE-ALIGN	Use STYLE-ALIGN-HORIZONTAL
STYLE-ALIGN-HORIZONTAL	Changes the horizontal alignment of labels and values
STYLE-ALIGN-ORIENTATION	Changes the orientation of data in a range
STYLE-ALIGN-VERTICAL	Aligns text within a cell whose height is greater than that of the largest typeface
STYLE-BACKGROUND-COLOR	Use STYLE-FONT
STYLE-BACKGROUND-PATTERN	Use STYLE-FONT
STYLE-BORDER	Controls borders for a range
STYLE-EDGE	Changes the color, style, and width of the edges of charts, chart elements, text blocks, drawn objects, OLE objects, and pictures created in other Windows applications
STYLE-FONT	Assigns a font to a range
STYLE-FONT-ALL	Assigns a font and adds boldface, italic, and underlining to a range
STYLE-FONT-ATTRIBUTES	Adds boldface, italic, or underlining to a range
STYLE-FONT-EMPHASIS	Use STYLE-FONT
STYLE-FONT-RESET	Restores to a range the default font, font size, attributes, and color
STYLE-FONT-SIZE	Assigns a point size to the fonts in a range
STYLE-FOREGROUND-COLOR	Use STYLE-FONT
STYLE-FRAME	Adds or removes a frame for a range
STYLE-GALLERY	Formats a range with one of 10 style templates
STYLE-INTERIOR	Adds colors and patterns to a range

VIII

Automating with Macros

(continues)

Table 37.12 Continued	
Command	**Action**
STYLE-LINE	Changes the color, style, and width of the selected line for drawn lines and chart lines
STYLE-NUMBER-FORMAT	Sets the display of values
STYLE-NUMBER-FORMAT-RESET	Resets the format of a range to the default format
STYLE-TEXT-COLOR	Use STYLE-FONT
UNPROTECT	Removes protection for a range

Commands That Manipulate Text Files

The commands described in table 37.13 enable macros to read from and write to text files.

Table 37.13 Commands That Manipulate Text Files	
Command	**Action**
CLOSE	Closes a text file and saves any changes
FILESIZE	Counts the number of bytes in an open text file
GETPOS	Reports the current byte-pointer position in the open text file
OPEN	Opens a text file for processing
READ	Copies bytes from the open text file to the worksheet
READLN	Copies lines from the open text file to the worksheet
SETPOS	Moves the byte pointer in an open text file
WRITE	Copies text to the open text file
WRITELN	Copies text to the open text file, and adds a carriage return and line feed

Tools Commands

Table 37.14 describes macro commands that work with add-ins, audit worksheets, spell-checking worksheets, and control SmartIcon sets.

Table 37.14 Tools Commands	
Command	**Action**
ADDIN-INVOKE	Starts an add-in application
ADDIN-LOAD	Reads an add-in into memory
ADDIN-REMOVE	Removes an add-in from memory
ADDIN-REMOVE-ALL	Removes all add-ins from memory
AUDIT	Reports on formulas, circular references, file links, or DDE links
MAP-NEW	Draws a map
MAP-REDRAW	Redraws all maps in the current file
REGISTER	Registers a procedure in a DLL as an add-in @function
SMARTICONS-USE	Selects a set of SmartIcons
SPELLCHECK?	Launches spell checking
UNREGISTER	Unregisters a procedure and removes it from memory

Commands That Manipulate the User Environment

Table 37.15 describes commands that manipulate the user environment, display dialog boxes, accept user input, and modify menus.

Table 37.15 Commands That Manipulate the User Environment	
Command	**Action**
?	Suspends macro execution until the user presses Enter; then enables the user to type any number of keystrokes
ALERT	Displays a message box and waits for the user to choose OK or Cancel
BREAKOFF	Disables Ctrl+Break while a macro is running
BREAKON	Restores the use of Ctrl+Break
CHOOSE-FILE	Displays a Windows common dialog box that contains a list of files and waits for the user to select one

VIII

Automating with Macros

(continues)

Table 37.15 Continued	
Command	**Action**
CHOOSE-ITEM	Displays a dialog box that contains a list of data items, waits for the user to select one and then to choose OK or Cancel, and enters the index number for the user's choice in the worksheet
CHOOSE-MANY	Displays a dialog box and waits for the user to select one or more check boxes and then choose OK or Cancel
CHOOSE-ONE	Displays a dialog box and waits for the user to select an option and choose OK or Cancel; then runs the macro associated with the option
CHOOSEFILE	Uses CHOOSE-FILE
CHOOSEITEM	Uses CHOOSE-ITEM
CHOOSEMANY	Uses CHOOSE-MANY
CHOOSEONE	Uses CHOOSE-ONE
DIALOG	Displays a custom dialog box created with the Lotus Dialog Editor
DIALOG?	Displays a 1-2-3 dialog box and waits for the user to choose OK or press Enter
FORM	Suspends macro execution temporarily so that the user can enter and edit data in unprotected cells
FORMBREAK	Ends a FORM command
GET	Suspends macro execution until the user presses a key; then records the keystroke
GET-FORMULA	Displays a dialog box that contains a text box, and enters the data from the text box in the worksheet when the user chooses Cancel or OK
GET-LABEL	Displays a prompt and accepts any user input
GET-NUMBER	Displays a prompt and accepts numeric user input
GET-RANGE	Displays a prompt and accepts range input
GETLABEL	Use GET-LABEL
GETNUMBER	Use GET-NUMBER
LOOK	Checks the type-ahead buffer and records the first keystroke

Command	Action
MENU-COMMAND-ADD	Adds a command to a pull-down menu
MENU-COMMAND-DISABLE	Disables a command in a custom menu
MENU-COMMAND-ENABLE	Enables a command disabled with MENU-COMMAND-DISABLE
MENU-COMMAND-REMOVE	Removes a command from a pull-down menu
MENU-CREATE	Replaces the 1-2-3 menu bar with a customized menu bar
MENU-INSERT	Adds a custom pull-down menu to the default 1-2-3 menu bar, between the **T**ools and **W**indow commands
MENU-RESET	Displays the default 1-2-3 menu bar
MENUBRANCH	Displays a dialog box that contains a list of menu commands, waits for the user to select one and then to choose OK or Cancel, and then branches to the macro instructions associated with the selected command
MENUCALL	Displays a dialog box that contains a list of menu commands, waits for the user to select one and then to choose OK or Cancel, and then performs a subroutine call to the macro instructions associated with the selected command
MENUCREATE	Uses MENU-CREATE
MENUINSERT	Uses MENU-INSERT
MENURESET	Uses MENU-RESET
MODELESS-DISMISS	Closes a modeless dialog box
MODELESS-DISPLAY	Displays a modeless dialog box
PLAY	Plays a file with a WAV extension
WAIT	Suspends macro execution for a specified period
WGETFORMULA	Uses GET-FORMULA
WGETLABEL	Uses GET-LABEL
WGETNUMBER	Uses GET-NUMBER

VIII

Automating with Macros

Commands That Manage Scenarios

The commands described in table 37.16 use the 1-2-3 for Windows Version Manager to manage scenarios. These macro commands provide strong what-if capabilities.

Table 37.16 Commands That Manage Scenarios	
Command	**Action**
RANGE-VERSION?	Provides access to Version Manager
SCENARIO-ADD-VERSION	Adds a version to a scenario
SCENARIO-CREATE	Creates a scenario
SCENARIO-DELETE	Deletes a scenario
SCENARIO-INFO	Modifies comment and sharing options for a scenario
SCENARIO-REMOVE-VERSION	Removes versions from a scenario
SCENARIO-SHOW	Displays a selected scenario
VERSION-CREATE	Creates a new version
VERSION-DELETE	Deletes a specified version
VERSION-INDEX-COPY	Copies Version Manager Index information to the Clipboard
VERSION-INDEX-MERGE	Copies versions and scenarios from another file
VERSION-INFO	Modifies style retention and sharing options for a version
VERSION-REPORT	Creates a version report
VERSION-SHOW	Displays a selected version
VERSION-UPDATE	Updates an existing version with new data

Commands That Enhance Programs

The commands described in table 37.17 can "dress up" a program by creating a better visual presentation or by speeding program execution.

Table 37.17 Commands That Enhance Programs	
Command	**Action**
APP-ADJUST	Moves and sizes the 1-2-3 window
APP-STATE	Minimizes, maximizes, or restores the 1-2-3 window
BEEP	Sounds one of four tones
BREAK	Clears the edit line and returns to Ready mode
INDICATE	Displays text in the title bar
PANELOFF	Freezes the control panel
PANELON	Unfreezes the control panel and the status line
VIEW-ZOOM	Decreases or increases the display size of cells
WINDOW-ACTIVATE	Makes a specified window the active window
WINDOW-ADJUST	Moves and sizes the active window
WINDOW-ARRANGE	Sizes and arranges open windows
WINDOW-STATE	Minimizes, maximizes, or restores the active window
WINDOWSOFF	Suppresses screen updates while a macro is running
WINDOWSON	Restores normal screen updates
WORKSHEET-TITLES	Freezes or unfreezes columns along the top of the worksheet, rows along the left edge of the worksheet, or both

VIII

Automating with Macros

From Here...

In this chapter, you learned about the powerful macro commands available in 1-2-3 Release 5 for Windows. The commands listed in this chapter enable you to create sophisticated applications that automate every aspect of 1-2-3 for Windows and make your worksheets much easier to use.

■ Chapter 35, "Writing 1-2-3 for Windows Macros," steps you through the basics of planning, writing, debugging, and running a macro.

■ Chapter 36, "Recording and Modifying Macros," introduces the Macro Transcript window, which records all your keystrokes so you can easily turn them into powerful, versatile macros. This chapter also explains how the Macro Translator updates your old 1-2-3 macros.

■ Chapter 38, "Exploring a Corporate Macro Example," analyzes a longer macro that lets 1-2-3 work with other applications.

Chapter 38

Exploring a Corporate Macro Example

The 1-2-3 for Windows macro language provides the power to create complex, sophisticated applications. But, you don't have to be an experienced programmer to create useful applications. With a little practice, you can use macros to build professional-looking applications that guide users through complicated or repetitive tasks.

In Chapter 36, you learned how to automate 1-2-3 for Windows by using macros. Chapter 37 introduced you to macro commands: Macro instructions that tell 1-2-3 for Windows to perform one of the built-in programming functions. In this chapter, you'll explore a macro-driven application that builds on the lessons learned in the two preceding chapters.

This chapter describes the macros used to create an expense report application. The application does the following:

- Displays a blank expense report form with embedded macro buttons

- Displays dialog boxes in which you fill expense account information

- Automatically calculates formulas, such as mileage allowance and total expenses

- Prints a copy of the expense report

- Mails an electronic copy of the expense report to an accounts payable representative in the Finance department

- Provides help and tips about using the expense report application

An Overview of the Expense Report Application

When a user opens the expense report application, EXPENSE.WK4, the worksheet looks like that shown in figure 38.1.

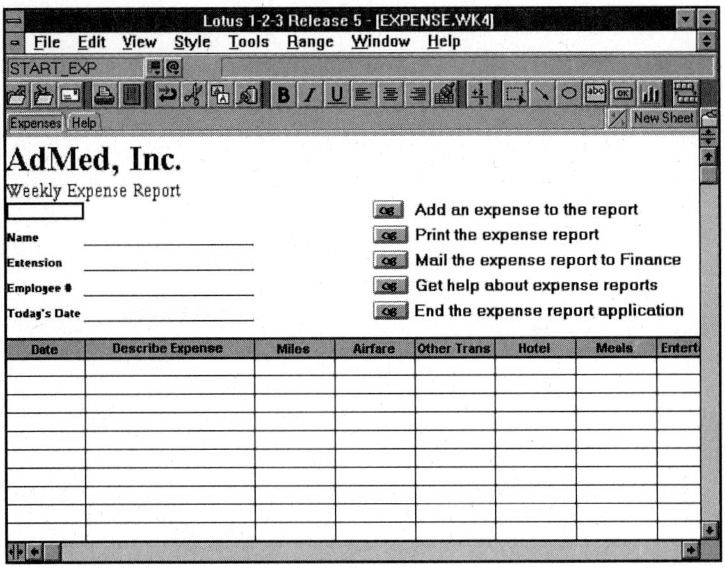

Fig. 38.1
The expense report worksheet.

Tip
Although the worksheet shown in figure 38.1 appears to be the first sheet in the file, it is actually worksheet B. Worksheet A, which contains the macros, has been hidden with the Style Hide command. Hiding the worksheet that contains your macros keeps users from accidentally altering or over-writing your macros.

The worksheet named "Help" contains instructions that your users can follow if they need additional information (see fig. 38.2). Users can get to this worksheet either by clicking on its tab or by clicking a macro button on the Expenses worksheet.

Now that you know how the expense report looks from the perspective of someone who will use it, read the following sections to learn how to build this application.

Planning the Application

Before you write a single macro, you must decide what you want your application to accomplish. First, decide on a generalized task. For example, the application described in this chapter fills in an expense report. Next, think about the steps needed to complete that task. For the expense report example, steps include getting expense information from the user, entering it into the worksheet, and calculating totals. Finally, think about tasks that users of your application would consider important, even though these tasks might not seem directly related to the primary task. For example, users might want to quickly print the expense report or send the completed report to someone else via electronic mail.

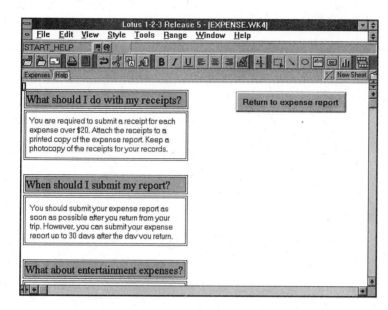

Fig. 38.2
This worksheet contains information about filling out the expense report.

Once you plan what your application does, you must plan what it will look like. Although you should freely experiment with different fonts and styles, remember that neat, uncluttered worksheets are almost always best for applications that you build for others to use.

Writing the Formulas

Formulas are an important part of many macro-driven applications. As you design the worksheets, plan what data the formulas should calculate and where the formulas should be located.

The expense report application uses formulas to total the expenses and to multiply the mileage allowance by the number of miles driven. Figure 38.3 shows the formulas that create the subtotal and grand total of expenses.

The expense report application also needs a formula that multiplies the mileage allowance, 30-cents per mile, by the number of miles driven.

Fig. 38.3
Formulas that
calculate total
expenses.

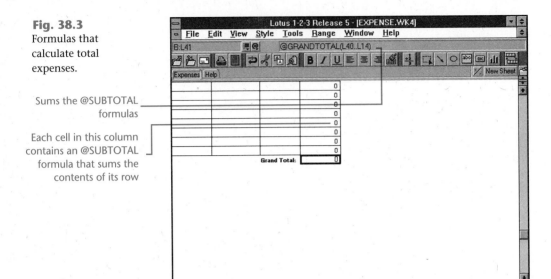

Sums the @SUBTOTAL
formulas

Each cell in this column
contains an @SUBTOTAL
formula that sums the
contents of its row

Adding Macro Buttons

Macro buttons are a good alternative to customized menus for less-experienced application developers. Macro buttons let users quickly and easily run your macros; the buttons also give your application a more polished, professional look.

The Expenses worksheet contains five macro buttons (see fig. 38.4) that users can click to perform various tasks in the expense report application.

◀ "Recording and Modifying Macros," p. 1059

You can add the macro buttons to the worksheet while you are designing the application. Later, after you have written and named the macros, you can go back and assign each button to a macro.

◀ "Advanced Macro Techniques," p. 1077

Writing the Macros

Once you've designed the worksheets that will make up your application, you're ready to write the macros that will control the application.

As you've learned, it's a good idea to store macros in a separate worksheet. In the expense report application, macros are stored in worksheet A. Because the macros are located before the worksheets where data is entered, they won't get written over. Hiding the macros worksheet further protects the macros from accidental damage (see fig. 38.5).

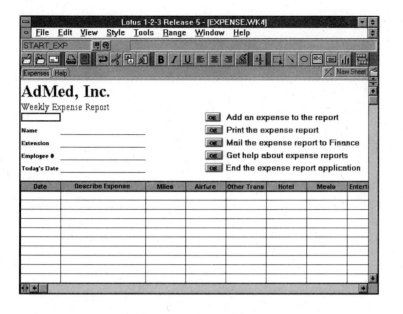

Fig. 38.4

These buttons run the macros for the expense report application.

Fig. 38.5

This worksheet contains macros for the expense report. When users see the application, this worksheet is hidden.

The following sections describe the macros that run the expense report application.

Starting the Application

The first macro in the expense report application is an autoexecute macro that 1-2-3 runs as soon as you open EXPENSE.WK4 (see fig. 38.6).

Fig. 38.6
Autoexecute macros are always named \0.

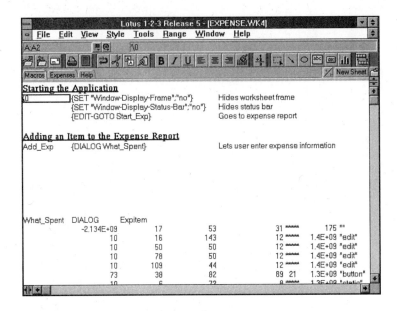

{SET "Window-Display-Frame";"no"} hides the worksheet frame so the user does not see the worksheet and column letters and row numbers. Hiding the worksheet frame gives the application a cleaner appearance, especially if you formatted the worksheets with many different row heights and column widths.

{SET "Window-Display-Status-Bar";"no"} hides the status bar. Hiding parts of the 1-2-3 window, such as the status bar, edit line, and SmartIcon bar, lets more of your worksheet show. Hiding these elements also helps keep users from getting distracted while they work in your application.

{EDIT-GOTO Start_Exp} moves the cell pointer to the first cell in the Expenses worksheet. Including this command in the autoexecute macro ensures that the expense report form will always be visible when the user starts the application.

Adding an Item to the Expense Report

When you create an application that requires users to enter data in a worksheet, it's often best to create a dialog box for them to enter the data into. That way, you control where the data goes. If you let users enter data directly into the worksheet, they might make mistakes or write over data they've already entered. You can use the Lotus Dialog Editor to create custom dialog boxes for user input (see fig. 38.7).

When users click the "Add an expense to the report" macro button, 1-2-3 runs a macro that displays a custom dialog box for them to fill in.

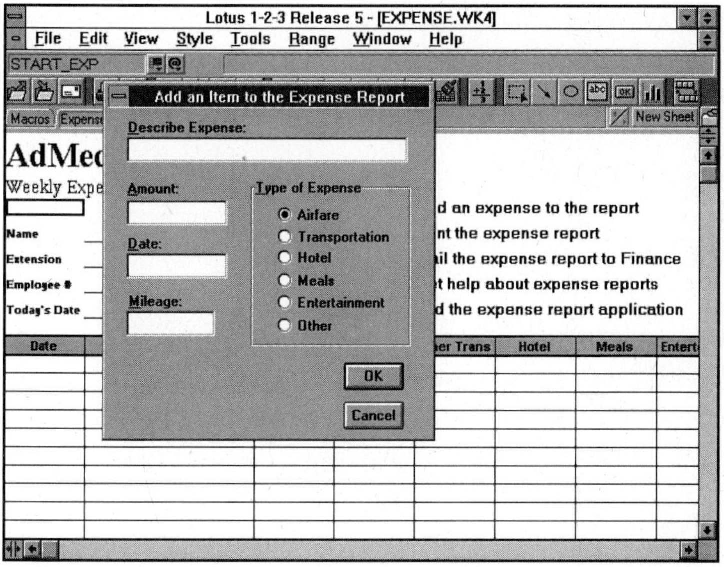

Fig. 38.7
A custom dialog box created with the Lotus Dialog Editor.

The following macro commands display the dialog box and add the user's data to the appropriate column in the expense report:

```
Start_Exp        {DIALOG Exp_Dialog}
        {IF Button_Val=0}{QUIT}
        {IF @CELL(Date_Val;"type")="b"}{Get_Date}
        {EDIT-GOTO Start_Exp}
        {BRANCH 1st_Blank}

Get_Date        {GET-NUMBER Message;Date_Val;@TODAY}

1st_Blank        {IF @CELLPOINTER("type")="b"}{BRANCH Date_Desc}
        {Look_Again}

Look_Again {D}{BRANCH 1st_Blank}

Date_Desc        {LET @CELLPOINTER("address");Date_Val}{R}
        {LET @CELLPOINTER("address");Desc_Val}{R}
        {IF @ISEMPTY(Mil_Val)=1}{R}{BRANCH Next_1}
        {LET @CELLPOINTER("address");+Mil_Val*0.30}
        {CALC}
        {QUIT}
```

```
Next_1   {R}{IF Air_Val=0}{BRANCH Next_2}
         {LET @CELLPOINTER("address");How_Much}
         {CALC}
         {QUIT}

Next_2   {R}{IF Trans_Val=0}{BRANCH Next_3}
         {LET @CELLPOINTER("address");How_Much}
         {CALC}
         {QUIT}

Next_3   {R}{IF Hotel_Val=0}{BRANCH Next_4}
         {LET @CELLPOINTER("address");How_Much}
         {CALC}
         {QUIT}

Next_4   {R}{IF Meals_Val=0}{BRANCH Next_5}
         {LET @CELLPOINTER("address");How_Much}
         {CALC}
         {QUIT}

Next_5   {R}{IF Meals_Val=0}{BRANCH Next_6}
         {LET @CELLPOINTER("address");How_Much}
         {CALC}
         {QUIT}

Next_6   {R}{IF Ent_Val=0}{BRANCH Next_7}
         {LET @CELLPOINTER("address");How_Much}
         {CALC}
         {QUIT}

Next_7   {R}{LET @CELLPOINTER("address");How_Much}
         {CALC}
         {QUIT}
```

An Overview of the Adding-an-Item Macro

The first section of the macro displays the dialog box, and if the user clicks the OK button, searches for the first blank row in the expense-report range. The macro then enters the date of the expense and a description of the expense in the appropriate columns.

Seven shorter macros check the cells in the eleventh column of the dialog description table that correspond to the six radio buttons in the 'Type of Expense' group box. The macros determine which radio button the user selected (Airfare, Hotel, Meals, etc.) and then enter the amount of the expense in the appropriate column of the expense report.

An In-Depth Look at the Adding-an-Item Macro

{DIALOG Exp_Dialog} displays the dialog box shown in figure 38.7. (Exp_Dialog is the name of the first cell of the dialog description table.) The user fills in the dialog box fields with the appropriate information. There is no time limit on how long 1-2-3 displays this dialog box; users can take as much time as they need to fill it in. 1-2-3 continues the macro only when the dialog's OK or Cancel button is clicked. 1-2-3 records the user's dialog-box entries and selections in the eleventh column of the dialog description table.

{IF Button_Val=0}{QUIT} ends the macro if the user clicked the Cancel button in the dialog box. Button_Val is the name of a cell in the dialog description table where 1-2-3 enters 1 if the user clicked the OK button or 0 if the user clicked the Cancel button. If the user clicked the OK button, 1-2-3 goes immediately to the next {IF} command.

{IF @CELL(Date_Val;"type")="b"}{Get_Date} verifies that the user entered a date for the expense by checking the cell Date_Val, where 1-2-3 enters the date from the dialog box. If Date_Val contains a date, the macro continues at the {EDIT-GOTO} command in the next cell. If Date_Val is blank (the user forgot to enter a date), 1-2-3 executes the subroutine **{Get_Date}**, which consists of the following {GET-NUMBER} command:

{GET-NUMBER Message;Date_Val;@TODAY} displays a dialog box with a message (in the range Message) that tells the user to enter a date for the expense. The current date is displayed in the dialog's edit box, by default. When the user enters a date in the edit box and clicks the OK button, 1-2-3 records the date in the cell named Date_Val. Because {Get_Date} is a subroutine, 1-2-3 returns macro control to the {EDIT-GOTO} command in the cell immediately following the {Get_Date} command.

{EDIT-GOTO Start_Exp} moves the cell pointer to the first cell in the Expenses worksheet.

{BRANCH 1st_Blank} branches—that is, transfers macro control—to the macro commands that start in the cell named 1st_Blank. These commands find the first blank row in the expense report.

{IF @CELLPOINTER("type")="b"}{BRANCH Date_Desc} checks to see if the current cell, Start_Exp, is blank. If Start_Exp is blank, the macro branches to the macro commands at Date_Desc. These commands enter a date and description for the expense. If Start_Exp is not blank, 1-2-3 skips the

{BRANCH} command and goes immediately to the subroutine, **{Look_Again}**, in the next cell. {Look_Again} consists of the following commands:

{D}{BRANCH 1st_Blank} moves the cell pointer down one row and branches back to the {IF} command in 1st_Blank. The macro continues this loop until it reaches a blank cell in the 'Date' column of the expense report.

{LET @CELLPOINTER("address");Date_Val}{R} enters the date stored in the cell Date_Val in the 'Date' column of the expense report. **{R}** moves the cell pointer one column to the right, to the 'Describe Expense' column.

{LET @CELLPOINTER("address");Desc_Val}{R} enters a description of the expense 'Description' column of the expense report. Desc_Val is the name of a cell in the dialog description table where 1-2-3 stores the description the user entered in the dialog box. **{R}** moves the cell pointer one column to the right, to the 'Miles' column.

{IF @ISEMPTY(Mil_Val)=1}{BRANCH Next_1} checks the cell named Mil_Val to see if it is empty. If it is empty, the user did not enter any mileage, so **{BRANCH}** transfers macro control to the commands located at Next_1. If Mil_Val is not empty, 1-2-3 moves to the {LET} command in the next cell.

{LET @CELLPOINTER("address");+Mil_Val*0.30} multiplies the number of miles the user entered by the mileage allowance, $0.30 per mile, and enters the result in the 'Miles' column.

{CALC} forces a recalculation. {LET} commands do not cause 1-2-3 to recalculate the worksheet, even if you set recalculation to Automatic. Including a {CALC} command ensures that all formulas in the expense report are updated.

{QUIT} ends the macro if a mileage figure was entered in the 'Miles' column.

Next_1. If Mil_Val is empty (the user did not enter a mileage figure), the macro branches to the commands that begin at the cell named Next_1.

{R}{IF Air_Val=0}{BRANCH Next_2} moves the cell pointer one cell to the right, to the 'Airfare' column, and then checks the cell named Air_Val to see if it contains 0 or 1. If it contains 0, the user did not select the 'Airfare' radio button, so **{BRANCH}** transfers macro control to the commands located at Next_2. If Air_Val contains 1, 1-2-3 moves to the {LET} command in the next cell.

{LET @CELLPOINTER("address");How_Much} enters the value in How_Much (the cost of the airline ticket) in the 'Airfare' column.

{CALC} forces a recalculation. {LET} commands do not cause 1-2-3 to recalculate the worksheet, even if you set recalculation to Automatic. Including a {CALC} command ensures that all formulas in the expense report are updated.

{QUIT} ends the macro if an amount was entered in the 'Airfare' column.

Next_2. If the 'Airfare' radio button was not selected, 1-2-3 checks to see if the next button, 'Transportation' was selected.

{R}{IF Trans_Val=0}{BRANCH Next_3} moves the cell pointer one cell to the right, to the 'Other Trans' column, and then checks the cell named Trans_Val to see if it contains 0 or 1. If it contains 0, the user did not select the 'Transportation' radio button, so **{BRANCH}** transfers macro control to the commands located at Next_3. If Trans_Val contains 1, 1-2-3 moves to the {LET} command in the next cell.

{LET @CELLPOINTER("address");How_Much} enters the value in How_Much (the cost of rental cars, train tickets, etc.) in the 'Other Trans' column.

{CALC} forces a recalculation. {LET} commands do not cause 1-2-3 to recalculate the worksheet, even if you set recalculation to Automatic. Including a {CALC} command ensures that all formulas in the expense report are updated.

{QUIT} ends the macro if an amount was entered in the 'Other Trans' column.

Next_3 through Next_7. If the 'Transportation' radio button was not selected, 1-2-3 checks to see if the next button, 'Hotel' was selected, and so on. 1-2-3 branches to Next_3 through Next_7 until it finds which radio button the user selected. The last possible radio-button selection is 'Other.' If none of the previous radio buttons has been selected, 1-2-3 branches to the commands in Next_7.

{R}{LET @CELLPOINTER("address");How_Much} enters the value in How_Much (miscellaneous expenses) in the 'Other' column.

{CALC} forces a recalculation. {LET} commands do not cause 1-2-3 to recalculate the worksheet, even if you set recalculation to Automatic. Including a {CALC} command ensures that all formulas in the expense report are updated.

{QUIT} ends the macro if an amount was entered in the 'Misc' column.

Printing the Expense Report

When users click the "Print the expense report" button, 1-2-3 sets several print settings, then prints the expense report on the default printer (see fig. 38.8).

Fig. 38.8
This macro prints the expense report.

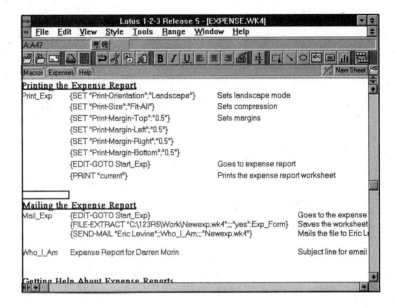

{SET "Print-Orientation";"Landscape"} sets the print orientation to landscape mode, so the expense report columns print across instead of down the page.

{SET "Print-Size";"Fit-All"} sets the print compression so that the whole worksheet fits on a single printed page. If you anticipate very long reports, omit this command; it could cause the printed data to be too small to read easily.

{SET "Print-Margin";"Top";"0.5"} sets the top print margin to half an inch.

{SET "Print-Margin";"Bottom";"0.5"} sets the bottom print margin to half an inch.

{SET "Print-Margin";"Right";"0.5"} sets the right print margin to half an inch.

{SET "Print-Margin";"Left";"0.5"} sets the left print margin to half an inch.

{EDIT-GOTO Start_Exp} moves the cell pointer to the first cell in the Expenses worksheet. Including this command in the print macro ensures that Expenses is the current worksheet before 1-2-3 starts printing.

{PRINT "Current"} prints the Expenses worksheet on the user's default printer.

Mailing the Expense Report

When users click the "Mail the expense report to Finance" button, 1-2-3 mails a copy of the expense report to an accounts payable representative in the Finance department (see fig. 38.9).

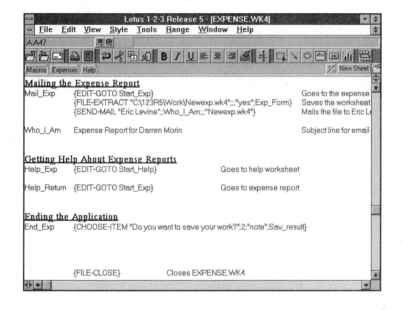

Fig. 38.9
This macro mails the expense report to the Finance department.

{EDIT-GOTO Start_Exp} moves the cell pointer to the first cell in the Expenses worksheet.

{FILE-EXTRACT "C:\123R5W\Work\Newexp.wk4";;;;Exp_Form} saves the worksheet Expenses (the entire worksheet is a range named Exp-Form) in a file named NEWEXP.WK4. The file is not saved with a password. If this macro has been run previously, and a file named NEWEXP.WK4 already exists in the specified directory, 1-2-3 creates a backup file.

{SEND-MAIL "Eric Levine";;Who_I_Am;;;"Newexp.wk4"} sends NEWEXP.WK4, as an attachment to an email message, to Eric Levine.

The subject line of the email is created by a text formula located in the cell Who_I_Am. The formula,

+"Expense Report for "&@INFO("Setup-User-Name")

looks for the user's name in the [User Name] section of the LOTUS.INI file, and then appends the name to the phrase "Expense Report for " If the user's mail application is not running when this macro is executed, 1-2-3 tries to launch the mail application.

Getting Customized Help

It's easy to provide users with customized help for the applications you write. Simply enter the help in a separate worksheet, then use {EDIT-GOTO} commands to display that worksheet (see fig. 38.10). You could also use separate {EDIT-GOTO} commands to display different parts of the help, located in different sections of the worksheet.

Fig. 38.10
This macro takes the user to a worksheet that contains Help for the expense report application.

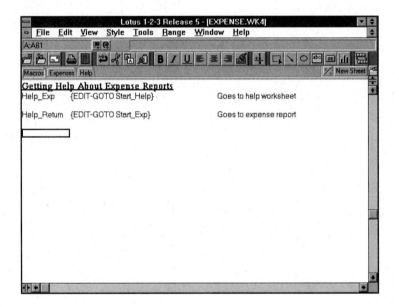

{EDIT-GOTO Start_Help} moves the cell pointer to the first cell in the worksheet named Help.

{EDIT-GOTO Start_Exp} moves the cell pointer to the first cell in the Expenses worksheet. A button in the Help worksheet runs this macro.

Ending the Application

When the user clicks the "End the expense report application" button, 1-2-3 displays a dialog box (see fig. 38.11) that lets the user choose whether to save the expense report before closing the file.

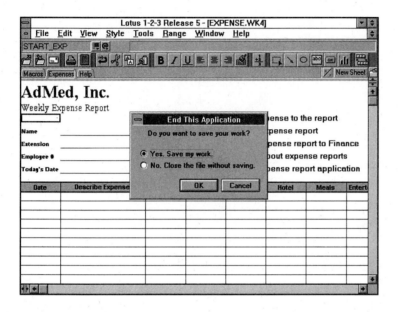

Fig. 38.11
This dialog box can be quickly created with a {CHOOSE-ONE} command.

Figure 38.12 shows the macro that displays the dialog box and saves or discards the user's changes.

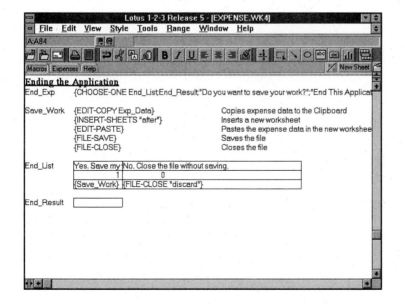

Fig. 38.12
If the user chooses not to save the expense report information, the {FILE-CLOSE "discard"} command closes EXPENSE.WK4 without saving any changes.

If the user wants to save the expense report information, the following macro commands, in the subroutine named {Save_Work}, save the data and close the file:

{EDIT-COPY Exp_Data} copies the range Exp_Data, which contains the expense data portion of the Expenses worksheet, to the Clipboard.

{INSERT-SHEETS "after"} inserts one blank worksheet after the Expenses worksheet. The new worksheet becomes the current worksheet, that is, the worksheet that contains the cell pointer.

{EDIT-PASTE} pastes the expense data from the Clipboard to the new worksheet.

{BLANK Not_Totals} clears any data the user entered in the expense report. The range Not_Totals consists of the cells in the Expenses worksheet where 1-2-3 enters the user's expense data. The range does not include the row that contains the totals formulas, so the formulas remain intact.

{FILE-SAVE} saves EXPENSE.WK4 in the user's default worksheet directory. The file is not saved with a password, and no backup file is created.

{FILE-CLOSE} closes EXPENSE.WK4.

Summary

It takes some time to create a well-planned, well-written macro application, but this time will be well rewarded. A good macro application has a long life, because it makes tasks easier for the people who use it, and gives users a sense of assurance while they work.

Take advantage of the graphical elements of the 1-2-3 macro language, such as macro buttons, and custom dialog boxes. These elements make your application look polished and they make your application easier to use. Remember: An easy-to-use application gets used more often! For more information about macros, read the following chapters:

From Here...

- Chapter 35, "Writing 1-2-3 for Windows Macros"

- Chapter 36, "Recording and Modifying Macros"

- Chapter 37, "Advanced Macro Techniques"

Appendixes

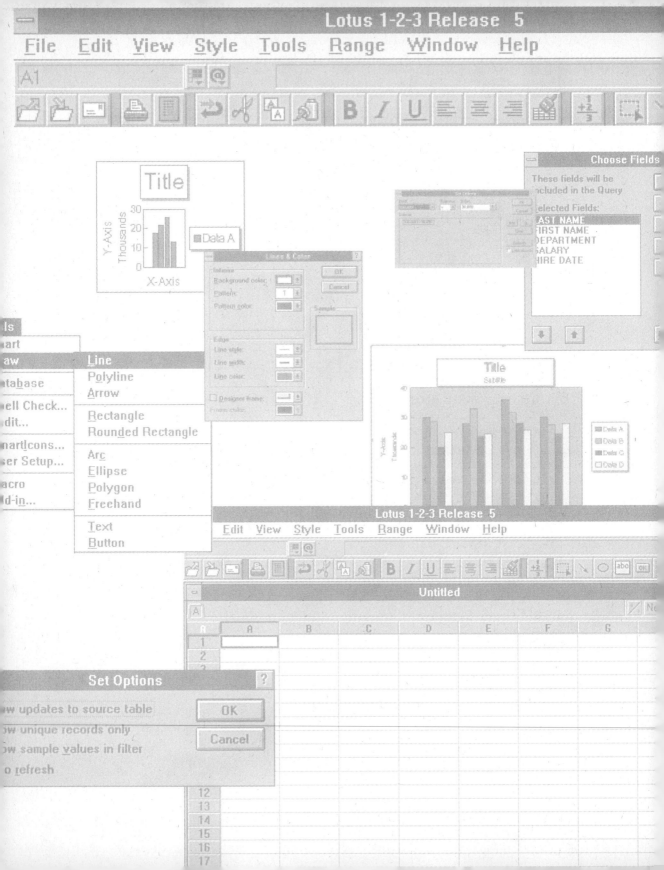

1-2-3 for Windows Support Services

It's your worst nightmare. You're scrambling to finish a financial report for an afternoon board meeting. Weird things start happening on-screen. Finally, your display freezes. You can still move the pointer, but nothing responds when you click it. What do you do?

What Help Is Available?

Lotus 1-2-3 for Windows includes a full menu of help items while you are using the program. You can choose any one of the commands from the Help menu at any time, or you can press F1 while you're in the middle of a procedure to get additional insight on what to do next.

◄ "Using the 1-2-3 for Windows Help System," p. 54

When you need more help than your computer can offer, try one of these services:

■ *Lotus PROMPT*. A call-in technical support program sponsored by Lotus Development Corporation. You are given a 90-day complimentary membership to Lotus PROMPT when you first purchase 1-2-3 for Windows. The phone number of Lotus PROMPT is (800) 386-8600 in the U.S. or (800) 265-6887 in Canada.

After your 90 days are up, you can choose to continue with PROMPT for a fee ($129 a year in the U.S., $99 in Canada). If you prefer, you can use the "pay-as-you-go" 1-900 option (the number is (900) 454-9009). You'll get the first minute free, but pay $2.00 a minute for every minute after that.

■ *Automated Services*. If you've got a touch-tone telephone, you can call the Lotus interactive, automated technical support line 24 hours a day, seven days a week. The number for Automated Services is (800) 346-3508 in the U.S. or (416) 364-7507 in Canada.

■ *Lotus FAX*. You can access technical support documents and have them faxed to you at your own fax number. This number is the same as the Automated Services. During the initial moments of connection you are prompted to choose a voice or fax communication.

Tip
Lotus also offers corporate techni-cal support pack-ages as well as training programs. Call (800) 343-5414 for more information.

■ *Lotus Bulletin Board*. You can use your modem to contact the Lotus bul-letin board and scan through Lotus CD/PROMPT, a CD-ROM that in-cludes an enormous library of documents on all Lotus products. Set your modem to a baud rate of 1200 or 2400 and, in the U.S., call (617) 693-7000. In Canada, call (416) 364-4941.

■ *Lotus on CompuServe*. Lotus also has a significant presence on CompuServe. You can put your questions on the electronic message board, write to technical support people, or browse the libraries for helpful information. To access the Lotus forum, type **GO LOTUS**.

What To Do Before You Call

If you are stuck in a procedure, look in the manual or press F1 to see whether further explanation can solve the problem.

If your screen appears to be locked up, try pressing Alt+Tab to switch to an-other application. If you are able to display the Program Manager, try closing any other open applications to free up more memory.

Write down any "symptoms" you think may be helpful to a technical support person.

Have your system information (like the type of microprocessor your com-puter uses, available RAM, hard disk space, and DOS version) and 1-2-3 for Windows manuals handy.

Stay at your computer and do not turn the system off. Leave the computer as it is, even if it is totally locked up. (The technical support person will walk you through procedures to try to solve the problem.)

You need your nine-digit PROMPT ID (on the Lotus Software Agreement in your Lotus 1-2-3 for Windows package). Each time you call for technical support, you will be asked for this ID number, so keep it somewhere safe.

Important Technical Support Numbers

(800) 386-8600	Technical support hotline
(800) 346-3508	Automated support line/fax
(617) 693-7000	Lotus BBS

SmartIcons Listing

SmartIcons are small on-screen buttons that allow you to select often-used procedures and settings easily. Instead of opening a menu and choosing a command, you can often accomplish the same task with a simple click of the mouse button on the appropriate SmartIcon.

1-2-3 for Windows includes more than 200 different SmartIcons, each with a different purpose. Nine palettes of SmartIcons are available when you begin using 1-2-3; one palette, called the Default Sheet palette, is displayed across the top of the worksheet area automatically. You can use the other SmartIcon palettes or you can create and save your own palette, customized to your particular needs.

◀ "SmartIcon Basics," p. 44

Table B.1 lists each of the SmartIcons you'll encounter in 1-2-3 for Windows. Remember that not all the icons appear on the screen at one time or in the order presented. The SmartIcons listed here are arranged by the menu to which their functions correspond.

Table B.1   SmartIcons Listing

SmartIcon	Name	Description
File Menu		
	Create File	Allows you to create a SmartMaster or a new worksheet file
	Quick New File	Displays a blank worksheet screen
	Open File	Displays the Open File dialog box
	Close Window	Closes the active window

(continues)

Appendixes

Table B.1 Continued		
SmartIcon	**Name**	**Description**
File Menu		
	Save File	Displays the Save As dialog box the first time the file is saved; otherwise, saves file without prompting
	Send Mail	Begins transmission of electronic mail
	Print Preview	Allows you to preview the current worksheet before printing
	Preview Next Page	Displays the next page in PREVIEW mode
	Preview Previous Page	Displays the previous page in PREVIEW mode
	Preview Multiple Pages	Shows multiple pages in PREVIEW mode
	Preview Facing Pages	Shows facing pages in PREVIEW mode
	Preview Single Page	Shows a single page in PREVIEW mode
	Page Setup	Lets you set up page header, footer, and margins
	Landscape	Sets landscape orientation
	Portrait	Sets portrait orientation
	Center Horizontally	Centers worksheet information horizontally on a page
	Center Vertically	Centers information vertically on a page
	Center All	Centers information horizontally and vertically on a page
	Fit All to Page	Fits printing on one page
	Fit Columns to Page	Fits all columns on one page for printing

SmartIcon	Name	Description
File Menu		
	Fit Rows to Page	Fits all rows on one page for printing
	Set Print Columns	Lets you choose the columns to print along the leftmost column
	Set Print Rows	Lets you choose the rows to print at the top of every page
	Range to Print	Allows you to choose the data you want to print
	Print	Displays the Print dialog box
	Quick Print	Prints the current selection
	Exit	Closes 1-2-3
Edit Menu		
	Undo	Reverses last command or action
	Cut	Removes selected item to the Windows Clipboard
	Copy	Copies selected item to the Windows Clipboard
	Paste	Pastes contents of Clipboard to the worksheet
	Delete	Deletes the selected item
	Delete Styles	Removes styles but leaves data
	Paste Data	Pastes only data from the Clipboard, without styles
	Paste Styles	Pastes only styles from the Clipboard, without data
	Paste Formula Results	Pastes only the result of a formula, not the formula itself

(continues)

Table B.1 Continued		
SmartIcon	**Name**	**Description**
Edit Menu		
	Paste Link	Pastes formula, file link, DDE, or OLE link
	Bring to Front	Moves object in front of other objects
	Send to Back	Moves object in back of other objects
	Flip Horizontal	Flips selected object horizontally
	Flip Vertical	Flips selected object vertically
	Rotate Object	Rotates object
	Group/Ungroup Objects	Puts together or separates selected objects
	Lock/Unlock Objects	Locks or unlocks chosen objects
	Attach Top and Bottom	Fastens a selected object to cells behind at the top left and bottom right
	Attach Top	Fastens a selected object to the top left cell
	Select Objects	Selects several objects at once
	Select All	Selects all drawn objects
	Copy Row	Copies row contents to fill selected area
	Copy Column	Copies column contents to fill selected area
	Copy Cell	Copies contents of the top left cell to fill selected area
	Insert Columns	Inserts one or more columns
	Insert Rows	Inserts one or more rows

SmartIcon	Name	Description
Edit Menu		
	Insert Range	Inserts a range at the specified location
	Insert Worksheet	Inserts a worksheet following the current worksheet
	Delete Columns	Deletes all columns in the highlighted range
	Delete Rows	Deletes all rows in the highlighted range
	Delete Range	Deletes the selected range
	Delete Worksheets	Deletes all worksheets in the highlighted range
	Find and Replace	Finds and replaces worksheet characters
	Select Object	Allows you to select a range, chart, drawing, or table
	Embed Data	Lets you create or embed data in the current worksheet
View Menu		
	Zoom In	Magnifies the window
	Zoom Out	Reduces the window
	Default Size	Returns display to default size
	Perspective View	Displays three grouped worksheets in perspective view
	Show/Hide Elements	Shows or hides elements on the worksheet
Style Menu		
	Default Currency	Applies default currency format to selected cells
	U.S. Dollars	Formats selected values in U.S. dollar currency format

(continues)

SmartIcon	Name	Description
Table B.1	**Continued**	
Style Menu		
£	British Pound	Formats selected values in British pound currency format
¥	Japanese Yen	Formats selected values in Japanese yen currency format
0,0	Comma 0	Formats values with thousands separator but no decimal places
%	Percent 2	Displays values as percentages with two decimal places
16	Date	Displays current date
aZ	Font & Attributes	Changes font, color, and style of selected data
N	Normal	Removes style attributes
B	Boldface	Adds or removes boldface
I	Italics	Adds or removes italics
U	Underline	Adds or removes underlining
U	Double-Underline	Adds or removes double-underline
	Lines & Color	Changes color, pattern, lines, and frames
	Drop Shadow	Draws cell or range outline and adds drop shadow
	Border	Adds border to selected cells
	Left Align	Left-aligns selected data
	Center	Centers selected data
	Right Align	Right-aligns selected data

SmartIcon	Name	Description
Style Menu		
	Even Align	Justifies selected data
	Center Across Columns	Center text across selected columns
	Angle Text	Displays text at an angle
	Style Gallery	Applies a style template to selected cells
	Named Style	Creates a named style
	Size Column	Resizes column to fit widest entry
	Horizontal Page Break	Inserts a horizontal page break
	Vertical Page Break	Inserts a vertical page break
	Fast Format	Copy styles in selected range to other ranges
Tools Menu		
	Create Chart	Creates chart with selected data
	Draw Map	Draws map with selected data
	Draw Line	Draws a line
	Draw Segmented Line	Draws a segmented line
	Draw Arrow	Draws line with a forward arrow
	Draw Double Arrow	Draws a double-headed arrow
	Draw Rectangle	Draws a rectangle or square

(continues)

Appendixes

Table B.1 Continued		
SmartIcon	**Name**	**Description**
Tools Menu		
	Draw Rounded Rectangle	Draws a rounded rectangle
	Draw Arc	Draws an arc
	Draw Ellipse	Draws an ellipse or circle
	Draw Polygon	Draws a polygon
	Draw Freehand	Creates a freehand drawing
	Text Block	Allows you to create a text block
	Macro Button	Lets you create a button for starting a macro
	Query Table	Creates query table
	Crosstab	Cross-tabulates values from a database table
	Spell Check	Starts the spelling checker
	Audit Cells	Audits selected cells
	Find Formulas	Allows you to look for specific formulas
	Find Precedents	Finds formula precedents
	Find Dependents	Finds formula dependents
	Find 1-2-3 Links	Finds links to 1-2-3 files
	Find DDE Links	Finds DDE links
	Arrange SmartIcons	Displays SmartIcons so you can change their arrangement

SmartIcon	Name	Description
Tools Menu		
	Select SmartIcons	Lets you choose from available SmartIcon sets
	Recalculate	Recalulates the worksheet
	Select Macro Command	Lets you select a macro command
	Run Macro	Runs selected macro
	Step Mode	Turns Step mode on or off
	Trace Mode	Turns Trace mode on or off
	Record Macro	Begins or stops recording a macro
	Show/Hide Transcript	Shows or hides the transcript window
	Database Form	Lets you select options for the form
	Database Report	Displays dialog box for creating report
	Database Crosstab	Enables you to create a dynamic crosstab
	Mailing Labels	Displays dialog box for mailing labels
Range Menu		
	Version Manager	Allows you to use the Version Manager to work with versions and scenarios
	Fill Range	Fills selected range with values
	Fill by Example	Fills range by example in first cell
	Sort Ascending	Sorts the range in ascending order

(continues)

Table B.1 Continued		
SmartIcon	**Name**	**Description**
Range Menu		
	Sort Descending	Sorts selected range in descending order
	Transpose Data	Transposes data from columns to rows or vice versa
	Create/Delete Range Name	Creates or deletes a range name
	Solver	Lets Solver find solutions
	Sum	Totals values in the selected range
Query Menu		
	Set Criteria	Sets the criteria for a query table
	Query Fields	Sets the fields to be included in a query table
	Sort Records	Sorts query table records
	Aggregate Values	Aggregates values in a query table
	Rename Field	Renames fields in a query table
	Update Query Table	Updates a query table
	Show Records	Shows all records in a query table
Chart Menu		
	Select Chart Type	Displays Chart Gallery
	Line Chart	Creates or changes selected chart to a line chart
	Area Chart	Creates or changes selected chart to an area chart

SmartIcon	Name	Description
Chart Menu		
	Vertical Bar	Creates or changes selected chart to a vertical bar chart
	Horizontal Bar	Creates or changes selected chart to a horizontal bar chart
	Horizontal Stacked Bar	Creates or changes selected chart to a horizontal stacked bar chart
	Vertical Stacked Bar	Creates or changes selected chart to a vertical stacked bar chart
	Pie Chart	Creates a pie chart
	XY Chart	Creates an XY chart
	HLCO Chart	Creates a high-lo-close-open chart
	Vertical Bar Comp	Creates a vertical bar chart with a comparison grid
	Unfilled Radar Chart	Creates an open radar chart
	Filled Radar Chart	Creates a filled radar chart
	3D Line Chart	Creates a 3D line chart
	3D Area Stacked	Creates a 3D area chart with stacked data series
	3D Area Chart	Creates a 3D area chart with overlapped data series
	3D Vertical Bar 1	Creates a 3D vertical bar chart with data series side by side
	3D Vertical Bar 2	Creates a 3D vertical bar chart with data series placed behind
	3D Pie Chart	Creates a 3D pie chart
	Mixed Chart	Enables you to mix chart styles

(continues)

Appendixes

SmartIcon	Name	Description
Table B.1 Continued		

Chart Menu

| | 100% Vertical Bar | Cretes a bar chart in which the bars fill the chart area vertically |
| | 100% Horizontal Bar | Creates a bar chart in which the bars fill the chart horizontally |

Transcript Menu

| | Play Transcript | Plays the contents of the transcript window |
| | Transcript Macro Button | Creates a macro button from commands in the Transcript window |

Window Menu

| | Tile | Arranges windows side by side |
| | Cascade | Overlaps windows so that only title bars show |

Navigation SmartIcons

	Next Worksheet	Moves to next worksheet in a file
	Previous Worksheet	Moves to previous worksheet in a file
	Home	Moves to cell A1 in current worksheet
	End Home	Moves to the bottom right corner of the active worksheet area
	End Up	Moves up to the next cell that contains data beside a blank cell
	End Down	Moves down to next cell that contains data beside a blank cell
	End Right	Moves right to next cell that contains data beside a blank cell
	End Left	Moves left to next cell that contains data beside a blank cell

SmartIcon	Name	Description
Navigation SmartIcons		
	Next Collection	Moves to first cell in range of collection
	Previous Collection	Moves to first cell in previous range of collection
Applications		
	Ami Pro	
	Approach	
	cc:Mail	
	DOS	
	Freelance Graphics	
	Improv	
	Lotus Dialog Editor	
	Lotus Notes	
	Macro Translator	
	Organizer	
	SmartPics	
	Windows File Manager	
	ScreenCam	

Appendix C

Index of Common Problems

Worksheet Basics	
If you have this problem...	**You'll find help here...**
1-2-3 beeps and won't enter a formula into a cell	p. 125
1-2-3 displays incorrect data when you enter a date or time	p. 342
1-2-3 doesn't accept a phone number with the area code in parentheses	p. 89
1-2-3 won't accept a function after you enter all of the required arguments	p. 140
Application icon for 1-2-3 doesn't appear in the Program Manager	p. 18
Asterisks appear when you type a number into a cell	p. 91
Can't find a 1-2-3 command to rename a file	p. 289
Can't find a 1-2-3 command to repeat borders, columns, or rows on each page	p. 380
Can't remember the password you created for a worksheet	p. 303
Can't seal one worksheet in a file that contains multiple worksheets	p. 303

(continues)

Worksheet Basics Continued

If you have this problem...	You'll find help here...
Dates: You accidentally typed a date into a cell and when you type a number into that cell, a strange date appears	p. 91
Dialog box options that you didn't choose seem to be active	p. 41
Drag-and-drop procedure doesn't work, and the hand pointer doesn't appear when you move the mouse pointer to the edge of a highlighted area	p. 256
Drag-and-drop procedure overwrites existing data	p. 257
ERR appears in place of certain formulas after you deleted a row from a worksheet	p. 112
Error message `File does not exist` appears when you click a file name listed at the bottom of the **F**ile menu	p. 296
Error message `No application is associated with this file` appears when you try to open a 1-2-3 file from the Windows File Manager	p. 296
Excel worksheet won't open in 1-2-3 Release 4 for Windows	p. 303
Filled range contains dates or percents instead of the numbers you expected	p. 99
Formulas in other worksheets evaluate to ERR when you delete a worksheet	p. 277
Global column width change does not affect all worksheet columns	p. 316
Grouped worksheets don't enable you to enter data simultaneously in multiple worksheets	p. 279
Header is not correctly centered over your report	p. 380
Hide dialog box doesn't enable you to unhide a hidden column	p. 374
Long entries are truncated when you type data in an adjacent column	p. 89

If you have this problem...	You'll find help here...
Menu option appears gray and nothing happens when you select it	p. 36
Named print settings you previously saved are no longer available	p. 374
Page Setup dialog box doesn't have an option for specifying the paper size	p. 380
Paste command appears gray when you try to use it	p. 269
Paste data procedure overwrites existing data	p. 257
Paste data procedure results in incorrect information copied into the cells	p. 257
Print dialog box doesn't enable you to select multiple print ranges	p. 374
Protection appears gray on the **S**tyle menu when you try to unprotect a cell range in a sealed file	p. 303
Range Fill By **E**xample filled an entire range with the same label you entered in the first cell of the range	p. 99
Range **F**ill only filled data in a portion of a selected range	p. 99
Range selector doesn't return you to the dialog box, so you can't complete a command	p. 277
Row height did not readjust when you deleted a long text entry from a cell that used the **W**rap Text option	p. 351
SmartIcon palette appears different than in figures	p. 23
SmartIcons you added to the palette do not appear on-screen	p. 989
SmartIcons: Nothing happens after you choose a SmartIcon	p. 989
Title bar doesn't appear in worksheet	p. 23

(continues)

Worksheet Basics   Continued

If you have this problem...	You'll find help here...
Worksheet entries don't line up correctly after accidentally inserting a cell instead of a row	p. 112
Worksheet tabs don't appear	p. 27
Worksheet window suddenly disappeared	p. 50
Wrap Text option filled the next few cells to the right instead of wrapping the data within the cell	p. 350
Zoom displays nothing on-screen when you zoom in while previewing a report	p. 367

Charts and Presentations

If you have this problem...	You'll find help here...
1-2-3 beeps when you try to copy a graphic from another program into your chart	p. 458
1-2-3 created a legend that you don't need	p. 424
Can't select worksheet data and two charts to print on a single page	p. 441
Chart has overlapping labels on the x-axis	p. 424
Chart option doesn't appear in the menu bar	p. 411
Clip-art image added to a worksheet does not display data in underlying cells	p. 542
Custom zoom percentage that you changed now appears in the **V**iew menu	p. 501
Data series in a bar chart printed on a black-and-white printer are difficult to distinguish	p. 441
Data series in a line chart are difficult to distinguish	p. 437
Designer frames added as slide borders appear dark and uninteresting	p. 543

If you have this problem...	You'll find help here...
Drawing objects added to a slide move when you insert columns or change column widths	p. 542
Frozen titles appear duplicated on the worksheet	p. 492
Gridlines change color instead of the outline color of a single cell	p. 492
Imported graphic appears in a box frame that you don't want	p. 458
Legends and x-axis labels appear to be reversed in an automatic chart	pp. 391-392
Maps: Can't add commas and currency symbols to the legend labels	p. 480
Maps: Can't find the mapcodes for each country	p. 480
Mixed chart type results in a chart that displays only bars	p. 455
Perspective view displays only one file when multiple files are open	p. 501
Pie slices aren't labeled	p. 424
Rectangle added to a worksheet blocks out portion of a chart	p. 513
Screen didn't split when you displayed the Split dialog box and clicked on **V**ertical	p. 495
Screen split resulted in column appearing on the wrong side of the split	p. 495
Text block characters do not appear as you are entering them in the text block	p. 508
Title frame does not fit in the chart frame after you enlarged the title frame	p. 401
XY chart ranges appear incorrect when you preselect the range and create an automatic chart	p. 455
Y-axis scale doesn't display dollar signs even though the numbers in the worksheet are formatted for currency	p. 437
Y-axis scale shows single digit numbers with a unit indicator of Thousands, but you would prefer to see the actual numbers	p. 437

Data Analysis

If you have this problem...	You'll find help here...
Can't incorporate a number from a value cell in a text formula	p. 557
`Circ` appears in the status bar	p. 627
Combine 1-2-3 File dialog box ignores your revisions when you make changes to the source file for a combine operation	p. 610
Merge Results dialog box does not appear when you merge versions and scenarios	p. 691
Solver report tables are difficult to read and interpret	p. 657
Version Manager doesn't enable you to track changes made by others on your computer	p. 676
Version Manager: **U**pdate button appears gray and does not respond when you click it	p. 676

Databases

If you have this problem...	You'll find help here...
1-2-3 prompts for a password when you try to open a Paradox database	p. 797
Aggregate command appears gray when you choose **Q**uery	p. 774
Cross-tabulation table contains errors (ERR)	p. 775
Database has more records and fields than can fit on-screen at one time	p. 708
Dates do not sort properly	p. 737
Error message `Ambiguous field reference in query` appears after you enter a field formula in the Formula dialog box	p. 747

If you have this problem...	You'll find help here...
Error message `Cannot join tables to a query that has an unnamed database table or a database table not in memory` appears when you try to join databases	p. 769
Error message `Invalid field name` appears when you try to append records using the **T**ools Data**b**ase **A**ppend Records command	p. 714
Formulas in your worksheet change to ERR when you disconnect from an external database file	p. 804
Frequency distribution results in zeros	p. 779
New records added to the bottom of a database don't print	p. 714
No drivers are listed or the driver you want is not listed when you choose **T**ools Data**b**ase **N**ew Query **E**xternal	pp. 796-797
No records show in the query table when you join two databases	p. 769
Numeric values change to labels when you parse data	p. 808
Query table contains too many records when you join two databases	pp. 769-770
Query table correctly joined two databases, but it shows two copies of the join field	p. 770
Query table doesn't display all records specified by criterion	p. 751
Query table lists all records when you use an asterisk in the criterion	p. 751
Query tables: Column heading for a calculated field contains a formula instead of a field name	p. 747
ZIP codes with leading zeros in your database appear without the zeros	p. 708

Application Integration

If you have this problem...	You'll find help here...
1-2-3 linked object does not update properly	p. 913
Can't embed a single object or group of objects from a Freelance page in 1-2-3	p. 862
Changing data in the source application does not change data in the destination application, even if the applications are linked	p. 833
Error message Cannot establish DDE link appears when linking a chart	p. 840
Paste Link command appears gray in the Edit menu, and DDE Link isn't one of the available formats after you choose Edit Paste Special	p. 829
Send Mail command doesn't appear in the File menu	p. 930
Text in a 1-2-3 object in Notes appears enlarged and causes wordwrapping	p. 913

Macros

If you have this problem...	You'll find help here...
Alt+*letter* macros do not work	p. 86
Auto-execute macro does not run when you open a worksheet	p. 51
Can't change the macro associated with a macro button, because selecting the button causes the macro to run	p. 71
Macro buttons disappear when you reopen a worksheet	p. 71
Macro you assigned to a SmartIcon does not run when you click the SmartIcon	p. 994
Macro you previously tested enters data in the wrong cells and generally causes problems	p. 88

If you have this problem...	You'll find help here...
Macros don't work as expected after you upgraded from 1-2-3 Release 1 for Windows	p. 76
Macros don't work correctly; instead of using the specified literal argument, they seem to be using information from the worksheet as arguments	p. 82
Macros translated using the 1-2-3 Macro Translator run incorrectly	p. 76
String of repeated zeros appears when you enter \0 as the macro name	p. 51
Syntax errors occur when you use commas as argument separators	p. 82

Index

Selecting Worksheet Areas

Selected Area/Location	Shortcut
Select cells	Shift+movement key
Select current row	Click on row number
Select current column	Click on column letter
Select entire worksheet	Click on worksheet letter
To beginning of worksheet	Home
To beginning of file	Ctrl+Home
To end of worksheet	End Home
To end of file	End Ctrl+Home

Editing Data

Operation	Shortcut
F2	Edit data in current cell/contents box
Undo last action	Alt+Backspace *or* Ctrl+Z
Insert column/row/sheet	Ctrl+ Gray+
Delete column/row/sheet	Ctrl+ Gray–
Del	Deletes selected data
Cut	Shift+Del *or* Ctrl+X
Copy	Ctrl+Ins *or* Ctrl+C
Paste	Shift+Ins *or* Ctrl+V

Formatting

Format	Shortcut
Bold on/off	Ctrl+B
Italics on/off	Ctrl+I
Underline on/off	Ctrl+U
Reset to normal text	Ctrl+N
Left align	Ctrl+L
Center align	Ctrl+E
Right align	Ctrl+R

Worksheet Operations

Task	Shortcut
Open a worksheet	Ctrl+O
Close a worksheet	Ctrl+F4
Save a worksheet	Ctrl+S
Print a worksheet	Ctrl+P
Exit 1-2-3	Alt+F4
Execute a macro	Ctrl+*letter*

The 1-2-3 Release 5 for Windows Screen

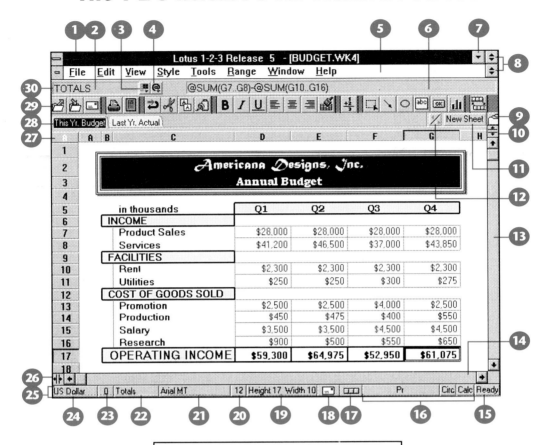

PARTS OF THE SCREEN

1. Title Bar	11. New Sheet Button	21. Font Selector
2. Selection Indicator	12. Tab Scroll Arrows	22. Style Selector
3. Navigator	13. Vertical Scroll Bar	23. Decimal Selector
4. @Function Selector	14. Horizontal Scroll Bar	24. Format Selector
5. Menu Bar	15. Mode Indicator	25. Status Bar
6. Contents Box	16. Status Indicators	26. Vertical Splitter
7. Minimize Button	17. SmartIcons Selector	27. Worksheet Letter
8. Maximize/Restore Buttons	18. Mail Button	28. Worksheet Tabs
9. Tab Button	19. Date/Time/Style Indicator	29. SmartIcons
10. Horizontal Splitter	20. Point-Size Selector	30. Edit Line